PENGUIN HANDBOOKS

THE PENGUIN GUIDE TO COMPACT DISCS YEARBOOK 1995

EDWARD GREENFIELD, until his retirement in 1993, was for forty years on the staff of the *Guardian*, succeeding Neville Cardus as Music Critic in 1975. He still contributes regularly to the record column which he founded in 1954. At the end of 1960 he joined the reviewing panel of *Gramophone*, specializing in operatic and orchestral issues. He is a regular broadcaster on music and records for the BBC, not just on Radios 3 and 4 but also on BBC World Service, latterly with his weekly programme, 'The Greenfield Collection'. In 1958 he published a monograph on the operas of Puccini. More recently he has written studies on the recorded work of Joan Sutherland and André Previn. He has been a regular juror on International Record awards and has appeared with such artists as Dame Elisabeth Schwarzkopf, Dame Joan Sutherland and Sir Georg Solti in public interviews. In October 1993 he was given a *Gramophone* Award for Special Achievement and in June 1994 received the OBE for services to music and journalism.

ROBERT LAYTON studied at Oxford with Edmund Rubbra for composition and with Egon Wellesz for the history of music. He spent two years in Sweden at the universities of Uppsala and Stockholm. He joined the BBC Music Division in 1959 and has been responsible for such programmes as *Interpretations on Record*. He has contributed a 'Quarterly Retrospect' to *Gramophone* for a number of years, and he has written books on Berwald and Sibelius and has specialized in Scandinavian music. He has written a monograph on the Dvořák symphonies and concertos for the BBC Music Guides, of which he was General Editor for many years. His translation of the first two volumes of Erik Tawastsjerna's definitive study of Sibelius was awarded the 1984 Finnish State Literary Prize. In 1987 he was awarded the Sibelius Medal and in the following year was made a Knight of the Order of the White Rose of Finland for his services to Finnish music. His *Guide to the Symphony* has recently been published as an Oxford paperback.

IVAN MARCH is a former professional musician. He studied at Trinity College of Music, London, and at the Royal Manchester College. After service in the Central Band of the RAF, he played the horn professionally for the BBC and travelled with the Carl Rosa and D'Oyly Carte opera companies. Now director of the Long Playing Record Library, the largest commercial lending library for classical music on compact discs in the British Isles, he is a well-known lecturer, journalist and personality in the world of recorded music. As a journalist, he contributes to a number of record-reviewing magazines, including *Gramophone*, where his regular monthly 'Collector's Corner' deals particularly with important reissues.

The Penguin Guide to Compact Discs Yearbook 1995

Edward Greenfield, Robert Layton and Ivan March

Edited by Ivan March

Penguin Books

PENGUIN BOOKS

Published by the Penguin Group
Penguin Books Ltd, 27 Wrights Lane, London W8 5TZ, England
Penguin Books USA Inc., 375 Hudson Street, New York, New York 10014, USA
Penguin Books Australia Ltd, Ringwood, Victoria, Australia
Penguin Books Canada Ltd, 10 Alcorn Avenue, Toronto, Ontario, Canada M4V 3B2
Penguin Books (NZ) Ltd, 182–190 Wairau Road, Auckland 10, New Zealand

Penguin Books Ltd, Registered Offices: Harmondsworth, Middlesex, England

First published 1995
10 9 8 7 6 5 4 3 2 1

Typeset, from data supplied, by Datix International Ltd, Bungay, Suffolk
Made and printed in Great Britain by
Clays Ltd, St Ives plc

Contents

Editor's Note

In the past we have used the *Penguin CD Yearbook* primarily as a means of updating the previous main *Penguin Guide to Compact Discs*, and the book you now hold in your hands certainly offers an appraisal of the year's most prominent records. But it also includes a substantial number of newer discs for which there simply was no room in our 1994 main volume.

In consequence this edition brings the most extensive coverage yet offered in a *Yearbook*, which becomes much more than a mere supplement and assumes the role of a new *Guide* in its own right (even though frequent references are still made to the 1994 survey).

Within its pages a huge amount of new repertoire is balanced by a treasure trove of reissues, often inexpensive and offering extraordinary value for money in the quality of the performances, the excellence of the recording and the generosity of content.

For the authors, one rewarding feature of the present comprehensive reassessment has been the unrestricted space available to us to discuss both the music and the calibre of these performances. Here we are not under the constraint of space limitations caused by relisting and discussing all the previous CDs of consequence, for we need refer back to the best of them only in relation to newer arrivals.

It is self-evident that only the *crème de la crème* of the recordings discussed here will be carried forward to our next main volume. There will be many CDs which are of great interest – because they offer rare repertoire or performances of outstanding interest, or both – which will inevitably have to be passed over. So the serious collector will continue to need access to the current text, independent of the surveys which will be found in future editions.

The musical riches (including the reappearance of so many outstanding earlier recordings) are surely reflected by the remarkably large number of Rosettes we have been stimulated to award within these pages.

Preface

Early vocal music

As always, the present volume introduces a number of fascinating new names to the composer index, including Guillaume Bouzignac, who may perhaps be described as the Charles Ives of the sixteenth century, and the Portuguese master of Renaissance polyphony, Duarte Lôbo (c. 1565–1646), who was an almost exact contemporary of the rather more familiar Manuel Cardoso.

Nicholas Ludford (1485–1557), one of the least-known of the great English Tudor composers, made his début in our last volume, and ASV have now put together a special package of four CDs covering some of his motets and many of his Masses (of which he was 'the most prolific of English composers'), superbly sung by the Cardinall's Musick, directed by Andrew Carwood. This inspiring group of singers have added to their laurels by following this up with a hardly less valuable and stimulating CD of the music of another neglected Elizabethan master, Robert Fayrfax.

Also contributing to the field of authentic performances of early vocal music is Gérard Lesne with his distinguished accompanying ensemble, Il Seminario Musicale, who is exploring seventeenth-century repertoire, including the very beautiful *Leçons de ténèbres* of Marc-Antoine Charpentier and some remarkably dramatic cantatas by Alessandro Scarlatti. Lesne's unique timbre, subtle control of vocal colour and feeling for decoration make him a true successor to Alfred Deller, who is well represented in our pages by a 14-CD Vanguard 'Deller Edition'. At the very last moment as we were going to press, the legendary Russell Oberlin, another real counter-tenor of exquisite quality, returned to the catalogue on the Lyrichord Early Music label, which we hope to explore more thoroughly next time.

The symphony

Modern symphonists whose names appear here for the first time include the doyen of New Zealand composers, Douglas Lilburn (born 1915), and two Russians: Boris Lyatoshynsky (1895–1968), whose works show early influences of Scriabin as well as of Shostakovich, and Moishei Vainberg (born 1919), in whom a direct Shostakovich inheritance does not prevent his symphonies from having an individual voice and being well worthy of exploration.

The Dutchman Lex van Delden (1919–88), inventive and intelligent, is another orchestral composer who leaves you wanting to hear more. His *Third Symphony* is really quite strong; while in Britain, Sir John Blackwood McEwan (1868–1948) is represented by the highly evocative *Solway Symphony* (of 1911), a very successful work which suggests that McEwan was far more than just an academic.

Chamber and keyboard music

Willan Pijper, a dominating influence in Holland between the wars, has left us some impressive string quartets; but an even more remarkable discovery in the world of chamber music has been a rare example of a successful female composer, the Venetian-born Maddelina Lombardini Sirmen (1745–1818). Her six string quartets had to be attributed as being written jointly with her husband (which they weren't) in order for them to be accepted for publication (in Paris in 1769).

The Florentine composer, Francesco Veracini (1690–1768), now also emerges from the shadows as a composer of suites for the famous Dresden orchestra of the time, and he also produced a set of highly individual violin sonatas. Handel's chamber music – meagrely represented in our main volume because of the deletions axe – is now covered on period instruments, by the expert L'Ecole d'Orphée; while his complete harpsichord music is splendidly played by Paul Nicholson on Hyperion. Other important keyboard surveys include Marie-Claire Alain's new 12-disc set of the organ music of Bach, and Kathleen Stott's complete Fauré piano music, while John McCabe's unique coverage of Haydn includes not only all the sonatas but also a remarkably effective keyboard transcription of *The Seven Last Words*.

The piano music of the Norwegian, Harald Sæverud (1897–1993), makes a refreshing CD début, often touching, and full of character, while in the USA – in Edgeworth, Pennsylvania, to be precise – through the sympathetic advocacy of Donna Amato (who grew up there herself) the works of Ethelbert Nevin (1862–1901) are brought out of obscurity. Yet his *Narcissus* was one of those nagging 'hit' tunes that almost anyone in Western Europe would have recognized instantly at any time in the last fifty years (and perhaps you will, too!).

More recent music

Closer to home, we encounter the minimalist with magnetic crossover appeal, Michael Nyman, who – rumour has it – is Decca's best-selling classical artist after Pavarotti. He has turned his famous score for Jane Campion's movie, *The Piano*, into a four-movement piano concerto. Its effectiveness is undeniable, and his other music on CD confirms the individuality and genuineness of emotion behind almost all his output.

Long-overdue amends are also being made to the work of the British composer, Benjamin Frankel (1906–73), who made his début in our main volume; while yet another completely new name is that of Harold Truscott (1914–92), himself no mean symphonist, but also the composer of a beautiful orchestral elegy, a kind of British equivalent of Barber's *Adagio*.

Those who wish that Ravel and Roussel had been more prolific should investigate some Marco Polo releases of the orchestral music of Fauré's talented pupil, Jean-Jules Roger-Ducasse (1873–1954), for he displays that elegance and feeling for atmosphere that always seem to distinguish Gallic *petits-maîtres*.

Concertos

Among a profusion of other novelties, there are new records of piano concertos by Eugen d'Albert, Arensky, Bortkovitch, and John Corigliano, a fine traditional violin concerto by Sir George Dyson (written as recently as 1941) and a comparably beautiful, more recent work by Howard Blake, both of which deserve to make their way into the mainstream concert repertoire.

A masterpiece which has belatedly achieved that distinction is Samuel Barber's *Violin concerto* (whose rapturous slow movement is every bit as memorable as his more famous *Adagio*). This concerto now receives two equally recommendable new recordings by Itzhak Perlman and Gil Shaham.

It might be thought that Beethoven's piano concertos could yield no new surprises, but (with the editorial help of the Beethoven scholar, Dr Barry Cooper) the Russian pianist, Mikail Kazakevich, together with the ECO under Mackerras, has recorded performances of the *Second* and *Fourth Piano concertos* in revised editions, taking into account the composer's own later alterations. These were made after Beethoven's own public perform-ances and, in the case of the second concerto, the amendments were inked into the autograph too late to be included in the printed score. As the performances are outstanding in their own right, this Conifer disc is not merely a curiosity but a viable coupling to recommend generally.

Choral music

There have been many fine choral discs, among which must be included DG's reissue of the three Bruckner Masses under Jochum's inspirational direction and, of course, the various tercentenary collections of the music of Purcell. However, Mackerras's vivid new record of the original score of Janáček's *Glagolitic Mass* stands out. But Karel Ančerl's thrilling account of the Dvořák *Requiem*, from the earliest days of stereo, is not to be missed either; nor is Fricsay's electrifying mono Verdi *Requiem*, about which absolutely no technical apologies need be made, while John Eliot Gardiner provides a new digital version of this same work which takes its place at the top of the list of modern versions.

Complete sets

Quite apart from the profusion of individual discs, complete sets are very much the order of the day. The RCA 'Symphony Edition' (currently available in the USA only as an import) has produced highly recommendable new bargain boxes of the complete symphonies of Beethoven and Brahms (both conducted by Günter Wand), Nielsen (Berglund) and Schumann (Levine), while Shostakovich enjoys two different integral series of interpretations, from Kondrashin on Melodiya and from Haitink via another bargain package, this time from Decca.

The complete Beethoven symphonies are also included in Sony's 'Bruno Walter Edition', and all but the *Ninth* are vibrantly conducted by Pierre Monteux on a pair of Double Decca reissues. But here we must not forget Rudolph Kempe's Berlin Philharmonic Brahms set on Testament (for Kempe was the Brahms conductor *par excellence*) or the revelatory début of the Schumann symphonies, played on period instruments, from Roy Goodman and the Hanover Band on Hyperion.

Naxos, in planning to record all Vivaldi's concertos, has begun impressively with all 27 cello concertos (including the double concerto), played with great flair by Raphael Wallfisch, with the City of London Sinfonietta under Nicholas Kraemer. Complete on four discs, they cost not too much more than a single premium-priced CD. Another valuable Vivaldi first is Scimone's excellent mid-priced Erato set, including many of the string sinfonias (or concertos for strings, the terms apparently being interchangeable).

One of the most valuable individual CDs which just missed inclusion in our main volume is an absolutely complete version of Walton's *Façade*, with the poems spoken by the irrepressible Pamela Hunter, accompanied by a group of Belgian musicians, directed by Van de Broeck. This comes on the appropriately named Discover super-bargain label, while EMI have just issued a five-CD 'Walton Edition', including all the composer's own recordings.

Opera

The year has been particularly rich in fine new opera recordings. Early music is well represented, notably by Minkowsky's new set of Lully's *Phaëton* and a single L'Oiseau Lyre disc from Philip Pickett which contains all three of Monteverdi's inspired opera-ballets, *Il ballo delle'Ingrate*, *Il combattimento di Tancredi e Clorinda* and *Tirsi e Clori*, each dominated by a superb contribution from Catherine Bott.

Decca's spectacular new Dutoit version of Berlioz's *Les Troyens* may not entirely supersede the classic Davis set but it remains a very fine achievement, while in the field of Russian opera Gergiev has given us outstanding new recordings of Borodin's *Prince Igor* and Rimsky-Korsakov's *Sadko*, a work full of glorious invention. Järvi's highly persuasive account of Tchaikovsky's *Mazeppa* reveals yet another, hitherto under-appreciated, masterpiece. Among the many novelties is a first complete recording of Chabrier's *Briseis*, made at the 1994 Edinburgh Festival, while Philip Glass's score for *La Belle et la Bête* is cleverly organized to act as a replacement soundtrack for the famous Cocteau movie of the same name.

Dame Ethel Smyth's *The Wreckers* turns out to be a slight disappointment, although it has its vigorous moments; on the other hand, her chamber music proves surprisingly attractive. George Lloyd's *Iernin*, written in the 1930s, is a recording of a worthy Radio 3 broadcast from 1988, conducted by the composer.

Goldschmidt's *Beatrice Cenci* makes a powerful début alongside Hans Schreker's *Die Gezeichneten*, which was banned by the Nazis in the 1930s as decadent, while Viktor Ullman's *Der Kaiser von Atlantis* was composed in a concentration camp before the composer went to the gas chambers. Its mixture of dark satiric irony and human feeling is deeply poignant.

On Teldec a new first choice for Humperdinck's fairy-tale opera, *Hänsel und Gretel*, marks the (CD) début on the rostrum of Donald Runnicles, while Jennifer Larmore (who plays Hänsel) is even more enchanting in the title-role of the new Covent Garden production of Rossini's *La Cenerentola* under Rizzi. A first-class new *Il Signore Bruschino* casts Kathleen Battle as the provocative heroine, while a superb new set of *Tancredi*, directed by Alberto Zedda on Naxos, brings Sumi Jo's dazzlingly clear coloratura in the role of Amenaide.

As an impressive celebration of the centenary of the birth of Karl Boehm, DG have issued a whole series of his Richard Strauss opera sets, often recorded live at the Salzburg Festival. Many appear on disc for the first time.

Plácido Domingo's third recording of Verdi's *Otello*, conducted by Myung-Whun Chung, proves to be his finest yet, and he also contributes to the recording premières of *Dona Francisquita* by Amadeo Vives (1871–1932), with Linda Mirabel and with Ainhoa Arteta in the title-role, and *El gato montes* by his contemporary, Manuel Penella (1880–1939).

The newest Wagner listings include Abbado's superb new version of *Lohengrin*, with Siegfried Jerusalem in glorious voice, while Barenboim's *Siegfried*, recorded at the 1992 Bayreuth Festival, takes its place at the top of the list as the finest of latterday digital recordings of this opera. Walton's *Troilus and Cressida* at last appears in a really excellent, modern recording of the Opera North production under Richard Hickox, rounding off the complete Chandos Walton Edition, while EMI have taken the opportunity to reissue the famous earlier version with Dame Janet Baker as Cressida. Surely at last this fine and tuneful opera should become established in the opera house.

'Live from the Vienna State Opera'
But the most remarkable operatic set of all comes in our Vocal Recitals section – 24 two-CD boxes 'recorded in the wings' of the Vienna State Opera during the decade from 1933 to 1943, featuring a huge, constantly changing cast of legendary voices and many famous conductors, not least Richard Strauss conducting his own arrangement of Mozart's *Idomeneo* and excerpts from *Salome*. Many of these recordings are technically inadequate, but the repertoire they contain offers endless fascination for the true opera buff willing to offer a 'creative ear'.

Special editions
Whereas in our main volume the space available for Collections had to be cut right back, this time we have plenty of room for an expanded coverage. Indeed, henceforth it will be our policy to include noteworthy collections, whether of orchestral, instrumental or vocal music, primarily in our *Yearbooks*, thereby freeing much-needed space in the biennial *CD Guides* to concentrate on music by specific composers. This year we have observed the presence of an extraordinary number of boxed sets featuring major artists celebrated with editions entirely their own.

On five CDs – one given free – Philips remember 50 years of recordings by the Beaux Arts Trio, with the pianist Menahem Pressler the bedrock, through various changes of personnel. The achievement of Frans Brüggen, the great recorder player who pioneered authentic performances of early music using original instruments, occupies 12 Teldec discs; Pablo Casals, creating his own special aura playing chamber music, brings a more modest offering on Sony (four CDs), while György Cziffra, a Hungarian-born pianist who could command virtuosity of the highest order but who could also be exasperatingly wilful, shows his range of repertoire on EMI (six CDs).

On Decca the 'Kirsten Flagstad Edition' (five CDs) brings a uniquely authoritative coverage of the songs of Grieg and Sibelius (among other Scandinavians), plus celebrated Wagner recordings. Sony's 'Glenn Gould Edition' covers 36 discs and, for all its inadequacies (and the vocalise), remains a remarkable achievement.

Philips celebrate eighteenth- and nineteenth-century piano music with the four-volume Clara Haskil 'Legacy' (spread over a further dozen CDs) and they cover an even wider range with the 'Sviatoslav Richter Edition' (21 CDs), while BMG/Melodiya have assembled a further fascinating ten-disc anthology of 'Great Pianists of the Russian Piano School', including Richter, Berman, Gilels and Kissin, among other names which are less familiar in the West. On the same label the 'Mravinsky Edition' brings ten CDs of outstanding Russian orchestral performances.

EMI celebrate Itzhak Perlman's achievement in most of the major and minor violin concertos and much else besides, spread over 20 CDs. Leopold Stokowski is not given a box of his own, but a number of his recordings, with various orchestras, have appeared simultaneously, which together give a fine representation of his orchestral magnetism.

The ten-CD DG box commemorating the under-valued Ferenc Fricsay highlights his work with contemporary composers, notably Bartók and Richard Strauss, while at the same time not ignoring his contributions, made in the 1950s and '60s, to both the classical and romantic repertoire. Especially remarkable in this set (each CD available separately) is the high technical quality of the engineering.

Lieder and French mélodie are already particularly well represented in the composer index – from Berlioz through to Hugo Wolf; even so, Vocal Collections bring many superb individual recitals (of opera and art songs). Here Gérard Souzay has a 4-disc collection to himself on Philips, while a DG recital of English songs from Bryn Terfel also stands out, alongside a dazzling programme of coloratura French opera and operetta by Sumi Jo, sung with breathtaking ease and virtuosity, in the spirit of Galli-Curci and, more recently, Rita Streich. Finally there is the extraordinary range of the Fischer-Dieskau Lieder Edition on 44 CDs, a worthy celebration of the great German baritone's seventieth birthday.

Historical collections

Among historical collections, a pair of recent CDs featuring two famous British singers are of special interest: a recital from 'The incomparable Heddle Nash' (which includes Beecham's complete 1935 recording in Italian of Act IV of *La Bohème*) and a 75-minute compilation revelling in the art of the 'unforgettable Isobel Baillie', whose autobiography was entitled *Never Sing Louder Than Lovely*. One could wish that certain other singers would follow this admirable advice! Both these discs are among the superb series of transfers made directly from LPs and 78-r.p.m. shellac discs by Mike Dutton Laboratories. Their quality continues to astonish – they are far ahead of any other historical CD transfers and almost always produce sound-quality which, instead of making the listener wince, gives pleasure in its own right – for truthfulness, smoothness, warmth and body of tone (subject, of course, to the originals' limitations, which usually seem to be remarkably few).

Further outstanding examples of this artistic use of modern technology include Anthony Collins' beautiful and passionate Decca mono recordings of the orchestral music of Delius with the LSO from the 1950s, and Decca's première LP recordings of Nielsen's *First* and *Fifth Symphonies* by the Danish State Radio Orchestra under Thomas Jensen from the same period. Even more remarkable is a set of 78-r.p.m. transfers of performances by the wartime National Symphony Orchestra, celebrating the launch of Arthur Haddy's *ffrr* (full frequency range recording) in 1944. The quality of the orchestral sound is little short of amazing. This is particularly valuable when one remembers that Decca's own transfers of early mono recordings very seldom match the originals in beauty of sound and all too often have an acidulated treble which ruins the violin timbre.

Other Dutton transfers draw on the EMI catalogue and include a superb CD of recordings made by Sir Hamilton Harty with the LPO on the Columbia label in 1933 and 1935. Beecham's remarkably vivid and very entertaining abridged set of Gounod's *Faust*, from 1929, his Sibelius *Seventh Symphony* with the NYPO (1942) and his wonderfully warm and graceful Schubert – the *Fifth* and *Sixth Symphonies* paired with the *Unfinished*, as performed on 78s by the LPO – are among the highlights.

DG's Originals

Heading the general collections is DG's set of 'Originals' – 29 CDs offered for the price of 26 (and all also available separately). These 'Legendary Recordings' from the back-catalogue have been remastered with great success and are engagingly presented with the upper surface of each CD made to simulate a vinyl LP, with its famous yellow label and the 'light' apparently reflecting on the black 'grooves'. As this collection covers repertoire of all kinds (orchestral, vocal and instrumental), we have placed it as a separate listing at the very beginning of the Collections section, although virtually all the individual record-ings have also been cross-indexed into the Composer section.

'The world of Borodin'

Last but not least comes a quite remarkable and inexpensive single Decca CD which, in the space of 76 minutes, sums up the overall musical achievement of that great Russian composer quite admirably. It includes a complete (1960) recording of the *Second Symphony*, directed by Jean Martinon, which has never since been surpassed.

Duos and Doubles

If DG's Originals are among the leaders in the faithful transfer to compact disc of older analogue stereo recordings, the steady improvement in the making of such transfers is notable from all sources, and especially so with the Philips Duos. Together with the Double Deccas and DG Doubles, and EMI's *Rouge et Noir* series, such reissues bring remarkable value in offering two discs (often packed full to the brim with music) for the cost of a single, premium-priced CD. Such bargains represent a clever marketing response by the majors to super-bargain labels like Naxos, and a very successful one at that.

EMI have now gone one step further by the introduction of their Seraphim logo, used to repackage what might be regarded from the Sales Department's point of view as 'second-line repertoire'. Seraphims are two-disc sets offered at the cost of one *medium-priced* CD. Artists on the Seraphim roster include Annie Fischer, Sir Yehudi Menuhin, Giulini and Rudolph Kempe, and the early stereo sound of the CD transfers is a great deal more than respectable. For the impecunious collector, these offerings at considerably less than full price represent performances and recordings of sufficient distinction to make many of them highly seductive. Documentation, however, is skimpy, and this still remains an area in which bargain and mid-priced (and sometimes even full-priced) repertoire is often very poorly served. If Naxos can provide adequate notes for brand-new CDs costing under £5, there is no reason why the major companies, offering back-catalogue which has already paid for itself, cannot do the same.

Yet in some ways such comments seem to be carping when today's music-lover lives in a golden age in which great performances of great music have never been more accessible or less expensive.

Edward Greenfield, Robert Layton and Ivan March

Introduction

As in previous editions, the object of the current *Penguin Guide to Compact Discs Yearbook* is to give the serious collector a comprehensive survey of the finest recordings of permanent music on CD. The present publication covers as many as possible of the important records (and, where available, cassettes) issued since our last main volume went into print. It also includes a fair number of CDs that missed inclusion therein for reasons of space, notably many concert and recital discs. It is obviously best used in conjunction with that 1994 complete survey. However, it can also be used independently, as we have included current 'best buy' recommendations for virtually all the major repertoire works, taking into account previous issues which remain available as well as the latest arrivals.

As most records are issued almost simultaneously on both sides of the Atlantic and use identical international catalogue numbers, this *Yearbook* should be found to be equally useful in Great Britain and the USA. The internationalization of repertoire and numbers now applies to almost all CDs issued by the major international companies and by many smaller ones too, while most of the smaller European labels are imported in their original formats into both the UK and the USA.

The sheer number of records of artistic merit now available causes considerable problems in any assessment of overall and individual excellence. While in the case of a single popular repertoire work it might be ideal for the discussion to be conducted by a single reviewer, it has not always been possible for one person to have access to every version, and division of reviewing responsibility becomes inevitable. Also there are certain works and certain recorded performances for which one or another of our team has a special affinity. Such a personal identification can often carry with it a special perception too. We feel that it is a strength of our basic style to let such conveyed pleasure or admiration for the merits of an individual recording come over directly to the reader, even if this produces a certain ambivalence in the matter of choice between competing recordings. Where disagreement is more positive, then readers will find an indication of this difference in the text. In the present edition, the new Dutoit Decca recording of *Les Troyens* of Berlioz is an obvious example of such divergence of views.

We have considered (and rejected) the use of initials against individual reviews, since this is essentially a team project. The occasions for disagreement generally concern matters of aesthetics, for instance in the manner of recording-balance, where a contrived effect may trouble some ears more than others, or in the matter of style, where the difference between robustness and refinement of approach appeals differently to listening sensibilities, rather than involving a question of artistic integrity. But over the years our views seem to grow closer together rather than to diverge; perhaps we are getting mellower, but we are seldom ready to offer strong disagreement following the enthusiastic reception by one of the team of a controversial recording, if the results are creatively stimulating. Our perceptions of the advantages and disadvantages of performances of early music on original (as against modern) instruments seem fairly evenly balanced; again, any strong feelings are indicated in the text.

EVALUATION
Most recordings issued today by the major companies are of a high technical standard and offer performances of a quality at least as high as is experienced in the concert hall. In adopting a starring system for the evaluation of records, we have decided to make use of from one to three stars. Brackets round one or more of the stars indicate some reservations

about its inclusion, and readers are advised to refer to the text. Brackets round all the stars usually indicate a basic qualification: for instance, a mono recording of a performance of artistic interest, where considerable allowances have to be made for the sound-quality, even though the recording may have been digitally remastered.

Our evaluation system may be summarized as follows:

*** An outstanding performance and recording in every way.
** A good performance and recording of today's normal high standard.
* A fair performance, reasonably well or well recorded.

Our evaluation is normally applied to the record as a whole, unless there are two main works or groups of works, and by different composers. In this case, each is dealt with separately in its appropriate place. In the case of a collection of shorter works we feel that there is little point in giving a separate starring to each item, even if their merits are uneven, since the record has to be purchased as a complete programme.

ROSETTES
To a very few records – although perhaps to more than usual in the present volume – we have awarded a Rosette: ⊛.

Unlike our general evaluations, in which we have tried to be consistent, a Rosette is a quite arbitrary compliment by a member of the reviewing team to a recorded performance which, he finds, shows special illumination, magic, or a spiritual quality, or even outstanding production values, that places it in a very special class. A key historical recording which springs to life with remarkable vividness because of an outstanding CD transfer could also earn our accolade. Occasionally a Rosette has been awarded for an issue that seems to us to offer extraordinary value for money, but that presupposes that the performance or performances are outstanding too. The choice is essentially a personal one (although often it represents a shared view), and in some cases it is applied to an issue where certain reservations must also be mentioned in the text of the review. The Rosette symbol is placed before the usual evaluation and the record number. It is quite small – we do not mean to imply an 'Academy Award' but a personal token of appreciation for something uniquely valuable. We hope that, once the reader has discovered and perhaps acquired a 'rosetted' CD, its special qualities will soon become apparent.

DIGITAL RECORDINGS
Nearly all new compact discs are recorded digitally, but an increasingly large number of digitally remastered, reissued analogue recordings are now appearing, and we think it important to include a clear indication of the difference:

Dig. This indicates that the master recording was digitally encoded.

BARGAIN AND SUPER-BARGAIN ISSUES
Since the publication of our last main volume we have seen a further huge expansion of the mid- and bargain-price labels from all the major companies. These are usually standard-repertoire works in excellent analogue recordings, digitally remastered. Often these reissue CDs are generous in playing time, increasing their value to the collector. There are also even cheaper classical CDs at super-bargain price, usually featuring performances by artists whose names are not internationally familiar, notably on the (now rightly famous) Naxos label. While many of these recordings derive from Eastern Europe, where recording costs have in the past been much lower than in the West, now this enterprising company is spreading its wings to embrace major orchestras and ensembles from Great Britain and Ireland and from overseas, too, even as far away as New Zealand.

A further super-bargain label, appropriately called Discover, has also appeared quite recently. Most of these inexpensive issues are digitally encoded, and some offer outstanding value, both technically and musically. The major companies have responded vigorously to this competition, not only by issuing super-bargain issues of their own (as under the DG

Classikon and Polygram Belart logos) but also by the introduction of Duos and Doubles: two CDs packaged back-to-back in a single jewel-case, generously filled with top-line repertoire and offered for the cost of a single premium-priced CD. The most recent addition to the bargain duos is on the EMI Seraphim label, where two CDs are offered for the cost of a single *medium-priced* disc. Thus the collector has plenty of scope in deciding how much to pay for a recorded performance, with a CD range from about £5 up to nearly three times that amount.

Our listing of each recording first indicates if it is not in fact in the premium-price category, as follows:

(M) Medium-priced label

(B) Bargain-priced label

(BB) Super-bargain label

See below for price structures for CDs and cassettes in the UK and the USA.

LAYOUT OF TEXT

We have aimed to make our style as simple as possible, even though the catalogue numbers of recordings are no longer as straightforward as they once were. So, immediately after the evaluation and before the catalogue number, the record make is given, often in abbreviated form (a key to the abbreviations is provided on pages xxii–xxiii). In the case of a set of two or more CDs, the number of units involved is given in brackets after the catalogue number, unless that catalogue number itself makes the fact explicit. Cassette numbers are still denoted by being given in italic type.

AMERICAN CATALOGUE NUMBERS

The numbers which follow in square brackets are US catalogue numbers, while the abbreviation [id.] indicates that the American number is identical to the European, which is increasingly becoming the case. Even BMG/RCA has recently moved over to completely identical numbers, although earlier issues have an alphabetical prefix in the UK which is not used by the *Schwann* catalogue in the USA.

There are certain other small differences to be remembered by American readers. For instance, a CBS/Sony number could have a completely different catalogue number on either side of the Atlantic, or it could use the same digits with different alphabetical prefixes, although this now seldom occurs. Both will be clearly indicated. EMI/Angel use extra digits for their British compact discs; thus the American number CDC 47001 becomes CDC7 47001-2 in Britain (the -2 is the European indication that this is a compact disc). We have taken care to check catalogue information as far as is possible, but as all the editorial work has been done in England there is always the possibility of error; American readers are therefore invited, when ordering records locally, to take the precaution of giving their dealer the fullest information about the music and recordings they want.

The indications (M), (B) and (BB) immediately before the starring of a disc refer only to the British record, as pricing systems are not always identical on both sides of the Atlantic.

Where no American catalogue number is given, this does not necessarily mean that a record is not available in the USA; the transatlantic issue may not have been made at the time of the publication of this *Yearbook*. Readers are advised to check the current *Schwann* catalogue and to consult their local record store.

ABBREVIATIONS

To save space, we have adopted a number of standard abbreviations in listing orchestras and performing groups (a list is provided below), and the titles of works are often shortened, especially where they are listed several times. Artists' forenames are sometimes omitted if they are not absolutely necessary for identification purposes. Also we have not usually listed the contents of operatic highlights and collections; these can sometimes be found in *The Classical Catalogue*, published by *Gramophone* magazine (177–179, Kenton Road, Kenton, Harrow, Middlesex, HA3 0HA, England).

We have followed common practice in the use of the original language for titles where it seems sensible. In most cases, English is used for orchestral and instrumental music and the original language for vocal music and opera. There are exceptions, however; for instance, the Johann Strauss discography uses the German language in the interests of consistency.

ORDER OF MUSIC

The order of music under each composer's name broadly follows that adopted by *The Classical Catalogue*: orchestral music, including concertos and symphonies; chamber music; solo instrumental music (in some cases with keyboard and organ music separated); vocal and choral music; opera; vocal collections; miscellaneous collections.

The Classical Catalogue now usually includes stage works alongside opera; in the main we have not followed this practice, preferring to list, say, ballet music and incidental music (where no vocal items are involved) in the general orchestral group. Within each group our listing follows an alphabetical sequence, and couplings within a single composer's output are *usually* discussed together instead of separately with cross-references. Occasionally and inevitably because of this alphabetical approach, different recordings of a given work can become separated when a record is listed and discussed under the first work of its alphabetical sequence. The Editor feels that alphabetical consistency is essential if the reader is to learn to find his or her way about.

CATALOGUE NUMBERS

Enormous care has gone into the checking of CD catalogue numbers and contents to ensure that all details are correct, but the editor and publishers cannot be held responsible for any mistakes that may have crept in despite all our zealous checking. This especially applies to a *Yearbook*, which includes all new recordings and where there has not been a passage of time when experience can reveal errors. When ordering CDs, readers are urged to provide their record-dealer with full details of the music and performers, as well as the catalogue number.

DELETIONS

Compact discs, especially earlier, full-priced issues not too generous in musical content, are now steadily succumbing to the deletions axe, and more are likely to disappear during the lifetime of this book. Sometimes copies may still be found in specialist shops, and there remains the compensatory fact that most really important and desirable recordings are eventually reissued, usually costing less!

Readers will note that EMI's new Special Import Service, which began in August 1995, means that the whole EMI international catalogue will be available to UK customers, restoring over 1,000 EMI and Virgin classical titles. EMI suggest that dealers should be able to get these special import discs in not more than eight days, and such records will probably cost about £1 more than in the UK catalogue.

COVERAGE

As the output of major and minor labels continues to expand, it will obviously be impossible for us to mention *every* CD that is available, even in an ongoing survey. We have to be carefully selective in choosing the discs to be included (although on rare occasions a recording has been omitted simply because a review copy was not available); anything which eludes us can always be included next time. However, we do welcome suggestions from readers about such omissions if they seem to be of special interest, and particularly if they are inexpensive. But borderline music on specialist labels that are not readily and reliably obtainable on both sides of the Atlantic cannot be given any kind of priority.

ACKNOWLEDGEMENTS

Our thanks, as ever, are due to Roger Wells, our copy editor, who has worked closely alongside us throughout the preparation of this book and, as a keen CD collector himself, also frequently made valuable creative suggestions. Kathleen March once again zealously checked the proofs for errors and reminded us when the text proved ambiguous, clumsily repetitive in its descriptive terminology, or just plain contradictory. Barbara Menard and Roy Randle contributed to the titling – never an easy task, and especially complicated in the many boxed anthologies involving a bouquet of different performers. Our team of Penguin proofreaders are also indispensable. Grateful thanks also go to all those readers who write to us to point out factual errors and remind us of important recordings which have escaped our notice.

Finally, we again welcome back to our cover the whimsical portrait of Nipper, the most famous dog in the world. He is associated with a deservedly world-famous trademark and reminds us that fine records have been available from this source for almost exactly one hundred years!

Price Differences in the UK and USA

Compact discs and cassettes in all price ranges are more expensive in Britain and Europe than they are in the USA but, fortunately, in nearly all cases the various premium-price, mid-price, bargain and super-bargain categories are fairly consistent on both sides of the Atlantic. However, where records are imported in either direction, this can affect their domestic cost. For instance, (British) EMI's Classics for Pleasure is in the mid-price range in the USA, whereas CfP is a bargain series in the UK. Naxos, a super-bargain digital label in the UK, is a bargain label in the USA. EMI Eminence is a full-price label in the USA, as is Mercury. Some Polygram issues (DG, Decca, Philips), both single CDs and sets, which are at mid-price in the UK are at full price in the USA.

Vox Boxes are exceptionally good value at super-budget price in America, while in Britain they are comparable with the Duos and 'two for the price of one' series. Of course retail prices are not fixed in either country, and various stores may offer even better deals at times, so our price structure must be taken as a guideline only. One major difference in the USA is that almost all companies make a dollar surcharge (per disc) for mid-priced opera sets (to cover the cost of librettos) and Angel apply this levy to all their boxed sets. The Carlton IMP compact disc series appear to be available only as a special import in the USA. The Vanguard CD label is upper-middle price in the USA ($12.19–$13.99) but lower-middle price in the UK. In *listing* records we have not used the major record companies' additional label subdivisions (like Decca/London's Ovation, DG's Galleria, EMI's Studio and Références, Philips's Concert Classics, Sony's Essential Classics and so on) in order to avoid further confusion, although these designations are sometimes referred to in the text of reviews.

Comparable prices in the UK and USA

Premium-priced CDs (although they cost less west of the Atlantic) are top-price repertoire the world over. Here are comparative details of the other price ranges:

(M) MID-PRICED SERIES (sets are multiples of these prices)
Includes: Chandos (Collect); Decca/London; DG; EMI/Angel (Studio and Références; Eminence, UK only); Erato/Warner (UK), Erato/WEA (USA); HM/BMG (UK), DHM/BMG (USA); Mercury (UK only); Philips; Saga; RCA; Sony; Teldec/Warner (UK), Teldec/WEA (USA); Unicorn (UK only).

   UK
   CDs: under £10; more usually £8–£9.50
   Cassettes: around £5–£6
   USA
   CDs: under $12 (usually $9.99, but sometimes $11.99)
   Cassettes: $5–$6.50 – but very few are available

(B) Duos – two CDs for the cost of one premium-priced CD, which results in an 'upper' bargain price per disc but compensates by offering exceptionally generous playing time.
Includes: EMI Rouge et Noir (CZS); Erato Bonsai Duos; Decca/London and DG Doubles; Philips Duos
(B) BARGAIN-PRICED SERIES (sets are multiples of these prices)
Includes: Decca/London; CfP (UK only); Harmonia Mundi Musique d'Abord; Hungaroton White Label; Philips; Carlton IMP (UK only); RCA; Sony.

UK

CDs: £5–£7.50

Cassettes: around £4

USA

CDs: under $7

Cassettes: around $4 – but very few are available

SPECIAL SETS: Vox Boxes cost only $5 per disc in the USA, but (alongside the Turnabout Doubles) are UK imports and are priced at around £5–£6 per disc in Britain, where available. EMI CZS multiple sets are also within the bargain range in the UK but may cost rather more in the USA.

Seraphim EMI doubles – 2 CDs for the price of 1 medium-priced disc (in both countries)

(BB) SUPER-BARGAIN SERIES – CDs

Includes: ASV (UK only); Discover; DG Classikon; Naxos; Polygram Belart; RCA Navigator (not yet available in the USA); Virgin (Virgo).

UK

CDs: under £5; some (including Discover) cost around £4

USA

CDs: $6

(In some cases, equivalent cassettes are available, usually costing slightly less than bargain cassettes.)

An International Mail-order Source for Recordings in the UK

Readers are urged to support a local dealer if he is prepared and able to give a proper service, and to remember that obtaining many CDs involves expertise and perseverance. However, because of the recession many specialist sources have disappeared and for that reason, if any difficulty is experienced in obtaining the CDs you want, we suggest the following mail-order alternative, which offers competitive discount, operates world wide and is under the direction of the Editor of *The Penguin Guide to Compact Discs*, whose advice on choice of recordings is always readily available to mail-order customers:

PG Dept
Squires Gate Music Centre
Squires Gate Station Approach
Blackpool
Lancashire FY8 2SP
England
Tel.: 01253 344360 Fax: 01253 406686

This organization patiently extends compact disc orders until they finally come to hand. A full guarantee of safe delivery is made on any order undertaken. Please write for further details, or make a trial credit card order, by fax or telephone.

❀ The Rosette Service

Squires Gate also offers a try-before-you-buy weekly loan service (within the UK only) so that customers can try out at home rosetted recordings, plus a hand-picked group of recommended key repertoire works, for a small charge, without any obligation to purchase. If a CD is subsequently purchased, it will be discounted and the trial charge waived. Full details sent on request.

Squires Gate Music Centre also offers a simple bi-monthly mailing, listing a hand-picked selection of current new and reissued CDs, chosen by the Editor of the *Penguin Guide*, Ivan March. Regular customers of Squires Gate Music Centre, both domestic and overseas, receive the bulletin as available, and it is sent automatically with their purchases.

An International Mail-order Source for Recordings in the USA

American readers seeking a domestic mail-order source may write to the following address, where a comparably expert and caring supply service is in operation (for both American and imported European labels). Please write for further details (enclosing a stamped, self-addressed envelope if within the USA) or make a trial order by letter, fax or phone to:

PG Dept
Serenade Records
1800 M St, N.W.
Washington DC 20036
USA
Tel.: (202) 638-5580 Fax: (202) 783-0372
Tel.: (for US orders only) 1-800-237-2930

Regular customers of Serenade Records, both domestic and overseas, will also receive the bi-monthly mailing, with a hand-picked selection of current new and reissued CDs chosen by the Editor of the *Penguin Guide*, Ivan March.

Abbreviations

AAM	Academy of Ancient Music	Hung.	Hungaroton
Ac.	Academy, Academic	L.	London
Amb. S.	Ambrosian Singers	LAPO	Los Angeles Philharmonic Orchestra
Ang.	Angel		
Ara.	Arabesque	LCO	London Chamber Orchestra
arr.	arranged		
ASMF	Academy of St Martin-in-the-Fields	LMP	London Mozart Players
		LOP	Lamoureux Orchestra of Paris
Bar.	Baroque		
Bav.	Bavarian	LPO	London Philharmonic Orchestra
BPO	Berlin Philharmonic Orchestra	LSO	London Symphony Orchestra
Cal.	Calliope		
Cap.	Caprice	Mer.	Meridian
CBSO	City of Birmingham Symphony Orchestra	Met.	Metropolitan
		MoC	Ministry of Culture
CfP	Classics for Pleasure	movt	movement
Ch.	Choir; Chorale; Chorus	N.	North, Northern
Chan.	Chandos	nar.	narrated
CO	Chamber Orchestra	Nat.	National
COE	Chamber Orchestra of Europe	NY	New York
		O	Orchestra, Orchestre
Col. Mus. Ant.	Musica Antiqua, Cologne	OAE	Orchestra of the Age of Enlightenment
Coll.	Collegium		
Coll. Aur.	Collegium Aureum	O-L	Oiseau-Lyre
Coll. Mus.	Collegium Musicum	Op.	Opera (in performance listings); opus (in music titles)
Concg. O	Royal Concertgebouw Orchestra of Amsterdam		
		orch.	orchestrated
cond.	conductor, conducted	ORTF	L'Orchestre de la radio et télévision française
Cons.	Consort		
DG	Deutsche Grammophon	Ph.	Philips
Dig.	digital recording	Phd.	Philadelphia
E.	England, English	Philh.	Philharmonia
ECCO	European Community Chamber Orchestra	PO	Philharmonic Orchestra
		Qt	Quartet
ECO	English Chamber Orchestra	R.	Radio
		RLPO	Royal Liverpool Philharmonic Orchestra
Ens.	Ensemble		
Fr.	French		
GO	Gewandhaus Orchestra	ROHCG	Royal Opera House, Covent Garden
HM	Harmonia Mundi France		
HM/RCA	Deutsche Harmonia Mundi	RPO	Royal Philharmonic Orchestra

RSO	Radio Symphony Orchestra	Sup.	Supraphon
S.	South	trans.	transcription, transcribed
SCO	Scottish Chamber Orchestra	V.	Vienna
Sinf.	Sinfonietta	Van.	Vanguard
SNO	Royal Scottish National Orchestra	VCM	Vienna Concentus Musicus
SO	Symphony Orchestra	VPO	Vienna Philharmonic Orchestra
Soc.	Society	VSO	Vienna Symphony Orchestra
Sol. Ven.	I Solisti Veneti	W.	West
SRO	Suisse Romande Orchestra		

Adam, Adolphe (1803–56)

Giselle (ballet): complete.
(BB) *** Naxos Dig. 8.550755/6 [id.]. Slovak RSO, Mogrelia.

Andrew Mogrelia is a ballet conductor to his fingertips and he has already given us a first-class Naxos set of Tchaikovsky's *Swan Lake* ballet. His complete *Giselle* is hardly less attractive, using the normal performing edition, including interpolated scenes by Friedrich Burgmüller, and by Minkus, which means that it offers some 1 hour 54 minutes of music. The orchestral playing has grace and elegance and plenty of life: the brass are not ashamed of the melodrama. The recording is resonantly full and warm in ambience, yet well detailed. Bonynge's performance on Decca is just that bit more strongly characterized and the Decca sound has a slightly sharper profile. That remains first choice (at mid-price – see our main volume), but this Naxos set costs considerably less. Certainly it upstages Mark Ermler's Royal Opera House, Covent Garden, version which, fine as it is, becomes uncompetitive at premium price. However, Michael Tilson Thomas's generous single CD selection with the LSO on Sony, which offers all the important music and was recorded, like Bonynge's set, in the Henry Wood Hall, is still worth considering, for the LSO playing is beautifully polished (SK 42450).

Le Diable à quatre (ballet; complete).
(M) *** Decca 444 111-2 [id.]. LSO, Richard Bonynge (with MASSENET: *La Navaraise: Nocturne.*
    Don César de Bazan: Sévillana. Les Erinnyes: Invocation; BIZET: *Don Procopio: Entr'acte to Act*
    II; GOUNOD: *Le Tribut de Zamora, Act III: Danse grecque* ***).

Here is an unmissable addition to Decca's new Ballet Gala series worthy to be set beside this company's sparkling Lanchbery record of Hérold's *La Fille mal gardée* (430 849-2 – see our main volume). Adam's *Le Diable à quatre* was recorded in the same vintage period (1964) and, as the opening Act immediately demonstrates, produces Decca's top ballet quality, with glowing horns and woodwind, and wonderfully vivid detail. This was the seventh of Adam's thirteen ballets, arriving in 1845, four years after *Giselle*. Throughout the score the composer's felicitous sense of orchestral colouring (perhaps even more sophisticated here than in *Giselle*) pleases the ear in this continuously melodic score. It may be inconsequential but, when Richard Bonynge points the elegant writing for the strings so seductively, it makes a splendid entertainment. Moreover, for this reissue Decca have found five equally winning *entr'actes* from their vaults (bringing the playing time up to 75 minutes), and these pieces are even more melodically characterful than the main work. Bizet's *Don Procopio* comes from his student days, yet the excerpt here audaciously pre-echoes *Carmen*, while Massenet's *Invocation* from *Les Erinnyes* brings a luscious cello solo (which turns out to be an old favourite, called *Elégie*). Douglas Cummings plays it with a combination of delicate grace, swooning romantic feeling and a fine sense of style. The closing *Sévillana* glitters with castanets and local Spanish colour, observed through a Gallic sensibility. Bonynge clearly relishes all these items and presents them with characteristic polish and spontaneity. The 1971 Decca sound is every bit as warm, richly hued and immediate as the complete ballet.

Adams, John (born 1947)

Chamber symphony; Grand pianola music.
*** Elektra Nonesuch/Warner Dig. 7559 79219-2 [id.]. L. Sinf., composer.

This Elektra coupling combines the *Grand pianola music*, one of the most immediately accessible and inspired examples of minimalism, with a piece that is initally more intractable, the *Chamber symphony*, written for 15 instruments and inspired by Schoenberg's Opus 9 (the choice of instrumentation is both comparable and different). Unlike the Schoenberg, this piece is in three clearly defined movements, requiring great virtuosity from its performers. The first, *Mongrel airs*, was originally entitled *Discipline et punire*, but the composer tells us that he changed it 'to honour a British critic who complained that my music lacked breeding'. The writing is spiky (with an additional Stravinskian flavour) but there is an underlying good-natured lyricism that offsets its abrasiveness, and the ear is bracingly stimulated. The second movement, a sombre *Aria with walking bass*, is sung by a melancholy solo horn, which resumes after various enigmatically intricate interruptions from its companions. *Roadrunner*, the bizarre, jazzy finale, with its constant *moto perpetuo* supply of energy, has a link with the composer's young son Sam's love of cartoons from the 1950s, and the work is dedicated to him. It is surely given a definitive performance here.
    Grand pianola music is in three sections, the first possessing the most fascinating aural detail, dominated by the piano filigree, but with vocal, woodwind, brass and percussive interjections making

up a kaleidoscopic texture which is hypnotically compulsive in its climactic progress. After a more serene central movement the finale builds to a huge climax, using a simple but unforgettably swinging semi-chorale as its basis. In the composer's hands this projects with overwhelmingly thrilling impact, and throughout the balancing of the composite elements, notably the three 'siren' soprano voices, is near ideal. With extensive and illuminating notes from John Adams himself, this is a key issue in the Adams discography.

Grand pianola music; Short ride in a fast machine (arr. for wind band by Lawrence T. Odom).
**(*) Chan. Dig. CHAN 9393 [id.]. Netherlands Wind Ens., Stephen Moscow – LANG: *Are you experienced?* etc. (***)

John Adams' *Short ride in a fast machine* ought to be his popular equivalent of Samuel Barber's *Adagio*, although it is utterly different. Marked 'Delirio', it is rocket-powered, has unstoppable exhilaration and, as presented here, does not go on for a moment too long. It sounds splendid in the clever arrangement for wind ensemble by Lawrence T. Odom. *Grand pianola music* also suits the Netherlands group as it is scored for two obbligato pianos, three sopranos and an ensemble of woodwind, brass and percussion. It is very seductively played and the glowing ambience adds to the colour of the first two movements, even if detail is less well defined than in the composer's own recording, notably the female voices, which are integrated into the texture (whereas, on the evidence of the Elektra Nonesuch version, Adams wants their siren call to be heard in its own right). Stephen Moscow's account of the last movement also misses some of the sheer physical exhilaration of the climax. The couplings, too, are a highly debatable proposition.

Addinsell, Richard (1904–77)

Film and theatre music: *Fire over England: suite. Goodbye Mr Chips: theme* (arr. Alwyn). *Journey to Romance* (radio feature): *Invocation. The Prince and the Showgirl:* selection (arr. Felton Rapley). *Ring round the Moon: Invitation waltz* (orch. Alwyn). (i) *A Tale of Two Cities: Theme* (arr. Gamley). *Tom Brown's Schooldays: Overture* (arr. Alwyn). (ii) *Trespass: Festival* (beguine). *The Isle of Apples;* (ii) *Smokey Mountain concerto;* (i) *Tune in G.*
**(*) Marco Polo Dig. 8.223732 [id.]. BBC Concert O, Kenneth Alwyn, with (i) Roderick Elms; (ii) Philip Martin.

Richard Addinsell was above all a tunesmith, and some older readers will remember the English cabaret songs he wrote in collaboration with Joyce Grenfell for her wartime one-woman revues, of which '*I'm going to see you today*' is the most famous. The romantic theme for the *Warsaw concerto* (not included here) was based on a rumba the composer had written in his undergraduate days. It was Roy Douglas (uncredited at the time) who constructed that memorable concert-piece, which is still as popular as ever after fifty years. Throughout his composing career Addinsell left the scoring and arrangements of his ideas to others, and the present recorded collection owes much to the skill of its conductor, Kenneth Alwyn, who has pieced a good deal of the material together – where original scores are lost, notably in the 'Overture' from the film music for *Tom Brown's Schooldays* and the charming introductory sequence for *Goodbye Mr Chips*. Not all Addinsell's invention is distinguished, and, as with most film music, there is a good deal of hyperbole, but the *Invitation waltz* for Christopher Fry's translation, *Ring round the Moon*, of Jean Anouilh's *L'Invitation au château* is quite haunting, as it the gentle idyll, *The Isle of apples*, and the simple *Tune in G* with its piano embroidery. These pieces, like the *Smokey Mountain concerto*, were independent compositions, and the latter in its slow movement, *Valley song*, brings another characteristically gentle tune with just a tinge of Rachmaninov. Addinsell asked Douglas Gamley to rearrange the title-theme of *A Tale of Two Cities* for piano and orchestra (as presented here), hoping it would repeat the success of the *Warsaw concerto* but – perhaps not surprisingly – it didn't. Perhaps Roy Douglas was needed to bring it off. Alwyn and the BBC Concert Orchestra are thoroughly at home in this repertoire and they present it all freshly. The recording, using the Golders Green Hippodrome, gives a suitably bright but rather brash sonority to the orchestra.

Aho, Kalevi (born 1949)

(i) *Symphony No. 8;* (ii) *Pergamon.*
*** BIS Dig. CD 646 [id.]. (i) Hans-Ola Ericsson; (ii) Pauili Pietiläinen, Lilli Paasikivi, Eeva-Liisa
Saarinen, Tom Nyman, Matti Lehtinen; Lahti SO, Osmo Vänskä.

The *Eighth Symphony* for organ and orchestra is an ambitious 50-minute piece of unusual design: it
consists of three Scherzo movements, linked by interludes in which the organ is a dominant
protagonist, and flanked by an introduction and epilogue. It is often imaginative and at times
imposing in its massive sonorities, and the integration of the organ into the orchestral texture is
masterly. It does not quite sustain its length and one is left wondering whether this music establishes a
sufficiently individual sound-world. Aho is highly gifted and the piece has a powerful sweep. The
filler is *Pergamon*, a pretentious multi-lingual setting (four narrators speak a text of Peter Weiss
simultaneously in German, Finnish, Swedish and Ancient Greek, with elaborate instrumental support)
to pretty negligible effect.

Albéniz, Isaac (1860–1909)

*Cantos de España: Cordoba, Op. 232/4; Mallorca (Barcarola), Op. 202. Suite española: Cataluña;
Granada; Sevilla; Cádiz, Op.47/1–4.*
⊛ (BB) *** RCA Navigator Dig. 74321 17903-2. Julian Bream (guitar) – GRANADOS: *Collection;*
RODRIGO: *3 Piezas españolas.* *** ⊛

Julian Bream is in superb form in this splendid recital (apparently his own favourite record), vividly
recorded in the pleasingly warm acoustic of Wardour Chapel, near his home in Wiltshire. The CD is
electrifying, giving an uncanny impression of the great guitarist sitting and making music just beyond
the loudspeakers. The playing itself has wonderfully communicative rhythmic feeling, great subtlety
of colour, and its spontaneity increases the impression that one is experiencing a 'live' recital. The
performance of the haunting *Córdoba*, which ends the group, is unforgettable. The new super-
bargain Navigator reissue includes additionally the *Tres piezas españolas* of Rodrigo. This is now the
finest single recital of Spanish guitar music in the catalogue and a bargain of bargains.

d'Albert, Eugen (1864–1932)

Piano concertos Nos. 1 in B min., Op. 2; 2 in E, Op. 12.
*** Hyp. Dig. CDA 66747 [id.]. Piers Lane, BBC Scottish SO, Alun Francis.

British-born (in Glasgow in 1864), but totally Germanized in his teens, Eugen d'Albert is best
remembered as composer of the opera, *Tiefland*, and a handful of piano pieces. But in his youth, as a
virtuoso pianist and a devotee of Liszt, he wrote these two formidable piano concertos, each in a
cyclical single movement, and here brilliantly performed by Piers Lane. D'Albert was a composition-
pupil of Sullivan and a protégé of both Hans Richter and Liszt, who invited him to Weimar and
proclaimed that he knew of 'no more gifted as well as dazzling talent than that of d'Albert'. The
young musician settled in Germany and briefly became the third husband of the celebrated virtuoso
Teresa Carreño. He succeeded Joachim as the director of the Berlin Hochschüle für Musik, where his
students included Backhaus and Dohnányi. The *Piano concerto No. 1 in B minor* (1884), the
inspiration of a twenty-year-old, is the more ambitious of the two works, a 45-minute span, written in
a style half-way between Liszt and Rachmaninov, a warmly lyrical mix, lacking only the sharp
memorability of a masterwork. There was an earlier essay in the form, in A major, written when
D'Albert was a boy of seventeen, the year in which Hans Richter took him to Vienna. The present
concerto was dedicated to Liszt. This, its first recording, is an unqualified success, and Piers Lane
plays with delicacy and virtuosity and is well supported by the BBC Scottish Symphony Orchestra.
Its musical substance may not be immediately memorable but is always pleasing, and almost (but not
quite) sustains its length. There is a rather extraordinary fugal outburst towards the end of the work.
Nevertheless for a nineteen-year-old it is a formidable achievement. The *Piano concerto No. 2 in E
major* is a one-movement piece, though in four sections, following the style of Liszt's concertos, and
was written in 1893, by which time d'Albert had embarked on the first of his twenty or so operas. His
was a cultured rather than a distinctive voice. The recording is expertly balanced by Tony Kime. In
Hyperion's outstanding 'Romantic Piano Concerto' series this is one of the most successful issues yet,
very well recorded.

Albert, Stephen (1941–92)

Cello concerto.
*** Sony Dig. SK 57961 [id.]. Yo-Yo Ma, Baltimore SO, David Zinman – BARTOK: *Viola concerto;*
BLOCH: *Schelomo.* ***

Stephen Albert was a New Yorker who came to wider notice in 1985 when his symphony *River-run* was awarded the Pulitzer Prize. He taught composition at the Juilliard School from 1988 until his death in a car accident in December 1992. The *Cello concerto* (1989–90) was written in response'to a commission from the Baltimore Symphony Orchestra for a 15-minute orchestral piece, but this subsequently became a *Cello concerto* for Yo-Yo Ma. The idiom is both tonal and distinctive, and should enjoy an appeal for those who like Bartók and Shostakovich, though Albert resembles neither. He is very much his own man and his music is both inventive and imaginative. Yo-Yo Ma and the Baltimore orchestra give a passionately committed account of it and are superbly recorded.

Albinoni, Tommaso (1671–1750)

Adagio in G min. for organ and strings (arr. Giazotto).
(B) *** Carlton Dig. PCD 2001. Scottish CO, Laredo (with String masterpieces ***).

This bargain-priced, digitally recorded Carlton (formerly Pickwick) account of Giazotto's Albinoni confection is strongly contoured and most responsively played by the Scottish Chamber Orchestra under Jaime Laredo. Other versions are listed in the Concerts section.

12 Concerti a cinque, Op. 5.
(M) *** Ph. Dig. 442 658-2 [id.]. Pina Carmirelli, I Musici.

Even today, after much exposure on CD, Albinoni remains unjustly overshadowed by many of his contemporaries (and doomed to be represented in the consciousness of the wider public by Giazotto's famous *Adagio* arrangement). Yet his invention is unfailingly fresh and vital, and this body of concertos has variety and resource to recommend it. Each is in three movements, with the finale fugal, but no simpler or jollier fugues can be found – if one discounts those in the *Concerti grossi* of Handel. I Musici with Pina Carmirelli as the solo player are every bit as fresh as the music, and they are afforded altogether first-rate digital sound. This is one of the best sets of its kind among recent reissues; those prepared to explore these concertos will be well rewarded.

Oboe concertos, Op. 7/3, 6, 9 & 12; Op. 9/2, 5, 8 & 11.
*** Chan. Dig. CHAN 0579 [id.]. Anthony Robson, Coll. Mus. 90, Simon Standage.

Like Sarah Francis before him (on Unicorn DKPC 9088), Anthony Robson plays all eight solo concertos from Op. 7 and Op. 9, but using a period oboe (a modern copy of a Stanesby, made in London in 1710). His tone is most appealing and his phrasing and musicianship are second to none. Simon Standage provides alert accompaniments, also using original instruments, and creates bright, athletic string-timbres. The effect has slightly less flexibility in matters of dynamic than is possible using a modern instrument, but it is still both pleasing and stimulating. Authenticists need not hesitate.

Concerti a cinque, Op. 9/2, 5, 8 & 11.
(M) *** Virgin/EMI Veritas Dig. VER5 61152-2 [id.]. Hans de Vries, Alma Musica Amsterdam,
Bob van Asperen – TELEMANN: *Oboe concertos.* ***

Hans de Vries plays a baroque oboe, made by Gottlob Crone in Leipzig around 1735, and produces a most appealing timbre, while his technique is remarkably assured and true. There are several fine collections of Op. 9, but none more authentic than this. There is one cavil: Michael Talbot in his excellent notes comments that the composer specified that these concerti are 'with' rather than 'for' oboe, in which case the solo balance seems a shade too forward, even though the interaction with the strings (which are well in the picture) is effectively managed. The accompaniments are as alert and stylish as the solo playing and there is not a trace of vinegar in the string-timbre. Albinoni's adagios are justly famous for their expressive feeling and that provided for Op.9/11 has a little in common with the most famous example, well known in Giazotto's spurious adaptation. However, it is played as the composer conceived it and is as refined as it is beautiful.

6 Sonate da chiesa, Op. 4; 12 Trattenimenti armonici per camera, Op. 6.
*** Hyp. Dig. CDA 66831/2 [id.]. Locatelli Trio.

What we know of Albinoni derives almost entirely from his concertos, so this Hyperion set offering some key chamber works is especially valuable. The set of '*Church' sonatas* was published in 1708 and, while it is possible that their publisher, Estienne Roger (of Amsterdam), gave these works their descriptive title, the presence of many expressive movements of particular poignancy, showing the composer at his most lyrically appealing, does contrast them with Op. 6. *Trattenimento* indicates 'Entertainment', suggesting a more secular style; and certainly the allegros of Op. 6 are strikingly lively and infectiously dance-like in character. The slow movements are often more formal, although never dull. Both sets of works are in the four-movement plan usual for *sonate da chiesa*: slow – quick – slow – quick, and in Op. 4 the opening *Adagio* movements are notably serene. Paul Nicholson, the excellent continuo player of the Locatelli Trio, understands this well enough and he uses a discreet and often touchingly understated organ continuo to support the violin and cello in Op. 4 and a harpsichord in Op. 6. The performances, using original instruments, are of high quality, well paced, sensitive and fresh, and the recording is well balanced and vivid.

Il nascimento dell'Aurora (festa pastorale; complete).
(B) **(*) Erato/Warner Dig. 4509 96374-2 (2) [id.]. Anderson, Zimmermann, Klare, Browne, Yamaj,
    Sol. Ven., Scimone.

Albinoni's instrumental music has ridden into popularity on the Baroque wave, but this is the first major vocal piece to have been recorded (in 1983) and its bargain-price reissue is welcome. Written as a court celebration, probably on the birth of Princess Maria-Theresa, daughter of Charles VI of Austria, its 26 movements, mostly brief and lively, make up a substantial and attractive two-hour stage entertainment or 'festa pastorale'. This well-balanced live recording, made in Vicenza, Italy, puts forward a persuasive case despite some roughness in the choral singing (which is particularly distracting in the first chorus) and some intrusive audience applause. Soloists are first rate and the orchestra generally stylish. The CD transfer is excellently managed, improving definition without ambient loss. With full libretto and translation included, this is well worth exploring.

Alfvén, Hugo (1872–1960)

A Legend of the Skerries, Op. 20; Swedish rhapsodies Nos. 1 (Midsummer watch), Op. 19; 2 (Uppsala rhapsody), Op. 24; 3 (Dala rhapsody), Op. 47; King Gustav Adolf II, Op. 49: Adagio.
*** Chan. Dig. CHAN 9313 [id.]. Iceland SO, Sakari.

There are several versions of Alfvén's masterpiece, *Midsommarvaka* (*Midsummer Vigil*) in the catalogue, and Neeme Järvi has recorded the other rhapsodies and *A Legend of the Skerries* as fill-ups to the symphonies. But for those who do not have (or perhaps do not want) all five symphonies, this disc will be ideal. Petri Sakari is a totally unaffected guide in this repertory and secures excellent playing from the Icelandic orchestra. *Midsummer Vigil* is quintessential Sweden and so, too, is the affecting *Elegy* from the incidental music to Ludwig Nordström's play about *Gustav II Adolf*. Sakari produces more musically satisfying results than his more glamorous countryman, Salonen, in the *Midsummer Vigil*, and this useful anthology can be warmly recommended. The Chandos sound is excellent.

Alkan, Charles (1813–88)

Alleluia, Op. 25; 4 Impromptus, Op. 32; Deuxième recueil d'impromptus, Op. 32; Rondeau chromatique, Op. 12; Salut, cendre du pauvre!, Op. 45; Super flumina Babylonis: Paraphrase on Psalm 137, Op. 52. Variations on a theme from Steibelt's Orage concerto, Op. 1.
*(*) Marco Polo Dig. 8.223657 [id.]. Laurent Martin.

Alkan's output was extraordinarily uneven, music of vision rubbing shoulders with ideas that are positively trite. His muse visits him sporadically – hardly at all in the first set of the *Quatre impromptus*, although the second set is more interesting. In the second volume of his study of the composer, Ronald Smith calls the latter 'one of the most curious collections ever published, and is the fruit of Alkan's encounter with the Zorcico, a basque dance in 5/4', and of the first he says, 'Had Grieg and Bartók conspired to write a mazurka for quintupeds they might have produced something like this.' Whatever the interest of these and some of the other pieces, it requires far more persuasive advocacy. Laurent Martin's playing, which we have admired in earlier issues, is at times imaginative but at others routine. However, he is handicapped by the unglamorous acoustic of the Clara Wieck Auditoriun in Heidelberg; the piano-sound tends to be shallow, and there is insufficient space round the aural image.

Esquisses, Op. 63.
*(*) Marco Polo Dig. 8.223352 [id.]. Laurent Martin.

The *Esquisses*, Op. 63, are Alkan's 'last and most important collection of miniatures' (Ronald Smith), 48 in all, traversing the complete cycle of keys twice and ending up in C. There is variety of mood and character. Some of them are remarkable, others banal, but all are worth hearing – albeit not at one sitting, given the quality of Marco Polo's recording, made in the somewhat cramped acoustic of the Tonstudio van Geest in Heidelberg. Laurent Martin's playing is good rather than transcendental (Smith recorded a handful of them rather more imaginatively), but the sound becomes shallow and hard when the dynamics rise.

Grande Sonate (Les quatre âges), Op. 33; Barcarolle; Le festin d'Esope; Sonatine, Op. 61.
*** Hyp. Dig. CDA 66794 [id.]. Marc-André Hamelin.

Under studio conditions, Marc-André Hamelin records works by Alkan with a virtuosity just as breathtaking as on his live Wigmore Hall disc, also for Hyperion (see our Recitals section, below). In his flair and brilliance he has rarely, if ever, been matched. Written six years before the Liszt *Sonata*, Alkan's *Grande Sonate* over its four massive movements represents the hero at various ages, with the second, *quasi-Faust*, the key one. The *Sonatine*, the most approachable of Alkan's major works, is just as dazzlingly done, with the hauntingly poetic *Barcarolle* and the swaggering *Festin d'Esope* as valuable makeweights.

Alwyn, William (1905–85)

Crépuscule for solo harp; Divertimento for solo flute; Clarinet sonata; Flute sonata; Oboe sonata; Sonata impromptu for violin and viola.
*** Chan. Dig. CHAN 9197 [id.]. London Haffner Wind Ens. (members), Nicholas Daniel; Julius Drake (piano).

The *Oboe sonata* is an inspired work; its *Andantino* has a melody which persists in the memory and is then charmingly elaborated by the oboe, while the waltz finale ends gently. It is beautifully played here by Nicholas Daniel and Julius Drake. The *Clarinet sonata* is a fantasy piece in which Joy Farrall combines extrovert freedom with a more thoughtful reserve, yet with wild excursions into the upper tessitura. By contrast the solo *Divertimento* for flute (the responsive Kate Hill) is neo-classical, featuring a fuguetta, variations on a ground, a *Gavotte, Musette,* and a sparkling *Gigue*. The *Crépuscule* for solo harp (Ieuan Jones), written in 1955, is a quiet evocation of a cold, clear and frosty Christmas Eve. The *Sonata for flute and piano* is characteristically inventive with another memorably tranquil slow movement, while the *Sonata impromptu for violin and viola* opens no less strikingly. Its second movement is a theme and variations, and the composer writes for the two instruments as if they were one. Alwyn demonstrates in all these works a natural skill in interweaving his part-writing and his usual ready flow of appealing melody. Overall this programme is consistently rewarding and the recording is very real and immediate.

Antill, John (1904–86)

Corroboree (ballet suite).
(*) Everest/Vanguard EVC 9007 [id.]. LSO, Sir Eugene Goossens – GINASTERA: *Estancia; Panambi *; VILLA-LOBOS: Little train of the Caipira. **(*)*

The ballet-score *Corroboree*, the best-known work by the Australian composer, John Antill, is based on an aboriginal dance ceremony. Its primitivism generates imaginatively exotic invention, very colourfully scored, to include an enticing *Dance to the Evening Star*, a strongly rhythmic *Rain dance* and a boisterously frantic *Closing fire ceremony*. The performance here generates plenty of energy, and if the recording is over-resonant it is immensely vivid. It is a pity that this Everest series is not in the mid-priced range, although it costs slightly less than the highest premium-priced CDs.

Arensky, Anton (1861–1906)

Piano concerto in F min., Op. 2; Fantasia on Russian folksongs, Op. 48.
*** Hyp. Dig. CDA 66624 [id.]. Coombs, BBC Scottsh SO, Maksymiuk – BORTKIEWICZ: *Piano concerto.* ***

Despite some moments of bombast and vulgarity, Arensky's *Piano concerto in F minor* is an endearing piece, highly Chopinesque in feeling and with some very appealing ideas. Although it has been recorded before, it has never been better served than in this Hyperion performance by Stephen Coombs and his Scottish forces. Coombs is an artist of great sensitivity and effortless virtuosity, and he makes out the best possible case for both the *Concerto* and the much shorter *Fantasia on Russian folksongs*. Good orchestral support and recording.

Piano trios Nos. 1 in D min., Op. 32; 2 in F min., Op. 73.
*** Ph. Dig. 442 127-2 [id.]. Beaux Arts Trio.

Piano trio No. 1 in D min, Op. 32.
**(*) Sony Dig. SK 53269 [id.]. Yefim Bronfman, Cho-Liang Lin, Gary Hoffman – TCHAIKOVSKY: *Piano trio.* **(*)

The Beaux Arts offer the more logical coupling. While the *D minor Trio* is well represented in the catalogue, its later companion is neglected, though there is a very acceptable version from the Borodin Trio, coupled with the Shostakovich Blok settings and Prokofiev's *Overture on Russian themes* on Chandos. However, the Beaux Arts is a first recommendation now: lively playing, full of engagement and sparkle, and very well recorded.

Yefim Bronfman, Cho-Liang Lin and Gary Hoffman give a strongly characterized performance of the delightful *First Trio* which would be a credible first choice, alongside the Beaux Arts, were it not for the recording. Bronfman is allowed to swamp his string partners, even though (as in the Scherzo) it is obvious that he is playing with delicacy. Both Cho-Liang Lin and Gary Hoffman are players of such refinement and insight that their contribution cannot fail to afford great pleasure. So does Yefim Bronfman, but he would have afforded more, had he been more discreetly balanced. If you can make allowances for this, there is really outstanding music-making here.

Suites for 2 pianos Nos. 1, Op. 15; 2 (Silhouettes), Op. 23; 3 (Variations), Op. 33; 4, Op. 62.
*** Hyp. Dig. CDA 66755 [id.]. Stephen Coombs, Ian Munro.

Arensky was enormously fluent and his invention proceeds with apparently effortless ease. Only the *Valse* from the *Suite No. 1* of 1888 is at all known, yet all the music here is endearingly fresh. Small wonder that he belonged for a time to Tchaikovsky's circle, for he has the same abundance of inspiration and natural warmth. The *Polonaise*, which ends this suite, would not disgrace a ballet by Tchai-kovsky. *Suite No. 2*, written four years later, is subtitled *Silhouettes*, and each of its five movements represents a different character, *Le Savant* ('The Scholar'), *La Coquette*, and so on. The middle movement, *Polichinelle*, is deliciously played by this remarkable duo partnership who show virtuosity and delicacy in equal measure. *Suite No. 3* comes from 1894 (the same year as the *Piano trio in D minor* (see above); it is a set of nine variations and is the most brilliant and pianistically resourceful of all four. *Suite No. 4* was written five years before the composer's death and is hardly less beguiling than its companions: its third movement, *La rêve*, would also grace a Tchaikovsky or Glazunov ballet. Two pianos are difficult to record (and the piano technician deserves special credit for maintaining them together as well as he has) and the recording, though too resonant, reproduces them very truthfully. Altogether delightful music and captivating playing. Were it not so resonant, it would have a Rosette.

Arnold, Malcolm (born 1921)

Carnival of the animals, Op. 72; (i) Concerto for 2 pianos, 3 hands (Concerto for Phyllis and Cyril), Op. 104; A Grand, grand overture, Op. 57; Symphony No. 2, Op. 40.
*** Conifer Dig. CDCF 240 [id.]. (i) David Nettle and Richard Markham; RPO, Vernon Handley.

Malcolm Arnold's *Double piano concerto* was originally the *'Concerto for Phyllis and Cyril'*, written in 1969 for Phyllis Sellick and Cyril Smith when Cyril lost the use of his left hand and he and his wife continued as a highly successful piano duo. The concerto opens with a grand gesture and has an engaging Ravelian slow movement and an exuberantly precocious jazzy finale which was encored at its Proms première – understandably, as it includes one of Arnold's most catchy tunes. The piano duo here, Nettle and Markham, are obviously captivated by the piece, which they play with much flair and understanding – the slow movement is quite haunting in their hands. The *Second Symphony* was written in 1953 and was first conducted by Sir Charles Groves, who has made a fine recording of it. The work is fresh and colourful, far more complex in structure than it may initially seem. Like Shostakovich, Arnold opts for an easy-going *Allegretto* to open (a winning tune on the clarinet that is to reach its powerful climax later on the trumpets); but its undemanding open-air manner conceals genuine symphonic purpose. So with the rest of the symphony, including a murmuringly lively Scherzo, offering homage to Sibelius, and a long, austerely beautiful slow movement – much the longest – where a haunting tune with a distant echo of the second subject of Tchaikovsky's *Pathétique* builds to a formidable, curiously Mahlerian climax and ends ethereally on strings and a long, nostalgic horn solo. The tension is released in the finale, which has all the assertive self-confidence of the composer's earlier writing. Vernon Handley is a thoroughly persuasive advocate, and the spectacular recording is especially effective in the moments of brassy flamboyance in the outer movements. The *Grand, grand overture* was written for the famous Hoffnung Festivals and comes up remarkably effectively in this spectacular modern recording. It has a characteristically high-spirited, Arnoldian tune but is mainly notable for its outrageous scoring, including three vacuum-cleaners and a floor-polisher! Their hoarse heavy-breathing is finally silenced when they are shot dead at the end by four rifles. Arnold's supplement to Saint-Saëns's *Carnival of the animals*, written for a Hoffnung memorial concert, fails to match the French whimsy it simulates, but individual numbers have a certain charm, notably the *Giraffe* and the cheeping *Mice*, while the cows moo to a Gershwin tune (or almost). However the *Jumbo* joke, to music of Delibes, is unashamedly vulgar.

Clarinet concertos Nos 1, Op. 20; 2, Op. 115; Divertimento for flute, oboe and clarinet, Op. 37; Fantasy for B flat clarinet, Op. 87; Clarinet sonatina, Op. 29; 3 Shanties for wind quintet.
*** ASV Dig. CDDCA 922 [id.]. Emma Johnson, Jaime Martin, Jonathan Kelly, Claire Briggs, Susanna Cohen, Malcolm Martineau; ECO, Ivor Bolton.

With the characterful Emma Johnson as the central figure in all five works, this makes a delightful collection of what is labelled as Arnold's 'Complete Works for Clarinet'. Above all, these performances bring out the fun in Arnold's music, his bluff sense of humour set alongside a vein of warm lyricism matched by few of his contemporaries. The clarinet as an instrument seems to bring those qualities out to the full, and did so from the start when in 1943 he wrote his three witty *Shanties for wind quintet*. Though Emma Johnson is the leader in this ensemble, she is matched in both expressive warmth and wit by her young colleagues, notably the flautist, Jaime Martin, and the horn player, Claire Briggs. Compared with Thea King on Hyperion in the concertos (CDA 66634 – see our main volume), Emma Johnson has a rather reedier tone, less smooth, and her speeds tend to be a little more relaxed. Choice can safely be left to preference over coupling. Ivor Bolton with the ECO (the same orchestra as for King) matches his soloist in the pointing of rhythm, though the recording of the orchestra is rather less transparent than in the rival versions. Otherwise first-rate sound.

Symphonies Nos. 1, Op. 22; 2, Op. 40.
*** Chan. Dig. CHAN 9335 [id.]. LSO, Richard Hickox.

Richard Hickox takes naturally to the Malcolm Arnold idiom and moves easily from geniality to angry intensity, as in the first movement of No. 1; and he is particularly impressive in the two slow movements, which are full of atmosphere, vividly coloured and strongly felt. The rumbustious finale of No. 2 brings a splendid release of tension, and throughout the LSO response is powerful and thoroughly committed. The recording is well up to the high standard we expect from this label and the spontaneity of the playing communicates the feeling of live music-making. A first-rate coupling.

Symphony No. 3, Op. 63.
**(*) Everest/Vanguard EVC 9001 [id.]. LPO, composer – VAUGHAN WILLIAMS: *Symphony No. 9.*
**(*)

Arnold made his first recording of the *Third Symphony* at Walthamstow in the late 1950s. In the outer movements the performance has a certain chimerical, spontaneous quality that balances out the deeper feelings which are beneath the music's surface. The result is uncommonly fresh, even if Hickox's later recording has more gravitas. The early stereo is remarkably spacious and the brass writing is given fine sonority, though the violins are less full-bodied than we would expect today. The record is offered at very slightly less than premium price.

PIANO MUSIC

Allegro in E min.; 2 Bagatelles, Op. 18; 8 Children's pieces, Op. 36; Children's suite, Op.16; 3
Fantasies; 3 Pieces (1937); *2 Pieces* (1941); *3 Pieces* (1943); *Prelude; Serenade in G; Sonata;*
Variations on a Ukranian folksong, Op. 9.
*** Koch Dig. 3-7162-2 [id.]. Benjamin Frith.

This splendid disc spans Malcolm Arnold's almost unknown piano output, from his earliest pieces
(including the *Allegro in E minor*) from 1937, dedicated to his mother and firmly neo-classical in the
manner of Bach, to the Three *Fantasies* of 1986, terse in structure and much more ambivalent in
expressive mood to match the composer's last symphonies. In between are some highly atmospheric
pieces with a strong popular influence: *Serenade* and *Day dreams* (1938) and the two (brief) *Piano
Pieces* (1941) retain the bluesy influence of Louis Armstrong (whom the young composer admired)
and also have an appealing, melodic simplicity. The *Sonata* (1942), succinct and strongly argued,
brings motoric pungency and in the finale a reminder of Prokofiev; the slow movement, however, still
has a popular ambience in its harmony and melodic style. The *Three Pieces* (1943), engagingly sultry,
continue in the popular vein, while the *Prelude* (1945) has a languorous Mediterranean feeling. Then
comes the formidable quarter-of-an-hour-long *Variations on a Ukranian theme* (1948), which makes a
bold contrast, its complexities demonstrating the composer imaginatively stretched. The two groups
of short pieces for children are very much in the spirit of Elgar's nursery music. Most of the
movements are only about a minute long and, while the *Suite* includes both a blues and a baroque
Trumpet tune, the eight *Children's pieces*, Op. 36, introduce a memorable *Dancing tune* of great
charm, a blazingly colourful, fanfare-like piece, *The Duke*, and an audacious finale, *The Buccaneer*.
The comparatively enigmatic, more sombrely coloured *Ballades* provide further contrast. Benjamin
Frith is clearly at home in all this music, presenting it discerningly and spontaneously in order of
composition, to make a thoroughly rewarding 72-minute recital. Arnold communicates in every bar,
and the piano recording is very fine indeed.

Arriaga, Juan (1806–26)

String quartets Nos. 1 in D min.; 2 in A; 3 in E flat.
**(*) Claves Dig. CD 50-9501 [id.]. Sine Nomine Qt.

Arriaga's three quartets stand at a pivotal point between the eighteenth and nineteenth centuries. At
times they have something of the world of Schubert alongside that of Haydn, and they certainly look
towards Beethoven. But the individual strength of the composer's personality is in no doubt. Until
now we have consistently recommended the stylish and illuminating performances of these outstanding
works by the Chilingirians on CRD (CRD 33123) and we continue to do so. But this involves a pair
of CDs (admittedly with an interesting coupling) and many collectors will now be looking for a single
disc containing the triptych. In many ways this new Claves set, by the excellent Sine Nomine Quartet,
fills the bill. One has only to listen to the raptly sustained opening of the *Pastorale Andantino* slow
movement of the *E flat Quartet* to find playing which is sensitive to the music's atmosphere and
which has appealing lyrical feeling. But as soon as the impetus becomes more impassioned, a degree
of aggressiveness is imparted to the string timbre, and one realizes that the microphones are
uncomfortably close. Yet at lower dynamic levels the sound is very real and present, and the group's
neat, firm articulation of the closing *Presto agitato* is very appealing, as is the light, rhythmic touch
on the opening *Allegro con brio* of the *A major Quartet*. This has a charming *Andante with variations*
as its slow movement, which is presented with much finesse, while the serenely sombre opening of the
slow movement of the *D minor*, fully worthy of Haydn, is most impressive. The playing has warmth
and subtlety, clean ensemble and plenty of verve, and those who do not object to the up-front sound-
image and the degree of edge on the leader's attack will count this worth having, for there is no lack
of ambience.

Aubert, Louis (1887–1968)

*Cinéma (six tableaux symphoniques); Dryade; Feuilles d'images; Offrande; Tombeau de
Chateaubriand.*
** Marco Polo 8.223531 [id.]. Rheinland-Pfalz PO, Leif Segerstam.

Louis Aubert studied harmony with Lavignac and composition with Fauré and also pursued studies
in the classical languages. A man of many gifts, an accomplished singer and pianist, as a boy he took

part in the première of Fauré's *Requiem*, and he was Ravel's choice to give the first performance of the *Valses nobles et sentimentales*. The pieces recorded here span the period from 1924, the year in which Aubert composed his tableau symphonique, *Dryade*, through to 1956, the year of the ballet, *Cinéma*. *Offrande* (1952) is a short tone-poem dedicated to the victims of war, strongly reminiscent of Florent Schmitt, and much of the music here recalls others: the first of the *Feuilles d'images* evokes *Le jardin féerique* from Ravel's *Ma Mère l'oye*. Accomplished though it is, the music as a whole is too derivative to maintain a hold on the repertory. It is well played and recorded.

Auric, Georges (1899–1983)

Violin sonata in G.
*** EMI Dig. CDC7 54541-2 [id.]. Frank Peter Zimmermann, Alexander Lonquich – FRANCAIX: *Sonatine;* MILHAUD: *Sonata No. 2;* POULENC: *Sonata;* SATIE: *Choses vues.* ***

Georges Auric and Louis Durey are the least known of *Le Groupe des Six*, and the *Violin sonata in G major* of 1936 shows why. It is quite attractive but completely inconsequential, and it leaves no strong impression on the listener. Frank Peter Zimmermann and Alexander Lonquich play it with great spirit and elegance and are well recorded, though the balance rather favours the piano.

Avison, Charles (1709–70)

12 Concerti grossi after Scarlatti.
*** Hyp. CDA 66891/2 [id.]. Brandenburg Consort, Roy Goodman.

Marriner and the ASMF pioneered a complete recording of these works by the Newcastle-upon-Tyne composer, Charles Avison, which he ingeniously based on the keyboard sonatas of Domenico Scarlatti, and Marriner's fine set, with Iona Brown leading the solo group, has much grace and style. It makes a fine bargain on a Philips Duo two-discs-for-the-price-of-one (438 806-2). Those seeking a period-instrument performance will find Roy Goodman's version has plenty of vitality. Fast movements fizz spiritedly, but the linear style of the slower movements, though not lacking expressive feeling, is altogether less smooth, and these performances are essentially for those totally converted to the authentic style. The recording is excellent.

Bacewicz, Grazyna (1909–69)

String quartet No. 4.
** ASV Dig. CDDCA 908 [id.]. Maggini Qt – SZYMANOWSKI: *String quartets Nos. 1–2.* **

As we implied in our main edition, the Polish composer Grazyna Bacewicz is one of those composers who inspire respect and admiration rather than love. She possessed a cultivated and resourceful mind rather than a strongly individual profile, and the 'general purpose' modernity to which she had recourse is much in evidence here. There are a number of recordings in current circulation, but this newcomer is not a prime recommendation. As in the Szymanowski quartets with which this comes, the playing is very good, certainly more than acceptable, but it remains untouched by distinction.

Bach, Carl Philipp Emanuel (1714–88)

(i) *Flute concertos: in A min., Wq.166; in B flat, Wq.167; in A, Wq.168; in G, Wq.169;* (ii; iii) *Oboe concertos: in B flat, Wq.164; in E flat, Wq.165;* (ii; iv; v) *Solo in G min., for oboe and continuo;* (v) *Solo in G for harp, Wq.139.*
(B) **(*) Ph. Duo 442 592-2 (2) [id.]. (i) Aurèle Nicolet, Netherlands CO, David Zinman; (ii) Heinz Holliger; (iii) ECO, Leppard; (iv) Rama Jucker; (v) Ursula Holliger.

All four *Flute concertos* derive from the 1750s and, as a glance at the Wotquenne numbers will show, they exist in alternative versions for cello and keyboard. The present arrangement was made at the behest of Frederick the Great. Nicolet uses a modern instrument and plays very well, but the effect with a rather heavy string accompaniment (partly the result of the acoustic) makes less of the music than the rival versions on Capriccio. But those are at full price, and the Philips Duo set offers a great deal more music. Holliger's accounts of the *Oboe concertos* are masterly. Both date from 1765, when Bach was still in Berlin, and both exist in keyboard versions. The E flat is thought to be originally for oboe; its companion derives from the harpsichord. Both slow movements show the depth and range of Bach's imagination, and Holliger plays them with great feeling and a wide range of tone-colour. In addition to the excellence of the support from the ECO under Leppard, the Philips engineering is distinguished. The sound is beautifully lifelike and admirably fresh. The bonuses for oboe and continuo (in this instance harp and cello) and Ursula Holliger's harp *Solo* also add to the attractions of this very generous set.

4 Hamburg sinfonias, Wq.183/1–4; String sinfonia in B min., Wq.182/5 (H661).
(M) *** Virgin Veritas/EMI Dig. VER5 61182-2 [id.]. O of Age of Enlightenment, Gustav
    Leonhardt.

Unlike the six *Hamburg sinfonias* which C. P. E. Bach wrote earlier for Baron von Swieten, these four later works involve wind as well as strings. The writing is just as refreshing in its unexpectedness and originality. Gustav Leonhardt's account of this second set, Wq.183, is the one to have if you want them on period instruments. They are lively and alert, and distinguished by fine musical intelligence. This set is to be preferred, albeit by a small margin, to that by Koopman and in any case includes an extra work.

*Essay on the True Art of Playing Keyboard Instruments: 6 Sonatas, Wq.63/1–6; 6 Sonatinas, Wq.63/
7–12.*
(M) *** O-L 444 162-2 [id.]. Christopher Hogwood.

This record contains the twelve keyboard sonatas that C. P. E. Bach published with the first part of his *Essay on the True Art of Playing Keyboard Instruments* in 1753. These were to wield enormous influence for the remainder of the century on composers such as Haydn, Mozart and Beethoven. Despite their didactic intention, they are pieces of expressive power and are played by Christopher Hogwood not only with virtuosity but with a rare vein of poetic feeling. He uses a 1761 Haas clavichord of great beauty and is recorded excellently, though the disc should be played at a low level: remember that the clavichord has a very limited upper range of dynamic.

Bach, Johann Christian (1735–82)

Sinfonias, Op. 3/1–6.
(BB) ** Naxos Dig. 8.553083 [id.]. Camerata Budapest, Gmür.

Bach's Op. 3 symphonies were first played in 1765 'at Mrs Cornely's' in Carlisle House, Soho Square. They are essentially three-part Italian overtures and are full of lyrical melody, often of considerable charm, as in the *Andantino, sempre piano* of Op. 3/4. These works break no barriers but they clearly influenced the young Mozart, and the writing is easy-going and fluent. The *cantabile* quality of the writing is well captured by these elegant and polished performances by the Camerata Budapest, and Hanspeter Gmür's pacing of allegros is well judged and lively. The recording, however, made at the Festetich Castle, is very resonant and, while the modern string textures are undoubtedly beautiful, they are also inflated and there is a lack of transparency. Yet horns and oboes are nicely integrated in a slightly recessed balance which is wholly natural.

Sinfonias, Op. 6/1–6.
(BB) **(*) Naxos 8.553084 [id.]. Camerata Budapest, Hanspeter Gmür.

The music of Op. 6 shows a distinct advance on Op. 3, with allegros more dramatic and often very spirited, and slow movements touchingly expressive. Affinities with Mozart are the more striking, and a link with Haydn is also suggested, particularly in the remarkable *G minor Symphony*, the last of the set, with its stormy outer movements suggesting *Sturm und Drang* and a darkly dramatic *Andante*. This is very strongly played here, as is the striking *E flat Symphony*, Op. 6/3; the weightiness of the recordings, which is very well balanced, suits the added gravitas of the performances, which retain also the music's 'singing' qualities.

*Sinfonias, Op. 9/1–4; Sinfonia concertante in A for violin and cello; Sinfonia concertante in E flat, for 2
violins, oboe and orchestra.*
(BB) **(*) Naxos 8.553085 [id.]. Camerata Budapest, Hanspeter Gmür.

The third disc in this promising Naxos series is of interest not so much for the symphonies as for the two *Sinfonias concertantes* which are beautifully played, with stylish and appealing contributions from the soloists, all drawn from the orchestra. Moreover the Naxos engineers seem now to have got the measure of the Festetich Castle acoustics and, although the effect remains resonant, detail emerges quite freshly with the solo instruments nicely focused and effectively balanced in relation to the orchestra. The solo writing in the *A major Sinfonia concertante* is quite elaborate, and in the *Andante* of the E flat work there is a surprise when the two solo violins introduce Gluck's *Che farò senza Euridice*, which is then taken up by the oboe. The Op. 9 symphonies are not perhaps as interesting overall as Op. 6, but the second of the set of four has a real lollipop *Andante con sordini*, presented over a pizzicato accompaniment.

Bach, Johann Sebastian (1685–1750)

The Art of fugue, BWV 1080; The Musical offering, BWV 1079.
(B) *** Ph. Duo 442 556-2 (2) [id.]. ASMF, Marriner.

How to perform *The Art of fugue* has always presented problems, since Bach's own indications are so sparse. The very fact that (with the exception of the items for two harpsichords) the whole complex argument can be encompassed by ten fingers on one keyboard points to that option, but there is no doubt that for the listener at large, not following the score, a more varied instrumentation is both easier on the ear and clearer in its presentation of the argument. Sir Neville Marriner in the edition he prepared with Andrew Davis has varied the textures most intelligently, giving a fair proportion of the fugues and canons to keyboard instruments, organ as well as harpsichord. In each instance the instrumentation has been chosen as specially suitable to that particular movement. So the opening fugue is given to plain string quartet, the second to full orchestra of strings and woodwind, and so on. The fugue for two harpsichords and its inversion are exhilarating as performed by Andrew Davis and Christopher Hogwood, while the final quadruple fugue, which Bach never completed, is left achingly in mid-air at the end, a valid procedure on record at least. Marriner's style of performance is profoundly satisfying, with finely judged tempi, unmannered phrasing and resilient rhythms, and the 1974 recording is admirably refined. Similarly, in *The Musical offering* Marriner uses his own edition and instrumentation: strings with three solo violins, solo viola and a solo cello; flute, organ and harpsichord. The performance here is of high quality, though some of the playing is a trifle bland. It is, however, excellently recorded and overall must be numbered among the most successful accounts of the work. With these two key Bach works reissued together and with the pair of CDs offered for the price of one, this set must receive a cordial welcome back to the catalogue.

Brandenburg concertos Nos. 1–6, BWV 1046/51.
*** Sony Dig. S2K 66289 (2) [id.]. Tafelmusik, Jeanne Lamon.
(B) *** Carlton Dig. PCD 2006 (*Nos. 1–3*); PCD 2009 (*Nos. 4–6*) [id.]. ECO, Ledger.
(M) *** Virgin/EMI Dig. CUV5 61114-2 (2) [id.]. Scottish Ens., Jonathan Rees.
**(*) HM/BMG Dig. 05472 77308-2 (2) [id.]. La Petite Bande, Sigiswald Kuijken.
(BB) **(*) EMI Seraphim CES5 68516-2 (2) [CDEB 68516]. Bath Festival CO, Sir Yehudi Menuhin.

Tafelmusik seldom disappoint, and their set of *Brandenburgs* is enjoyably robust and spontaneous, if inevitably not always as polished as the best versions on modern instruments. Many will find this more infectious than Pinnock (DG 410 500/1-2), with the horn soloists in No.1, Ab Koster and Derek Conrod, playing mid-eighteenth-century hand horns with lustily extrovert vigour and bravura, so that one does not mind that intonation is not always exact. Crispian Steele-Perkins, the trumpet soloist in No. 2, plays a modern copy of a 1667 instrument with remarkable sophistication. Tempi are brisk (the finale of No. 3 is most invigorating) but never hurried, and slow movements relax warmly as they should, with bulges in phrasing fairly minimal. The recording is excellent.

On Carlton, Ledger has the advantage of fresh and detailed digital recording. He directs resilient, well-paced readings of all six concertos on modern instruments, lively yet never over-forced. The slow movements in particular are most beautifully done, persuasively and without mannerism. Flutes rather than recorders are used in No. 4.

From Virgin an excellent new Scottish set of *Brandenburgs*, directed with much spirit by Jonathan Rees, freshly played and with a warm yet clear recording, with excellent internal balance. The tempi seem very apt when the players so convey their enjoyment and the sound has such a pleasing bloom. A fine new mid-priced recommendation using modern instruments to put alongside the 'authentic' Halstead/Hanover Band set on EMI Eminence which is comparably joyful (CD-EMX 2200/2201).

La Petite Bande under Kuijken are stylish and musical and they are well recorded. The performance of No. 5 shows the group at its finest, with some particularly fine playing in the slow movement. But elsewhere, although the performances bring both vigour and polish, they have a less strong profile than Tafelmusik, whose performance of the first two concertos is much more compulsively alive. An enjoyable set, but not a distinctive one.

Menuhin's stylish 1959 set of *Brandenburgs* has stood the test of time. It is played by the chamber-sized Bath Festival Orchestra, which includes gambas – Dennis Nesbitt and Ambrose Gauntlett – and recorders. Rhythms are sprung lightly and joyfully, and tempi are uncontroversially apt. The excellent soloists (unnamed in the current – inadequate – documentation) include Barry Tuckwell, Janet Craxton and Michael Dobson, while Dennis Clift is the first-rate trumpeter. Throughout there is a spontaneity that is consistently refreshing. Although the current remastering brings a degree of astringency to the violins, some ears may feel that the effect is now very near to that of a period performance. There is no lack of ambient warmth and the balance is impressive. Apart from a hint of overloading from the horns in No. 1, inner detail is clear, and the harpsichord, splendidly played by George Malcolm, comes through naturally in the solo passages in No. 5. In No. 3, Menuhin very effectively interpolates a slow movement, using an arrangement for violin, viola and continuo by Benjamin Britten of the *Adagio* from the organ *Trio sonata*, BWV 530. With the pair of CDs offered for the price of one mid-priced disc, this is the least expensive among 'the more distinguished recordings of these much-recorded works.

(i) *Brandenburg concertos Nos. 1–6;* (ii) *Flute concerto in G min.* (from *BWV 1056*); *Double concerto for violin, oboe and strings in D min.* (from *BWV 1060*).
(B) *** Decca Double 443 847-2 (2) [id.]. (i) ECO, Britten; (ii) ASMF, Marriner.

Britten made his recordings in the Maltings concert-hall in 1968, not long before the serious fire there. The engineers had not quite accustomed themselves to the reverberant acoustic and, to compensate, they put the microphones rather close to the players. The result is a fairly ample sound that in its way goes well with Britten's interpretations. There is some lack of textural delicacy in the slow movements of Nos. 1, 2, 4 and 6; but the bubbling high spirits of the outer movements are hard to resist, and the harpsichordist, Philip Ledger, follows the pattern he had set in live Britten performances, with Britten-inspired extra elaborations a continual delight. The CD transfer is very successful, the sound both full and bright, and the effect of these performances is joyfully life-enhancing. As a makeweight for the Double Decca reissue, two more of Marriner's stylish perform-ances of reconstructions of Bach's harpsichord concertos for alternative instruments have been added. Christopher Hogwood's realizations are very effective indeed. BWV 1056 is the *F minor Harpsichord concerto*, BWV 1060 is the *Double harpsichord concerto in C minor* (here for violin and oboe), and many ears may find this latter work more attractive in the present format, when the playing sparkles as it does here. First-class (originally Argo) recording, too.

Brandenburg concertos Nos. 1–3; (i) *Violin concertos Nos. 1 in A min.; 2 in E, BWV 1041/2.*
(M) *** Ph. 442 386-2 [id.]. ECO, Leppard; (i) with Arthur Grumiaux.

Brandenburg concertos Nos. 4–6; (i) *Triple concerto in A min. for violin, flute and harpsichord, BWV 1044.*
(M) *** Ph. 442 387-2 [id.]. ECO, Leppard; (i) with Grumiaux, Garcia & Adeney.

Leppard's mid-1970s Philips set with the ECO is higher-powered than the Rees Scottish performances, whose relaxed manner will for many be easier to live with. But the exhilaration of the Leppard set is undeniable: there is much to enjoy here and the soloists include John Wilbraham's trumpet in No. 2 and a piquant recorder contribution from David Munrow in No.4. The remastered sound is fresh and full. Moreover Leppard offers considerable bonuses. Grumiaux's accounts of the two solo concertos come from 1964, but the warmly resonant recording does not sound dated. This playing from one of the most musical soloists of our time is extremely satisfying. It has a purity of line and an expressive response that communicate very positively, and Leppard's stylish accompaniments have striking buoyancy. The *Triple concerto* (recorded two decades later) has plenty of vitality, too; although the balance is a little contrived, the effect is certainly vivid.

Brandenburg concertos Nos. 1–6, BWV 1046/51; A musical offering, BWV 1079.
(M) *** Virgin Veritas/EMI Dig./Analogue VED5 61154–2 (2) [id.]. Linde Consort, Hans-Martin Linde.

With sprung rhythms and generally well-chosen tempi, the Linde Consort deserve to rank alongside Pinnock's set. But, quite apart from the considerable bonus of the *Musical offering*, many will prefer their version of the *Brandenburgs*, for the 1981 EMI recording is rather fuller than the DG Archiv sound, with the strings very slightly less immediate. Linde is as stylish and accomplished as any of his rivals, and he and his six colleagues offer the preferred version of this work using original instruments. They are again warmly as well as clearly recorded. *Concertos* Nos. 1–4 and 6 are on the first CD, and No. 5 with the *Musical offering* on the second.

Brandenburg concertos Nos. 1–6; Orchestral suites Nos. 3–4, BWV 1067–8.
(M) *(*) Teldec/Warner Dig. 4509 95980-2 (2) [id.]. VCM, Harnoncourt.

It is a sign of the maturing art of authentic performance that Harnoncourt's digital set of *Branden-burgs*, recorded in the early 1980s, sounds so laboured. Speeds are slow and rhythms heavy. There is some expert playing, both solo and ensemble, but the artificially bright and clinically clear recording gives an aggressive projection to the music-making. The pair of *Orchestral suites*, too, are sadly lacking in finesse. His earlier, analogue versions of all these works are preferable, but even these have been upstaged by more recent versions.

Harpsichord concertos Nos. (i) *1 in D min;* (ii) *2 in E; 3 in D; 4 in A; 5 in F; 6 in F* (for harpsichord, 2 recorders & strings); *7 in G min., BWV 1052/8; 8 in D min, BWV 1059* (reconstructed for harpsichord, oboe & strings); (ii; iii) *Double harpsichord concertos Nos. 1 in C min., BWV 1060; 2 in C, BWV 1061; 3 in C min., BWV 1062;* (iv) *Triple harpsichord concertos Nos. 1 in D min., BWV 1063; 2 in C, BWV 1064; Quadruple harpsichord concerto in A min., BWV 1065.*
(M) ** Teldec/Warner 4509 97452-2 (3) [id.]. (i) Herbert Tachezi, VCM, Harnoncourt; (ii) Gustav
   Leonhardt, Leonhardt Consort; with (iii) Edward Müller or Anneke Uittenbosch; (iv)
   Uittenbosch; Alan Curtis; (v) Uittenbosch; Müller; Janny van Wering.

Leonhardt's integral survey of the Bach keyboard concertos has many fine qualities. The recordings are very well balanced and reproduce smoothly and transparently without jangle; indeed the composite works are very successful in this respect. For some reason the *First Concerto in D minor*, BWV 1052, is played by Herbert Tachezi, a somewhat self-effacing soloist, but Harnoncourt with his VCM provides a lively accompaniment, taking care not to drown the harpsichord. Leonhardt's performances are alive and scholarly, with slow movements often thoughtful, if not inspired. Of the solo concertos, the *F major*, BWV 1057, an arrangement of the *Fourth Brandenburg concerto* (where Bach transferred the violin part to the harpsichord), is heard with its original recorder parts, and is one of the more striking of the performances. Only the first nine bars of the *D minor Concerto*, BWV 1059, have survived, but Bach seemingly used the first movement in 1726 as the sinfonia in the first section of his *Cantata No. 35: Geist und Seele sind verwirret*, featuring a solo organ. Thus the cantata's first aria (with obbligato organ) and its second sinfonia may have derived from the concerto, and Leonhardt has made a reconstruction using the sinfonias as outer movements. However, it was found impossible to turn the aria into the slow movement, 'without making unacceptably far-reaching alterations', so a simple cadential improvisation has been substituted. This set is comprehensive, decoration cannot be faulted; pacing is nicely judged and allegros are alert. Yet, all things considered, the result is something of a disappointment, lacking the final degree of spontaneity and imagination. First choice for this repertoire rests with Trevor Pinnock on harpsichord (DG 415 991-2 and 415 992-2) or András Schiff on piano (Decca 425 676-2) – see our main volume.

(i) *Violin concertos Nos. 1 in A min.; 2 in E;* (i; ii) *Double violin concerto in D min., BWV 1041/3;* (i; iii) *Double concerto for violin and oboe in D min., BWV 1060. Orchestral Suites Nos. 1 in C;* (iv) *2 in B min.* (for flute and strings); *3 in D, BWV 1066/68.*
(BB) *** EMI Seraphim CES5 68517-2 (2) [CDEB 68517]. (i) Y. Menuhin; (ii) Christian Ferras; (iii)
   Leon Goossens; (iv) Elaine Schaffer; Bath Festival CO, Sir Yehudi Menuhin.

This is one of the very best bargains in the EMI/Seraphim catalogue, offering a pair of discs for the cost of one premium-priced CD. The documentation – or lack of it – is no credit to the famous old EMI trademark, but the music-making is of the highest order. The *Violin concertos* date from 1960 and, played as they are here by Menuhin (in very good form), both the solo concertos take flight, for their balance of warmth, humanity and classical sympathy is very appealing. The smaller points of style are well catered for, yet the effect sounds perfectly spontaneous. In the *Double violin concerto* Ferras matches his timbre beautifully to that of Menuhin and the duet is a real partnership, with the slow movement especially fine. Leon Goossens makes a ravishing contribution to the *Adagio* of the *Concerto for violin and oboe*, the only slight snag being that the oboe is too backwardly balanced in the outer movements. To complete this attractive Menuhin/Bach package, we are offered three of the four *Orchestral Suites*, including the two favourites, the *B minor*, BWV 1067, in which Elaine Schaffer is a very pleasing soloist, not seeking to impose her personality above that of the composer, and the *D major*, BWV 1068, where the famous *Air* is played with appealing refinement and grace. Indeed, throughout these performances Menuhin finds an admirable balance between freshness and warmth, conveying the music's spirit and breadth without inflation. The *Suites* date from 1961 and the *Concerto for violin and oboe* from 1962; and the current remastering brings sound which is quite full, yet clear. However, the Grumiaux recordings of the *Violin concertos* are rather special (Philips 420 700-2) – see our main volume.

Violin concertos Nos. 1 in A min. 2 in E; in G min. (from *Harpsichord concerto, BWV 1056*); (i)
Double violin concerto in D min., BWV 1043; (ii) *Double concerto for violin and oboe in D min., BWV
1060.*
(M) ** Teldec/Warner 4509 95518-2 [id.]. Alice Harnoncourt, with (i) Walter Pfeiffer; (iii) Jürg
    Schaeftlein; VCM, Harnoncourt.

This Teldec offering is generous, but the performances will appeal only to those willing to accept the
wiry timbre of Alice Harnoncourt's baroque violin and her line in slow movements which, if often
uneven, is notably insubstantial in the *Largo* of the *G minor Concerto*. Slight tonal bulges also affect
the interchanges in the slow movement of the *Double concerto*. Nicholas Harnoncourt is for the most
part lively with his accompaniments but can be heavy-handed (as at the introduction of the
transcription of BWV 1056). The most enjoyable work here is the *Double concerto for violin and oboe*;
even if the oboe dominates, one relishes the engaging sounds from Jürg Schaeftlein. The sound itself
is good, admirably clear, but with no lack of ambience.

Orchestral suites Nos. 1–4, BWV 1066/9.
(M) *** EMI Dig. CDM5 68331-2 [id.]. Linde Consort, Hans-Martin Linde.

*Orchestral suites Nos. 1–4; Concerto movement in D, BWV 1045; Sinfonias from Cantatas Nos. 29;
42; 209.*
*** Hyp. Dig. CDA 66701/2 [id.]. Brandenburg Consort, Roy Goodman.

Orchestral suites Nos. 1 in C, 2 in B min., BWV 1066/7; Cantatas No. 42, 209: sinfonias.
*** Hyp. Dig. CDA 66501 [id.]. Brandenburg Consort, Roy Goodman.
*Orchestral suites Nos. 3 in D, 4 in D, BWV 1068/9; Concerto movement in D, BWV 1045; Cantata
    No. 29: sinfonia.*
*** Hyp. Dig. CDA 66502 [id.]. Brandenburg Consort, Roy Goodman.

Roy Goodman directs brisk and stylish readings of the four Bach *Orchestral Suites*, which are aptly
supplemented by four *Sinfonias*, each following a suite in the same key. Three are from recognized
cantatas – one of them Bach's dazzling arrangement of the *Prelude* to the solo *Violin partita No. 3* –
and the fourth is a concertante movement presumed to be the sinfonia for a lost cantata. Though in
the *Suites* Goodman in eagerness occasionally chooses too breathless a tempo for fast movements,
the lightness of rhythm and the crispness of ensemble are consistently persuasive, with textures
cleanly caught in excellent, full-bodied sound. These are among the finest versions on a long list, with
Rachel Brown an exceptionally warm-toned flautist in No. 2. One movement to sample is the most
celebrated of all, the *Air* from the *Suite No. 3*, which flows easily and fluently with the violinist, Pablo
Beznosiuk, sweeter than most rivals, ornamenting repeats very stylishly. Unlike many alternative
versions, Goodman observes all repeats, making the opening overtures longer than usual. As
indicated above, the discs are available either separately or in a box.

The previous issue of the Linde performances was also on a single (full-priced) CD, but it omitted
the *Second suite*. Now it is added and the price reduced, making this reissue very competitive and
recommendable alongside Marriner (Decca 430 378-2; *430 378-4*), who also offers the four *Suites* on a
single analogue-sourced CD, but using modern instruments (very stylishly). As with the companion
set of *Brandenburgs*, for those wanting period instruments and digital sound Linde should make an
excellent choice. The string style is less abrasive than that of the English Concert (currently on two
full-priced CDs) and the rhythmic spring in allegros generally lighter. Nor is the grandeur of the
music missed for, against a warm acoustic, the intimate scale readily accommodates the panoply of
trumpets in Nos. 3 and 4. The famous *Air* is pointed and elegant. The acoustic is warm, the recording
cleanly focused.

CHAMBER MUSIC

(Unaccompanied) *Cello suites Nos. 1–6, BWV 1007/12.*
⊛ *** EMI Dig. CDS5 55363-2 (2) [id.]. Mstislav Rostropovich.
*** DG Dig. 445 373-2 (2) [id.]. Mischa Maisky.

Rostropovich, the most intrepid of cellists, ever eager to tackle concertos by the score, has nevertheless
approached these supreme masterpieces of the solo cello repertory with caution. He played them all
in his teens but, until the 1990s, refrained from recording them as a complete cycle. The result is
revelatory, in many ways the most powerful recording of all, positive and personal, full of individual
perceptions. Rostropovich verbally characterizes each one of the series: 'No. 1, lightness; No. 2,
sorrow and intensity; No. 3, brilliance; No. 4, majesty and opacity; No. 5, darkness; and No. 6,
sunlight'. True to his word, more than usual he draws distinctions between each, also reflecting the

point that the structure of each suite grows in complexity. He pays tribute to the example of Casals (EMI CHS7 61027-2) and, like Casals, Rostropovich takes a broadly romantic view but, far more than that master, he keeps the basic rhythm of each movement clearly defined, whatever his expressive freedom. The results are both moving and strong with the sound of the cello, as recorded in a warm acoustic, full and powerful. He is just as positive in his choice of speeds, often fast and volatile, vigorously sprung, but with the slow sarabande in each suite made to represent the inner heart. His dynamics are romantically free but always compelling, making one hear the music afresh, with pianissimo repeats magically achieved. Anyone who has ever been daunted by solo cello music will find its range of expression astonishingly expanded by Rostropovich.

Mischa Maisky's 1985 set, originally on three CDs, now reappears, remastered on to two, but still at full price. Maisky's performances are beautifully cultured and at a high emotional temperature. He is rather less inclined to let the music speak for itself than some of his rivals and is at times even self-indulgent. The *Sarabande* of the *D minor Suite* is a little narcissistic and the impatient may find it interminable; nor is that of *No. 5 in C minor* free from affectation. There are times in the quicker dance movements when one longs for him to move on. However, there is no doubt that he makes an absolutely glorious sound and commands an unusually wide range of colour and tone.

(i) *Viola da gamba sonatas Nos. 1–3, BWV 1027/9;* (ii) *Violin sonatas* (for violin and harpsichord) *Nos. 1–6, BWV 1014/19.*
(M) ** Sony SM2K 52615 (2) [id.]. (i) Leonard Rose or (ii) Jaime Laredo; Glenn Gould (piano).

Leonard Rose does not project a larger-than-life instrumental personality like Rostropovich, but his tone is subtly coloured and beautifully focused, his playing shows a fine sensibility, and his slightly introvert style is admirably suited to the *Viola da gamba sonatas* of Bach. Moreover, he and Glenn Gould achieve a very close partnership indeed, although some of Gould's ornamentation is question-able. The cello is well forward with the piano behind, but the matching is nigh perfect, and the playing throughout is live and spontaneous. At times Glenn Gould's clean, staccato articulation in outlining the rhythm of slow movements (usually taken very slowly) seems a shade eccentric, but when both artists do it together, as in the *Andante* of BWV 1027, the effect is both individual and pleasing. In allegros, the music-making has splendid vitality, and altogether these performances are rewarding, if highly idiosyncratic. In the *Violin sonatas* Jaime Laredo is also brought forward by the close balance, and this brings a degree of edge to his timbre, though the effect is not unpleasing; indeed it has an 'authentic' feel. But the close microphones do not spoil the dynamic range and there is some lovely quiet lyrical playing from Laredo. Again Gould's unforced staccato style is very apparent in slow movements, but the violin line floats serenely above (try the *Andante un poco* of BWV 1015), and again faster movements are enjoyably spirited. There is undoubtedly pleasure to be had from this pair of discs, for all the unconventionality of Gould's contribution.

(Unaccompanied) *Violin sonatas Nos. 1–3, BWV 1001, 1003, & 1005; Violin partitas Nos. 1–3, BWV 1002, 1004, & 1006.*
(M) ** DG Dig. 445 526-2 [id.]. Shlomo Mintz.
** Virgin/EMI Dig. VC5 45089-2 (2) [id.]. Christian Tetzlaff.

Schlomo Mintz takes all the technical difficulties in his stride and his excellently recorded accounts give much musical satisfaction. His playing has youthful vitality and power, but the famous *Chaconne* from the *D minor Partita* finds him wanting. Intonation is generally secure but goes seriously awry in the middle of the *G minor Fugue*. The recording has a remarkably vivid presence (although the ear is conscious of the presence of the microphones), and this set (originally on three full-priced CDs) is now much more economically priced on two. But this would not be a first choice.

Christian Tetzlaff is a very talented player and he has already made several fine records. But on the evidence of this very real and truthful recording of the unaccompanied works for violin, he has tackled Bach too early. These performances have a curious lack of profile, and his lyrical manner, with its hints of portamento, is semi-romantic in effect. In the dazzling *Presto* which forms the last movement of the *First Sonata in G minor*, Tetzlaff's smooth bowing, for all the ready control of light and shade, loses the music's bracing character, as if it were a Paganini study. The *Allemanda and Double* which begins the *First Partita* is a ready example of the blandness of Tetzlaff's style, and in the *D minor Partita* the comparatively flabby opening of the *Chaconne* does not bode well for an account that seems unable to convey the sense of his observing the structure as a whole. The playing is technically very assured indeed, but this is not a set we should choose to live with, like those of Perlman (EMI CDS7 49483-2), Shumsky (ASV CDDCD 454) or Milstein (DG 423 294-2). These are all discussed in our main volume, and readers will note that the Erato version by the inestimable (and late) Oleg Kagan, to which we gave a Rosette, has alas, been withdrawn by the manufacturers through lack of public support.

KEYBOARD MUSIC

Chaconne in D min. (arr. Busoni from (unaccompanied) *Violin partita No. 2 in D min., BWV 1004).*
(M) *** RCA 09026 62590-2 [id.]. Artur Rubinstein – FRANCK: *Prelude, chorale and fugue* ***;
    LISZT: *Piano sonata in B min.* **(*)

Busoni's arrangement of the celebrated *Chaconne* for solo violin is a piece which has to be presented
with flair as virtuoso piano music, and Rubinstein is an ideal choice of pianist. He recorded this
performance in Rome in 1970, when he was already in his eighties, but the freshness and spirit are a
delight. The transfer of the 1970 recording is just a little clangy, but not unpleasantly so.

*Chromatic fantasia and fugue in D min., BWV 903; Chorale Preludes: Ich ruf zu dir, BWV 639; Nun
komm' der Heiden Heiland, BWV 659* (both arr. Busoni); *Fantasia in A min., BWV 922; Fantasia
and fugue in A min., BWV 904; Italian concerto in F, BWV 971.*
(M) *** Ph. 442 400-2 [id.]. Alfred Brendel.

Brendel's fine Bach recital originally appeared in 1978. The performances are of the old school, with
no attempt made to strive after harpsichord effects and with every piece creating a sound-world of its
own. The *Italian concerto* is particularly imposing, with a finely sustained sense of line and beautifully
articulated rhythms. The recording is in every way truthful and present, bringing the grand piano
very much into the living-room before one's very eyes. Masterly.

English suites Nos. 1–6, BWV 806/811.
(M) *** Virgin Veritas/EMI Dig. VER5 61157-2 (2) [id.]. Gustav Leonhardt (harpsichord).
(M) ** Sony SM2K 52606 (2) [id.]. Glenn Gould (piano).

Gustav Leonhardt uses a 1755 instrument by Nicholas Lefébre of Rouen, recently restored by Martin
Skowroneck, and very beautiful it sounds too in this clear but not too forwardly balanced recording.
The *English suites* are thought to come from 1715, the year of Carl Philipp Emanuel's birth, or
possibly a few years later, and to predate the *French suites*. Leonhardt's playing here has a flair and
vitality that one does not always associate with him, and there is no doubt that he makes the most of
the introspective *Sarabande* of the *G minor Suite*. He is better served by the EMI engineers than when
he last recorded these for Philips, where he was too forward; his performances, too, are more flexible
and relaxed. The CD transfer retains the atmospheric sound-balance; the harpsichord is present
without being right on top of the listener.

   Glenn Gould often inspires the adjective 'wilful', and certainly these performances have much that
is eccentric. At the same time there is undoubtedly a strong musical personality to which the listener
cannot remain indifferent. The vocalizations are tiresome and, although phrasing is often imaginative,
there is some bizarre ornamentation and accentuation and the piano sound tends to be dry and
unappealing, although it represents the effect intended by Gould himself.

French suites Nos. 1–6, BWV 812/17.
*** DG Dig. 445 840-2 [id.]. Andrei Gavrilov (piano).

Like most of his instrumental works, the *French suites* belong to Bach's time in Cöthen (1717–23), the
last, in E minor, being added in 1724. Andrei Gavrilov, quoted in the booklet about playing Bach on
the piano or the harpsichord, says: 'the piano has to win every time. It has such a variety of sounds,
allowing one to "paint" different voices of the music in contrasting timbres, and its great power is
perfectly suited to the grandeur in Bach's music.' Certainly Gavrilov conveys the enormous inner
vitality of these suites and makes this music vibrant. Such is the conviction he conveys that while he is
playing one feels there is no other way to play this music and no other instrument to play it on. Very
good sound.

French suites Nos. 1–6, BWV 812/17; Partita No. 7 in B min., BWV 831.
(M) ** Sony SM2K 52609 (2) [id.]. Glenn Gould (piano).

Brilliant though Glenn Gould's playing is, it is far too idiosyncratic to justify an unqualified
recommendation. Needless to say, there are revealing touches, marvellously clear part-writing and
some impressive finger dexterity. There are some odd tempi and a lot of very detached playing that
inspires more admiration than conviction. The sound is clear and clean and is acceptably transferred.

Goldberg variations, BWV 988.
(M) *** Virgin Veritas/EMI Dig. VER5 61153-2 [id.]. Maggie Cole (harpsichord).
(M) *** DG 439 978-2 [id.]. Wilhelm Kempff (piano).

Maggie Cole plays a copy by Andrew Warlick of an instrument by J. C. Goujon of 1749. She is recorded with great clarity; as so often, the playback level needs to be reduced if a truthful and realistic effect is to be made. Her playing is completely straightforward and she holds the listener's interest throughout. At mid-price this make a very strong recommendation for those wanting a digital harpsichord version of this work.

Kempff's version is not for purists, but has a special magic of its own. Ornaments are ignored altogether in the outlining of the theme and the instances of anachronisms of style are too numerous to mention. Yet, for all that, the sheer musicianship exhibited by this great artist fascinates and his playing is consistently refreshing. Even where he seems quite wilfully nineteenth century in his approach, there is a unique musical impulse and conviction behind it. Readers should certainly hear this for themselves. The 1969 recording is very natural. Rosalyn Tureck's version, however, remains very special indeed (VAI Audio VAIA 1029) – see our main volume.

Goldberg variations, BWV 988; Fantasia in C min., BWV 906; Fantasia and fugue in F min., BWV 904; Italian concerto in F, BWV 971.
(M) **(*) DG 439 465-2 [id.]. Ralph Kirkpatrick (harpsichord).

Ralph Kirkpatrick's recording of the *Goldberg variations* comes from the late 1950s, but it sounds extremely fresh in the present CD transfer. He is at his best in this work, providing light and subtle registration, and the music benefits both in clarity and in colour. The playing is lively when it should be, controlled and steady in the slow, stately, contrapuntal variations. He is a scholarly rather than an intuitive player and his thoughts are rarely without interest. Though not a first choice, this version is still worth considering, particularly as the CD includes three extra items where he uses his modern Neupert harpsichord to good effect, while sounding more pedantic, particularly in the *Italian concerto*.

Goldberg variations (trans. for strings by Dmitry Sitkovetsky).
*(*) Nonesuch/Warner Dig. 7559 79341-2 [id.]. NES CO, Sitkovetsky.

It was a fascinating idea to arrange Bach's famous set of variations for string orchestra, but it does not work. The opening aria sounds serenely beautiful but thereafter the music's depth of argument simply evaporates, and the piece sounds like a string divertimento. Good playing and recording.

Partitas Nos. 1–6, BWV 825/30; Partita in B min. (Overture in the French style), BWV 831.
(B) *** Ph. Duo 442 559-2 (2) [id.]. Blandine Verlet (harpsichord).

Blandine Verlet's Philips Duo set is not only inexpensive, it is the only set of the *Partitas* to include the later *Overture in the French style*, BWV 831, which is played with much character. Indeed the performances throughout are direct and spontaneous, thoughtful and strongly characterized. The harpsichord in use is unnamed but is very suitable for this repertoire. It is given a good presence, without clangour, within an acoustic that is not too confined but which is not over-reverberant either. Not an out-and-out first choice, which lies with Christophe Rousset on Oiseau-Lyre (440 217-2 – see our main volume). But he does not give us the *B minor Partita* and, in its price range, Verlet can certainly be strongly recommended.

8 Preludes for W. F. Bach, BWV 924/31; 6 Little Preludes, BWV 933/8; 5 Preludes, BWV 939/43; Prelude, BWV 999; Prelude, fugue and allegro in E flat, BWV 998; Preludes and fughettas: in F & G, BWV 901/2; Fantasia in C min., BWV 906; Fantasia and fugue in A min., BWV 904.
(M) **(*) DG Dig. 447 278-2 [id.]. Kenneth Gilbert (harpsichord).

Splendid artistry from this scholar-player; he is predictably stylish and authoritative. He uses a harpsichord by a Flemish maker, Jan Couchet, enlarged by Blanchet in 1759 and by Taskin in 1778, overhauled by Hubert Bédard. Even played at the lowest setting, the sound seems a bit unrelieved and overbright. This really has 'presence' with a vengeance. The excellence of the playing however is not in question.

The Well-tempered Clavier, Book II, Preludes & fugues Nos. 25–48, BWV 870/893.
(BB) *** Naxos Dig. 8. 550970/1 (2) [id.]. Jenö Jandó (piano).

Like András Schiff on Decca (414 388-2 and 417 236-2), Jandó sees the *Well-tempered Clavier* in pianistic terms; he varies his touch from boldly assertive, as in the very first Prelude of Book II, to a light staccato (as in the second) or a more mellow, expressive style (as in the third). He can also be thoughtful, almost improvisatory, as in the fourth, and then commanding, as in the fifth, or almost motoric as in the sixth. He uses light and shade judiciously, as in the seventh. His approach brings great variety to the music and, like his choice of tempi, seems apt, although some listeners may not always agree with his choices. The piano timbre is firm, clear and realistic without spreading too richly, and this makes a thoroughly recommendable super-bargain alternative to Schiff, who remains rather special.

ORGAN MUSIC

Complete organ music

Marie-Claire Alain Erato series
(M) **(*) Erato/Warner Dig. 4509 96358-2 (14) [id.]. Marie-Claire Alain.

Marie-Claire Alain's series has much to offer the lover of Bach's organ music, and she plays to excellent effect on some splendid instruments. The complete set of fourteen records is available in a slipcase at a small saving in cost, and admirers of this artist should not be disappointed with such an investment. But competition is strong, and for most collectors a choice from among the separate issues, all at mid-price, would seem more sensible.

Volume 1: *Leipzig chorale preludes: An Wasserflüssen Babylon, BWV 653; Schmücke dich, o liebe Seele, BWV 654; Von Gott will ich nicht lassen, BWV 658; Triple chorale (with Trio): Allein Gott in der Höh' sei Ehr', BWV 662/4; Preludes and fugues: in B min., BWV 544; in E min., BWV 548.*
(M) **(*) Erato/Warner Dig. 4509 96718-2 [id.]. Marie-Claire Alain (organ of Martinikerk, Groningen).

Marie-Claire Alain began recording her new Bach survey in 1985, using several different period organs which had been successfully restored. She comments: 'The historical organ cannot be rushed: it issues its orders and the artist bends to its will. Tempi are determined by the relatively heavy touch and by the unpredictability of the wind. Such organs command respect ... but provide much enchantment in sound.' Volume 1 is recorded on the Martinikerk organ in Groningen and the results are not entirely satisfactory, for the engineers obtain a rich, weighty sound as in the opening *E minor Prelude and fugue*, but the resonance makes the result rather opaque, which does not enable Alain to clarify detail. The fugue, however, is measured and powerful. This whole programme bears out her comments about tempi, which are essentially relaxed. The *Leipzig chorales* are serene and pleasingly voiced, with *Schmücke dich, o liebe Seele* bringing delightfully fresh registration. One feels, however, that after the brightly registered *Prelude in B minor*, the fugue plods on. The triple setting of the chorale, *Allein Gott in der Höh' sei Ehr'*, with its cantus firmus first in the treble and then in the tenor, offers undoubted poise, but it is the decoration in the final Trio which brings the music fully to life.

Volume 2: *Orgelbüchlein: Chorale preludes, BWV 618–32; Prelude and fugue in G min., BWV 535; Toccatas and fugues: in D min. (Dorian), BWV 538; in C, BWV 566.*
(M) **(*) Erato/Warner Dig. 4509 96719-2 [id.]. Marie-Claire Alain (organ of Freiburg Cathedral).

Volume 2 was recorded in 1991 on the early eighteenth-century Silbermann organ at Freiburg, and the sound is immediately more vivid and clear. The opening *Dorian Toccata in D minor* is brightly registered and lively and, if the fugue is unhurried, the tension is well sustained. The *C major Toccata*, however, is one of the finest performances in the cycle. The presentation of the *Toccata* is firm and positive rather than especially flamboyant, but the organ sonority is glorious; then the fugue opens piquantly, using flute stops, and is lightly registered so that the return of the modified *Toccata* is the more impressive and the expansive closing section very satisfying indeed. Alain presents the earlier chorales from the *Orgelbüchlein* gently and persuasively. She adopts a curiously staccato decorative effect for *O Lamm Gottes unschuldig*; on the other hand the downward scale in *Christe, du Lamm Gottes* is nicely poised. Generally these simple pieces come off very well, although she does not always make the cantus firmus stand out and in *Hilf Gott, dass mir's gelinge* it becomes almost buried in the flowing melisma which surrounds it. The second group of chorales, BWV 625/630, are richly textured until *Erschienen ist der herrliche Tag*, BWV 629, which makes an engaging lighter contrast. The *Prelude in G minor* is commanding and swirls with colour, and the fugue, if not assertive, begins brightly and gathers weight, although the flourishes at the end could have been more extrovert.

Volume 3: *Allabreve in D, BWV 589; Canzona in D min., BWV 588; Fugues: in C min., BWV 575; in G, BWV 577; Fugue sopra 'Meine Seele erhebet den Herren'; Kirnberger chorale preludes: Wo soll ich fliehen hin, BWV 694; Wir Christenleutt hab'n jetz und Freud, BWV 710; Kleines harmonisches Labyrinth, BWV 591; Partita sopra 'O Gott, du frommer Gott', BWV 767; Preludes and fugues: in D min., BWV 539; in C, BWV 545; in A min., BWV 551.*
(M) **(*) Erato/Warner Dig. 4509 96720-2 [id.]. Marie-Claire Alain (organ of Freiburg Cathedral).

The Freiburg organ is again used in Volume 3 (also recorded in 1991) and Alain uses its fullest sonority for her weighty presentation of the opening *Prelude and fugue in C*. However, the following *G major fugue* (better known as the *Fugue à la gigue* and of questionable authenticity) is impossibly slow and heavy. Alain is much more impressive in the *D minor fugue*, BWV 539, which is cleanly pointed and rhythmically positive. The extended *Partita* on *O Gott, du frommer Gott* opens with a suitably grand presentation of the chorale, and then the variations begin lightly and pleasingly, and throughout the organ's palette is explored imaginatively, with the style becoming more robust only towards the close. The *Canzona in D minor* is relaxed but not dull, effectively embellished in the French style. The splendid virtuoso *Fugue in C minor* (which reminds one of the more famous *D minor*, BWV 565) is fluent and quite dramatic at the end, while in the fugue, based on the *Magnificat*, Alain uses the pedals impressively to build a most powerful climax. The *Kleines harmonisches Labyrinth* has sounded more original in other hands, but here the registration is certainly interesting. The closing *Prelude in A minor* seems a bit staid, but the fugue is tangy in colouring and proceeds through its somewhat awkward changes of style with a fair degree of momentum. Throughout the sound of the organ is a pleasure in itself.

Volume 4: *Chorale preludes: BWV 711, 714–18, 722, 724–32, 734, 737–9, 765; Fantasia in B min., BWV 563; Preludes and fugues: in C, BWV 531; in E min., BWV 533.*
(M) **(*) Erato/Warner Dig. 4509 96721-2 [id.]. Marie-Claire Alain (organ of Georgenkirche, Rötha).

The Silbermann organ at Rötha (still 1991) proves ideal for this repertoire, and it stimulates Alain to some of her most spontaneous performances so far in this variable series. After a robust *Prelude and fugue in E minor*, Marie-Claire Alain is at her most chimerical in the Christmas chorale, *Nun freut euch, lieben Christen g'mein*, with the registration like tinkling bells. The two settings of *Liebster Jesu* then seem rather staid and solemn, and *In dulci jubilo* is very grand indeed. Alain clearly revels in the elaborate passage on the pedals which opens the *Prelude in C*, BWV 531, and even conveys exuberance (not a quality for which her Bach playing is notable), while the fugue is equally alive and vivid. The decoration on the first presentation of the chorale *Allein Gott*, BWV 711, also sparkles, and the melody is sharply etched. Then, after a more grandiloquent re-statement against swirling roulades (BWV 715), there is a neat fugue and finally a light-hearted gigue on the same subject, all played with considerable élan. In *Christ lag in Todesbanden*, BWV 718, the trumpet stop is used for the chorale, presented against a complex fantasia which Alain balances very well indeed, and she is almost equally good in the *Fantasia con imitazione*, used to make a serene contrast. The third group of chorales are almost all boldly registered (though not the touchingly hushed *Wir glauben all'einen Gott*, BWV 765). The contrapuntally grand *Herr Gott, dich loben wir* ends the recital massively, and here one feels Alain could have moved the music on a bit. But there is no doubt that Alain is really enjoying this organ, which sounds as if it answers readily to her touch.

Volume 5: *Chorale preludes: BWV 690–91, 695, 700, 706, 709, 712, 721; Fantasia ('Jesu, meine Freude'), BWV 713; Fugue (on a theme of Corelli) in B min., BWV 579; Kirnberger chorale preludes for Christmas, BWV 696–704; Partita sopra 'Christ, du bist der helle Tag', BWV 766; Preludes and fugues: in C min., BWV 537; in C min., BWV 549.*
(M) **(*) Erato/Warner Dig. 4509 96722-2 [id.]. Marie-Claire Alain (organ of Georgenkirche, Rötha).

Alain opens Volume 5 with the early *Prelude and fugue in C minor* (1703/4) using the Rötha organ's pedals to bravura effect, following with a fairly spontaneous account of the jolly fugue. The first chorale, *Herr Jesus Christ, dich zu uns wend*, BWV 709, is full of gleaming sunshine, while *Erbarm' dich mein O Herre Gott* brings that dedicated feeling of repose which Alain manages so well. The *Prelude* (or *Fantasia*) in *C minor*, BWV 537, opens with a massive pedal effect which sounds superb, and the fugue is presented simply and strongly. The *Partita sopra 'Christ, du bist der helle Tag'* brings six variations (it is a pity they are not separately cued) and Alain finds an orchestral range of colour for them, with a gigue movement finally leading to a majestic close. The seven *Fughettas* for the Christmas season are brief and to the point; some of the tempi here seem too slow and deliberate, and this surely also applies to the *Fugue on a theme by Corelli*, BWV 579.

Volume 6: *Canonic variations: Vom Himmel hoch, BWV 769; Chorale preludes: BWV 669–79; Clavier-Ubung, Part 3: German organ Mass: Prelude in E flat, BWV 552; Prelude and fugue in C, BWV 547.*
(M) **(*) Erato/Warner Dig. 4509 96723-2 [id.]. Marie-Claire Alain (organ of Martinikerk, Groningen).

Volume 6 was one of the earlier sets of recordings, made in 1985 in Groningen, but the organ is beautifully focused and detail hardly ever clouds. If the *C major fugue*, BWV 547, proceeds on its way somewhat remorselessly, the *Canonic variations* (as with other similar, expansive sets of divisions) bring out the very best in Marie-Claire Alain, and the opening presentation, in which the Christmas chorale cantus firmus subtly creeps through the flowing decorative lines, is very cunningly managed, while the intricate contrapuntal writing remains clear throughout. It is again a pity that there are not inner cues, for the fourth variation ingeniously includes Bach's own signature (B-A-C-H), which returns at the final grandiloquent flourish. The *Prelude in E flat* (with its biblical associations and connection with the so-called Lutheran organ Mass) is given a powerfully monolithic performance, and the chorales which follow have plenty of variety in presentation and mood. Few will fail to respond to the piquant piping in the *Allein Gott* fughetta, BWV 677.

Volume 7: *Chorale preludes: 'Herr Jesu Christ, dich zu uns wend', BWV 655; 'Vor Deinen Thron tret' ich', BWV 668; Clavier-Ubung, Part 3: German organ Mass: Chorale preludes, BWV 680–89; 4 Duets, BWV 802–5; Fugue in E flat, BWV 552.*
(M) *** Erato/Warner Dig. 4509 96724-2 [id.]. Marie-Claire Alain (organ of Martinikerk, Groningen).

Marie-Claire Alain returned to the Groningen organ in 1990, having decided that its range of colours was especially suitable for this collection of chorales, plus the four *Duets* and *Fugue in E flat* which make up the so-called 'German organ Mass'. (Its opening *Prelude in E flat* had already been included in the previous volume.) This is repertoire which finds Alain at her very finest, for her performances of the chorales clearly identify with their spiritual implications. After the gentle *Christ, unser Herr, zum Jordan kam*, the power of *Aus tiefer Not schrei' ich zu dir* (BWV 686) is gripping, while the spacious tempo for the fugue on *'Jesus Christus, unser Heiland'*, BWV 589, brings out the music's devotional dimension. The spirited, lightly articulated *Four Duets* are thought to represent the four elements: Water, Air, Fire and Earth. The closing fugue on 'O God, our help in ages past' opens very majestically indeed, and develops a fine flowing impetus, while the dénouement is very powerful. The programme is rounded off with two further chorales, the one lively, the other, *Vor deinen Thron tret' ich* ('Before your throne I now appear'), deeply felt and movingly communicated. It surely sums up the feeling which pervades Alain's approach throughout. Splendid recording: this can be strongly recommended.

Volume 8: *Chorale preludes: Orgelbüchlein Nos. 35–46, BWV 633–44; Fantasia in C, BWV 570; Partita sopra 'Sei gegrüsset, Jesu gutig', BWV 768; Preludes and fugues: in F min., BWV 534; in C min., BWV 546.*
(M) **(*) Erato/Warner Dig. 4509 96725-2 [id.]. Marie-Claire Alain (organ of St Laurentskerk, Alkmaar).

The famous Schnitger organ at Alkmaar has stimulated many Bach perfomers on record, but one has to say that Alain's opening *Prelude and fugue in C minor* is rather stoic, though it is certainly a powerful utterance. The dozen chorale preludes from the *Orgelbüchlein* bring the usual simplicity and variety, but it is the Partita on *'Sei gegrusset, Jesu gütig'* which really excites Alain's imagination – not surprisingly, as it is one of Bach's very finest set of keyboard variations; again one laments that there is no separate cueing for this expansive work (19 minutes 50 seconds) which reaches such a stunning apotheosis here. The other pieces come as something of an anticlimax, though the *F minor Fugue* is massively structured and the early *Fantasia in C* makes a reflective coda – Alain at her most responsive. The recording dates from 1990.

Volume 9: *Chorale preludes: Orgelbüchlein Nos. 1–19, BWV 599–617; 'Valet will ich dir geben', BWV 735; Fantasias: in C min., BWV 562; in G, BWV 572; Fugue on a theme of Legrenzi in C min., BWV 574.*
(M) **(*) Erato/Warner Dig. 4509 96742-2 [id.]. Marie-Claire Alain (organ of St Laurentskerk, Alkmaar).

The *Très vitement* opening of the *G major Fantasia* is always appealing, and Alain plays it perkily enough, then returning to her full-bodied style for the *Gravement–Lentement*, which she takes very literally. The first of the Orgelbüchlein chorales included here, *Nunn komm' der Heiden Heiland*, BWV 599, is also very fully orchestrated, but in *Gottes Sohn ist kommen*, BWV 600, the balance between decoration and chorale is felicitous (something Alain does not always manage ideally). Again in *Vom Himmel hoch*, BWV 606, one feels that the organ sound is excessively massive, and the same comment also applies to *Christum wir sollen loben schon*, BWV 611. The host of ascending and descending angels in BWV 606 is evocatively pictured, and the complex setting of *In dulci jubilo*,

BWV 608, is sorted out reasonably well, but it is in a quietly reflective piece like *Das alte Jahr vergangen ist*, BWV 614, that Alain is at her finest. The closing *Variations on a theme by Giovanni Legrenzi* are fluent but little else.

Volume 10: *Leipzig chorale preludes: BWV 651–2, 656–7, 659–61, 665–7; Prelude and fugue in D, BWV 532; Trio in D min., BWV 583.*

(M) **(*) Erato/Warner Dig. 4509 96743-2 [id.]. Marie-Claire Alain (organ of St Laurentskerk, Alkmaar).

There is no denying the grandeur of Alain's opening *D major Prelude*, BWV 532, and the fugue is ebullient. The *Trio in D minor* provides a comparatively lightweight transition to a further extended grouping of Bach's splendid Leipzig chorales, including three different settings of *Nun komm der Heiden Heiland*, and two each of *Komm, heiliger Geist* and *Jesus Christus, unser Heiland*. They definitely suit the panoply of colour possible with the Alkmaar organ, and Alain is generally very persuasive. Recording date: again 1990.

Volume 11: *Concertos (for solo organ): Nos. 1 in G (after ERNST); 2 in A min. (after VIVALDI: Concerto, Op. 3/8); 3 in C (after VIVALDI: Concerto, Op. 7/11); 4 in C (after ERNST); 5 in D min. (after VIVALDI: Concerto, Op. 3/11), BWV 592/6; Aria in F, BWV 587; Chorale prelude 'An Wasserflüssen Babylon', BWV 653b; Preludes and fugues: in A, BWV 536; in G, BWV 550; Trio in G min., BWV 584.*

(M) *** Erato/Warner Dig. 4509 96744-2 [id.]. Marie-Claire Alain (organ of St Martin, Masevaux).

For Volume 11 (recorded in 1992) Marie-Claire Alain went to France, and this splendid Müller organ with its bright, sunny reeds sounds just right for Bach's vivacious Vivaldi transcriptions. Moreover the manuals and pedals have a compass sufficiently wide for these arrangements to be played as Bach conceived them, which is not possible on certain of the other organs in use for this series. Alain opens the *A minor Concerto*, BWV 592, in high spirits, and clearly enjoys this repertoire, and so do we. Her account of the *Largo* of the *D minor*, BWV 596, is exquisitely poignant. The works by Johann Ernst, BWV 592 and BWV 595, are also most rewarding, especially the voicing in the touching *Grave* central movement of the *G major*. Alain's tempi are apt; allegros are not raced, but they are certainly infectious. The *Aria in F* is a Couperin transcription (from *Les Nations*). The two *Preludes and fugues* are also comparatvely lightweight, although still first-class Bach, from the early Weimar period. They are given attractively lively performances. The *Trio in G minor*, an arrangement of a tenor aria from *Cantata No. 166*, makes a pleasing encore. A splendid disc and an ideal sampler to show this artist at her most perceptive.

Volume 12: *Pastorale, BWV 590; Prelude (Fantasia) and fugue in G min., BWV 542; Prelude and fugue in A min., BWV 543; Toccatas: in C, BWV 564; in D min., BWV 565; Toccata and fugue in F, BWV 540.*

⊛ (M) *** Erato/Warner Dig. 4509 96745-2 [id.]. Marie-Claire Alain (organs of St Bavokerk, Haarlem; Jakobijnkerk, Leeuwarden).

Using a pair of magnificent Dutch organs, Marie-Claire Alain here (in 1992) surveys an ideally chosen group of Bach's organ works on the largest scale, and she is not found wanting. The pedal solo in the *Toccata in F* is spectacular indeed, while the *Fantasia and Fugue in G minor*, BWV 542, is particularly imposing, with the fugue given a thrilling impetus. The famous *Toccata and fugue in D minor* is a shade resonant – there have been clearer-focused versions – but the performance certainly does not lack panache. The *Prelude and fugue in A minor*, too, has unquestioned flair, while in the *Toccata, Adagio and fugue in C* the clarity of articulation (again with the pedals used spectacularly) is very commanding indeed, and the lyrical feeling in the *Adagio* provides fine contrast. This performance climaxes a recital of the very highest calibre, superbly recorded.

Volume 13: *6 Trio sonatas, BWV 525–30.*

(M) **(*) Erato/Warner Dig. 4509 96746-2 [id.]. Marie-Claire Alain (organ of Aa Kerk, Groningen).

Marie-Claire Alain decided to use the the 'other' (Schnitger) organ in Groningen for the *Trio sonatas* and in the notes she tells us why: 'The action is reliable if noisy. I hope that organ lovers will not take offence at this. There are also irregularities in the intensity or attack of certain stops, notably in the bass, while the hum of the motor is due to sheer overwork. However, the voicing of the old stops does not appear to have been altered . . . and the variety of the individual tone-colours and the instrument's ability to bring out the separate lines of the polyphonic writing seems to me to be admirably suited to such finely wrought and intimate works as the Six Sonatas.' However, to our ears the organ sounds very good indeed and, if there is a criticism of the sound, it is its relative lack of intimacy as recorded.

Alain plays these Italianate works with considerable flair, and she is particularly appealing in slow movements. Just occasionally the running passages of the outer movements seem almost too mellifluous but for the most part these are fresh and highly enjoyable performances that do justice to this splendid old instrument.

Volume 14: *Adagio (& Allegro), BWV 1027; Chorale prelude, 'Ein feste Burg ist unser Gott', BWV 720; Fugue in G min., BWV 578; Passacaglia and fugue in C min., BWV 582; Preludes: in G, BWV 568; in A min., BWV 569; Prelude and fugue in G, BWV 541; Ricercare a 6, BWV 1079; 6 Schübler chorale preludes, BWV 645/50.*
(M) **(*) Erato/Warner Dig. 4509 96747-2 [id.]. Marie-Claire Alain (organ of Stiftskirche, Goslar).

The famous *Schübler chorales* are the highlight of Marie-Claire Alain's final volume. They are particularly imaginative and pleasing. *Wachet auf* entirely avoids the jerky rhythm that is affected by some players, the cantus firmus sings out strongly and *Kommst du nun* is beautifully registered. The action of the Goslar organ is more audible than in some of this series, but that is hardly a problem. Alain takes the famous *Passacaglia in C minor* very spaciously, and here she miscalculates slightly, for she does not quite generate a high enough degree of tension to carry it at such a slow speed. The *Fugue in G minor* is a little didactic, too – although again very effectively registered. On the other hand, the *Prelude and fugue in G minor* is a considerable success, and the *Prelude in G* is also a fine performance. The *Adagio* (and *Allegro*) *in G* is a transcription of movements from the *Viola da gamba sonata*, BWV 1027, and is effective enough in its organ format. The *Ricercare* from the *Musical offering* is taken very slowly, again without quite enough concentration, while the *Prelude in A minor* is a curious choice as a final item.

Canzona in D min., BWV 588; Fantasie in G, BWV 572; Passacaglia and fugue in C min., BWV 582; 6 Schübler chorales, BWV 645/50; Toccatas and fugues in F, BWV 540; in D min., BWV 565.
(B) **(*) DG Dig. 439 477-2 [id.]. Ton Koopman (various organs).

Ton Koopman uses two different organs here, principally that of the Grote Kerk, Masslius, but the *Schübler chorales* are recorded on the Waalse Kerk, Amsterdam, whose reeds are brightly and colourfully projected. The recital opens with the famous *Toccata and fugue in D minor*, BWV 565, and this performance has an engaging eccentricity in that Koopman introduces decoration into the opening flourishes. The performance has an excitingly paced fugue and is superbly recorded. Contrast is provided by the *Canzona in D minor*, a slow and rather solemn contrapuntal exercise. Overall the performances are well structured and alive, if sometimes rather considered in feeling. The recital ends with the mighty *Passacaglia and fugue in C minor*, BWV 582.

Chorale preludes: Herzlich tut mich verlangen, BWV 727; In dulci jubilo, BWV 729; Liebster Jesu, wir sind hier, BWV 730; Nun freut euch, lieben Christen g'mein, BWV 734; Nun komm, der Heiden Heiland, BWV 659; Wachet auf, ruft uns die Stimme, BWV 645; Wo soll ich fliehen hin, BWV 694; Fantasias: in C min., BWV 562; in G, BWV 572; Fantasia and fugues: in C min., BWV 537; in G min., BWV 565; Passacaglia and fugue in C min., BWV 582; Preludes and fugues: in A min., BWV 543;in D, BWV 532; in E flat (St Anne), BWV 552; Toccata, Adagio and fugue in C, BWV 564; Toccatas and fugues in D min.,(Dorian), BWV 538; BWV 565.
(B) *** Decca Duo 443 485-2 (2) [id.]. Peter Hurford (organs of Ratzeburg Cathedral; Knox Grammar School, Sydney, Chapel; Church of Our Lady of Sorrows, Toronto; New College, Oxford, Chapel; All Souls' Unitarian Church, Washington, DC).

A generous 146-minute collection of major Bach organ works, taken from Peter Hurford's complete survey (see our main volume), brings two separate recitals, each framed by major concert pieces, with the beautifully played chorales used in between the large-scale pieces to add contrast. The current bright transfers seem to have added an extra sharpness of outline to the sound of some of the big set pieces, but this is something which will be more noticeable on some reproducers than on others, and the various organs are caught with fine realism and plenty of depth.

VOCAL MUSIC

Cantatas Nos. 1–14; 16–17; 19–52; 54–69; 69a; 70–117; 119–140; 143–159; 161–188; 192; 194–199 (complete).
(B) *** Teldec/Warner Analogue/Dig. 4509 91765-2 (60) [id.]. Treble Soloists from V. Boys' & Regensburg Choirs, Esswood, Equiluz, Van Altena, Van Egmond, Hampson, Nimsgern, Van der Meer, Jacobs, Iconomou, Holl, Immler, King's College, Cambridge, Ch., V. Boys' Ch., Tölz Boys' Ch., Ch. Viennensis, Ghent Coll. Vocale, VCM, Harnoncourt; Leonhardt Consort, Leonhardt.

Cantatas: Nos. 1–14; 16–17; 19.
(M) *** Teldec/Warner 4509 91755-2 (6) [id.]. Soloists & Choruses, VCM, Harnoncourt; Leonhardt Consort, Leonhardt.

Cantatas Nos. 20–36.
(M) *** Teldec/Warner 4509 91756-2 (6) [id.]. Soloists & Choruses, VCM, Harnoncourt; Leonhardt Consort, Leonhardt.

Cantatas Nos. 37–52; 54–60.
(M) *** Teldec/Warner 4509 91757-2 (6) [id.]. Soloists & Choruses, VCM, Harnoncourt; Leonhardt Consort, Leonhardt.

Cantatas Nos. 61–69; 69a; 70–78.
(M) **(*) Teldec/Warner 4509 91758-2 (6) [id.]. Soloists & Choruses, VCM, Harnoncourt; Leonhardt Consort, Leonhardt.

Cantatas Nos. 79–99.
(M) **(*) Teldec/Warner 4509 91759-2 (6) [id.]. Soloists & Choruses, VCM, Harnoncourt; Leonhardt Consort, Leonhardt.

Cantatas Nos. 100–117.
(M) *** Teldec/Warner 4509 91760-2 (6) [id.]. Soloists & Choruses, VCM, Harnoncourt; Leonhardt Consort, Leonhardt.

Cantatas Nos. 119–137.
(M) **(*) Teldec/Warner 4509 91761-2 (6) [id.]. Soloists & Choruses, VCM, Harnoncourt; Leonhardt Consort, Leonhardt.

Cantatas Nos. 138–140; 143–159; 161–162.
(M) **(*) Teldec/Warner Analogue/ Dig. 4509 91762-2 (6) [id.]. Soloists & Choruses, VCM, Harnoncourt; Leonhardt Consort, Leonhardt.

Cantatas Nos. 163–182.
(M) **(*) Teldec/Warner Dig. 4509 91763-2 (6) [id.]. Soloists & Choruses, VCM, Harnoncourt; Leonhardt Consort, Leonhardt.

Cantatas Nos. 183–188; 192; 194–199.
(M) **(*) Teldec/Warner Dig. 4509 91764-2 (6) [id.]. Soloists & Choruses, VCM, Harnoncourt; Leonhardt Consort, Leonhardt.

The remarkable Teldec project, a recording of all Bach's church cantatas, began in the 1970s and reached completion in time for our main volume to list the detailed separate issues. These were originally offered in 45 volumes, each usually combining two CDs at upper-mid-price. Now – although those separate issues currently remain available – the whole series has been repackaged and is offered in two further alternative choices: as a 60-CD box (with more music on each disc) at bargain price or as a series of ten separate collections, each of six CDs, at mid-price.

The recordings got off to a very good start but, later in the project, various flaws of intonation, and sometimes a feeling that the ensemble would have benefited from more rehearsal, plus occasionally sluggish direction, slightly undermined the overall excellence. However, the authentic character of the performances is in no doubt. Boys replace women not only in the choruses but also as soloists (which brings occasional minor lapses of security), and the size of the forces is confined to what we know Bach himself would have expected. The simplicity of the approach brings its own merits, for the imperfect yet otherworldly quality of some of the treble soloists refreshingly focuses the listener's attention on the music itself. Less appealing is the quality of the violins, which eschew vibrato and, it would sometimes seem, any kind of timbre! Generally speaking, there is a certain want of rhythmic freedom and some expressive caution. Rhythmic accents are underlined with some regularity and the grandeur of Bach's inspiration is at times lost to view. Nevertheless, overall this is an astonishing achievement, and there is much glorious music here which, to do justice to Harnoncourt and Leonhardt, usually emerges freshly to give the listener much musical nourishment. The CD transfers of the earlier analogue recordings are first class. There is no background noise to speak of and the sound is clarified and refined to bring striking presence to voices and accompaniment. The acoustic is usually not too dry – and not too ecclesiastical, either – and the projection is realistic. The later digital recordings are altogether excellent, and this is an infinitely rewarding series.

Cantatas Nos. 140: Wachet auf; 147: Herz und Mund und tat und Leben.
(M) **(*) Teldec/Warner Dig./Analogue 4509 95987-2 [id.]. Bergius, Rampf, Esswood, Equiluz,
  Hampson, Tölz Boys' Ch., VCM, Harnoncourt.

This separate reissue accompanies the complete cantata series, offering a coupling of two familiar
cantatas, both made famous by their chorales. In No. 147, some may be a little disconcerted by the
minor swelling effect in the phrasing of *Jesu, joy of man's desiring*, but otherwise the authentic
approach brings much to enjoy. In No. 140 there are two beautiful duets between treble and bass
soloists, representing dialogues between Jesus and the human soul, which are memorably sung. The
production and recording are well up to the usual Telefunken standard. However, John Eliot
Gardiner's highly accomplished performances on DG Archiv are well worth the extra money. The
instrumental playing is more polished and the soloists are even finer (DG 431 809-2).

*Cantatas Nos. 208: (i) Was mir behagt ist nur die muntre Jagd! (Hunt); 212: Mer hahn en neue
Oberkeet (Peasant).*
(M) *** Teldec/Warner Dig. 4509 97501-2 [id.]. Angela Maria Blasi, Robert Holl; (i) with Yvonne
  Kenny, Kurt Equiluz; Arnold Schoenberg Ch., VCM, Harnoncourt.

Harnoncourt tops off the complete Teldec set of Bach's church cantatas with admirably ebullient
accounts of a pair of Bach's secular cantatas, celebrating the name-days of two local dignitaries. The
cantata numbers indicate the order in which they were published by the editors of the Bach
Gesamtausgabe and have no chronological significance. The delightful *Hunt cantata* comes from
1713, when Bach was in his twenties, and celebrates the birthday of the Duke of Saxe-Weissenfels,
whose passion was hunting, It is a cantata rich in melodic invention of the highest quality, including
the famous aria, *Schafe können sicher weiden*, with its obbligato for a pair of flutes, better known as
'Sheep may safely graze', sung here quite gloriously by Angela Maria Blasi. Indeed the solo
contributions in both works are splendid, and Blasi and the robust Robert Holl both enjoy
themselves hugely in the boisterous *Peasant cantata* in their alternating bursts of extravagant praise,
lyrical and exuberant, for Carl Heinrich von Dieskau, Chamberlain at the Court of the Elector of
Saxony and Lord of the Manor, written three decades later in 1742. The libretto, by Christian
Friedrich Henrici, known as Picander, begins with a duet in Upper-Saxon peasant dialect, 'The
Chamberlain has been our new Squire. His beer makes our heads spin', but after that continues in
High German. It concerns itself with earthly pleasures, dealing in love ('Ah how delightful it is if two
people are affectionate'), paying taxes ('Our master is kind, but the tax collector is the very devil') and
even the military draft; but mostly it celebrates ('Our excellent beloved Chamberlain, an affable man
with whom no one can find fault'). This latter lyrical eulogy from the soprano is introduced by a
quotation of the famous *La Folia*, and the musical interest of this remarkably inspired cantata
(considering its ragbag of a text) is Bach's use of various old melodies familiar to his audience; and
indeed the Overture is a patchwork, almost a musical swatch of such tunes. The exuberance of the
performance carries over to Harnoncourt's accompaniments – no scholarly rectitude here – and the
recording is first rate.

*Cantatas Nos. 8: Liebster Gott, wenn werd ich sterben; 99: Was Gott tut, das ist wohlgetan, BWV 99;
106: Gottes Zeit ist die allerbeste Zeit (Actus tragicus); 131: Aus der Tiefen rufe ich, Herr zu dir.*
(M) *** O-L Dig. 444 166-2 [id.]. Monoyios, Baird, Rickards, Fast, Brownless, Kelley, Opalach, Bach
  Ens., Joshua Rifkin.

Rifkin's performances opt for the one-to-a-part principle not only in his instrumental ensemble but
also as far as the choruses are concerned. He opts for female sopranos rather than boy trebles but
uses adult male altos. Not all will find his solutions congenial and the use of one voice to a part in the
chorales is not convincing. But there is some good singing in this series, and the playing is lively
enough. Rifkin strips away much of the received convention about Bach performance practice. Of the
four cantatas included here Nos. 106 and 131 are of particular interest in probably coming from the
early months of Bach's tenure as organist at Mulhausen in 1707. The opening of *Gottes Zeit* is one of
the most beautiful moments in all Bach cantatas and it is beautifully done here. Even those for whom
the avoidance of vocal vibrato seems an unnatural constraint may find themselves persuaded by this
performance and, indeed, by the others included here. *Aus der Tiefen* is hardly less fine, and the
singers are all first class. One feels the need for greater weight and a more full-blooded approach at
times, but this is outweighed by the sensitivity and intelligence that inform these excellently balanced
recordings.

Cantatas Nos. 51: Jauchzet Gott in allen Landen; 78: Jesu, der du meine Seele; 140: Wachet auf, ruft uns die Stimme.
(M) *** O-L Dig. 443 188-2 [id.]. Baird, Minter, Fast, Thomas, Kelley, Opalach, Bach Ens., Rifkin.

Wachet auf, ruft uns die Stimme is placed first and gives pleasure, for the artists seem to be enjoying themselves. As in his other Bach records, Joshua Rifkin goes for the one-to-a-part principle in his instrumental ensemble (save for the violins), resting his case on the number of copies of the parts surviving at Leipzig. Rifkin uses a later Leipzig text for *Jauchzet Gott*. The very opening is somewhat measured and bloodless and does not ring out as it does on some rival versions; generally speaking, his account is too judicious in spirit. Julianne Baird is an excellent singer who possesses a pleasing voice and has commendable technique. The recording is excellent. For the reissue *Jesu, der du meine Seele* has been added, another very fine work which shows all the four soloists (here Julianne Baird, Allan Fast, Frank Kelley and Jan Opalach) to good advantage.

Cantatas Nos. (i) *51: Jauchzet Gott in allen Landen;* (ii; iii; iv; v; vi) *80: Ein feste Burg is unser Gott;* (vii; viii) *82: Ich habe genug;* (ix; iv; vi) *106: Gottes Zeit ist die allerbeste Zeit (Actus tragicus);* (ii; iii; iv; v; vi) *140: Wachet auf, ruft uns die Stimme;* (x; viii) *147: Herz und Mund und Tat und Leben.*
(B) **(*) EMI Analogue/Dig. (No. 51) CZS5 68544-2 [CDZB 68544]. (i) Donath, ASMF, Marriner; (ii) Ameling; (iii) J. Baker, (iv) Altmeyer; (v) Sotin; (vi) S. German Madrigal Ch. & Consortium Musicum, Gönnenwein; (vii) Souzay; (viii) Geraint Jones O, Jones; (ix) Mathis, Michelow, Crass; (x) Sutherland, Watts, Wilfred Brown, Hemsley, Geraint Jones Singers.

This quite arbitrary collection has been compiled by EMI France, gathering six of what are described as '*Les grandes cantates*' recorded between 1957 (BWV 147) and 1983 (BWV 51), in Stuttgart or at Abbey Road. Although by today's authentic standards these now sound to be rather old-fashioned Bach performances, they are certainly not unstylish. Gönnenwein is thoroughly reliable and *Eine feste Burg* achieves generally high standards. Trumpets are used (which some authorities believe to have been added after Bach's death). *Wachet auf* is equally attractive and Janet Baker's contribution, though small, is distinguished. The singing throughout is admirable, as it is in *Gottes Zeit*, Bach's funeral cantata, which has different soloists. It probably owes its existence to the death of Bach's uncle, Tobias Lämmerhirt, in 1707. Bach's feelings must have been mixed as he was left a small legacy. At any rate, if this was for the uncle, Bach did him proud, with inspired writing of great poignancy. Gönnenwein secures highly musical results on the whole but misses the last ounce of inspiration.

For the solo cantata, *Jauchzet Gott*, Helen Donath has Maurice André, no less, to provide the trumpet obbligato; but her performance, though fresh, is slightly marred by her close vibrato. When one turns to *Ich habe genug*, it is to encounter artistry of a very high order indeed. Gérard Souzay, recorded at his peak in 1958, gives an intimate, wonderfully dedicated performance which is surely one of the finest recorded accounts of any of Bach's solo cantatas. Geraint Jones accompanies most sensitively and the recording is excellent.

Joan Sutherland is not usually associated with Bach, but in the famous *Herz und Mund und Tat und Leben*, dating from the very beginning of her recording career, she displays an unfamiliar facet of her vocal facility, making of Bach's tricky lines a memorably beautiful impression, rich in ornament and variety of timbre. Helen Watts is impressive too, and the other soloists also sing with heart as well as the voice. Their German is excellent. Thomas Hemsley deserves special praise in this respect, and he is almost matched by the impeccable clarity of Wilfred Brown's diction. The Geraint Jones Singers and Orchestra give firm and buoyant support and the famous chorale, *Jesu joy of man's desiring*, is beautifully sung. Good, vivid recording.

Magnificat in E flat, BWV 243a (original version).
(M) *** O-L 443 199-2 [id.]. Nelson, Kirkby, C. Watkinson, Elliot, D. Watkinson, Christ Church Ch., AAM, Preston – KUHNAU: *Der Gerechte kommt um;* VIVALDI: *Nisi dominus; Nulla in mundo pax sincera.* ***

The original version of the *Magnificat* is textually different in detail (quite apart from being a semitone higher) and has four interpolations for the celebration of Christmas. Preston and the Academy of Ancient Music present a characteristically alert and fresh performance, and the Christ Church Choir is in excellent form. One might quibble at the use of women soloists instead of boys, but these three specialist singers have just the right incisive timbre and provide the insight of experience. The reissue is now joined with two Vivaldi motets and an interesting piece by Kuhnau, which is much more generous than the old full-priced coupling.

Mass in B min., BWV 232.
**(*) Erato/Warner Dig. 4509 98478-2 (2) [id.]. Schlick, Wessel, De Mey, Mertens, Amsterdam Bar. Ch. & O, Ton Koopman.

(M) **(*) Teldec/Warner 4509 95517-2 (2) [id.]. Hansmann, Iiyama, Watts, Equiluz, Van Egmond, V.
    Boys' Ch., Ch. Viennensis, VCM, Harnoncourt.

(B) **(*) Decca Duo 440 609-2 (2) [id.]. Ameling, Minton, Watts, Krenn, Krause, V.
    Singakademiechor, Stuttgart O, Münchinger.

(B) ** DG Double 439 696-2 (2) [id.]. Janowitz, Ludwig, Schreier, Kerns, Ridderbusch, V. Singverein,
    Karajan.

** Collins Dig. 7032-2 (2) [id.]. Dubosc, Denley, Bowman, Ainsley, George, The Sixteen & O,
    Christophers.

(BB) ** Naxos Dig. 8.550585/6 [id.]. Wagner, Schäfer-Subrata, Koppelstetter, Schäfer, Elbert, Slovak
    Philharmonic Ch., Capella Istropolitana, Christian Brembreck.

Ton Koopman directs a purposeful, consistently persuasive account of the *B minor Mass* with four
excellent, stylish soloists. With keenly responsive choral singing – as recorded, rather soft-grained – it
is warmer than most period performances but lacks some of the brightness and bite that mark the
very finest versions. So in Koopman's reading the opening fugue of the *Credo* starts softly and
gently, building up its affirmation of faith only later. The great censer-swinging motif in the *Sanctus*
is easy and persuasive, but neither the alto solo of the *Agnus Dei* (Kai Wessel the assured counter-
tenor) nor the final *Dona nobis pacem* has quite the devotional quality one finds, for example, in
Gardiner's outstanding version, an even clearer recommendation (DG 415 514-2 – see our main
volume).

Harnoncourt's version marked a breakthrough in the development of the authentic movement. It
confirms that, in parallel with his account of the *Christmas oratorio*, this is one of his most effective
Bach performances on a chamber scale, with the choir, including boys' voices, projecting keenly.
Rhythmically he is not as imaginative as his finest authentic rivals, and the brisk *Sanctus* is
disappointing, but he rises warmly to the final *Dona nobis pacem*, given a real sense of occasion. First-
rate solo singing, notably from Helen Watts, aptly firm and even. Nicely balanced recording, good
for its late-1960s vintage.

Münchinger's is a strong, enjoyable performance with an exceptionally fine quintet of soloists and
very good recording. On balance it makes a fair recommendation; however, with fastish tempi and a
generally extrovert manner it is efficient rather than inspiring. The chorus sings well but is placed
rather backwardly. The recording dates from 1971 and has been successfully remastered. The chorus
sounds vibrant and clear and the trumpets offer no transfer problems. Good value in Decca's Duo
series, but not a first choice.

Karajan conveys intensity, even religious fervour, and the very opening brings an impressive first
entry of the choir on *Kyrie*. But then, after the instrumental fugue, the contrapuntal entries are sung
in a self-consciously softened tone. There is a strong sense of the work's architecture, and the highly
polished surfaces do not obscure the depths of the music, but (despite a fine solo team) this is hardly
a first choice, although in its two-for-the-price-of-one format it is certainly reasonably priced.

Harry Christophers, with the Sixteen expanded to 26 singers, gives a fresh, direct period
performance, marked by well-chosen speeds and bright choral singing. It wears its period manners
easily, which many will welcome. The stylistic plainness, less detailed in such matters as appoggiaturas,
is certainly refreshing but rarely allows the sharply distinctive characterization which marks such
outstanding versions as Gardiner's on DG Archiv. The great *Sanctus* lacks a little in gravity, and the
slightly distanced recording takes some of the impact from bright, vigorous movements, where
trumpets are less forward than usual. Though Catherine Dubosc's vibrato is obtrusive at times, the
soloists make an excellent team.

There is certainly room for a bargain digital version of the *B minor Mass*, and the Naxos set offers
a chamber-scale performance on modern instruments. With generally well-chosen speeds it offers a
good middle-of-the-road approach, and the orchestral playing is first rate, very well recorded, with
string-playing finely detailed and with trumpets braying out superbly to bring out the joy of such
numbers as the *Gloria*. The soloists are a reliable team, with the contralto, Martina Koppelstetter,
outstanding in her two big solos, *Qui tollis* and *Agnus Dei*, the latter taken broadly with fine
concentration. In this of all Bach's choral works the chorus is central to any performance, and sadly
the backward placing of the chorus takes away bite from the singing except in the big, extrovert
moments like the very opening of the *Kyrie* and the *Sanctus*, where the singers suddenly seem more
confident.

St John Passion, BWV 245.
*** Teldec/Warner Dig. 9031 74862-2 (2) [id.]. Blasi, Lipovšek, Rolfe Johnson, Holl, Scharinger,
    Arnold Schoenberg Ch., VCM, Harnoncourt.

*** Virgin/EMI Dig. VCD5 45096-2 (2) [id.]. Covey-Crump, Thomas, Bonner, Van Evera, Trevor, Taverner Consort & Players, Parrott.

Harnoncourt's 1993 recording brings an astonishing contrast with his pioneering set of 22 years earlier. Where the earlier one used all-male forces, with boy trebles in the choir as well as singing soprano and alto arias, here Harnoncourt opts for an outstanding professional mixed chorus, the Arnold Schoenberg Choir, singing with biting incisiveness, helped by close balance and – like the Parrott version – a relatively dry acoustic. The soloists too include characterful, finely focused women singers, Angela Maria Blasi and Maria Lipovšek, with Anthony Rolfe Johnson a searchingly expressive Evangelist, as he is also for Gardiner on DG Archiv. Consistently Harnoncourt's speeds are faster than before, markedly so in the chorales, and though the performing style is lighter and more detached the thrust is keener. Gardiner is more resilient in his rhythms, leading the ear on; but, for a period performance using modest forces, this is another outstanding recommendation.

Andrew Parrott's version offers an intimate view that yet has sharp focus and plenty of power. Though speeds are generally fast and rhythms resilient, he allows himself a broader tempo for the great final chorus and the concluding *Chorale*, giving them an aptly expressive weight. The Taverner Consort here has only two choristers per part, with soloists included among the singers, while Rogers Covey-Crump as the Evangelist, light and alert, also sings the tenor arias, and David Thomas as Jesus sings the bass arias. The soprano soloists, Tessa Bonner and Emily van Evera, are both bright-toned and boyish, while the alto, Caroline Trevor, has a counter-tenor-like timbre. In compensation for any lack of weight from the scale of forces, the recording balance keeps the voices well forward, both in solo and in choral work. The dramatic bite of the performance is also enhanced by the relatively dry acoustic, not of a church but of a large studio, with fair bloom on the voices. An outstanding recommendation for those who fancy an intimate but powerfully dramatic view.

St John Passion, BWV 245 (sung in English).

⊛ (B) *** Decca Double 443 859-2 (2) [id.]. Peter Pears, Heather Harper, Alfreda Hodgson, Robert Tear, Gwynne Howell, John Shirley-Quirk, Wandsworth School Boys' Ch., ECO, Britten.

Benjamin Britten directed live performances of this, the more dramatic of Bach's *Passions*, at the Aldeburgh Festival and elsewhere, which culminated in this wonderfully vivid recording, made at The Maltings in April 1971. A quarter of a century later, with a superb CD transfer, it still sounds marvellous, demonstration analogue sound indeed, with the glowing Maltings acoustic casting its benevolent aura over soloists and chorus alike, in perfect balance with the orchestra. Yet every word of Peter Pears's superbly vibrant assumption of the role of Evangelist is absolutely clear. Britten characteristically refuses to follow any set tradition, whether baroque, Victorian or whatever; and, with greater extremes of tempo than is common (often strikingly fast), the result makes one listen afresh. The soloists are all excellent, Heather Harper radiant, and though the Wandsworth School Boys' Choir has its rough edges, it reinforces the freshness of the interpretation. The excellent accompaniments from the English Chamber Orchestra resonate grandly, and the ear relishes the richly resilient textures of modern string instruments giving splendidly full support to the singers, while there is also outstanding continuo playing from Philip Ledger. A superb bargain.

St Matthew Passion, BWV 244.

*(*) Vanguard 99070 (3) [id.]. Kirkby, Covey-Crump, George, Chance, Hill, Thomas, King's College and Jesus College Choirs, Brandenburg Consort, Stephen Cleobury.

Recorded in King's College, Cambridge, Chapel with the College Choir (the sopranos of Jesus College providing the treble descant) and with an outstanding team of soloists, the Vanguard version deserves to be more successful than it is. With Stephen Cleobury conducting, it is a well-mannered but dull performance. Perhaps in compensation, the soloists sound more effortful than they usually are, even Michael Chance – whose singing in *Erbarme dich* is far less persuasive than in the Gardiner recording. Rogers Covey-Crump is also too effortful as the Evangelist, far less successful here than he is in the Parrott version of the *St John Passion*, issued simultaneously. Maybe he and the others are worried by the reverberant acoustic, though Emma Kirkby proves a shining exception, producing not just bright but golden tone. Despite the reverberation, the recording otherwise seems to exaggerate tonal unevenness in the solo singing. The recording also balances the choir rather backwardly: with trebles on the top line and with limited numbers, the result lacks the power and bite needed even for a period performance of this masterpiece. First choice remains with Gardiner's intensely dramatic DG set (427 648-2) – see our main volume.

St Matthew Passion: Arias and choruses.

(B) **(*) DG 439 447-2 [id.] (from complete recording with Schreier, Fischer-Dieskau, Mathis, J. Baker, Salminen, Regensburger Domspatzen, Munich Bach Ch. & O, Karl Richter).

Many collectors who have another complete set will be glad to have this 73-minute Classikon bargain selection from Richter's dedicated second (1979) stereo recording, particularly as Dame Janet Baker's *Erbarme dich* is included.

Baird, Tadeusz (1928–81)

Colas Breugnon: suite.
(M) *** EMI CDMS5 65418-2 [id.]. Polish CO, Jerzy Maksymiuk – SZYMANOWSKI: *Violin concertos Nos. 1–2.* **(*)

Baird's delightful neo-classical suite (for flute and strings) has much in common with Warlock's *Capriol suite*. It is beautifully played and recorded.

Balakirev, Mily (1837–1910)

Islamey.
** Decca Dig. 436 255-2 [id.]. Olli Mustonen – MUSSORGSKY: *Pictures* **; TCHAIKOVSKY: *Children's album.* *(*)

Islamey is much the most successful item in Olli Mustonen's otherwise slightly disappointing recital. Here he is in excellent form and plays with flair and panache.

Barber, Samuel (1910–81)

Adagio for strings, Op. 11; Knoxville, Summer of 1915; Songs, Op. 13: Nocturne; Sure on the shining night.
*** EMI Dig. CDC5 55358-2 [id.]. Barbara Hendricks, LSO, Tilson Thomas – COPLAND: *Quiet city* etc. ***

Few discs of American music can match this for sheer beauty. Between them, Tilson Thomas and Barbara Hendricks have devised a programme of Copland as well as Barber with both composers at their most radiantly inspired. *Knoxville*, to a poem by James Agee, is one of the most magically evocative pieces of its kind, and is the more magical here for the authentically American inflexions that Hendricks gives it, together with glowing string-tone. The high violin entry after '*a quiet auto*' is breathtaking. The two songs which Barber orchestrated from his Opus 13 are most beautifully done too, while the celebrated *Adagio* is taken at a flowing tempo with no self-indulgence or sentimentality at all. A radiant disc.

Violin concerto, Op. 14.
⊛ *** DG Dig. 439 886-2 [id.]. Gil Shaham, LSO, Previn – KORNGOLD: *Violin concerto* etc. *** ⊛
*** EMI Dig. CDC5 55360-2 [id.]. Perlman, Boston SO, Ozawa – BERNSTEIN: *Serenade;* FOSS: *Three American pieces.* ***
** Nimbus Dig. NI 5329 [id.]. Hu Kun, ESO, William Boughton – BERNSTEIN: *Serenade.* **(*)

Though the conjunction of Barber and Korngold might not seem pointful, it works splendidly when the performer is the fine Israeli violinist, Gil Shaham. The performance of the Barber has great virtuosity and is a reading of strong profile, with every moment of dramatic intensity properly characterized. The effect is warm and ripe, with the sound close and immediate, bringing out above all the work's bolder side, allowing moments that are not too distant from the world of Hollywood music (no disparagement there), and aptly the Korngold emerges as a central work in that genre. There have been subtler readings of Barber's lovely *Concerto*, with the soloist not always helped by the close balance, but it is good to have a sharp distinction drawn between the purposeful lyricism of the first movement, marked *Allegro*, and the withdrawn, tender lyricism of the heavenly *Andante*. In the *moto perpetuo* finale Shaham brings out the fun behind the movement's manic energy, with Previn pointing the Waltonian wit. This really *is* good – and worthy to rank alongside the Stern/Bernstein (Sony). Indeed it is to be preferred to the richly extrovert Perlman account.

Perlman on his American album plays not just with unrivalled power but with rare passion in what are arguably the two finest concertante works for violin written by American composers, adding an attractive makeweight in the colourful Foss *Pieces*. For Perlman the kernel of the Barber *Concerto* lies in the central slow movement. When the soloist enters after the extended orchestral introduction, he plays with a warmth and intensity that even he has rarely matched, making the return of the main theme on the G-string a wonderful resolution, with vibrato so perfectly controlled that there is no hint of soupiness. Weight, power and virtuoso brilliance then come together in Perlman's dazzling account of the finale. Though orchestral textures could be more open, the rich tapestry of the Boston sound is moulded beautifully to the fullness of Perlman's violin.

Born in China in 1963, Hu Kun has established himself as an exceptionally sensitive violinist, who is at his most impressive in reflective music. Here in the Barber *Concerto* he brings to the lyricism of the first two movements an inner depth, while playing the brilliant third movement with mercurial lightness. This is the antithesis of Perlman's powerful, upfront reading with the same Bernstein coupling; it is a pity that the Nimbus recording is rather distant and misty, which seriously dims the responsive playing of the orchestra.

Symphony No. 1, Op. 9.
(M) (**) Bruno Walter Edition: Sony mono SMK 64466 [id.]. NYPO, Bruno Walter (with DVORAK: *Slavonic dance, Op. 46/1*) – R. STRAUSS: *Death and transfiguration* etc. (**(*))

Walter is an unexpected conductor in the music of Samuel Barber, but he recorded the *First Symphony* in 1945, two years after the composer had revised his score. It is a fresh, powerfully intense reading, let down by harsh, two-dimensional, mono sound.

(i; ii) *Canzone for flute and piano, Op. 38;* (iii; ii) *Cello sonata, Op. 6;* (iv) *Summer music* (for wind quintet), *Op. 31;* (ii) (Piano) *Excursions, Op. 20; Nocturne (Homage to John Field), Op. 33; Souvenirs, Op. 28: Pas de deux; Two-step.*
*** EMI Dig. CDC5 55400-2 [id.]. (i) Jeanne Baxtresser; (ii) Israela Margalit; (iii) Alan Stepansky; (iv) Baxtresser, Robinson, Drucker, Le Clair, Myers.

The only chamber music of Barber that is at all well known is the *String quartet* (from which derives the famous *Adagio*) and the delightfully evocative *Summer music*, which is most beautifully played here by this superbly balanced and tonally well-matched wind ensemble. The collection, presented by members of the NYPO, is one of the first issues in EMI's enterprising Anglo-American Chamber Music series. The performances are warmly spontaneous in feeling, readily demonstrating that these players have lived with this music before recording it. The *Canzone for flute and piano* has an Elysian, soaring melody (slightly French in atmosphere). It was written in 1959 and was later orchestrated to form the second movement of Barber's *Piano concerto*. Jeanne Baxtresser plays it very beautifully and convinces the listener that it sounds best in its original format. The splendid *Cello sonata*, boldly romantic yet by no means backward-looking, is hardly less memorable in its melodic invention, especially in its central *Adagio-Presto*. It has a powerful impulse and is given the most eloquent advocacy here, although Alan Stepansky and Israela Margalit are not helped by a rather too resonant acoustic. But better this than a dry studio, and the finely played piano works are beautfully full in timbre. The four *Excursions* have wit and elegance, and the *Nocturne* for John Field is quite charming, recalling that composser's own melodic simplicity and the way he anticipated the filigree decoration which Chopin was later to make famous. The concert closes with the gently sombre *Pas de deux* (which has something of Ravel in its poise and colouring) and the audacious and witty *Two-step*, both from the ballet *Souvenirs*. They originated as piano pieces (in 1951), but were written for four hands. Israela Margalit manages admirably with only two. Overall, this hour-long concert is very rewarding indeed and it cannot be too highly recommended.

(i) *Serenade for string quartet, Op.1; String quartet Op. 11;* (i; ii) *On Dover Beach, Op. 3;* (ii; iii) *3 Songs, Op. 2; 3 Songs, Op. 10; Sure on this shining night; Nocturne; Despite and still* (from *Op. 13*); *Solitary hotel, Op. 41/4; 3 Songs, Op. 45.*
*** Virgin/EMI Dig. VC5 45033-2 [id.].(i) Endellion Qt; (ii) Thomas Allen; (iii) Roger Vignoles.

This is a beautifully varied disc to recommend to anyone wanting to investigate Barber beyond the celebrated *Adagio*. Where the DG set of his complete songs centred round John Browning at the piano, this single disc is geared to the Endellion Quartet, both as accompanist in *Dover Beach* and in the two early string quartet works. The *Serenade*, Op. 1, was written when Barber was only nineteen, with the first two of its three brief movements belying any idea of a lightweight work, even bringing echoes of late Beethoven. The Endellion Quartet play with the hushed gravity and clear intensity that it deserves, and their reading of the Opus 11 *Quartet* – best known as the original source of Barber's celebrated *Adagio for strings* – has points of advantage over even the finest rivals, with more mystery and variety of expression, and with the *Adagio* kept flowing. With Thomas Allen a superb soloist, this account of *Dover Beach* not only conveys more mystery and a keener feeling for atmosphere than current rivals, it builds to a thrilling climax on the poet's expression of love. In the solo songs Allen and Vignoles opt consistently for speeds on the fast side, so that the slow tango of the Joyce setting, *Solitary hotel*, is more clearly established. If Vignoles cannot quite match the velvety persuasiveness of Browning's spontaneous-sounding accompaniments in the DG set, Allen compensates in singing that is even more consistently purposeful and varied in expression than Hampson's, and no less beautiful in tone.

Bartók, Béla (1881–1945)

Concerto for orchestra.
** Everest EVC 9008 [id.]. Houston SO, Stokowski – KODALY: *Psalmus hungaricus.* **

Opening atmospherically, Stokowski the exhibitionist gives an extrovert, highly romantic – not to say romanticized – reading of Bartók's most exhibitionist work, and with playing of such warmth it can be recommended except to those who are concerned for the last of Bartók's score details to be observed. The early stereo is made to seem much more flattering than the early LP, but this CD would have been more tempting at mid-price.

Concerto for orchestra; Kossuth.
*** Decca Dig. 443 773-2 [id.]. San Francisco SO, Blomstedt.

Written in 1903, after the young Bartók had heard and admired Strauss's *Ein Heldenleben*, the symphonic poem *Kossuth* was inspired by the Hungarian revolutionary hero in the 1848 uprising. Except in the Hungarian rhythms it may give little indication of the mature Bartók, but in its opulence it makes a most satisfying piece. A modern recording has been badly needed that would do justice to its refinement as well as to its vigour. Blomstedt fills the gap very well indeed – the only other current version offers a rushed and crudely loud account. In the *Concerto for orchestra* Blomstedt takes an equally refined view, missing some of the fire but genially bringing out not just the exotic colours but the warm lyricism of this late masterpiece.

Concerto for orchestra; (i) *The Miraculous Mandarin* (complete ballet).
(M) **(*) Virgin/EMI Dig. CUV5 61192-2 [id.]. (i) Dumont Singers; Melbourne SO, Iwaki.

Iwaki and the Melbourne orchestra have an obvious advantage over their direct mid-priced and bargain rivals in presenting the complete *Miraculous Mandarin* ballet, not just the suite, as coupling for the *Concerto for orchestra*. The recording is excellent, spacious and full, though transferred at a rather low level. The playing is finely pointed but is often too well-mannered for Bartók, lacking something in fierceness and excitement. The ballet is generously indexed with tracks.

(i) *Concerto for orchestra;* (ii) *Music for strings, percussion and celesta.*
**(*) Chant du Monde Praga PR 254047 [id.].(i) Czech PO, Lehel; (ii) Leningrad PO, Mravinsky.

The *Music for strings, percussion and celesta* was recorded at a concert during the Prague Spring in 1967. If anything, it has even greater intensity than Mravinsky's earlier (1965) performance, coupled (among other things) with Sibelius's *Seventh Symphony* on the Olympia label. In this performance the slow movement has tremendous mystery and intensity, and it makes one regret the rather less than opulent sound. The *Concerto for orchestra* is of later provenance, being made at a live concert in 1979 conducted by one of the most underrated of modern conductors; György Lehel's account of the *Dance suite* on DG, way back in the 1960s, left a strong and lasting impression. Like Janos Ferencsik, Lehel was able to evoke a tremendous poetic feeling, and the high expectations aroused by that disc are not disappointed by this performance of the *Concerto for orchestra*. It is highly atmospheric and has both a magisterial sweep and a sensitive ear for detail. Even in a catalogue rich in versions of this work (and from such celebrated names as Karajan, Solti, Bernstein) this deserves a special place. While it is not superior to such classic accounts as Reiner nor as well recorded as Jansons (see our main volume), it is completely gripping in its atmosphere. Artistically it deserves a three-star grading, though the recording is not quite comparable in quality with the very best. Nevertheless it is warm and spacious and truthfully balanced – and infinitely superior to that accorded Mravinsky.

Piano concertos Nos. 1–3.
(M) *** DG 447 399-2 [id.]. Géza Anda, Berlin RSO, Ferenc Fricsay.
(BB) **(*) Naxos Dig. 8.550771 [id.]. Jenö Jandó, Budapest SO, András Ligeti.

The Géza Anda recordings with Fricsay from the beginning of the 1960s are rather special. Both artists show a special feeling for the music's inner world and its colouring, which is especially magnetic in the slow movements. The performances are refined yet urgent, incisive but red-blooded too. They make a worthy addition to DG's series of 'Originals'. The recording, from the beginning of the 1960s, is vivid and remarkably atmospheric, yet still tangible in detail at lower dynamic levels in these new CD transfers. It compares remarkably favourably with the EMI sound for Donohoe (CDC7 54871-2), while the DG disc has a distinct price advantage.

With an all-Hungarian cast, Naxos offers invigorating accounts of the three Bartók *Piano concertos* with Jandó on top form, playing with exciting bravura throughout. The energy of the motoric *First Concerto* is not brutalized; and in the slow movement with its important percussion parts and the haunting 'Night music' of the *Second* the resonance of the recording ensures that there is plenty of atmosphere, even if in outer movements the violent brass interjections could be more cleanly focused. The *Third Concerto* opens genially, swinging along agreeably, and the scherzando section of the central movement with its exotic bird calls is piquantly observed by pianist and orchestra alike, while the momentum and good humour of the finale bring a scintillating and rousing conclusion. Apart from the excess of resonance, the recording is vivid and well balanced.

(i) *Piano concertos Nos. 1–3. Allegro barbaro; 14 Bagatelles, Op. 6; 4 Dirges, Op. 9a; 2 Elegies, Op. 8b; First term at the piano; For Children, Books I–IV; 3 Hungarian folksongs from Csík; 3 Hungarian folk tunes; Rumanian Christmas carols; 6 Rumanian folk tunes; 2 Rumanian dances, Op. 8a; 3 Rondos on folk tunes; Sonatina; 3 Studies, Op. 18; Suite, Op. 14.*
*** Ph. Dig. 446 368-2 (4) [id.]. Zoltán Kocsis; (i) Budapest Festival O, Iván Fischer.

The calibre of this Philips set cannot be denied, but it is expensive: four full-price CDs for the price of three. Kocsis's recordings of the three concertos are as idiomatic as they are vibrant, and the *Third* is superbly done, among the finest on record. The Philips recording is admirably bold and full-bodied. But there are other fine versions which cost less (notably Anda), and many may prefer to approach the solo piano music separately. The two major Kocsis recitals are available as individual issues; the first, including the *Bagatelles* and *Sonatina* (434 104-2), received a Rosette in our main edition. The second is listed and discussed below, as is the music *For Children*. The Philips box is, of course, not comprehensive and does not include the *Piano sonata*, the *Burlesques, Out of doors* or any of the *Mikrokosmos*. A reminder then, that Michel Béroff's two-CD set on EMI (CZS5 68101-2), listed in our main volume, does include the *Sonata* and, although he does not command quite the same earthiness one finds in the Kocsis set, his collection makes an admirable alternative for those who cannot afford the outlay involved, while Anda makes an impressive alternative in the concertos.

(i) *Piano concerto No. 3. Sonatine.*
(B) (**) DG Double mono 439 666-2 (2) [id.]. Monique Haas, (i) RIAS SO, Berlin, Ferenc Fricsay –
    DEBUSSY: *Préludes, Books I and II.* RAVEL: *Piano concertos.* **(*)

This is part of a very generous compilation, and these Bartók performances are a good deal more than serviceable. With Fricsay at the helm, the performance of the *Concerto* has a distinct, Bartókian character. The first movement is lightweight, but attractively so, and the *Adagio* has both atmosphere and concentration. The account of the *Sonatine* is fully acceptable and, in both, the mono recording from the 1950s is of natural quality and well transferred.

Viola concerto.
*** Sony Dig. SK 57961 [id.]. Yo-Yo Ma, Baltimore SO, David Zinman – ALBERT: *Cello concerto;*
    BLOCH: *Schelomo.****

Yo-Yo Ma had originally intended to record the cello version of the Bartók concerto which Tibor Serly made at the instigation of the Bartók Estate; but eventually he discovered he could play it at the correct pitch on the alto violin or vertical viola, in which the instrument is fitted with a long end-pin and played upright like a cello. His performance has characteristic finesse and eloquence, and it gains from the transparent sound which Zinman draws from the Baltimore orchestra. This does not displace Tabea Zimmermann on EMI (CDC7 54101-2) but makes a useful makeweight for Stephen Albert's impressive *Cello concerto*.

(i) *Dance suite;* (ii) *Music for strings, percussion and celesta;* (i) *The Wooden Prince* (complete), *Op. 13.*
(M) **(*) Sony SM2K 64100 (2) [id.]. (i) NYPO; (ii) BBC SO; Boulez – SCRIABIN: *Poème de l'exstase.* ***

In *The Wooden Prince* Bartók adopted his sweetest manner to match a fairy story which, for all its unintended Freudian overtones, essentially has a warm simplicity. Boulez is the most compelling of advocates, maintaining his concentration throughout; the *Dance suite* brings a performance just as warm, but a degree less precise. The 1975 analogue recording, originally among CBS's best, emerges vividly on CD with plenty of atmosphere, although the upper strings could be more expansive. The *Music for strings, percussion and celesta* was made in Walthamstow two years later and was one of

Boulez's finest records of that period. He gives an admirably hushed account of the opening and conveys its sense of mystery, while the quick movements have plenty of attack and rhythmic vitality. The BBC Symphony Orchestra respond with genuine enthusiasm and their playing is often most sensitive. Unfortunately the recording suffers from the artificial balance sometimes favoured by CBS, so that in the second movement a jumbo piano suddenly looms into the foreground, and the perspective elsewhere is not ideal. However, for those who can overlook this there are genuine rewards in this magnetic music-making, and the Scriabin coupling is quite superb.

Divertimento for strings; Rumanian folk dances.
(M) **(*) DG Dig. 445 541 [id.]. Orpheus CO – STRAVINSKY: *Dumbarton Oaks Concerto* etc.

The American Orpheus Chamber Orchestra give an eminently well-prepared account of the *Divertimento*. A good performance with a sense of mystery and intensity of feeling, if not entirely idiomatic. The recording is very clean and well balanced. The *Rumanian folk dances* are also attractively done, and the recording is fresh and immediate.

(i) *The Miraculous Mandarin* (complete ballet); (ii) *2 Portraits, Op. 5.*
(M) *** DG Dig. 445 501-2 [id.]. LSO, Abbado; (i) with Ambrosian S.; (ii) Shlomo Minz –
    JANACEK: *Sinfonietta.* ***

Abbado directs a fiercely powerful performance of Bartók's barbarically furious ballet – including the wordless chorus in the finale – but one which, thanks to the refinement of the recording, makes the aggressiveness of the writing more acceptable while losing nothing in power. The Janáček coupling is highly appropriate and equally successful; before that, however, the ear is sweetened by Minz's warmth in the *Portraits*.

CHAMBER MUSIC

(i; ii) *Contrasts;* (ii) *2 Rhapsodies; Rumanian folk dances.* (Solo) *Violin sonata.*
*** Hyp. Dig. CDA 66415 [id.]. Krysia Osostowicz; with (i) Michael Collins; (ii) Susan Tomes.

Hyperion's coupling of the Bartók *Contrasts*, *Rhapsodies* and the *Sonata for solo violin* is a distinguished and well-recorded issue which finds all these artists on excellent form. Krysia Osostowicz is as good as any of her rivals in the *Sonata for solo violin*, and the remainder of the programme is hardly less impressive. Michael Collins is as impressive as one expects, and the rapport between Osostowicz and Susan Tomes is exemplary. Those wanting this coupling can buy it with confidence.

(i) *Contrasts. Violin sonatas Nos. 1–2.*
(BB) *** Naxos Dig. 8.550749 [id.]. György Pauk, Jenö Jandó; (i) with Kálmán Berkes.

The appearance of both the *Violin sonatas*, together with *Contrasts* for clarinet, violin and piano, making 75 minutes of music for less than £5 (or its equivalent), will cause a stir, particularly when they are played by such an experienced artist as György Pauk and his fellow Hungarian, Jenö Jandó. Given the refinement and subtlety of Pauk's playing here, it would be churlish not to give it a three-star recommendation, the only very small qualification being the balance, which favours the piano too much in both sonatas. In the superb account of *Contrasts*, in which Kálmán Berkes joins them, the balance is better. Outstanding value.

44 Duos for 2 violins.
** Hyp. Dig. CDA 66453 [id.]. Ferenc Balogh and András Kiss.

'There is only one thing worse than having to suffer a solo violin recital – and that is a two-violin recital' (as one British composer once said). And to be frank, the present issue is not what many readers would think of as easy listening. The *44 Duos* are very much to violinists what *Mikrokosmos* is to pianists, but although they were educational in origin and purpose they were also intended (as was *Mikrokosmos)* for concert performance. Ferenc Balogh and András Kiss are the violinists of the New Budapest Quartet and give a very good account of themselves, though they are heard in a somewhat resonant acoustic environment. Their disc can be recommended, albeit not in preference to Sandor Végh and Albert Lysy (on the Astrée label), who brought greater expressive meaning to these pieces.

String quartets Nos 1–6.
** Hyp. Dig. CDA 66681/2 [id.]. New Budapest Qt.

The New Budapest Quartet offer a meticulously prepared and beautifully recorded survey of the six Bartók *Quartets* and accommodate them on two CDs. But ultimately they are curiously uninvolving, and by the side of the Tokyo Quartet (DG 445 241-2), the Alban Berg (EMI CDS7 47720-8) or the

Novák (Philips Duo 442 284-2) they are just a shade undercharacterized. One does not necessarily want the jet-set overprojection of the Emerson but one needs to be drawn into this compelling world, and the New Budapest Quartet is just a little too unexcited. The performances are sound but, by the tough benchmarks of the gramophone, they fall short of distinction while remaining more than just routine. The presentation material is particularly good.

Violin sonata No. 1; Sonatina (trans. André Gertler); *Rhapsody No. 2 for violin and piano; Hungarian folksongs* (trans. Tivadar Országh); *Hungarian folk-tunes* (trans. Jozsef Szegeti).
*** ASV Dig. CDDCA 883 [id.]. Susanne Stanzeleit, Gusztáv Fenyö.

We were full of praise for the earlier CD of Bartók's violin and piano music that these artists gave us (see our main volume). Susanne Stanzeleit has a distinguished pedigree, having studied with Kogan, Parachkevov, Milstein, Sándor Végh and practically every great violinist or violin teacher you care to think of. She and her partner, Gusztáv Fenyö, are completely inside the idiom – as you might expect, since the latter is related to Jelly d'Arányi, for whom Bartók composed the sonatas. The *Violin sonata No. 1* and the *Rhapsody No. 2* are every bit as well played and recorded as on the companion disc, and this makes a worthy successor. Strongly recommended.

Sonata for 2 pianos and percussion.
*** DG Dig. 439 867-2 [id.]. Martha Argerich, Nelson Freire, Peter Sadlo, Edgar Guggeis – RAVEL: *Ma Mère l'oye* etc. ***

Martha Argerich recorded the Bartók *Sonata* with Stephen Bishop-Kovacevich in the late 1970s, and this performance with Nelson Freire and the percussionists, Peter Sadlo and Edgar Guggeis, is a worthy successor artistically. It has tremendous fire and intensity. The aural image is not quite as fresh or open as the sound Philips produced for the earlier recording, though it is still very good and discreetly balanced. It comes with two Ravel transcriptions made by Peter Sadlo which, though of interest, are ultimately less satisfying than the originals.

PIANO MUSIC

Allegro barbaro; 4 Dirges, Op. 9a; First term at the piano; 3 Hungarian folksongs from Csík; Romanian Christmas carols; 2 Romanian dances, Op. 8a; 3 Rondos on folk tunes; 3 Studies, Op. 18; Suite, Op. 14.
*** Ph. Dig. 442 016-2 [id.]. Zoltán Kocsis.

Zoltán Kocsis recorded some of these pieces (the *Allegro barbaro*, the *Quatre Nénies* ('Dirges') and the *3 Hungarian folksongs from the Csík district*) for Philips way back in the last days of LP, and these performances are no less immaculate. This is every bit as impressive as the first CD (reviewed in our main volume) in what is to be a complete survey of the piano music from him. Like Perahia in his CBS recital and Bishop-Kovacevich on Philips (now deleted), Kocsis penetrates to the very centre or soul of this music more deeply than almost any other rival – certainly such pioneering artists as György Sándor or Andor Foldes. This is likely to be the classic set for a long time to come, and the recorded sound is altogether natural and realistic. The disc is also included with the concertos in the four-CD box listed above.

For Children, Books I–IV.
*** Ph. Dig. 442 146-2 [id.]. Zoltán Kocsis.

As in the earlier volumes, Zoltán Kocsis has been scrupulously attentive to Bartók's own wishes as expressed not only in autographs and revised editions of the published scores but as expressed on record. Kocsis's playing is both more subtle and refined (and better recorded) than his earlier, Hungaroton set. As we said of his first disc, one is reminded of Bartók's own injunction that performances must be 'beautiful but true'. Bartók playing doesn't come much better than this.

Mikrokosmos, Books I–VI (complete).
** Koch Schwann Dig. 3-1218-2 (2) [id.]. Jenö Jandó.

Coming to this music immediately after hearing the latest instalment in Zoltán Kocsis's survey of Bartók piano music perhaps shows Jenö Jandó to disadvantage. His playing is far from unimaginative but he does not command the diversity of colour, keenness of response or quite the authority of his countryman. Part of this impression may be due to the quality of the recordings, made in the studios of Saarländischer Rundfunk at Saarbrücken, which do not have the depth of perspective or realism that Philips give Kocsis. All the same, these are vital and far from insensitive performances, and are perfectly recommendable if you can't wait until Kocsis and Philips reach this (not always rewarding) collection.

OPERA

Bluebeard's Castle (complete).
(M) *** Sony SMK 64110 [id.]. Nimsgern, Troyanos, BBC SO, Boulez.
(M) *** Decca 443 571-2 [id.]. Berry, Ludwig, LSO, Kertész.

Bartók's idea of portraying marital conflict as an opera was as unpromising as could be, but in the event *Bluebeard's Castle* is an enthralling work with its concentration on mood, atmosphere and slow development, as Bluebeard's wife finds the key to each new door. Its comparative absence of action makes it ideal for the gramophone. Boulez reveals himself as an impressively warm Bartókian, the soloists are vibrantly committed and the recording is outstandingly vivid, presenting the singers in a slightly contrasted acoustic as though on a separate stage. Boulez has rarely if ever made a finer Bartók record. A superb mid-priced alternative to the Fischer and Solti versions discussed in our main volume. A full libretto is provided.

In 1965 Kertész set new standards in his version of *Bluebeard's Castle* with Christa Ludwig and Walter Berry, not only in the playing of the LSO at its peak, in the firm sensitivity of the soloists and the brilliance of the recording, but also in the natural Hungarian inflexions inspired by the conductor. This reissued recording was one of the first in Decca's new Classic Sound series and is admirably transferred to CD; a full libretto is included. At mid-price it is recommendable alongside the Boulez version; there is still a strong case for preferring the reading conducted by a Hungarian, especially as the Decca sound approaches demonstration standard, but on performance the later, Sony CD has the balance of advantage.

Beethoven, Ludwig van (1770–1827)

Piano concertos Nos. 1–5.
**(*) DG Dig. 439 770-2 (3) [id.]. Pollini, BPO, Abbado.

Piano concertos Nos. 1–2.
**(*) DG Dig. 445 852-2 [id.]. Pollini, BPO, Abbado.

Piano concertos Nos. 3–4.
**(*) DG Dig. 445 850-2 [id.]. Pollini, BPO, Abbado.

Piano concerto No. 5 (Emperor).
**(*) DG Dig. 445 851-2 [id.]. Pollini, BPO, Abbado.

Recorded live in December 1992 and January 1993, Pollini's second Beethoven cycle for DG provides an alternative rather than a replacement for his earlier series, recorded in Vienna (419 793-2), with Eugen Jochum conducting Nos. 1 and 2, Karl Boehm the rest and including also the *Choral Fantasia*. One problem is that the piano sound in the later recording is often shallower than that on the earlier set (digital in Nos. 1 and 2, analogue in the rest). On balance, the newer performance of No. 4 has keener concentration, but otherwise only occasionally do the later performances bring a clear advantage, as in the rapt intensity of Pollini's playing in the slow movements of Nos. 2 and 3, more hushed than before. The new performance of No. 1 has less sparkle than the old, which was also recorded live and has a keener sense of spontaneity. In the finale Pollini fails in the Berlin recording to articulate the anapaestic rhythm of the main theme with the precision and clarity he achieved before. In the *Emperor* too, less explicably, the earlier performance, though recorded in the studio, sounds more spontaneously expressive, with a vein of poetry that is largely missing in the live recording. On balance the earlier set is preferable, particularly when the orchestral sound on the Berlin recording tends towards harshness in tuttis, lacking bloom. But Perahia and Haitink remain first choice for a complete set of the Beethoven piano concertos (Sony M3K 44575).

(i) *Piano concertos Nos. 1–4;* (ii) *Romances for violin and orchestra Nos. 1–2, Opp. 40 & 50.*
(B) *** Ph. Duo 442 577-2 (2) [id.]. (i) Steven Kovacevich, BBC SO, Sir Colin Davis; (ii) Arthur
    Grumiaux, Concg. O, Haitink.

The first four concertos bring characteristically crisp and refreshing readings from Kovacevich and Davis which convey their conviction with no intrusive idiosyncrasy, while Nos. 3 and 4 would be top recommendations even if they cost far more. These are model performances and, throughout, the playing of Kovacevich has a depth and thoughtful intensity that have rarely been matched. The recording, from the early 1970s, is refined and well balanced and has been admirably transferred to CD. Grumiaux's *Romances* date from a decade earlier, but the Concertgebouw acoustic brings a characteristic fullness, and the solo playing is peerless.

Piano concertos Nos. 1 in C, Op. 15; 2 in B flat, Op. 19.
(M) *** DG Dig. 445 504-2 [id.]. Martha Argerich, Philh. O, Sinopoli.

The conjunction of Martha Argerich and Giuseppe Sinopoli in Beethoven produces performances which give off electric sparks, daring and volatile. Argerich's contribution in phrase after phrase brings highly individual pointing. She is jaunty in allegros rather than lightweight – one might even ask for more pianissimo – and slow movements are songful, not solemn. Very distinctive and stimulating performances, given full, vivid – albeit not ideally balanced – sound in a rather reverberant acoustic.

Piano concertos Nos. (i) 2 in B flat, Op. 19; (ii) 3 in C min., Op. 34; (i) 4 in G, Op. 58; (iii) 5 in E flat (Emperor), Op. 73. Piano sonata No. 14 in C sharp min. (Moonlight), Op. 27/2.
(M) (**(*)) EMI mono CHS5 65503-2 (2) [CDHB 65503]. Solomon; (i) Philh. O, Cluytens; (ii) BBC SO, Boult; (iii) Philh. O, Menges.

EMI Références have chosen to restore Solomon's 1944 Bedford recording of the *C minor Piano concerto* to circulation in preference to the 1956 version with Herbert Menges, which was recorded in stereo. This is logical enough, in that both the *First* and *Third Concertos* with Menges are available in EMI's two-CD Artist Profile series (CZS7 67735-2 – see our main volume). Solomon's playing is, as always, impressive in its total dedication and aristocratic finesse. Solomon's entry in the *Third Piano concerto* is marvellously imperious and the performance is every bit as good as the later version with Menges, even if the recording is not. The Dutton transfer of this concerto (reviewed below) is, however, vastly superior to theirs. This has an attenuated quality at the top end of the range; the strings sound tizzy. The later recordings, including the delightful account of the *B flat Concerto* with André Cluytens conducting, come up very well indeed. Such is the artistic quality of these performances that they deserve the strongest recommendation.

Piano concertos Nos. 2 in B flat, Op. 19; 4 in G, Op. 58 (with the composer's final revisions).
*** Conifer Dig. CDCF 237 [id.]. Mikhail Kazakevich, ECO, Mackerras.

It is surprising how flawed the texts often are of the regular editions of Beethoven, and not just of the symphonies. With the help of the Beethoven scholar, Dr Barry Cooper, the Russian pianist, Mikhail Kazakevich, has come up with fascinating new recordings of the *Second* and *Fourth Piano concertos* in revised editions. Dr Cooper, whose earlier researches into Beethoven's sketchbooks gave us an illuminating reconstruction of the fragmentary *Tenth Symphony*, has here investigated Beethoven's amendments on a score the composer himself used for a public performance of the *Fourth Piano concerto*. Though the differences are relatively minor, it is fascinating to find Beethoven regularly adding virtuoso figuration to the solo part, making the result sparkle even more brightly. The poetry of Kazakevich's crisply articulated playing is then heightened, not least in the dialogue of the slow movement, by the sharply dramatic conducting of Sir Charles Mackerras with the ECO. In the *Second Piano concerto* the amendments come only in the first movement – inked into the autograph too late to be included in the published score. They involve the orchestra as well as the solo part, and include cuts of ten complete bars, tautening and clarifying the result. However incidental the changes may seem, this disc has one listening with extra attention to the detailed text and marvelling the more. This is not just a curiosity but a viable coupling to recommend generally, for the performances, particularly of the *G major Concerto*, are memorable in their own right.

Piano concertos Nos. 3 in C min., Op. 37; 4 in G, Op. 58; 5 in E flat (Emperor), Op. 73; (i) Choral Fantasia in C min., Op. 80.
(B) **(*) Decca Double 440 839-2 (2) [id.]. Julius Katchen, LSO, Piero Gamba; (i) with London Symphony Ch.

Julian Katchen's account of the *C minor Concerto* dates from 1958, the *G major* from five years later. Both were well recorded (by Decca), though remastering reveals their early dates by the sound of the violins (in No. 3 they are somewhat thin); the piano image, however, is most real, and there is a good balance and plenty of ambient warmth. The first movement of No. 3 takes a little while to warm up but, when Katchen enters, the whole performance springs splendidly to life. The slow movement is sustained with considerable tension, its beauty readily conveyed, and there is plenty of vigour and sparkle in the finale. Katchen is less penetrating in No. 4. Gamba opens sensitively, the pianist's virtuosity, tempered with restraint, is remarkable, and the performance is by no means without feeling, but Kempff and Kovacevich find more expressive depth in this work than Katchen does. Katchen's *Emperor* is an excellent performance, full of characteristic animal energy and superbly recorded (and remastered). The first and last movements are taken at a sparkling pace, but not so fast that Katchen sounds at all rushed. Plainly he is enjoying himself all the way through, and so are we.

With this pianist, who has sometimes seemed too rigid in his recorded playing, it is good to find that here he seems to be coaxing his orchestra to match his own delicacy. The slow movement is very relaxed – as in the *Third Concerto* – but, with the tension admirably sustained, it contrasts well with the bravura of the finale. Overall, this is an enjoyable set of recordings and is undoubtedly good value. The performance of the *Choral Fantasia*, Beethoven's curious hybrid work for piano, chorus and orchestra so obviously anticipating the *Choral Symphony*, is highly compelling. Katchen is very commanding in the opening cadenza, and later in the work there are some delightfully light touches from the orchestra. Very well recorded in 1965, it remains among the freshest versions in the catalogue.

(i) *Piano concerto No. 3 in C min., Op. 37;* (ii) *Piano trio No. 7 (Archduke), Op. 97.*
(M) (***) Dutton Lab. mono CDLX 7015 [id.]. Solomon; (i) BBC SO, Boult; (ii) Henry Holst,
   Anthony Pini.

There is simply no comparison between the Dutton transfer of the 1944 account of the *Third Piano concerto* and the one offered on the EMI Références set. The latter does not tame the tizz on the top, nor does it reproduce as warm a sound from the wind or as firm a piano-sound. The performance was recorded in Bedford, whither the BBC Symphony Orchestra was evacuated in 1944 when London was under attack by V-bombs. Solomon's performance is one of the great interpretations of this concerto. He holds the listener in the palm of his hand from his entry throughout the whole; every phrase is alive and sharply and compellingly characterized, yet at no time is it for the glory of Solomon. Another point of interest is that he plays the Clara Schumann cadenza in the first movement. Sir Adrian gets a very good response from the orchestra. It is doubtless a counsel of perfection, but the difference is so great that it is almost worth paying the extra and supplementing the EMI set. The Dutton CD brings another wartime performance, from 1943, of the *Archduke Trio* with Henry Holst and Anthony Pini – not really in the same class, but Solomon himself is in very good form.

Piano concertos Nos. 4 in G, Op. 58; 5 (Emperor), Op. 73.
(M) *** DG 447 402-2 [id.]. Wilhelm Kempff, BPO, Leitner.
(BB) **(*) RCA Navigator Dig. 74321 17890-2. Emanuel Ax, RPO, Previn.

The Kempff/Leitner performances, now reissued in DG's 'Originals' series, bring an outstanding mid-priced recommendation for this particular coupling. The digital remastering has perceptibly enhanced the sound, with the most natural balance in the *Fourth Concerto*. Here Kempff's delicacy of fingerwork and his shading of tone-colour are as effervescent as ever, and the fine control of the conductor ensures the unity of the reading. Although Kempff's version of the *Emperor* is not on an epic scale, it has power in plenty, and excitement, too. As ever, Kempff's range of tone-colour is extraordinarily wide, from the merest half-tone, as though the fingers were barely brushing the keys, to the crisp impact of a dry fortissimo. Leitner's orchestral contribution is of high quality and the Berlin orchestral playing has vigour and warmth. Here some reservations need to be made about the quality of the remastered CD. The bass is somewhat over-resonant and the orchestral tuttis are very slightly woolly; the piano timbre is natural but the slight lack of firmness in the orchestral focus is a drawback, though it does not seriously detract from the music-making.

   Emanuel Ax's thoughtful, lightweight Beethoven style is entirely suited to the *G major Concerto* and this somewhat reticent performance is most enjoyable in its way, bringing out the work's expressive lyricism appealingly, with Previn providing sympathetic support and no lack of sparkle in the finale. The *Emperor* is less suitable for such an approach, although again Previn's understanding of Ax's lack of forcefulness is a plus point. The relaxed quality of the solo playing however makes this a less bitingly compelling version than many, with the first movement less of a contest than it can be; while the flowing speed for the slow movement and the scherzando quality in the finale make it less weighty than usual, powerful as Ax's articulation is. Unexceptional digital recording, the orchestra appropriately mellow.

(i) *Piano concerto No. 5 (Emperor);* (ii) *Piano concerto in E flat, WoO 4* (arr. & orch. Willy Hess);
(iii) *Violin concerto in D, Op. 61;* (iv) *Triple concerto for violin, cello and piano in C, Op. 56.*
(B) *** Ph. Duo 442 580-2 (2) [id.]. (i) Kovacevich, LSO, Sir Colin Davis; (ii) Lidia Grychtolowna,
   Folkwang CO, Heinz Dressel; (iii) Herman Krebbers, Concg. O, Haitink; (iv) Szeryng, Starker,
   Arrau, New Philh. O, Inbal.

Kovacevich is unsurpassed today as an interpreter of the *Emperor concerto*. This superb 1969 account with Davis set a model for everyone and, while his newer, Eminence version (CD-EMX 2184) with the soloist directing from the keyboard is sharper and tauter and the digital piano recording is aptly brighter and more faithful, the earlier version is given an excellent analogue sound-balance and remains highly recommendable. It is part of an attractive Duo compilation which includes also the early *E flat Piano concerto* (WoO 4) which the composer wrote when he was only fourteen. The work survives in a copy manuscript containing only the piano score plus an indication that the orchestral passages were scored for two flutes, two horns and strings. The present performance uses a reconstruction by Willy Hess in which the dominating flute colouring of the orchestration is hardly characteristic and not helped by less than distinguished playing from the wind section of the Folkwang Chamber Orchestra. The performance is spirited, especially the finale; but the piece sounds more like a concerto in the style of the sons of Bach rather than showing much evidence of the pen of even an immature Beethoven. Krebbers' 1974 recording of the *Violin concerto* is distinguished and will disppoint no one. As a soloist he has not quite the commanding 'star' quality of David Oistrakh, Menuhin or even Grumiaux, but he plays with an appealing naturalness and a totally unforced spontaneity. In his hands the slow movement has a tender simplicity which is irresistible, and it is followed by a delightfully relaxed and playful reading of the finale. In the first movement Haitink and his soloist form a partnership which brings out the symphonic strength more than almost any other reading. If the balance of the soloist is a shade too close, the recording is otherwise excellent, and it has transferred with vivid fullness to CD. The companion account of the *Triple Concerto* with Arrau, Szeryng and Starker again brings full and spacious Concertgebouw recording (dating from four years earlier), but Arrau and his colleagues are less strongly projected and, by adopting very unhurried tempi, they run the risk of losing concentration. The central brief *Largo* is exquisitely done, and Starker's dedicated and spacious reading of the great cello solo has rarely been matched; but the outer movements, with the solo playing almost on a chamber scale, lack the bite and bravura of the finest rivals. However, at 'two CDs for the price of one', this set remains well worth consideration for both the *Emperor* and the *Violin concerto*.

(i) *Piano concerto No. 5 (Emperor);* (ii) *Violin concerto in D; Romances Nos. 1–2, Opp. 40 & 50.*
(BB) **(*) EMI Seraphim Dig./Analogue CES5 68520-2 (2) [CDEB 68520]. (i) Youri Egorov, Philh. O, Sawallisch; (ii) Josef Suk, New Philh. O, Boult, or ASMF, Marriner – MOZART: *Piano concerto No. 20.* **(*)

Youri Egorov in his first concerto recording, made in the early 1980s, gives a refreshingly direct but still individual account of the opening allegro of the *Emperor*, helped by authoritative conducting from Sawallisch, and the finale, too, has splendid drive and attack, supported by bright yet full, digital sound. The slow movement is the controversial point, taken at a very measured *Adagio* which might have flowed better had Egorov adopted a more affectionate style of phrasing. Suk also chooses a very measured tempo for the first movement of the *Violin concerto* which is unusually slow, and some may feel that there is not enough urgency and concentration to sustain the interpretation, especially as Suk's tone, as recorded, is on the small side. But otherwise the analogue recording, from the beginning of the 1970s, is excellent, and Suk's playing is both noble and spacious. The performance is classical in style, though Suk, like Kreisler, pulls back at the G minor section in the development of the first movement. It is the breadth and grandeur of design that emerge and Sir Adrian observes certain revisions in the score, made in Alan Tyson's relatively recent edition. The eloquence of the slow movement and the lightness and sparkle of the finale are in no doubt; and the *Romances* are very successful, too. Good value at EMI's bargain-basement price for the two discs.

(i) *Piano concerto No. 5 (Emperor); Piano sonata No. 32 in C min., Op. 111.*
(BB) **(*) Discover DICD 920160 [id.]. Jasminka Stancul, (i) Belgian R. & TV O, Rahbari.

As in the rest of her enjoyable super-bargain series of Beethoven concertos with Rahbari (see our main volume), Jasminka Stancul offers a thoroughly alive, keenly articulated *Emperor*, well supported by the Belgian Radio and TV Orchestra. The slow movement is expressively satisfying and the finale sparkles. She follows Kovacevich's example on his individual Philips disc by offering a late sonata as coupling, and her performance is particularly thoughtful and individual in the second-movement Arietta with variations. This bright, well-balanced CD is not a first choice but is excellent value and caps her cycle impressively.

Violin concerto in D, Op. 61.
ꙮ (M) *** DG 447 403-2 [id.]. Schneiderhan, BPO, Jochum – MOZART: *Violin concerto No. 5.* ***

(i) *Violin concerto in D; Coriolan overture, Op. 62.*
(M) **(*) Virgin/EMI Dig. CUV5 611117-2 [id.]. (i) Mayumi Seiler, City of L. Sinfonia, Hickox.

Violin concerto in D: Romances Nos. 1-2, Opp. 40 & 50.
(M) **(*) Ph. 442 398-2 [id.]. Henryk Szeryng, Concg. O, Haitink.

Wolfgang Schneiderhan's stereo version of the *Violin concerto* is among the greatest recordings of this work: the serene spiritual beauty of the slow movement, and the playing of the second subject in particular, have never been surpassed on record; the orchestra under Jochum provides a background tapestry of breadth and dignity. As an added point of interest, Schneiderhan uses cadenzas that were provided for the transcription of the work for piano and orchestra. This makes an entirely justified reissue in DG's 'Legendary recordings' series, and the current transfer of the well-balanced (1962) analogue recording is fresh and realistic. Moreover the new Mozart coupling is both more appropriate and more generous. Among modern digital versions, Kremer's Teldec account with Harnoncourt remains commandingly spontaneous (9031 74881-2), while Perlman's Berlin recording with Barenboim is also highly recommendable (EMI CDC7 49567-2).

Szeryng's 1974 recording with Haitink brings a superb balance between lyricism and power. The orchestral introduction is immediately riveting in its breadth and sense of scale, and throughout the first movement Szeryng's playing has great beauty. His use of the Joachim cadenza is an added attraction. The slow movement blossoms with a richly drawn line, the glorious second subject phrased with great intensity; after this emotional climax, the link into the finale is managed with a fine sense of spontaneity. The dance-like mood which follows completes an interpretation that is as satisfying in its overall shape as in its control of mood and detail. The recording is full and resonant – inner orchestral definition is not always absolutely sharp – but the ambience is attractively warm. However, the CD transfer adds a very slightly febrile quality to the soloist's upper range; one must comment that, while the *Romances* (recorded two years earlier) make a fine bonus, for very little more one can get the Grumiaux Philips Duo set which includes also the Brahms, Mendelssohn and Tchaikovsky concertos (442 287-2).

An impressive account of the *Violin concerto* from Mayumi Seiler which stands up well against distinguished mid-priced competition. Hickox is slightly below his finest form (in the overture as well as the concerto) and is slightly stiff at the opening of the first movement, but his soloist soars lyrically and is movingly serene in the slow movement, creating an ethereal thread of sound for the secondary theme; she then dances away in the finale. Max Rostal's cadenzas are used, which include the timpani parts used in Beethoven's transcription of the work for piano and orchestra. Excellent recording.

(i) *Triple concerto for violin, cello and piano, Op. 56. Piano trio No. 5 in D (Ghost), Op. 70/1.*
(M) ** Teldec/Warner Dig. 4509 97447-2 [id.]. Trio Fontenay, (i) with Philh. O, Inbal.

The *Triple concerto* is convincingly balanced on Teldec and the performance of the opening movement spaciously conceived. The Trio Fontenay make a convincing group contribution, but the slow movement is robbed of warmth by the rather unglamorous sound; this is even more striking in the generally well-played *Trio*, where again the *Largo* very evidently lacks atmosphere.

The Creatures of Prometheus: Overture and ballet music, Op. 43 (complete).
*** Hyp. Dig CDA 66748 [id.]. SCO, Sir Charles Mackerras.
**(*) Teldec/Warner Dig. 4509 90876-2 [id.]. COE, Harnoncourt.

The 18 numbers of Beethoven's early ballet about Prometheus, the bringer of fire, are recorded all too rarely. Here in fresh, vigorous performances Sir Charles Mackerras and the Scottish Chamber Orchestra bring out not only the drama of the piece but those colourful qualities which made Beethoven a great composer of light music. Exceptionally for him, he included an important part for the harp, and the ballet ends with the number that gave him one of his most fruitful themes, ultimately used for the finale of the *Eroica Symphony*. Recommended alongside the fine alternative version by the Orpheus Chamber Orchestra (DG 419 608-2 – see our main volume).

Harnoncourt's comparative gruffness in the *Overture*, with its bold opening chords, prepares the listener for robust accents and strongly rhythmic allegros, and his performance reminds the listener more than usual of Beethoven the symphonist, most appropriately so in the finale. The solo playing from the COE is peerless; no one could complain that the *Adagio*, with its harp scoring and flute, bassoon and cello solos, lacks romantic feeling, while at times there is beautifully light articulation from the violins. Excellent, resonant recording and a performance which is full of individuality and character.

Overtures: *Coriolan; Creatures of Prometheus; Egmont; Fidelio; Leonora No. 1; Leonora No. 3; The Ruins of Athens.*
(BB) *** RCA Navigator 74321 21281-2. Bamberg SO, Eugen Jochum.

Not surprisingly, Jochum provides a superb collection of overtures, naturally spontaneous and full of warmth and drama. The finest performance of all is *Leonora No. 3*, which makes a thrilling end to the programme. The Bamberg Symphony Orchestra are in excellent form and the recording has a full, spacious acoustic with a natural brilliance. A real bargain.

Overtures: *Coriolan, Op. 62; Leonore No. 2, Op. 72.*
(M) (***) EMI mono CHS5 65513-2 (3) [id.]. BPO or VPO, Furtwängler – BRAHMS: *Symphonies Nos 1–4* etc. (**(*))

These studio recordings of Beethoven overtures, the one from Vienna in 1947, the other from Berlin in 1954, make a good supplement to Furtwängler's Brahms cycle, with Vienna mellower-sounding than Berlin, but both less harshly recorded than on the Brahms broadcasts.

Symphonies Nos. 1-9.
(B) *** RCA Dig. 74321 20277-2 (5). N. German RSO, Günter Wand (with Edith Wiens, Hildegard Hartwig, Keith Lewis, Roland Hermann, combined Ch. from Hamburg State Op. and N. German R.in *No. 9*).
**(*) Everest/Vanguard EVC 9010/14 (5) [id.]. Vyvyan, Verrett, Petrak, Bell, BBC Ch. (in *No. 9*); LSO, Krips.
** Ph. Dig. 442 156-2 (5) [id.]. Dawson, Van Nes, Rolfe Johnson, Schulte, Gulbenkian Ch. (in *No. 9*); O of 18th Century, Brüggen.

Wand's digital set with the North German Radio Orchestra, recorded between 1985 and 1988, makes a first class bargain choice, and indeed is thoroughly recommendable irrespective of cost, offering performances without idiosyncrasy yet full of character that are consistently satisfying to live with. There is a directness about Wand's approach to Beethoven, both early and mature, which is the opposite of dull or stuffy. Throughout the orchestral playing is of the highest quality and the recording is superb, both clean and atmospheric, and admirably transparent (witness the very opening of the first movement of No. 9). The *First Symphony* is strikingly fresh, with briskly vivacious allegros matched by those in the *Fourth*, which is particularly attractive and has splendid rhythmic bounce. No. 2 and the vigorous No. 8 have hardly less vitality, while slow movements have a simple eloquence and warmth that are most satisfying. Wand is generous with exposition repeats. In the *Seventh* – with the horns beautifully balanced in textures both clear and full-bodied – every single repeat is observed; yet, although tempi are relatively steady, the propulsion remains unflagging from first to last. The *Eroica* is admirably paced, a strong reading with plenty of underlying lyrical feeling, and again the horns are impressive in the Trio of the Scherzo and in the joyous finale. The *Pastoral*, taken rather steadily, does not have a very resonant bass, but the cello line is full and warm and the finale radiant. It is far preferable to the Karajan account in his 1961–2 analogue set and, while at times those performances may have a more dramatic edge, there is no lack of urgency and adrenalin flow with Wand; and the added fullness and naturalness of the RCA recording are especially telling in the even-numbered symphonies. The *Fifth* makes a powerful statement and, with its fine slow movement (bringing a neat coda to lead to the Scherzo) and compulsive finale, can be mentioned alongside Giulini's Los Angeles version – see below. The whole series is capped by a powerful account of the *Ninth* with weight and rhythmic bite in equal measure and here, like the *Eroica*, the *Adagio* is movingly intense. The finale is led by a fine team of soloists with the tenor, Keith Lewis, appealingly ardent and the soprano, Edith Wiens, notably secure in her big moment. The combined choruses of North German Radio and Hamburg State Opera, very effectively balanced, sing with fervour, and after Wand's spacious broadenening at the centre of the movement the closing pages bring a thrilling culmination. You can't better this if you want a complete set of the Beethoven symphonies played on modern instruments. As we go to press, RCA have made Wand's discs available separately at mid-price: *Symphonies Nos. 1* and *6* (74321 20278-2); *Symphonies Nos. 2* and *7* (74321 20279-2); *Symphonies Nos. 3* and *8* (74321 20280-2); *Symphonies Nos. 4–5* (74321 20281-2); *Symphony No. 9* (74321 20282-2).

In 1960, well before Karajan and the Berlin Philharmonic made their pioneering cycle of the Beethoven symphonies for DG, Josef Krips and the LSO recorded one for Everest, similarly completed over a short span and issued in 1960. It did not get nearly as wide a circulation as it deserved, which makes this CD transfer doubly welcome, for this is an exceptionally fresh and alert series, conveying a sense of cohesion and spontaneity, only occasionally at the expense of polish. In 1960 the LSO was in process of rising to a new peak, having acquired such outstanding players as Barry Tuckwell and Gervase de Peyer, and the response here to a challenge is consistently clear. As a Beethoven interpreter Krips is in the central tradition, with speeds well chosen if rather broader than has latterly become the rule. In such a symphony as the *Pastoral* or the *Eighth*, one regularly registers that here is a great Schubertian, for Krips makes the music sing, giving it a glow of warmth. That is not to say that the performances lack dramatic bite. No. 4, for example, is given with great flair and panache, with the syncopations in the first movement sharply driven home and the great violin melody of the slow movement flowing sweetly. In the great opening movements of the *Eroica* and No. 9, weight and incisiveness go together, helped by the sharp focus of the 1960 sound, transferred from the original masters to give a fine sense of presence, though often with an acid edge on high violins in tuttis. Otherwise one would hardly register that these are vintage recordings. The *Funeral march* in the *Eroica*, against the general rule, is taken fast at a speed one nowadays associates with period performances, making its march-like qualities clearer without sounding perfunctory. After the sunny and lyrical performance of No. 8, the cycle is crowned by the *Ninth*, particularly the choral finale which, with excellent soloists and chorus, builds to a thrilling climax, giving the illusion of live performance. Only No. 5 is a degree disappointing, well shaped and pointed but too relaxed, lacking some of the tensions needed. In the manner of the time, exposition repeats are not observed in Nos. 3, 6 and 7, and neither repeat is observed in the finale of No. 5. This remains a highly stimulating set, but it is much more expensive than the superb Wand set – indeed, with the discs costing only a little below premium price, and bearing in mind the edge on the violin timbre, it cannot be regarded as a primary recommendation until the cost is reduced.

Brüggen conducts the period instruments of the Orchestra of the 18th Century in a Beethoven cycle more intimate than its direct rivals. The best is first, for not only is the scale of Brüggen's approach very apt for No. 1, but the Philips recording is at its fullest and most vivid. No. 2, by contrast, similarly sympathetic as an interpretation, is marred by thin sound, rather fizzy in tuttis. The recordings were made over an extended period between 1984 and 1992, with Nos. 4, 6 and 9 given studio recordings but the rest recorded live, adding to the discrepancies both of performances and of sound. Too often the violin tone is thin and scrawny, even by the standards of period performance. Those who fancy period readings with more relaxed manners than in the main rival sets may well respond to Brüggen, but his tendency to vary speeds erratically is distracting, making this an issue to approach with caution. The soloists in No. 9 are first rate, but the chorus lacks bite and intensity. The five discs come in a single compact box.

Symphonies Nos. 1 in C, Op. 21; 3 in E flat (Eroica); 6 in F (Pastoral); 8 in F, Op. 93.
(B) **(*) Decca Double 440 627-2 (2) [id.]. VPO, Pierre Monteux.

Symphonies Nos. 2 in D, Op. 36; 4 in B flat, Op. 60; 5 in C min., Op. 67; 7 in A, Op. 92; Overtures: Egmont; King Stephen.
(B) *** Decca Double 443 479-2 (2) [id.]. LSO, Pierre Monteux.

Pierre Monteux, recording for Decca in his last years, did not include the *Choral Symphony* (the company turned to Ansermet and Stokowski instead). But he recorded all the rest, and with distinction. Listening to these performances together as a sequence, the listener discovers the continuing thread of life-enhancing energy that brings all Monteux's music-making to life, together with consistent imagination in his phrasing and glowing treatment of the detail of slow movements. The Double Decca reissues have been sensibly divided into the performances with the VPO and those with the LSO and thus provide an obvious first choice for those not wanting both sets.

For some reason, the 1960 VPO coupling of Nos. 1 and 8 brings a hint of discoloration in the woodwind. But the ear soon adjusts when in both works Monteux steers an ideal course, neither underestimating the weight nor making the music too heavy. The first movement of the *Eighth* is especially exhilarating, and the fast tempo of the *Allegretto* which follows (feather-light in articulation and more scherzando in effect than usual) demonstrates the conductor's individuality. The *Eroica* was the first to be recorded (in 1957) and again it is as masterly as it is individual. The first movement (without exposition repeat) is superbly dramatic – the climax of the development wonderfully built up – and only in the *Funeral march* are there any real reservations. A slower speed would have allowed a greater sense of tragedy; and his oboe soloist is on the flat side, though never beyond tolerance. The early stereo is relatively coarse and does not allow a real pianissimo. The *Pastoral* dates from only a year later, yet the recording is strikingly better, full, warm and vivid. The performance emerges as finer than we had remembered it, even if the VPO were not on the form they were for the *Eroica*. The first movement is invigoratingly strong and direct rather than lilting, with trumpeting horns, but the brook flows agreeably, and the finale brings a burst of sunshine; the coda, however, might have displayed more contrasting repose.

At the beginning of the 1960s Monteux achieved a special understanding with the players of the LSO, and his 1960 coupling of Nos. 2 and 4 shows this genial rapport to rewarding effect. The performance of No. 2 is essentially light in style, but the alertness of the LSO playing makes it strong and enjoyable. No. 4 is hardly less successful. You have only to listen to the way Monteux leads into the second subject or the way he floats the high violin melody in the slow movement to realize that a master is at work. The finale is exhilaratingly hectic in the fast, flying manner that he tends to adopt in Beethoven finales: it is very exciting when played with such precision. Perhaps it was this movement that prompted his famous remark to the LSO players: 'Gentlemen, you may think this is too fast, but it is how the critics like it.' What he meant was that he revelled in risk-taking in the recording studio.

In a hardly less memorable performance of the *Fifth*, the volatile Frenchman plays his part. Where hitherto these Beethoven performances have tended to be straight and direct, here there is not only strength and drive but an element of waywardness. Unashamedly Monteux presents the fate theme at the very start more slowly and weightily than the very fast basic tempo of the movement, an effect which requires sleight-of-hand, both there and elsewhere. It is a personal reading, but a compelling one in all four movements, with fine articulation from the LSO, unashamedly strong, even aggressive in the finale. The *Egmont Overture* has comparable urgency but less polish; the *King Stephen overture* brings a Gallic twinkle.

The series is capped by an unforgettable account of the *Seventh Symphony*. Monteux opens with a powerful slow introduction, followed by a hard-driven 6/8 *Allegro* but with the rhythms nicely pointed, and a fast *Allegretto* to recall the famous early mono LP by Erich Kleiber. Then comes a wide speed-change for the trio after the Scherzo and an absolute headlong finale, out-Toscanini-ing Toscanini in its incandescent excitement, with the horns singing out flamboyantly at the close. Throughout, the full, atmospheric recording adds just the right degree of weight, and this Monteux/ LSO box offers Beethoven performances as stimulating as any available.

Symphonies Nos. 1 in C; 2 in D, Op. 36; Overture Coriolan.
(M) *** Bruno Walter Edition: Sony SMK 64460 [id.]. Columbia SO, Bruno Walter.

Bruno Walter's CBS recordings of the Beethoven symphonies now reappear on a series of mid-priced discs as part of the Bruno Walter Edition. They were recorded in 1958/9 in the American Legion Hall in Hollywood, which provided an attractive ambient warmth, while the upper-string timbre remained fresh and lively. The Columbia Symphony was a pick-up orchestra of outstanding musicians whom Walter moulded into a cohesive body of players of some distinction. In the *First Symphony* Walter achieves a happy medium between the eighteenth-century quality of Karajan's analogue versions and the turgidity of Klemperer. The most controversial point about his interpretation of the *Second Symphony* is the slow movement, which is taken very slowly indeed, with plenty of rubato. But the rich warmth of the recording makes the effect very involving. For the rest, the speeds are well chosen, with a fairly gentle allegro in the finale which allows the tick-tock accompaniment to the second subject to have a delightful lift to it. On technical grounds this reissue can stand alongside most of the more recent competition, and the remaining hiss is not disturbing. The *Coriolan Overture* is equally impressive, spacious, warm and dramatic, and the sound-balance is remarkably telling.

Symphonies Nos. 1 in C, Op. 21; 3 (Eroica).
**(*) EMI Dig. CDC7 54501-2 [id.]. Concg. O, Sawallisch.
**(*) Decca Dig. 430 515-2 [id.]. San Francisco SO, Blomstedt.

The *First Symphony* sounds fresh and vibrant in Sawallisch's hands and the textures are clean and transparent in this splendidly engineered EMI recording. However, it is the *Eroica* for which collectors will buy this disc, and this new one is among the best to have appeared in recent years. It is a performance of some stature and has breadth and dignity; the orchestral playing is a joy in itself. The recording, too, is very good, though the violins above the stave have a very slight hardness that one did not encounter from softer-grained analogue sound.

Very well recorded in Decca sound that is both full-bodied and transparent, Blomstedt's coupling provides satisfyingly weighty and strong performances, superbly played with outstanding wind solos (notably from the oboe in the *Funeral march*). These are most satisfying, sharply focused readings, notably of the *Eroica*, lacking only a little in Beethovenian dynamism. Speeds are relatively broad, but brisk enough for the exposition repeat to be observed in the *Eroica* first movement and for repeats to be included in the da capo of the Scherzo of the *First Symphony*. There are more revelatory and individual readings than this, but in its central way this is very enjoyable.

(i) *Symphonies Nos. 1 in C, Op. 21; 3 in E flat, Op. 55; 5 in C min., Op. 67;* (ii) *Overtures: Creatures of Prometheus; Egmont; Fidelio.*
(BB) **(*) EMI Seraphim CES5 68518-2 (2) [CEDB 68518]. (i) Munich PO; (ii) BPO; Rudolf Kempe.

Kempe's cycle of Beethoven symphonies originally had the distinction of being the first to be issued in quadraphonic form on LP, and the warm breadth of the early-1970s analogue sound reflects that.

Now it has another distinction in being used to launch EMI's Seraphim label, which offers two CDs for the price of one *medium-priced* disc, thus competing in the Naxos price-range. However, the documentation is minimal and cannot compare with the musical notes Naxos provide with their super-bargain discs. Kempe's performances were recorded over a relatively brief period, and this shows in their merits as well as their limitations. Plainly the Munich orchestra responded to this challenge, producing fresh, spontaneous-sounding playing, not always perfectly disciplined but natural and communicative. Kempe as a Beethovenian believes in letting the music speak for itself at sensitive and unexaggerated tempi, so that even the introduction of No. 1 is weighty. Otherwise the crisp articulation of the Munich woodwind makes for refreshing results in the allegros, with the Munich strings producing sweet tone in the slow movement. Not all the symphonies sound as intense as they might – No. 5, for example. But even here the performance is warmly enjoyable, if not electrifying. Exposition repeats are normally observed, though not in the *Eroica*. Here Kempe takes a spacious view of the first movement. Initially it may sound unexciting, but then (as with Klemperer) the structure builds up strongly and compellingly. The *Funeral march* is subdued and inward, spontaneous-sounding in its concentration up to the hushed distintegration of the main theme. The oboe solos (Kempe himself was an oboist before he became a conductor) are beautiful. Fast speeds and fine articulation in the last two movements, although here the violins lose just a little of their bloom. The overtures feature the Berlin Philharmonic and are very well played indeed. Good value.

Symphonies Nos. 2 in D, Op. 36; 8 in F, Op. 92.
*** EMI Dig. CDC7 54502-2 [id.]. Concg. O, Sawallisch.

A lovely, alert account of both symphonies from Sawallisch that gives much pleasure. The *Second Symphony* in particular sounds beautifully fresh; the orchestral playing is of the high standard one expects from this great orchestra and Sawallisch has a fine sense of proportion. The recording is first class.

Symphony No. 3 in E flat (Eroica), Op. 55.
*** DG Dig. 439 862-2 [id.]. Met. Op. O, Levine – SCHUBERT: *Symphony No. 8.* ***

As he shows in his dedicated reading of the *Missa solemnis*, James Levine can on occasion expand his usual image and interpret Beethoven with a rare depth and intensity. This account of the *Eroica*, recorded with his own opera orchestra, provides a clear instance, a reading that in its high drama and extremes of dynamic and tempo seems to reflect the influence of Toscanini. The first movement at a brisk speed is bright and bold, leading up powerfully to the great dissonances of the central development section. The *Funeral march* is taken spaciously, with concentration never slipping and with the measured tread of the central fugato as tense as in a Toscanini performance. There is plenty of fire in the last two movements, to confirm this as a first-rate recommendation for anyone wanting this unusual and generous coupling. Full-bodied sound, with more reverberation than you normally have in the Manhattan Center.

Symphonies Nos. 3 (Eroica); 8 in F, Op. 93.
(M) **(*) Bruno Walter Edition: Sony SMK 64461 [id.]. Columbia SO, Bruno Walter.

It is a pleasure to turn from other accounts of the *Eroica* and hear as beautiful and sympathetic a performance as Walter's. He is not monumental in the different ways of Klemperer and, before him, Toscanini; but this interpretation has all the ripeness of the best of Walter's work with the Vienna Philharmonic Orchestra between the wars. The digitally remastered recording has all the amplitude one needs for such a reading: its expansive qualities bring rich horns as well as full-bodied strings. The coupled *Eighth* has comparatively slow speeds, especially in the inner movements. The first goes well enough, but after that the pacing hampers the sustaining of any high degree of intensity. The reading is of course interesting and sympathetic, but there is a lack of grace, as though the players were not strongly involved; and the finale, though revealing many points with unusual clarity, has a tendency to dullness. The sound is full and well balanced.

Symphonies Nos. 3 (Eroica); (i) 9 in D min. (Choral). Overtures: *Coriolan; Creatures of Prometheus; Egmont.*
(B) ** DG Double 437 368-2 (2) [id.]. VPO, Karl Boehm; (i) with Gwyneth Jones, Troyanos, Thomas, Ridderbusch, V. State Op. Konzertvereinigung.

Except in the *Funeral march*, Boehm was not at his finest in his VPO *Eroica*, made in the early 1970s. His Berlin Philharmonic version, recorded a decade earlier, had greater spontaneity. The Vienna version has sanity and good sense, but its sobriety undermines the intensity of the playing. But the *Funeral march*, without undue moulding of phrase, is still deeply devotional. The *Ninth* is a good deal more successful, although again Boehm was to record a further, even more intense (digital) version just before he died. Yet this Vienna performance made a fine culmination to his earlier cycle. Even in this titanic work the natural, unforced quality about Boehm's interpretation commands respect. In the slow movement you may well feel that his view is too straight – that quality is underlined when he chooses slow tempi for both the *Adagio* and *Andante* themes, which are therefore given less contrast than usual. But the tone of voice is dedicated, and the work ends with a superbly dramatic yet controlled account of the finale, with excellent playing and singing all round. There is some forward balance of soloists in the finale of No. 9, but otherwise the recording of both symphonies is excellent.

Symphonies Nos. 4 in B flat, Op. 60; 5 in C min., Op. 67.
(M) *** O-L Dig. 444 164-2 [id.]. AAM, Hogwood.

Hogwood's generous coupling of Nos. 4 and 5 presents excellent versions for anyone wanting performances on period instruments. Dramatic contrasts are strongly marked, with no feeling of miniaturization, and the clarity of textures is admirable, with natural horns in particular braying out superbly. This is now the more tempting at mid-price.

Symphonies Nos. 4 in B flat; 6 (Pastoral).
⊛ (M) *** Bruno Walter Edition: Sony SMK 64462 [id.]. Columbia SO, Walter.

For those collectors wanting a sampler of Bruno Walter's Beethoven series of the late 1950s, the coupling of the *Fourth* and *Sixth Symphonies* is the one to go for. Walter's reading of the *Fourth* is splendid, the finest achievement of his whole cycle. There is intensity and a feeling of natural vigour which makes itself felt in every bar. The first movement may not have quite the monumental weight that Klemperer gives it, but it is livelier. The slow movement gives Walter the perfect opportunity to coax a genuinely singing tone from his violins as only he knows how; and the finale allows the wind department its measure of brilliance. All aspects of this symphony – so much more varied than we have realized – are welded together here and show what depths it really contains. The recording is full, yet clear, sweet-toned with a firm bass. The pairing with the *Pastoral* is apt. It was the only Beethoven symphony Walter recorded twice in the 78-r.p.m. era (although his second version with the Philadelphia Orchestra was disappointing). The present version dates from the beginning of the 1960s and, like his recording of the *Fourth Symphony*, it represents the peak of his Indian summer in the American recording studios. The whole performance glows, and the gentle warmth of phrasing is comparable with Klemperer's famous version. The slow movement is taken slightly fast, but there is no sense of hurry, and the tempo of the *Peasants' merrymaking* is less controversial than Klemperer's. It is an affectionate and completely integrated performance from a master who thought and lived the work all his life. The sound is beautifully balanced, with sweet strings and clear, glowing woodwind, and the bass response is firm and full.

Symphony No. 5 in C min. Op.67.
(M) *** DG Dig. 445 502-2 [id.]. LAPO, Giulini – SCHUMANN: *Symphony No. 3 (Rhenish).* ***
(BB) **(*) Tring Dig. TRP 022 [id.]. RPO, Claire Gibault – SCHUBERT: *Symphony No. 8 (Unfinished).* **

Giulini's 1982 Los Angeles recording of Beethoven's *Fifth* is among the finest performances this symphony has ever received on record. The performance possesses majesty in abundance and conveys the power and vision of this inexhaustible work. The slow movement is glorious; the horn entry in the Scherzo is stunning and the finale almost overwhelming in its force and grandeur. Giulini also has the advantage of outstanding digital sound, clear, full and splendidly balanced, and the Schumann coupling is hardly less distinguished.

Claire Gibault's career has centred on the opera house. She was assistant conductor to John Eliot Gardiner at Lyon, where she gained wide experience, and she has conducted *Pelléas et Mélisande* at Covent Garden. But she has much concert-hall experience and, as this record suggests, she is a formidable exponent of Beethoven. The *Fifth Symphony* is not an easy work to bring off on record, but her performance with the RPO is admirably paced, direct and powerful. She has the advantage of excellent, full-bodied recording and it is a pity that in the Schubert coupling her tempo for the second movement is not entirely convincing.

Symphonies Nos. 5 in C min.; 6 in F (Pastoral).
(M) **(*) Ph. Dig. 442 404-2 [id.]. Concg. O, Haitink.

Haitink's recordings come from his 1987 cycle, his swan song as musical director of the Concert-gebouw Orchestra. Both are fresh and unmannered readings with plenty of impetus. He observes exposition repeats in first movements but not in the finale of the *Fifth*. The recording is well balanced but falls short of the highest Concertgebouw standards, as does the playing in the *Pastoral*. Though the string-tone is as sweet as ever – the opening of the finale caresses the ear – the ensemble is often surprisingly slack, and the sound fails to expand in tuttis, growing opaque, as in the fortissimos of the *Storm*, with odd balances of individual instruments.

Symphonies Nos. 5 in C min.; 7 in A.
⊛ (M) *** DG 447 400-2 [id.]. VPO, Carlos Kleiber.
(M) **(*) Bruno Walter Edition: Sony SMK 64463 [id.]. Columbia SO, Bruno Walter.
(M) *(*) EMI Dig. CDM5 68332-2 [id.]. Philh. O, Kurt Sanderling.

If ever there was a legendary recording, it is Carlos Kleiber's version of the *Fifth* from the mid-1970s. In Kleiber's hands the first movement is electrifying but still has a hushed intensity. The slow movement is tender and delicate, with dynamic contrasts underlined but not exaggerated. In the Scherzo the horns, like the rest of the VPO, are in superb form, and the central section has enormous energy; the finale, even more than usual, releases the music into pure daylight. Indeed the gradation of dynamics from the hushed pianissimo at the close of the Scherzo to the weight of the great opening statement of the finale has not been heard on disc with such overwhelming effect since Toscanini. The latest remastering has certainly enhanced the sound. Textures are drier than with Giulini's somewhat more expansive account with the Berlin Philharmonic, but the upper range of the strings has more body than before, and there is little to complain of when this is undoubtedly one of the greatest performances of the work ever put on record.

When it was first issued, a year after the *Fifth*, Carlos Kleiber's *Seventh* excited considerable controversy, and certainly this is a performance where symphonic argument never yields to the charm of the dance. Kleiber's incisively dramatic approach is marked instead with sharp dynamic contrasts and thrustful rhythms. Another controversial point is that Kleiber, like his father, maintains the pizzicato for the strings on the final phrase of the *Allegretto*, a curious effect. The current digital remastering has again greatly improved the sound, with the constriction noted on the original LP now opened up so that the effect is much more spacious than before, with more resonance and weight in the middle strings – and how gloriously the horns come through in the tuttis of the outer movements.

In Bruno Walter's reading of the *Fifth*, the sound-balance is richer and more satisfying than in many more modern recordings. The first movement is taken very fast, yet it lacks the kind of nervous tension that distinguishes Carlos Kleiber's famous version. The middle two movements are contrastingly slow. In the *Andante* (more like an *adagio*) there is a glowing, natural warmth, but the Scherzo at this speed is too gentle. The finale, taken at a spacious, natural pace, is joyous and sympathetic, but again fails to convey the ultimate in tension. Walter's *Seventh* has a comparatively slow first-movement allegro, but he had rehearsed his players well in the tricky dotted 6/8 rhythm and the result dances convincingly, even if the movement seems to lumber somewhat. The *Allegretto* also seems heavier than usual (partly because of the rich, weighty recording). It is rather mannered, with *marcato* emphases on most of the down beats, but the important point is that genuine tension is created with the illusion of an actual performance. The Scherzo is also rather wayward: after a slow start, Walter suddenly livens up the middle with a faster pace, and this speed-change occurs in each repetition of the Scherzo section. The Trio also takes its time, but in contrast the finale goes with a splendid lift to the playing and very brilliant horns and trumpets in the exciting coda.

Sanderling's reading of the *Fifth* is powerful and direct, lacking a little in rhythmic subtlety, almost too plain, but generally conveying a Klemperer-like ruggedness. A point of detail is that Sanderling at the start has – with fair justification – a shorter pause after the first knock of fate than after the second. The opening statement of the finale is massive rather than incisively dramatic. The early-1980s digital recording is bold and clear, but the snag to this reissue is the unattractive coupling. Sanderling's *Seventh* is disappointingly unsprung, heavy to the point of turgidity in the first movement and lacking intensity elsewhere – with generally slow speeds.

(i) *Symphonies Nos. 6 (Pastoral); 7 in A, Op. 92; 8 in F, Op. 93;* (ii) Overtures: *Fidelio; Leonora No. 3.*
(B) **(*) DG Double 437 928-2 (2) (i) VPO; (ii) Dresden State O; Karl Boehm.

Boehm's beautiful, unforced reading of the *Pastoral* from the beginning of the 1970s has long been famous alongside Bruno Walter's version, with which it has much in common. In the first movement Boehm observes the exposition repeat (not many analogue versions do); though the dynamic contrasts are never underplayed and the phrasing is affectionate, there is a feeling of inevitable rightness about Boehm's approach, no sense of an interpreter forcing his will. Only the slow movement with its even stressing raises any reservation, and that very slight. The other works are not quite as memorable as this, but are still rewarding. In the *Seventh* the conflict between symphony and dance is convincingly balanced, slightly in favour of the former. Tempi are never hectic but, with well-articulated playing throughout, the effect is not heavy and the slow movement is eloquent. Boehm's straight approach is most striking in the finale, a performance that keeps within itself. But on its own terms this is satisfying, as is the comparable reading of the *Eighth*. The recording is full and does not sound too dated.

Symphonies Nos. 6 in F (Pastoral), Op. 68; 8 in F, Op. 93.
(M) ** DG Dig. 445 542-2 [id.]. VPO, Abbado.

Abbado's reading of the *Pastoral* is unexceptionable, slowish and easy-going in the first movement, fresh but unmagical in the slow movement and finding full inspiration only in the finale. It is not helped by dull, rather thick, if quite agreeable sound. However, the *Eighth* is an incandescent performance, fresh and rhythmic. The sound is full and atmospheric and, with such weight, it is instantly established as more than a little symphony. Speeds are beautifully judged, and the tensions of a live occasion are vividly conveyed.

Symphonies Nos. (i) *6 in F (Pastoral); 8 in F, Op. 93;* (ii) *9 in D min. (Choral), Op. 125.*
(BB) **(*) EMI Seraphim CES5 68519-2 (2) [CDEB 68519]. (i) Munich PO, Rudolf Kempe; (ii) Armstrong, Reynolds, Tear, Shirley-Quirk, London Symphony Ch., LSO, Giulini.

Kempe's performance of the *Pastoral* is one of the most genially satisfying in the set. With warm, reverberant sound, few will be disappointed with either this or the comparable No. 8 (first-movement exposition repeat included), although there are even finer versions available of both symphonies in the bargain range. For the *Choral Symphony* EMI turned to Giulini's LSO account, also from the early 1970s. This is affected positively by the recording acoustic: close, immediate and full. Giulini's tempo in the first movement is unusually slow. He insists on precise sextuplets for the opening tremolando, with no mistiness – and he builds the architecture relentlessly, finding the resolution only in the concluding coda. The Scherzo is lithe and powerful, with shattering timpani. The slow movement is warm and Elysian rather than hushed, while the finale, not always quite perfect in ensemble, is dedicatedly intense, with excellent contributions from chorus and the solo team.

Symphony No. 9 (Choral), Op. 125.
(M) *** DG Dig. 445 503-2 [id.]. Norman, Fassbaender, Domingo, Berry, V. State Op. Ch. Soc., VPO, Karl Boehm.
**(*) RCA Dig. 09026 60363-2 [id.]. Alexander, Quivar, Lakes, Plishka, Amb. S., RPO, Previn.
(M) *(*) Bruno Walter Edition: Sony SMK 64464 [id.]. Cundari, Rankin, Da Costa, Wilderman, Westminster Ch., Columbia SO, Bruno Walter.

Symphony No. 9 (Choral); Overture: Coriolan.
(M) *** DG 447 401-2 [id.]. Janowitz, Rössl-Majdan, Kmentt, Berry, V. Singverein, BPO, Karajan.

This is Karajan's 1962 version, one of three stereo recordings he made of the *Ninth*. Though less hushed and serene in the slow movement than either of his two later versions, the finale blazes even more intensely, with Janowitz's contribution radiant in its purity. This reflected the electricity of the Berlin sessions, when it rounded off a cycle recorded over two weeks. Even so, it is strange that DG chose this recording rather than the 1977 account for reissue in their 'Originals' series of legendary recordings, as the latter version is even finer (415 832-2). The *Coriolan* coupling is an added bonus.

Karl Boehm's reading is spacious and powerful, and in its broad concept it has much in common with Klemperer's version. Yet overall there is a transcendent sense of a great occasion; the concentration is unfailing, reaching its peak in the glorious finale, where ruggedness and strength well over into inspiration. With a fine, characterful team of soloists and a freshly incisive chorus formed from singers of the Vienna State Opera, this is strongly recommendable.

The heart of André Previn's reading on RCA lies in the rapt, spacious account of the great *Adagio*, with mystery evoked in the hushed, inner accounts of the two variation themes. The Scherzo is exhilaratingly sprung and the choral finale brings cleanly articulated singing both from the soloists – a distinguished American quartet – and from the professional chorus. The recording balances the chorus more forwardly than usual, giving it necessary weight, and it is good to hear the piccolo clearly defined in the coda. Where the recording falls down is in the first movement, where the slightly distanced violins take away dramatic bite from a broad, weighty reading.

Walter's *Ninth* has many fine moments but suffers from slow tempi and a comparatively low level of tension. The first three movements were recorded in California in January 1959 and the finale in New York City four months later. Somehow the interpretation went off the boil and the choral finale fails to rise to the sense of occasion that a really great *Ninth* should have. The soloists are not particularly impressive and the choir finds it hard to sound alert at Walter's slow tempi, all of which shows up most strikingly in the work's closing pages. Needless to say, there are many typical Walter touches, particularly in the slow movement, and the jog-trot speed for the Scherzo sustains itself by the beauty and thoughtfulness of the general shaping; but one cannot get away from the feeling that this is a rather disappointing end to a fine cycle. Those interested in discovering Walter's methods of preparation for the final performances will be glad to know that there is a separate disc including recorded excerpts from the rehearsals of symphonies 4, 5, 7, and 9 (SMK 64465).

CHAMBER MUSIC

(i) *Cello sonatas Nos. 1–5;* (ii) *7 Variations on 'Bei Männern, welche Liebe Fühlen'* (from Mozart's *Die Zauberflöte*), *Op. 46; 12 Variations on 'Ein Mädchen'* (from Mozart's *Die Zauberflöte*), *WoO 66; 12 Variations on 'See the conqu'ring hero comes'* from Handel's *Judas Maccabaeus*), *WoO 45.*
(B) *** Ph. Duo 442 565-2 (2) [id.]. (i) Mstislav Rostropovich, Sviatoslav Richter; (ii) Maurice Gendron, Jean Françaix.
(B) *** EMI CZS5 68348-2 (2). Paul Tortelier, Eric Heidsieck.

Made in the early 1960s, the classic Philips performances by Mstislav Rostropovich and Sviatoslav Richter, two of the instrumental giants of the day, have withstood the test of time astonishingly well and sound remarkably fresh in this transfer. The performances of the *Variations* by Maurice Gendron and Jean Françaix have an engagingly light touch and are beautifully recorded. Indeed by their side the Rostropovich/Richter recording is noticeably drier and less vivid. But at its new price this reissue is very tempting.

The Tortelier set with Eric Heidsieck dates from the early 1970s and has the advantage of more modern and perhaps slightly better sound than the earlier Philips set. The performances are distinguished and make a useful alternative, as the style is bolder than the way of Fournier and Kempff on DG, and less chimerical, too; indeed Tortelier and Heidsieck are nearer to Rostropovich and Richter, although they have their own insights. The variations have been added and make a bonus for the reissue, which comes at two CDs for the price of one. The CD transfer is admirably natural and clean, with the variations sounding particularly fresh.

Notturno, Op. 42.
*** EMI Dig. CDC5 55166-2 [id.]. Caussé, Duchable – REINECKE: *Fantasiestücke ***; SCHUBERT: Arpeggione sonata. **(*)

Beethoven's *Notturno* is an 1803 arrangement by Franz Xaver Kleinheinz of the *Serenade*, Op. 8, for string trio. Kleinheinz had come to Vienna the preceding year to study with Beethoven's former tutor, Albrechtsberger, and Beethoven himself sanctioned (and made some alterations to) the transcription. It is a slight work, but Gérard Caussé and François-René Duchable give a nicely turned and musicianly account of it. Exemplary recording.

Octet in E flat, Op. 103.
*** Decca Dig. 436 654-2 [id.]. Vienna Wind Soloists – MOZART: *Serenades. ***

Nothing much to say about the new recording by the Vienna Wind Soloists on Decca. This is delightful playing, fresh and natural – as is the recorded sound. If the two Mozart *Serenades* the disc offers are what you want for your collection, there is no need to hesitate.

Septet in E flat, Op. 20; Clarinet trio, Op. 11.
(M) *** Virgin/EMI Dig. CUV5 61233-2 [id.]. Nash Ens.

There is sheer magic in these performances on the Virgin Ultraviolet label, with the members of the Nash Ensemble conveying their own enjoyment in the young Beethoven's exuberant inspiration. So the *Clarinet trio* finds each player, not just the fine clarinettist Michael Collins but also the pianist Ian Brown and the cellist Christopher van Kampen, pointing rhythms and phrases as a friendly challenge to be answered and capped by colleagues, the spontaneous interplay of the moment. It is a happy phenomenon, too rarely evident on record but delectably present here. An apt sense of fun also infects the *Septet*, though the allegros in the outer movements, exhilaratingly fast, would have been even more winning at speeds a shade more relaxed. But here too the performance brims with joy. Good, atmospheric sound. This is an obvious first choice at mid-price for this coupling.

(i) *Septet in E flat, Op. 20;* (ii) *Wind sextet in E flat.*
*** Decca Dig. 436 653-2 [id.]. (i) Vienna Octet; (ii) Vienna Wind Soloists.
(M) *** Teldec/Warner Dig. 4509 97451-2 [id.]. Berlin Soloists – MOZART: *Horn quintet. **(*)

Over the years the Vienna Octet have been justly famous for their recordings of Beethoven's *Septet* for Decca, and the newest version is no disappointment. Brio and good humour mark the performance with a warmly elegant account of the slow movement to offset the high spirits of the Minuet and Scherzo with its galumphing horn playing. The finale is no less infectious. The recording is wonderfully warm and real, and the *Wind sextet*, equally cultured and spontaneous, makes a good encore.

The Teldec Berlin recording is somewhat richer and more expansive in its bass resonance than the competing Vienna version on Decca, but that does not inhibit the vivacity of the playing. The opening movement (exposition repeat included) sets off with a sparkling tempo, and such verve is irresistible. The *Adagio* has a gloriously rich melodic flow, offset by the elegantly measured minuet. The *Theme and variations* has the most delightfully perky rhythmic lightness from the very opening, and the fun of the Scherzo is appreciated by one and all, not least the solo horn. The finale has spendid impetus and a glowing warmth of timbre. This is all very enticing indeed, and the recording is appealingly atmospheric. Perhaps the Vienna account occasionally has a touch more rustic charm, but this Teldec version (dating from 1990) is equally enjoyable in its slightly more sumptuous way.

STRING QUARTETS

String quartets Nos. 1 in F; 2 in G; 3 in D; 4 in C min.; 5 in A; 6 in B flat, Op. 18/1–6; 7 in F; 8 in E min.; 9 in C, Op. 59/1–3; 10 in E flat, Op. 74; 11 in F min., Op. 95; 12 in E flat, Op. 127; 13 in B flat, Op. 130; 14 in C sharp min., Op. 131; 15 in A min., Op. 132; 16 in F, Op. 135; Grosse fugue, Op. 133.
*(*) Delos Dig. DE 3039 (8) [id.]. Orford Qt.

The box proclaims the *New York Times*'s verdict that 'the Orford Beethoven Series sets a standard for others to emulate', and *The Times* newspaper of London hailed the group as showing 'a consistency in depth and variety of tone, in musical concentration and sheer freshness of interpretation, which makes other digital cycles seem pale by comparison'. Our impressions are very different: true, theirs are immaculately played, highly polished and strongly projected readings, but they consistently exaggerate dynamic markings and rarely seem to penetrate far below the surface. Expression is painted on rather than organically inherent in their readings. In terms of quartet-playing they achieve a high level of distinction, and their ensemble and intonation cannot be faulted; but in terms of humanity or vision they are no match for the Végh (Valois V 4400), the Lindsays (see below) or the Quartetto Italiano (see our main volume), and don't let anyone tell you that they are. If pressed to make a first choice, we would probably plump for the Végh, with the Lindsays a very worthwhile alternative.

String quartets Nos. 1, 3 & 4, Op. 18/1, 3 & 4; 7 (Rasumovsky No. 1), Op. 59/1; 10 (Harp), Op. 74; 13, Op. 130; 14, Op. 131.
*** EMI Dig. CDS7 54587-2 (4) [Ang. ZDCD 54587]. Alban Berg Qt.

String quartets Nos. 2, 5 & 6, Op. 18/2, 5 & 6; 8–9 (Rasumovsky Nos. 2–3), Op. 59/2–3; 11, Op. 95; 15, Op. 132; 16, Op. 135; Grosse Fuge, Op. 133; Cavatina from Op. 130.
*** EMI Dig. CDS7 54592-2 (4) [Ang. ZDCD 54592].Alban Berg Qt.

The Alban Berg's studio recordings of the Beethoven quartets in the late 1970s/early 1980s set high standards, but there are some of us who thought the late quartets too clinical and well prepared and, as a result, lacking in mystery. The new set originates at public concerts and is, perhaps, an attempt to ensure that the greater intensity and spontaneity generated in the presence of an audience finds its way on to records. Generally speaking it does; on balance, these performances, when listened to alongside the earlier set, are freer and more vital. But the differences are small and readers already happy with the studio version need not feel it necessary to go to the expense of replacing it. It may seem perverse to say so, but even now there is perfection of ensemble and sheer beauty of sound that will not strike all listeners as altogether appropriate in this repertoire. However, these are not by any means superficial or slick – and admirers of this ensemble need have no hesitation in acquiring them.

String quartets Nos. 1–6, Op. 18/1–6; 10 in E flat (Harp), Op. 74; 11 in F min., Op. 95.
(M) *** ASV CDDDCS 305 (3) [id.]. Lindsay Qt.

It is good to have the Lindsay recordings now reissued at mid-price (retaining their old catalogue numbers). Their great merit in Beethoven lies in the natural expressiveness of their playing, most strikingly of all in slow movements, which brings a hushed inner quality too rarely caught on record. The sense of spontaneity necessarily brings the obverse quality: these performances are not as precise as those in the finest rival sets; but there are few Beethoven quartet recordings that so convincingly bring out the humanity of the writing, its power to communicate. The recording of Op. 18, set against a fairly reverberant acoustic, is warm and realistic; the transfers reflect the fact that the recordings are more modern and rather fuller than the remastered Philips quality for the Italian group (426 046-2).

String quartets Nos. 1 in F; 2 in G; 3 in D; Op. 18/1–3.
** Telarc Dig. CD 80382 [id.]. Cleveland Qt.

In terms of finesse and tonal elegance, the Cleveland Quartet are comparable with (and perhaps superior to) any ensemble now before the public. Their account of the first three Op. 18 quartets could hardly be improved upon in terms of technical address. At the same time, such spontaneity as they show seems all too over-rehearsed and they leave the listener feeling admiration for them rather than affection for the music. The recording is very clear and clean (a bit too forward) but, for all their perfection, these are not very likeable perfomances. A disc to be praised rather than played.

String quartets Nos. 1 in F; 2 in G; 3 in D; 4 in C min.; 5 in A; 6 in B flat, Op. 18/1–6.
*(*) Ph. Dig. 432 115-2 (3) [id.]. Guarneri Qt.

The Guarneri set, recorded in 1991, comes on three CDs at full price. So, of course, do the Tokyo, but they offer the *String quintet in C major* and the F major transcription of the *Sonata in E*, Op. 14, No. 1, as a bonus (RCA 09026 61284-2). The Guarneri performances are better characterized than the late quartets which Philips issued in 1988–90 but, immaculately played and well recorded though they are, they fail to engage the enthusiasm of the listener. One listens with much admiration but rather less enjoyment.

(i) *String quartets Nos. 1 in F, Op. 18/1; 9 in C, Op. 59/3; 11 in F min., Op. 95; 12 in E flat, Op. 127; 14 in C sharp min., Op. 131; 15 in A min., Op. 132; 16 in F, Op. 135;* (ii) *Violin sonata No. 3 in E flat, Op. 12/3.*
⊛ (M) *** EMI mono CHS5 65308-2 (4) [id.]. (i) Busch Qt; (ii) Adolf Busch, Rudolf Serkin –
SCHUBERT: *String quartet No. 8.* ***

Beethoven's greatest music, it is often rightly said, is better than any performance of it can ever be. Listening to the Busch Quartet's pre-war HMV accounts of the quartets, however, one is almost tempted to doubt this received wisdom. Certainly no group since has ever penetrated deeper into the heart of these scores. And one is also tempted to say that the (very occasional) technical imperfections (or frailties of intonation in Op. 132) are of greater musical interest than the meticulous perfection of most modern ensembles. In addition to the Beethoven quartets there is a bonus in the form of the *Violin sonata in E flat*, Op. 12, No. 3, from Busch and Serkin, playing of warmth and humanity, and a sparkling account of the early *B flat Quartet*, D.112, of Schubert. These are classics of the gramophone and not to be missed, and they are excellently remastered and transferred.

String quartets Nos. 1 in F, Op. 18/1; 14 in C sharp min., Op. 131.
*** Capriccio/Target Dig. 10510 [id.]. Petersen Qt.

Quite easily the best account of the Op. 131 *Quartet* to have appeared in recent years. The Petersen Quartet began playing when they were students in 1979 in Berlin. They need not fear comparison with the most starry groups now on record and can match any of them in terms of ensemble and finesse. But, more unusually, they are not interested in impressing the listener with their beauty of sound or impeccable tuning, but in presenting this music pure and complex. Both here and in the less successful *F major Quartet*, Op. 18, No. 1, they prove dedicated and charcterful. (The first movement is a bit rushed and the *Adagio* does not have the depth of the Végh, but it is still a very good performance.) For those who are unduly worried by the odd blemish in the Végh (or the leader's intakes of breath) or who do not care for the slightly dryish, bottom-heavy sound in the Talich, this could well be a satisfying alternative recommendation.

String quartets Nos. 1–2, Op. 18/1–2.
** Hyp. Dig. CDA 66401 [id.]. New Budapest Qt.

String quartets Nos. 3, 4 & 6, Op. 18/3, 4 & 6.
*** Hyp. Dig. CDA 66402 [id.]. New Budapest Qt.

String quartets Nos. 8–9 (Rasumovsky Nos. 2–3), Op. 59/2–3.
*** Hyp. Dig. CDA 66404 [id.]. New Budapest Qt.

String quartets Nos. 10 in E flat (Harp), Op. 74; 14 in C sharp min., Op. 131.
*** Hyp. Dig. CDA 66405 [id.]. New Budapest Qt.

String quartets Nos. 11 in F min., Op. 95; 15 in A min., Op. 132.
*** Hyp. Dig. CDA 66406 [id.]. New Budapest Qt.

String quartets Nos. 12 in E flat, Op. 127; 16 in F, Op. 135.
*** Hyp. Dig. CDA 66408 [id.]. New Budapest Qt.

String quartet No. 13 in B flat, Op. 130; Grosse Fuge, Op. 133.
*** Hyp. Dig. CDA 66407 [id.]. New Budapest Qt.

Although we have heard the New Budapest Quartet cycle as and when issues have appeared, we have commented only on two of the late *Quartets*, Opp. 127 and 135, in our main volume (and have listed them here for the sake of completeness). Generally speaking, the quartet produces fine results not only in the Op. 127, which we much liked, but also in the companions in the series. Throughout the cycle their playing is distinguished by consistent (but not excessive) refinement of sonority, spot-on intonation, excellent ensemble and tonal blend. Their performances are never less than intelligent and are often touched by considerable insight. Given their first-class technical credentials and musicianship, as well as the excellence of the Hyperion recording, there is no justification for withholding a third star, except in the case of Op. 18/1–2 which are somewhat lacking in vitality. Yet the fact remains that the temptation to return to them for pleasure is not strong. Is it because they are somehow too clean and occasionally a shade characterless? They are certainly less searching than the Talich, the Lindsays, the Tokyo (in Opp. 18 and 59) – and, above all, the Végh (available together in a mid-priced Valois box of eight discs – V 4400) or, in Op. 131, the new Peterson Quartet version on Capriccio. Recommendable, then, but not with the same enthusiasm as rival sets.

String quartet No. 3 in D, Op. 18/3.
(*) Orfeo mono 361 941 [id.]. Végh Qt – DEBUSSY: *Quartet;* HAYDN: *Quartet in F.* (*)

There is, of course, always something to learn from a performance by the Végh Quartet, but this Austrian Radio recording, made at the 1961 Salzburg Festival, is far from ideal. Their later commercial recording is in every way superior and has much greater finish. The sound here is distinctly scrawny.

String quartets Nos. 3 in D, Op. 18/3; 7 in F, (Rasumovsky) Op. 59/1.
*** Channel Classics Dig. CCS 6094 [id.]. Orpheus Qt.

The Orpheus Quartet are first class in every way. Their account of the *First Rasumovsky quartet* is among the best to have appeared in recent years; the best, in fact, since the Tokyo account on RCA. They do not surpass the latter in the first movement, which has an impressive symphonic breadth, or go deeper in the slow movement than the Végh or the Talich. But their playing is far removed in spirit from the characterless, jet-setting versions we have had from the glossy and glamorous. This is real music-making: the finale of the *D major Quartet*, for example, is not rushed off its feet, as is so often the case nowadays. This playing is more in harmony with the horse-drawn rather than the jet-driven, with candlepower rather than strip-lighting; in short, this group are attuned to the sensibility of the period. This is very natural playing; much felt without being over-intense. The recording has clarity and presence.

String quartets Nos. 7 in F; 8 in E min.; 9 in C (Rasumovsky), Op. 59/1–3.
(M) *** ASV Dig. CDDCS 207 (2) [id.]. Lindsay Qt.
*(*) Ph. Dig. 432 980-2 (2) [id.]. Guarneri Qt.

The Lindsay set contains performances of real stature; and though they are not unrivalled in some of their insights, among modern recordings they are not often surpassed. As a recording, this set is comparable with most of its competitors and superior to many; artistically, it can hold its own with the best. They are now reissued in a box, retaining the old catalogue number, but with further reduction to upper mid-price.

On the Philips/Guarneri set of *Rasumovsky Quartets* the *F major* and *E minor Quartets* are accommodated on the first disc while the *C major*, Op. 59, No.3, occupies the second on its own. There is a high gloss on the finish and the playing has all the proficiency and unanimity of ensemble one could ask for. Some listeners may feel differently, but to us the performance seems as highly accomplished as it is ultimately uninteresting. When one turns to recent (Tokyo Quartet) and older (Talich, Végh and Lindsay) rivals, one realizes that one has not fallen out of love with this music.

String quartet No. 7 in F (Rasumovsky), Op. 59/1; (ii) *Violin sonata No. 9 in A (Kreutzer), Op. 47.*
(B) **(*) DG 439 453-2 [id.]. (i) Amadeus Qt; (ii) Sir Yehudi Menuhin, Wilhelm Kempff.

An unusual coupling that might well appeal to impecunious collectors. There is some splendid playing from the Amadeus in the *First Rasumovsky Quartet*. Perhaps they do not uncover all its secrets, but the self-assurance and polish of the playing does not mean that the *Adagio* is unfeeling. The 1959 recording sounds well (with a touch of thinness on top), and the same comment might apply to the 1970 *Kreutzer Sonata*, although the sound is obviously more modern. Here the Kempff/ Menuhin partnership is unique. In many ways it is not as immaculate as earlier accounts, but the spontaneous imagination of the playing, the challenging between great artists on the same wavelength, is consistently present.

String quartets Nos. 10 in E flat (Harp), Op. 74; 11 in F min., Op. 95.
** Telarc Dig. CD 80351 [id.]. Cleveland Qt.

As with the first three Op. 18 quartets (see above), there can be no quarrels with the playing as such. Here, as there, we have the same finesse and elegance. Tonally and technically, the Cleveland Quartet are comparable with the best, though their spontaneity seems a trifle calculated and does not ring true. But this coupling, though standard in the balmy days of LP, does not seem generous nowadays.

String quartets Nos. 12-16.
(M) *** ASV Dig. CDDCS 403 (4) [id.]. Lindsay Qt.

The Lindsays get far closer to the essence of this great music than most of their rivals. They have the benefit of very well-balanced recording; the sound of the ASV set is admirably present. They seem to find tempi that somehow strike the listener as completely right and which enable them to convey so much of both the letter and the spirit of the music. They bring much rich musical characterization and musical strength. Taken overall, these are among the very finest versions to have been made in recent years. They now reappear, their catalogue number unchanged, but at lower mid-price – excellent value.

VIOLIN SONATAS

Clara Haskil: The Legacy, Volume 1: Chamber music

Violin sonatas Nos. 1–10.
(M) (***) Ph. mono 442 625-2 (5) [id.]. Arthur Grumiaux, Clara Haskil – MOZART: *Violin sonatas.*
   (***)

Violin sonatas Nos. 1 in D; 2 in A; 3 in E flat, Op. 12/1–3; 4 in A min., Op. 23.
(M) (***) Ph. mono 442 626-2. Arthur Grumiaux, Clara Haskil.

Violin sonatas Nos. 5 in F (Spring), Op. 24; 6 in A; 7 in C min., Op. 30/1–2.
(M) (***) Ph. mono 442 627-2. Arthur Grumiaux, Clara Haskil.

Violin sonatas Nos. 8 in G, Op. 30/3; 9 in A (Kreutzer), Op. 47; 10 in G, Op. 96.
(M) (***) Ph. mono 442 628-2. Arthur Grumiaux, Clara Haskil.

Arthur Grumiaux and Clara Haskil made their celebrated recordings in 1956–7 and these versions sound remarkably well for their age. The performances are wonderfully civilized and aristocratic, and no one investing in them will regret it. They accommodate all ten *Sonatas* on three CDs at mid-price, as opposed to the four of Perlman and Ashkenazy, but they come in harness with two further CDs (equally desirable) of Mozart's mature *Violin sonatas*, as part of the 'Clara Haskil Legacy'. The discs are not at present available separately.

SOLO PIANO MUSIC

Piano sonatas Nos. 1–32 (complete).
*** Elektra Nonesuch/Warner Dig. 7559 79328-2 (10). Richard Goode.
(B) *** Decca 443 706-2 (10) [id.] (with *Andanti favori*). Vladimir Ashkenazy.

After years of concentrating on chamber music, the American pianist Richard Goode has emerged in his own right as one of the most searching Beethoven interpreters today. This cycle of the 32 sonatas was recorded over a period of years – the late sonatas were available earlier – and after Goode had given a number of cycles in live concert. In America, Goode has often been likened to Schnabel or Serkin, rugged Beethovenians, but that is misleading. It is not just the power of Goode's playing that singles him out, but the beauty, when he has such subtle control over a formidably wide tonal and dynamic range. Even at its weightiest, the sound is never clangorous. Particularly in the early sonatas Goode brings out the wit and parody, while slow movements regularly draw sensuously velvety legato. Helped by an unusually full and clear recording, with no haze of reverberation, the clarity of his articulation is breathtaking, as in the running semiquavers of the finale of the *Appassionata sonata*. Above all, Goode has a natural gravity which compels attention. One has to go back to the pre-digital era to find a Beethoven cycle of comparable command and intensity – to the earlier of

Barenboim's two cycles (EMI CZS7 62863-2), daringly spacious in its speeds, or to the jewelled clarity of Wilhelm Kempff (DG 429 306-2). We feel this is now a clear first choice for those wanting a modern digital cycle.

Decca have now reissued Ashkenzy's set which occupied him over a decade from 1971 until 1980, with the *Andante favori* added on as an encore in 1981. He brings to the early sonatas the concentrated, unaffected qualities which make his recordings of the *Violin sonatas* with Perlman so eminently compelling. Interpretatively the manner is strong and direct, treating the young Beethoven rightly as a fully mature composer, no imitator of Haydn and Mozart; but the important point is that, whether in fast music or slow, he conveys the feeling of new discovery and ready communication. As the cycle proceeds, at times the tempi are questionably fast (the finale of Op. 10/2) or slow (the first movement of the *Pastoral*, Op. 28), but Ashkenazy's freshness of manner silences criticism and he gives a thoughtful and masterly account of the *D major Sonata*, Op. 10/3. He is also especially persuasive in the two Op. 14 sonatas (Nos. 9 and 10). Among the famous named sonatas, there is much to admire in the *Moonlight* and, if his *Pathétique* is perhaps understated for so youthfully ebullient a work, the finale, unusually gentle, conveys the underlying power. He gives a deeply satisfying reading of the *Waldstein sonata*, where the degree of restraint, the occasional hesitations, intensify his thoughtful approach, never interrupting the broader span of the argument. There are some fine things in Op. 26 (the so-called *Funeral march Sonata*) even if here Ashkenazy does not seek out the subtleties of the opening variation movement as does Gilels. The Op. 31 *D minor Sonata*, nicknamed *Tempest*, and its companion in E flat, Op. 31/3, are among the best of his cycle. He brings concentration of mind, together with a spontaneity of feeling, that illumines both works. The command of keyboard colour is as always impressive and, in terms of both dramatic tension and the sense of architecture, these are thoroughly satisfying performances. *Les Adieux* has a vehement first movement and memorable concentration, while the *Appassionata* is superb. His readings of the other middle-period sonatas are as masterly and penetrating as anything he has given us, and he is pretty impressive in the late sonatas. There is an rapt sense of repose in the slow movement of Op. 109 (*No. 30 in E major*) and the last two sonatas are played with a depth and spontaneity which put these readings among the finest available. In the slow movement of Op. 111 Ashkenazy matches the concentration, at the slowest possible speed, which marks the reading of his friend, Barenboim, but there is an extra detachment. If anything, the interpretation of Op. 110 is even more remarkable. However, the *Hammerklavier*, one of the last to be recorded, is not quite on this level. Curiously, it is coupled with the *Andante favori* (which comes first on the CD). The performance of the sonata is fresher and more spontaneous-sounding than in his earlier Decca version, not quite so immaculate in the playing, but still strong and direct, with power and speed in the outer movements; but the total experience is less than monumental and, though the recording is very good, it occasionally clangs a bit. Overall the sound is excellent, vivid and present, if not always quite as full and natural as Barenboim's alternative and highly recommendable bargain-priced EMI set.

Piano sonatas Nos. 8 in C min. (Pathétique), Op. 13; 14 in C sharp min. (Moonlight), Op. 27/2; 21 in C (Waldstein), Op. 53; 23 in F min. (Appassionata).
(M) *** DG 447 404-2 [id.]. Wilhelm Kempff.

Kempff's masterly recordings are truly legendary and make a fitting contribution to DG's series of 'Originals'. Each performance here shows so well his ability to rethink Beethoven's music within the recording studio. Everything he does has his individual stamp; above all, he never fails to convey the deep intensity of a master in communication with Beethoven. The slow movement of the *Pathétique*, for example, is slower and more expressively romantic than is usual in a classical performance, but is still restrained. The opening of the *Moonlight* is calmly atmospheric, the Scherzo poised and with admirable contrast in the finale. In the *Waldstein*, although the opening movement is dramatic, Kempff's preparation for the great theme of the finale is gentle, and when it appears the effect is to give the melody a less joyous quality than we are used to. But the result is magical, for there is a compensating spiritual quality and, with the suggestion of a more restrained forward momentum, the finale gains in breadth and boldness what it loses in sheer vivacity. The *Appassionata* is characteristically clear and classically straight. Although less weightily dramatic than in other readings, the concentration is irresistible. The recording has undoubtedly gained in firmness with the clean sound of the digital remastering, and there is plenty of warmth and colour at lower dynamic levels.

Piano sonatas Nos. 21 in C (Waldstein), Op. 53; 23 in F min. (Appassionata), Op. 57; 26 in E flat (Les Adieux), Op. 81a.
(M) *** Virgin Veritas/EMI Dig. VER5 61160-2 [id.]. Melvyn Tan (fortepiano).

Melvyn Tan's playing is for those yet unconverted to the fortepiano and who find its exponents tame.

In all three sonatas he exhibits consummate artistry and real temperament and fire. Nor is there any want of poetic feeling. The EMI recording is excellent; in short, an outstanding issue.

Miscellaneous Piano Music

Allegretto in C min., WoO 53; Andanti favori, WoO 57; 'Für Elise', WoO 59; 6 Variations on an original theme in F, Op. 34.
(M) *** Virgin Veritas/EMI Dig. VER5 61161-2 [id.]. Melvyn Tan (fortepiano) – SCHUBERT: *Moments musicaux* etc. ***

Melvyn Tan is a spirited artist and an enormously persuasive exponent of the fortepiano. The *F major Variations* come off splendidly; this is a thoroughly enjoyable recital and is recorded with great realism and presence in the Long Gallery, Doddington Hall, Lincolnshire.

Allegretto in C min., WoO 53; 6 Ecossaises, WoO 83; 6 Easy variations on a Swiss air in F; Für Elise; Polonaise in C, Op. 89; Rondo in G, Op. 51/2; Piano sonatas Nos. 4 in E flat, Op. 7; 20 in G, Op. 49/ 2; 5 Variations on 'Rule Brittania' in D, WoO 79; 6 Variations on an original theme in F, Op. 34; 6 Variations on a theme from The Ruins of Athens, Op. 76; 6 Variations on an original theme, in G, WoO 77; 7 Variations on 'God save the King' in D; 8 Variations on Grétry's air 'Une fièvre brûlante' in C; 9 Variations on Paisiello's Air 'Quant è piu bello' in A, WoO 69; 12 Variations on a Russian dance from Wranitsky's ballet 'Das Waldmädchen' in A; 15 Variations and a fugue on a theme from Prometheus in E flat (Eroica variations), Op. 35.
(B) ** Vox Box 11 59212 (2) [CD3X 3017]. Alfred Brendel.

It is good to have Brendel's Vox recordings of the variations back in the catalogue, even if the recording is too close and rather hard. As in his early set of the Beethoven sonatas on the same label, his manner is strong and purposeful. Sometimes the toughness may seem too keen for these miniature pieces, but Brendel's naturally spontaneous manner brings out many felicities and the playing is never matter-of-fact. The well-known set of variations on the *Prometheus* theme is done with directness and brilliance and muscular fingerwork, and the inclusion of the other incidental pieces is also valuable. Brendel throws off the *Ecossaises* splendidly, and the *Polonaise* (not in the least characteristic) is given a flexible rubato. The variations on the two famous British national airs also come off splendidly. Of the two sonatas included as makeweights, Op. 7 comes off the better. Brendel's concentration underlines the strength, and in the orchestral textures of the first movement his directness is particularly impressive. He is less persuasive in the 'little' *G major Sonata*, which lacks charm, not helped by the unglamorous sound.

33 Variations on a waltz by Diabelli, Op. 120.
*** Hyp. Dig. CDA 66763 [id.]. William Kinderman.
** Erato/Warner Dig. 4509-94810-2 [id.]. Daniel Barenboim.

33 Variations on a waltz by Diabelli, Op. 120; Piano sonata No. 28 in A, Op. 101.
*** EMI Dig. CDC7 54792-2 [id.]. Peter Donohoe.

The *Diabelli* is the greatest set of variations ever written, the only possible challenger being the *Goldberg*, and even they, though peerless in musical ingenuity, do not match the range, scale and depth of the Beethoven. (Brendel called them 'the greatest of all piano works'.) William Kinderman's version on Hyperion is really in a class of its own, remarkably fresh and well thought out. Some years ago Kinderman published a monograph on the *Variations* (Oxford University Press), which was received with great acclaim. It is almost worth buying the present disc for the sake of his illuminating liner-notes. Although a reputable scholar, however, his is playing of real temperament and psychological insight. He is not excessively judicious in his interpretative judgements, carefully weighing one view against another, but is sparkling with life and character. He is very well recorded, too. The most outstanding *Diabelli variations* to have appeared for ages.

Peter Donohoe's EMI recording enjoys one advantage over its immediate rivals: it offers an additional work, the *A major Sonata*, Op. 101. (Not that the presence of a fill-up is likely to sway the collector greatly one way or the other, so extraordinary is this masterpiece.) Donohoe also has the advantage of excellent recorded sound, realistic and fresh in equal measure. His performance of both pieces is intelligent and vigorous, eminently recommendable, if not quite the equal of Kinderman (Hyperion), Kovacevich (Philips) or Brendel (Vox/Turnabout). Nor does he penetrate the depths as do they, or as did Schnabel's celebrated pioneering set (which periodically resurfaces in historic editions). But there is no want of characterization and he has a good feeling for Beethoven's humour. No reason to withhold a third star, but this is not a first recommendation.

Daniel Barenboim recorded the variations in the late 1960s and is no stranger to their mystery.

His Erato account has much to recommend it, and his admirers need not doubt that he is a thoughtful and serious guide in this masterpiece. Yet William Kinderman's account on Hyperion is really in a different league.

VOCAL MUSIC

Missa solemnis.
(B) *** Sony SBK 53517 [id.]. Arroyo, Forrester, Lewis, Siepi, Singing City Choirs, Phd. O, Eugene Ormandy.
(M) **(*) DG Dig. 445 543-2 (2) [id.]. Cuberli, Schmidt, Cole, Van Dam, V. Singverein, BPO, Karajan – MOZART: *Mass No. 16.* **(*)
** Decca Dig. 444 337-2 [id.]. Varady, Vermillion, Cole, Pape, Berlin R. Ch., BPO, Solti.

On a single disc in Sony's Essential Classics series at budget price, Ormandy's 1967 Philadelphia recording makes an excellent bargain. Ormandy takes a bold and firm view of this masterpiece. It may not plumb all the spiritual depths of the work but, with four outstanding soloists and an excellent, well-focused choir, this is an account which takes you magnetically through the drama of Beethoven's personal view of the liturgy. The vintage recording gives plenty of body to the sound, both of voices and of orchestra, not least the bright-toned trumpets.

Karajan conducts a powerful reading marked by vivid and forward recording for orchestra and soloists, less satisfactory in rather cloudy choral sound. This was one of Karajan's recordings made in conjunction with a video film, and that brings both gains and losses. The sense of spontaneity, of a massive structure built dramatically with contrasts underlined, makes for extra magnetism, but there are flaws of ensemble and at least one serious flaw of intonation in the singing of Lella Cuberli, otherwise a full, sweet-toned soprano. First choice still rests with Levine (DG 435 770-2) or Gardiner (DG 429 779-2), the latter on a single CD – see our main volume.

Unlike his earlier Chicago recording of 1977, Solti's Berlin version of 17 years later, recorded live, is squeezed on to a single disc. Speeds are consistently a degree faster and textures lighter, helped by the recording, made in the Philharmonie. As well as being brisker, Solti is often a degree more warmly expressive; but, against that, the newer performance is less intense, less dedicated and less sharply focused. The soloists too are more variable, with René Pape disappointing in the bass solo opening the *Agnus Dei.*

Missa solemnis; (i) *Choral Fantasia, Op. 80.*
*(*) BMG/RCA Dig. 09026 60967-2 (2) [id.]. Orgonasova, Rappé, Heilmann, Rootering; (i) Oppitz; Bav. R. Ch. & SO, Sir Colin Davis.

At speeds more spacious than on any rival version, Davis with his Bavarian forces aims at a serene vision of this masterpiece, largely missing the drama behind Beethoven's very personal re-thinking of the liturgy. Tensions are low and they are not helped by the distant balance of the chorus, set against slightly hazy sound. Devotees of Davis should stand by his earlier, Philips version, which has a better coupling in the *Mass in C*, where here the *Choral Fantasia* lacks the bite this episodic work needs.

OPERA

Fidelio (complete).
⊛ *** EMI CDS5 55170-2 (2). Ludwig, Vickers, Frick, Berry, Crass, Philh. Ch. & O, Klemperer.
(M) *** EMI CMS7 69290-2 (2) [CDMB 769290]. Dernesh, Vickers, Kélémen, Ridderbusch, German Op. Ch., BPO, Karajan.
(M) *(*) RCA Dig. 74321 25278-2 (2). Adam, Nimsgern, Jerusalem, Altmeyer, Meven, Nossek, Wohlers, Leipzig R. Ch. & GO, Masur.

Klemperer's great set of *Fidelio* is now reissued, but at full price. However, it has been superbly remastered. The sound has a depth, beauty and realism far beyond any previous incarnation of this splendid 1962 Kingsway Hall recording. The result is a technical triumph to match the unique incandescence and spiritual strength of the performance, with wonderful contributions from all concerned and a final scene in which, more than in any other recording, the parallel with the finale of the *Choral Symphony* is underlined. It remains first choice; but the price rise is a move in the wrong direction, even though the reissue has been repackaged with an admirably clear libretto. We have to say, however, that it is well worth its cost.

Comparison between Karajan's strong and heroic reading and Klemperer's version is fascinating. Both have very similar merits, underlining the symphonic character of the work with their weight of utterance. Both may miss some of the sparkle of the opening scene, but it is better that seriousness should enter too early than too late. Since seriousness is the keynote, it is rather surprising to find Karajan using bass and baritone soloists lighter than usual. Both the Rocco (Ridderbusch) and the Don Fernando (Van Dam) lack something in resonance in their lower range. Yet they sing dramatically and intelligently, and there is the advantage that the Pizarro of Zoltan Kélémen sounds the more biting and powerful as a result – a fine performance. Jon Vickers as Florestan is, if anything, even finer than he was for Klemperer; and although Helga Dernesch as Leonore does not have quite the clear-focused mastery of Christa Ludwig in the Klemperer set, this is still a glorious, thrilling performance, outshining lesser rivals than Ludwig. The orchestral playing is superb.

Masur's version (previously issued on Eurodisc) is offered in well-balanced, modern, digital sound. It is played very well by the Leipzig orchestra, but this is a surprisingly small-scale view, lacking the full dramatic bite needed in this towering masterpiece. Neither Jeannine Altmeyer nor Siegfried Jerusalem had achieved their peak when they made the recording in 1982 and, though there is fine singing from the male members of the cast, the Marzelline of Carola Nossek is thin and unsteady. The whole performance has the feeling of a well-behaved run-through.

Fidelio: highlights.
(M) *** DG 445 461-2 [id.] (from complete set, with Janowitz, Kollo, Sotin, Jungirth, Fischer-
  Dieskau, Popp; cond. Bernstein).

It is good to have a set of highlights from the Bernstein set, recorded in conjunction with live performances at the Vienna State Opera and full of dramatic flair, yet which presents the drama on a human scale, less monumental than with Klemperer. Janowitz sings most beautifully as Leonore and, although Hans Sotin is not an especially villainous Pizarro, his vocal projection is impressive, Kollo is an intelligent and musicianly Florestan and Lucia Popp is at her delightful best as Marzelline. The selection is generous (71 minutes), including the *Overture* and the final scene, and contains a cued synopsis of the narrative.

Bellini, Vincenzo (1801–35)

I Capuleti ed i Montecchi (complete).
(M) **(*) EMI Dig. CMS7 64846-2 (2) [CDMB 64846]. Baltsa, Gruberová, Raffanti, Gwynne
  Howell, Tomlinson, ROHCG Ch. & O, Muti.

Bellini's adaptation of the famous Shakespearean story of the star-crossed lovers has its own variations on the original, with Tybalt still Romeo's rival, but with Lorenzo, physician to the Capulets, persuading Juliet to take the sleeping draught. After that, the nemesis of the plot continues. Romeo, finding Juliet, thinks she is dead and takes poison. Juliet awakens, only to suffer Romeo dying in her arms. She then dies from grief.

Muti's set was recorded live at a series of performances at Covent Garden when the production was new, in March 1984. With the Royal Opera House a difficult venue for recording, the sound is hard and close, far less agreeable and well balanced than in the previous EMI version of this opera, recorded in the studio with Beverley Sills and Dame Janet Baker and now deleted. On the later version, Agnes Baltsa makes a passionately expressive Romeo and Edita Gruberová a Juliet who is not just brilliant in coloratura but also sweet and tender. It is an unlikely but successful matching of a Carmen with a Zerbinetta; but it is the masterful conducting of Muti that, more than anything, makes one tolerant of the indifferent sound. If (for good reasons) he has often been considered something of a sprinter in opera, here he is superb with the pacing, balancing fast and incisive choruses against passages of warmth, relaxation and repose. That mastery is especially striking at the end of Act I, when the five principals sing a hushed quintet in which Romeo and Juliet musically reveal their understanding, singing sweetly in thirds. With excellent contributions from the refined tenor Dano Raffanti (as Tebaldo), Gwynne Howell and John Tomlinson, it is a performance to blow the cobwebs off an opera that – even in the earlier recording – seemed one of Bellini's less compelling pieces.

I Puritani (complete).
(M) **(*) EMI CMS7 69663-2 (2) [Ang. CDMC 69663]. Caballé, Kraus, Manuguerra, Hamari,
  Ferrin, Amb. Op. Ch., Philh. O, Muti.

In the EMI version of *I Puritani*, Riccardo Muti's contribution is most distinguished. As the very opening demonstrates, his attention to detail and pointing of rhythm make for refreshing results, and the warm but luminous recording is excellent. But both the principal soloists – Bellini stylists on their day, but here below form – indulge in distracting mannerisms, hardly allowing even a single bar to be presented straight in the big numbers, pulling and tugging in each direction, rarely sounding spontaneous. The big ensemble, *A te, o cara*, in its fussiness at slow speed loses the surge of exhilaration which the earlier Decca set with Sutherland and Pavarotti shows so strongly (Decca 417 588-2 – see our main volume).

Berg, Alban (1885–1935)

Chamber concerto.
(M) *** DG 447 405-2 [id.]. Barenboim, Zukerman, Ens. Intercontemporain, Boulez – STRAVINSKY: *Concerto in E flat* etc. ***

Boulez sets brisk tempi in the *Chamber concerto*, seeking to give the work classical incisiveness; but the strong and expressive personalities of the pianist and violinist tend towards a more romantic view. The result is characterful and convincing, though unaccountably Boulez omits the extended repeat in the finale. The recording is attractively atmospheric, and those who regard this as a difficult work will find the music-making here not in the least intimidating. For this reissue in DG's 'Legendary Recordings' series the concerto is aptly coupled with *Dumbarton Oaks* and two other Stravinsky pieces.

Violin concerto.
*** Teldec/Warner Dig. 4509 97449-2 [id.]. Zehetmair, Philh. O, Holliger – HARTMANN: *Concerto funèbre;* JANACEK: *Violin concerto.* ***

The Teldec recording by Thomas Zehetmair and the Philharmonia Orchestra under Heinz Holliger is one of the best to appear for a long time. Zehetmair plays with great sensitivity and a natural eloquence that many will prefer to the much (and rightly) admired account by Mutter on DG. That has tremendous brilliance and panache, but the glitzy elegance and slight coolness are less affecting than Zehetmair's reading. His version is less sensational and brings you closer to the heart of this poignant music. It offers more interesting couplings in the form of the Hartmann *Concerto funèbre* and the fragmentary Janáček *Concerto* of 1927–8. The recording, made at The Maltings in Snape, is of exemplary clarity and has great presence. At mid-price this is very desirable indeed.

(i) *Violin concerto;* (ii) *Lyric suite: 3 Pieces; 3 Pieces for orchestra, Op. 6.*
(B) *** DG 439 435-2 [id.].(i) Szeryng, Bav. RSO, Kubelik; (ii) BPO, Karajan.

Another outstanding version of Berg's *Violin concerto* comes from Henryk Szeryng, who gives a persuasive, perceptive and sympathetic account of this fine work and is well accompanied by the Bavarian orchestra under Kubelik. Superb playing, and a recording that has transferred well to CD. It is perhaps remarkable that, for their bargain Classikon reissue, DG have chosen to add to this two of Karajan's key recordings of Berg's orchestral music. Karajan's purification process gives wonderful clarity to these often complex pieces, with expressive confidence bringing out the romantic overtones. No more persuasive view could be taken – though, next to Schoenberg and Webern, Berg appears here as a figure who overloaded his music rather than as the most approachable of the Second Viennese School. A beautiful, refined recording, admirably transferred to CD.

Lyric suite; String quartet, Op. 3.
*** EMI Dig. CDC5 55190-2 [id.]. Alban Berg Qt.

The eponymous Alban Berg Quartet give masterly and authoritative accounts of the early *String quartet* of 1910 and of the *Lyric suite*. It is difficult to imagine these works being better played or recorded. There is room for another work – say, the Webern 1905 *Quartet* – the playing time is no more than 47 minutes; but if it is short on quantity, it is emphatically not on quality. Of the ten or so versions now on the market, this *Lyric suite* is a good first choice, and that of the Op. 3 *Quartet* is arguably the best ever. The recording has a comparable finesse and is realistic and truthful.

Berio, Luciano (born 1925)

(i) *Recital I (for Cathy);* (ii) *Folk-song suite;* (iii) *3 Songs by Kurt Weill* (arr. Berio).
(M) *** RCA 09026 62540-2 [id.]. Cathy Berberian, with (i) L. Sinf.; (ii, iii) Julliard Ens.; all cond. composer.

Recital I is the most elaborate, colourful work that Berio ever wrote for Cathy Berberian. Against fragmentary accompaniment from the instrumental band, the soloist in this semi-dramatic piece (presented in live performances as music theatre) thinks back through her repertoire as a concert-singer from Monteverdi to the present day. The end-product is a collage of musical ideas of a kind that Berio has always handled most skilfully and, with Berberian at her most intense, the result is very compelling. As the music progresses, one realizes that the singer is in fact represented as a patient in a mental home, her mind unbalanced – the twilight world between past memory and living present very much the source of evocation here. It is not always a comfortable work but, more than most of the avant-garde, it is a dramatic and eventful one. Excellent recording. Also included is a first-rate recording of an enchanting collection of folksongs arranged with twinkling ingenuity by Berio, again with Berberian very much in mind. The record concludes with three Kurt Weill songs, arranged by Berio, including the *Song of sexual slavery* intended for *The Threepenny Opera* but with the third verse cut as being 'too raw'; it ends with the spoken works: 'There's no getting away from it: all men are pigs!' Cathy Berberian relishes every word, and she sings *Surabaya Johnny* with comparable enjoyment to Berio's effective scoring.

Berlioz, Hector (1803–69)

Harold in Italy, Op. 16.
(M) *(*) RCA 09026 62582-2. William Primrose; Boston SO, Charles Munch – D'INDY: *Symphonie pour un chant montagnard français.* **(*)

(i) *Harold in Italy, Op. 16. Overture: Le carnaval romain, Op. 9; La damnation de Faust, Op. 24: Minuet of the Will-o'-the-wisps; Dance of the Sylphs; Hungarian march.*
(*) Biddulph mono WHL 028 [id.]. (i) William Primrose; Boston SO, Koussevitzky.

The Primrose–Koussevitzky account of *Harold in Italy*, Berlioz's symphony with viola obbligato commissioned by Paganini, was the very first commercial recording of the work. Its fires burn undimmed even now, so passionate and involving is this wonderful playing. For many musicians, it has never been surpassed, even though successors have not been few, the best being from Koussevitzky's protégé, Bernstein. His second recording with Donald MacInnes and the French Radio Orchestra has something of Koussevitzky's incandescence (CDM7 64745-2 – see our main volume). But the present transfers do not do these performances justice. The enormous tonal lustre these artists commanded is little in evidence. The sound is shrill and shallow. Perhaps nostalgia has clouded one's judgement and memories have been too rosy, but put this alongside the RCA LP transfer of the 1960s, and the ear notices greater richness and smoothness, while the original 78s reveal a much greater presence and a much firmer bass. There is an octave or so more on the originals, and greater definition. Tinkering with the controls produces some improvement, but it is difficult to recommend this with the enthusiasm the performances naturally engender.

Primrose recorded *Harold in Italy* on three occasions (and there is a fourth, off-air version with Toscanini, made in 1939). The first with Koussevitzky has never been surpassed by anyone, and we await a satisfactory transfer of it (see above). There was a second with Beecham, now reissued on Sony, which shows neither artist at their distinguished best; and, finally, the present issue, dating from 1958. At times Munch is positively coarse and hard-driven and Primrose not on form. Of course there are good things, but for the most part this is a disappointment.

(i) *Harold in Italy, Op. 16. Overtures: Le carnaval romain, Op. 9; Le corsaire, Op. 21; Symphonie fantastique;* (ii) *Symphonie funèbre et triomphale, Op. 15.*
(B) ** Ph. Duo 442 290-2 (2) [id.]. (i) Nobuko Imai; (ii) John Alldis Ch.; LSO, Sir Colin Davis.

Although the CD transfers are very well managed and this Berlioz Duo set is obviously good value, it would be perverse to recommend it when Sir Colin Davis's 1974 Concertgebouw recording of the *Symphonie fantastique* at full price (Philips 411 425-2) is so obviously superior to his earlier, LSO version, good though that is. The fine account of *Harold in Italy* with Nobuko Imai is also available (again at full price) with very successful alternative couplings (see our main volume), and the rather less persuasive *Symphonie funèbre* comes alternatively paired with the *Grand messe des morts.* The overtures are impressive, but overall this set is for bargain-hunters only.

Rêverie et caprice, Op. 8.
(M) *** DG Dig. 445 549-2 [id.]. Perlman, O de Paris, Barenboim – LALO: *Symphonie espagnole;* SAINT-SAENS: *Concerto No. 3.* ***

Berlioz's short concertante work for violin and orchestra uses material originally intended for *Benvenuto Cellini.* Perlman's ripely romantic approach to the *Rêverie* brings out the individuality of the melody and, with a sympathetic accompaniment from Barenboim, the work as a whole is given considerable substance. First-rate digital recording.

Symphonie fantastique, Op. 14.
(M) **(*) Telarc Dig. CD 82014 [id.]. Cleveland O, Lorin Maazel.
(M) **(*) DG 447 406-2 [id.]. LOP, Markevitch (with: CHERUBINI: *Anacréon: overture;* AUBER: *La Muette de Portici: overture* (**)).

(i) *Symphonie fantastique;* (ii) *Overtures: Béatrice et Bénédict; Le carnaval romain; Le Corsaire.*
(BB) **(*) RCA Navigator 74321 21283-2. Boston SO, (i) Prêtre; (ii) Munch.

(i) *Symphonie fantastique, Op. 14;* (ii) *Overture: Benvenuto Cellini.*
(B) ** BBC Radio Classics BBCRD 9117 [id.]. (i) Leningrad PO, Rozhdestvensky; (ii) RPO, Lawrence Foster.

Symphonie fantastique; Overture, Le carnaval romain, Op. 9.
**(*) Ph. Dig. 438 939-2 [id.]. O. de Paris, Bychkov.

Philips provide superb recording quality for the Orchestre de Paris and Semyon Bychkov in the *Symphonie fantastique* and it must be said that the quality of the orchestral response is very high. As an interpretation it is rather less impressive, and such wonderful performances as Beecham, Davis, Bernstein (EMI CDM7 64630-2) and Martinon (with *Lélio*: EMI CZS7 62739-2) need not fear that the newcomer will displace them. Bychkov freely indulges in some wilful agogic touches, only some of which strike an idiomatic note. While it is far from being a front runner, Bychkov's is not a negligible account either – and the fine recording may well sway some collectors. However, first choice remains with Sir Colin Davis (Philips 411 425-2) or, for those wanting period instruments and modern, digital sound, John Eliot Gardiner and his Orchestre Révolutionnaire et Romantique (Philips 434 402-2).

Prêtre's excitingly chimerical Boston account was recorded in 1969, and the upper range is far from full. However, the Boston ambience brings weight and the sound is otherwise resonantly spacious, with exciting projection for the brass. It is a highly volatile performance but Prêtre's sense of neurosis is convincing, and the finale combines an element of the grotesque with high adrenalin flow. An individual and involving account. Munch's famous accounts of the three *Overtures* make a thrilling bonus, but here the sound tends to shrillness.

Maazel's Telarc version dates from 1982, and the spectacular Severance Hall recording brings some superbly tangible brass sounds in the last two movements, not only in the clipped rhythms of the *March to the scaffold* but, notably, at the powerful entry of the *Dies irae* in the finale. Apart from this emphasis, the refined recording has a warm concert-hall perspective and the performance is naturally expressive in a spontaneous-sounding way without losing anything in precision of ensemble. Even so, this rather plain reading competes with the finest rivals only in its demonstration-worthy sonics and, with no fill-up, the disc has a playing time of only 49 minutes.

Igor Markevitch's recording of the *Symphonie fantastique* was technically among the best available in 1962, and in the transfer to CD the sound is remarkably good, rich and clear and with plenty of bloom. The strings in the slow movement can be made to sound particularly fresh and pleasing. The performance is impulsive, and if the reading falls just short of the standard set by the very finest versions it is still very convincing and the orchestral playing is excellent. For some, the extra clarity of the orchestral sound may be what especially commends it. However, the two *Overtures* are not really an asset: both are fiercely recorded and cannot compare in sound with the *Symphony*. Markevitch is very dramatic in *Anacréon* and gives an exciting account of the Auber bandstand showpiece; but the reproduction is not flattering enough for either to be really enjoyable, and this is a very doubtful candidate for reissue in DG's 'Originals' series of legendary recordings.

This BBC recording of the *Symphonie fantastique* was made at the Royal Albert Hall when, in September 1971, the Leningrad Philharmonic visited the Proms. The *Benvenuto Cellini overture* is a Festival Hall broadcast of the preceding year, and this bargain reissue prompts some difference of opinion. For EG the high-voltage electricity of the occasion is severely muted by the thin, distanced sound, making this version of the *Symphony* uncompetitive. To his ears the sound for the *Overture* has far more body, but the performance has less tension. RL, however, responds very positively to what he describes as some wonderful playing from this great orchestra, which prompts a boisterous roar of applause from the Promenaders – and rightly! The resonant acoustic and recessed but pleasing balance do not enable detail to register as well as it might in studio conditions: it does not compare well with, for instance, Rozhdestvensky's later, digital recording for Chandos, listed in our main volume. But that is a less convincing performance, offered at full price; this BBC recording is much less expensive and is worth considering, as there is a good sense of perspective and of space. RL also finds plenty of fire in the *Benvenuto Cellini overture* but comments that the well-filled Festival Hall produces a drier acoustic.

(i) *Symphonie fantastique;* (ii) *Lélio, ou Le Retour à la vie, Op. 14b;* (iii; iv) *La Mort de Cléopâtre;* (iii–v) *Les Nuits d'été, Op. 7;* (vi) *Béatrice et Bénédict: Overture & Entr'acte; Overtures: Benvenuto Cellini; Le carnaval romain, Op. 9; Les Troyens: Royal hunt and storm.*
(M) *** Sony SM3K 64103 (3) (i) LSO; (ii) with Jean-Louis Barrault (narrator), John Mitchinson, John Shirley-Quirk, L. Symphony Ch.; (iii) Yvonne Minton; (iv) BBC SO; (v) Stuart Burrows; (vi) NYPO; all cond. Boulez.

A thoroughly worthwhile Berlioz anthology, spanning a decade of Boulez recordings for CBS from 1967 (the *Symphonie* and *Lélio*) to 1976 (the two song-cycles). Even by Berlioz's standards, *Lélio* is a strange work. He intended it as a sequel to the *Fantastic symphony*, which made the original two-disc LP issue very apt. As so often with a dotty work, the gramophone tones down the oddity, allowing one to appreciate genuine merits more clearly than in a live performance. Though the spoken dialogue remains obtrusively long (even when spoken most beautifully by M. Barrault), the individual cueing on CD allows one access to the music itself and the six numbers make a fascinating suite, ranging as they do from a Goethe ballad through such pieces as a *Chanson de Brigands* to an extended fantasy on Shakespeare's *The Tempest*. Coupled with a unique reading of the *Fantastique* (clear-headed and intense rather than atmospheric), it shows Boulez at his most searchingly convincing. Very good recording, except for the difference of levels in *Lélio* between speech (loud and forward) and music. The dramatic scena, *La Mort de Cléopâtre*, an early work which yet gives many hints of the mature Berlioz, makes a particularly suitable companion, as it offers specific quotations of material later used in the *Symphonie fantastique* (the *idée fixe*) and the *Roman carnival overture* (the melody of the introduction). Yvonne Minton's account is dramatically incisive, less varied of expression than Dame Janet Baker's famous recording, but strongly committed. When Berlioz orchestrated *Les nuits d'été* he specified the use of more than one voice in the score, and here the cycle is shared by Minton and Stuart Burrows, with Minton's passionate response showing her at her most movingly eloquent and Burrows also at his finest. The 1972 New York collection of Overtures and Entr'actes was originally recorded quadrophonically in the Avery Fisher Hall, but not all the richness of tone and ambience was carried over into the stereo master. The performances are warmer, less concerned with sharpness of detail than the earlier recordings, yet they still show toughness taking priority over flexible brilliance and the sound-balance matches the readings in its brightness, although it also has weight and atmosphere. Overall this is strongly recommended to Boulez admirers, and others will find it highly stimulating.

VOCAL MUSIC

La damnation de Faust, Op. 24 (complete).
(B) *** DG Double 437 931-2 (2) [id.]. Rubio, Verreau, Roux, Mollet, Elisabeth Brasseur Ch., RTF Children's Ch., LOP, Markevitch.

Reissued as a bargain DG Double, Markevitch's recording is very competitive indeed. It deservedly won a *Grand Prix du Disque* in 1960. The performance is extremely dramatic and vivid, and the recording, which dates from the very end of the 1950s, sounds remarkably fresh, with an attractive bloom on the sound and no lack of atmosphere. The orchestral contribution emerges with fine colour and Markevitch draws the full effect from Berlioz's quirky touches of scoring. Richard Verreau, a distinctly Gallic tenor, as Faust, is especially impressive among the soloists, but Consuelo Rubio is also very good, as is Pierre Mollet, and Michel Roux makes an effective Mephistopheles. The choral contribution is very French, not always too sophisticated but committed and vibrant, with plenty of character. In short, this is very stimulating and enjoyable, and one notices especially some lovely sounds from the orchestral strings in the score's more expressive moments. The vivid CD transfer gives the performance all the immediacy of a live performance.

(i; ii) *L'enfance du Christ;* (ii; iii) *Méditation religieuse; La mort d'Ophélie; Sara la baigneuse;* (iii; iv) *La mort de Cléopâtre.*
(B) *** Double Decca 443 461-2 (2) [id.]. (i) Pears, Morison, Cameron, Rouleau, Frost, Fleet, Goldsbrough O; (ii) St Anthony Singers, (iii) ECO; (iv) Anne Pashley; Sir Colin Davis.

Davis's 1961 recording of *L'enfance du Christ* (originally made for L'Oiseau-Lyre) is by no means inferior to his later, Philips set. At times the earlier performance was fresher and more urgent, and Peter Pears was a sweeter-toned, more characterful narrator. Elsie Morison and John Cameron are perfectly cast as Mary and Joseph, and Joseph Rouleau makes an impressive contribution as the

Ishmaelite Father. Not all the French pronunciation is immaculate, but Davis and his singers revel in the sheer originality of the melody. Such moments as the famous *Shepherds' chorus* and the angelic hosannas which end Part 2 are ravishingly beautiful, particularly when the recording has transferred so freshly and atmospherically to its new format. Moreover this Decca reissue offers (on a Double Decca set with two CDs for the price of one) the entire contents of a third LP, issued in 1968 and also sounding freshly minted. This is an invaluable collection of off-beat vocal works, with fine choral singing and a splendid contribution from Anne Pashley. In a wonderfully intense account of the early scena, *La mort de Cléopâtre*, she even manages to rival Dame Janet Baker's version; in this most substantial of pieces Miss Pashley is if anything the more dramatic: the closing section, where Cleopatra in her death throes can merely mutter disconnected phrases, is most affectingly done. The other three pieces are for chorus: the gentle *Méditation religieuse* is a setting of Thomas Moore in translation; *La mort d'Ophélie*, for women's chorus, brings overtones of the choruses in *Roméo et Juliette*; and *Sara la baigneuse* is a strong, flowing setting of a Victor Hugo poem.

(i) *Herminie; La mort de Cléopâtre*. Overtures: *Béatrice et Bénédict; Le roi Lear*.
** ASV Dig. CDDCA 895 [id.]. (i) Rosalind Plowright; Philh. O, Jean-Philippe Rouchon.

Rosalind Plowright is a fine, positive soprano who should appear on disc more often, and here she chooses rare and valuable repertory, two of the cantatas that the young Berlioz wrote as his entries in successive years (1828 and 1829) for the Prix de Rome. The music proved too adventurous for the judges, but in juxtaposition here one finds how much Berlioz had progressed towards an individual style in those twelve months. Though *Herminie* starts with the strikingly original theme which became the *idée fixe* in the *Symphonie fantastique*, it is relatively conventional in its ground plan, revealing the mature Berlioz only occasionally, as in the *Prière*. *La mort de Cléopâtre* is more striking, with many masterly touches, not least in the final death scene, where Plowright movingly stills the vibrato in her voice to produce a drained tone. Sadly, the accompaniment fails to match her involvement. Like the performances of the two Shakespearean overtures, it lacks the tautness and bite needed for this music with its frequent declamations. The distancing of both voice and orchestra in a reverberant acoustic does not help either.

Mélodies: *Adieu Bessy; Amitié, reprends ton empire; La belle Isabeau; La belle voyageuse; Boléro; Canon libre à la quinte; La captive; Les champs; Chanson à boire; Chansonette de M. Léon de Wailly; Le chant des bretons; Chant guerrier; Le chasseur danois; Je crois en vous; Elégie en prose; Hélène; Le jeune pâtre breton; Le matin; Le Maure jaloux; Le Montagnard exilé; La mort d'Ophélie; Nocturnes à deux voix; L'Origine de la harpe; Pleure, pauvre Colette; Prière du matin; Le roi de Thulé; Sara la baigneuse; Sérénade de Méphistophélès; Le Trébuchet; Zaïde*.
*** DG Dig. 435 860-2 (2) [id.]. Françoise Pollet, Anne Sofie von Otter, John Aler, Thomas Allen, Cord Garben (with Bernd Schenk, Christine Mühlbach, Göran Söllscher, Torleif Thedéen, Thomas Lutz, Royal Op. Ch., Stockholm (members)).

Starting magically with a little duet for soprano and mezzo to guitar accompaniment, this collection of 29 of Berlioz's songs and ensembles includes many rarities previously unrecorded. With four outstanding soloists, it makes a unique and attractive collection which no Berlioz enthusiast should ignore, despite piano accompaniment from Cord Garben that is often rhythmically too square . That does not prevent the many strophic songs in the first half of the collection, the early works written before 1830, from revealing their fresh charm. Even the settings of Thomas Moore that Berlioz in 1829 grouped under the title *Irlande* (he was in love with Harriet Smithson at the time) reveal only occasional flashes of the distinctive Berlioz. Seven of the nine are included here. But no one will miss the Berlioz flavour in the first drafts, included here, of two numbers later celebrated in *La damnation de Faust, Le roi de Thulé* and *Mephistopheles' serenade* – for tenor here, not bass. The second disc includes many fine songs that are familiar, notably *La captive* (here with Berlioz's cello obbligato), *La mort d'Ophélie* and *Sara la baigneuse*. Such a witty little duet for tenor and baritone as *Le trébuchet* ('The snare') proves a charmer with its bird-like accompaniment, and so does the *Boléro*, with castanets as well as piano. *Le matin*, Berlioz's last song, was written as early as 1850, and it makes one regret that from then on he ignored the genre. Though the recordings were made in different venues over several years, they present a consistent series, and one specially values the rare opportunity of having such fine singers as these in duets and ensembles as well as solo songs.

Mélodies: (i) *La belle Isabeau; La belle voyageuse; La captive; Le matin; La mort d'Ophélie*. (ii) *Nuits d'été* (song-cycle); (ii; iii) *Roméo et Juliette: Prologue: Premiers transports (Strophes)*.
*** DG Dig. 445 823-2 [id.]. Anne Sophie von Otter, with (i) Royal Stockholm Op. Ch.; Cord Garben; (ii) BPO, Levine; (iii) Berlin RIAS Chamber Ch.

This is an excellent, most attractive compilation, bringing together von Otter's outstanding contributions both to DG's Berlioz song collection and to the Levine set of *Roméo et Juliette*, which had *Nuits d'été* as a fill-up. It allows those who do not want those bigger sets to savour von Otter's masterly singing. Hers is the most strikingly warm and characterful contribution to the song series, and the five solo songs here are among the most moving and individual of all, notably *La mort d'Ophélie*, the most extended of the songs. In *Les nuits d'été* von Otter is fresh and radiant, bringing out the dramatic contrasts between the songs, and the poise and weight of *Strophes* from *Roméo* is magical.

OPERA

Les Troyens (complete).
⊕ *** Decca Dig. 443 693-2 (4) [id.]. Lakes, Pollet, Voigt, Montreal Schubert Ch. & SO, Dutoit.

There is controversy among us about the impressive new Decca set of *Les Troyens*; in determining a choice between this and the older, Davis set, readers are invited to consider the following conflicting viewpoints. For EG (at whose request the Rosette has been appended), Dutoit and the Montreal Symphony Orchestra, second to none in the French repertory, here confirm their idiomatic responsiveness to the music, coupled with the consistent warmth and richness of the sound. Add to that a largely French-speaking cast here, on balance even more sensitive and tonally more beautiful than Davis's in his classic set of 25 years earlier, plus two minor but valuable textual additions, and the practical advantage of the new over the old is clear. This was the swan-song of Decca's veteran record-producer, Ray Minshull, and he could not have had a more glorious monument to celebrate his career. The recording was linked to two concert performances of each of the parts of the opera, *La prise de Troie* and *Les Troyens à Carthage*. The church of St Eustache, the orchestra's regular recording venue, was not big enough to accommodate all the separate ensembles and choirs in the *Trojan march* at the end of Act I, and to synchronize everything they needed 64 tracks. Interpretatively, the contrasts between Dutoit and Davis are quickly established at the very start of *La prise de Troie*. Dutoit launches in at high voltage, more volatile than Davis, conveying exuberance, consistently preferring faster speeds. Davis may be marginally less exciting, but he often compensates in the extra crispness and clarity of the playing of the Covent Garden Orchestra. The advantage of Dutoit's faster speeds – reflecting the metronome markings – comes not just in thrilling allegros but also in flowing andantes. So Cassandra's first solo is more persuasively moulded at a flowing speed, with Deborah Voigt far warmer than Berit Lindholm for Davis, both in her beauty of tone and in her espressivo phrasing. Lindholm is accurate, but her tone too readily becomes raw and throaty under pressure, where Voigt's portrait is far more feminine and movingly vulnerable. She crowns her performance at the end of Act II, triumphantly leading the final ensemble of defiant Trojan women, more impetuous than her rival.

In *La prise de Troie*, such a moment as the clash of arms within the Trojan horse comes over more dramatically with Dutoit, thanks to his timing, and there is more mystery before the arrival of Hector's ghost at the beginning of Act II. For completeness, Dutoit includes the brief prelude that Berlioz wrote for the garbled 1863 performances of the second part of the opera, but not intended to be given in the full five-Act version. The other textual addition comes in Act I. After the Andromache scene – with a clarinet solo of breathtaking gentleness from the Montreal player – there is an extra scene, lasting six minutes, which the Berlioz scholar, Hugh MacDonald, editor of the Barenreiter score, has orchestrated from the surviving piano score.

The role of Chorebus, Cassandra's lover, in the first part of the opera is very well taken in both sets, by Peter Glossop for Davis, by Gino Quilico for Dutoit, both in rich, firm voice. As Aeneas, Gary Lakes may not have as richly heroic a voice as Jon Vickers for Davis, being rather more easily stressed at the top; among today's tenors, however, he is the most experienced of all in this role, having sung it close on two dozen times on both sides of the Atlantic. His big advantage over Vickers, most of all in the great love scene with Dido in Act IV, is that he shades his voice far more subtly. Though the role of Dido very often goes to a mezzo – Josephine Veasey in the Davis set, Dame Janet Baker in EMI's set of excerpts, with Sir Alexander Gibson conducting – here Decca firmly opts for a soprano, Françoise Pollet. One of the most exciting French singers to have appeared in years, she is in many ways an ideal choice. Very much attuned to the idiom, she sings consistently with full, even tone, so that, matching Dutoit's expressiveness and the richness of the Montreal sound, she brings out the feminine sensuousness of the role more than a mezzo normally would. Anna is very well taken by another French singer, Hélène Parraguin, with her firm, rich mezzo providing a clear contrast with Pollet. Where there is a disadvantage in having a soprano as Dido is in the darker passages. Pollet has a formidable chest register, but at the start of Dido's final monologue, *Je vais mourir*, she does not convey the heart-aching desolation that the finest mezzos achieve. She sounds purposeful instead of resigned, and the lyrical section that follows, '*Adieu, fière cité*', brings a tender contrast, with the reference back to the love duet most poignant. Then, in the final solo, Pollet portrays the distraught Dido, all purpose gone in the disjointed recitative. She may not have the dark colourings of a Baker or a Veasey, but her dramatic power is just as intense.

There is barely a weak link in the rest of the huge cast. Catherine Dubosc makes a breathily boyish Ascanius, and Gregory Cross sings with sharp clarity in the tenor role of the spy, Sinon. John Mark Ainsley, though not quite so free of tone as usual on top, makes a sensitive Hylas in the sailor song of Act V, though the high tessitura of the other tenor role, Iopas, strains Jean-Luc Maurette uncomfortably at the top, bringing unsteadiness. As recorded, Michel Philippe as Pantheus also sounds unsteady, but that is very much the exception. Though on balance the Covent Garden Chorus in the Davis set sing with even crisper ensemble, the passionate commitment of the performance matches the fire of Dutoit's whole reading. This is a thrilling set, to have one marvelling afresh at the electric vitality of Berlioz's inspiration – and marvelling too that the formidable problems of recording so massive a work have been accomplished so confidently.

For RL, however, the ambitious new Decca recording was something less than a whole-hearted triumph. It is not so much the cast, though there are reservations here, but above all the conducting which he feels is the problem. This score depends on the spell that the conductor can cast over orchestra and thus on audience, and Dutoit is far from magical. For RL, allegiance to Sir Colin's set remains unchanged (Philips 416 432-2).

Bernstein, Leonard (1918–90)

Candide: overture; Facsimile (choreographic essay); *Fancy free* (ballet); *On the Town: 3 Dance episodes.*
(M) **(*) EMI Eminence CD-EMX 2242; *TC-EMX 2242* [id.]. St Louis SO, Slatkin.

Though Slatkin cannot quite match Bernstein himself in the flair he brings to his jazzier inspirations, this is an attractive and generous collection. Next to Bernstein, Slatkin sounds a little metrical at times, but it is a marginal shortcoming, and he directs a beautiful, refined reading of the extended choreographic essay, *Facsimile*. As a gimmick, the song 'Big Stuff' before *Fancy Free* is recorded in simulation of a juke-box, complete with 78-r.p.m. surface-hiss and a blues singer (Jean Kittrell) with very heavy vibrato. The sound otherwise is full rather than brilliant, set in a helpful, believable acoustic.

Serenade after Plato's Symposium (for solo violin, string orchestra, harp & percussion).
*** EMI Dig. CDC5 55360-2 [id.]. Perlman, Boston SO, Ozawa – BARBER: *Violin concerto;* FOSS:
    Three American pieces. ***
**(*) Nimbus Dig. NI 5329 [id.]. Hu Kun, ESO, William Boughton – BARBER: *Violin concerto.* **

Perlman may initially seem almost too confident, missing an element of fantasy in Bernstein's personalized meditation on Plato's *Symposium*, where the more reticent view of Gidon Kremer with the composer conducting (DG 445 245-2) seems to delve deeper. Yet increasingly through the five contrasted movements the purposefulness as well as the masterful power of Perlman's playing adds to the work's impact, eliminating any thought that the piece might be too episodic. He brings it home the more tellingly how each movement leads thematically out of the preceding one, until the final movement, much the longest, completes the circle in its references back to the opening. He makes it seem a warmer piece too, thanks to his range of incomparably rich tone-colours. The richness of the Boston string-sound is beautifully set against the fullness of Perlman's violin.

As in the Barber *Concerto* with which it is coupled, Hu Kun, born in China in 1963, gives a deeply reflective account of Bernstein's Plato-inspired work for intimate forces: violin, strings, harp and percussion. Again the bravura passages lack impact, thanks to the distant, rather dim recording, but that shortcoming is less serious in a work where thoughtfulness is far more important than display. A possible alternative to Perlman's American album, powerful and intense, though there is no make-weight in addition to the Bernstein and Barber.

Berwald, Franz (1797–1868)

Symphonies Nos. 1 in G min. (Sérieuse); 3 in C (Singulière); Play of the elves (Elfenspiel).
(M) **(*) EMI CDM5 65303-2 [id.]. RPO, Björlin.

This CD continues EMI's CD reissues from a 1976 boxed set of LPs containing all Berwald's important orchestral music. The composer's reputation rests largely on the symphonies, and they possess a refreshing vigour and an imaginative vitality that step well outside the comparatively pale atmosphere of the Scandinavian musical world of the 1840s. Their originality in matters of form is well known; what cannot be stressed too often is that all four have a sparkle and freshness of vision that deserve wider recognition and a more secure foothold in the international concert repertoire. The performances here are thoroughly sympathetic and certainly worth considering at mid-price. They sound warm and fresh, though the orchestral playing under the late Ulf Björlin is a little deficient in vitality; the recordings were made during a heatwave. Both Järvi and Erling with the LSO are more vital and alert in the *Singulière*, and the former's account of the *Sérieuse* is comparably rewarding (see our main volume). By their side, Björlin does not succeed in creating the same degree of tension in shaping melodic lines. The tone-poem, *Play of the Elves*, is a delightful piece under whose deceptively Mendelssohnian surface resides an inventive and original mind. There is no current alternative at present, so this CD is by no means to be written off by those with limited budgets, as the EMI engineers have provided excellent recording, well transferred to CD. For the set of four symphonies, first choice rests with the Gothenburg Symphony Orchestra under Järvi (DG 415 502-2).

Biber, Heinrich (1644–1704)

Harmonia artificiosa-ariosa (7 Partitas), Nos. 1–3 & 5 for 2 scordatura violins & continuo; 4 for scordatura violin, viola di braccio & continuo; 6 for 2 violins & continuo; 7 for 2 violas d'amore & continuo (complete).
*** Sony Dig. SK 58920 [id.]. Tafelmusik, Jeanne Lamon.
(M) *** Chan. Dig. 0575/6 [id.]. Purcell Quartet with Elizabeth Wallfisch.

Two complete recordings of Biber's masterly *Harmonia artificosa-ariosa*, equally distinguished, show us the amazing range of these seven partitas (or suites), which were published posthumously in 1712. (The term *scordata*, incidentally, indicated a different system of tuning.) Each work consists of a very free opening *Prelude* or a more structured *Sonata* (slow–fast–slow), usually improvisational in feeling, and includes the usual dance forms of *Allemande* and *Sarabande*, plus an *Aria* with divisions, and often closes with a lighthearted *Gigue*, although the *Third* ends with a remarkable *Canon in uniso*, liberally decorated with violin cascades, which readily relates to the more famous piece by Biber's contemporary, Pachelbel. The *Fifth Sonata in G* ends with a splendid *Passacaglia*. The *Aria* in the *Sixth* has thirteen variations plus finale, and, including all repeats, the Purcell performance extends this remarkable movement to over 13 minutes, with playing of the highest order to hold the listener's attention readily throughout; the Tafelmusik account is half as long. But in many ways the two sets of performances are alike, and they certainly share the spontaneity and scholarship of the very best period-instrument performances. Tempi are usually similar, although the Purcell Consort tend to bring a slightly more spacious espressivo to slower movements. Their extra weight (with use of organ continuo) is especially telling in the passacaglias. On the other hand, the airy sprightliness of Tafelmusik, especially in the *Gigues*, often more dashing, is very attractive. The *G minor Partita* (No. 5) is particularly successful in the Chandos performance, while in the *Sixth* Tafelmusik are at their finest, using the organ continuo effectively as a basis for the busy violin fireworks in the opening movement. The final work, scored for two violas d'amore, brings a much warmer, fuller sound from Elizabeth Wallfisch and Richard Boothby (again with organ continuo) than their Tafelmusik colleagues, Thomas Georgi and Elli Winer, who use a harpsichord and create much leaner textures. On Chandos (in No. 7) the organ is again used very tellingly at the sombre opening of the closing *Arietta*, with its eleven divisions on a ground (in essence another inspired chaconne), which makes such a satisfying end to the set and which, it must be said, Tafelmusik also present with considerable gravitas – even if the textural effect is lighter. In short, you cannot go wrong with either of these recordings, which are both splendidly balanced and truthful. We have listed Tafelmusik first as (for some of the reasons stated above) Sony squeeze all seven partitas on to a single CD. Chandos have been forced to use a pair, playing for 43 minutes and 47 minutes respectively. But the cost has been reduced accordingly, and this set retails at upper-mid-price, probably costing slightly under £20 for the two CDs.

8 Violin sonatas (for violin and continuo) (1681); *Sonata pastorella; Sonata representativa in A* (for solo violin); *Passacaglia for solo violin; Passacaglia for lute*.
*** HM Dig. HMU 907134/5 (2) [id.]. Romanesca (Andrew Manze, Nigel North, John Toll).

As a performer, Biber was obviously a virtuoso of the highest order, for these phenomenally difficult *Sonatas*, with their chimerical upper tessitura and sometimes bizarre effects, could be played only by a violinist of remarkable technical gifts. Such is Andrew Manze, whose baroque violin encompasses all the demands made on it with consummate mastery. He conveys to the full the tension which always springs from strong performances of technically demanding music, yet at the same time retains an essentially expressive style. For with all the extraordinary decorative divisions inherent in Biber's writing, it is esentially melodic, and the tunes come out fast and furious. He is an unashamed borrower, using *La Folia* readily enough and drawing on other composers' ideas without shame (Schmelzer among them). What is remarkable in these superbly played performances is the conveyed improvisatory feeling in the writing, to say nothing of its sublimely volatile unpredictability. We already know (from the earlier, BIS performances) the remarkable solo violin *Passacaglia*, an essentially melancholy piece, and the contrasting *Sonata representativa* with its variety of bird imitations (plus a weird croaking frog and a glissando cat). Although the solo lute *Passacaglia*, which is a simplified piece, does not give him much of a chance to shine, Nigel North's often plangent continuo on lute and theorbo makes a major contribution to the imaginative vitality of the music-making, and John Toll is a good keyboard partner (for instance, the organ underpinning of the *Passacaglia* which opens the *Sixth Sonata*). But it is Andrew Manze who makes these performances so exciting and stimulating: surely the composer himself must have played them like this. The recording has a fine, spacious acoustic, and only those who find the abrasiveness of authentic fiddling aurally difficult should stay away from this highly stimulating pair of discs.

Binge, Ronald (1910–79)

Las Castañuelas; (i) *Concerto for E flat saxophone. Dance of the snowflakes; Elizabethan serenade; Faire Frou-Frou; High stepper; Madrugado; Miss Melanie; The red sombrero; Sailing by; Scherzo; Scottish rhapsody; String song; Trade winds; Venetian carnival; The watermill;* (ii) *The whispering valley: Prelude.*
** Marco Polo Dig. 8.223515 [id.]. Slovak RSO (Bratislava), Ernest Tomlinson; (i) with Kenneth Edge; (ii) Silvia Cápová.

Ronald Binge began his career accompanying silent films, then moved on to the end-of-the-pier orchestral world of the 1930s, working at Great Yarmouth until the pier burned down! In 1935 he began his association with Mantovani, and after his war service (with the RAF in Blackpool, where he continued music-making with the help of Sidney Torch), he renewed this association. In 1951, at the behest of the Decca Record Company, Binge created the Mantovani 'sound', a cascading string effect cleverly achieved not by studio reverberation alone but by overlapping the part-writing for the violins. (Glazunov had already hinted at how it could be done in his *Seasons* ballet.) Binge's ingenious arrangement helped to make *Charmaine* one of the great post-war instrumental hits. Later he went on to use this effect, slightly modified, in one of his own pieces – pointing the string phrasing with the harp, in *The dance of the snowflakes*. Then came his own great personal success, *Elizabethan serenade* (first called simply 'Andante cantabile'), which Mantovani premièred in 1951. It immediately caught the public fancy and became a signature-tune *par excellence*. Binge's other striking lyrical success was *Sailing by*, but his most delectable miniature is undoubtedly *The watermill*. The jaunty *High stepper*, a TV signature-tune, opens with a whiff of the Litolff *Scherzo* from the *Concerto symphonique*. The *Saxophone concerto* is lively enough, with the finale the most striking movement. It is given a first-rate performance by Kenneth Edge but is not as memorable as the Eric Coates *Rhapsody*. Other attractive novelty numbers here include *Miss Melanie* (which reminds one a little of Ron Goodwin's *Miss Marple theme*), the chirpy *Faire Frou-Frou* – more English music-hall than French can-can – and the rhapsodically atmospheric *Trade winds*. The whole programme is freshly played by this excellent Slovak orchestra under the sympathetic Ernest Tomlinson, although he phrases the *Elizabethan serenade* rather angularly. The one snag is that the microphones have been placed too close to the violins, which produces an unflattering, grainy patina of string-tone. The conductor provides nine pages of biography and excellent descriptive notes.

Bizet, Georges (1838–75)

(i) *L'Arlésienne: suites Nos. 1–2; Carmen: suites Nos. 1–2;* (ii) *Jeux d'enfants; The Fair Maid of Perth: suite; Symphony in C;* (iii) (Piano) *Variations chromatiques;* (iv) *Agnus Dei;* (v) *Chanson d'avril;* (vi) *Carmen: excerpts;* (vii) *Les Pêcheurs de perles: Duet: Au fond du temple saint.*
(B) ** Ph. Duo 442 272-2 (2) [id.]. (i) LOP, Dorati; (ii) LSO, Roberto Benzi; (iii) Marie Françoise

Bucquet; (iv) José Carreras; (v) Gérard Souzay, Dalton Baldwin; (vi) Jane Rhodes, Albert Lance, Paris Op. Ch. & O, Benzi; (vii) Léopold Simoneau, René Biano.

Roberto Benzi has made too few records. He has the gift of bringing music fully alive in the recording studio, and his 1965 LSO version of the Bizet *Symphony* is most attractive, standing comparison with the finest versions. He is supported by first-rate LSO playing, with the oboe distinctive in the slow movement. The personality of the orchestra comes through strongly in the couplings and the performance of the surprisingly rare *Jolie fille de Perth suite* approaches Beecham in finesse. In *Petit mari, petite femme* from *Jeux d'enfants* (another successful performance), the leading string parts are played as cello and violin solos, which is not the composer's idea but works very well. The sound is admirable. The earlier Lamoureux Orchestra recordings of the *Carmen suites* (1959) and *L'Arlésienne* (1960) are extremely lively under Dorati (especially the latter, where pacing is very alert and brisk) but the sound is a little dated. Apart from the song provided by Souzay and Baldwin, the vocal items are not really an asset, and the three popular excerpts from *Carmen* are undistinguished. The performance of the *Variations*, too, is a routine one. But the set is very nearly worth getting for the Benzi performances alone.

Roma suite; Patrie overture, Op. 19; Symphony in C.
**(*) EMI Dig. CDC5 55057-2 [id.]. Capitole Toulouse O, Michel Plasson.
(BB) **(*) ASV Dig. CDQS 6135 [id.] (without *Patrie*). RPO, Enrique Bátiz.

Roma was written over a period, some years after the *Symphony in C*. Bizet originally called the work (first performed without the Scherzo) a *Fantastique symphonique* with its four movements labelled *Rome, Venice, Florence* and *Naples*. It has not the overall spontaneity of the *Symphony* and is uneven in quality, but it remains a piece easy to indulge if you are a lover of Bizet's feeling for the orchestral palette. The warmth of the opening horn chorale and the gaiety of the finale, with its pleasing secondary tune, are brought out enjoyably in Toulouse and the orchestral playing is excellent. The recording, too, is very good, vividly coloured, if not of demonstration standard. *Patrie*, too, comes over with plenty of gusto, and again its lyrical theme is warmly presented. The *Symphony* is lively and well played (with an imaginative oboe soloist) and is certainly enjoyable if not distinctive. Martinon's version (see below) has more sheer *joie de vivre* and Prêtre's slightly more character. But the disc is worth considering for *Roma*.

Bátiz's performances are also attractive, with very good playing from the RPO. As with the Plasson account of *Roma*, it is the first and last movements which come off the most effectively. Although he omits *Patrie*, Bátiz has a considerable price advantage and he receives excellent (1990) digital recording, engineered by Brian Culverhouse. In the *Symphony* the sound is noticeably full and weighty, and this adds to the impression that the performance is less lighthearted than usual in the first movement (repeat included), though there is no lack of vitality and, with its more serious manner, it is still both effective and enjoyable.

Symphony in C; L'Arlésienne: suites Nos. 1–2: excerpts; Carmen: suites Nos. 1–2: excerpts.
(BB) *** RCA Navigator 74321 17901-2. Bamberg SO, Georges Prêtre.

A most enjoyable and generous super-bargain disc, originating from the Eurodisc catalogue, very warmly and naturally recorded, most elegantly played and offering 77 minutes of music. The most important numbers are included in the two orchestral suites and, if the playing in *L'Arlésienne* is a little low-key, the *Carmen* vignettes alternate vividness with pleasing instrumental delicacy. The performance of the *Symphony*, complete with exposition repeat, is alert, yet has much refinement as well as warmth, the oboe solo in the slow movement played most engagingly. There is plenty of vigour in the outer movements and, although the ambience is resonant, it does not cloud detail.

Symphony in C; Jeux d'enfants; La jolie fille de Perth: suite.
(B) **(*) DG Double 437 371-2 (2) [id.]. Fr. R. & TV O, Jean Martinon – LALO: *Cello concerto; Namouna* etc. **(*)
(BB) ** Naxos Dig. 8.553027 [id.] (without *Jolie fille Sérénade*). New Zealand SO, Donald Johanos.

Although Martinon's performance' has not quite the magic of the Marriner (Decca) or Beecham (EMI CDC7 47794-2) accounts, it is still very good indeed, with both charm and sparkle, and the couplings make this Double DG set worth considering, even though the early-1960s string timbre is somewhat lacking in allure. However, the finest current version of the Bizet *Symphony* is by the Orpheus Chamber Orchestra (DG 423 624-2 – see our main volume).

On Naxos, Johanos secures some sprightly playing from his New Zealand group, with a nice oboe solo in the slow movement. But string textures are a little lean and it is a distinct drawback that the *Fair maid of Perth suite* is without the famous *Serenade*.

Carmen (complete).

(B) **(*) DG 427 885-2 (3) [id.]. Berganza, Domingo, Cotrubas, Milnes, Amb. S., LSO, Abbado.

(B) **(*) CfP CD-CFPD 4454 (2). Grace Bumbry, Jon Vickers, Mirella Freni, Les Petites Chanteurs à la Croix de Bois, Paris Op. Ch. & O, Frühbeck de Burgos.

(M) *(*) RCA 74321 25279-2 (2). Moffo, Corelli, Donath, Cappuccilli, Augér, Schönberg Boys' Ch., German Op. Ch. & O, Berlin, Maazel.

(B) * Decca Double 443 871-2 (2) [id.]. Regina Resnik, Del Monaco, Sutherland, Krause, Geneva Grand Theatre Ch., SRO, Schippers.

Superbly disciplined, Abbado's performance nails its colours to the mast at the very start with a breathtakingly fast account of the opening prelude. Through the four Acts there are other examples of idiosyncratic tempi, but the whole entertainment hangs together with keen compulsion, reflecting the fact that these same performers – Sherrill Milnes as Escamillo excepted – took part in the Edinburgh Festival production directly associated with this recording project. Conductor and orchestra can take a large share of credit for the performance's success for, though the singing is never less than enjoyable, it is on the whole less characterful than on some rival sets. Teresa Berganza is a seductive if somewhat unsmiling Carmen – not without sensuality, and producing consistently beautiful tone, but lacking some of the flair which makes for a three-dimensional portrait. If you want a restrained and thoughtful view, then Tatiana Troyanos in Solti's set, also opposite the admirably consistent Plácido Domingo, is preferable. Ileana Cotrubas as Micaëla is not always as sweetly steady as she can be; Milnes makes a heroic matador. The spoken dialogue is excellently produced, and the sound is vivid and immediate, with the CDs hardly betraying the fact that the sessions took place in different studios (in London as well as Edinburgh). Nevertheless this makes a possible bargain alternative to the Bernstein set with Marilyn Horne and James McCracken, although Horne's portrait of Carmen has more guts and fire (DG 427 440-2). At full price, Karajan's set with Baltsa, Carreras and Van Dam remains first choice (DG 410 088-2).

Frühbeck's version of 1970, made before the Oeser edition appeared, was the first to use the original (1875) version of Bizet's score without the cuts that were made after experience in the theatre, and with spoken dialogue instead of the recitatives which Guiraud composed after Bizet's early death. Well recorded on two bargain-priced discs, it makes a fair recommendation, though Grace Bumbry gives a generalized portrait of the heroine, singing with firm tone but too rarely with musical or dramatic individuality. Vickers makes a strong, heroic Don José; and though, surprisingly, Frühbeck's conducting lacks sparkle, it is very well paced. Paskalis makes a gloriously rich-toned Escamillo and Freni an exquisite Micaëla.

At mid-price on only two discs, Maazel's 1979 RCA version (previously on Eurodisc), using the expanded Oeser edition, makes a doubtful bargain. The casting is starry – with such celebrated singers as Arleen Augér and Jane Berbié in the small roles of Frasquita and Mercedes – but almost totally non-French and not always apt. Anna Moffo, lacking mezzo weight, is hardly an ideal Carmen, and she makes up for that by underlining her characterization too heavily. Franco Corelli too is heavy-handed as Don José, not as effective as he was for Karajan in his earlier recording. Helen Donath makes a charming Micaëla, light and sweet, while Piero Cappuccilli as Escamillo produces a stream of strong, firm tone, even if – like others in the cast – his French is not his strong point. As in his later, Erato version (the one used in Franco Rosi's film), Maazel directs a bright and forceful performance, dramatically tense, exaggerated by the fierceness of the recorded sound in tuttis. Otherwise the recording (not digital) is reasonably atmospheric.

Even at Double Decca price and despite brilliant engineering of a 1963 recording, produced by John Culshaw, the Schippers set is not recommendable. It is very variable. Resnik has a big, fruity tone, but her aim is wild. Del Monaco sings coarsely, and vocally the main joy is having Sutherland as Micaëla, even if it sounds as though Lucia had strayed into the wrong opera. Schippers drives very hard indeed. There is no libretto and the synopsis is not related to the cueing of each separate number.

Carmen: highlights.

(B) **(*) DG 439 496-2 [id.] (from above set with Berganza, Domingo; cond. Abbado).

The bargain highlights selection on DG Classikon offers a generous sampler of the Berganza/Domingo/Abbado set with some 69 minutes of well-chosen excerpts, including all the hits. The documentation relates the music to the narrative in a brief but succinct synopsis.

Blake, Howard (born 1938)

(i) *Violin concerto (Leeds); A Month in the Country* (film incidental music): *suite; Sinfonietta for brass.*
*** ASV Dig. CDDCA 905 [id.]. (i) Christiane Edlinger; E. N. Philh., Paul Daniel.

It was the success of his music for *The Snowman* that gave Howard Blake the encouragement and the artistic breathing-space to write more 'tonal music in the post-modern era' for the concert hall, and his beautiful and stimulating *Violin concerto* (commissioned by the Leeds City Council for the city's 1993 centenary celebrations) is the encouraging result. Christiane Edlinger, who gave its première, is the soloist in what proves to be an inspired performance, caught 'on the wing' to join a select group of very special first recordings made over the years. The work, written in the received tradition of Elgar, Vaughan Williams, Walton and, more recently, Christopher Headington, has a ready and appealing melodic impulse, and the playing here is as intense and communicative as it is spontaneous. The slow movement, like the haunting close of the opening movement, brings some exquisitely tender pianissimo playing from the soloist (matched by the orchestra), and she is equally at home in the vigorously extrovert dancing finale which has much in common with the last movement of Dvořák's concerto. The only snag is the very wide dynamic range of the recording; this means that the spectacular bursts of percussion interrupting the reverie, which opens the first movement and which reappears at the climax of the *Adagio*, are almost overwhelming when one has set the volume level to accommodate the music's quieter moments. The microphones are not always entirely flattering to the solo violin; but, in spite of these criticisms, this recorded performance is a heartwarming experience. Blake's suite of string music written for the film, *A Month in the Country*, brings moments of comparable bitter-sweet elegiac feeling. It is most sensitively played, as is the brass *Sinfonietta*, sonorous and jolly by turns. In terms of overall concert-hall realism the recording is impressive and this record is strongly recommended; it would have earned a Rosette, were it not for the (not entirely insoluble) problem of accommodating both the loudest and quietest music on a single volume setting for comfortable domestic listening.

Bliss, Arthur (1891–1975)

(i) *A Colour Symphony; Introduction and allegro;* (ii) *Men of Two Worlds: Baraza;* (i) *Things to come* (film music): *suite* and excerpts: *Ballet for children; Pestilence; Attack; The world in ruins.*
(M) (***) Dutton Lab. CDLXT 2501 [id.]. (i) LSO, composer; (ii) Eileen Joyce, Ch. & Nat. SO, Muir Mathieson.

A Colour Symphony was the work that brought Bliss fame as an *enfant terrible*, but nowadays its flavour seems more Elgarian than modern, with the merest hint that Bliss knew his early Stravinsky. The sounds are attractive and the recording (1956 vintage) captures them well (courtesy of Mike Dutton's admirably faithful CD transfer of Decca's excellent Kingsway Hall recording). But, as with so much of this composer's output, in all honesty the thematic material is never very memorable. The most immediately appealing movement is the Scherzo, representing *Red – the colour of rubies, wine, revelry, furnaces, courage and magic*. But the music itself is less exotic than that description would merit. The *Introduction and allegro*, written for Stokowski (also in the early 1920s), is another well-constructed, completely professional but unmemorable work. When we turn to the film music, matters improve. The film *Men of Two Worlds: Baraza* has a preposterously patronizing story about an African composer/pianist who comes from his Tanganyikan village to Europe to write his Concerto. Its title means a dialogue between a village chief and the head-man. Eileen Joyce was recruited to the the piano part of a score of which only a snippet survives, including a chorus and some touches of syncopation. It is quite vigorous if at times somewhat coarse, even embarrassing in its pseudo-African ideas; it is nevertheless rather endearing. Again, the 1946 recording in Dutton's vivid transfer sounds astonishingly good, like a broadcast transcription rather than an old record, only with more ambience. But Bliss's masterpiece was his incidental music for Korda's H. G. Wells film, *Things to come*. Nowhere near all of it was used in the movie, and what was featured had to be heavily edited (by Lionel Salter, under the eagle eye of Muir Mathieson); but Bliss rescued his material and recorded an early set of four excerpts for Decca on 78-r.p.m. discs in 1936. This included a section called *The world in ruins*, missing from the final orchestral suite, which the composer published and recorded later in stereo in 1957. In terms of memorability of ideas, Bliss never surpassed this music. Even if the opening *Ballet* faintly recalls Debussy's *Petite suite*, *Reconstruction* brings a genuine Elgarian nobilmente theme, and the *March* is unforgettable in its gutsy, flamboyantly tuneful vitality.

Things to come: suite; Welcome the Queen.
(BB) ** Belart 450 143-2 [id.]. LSO, composer – ELGAR: *Pomp and circumstance marches 1–5.* **

The composer's own excellent (1957) recording of his *Things to come suite* is additionally available on a super-bargain Belart reissue, offering its original couplings of *Welcome the Queen* and Elgar's five *Pomp and circumstance marches.* The former was an occasional piece, written by Bliss in his role as Master of the Queen's Musick, to celebrate the return of the Queen from her Commonwealth tour in 1954. In the Elgar tradition of pageantry, the piece is of no particular distinction except for a very gracious middle tune. The performance could hardly be more authentic but the (originally very good) recording is not flattered by the current transfer, which is excessively bright and thin on top.

Bloch, Ernest (1880–1959)

Schelomo (Hebraic rhapsody) (for cello and orchestra).
(M) *** Virgin/EMI Dig. CUV5 61125-2 [id.]. Steven Isserlis, LSO, Hickox – ELGAR: *Cello concerto.* **(*)
*** Sony Dig. SK 57961 [id.]. Yo-Yo Ma, Baltimore SO, David Zinman – ALBERT: *Cello concerto;*
   BARTOK: *Viola concerto.* ***

The dark intensity of Isserlis's solo playing and the sharp, dramatic focus of Hickox in the big climactic orchestral tuttis are here magnetic, preventing Bloch's youthful outpouring on Solomon and the Song of Songs from sounding self-indulgent. Warm, refined recording.

Collectors accustomed to the impassioned playing of Emanuel Feuermann on the pioneering (1940) Philadelphia Orchestra version with Stokowski or such successors as Nelsova–Ansermet and Rostropovich–Bernstein will find this a more introspective account, though it benefits from excellent playing from the Baltimore orchestra and first-class Sony engineering. Yo-Yo Ma is more cultured and refined than many of his current rivals, but there are moments when Solomon drops his voice, as it were, and dispenses his wisdom in a whisper rather than in full-throated fervour. It comes with an interesting first recording of a rewarding *Cello concerto* by the New York composer, Stephen Albert.

Boccherini, Luigi (1743–1805)

Cello concertos Nos. 4 in C, G.477; 6 in D, G.479; 7 in G, G.480; 8 in C, G. 481.
(M) *** Teldec/Warner Dig. 9031 77624-2 [id.]. Anner Bylsma, Concerto Amsterdam, Schröder.

These concertos were originally published as Nos. 1–4 but are numbered as above in the Gérard catalogue. They are scored for strings with the addition of simple horn parts in Nos. 4 and 8 and are agreeable works which sit easily between the galant and classical styles. There are few moments of routine in the writing, and it is always elegant and pleasing. *No. 6 in D major* is a particularly fine work, while the finale of No. 8 is very jolly. Anner Bylsma is a fine player and seems eminently suited to this repertoire, while Schröder's accompaniments are most stylish and full of vitality. Charm, too, is an important element and it is not missing here, while the sombre *Adagio* of No. 7 has undoubted eloquence and is ideally paced to contrast with the sprightly and tuneful finale. The 1965 recording is first class and, like so many of Teldec's *Das Alte Werk* series, the immaculate CD transfer makes the very most of the sound.

(i) *Cello concertos Nos. 6 in D, G.479; 7 in G, G.480;* (ii) *9 in B flat, G.482; 10 in D, G.483.*
(M) *** Erato/Warner 4509 97408-2 (2) [id.]. Frédéric Lodéon, (i) Lausanne CO, Jordan; (ii)
   Bournemouth Sinf., Guschlbauer.

This set combines two sets of performances, recorded four years apart. Lodéon was in his thirties at the time and plays splendidly throughout. His playing has genuine style and real eloquence and in the *G major concerto*, G.480, originally unearthed by Maurice Gendron, he is wonderfully fresh and fervent; in his hands the better-known *D major Concerto*, G.479 (also recorded by Bylsma and Rostropovich), has genuine tenderness and depth. He is well accompanied by both groups, but the two Lausanne performances (1981) have slightly superior sound and the balance of the soloist is less obviously spotlighted. The snag to this pair of records is the playing time of only 85 minutes, whereas the competing Bylsma collection manages to get four concertos (including G.479 and 480) on a single CD.

String quartets, Op. 32/1–6.
(M) *** Teldec/Warner 4509 95988-2 (2) [id.]. Esterházy Qt.

There are more than 130 Boccherini quintets and his fecundity in the quartet medium is scarcely less.

This set dates from 1780, about the same period as Haydn's Op. 33. They may ultimately lack the depth and vision of Haydn and Mozart, but to listen to this pioneering recording is to be amazed that music of this quality has been so long neglected. Its originality and the quality of the inspiration, its freshness and grace can scarcely be exaggerated, and these performances on original-period instruments are both committed and authoritative, with no want of charm to boot. The Esterházy Quartet are led by Jaap Schröder and theirs is thoroughly rewarding music-making. The Quartet was beautifully recorded in Haarlem, Holland, in 1976 and the CD transfer and excellent documentation of this Das Alte Werke reissue are both commendable. The only snag is the short overall playing time of the pair of CDs – 89 minutes, but every one of them is enjoyable.

Boeck, August de (1865–1937)

Symphony in G.
(BB) *** Discover Dig. DICD 920126 [id.]. Brussels BRT PO, Karl Anton Rickenbacher – GILSON: *De Zee*. ***

The *Symphony in G* of August de Boeck, like Paul Gilson's suite, *De Zee*, with which it is coupled, is a ripely exotic work, full of Russian echoes. You might describe it as the Borodin symphony that Borodin didn't write, sharply rhythmic in the fast movements and sensuous in the slow movement, brilliantly orchestrated and full of tunes that are only marginally less memorable than those of the Russian master. Gilson's work is a series of four seascapes, half-way between Wagner's *Flying Dutchman* and Debussy's *La Mer*, with Rimsky-Korsakov's *Scheherazade* mixed in. Well played and recorded and, at Discover International's super-bargain price, an ideal disc for experimenting with.

Bononcini, Antonio (1677–1726)

Stabat Mater.
(B) *** Decca Double 443 868-2 (2) [id.]. Palmer, Langridge, Esswood, Keyte, St John's College,
   Cambridge, Ch., Philomusica, Guest – PERGOLESI: *Magnificat in C; Stabat Mater* **(*);
   D. SCARLATTI: *Stabat Mater;* A. SCARLATTI: *Domine, refugium factus es nobis; O magnum
   mysterium;* CALDARA: *Crucifixus;* LOTTI: *Crucifixus*. ***

This fascinating Double Decca collection centres on three different settings of the *Stabat Mater dolorosa*, a medieval poem describing the anguish of Mary during her son's crucifixion, an experience with which women, especially, have readily identified down through the ages. Although its origins date from the end of the thirteenth century, it was not until 1727 that it became part of the Roman liturgy.

Antonio Bononcini is not to be confused with Handel's rival, Giovanni (1670–1747), his older brother. At the age of twenty-one he wrote an opera, *Il trionfo di Camilla, regina dei Volsci*, that became a great success not only in Italy but also in London. His *Stabat Mater* appears to have been composed in Vienna before he returned to Modena in 1716. It is a work of genuine melodic distinction and affecting tenderness; there are some striking harmonies, even moments of drama, and in general a nobility and simple expressiveness that leave a strong impression. The St John's performance is wholly admirable and is very well recorded. The work is ambitious in scale (36 minutes) and stands out among the three settings included in this fine survey. It is a pity that a translation of the Latin words was not included.

Borodin, Alexander (1833–87)

'The World of Borodin': (i) *In the Steppes of Central Asia; Prince Igor:* (ii) *Overture;* (ii–iii) *Polovtsian dances;* (iv) *Symphony No. 2 in B min.;* (v) *String quartet No. 2: Nocturne;* (vi) *Scherzo in A flat;* (vii, viii) *Far from the shores of your native land;* (vii, ix) *Prince Igor: Galitzky's aria.*
(M) *** Decca Analogue/Dig. 444 389-2; *444 389-4.* (i) SRO, Ansermet; (ii) LSO, Solti; (iii) with
   London Symphony Ch.; (iv) LSO, Martinon; (v) Borodin Qt.; (vi) Ashkenazy; (vii) Nicolai
   Ghiaurov; (viii) Zlatina Ghiaurov; (ix) London Symphony Ch. and LSO, Downes.

An extraordinarily successful disc that will provide for many collectors an inexpensive summation of the art of Borodin. The compilation, which was originally offered on LP, has been updated and extended, with the changes of performers all to advantage. There can be few if any other collections of this kind that sum up a composer's achievement so succinctly or that make such a rewarding and enjoyable 76-minute concert. Solti's *Prince Igor overture* is unexpectedly romantic, and very exciting too; there is no finer account in the current catalogue, and the same can be said for the *Polovtsian dances*, with splendid choral singing – even if the chorus takes a little longer to warm up than in the famous Beecham version. Both recordings date from 1966 and have vintage Decca sound. The *Nocturne* follows the *Overture* so effectively that one might have thought it the composer's own plan. Then comes *Galitzky's aria* (complete with chorus), where the sound is over-bright, but no matter, and the *Scherzo in A flat* follows – with Ashkenazy in fine form – before the choral *Polovtsian dances*. Ansermet's *In the Steppes of Central Asia* is warmer and more atmospheric than we had remembered it and, if the Suisse Romande violins fail to do its voluptuous main theme full justice, Ansermet's interpretation is spacious and vivid. After Nicolai Ghiaurov has reminded us of the melancholy side of the Russian spirit, we come finally to Martinon's unsurpassed 1960 LSO performance of the *B minor Symphony*, notable for its fast tempo for the famous opening theme. The strong rhythmic thrust suits the music admirably, the Scherzo has vibrant colouring and the slow movement, with a beautifully played horn solo, is most satisfying. The sound has remarkable presence and sparkle, and only in the massed violin tone (which is good) is there a suggestion that the recording is not modern.

Prince Igor: Overture and Polovtsian dances.
(M) *** Virgin/EMI Dig. CUV5 61135-2 [id.]. Royal Liverpool PO. Ch. & O, Mackerras –
MUSSORGSKY: *Night* etc. **

Prince Igor: Polovtsian dances.
(M) ** Carlton Dig. IMGCD 1610 [id.]. RPO, Bátiz – STRAVINSKY: *Petrushka* etc.

A splendid account of the *Prince Igor overture*, with the brilliant, jaggedly thrusting imitation in the allegro given plenty of bite and the lyrical secondary melody glowingly phrased by principal horn and strings alike. The *Polovtsian dances* proceed with comparable brilliance and fervour, with the Royal Liverpool Philharmonic Choir producing expansive lyrical tone and joining in the frenzy of the closing section with infectious zest. Excellent recording too, vivid and full; if only the Mussorgsky coupling had produced comparable electricity, this record would have been a world-beater.

Bátiz's performance has more energy than finesse, although it does not lack languor. It is vividly recorded, but not distinctive.

Piano quintet in C min.
** Auvidis Valois Dig. V 4702 [id.]. Monte Carlo Pro Arte Quintet – SHOSTAKOVICH: *Piano quintet.*
**

Borodin's *Piano quintet in C minor* is an early and uncharacteristic piece, without the technical finesse that distinguished his mature work. Ideally it needs a rather more mercurial touch than this team bring to it. The recording is perhaps a bit two-dimensional with little back-to-front depth, but there is currently no alternative. It is coupled to a very good account of the Shostakovich *Piano quintet.*

String quartets Nos. 1 in A; 2 in D.
(BB) ** Naxos Dig. 8.550850 [id.]. Haydn Qt of Budapest.

Borodin's two *Quartets* are very romantic and very Russian. They have brilliantly infectious Scherzi, vivaciously presented here, and plenty of ripe tunes; the beautiful *Notturno* second movement of the *Second Quartet* (which could well be subtitled 'Kismet') is justly famous in its own right. The Haydn Quartet of Budapest play both works with a passionate display of Slavonic temperament. Their playing does not lack light and shade but the Unitarian Church acoustic makes their agreeably sumptuous textures seem forwardly orchestral, and the close microphones restrict the dynamic range. Perhaps that will not be a drawback for some listeners, and such opulence of tone suits the music, even if it robs the performances of subtlety. First choice for these works remains with the Borodin Quartet (EMI CDC7 47795-2 – see our main volume).

String quartet No. 2 in D.
(***) Testament mono SBT 1061 [id.]. Hollywood Qt – GLAZUNOV: *5 Novelettes;* TCHAIKOVSKY:
String quartet No. 1. (***)
(M) *(*) DG Dig. 445 551-2 [id.]. Emerson Qt – DVORAK: *Quartet No. 12* **; TCHAIKOVSKY:
Quartet No. 1. *(*)

At the time when the Hollywood Quartet's version of the Borodin *Second Quartet* first appeared in 1953, there were complaints that the sound was steely and hard. At the same time, the work itself was in the doldrums – 'the Hollywood Quartet do all that is possible to revive the faded colours of this melodious but weak composition,' was one verdict. Although, for once, it is possible to speak of later recordings (most notably by the eponymous Borodin Quartet) as matching – and even surpassing –

the Hollywood group, this is still a performance that has a freshness and ardour which are very persuasive. The sound has been improved, and the addition of the Glazunov, which is new to the catalogue, enhances the disc's value. The playing-time runs to one second short of 80 minutes, and the sleeve warns that some CD players may have difficulty in tracking it. We have not found this to be the case, but some caution may be necessary on the part of readers with older players.

The Emerson Quartet are unrivalled in terms of technical expertise. It seems curmudgeonly not to respond to their superlative playing, but it is all very chromium-plated. Good, if very present, DG recording.

Petite suite.
** Chan. Dig. CHAN 9309 [id.]. Luba Edlina – TCHAIKOVSKY: *The seasons.* **

Borodin's charming *Petite suite*, once so often played, has rather fallen from view. The current catalogues list only two alternative versions of the piano version (Tatiana Nikolaieva and Dirk Joeres), so Luba Edlina's well-recorded version is welcome. Her playing is forthright and intelligent, albeit not always as charming as she can be. Her substantial coupling, Tchaikovsky's suite *The Seasons*, is also well pláyed but is no challenge to Pletnev's outstanding performance on Virgin.

Prince Igor (complete).
*** Ph. Dig. 442 537-2 (3) [id.]. Kit, Gorchakova, Ognovienko, Minjelkiev, Borodina, Grigorian,
    Kirov Ch. & O, St Petersburg, Gergiev.

Gergiev has been an inspired musical director of the Kirov company in St Petersburg, and this electrifying account of Borodin's epic opera reflects not only his own magnetic qualities as a conductor but also the way he has welded his principal singers as well as the chorus and orchestra into a powerful team. Textually the oddity of this version is that Acts I and II are given in reverse order from the usual, with the substantial Prologue here followed by the first Polovtsian scene and its spectacular dances. Only then do you get the scene at Prince Galitsky's court, normally Act I, leading up to Yaroslavna's great lament, here superbly sung by Galina Gorchakova. The reordering works well, with contrasting elements better separated, and Gergiev has authority on his side, when he has discovered an outline made by Borodin in 1883, proposing such an alternation of Russian and Polovtsian Acts. Acting on that seems reasonable enough, when Borodin failed to complete this magnificent score and much of it, not just the scoring, was left to be filled out by the composer's friends and colleagues, Glazunov and Rimsky-Korsakov. Otherwise Gergiev generally follows that well-established edition, but has included material they omitted from Borodin's copious sketches, notably an extended monologue of lament for Igor himself as a prisoner of Khan Konchak in Act III, '*Why did I not fall on the field of battle*'. It may not be as fine as the aria Igor sings in the first Polovtsian scene, using the great melody introduced in the overture, but that and other supplementary passages are very welcome. That alone puts this ahead of the fine rival Sony recording from Tchakarov with Bulgarian forces, and Gergiev is even more sharply dramatic, generally adopting faster speeds. The Philips recording too is weightier than the Sony, with the chorus in particular sounding satisfyingly large as well as incisive. On the solo casting, honours are much more even. The two principal women here, not just Gorchakova but Olga Borodina too as Konchak's daughter, Konchakovna, are both magnificent, even finer than their Bulgarian rivals, but neither principal bass, Vladimir Ognovienko as Galitsky and Bulat Minjelkiev as Konchak, can match the vocal richness or character of the Bulgarians, Ghiuselev and Ghiaurov, both older-sounding but still compelling. Gegam Grigorian in the tenor role of Igor's son gives a lusty performance, while Mikhail Kit as Igor himself, though often gritty and even fluttery of tone, sings thoughtfully and intelligently, making him a fair match for his Bulgarian rival. Yet in the end the overall control of this massive score is what matters, and there Gergiev, with a finer and more polished orchestra, clearly takes the palm.

Bortkiewicz, Serge (1877–1952)

Piano concerto No. 1 in B flat min., Op. 16.
*** Hyp. Dig. CDA 66624 [id.]. Coombs, BBC Scottish SO, Maksymiuk – ARENSKY: *Piano
    concerto.* ***

Serge Bortkiewicz studied in St Petersburg and Leipzig and spent the last three decades of his life teaching in Berlin, Constantinople (as Istanbul was then known) and Vienna, where he settled in 1922. He was not an accomplished enough pianist to make an international career, though he wrote effectively for the instrument. His concerto is conservative in idiom, a conventional, romantic, virtuoso offering without much individual flavour. Older collectors will recall Marjorie Mitchell's LP of Bortkiewicz's *First Piano concerto* (coupled with Busoni's *Indian Fantasy* on Brunswick) but this present version is uncut. Stephen Coombs takes its considerable difficulties in his stride and plays the work as if it is great music, and at times he almost persuades one that it is; and he receives excellent support from the BBC Scottish Orchestra under Jerzy Maksymiuk, and good recording quality.

Bottesini, Giovanni (1821–89)

(i) *Double-bass concertino in C min.;* (i; ii) *Duo concertante on themes from Bellini's 'I Puritani' for cello, double-bass and orchestra;* (i) *Elégie in D;* (i; iii) *Passioni amorose* (for 2 double-basses); *Ali Baba overture; Il Diavolo delle notte; Ero e Leandro: Prelude.*
*** ASV Dig. CDDCA 907 [id.]. (i) Thomas Martin; (ii) Moray Welsh; (iii) Francesco Petracchi; LSO, Petracchi, or (iii) Matthew Gibson.

Bottesini must have been a double-bass player *extraordinaire*! A contemporary said of his playing: 'Under his bow the double-bass sighed, cooed, sang, quivered,' and it does all those things here on the flamboyant bow of Thomas Martin, himself a musician of the strongest personality. He 'coos' mellifluously in the *Elégie*, a conventional piece but agreeably melodic; then he sings the yearning cantilena which forms the slow movement of the *Concertino* with a grace unexpected from his comparatively unwieldy instrument. He certainly quivers with bravura in its genial finale, while the orchestral violins respond with their own frolicking above. In this work the composer resourcefully commands the soloist to tune his instrument a minor third above the orchestra, which increases the instrument's projection. For the *Passioni amorose* the conductor, Francesco Petracchi (professor of the double-bass at the Geneva Conservatoire), exchanges his baton for another bow to join his colleague, first establishing a close, decisive partnership; then they swoon together in the shared theme of the *Andante* and let their hair down in the finale. Further contrast is provided when Moray Welsh successfully interweaves with his larger instrumental cousin in the *Duo concertante* on melodies of Bellini. To prevent the ear from being over-lubricated with sounds from the orchestral basement, the programme is interspersed with colourful orchestral miniatures. The *Prelude to Ero e Leandro* has a distinctly Neapolitan flavour (and a nice oboe solo); the *Sinfonia, Il Diavolo della notte*, turns naturally from warm lyricism to galloping liveliness, and the brief *Ali Baba overture* brings a spirited whiff of Rossini. The recording engineers have done marvels to balance everything so convincingly; thus the persuasive Thomas Martin can play with delicacy and easy virtuosity within his instrument's little-heard upper tessitura and be sure he is clearly audible. His intonation is remarkably true, and this programme is surprisingly rewarding and entertaining, far more than a specialist collection for the musically curious.

Bouzignac, Guillaume (c. 1590–c. 1640)

Te Deum. Motets: *Alleluia, venite amici; Ave Maria; Clamant clavi; Dum silentium; Ecce Aurora; Ecce festivitas; Ecce homo; Flos in flores; Ha! Plange; In pace, in idipsum; Jubilate Deo; Salve Jesu Piisime; Tota pulchra est; Unus ex vobis; Vulnerasti cor meum.*
⊛ *** HM Dig. HMC 901471 [id.]. Les Pages de la Chapelle, Les Arts Florissants, William Christie.

You might call Bouzignac the Charles Ives of the sixteenth century. His music was almost totally forgotten for 250 years until rediscovered by a scholar at the beginning of this century. On record he has continued to be neglected, and this pioneering disc brings a revelation. The great refreshing quality of Bouzignac for the modern ear is that consistently he responds vividly and unpredictably to the texts of each of these motets. Often his response is so wildly individual that you would be unlikely to deduce which century the music came from, let alone which country. Vigour is the essence, as in the exuberantly light-hearted setting of *Jubilate Deo*, yet such a motet as *In pace, in idipsum* in its sustained lines has a rare meditative beauty, and the dialogue of *Unus ex vobis* even brings echoes of Russian Orthodox music. The response of William Christie, always a vivid interpreter of early music, brings out the colour in all its variety, for once with boy trebles (Les Pages de la Chapelle) added to the finely disciplined forces, vocal and instrumental, of Les Arts Florissants. This will be a thrilling discovery for many, helped by vividly immediate sound.

Boyce, William (1710–79)

Symphonies Nos. 1–8, Op. 2.
(M) *** Decca 444 523-2 [id.]. ASMF, Marriner.

Marriner treats these superb examples of English baroque to exhilarating performances, with the rhythmic subtleties in both fast music and slow guaranteed to enchant. The recording was made in 1978 at St John's, Smith Square, and it has plenty of ambience, while the digital remastering ensures brighter lighting to the upper strings in a beneficial way. The listener now experiences more of the bite one would expect from an authentic version, yet the expressive style of modern instruments and the absence of bulges in the phrasing bring an approach that should satisfy most ears. Those requiring a period performance should turn to Hogwood (Oiseau-Lyre 436 761-2).

Bræin, Edvard Fliflet (1924–76)

Anne Pedersdotter (opera; complete).
*** Simax Dig. PSC3121 (2) [id.]. Ekeberg, Handssen, Carlsen, Sandve, Thorsen, Norwegian Nat.
  Op. Ch. & O, Per Ake Andersson.

Edvard Fliflet Bræin was a highly talented Norwegian composer who died in his early fifties. His musical speech is predominantly diatonic and, apart from the obvious Nordic debts, owes much to Shostakovich. Hence, like Bo Linde and Eduard Tubin in Sweden, he made little headway during the 1960s when interest largely came to focus on the post-serialist avant-garde. His high-spirited *Concert overture*, Op. 2, has gained some currency outside Norway, and his fine craftsmanship and innate musicality shine through everything he did. His opera, *Anne Pedersdotter* (1971), is based on the most famous of witchcraft trials in Norway, the burning of Anne Pedersdotter in Bergen in 1590. Fliflet Bræin called it 'a symphonic opera' and, like Schoeck's *Venus*, its invention unfolds in an effortlessly organic fashion; in other words, his is the art that conceals art. He also evokes a strong atmosphere and possesses a lyrical impulse rare in our day and age. It is effective music-theatre, and many of its ideas, as is so often the case with this composer, are memorable. The characters may not be drawn with the greatest musico-dramatic subtlety but the opera has a lot going for it. It also gets an eminently serviceable performance, with good singing from Kjersti Ekeberg as the eponymous heroine, Svein Carlsen as her husband, Absolon Pedersøn-Beyer, and Kjell Magnus Sandve as his son by his first marriage. The Norwegian Opera forces under the baton of Per Ake Andersson are excellent, and the recording, produced by Michael Woodcock, is very good indeed. Whether Fliflet Bræin is really a powerful enough musical personality for *Anne Pedersdotter* to reach the international stage is another matter, but it is stronger musically than, say, Sallinen's pretentious *The King goes forth to France*, and it has warmth, is full of good and memorable ideas and will reward those who invest in it. Strongly recommended.

Brahms, Johannes (1833–97)

Piano concertos Nos. (i) 1 in D min., Op. 15; (ii) 2 in B flat, Op. 83. Variations and fugue on a theme of Handel, Op. 24; Variations on a theme of Paganini, Op. 35.
(B) **(*) Decca Double 440 612-2 (2) [id.]. Julius Katchen; (i–ii) LSO; (i) Pierre Monteux; (ii) János Ferencsik.

Julius Katchen was one of Decca's star pianists in the early 1960s and it is good to have a reminder of his considerable achievement, recording the music of Brahms. In the *First Concerto* he was not particularly well served by the balance provided by the Decca engineers, but he plays superbly, particularly in the first movement, and is sonorously matched by some fine playing by the LSO under Monteux. Again in No. 2 he gives an impassioned and exciting account of the solo piano part, combining great drive with the kind of ruminating delicacy Brahms so often calls for in his piano writing. The first movement and finale are particularly successful, and both soloist and orchestra under János Ferencsik are in perfect accord. In the slow movement there is occasionally a tendency to linger in purely decorative passages, but the music's flow is not seriously impeded. The balance places the piano well within the orchestral framework and the sound is not too dated. The sets of solo variations, brilliant though they are, are not among the most compelling of Katchen's solo Brahms recordings for Decca. Oddly enough, for all their sheer pyrotechnical display, they sound comparatively unspontaneous.

Piano concerto No. 1 in D min., Op. 15.

(M) *** Decca 425 082-2 [id.]. Clifford Curzon, LSO, Szell – FRANCK: *Symphonic variations;* LITOLFF: *Scherzo.* ***

*(*) Nimbus Dig. NI 5349 [id.]. Mark Anderson, Hungarian State SO, Adám Fischer – DOHNANYI: *Variations on a Nursery Song.* *(*)

(i) *Piano concerto No. 1 in D min., Op. 15; 4 Ballades, Op. 10.*

(M) *** DG 439 979-2 [id.]. Gilels; (i) BPO, Jochum.

Gilels's reading of the *D minor Concerto* has a magisterial strength blended with a warmth, humanity and depth that are altogether inspiring. Jochum is a superb accompanist and the remastered 1972 recording has a better focus on CD. The *Ballades* have never been played so marvellously on record, and the recording is very believable.

Clifford Curzon's 1962 recording, produced by John Culshaw in Kingsway Hall, returns to the catalogue, carefully remastered by the Decca engineers. The fierceness of attack in the upper strings, especially in the powerful opening tutti, sounds naturally focused on CD, adding a leonine power to Szell's orchestral contribution, and the piano tone is admirably natural. Curzon has the full measure of Brahms's keyboard style and penetrates both the reflective inner world of the slow movement and the abundantly vital and massive opening movement. The piano balance is most satisfying. For this generous reissue in Decca's Classic Sound series, the Franck *Symphonic variations* and Litolff *Scherzo* have been added.

Mark Anderson is an American pianist who was a finalist at the 1993 Leeds Piano Competition (and was the TV Audience Choice – not, mind you, the jury's, who sat through everything, not just the final round). He is an accomplished pianist and this account of the *D minor Concerto* is well played, though he pulls back rather unconvincingly at the second subject group. But there is not enough personality here. Decent but not first-class recording, and in no way a match for the best.

(i) *Piano concerto No. 2 in B flat, Op. 83; 4 Ballades, Op. 10.*

(M) *** DG 439 466-2 [id.]. Gilels; (i) BPO, Jochum.

(i) *Piano concerto No. 2;* (ii) *5 Lieder, Op. 105.*

*** EMI Dig. CDC5 55218-2 [id.]. (i–ii) Stephen Kovacevich; (ii) Ann Murray; (i) LPO, Wolfgang Sawallisch.

The partnership of Gilels and Jochum produces music-making of rare magic and the digital remastering has improved definition: the sound is full in an appropriately Brahmsian way. Readers will note that this reissue is now recoupled with the *4 Ballades,* Op. 10 (instead of the *Fantasias,* Op. 116), which seems perverse when the Gilels version of the *First Concerto* has the same coupling.

After his noble and dedicated account of the *First Piano concerto* with Wolfgang Sawallisch and the LPO, Stephen Kovacevich's version of its successor brings admiration tinged with disappointment. Not that his playing is anything other than magisterial – indeed, it is difficult to find a flaw in the performance in any respect. Although it is among the finest to have appeared in the 1990s, it does not match this partnership's *First.* This does not take wing or catch fire in quite the same way; and memories of Gilels and Jochum, still our first recommendation for this concerto, and the phenomenal Solomon (Testament), are not displaced. Some have been disappointed with the sound, which will naturally give diverse results in different acoustic environments. However, on most equipment the recording reproduces well, though it is perhaps not quite as refined or as transparent as the *D minor.*

Violin concerto in D, Op. 77.

(M) *** DG Dig. 445 515-2 [id.]. Anne-Sophie Mutter, BPO, Karajan – MENDELSSOHN: *Violin concerto.* ***

(M) **(*) Ph. Dig. 438 998-2 [id.]. Viktoria Mullova, BPO, Abbado.

In many ways the playing of Anne-Sophie Mutter combines the unforced lyrical feeling of Krebbers with the flair and individuality of Perlman. There is a lightness of touch, a gentleness in the slow movement that is highly appealing, while in the finale the incisiveness of the solo playing is well displayed by the clear (yet not clinical) digital recording. Needless to say, Karajan's accompaniment is strong in personality and the Berlin Philharmonic play beautifully; the performance represents a genuine musical partnership between youthful inspiration and eager experience. The recording balance places the soloist rather close, but on this newly remastered CD the orchestral sound, while retaining its vivid presence, is smoother on top. The coupling is hardly less attractive. This is recommendable alongside Tasmin Little on EMI Eminence CD-EMX 2203, coupled with the Sibelius concerto (see our main volume).

Mullova's is a commanding performance, recorded at a concert the Berlin Philharmonic gave in

Suntory Hall, Tokyo, in 1992. She plays with breathtaking assurance, pure and true throughout, made the more compelling by the spontaneous expressiveness that goes with live performance. Her admirers need not hesitate for, apart from over-prominent timpani, the recording is first rate, and Abbado and the Berlin Philharmonic here match their Brahmsian achievement in the DG symphony cycle. With the solo instrument not spotlit, the wide dynamic range of Mullova's playing is the more telling, with the many reflective passages in the first movement, as well as the central *Adagio*, given a rapt intensity at a true pianissimo. The only snag is the disc's short measure.

(i) *Violin concerto in D;* (ii) *Hungarian dances Nos. 1 & 3* (orch. Brahms); *5–6* (orch. Schmedling); (iii; iv) *Symphony No. 4 in E min., Op. 98;* (v; iv) *Variations on a theme of Haydn (St Anthony chorale), Op. 56a.*
(BB) ***** EMI Seraphim CES5 68526-2 (2) [CDEB 68526]. (i) Sir Yehudi Menuhin, BPO, Kempe; (ii) RPO, Kubelik; (iii) New Philh. O; (iv) Giulini; (v) Philh. O.

Reissued in EMI's Seraphim series (two CDs for the cost of one mid-priced disc), Menuhin's recording from the end of the 1950s can be given the strongest recommendation. He was in superb form, producing tone of great beauty, while the reading is memorable for its warmth and nobility. He was splendidly accompanied by Kempe, and the Berlin Philharmonic was inspired to outstanding playing – the oboe solo in the slow movement is particularly fine. The sound remains satisfyingly well balanced, and now compares very favourably indeed with any of the top recommendations for this work. Giulini's account of the *Fourth Symphony* was part of a cycle begun in the early 1960s, which was finally published as a set in the early 1980s – so its recording date is uncertain; it was one of the last to be recorded, for by then the Philharmonia had become the New Philharmonia. The performance shows Giulini as a typically thoughtful and direct Brahmsian, using measured tempi: the very opening of the work has a coaxing warmth which is persuasive. The slow movement is beautifully played too, and the finale is strong. This was undoubtedly one of the best of the cycle, and the only snag is the relative absence of bloom on the violins, although the recording itself is full and expansive. The *St Anthony variations* date from 1962 and show Giulini and the Philharmonia on their very finest form. The challenge of variation form obviously suited him, and it certainly demonstrates the superb quality of the Philharmonia Orchestra of the early 1960s. The freshness of the performance is matched by Giulini's control of the overall structure: the finale has a memorable culminating inevitability. The recording still sounds well, and this pair of discs is more than worth its modest cost.

Hungarian dances Nos. 1 in G min.; 3 in F; 10 in E; & 17 in F sharp min.
(M) (*****) Bruno Walter Edition: Sony mono SMK 64467 [id.]. NYPO, Bruno Walter – SMETANA: *Vltava* (**); J. STRAUSS: *Overtures; Waltzes.* (***)

Walter's performances have a warmly affectionate Viennese lilt, and the 1951 mono recording is surprisingly full and pleasing.

Serenade No. 1 in D, Op. 11.
*** Sony Dig. SK 57973 [id.]. La Scala O, Muti – ELGAR: *In the South.* ***

The neglect of the Brahms *Serenades* in the concert hall is difficult to understand, for they are glorious, lyrical works, every bit as masterly as the symphonies and more genial and easy-going. Generally speaking, they have been better served on records: Sir Adrian Boult recorded both on LP, and so has Bernard Haitink, who accommodates them on one mid-price CD (Philips 432 510-2), good value at mid-price; and there is a fine bargain version on Carlton by the West German Sinfonia under Dirk Joeres (PCD 1024). Michael Tilson Thomas has also recorded both for Sony (SK 45932 and SK 47195), and he couples them separately with other Brahms orchestral pieces (see our main volume). Riccardo Muti, so often tempted into overdrive, offers here an unhurried yet alert, strong and expressive performance, full of insights and character, which can be recommended to anyone who fancies the unexpected linking of early Brahms with mature Elgar. Muti's reading of the Brahms brings out the fun and beefy good humour over the six movements, but the recording is very good and is well focused, if with a weighty bass and less body given to the high violins. Even so, the rustic quality of many of Brahms's ideas is well caught, with some outstanding wind solo playing, and with Muti giving the central *Adagio*, much the longest movement, a tender expressiveness. A most winning account of this endearing and high-spirited music.

Symphonies Nos. 1–4.
(B) **(*) RCA Dig. 74321 20283-2 (2). N. German RSO, Günter Wand.

Symphonies Nos 1–4, Hungarian dances Nos. 1, 3 & 10; Variations on a theme of Haydn (St Anthony chorale).
(**(*)) EMI CHS5 65513-2 (3). BPO or VPO, Furtwängler – BEETHOVEN: *Overtures.* (***)

Symphonies Nos. 1 in C min., Op. 68; 2 in D, Op. 73; 3 in F, Op. 90; 4 in E min., Op. 98; Tragic
overture, Op. 81; Variations on a theme by Haydn, Op. 56.
(***) Testament mono/stereo SBT 3054 (3) [id.]. BPO, Rudolf Kempe.

As with his companion box of Beethoven symphonies, Günter Wand's Brahms set, now reissued on a
pair of CDs, is highly recommendable for providing spontaneously compelling readings of all four
works, very well played. The snag is that the early digital recording (1982/3) brings a degree of
fierceness on violin tone in all but No. 2 and verges on shrillness in No. 3. Wand's is a consistently
direct view of Brahms, yet the reading of each symphony has its own individuality. In the opening
movement of the *First*, like Toscanini he brings great intensity to the slow introduction by choosing
an unusually fast speed, then leading naturally by modular pacing into the main allegro. The extra
unity is clear. There is a comparable dramatic intensity in the finale, although his choice of a tempo
for the main marching melody, far slower than the rest, brings uncomfortable changes of gear. Yet
the performance is made convincing by its spontaneity. Even though he does not observe the
exposition repeat, Wand's reading of the *Second* is the pick of his Brahms series, a characteristically
glowing but steady reading, recorded with a fullness and bloom that are missing in the companion
issues. His unsensational approach exactly matches this sunniest of symphonies. Its lyricism is made
to flow freely, and the slow movement is robust, its melancholy underplayed. The third movement is
light and fresh, the finale warm and exhilarating. In the *Third Symphony* Wand does observe the
exposition repeat and his wise way with Brahms, strong and easy and steadily paced, works
beautifully here, bringing out the autumnal moods, ending with a sober view of the finale. The bright
sound underlines the reedy twang of the Hamburg woodwind – rather rough in the slow movement –
while the horn could be more secure in his solo in the third movement. By contrast, the reading of
No. 4 initially seems understated. At a fastish speed, the first movement is melancholy rather than
tragic, while the slow movement, similarly steady and flowing, makes no great expansion for the big
melody of the counter-subject. The third movement in jollity has plenty of light and shade, and the
finale is rather brisk and tough, with the great flute passage in the passacaglia tender but not drawn
out. It is quite a strong reading and, though the recording is less than ideally clear, it provides a
generally satisfying culmination to an inexpensive modern set of the four symphonies and is well
worth considering. As we go to press, Wand's recordings have been made available separately at mid-
price: *Symphonies Nos. 1* and *3* (74321 20284-2); *Symphonies Nos. 2* and *4* (74321 20285-2).

Kempe's magnetism in Brahms lies very much in his compelling ability to draw out the lyrical
warmth of the writing. He has one's ear following the melodies so naturally that one hardly registers
the strength of the structure underlying them. Like Furtwängler, Kempe is freely expressive, but his
freedom is very different, with far less extreme tempo changes. Speeds and timings are often very
similar, but results are strikingly different, with Kempe's Brahms above all glowing with warmth and
beauty. This conductor also brought great fire to the quicker movements and a tremendous sense of
breadth. First and foremost, Kempe has his finger on the natural flow and pulse of these symphonies
in a way which calls to mind only the most exalted comparisons. There is the same search for the
unadorned truth that distinguished Weingartner, the dramatic fire that Toscanini commanded and
the warmth of Bruno Walter. The *First* and *Third* were recorded in 1959 and 1960 in stereo, and are
accommodated on the first disc; the *Second* and the *Fourth* (from 1955 and 1956 respectively) are
both mono, and the sound is less transparent and fresh – but, ironically, they are at least as vivid and
are rather better focused. The *Tragic Overture* is one of the best ever committed to disc. The noble
performance of the *St Anthony chorale variations* was never issued in the UK and comes from 1957.
The recording venue is the same throughout, the Grünewaldkirche in Berlin. Excellent transfers.

The valuable EMI compilation brings together the studio recording of the *First Symphony* that
Furtwängler made with the Vienna Philharmonic in 1949 and live recordings of the remaining three
symphonies. All were made with the Berlin Philharmonic in 1948 and 1952, presumably taken from
radio sources. The sound is disappointingly thin, lacking in body and with some harshness in the live
recordings; but the electricity of Furtwängler in Brahms is vividly captured. His freedom of expression,
with speeds varied far more extremely than by any latterday conductor, is essentially a spontaneous
style, however carefully planned. Set in aspic in the studio, it can easily sound self-conscious – though
not in the *First Symphony* here. Furtwängler's regular habit of starting a movement very slowly and
then suddenly speeding up is heard in context. Particularly when it is a hushed opening, as in the
finales of both *Symphonies Nos. 2* and *3*, the concept of having the opening pages as an introduction,
launching into an allegro, seems very natural. Far from making the symphonies seem rhapsodic, with
structure undermined, the results are totally cohesive, thanks also to Furtwängler's magnetic
concentration. Though his moulding of phrase is affectionate, with rubato freely used (rather more
than tenuto), these are not performances that set Brahmsian lyricism above drama. Despite the

limitations of the sound, lacking in body but with plenty of detail, and despite the bronchial audiences in Nos. 2, 3 and 4, this is an inspirational set, with the makeweights an added attraction.

Symphony No. 1 in C min., Op. 68.
(M) *** DG 447 408-2 [id.]. BPO, Karajan – SCHUMANN: *Symphony No. 1.* ***
(BB) *** Virgin/EMI Dig. VJ7 91566-2 [id.]. RPO, Litton.
**(*) Decca Dig. 436 289-2 [id.]. Cleveland O, Ashkenazy (with DVORAK: *Othello* **(*)).
(M) ** DG Dig. 445 505-2 [id.]. VPO, Bernstein (with BEETHOVEN: *Overtures: Coriolan; Egmont* **).
*(*) BMG/RCA Dig. RD 60428 [60428-2 RC]. Chicago SO, Wand.

Symphony No. 1; Academic festival overture, Op. 80.
(B) *** Carlton Dig. PCD 2014 [id.]. Hallé O, Skrowaczewski.

Karajan's 1964 recording of Brahms's *First Symphony* (the conductor's third version of five) seems by general consensus to be regarded as his finest. With his previous recording, made for RCA in Vienna, the total result did not quite add up, whereas in Berlin Karajan is entirely at home. The control of tension in the first movement is masterly and, as in his previous versions (not just the RCA), Karajan allows himself a fair latitude of tempo, both here and in the last movement. The orchestral playing is of superlative quality and the result is very powerful, with the finale a fitting culmination. The remastering has restored the original full, well-balanced, analogue sound, with plenty of weight in the bass (as is obvious at the timpani-dominated opening), yet detail is firmer. The coupling with Schumann's *First Symphony* makes this a very desirable record indeed – an obvious candidate for inclusion in DG's set of legendary 'Originals'.At full price, Abbado and the BPO still head the list of digital recommendations (DG 431 790-2).

Litton conducts a fresh, intense reading of Brahms's most dramatic symphony, helped by full, weighty sound that is both rich and clear, letting you hear the double bassoon clearly, for example, in the introduction to the finale. Litton takes a relatively spacious view in all four movements, but tension is well maintained, consistently giving you the impression of live communication, with the RPO challenged to produce crisp, alert playing. It is a good recommendation for a modern digital version in the lowest price-range.

Skrowaczewski conducts the Hallé in a powerful performance of No. 1, both warmly sympathetic and refined, with sound which is fresh, bright and clear and with a good, open atmosphere. The first movement is ideally paced, but without the exposition repeat. His view of the finale is big and bold, but with a rather old-fashioned slowing for the final appearance of the chorale theme in the coda. Nevertheless it makes an excellent bargain-price digital choice.

Ashkenazy, with full, weighty recording of an exceptionally rich and resonant orchestra, gives a strong, warmly expressive reading, with no self-indulgence. If the slow movement lacks a little in hushed intensity, the freshness of the rest compensates, and the disc could be considered by anyone fancying the unusual Dvořák coupling, equally well played and recorded.

The finale in Bernstein's version brings a highly idiosyncratic reading with the great melody of the main theme presented at a speed very much slower than the main part of the movement. On reprise it never comes back to the slow tempo, until the coda brings the most extreme slowing for the chorale motif. These two points are exaggerations of accepted tradition and, though Bernstein's electricity makes the results compelling, this is hardly a version for constant repetition. The remastered sound is fully acceptable.

Wand recorded his Chicago performance of the *First Symphony* live in 1989, consistently adopting broader speeds than in his earlier version with his own North German Radio Orchestra. Negating the advantages of live recording, the Chicago performance is noticeably less tense and compelling than the Hamburg one, with the recording less clear and with violins edgier. At full price and without a coupling, it is uncompetitive when, on two bargain-priced discs in RCA's Symphony Edition, together costing not much more than this, you can get Wand's outstanding earlier recordings of all four Brahms symphonies (see above).

Symphony No. 2 in D; Academic festival overture.
(M) ** DG Dig. 445 506-2 [id.]. VPO, Bernstein.

Abbado's splendid Berlin Philharmonic version remains our top recommendation for Brahms's *Second Symphony*, coupled with the *Alto rhapsody* (DG 427 643-2 – see our main volume).

Bernstein in his live recording directs a warm and expansive account, notably less free and idiosyncratic than the *C minor Symphony*, yet comparably rhythmic and spontaneous-sounding. Considering the limitations at a live concert, the recording sounds well. But this is by no means a first choice, even at mid-price, especially remembering that Karajan's 1964 account is available, coupled with the *Third Symphony*, on DG's bargain label (429 153-2). However, Abbado's BPO recording continues to dominate modern digital versions of the *Second Symphony* (DG 427 643-2).

Symphony No. 3 in F, Op. 90.
(M) *** RCA 09026 61793-2 [id.]. Chicago SO, Fritz Reiner – SCHUBERT: *Symphony No. 5.* ***

Symphony No. 3; Tragic overture, Op. 81; (i) *Alto rhapsody, Op. 53.*
*(*) DG Dig. 439 887-2 [id.]. (i) Anne Sofie von Otter, Arnold Schoenberg Ch.; VPO, Levine.

Symphony No. 3; Variations on a theme of Haydn, Op. 56a.
(*) Decca Dig. 433 548-2 [id.]. Cleveland O, Ashkenazy (with DVORAK: *Carnival overture* *).
(M) *(*) DG Dig. 445 507-2 [id.]. VPO, Bernstein.

Symphony No. 3 in F, Op. 90; (i) *Alto rhapsody, Op. 53.*
**(*) Ph. Dig. 442 120-2 [id.]. (i) Jard van Nes, Tanglewood Festival Ch.; Boston SO, Haitink.

Reiner's magnificent performance dates from 1956. It is a glowing, marvellously proportioned account, exposition repeat included, and prepared in masterly fashion, and with the close of the work given a touchingly gentle, valedictory feeling. Yet there is no want of momentum in the outer movements and the lyrical intensity and warmth in the slow movement are equally memorable. Here the Chicago ambience adds to the atmosphere and it is a pity that in tuttis there is some loss of refinement in the upper strings. This has been improved in the CD transfer and the balance is good, so this should not be enough to deter the serious collector, for this is a reading of stature and the Chicago orchestra has never been better than it was in the days of Reiner. Besides the estimable Schubert coupling there is an exciting account of Mendelssohn's *Fingal's Cave overture*.

The weight and resonance of the Cleveland Orchestra as recorded by the Decca engineers helps to make Ashkenazy's version a strongly competitive one for anyone who fancies the coupling, not just the *Haydn Variations* but with the Dvořák overture as an extra. In the *Symphony* Ashkenazy takes a direct view, characteristically fresh and lacking in mannerism but with plenty of dramatic tension, helped by clean, incisive playing.

We are somewhat in two minds as to the attractions or otherwise of Haitink's reading of the *Third Symphony*. For EG, Haitink's mellow reading with the Boston Symphony Orchestra cannot compare in bite or intensity with his earlier, Concertgebouw recording for Philips, latterly available at mid-price, coupled with No. 2 (426 632-2). The first movement of the Boston version in particular sounds lethargic and, though the recorded sound is full and weighty (if with rather edgy violins), there is less clear focus on internal details of Brahms's instrumentation. Beautifully moulded and refined as the playing is, the result too often sounds self-conscious. However, for RL, Haitink's recording of the *Third Symphony* is impressive in its directness and want of any kind of artifice. Here is Brahms pure and simple, the music left to speak for itself. Haitink draws playing of exemplary culture from the Boston orchestra, and the Philips recording is judiciously balanced and truthful. Some may feel that the first movement in particular could be more urgent in feeling; although there have been more highly charged accounts from Koussevitzky, Kempe and Walter, this is an eminently sane and civilized performance. About this version of the *Alto rhapsody* we are agreed: it is an exceptionally broad account which is better played than it is sung; Jard van Nes has too wide a vibrato.

The best thing on James Levine's record is the *Alto rhapsody*, beautifully sung by Anne Sofie von Otter. By the side of Reiner or Kempe, Levine's account of the *Symphony*, recorded at a public concert in the Musikverein in 1992, does not rise far above the routine. As one might expect, it is very well played, but ultimately the performances of both the *Third Symphony* and the *Tragic overture* have little real personality. To play Reiner immediately afterwards is to enter a totally different world. Levine does observe the first-movement exposition repeat. The engineering is goodish, though the Vienna Philharmonic strings sound far more transparent in the flesh; the overall texture is generally opaque. The *Alto rhapsody* is worth having for von Otter, but the rest is very ordinary.

Bernstein's 1981 account of the *Third* was recorded live, like the others in the series; but, with speeds in the first three movements so slow as to sound sluggish, it lacks the very quality of flow one hopes to find in a concert performance. The result is disappointingly self-conscious, and only the finale at an aptly fast speed brings Bernstein's usual incisiveness. Abbado's glowingly affectionate BPO performance remains first choice among modern recordings (DG 429 765-2).

Symphony No. 4 in E min., Op. 98.
(BB) **(*) BBC Radio Classics BBCRD 9107 [id.]. New Philh. O, Stokowski (with Concert) –
    VAUGHAN WILLIAMS: *Tallis Fantasy;* RAVEL: *Rapsodie espagnole.* **(*)

Symphony No. 4 in F min.; Tragic overture.
(M) *** DG Dig. 445 508-2 [id.]. VPO, Bernstein.

Bernstein's 1981 Vienna version of Brahms's *Fourth*, recorded live, is exhilaratingly dramatic in fast music, while the slow movement brings richly resonant playing from the Vienna strings, not least in the great cello melody at bar 41, which with its moulded rubato comes to sound surprisingly like Elgar. This is easily the finest of Bernstein's Vienna cycle and, with generally good sound, is well worth considering. However, Abbado's Berlin recording (DG 435 349-2) remains first choice for this much-recorded symphony at full price.

Part of a live concert, recorded at the Royal Albert Hall in May 1974, Stokowski's is a masterly reading of pretty high voltage, with notably fast tempi in outer movements but never sounding hurried; he pulls back, as he always did, just before the end of the exposition of the first movement but, generally speaking, this is pretty free from exaggeration. The playing has you sitting on the edge of your seat. Even if at times ensemble could be more precise, the performance is thrilling with the New Philharmonia playing with great eloquence. There is intrusive applause at the end of the first movement (over the last chord); the recording is inclined to be opaque and it is a pity that the reverberant acoustic has brought close microphones, which are not entirely flattering to the violins. All the same, this is a disc well worth investigating in this new series from the BBC's archives.

CHAMBER MUSIC

Cello sonatas Nos. 1 in E min., Op. 38; 2 in F, Op. 99.
** RCA Dig. 09026 61562-2 [id.]. Janos Starker, Rudolf Buchbinder – SCHUMANN: *Adagio and allegro.* **

Janos Starker's recording of the two *Sonatas* with Rudolf Buchbinder is impressive artistically but suffers from an overlit recording. The piano is very much the dominant partner in the picture and the listener is consistently close, with resulting aural fatigue. As anyone who has heard him in the flesh knows, Starker produces a small tone and, though he plays with impeccable taste and musicianship, it is a pity that Buchbinder does not scale down his tone. This does not displace Rostropovich and Serkin on DG (410 510-2 – see our main volume).

Cello sonata in D (arr. of *Violin sonata, Op. 78*).
** RCA Dig. RD 60598 [09026 60598-2]. Janos Starker, Shigeo Neriki – SCHUMANN: *Fantaisiestücke;* RACHMANINOV: *Sonata.* **

The arrangement for cello of the *Violin Sonata in G major* is the composer's own. Recorded in Manhattan in 1990, the sound is eminently vivid but unremittingly close. Those undeterred by sitting, as it were, in the front row, need have no hesitations: Starker's artistry is always strongly in evidence, and his pianist, though too prominent, is a responsive player.

(i) *Clarinet quintet in B min., Op. 115;* (ii) *Piano quintet in F min., Op. 34; String quintets Nos. 1 in F, Op. 88; 2 in G, Op. 111.*
(B) *** Ph. Duo 446 172-2 (2) [id.]. (i) Herbert Stähr; (ii) Werner Haas; Berlin Philharmonic Octet (members).

The Berlin performance of the *Clarinet quintet* is both beautiful and faithful to Brahms's instructions, an outstanding version in every way. The delicacy with which the 'Hungarian' middle section of the great *Adagio* is interpreted gives some idea of the insight of these players. It is an autumnal reading, never overforced, and is recorded with comparable refinement. The two *String quintets* are also admirably served by these same players (with Dietrich Gerhard, viola, replacing the clarinettist, Herbert Stähr). The performances are searching and artistically satisfying, combining freshness and polish, warmth with well-integrated detail. For the *Piano quintet* Werner Haas joins the group, and they give a strongly motivated, spontaneous account of this splendid work that is in every way satisfying. The piano is most convincingly balanced. The recordings come from the early 1970s and the sound is remarkably full and warm, the richness of texture suiting the *String quintets* especially well. This is among the finest bargains in the Philips Duo list.

Clarinet sonatas Nos. 1 in F min.; 2 in E flat, Op. 120/1–2.
*** Decca Dig. 430 149-2 [id.]. Cohen, Ashkenazy – SCHUMANN: *Fantasiestücke.* ***

Franklin Cohen and Vladimir Ashkenazy give an eloquent account of both sonatas. What glorious pieces they are, and how well they sound here. The Decca recording has an exemplary balance and, although the clarinettist is not as imaginative or as sensitive as Hein Wiedijk (see our main volume), the overall sound-picture is richer, and Ashkenazy has a better instrument than Frank van der Laar. Instead of the Schumann, the latter disc offers the *Clarinet trio*, with Peter Wispelwey, an even more appropriate coupling (Gutman CD 931).

(i) *Piano quartet No. 1 in G min., Op. 25. 4 Ballades, Op. 10.*
(M) **(*) DG 447 407-2 [id.]. Gilels, (i) with Amadeus Qt.

As might be expected, Gilels' account of the *G minor Quartet* with members of the Amadeus has much to recommend it. The great Soviet pianist is in impressive form, and most listeners will respond to the withdrawn delicacy of the Scherzo and the gypsy fire of the finale. The slow movement is perhaps somewhat wanting in ardour and the Amadeus do not sound as committed or as fresh as their keyboard partner. At medium price, however, this version enjoys an advantage, and the 1971 DG recording is well balanced and sounds very natural in its new transfer. Moreover in the *Ballades* Gilels offers artistry of an order that silences criticism. In terms of imaginative vitality and musical insight it would be difficult to surpass these readings. It goes without saying that at no time is one's attention drawn to Gilels' keyboard mastery for, so complete is his identification with the musical inspiration, one thinks only of Brahms. The *Ballades* have never been so marvellously played on record, and the 1976 recording is also first class. This certainly is a recording worthy of inclusion in DG's legendary series of 'Originals'.

Piano quintet in F min., Op. 34.
** DG Dig. 437 804-2 [id.]. Paul Gulda, Hagen Qt – SCHOENBERG: *Chamber symphony No. 1* (arr. for piano quintet). **
* Sony Dig. SK 58954 [id.]. Artis Qt, with Stefan Vladar – SCHUMANN: *Piano quintet.* *

Paul Gulda and the Hagen Quartet give a vivid, well-projected account of the *F minor Piano quintet*. This is a highly accomplished and eminently polished account which, if it were less self-aware, would have been a strong recommendation. However, these players are not always content to leave things to speak for themselves, and there is some loss of that natural unforced eloquence so essential in chamber-music-making.

Sony's recording with Stefan Vladar and the Artis Quartet has regretfully to be ruled out of court. The balance appears to place the listener on the platform on the piano side: not only is the piano sound larger than life and bottom-heavy, but the strings are swamped. There is some ardent if not always subtle playing (the pianist is not strong on finesse) but the disc as a whole is unlikely to give much pleasure, and the Naxos version by Jandó and the Kodály Quartet (coupled with Schumann) is far more recommendable (8.550406).

Piano trios Nos. 1 in B, Op. 8; 2 in C, Op. 87; 3 in C min., Op. 101; in A, Op. posth.
* EMI Dig. CDS7 54725-2 (2) [id.]. Vladimir Ashkenazy, Itzhak Perlman, Lynn Harrell.

This is high-powered stuff – and that is not meant as a compliment. In addition to the three *Piano trios*, Perlman, Ashkenazy and Harrell also offer the posthumously published *A major*, which is an undoubted plus. Otherwise their playing is full of tension and over-projection: nothing is ever left to speak for itself. Perlman plays pretty loudly, which forces similarly high-voltage responses from his partners. To put it bluntly, this is all strip-lighting rather than the gentler light to which Brahms would have been accustomed; it is music-making for a large concert hall rather than domestic surroundings. The civilized discourse and natural give-and-take of chamber-music-playing are little in evidence. These performances are thrustful and driven and, for all the eminence of these artists, give little pleasure. First choice remains with the Trio Fontenay (Teldec 9031 76036-2 – see our main volume).

String quartets Nos. 1 in C min.; 2 in A min., Op. 51/1–2.
** Telarc Dig. CD 80346 [id.]. Cleveland Qt.

String quartets Nos. 1–2, Op. 51/1–2; 3 in B flat, Op. 67.
(M) *** Teldec/Warner 4509 95503-2 (2) [id.]. Alban Berg Qt – DVORAK: *String quartet No. 13.* ***
(M) ** EMI Dig. CMS5 65459-2 (2). Britten Qt.

We have commented on the Alban Berg performances in earlier editions. They were made in the mid-1970s when the quartet was on peak form, highly polished yet completely fresh in their musical responses. The recording is very good: the sound of the *B flat*, Op. 67, made in a Swiss church, is superior but not overwhelmingly so; the *A minor* was recorded in Palais Yusopov in St Petersburg. The Teldec performances have the inestimable advantage of being economical in price and also space; they are accommodated in the now-popular two-in-one jewel-case. This set is strongly recommended and can stand alongside the best in the catalogue.

The Britten Quartet also comes at mid-price, though the recording is brand new; no doubt the absence of a coupling has prompted the competitive pricing. The Brittens are a quartet of high accomplishment and have the benefit of very fine recorded sound. The *C minor* is accommodated on the first disc, the *A minor* and *B flat* on the second. The venue, so the insert leaflet tells us, is St

George's, Brandon Hill, Bristol, which helps to enhance the fine tonal lustre this ensemble commands. All the same, for all their technical aplomb, their performances are not really in the same league as the Borodins or the early Alban Berg listed above. While they cannot be accused of being on autopilot, their music-making does not convey the same meaning or expressive urgency of the greatest players. Polished and musicianly, but without having quite that inner commitment so necessary to turn an accomplished performance into a distinguished one.

The Cleveland Quartet makes an impressive sound, and their ensemble, intonation and surface sheen are of the highest order. They are fine musicians but tend to wear their hearts on their sleeves and go for big, romantic gestures. They rarely give the impression of spontaneous feeling. Others may enjoy them more, but it is a set which offers less satisfaction than either of the Alban Berg versions or the Borodins. They are well recorded, and those on the Cleveland wavelength have no need to hold back.

String quartet No. 2 in A min., Op. 51/2.
*** ASV Dig. CDDCA 712 [id.]. Lindsay Qt – MENDELSSOHN: *String quartet No. 6.* ***

A straightforward, sane performance, free of gloss and schmaltz. No one trying this is likely to be disappointed either with the Lindsays' musicianship or with the ASV recording.

String quartet No. 2 in A min., Op. 51/2.
*** RCA Dig. 09026 61866-2 [id.]. Vogler Qt – SCHUMANN: *String quartet No. 3.* ***

String quartet No. 3 in B flat, Op. 67.
*** RCA Dig. 09026 61438-2 [id.]. Vogler Qt – SCHUMANN: *String quartet No. 1.* ***

The Vogler is an extremely fine ensemble who have been engaged on recording the Brahms and Schumann quartets, as the Quartetto Italiano did on LP in the 1970s. Tough luck if you already have one and want the other (though there is no lack of alternatives) but, if you do want both in modern, digital recordings, it would be difficult to improve on them. They have the advantage of a rich and beautifully blended sonority and refined musicianship. Moreover the RCA recording is very good indeed. Recommended with enthusiasm. If the remaining disc (which will couple the Brahms *C minor*, Op. 51, No. 1, with the Schumann *F major*, Op. 41, No. 2) is their equal, this is likely to be a first recommendation for years to come.

String sextet No. 1 in B flat, Op. 18.
(***) Biddulph mono LAB 093 [id.] Pro Arte Qt, with Hobday, Pini – SCHUBERT: *String quintet in C.* (***)

Although they enjoyed much renown in the concert hall, the Pro Arte Quartet were rather overshadowed in the recording studios of the 1930s by the Busch and Budapest Quartets. True, they were allocated the task of recording what was to have been a complete cycle for the Haydn Quartet Society, but this was a subscription set. They made a handful of other discs, including some Mozart (K.428 and, with Alfred Hobday, the *G minor Quintet*, K.516), which were classics of their day. They also recorded Bartók's *First Quartet* and championed the new music of the time (Honegger, Roussel, Tansman and Milhaud). Their impeccable technical address shows here, and their warmth and finesse make their Brahms as satisfying as any account recorded since. Needless to say, some allowance has to be made for the 1935 recording, eminently well transferred though it is.

PIANO MUSIC

4 Ballades, Op. 10; Piano sonata No. 3 in F min., Op. 5.
(BB) **(*) Naxos Dig. 8.550352 [id.]. Idil Biret.

Idel Biret turns from Chopin to the solo piano music of Brahms. As a pupil of Kempff, she has a fine understanding of this repertoire, although her approach is more muscular than Kempff's. Thus the first of the *Four Ballades* opens with enticing lyrical feeling but has the most powerfully dramatic climax, to match the feeling of the Scottish ballad, *Edward*, on which it is based. The *Fourth Ballade* is gravely beautiful and shows her at her finest. The *Sonata* opens commandingly and its lyrical side is well balanced; the second movement has a gentle *grazioso* which is very appealing, and the Intermezzo is equally sensitve. The Scherzo is heavily accented, while the finale is comparatively lightweight: its great descending choral theme is nevertheless very tellingly introduced. These performances are full of character. Good recording, made in the Heidelberg studio.

(i) *Fantasias, Op. 116; Intermezzi, Op. 117;* (ii) *Pieces, Op. 76;* (i) *Pieces, Opp. 118/119;* (ii) *Rhapsodies Nos. 1 in B min.; 2 in G min., Op. 79/1–2;* (i) *Variations and fugue on a theme by Handel, Op. 24;* (iii) *Variations on a theme by Paganini, Op. 35.*
(B) *(**) Ph. Duo Analogue/Dig. 442 589-2 (2) [id.]. (i) Stephen Kovacevich; (ii) Dinorah Varsi; (iii) Adam Harasiewicz.

The performances by Stephen Kovacevich can receive the strongest recommendation. He finds the fullest range of emotional contrast in the Op. 116 *Fantasias,* but is at his finest in the Op. 117 *Intermezzi* and the four *Klavierstücke,* Op. 119, which contain some of Brahms's most beautiful lyrical inspirations for the keyboard, while the *Allegro risoluto* of the final *Rhapsodie* of Op. 119 has splendid flair and presence. On the second CD the *Handel variations* are also impressive and it seems perverse that Philips then turned to recordings by Dinorah Varsi of the two *Rhapsodies* and eight *Klavierstücke,* Op. 76, when Kovacevich has also recorded them. However, these are already available, coupled with the two piano concertos, on another Duo (442 109-2) – see our main volume. Varsi's playing is at times very impulsive (as in the Op. 79 *Rhapsody*) and her performances of the *Klavierstücke* also lack the necessary degree of poise. Adam Harasiewicz, however, plays the *Paganini variations* with some flair and towards the end produces some exciting bravura. Generally the recordings are very good; Kovacevich's Op. 116 and Op. 118 are digital.

7 Fantasies, Op. 116; 8 Pieces, Op. 76; 2 Rhapsodies, Op. 79.
(BB) **(*) Naxos Dig. 8.550353 [id.]. Idil Biret.

Biret opens her programme strongly with the agitato *Capriccio in F sharp minor* (the first of the Op. 76 group), and then articulates the second lightly and engagingly. She readily captures the graceful intimacy of the *A flat* and *B flat Intermezzi.* Of the two *Rhapsodies,* the first is very impulsive indeed, but the second is particularly fine, boldly spontaneous, its dark colouring caught well. The *Fantasias,* Op. 116, bring some beautifully reflective playing, notably in the three *Intermezzi* grouped together (in E major and E minor), while the framing *G minor* and *D minor Capriccios* are passionately felt, the latter ending the recital strongly. This is all impressively characterized Brahms playing, and the recording does not lack sonority.

Theme and variations in D min. (1860); *Variations and fugue on a theme by Handel, Op. 24; Variations on a Hungarian song, Op. 21; Variations on a theme by Schumann, Op. 9.*
*** EMI Dig. CDC5 55167-2 [id.]. Mikhail Rudy.

The Russian pianist Mikhail Rudy proves to be a Brahms interpreter of considerable insight. He keeps a firm grasp on the musical structure of each of these sets of variations, not least the 1860 D minor transcription of the slow movement of the *Sextet in B flat,* Op. 18, whose use (in its original form) in Louis Malle's *Les Amants* did so much to further Brahms's cause in France – and elsewhere for that matter; and he produces a sonority of consistent beauty. The *Handel variations* do not obliterate memories of Solomon (now reissued on Testament), Stephen Bishop-Kovacevich (now on a Philips Duo set) or other great performances on record, but they are the best to appear more recently. Very good sound.

VOCAL MUSIC

German Requiem, Op. 45.
(M) **(*) DG Dig. 445 546-2 [id.]. Bonney, Schmidt, V. State Op. Ch., VPO, Giulini.

Giulini directs a deeply dedicated performance of the *German Requiem* but one which, at spacious speeds, lacks rhythmic bite. Meditation is a necessary part of Brahms's scheme; but here, with phrasing smoothed over and the choral sound rather opaque, there is too little contrast. Gardiner's version with his Monteverdi Choir remains a clear first choice for this work (Philips 432 140-2).

(i) *German Requiem;* (ii) *Alto rhapsody, Op. 53.*
(M) (**(*)) Bruno Walter Edition: Sony mono/stereo SMK 64469 [id.]. (i) Seefried, London, Westminster Ch., NYPO; (ii) Mildred Miller, Occidental College Concert Ch., Columbia SO; Bruno Walter.

In spite of opaque, if full-bodied, choral sound, Bruno Walter's 1954 mono recording of the *German Requiem* still grips the listener. *Denn alles Fleisch, es ist wie Gras* brings a dark, atmospheric frisson that all but sends a shiver to the nape of the neck, and the work's closing section is exultant. Of the soloists, Irmgard Seefried makes the stronger impression and, though the choral singing is at times ill-focused, the nobility and power of the music is communicated. In the *Alto rhapsody* Mildred Miller is a fresh rather than an inspirational soloist and, despite coaching from Walter (who had decided views on the interpretation of this fine work), she gives a somewhat strait-laced account of the opening pages. However, the fine choral singing shows that Walter's directing hand again had a special contribution to make. The stereo recording is far superior to the coupling.

Bridge, Frank (1879–1941)

3 Idylls (for string quartet).
*** Hyp. Dig. CDA 66718 [id.]. Coull Qt – ELGAR: *Quartet* **(*); WALTON: *Quartet.* ***

The *Three Idylls* date from 1906, soon after Bridge's first regular quartet. As this superb, purposeful performance shows, the separate pieces, each marked by sharp changes of mood as a phantasie-form, make up a satisfying whole, a quartet in all but name. They provide a superb bonus to a fine performance of the Elgar and an outstanding performances of the Walton *Quartet*. Excellent sound.

Cello sonata.
(M) *** Decca 443 575-2 [id.]. Rostropovich, Britten – SCHUBERT: *Arpeggione sonata.* **(*)

Bridge wrote his *Cello sonata* during the First World War. At first sight it bears all the imprints of the English pastoral school, with its pastel colourings and gentle discursive lines, as well as a nod in the direction of Debussy. Nevertheless it has a sturdy independence of outlook and a personality to which one increasingly warms. The craftmanship is distinguished and the lines delicately traced, and the modulations are often personal. The playing is of an altogether rare order, even by the exalted standards of Rostropovich and Britten, and the recording, made at The Maltings in 1968, has immediacy, warmth and great response. The reissue reappears with its original coupling in Decca's Classic Sound series.

Britten, Benjamin (1913–76)

An American overture; Ballad of heroes; The building of the house; Canadian carnival; (i) *Diversions for piano (left hand) and orchestra. Occasional overture; Praise we great men; Scottish ballad; Sinfonia da Requiem; Suite on English folk tunes; A time there was . . .; Young Apollo;* (ii) *4 Chansons françaises.*
*** EMI Dig. CDS7 54270-2 (2) [CDCB 54270]. (i) Peter Donohoe; (ii) Jill Gomez; CBSO, Rattle.

A valuable compilation from the various recordings of Britten's music, most of it rare, which Rattle has made over the years. It is good to have the *Diversions for piano (left-hand) and orchestra* with Peter Donohoe as soloist, amazingly the first version in stereo; and the most cherishable item of all is the radiant performance given by Jill Gomez of the *Four Chansons françaises*, the amazing and tenderly affecting settings of Hugo and Verlaine composed by the fifteen-year-old Britten. Sadly, this collection of reissues is offered at full rather than medium price, but it is worth it.

Piano concerto, Op. 13.
(M) **(*) Hyp. Dig. CDA 66293 [id.]. Servadei, LPO, Giunta – KHACHATURIAN: *Piano concerto.*
     **(*)

Now that Decca have brought out Sviatoslav Richter's recording of the Britten *Piano concerto* with the composer conducting (417 308-2 – see our main volume), others are likely to be outshone; but, with its exceptionally generous coupling, no one will be too seriously disappointed with this Hyperion alternative. With good, well-balanced digital recording, Annette Servadei gives a strong, dedicated, muscular performance. South-African born but trained mainly in Italy, Servadei is nevertheless a devotee of British music. She is particularly impressive in the hushed and sustained passacaglia, entitled *Impromptu*, which makes up for the slow movement and provided Walton with the theme of his *Variations on an Impromptu of Britten*.

(i; ii) *Lachrymae (Reflections on a song by Dowland);* (i) *Prelude and fugue, Op. 29; Simple Symphony, Op. 4; Variations on a theme of Frank Bridge, Op. 10;* (ii) *Elegy for solo viola.*
⊛ *** Virgin/EMI Dig. VC5 45121-2 [id.]. (i) Norwegian CO, Iona Brown; (ii) Lars Anders Tomter.

In 1981 Iona Brown moved on from being leader/director of the ASMF to principal conductor of the Norwegian Chamber Orchestra. In her first Virgin record with these excellent string players, made in Oslo's Uranienborg Church between 1988 and 1991, she gives performances of the *Simple Symphony* and the *Frank Bridge variations* to match and even surpass the composer's own. The *Simple Symphony* fizzes with youthful energy, yet Iona Brown brings an unusually wide dynamic and expressive range to the first movement and the poignant *Sentimetal sarabande*, which elevates Britten's writing far beyond any suggestion of juvenilia. The *Playful pizzicato* has a splendid bounce.

The *Frank Bridge variations* have never sounded more emotionally powerful on record and, after the opening flourish, the raptly quiet playing of the solo strings draws a parallel with the Vaughan Williams *Tallis fantasia*. There are many insights of imaginative detail, not least in the *Wiener waltzer* which, with its surprisingly poignant feeling and subtle control of dynamic and rubato, is the very opposite of trivial. The starkness of the *Funeral march* compares with the famous Karajan/Philharmonia version in its intensity, and in the following *Chant* the Norwegian players show they understand all about icy landscapes. The finale brings a release of the utmost virtuosity, crisp ensemble, and then great tenderness, leading to a hushed pianissimo from the violins to surpass even the opening solo passages. In the *Lachrymae* Lars Anders Tomter is an outstanding soloist, not least in the touching full presentation of Dowland's tune, *If my complaints could passions move*, in the haunting coda. He follows the *Lachrymae* with an ardent account of the solo *Elegy*. The recording is in the demonstration bracket, and this fine concert throughout conveys the natural spontaneity of seemingly live music-making.

Matinées musicales; Soirées musicales.
(M) *** Decca Dig. 444 109-2 [id.]. Nat. PO, Bonynge – ROSSINI: *La Boutique fantasque*. ***

Britten wrote his *Soirées musicales* for a GPO film-score in the 1930s; the *Matinées* followed in 1941 and were intended as straight ballet music. Both are wittily if rather sparsely scored, deriving their musical content directly from Rossini. Bonynge's versions are brightly played and extremely vividly recorded in the best Decca manner, and are now reissued at mid-price in this company's Ballet Gala series.

Sinfonia da Requiem, Op. 20; The Young person's guide to the orchestra, Op. 34; Peter Grimes: 4 Sea interludes & Passacaglia, Op. 34.
(M) **(*) Virgin/EMI Dig. CUV5 61195-2 [id.]. RLPO, Libor Pešek.

Though Pešek fails to convey the full ominous weight of the first movement of the *Sinfonia da Requiem*, he then directs a dazzling account of the central *Dies Irae Scherzo*, taken breathtakingly fast, and finds an intense repose in the calm of the final *Requiem aeternam*. The *Sea interludes* sound very literal, not ideally atmospheric. The *Young person's guide* lacks a degree of tension, with the fugue not dashing enough. The recording is comfortably reverberant.

(i) *Simple Symphony, Op. 4; Variations on a theme of Frank Bridge, Op. 10;* (ii) *Young person's guide to the orchestra, Op. 34; Peter Grimes: 4 Sea interludes.*
(M) **(*) Nimbus NI 7017 [id.]. (i) E. String O; (ii) E. SO, Boughton.

An attractive and generous 75-minute Britten anthology, very well played and showing the sumptuous Nimbus recording style at its most effective. The *Simple Symphony* and *Frank Bridge variations* were recorded in the Great Hall of Birmingham University in 1985 and are most sympathetically played (the *Playful pizzicato* has a resonance to match the composer's own version). The *Young person's guide* and *Sea interludes* were recorded in Birmingham's new Symphony Hall in 1991 and, while equally rich in texture, have even better definition. The famous *Variations* are amiably colourful, but Boughton is fired with a strongly emotional response to the *Sea Interludes*, bringing out the inner tensions in *Moonlight* most involvingly, while the powerful *Storm* sequence is highly spectacular.

Young person's guide to the orchestra (Variations and fugue on a theme of Purcell), Op. 34.
(B) ** CfP CD-CFP 185; *TC-CFP 185*. Richard Baker, New Philh. O, Leppard – PROKOFIEV: *Peter and the Wolf*. **

The rather cosy narration by Richard Baker on this Classics for Pleasure reissue tends to hold up the flow of the music. The orchestral playing is lively and the recording good, but one feels that there are too many words here. This is not a version to stand constant repetition, although it would be suitable for school use.

CHAMBER MUSIC

(i) *Cello sonata in C, Op. 65;* (ii) *Elegy for solo viola;* (iii) *6 Metamorphoses after Ovid, for solo oboe, Op. 49;* (iv) *Suite for violin and piano, Op. 6.*
*** EMI Dig. CDC5 55398-2 [id.]. (i) Moray Welsh, John Lenehan; (ii) Paul Silverthorne; (iii) Roy Carter; (iv) Alexander Barantschick, John Alley.

This collection is part of an ongoing EMI Anglo-American chamber music series, played respectively by soloists from the LSO and NYPO. The present disc (from the London musicians) makes an admirable companion to its equivalent American recital of the music of Samuel Barber, which also centres on an inspired *Cello sonata*. In the Britten, Moray Welsh and John Lenehan make no attempt to ape the famous Rostropovich account, but instead choose their own approach, thoughtful, ardent (especially in the central *Elegia*) and strong (as in the *Marcia* – very *echt*-Shostakovich) and highly spontaneous. The *moto perpetuo* finale has great energy and develops a vibrant intensity at the close, and the whole performance is very immediate. Paul Silverthorne gives a touchingly valedictory account of the *Elegy* and Roy Carter is rhapsodically free in the six piquant oboe miniatures, capturing their wistful innocence to perfection. But perhaps most memorable of all is the compellingly alive account of the early *Suite for violin and piano*, written between 1934 and 1936. As if anticipating the *Cello sonata*, the five movements are beautifully contrasted, either full of imaginative vitality or, as in the *Lullaby* – marked *Lento tranquillo* – bringing a serene repose. Here the result is quite ravishing. Throughout, the recordings, made in the Conway Hall, have a pleasing degree of resonance: the effect is real and present in the most natural way.

(i) *String quartets Nos. 1 in D, Op. 25; 2 in C, Op. 36; 3, Op. 94; String quartet in D; Quartettino; Alla marcia; 3 Divertimenti; Rhapsody* (all for string quartet); (ii) *Elegy for solo viola;* (i; iii) *Phantasy for oboe and string trio, Op. 2;* (i; iv) *Phantasy in F min. for string quintet.*
(M) *** EMI Dig. CMS5 65115-2. (i) Endellion Qt; (ii) Garfield Jackson; (iii) Douglas Boyd; (iv) Nicholas Logie.

In addition to the three mature *Quartets* which are familiar to collectors, this set brings a number of early works, many of which are completely new (although some have appeared in alternative versions since this EMI compilation first appeared in 1987). The early *Rhapsody* (1929) is followed on the first disc by the remarkable three-movement *Quartettino* (1930) which is at times almost Berg-like and shows how exploratory were Britten's musical instincts and how keenly he responded to the stimulus of Frank Bridge. (As John Evans puts it in his notes, 'Here is the Bridge of the *Third Quartet* (1926) and more besides!') Also offered is the *Quartet in D* (1931) which the composer later reworked when he was convalescing from open-heart surgery. Originally Bridge had complained that its counterpoint was too vocal, but there is much that is characteristic in this fluent and well-crafted piece, which was published in the last year of Britten's life. The *Elegy* for solo viola, Britten's own instrument, was one of the last pieces he wrote before taking up his scholarship at the Royal College of Music in London in 1930. The *Phantasy quintet* for strings comes from 1932, the same year as the eloquent *Oboe Phantasy quartet*. Britten may have looked back self-deprecatingly on this early work ('Here was no early Mozart, I'm afraid') but, listening again to this Op. 2, one is taken aback by the sheer fertility of its invention and the abundance of his imagination. The *Alla marcia* followed a year afterwards and resurfaced in 1939 in 'Parade' in *Les illuminations*. The three *Divertimenti* date from 1936 and derive from a suite of contrasting character movements entitled *Alla quartetto serioso*, written three years earlier. Then in 1941 came Britten's first published quartet, written in response to a commission from Elizabeth Sprague Coolidge.

Overall this survey affords a valuable insight into the young Britten and is of importance, not merely in showing us 'the father to the man', but as a rewarding musical experience in its own right. Before undertaking these recordings, the Endellions had established themselves as one of the finest quartets in the country and their playing is as responsive and intelligent as one could wish for. In the three published *Quartets* both performances and recordings are exemplary and the *Second* and *Third* can match the much (and rightly) admired pioneering accounts by the Zorian and Amadeus groups.

VOCAL MUSIC

The Company of Heaven. Paul Bunyan: Overture; Inkslinger's aria; Lullaby of dream shadows.
*** Virgin/EMI Dig. VC5 45093-2 [id.]. Allen, Barkworth (narrators), Pope, Dressen, LPO Ch., ECO, Brunelle.

Britten wrote the big cantata, *The Company of Heaven*, for radio in 1937 as an offering for the Feast of St Michael and All Angels, but the score was lost for many years. The music, some half-hour of it, links extensive readings from texts on the theme of angels, and there is much that echoes such works of the time as the *Frank Bridge variations* and *Les illuminations*, with Britten's use of a congregational hymn in the last item anticipating both *Noye's Fludde* and *St Nicholas*. It was here too that Britten wrote, with the voice of Peter Pears in mind, a jaunty setting of Emily Brontë. Also very striking is the movement, *War in heaven*, with the men in the chorus delivering the words in sing-speech. Philip Brunelle made this recording soon after the first concert performance at The Maltings in 1989, using the same excellent forces, with the spoken contributions more effective on record than in concert. The brief excerpts from *Paul Bunyan* include an infectious 'Overture' (completed, from sketches, by Colin Matthews) and a rather engaging *Lullaby*, here performed most persuasively. The recording throughout is excellent, spacious and with fine balance and presence.

Folksong arrangements (complete).

**(*) Hyp. Dig. CDA 66941/2 [id.]. Lorna Anderson, Regina Nathan, Jamie MacDougall, Malcolm
   Martineau, Bryn Lewis, Craig Ogden.

Some of Britten's folksong arrangements are among his most popular pieces, notably *The foggy dew*
and *The ploughboy*. Unlike most similar arrangements, Britten's consistently reflect the individual
character of the arranger, often in accompaniments that disconcertingly clash with the solo line. Some
of them add unexpected asperity, as in the setting of the *Lincolnshire poacher*, which is bitter, not jolly
at all. It is valuable to have all 53 settings in this two-disc set, freshly and clearly sung if without quite
the character and imagination which marked the various recordings of Peter Pears with the composer
at the piano. Jamie MacDougall's sweetly agreeable tenor is not always flattered by the recording,
which exaggerates his vibrato at times and brings out a roughness under pressure. Lorna Anderson's
fresh, clear soprano is better caught, though her contributions are fewer. They include roughly a third
of the main collections of songs and one each of the groups with guitar accompaniment (*Bonny at
morn*, the song which Pears did not record) and with harp accompaniment (*The false knight*). Jamie
MacDougall sings the folksong, *David of the white rock*, in the original Welsh. Regina Nathan's
contribution is limited to ten songs at the end, setting Moore's Irish melodies, including *Oft in the
stilly night* and *The last rose of summer*. Hers is a soprano as fresh as Lorna Anderson's, but slightly
warmer.

Orchestral song-cycles: (i) *4 Chansons françaises (1928);* (ii) *Our Hunting Fathers, Op. 8;* (i) *Les
illuminations, Op. 18;* (iii) *Nocturne, Op. 60;* (iv) *Phaedra, Op. 93;* (iii;v) *Serenade for tenor, horn and
strings, Op. 31.*

*** Collins Dig. 7037-2 (2) [id.]. (i) Felicity Lott; (ii) Phyllis Bryn-Julson; (iii) Philip Langridge; (iv)
   Ann Murray; (v) Frank Lloyd; ECO or (in *Nocturne*) N. Sinf., Steuart Bedford.

Steuart Bedford, successor to Britten himself as conductor, here offers fresh, clear readings of the five
orchestral song-cycles, plus the scena, *Phaedra*, written in 1975 long after the rest. In that Ann
Murray may not match the dedicatee, Janet Baker, but the dramatic bite is intense. Similarly in the
anti-blood-sports cantata, *Our Hunting Fathers*, Phyllis Bryn-Julson is refreshingly fluent and agile.
In the even earlier cycle, *Quatre chansons françaises*, Felicity Lott could be warmer, but she is
masterly in the Baudelaire cycle, *Les illuminations*. Best of all, with Philip Langridge the characterful,
heady-toned tenor, are the two most popular cycles, the *Serenade* (horn soloist Frank Lloyd) and the
Nocturne. Bright, forward sound.

(i) *Les Illuminations* (song-cycle), *Op. 18;* (ii) *Phaedra, Op. 93;* 5 French folksong arrangements: *La
belle est au jardin d'amour; Eho! Eho!; Fileuse; Quand j'étais chez mon père; Le roi s'en va-t'en chasse.*

(M) *** EMI Dig. CDM5 65114-2 [id.]. (i) Jill Gomez; (ii) Felicity Palmer; Endymion Ens.,
   Whitfield.

Sir Peter Pears was such a dominant interpreter of Britten's vocal music that the original inspiration
of the orchestral cycle, *Les Illuminations*, using a soprano has rather been forgotten. Though Heather
Harper recorded a fine performance, Jill Gomez, ably backed by John Whitfield and the Endymion
Ensemble, is far more seductively sensuous, with the soloist bringing out a gorgeous feminine beauty,
matching the exotic quality of the Baudelaire poems. Felicity Palmer, contrasting strongly, gives
strong, intense performances both of the late dramatic cantata, *Phaedra* (tougher and less tender than
the dedicatee, Janet Baker), and of the five French folksong arrangements not previously recorded in
this colourful orchestral form. Vivid, well-balanced recording.

Serenade for tenor, horn and strings, Op. 31.

(B) *** DG 439 464-2 [id.]. Robert Tear, Dale Clevenger, Chicago SO, Giulini – DELIUS: *On hearing
   the first cuckoo; Summer night on the river;* VAUGHAN WILLIAMS: *Greensleeves; Lark ascending.*
   ***

Robert Tears' 1977 interpretation of the *Serenade* is very much in the Aldeburgh tradition set by
Pears, and Giulini has long been a persuasive advocate of Britten's music. He presents the cycle as a
full-scale orchestral work and Tear is at his finest, more open than in his earlier, EMI recording.
Dale Clevenger is a superb horn player, and though in places some may find him unidiomatic it is
good to have a fresh view of the music, especially when inexpensively coupled with fine performances
of music by Delius and Vaughan Williams.

(i) *Spring Symphony, Op. 44. Young person's guide to the orchestra, Op. 34; Peter Grimes: Four Sea
interludes.*

(M) (**) Decca mono 440 063-2 [id.]. (i) Vincent, Ferrier, Pears, St Willibrorduskerk Boys' Ch.,
   Netherlands R. Ch.; Concg. O, Eduard van Beinum.

The major item here is a historic radio recording of the first performance in Amsterdam in July 1949 of the *Spring Symphony*. The sound is far worse than would ever be normally acceptable on disc, with a scrunching background noise throughout the work and with frequent relapses into fuzzy focus. The subtle pianissimo textures of the very opening are hardly even identifiable, yet with Kathleen Ferrier singing with heartfelt intensity, with Peter Pears showing a youthful freshness quite distinct from his later performance on record, and with Jo Vincent a bright, clear soprano soloist, there is much to cherish. Eduard van Beinum was an impassioned interpreter of Britten, and that comes out even more clearly in the other two items, both recorded for Decca in the studio, and here transferred brightly rather than with full body. Rarely have the *Four Sea interludes* from *Peter Grimes* been recorded with such bite and dramatic flair as here and, though the *Young person's guide* brings some wildness in the playing, the excitement of this performance makes it well worth hearing.

OPERA

(i) *The Little Sweep, Op. 45;* (ii) *Rejoice in the Lamb* (festival cantata), *Op. 30.*
(M) *** EMI CDM5 65111-2 [id.]. (i) Robert Lloyd, Robert Tear, Sam Monck, Heather Begg, Catherine Benson, Mary Wells, Finchley Children's Music Group, Choral Scholars of King's College, Medici Qt, Constable, Grier, Fry; (ii) James Bowman, Richard Morton, Marcus Creed, King's College Ch.; Philip Ledger.

The composer's own recording of *The Little Sweep* – the operatic second half of the entertainment, *Let's make an opera* – is available in mono only (Decca 436 393-2 – see our main volume), and one principal gain in this 1977 analogue stereo recording directed by Britten's longtime collaborator at the Aldeburgh Festival is the vividness of atmosphere. The game of hide-and-seek sounds much more real, and though the words are not always ideally clear, there is a good illusion of having an audience and not a trained choir singing them. In the cast Sam Monck as the Little Sweep himself is delightfully fresh-toned and artless – less expressive than the star-to-be, David Hemmings, on Britten's record, but just as appealing – and among the others the outstanding contributor is Heather Begg as the dragon-like Miss Baggott, bringing out the occasional likenesses with Gilbert and Sullivan in some of the patter ensembles. Apart from the cast of grown-ups, the solos are taken by members of the Finchley Children's Music Group, and Ledger's direction follows very much in the tradition set by the composer himself, without lacking impetus. To make a more generous reissue, EMI have added, very appropriately, Philip Ledger's 1974 version of the cantata, *Rejoice in the Lamb*, with timpani and percussion added to the original organ part. Here the biting climaxes are sung with passionate incisiveness, while James Bowman is in his element in the delightful passage which tells you that 'the mouse is a creature of great personal valour'. Excellently transferred King's sound.

Bruch, Max (1838–1920)

Violin concerto No. 1 in G min., Op. 26.
(M) *** Sony Dig. SMK 64250 [id.]. Cho-Liang Lin, Chicago SO, Slatkin – MENDELSSOHN: *Concerto;* VIEUXTEMPS: *Concerto No. 5.* ***
(B) *** Carlton Dig. PCD 2005 [id.]. Jaime Laredo, SCO – MENDELSSOHN: *Concerto.* ***
(BB) *** EMI Seraphim CES5 68524-2 (2) [CEDB 68524]. Sir Yehudi Menuhin, LSO, Boult – MENDELSSOHN: *Violin concerto* etc. ***

There have been few accounts on record of Bruch's slow movement that begin to match the raptness of Lin. He is accompanied most sensitively by Slatkin and the Chicago orchestra, and this reading is totally compelling in its combination of passion and purity, strength and dark, hushed intensity. The addition of the attractive *Fifth Concerto* of Henri Vieuxtemps makes this CD more attractive than ever. The recording is excellent.

Jaime Laredo with consistently fresh and sweet tone gives a delightfully direct reading, warmly expressive but never for a moment self-indulgent. The orchestral ensemble is particularly impressive, when no conductor is involved. With first-rate modern digital recording, this is a highlight of the Carlton (formerly Pickwick) budget-price catalogue.

Menuhin's second stereo recording of the Bruch *Concerto* was made in the early 1970s. While he is obviously on familiar ground, there is no sign of over-familiarity and the lovely slow movement is given a performance of great warmth and humanity. Boult accompanies admirably, and the recording is obviously fuller and more modern than the earlier version with Susskind, even if the solo playing is technically less immaculate and the solo timbre a little spare. On EMI's bargain-basement Seraphim label, this coupling with Mendelssohn remains very attractive.

Scottish fantasy for violin and orchestra, Op. 46.
** Sony Dig. SK 58967 [id.]. Midori, Israel PO, Mehta – SIBELIUS: *Violin concerto.* **

As in the Sibelius coupling, Midori gives a commanding performance, at once pure in tone and warmly expressive, with the live recording allowing rather more bloom. The cleanness of the articulation, not least in heavy double-stopping, makes for a lighter, less overtly romantic approach, less fat in tone than usual, with the lightness bringing a sense of fantasy. The rapt intensity of Midori's very first pianissimo entry in the slow introduction to the first movement is evidence enough of that, and there are many such magic moments. Plainly, we should have more live recordings of Midori, but preferably not from the Mann Auditorium, used here. Midori's playing deserves rather better than this, for although the orchestral contribution is not the last word in subtlety it is perfectly acceptable. But the sound is lacking in bloom and the orchestral climaxes are lacking in transparency so that, however excellent the playing may be, this is no match for its rivals recommended in our main volume.

Bruckner, Anton (1824–96)

SYMPHONIES
The Bruckner symphonies as a set are well served, notably by either Karajan (DG 429 648-2) or Jochum (DG 429 079-2). Both are on nine mid-priced discs and represent outstanding value.

Symphony No. 4 in E flat (Romantic).
*** Decca Dig. 443 327-2 [id.]. San Francisco SO, Herbert Blomstedt.
(BB) **(*) RCA Navigator 74321 17895-2. Leipzig GO, Kurt Masur.
** Teldec/Warner Dig. 4509 93332-2 [id.]. NYPO, Kurt Masur.

Symphony No. 4 in E flat; Overture in G min.
(***) Testament mono/stereo SBT 1050 [id.]. Philh. O, Lovro von Matačić.

Symphony No. 4 in E flat; (i) *Psalm 150.*
(B) *(*) DG Classikon 439 448-2 [id.]. Chicago SO, Barenboim; (i) with Ruth Welting, Chicago
    Symphony Ch.

The new Blomstedt account with the San Francisco orchestra is, as always with this conductor, a performance of the old school. He uses the Haas edition with a few minor adjustments that Bruckner made for the New York première of 1886. The acoustic of the Davies Symphony Hall does not have the opulence or warmth of the Lukaskirche in Dresden where Blomstedt made his 1981 recording with the Staatskapelle (on Denon C37 7126 – see our main volume); nor are the strings as rich and luxuriant. But this is an admirably direct and at times moving performance and is cleanly recorded. Put alongside his earlier account, this 1993 reading may strike some as a bit cool; it certainly does not displace the former, nor the Karajan (DG 439 522-2) or Jochum, but those who cannot find copies of the Denon are unlikely to feel much disappointment with this.

Lovro von Matačić's Philharmonia account of the *Fourth Symphony* dates from 1954, and older readers will recall that it had the misfortune to appear on three LP sides with the fourth blank and, like Knappertsbusch on Decca which came out at the same time, used the Franz Schalk–Karl Loewe edition of 1889. Apart from retouching the orchestration, it involved a cut of some 70 bars in the repeat of the Scherzo and half that number from the finale. Its 3-sides/1-blank format quickly ensured its disappearance from the catalogue. Its Testament transfer is tribute to the fine ears of the Walter Legge/Douglas Larter recording team; every detail in the orchestral texture is transparent and finely delineated and the sound beautifully blended. When it was issued in the USA, the *Overture in G minor* was added two years later, and this was also recorded in stereo. It is state-of-the-art recording for its period, and impressive even now. The performance has both lucidity and majesty, and Dennis Brain's horn-playing is a source of great pleasure.

In RCA's super-bargain Navigator series, Masur with the Leipzig orchestra is obviously a sound guide in Bruckner (no pun intended) and after opening poetically he shapes individual movements spaciously and convincingly and his conception of the overall span is impressive. The horns roister appropriately in the hunting Scherzo and the *Andante* has a gentle concentration and genuine atmosphere. The resonant Leipzig recording has brought some problems with the digital remastering:

there is at times an element of minor coarseness in fortissimos, but at super-bargain price one can make allowances when the interpretation is so instinctively sympathetic.

Kurt Masur's New York later account, recorded at Avery Fisher Hall, comes from 1993 and has all the breadth and much of the finesse one could ask for. Those with keen memories of the Mehta years can be assured that the orchestra now produces a far more cultured and refined sound. Masur's command of the architecture of the piece is undoubtedly impressive and there is no want of feeling. The weakness is perhaps in the slow movement, where concentration flags, certainly among the audience. Very decent recorded sound but not a first recommendation, given the competition.

Although it is linked to a majestic account of *Psalm 150* with the Chicago Chorus and orchestra playing with heart-warming resonance (even if Ruth Welting's contribution is too shallow), this DG Classikon coupling must be passed over. Barenboim's 1972 performance of the symphony offers good analogue sound, and the Chicago orchestra play magnificently, but Barenboim's reading is very mannered and its insights confined to the surface.

Symphonies Nos. 4 in E flat; 9 in D min.
(BB) *** EMI Seraphim CES5 68527-2 (2) [CDEB 68627]. Dresden State O, Jochum.

As a Brucknerian, Eugen Jochum has a special magnetism. Whatever the reservations that may be made on detailed points of style – Jochum believes in a free variation of tempo within a movement – his natural affinity of temperament with the saintly, innocent Austrian gives these massive structures an easy, warm, unforced concentration which brings out their lyricism as well as their architectural grandeur. So it is in these fine performances with the Dresden orchestra, made at the beginning of the 1980s. As in his earlier cycle with the Berlin Philharmonic and Bavarian Radio orchestras, he uses the Nowak edition. In No. 4 the playing of the Dresden orchestra cannot always quite match that of the West German rival of a decade and more earlier, and that earlier Berlin Philharmonic record (DG 427 200-2) has a special claim on the collector for its subtlety and persuasiveness. But the newer version is very fine too – the misty opening with its gentle horn-call is magical – and both this and No. 9 have the advantage of a more modern and somewhat more opulent yet wide-ranging recording, although the remastering has brought extra brightness on top which is not entirely natural. The Dresden account of the last, uncompleted symphony shows the newer combination at its most persuasive, giving an impression of spontaneity such as you would expect in the concert hall; it is a splendid example of Jochum's art, with the Dresden strings sounding full and sonorous. On Seraphim, the two discs are offered together for the cost of a single medium-priced CD.

Symphony No. 5 in B flat.
*** EMI Dig. CDC5 551255 [id.]. LPO, Franz Welser-Möst.

Welser-Möst's account of the *Fifth Symphony* deserves a fairly high placing among the two dozen or so versions that now enrich the catalogue, even if first choice remains with Chailly on Decca (435 819-2). However stormy their relations may or may not have been, the London Philharmonic play well for Franz Welser-Möst on this occasion. They were recorded at the Konzerthaus, Vienna, in late May–early June 1993 before an attentive and silent audience whose presence emerges only at the very end. The applause is deserved. Whether or not one shares Welser-Möst's interpretative convictions in every respect, the performance leaves one in no doubt that he does at least have convictions. There are some potentially disruptive agogic touches, but he succeeds in persuading you that they have some logical motivation. There is nothing bland or 'general purpose' about this reading, and the LPO play with an impressive eloquence and radiance. The wide-ranging dynamics are well captured by the engineers.

Symphony No. 7 in E (original edition).
(M) *(*) Teldec/Warner Dig. 4509 92686-2 [id.]. Frankfurt RSO, Inbal.

Inbal uses the original score, published by Nowak, which omits the famous cymbal strokes which cap the climax of the slow movement. Alas, the tension level here is not high enough to manage without them, and overall this is a sound, well-played reading, given excellent mid-1980s digital recording, which fails to rise to the occasion.

Symphony No. 7 in E.
*** DG Dig. 437 518-2 [id.]. VPO, Abbado.
(M) ** Teldec/Warner Dig. 4509 97437-2 [id.]. NYPO, Kurt Masur.
(BB) *(*) ASV Dig. CDQS 6154 [id.]. Philh. O, Francesco D'Avalos.
(M) (*) Sony mono SMK 47646 [id.]. VPO, George Szell.

It is difficult to fault Claudio Abbado's DG account, which brings playing of great eloquence from the Vienna Philharmonic. The sound has splendid lustre and the architecture is impressively realized.

No one listening to it is likely to feel short-changed – but at the same time one comes away from it with the sense that, despite its tonal finesse and opulent recording, there are depths undiscovered and terrain unexplored. They are to be found in such outstanding versions as those by Karajan, Blomstedt and Haitink (listed in our main volume), all of which are to be preferred. Nevertheless, given its many splendours, the fine playing and recording, it would be curmudgeonly to withhold a third star. But first choice remains with Haitink at mid-price (Philips 434 155-2).

Kurt Masur's account with the New York Philharmonic comes from a live concert, given in September 1991 when their relationship was in the bloom of youth and he was working hard to banish the unrefined sonority that distinguished so many of their recordings with Mehta. They certainly produce a more cultured and better-blended sound than before. His opening is very spacious and expansive, with consequent accelerandi later on. The performance is arguably more characterful than his Leipzig account from the 1970s and has quite a lot going for it – albeit not quite enough to overcome the unpleasing acoustic of Avery Fisher Häll, hardly a Bruckner venue, and certainly not enough to effect a challenge to the front recommendations.

Francesco D'Avalos on a super-bargain ASV issue has the advantage of the Philharmonia Orchestra in his 1988 recording, but otherwise its claims are slender. D'Avalos does not give us a reading of any real character or personality and, given the rival versions now to be had at all price levels, this is really a non-starter.

Szell's VPO account was recorded 'live' by Austrian Radio at the Salzburg Festival in 1968 and, curiously, the first two movements uncharacteristically fail to ignite. The Scherzo is lively enough, but the same, rather studied approach affects the finale, although here the brass are given their head. The note with this CD tells us that Szell's exacting rehearsal methods did not find favour with the Viennese players, and there is certainly little enthusiasm evident here. The mono recording is generally very satisfactory, with only a hint of congestion at climaxes.

Symphony No. 8 in C min.
(M) *** DG 439 969-2 (2) [id.]. BPO, Karajan – WAGNER: *Siegfried idyll.****
*** RCA Dig. 09026 68047-2 (2) [id.]. N. German RSO, Wand.

Karajan's last (digital) version of Bruckner's *Eighth* with the VPO remains unsurpassed (DG 427 611-2), but this earlier (1975) Berlin Philharmonic recording sounds very impressive in the current CD transfer. Moreover it has the advantage, not only of a lower price, but also of a first-class coupling in Wagner's *Siegfried idyll*. The analogue recording of the symphony has fine body and refinement of texture. Sonically it does not perhaps quite match the later, Vienna Philharmonic account but there is very little in it, and no one investing in this noble account is likely to be disappointed. The reading is majestic, massive in scale, yet immaculate in detail. Excellent value.

Günter Wand is as far removed from the jet-set maestro as it is possible to get, and his new recording of the *Eighth Symphony* has a patrician eloquence that is impressive. It is the product of three live concerts from December 1993, and is a straightforward, selfless reading of integrity and vision. All the same, it does not significantly add to his view of the work as exemplified in his earlier cycle. The Hamburg orchestra is a fine body, though it does not quite possess the tonal lustre of the Berlin Philharmonic or Concertgebouw. This comes on two CDs, packaged as one and costing as much. Given its artistic claims and the very truthful sound, it is certainly worth considering.

Symphony No. 8 in C min. (Scherzo; Adagio; Finale only).
(***) Koch Schwann mono/stereo 314482 [id.]. Prussian State O, Karajan.

Who would ever have thought that a Bruckner symphony *without its first movement* would ever score so resounding a success? Karajan's 1944 recording, made at a time when the war was at so crucial a stage, was among those which were spirited off to the then Soviet Union after the Nazi collapse. Technically the sound is quite astonishing – and in the finale, an early example of stereo, is little short of incredible. ('It beggars belief' was one verdict.) Not only is it extraordinary in terms of sound, it is also of exceptional artistic interest. The finale has a breadth and spaciousness, a grandeur and, above all, a sense of repose, that Karajan does not surpass in his later recordings with the Berlin Philharmonic (1957 and 1975) or the Vienna Philharmonic (1987). The slow movement is also more intense, yet natural in feeling, than subsequent performances. It is amazing that such artistic and technical results could have been achieved under wartime conditions.

CHAMBER MUSIC

String quintet in F; Intermezzo in D min.; Rondo in C min.; String quartet in C min.
*** Sony Dig. SK 66251 [id.]. L'Archibudelli.

String quintet in F; Intermezzo for string quintet.
(*) Hyp. Dig. CDA 66704 [id.]. Raphael Ens. – R. STRAUSS: *Capriccio: Sextet.* *
**(*) CRD Dig. CRD 3456 [id.]. Alberni Qt.

Sony's newest version of the beautiful Bruckner *String quintet* as played by L'Archibudelli has much going for it. Unlike the Decca version by the VPO Quintet, listed in our main volume (which is coupled with Schmidt), it includes three more Bruckner works. However, its appeal rests not so much in terms of the interest of the early and uncharacteristic *String quartet in C minor*, a student work lasting over twenty minutes to which few are likely to return, but in the care these players exercise over matters of phrasing and dynamics. As usual (as is the case with the symphonies) there is no escape from editions here: L'Archibudelli give us the later, longer version which Novak edited, whereas rivals give us the shorter coda. They use gut strings, which initially give the impression of being under-projected – or would do, were it not for the careful dynamic perspective.

The Raphael Ensemble, coupling their performance with the *Intermezzo in D minor* and the opening *Sextet* from Strauss's *Capriccio*, are more full-blooded, more obviously ardent and they have the benefit of rich recorded sound. Theirs is an eloquent account which, coming after the Sony, could seem over-stated.

The Alberni version comes from the early 1980s without any additional fill-up. It is nicely played without affectation and, taken in isolation, provides considerable musical satisfaction. However, where the above rivals are to be found, they should probably take precedence.

VOCAL MUSIC

Masses Nos. (i) *1 in D min.* (for soloists, chorus and orchestra); *2 in E min.* (for 8-part chorus and wind ensemble); (ii) *3 in F min.* (for soloists, chorus and orchestra).
⊛ (M) *** DG 447 409-2 (2) [id.]. (i) Mathis, Schiml, Ochman, Ridderbusch; (ii) Stader, Hellman, Haefliger, Borg; Bav. R. Ch. & O, Jochum.

Bruckner composed his three *Masses* between 1864 and 1868, although all three works were revised two decades later. Each contains magnificent music; Eugen Jochum is surely an ideal interpreter, finding their mystery as well as their eloquence, breadth and humanity. The *Kyrie* of the *E minor* swelling out gloriously from its gentle opening is quite breathtaking, while the fervour of the passionate *F minor* work is extraordinarily compelling, with all the intensity and drive of an inspirational live performance. But throughout all three works the scale and drama of Bruckner's inspiration are fully conveyed. In these outstanding new transfers, the analogue recordings from the early 1970s are given remarkable vividness and presence, while the warm atmosphere is fully retained. A remarkable achievement and a splendid choice for DG's 'Original' series of Legendary Recordings.

Bull, John (1562/3?–1628)

Keyboard music: *Canon in subdiapente, two parts in one with a running basse ad placitum; Dr Bull's my-selfe; Dutch dance; Fantasias X & XII; Fantastic pavan and galiarda; Germain's alman; In nomine IX & XII; The King's hunt; The Queen Elizabeth's chromatic pavan and galliard.*
(M) **(*) Teldec/Warner Dig. 4509 95532-2. Bob van Asperen (harpsichord).

John Bull is handsomely pictured in the booklet which accompanies this most rewarding collection; his features are aristocratic, with an almost Spanish character to the eyes, the gaze slightly saturnine but revealing nothing. His brief self-descriptive piece, robust and extrovert, also tells us nothing. He travelled a great deal 'without licence', and finally left the country for good, working as organist in Antwerp Cathedral, where he was buried, so the enigma of his life-style remains unsolved. Apart from the justly famous, rhythmically vigorous *King's hunt*, most of his music is unfamiliar compared to that of his contemporaries, yet he wrote for the keyboard expressively and with intellectual command (witness the *In Nomine IX* and the impressive *Canon*) and many of his pieces demand great bravura from their exponents. (Thomas Tomkins described his keyboard writing as 'for the hand' as distinct from Byrd's which was 'for substance'.) Yet Bull could write with simple charm, as in the two vignettes in the treble clef, *Germain's alman* and the engaging *Dutch dance*. The performances here are distinguished in every way, as we expect from Bob van Asperen; but his 1624 Ruckers harpsichord is too closely observed and made to sound metallic. Nevertheless, at a low volume setting, fully acceptable results can be achieved.

Caldara, Antonio (c. 1670–1736)

Crucifixus.
(B) *** Decca Double 443 868-2 (2) [id.]. Palmer, Langridge, Esswood, Keyte, St John's College,
   Cambridge, Ch., Philomusica, Guest – BONONCINI: *Stabat Mater* ***; PERGOLESI: *Magnificat in
   C; Stabat Mater* **(*); D. SCARLATTI: *Stabat Mater;* A. SCARLATTI: *Domine, refugium factus es
   nobis; O magnum mysterium;* LOTTI: *Crucifixus.* ***

Antonio Caldara settled in Vienna and established an enviable reputation as a master of opera – he
composed nearly a hundred! The *Crucifixus* is an elaborate sixteen-part setting of great eloquence,
texturally rich and concentrated into a few seconds short of five minutes. It follows on naturally after
Bononcini's beautiful *Stabat Mater*. The treble lines have some moments of insecurity but otherwise
the performance is impressive and the (originally Argo) recording first class.

Campra, André (1660–1744)

Idoménée (opera): highlights.
*** HM Dig. HMC 901506 [id.] (from complete set with Delétré, Piau, Zanetti, Fouchécourt,
   Boyer, Les Arts Florissants, Christie).

Here is some 70 minutes, with items well balanced to include the Overture, a brief reminder of the
Prologue and excerpts from all five Acts. Christie and his Arts Florissants present the music with a
taut feeling for its dramatic qualities. The complete work runs to three CDs, and this makes a very
useful sampler. A full translation is provided.

Canning, Thomas (born 1911)

Fantasy on a hymn tune by Justin Morgan (for double string quartet and string orchestra).
*** Everest EVC 9004 [id.]. Houston SO, Stokowski – R. STRAUSS: *Don Juan* etc. ***

The Pennsylvanian composer, Thomas Canning, has clearly modelled his *Fantasy* on the Vaughan
Williams *Tallis fantasia*. Although the contrast with the secondary string group is less ethereal, in
Stokowski's hands the work reaches a thrilling climax, and this fine if derivative piece is well worth
having on disc when the recording is so rich and well focused. This CD is offered at slightly under
premium price.

Cardoso, Frei Manuel (c. 1566–1650)

Missa pro defunctis.
(BB) *** Naxos Dig. 8.550682 [id.]. Oxford Schola Cantorum, Jeremy Summerly – LOBO: *Missa pro
   defunctis.* ***

Cardoso's *Missa pro defunctis* is not as dramatic in its contrasts as the coupled setting of Duarte
Lôbo, but its polyphony is characteristically long-breathed and expressively powerful. As with the
Lôbo performance, a solo treble makes a brief but effective introduction for each movement, a device
which works very touchingly. Here it is the *Sanctus* that one especially remembers as being gloriously
rich in expressive feeling, although the *Communio* closes the work with rapt intensity. The performance
by Jeremy Summerly and his Oxford Schola Cantorun is beautifully paced and the calibre of the
singing itself is very impressive indeed, as is the Naxos recording.

Carulli, Ferdinando (1770–1841)

Guitar concerto in A.
(M) **(*) DG 439 984-2 [id.]. Siegfried Behrend, I Musici – GIULIANI: *Concerto in A* ***; VIVALDI:
   Guitar concertos **(*).

The Italian virtuoso Ferdinando Carulli made his reputation in Paris, where this innocent post-
Mozartian one-movement piece was written. It is elegantly played by Behrend and I Musici and
immaculately recorded. A touch more vitality would have been welcome, but this is enjoyable
enough.

Cavalli, Francesco (1602–76)

La Calisto (complete).
**(*) HM Dig. HMC 901515/17 (3) [id.]. Bayo, Lippi, Keenlyside, Pushee, Mantovani, Concerto Vocale, René Jacobs.

This opera brought the name of Cavalli to the fore back in the 1970s, when at Glyndebourne (and, later, on disc) Raymond Leppard prepared a much-modified edition for a production by Sir Peter Hall that was both witty and magical. Purists objected, but any more authentic realization is likely to bring its disappointments, not least for the lack of the sensuously beautiful arias that Leppard borrowed from other Cavalli operas. Jacobs directs a lively account, recorded in vivid, immediate sound, readily sustaining the extra length of the original score (2 hours 45 minutes), helped by some characterful, generally well-sung solo performances. In the title-role Maria Bayo has a sweet and fresh, very girlish-sounding soprano, and Alessandra Mantovani as Diana sings warmly, though with some unsteadiness. The disappointment, remembering the Leppard reading with Dame Janet Baker, is that when Jove is disguised as Diana, the part is sung by the weighty baritone, Marcello Lippi, taking the role of Jove, in a piping falsetto. Graham Pushee, a reliable but hooty counter-tenor, takes the role of Endimione and, as at Glyndebourne, the comic role of the nymph, Linfea, is taken by a male singer, Gilles Ragon, capable but nowhere near as characterful as Hugues Cuénod at Glyndebourne. However inauthentic the Leppard version is, it conveys more intense enjoyment than this and, though the vigour and variety of Cavalli's inspiration are brought out well by Jacobs and his team, the Decca mid-priced reissue is the one to go for (436 216-2 – see our main volume).

L'Ormindo (opera): complete (ed. Raymond Leppard).
(M) *** Decca 444 529-2 (2) [id.]. Wakefield, Howells, Runge, Garcisanz, Berbié, Cuénod, Van Bork, F. Davis, Alister, Van Allan, LPO, Leppard.

We owe it above all to Raymond Leppard that the name of Francesco Cavalli has become famous again. He discovered the long-forgotten score of this fascinating opera and subjected it to his own magical Leppardization process, to produce one of the most enchanting of Glyndebourne entertainments. The gaiety of Glyndebourne is superbly caught, for wisely Decca (or, rather, Argo) opted to record the work on the editor's home ground in Sussex, using the Organ Room for studio instead of the excessively dry acoustic of the old opera house. With modern instruments in the orchestra, the sounds are nothing short of luscious, often almost Straussian in their opulence, and Leppard's array of continuo instruments constantly charms the ear. Anne Howells makes a fine Erisbe, so pure-sounding one scarcely credits the blatant immorality of the story. Indeed the whole point is that one should not question it but accept it as a product of the permissive society of 1650. Excellent contributions from the whole team, with special mention required for the veteran Hugues Cuénod in the 'drag' part of the maid, Erice. The gloriously full recorded quality has not been lost in the CD transfer.

Chabrier, Emmanuel (1841–94)

Bourrée fantasque; España (rhapsody); *Gwendoline overture; Marche joyeuse; Le Roi malgré lui: Danse slave. Suite pastorale.*
(M) *** Erato/Warner Dig. 4509 96730-2 [id.]. Fr. Nat. PO, Armin Jordan.

A sparkling collection which (originally) provided Chabrier's CD début. The playing is admirably spirited, even boisterous in the *Marche joyeuse*, and the melodramatic *Gwendoline overture* is relished with proper gusto. Perhaps Paray's account of the engaging *Suite pastorale* (on Mercury 434 303-2) is that bit more distinctive, but here the tempo of the third movement, *Sous bois*, is less controversial. *España* has infectious élan, yet rhythms are nicely relaxed so that the gaiety is never forced. The recording is generally first class, with the body and range especially telling.

PIANO MUSIC

(i) Piano music, four hands: *Cortège burlesque; Joyeuse marche; Souvenirs de Munich (Quadrille* on themes from Wagner's *Tristan und Isolde*); *3 Valses romantiques.* (Piano): *Air de ballet; Bourrée fantasque; Capriccio* (finished by Maurice le Boucher); *Habañera; Impromptu; Marche des Cipayes; Petite valse; 5 Pièces (Ballabile; Feuillet d'album; Aubade; Caprice; Ronde champêtre); 10 Pièces pittoresques; Souvenirs de Brunehaut (Grand valse); Suite de valses.*
(M) **(*) Erato/Warner 4509 95309-2 (2) [id.]. Pierre Barbizet; (i) with Jean Hubeau.

(B) ** Vox Box 116019-2 (2) [CDX 5108] (without *Petite valse; Souvenirs de Brunehaut*). Rena
  Kyriakou; (i) with Walter Klien.

Chabrier's piano music is little known outside France and so these two surveys are especially
valuable. The most striking solo work is the set of ten *Pièces pittoresques*: these are the source of
Chabrier's charming orchestral *Suite pastorale*. Like much twentieth-century French piano music, the
medium seems interchangeable without too much loss either way. Some of the other music is trivial, if
engaging (the *Air de ballet*, for instance), but the music for piano, four hands, is particularly enticing.
The delectable Gallic joke of doing quadrilles on themes from Wagner's *Tristan* could be what first
attracts the new listener to this repertoire, and Barbizet recorded for the first time another Wagner
joke, an elaborate waltz called *Souvenirs de Brunehaut* (Brünnhilde). Vigorous, jolly music makes up a
high proportion of this collection and Barbizet in his tough, brightly rhythmic style is excellently
suited, recorded in clear, vivid sound with the piano close and real.

   The alternative recording on Vox is not so closely balanced, and many may prefer this, although
the sound is also more reverberant so the focus is less clear, especially in the duet music. Rena
Kyriakou is spontaneous enough (some may find her more so than Barbizet) but she is also a highly
impulsive player. There is temperament in excess, and she tends to get carried away by the music
instead of staying in firm rhythmic control. Nevertheless she uses a wide range of dynamic, and some
of the vignettes are beguilingly done, the sultry *Habañera*, for instance. In the music for four hands
she is joined by Walter Klien (although he is not credited) and the playing has splendid panache,
especially in the *Cortège burlesque* and of course the highly disrespectful *Souvenirs de Munich*. Both
sets have extensive notes. Clearly the Erato issue is first choice, but the Vox Box may tempt some
readers by its very inexpensiveness and should not be written off, though music of this kind needs
poise. Chabrier can be a poet too, and that point is not missed by Miss Kyriakou; perhaps the only
warning to give is that neither collection should be played at one sitting.

Music for piano duet: *Air de ballet; Cortège burlesque; Prélude et marche française; Souvenirs de
Munich; Suite des valses*. Music for 2 pianos: *España; 3 Valses romantiques*.
  (BB) ** Naxos Dig. 8.550380 [id.]. Georges Rabol, Sylvie Dugas.

The works for two pianos come off with much more flair than the solo items in the Naxos series, and
the acoustic is more open: indeed the recording is more than satisfactory. The programme opens with
España, which has plenty of gusto (and distinct touches of orchestral colouring) while the *Marche
française* (better known as the *Marche joyeuse*) is also ebullient. The second of the *Trois valses
romantiques* displays real charm, while the *Cortège burlesque* and *Souvenirs de Munich* are lively and
spirited. The exaggerated parody rubato in the *Air de ballet* is a minus point, and *Suite des valses* is
also rhythmically self-conscious, but not unredeemably so.

*Aubade; Capriccio; Impromptu in C; Julia (valse), Op. 1; Marche des Cipayes; Ronde champêtre;
Souvenir de Brunehaut (valse)*.
  (BB) * Naxos Dig. 8. 553010 [id.]. Georges Rabol.
*Ballabile; Bourrée fantasque; Caprice; Feuillet d'album; Habañera; Petite valse; 10 Pièces
  pittoresques*.
  (BB) * Naxos Dig. 8.553009 [id.]. Georges Rabol.

Georges Rabol's solo performances are just about acceptable at super-bargain price but they lack the
imaginative touches that make this music spring to life, although some of the shorter pieces are
modestly effective. But the *Pièces pittoresques* are disappointing. Rabol makes comparatively little of
Sous-bois and, although the *Danse villegeoise* is cleanly articulated, he almost gabbles the closing
Scherzo-waltz. On the second disc, the *Marche des Cipayes* has character, but the rubato in the *Julia
waltz* is unspontaneous and elsewhere the impulsive manner finds little charm in the music, with the
Ronde champêtre hardly sparkling as its name might suggest, and the *Souvenir de Brunehaut* at times
rather heavy going. The piano tone is clear and faithful but the acoustic is unflatteringly dry and
studio-ish.

Aubade; Ballabile; Caprice; Feuillet d'album; Impromptu; Pièces pittoresques; Ronde champêtre; (i) *3
Valses romantiques*.
*** Unicorn-Kanchana DKPCD 9158 [id.]. Kathryn Stott, (i) with Elizabeth Burley.

It is good to see Chabrier's piano music receiving the attention of the record companies. In its day it
exerted quite an influence over Ravel, Debussy, Poulenc and others. While some readers will be
drawn to the complete surveys listed above, for those wanting a representative single-CD selection,
Kathryn Stott provides the ideal answer. She plays this long-neglected but rewarding repertoire with
intelligence, wit and elegance. Perhaps the very last ounce of charm is missing, but there is enough of

it to provide delight. She is moreover recorded with great presence and fidelity; the piano-sound is very alive, natural and fresh.

OPERA

Briseis (complete).
⊛ *** Hyp. Dig. CDA 66803 [id.]. Rodgers, Padmore, Keenlyside, Harries, George, BBC Scottish SO, Jean-Yves Ossonce.

Starting with a ripely seductive sailors' chorus, few operas are as sensuous as *Briseis*, subtitled 'The Lovers of Corinth'. Chabrier, with his flair for colour in vocal and instrumental sound, completed the long first Act of this tale of conflict between early Christianity and pagan indulgence, then hit a block. The piece remained unfinished when he died, but Richard Strauss, no less, conducted the first staging, and it plainly influenced him when later he was writing *Salome*, built on a similar conflict. This passionate performance was recorded live at the 1994 Edinburgh Festival, the first-ever hearing in Britain. On disc it matters little that this is a torso. The writing is not just sensuous but urgent, a warm bath of sound that is also exhilarating. Casting is near ideal, with Joan Rodgers in the title-role rich and distinctive, and with Mark Padmore as the sailor, Hylas, equally warm, producing heady, clear tenor tone. Symbolizing the forces of Christian good, Simon Keenlyside as the Catechist and Kathryn Harries as the mother of Briseis, cured through faith, both sing with character and apt resonance. Full, atmospheric sound.

Chadwick, George (1854–1931)

Symphony No. 2 in B flat; Symphonic sketches.
*** Chan. Dig. CHAN 9334 [id.]. Detroit SO, Neeme Järvi.

We had a warm welcome for the Detroit version of Chadwick's *Third Symphony* (CHAN 9253 – see our main volume) and find this newcomer equally fresh and appealing. It dates from the early 1880s, though its delightful Scherzo was premièred two years ahead of the rest of the work. When this was first heard, it had to be encored, which is hardly surprising. It has an engaging, cheeky quality (one contemporary review in the *Boston Transcript* wrote that 'it positively winks at you'). Generally speaking, Chadwick's music inhabits much the same world as Dvořák or Svendsen. The *Symphonic sketches* are later, occupying the composer over the best part of a decade (1895–1904). Neither work is a masterpiece but both are pleasing, and the Detroit orchestra under Neeme Järvi make out a very persuasive case for it. This supersedes the 1985 account from the Albany Orchestra listed in our main volume.

Chaminade, Cécile (1857–1944)

Piano trio No. 1 in G min., Op. 11.
(*) Dorian Dig. DOR 90187 [id.]. Rembrandt Trio – RAVEL: *Piano trio;* SAINT-SAENS: *Piano trio No. 1.* (*)

This slight music needs much stronger advocacy if its charms are to have their full effect. In the Rembrandt Trio the pianist Valerie Tryon is the dominant partner but the playing of Gérard Kantarjian and Coenraad Bloemendal is not characterized strongly enough and they sound a little too colourless by her side.

Charpentier, Marc-Antoine (1634–1704)

9 Leçons de ténèbres, H.120–125; H.135–137.
(M) **(*) Erato/Warner Dig. 4509 96376-2 (2) [id.]. Widmer, Verschaeve, Crook, Caals, De
    Meulenaere, Ruyl, Musica Polyphonica, Louis Devos.

The first six *Leçons de ténèbres* for solo voices included here (H.120–125) come from Volume XXIII and were probably written in 1680 for the Abbaye-aux-Bois; the remainder are for three voices and, though not unrelated to the earlier ones, are later still. Neither set duplicates the repertoire already covered in our main volume by the Harmonia Mundi and Virgin issues; but the performances here, although sensitive and lyrically eloquent, lack something in vitality. In that respect the solo works are rather more positive than those for three voices. The stylish instrumental accompaniments using original instruments are suitably pastel-shaded and the recording is excellent; but one feels that a rather stronger characterization would have made these performances even more appealing.

Leçons de ténèbres for Wednesday in Holy Week.
(M) *** Virgin/EMI VC5 45107-2 [id.]. Catherine Greuillet, Caroline Pelon, Gérard Lesne, Christopher Purves, Il Seminario Musicale.

Leçons de ténèbres for Maundy Thursday.
(M) *** Virgin/EMI VC5 45075-2 [id.]. Sandrine Piau, Gérard Lesne, Ian Honeyman, Peter Harvey, Il Seminario Musicale.

This continuing series of Charpentier's *Leçons de Ténèbres* from Il Seminario Musicale offers music of great variety and beauty, featuring soloists who are naturally attuned to this repertoire. The accompaniment is provided by a varied instrumental group, including recorders, treble and bass viols, with a continuo of theorbo, bass viol and organ, and their use is consistently imaginative and refreshing to the ear. The Psalms are sung by a small choral group. The effect is warm yet refined and the lyrical melancholy of much of this music is quite haunting. It is difficult to imagine these inspired and highly expressive settings being presented more persuasively or better balanced, and the acoustic of L'Abbaye Royale de Fontevraud is ideal for the music. The documentation is first class. Charpentier's settings were enormously admired in his own time, and rightly so. No collection is complete without at least one of these CDs.

Messe pour les Trépassés, H.2; Dies irae, H.12; Motet pour les Trépassés, H.311.
(M) **(*) Erato/Warner 4509 92738-2 [id.]. Rosat, Jennifer Smith, Schaer, Elwes, Serafim, Huttenlochwer, Brodard, Gulbenkian Foundation Ch. & O, Lisbon, Corboz.

The *Messe pour les Trépassés* (Mass for All Souls' Day) is scored for large forces: soloists, double-chorus and orchestra. In this account a *Dies irae* and a motet are inserted into its course. They were all recorded in 1972 and, for ears attuned to period-instrument performances, will sound distinctly old-fashioned. Readers who welcome the opportunity to hear this music on modern instruments, however, will find much to reward them. Corboz draws some lively singing from both soloists and choir, and the generous acoustic in which the recording was made serves to give a pleasing effect. The music itself dates from the 1670s, not long after Charpentier's return from Italy, and is both powerful and eloquent. The recorded sound, if not up to the best modern standards, is eminently acceptable.

Médée (complete).
*** Erato/Warner Dig. 4509 96558-2 (3) [id.]. Hunt, Padmore, Delétré, Zanetti, Salzmann, Les Arts Florissants, William Christie.

Barely ten years after making his prize-winning recording of this rare opera for Harmonia Mundi, Christie, again with his group, Les Arts Florissants, has recorded it again. He explained in a note that ten years of experience actually staging this and other operas had modified his view. The earlier set was 'a brave beginning' but, with experience, the orchestra had learnt above all to respond in a livelier way. He was also glad to be able to open out the small cuts that were made before so as to fit the LP format. Christie's claims are readily borne out in the finished performance, which easily surpasses the previous one in its extra brightness and vigour, with consistently crisper and more alert ensembles, often at brisker speeds, with the drama more clearly established. With a libretto by Thomas Corneille, younger brother of the celebrated dramatist, Pierre, this is a powerful and moving piece, readily matching the finest of the exploratory operas of Charpentier's predecessor, Lully.

The casting is first rate, with Lorraine Hunt outstanding in the tragic title-role. Her soprano has satisfying weight and richness, as well as the purity and precision needed in such classical opera; and Mark Padmore's clear, high tenor copes superbly with the role of Jason, with no strain and with cleanly enunciated diction and sharp concern for word-meaning. The others follow Christie's pattern of choosing cleanly focused voices, even if the tone is occasionally gritty.

Chopin, Frédéric (1810–49)

Piano concertos Nos. (i) 1 in E min., Op. 11; (ii) 2 in F min., Op. 21.
*** Conifer Dig. 76505 51247-2 [id.]. Martino Tirimo, Philh. O, Fedor Glushchenko.
(BB) *** RCA Navigator 74321 17892-2. Emanuel Ax, Phd. O, Ormandy.
(M) **(*) Sony Analogue/Dig. SMK 64241 [id.]. (i) Hiroko Nakamura, LSO, Fistoulari; (ii) Cécile Licad, LPO, Previn.
** Collins Dig. 3015-2 [id.]. Fou Ts'song, Sinfonia Varviso, Muhai Tang.
(BB) *(*) ASV Dig. CDQS 6141 [id.]. Tamás Vásáry, N. Sinfonia O.

Among the newer couplings of the two Chopin *Concertos*, Martino Tirimo's Conifer record is in a class of its own, and these performances are worthy to rank alongside those of Perahia (Sony SK 44922) and Zimerman (DG 415 970-2). Poetic feeling is paramount: Tirimo's readings often bring exquisite delicacy and they are totally without barnstorming, yet there is spontaneity in every bar. The gentle presentation of the secondary theme by the pianist in the *F minor Concerto* is a moment of magic, and both slow movements bring playing where one has an impression of musing reverie. In outer movements passage-work is scintillatingly alive, and both finales have a beguiling rhythmic lift. There is strong orchestral support and, after a bold tutti from Glushenko, Tirimo's answer is always spirited. He sets off into the last movement of the *E minor* with a particularly delightful lilt, where in the *F minor* there is an engaging hint of initial reticence before the sparkling dance rhythms assert themselves.

Emanuel Ax offers fine performances of both concertos at super-bargain price. His account of the *F minor* has admirable taste and finesse, though not quite the sense of character of his finest full-priced rivals – Rubinstein for instance. Nevertheless this is genuinely poetic playing and the finale with its light, chimerical touch is particularly pleasing. This is a digital recording and not quite top-drawer in the matter of transparency. Yet it provides a fuller and more flattering sound for the Philadelphia Orchestra than on many of their recent records. Ormandy is a highly sensitive accompanist in both works and in the analogue *E minor* (made two years earlier, in 1978) these artists are well served by the engineers and the performance is fresh and full of character. Overall there is a great deal to admire here and this Navigator reissue, with its frontispiece map to show the source of the music, is well worth its modest price.

The Sony coupling is also an attractive proposition at mid-price. Fistoulari never lets one down and, though he provides a comparatively gentle tutti in the first movement of No. 1, he sets the scene for a pleasingly delicate and poetic contribution from his young Japanese soloist, while there is plenty of rhythmic life in the finale. Cécile Licad gives a very impressive account of the *F minor Concerto*: she has the appropriate fire and delicacy. Comparisons with the most distinguished versions are not to her disadvantage; moreover her sense of style earned her the imprimatur of the International Chopin Competition in Warsaw, who chose this for their concerto record prize in 1985. She has excellent support from the LPO under Previn and the benefit of very natural recording.

Fou Ts'ong is also an estimable Chopin player and his contribution to the Collins coupling has no want of poetry, particularly in the slow movement of the *F minor*, where he plays very beautifully. However, the very relaxed style of the interpretations here does not aid the feeling of spontaneity, particularly in the passage-work, and this is not a front runner in a very competitive field.

Vásáry's coupling on ASV, in which he not only plays but directs the Northern Sinfonia from the keyboard, has the advantage of full and well-balanced sound but, while the solo playing has much delicacy and refinement, neither concerto is as boldly characterized or as full of ardour and flair as were his earlier accounts for DG. The *F minor* comes off well enough, but the *E minor* (which understandably is placed second on the CD) does not spring so readily to life, and the orchestral contribution is pale beside that of the Berlin Philharmonic on his earlier record.

Cziffra Edition, Volume 2: (i) *Piano concerto No. 1 in E min., Op. 11. Ballade No. 4 in F min., Op. 52; Etudes: in E; in A flat, Op. 10/3 & 10; in A flat & F min., Op. 25/1–2; Impromptu No. 1 in A flat, Op. 29; Nocturne No. 2 in E flat, Op. 9/2; Polonaise in A (Military), Op. 40/1.*
(M) ** EMI CDM5 65251-2 [id.]. György Cziffra; (i) O de Paris, György Cziffra, Jr.

(i) *Piano concerto No. 1 in E min. Barcarolle in F sharp, Op. 60; Preludes, Op. 28/1, 3, 6, 10, 15–17, 20–21 & 24; Scherzo No. 3 in C sharp min., Op. 39.*
(B) **(*) DG 439 459-2 [id.]. Martha Argerich; (i) LSO, Abbado.

Martha Argerich's recording dates from 1968 and helped to establish her international reputation. The distinction of this partnership is immediately apparent in the opening orchestral ritornello with Abbado's flexible approach. Argerich follows his lead and her affectionate phrasing provides some lovely playing, especially in the slow movement. Perhaps in the passage-work she is sometimes rather too intense, but this is far preferable to the rambling style we are sometimes offered. The recording was originally of high quality, and it sounds remarkably fresh in its CD format. Definition is still good, and the ambient warmth of the analogue recording is preserved, although there is very slight recession of the image in pianissimo passages. There is very little background noise. For the Classikon reissue a miscellaneous programme of encores has been added, showing well the impulsive qualities of her solo playing; however, the offering of just a (well-chosen) selection of the *Préludes* may not suit collectors who would prefer to invest in a complete set.

Cziffra's account of the Chopin *E minor Concerto* has plenty of life, helped by a robust orchestral contribution from his son, who yet opens the central *Romance* with some delicacy. There are moments of genuine poetry, and the first movement's secondary theme is coaxed seductively. But the reading as a whole is characteristically extrovert. The finale has plenty of lift and rhythmic impetus, passage-work never drags and one cannot but admire the soloist's glittering dexterity. But the solo performances are less attractive and, despite much deft articulation, too often sound calculated. Cziffra creates a powerful metallic clatter at his climax of the famous *E major Etude*, Op. 10/3; the performance of the famous *Military Polonaise* is somewhat mannered, and the equally familiar *Nocturne in E flat* which ends the programme is disappointingly unspontaneous. Fair recording, using the Paris Salle Wagram. The concerto dates from 1968 and the rest from over the next decade.

(i) *Piano concerto No. 2 in F min., Op. 21. Mazurkas Nos. 5 in B flat; 7 in F min., Op. 7/1 & 3; 15 in C; 17 in B flat min., Op. 24/2 & 4; 20 in D flat; 21 in C sharp min., Op. 30/3–4; 22 in G sharp min.; 23 in D; 25 in B min., Op. 33/1, 2 & 4; 27 in E min., Op. 41/2; 32 in C sharp min., Op. 50/3; 41 in C sharp min., Op. 63/3; 45 in A min., Op. 67/4; 47 in A min.; 49 in F min., Op. 68/2 & 4; Piano sonata No. 3 in B min., Op. 58; Waltzes Nos. 1–14.*

(b) **(*) EMI CZS5 68226-2 (2). Witold Malcuzynski; (i) with LSO, Walter Susskind.

Malcuzynski had a fairly brief recording career with EMI in the early days of stereo, and the present recordings were made between 1959 and 1961. They project his musical personality with great intensity. This is especially apparent in his brilliant and highly individual collection of the fourteen *Waltzes* (a favourite of im's), which glitter and sparkle whenever they should – and sometimes when they should not. Yet the crisp, assured playing is undeniably attractive, especially in the more extrovert numbers, thrown off with splendid panache, every moment of rubato skilfully calculated to give the maximum degree of polish and precision. In the quieter, more reflective waltzes the pianist does not penetrate too deeply below the surface but he is never dull, and there is no doubt that these performances show Malcuzynski's art to good advantage, especially as the recording has such immediacy. But his finest EMI LP was his collection of *Mazurkas*, brilliantly successful in every way. The playing is again immensely polished, yet finds an infinite range of mood and expression in a very well-chosen programme. The personality of the artist comes out as intensely as ever and the assurance of the readings is very persuasive. The excellent, vivid recording was perhaps the best he ever received. The performance of the *B minor Sonata* is undoubtedly commanding, mannered perhaps, sometimes glittering, and certainly not insensitive. But there is a dimension missing compared with Rubinstein. The concerto is a disappointment. Again Malcuzynski offers confident, extrovert playing which inevitably provides much excitement, but this is altogether too glittering to be an ideal account of Chopin's delicate inspiration. It is an object lesson to compare Malcuzynski in the second subject of the first movement with Rubinstein, for the older's maestro's rubato is infinitely subtler. However, it would be wrong to suggest that Malcuzynski's *Larghetto* lacks poetic feeling, and the finale has much dash and fire. The LSO under Susskind provide good support and the recording is bold, rather loud and rather over-projected to suit the brilliant music-making. For all one's reservations, there is nothing pallid or routine about this Chopin playing, and this inexpensive 'Profile' is a thoroughly worthwhile reissue and worth seeking out before it disappears back into the EMI vaults.

Ballades Nos. 1–4; Etudes: in E; C sharp min., Op. 10/3–4; Mazurkas: in F min., Op. 7/4; in A min., Op. 17/4; in D, Op. 33/2; Nocturne in F, Op. 15/1; Waltzes: in E flat (Grand valse brillante), Op. 18; in A flat, Op. 42.
⊕ *** Sony Dig. SK 64399 [id.]. Murray Perahia.

Murray Perahia was absent from the concert platform for much of 1992/3, and this is his first record for some time. Chopin playing does not come better than this, and this set of the *Ballades* is unlikely to be surpassed. One has to go back to Hofmann, recorded in 1937, to find a more searching or poetic account of the *G minor Ballade*, and the *Waltzes* not only prompt thoughts to turn to the classic post-war Lipatti set, but comparison does not find Perahia less poetic. Moreover the Sony engineers do him justice. In every respect a masterly recital that is in a class of its own and which readers should not miss.

Ballades Nos. 1 in G min., Op. 23; 2 in F, Op. 38; 3 in A flat, Op. 47; 4 in F min., Op. 52. Grande Polonaise Brillante, Op. 22; Polonaise fantaisie, Op. 61.
** Chan. Dig. CHAN 9353 [id.]. Míceál O'Rourke.

As earlier releases have shown, Míceál O'Rourke, impressive in the music of John Field, is a sensitive and intelligent player. But he proves disappointing in Chopin. The measured opening of the *G minor Ballade* sounds unspontaneous, and his rubato does not convince; a similar thoughtfulness at the beginnings of the other works brings a feeling of poetic lethargy. There is evidence of real artistry, but the overall impression is one of disappointment despite the excellence of the Chandos sound.

Ballades Nos. 1–2; Scherzi Nos. 1–4; Waltzes Nos. 1–19.
(M) *(**) Teldec/Warner Dig.4509 95499-2 (2) [id.]. Cyprien Katsaris.

Cyprien Katsaris is a player with an impressive technique and considerable power. He is a fiery interpreter of Chopin but displays no lack of poetic feeling in the *Ballades* and *Scherzi*. The *B minor Scherzo* is very brilliant indeed, although the virtuosity never distracts attention away from composer to interpreter. Unlike Gilels or Perahia, here one is quite aware that the piano has hammers! The LP of the performances of the *Ballades* and *Scherzi* was awarded a prize in the 1985 Warsaw Chopin competition as 'the finest recital of the last five years' (though one does not know what other Western recordings were available to the jury). As piano playing it is certainly very good, at times even distinguished, but the recording as such leaves much to be desired. The acoustic is not really big enough and the disc is best heard at not too high a volume level. At times one has the feeling that the attention of a tuner might not have come amiss. Moreover, for the reissue as a Double this CD is paired with a disc of the *Waltzes*, and here the playing, although brilliant, is much less sympathetic. There are moments of poetry, of course, but the aristocratic quality that a Zimerman, Ashkenazy or Lipatti brings to this repertoire is missing, and again the sound does not compare with the best piano recording from Philips or Decca.

Barcarolle in F sharp, Op. 60; Berceuse in D flat, Op. 57; Fantaisie in F min., Op. 49; Nocturne No. 4 in F, Op. 15/1; Polonaise No. 4 in C min., Op. 40/2; Sonata No. 3 in B min., Op. 58.
(B) **(*) Carlton Dig. PCD 2008 [id.]. John Ogdon.

John Ogdon's collection presents fresh and thoughtful performances, not as electrifying as some he recorded earlier in his career but often bold and full of individual insights. His speeds for the slower pieces are at times daringly extreme, but he sustains them well and the delicacy of much that he does is a delight, set in contrast to his natural strength in bravura. Bright, clear, realistic recording, giving the piano a powerful presence.

Etudes, Op. 10/1–12; Op. 15/1–12.
(M) *(**) Saga EC 3351-2 [id.]. Vladimir Ashkenazy.

Ashkenazy's set first appeared in the early 1960s on the Chant du Monde label. The playing is unfailingly rewarding and demonstrates a prodigious virtuosity completely at the service of the composer, and the poetic feeling is never in doubt. The sound is perfectly acceptable if not distinguished, and this pianist's admirers will be glad to discover Ashkenazy's potential before he was signed by Decca. It is a pity that this Saga reissue is not at bargain price, when the recommendation could have been less qualified. The Decca set is far preferable (414 127-2) and well worth its extra cost.

Mazurkas Nos.1–53, Opp. 6–7; 17; 24; 30; 33; 41; 50; 56; 59; 63; 67–8 & Op. posth.; Berceuse, Op. 57; Impromptus Nos. 1–3; Fantaisie-impromptu, Op. 66.
(B) ** Ph. Duo 442 574-2 (2) [id.]. Alexander Uninsky.

Alexander Uninsky offers an inexpensive complete survey of the *Mazurkas*, including the four published posthumously plus the *Impromptus*. His playing is sympathetic but not especially individual or imaginative, and after a while his rubato and control of dynamic nuance become rather predictable. Even so, many of the performances are effective and musical, especially the later works: Op.56/1, for instance, which opens the second CD, has a pleasing poise and intimacy of feeling, although just occasionally elsewhere he tends to rush his fences. The recordings were made in three groups, dating from 1959, 1961 and 1971, but the realistic sound remains remarkably consistent, a tribute to the Philips engineering. The programme ends with the lovely *Berceuse*, which is played persuasively. However, Rubinstein's set remains unsurpassed (RCA RD 85171).

Nocturnes Nos. 1–21 (complete).
(B) *** DG Double Dig. 437 464-2 (2). Daniel Barenboim.
(M) ** Ph. 438 967-2 (2). Jan Smeterlin.
* EMI Dig. CDS5 55073-2 (2) [Ang. ZDCB 55073]. Maria Tipo.

Nocturnes Nos. 1–4; 7–10; 12–13; 15; 18–19.
(B) *** DG Dig. 439 497-2 [id.]. Daniel Barenboim.

Re-listening to Barenboim's performances, which are beautifully recorded, gave much pleasure. His phrasing is beautifully moulded, the nuancing of tempi thoughtful and poetic, yet seemingly spontaneous. While the mercurial dimension of Rubinstein's performances (RCA RD 89563) gives them a special claim on the listener, Barenboim's set will give genuine satisfaction, his style essentially relaxed, only becoming really impetuous in the music's more passionate moments. There is an excellent, well-chosen single-disc selection on DG's bargain label which offers 72 minutes of music and scores thirteen out of the total of twenty-one. The recording remains first class.

Jan Smeterlin, born in Poland in 1892, very much belongs to an earlier generation of Chopin interpreters, studying under Godowsky, who liked to elaborate Chopin's decorative effects further. So it is not surprising that Smeterlin's style is individually volatile, at times to the point of fantasy – though occasionally, as in the famous *E flat Nocturne*, Op. 9/2, he can be curiously stiff. But for the most part these performances have considerable poetry, and the rubato, if personalized, is usually convincing. There are moments of real magic, as at the ruminative opening of the *F sharp Nocturne*, Op. 15/2, but later this performance becomes very impulsive, as does the *C sharp minor*, Op. 27/1. The very early stereo recording (1954) is surprisingly good, though sometimes the piano-tone is dry in the bass at higher dynamic levels.

Maria Tipo is languorous to the point of lethargy. She takes 6 minutes 52 seconds for the opening *B flat minor Nocturne*, Op. 9/1, as against Smeterlin's 4 minutes 59 seconds; the following *E flat major* is timed at 5 minutes 25 seconds compared with 3 minutes 50 seconds; while the *B major*, Op. 9/3, runs to 8 minutes 11 seconds against Smeterlin's 5 minutes 37 seconds. Such indulgent romanticism might work for a single item at a live concert, but in a complete set like this it is not acceptable. The recording is of only fair quality.

Scherzos Nos. 1–4; Polonaise-fantaisie, Op. 61.
(M) *** Ph. Dig. 442 407-2 [id.]. Claudio Arrau.

Arrau's last recording of the four *Scherzi* was made in Munich, just after the artist's eightieth birthday. There is little sign of age, even if he would have produced a greater weight of sonority at the height of his powers. However, these accounts are full of wise and thoughtful perceptions and remarkable pianism, recorded with great presence and clarity. The middle section of the *First Scherzo* may strike some collectors as unusually slow and a trifle mannered, but there are magical things elsewhere, notably in the *Fourth*. Arrau's fire may have lost some of its youthful charisma, but the gains in wisdom and delicacy of feeling are adequate compensation. The Philips engineers seem to produce piano quality of exceptional realism. However, this is short measure (55 minutes).

Piano sonata No. 3 in B min., Op. 58; Mazurkas, in A min., Op. 17/4; in B flat min., Op. 24/4; in D flat, Op. 30/3; in D, Op. 33/2; in G; in C sharp min., Op. 50/ 1 & 3; in C, Op. 56/2; in F sharp min., Op. 59/3; in B; in F min.; in C sharp min., Op. 63/1–3; in F min., Op. 68/4.
*** RCA Dig. 09026 62542-2 [id.]. Evgeny Kissin.

Evgeny Kissin's second Chopin recital at Carnegie Hall is hardly less distinguished than the wonderful programme that RCA issued in time for our main edition. Kissin plays not only with an effortless mastery but with a naturalness and freshness that silence criticism. His sense of poetry and his idiomatic rubato are combined with impressive technical address and impeccable taste. Along with Perahia's recent set of the *Ballades*, this is one of the best Chopin recitals to have appeared this year.

Miscellaneous Recitals

'The best of Chopin': Ballades Nos. (i) *1 in G min., Op. 23;* (ii) *4 in F min., Op. 52;* (iii) *Barcarolle in F sharp min.;* (iv) *Berceuse, Op. 57;* (v) *Etudes, Op. 10/3, 5 & 12; Op. 25/1 & 9; Impromptus Nos.* (vi) *1 in A min., Op. 29;* (iii) *3 in G flat, Op. 51;* (vi) *4 (Fantaisie-impromptu),Op. 66;* (v) *3 Mazurkas, Op. 59;* (iii) *3 Mazurkas, Op. 63; Nocturnes Nos.* (ii) *8 in D flat, Op. 27/2;* (iii) *17 in B; 18 in E, Op. 62/1– 2;* (vii) *Polonaises Nos. 6 in A flat, Op. 53;* (iii) *7 (Polonaise-fantaisie), Op. 61.* (v) *Préludes, Op. 28/4, 7, 9 & 15;* (iv) *Scherzo No. 2 in B flat min., Op. 31; Sonata No. 2 in B flat: Funeral march* (only). (viii) *Waltzes: Nos. 5 in A flat, Op. 42; 6 in D flat; 7 in C sharp min., Op. 64/1–2.*
(B) **(*) Ph. Duo Analogue/Dig. 446 145-2 (2) [id.]. (i) Harasiewicz ;(ii) Arrau; (iii) Kovacevich; (iv) Orozco; (v) Magaloff; (vi) Davidovich; (vii) Cziffra; (viii) Kocsis.

'The Best of Chopin' is a hard sobriquet to live up to, but what makes the Philips Duo compilation distinctive is that at its heart is an outstanding complete 49-minute continuing recital which Stephen Kovacevich recorded in 1972. The opening bars of his *Barcarolle in F sharp minor* immediately establishes this as Chopin playing of the highest order, and the two following Opus 62 *Nocturnes, in B major* and *E major*, are equally poetic. Here Kovacevich shows it is possible to adopt very spacious tempi and, unlike Maria Tipo (see above), spin magic in every bar. Then comes the *Third Impromptu in G flat* and three engagingly contrasted *Mazurkas*, Op. 63, and the recital ends with a wonderfully imaginative account of the *Polonaise-fantaisie*, Op. 61, full of exquisite touches. The other perform-ances are all reliable, especially those from Nikita Magaloff who has his own insights to offer, though Zoltán Kocsis treats his three *Waltzes* primarily as opportunities for dazzling bravura display. Arrau contributes a characterful *Nocturne in D flat*, Op. 27, No. 2, but here, as in his *F minor Ballade*, the playing seems too considered; and Adam Harasiewicz subsequently demonstrates just how it can be done with a romantically impulsive *Ballade in G minor*. The programme ends with Cziffra in impressive form in the *A flat Polonaise*, Op. 53. Good sound throughout; although the recordings were made over a long period, between 1962 and 1982, the consistency of quality is remarkable.

Cimarosa, Domenico (1749–1801)

(i) *Requiem* (revised Vittorio Negri); *Concertante in G for flute, oboe and orchestra* (arr. Holliger).
(M) *** Ph. Analogue/Dig. 442 657-2 [id.]. (i) Ameling, Finnilä, Van Vrooman, Widmer, Montreux Festival Ch., Lausanne CO, Negri; (ii) Nicolet, Holliger, ASMF, Sillito.

Cimarosa's *Requiem*, an impressive, even formidable work, puts an unexpected slant on the composer of the brilliant comic opera with which his name is usually associated. The choral writing, whether in the big contrapuntal numbers or in the more homophonic passages with solo interpolations, is most assured. The singing here by the Montreux Festival Choir conveys a feeling of spacious eloquence and it is a pity that the recording is rather too reverberant to produce an incisive edge to the choral sound; its warm atmosphere, however, adds to the feeling of weight and serenity. The soloists are very good, though some might find the tenor, Richard van Vrooman, a trifle histrionic in the *Preces meae*. Elly Ameling's lovely singing more than compensates, and the bass, Kurt Widmer, is impressive in the *Inter oves*. Vittorio Negri secures excellent playing from the Lausanne orchestra, best known for its contribution to Haydn opera recordings under Dorati, and the CD transfer, as usual with Philips, greatly enhances a 1969 recording which does not sound dated. What makes this reissue especially attractive is the inclusion of Cimarosa's best-known concertante work. This engaging *Concertante* is aptly operatic in feeling. The music is not without substance, but the singing, lyrical secondary theme in the first movement and the interplay of flute and oboe in the *Largo* show a distinct vocal style. With such superb playing from Nicolet and Holliger, nicely turned accompani-ments and first-rate digital recording, this CD, with its attractive coupling, is most entertaining.

Ciurlionis, Mikolajus (1875–1911)

Symphonic poems: *Miške (In the forest); Jūra (The sea). 5 preludes for string orchestra.*
** Marco Polo Dig. 8.223323 [id.]. Slovak PO, Jouozas Domarka.

Mikolajus Ciurlionis was endowed with many talents (he was also a painter and poet) but too short a life in which to develop them. His music has made little headway outside his native Lithuania. His tone-poem, *In the Forest*, made a brief appearance as a fill-up to Balakirev's *Second Symphony* on an EMI/Melodiya LP, but otherwise his music has suffered total neglect. Ciurlionis studied at first in Warsaw, before becoming a pupil of Reinecke in Leipzig. The orchestral tone-poems are highly accomplished in their way, though it is difficult to discern a strongly individual voice in either of them. The nearest approximation would be, perhaps, the lush, early orchestral music of Scriabin, though Ciurlionis remained relatively uninfluenced by the more mature music of the Russian master, who was the standard-bearer of modernity by the first decade of the century. Decent performances by the Slovak Philharmonic under Jouozas Domarkas and more than adequate recording. It is well to note that an alternative version of the two tone-poems (which we have been unable to hear) from the USSR Radio TV Symphony Orchestra under Vladimir Fedoseyev is available on Harmonia Mundi LDC 288004, but the *Five preludes for string orchestra* are replaced by his unfinished *String quartet*.

Chansonette, VL 199; Humoresque, VL 162; Impromptu, VL 181; Mazurkas, VL 222 & 234; Nocturnes, VL 178 & 183; Preludes, VL 164, 169, 182a, 184–188, 197 & 230; Sonata, VL 155.
** Marco Polo Dig. 8.223549 [id.]. Mûza Rubackyté.

Fugue in B flat min., VL 345; 3 Pieces on a theme, VL 269–271; Preludes, VL 239, 241, 256, 259, 294–295, 298, 304, 325, 327, 330, 335, 338, 340, 343 & 344; String quartet (transcribed Rubackyté).
** Marco Polo Dig. 8.223550 [id.]. Mûza Rubackyté.

During his studies in Warsaw and Leipzig, Ciurlionis was brought under the spell of Chopin and Schumann, both of whom left their mark on his keyboard music. The most substantial piece on the first of Mûza Rubackyté's two discs is the *Piano sonata* of 1898, a well-wrought and often inventive four-movement piece which she plays with admirable sympathy and sensitivity. The first disc covers Ciurlionis's output up to 1902, and the second from the middle part of the decade to his death in 1911. Incidentally the VL numbers stand for Vytautus Landsbergis, the musicologist who became Prime Minister of Lithuania during the period leading to the break-up of the Soviet Union. The chances of any British composer's works bearing Margaret Thatcher or John Major numbers are as remote as the possibility of any British musicologist becoming Prime Minister. Be that as it may, many of these pieces are of considerable interest and some are of real poetic feeling and a quiet individuality. Mûza Rubacktyé has also transcribed – and very effectively – the *String quartet* – or, rather, the three movements of it that Ciurlionis completed, for piano.

Coates, Eric (1886–1958)

Calling all workers march; Dambusters march; The Jester at the wedding; London suite; The Merrymakers overture; The Three Elizabeths; (i) The Green hills; Stonecracker John.
(B) ** BBC Radio Classics BBCRD 9106 [id.]. BBC Concert O, Sir Adrian Boult; (i) with Ian Wallace.

An exceptionally generous collection (76 minutes) of Eric Coates favourites, including the three best-known marches, *Dambusters*, *Knightsbridge* (once used as the introduction to the BBC's vintage radio chat show, 'In Town Tonight') and *Calling all workers*, specifically written as the signature-tune for later wartime broadcasts of 'Music while you work'. Most importantly, the programme includes Coates' finest orchestral work, *The Three Elizabeths* (1944), in which the Queen Mother (*Elizabeth of Glamis*) got the best tune – scored for the oboe, and with a delightful, Scottish snap (although as played here it does not beguile the ear as much as it can). Queen Elizabeth II (then a princess) was celebrated with yet another swinging march. The charming and little-known ballet suite, *The Jester at the wedding*, is played quite delightfully and Boult sees that the marches have plenty of rhythmic swing. The fine bass-baritone, Ian Wallace, is also on hand to give resonant accounts of two of Coates' most successful ballads. The orchestral playing is lively enough, if not immaculate; but the recording, although quite satisfactorily balanced in the Hippodrome Studio, Golders Green, does not flatter the violins and suggests that there were not too many of them. Good value, nevertheless.

Copland, Aaron (1900–90)

Appalachian spring (ballet).
*** Everest/Vanguard EVC 9003 [id.]. LSO, Walter Susskind – GOULD: *Spirituals* ***; GERSHWIN: *American in Paris*. **(*)

Susskind's dramatic and sympathetic reading of what is perhaps Copland's finest orchestral score is most spaciously and vividly recorded. Although it is an English performance, it compares very favourably indeed with the composer's own – see below – and the American-style engineering with wide dynamics adds plenty of drama, but not at the expense of amplitude. Susskind conducts the piece in a completely spontaneous way, the string ostinatos have the proper rhythmic bite, the quieter, more reflective pages bring serenity, and the unfolding of the Shaker variations is managed with a simplicity of great charm. With its apt Gould coupling – no less well done – this is an outstanding reissue. It is a pity that it is offered at only slightly less than full price, but it is worth its cost.

(i) *Appalachian spring;* (ii) *Billy the Kid* (suite); *Rodeo* (suite).
(BB) *** RCA Navigator 74321 21297-2. (i) Boston SO, composer; (ii) Morton Gould and his Orchestra.

Copland's first recording of *Appalachian spring* is special. It was recorded in Boston in 1959 and is alone worth the modest price of this disc. The performance has an appealing breadth and warmth of humanity, helped by the Symphony Hall resonance: the Shaker climax is wonderfully expansive. Morton Gould, a talented composer himself, conducts the other two ballets with enormous zest and vitality, and 'his' orchestra play as if their very lives depended on it. The early (1957) stereo is a little dated but remains arrestingly spectacular (the *Gun battle* stands up remarkably well against the famous Mercury version) and the quieter, evocative writing is haunting, distilling a special combination of tender warmth and underlying tension. The *Corral Nocturne* and wistful *Saturday night waltz* in *Rodeo* are especially fine, and here Gould also includes the *Honky-tonky interlude* on an appropriate piano. The closing *Hoe-down* is refreshingly folksy and has great rhythmic energy. The Navigator reissue features an 1896 map of Greater New York, but why not have used the Appalachian mountain area?

(i) *Grogh* (complete ballet); (ii) *Hear ye!, hear ye!* (ballet; complete version for small orchestra); *Prelude for chamber orchestra.*
*** Argo Dig. 443 203-2 [id.]. (i) Cleveland O; (ii) L. Sinf., Oliver Knussen.

Copland's full score for *Grogh* was apparently lost; then Oliver Knussen found it, hidden away in the Library of Congress. Inspired by the images of the German horror film, *Nosferatu*, it is a strange early score (1922–5, revised 1932), given a superbly played, atmospheric performance here. *Hear ye!, Hear ye!* is a curious burlesque, about a nightclub murder, set in a courtroom, with all kinds of influences, including jazz and even a parody of Mendelssohn's *Wedding march* on four violins. The *Prelude for chamber orchestra* uses material from the *Symphony for organ and orchestra* in a very succinct form. Excellent performances of not always entirely convincing music, given first-class recording.

Quiet city; (i) *8 Poems of Emily Dickinson.*
*** EMI Dig. CDC5 55358-2 [id.]. (i) Barbara Hendricks; LSO, Tilson Thomas – BARBER: *Adagio for strings* etc. ***

Tilson Thomas and Barbara Hendricks have between them devised a programme of Copland as well as Barber, with both composers at their most radiantly inspired. This is an intensely beautiful disc that in its deep thoughtfulness belies the conventional idea of American culture being brash. Tilson Thomas describes *Quiet city*, adapted from film music, as 'Mahler in Manhattan', but that hardly gives a fair idea of its rapt individuality, with solo trumpet and cor anglais (superbly played by Maurice Murphy and Christine Pendrill) adding atmospheric intensity. Copland himself orchestrated eight of his twelve settings of Emily Dickinson poems for chamber orchestra for his seventieth birthday concert, and Tilson Thomas as a young conductor was in charge. The freshness and sharp imagination of the accompaniments are enhanced in support of vocal lines lovingly matched to Dickinson's distinctive poetic style. Radiant singing from Hendricks, and equally sensuous sounds from the orchestra.

PIANO MUSIC

Down a country lane; In the evening air; Midday thoughts; Midsummer nocturne; 3 Moods; Night thoughts (Homage to Ives); Passacaglia; Petite portrait; 4 Piano Blues; Piano fantasy; Proclamation; Piano variations; Scherzo humoristique: The cat and the mouse; Sentimental melody (Slow dance); Sonata; Sunday afternoon music; The Young Pioneers.
(M) *** Sony Analogue/Dig. SM2K 66345 (2) [id.]. Leo Smit.

The sound-quality here may not be ideal – the piano is recorded in a rather small acoustic – but this is nevertheless an important and valuable set. Much of it was recorded in 1978 with a grant from the Ford Foundation, and the remaining half-dozen pieces were added in 1993. The result is a collection of all Copland's important piano music from the very earliest pre-Boulanger days – the abrasively impressionistic *Scherzo, The cat and the mouse* (1920) – right down to his most recent works, *Midday thoughts* and *Proclamation* completed in November 1982 and based on earlier material, which are within the 1993 supplement. The original analogue set ended with the hauntingly atmospheric yet audaciously conceived *Night thoughts*, composed in 1972 as an apt tribute to Ives. The three most important works, the *Variations* (1930), the *Sonata* (1941) and the *Fantasy* (1957), were not otherwise available at the time Smit's recordings were made. Now the catalogue has expanded. Their complexity and seriousness of purpose are summed up by Leonard Bernstein's comment about the *Variations*: 'a synonym for modern music – so prophetic, harsh and wonderful, and so full of modern feeling and thinking'. Copland's own response when questioned about the three works was: 'I think that has a lot to do with the quality of the piano itself and with the kind of sound – lean, percussive and rather harmonically severe – that I like to make at the keyboard.' But of course not all this writing is uncompromising. Apart from the bluesy and jazzy pieces, the wistful *In the evening air* and *Midday thoughts* (deriving from sketches for a *Ballade for piano and orchestra*, conceived and abandoned at the time of writing *Appalachian spring*) have something of the evocation of the atmospheric writing in the three great ballets, and *Down a country lane* brings a comparable brand of pastoralism. Both are played very sympathetically. Leo Smit has been closely associated with Copland's music over the years (the first of the *Four Piano blues* and the *Midsummer nocturne* of 1947 were here receiving their first recording and both are dedicated to Smit), and he recorded the *Sonata* in the days of 78s. It would be difficult to find anyone who is more inside the idiom and whose command of nervous energy so well matches the needs of this vital music. Authoritative, stimulating and vivid performances.

Corelli, Arcangelo (1653–1713)

12 Concerti grossi, Op. 6.
*** HM Dig. HMC90 1406/7 [id.]. Ensemble 415, Banchini.
*** Hyp. Dig. CDA 66741/2 [id.]. Brandenburg Consort, Goodman.
(B) **(*) Decca Double 443 862-2 [id.]. ASMF, Marriner.

For a long time relatively (though not entirely) neglected in the days of LP and the early days of CD, Corelli's glorious set of *Concerti grossi*, Op. 6, is at long last gaining more than a foothold in the catalogue. In fact one really can't go far wrong with any of the three-star listings in our main volume. Apart from the excellent performance from the Guildhall Strings, using modern instruments (RCA RD 60071), there are two period-instrument competitors: the spacious, at times slightly rigid, but very alive English Concert set under Trevor Pinnock on Archiv (DG 423 626-2) and the excellent mid-priced alternative from La Petite Bande. Now we have three further sets. Decca have restored Marriner's eminently recommendable account with the Academy of St Martin-in-the-Fields to circulation among their two-CD sets packed as one, which makes it a real bargain. For those who want period instruments, there are now two more alternatives to list alongside (and in some ways in preference to) Pinnock. Annoying though it may be for readers who want a definite preference declared for one or the other (or for us, who like to give clear-cut recommendations), the two newcomers are both almost equally recommendable in different ways. One can invest in either with confidence.

Roy Goodman and the Brandenburg Consort use the smaller forces (17 string players) plus harpsichord continuo, archlute and organ; Harmonia Mundi's Ensemble 415, with Chiara Banchini and Jesper Christensen, number 32 strings and a comparably larger continuo section with several archlutes, chitarrone, harpsichords and organ. The richer bass and altogether fuller sonority may cause some readers to prefer it (if pressed, we would incline towards it for its greater splendour and the imaginative use of continuo instruments). However, there is a sense of style and a freshness of approach in the Goodman that is very persuasive. In both instances the recorded sound is first class. Choice will largely rest on whether you want a more chamber-like approach, as on Hyperion, or the richer sonority the Harmonia Mundi set offers.

The reissued ASMF version uses a performing edition by Christopher Hogwood and has been prepared with evident thought and care; if one cavils it is only at two small points: some fussy continuo playing here and there, and a certain want of breadth and nobility of feeling in some of the slow movements. These are perhaps small points when weighed alongside the liveliness and intelligence of these performances, so expertly played. Yet compared to the three issues mentioned above, there is at times a hint of blandness, and those wanting a bargain version should turn to the Naxos recording by the excellent Capella Istropolitana under Jaroslv Kr(e)chek, which is even more vital and has first-rate, modern, digital sound (8. 550402/3).

Corigliano, John (born 1938)

Piano concerto.
*** Koch 3-7250-2 [id.]. Alain Lefevre, Pacific SO, Carl St Clair - TICHELI: *Postcard* etc. ***

Dating from 1968, long before Corigliano's Aids-inspired *Symphony No. 1* and the brilliantly successful Met. opera, *The Ghosts of Versailles*, this *Piano concerto* communicates with similar immediacy. Starting with an expansive Allegro, it is in four sharply contrasted movements. Here, as later, Corigliano unashamedly uses a freely eclectic style, positive and energetic, with Gershwin and jazz among the influences, and with the lyrical slow movement bringing repose. It is well coupled with two similarly unproblematic works by Frank Ticheli, composer-in-residence to this orchestra of musicians from the film studios. First-rate performances and sound.

Couperin, François (1668–1733)

Harpsichord suites, Book 1, Ordres 1–5.
*** HM Dig. HMC 901450/2 [id.]. Christophe Rousset (harpsichord).

(i) *Harpsichord suites, Book 2, Ordres 6–12. L'Art de toucher le clavecin.*
*** HM Dig. HMC 901447/9 [id.]. Christophe Rousset (harpsichord), (i) with William Christie.

These two boxes complete Rousset's distinguished series of the *Pièces de clavecin*, including *L'Art de toucher le clavecin*, using appropriate instruments: in the case of Book 1 a 1624 Ruckers, while in Book 2 he plays a 1671 Couchet-Taskin. In Book 2 he is joined in certain pieces (the *Allemande* which opens Ordre No. 9 is for two harpsichords) by the estimable William Christie, who uses an Albert Delin of 1678. One could carp here and there about choice of tempi and so on, but Couperin wanted his music to be played creatively and flexibly, and that is what Christophe Rousset does – and with total spontaneity, too. He is beautifully recorded within an open but not too resonant acoustic, and this series can be welcomed very cordially indeed. The companion volumes are discussed in our main volume (Book 3 is offered, together with the *Concerts royaux*, on HMC 901442/4; Book 4 on HMC 901445/6). Bargain hunters will note that Kenneth Gilbert's earlier, analogue set is still available and can be recommended as a much less expensive alternative (HMA 190351/3 (Book 1); HMA 190354/6 (Book 2); HMA 190357/8 (Book 3) and HMA 190359/60 (Book 4) – see our main volume).

3 Leçons de ténèbres; Motet pour le jour de Pâques.
(M) *** O-L 444 169-2 [id.]. Nelson, Kirkby, Ryan, Hogwood – MONTECLAIR: *Cantatas.* ***.

The *Trois leçons de ténèbres* were written for performance on Good Friday and were the only ecclesiastical music Couperin published during his lifetime. Unlike Bach's cantatas, Couperin's settings had female voices in mind, and he could scarcely have hoped for more ethereal timbres than those of Judith Nelson and Emma Kirkby. Purity and restraint rather than warmth and humanity are the keynote of these performances, but few are likely to complain of the results. The recordings are admirably vivid, and the *Easter motet* is another attraction. But what makes this reissue especially appealing is the additional coupling of two delightful cantatas by Michel Pignolet de Montéclair, a bass viol player at the Opéra who was also employed to teach Couperin's daughters. His setting of the story of *Pan et Syrinx* is particularly graphic, both lyrically and dramatically.

Couperin, Louis (c. 1626–61)

Harpsichord suites: in A min.; C; D; F (including Le Tombeau de M. de Blancrocher).
(BB) *** Naxos Dig. 8.550922 [id.]. Laurence Cummings.

Harpsichord suites: in C min.; D min.; F.
(M) **(*) O-L Dig. 443 189-2 [id.]. Christopher Hogwood (harpsichord).

Christopher Hogwood plays a Couchet harpsichord of 1646. Louis Couperin's teacher, Chambonnières, used such an instrument, although the one used for these recordings was modified (probably at the turn of the century) for playing later music. Tuned to the mean-tone temperament, it is in excellent condition and, observed not too closely in a pleasing acoustic, it sounds beautiful. Hogwood plays expertly and these performances give pleasure. The *Tombeau de Monsieur de Blancrocher* which ends the *F major Suite* and the *Chaconne la bergeronette* which closes the *C minor* are characteristic of his style, thoughtful and with unexaggerated rubato, but here, as in the more lively movements, a little more panache would have been welcome.

Laurence Cummings was an organ scholar at Christ Church, Oxford, and he seems quite as much at home in this repertoire as Hogwood. He plays a modern copy of a Ruckers, which is very well recorded by Naxos. His selection is more generous than Hogwood's and he arranges his own groupings. His decoration is convincing and he plays with more spontaneity and flair than his illustrious colleague. The CD offers some 75 minutes of music and is one of Naxos's best bargains.

Coward, Noël (1899–1973)

After the ball: I knew that you would be my love. Bitter Sweet: I'll see you again; Zigeuner.
Conversation piece: I'll follow my secret heart; Never more; Melanie's aria (sung in French); Charming.
Operette: Dearest love; Where are the songs we sung? Countess Mitzi. Pacific 1860: Bright was the day; This is a changing world.
(BB) *** Belart 450 014-2. Dame Joan Sutherland, Noël Coward, soloists, Ch. & O, Richard
     Bonynge.

It is fairly easy to criticize this disc on the grounds that a full operatic style does not always suit Noël Coward and that Joan Sutherland does not always get right inside the characters Coward created (she tries very hard with Countess Mitzi). But all this is swept aside in the sheer pleasure of hearing such a wonderful voice sing such delightful music. *I'll see you again* is one of the great tunes of the twentieth century and, like Flanagan and Allen's *Underneath the arches*, excites a piercing nostalgia for a period of recent English history, now gone. Dame Joan Sutherland's tonal lustre and sense of line in *I'll see you again* are incomparable, as is her display of fireworks in *Ziguener*, and her gentle delicacy in *I knew that you would be my love*, with its ravishing final cadence. Noël Coward's own vocal contributions are quite small but they magically create atmosphere, and Richard Bonynge's affectionate and stylish conducting is a model. The recording is superb and marvellously transferred, and is surely a collector's item – especially at super-bargain price. Only regrettable is the omission of IM's favourite, *If love were all*, but that is perhaps not a song best suited to an 'operatic' voice.

Creston, Paul (1906–85)

String quartet, Op. 8.
(***) Testament mono SBT 1053 [id.]. Hollywood Qt – DEBUSSY: *Danse sacrée* etc. RAVEL: *Intro & allegro;* TURINA: *La Oración del torero;* VILLA-LOBOS: *Quartet No. 6.* (***)

The *String quartet*, Op. 8, was written in 1938. It is a pleasing, well-fashioned piece, slightly Gallic in feeling but not possessed of strong individuality. The *Adagio* is perhaps the most memorable of the four movements, and its argument unfolds with eloquence. It could not be better served than it is by the Hollywood Quartet, recorded in 1953: the playing is stunning, and the recording, too, is very good for its period, even if the acoustic is on the dry side.

Debussy, Claude (1862–1918)

2 Arabesques (orch. Mouton); (i) *La cathédrale engloutie* (orch. Stokowski); *La mer; Petite suite* (orch. Henri Büsser); *Pagodes* (orch. Grainger). *Première rapsodie for clarinet and orchestra; Suite bergamasque: Clair de lune* (orch. Caplet).
*** Cala Dig. CACD 1001 [id.]. (i) James Campbell; Philh. O, Geoffrey Simon.

This is one of those interesting discs which we have been unable to include before; we do so now not so much for the sake of Geoffrey Simon's account of *La mer*, though that is by no means negligible, but rather for the interest of its companions. Stokowski's masterly orchestration of *La cathédrale engloutie* is well worth having – as, of course, is André Caplet's relatively conventional and highly effective *Clair de lune*. Of greatest curiosity value is Grainger's arrangement of *Pagodes*, the first of the *Estampes*, for thirteen percussion instruments, harmonium, celeste, dulcitone and four pianos, an imaginative re-creation of the kind of gamelan sonorities Debussy might have heard at the Paris Universal Exhibition in 1889 and which inspired this piece – a first recording. The programme also includes a highly sensitive account of the *Première rapsodie* for clarinet and orchestra by James Campbell. Geoffrey Simon's *La mer*, though often sensitive, does not quite match first recommendations in terms of grip or inner tension, and *Jeux de vagues* is a bit too fast. Very good recording quality enhances the value of this eminently recommendable disc.

Danse (Tarantelle styrienne); Sarabande (orch. Ravel).
(M) *** Virgin/EMI Dig. CUV5 61206-2 [id.]. Lausanne CO, Zedda – MILHAUD: *Création du monde;* PROKOFIEV: *Sinfonietta.* ***

Zedda's performances with the Lausanne Chamber Orchestra are neat and polished, full of character and well recorded. But it is the couplings that make this disc especially attractive.

Danse sacrée et danse profane (for harp and string orchestra).
(***) Testament mono SBT 1053 [id.]. Anne Mason Stockton, Concert Arts Strings, Slatkin – CRESTON: *Quartet;* RAVEL: *Intro & allegro;* TURINA: *La Oración del torero;* VILLA-LOBOS: *Quartet No. 6.* (***)

Felix Slatkin and his Hollywood colleagues give as atmospheric an account of the *Danse sacrée et danse profane* as any on record, and Anne Mason Stockton is the excellent harpist. The mono recording dates from 1951 but is uncommonly good. This comes as part of a remarkably fine anthology of Hollywood Quartet recordings.

Images (complete).
**(*) Sony Dig. SK 53284 [id.]. BPO, Levine – ELGAR: *Enigma variations.* **(*)

This is hardly central repertory for the Berlin Philharmonic and it brings a degree of controversy among us. For EG, Levine draws thrilling, intense performances from the players, clear-cut rather than atmospheric, making an unexpected but exciting coupling. Unlike *Enigma*, this was recorded under studio conditions, offering sound as full and immediate as has ever been achieved in the Philharmonie. RL feels that the sonority produced by the Berlin Philharmonic is much changed since Karajan's days and, although these fine players are incapable of falling below a certain standard, the orchestra's corporate personality of the previous era is here replaced by a general-purpose sound such as any orchestra of the first rank might produce. The recording is very good indeed, with good definition and dynamic range. By the side of Abbado, Levine is no Debussy stylist and, while it would be going too far to call the performance characterless, for RL the reading remains moderately unmemorable.

Images: Ibéria. La Mer; Prélude à l'après-midi d'un faune.
(M) *** Mercury 434 343-2 [id.]. Detroit SO, Paray – RAVEL: *Ma Mère l'oye.* ***

Paray's collection, (unbelievably) dating from as early as 1955, gave us the first stereo recording of *La Mer*. This may not quite match Karajan's famous analogue version in evocative grip, but it remains very distinctive with some fine pianissimo playing to match the expansive climaxes in the finale, which is very exciting, balancing powerful evocation and firm overall control. The balance is slightly recessed, which provides plenty of atmosphere and a hazy warm sentience to the sound, adding luminosity to *Les parfums de la nuit* from *Images* and Paray's glowingly voluptuous account of *L'après-midi* with its ardently beautiful string climax. The recording was made in Detroit's Old Orchestra Hall, where the resonance adds great warmth but prevents sharply delineated detail. Yet for body, natural concert-hall balance and richness of orchestral colour there are few stereo recordings made in the mid- to late-1950s to match this.

Jeux; La Mer; (i) *Nocturnes;* (ii) *Première rhapsodie for clarinet and orchestra.*
**(*) DG Dig. 439 896-2 [id.].(i) Cleveland O Ch.; (ii) Franklin Cohen; Cleveland O, Boulez.

It is difficult to offer guidance in the case of the new Boulez account of *La Mer* and the *Nocturnes*. Readers who normally respond to this conductor will probably like all these performances. It is difficult not to admire the clarity of his readings, the meticulous balance and lucidity of his textures. At the same time there is a cool, neutral quality about these readings. Hans Keller once spoke of a Boulez performance as 'music without phrasing', and there is a certain detachment about his approach, as if he was involved in an act of analysis and dissection. The orchestra play well for him and the sound is admirably balanced; there is even some atmosphere at times, but little sense of mystery or discovery. The *Jeux* is no match for such rivals as André Cluytens, Bernard Haitink or Simon Rattle; and in *La Mer* Karajan, Giulini, Reiner, Baudo and Ormandy are greatly to be preferred. As we said of his 1994 *Images, Printemps* and *Prélude à l'après-midi d'un faune*: atmosphere, yes – but magic, no.

La Mer.
(M) *** DG 447 426-2 [id.]. BPO, Karajan – MUSSORGSKY: *Pictures;* RAVEL: *Boléro.* ***
(M) *** RCA 0926 68079-2 [id.]. Chicago SO, Fritz Reiner – RESPIGHI: *Fountains & Pines of Rome.*
    *** ⊛

After three decades, Karajan's 1964 account of *La Mer*, now reissued in DG's Legendary Recordings series, is still very much in a class of its own. So strong is its evocative power that one feels one can almost see and smell the ocean. It enshrines the spirit of the work as effectively as it observes the letter, and the superb playing of the Berlin orchestra, for all its virtuosity and sound, is totally self-effacing. For CD reissue, the performance is coupled with Karajan's outstanding (1966) record of Mussorgsky's *Pictures at an exhibition* and a gripping account of Ravel's *Boléro*.

Reiner's 1960 recording is also available coupled with Rimsky-Korsakov's *Scheherazade* (GD 60875). It has all the warmth and atmosphere that make his version of *Ibéria*, recorded at about the same time (GD 60179), so unforgettable. The pianissimo opening has enormous evocative feeling and the *Jeux des vagues* has the same haunting sense of colour. Of course the marvellous acoustics of the Chicago Hall contribute to the appeal of this superbly played account: the effect is richer and fuller than in Karajan's remastered DG version, and Reiner's record gives no less pleasure. With Karajan, one could picture the bracing air of the northern Atlantic, whereas with Reiner, although the dialogue of the wind and waves is no less powerful, one senses a more southerly latitude. The new coupling with Resphigi is surely ideal, for Reiner's magical Roman evocations are among the most unforget-tably evocative recorded performances the gramophone has to offer.

La Mer; Nocturnes: Nuages; Fêtes (only). *Prélude à l'après-midi d'un faune. Printemps* (symphonic suite).
(BB) *** RCA Navigator 74321 21293-2. Boston SO, Munch.

The new CD transfers have completely transformed these Munch recordings, the Boston acoustic now casting a wonderfully warm aura over the orchestra; and the sound, hitherto rather fierce in its original LP format, is gloriously expansive and translucent. The result is that the opening of *Printemps* is ravishingly sensuous and the 1956 *La Mer* has plenty of atmosphere to match its undoubted excitement. There is marvellous Boston playing here, especially from the violins, and the climax of the former is driven very hard indeed (*Fêtes* is similarly pressed on with comparable emotional force). Munch's inclination to go over the top may not appeal to all listeners, but the results are very compelling when the orchestral bravura is so thrilling. The *Prélude*, placed after *La Mer*, makes a ravishing interlude, expanding to a rapturous climax.

CHAMBER MUSIC

Cello sonata.
** Globe Dig. GLO 5057 [id.]. Ferschtman, Baslawskaya – FAURE: *Après un rêve* etc.; FRANCK: *Cello sonata.* **
(M) ** Virgin/EMI Dig. CUV5 61198-2 [id.]. Steven Isserlis, Pascal Devoyon – FRANCK; POULENC: *Cello sonatas.* **

Dmitri Ferschtman and Mila Baslawskaya are a Russian partnership now based in the Netherlands, where they both teach. Alert playing and with some imaginative touches, particularly in the finale, and decently recorded. Ferschtman, as represented here, does not possess a particularly big tone, though he is a responsive player – as, indeed, is his partner. However, in terms of musical personality and quality of sound, this is no match for such outstanding versions as the Rostropovich–Britten (Decca 417 833-2) and Gendron–Françaix (Philips 422 839-2) partnerships.

Steven Isserlis and Pascal Devoyon also make a well-matched partnership, though the latter is ill-served by the engineers. His piano entry sounds pretty thunderous, though both these fine players are exposed to rather too close a scrutiny. Isserlis brings great intensity to the middle movement, and there are many things to admire throughout this extraordinarily concentrated masterpiece; but this is not a first recommendation.

Danse sacrée et danse profane; Sonata for flute, viola and harp; Petite suite: En bateau.
** EMI Dig. CDC7 54884-2 [id.]. Klinko, Soloists from Paris-Bastille Op. O (with SATIE & FAURE) – RAVEL: *Introduction and allegro* etc. **

Markus Klinko and his colleagues from the Orchestre de l'Opéra de Paris-Bastille give a fine account of the Debussy *Sonata for flute, viola and harp*, spoilt only by the balance which makes this other-worldly music sound at times just a little too lush. They take as long as nineteen minutes over it! The playing here and in the glorious *Danse sacrée et danse profane* is very persuasive. Apart from the Debussy and Ravel (see separate entry), there are arrangements of the Fauré *Berceuse* and the Satie second *Gymnopédie*, which account for barely five minutes. The flute and harp arrangement of the Satie is more acceptable than the *Berceuse*, which is uninvitingly played by Frédéric Laroque.

Le petit nègre; Petite pièce; Première rapsodie; Rapsodie for cor anglais; Rapsodie for saxophone; Sonata for flute, viola and harp; (i) Syrinx.
(B) *** Cala Dig. CACD 1017 (2) [id.]. William Bennett, Nicholas Daniel, James Campbell, Rachael Gough, (i) Simon Haram & Ens. – SAINT-SAENS: *Chamber music.* ***

Another two-CD set for the price (and shape) of one, the first volume of French chamber music for woodwind. The *Rapsodie for cor anglais* with which it opens is more familiar in its form for alto saxophone, which was originally to have been called *Rapsodie Mauresque*. As Nicholas Daniel explains in his excellent note, it was written for Elise Hall, the wife of an American surgeon, to aid an asthmatic complaint; but when she was unable to sustain some of the long phrases, Debussy was forced to modify long sections of the solo part and work them into the piano part. Debussy himself suggested the cor anglais as an alternative, and Daniels plays it with great sensitivity. It is also heard in its alternative form, splendidly played by Simon Haram. The performance of the *Sonata for flute, viola and harp* is not quite as wayward as the highly sensitive but rather lush account from Markus Klinko (William Bennett, Roger Tapping and Ieuan Jones take 15 minutes 48 seconds as opposed to the French group's 19 minutes 10 seconds).

Piano trio in G (1880).

(*) Ara. Dig. Z 6643 [id.]. Golub Kaplan Carr Trio – FAURE: *Piano trio* *; SAINT-SAENS: *Piano trio.* **(*)

** RCA Dig. 09026 68062-2 [id.]. Previn, Rosenfeld, Hoffman – RAVEL: *Trio.* **

* Erato/Warner Dig. 2292 44937-2 [id.]. Trio Fontenay – FAURE: *Piano trio* **; RAVEL: *Piano trio.* *

The *Piano trio in G major* was composed when Debussy was eighteen and still a student, but the score only appeared during the 1970s. It is not good Debussy, and in a way it does not deserve the representation it enjoys in the catalogue. The Golub–Kaplan–Carr Trio give as good an account as any of this slender piece, and they are decently recorded.

It is a pity that RCA offer such short measure and handicap their Ravel *Trio* by giving it only one coupling. It makes it quite uncompetitive at full price.

The Trio Fontenay are not at their best here and do not make very much of this immature work. Part of the problem is the close balance and over-lit aural image, which does not enhance the atmosphere.

String quartet in G min., Op. 10.

**(*) RCA Dig. 09026 62552-2 [id.]. Tokyo String Qt – RAVEL: *Introduction and allegro; Quartet.* **(*)

** Erato/Warner Dig. 4509 96361-2 [id.]. Keller Qt – RAVEL: *Quartet.* **

(M) ** DG Dig. 445 509-2 [id.]. Emerson Qt – RAVEL: *Quartet.* **

(*) Orfeo mono 361 941 [id.]. Végh Qt – BEETHOVEN: *Quartet in D;* HAYDN: *Quartet in F.* (*)

The Tokyo Quartet play with great beauty and sweetness of tone. Their tonal refinement and perfect ensemble are a joy in themselves and are heard to great advantage in the inner movements. Unfortunately the first movement is pulled around rather more than is acceptable on a disc designed for repeated hearing, and some listeners will find this problematic. First choice remains with the Hagen Quartet on DG (437 836-2).

The Keller Quartet are a youngish Hungarian group, formed when the players were still studying in Budapest. They came to wider attention when they won a number of international prizes in 1990, including the Evian competition. They offer the Debussy and Ravel quartets alone (there is usually a bonus nowadays), and rush and overdramatize its first movement. In fact the whole work is rather hurried along (23 minutes 34 seconds, as opposed to the Tokyo Quartet's 26 minutes 3 seconds). There is just a little too much paprika here to make this a three-star recommendation.

The Emersons play with amazing precision and body of sound on DG, but their performances are too high-powered to do full justice to the sensibility of Debussy's score. The playing dazzles – but then, so does strip-lighting!

There is much that is perceptive in the Végh Quartet's account, but this Austrian Radio recording, made at the 1961 Salzburg Festival, is no match for the current competition. The slow movement has many beauties but needs greater finish. Intonation is not flawless and the mono sound is a bit hard and scrawny.

Violin sonata in G min.

* RCA Dig. 09026 62697-2 [id.].Pinchas Zukerman, Marc Neikrug. – FAURE; FRANCK: *Violin sonatas.* *

Though they are well recorded, Zukerman and Neikrug do not compete with first recommendations. The playing is highly finished and masterful but full of self-conscious touches, and on occasion Zukerman leaves himself open to the charge of schmaltz. Kyung-Wha Chung's version with Radu Lupu remains a clear front runner (Decca 421 154-2 – see our main volume).

PIANO MUSIC

2 Arabesques; Children's corner; Estampes; Images, Books I–II; L'Isle joyeuse; Pour le piano; Préludes, Book I; Rêverie; Suite bergamasque.

(B) *** Decca Double 443 021-2 (2) [id.]. Pascal Rogé.

Pascal Rogé's playing is distinguished by a keen musical intelligence and sympathy, as well as by a subtle command of keyboard colour, and this Double Decca set must receive the warmest welcome. *Children's corner* is played with neat elegance and the characterization has both charm and perception, while the *Suite bergamasque* brings crisp, well-articulated playing in the *Passepied* and genuine poetry in the famous *Clair de lune*. *Pour le piano* is no less distinguished, and the *Images* are full of evocative imagery. In *Estampes* one feels that in *La soirée dans Grenade* a shade more atmosphere might not be out of place and there are occasional moments when the listener senses the need for more dramatic projection. In the earlier part of *L'Isle joyeuse* Rogé tends to understate a little, but he brings genuine poetic feeling to the first book of the *Préludes*. Here he communicates atmosphere and character in no small measure and has greater warmth than Michelangeli and Zimerman, perhaps partly the effect of the 1978 recording, which has a slightly fuller recording in the bass than the rest of the programme. The other recordings were made in 1977 and 1979 and the CD transfers are clear and firm.

Children's corner; Estampes; La fille aux cheveux de lin; L'Isle joyeuse; La plus que lente; Suite bergamasque.
(M) DG 445 547-2 [id.]. Alexis Weissenberg.

Why DG should have chosen to reissue this in the Masters series is inexplicable. The recording is one of the most insensitive – indeed brutal – accounts of Debussy to have been committed to disc. Dynamic nuances are totally ignored and such subtleties as pianissimo unknown. Totally unacceptable artistically, though well enough recorded. Not recommended.

Estampes; Pour le piano.
** DG Dig. 439 927-2 [id.]. Lilya Zilberstein – RAVEL: *Miroirs* etc. **

This fine pianist is not altogether convincing in this repertoire, even if there are many details that command admiration including a strongly characterized *Jardins sous la pluie*. Though eminently present, her recording is overlit and close.

Etudes: Pour les degrés chromatiques; Pour les arpèges composés. Estampes: Jardins sous la pluie. L'isle joyeuse; Pour le piano; Poissons d'or. Préludes: Les collines d'Anacapri; Ce qu'a vu le vent d'Ouest; Feuilles mortes; Feux d'artifice.
** Berlin Classics Dig. BC 2171-2 [id.]. Cécile Ousset.

The distinguished French pianist is recorded in 1967, though so well are these performances remastered that one would scarcely know. Mind you, it is a bit steep to ask full price for a recording of this vintage, particularly as it offers hardly more than 50 minutes. The playing is generally full of character and there are many poetic touches. Admirers of this artist need not hesitate, though there are better introductions to Debussy's piano music, notably Pascal Rogé's Double Decca compilation (see above), which offers consistently more sensitive playing. It is the equivalent of three LPs for the same price as this one CD.

Préludes, Books I and II.
(B) **(*) DG Double mono/stereo 439 666-2 [id.]. Monique Haas – BARTOK: *Piano concerto No. 3* etc. (**); RAVEL: *Piano concertos.* **(*)

Although Gieseking reigns supreme in this repertoire (EMI CDH7 61004-2), Monique Haas's account of the two books of *Préludes* still occupies a fairly strong position in the lower price-range. Refined, classical playing, naturally recorded; a trifle cool, perhaps, for she is not as imaginative or atmospheric as Tirimo, but eminently sound and recommendable. Coupled with the Bartók and Ravel performances, this DG set offers an ample and varied programme of music which may well find a welcome in smaller collections.

(i) *Préludes,* Book I: *Le vent dans la plaine; Les sons et les parfums tournent dans l'air du soir; Les collines d'Anacapri; Ce qu'a vu le vent d'ouest; La fille aux cheveux de lin; La cathédrale engloutie; Minstrels;* Book II: *Feuilles mortes; La puerta del vino; General Lavine – eccentric; La terrasse des audiences du clair de lune; Feux d'artifice.* (ii) *Suite bergamasque.*
(B) ** DG 439 442-2 [id.]. (i) Dino Ciani; (ii) Tamás Vásáry.

A perceptively chosen selection taken from both Books of Debussy's *Préludes*. Dino Ciani has a fine technique (witness *Feux d'artifice*) and plays with intelligence and taste. Moreover she is very well recorded. However, it is possible to fit all the Preludes on to a single CD and, while Vásáry's *Suite bergamasque* is in every way distinguished, both stylish and poetic, this CD can only be regarded as a supplement to a collection already containing both Books of *Préludes*.

Préludes, Book 2.
(M) **(*) Saga EC 3347-2 [id.]. Lívia Rév.

Lívia Rév's Saga recording of the second book of *Préludes* comes from the 1970s. We thought quite highly of it at the time, giving it a full three-star grading. The playing has great polish and finesse, and it gives pleasure. However, at 39 minutes it is no bargain, even were it at super-bargain rather than mid-price. Book 2 is less well represented in the catalogue than its companion, but we do not lack for excellent packages that offer both books in distinguished performances which are worth the extra outlay (Gieseking, Werner Haas etc).

VOCAL MUSIC

3 Chansons de Charles d'Orléans.
*** Ph. Dig. 438 149-2 [id.]. Monteverdi Ch., O Révolutionnaire et Romantique, Gardiner – FAURE: *Requiem;* RAVEL; SAINT-SAENS: *Choral works.* ***

With Gardiner and his period forces bringing out the medieval flavour of these charming choral settings, this adds to a generous and unusual coupling for Gardiner's expressive reading of the Fauré *Requiem.*

OPERA

Pelléas et Mélisande (complete).
(***) Testament mono SBT 3051 (3) [id.]. Jansen, De los Angeles, Souzay, Froumenty, Collard, French Nat. R. O, Cluytens.

It is good to see this 1956 recording return to currency. On its first appearance it was compared unfavourably to the first Ansermet account on Decca, and Jacques Jansen's Pelléas was thought less successful than his earlier account of the role in the wartime set under Roger Desormière. While Decca left their four-LP set of the opera in the catalogue until the mid-1960s, EMI quickly removed the Cluytens set; it had disappeared from the catalogue after about two years in spite of the presence of Victoria de los Angeles as Mélisande and Gérard Souzay as Golaud. In fact de los Angeles is often affecting and always sings the role exquisitely, and readers will obviously want the set for her. Souzay's Golaud is also magnificent vocally – he was thought cooler and more austere at the time, though his conception of the part is, on its own terms, perfectly convincing. André Cluytens gets superior playing from the Orchestre National de la Radiodiffusion Française, an altogether finer and more polished ensemble than the 1950s' Suisse Romande Orchestra – with far truer woodwind intonation. And without disrespect to Ansermet (or, for that matter, to Fournet on Philips), Cluytens, too, casts a strong spell even if he does not always distil as powerful an atmosphere. The transfer is altogether exemplary, a model of its kind, and the well-focused mono sound gives unalloyed pleasure. Recommended alongside the first Ansermet set (Decca 425 965-2 – see our main volume), while Abbado's set stands supreme among more modern versions (DG 435 444-2).

Delalande, Michel-Richard (1657–1726)

Cantate Domino; De profundis; Regina coeli.
*** ASV/Gaudeamus Dig. CDGAU 141 [id.]. Ex Cathedra Chamber Ch. & Bar. O, Skidmore.

Jeffrey Skidmore with his fine, Birmingham-based choir and orchestra presents vividly characterized performances of three of Delalande's *'grands motets'*, written to be performed simultaneously with the daily celebration of Mass at Louis XIV's court. *De profundis* was originally composed in 1689 but was radically revised and developed over the years, with the most elaborate version prepared for the King's funeral in 1715. It is a magnificent piece, as are the two lighter, joyful motets. As the title indicates, *Regina coeli* has a Marian text and was intended as a celebratory Easter antiphon, the shortest of the *grands motets*, while *Cantate Domino*, probably the best known, dates from 1707, representing the peak of Delalande's long career. With their sequences of brief, sharply contrasted movements, these motets, in performances as lively and sensitive as these, can be warmly recommended to many more than baroque specialists. Warm, full sound.

3 Leçons de ténèbres.
(M) *** Erato/Warner 4509 98528-2 [id.]. Etcheverry, Charbonnier, Boulay.

A very different Delalande appears here from the one we know from the more celebrated *Sinfonies pour les soupers du roi*. These *Leçons de ténèbres* are for the relatively austere combination of voice and continuo favoured in France at this time and perhaps best known from their use by Couperin and Charpentier. Delalande brings a distinctive personal stamp to these settings and is no less a master of the ariosa style than his contemporaries; indeed, in melodic richness some of this is even finer than the Couperin version. And the continuo realization (viola da gamba; harpsichord; chamber organ) was spontaneous and not prepared in every detail beforehand; it sounds fresh and immediate without having the fussiness that often marks continuo realizations. Micaëla Etcheverry is an excellent soloist; she sings with considerable lyrical beauty, and the artists are eminently well balanced and recorded. A welcome reissue.

Delden, Lex van (1919–88)

(i) *Concerto for double string orchestra, Op. 71; Piccolo concerto, Op. 67*; (ii) *Musica sinfonica, Op. 93*; (iii) *Symphony No. 3 (Facets), Op. 45.*
*(**) Etcetera stereo/mono KTC 1156 [id.]. Concg. O; (i) Eugen Jochum; (ii) Bernard Haitink; (iii) George Szell.

The Dutch composer, Lex van Delden, is little known outside his native country – though, judging by the roll-call of conductors who have conducted his music, he is obviously highly regarded. He is largely self-taught, though he studied briefly with Cor de Groot and the composer, Sem Dresden. He abandoned his medical studies during the war as a result of injuries and played a distinguished role in the Dutch resistance. His idiom is predominantly tonal and his style offers occasional reminders of Roussel, Honegger and Stravinsky. The strongest of the works here are the *Third Symphony* and the brilliant *Piccolo concerto* for twelve wind instruments, timpani, percussion and piano. Van Delden is inventive and intelligent, and these four pieces leave you wanting to hear more. The recordings were made at various times and are of varying quality, all in the Concertgebouw Hall and taken from various broadcast tapes, the two concertos conducted by Jochum in 1968 and 1964 respectively (the latter is mono), the *Musica sinfonica* with Haitink in 1969, and the *Third Symphony* with Szell, again mono, in 1957.

Delibes, Léo (1836–91)

Coppélia (ballet) extended excerpts: Act I, Nos. 1–2, 6–8, 10; Act II, Nos. 12, 14, 15–20, 22; Act III, Nos. 23–8, 30, 32, 34–6.
*** Erato/Warner 4509 96368-2 [id.]. Lyon Opéra O, Kent Nagano.

A very comprehensive selection from our top recommendation for Delibes' delightful score for *Coppélia*, which Tchaikovsky admired so much. The whole set on two CDs (4509 91730-2) plays for only 99 minutes and here are 74 minutes 35 seconds of them. Every bar of the music-making is of the highest quality, and the recording, with its nicely judged acoustic, is as attractive as the playing. Self-recommending.

Delius, Frederick (1862–1934)

The Delius Collection

Volume 1: (i–ii) *Dance rhapsody No. 1* (ed. Beecham); (i; iii) *Dance rhapsody No. 2; Fantastic dance;* (iv) (Piano) *Preludes Nos. 1–3; Zum carnival* (polka); (v; i; iii) *Song of the high hills.*
⊛ (M) *** Unicorn Dig. UKCD 2071 [id.]. (i) RPO; (ii) Del Mar; (iii) Fenby; (iv) Parkin; (v) Amb. S.

The *Dance rhapsody No. 1*, written in 1908, is unexpectedly ambitious, being scored for two orchestras, the second 'piccolo orchestra' drawn from the first. Norman Del Mar, a natural Delian, gives a spontaneously volatile performance, and the spacious recording with its wide dynamic range captures well the music's sudden mood-changes and the kaleidoscopic character of the chimerical series of variations. The *Dance rhapsody No. 2* is not much more than half as long but, even more than the first, it gives the lie to the idea of Delius as an unrhythmic composer, written almost throughout in 3/4 tempo, though certainly not a waltz. Fenby's performance is both fluid and crisply sprung. The *Fantastic dance* is an agreeable late miniature, derived from a fragmentary sketch and owing its existence to Fenby during his period as the composer's devoted amanuensis and dedicated to him. Eric Parkin also breathes Delian air naturally. The *Preludes* for piano are typical miniatures, the *Polka* an oddity. The piano is naturally caught. But the highlight of this well-planned programme is *The Song of the high hills*, written in 1911. Fenby, the composer's life-long advocate, draws a richly atmospheric performance from Beecham's old orchestra in what proves to be one of the most ravishingly beautiful of Delius's choral works. Inspired by the hills of Norway, Delius evocatively conveys the still, chill atmosphere above the snowline with episodes for wordless chorus, here finely balanced within an evocative sound-picture, ideally warm yet with the most delicate pianissimo detail.

Volume 2: (i–ii) *Piano concerto;* (iii–iv) *Violin concerto;* (v) *Irmelin: Prelude; A Late lark; A Song of summer.*
(M) *** Unicorn Dig. UKCD 2072 [id.]. RPO; (i) Fowke; (ii) Del Mar; (iii) Holmes; (iv) Handley; (v) Fenby.

Philip Fowke rides confidently over the orchestra in this impassioned account of the one-movement *Piano concerto*, a work admired by Busoni. As ever, Del Mar is the responsive accompanist, and he and Fowke join to give a spaciously rapt account of the lovely central *Largo*, with its gentle reverie all but eclipsed by the romantic bravura of the final section. The piano balance is well judged, with the soloist forward yet integrated into the warmly resonant, perhaps slightly over-resonant sound-picture. Ralph Holmes and Vernon Handley form a comparable symbiosis in their strong and beautiful account of the *Violin concerto*, one of Delius's supreme masterpieces, recorded shortly before the premature death of the soloist. Though its structure may seem rhapsodic, it is in fact closely co-ordinated, as the late Deryck Cooke amply illustrated. Holmes and Handley together bring out the Delian warmth in their shaping of phrase and pointing of rhythm while keeping firm overall control. Holmes's beautifully focused playing is nicely balanced against the wide span of the orchestra behind him, and here the resonance seems just right. *A Late lark* was the last composition which Delius was able to finish, except for a few bars, before the arrival of Eric Fenby; while *A Song of summer* is the finest of the works which Fenby subsequently took down from the dictation of the blind, paralysed and irascible composer; the performance is loving and dedicated. The programme opens with a ravishingly atmospheric account of the *Irmelin Prelude*, arranged by Fenby with the composer's approval, taking material from an opera at a time when it seemed it would never receive a full performance.

Volume 3: (i) *Koanga: La Calinda;* (i–iii) *Idyll;* (i–iv) *Songs of sunset;* (v) *A Village Romeo and Juliet: Walk to the Paradise Garden.*
(M) *** Unicorn Dig. UKCD 2073 [id.]. RPO; (i) Fenby; with (ii) Felicity Lott, (iii) Thomas Allen; (iv) Sarah Walker, Amb. S. (v) Del Mar.

In this continuing series, conducted for the most part by Eric Fenby – without whose help for the blind and paralysed composer the later Delius works would never have existed – Volume 3 is particularly valuable. The love scene entitled *Idyll* was rescued from an abortive opera project (*Margot la rouge*) and the composer reworked the music to words of Walt Whitman, arranged by Robert Nichols. It becomes a beautiful, extended duet in this impressive performance by Felicity Lott and Thomas Allen. Allen is no less persuasive in the *Songs of sunset*, where he is joined by Sarah Walker, and this fine recording brings ravishing sounds from the Ambrosians, with both soloists deeply expressive. The concert opens with Norman Del Mar's languorously brooding yet passionate account of the *Walk to the Paradise Garden* and ends with Fenby's expansive performance of *La Calinda*, which begins with deceptive delicacy. First-class digital sound throughout.

Volume 4: (i) *Cello sonata;* (ii) *Violin sonatas Nos. 1–3.*
(M) *** Unicorn Dig./Analogue UKCD 2074 [id.]. (i) Julian Lloyd Webber; (ii) Ralph Holmes; Eric Fenby.

(i) *Cello sonata; Violin sonatas Nos.* (ii) *1–2;* (iii) *3.*
*** EMI Dig. CDC5 55399-2 [id.]. (i) Moray Welsh; (ii) Janice Graham; (iii) Alexander Barantschick; (i–iii) Israela Margalit.

The *Cello sonata* dates from the fruitful period of the First World War, when Delius wrote a sequence of richly lyrical and imaginative works – concertos as well as sonatas – in what ostensibly were conventional forms but which in fact he moulded to his very own personal expression. Lloyd Webber is a warmly persuasive advocate and Fenby partners him admirably. The three *Violin sonatas*, particularly the last, which we owe entirely to Eric Fenby's ability to transcribe the totally incapaci-tated composer's inspirations, are also among the finest of Delius's chamber works. Though Fenby as pianist may not be a virtuoso, the natural affinity of his playing and that of Ralph Holmes with the composer's muse makes this one of the most treasurable and moving of Delius recordings. The *Cello sonata* was recorded digitally in 1981 and is set in a natural and pleasing acoustic. The *Violin sonatas*, dating from a decade earlier, are also atmospheric in ambience, but the violin timbre has just a hint of thinness on top.

Those looking for modern digital recordings of these same four works will find that the performances by members of the LSO, in EMI's Anglo-American Chamber Music series, are in every way satisfying. Moray Welsh provides warm tone and much depth of feeling in the *Cello sonata* and Janice Graham's passionate advocacy in the earlier *Violin sonatas* matches that of Alexander Barantschik in the *Third*, which opens the record. Israela Margalit's pianism in all four works is full of personality. The recording is both resonant and forwardly balanced, and satisfyingly full.

(i) *Brigg Fair; La Calinda* (arr. Fenby); *In a summer garden; Intermezzo from Fennimore and Gerda; Intermezzo* and (iii) *Serenade* from *Hassan* (arr. Beecham); (ii) *Irmelin prelude;* (i) *Late swallows* (arr.

Fenby); *On hearing the first cuckoo in spring; A song before sunrise;* (ii) *A song of summer;* (i) *Summer night on the river;* (ii) *A Village Romeo and Juliet: Walk to the Paradise Garden* (arr. Beecham); (i; iv) *Appalachia* (with brief rehearsal sequence).
(M) *** EMI CMS5 65119-2 [Ang. ZDMB 65119]. (i) Hallé O; (ii) LSO, Sir John Barbirolli; (iii) with Robert Tear; (iv) Balun Jenkins, Amb. S.

Atmospheric and loving performances of these colourful scores. Sir John shows an admirable feeling for the sense of light Delius conjures up and for the luxuriance of texture his music possesses. The languor of the string and horn tune in *Brigg Fair* is matched by the almost Mediterranean feeling of the works evoking summer, whilst the gentle evocation of *La Calinda* contrasts with the surge of passionate Italianate romanticism at the arching string-phrases of the climax of *The walk to the Paradise Garden*. Barbirolli's style is evanescent in repose and more romantic than the Beecham versions but, with lovely playing from both the Hallé and the LSO, the first-rate analogue sound from the mid- to late 1960s adds to the listener's pleasure. In *Appalachia*, perhaps Barbirolli dwells a little too lovingly on detail to suit all tastes, but for the most part he gives an admirably atmospheric reading that conveys the work's exotic and vivid colouring.

Brigg Fair; In a summer garden; Paris (The song of a great city); On hearing the first cuckoo in spring; A song of summer; Summer night on the river.
(M) (***) Dutton Lab. CDLXT 2503 [id.]. LSO, Anthony Collins.

Mike Dutton works another of his miracles here, achieving colour, body and translucence for these 1953 Decca recordings and revealing why they were so much admired in their day. Made in the Kingsway Hall, the ambient warmth of that famous venue means that the usual flatness of mono perspective all but disappears except in the complex fortissimos, and the glow of the sound, so essential in Delius, makes listening to this CD a real pleasure, with no apologies necessary for the body of string-tone. In their day Collins's two Delius LPs, which are here combined (but without the *Walk to the Paradise Garden*), rested under the shadow of Sir Thomas Beecham. Yet this Collins performance of *Paris*, so spontaneously full of passionate evocation, confirms the younger man as an inspired and individual Delian in his own right, able to create a subtle control of mood and texture reminiscent of Debussy in its atmospheric impressionism. But *Brigg Fair*, for all its ardour, is totally English in feeling. The delicate woodwind playing at the opening is most beautiful, while the hazy languor of the string theme, echoed by the horn, is wonderfully gentle in its sentience. Indeed there is lovely string and exquisite wind playing throughout; *First cuckoo* is not less luminous in its woodwind detail. The recording shows how far Decca's engineers were ahead of the competition with their *ffrr* (full frequency range recording) technique, even in the earliest days of LP.

Dance rhapsodies Nos. 1–2; In a summer garden; North country sketches; A Village Romeo and Juliet: Walk to the Paradise Garden.
**(*) Chan. Dig. CHAN 9355 [id.]. Bournemouth SO, Richard Hickox.

Hickox is a sensitive and flexible Delian and the Bournemouth orchestra play passionately for him, especially in the *Walk to the Paradise Garden*. The *Dance rhapsodies* are impulsively volatile and attractively so, but they are not held together quite so persuasively as by Eric Fenby, who also has the advantage of smoother and more natural string recording. *In a summer garden* is both ardent and luxuriant in its shimmering summer heat-haze, while the wintry landscape of the *North country sketches* brings almost crystalline iciness from the violins. The *March of spring* with its 'light, lively and throbbing movement' is chimerically spontanenous in unfolding its kaleidoscopic detail. But the recording, made in the Winter Gardens, Bournemouth, although basically full and spacious, brings a somewhat two-dimensional effect in catching the fervent sweep of violin-tone, as if the microphones were a little too close.

On hearing the first cuckoo in spring; Summer night on the river.
(B) *** DG 439 464-2 [id.]. ECO, Barenboim – BRITTEN: *Serenade*; VAUGHAN WILLIAMS: *Greensleeves; Lark ascending.* ***

Hazily sensuous in the summer sunshine, Barenboim's performances are warmly and enticingly recorded as part of a fine bargain collection of English music.

VOCAL AND CHORAL MUSIC

Sea drift.
(M) ** EMI CDM5 65113-2 [id.]. John Noble, R. Liverpool PO Ch. & O, Ch, Groves – STANFORD: *Songs of the sea* etc. **(*)

Sir Charles Groves could be a persausive Delian, but his 1973 recording of *Sea drift* is rather too matter-of-fact, failing to convey the surge of inspiration that so exactly matches the evocative colours of Walt Whitman's poem about the seagull, a solitary guest from Alabama. The recording is generally very good.

Denisov, Edison (born 1929)

Variations on Haydn's Canon, 'Tod ist ein langer Schlaf' (Death is a long sleep).
*** RCA Dig. 09026 68061-2 [id.]. Moscow Virtuosi, Vladimir Spivakov – SHOSTAKOVICH: *Chamber symphony No. 2;* PART: *Collage on B-A-C-H* etc.; SHCHEDRIN: *Stalin cocktail.* ***

The Soviet composer Edison Denisov kept a low enough profile to survive the Zhdanov witch-hunt and, like his contemporary, Alfred Schnittke, was later able to write experimental music. His *Variations* celebrated the 250th anniversary of Haydn's birth in 1982, and one wonders what Haydn would have made of this 13-minute concertante cello piece. The soloist's eloquent soliloquy reaches a climax against weird slithers and oscillations from the strings and woodwind, then finally vanquishes their intrusions and breaks free into a touching unaccompanied elegy. The piece closes with three gentle bell-strokes, thus preparing the way for the Arvo Pärt *Cantus*, which follows in this well-planned, very well-played and admirably recorded concert.

Devreese, Frédéric (born 1929)

Belle; Benvenuta (suite); *L'œuvre au noir* (suite); *Un soir, un train.*
** Marco Polo Dig. 8.223681 [id.]. Belgian R. & TV PO (Brussels), composer.

Effective and at times appealing film scores by an accomplished composer, the son of Godfried Devreese. They do not amount to anything more than what they set out to do, which is to provide atmospheric background to events on the screen. Taken out of context, they provide some pleasure but little substance. They are well played by the Belgian Radio and Television Philharmonic under the composer's own direction, and are very well recorded, too.

Piano concertos Nos. 2–4.
** Marco Polo Dig. 8.223505 [id.]. Daniel Blumenthal, Belgian R. & TV PO (Brussels), composer.

There is a lot of Prokofiev in the *Piano concerto No. 2*, and there are also similarities with, say, Malcolm Arnold. The writing is effective, without being in any way memorable. There are occasional reminders of the Honegger of the middle movement of the *Concerto* as well as Prokofiev in the *Piano concerto No. 3*. Nearly three decades separate it from the shorter and rather Bartókian *Piano concerto No. 4*, which is in two movements – *Introduction and variations* and *Finale*. It was commissioned for the International Queen of the Belgians Competition to be played as the set piece. Daniel Blumenthal, who was one of the contestants, plays this and the earlier concertos brilliantly and is well supported by the excellent Belgian Radio and Television Orchestra under the composer's direction. Well-crafted, literate music and, if it is of no great individuality, it is still worth hearing.

Devreese, Godfried (1893–1972)

(i) *Cello concertino;* (ii) *Violin concerto No. 1. Tombelène* (choreographic suite).
*** Marco Polo Dig. 8.223680 [id.]. (i) Viviane Spanoghe, (ii) Guido de Neve. Belgian R. & TV PO (Brussels), Frédéric Devreese.

Godfried Devreese is a Belgian composer whose work is little known outside his native country. He was for many years a member of the Concertgebouw Orchestra in Amsterdam and was violist in the Concertgebouw Quartet, before becoming Principal of the Mechelen Conservatoire. The ballet, *Tombelène*, dates from 1925–6 and was premièred under Gabriel Pierné. It is rather derivative – but none the worse for that – close in atmosphere and idiom to early Stravinsky and Florent Schmitt's *Tragédie de Salomé*. But Devreese is imaginative as well as a gifted and colourful orchestrator, and this suite gives pleasure. His *Violin concerto No. 1* sounds balletic in inspiration (the composer spoke of it as semi-Apollonian, semi-Dionysian in conception), and if you respond to the Bloch and Delius concertos, you would find much here to engage your sympathies. The *Cello concertino* (1930) originally appeared scored for 15 wind instruments, celesta, harp, six double-basses and variously tuned side-drums. The present version is rescored by his son for more practical forces; it, too, is imaginative without possessing a strong individual voice. Very good performances and vivid, well-detailed recording.

Diamond, David (born 1915)

Symphony No. 8; Suite No. 1 from the ballet, Tom; (i) *This sacred ground.*
*** Delos Dig. DE 3141 [id.]. (i) Erich Parce, Seattle Ch., Seattle Girls' Ch., NorthWest Boys' Ch.; Seattle SO, Gerard Schwarz.

It is good to note the increasing representation on CD of this long-neglected and civilized composer. The earliest work is the *First Suite from the ballet, Tom.* The scenario, by e. e. cummings, was based on Harriet Beecher Stowe's famous abolitionist novel for the twenty-year-old composer, but it was never staged. It is often powerful and inventive, and inhabits much the same musical world as Aaron Copland, Diamond's mentor and friend, for whose sixtieth birthday the *Eighth Symphony* was composed. Although it makes use of serial technique, it will still present few problems to those familiar with Diamond's earlier music, for it remains lyrical and thought-provoking. It culminates in a double fugue of considerable ingenuity. *This sacred ground* is a short setting for soloist, choirs and orchestra of the Gettysburg address, which may not travel so well. Much of it finds his muse on auto-pilot. Well worth investigating for the ballet and the symphony. Committed performances and excellent, natural, recorded sound.

Diepenbrock, Alphons (1862–1921)

Im grossen Schweigen.
*** Decca Dig. 444 446-2 (2) [id.]. Hagegård, Concg. O, Chailly – MAHLER: *Symphony No. 7.* **(*)

A contemporary and friend of Mahler, similarly short-lived, the Dutch composer Diepenbrock wrote his colourful setting of Nietzsche, *Im grossen Schweigen* ('In the great silence'), around the same time as Mahler wrote his *Symphony No. 7*, making it an unusual and apt coupling for that work. The words are a prose meditation inspired by the sea, and Diepenbrock sets them in a colourful, evocative way with many Mahlerian overtones and superb orchestration. Håkan Hagegård is the firm, expressive soloist, and both performance and recording are outstanding.

Dieupart, Charles (after 1667–1740)

Frans Brüggen Edition, Volume 6: *Suites in G min. and A.*
(M) *** Teldec/Warner 4509 97468-2 [id.]. Frans Brüggen, Kees Boeke, Nikolaus Harnoncourt, Anner Bylsma, Gustav Leonhardt – HOTTETERRE: *Suite No. 1.* ***

These two suites by Dieupart (a French-born musician who taught in London around 1700 and whose harpsichord suites influenced Bach) are very much cast in the style favoured by Telemann, with an *Overture* and a collection of colourful dances, and they have a distinctive French elegance and charm. Both are ingeniously contrived so that each movement is derived from the opening phrase of the music first heard in the *Overture*: the result is like an ingenious set of divisions, although each dance has its own completeness. Brüggen uses a different instrument for each suite. For the *G major* he chooses a bright, early eighteenth-century English Bressan recorder, but the 'voice flute' used in the *A major Suite* is another Bressan with a paler personality. Brüggen's usual team provide thoroughly stylish accompaniments and the early-1970s recording is excellent.

Dohnányi, Ernst von (1877–1960)

Variations on a nursery song, Op. 25.
*(*) Nimbus Dig. NI 5349 [id.]. Mark Anderson, Hungarian State SO, Adám Fischer – BRAHMS: *Piano concerto No. 1.* *(*)

A goodish performance of the perennially fresh *Nursery song variations* from the young American pianist, Mark Anderson, and the Hungarian State Symphony Orchestra under Adám Fischer. Not touched by sufficient distinction as performance or recording to displace existing recommendations.

(i; ii) *Piano quintets Nos. 1 in C min., Op. 1; 2 in E flat min., Op. 28;* (i) *Suite in the old style, Op. 24.*
*** ASV Dig. CDDCA 915 [id.]. (i) Martin Roscoe; (ii) Vanbrugh Qt.

When nowadays even Dohnányi's witty *Nursery variations* are neglected, it is good to have three works that winningly bring out the composer's lyrical warmth and his keen instrumental mastery. He wrote the first of his two *Piano quintets* when still in his teens, ripely Brahmsian, built strongly on memorable themes. The *Second quintet*, dating from twenty years later, just after the *Nursery variations*, is sharper and more compact, with Hungarian flavours more pronounced, if never Bartókian. The *Suite in the old style*, for piano alone, is an amiable example of pre-Stravinsky neo-classicism, again beautifully written for the instrument. The prize-winning Vanbrugh Quartet is well matched by Martin Roscoe in keen, alert performances, warmly recorded.

Donizetti, Gaetano (1797–1848)

Ballet music from: *L'assedio di Calais; Dom Sébastien; La favorita; Les martyres.*
(B) *** Ph. Duo 442 553-2 (2) [id.]. Philh. O, Antonio de Almeida – ROSSINI: *Ballet music.* **(*)

Music from the baroque period has given us dozens of records which are validly used for aural wallpaper. The ballet music from four of Donizetti's operas which were presented in Paris provides a nineteenth-century equivalent, sparkling, refreshing dances of no great originality, delivered here with great zest and resilience and fine solo playing, and excellently recorded. The Rossini coupling offers even more characterful music, and if the playing of the Monte Carlo Orchestra cannot match that of the Philharmonia, this is still very enjoyable.

String quartet in D (arr. for string orchestra).
(B) *** Decca Double 443 838-2 (2) [id.]. ASMF, Marriner – ROSSINI: *String sonatas Nos. 1–6* (with CHERUBINI: *Etude No. 2 for French horn and strings* (with Barry Tuckwell); BELLINI: *Oboe concerto in E flat* (with Roger Lord) ***).

This delightful 'prentice work has a sunny lyricism and a melodic freshness that speak of youthful genius. The composer's craftsmanship is obvious and the writing is such that (unlike Verdi's *String quartet*) it lends itself readily to performance by a string orchestra, especially when the playing is so warm-hearted and polished and the recording transferred so immaculately to CD. A fine bonus for the irresistible Rossini *String sonatas.*

String quartets Nos. 7 in F min.; 8 in B flat; 9 in D min.
* CPO Dig. CPO 999170-2 [id.]. Revolutionary Drawing Room.

If would be useful to have a recommendable CD of the Donizetti *String quartets*, but this will not do. The players here may be revolutionary in their approach to authenticity, but the Gillette-edged timbre of the leader would not be welcome in an elegant nineteenth-century drawing-room. Its thin penetration dominates the texture to such an extent that any convincing overall blend of sonority between the four instruments seems possible only very occasionally.

OPERA

Don Pasquale (complete).
*** RCA Dig. 09026 61924-2 (2) [id.]. Bruson, Mei, Allen, Lopardo, Bav. R. Ch., Munich R. O, Roberto Abbado.
(M) * Ph. 442 090-2(2) [id.]. Capecchi, Rizzoli, Valdengo, Munteanu, Teatro di San Carlo di Napoli Ch. & O, Molinari-Pradelli.

In vivid, immediate sound and with voices balanced well forward, Roberto Abbado's Munich set for RCA is on balance the finest modern version of Donizetti's sparkling comedy. Not only does Abbado spring rhythms cleanly and lightly, they are made the more infectious by the clarity of focus. The cast has no weak link. Renato Bruson may accentuate Pasquale's comic lines with little explosions of underlining, but that helps to distinguish him sharply as a *buffo* character from his opposite number, Malatesta, here sung with rare style and beauty by Thomas Allen, as well as with a nicely timed feeling for the comedy. In their celebrated patter duet in Act III they convey the jollity without resorting to exaggeration. Trained on Rossini as well as Donizetti, Frank Lopardo as Ernesto shades his clear tenor most sensitively, singing his *Serenade* with far more refinement than most latterday rivals. Eva Mei sings the role of Norina with an apt brightness and precision (including an excellent trill), even if others have presented a more characterful heroine.

Dating from the mid-1950s, the Philips set from Naples is disappointing. Renato Capecchi was renowned in *buffo* roles but, for all the clarity of articulation, his performance sounds gruff, with little fun in it, and Giuseppe Valdengo is a one-dimensional Malatesta. Bruna Rizzoli with her shallow, if cleanly produced, soprano is an unappealing Norina, and the vocal joys of the set lie almost entirely in the singing of the Romanian, Petre Munteanu, as Ernesto, singing sweetly and stylishly.

L'Elisir d'amore (complete).
(B) **(*) Decca Double 443 542-2 (2) [id.]. Gueden, Di Stefano, Corena, Capecchi, Mandelli, Maggio Musicale Fiorentino Ch. & O, Molinari-Pradelli.
(M) **(*) RCA Dig. 74321 25280-2 (2) [id.]. Popp, Dvorský, Weikl, Nesterenko, Munich R. Ch. & O, Wallberg.

With Hilde Gueden at her most seductive – an enchanting, provocative Adina, characterfully using her golden tone to bring out the minx-like qualities of the heroine – this very early (1955) stereo recording offers a delightful, spontaneous-sounding performance. Not just Gueden but also the other soloists are strikingly characterful, with Giuseppe di Stefano at his most headily sweet-toned, singing with youthful ardour, Fernando Corena a strong and vehement Dulcamara and Renato Capecchi well contrasted as Sergeant Belcore, though not quite so firm of tone, but both splendidly comic. A totally happy set, well transferred, if with some thinness on top, making high violins a little wiry. Even without a libretto it makes a good bargain, with two CDs offered for the price of one.

Wallberg conducts a lightly sprung performance of Donizetti's sparkling comic opera, well recorded and marked by a charming performance of the role of Adina from Lucia Popp, bright-eyed and with delicious detail both verbal and musical. Nesterenko makes a splendidly resonant Dr Dulcamara with more comic sparkle than you would expect from a great Russian bass. Dvorský and Weikl, both sensitive artists, sound much less idiomatic, with Dvorský's tight tenor growing harsh under pressure, not at all Italianate, and Weikl failing similarly to give necessary roundness to the role of Belcore. Like other sets recorded in association with Bavarian Radio, the 1982 sound is excellent, naturally balanced and with voices never spotlit. Though this RCA set (previously on Eurodisc) does not displace the Sutherland/Pavarotti/Bonynge set on Decca (414 461-2), it makes a viable alternative, especially for admirers of Lucia Popp.

Lucia di Lammermoor: highlights
** Teldec/Warner Dig. 4509 93692-2 [id.] (from recording with Gruberová, Shicoff, Agache; cond. Bonynge).

This 72-minute selection comes from a very disappointing complete performance, with Gruberová tending to sound emotionally over the top and self-consciously so. Schicoff is a strong but coarse Edgardo. Bonynge's alternative Decca highlights with Sutherland and Pavarotti is far superior (421 885-2).

Dufay, Guillaume (c. 1400–1474)

Missa L'homme armé; Motet: *Supremum est mortalibus bonum.*
(BB) *** Naxos Dig. 8.553087 [id.]. Oxford Camerata, Jeremy Summerly.

Jeremy Summerly and his Oxford Camerata give a powerfully expressive and wholly convincing account of Dufay's masterly cyclic Mass using a Burgundian chanson as its basis. We hear this sung first in its original format as an introduction, and its message, 'The armed man should be feared', makes a dramatically appropriate contrast with the motet, *Supremum est mortalibus* which is a peace song. The latter was written some 30 years earlier, yet shows just as readily the remarkable inventiveness and eloquence of this fifteenth-century French composer. The Mass movements are interspersed with plainchant in the same Dorian mode. With vivid yet atmospheric recording, this can be given the strongest recommendation.

Dussek (Dusik), Jan Ladislav (1760–1812)

Keyboard sonatas: in D, Op. 31/2; in B flat; in G; in C min., Op. 35/1–3.
*** HM/BMG Dig. 05472 77286-2 [id.]. Andreas Staier (fortepiano).

The four sonatas in Andreas Staier's recital come from Dussek's London years in the 1790s, when he was befriended by Haydn and John Broadwood, the piano-maker, for whose five-and-a-half-octave grand the three sonatas of Op. 35 (1797) were written. Staier's exhilarating recital is recorded on a Broadwood of 1806, restored by Christopher Clarke, who describes it as 'loud, sonorous, dramatic, a little vulgar'. It has all the weight to cope with the dramatic flair which Staier brings to these highly interesting and occasionally prophetic sonatas. At one point the *B flat Sonata*, Op. 35/1, anticipates Schubert, and the *C minor*, Op. 35/3, has often been compared with the Beethoven *Pathétique*.

Dutilleux, Henri (born 1916)

(i) *Métaboles;* (ii) *Mystère de l'instant;* (i) *Timbres, Espace, Mouvement (La nuit étoilée)*.
** Erato/Warner 2292 45626-2 [id.]. (i) O Nat. de France, Rostropovich; (ii) Coll. Mus., Paul Sacher.

The *Métaboles* is the earliest work here and is now well represented in the catalogue. *Timbres, Espace, Mouvement*, inspired by van Gogh's painting *La nuit étoilée*, is highly imaginative, and it is good to have it under the baton of Rostropovich, who commissioned it. Both performances date from 1982 and are analogue. The most important piece, *Mystère de l'instant*, dates from 1989 and was composed to a commission by Paul Sacher. It is a set of ten miniatures, 'snapshots' of both subtlety and ingenuity, splendidly played by the Collegium Musicum under Sacher and digitally recorded. Given the date of the recording of the two main works and the short playing time (46 minutes), this would have been more competitively priced at less than full price.

(i) *Ainsi la nuit* (for string quartet); (ii) *Les Citations* (diptyque for oboe, harpsichord, double-bass & percussion); (iii) *3 Strophes sur le nom de Sacher* (for unaccompanied cello); (iv) *Figure de résonances* (for two pianos); (v) *3 Préludes; Sonate;* (vi) *2 Sonnets de Jean Cassou*.
*** Erato/Warner Dig. 4509 91721-2 (2) [id.]. (i) Quatuor sine Nomine; (ii) Bourgue, Dreyfus, Cazauran, Balet; (iii) Geringas; (iv–v) Joy; (iv) composer; (vi) Cachemaille.

These two Erato CDs afford an excellent survey of Dutilleux's chamber and instrumental music in this, his eightieth year. They include the *Sonata* of 1947, played by the pianist most closely associated with it over the years, Geneviève Joy – and played with great zest and panache, too! Although Ogdon recorded it on LP (and it is already represented on CD by Donna Amato, coupled with the Balakirev *B flat minor Sonata*), this French version has obvious authority. Joy is no less excellent in the *Préludes*. Dutilleux is a composer of keen imaginative awareness and consistent inventive quality, who always holds the listener – *Les Citations* for oboe, harpsichord, double-bass and percussion is a case in point. *Ainsi la nuit* is fairly well represented on CD now and those who already have it, coupled with the Debussy and Ravel quartets (as it is by the Juilliard), may want to think twice before buying this full-price two-CD set, which offers 40-odd minutes a disc. Those coming to it afresh need not hesitate. The performances and recording are very fine and the music stimulating and rewarding.

Dvořák, Antonín (1841–1904)

Czech suite.
(M) **f Ph. 442 660-2[id.]. ECO, Mackerras – JANACEK: *Sinfonietta* etc. (*)

Mackerras gives a fresh, lively performance of a lesser-known Dvořák orchestral work, and the 1980 Philips recording is naturally balanced. Alas, the coupling is a non-starter.

Cello concerto in B min., Op.104.
⊛ (M) *** DG 447 413-2 [id.]. Rostropovich, BPO, Karajan – TCHAIKOVSKY: *Variations on a rococo theme*. *** ⊛

There have been a number of distinguished recordings of both the Dvořák *Concerto* and its equally seductive Tchaikovsky coupling over the two and a half decades since this DG record was made, but none to match it for intensity of lyrical feeling and the spontaneity of the partnership between Karajan and Rostropovich. Any moments of romantic indulgence from the soloist, who is clearly deeply inside the music, are set against Karajan's overall control, which provides a firm yet supple bass. The orchestral playing is glorious, as instanced by the beautiful introduction of the secondary theme of the first movement by the principal horn. Moreover the analogue recording, made in the Jesus-Christus Kirche in September 1969 and produced by Otto Gerdes and balanced by Günter Hermann, is as near perfect as any made in that vintage analogue era. The CD transfer has freshened the original, and the metaphor of 'cleaning an Old Master' readily applies to a sound-picture which projects the soloist with remarkable presence and realism and loses only a little allure in the vibrant fortissimo violins and just a degree of resonance in the bass. This provides an ideal choice at the summit of DG's 'Legendary Originals' series and for once the sobriquet is absolutely justified. Engagingly, the CD itself is made to look like a miniature reproduction of the famous yellow-label LP, complete with a glossy light reflecting on the black vinyl surface.

(i) *Cello concerto; Symphony No. 8 in G, Op.35.*
(BB) **(*) RCA Navigator 74321 2189-2. (i) Piatigorsky; Boston SO, Munch.

When it first appeared on LP, we were inclined almost to dismiss Piatigorsky's 1960 recording because the sound was so shallow. It has been improved remarkably for this CD and, although the balance is still too close and not always flattering to the soloist, with tuttis still inclined to be somewhat two-dimensional, the quality is now fully acceptable. There is no lack of orchestral colour and the acoustic of Symphony Hall is conveyed behind the music-making. The performance is the very opposite of routine, with Piatigorsky and Munch in complete rapport, producing a consistently spontaneous melodic flow, moving from introspective thoughtfulness to expressive warmth and ardour. Tuttis blaze up in the orchestra, yet the soloist brings moments of rapt meditation; although there are also moments when intonation is less than immaculate, the inspiration of the performance carries the day. This is well matched by Munch's account of the *G major Symphony*, recorded a year later. As in the *Concerto*, the improvement in the recorded sound is remarkable and the work is made to sound extremely vivid against the spacious Boston acoustic. Munch's reading is strongly character-ized and, though he occasionally presses hard, the thrust comes from a natural ardour. The performance undoubtedly adds a degree of fierceness to Dvořák's sunny masterpiece but it is very firmly held together and, as always with this conductor, there is a splendid sense of line and momentum. Some might feel the finale a bit overdriven, but there is plenty of feeling in the slow movement and few would fail to respond to the passionate blossoming in the strings of the inspired lyrical theme that forms the centrepiece of the third-movement *Allegretto*.

(i) *Cello concerto;* (ii) *Symphony No.9 (New World).*
(M) *** Ph. 442 401-2 [id.]. (i) Heinrich Schiff; Concg. O; (i) Sir Colin Davis; (ii) Antal Dorati.

(i) *Cello concerto;* (ii) *Symphony No. 9 (New World); Carnaval overture, Op. 92; Scherzo capriccioso, Op. 66.*
(BB) *** EMI Seraphim CES5 68521-2 (2) [CEDB 68521]. (i) Paul Tortelier, LSO, Previn; (ii)
    Philh. O, Giulini – TCHAIKOVSKY: *Variations on a Rococo theme.* ***

The two Philips performances are fascinatingly different in character. Schiff's reading of the *Concerto* (from the beginning of the 1980s) brings an unexaggerated vein of poetry akin to the approach of Yo-Yo Ma – its range of emotion is on a relatively small scale, though satisfying in its intimacy. This performance remains among the very top choices for the *Cello Concerto*, refreshingly different from the more extrovert Rostropovich account. It sounds extremely well in its CD transfer. Dorati's *New World* is characteristically vibrant and extrovert, less subtle but compelling in its direct way; indeed the level of tension is high in the outer movements and the finale ends with a thrilling surge of adrenalin. Because of the rich Concertgebouw acoustic, the forwardly balanced recording from the late 1950s does not sound too dated; indeed the woodwind glow attractively in the *Largo*.

The richness of Tortelier's reading of Dvořák's *Cello concerto* has long been appreciated on record; his 1978 recording with Previn has a satisfying centrality, not as passionately romantic as Rostropovich's recording on DG, but with the tenderness as well as the power of the work held in perfect equilibrium. What is rather less perfect is the balance of the recording, favouring the cellist too much, and, although the digital remastering has improved overall clarity, the microphones are obviously rather too near the soloist. Giulini's recording of the *New World Symphony* was made when the Philharmonia was at its peak in 1962. The result has a refinement, coupled to an attractive directness, which for some will make it an ideal reading. The remastering gives the sound plenty of warmth and projection and, if the performance is not as physically exciting as some versions, like Reiner's Chicago account, the playing, with its beautiful moulding of phrase, is very refreshing. With two attractive bonuses (the lyrical side of the *Scherzo capriccioso* appealingly affectionate), this is a bargain on EMI's new Seraphim series, offering two discs for the cost of one medium-priced CD, for the Tchaikovsky *Rococo variations* is also well worth having.

(i) *Piano concerto in G min., Op. 33; The Water Goblin (symphonic poem), Op. 107.*
(BB) *** Naxos Dig. 8.550896 [id.]. (i) Jenö Jandó; Polish Nat. RSO, Antoni Wit.

An infectiously fresh and warmly lyrical account from Jandó and the highly supportive Polish National Radio Orchestra under Antoni Wit, which makes it difficult to understand why the piece is not a popular favourite. The first movement is based on two memorable yet contrasted ideas, the lovely *Andante* opens with the solo horn poetically giving us just an anticipatory whiff of the *Largo* from the *New World Symphony*, and the finale ripples along with an irrepressible lightness of spirit. Jandó plays with engaging freshness and conveys his own pleasure, and Wit's accompaniment glows with colour; he then offers a splendidly vibrant and colourful portrayal of *The Water Goblin*, one of the composer's most vividly melodramatic symphonic poems. The recording is admirably spacious and realistically balanced. The violins are a shade overbright, but otherwise the sound is first class. Very enjoyable and well worth its modest cost.

Violin concerto in A min., Op. 53.
*** Virgin/EMI Dig. VC5 45022-2 [id.]. Christian Tetzlaff, Czech PO, Pešek – LALO: *Symphonie espagnole.* ***
*** EMI Dig. CDC7 54872-2 [id.]. Zimmermann, LPO, Welser-Möst – GLAZUNOV: *Concerto.* ***

Violin concerto in A min., Op. 53; Romance in F min., Op. 11.
(BB) *** Naxos Dig. 8.550758 [id.]. Ilya Kaler, Polish Nat. RSO (Katowice), Camilla Kolchinsky – GLAZUNOV: *Concerto.* ***

Adding to the list of excellent new recordings of the Dvořák *Violin concerto*, Tetzlaff's version brings not only a unique and generous coupling in the Lalo *Symphonie espagnole* but an obvious advantage in having the composer's compatriots accompanying, with crisp ensemble and rhythms deliciously sprung. Tetzlaff's performance, distinguished by quicksilver lightness in the passage-work, is both full of fantasy and marked by keen concentration and a sense of spontaneity. With the violin balanced naturally, not spotlit, the slow movement has a hushed intensity at the opening, which gives extra poignancy to Tetzlaff's tender, totally unsentimental phrasing. In romantic freedom of expression Tetzlaff comes somewhere between Midori and Chung on the one hand and the restrained Zimmermann on the other. Characteristically, Pešek makes orchestral textures clear, bringing out extra detail even in the heaviest tuttis, despite reverberant recording. Very recommendable.

Frank Peter Zimmermann's account of the Dvořák concerto is fresh and full of spirit. His rhythms are lightly sprung and he conveys great delight in this genial yet underrated score. There are some twenty or so accounts in the catalogue, and this belongs among the best. Certainly the LPO under Franz Welser-Möst are supportive, and the EMI recording is first class.

The performance of the Russian violinist, Ilya Kaler, has great romantic warmth and natural Slavonic feeling, and he is given excellent support by Kolchinsky and the Polish orchestra. In short this is first class in every way, irrespective of cost, with a richly sustained *Adagio* and a sparkling finale. The one snag, if snag it be, concerns the very resonant acoustics of the recording, made in the Concert Hall of Polish Radio, which (with fairly close microphones) give the soloist a somewhat larger-than-life image against a widely resonant orchestral backcloth. But the effect is easy to enjoy when the playing is so ardent; moreover these artists tend to trump the opposition by offering the *Romance in F minor* as a considerable (13-minute) bonus, and that is also beautifully played.

Czech suite, Op. 39; A Hero's song, Op. 111; Festival march, Op. 54; Hussite overture, Op. 67.
(BB) **(*) Naxos Dig. 8.553005 [id.]. Polish Nat. RSO (Katowice), Antoni Wit.

Antoni Wit, who has already given us a memorable performance of Smetana's *Má Vlast*, is almost equally impressive in *A Hero's song*, written in 1897 and first performed in Vienna under Mahler the following year. It opens atmospherically and produces a characteristically Slavonic melodic flow, with some lovely writing for strings and horns. There is an outburst of patriotic hyperbole towards the close (with thundering trombones), which is considerably inflated by the resonant acoustics of the Concert Hall of Polish Radio, which have a similar effect on the *Hussite overture* and *Festival march*; however, no one could grumble that the result lacks spectacle, and Antoni Wit generates excitement without letting things get out of hand. The performance of the *Czech suite* is warm and relaxed, nicely rustic in feeling, but again is affected by the resonance.

Legends Nos. 1–10, Op. 59; Nocturne for strings; (i) Romance in F min., Op. 11.
(M) *** EMI Dig. CD-EMX 2232; *TC-EMX 2232* [id.]. (i) Stephanie Gonley; ECO, Mackerras.

Dvořák in lighter mood inspires a charmer of a record, perfect for relaxed listening. The ten *Legends*, like the *Slavonic dances*, were originally written for piano duet and were orchestrated later, easy-going pieces given winningly pointed performances by Mackerras and the ECO, helped by glowing recorded sound. The critic Eduard Hanslick, so far from acting like Beckmesser (as Wagner portrayed him in *Meistersinger*), was delighted to receive the dedication. The ECO strings play with similar refinement in the early *Nocturne*, and Stephanie Gonley, the ECO's leader, is the characterful soloist in the longest of the pieces, the haunting *Romance* for violin and orchestra.

Serenade for strings in E, Op. 22.
(M) **(*) Ph. Dig. 442 402-2 [id.]. Bav. RSO, Sir Colin Davis – TCHAIKOVSKY : *Serenade.* **(*)
(M) *(*) EMI CDM5 68343-2 [id.]. BBC SO, Rudolf Schwarz – TCHAIKOVSKY; WIREN: *Serenades.* ***

Sir Colin Davis in his version with the Bavarian Radio Symphony Orchestra gives a heavyweight performance, marked by speeds on the slow side, particularly in the first movement. With the Bavarian string-sound rich and silky and a well-upholstered bass, it is warmly enjoyable, with the dance rhythms subtly sprung, but it misses some of the spring-like freshness of the work's inspiration.

Schwarz is spaciously recorded; the wide acoustic, plus fine string playing, do more for the music than does the conductor, who is heavy and stolid. There is an airy grace to this lovely *Serenade* which he barely hints at.

Slavonic dances Nos. 1–8, Op. 46; 9–16, Op. 72.
*** Ph. Dig. 442 125-2 [id.]. VPO, André Previn.

Previn with his rhythmic flair brings out the playfulness of the *Slavonic dances* as few others do. One is regularly reminded of the closeness of Dvořák's Bohemia to Vienna, when in the warm Musikverein acoustic these dances become first-cousins to the waltzes and polkas of the Strauss family. In their different ways both Szell, with superbly exuberant playing on Sony (SBK 48161), and Dohnányi on Decca (430 171-2) are more brilliant and more robust than Previn, with their recordings adding richness and weight of sound (the Decca is especially fine). Helped by the Vienna ambience, however, Previn has more light and shade. Whatever the contrasts, all three are outstanding versions, with Previn's the most genial, although Dohnányi's rhythmic flexibility and the ebb and flow of his rubato are a constant delight.

SYMPHONIES

For a complete set of the Dvořák symphonies, one can turn to Järvi, with six full-price discs offered for the price of four (Chandos CHAN 9008/13), while Kertész and the LPO represent an excellent bargain alternative (Decca 430 046-2); they are well worth their modest cost. For individual super-bargain recordings, Gunzenhauser with the Czecho-Slovak Radio Symphony Orchestra or the Slovak Philharmonic Orchestra on Naxos will not disappoint: *Symphony No. 1* (8.550266); *Symphony No. 2* (8.550267); *Symphonies Nos. 3* and *6* (8.550268); *Symphonies Nos. 4* and *8* (8.550269); *Symphonies Nos. 5* and *7* (8.550270). An individual record of the *Fifth Symphony* by the Oslo Philharmonic Orchestra under Jansons stands out and was given a Rosette in our main edition (EMI CDC7 49995-2).

(i) *Symphonies Nos. 7 in D min., Op. 70; 8 in G, Op. 88; 9 in E min. (From the New World), Op. 95;*
(ii) *The Wood dove, Op. 110.*
(B) *** DG Double 439 663-2 (2) [id.].(i) BPO, (ii) Bav RSO; Kubelik (with SMETANA: *Má Vlast: Vltava* (with Boston SO) ***).
(M) ** Teldec/Warner Dig. 4509 95497-2 (2) [id.]. Philh. O, Inbal.

Symphonies Nos. 8 in G, Op. 88; 9 in E min. (From the New World), Op. 95.
(M) *** DG 447 412-2 [id.]. BPO, Kubelik.

Rafael Kubelik's performances of the last Dvořák symphonies are among the finest ever recorded. The recordings sound admirably fresh, full yet well detailed, the ambience attractive. Kubelik gives a glowing performance of the *Seventh*, one of Dvořák's richest inspirations. His approach is essentially expressive, but his romanticism never obscures the overall structural plan and there is no lack of vitality and sparkle. The account of the *Eighth* is a shade straighter, without personal idiosyncrasy, except for a minor indulgence for the phrasing of the glowingly lyrical string-theme in the trio of the Scherzo. Throughout both works the playing of the Berlin Philharmonic Orchestra is most responsive, with the polish of the playing adding refinement. The orchestral balance in the *G major Symphony* is particularly well judged. The recordings come from 1971 and 1966 respectively. Kubelik's marvellously fresh *New World*, recorded in the Jesus-Christus Kirche and dating from 1972, also remains among the top recommendations, providing one does not mind the omission of the first movement's exposition repeat. There is a choice of formats. The best buy is surely the DG Double, which includes a comparably fine Bavarian Radio Orchestra performance of *The Wood dove*, plus Smetana's *Vltava*, recorded in Boston. However, the *Eighth* and *Ninth Symphonies* are also reissued as 'Legendary Recordings' in DG's 'Originals' series at mid-price, and the *New World* is additionally available on a DG Classikon bargain CD (439 436-2), coupled with five sparkling *Slavonic dances* (see our main volume).

The *Seventh* is marginally the finest of Inbal's performances of the last three symphonies, nicely relaxed and full of idiomatic feeling, the Scherzo gently lilting and the finale gathering force at the end. The *Eighth* is also a very attractive performance, with refined playing from the Philharmonia woodwind and strings alike. A ready comparison might be made here with Previn's account on

Telarc, and this is not to Inbal's disadvantage: his reading is at times sharper in its idiomatic feeling and his finale makes a particularly satisfying conclusion. The *New World* is less distinctive, very well played (especially the beautiful *Largo*), but the first movement does not include the exposition repeat, and Inbal's introduction of the secondary theme is somewhat mannered. Throughout, the recording can hardly be faulted, with a vivid presence and a realistic balance.

Symphonies Nos. 7 in D min., Op. 70; 8 in G, Op. 88.
(M) **(*) Telarc Dig. CD 82018 [id.]. LAPO, André Previn.

Previn directs a tautly rhythmic account of the *Seventh Symphony*. Rather than developing Slavonic atmosphere, he tends to bring out the symphonic cohesion. The opening could be more mysterious but the toughness of the argument is immediately clear, with the timpani dramatically prominent. The slow movement is warmly done, with fine horn solos; but some of the lightness of the last two movements is lost – notably in the lilting Scherzo – with such rhythmic emphasis. The *Eighth*, too, is sharply rhythmic but rather more idiomatic in feeling, and Previn's use of rubato brings affectionate moulding of phrase and rhythm, generally kept within a steady pulse. Warmth and freshness here go with the finest orchestral sound yet achieved by this orchestra in Royce Hall, full and with a vivid sense of presence that allows fine inner quality. In the *Seventh Symphony* the upper range has marginally less bloom.

Symphonies Nos. 8 in G, Op. 88; 9 (New World), Op. 95.
(M) ** DG Dig. 445 510-2 [id.]. VPO, Lorin Maazel.

Although Maazel's *Eighth* opens well, it is a fierce performance, lacking the glow of warmth one associates with this work. Despite excellent incisive playing, the hardness of the reading is underlined by the recording balance, which favours a bright treble against a rather light bass. Though the trumpet fanfare heralding the start of the finale is wonderfully vivid, the sound lacks something in body. The *New World* is similarly high-powered, incisive to the point of fierceness. It is superbly played and has moments of affection, most strikingly in the poised and pure account of the slow movement. But there are far more recommendable versions of this coupling.

Symphony No. 9 in E min.(From the New World), Op. 95.
(M) ** Virgin/EMI Dig. CUV5 61124-2 [id.]. Houston SO, Christoph Eschenbach – TCHAIKOVSKY: *Francesca da Rimini.* **

Symphony No. 9 (New World), Op. 95; Carnival overture.
(M) *** RCA 09026 62587-2 [id.]. Chicago SO, Fritz Reiner – SMETANA: *Bartered Bride overture;* WEINBERGER: *Schwanda polka and fugue.* ***

Symphony No. 9 (New World); Scherzo capriccioso.
(BB) *(*) RCA Navigator 74321 17898-2. Phd. O, Ormandy (with SMETANA: *Vltava*: Bamberg SO, Kuhn *).

We don't recall hearing Reiner's 1957 *New World* before, but it is an essentially lyrical performance without idiosyncratic disturbances. There is no first-movement exposition repeat, but how naturally the second subject is ushered in and how well the music flows, both here and in the *Largo*, with consistently lovely playing, especially in the rapt closing section. The Scherzo sparkles and its lilting rustic interlude is especially beguiling, while there is no lack of excitement in the finale. Typically warm Chicago sound, well balanced if not especially brilliant. What makes this disc the more attractive are the fill-ups, not just the brilliant *Carnival overture*, which bursts with energetic orchestral bravura and yet has ravishing Slavonic feeling in the middle section. However, first choice at mid-price still rests with Kondrashin and the VPO (Decca 430 702-2), appropriately coupled with the *American suite*.

Eschenbach's reading with the Houston orchestra is strong and often thoughtful, played and recorded with refinement, but it often sounds self-conscious and over-prepared, not at all idiomatic, with a very slow tempo indeed for the *Largo*. That brings out the refined beauty of the Houston string-tone and generally ensemble is excellent. It would have been much better to have this under-appreciated orchestra in music less frequently recorded than the *New World*.

There is nothing special about Ormandy's RCA version. He, too, omits the first-movement exposition repeat and is fairly easy-going, though he takes affectionate care over detail in the *Largo*. The remastered sound is not very refined. The *Scherzo capriccioso* is more enjoyable and much better recorded, but Kuhn's Bamberg performance of Smetana's *Vltava*, which opens the CD, is a very low-key affair.

String quartet No. 12 in F (American), Op. 96.

(M) ** DG Dig. 445 551-2 [id.]. Emerson Qt – BORODIN: *String quartet No. 2;* TCHAIKOVSKY: *Quartet No. 1.* *(*)

This is much the most enjoyable performance among the three on this well-filled CD (78 minutes). As a quartet, the Emersons are technically in a class of their own. They can produce the sonority of a full orchestra and their virtuosity in terms of ensemble and attack is matchless. They are undoubtedly involved in the music, particularly in the lyrical secondary material of the first movement and in the *Lento*. The Scherzo and finale, too, are brilliantly played, and few could fail to respond to the genuine excitement of the bravura articulation in the last movement. But the vivid and present DG recording is not entirely flattering and gives a feeling of overprojection, even of slickness at times. First choice rests with the Lindsay coupling of Opp. 96 and 106 on ASV (CDDCA 797).

String quartet No. 13 in A, Op. 106.

(M) ** Teldec/Warner 4509 95503-2 (2). Alban Berg Qt – BRAHMS: *String quartets Nos.1–3.* **

An expert performance, full of sophistication in the matter of blending of timbre and control of tempo and offering immaculate ensemble. There is much to admire, although there is a degree of surface gloss which robs the music-making of its full intimacy. Even so, the panache of the finale is easy to admire. It obviously has moments of conveyed feeling but, for all its brilliance, does not sound completely spontaneous. The sound is smoother than in the Brahms couplings.

CHORAL MUSIC

(i) *Requiem, Op. 89;* (ii) *6 Biblical songs from Op. 99.*

⊛ (B) *** DG Double 437 377-2 (2) [id.]. (i) Maria Stader, Sieglinde Wagner, Ernst Haefliger, Kim Borg, Czech PO & Ch., Karel Ančerl; (ii) Dietrich Fischer-Dieskau, Joerg Demus.

This superb DG set from 1959 brings an inspired performance of a work that can sound relatively conventional but which here emerges with fiery intensity, helped by a recording made in an appropriately spacious acoustic that gives an illusion of an electrifying live performance, without flaw. The passionate singing of the chorus (in the *Hostias* and *Sanctus*, for instance) is unforgettable, and the soloists not only make fine individual contributions but blend together superbly in ensembles. Dvořák's *Requiem* was first performed in 1890, some eight years after Wagner's *Parsifal* and twenty-two after Verdi's *Requiem*. If one mentions these two works, it is because of obvious influences that they have had on Dvořák's writing here. The charming opening of the *Recordare* (beautifully sung by Haefliger) is typical Dvořák, and the *Pie Jesu*, with its brief cor anglais interjections, is equally affecting, but much of the more intense writing would be hard for anyone not knowing the music to pin down. The *Dies irae*, for example, has some strong and vital unison writing for chorus, accompanied *à la* Berlioz by really big-scale orchestral writing. Yet typical of Dvořák or not, this is a wonderfully rich work which repays the closest study, especially in a performance as vigorous as this. Ančerl controls his forces with expert precision and the Czech chorus responds to the manner born. Apart from the fervour, the hushed singing towards the close of the *Agnus Dei* is frisson-creating, preparing for the entry of the soloists before the work ends quite darkly. It was a good idea to choose good German soloists rather than Czech ones, who might have sounded uncouth in comparison with chorus and orchestra. Haefliger and Borg are particularly fine. Haefliger's voice does not quite have its usual timbre – the oddity of the recording perhaps? – but his unfailing musicality is a delight. Borg sounds even better. The tone-colour is gloriously dark and dramatic and the manner sharp and authoritative, which is particularly suitable for this work. The recording is magnificent. The first entry of the chorus moaning away to a gentle '*Requiem aeternam*' suggests that the balance is going to favour the orchestra, but this is all part of the deliberate control of acoustic in which the balance between soloists, chorus and orchestra is particularly well handled in DG's best analogue manner. (Was the recording made in the Berlin Jesus-Christus Kirche, we wonder.) It is a pity that the trumpet which heralds in the *Tuba mirum* sounds much more like a cornet than the last trump, but that is entirely the fault of the player's loose vibrato, and it is a small flaw in a performance which in every way is an outstanding achievement. As if that were not enough, DG have added Fischer-Dieskau's 1960 recordings of six excerpts from Op. 99. He is at his superb best in these lovely songs. Brimming over with melody and never in the least sanctimonious, they deserve to be more generally known. (The numbers included are: *Rings an den Herrn; Gott, erhöre meine inniges Flahen; Gott ist mein Hirte; An den Wassern zu Babylon; Wende dich zu mir;* and *Singet ein neues Lied.*) Joerg Demus accompanies sensitively, and the recording balance is most convincing.

OPERA

Dimitrij (complete).
**(*) Sup. Dig. 11 1259-2 (3) [id.]. Vodička, Drobková, Hajossyová, Aghová, Mikulas, Prague R.
Ch., Czech PO Ch. and O, Albrecht.

Dimitrij, Dvořák's attempt to write a really grand opera, might be regarded as a sequel to *Boris Godunov*, following the career of the character who in Mussorgsky's opera is the Pretender who usurps Boris's throne. Here, with Schiller and Ferdinand Mikovec as sources rather than Pushkin, Dimitrij is an honourable rather than a devious character, believing sincerely in his legitimacy. Marfa, widow of Ivan the Terrible and mother of the murdered legitimate successor, pretends to recognize him as her son, hoping to worst her enemies. Dimitrij marries Marina, but then falls in love with Xenia, daughter of Boris. Dimitrij is finally killed by Shuisky, when Marfa admits her deception. As in Mussorgsky but in a less rugged way, Dvořák contrasts large-scale ensemble scenes with intimate ones full of lyrical ideas as ripely inspired as he ever conceived for an opera. The title-role is taken by the tenor, Leon Marian Vodička, whose Slavonic timbre is very apt for the music, even if he is strained at times. Drahomira Drobková as Marfa and Magdalena Hajossyová as Marina sing strongly, but it is Livia Aghová as Xenia who with sweet, pure tone brings out the beauty of Dvořák's melodies more than anyone. The male principals are more variable, though characterful enough. Gerd Albrecht draws brilliant playing from the Czech Philharmonic, though the choral singing is less well disciplined. With the four Acts contained on three CDs, each with well over an hour of music, this recording follows a reconstruction of Dvořák's original score of 1882, which he was persuaded – many think misguidedly – to revise and cut in a long sequence of alterations. So it is that this set contains sections of the score never previously heard this century.

The Jacobin.
*** Sup. 11 2190-2 (2) [id.]. Zítek, Sounová, Přibyl, Machotková, Blachut, Prusa, Tuček, Berman, Katilena Children's Ch., Kuhn Ch., Brno State PO, Pinkas.

The Jacobin dates from the most contented period of Dvořák's life and, though the background to the piece is one of revolt and political turmoil, he was more interested in individuals, so this is more a village comedy than a tract for the times. Starting with a jolly waltz-like prelude, the inconsequential tale – of a son (Bohus), the Jacobin of the title, at odds with his noble father, and of a young gamekeeper in love with the schoolmaster's daughter – inspired Dvořák to some of his most enchanting music. Though the drama is minimal, the sequence of exuberant, tuneful numbers, dances and choruses as well as arias, is more than enough to make the piece a delight on disc. Originally written in 1888, the opera was substantially revised nearly ten years later, and in Czechoslovakia has remained second in popularity among Dvořák's operas only to *Rusalka*. From this fine performance, recorded in 1977, one can understand why. Jiři Pinkas draws lively and idiomatic performances from a first-rate cast, including such stalwarts as Vilem Přibyl as the hero (a little old-sounding but stylish) and the veteran tenor Beno Blachut giving a charming portrait of the heroine's father. Václav Zítek sings the heroic part of the Jacobin himself with incisive strength and Daniela Sounová is bright and clear as the heroine. The analogue sound is clear and firmly focused. On CD, the three Acts are squeezed on to two extremely well-filled discs, with minimum inconvenience from having the break between discs in the middle of the second Act. The CD transfer is most vivid, and a full libretto/translation is included.

The Jacobin: highlights.
(M) **(*) Sup. 11 2250-2 [id.] (from above complete recording, cond. Pinkas).

The highlights disc is at medium price and, with 62 minutes' playing time, makes a good sampler. However, there is no libretto included, not even a synopsis, which is unhelpful in an unfamiliar work of this kind.

Kate and the Devil (complete).
**(*) Sup. 11 1800-2 (2) [id.]. Barová, Ježil, Novák, Sulcová, Suryová, Horáček, Brno Janáček Op.
Ch. & O, Pinkas.

Attracted by the combination of folk element and fairy-tale, Dvořák began composing this opera in 1898, a charming comic fantasy about the girl who literally makes life hell for the devil who abducts her, where the music has more in common with Smetana and *The Bartered Bride* than with Wagner, whose techniques Dvořák – writing towards the end of his career – was here consciously using. It inspired a score that might almost be counted an operatic equivalent of his *Slavonic dances*, full of sharply rhythmic ideas, colourfully orchestrated. The jolly folk atmosphere of the opening is established in peasant choruses, with the tenor hero (a shepherd) slightly tipsy. The devil appears in the guise of a handsome gamekeeper, and his wooing brings obvious Wagnerian references. It is charmingly effective to have the supernatural represented in more chromatic music and to have a distant imitation of Wagner's *Nibelheim* music for the scene in hell in Act II. That the opera has not achieved much success outside Czechoslovakia is due not to the music but largely to the episodic plot, which spins out a delightful concept too thinly.

Kate, finding herself consigned to be a wallflower in her village, declares she would dance with the devil himself. A minor devil, Marbuel, appears and, spinning fantastic tales, persuades her to come away with him. She is whisked off to Hell, with the shepherd Jirka gallantly going off to save her. Not that she needs much help, for she defies Marbuel so successfully that he, Lucifer and the other devils are only too glad to be rid of her. The weakness of the plot then lies in the fact that the leading soprano appears only in Act III, a Princess who through Jirka and Kate is saved from the clutches of the Devil, repenting of her earlier misrule of her country. At the end the Princess makes Jirka her supreme counsellor, while Kate is happily settled in a house of her own. The role of Kate is very well taken by Anna Barová, firm and full-toned, with Jirka sung attractively by Miloš Ježil, though his Slavonic tones are strained on top. The snag is the ill-focused singing of Richard Novák as the Devil, characterful enough but wobbly. Jiři Pinkas persuasively brings out the fun and colour of the score, drawing excellent singing from the chorus; and the 1979 recording has plenty of space. Though the orchestra is a little distanced, the voices are well caught. The originally edgy top has been tamed in the CD transfer; the upper focus of the chorus is not quite true and the violins too lack something in fullness, but basically the sound is agreeably warm and atmospheric. The libretto is well produced and clear, but assumes that the set is on three CDs instead of two with Acts II and III together on the second.

Rusalka: highlights.
(M) **(*) Sup. Dig. 11 2252-2 [id.] (from complete recording, with Benacková, Novák, Ochman, Czech PO Ch. & O, Neumann).

This is a first-class selection, including, of course, the famous *Invocation to the moon* and offering an hour of music. But the current mid-priced reissue has neither libretto nor synopsis, merely a list of the excerpts.

Dyson, George (1883–1964)

(i)*Violin concerto. Children's suite* (after Walter De La Mare).
⊛ *** Chan. Dig. CHAN 9369 [id.]. (i) Mordkovitch; City of L. Sinfonia, Hickox.

Completed in 1941, Dyson's *Violin concerto* is a richly inspired, warmly lyrical work that readily sustains its 43-minute span. It was written for Albert Sammons, who gave the first performance, but it was then forgotten until the present recording, largely, one suspects, because it defies what one would expect of a work written at that time and place, with no hint of wartime tensions. Rather this reflects Dyson's contentment in his last position as Director of the Royal College of Music in London. Not that the extended first movement, *Molto moderato*, lacks dark undercurrents. The broad theme which opens the orchestral tutti has Elgarian nobility in it as well as melancholy, pointing the way to a movement built largely on seamless melody, not aimless but finely controlled, with bravura passages for the soloist that act as landmarks. The idiom in all four movements is warm and distinctive, with the second-movement Scherzo and the finale both exhilarating, regularly veering towards waltz-rhythms. The third-movement *Andante* for violin and muted strings, divided into variations, brings a rare hushed beauty, superbly achieved in this dedicated performance. Lydia Mordkovitch, as in so many neglected concertos, not a few of them by British composers, makes light of the formidable technical difficulties to give a reading both passionate and deeply expressive. It is time such a fine work was revived in the concert hall. The *Children's suite* of 1924 has four sharply characterized movements, inspired by De La Mare poems. In its lighter way it reflects similar qualities to those in the concerto, not least a tendency to switch into waltz-time and a masterly ability to create rich and transparent orchestral textures, beautifully caught in the opulent Chandos recording. Two rarities to treasure.

Elgar, Edward (1857–1934)

Caractacus, Op. 35: Triumphal march. Carillon, Op. 75. Dream children, Op. 43/1 and 2. Elegy for strings, Op. 58. Grania and Diarmid, Op. 42: Funeral march. Polonia, Op. 76. Funeral march (Chopin, orch. Elgar).
(M) *** EMI CDM5 65584-2 [id.]. LPO, Boult – WALTON: *Crown Imperial* etc. ***

The main interest here is provided by two pieces Elgar wrote at the beginning of the First World War as a gesture to help refugees from Belgium and Poland. The *Carillon*, written for 'gallant little Belgium', is rather effective and one can imagine its success at the time; the *Polonia* has character too, and both show the composer's flair for flag-waving orchestral sounds. The rest of the programme, although it displays a good sprinkling of Elgarian fingerprints, is uneven in quality and does not seem to fire Sir Adrian to his more persuasive advocacy. Even the *Dream children* seem on the cool side, although some will undoubtedly like the restraint which Boult provides. The orchestration of Chopin's *Funeral march* is moderately effective. The sound is full.

Caractacus: Triumphal march; Cockaigne overture, Op. 40; Coronation march (1911); *Empire march* (1924); *Imperial march, Op. 32; Pomp and circumstance marches Nos. 1–5.*
(M) **(*) Virgin/EMI Dig. CUV5 61199-2 [id.]. RPO, Sir Yehudi Menuhin.

Menuhin brings out the *nobilmente* in this patriotic programme, but there is certainly no lack of spirit. Tempi are at times extreme; thus the *First* and *Second Pomp and circumstance marches* are pressed on with such gusto that the orchestral ensemble is less crisp than it might be, while the *Coronation march* is very slow and grandiloquent, sustained by its rich sonority and expansive organ pedals. *Cockaigne* (which comes last in a generous programme) has plenty of life and colour, but Menuhin's lyrical broadening at the end may strike some ears as being not wholly spontaneous. The recording, made at EMI's Abbey Road Studio, has a convincing concert-hall effect without too much resonance, and the brass are resplendent, especially in the *Triumphal march* from *Caractacus.*

Cello concerto in E min., Op. 85.
*** BIS Dig. CD 486 [id.]. Torleif Thedéen, Malmö SO, Markiz – SCHUMANN: *Concerto.* ***
*** Finlandia Dig. 4509 95768-2 [id.]. Arto Noras, Finnish RSO, Saraste – LALO: *Cello concerto.*
***
(M) **(*) Virgin Dig. CUV5 61125-2 [id.]. Steven Isserlis, LSO, Hickox – BLOCH: *Schelomo.* ***

Two Nordic views of the Elgar *Cello concerto* come from BIS and Finlandia. The former offer the young Swedish virtuoso, Torleif Thedéen, splendidly recorded with the Malmö orchestra; and the latter brings his Finnish colleague, Arto Noras, with Finnish Radio forces. Choice will probably be determined by the coupling desired (Schumann on Thedéen's disc and the Lalo on Finlandia) but, as far as the Elgar is concerned, both artists seem completely attuned to the Elgar sensibility. Thedéen has a nobility and reticence that are strongly appealing and Noras is hardly less impressive. Neither will disappoint; both enrich and do justice to the Elgar discography, even if the famous Du Pré/Barbirolli recording remains unsurpassed (EMI CDC7 47329-2).

The most distinctive point about Steven Isserlis's version of Elgar's *Cello concerto* on Virgin is his treatment of the slow movement, not so much elegiac as songful. Using a mere thread of tone, with vibrato unstressed, the simplicity of line and the unforced beauty are brought out. The very placing of the solo instrument goes with that, rather more distant than is usual, with the refinement of Elgar's orchestration beautifully caught by both conductor and engineers.

(i) *Cello concerto in E min., Op. 85;* (ii) *Violin concerto in B min., Op. 61.*
(**(*)) EMI mono CDC5 55221-2 [id.]. (i) Beatrice Harrison. New SO; (ii) Sir Yehudi Menuhin, LSO; composer.

The 1932 Menuhin/Elgar recording of the *Violin concerto* emerges on CD with a superb sense of atmosphere and presence. As for the performance, its classic status is amply confirmed: in many ways no one has ever matched – let alone surpassed – the seventeen-year-old Menuhin in this work, even if the first part of the finale lacks something in fire. The performance of the *Cello concerto* has nothing like the same inspiration when Beatrice Harrison's playing is at times fallible, and there are moments which seem almost perfunctory; but there is still much Elgarian feeling. Readers will note that this reissue in EMI's Composer in Person series puts this coupling into the premium-price range.

(i) *Cello concerto in E min., Op. 85; Enigma variations, Op. 36; Serenade for strings, Op. 20.*
(M) *** DG Dig. 445 511-2 [id.]. (i) Mischa Maisky; Philh. O, Sinopoli.

Maisky is highly persuasive in the *Cello concerto* and, with Sinopoli a willing partner, gives a warmly nostalgic performance, essentially valedictory in feeling. The slow movement is deeply felt, but not in an extrovert way, and the soloist's dedication is mirrored in the finale. The mood of the *Concerto* is carried over into the other works here. The lyrical variations of *Enigma* are expressively relaxed and *Nimrod* has a simple, direct nobility. Though Sinopoli avoids the usual speeding-up at the end of the finale, the thrust of that and the other vigorous climaxes is pressed home passionately. The *Serenade* is similarly expansive, and some may feel that the *Larghetto*, for all its sympathetic feeling, is too measured. The rich recording adds to the character of the readings, with the Philharmonia strings in particular playing superbly.

(i) *Cello concerto in E min., Op. 85. Falstaff, Op. 68.*
(M) *(*) Chan. Dig./Analogue CHAN 6607 [id.]. (i) Ralph Kirshbaum; SNO, Gibson.

Kirshbaum, a fine cellist, is disappointing here. At the very start the great double-stopped chords are anything but commanding, not helped by recessed recording, and the whole performance sounds tentative rather than expressing spontaneity. Originally issued as an analogue disc, this was displaced by a digital version, which is crisper in outline but cannot cure the balance. The CD transfer improves detail further, but the effect is marginal: this is not a commanding version. Sir Alexander Gibson's highly spontaneous performance of *Falstaff* is another matter. It is one of the very finest of the recordings he made for Brian Couzens (who was subsequently to found Chandos) in the late 1970s. Gibson generates a strong forward momentum from the very opening bars, yet detail is consistently imaginative and the closing section is most touchingly played. The Scottish orchestra are in excellent form and play with character and commitment. The 1978 recording, made in Glasgow City Hall, has a natural perspective and has been most successfully remastered for CD. The sound has some lack of opulence but is truthful in all other respects. However, there is no internal access to *Falstaff*, which is a considerable drawback.

Violin concerto in B min., Op. 61.
(***) Beulah mono 1PD 10 [id.]. Alfred Campoli, LPO, Boult – MENDELSSOHN: *Violin concerto.* (***)

Campoli gives a deeply felt but highly individual account of Elgar's great concerto. One can judge one's reaction to this performance by the control of vibrato on the opening phrase of his first entry. This is an essentially romantic approach, full of warmth, but there is no indulgence; indeed his phrasing, both of the memorable second subject of the first movement and in the slow movement, is most beautiful. In the finale Campoli lacks the authority of Menuhin, but again the secondary theme is ravishingly played and when the composer looks back at the earlier movement, the air of sweet nostalgia is very affecting. Campoli's reading is based on an impeccable technique and he applies himself here with dedication to a work he obviously loves, and the result – with Boult securely and compellingly at the helm – is most rewarding. The 1954 Kingsway Hall recording has been impeccably transferred 'from the *ffrr* master tape' by Tony Hawkins at the Decca studios. With its outstanding Mendelssohn coupling this is a fully worthy memento of a strikingly fine soloist. First choice among modern recordings of the Elgar remains with Nigel Kennedy (EMI CD-EMX 2058).

Enigma variations, Op. 36.
(*) Sony Dig. SK 53284 [id.]. BPO, Levine – DEBUSSY: *Images.* *
(***) EMI mono CDC7 54837-2 [id.]. Royal Albert Hall O, composer – HOLST: *The Planets.* (***)
(B) **(*) BBC Radio Classics BBCRD 9104 [id.]. BBCSO, Sir Malcolm Sargent – HOLST: *Planets* **(*)

A new version of the *Enigma variations* and from the Berlin Philharmonic is of some interest, for they have not recorded it before. Karajan, whose repertoire included Vaughan Williams and Britten, never recorded it with them. However, we are to some extent divided about the results. For EG, Levine and the Berlin Philharmonic may not be idiomatic but their live recording has a thrust and passion that are hard to resist, least convincing at the start, but spacious and unhurried in *Nimrod* and thrillingly powerful in the final variation, which draws cheers from the Berlin audience. For RL, it is a pity that the orchestra did not record it with a conductor of more distinctive personality, and for him this is a general-purpose account with little to say. He wonders what has happened here to the wonderful sonority this famous orchestra once produced and still can under a great conductor.

Elgar's own 1928 recording is too well known to require further comment. It was included in the comprehensive Elgar Edition, which came out a few years ago. Now it represents Elgar in the 'Composers in Person' series and comes in harness with Holst's own version of *The Planets*. Both are remarkable in their different ways and are self-recommending. Although allowances have to be made for the sound, they are remarkably few.

With the BBC engineers capturing the atmospheric thrill of a Prom performance in the Royal Albert Hall, Sir Malcolm Sargent's account of Elgar's *Enigma variations* gives a better idea of why he was such a Proms favourite, with the result more spontaneous than almost any of his studio recordings. The live performance may be a degree less polished, but its thrust and urgency are irresistible, building up superbly to the final variation, in which the BBC brass and the obbligato organ convey an extra frisson, even if the sound is pretty opaque and there are too many extraneous noises. But this is an inexpensive disc and, with an equally warm and expressive account of *The Planets* as the generous coupling, in some ways this makes a more persuasive case for the conductor than the mid-price EMI pairing of Sargent's studio recordings of the same works.

Enigma variations, Op. 36; Falstaff, Op. 68; Grania and Diarmid: Funeral march.
* EMI CDC5 55001-2 [id.]. CBSO, Simon Rattle.

In *Enigma*, Rattle and the CBSO are both powerful and refined, overwhelming at the close, and they offer a generous and ideal coupling. *Falstaff* is given new transparency in a spacious reading, deeply moving in the hush of the final death scene, with the *Grania and Diamid* excerpts as a valuable makeweight.

In the South (Alassio), Op. 50.
* Sony Dig. SK 57973 [id.]. La Scala PO, Milan, Muti – BRAHMS: *Serenade No. 1.* *****

Muti's account of Elgar's *Alassio* or *In the South* is an almost unqualified success. The Straussian ebullience and Elgarian sentiment are nicely balanced and the music glows with the confidence of Edwardian Elgar, tinged with hints of melancholy forebodings. Like his compatriot, Sinopoli, Muti has a natural feeling for Elgarian rubato in this overture, and he too takes an expansive view. The Scala viola principal plays the wonderful solo in the *Canto popolare* very beautifully, with perfect intonation, but, surprisingly for an Italian in Italian-inspired music, he is emotionally reticent. And though Muti is warmly expressive, he fails to thrust the surging coda home as excitingly as he has done in the concert hall in Britain. Yet he certainly seems inside this idiom and should give us more. The Orchestra of La Scala, too, sound both convinced and committed. The performance of the Brahms *D major Serenade*, with which this is coupled, is also touched by distinction. The recording in both scores is natural and well focused, and the Milan acoustic treats the Elgar more kindly than the Brahms, though the violins are still somewhat lacking in opulence. But for anyone attracted to this coupling, these reservations will be insignificant.

Pomp and circumstance marches Nos. 1–5.
(BB) ****** Belart 450 143-2 [id.]. LSO, Bliss – BLISS: *Things to come* etc. ******

Sir Arthur Bliss was an admirable conductor for this music. He plays the marches with a rumbustious vigour, yet preserves a sense of style so that the *nobilmente* is never cheapened. The recording is bright but has less sonority than when it first appeared in 1959, and the upper range is thin.

Symphonies Nos. 1–2; Overtures: Cockaigne; In the South.
(B) ***** Decca Double 443 856-2 (2) [id.]. LPO, Solti.

Solti's recordings of the two Elgar symphonies are now offered very economically together as a Double Decca. In the *First Symphony* Solti's thrusting manner will give the traditional Elgarian the occasional jolt, but his clearing away of the cobwebs stems from the composer's own 78-r.p.m. recording. The modifications of detailed markings implicit in that are reproduced here, not with a sense of calculation but with very much the same rich, committed qualities that mark out the Elgar performance. Again modelled closely on the composer's own surprisingly clipped and urgent reading, the *Second Symphony* benefits from virtuoso playing from the LPO and full, well-balanced sound. Fast tempi bring searing concentration, yet the *nobilmente* element is not missed and the account of the finale presents a true climax. The effect is magnificent. The CD transfers bring out the fullness satisfyingly as well as the brilliance of the excellent 1970s sound, and this applies also to the sharply dramatic account of *Cockaigne. In the South*, recorded in 1979, is less successful, if still exciting. But the result is nervy and tense, although the playing is excellent. Here Solti is not helped by Decca recording in which the brilliance is not quite matched by weight or body (an essential in Elgar).

Symphony No. 1 in A flat, Op. 55.
⊛ (B) ***** Carlton Dig. PCD 2019 [id.]. Hallé O, James Judd.

James Judd, more than any rival on disc, has learnt directly from Elgar's own recording of this magnificent symphony. So the reading has extra authenticity in the many complex speed-changes (sometimes indicated confusingly in the score), in the precise placing of climaxes and in the textural balances. Above all, Judd outshines others in the pacing and phrasing of the lovely slow movement which in its natural flowing rubato has melting tenderness behind the passion, a throat-catching poignancy not fully conveyed elsewhere but very much a quality of Elgar's own reading. The refinement of the strings down to the most hushed pianissimo confirms this as the Hallé's most beautiful disc in recent years, recorded with warmth and opulence.

Symphony No. 2 in E flat, Op. 63; (i) *Sea pictures* (song-cycle), *Op. 37.*
**(*) Argo Dig. 443 321-2 [id.]. RPO, Sir Charles Mackerras; (i) with Della Jones.

Mackerras's strong and sympathetic Argo version of the *Second Symphony* may not be a first choice, but it has special claims, both as an interpretation and for the generous coupling it offers. In the outer movements Mackerras's speeds are markedly faster than on most modern versions, yet there is no feeling of rush. It may not be the most brilliantly played version of Elgar's *Second Symphony*, but the energetic thrust goes with an idiomatic feeling for Elgarian rubato. And though the recording is finely detailed, it still has plenty of body. As in most of her later recordings, Della Jones gives a commanding performance of the *Sea pictures.* As recorded, hers may not be a velvety voice, but its firm projection and tonal variety give a welcome toughness to a work which, thanks to the poems chosen, can fall into sentimentality. Excellent, well-detailed sound. However, Vernon Handley's version of the *First Symphony* (CfP CD-CFP 4544) remains unsurpassed, and Dame Janet Baker's set of the *Sea pictures* is uniquely inspirational (EMI CDC7 47329-2).

(i) *Piano quintet in A min., Op. 84; String quartet in E min., Op. 83.*
**(*) Medici Qt MQCD 7002 [id.]. Medici String Qt, (i) with John Bingham.

(i–ii) *Piano quintet in A min.;* (i) *String quartet in E min.;* (ii–iii) *In moonlight (Canto popolare for viola and piano).*
(M) *** EMI Dig. CD-EMX 2229 [id.]. (i) Vellinger Qt; (ii) Piers Lane; (iii) James Boyd.

The Vellinger Quartet, winner of the London International Quartet Competition in 1994, is an unusually characterful group for whom contrasts of ensemble are as important as blending. In this first recording, the Vellinger approach to Elgar is impulsive, with allegros taken faster than in rival versions, to make the finale of the *Quintet* bold and thrusting and the finale of the *Quartet* light and volatile. The middle movement of the *Quartet* is light and flowing too, like an interlude rather than a meditation; but the central *Adagio* of the *Quintet* is by contrast very slow and weighty, not as thoughtful as in other versions. What crowns the disc is the little fill-up, a ravishing performance of the magical interlude which Elgar arranged for viola and piano from the central *Nocturne* passage from his *Overture In the South.* James Boyd, the Vellinger viola, plays with a richness and firmness of intonation that make one long to hear him in more solo work.

John Bingham and the Medici Quartet play with a passionate dedication and bring an almost symphonic perspective to the *Piano quintet,* and there is no denying their ardour and commitment, particularly in the slow movement. They also give a fine and thoroughly considered account of the *Quartet,* and overall their reading is full of perceptive and thought-provoking touches. Unfortunately they are far too close in the *Quartet* (though less so in the *Quintet*) and it still remains difficult for a real *pp* to register, while tone tends to harden somewhat on climaxes. This is a straight reissue of a coupling previously available on Meridian, and it omits the extra item which makes the newer Eminence issue so enticing.

Piano quintet in A min., Op. 84; Violin sonata in E min., Op. 82.
*** Hyp. Dig. CDA 66645 [id.]. Nash Ens. (members).

With the violinist, Marcia Crayford, and the pianist, Ian Brown, as both the duo in the *Sonata* and the key players in the *Quintet,* these are performances, more volatile than usual, that bring out the fantasy behind these late chamber works of Elgar. The dedication behind the playing, the understanding of Elgarian rubato born of long study and affection, comes out in each movement, but the slow movements above all are what mark these performances as exceptional. Crayford's little pizzicato commentaries in the central *Romance* of the *Sonata* are deliciously pointed, intensifying the tenderness. The central *Adagio* of the *Quintet,* far slower than usual, then brings the most dedicated playing of all, making this not just a lyrical outpouring but an inner meditation. Warm, immediate recording.

String quartet in E min.
(*) Hyp. Dig. CDA 66718 [id.]. Coull Qt – BRIDGE: *3 Idylls;* WALTON: *Quartet.* *

The Elgar and Walton *Quartets,* both with elegiac qualities, make an apt and attractive coupling; here, generously, they come with a splendid bonus in the Bridge *Idylls.* Though in the Elgar the Coulls sound almost too comfortable, less successful at conveying the volatile mood-changes than the Vellinger Quartet on EMI Eminence (see above), their relaxed warmth is still very persuasive; and the Walton performance, with the melancholy of the slow movement intensified, compares very favourably even with that of the Brittens. Excellent sound.

(i) *The Music Makers, Op. 69. Chanson de matin; Chanson de nuit, Op. 15/1–2; Dream children, Op. 43; Elegy, Op. 58; Salut d'amour, Op. 12; Sospiri, Op. 70; Sursum corda, Op. 11.*

**(*) Teldec/Warner Dig. 4509 92374-2 [id.]. (i) Jean Rigby, BBC Symphony Ch.; BBC SO, Andrew Davis.

The Music Makers, Op. 69; Sea pictures, Op. 37.
*** Chan. Dig. CHAN 9022 [id.]. Linda Finnie, LPO Ch., LPO, Bryden Thomson.

On Chandos, the song-cycle and the neglected cantata make a good coupling, with a contralto soloist as the key figure in each work. *The Music Makers* is a work which, with its O'Shaughnessy text and plentiful self-quotations, has often been treated less seriously than it deserves. Bryden Thomson directs warmly expressive, spontaneous-sounding performances of both works, easily flexible in an idiomatic way. There are versions of both with crisper ensemble, and such a song as *Where corals lie* in *Sea pictures* is not as delicate as it might be, but the illusion of live communication is what matters, and this now makes a first choice among modern recordings. The recording, full and atmospheric, with the chorus well balanced and with the organ obbligatos richly caught in both works, yet brings out an unevenness in Linda Finnie's strong, forthright voice, giving a hint of flutter.

Andrew Davis conducts a dedicated, refined reading of *The Music Makers*, giving a rare intensity to the quotations from such earlier works as the symphonies and the *Enigma variations*, making one catch the breath. The crisp ensemble, both in the singing and the playing, goes with freely flexible speeds and warm understanding of Elgarian rubato. Jean Rigby, though she hardly matches the heartfelt gravity of Dame Janet Baker in Boult's classic reading, sings with clear, firm focus. The rather backward balance of the chorus prevents the performance from having the full impact it deserves; but the sound, both refined and atmospheric, consistently brings out the beauty of Elgar's orchestration, both in the cantata and in the very generous and imaginative selection of shorter pieces which come as coupling. Among the encores, the early *Sursum corda*, Op. 11, for brass, organ and strings, stands well between the two masterly elegiac pieces of his high maturity, *Elegy* and *Sospiri*.

Falla, Manuel de (1876–1946)

(i) *El amor brujo* (complete ballet); (ii) *Nights in the gardens of Spain*.
(B) **(*) DG 439 458-2 [id.]. (i) Teresa Berganza, LSO, Navarro; (ii) Margrit Weber, Bav. RSO, Kubelik – RODRIGO: *Concierto de Aranjuez*. **

(i) *El amor brujo* (complete ballet); (ii) *Nights in the gardens of Spain; Three-cornered hat: Dance of the Neighbours; Dance of the Miller; Finale (Jota)*.
(BB) **(*) RCA Navigator 74321 24215-2. (i) Mistral; (ii) Achurcarro; LSO, Mata.

(i) *El amor brujo* (complete ballet); *Three-cornered hat: Dance of the Miller's wife; Dance of the Neighbours; Dance of the Miller; Finale (Jota)*.
(M) ** DG 447 414-2 [id.]. (i) Bumbry; Berlin RSO, Maazel – STRAVINSKY: *Firebird suite*. ***

Navarro conducts a vibrantly atmospheric account of *El amor brujo* and Terasa Berganza is a strong, dark-throated soloist. The LSO are on top form, especially in the *Ritual fire dance*, and the recording (made in the Henry Wood Hall) is both vivid and evocative. The performance of *Nights in the gardens of Spain* is similarly compelling. With Margrit Weber giving a brilliant account of the solo part, particularly in the latter movements, the effect is both sparkling and exhilarating. A little of the fragant nocturnal essence is lost, particularly in the opening section (where de Larrocha on Decca (430 703-2) is gentler), but the performance, with its strong sense of drama, is certainly not without its evocative qualities. A stimulating pairing; a pity the Rodrigo coupling is less recommendable.

The late Eduardo Mata made some fine recordings for RCA in Dallas during the early digital era, notably of the music of Ravel (see below), but his Falla sessions are analogue and date from the previous decade. His account of *El amor brujo* is much more exciting than Maazel's; although the famous *Ritual fire dance* is measured, it does not lack rhythmic force. Mata, too, has an uninhibited vocal soloist in Nancy Mistral and her singing is, if anything, even more earthy than Bumbry's. *Nights in the gardens of Spain* brings a highly sympathetic contribution from Joachim Achurcarro, and the performance is both evocative and exciting, if not as delicately refined as the Del Pueyo/Martinon account. The sound throughout is warmly atmospheric and vivid. The dances from the *Three-cornered hat* are more rhythmically subtle than Maazel's, although here the LSO violin timbre sounds thinner. A good super-bargain triptych, nevertheless.

The most striking thing about Maazel's *El amor brujo* is the splendid contribution of Grace Bumbry. This black singer was an unexpected choice in music by Falla, but in fact she catches the flamenco style vibrantly and her dark timbre has an idiomatic 'throaty' clang. Unfortunately the rest of the performance, though warm and often vivid, is not really memorable and the four famous dances from the *Three-cornered hat* fail to take off.

Nights in the gardens of Spain.
⊛ (M) *** Ph. 442 751-2 (2) [id.]. Eduardo del Pueyo, LAP, Jean Martinon – GRANADOS: *Danzas españolas* etc. ***

Dating from 1955, Del Pueyo's *Nights in the gardens of Spain* was one of the very first performances to be recorded in stereo, and it has never been surpassed. Martinon's magically evocative orchestral opening is matched by the delicacy of the solo entry, and the continuing dialogue between piano and the Paris orchestra brings incandescent subtlety of colour. The thrilling climax of *En la Generalife* has a glowing, spacious rapture and the following *Danza lejana* brings an almost dream-like quality. Somehow the vibrato of the (French) horn playing is not intrusive, and the slightly diffuse orchestral tapestry presented by the early stereo suits the music admirably. After the brilliance of *En los jardines de la Sierra de Córdoba* the music sinks gently back into the repose of its closing cadence. Unforgettable.

The Three-cornered hat (complete ballet).
* Everest/Vanguard EVC 9000 [id.]. Barbara Howitt, LSO, Jorda – BARTOK: *Dance suite.* **

Jorda made some excellent Decca 78s of this music, but this later complete ballet is disappointing. The opening is most vivid and Barbara Howitt's short contribution is a vibrant one. But after that the performance refuses to flame up. The conducting is colloquial, but everything is too literal and there is no sense of urgency, which will not serve such a dramatic and colourful score. The recording is clear and immediate.

The Three-cornered hat (complete ballet); *Homenajes; La vida breve: Prelude and dance.*
(M) **(*) Telarc Dig. CD 82017 [id.]. Florence Quivar; Men of the May Festival Ch., Cincinnati SO, Jesús López-Cobos.

Telarc's recording is quite different from Decca's for Dutoit (410 008-2), with the proceedings cushioned by wider reverberation so that the opening of the ballet with its '*Olés!*' and castanets underlined by insistent timpani is much less sharply defined; elsewhere the warm ambience, with the orchestra set back in a concert-hall balance, is pleasingly atmospheric. But although the Cincinnati orchestra provides much felicitous detail (the violins in the *Grapes* sequence and the wit of the bassoon making fun of the Corregidor, for instance) this is overall a less distinctive and less dramatic reading than Dutoit's. The four *Homenajes* are impressively sombre, while the excerpts from *La vida breve* make an enjoyably contrasting end-piece. In the ballet, Florence Quivar's vocal contribution might with advantage have been earthier – it has more the feeling of the opera house than a gypsy encampment. However, with an hour of music, offered on Telarc's Bravo! mid-priced label, this is worth considering, for the sound is really very pleasing.

Fauré, Gabriel (1845–1924)

Ballade in F sharp for piano and orchestra, Op. 19.
(BB) **(*) Naxos 8.550754 [id.]. Thiollier, Nat. SO of Ireland, Antonio de Almeida – FRANCK: *Symphonic variations*; D'INDY: *Symphonie sur un air montagnard français.* **(*)

Naxos offer an intelligently planned coupling: none of these works is a concerto and all are written within a relatively brief time-span. François-Joël Thiollier shows some imagination and sensitivity in Fauré's lovely *Ballade*, which is not represented as generously on CD as it should be. The orchestral playing is perfectly acceptable, without being in any way out of the ordinary; likewise the recording. All the same, it is worth the money. First choice probably rests with Louis Lortie on Chandos (CHAN 8773), if the coupling of the Ravel concertos is suitable.

CHAMBER MUSIC

(i) *Allegretto moderato for two cellos;* (ii) *Andante. Elégie, Op. 24; Papillon, Op. 77; Romance, Op. 69; Sérénade, Op. 98; Sicilienne, Op. 78; Sonatas Nos. 1 in D min. Op. 109; 2 in G min., Op. 117.*
**(*) RCA Dig. 09026 68049-2 [id.]. Steven Isserlis, Pascal Devoyon; with (i) David Waterman; (ii) Francis Greer.

Steven Isserlis and Pascal Devoyon recorded the *Second sonata* but not the *First* for Hyperion, and we found it 'as short on quantity as it is strong on quality'. The present issue, more logically, presents Fauré's complete output for cello and piano and includes an *Allegretto moderato* for two cellos (which takes under a minute) and an *Andante* for cello and organ, which is the original version of the *Romance*. Steven Isserlis understands the essential reticence and refinement of Fauré's art and contributes perceptive notes on the music. Perhaps he is at times a shade too reticent in the music and could allow himself to produce a more ardent and songful tone. Maybe the balance, which slightly favours his partner, contributes to this impression. Pascal Devoyon is a no less perceptive and sensitive artist; were he less so, this imperfect balance would present greater problems. A welcome, then, for the artistry of these performances, but tinged with slight disappointment at the less than ideal balance.

Après un rêve, Op. 7/1 (trans. Casals); *Elégie, Op. 24; Papillon, Op. 77; Sicilienne, Op. 78.*
** Globe Dig. GLO 5057 [id.]. Ferschtman, Baslawskaya – DEBUSSY: *Cello sonata;* FRANCK: *Cello sonata.* **

Dmitri Ferschtman and Mila Baslawskaya are a Russian partnership now based in the Netherlands. They play these Fauré miniatures with appropriate lightness of touch. The *Sicilienne* is familiar from the *Pelléas et Mélisande* incidental music. Not highly competitive in terms of playing time or coupling, but there is some musicianly playing on this CD, and the recording is acceptable.

Cello sonatas Nos. 1 in D min., Op. 109; 2 in G min., Op. 117; Après un rêve, Op. 7/1 (trans. Casals); *Elégie, Op. 24;* (i) *Morceau de lecture; Papillon, Op. 77; Romance, Op. 69; Sérénade, Op. 98; Sicilienne, Op. 78.*
** Bridge Dig. BCD 9038 [id.]. Steven Doane, Barry Snyder, (i) Kurt Fowler.

Steven Doane is Professor of Cello at the Eastman School in Rochester, where his partner, Barry Snyder, also teaches. He plays with great artistry and has the full measure of the reticence and subtlety of the Fauré sonatas. In fact he is almost too restrained; his tone is not big and one longs for a little more fervour. Admittedly the balance does not favour him: he has an equally subtle and sensitive partner in Snyder. Intelligent and refined performances.

(i–ii) *Piano quartets Nos. 1 in C min., Op. 15; 2 in G min., Op. 45;* (i; iii) *Piano quintets Nos. 1 in D min., Op. 89; 2 in C min., Op. 115;* (i–ii) *Piano trio in D min., Op. 120;* (iii) *String quartet in E min., Op. 121.*
(M) ** Erato/Warner 4509 96953-2 [id.]. (i) Jean Hubeau; (ii) Raymond Gallois-Montbrun, Colette Lequien, André Navarra; (iii) Quatuor Via Nova.

A few years ago EMI issued this repertoire from Jean-Philippe Collard, Augustin Dumay, Frédéric Lodéon and the Parrenin Quartet on a pair of Rouge et Noir, two-for-the-price-of-one CD sets, which also enabled them to include both the two *Violin* and *Cello sonatas* (EMI CMS7 62548-2). Those who were wise enough to invest in them (or who find them still on sale) need read no further, as the present performances do not match them. These come from the late 1960s and were part of a five-LP box which also included the *Violin* and *Cello sonatas* as well as the perceptive notes by Harry Halbreich, reproduced again here. The performances are all musicianly and dedicated but workmanlike rather than subtle, intelligent but not inspired. Jean Hubeau has nowhere near the imagination or feeling for phrasing and dynamic nuance that distinguishes Collard. The digitally remastered analogue recordings are perfectly acceptable – decent but no more.

Piano quartets Nos. 1 in C min., Op. 15; 2 in G min., Op. 45.
(BB) ** Discover Dig. DIDC 920231 [id.]. Sheuerer Piano Qt.
** Carlton Dig. MCD 66 [id.]. Los Angeles Piano Qt.

The Sheuerers (four siblings) display a real feeling for Fauré's elusive world, and the *C minor Quartet* is certainly successful in achieving an ardent, romantic flow in the outer movements, contrasted with a nimble Scherzo and a warm yet serene *Adagio*. Gertraud Scheurer, the pianist, firmly recorded, plays with much character and holds the music-making together, and if her brother Franz leads the strings with a somewhat meagre timbre in the upper range, both viola and cello are more generous in tone, and the resonance of the Winterthur Studio provides plenty of fullness. Indeed it prevents real clarity of focus in the more passionate moments and in the G minor work means that in the Scherzo the piano tends to be over-dominant. But here the thoughtful slow movement is again successful and the finale has a strong impulse, even if there is some roughness from the principal violin. While the recordings by Domus on Hyperion (CDA 66166) are in a class of their own, we hope this inexpensive Discover disc may tempt newcomers to sample these lovely works.

   Musicianly and enjoyable performances of both *Piano quartets* come from the Los Angeles Piano Quartet which fall short of the best, but nevertheless have some artistic merits. The Scherzo of the *G minor Quartet* is a bit heavy-handed. The recording is not in the first rank in terms of definition, and is too resonant.

Piano quintets Nos. 1 in D min., Op. 89; 2 in C min., Op. 115.
⊛ *** Hyp. Dig. CDA 66766 [id.]. Domus, with Anthony Marwood.

The brilliant piano quartet group, Domus, joined by the violinist, Anthony Marwood, offer warm, poetic readings of two of Fauré's most unjustly neglected chamber works. Both dating from well after the two *Piano quartets*, they have never achieved the same popularity, perhaps because of the reticent use of the piano. The playing of Domus in these two masterpieces is as light, delicate and full of insight as one would expect. They make one fall for this music all over again. The first and more elusive of the two took Fauré many years to write but, as Domus's rapt performance demonstrates, the slow movement shows the composer at his most deeply reflective. Broader and more outward-going, the second is among the masterpieces of Fauré's Indian summer as he approached his eighties. As this concentrated performance suggests, its autumnal lyricism brings likenesses to late Elgar, with the pianist, Susan Tomes, at her most sparkling in the mercurial Scherzo. Excellent sound. Indeed, if anything, this is better recorded than the earlier Domus account of the two *Piano quartets*, to which we also accorded a Rosette in our main volume. Arguably this is the best-ever version of these two pieces.

Piano trio in D min., Op. 120.
*** Ara. Dig. Z 6643 [id.]. Golub Kaplan Carr Trio – DEBUSSY: *Piano trio* ***; SAINT-SAENS: *Piano trio.* **(*)
** Erato/Warner Dig. 2292 44937-2 [id.]. Trio Fontenay – DEBUSSY; RAVEL: *Piano trios.* *

David Golub, Mark Kaplan and Colin Carr give as understanding and idiomatic a performance of the sublime Fauré *Trio* as is to be found. They convey its understatement and subtlety of nuance to perfection, and the interplay among them is a model of the finest chamber-music-making. The recording is very good indeed, with plenty of warmth.

The Trio Fontenay are rather closely and brightly recorded and, though their Fauré is a good deal better than the Ravel (and the Debussy) with which it is coupled, it does not challenge its main competitors.

Violin sonata No. 1 in A, Op. 13.
** Carlton Dig. MCD 37 [id.]. Hasson, Ivaldi – DEBUSSY: *Violin sonata;* FRANCK: *Violin sonata.***
* RCA Dig. 09026 62697-2 [id.]. Pinchas Zukerman, Marc Neikrug. – DEBUSSY; FRANCK: *Violin sonatas.* *

A very musicianly and intelligent account of the Fauré *Violin sonata* from Maurice Hasson and Christian Ivaldi. It is well worth considering, given the fact that it is at less than full price and offers two other great French sonatas. The pianist is not balanced to best advantage but the performances are very satisfactory indeed, even if the new Amoyal–Rogé account on Decca (see below) is worth the extra outlay.

Zukerman and Neikrug give us a rather overdramatized, overheated and glamorized account of this lovely sonata. Their playing is enormously accomplished and polished, and there is much to be said for emphasizing its virility. But they both play the sonata as a virtuoso display piece and little else. There is much sweet tone from Zukerman, but the playing is pretty self-conscious and it is a relief to get back to such stylists as Grumiaux–Crossley, Amoyal and Rogé, and Osostowicz and Tomes.

Violin sonatas Nos. 1 in A, Op. 13; 2 in E min., Op. 108; Andante, Op. 75; Berceuse, Op. 16; Morceau de concours – Romance, Op. 28.
⊛ *** Decca Dig. 436 866-2 [id.]. Pierre Amoyal, Pascal Rogé.

Readers wanting a modern recording of the two Fauré *Violin sonatas* need look no further. Pierre Amoyal and Pascal Rogé play them as to the manner born. As one would expect, they are totally inside the idiom and convey its subtlety and refinement with freshness and mastery. There are admirable alternatives from Grumiaux and Crossley at mid-price (Philips 426 384-2) and from Krysia Osostowicz and Susan Tomes (Hyperion CDA 66277), but Amoyal and Rogé more than hold their own against them and throw new light on the three slight miniatures that they offer as a bonus. Impeccable recording, too. A lovely disc.

Complete piano music

Ballade in F sharp, Op. 19; Barcarolles Nos. 1–13; (i) Dolly, Op. 56. Impromptus Nos. 1–5; Impromptu, Op. 86; Mazurka in B flat, Op. 32; 13 Nocturnes; Pièces brèves Nos. 1–8, Op. 84; 9 Préludes, Op.

103; Romances sans paroles Nos. 1–3; (i) *Souvenirs de Bayreuth. Theme & variations in C sharp min., Op. 73; Valses-caprices Nos. 1–4.*

🔊 *** Hyp. CDA 66911/4 (4) [id.]. Kathryn Stott, (i) with Martin Roscoe.

This four-disc set, issued to coincide with the 150th anniversary of the composer's death, is a revelation. Both the *13 Barcarolles*, written between 1880 and 1921, and the *13 Nocturnes*, from an even wider period between 1875 and 1921, give a most illuminating view of Fauré's career, gentle and unsensational like the music itself, but with the subtlest of developments towards a sparer, more rarefied style. That comes out all the more tellingly when, as here, they are given in succession and are played with such poetry and spontaneous-sounding freshness. Stott earlier recorded for Conifer a generous selection of Fauré piano music (see below) but, quite apart from the warmer, clearer and more immediate sound on the Hyperion issue, allowing for velvet tone-colours, the later performances are more winningly relaxed, ranging wider in expression. Each of the four discs contains well over 70 minutes of music, logically presented, with the second containing the *Barcarolles* and the early *Ballade* (more taxing than the later version with orchestra) and with the *Nocturnes* spread between the third and fourth discs, framing the lighter pieces, including such duets as the witty Wagner quadrille, *Souvenirs de Bayreuth*, and the ever-fresh *Dolly suite*, both with Stott ideally partnered by Martin Roscoe. Then, in preparation for the superb last six *Nocturnes* come the elusively poetic *9 Préludes* of 1910/11 and the solitary *Mazurka* of 1878 which, unlike the *Nocturnes* and *Barcarolles*, finds Fauré's gentle individuality rather submerged by the ever-present Chopin influence. A masterly set.

Barcarolles Nos. 1 in A min., Op. 26; 2 in G, Op. 41; 4 in A flat, Op. 44; 5 in F sharp min., Op. 66; 6 in E flat, Op. 70; 7 in D min., Op. 90; 11 in G min., Op. 105; 12 in E flat, Op. 106; Impromptus Nos. 1 in E flat, Op. 25; 2 in F min., Op. 31; 3 in A flat, Op. 34; in D flat, Op. 86; Mazurka in B flat, Op. 32; Nocturnes Nos. 1 in E flat min., Op. 33/1; 4 in E flat, Op. 36; 6 in D flat, Op. 63; 8 in D flat, Op. 84/ 8; 9 in B min., Op. 97; 10 in E min., Op. 99; 11 in F sharp min., Op. 104/1; 3 Romances sans paroles, Op. 17; Valse-caprice No. 4 in A flat, Op. 62.
**(*) Conifer 75605 51751-2 (2). Kathryn Stott.

Kathryn Stott's earlier, more limited survey for Conifer first appeared in the form of two separate CD recitals in 1987 and 1988. They are now reissued together as a two-CD set, and it would have been prudent of Conifer – considering the availability of Stott's newer complete survey – to have offered these discs at two-for-the-price-of-one, instead of at premium price. Even so, this might be considered by those collectors wanting a shorter survey, although it was a pity that the much-loved *Theme and variations in C sharp minor* was not part of the otherwise well-chosen selection. Undoubtedly the playing demonstrates Stott's strong artistic personality and shows she has thought deeply and to good purpose about this music. Her playing is highly sensitive throughout, with not only a wide range of dynamic nuance but also with a subtle variety of colour. The recording is excellent in its own right, but there are only just over two hours of music here, against nearly three hours' playing time on the Hyperion four-disc set.

Requiem, Op. 48; Cantique de Jean Racine Op. 11; Messe basse.
(BB) *** Naxos Dig. 8.550765 [id.]. Beckley, Gedge, Schola Cantorum of Oxford, Oxford Camerata, Summerly (with DE SEVERAC: *Tantum ergo;* VIERNE: *Andantino;* with Colm Carey, organ ***).

This Naxos version makes an excellent bargain choice for the *Requiem* in its original orchestration. The fresh, forward choral tone goes with a direct, unmannered interpretation from Jeremy Summerly, with soloists comparably fresh-toned and English-sounding. The excellent recording brings out the colourings of the orchestra in sharp detail, with the organ and brass vividly caught. The performance of the *Messe basse* is comparably direct, made to sound a little square at times, but *Le cantique de Jean Racine* is most winningly done. The little meditative organ piece by Vierne and the unaccompanied motet by de Severac are pleasing makeweights.

(i; ii; iv) *Requiem, Op. 48;* (ii; iii) *Les Djinns, Op. 12;* (ii) *Madrigal, Op. 35.*
*** Ph. Dig. 438 149-2 [id.]. (i) Catherine Bott, Gilles Cachemaille; (ii) Monteverdi Ch., Salisbury Cathedral Boy Choristers; (iii) Sabine Vatin; (iv) O Révolutionaire et Romantique, Gardiner – DEBUSSY: *3 Chansons de Charles d'Orleans;* RAVEL: *3 Chansons;* SAINT-SAENS: *3 songs.* ***

John Eliot Gardiner with period forces also chooses the version of the *Requiem* with the original instrumentation, using only the lower strings, plus a solo violin, and without woodwind. The darkness matches Gardiner's view of the work which, with expressive moulding and flexible rhythm and phrasing, he makes more dramatic than it often is. The mellow recording takes away some of the bite but, with excellent soloists – Catherine Bott radiantly beautiful in the *Pie Jesu*, Gilles Cachemaille vividly bringing out word-meaning – and a generous, unusual coupling, it makes an excellent choice. Fauré's atmospheric setting of Hugo's *Les Djinns* is specially welcome, with piano accompaniment on a gentle-toned Erard of 1874; and all the other pieces, including Fauré's enchanting *Madrigal*, are in various ways inspired by early French part-songs, with the medieval overtones brought out in the Debussy and with the humour of the Ravel nicely underlined.

Requiem, Op. 48; Maria Mater gratiae, Op. 47/2; Tantum ergo, Op. 65/2.
(B) **(*) Carlton Dig. PCD 2015. Aidan Oliver, Harry Escott, David Wilson-Johnson, Westminster
   Cathedral Ch., City of L. Sinfonia, David Hill.

Using the full orchestral score, David Hill yet gives a performance which keeps a modest scale, set within a warm church acoustic – St Jude's, Hampstead, not Westminster Cathedral itself. Its special quality among current versions is that it uses boy trebles and male altos from the cathedral choir instead of women's voices. There is a very boyish, earnest quality to Aidan Oliver's singing of the *Pie Jesu* which is most winning, even if there are still more angelic accounts. The snag is that the choir is set at rather too great a distance in relation to the orchestra.

Fayrfax, Robert (1464–1521)

Ave Dei patris filia; Missa O quam glorifica; O quam glorifica (hymnus); Orbis factor (Kyrie). 3
secular songs: *Sumwat musyng; That was Joy; To complayne me, alas.*
⊛ *** ASV/Gaudeamus Dig. CDGAU 142 [id.]. Cardinall's Musick, Andrew Carwood.

Remembered in the history books as the father of Tudor music, the most celebrated composer of his day in England, a key figure at the great State occasions of the time, Robert Fayrfax has nevertheless been seriously neglected on disc. Previously he was represented by a mere handful of items but, following up their success in bringing to light the inspired church music of Nicholas Ludford, Cardinall's Musick, directed by Andrew Carwood, using editions specially prepared by David Skinner, here embark on another exciting voyage of discovery. As Skinner's notes explain, the Mass, *O quam glorifica*, is the most complex that Fayrfax ever wrote. It is elaborate not just in its amazingly involved musical arguments, with numerical relationships worked out to match any twentieth-century serialist, but in its very length. Who would believe that a Mass written around 1500 would last, even with a chanted rather than a fully composed *Kyrie*, some 50 minutes, as here? The rhythmic complexities, too, are wonderfully fresh for the modern ear, with conflicting speeds often involving bold cross-rhythms, parading the composer's closely controlled freedom before bar-lines applied their tyranny. Above all, whatever the complexity, this is music immediately to involve one in its radiant beauty. The separate antiphon or motet, *Ave Dei patris filia*, is comparably adventurous and beautiful, and that church music is well supplemented by three secular part-songs for male voices. They even anticipate the Elizabethan madrigal, notably the third and most poignant, *To complayne me, alas.* As in Ludford, Carwood draws inspired performances from his singers, crisp and dramatic as well as beautifully blended, and most atmospherically recorded in the Fitzalan Chapel at Arundel Castle.

Field, John (1782–1837)

Piano concertos Nos. 1 in E flat; 2 in A flat.
*** Chan. Dig. CHAN 9368 [id.]. Miceál O'Rorke, L. Mozart Players, Bamert.

Miceál O'Rorke embarks on what appears to be a complete cycle of the Field concertos with hardly less success than with his first disc of solo piano music (see below). The music of the present pair of concertos is uneven, but the first movement of No. 1 opens with a nice, tripping idea (a bit like Hummel) and has a charming, fairy-like second subject on the violins. Its Scottish slow movement features the folk tune '*Within a mile of Edinburgh town*' rather winningly, while the characteristically ingenuous *Poco adagio* of No. 2 is followed by a *Moderato innocente* – another Field rondo with an engaging principal theme which becomes catchier as it is given more rhythmic treatment. Perhaps the movement is a shade over-extended, but the soloist is very persuasive, and he receives admirable support from Bamert and the London Mozart Players. First-class, naturally balanced recording. It is a pity that this fine record duplicates the *Second Concerto*, already available (coupled with No. 3) on an equally recommendable Telarc CD by John O'Conor (CD 80370 – see our main volume).

*Air du bon roi Henri IV; 2 Album leaves in C min.; Andante inédit in E flat; Fantaisie sur un air russe,
'In the garden'; Fantaisie sur l'air de Martini; Irish dance: 'Go to the devil'; Marche triomphale;
Nocturne in B flat; Nouvelle fantaisie in G; Polonaise en rondeau; Rondeau d'écossais; Rondo in A*

flat; Sehnsuchtswalzer; Variations in D min. on a Russian song, 'My dear bosom friend'; Variations in B flat on a Russian air: Kamarinskaya.
*** Chan. Dig. CHAN 9315 [id.]. Míceál O'Rourke.

Míceál O'Rourke is as sympathetic and sensitive an advocate of these rarities as one could wish for. He avoids any attempt to invest this music with more significance than it has, and presents this (nearly 80-minute) recital with intelligence and taste. Most of this repertory is not otherwise available, and much of it has the quiet charm one expects from this delightful composer. Whether it is in the *Andante inédit*, possibly Field's last composition, or the captivating *Sehnsuchtswalzer*, also published posthumously, Míceál O'Rourke proves a dedicated interpreter of real artistry. Recorded at The Maltings, Snape, he is admirably served by the Chandos team.

Finzi, Gerald (1901–56)

(i) *Clarinet concerto;* (ii) *Introit for violin and orchestra.*
(B) **(*) BBC Radio Classics BBCRD 9119 [id.]. (i) Janet Hilton, BBC Northern SO, Bryden Thomson; (ii) Gerald Jarvis, LPO, Boult (with Concert). **(*)

The *Clarinet concerto* is well played, recorded in Milton Hall, Manchester, in 1978. Janet Hilton is the nimble soloist, with the performance of the lovely *Adagio* memorably intense. Though the quality is not as fresh or transparent as with such rivals as Thea King (Hyperion CDA 66001) and Emma Johnson (ASV CDDCA 787), and the transfer gives the solo instrument a flutter in the finale, the sound is otherwise acceptable. The virtually unknown *Introit for violin and orchestra* brings another memorable theme and is well worth having; it originally formed the middle movement of a larger work whose outer movements Finzi withdrew. It is a meditative, thoughtful work, very well played by Gerald Jarvis and the LPO under Sir Adrian Boult in 1969, even if the timbre of the solo violin as recorded could be sweeter. The recording holds up well but does not have the transparency or dynamic range one would expect from a commercial recording of this period. However, this is part of a 77-minute concert of English music, including the *Harpsichord concertino* of Walter Leigh, which is well worth having at so modest a cost.

Floyd, Carlisle (born 1926)

Susannah (opera; complete).
*** Virgin/EMI Dig. VCD5 45039-2 (2) [id.]. Cheryl Studer, Samuel Ramey, Jerry Hadley, Lyon Op. Ch. & O, Kent Nagano.

With claims to be the most successful American opera ever, Carlisle Floyd's *Susannah* clocked up no fewer than 150 productions in the United States in the 40 years following its first performance in 1955. Aged only twenty-nine when it appeared, Floyd had had no previous experience of writing a full-length opera, yet with a subject which related directly to his own background – the son of a Methodist minister in South Carolina – and with a simple, highly melodramatic story involving straightforward characterization, his formula worked immediately and powerfully with American audiences, not least in music college performances throughout the country.

This is an updating of the story of Susanna and the Elders in the Apocrypha, which readily adapts to the background of a traditional community in the Appalachian mountains. The hypocrisy of the Bible-thumping minister, Blitch, and of the elders of the church makes for an effective narrative-line, even if the dénouement goes over the top in melodrama. The idiom is tuneful and unashamedly tonal, influenced by American folk-music, just as atmospherically as in Copland (if far less distinctively). With echoes of Puccini on the one hand, of the American musical on the other, you might describe it as a cross between *Fanciulla del West* and *Carousel*. It is a pity that the musical invention is not more distinguished and that the words of the libretto are too often banal. The big dramatic climaxes quickly come to sound corny and a recording, even more than a live performance, makes one well aware of that. Most effective are the two big solos for the heroine, one in each of the compact Acts, both gloriously sung by Cheryl Studer, who as a native American sounds easily in character, taking to the idiom naturally. Samuel Ramey is similarly at home in this music, singing strongly with his richest tone, even if one can hardly believe in him as a vile hypocrite. With Jerry Hadley ideally cast as the tenor hero, Sam, Susannah's brother, who finally murders the predatory Blitch, the rest of the cast is first rate. The chorus and orchestra of the Lyon Opera are also inspired by their American conductor to give heartfelt, idiomatic performances. Excellent sound, as in previous Lyon Opera recordings with Nagano. It is surprising that an opera which has become such a favourite in America (even if it has so far failed to travel abroad) was not recorded earlier, but this set could not be more successful in filling the gap.

Foerster, Josef Bohuslav (1859–1951)

Symphony No. 4 in C min. (Easter), Op. 54; Springtime and desire, Op. 93.
*** Sup. Analog/Dig. 111 822-2 [id.]. Prague SO, Smetáček.

Strange that this beautiful if overlong symphony has enjoyed such little exposure. Kubelik recorded it on six 78-r.p.m. records immediately after the war, but Václav Smetáček's 1968 LP is its only successor. Yet it is dignified and noble, and its Scherzo is infectiously memorable and could be as popular as any of the *Slavonic dances* if only it were known. It dates from 1905, though it was not first performed until 1912. Foerster was devout, and the symphony has a religious programme; its first movement, *Calvary*, has great depth of feeling and spaciousness, and the titles of the remaining three movements, *A child's Good Friday, The charm of solitude* and *Holy Saturday victorious*, indicate its character. The idiom is best described as being close to that of Josef Suk, and the same elements that served to mould Suk's musical personality – Dvořák, Mahler and even Bruckner – are to be found here. Above all, Foerster has a feeling for architecture and there is a sweep to the first movement that is most impressive. The finale is the least successful of the four movements, and here attention flags. All the same, the symphony wears well and it is good to have it on CD, even if it would have been even better had we been given a new recording under, say, Bělohlávec. To this analogue recording Supraphon add a 1985 account, digitally recorded, of his *Springtime and desire*, a symphonic poem with a strong emphasis on the symphonic. Foerster has an inborn feeling for the natural growth of ideas. It was first performed by Weingartner in 1915 and, like the symphony, is a most welcome addition to the catalogue. Good performances, decent recording.

Foss, Lucas (born 1922)

3 American pieces.
*** EMI Dig. CDC5 55360-2 [id.]. Perlman, Boston SO, Ozawa – BARBER: *Violin concerto;*
BERNSTEIN: *Serenade.* ***

Foss's *Three American pieces* provide an attractive makeweight for Perlman's coupling of the two major works by Barber and Bernstein. As the title suggests, they have a strong element of Copland-like folksiness, married to sweet, easy lyricism and with some Stravinskian echoes. Skilfully orchestrated for a small orchestra with prominent piano, all three of the pieces, not just the final allegro, *Composer's holiday*, but the first two, *Early song* and *Dedication*, have a way of gravitating into hoe-down rhythms, often with a suddenness to remind one of the sharp contrasts in Bohemian *dumkas*.

Françaix, Jean (born 1912)

Violin sonatine.
*** EMI Dig. CDC7 54541-2 [id.]. Frank Peter Zimmermann, Alexander Lonquich – AURIC:
Sonate; MILHAUD: *Sonata No. 2;* POULENC: *Sonata;* SATIE: *Choses vues.* ***

Jean Françaix's engaging *Sonatine* for violin and piano of 1934 is a delight, and it is played with great sparkle and Gallic charm by Zimmermann and Lonquich. Beautifully present and lively recording.

Wind quintets Nos. 1 & 2; (i) L'heure du berger.
*** Priory/MDG Dig. 603 0557-2 [id.]. Kammervereinigung Berlin; (i) Frank-Immo Zichner.

These Berliners put over Françaix's delightful *Wind quintets* with great charm and delicacy. These are performances that radiate freshness and fun and, apart from the virtuosity of the performances, the naturalness of the recording and the balance are a continuing source of delight. The *Wind quintet No. 1* was written for the wind soloists of the French Radio Orchestra in 1948 and its ideas are abundant and full of wit. *L'heure du berger* comes from the preceding year and is a piano and wind sextet, which readers may recall from Decca's French chamber-music anthology with Pascal Rogé and friends (see our main volume), but this is as good in its different way. The *Wind quintet No. 2* is a later but hardly less charming piece, composed for the Aulos Ensemble in 1987. Delicious playing and enchantingly light-hearted music.

Franck, César (1822–90)

Symphonic variations for piano and orchestra.

(M) *** Decca 425 082-2 [id.]. Clifford Curzon, LPO, Sir Adrian Boult – BRAHMS: *Piano concerto No. 1;* LITOLFF: *Scherzo.* ***

(BB) **(*) Naxos 8.550754 [id.]. Thiollier, Nat. SO of Ireland, Antonio de Almeida – FAURE: *Ballade;* D'INDY: *Symphonie sur un air montagnard français.* **(*)

(BB) *(*) EMI Seraphim CES5 68522-2 (2) [CDEB 68522]. John Ogdon, Philh. O, Barbirolli – GRIEG: *Concerto* *(*); *Peer Gynt* ***; SCHUMANN: *Concerto.* *(*)

Curzon's Decca performance of the *Symphonic variations* has stood the test of time. It is an engagingly fresh reading, without idiosyncrasy, and the early (1955) Kingsway Hall recording is particularly clear and vivid. It can be recommended unreservedly, particularly as the couplings are so attractive for this reissue in Decca's Classic Sound series.

Naxos's coupling is intelligent enough: none of these works are concertos and all are written within a relatively brief time-span. But it would be idle to pretend that their anthology offers playing as distinguished as, say, Curzon or Jean-Philippe Collard or Pascal Rogé's account with Maazel and the Cleveland Orchestra, which ought to be reissued. François-Joël Thiollier shows some imagination, and the orchestral playing is perfectly acceptable without being in any way distinguished. All the same, many will find it tempting at this price.

John Ogdon opens in improvisatory style and the result is curiously unspontaneous; the best section is the finale, where a certain rhythmic spring catches the listener's previously flagging interest. Good 1963 recording.

(i) *Symphonic variations for piano and orchestra;* (ii) *Symphony in D min.; Les Eolides;* (iii) *Violin sonata in A;* (iv) (Piano) *Prélude, choral et fugue;* (v) (Organ) *Cantabile in B; Choral No. 2; Pièce héroïque in B min.;* (vi) *Panis angelicus.*

(B) **(*) Ph. Duo 442 296-2 (2) [id.]. (i) Bucquet, Monte Carlo Op. O, Capolongo; (ii) Concg. O, Otterloo; (iii) Arthur Grumiaux, István Hajdu; (iv) Eduardo del Pueyo; (v) Pierre Cochereau (organ of Notre-Dame de Paris); (vi) José Carreras.

Although the performances are variable, this Philips Duo set is certainly worth its asking price. Its highlights are Otterloo's splendid (1964) account of the *Symphony* (plus *Les Eolides*) and the Grumiaux/Hajdu performance of the *Violin sonata.* Otterloo's reading of the *Symphony* has tremendous thrust. Indeed the whole performance moves forward in a single sweep and its romantic urgency is impossible to resist when the orchestral playing is so assured. A most exciting performance, if not strong on subtlety. *Les Eolides* – not otherwise available – is a welcome bonus. The composer's holiday experience of a mistral wind in the Rhône valley in 1875 prompted the work's composition. The Aeolids were the breezes which aided Odysseus on his voyage and here they blow briskly and demand considerable virtuosity from the Concertgebouw strings. Grumiaux's account of the *Violin sonata* has both nobility and warmth, and if his partner is not quite his match this is still a memorable performance, most naturally recorded. Marie-Françoise Bucquet gives a perfectly satisfactory account of the *Symphonic variations,* and Carreras sings his heart out in *Panis angelicus.* But Pueyo's piano contribution is a routine one and Cochereau's organ pieces are also unmemorable, not helped by wheezily unflattering sound.

Symphony in D min.

(M) **(*) DG Dig. 445 512-2 [id.]. O Nat. de France, Bernstein – ROUSSEL: *Symphony No. 3.* **(*)

Symphony in D min.; Le chasseur maudit.

(M) **(*) EMI Eminence Dig. CD-EMX 2236; *TC-EMX 2236* [id.]. Phd. O, Riccaro Muti.

Bernstein conducts a powerful, warmly expressive performance which, thanks in part to a live recording, carries conviction in its flexible spontaneity. It has its moments of vulgarity, but that is part of the work; the reservations are of less importance next to the glowing, positive qualities of the performance. The recording is vivid and opulent, but with the brass apt to sound strident.

Muti's is a strongly committed but unsentimental reading. The cor anglais solo in the *Allegretto* is most beautiful and the finale is particularly refreshing in its directness. The fill-up is welcome, a vividly dramatic symphonic poem, strongly presented; but with Karajan's version, which includes the *Symphonic variations,* also at mid-price (EMI CDM7 64747-2), this is not especially competitive, except for those seeking a digital master. The 1983 recording, robust and vivid, is certainly improved in its CD format, generally well integrated and among EMI's better Philadelphia records made in the 1980s. However, first choice remains with Dutoit (Decca 437 278-2) or Monteux on RCA (9026 61697-2) – see our main volume.

Symphony in D min.; (i) Symphonic variations for piano and orchestra.
* Sony Dig. SK 58958 [id.]. (i) Paul Crossley; VPO, Carlo Maria Giulini.

The combination of Giulini and the Vienna Philharmonic is on the face of things attractive but, oh dear, this is much the slowest account of the *Symphony* to have appeared in the last few years: it is slower even than Giulini's 1987 DG account with the Berlin Philharmonic. Nor in the *Symphonic variations* does Paul Crossley resist the temptation to indulge in point-making. There are much more recommendable versions of both works now before the public.

CHAMBER MUSIC

String quartet in D.
** Koch Dig. 3-1053-2 [id.]. César Franck Ens.

While the Fitzwilliam account of the *String quartet* (Decca 425 424-2) remains in currency – see our main edition – the Koch version by the César Franck Ensemble is not a strong competitor. The playing has no want of enthusiasm – nor, for that matter, does it lack finesse; but the quality of the recording may pose problems for some collectors. The quartet is placed fairly close to us, so that *pianissimo* markings do not register to full effect, and the acoustic has too much resonance. Still, there is more to admire in this issue than to cavil at, and it deserves its two stars.

Violin sonata in A.
** Carlton Dig. MCD 37 [id.]. Hasson, Ivaldi – DEBUSSY: *Violin sonata;* FAURE: *Violin sonata No. 1.*
**
* RCA Dig. 09026 62697-2 [id.]. Pinchas Zukerman, Marc Neikrug – DEBUSSY; FAURE: *Sonatas.* *

Musicianly and intelligent playing comes from Maurice Hasson and Christian Ivaldi on the less-than-full-price Carlton (formerly Pickwick) label. It is worth considering, given the fact that it comes with two other great French sonatas. However, the pianist is not balanced to best advantage and the performances need greater eloquence and fire; so this version, whatever its merits, is not a first choice, which remains with Kyung-Wha Chung on Decca 421 154-2.

With Pinchas Zukerman and Marc Neikrug, one feels that the Franck *Sonata* is a vehicle for their virtuosity rather than that they are its servants. There is a very self-conscious whispered opening from Zukerman; but it does not stop there: few phrases are allowed to speak naturally. Glamour rather than eloquence is the keynote here. Perhaps the turbulence of the Scherzo suits them best but, generally speaking, those with low tolerance for schmaltz should give this a wide berth.

Cello sonata (arr. of *Violin sonata in A*).
(M) ** Virgin/EMI Dig. CUV5 61198-2 [id.]. Isserlis, Devoyon – DEBUSSY; POULENC: *Cello sonatas.*
**
** Globe Dig. GLO 5057 [id.]. Ferschtman, Baslawskaya – DEBUSSY: *Cello sonata;* FAURE: *Après un rêve* etc. **

There is some good playing from Steven Isserlis and Pascal Devoyon, but the partnership is somewhat let down by a rather overbearing recording which places both artists far too close to the microphone. Although the Franck *Sonata* really does sound better on the violin, these fine players make out as good a case as any for the transcription which the composer himself sanctioned.

Dmitri Ferschtman and Mila Baslawskaya offer a convincing and musicianly account of the transcription for cello of the *Violin sonata*. Not highly competitive in terms of playing time, nor wildly attractive as a coupling, but it is very decently recorded.

PIANO MUSIC

Danse lente; Chorale No. 3 (arr Crossley); *Prélude, chorale et fugue; Prélude, aria et final; Prélude, fugue et variation, Op. 18.*
*(*) Sony Dig. SK 58914 [id.]. Paul Crossley.

This is very different from the excellent Fauré/Franck recital Paul Crossley recorded for Oiseau-Lyre way back in the 1970s. This fine pianist makes a consistently beautiful sound for Sony and has impeccable technical address, but he is reluctant to leave the music unadorned, and he pulls far too many phrases out of shape. He is very well recorded, but the performances will prove too mannered for frequent repetition.

Prelude, chorale and fugue.
(M) *** RCA 09026 62590-2 [id.]. Artur Rubinstein – BACH: *Chaconne* ***; LISZT: *Sonata.* **(*)

In music like this, strangely poised between classical form and Romantic expression, between the piano and the organ-loft, no one is more persuasive than Rubinstein. This performance, recorded (like the Bach) in 1970, has fire and spontaneity. The piano-tone is firm and clear: its brightness suits the music.

Frankel, Benjamin (1906–73)

(i) *The Aftermath, Op. 17. Concertante lirico, Op. 27; 3 Sketches for strings, Op. 2; Solemn speech and discussion, Op. 11; Youth music, Op. 12.*
*** CPO Dig. 999 221-2 [id.]. (i) Robert Dan; Northwest CO, Seattle, Alun Francis.

Long overdue amends are being made to the work of Benjamin Frankel, whose name has been kept alive up to now by his prolific and distinguished output of film scores. All the works recorded here are for string orchestra and, with the exception of the *Concertante lirico*, all were composed before the *Violin concerto* of 1951, which was dedicated to the memory of the victims of the holocaust and which made so strong an impression at its première by Max Rostal. One of the strongest pieces here is *The Aftermath*, a song-cycle for tenor, strings and off-stage trumpet and timpani, to words of Robert Nichols. It is an evocative and imaginative piece. Frankel's craftsmanship is always of the highest order and his invention and imagination are more often impressive than not. The *Violin concerto* should appear in the lifetime of this book, but in the meantime this issue, like others in this series, is recommended to all with an interest in contemporary music that has real individuality and eschews trendiness like the plague. The notes are exceptionally helpful and informative.

Symphonies Nos. 2, Op. 38 (1962); 3, Op. 40 (1964).
⊛ *** CPO Dig. 999 241-2 [id.]. Queensland SO, Werner Andreas Albert.

The eight symphonies of Benjamin Frankel enjoyed some exposure in the 1960s and early 1970s, thanks to the Third Programme, but subsequently they went underground. His rediscovery now is as welcome as it is long overdue. In his early career Frankel earned a living in light music, playing in the Savoy Orpheans and the Henry Hall band before developing into one of the most sought-after and successful composers for the cinema, where his fine musicianship and distinctive individuality made his voice immediately recognizable. He composed some impressive quartets and came relatively late to the symphony. Like the *First*, his *Second Symphony* is a powerfully concentrated and finely argued piece which has a constant feeling of onward movement. His music has something of the strength of Sibelius combined with a post-Mahlerian expressive language, and his serialism, like that of Frank Martin, was never doctrinal but pragmatic, never undermining fundamental tonal principles – a well-argued and impressive score. While the *Second* springs from painful emotions, the *Third Symphony* with its almost Stravinskian opening is a compact one-movement work, predominantly positive in expression and compelling in its sense of purpose. Each symphony is prefaced by a paragraph or so of spoken introduction that the composer recorded at the time he conducted the first performance of these symphonies on the Third Programme. It is also supplemented by documentation and notes of exceptional quality. As was the case in the *First* and *Fifth Symphonies*, the playing of the Queensland Orchestra is excellent, and so, too, is the recording. We look forward to the appearance of his *Fourth* (and possibly finest) *Symphony*, which the BBC Radio Archive series should have issued in the composer's own performance.

Fux, Johann (1660–1741)

Concentus musico instrumentalis (1701): Serenada a 8; Rondeau a 7; Sonata a 4.
(M) *** Teldec/Warner 4509 95989-2 (2) [id.]. VCM, Harnoncourt – SCHMELZER: *Sonatas.* **

Johann Fux was Kapellmeister to Emperor Charles VI at the Habsburg Court; until recently, the common view of him was as a dull academic. But the present collection suggests entirely the contrary. The *Serenada* consists of 17 (mostly brief) movements and is amazingly inventive. Scored for two clarinos (high trumpets), two oboes, bassoon, two violins, viola and basso continuo (but not horns), it is surely an early anticipation of Handel's *Water music* – a group of lively, contrasting dances: gigues, bourrées, rigadons, ciacona plus arias, which are very entertaining indeed. There is some highly original writing for the trumpets and a most beautiful Minuet. The other works are attractive too, and the performances show Harnoncourt at his finest, full of vitality, and his players convey their enjoyment. As usual with this Das Alte Werk series, the recording (1970) is first class. The drawback is that this 48-minute programme comes in harness with music by another Habsburg

Kapellmeister, Johann Schmelzer, and his music is more uneven. It is a great pity that a shorter selection of Fux's music, including his string sonatas, was not used to fill out these discs, for the two CDs together play for only 96 minutes.

Gade, Niels (1817–90)

Abenddämmerung, Op. 34/4; Allegro vivace; Canzonetta, Op. 19/3; Capriccio in A min.; Elegie, Op. 19/1; Fantasiestücke, Op. 43; Scherzo, Op. 19/2; Volkstänze im nordische charakter.
* Kontrapunkt Dig. 32184 [id.]. Elbæk, Westenholz.

Not a long programme and perhaps, at under 45 minutes, not good value. All the same, there is little of Gade's violin music available on disc and, although these pieces are mostly rather slight and bland, they are well crafted. No grumbles about the playing of Søren Elbæk or Elisabeth Westenholz, but the engineering leaves something to be desired. The soloist is very forward and thus any pianissimo tone has difficulty in registering.

Comola, Op. 12.
** Kontrapunkt Dig. 32180 [id.]. Dahl, Halling, Katagiri, Mannov, Canzone Ch., Sønderjylland SO, Frans Rasmussen.

Comola was Gade's first choral work and dates from 1846 when he was living in Leipzig. In this genre of secular oratorio or romantic cantata, his models were the Mendelssohn of *Die erste Walpurgisnacht* or Schumann's *Das Paradies und die Peri*, written three years earlier. As always with Gade, the music is expertly crafted and the invention heavily indebted to Mendelssohn. There is a certain nobility and warmth about much of it, and one can understand why it enjoyed such popularity during his lifetime. All the same, inspiration flows less generously or naturally than in *Elverskud* or the *Fifth Symphony* for piano and orchestra. Like his Op. 1 *Overture*, the work draws on Ossian, and it receives a well-prepared and persuasive performance from both soloists and instrumentalists alike. The recording is decent rather than distinguished.

Gershwin, George (1898–1937)

An American in Paris.
(*) Everest/Vanguard EVC 9003 [id.]. Pittsburgh SO, Steinberg – COPLAND: *Appalachian spring*; GOULD: *Spirituals.* *

The recorded sound is rather dry and unexpansive, but otherwise vivid. Steinberg's performance is lively, idiomatic and convincing. The central blues tune is pleasingly sultry. Incidentally, the sleeve-note points out that the Parisian taxi horns that Gershwin took home with him to use in the orchestra and which Steinberg adopts now date the piece irretrievably, as horn-tooting is now forbidden in Paris by law.

An American in Paris; (i) *Piano concerto in F; Rhapsody in blue.*
(M) *** Ph. 442 395-2 [id.]. (i) Werner Haas; Monte Carlo Op. O, De Waart.

In Monte Carlo the *Concerto* is particularly successful; its lyrical moments have a quality of nostalgia which is very attractive. Werner Haas is a volatile and sympathetic soloist, and his rhythmic verve is refreshing. Edo de Waart's *An American in Paris* is not only buoyant but glamorous too – the big blues melody is highly seductive and, as with all the best accounts of this piece, the episodic nature of the writing is hidden. There is a cultured, European flavour to this music-making that does not detract from its vitality, and the jazz inflexions are not missed, with plenty of verve in the *Rhapsody*. Very good sound.

An American in Paris; (i) *Piano concerto in F; Rhapsody in blue; Variations on 'I got rhythm'.*
(BB) *** RCA Navigator 74321 17906-2. (i) Earl Wild; Boston Pops O, Arthur Fiedler.

This super-bargain CD on RCA's Navigator label is particularly generous (70 minutes) in including, besides the usual triptych, the *'I got rhythm' variations*, given plenty of rhythmic panache. Indeed these are essentially jazzy performances: Earl Wild's playing is full of energy and brio, and he inspires Arthur Fiedler to a similarly infectious response. In many ways these performances are as fine as any; if the *Rhapsody* has not the breadth of Bernstein's highly recommendable account (Sony SMK 47529), it is nearer the Paul Whiteman original and is rewarding in quite a different way. The outer movements of the *Concerto* are comparably volatile and the blues feeling of the slow movement is strong. At the end of *An American in Paris* Fiedler (like Steinberg) adds to the exuberance by bringing in a bevy of motor horns. The brightly remastered recording suits the music-making, though the resonant Boston acoustics at times prevent absolute sharpness of focus, but the current transfer gives a convincing overall sound-picture.

(i) *Piano concerto in F; Rhapsody in blue. Cuban overture.*
(M) ** Mercury 434 341-2 [id.]. (i) Eugene List; Eastman-Rochester O, Howard Hanson (with SOUSA: *Stars and Stripes forever* **).

Quite highly regarded in its day, this is one Mercury reissue which sounds dated. The dry acoustics of the Eastman Theatre in Rochester are not flattering and the orchestral strings sound thin to today's ears. List and Hanson are both at home in this repertoire, but it is the scherzando element in the *Rhapsody* that one most remembers and, for the same reason, the finale of the *Concerto* is the most effective movement. The *Cuban overture* is probably the most successful piece here and *The Stars and Stripes forever* (credited to the Eastman Philharmonia) is robustly gutsy rather than particularly peppy.

Gilson, Paul (1865–1942)

De Zee (suite).
(BB) *** Discover Dig. DICD 920126 [id.]. Brussels BRT PO, Karl Anton Rickenbacher – DE BOECK: *Symphony in G.* ***

Like August de Boeck, also represented on this disc, Paul Gilson was a Belgian composer, born in 1865. His suite, *De Zee*, like de Boeck's *Symphony* is full of Russian echoes. It is a series of four sea-scapes half-way between Wagner's *Flying Dutchman* and Debussy's *La Mer*, with Rimsky-Korsakov's *Scheherazade* mixed in. Well played and recorded and, at Discover International's super-bargain price, an ideal disc for experimenting with.

Ginastera, Alberto (1865–1936)

Estancia (ballet suite); *Panambi* (choreographic legend).
*** Everest EVC 9007 [id.]. LSO, Sir Eugene Goossens – ANTILL: *Corroboree*; VILLA-LOBOS: *Little train of the Caipira.* **(*)

These vivid recordings of the music of Ginastera are a highlight of an anthology conducted with verve and commitment by a conductor who championed much music at the edge of the repertoire. Both these brightly hued scores bring a high standard of invention. *Panambi* is the earlier – written when the composer was only twenty. It opens with a haunting picture of *Moonlight on the Panama* and the *Lament of the Maidens* is gently touching, while the *Invocations of the Powerful Spirits* and *Dance of the Warriors* are powerfully primitive. *Estancia* dates from a slightly later period. Again the scoring is exotic and impressive, and the lively dances are full of primeval energy, notably the closing *Malambo*, while the lovely *Wheat dance* brings another nostalgic interlude. The performances are in every way first class and the atmospheric recording brilliantly captures the composer's imaginatively varied sound-world.

Giordano, Umberto (1867–1948)

Andrea Chenier (complete).
(M) **(*) EMI CMS5 65287-2 (2) [Ang. CDMB 65287]. Corelli, Stella, Sereni, Rome Op. Ch. & O, Santini.

The glory of the 1964 EMI version is the Chénier of Franco Corelli, one of his most satisfying performances on record with heroic tone gloriously exploited. The other singing is less distinguished. Though Antonietta Stella was never sweeter of voice than here, she hardly matches such rivals as Scotto or Caballé. The 1960s recording is vivid, with plenty of atmosphere, and has been transferred to CD most naturally, but the RCA set in the same price range, with Domingo and Scotto, remains a clear first choice (GD 82046).

Giuliani, Mauro (1781–1828)

Guitar concerto in A, Op. 30.
(M) *** DG 439 984-2 [id.]. Siegfried Behrend, I Musici – CARULLI: *Concerto in A ***; VIVALDI:
Guitar concertos. **(*)

Giuliani's *A major Concerto* is presented here with much elegance and finesse and is immaculately
recorded. Its catchy main theme is endearing; though the music overall is slight, it is nicely crafted.

Glass, Philip (born 1937)

String quartets Nos. 2 (Company); 3 (Mishima); 4 (Buczak); 5.
*** Elektra-Nonesuch/Warner Dig. 7559 79356-2 [id.]. Kronos Quartet.

Happily, the quartets here are presented in reverse order, for the last of the four, No. 5, dating from
1991, presents Glass at his most warmly expressive and intense, the more moving for being
conventionally beautiful in a way that for so long he tended to avoid. Textures are luminous,
shimmering in their repetitions rather than thrusting them home relentlessly. The Kronos Quartet, for
whom the work was written, give a heartfelt performance, as they do of the *Quartet No. 4* (1990),
written in memory of Brian Buczak, who died of AIDS. The manner of the three substantial
movements is far darker, with the first presenting a strong, chorale-like theme. The valedictory mood
is intensified by a lyrical and poignantly beautiful middle movement, leading to a noble finale. The
Quartet No. 2 (1983) consists of four brief movements originally written to accompany the staged
soliloquy of a dying man, entitled *Company*. Again it is valedictory in tone but is far less tender. The
Quartet No. 3 (1985) similarly has its roots in music originally written for a dramatic entertainment,
the Paul Schrader film on the Japanese poet, Mishima, and his spectacular suicide. As in No. 2, the
idiom is repetitive in the characteristic Glass manner, this time with six brief movements. Though
Nos. 4 and 5 most clearly reveal the hand of a master, the earlier works also represent Glass at his
most approachable, the more so when they are treated to magnetic performances by the Kronos
Quartet, superbly recorded.

OPERA

Le Belle et la Bête (opera based on the film of Jean Cocteau): complete.
*** Nonesuch-Elektra/Warner Dig 7559 794347 [id.]. Felty, Purnhagen, Kuether, Martinez, Neill,
Zhou, Philip Glass Ens., Michael Riesman.

Philip Glass first saw Cocteau's films in Paris in 1954 at the age of seventeen, and he was so
profoundly impressed that three of his works have been directly inspired by them: *Orpheé* and *Les
enfants terribles*, as well as this most recent one. With *La Belle et la Bête* the composer tells us 'the
story interests me less as a fairy tale than as a love story', and the tender emotions behind the score,
as well as its evocative beauty, bear witness to that. What Glass has done is to provide a new musical
accompaniment to a showing of the 90-minute film, dispensing with Auric's original film-music and
synchronizing the singing-parts with the speech of the actors in the film. In the opening scenes the
music is far lighter and more conventionally beautiful than most Glass, but then the poignancy of the
story is more and more reflected in the score, both tender and mellifluous. Glass and Riesman had to
use computers in the end in order to synchronize the vocal line and the actors' lips perfectly, but what
matters on the disc is that the hypnotic quality of Glass's repetitions helps to enhance the magical
atmosphere, while the use of the original French film-script prompts Glass to be more warmly
melodic than usual. Glass himself recognizes that his score might be regarded as either presumptuous
or gimmicky, but the justification lies in the intensity of the score overall, with Janice Felty and
Gregory Purnhagen both clearly focused in the central roles, though Purnhagen's baritone suggests
from the start a heroic, not a bestial, figure. Vividly atmospheric sound.

Einstein on the Beach (complete).
*** Teldec/Warner Dig. 7559 79323-2 (3) [id.]. Soloists, Philip Glass Ens., Riesman.

Glass himself explains the need for a new recording of this bizarre and relentless opera – as the
surreal title implies, more dream than drama. 'To begin with, the new recording is almost 190 minutes
long, as opposed to some 160 minutes in 1978 . . . and length is not a trivial matter in a performance
of *Einstein* but part of the total experience'. Where the earlier recording of this opera had an abrasive
edge, this new one is more refined, melding the different elements, electronic alongside acoustic, more
subtly and persuasively than before. Even so, the first train episode, over 20 minutes long, remains
mind-blowing in its relentlessness. The impact is heightened by the vividness of the recording, with

spoken voices in particular given such presence that they startle you as if someone has burst into your room. The vision remains an odd one, and other examples of Glass's minimalist operatic style remain more immediately appealing, but, with a formidable group of vocalists and instrumentalists brilliantly directed, often from the keyboard, by Michael Riesman, the new recording certainly justifies itself.

Glazunov, Alexander (1865–1936)

Violin concerto in A min., Op. 82.
*** EMI Dig. CDC7 54872-2 [id.]. Zimmermann, LPO, Welser-Möst – DVORAK: *Violin concerto.*
     ***
(BB) *** Naxos Dig. 8.550758 [id.]. Ilya Kaler, Polish Nat. RSO (Katowice), Kolchinsky – DVORAK: *Concerto* etc. ***

The Glazunov comes up sounding delightfully fresh in Frank Peter Zimmermann's hands. There is no lack of competition, particularly from such classics as the Heifetz–Barbirolli (EMI CDH7 64030-2 – see our main edition) and the magisterial and glowing Milstein account (available only as part of a six-CD set that also includes his wonderful Brahms). Among recent versions, however, Zimmermann can hold his head high: he plays with effortless virtuosity, great polish and great beauty of tone. Franz Welser-Möst provides excellent support, and the recording is outstandingly natural and realistic.

The Russian violinist Ilya Kaler gives a rapturously lyrical performance, and Camilla Kolchinsky's accompaniment is equally warm and supportive. The resonant acoustic of the Concert Hall of Polish Radio gives a big, spacious orchestral sound, but Ilya Kaler's tone is full to match, and the violin playing can certainly accommodate the scrutiny of the fairly close microphones. The Dvořák *Concerto* is hardly less successful, and the delightful *Romance* is thrown in for good measure.

The Seasons (complete ballet), *Op. 67.*
(***) EMI mono CDC5 55223-2 [id.]. O, composer – PROKOFIEV: *Piano concerto No. 3* etc. (***)
*(*) Russian Disc mono RDCD 11155 [id.]. Leningrad PO, Mravinsky – KALINNIKOV: *Symphony No. 2.* (*)

As readers who acquired it in its earlier, LP transfer on Pearl will have already discovered, Glazunov's 1929 recording is of remarkable quality, vastly superior to, say, Pfitzner's *Palestrina Preludes*, recorded two years later and reissued in the same batch of EMI's 'Composers in Person' releases. *The Seasons* was recorded at the Portman Rooms in London's Baker Street, and a newspaper reporter present at the sessions described Glazunov as resembling 'a wealthy, retired tea-planter . . . with parchment-coloured skin . . . around his neck what appeared to be an untidy piece of handkerchief, really a stiff collar melted into disorder'. He appears to have charmed audiences when he later visited England in 1931, and he certainly charmed his players at these sessions, if the results are anything to go by. The playing is marvellously phrased and has great inner life and, above all, warmth and grace. Although, as one would expect from the period, the frequency range is limited, the actual orchestral texture is quite remarkably well detailed throughout the spectrum, and the present transfer does it justice. Strongly recommended, this comes with all of Prokofiev's commercial recordings as a pianist. An indispensable issue.

Oddly enough, the sound-quality of Russian Disc's 1952 Leningrad concert performance, conducted by Mravinsky, calls for less tolerance than one might expect, given its date and source. There is some distortion on climaxes but it is surprisingly clean elsewhere. The performance is obviously a good one, too, but at full price it is distinctly uncompetitive. The Kalinnikov coupling is of later provenance but is mono, and the sound is not really acceptable, suffering from considerable congestion, discoloration and, as far as the strings are concerned, a meagre sound above the stave.

(i) *Symphony No. 3 in D, Op. 33;* (ii) *Serenades Nos. 1 in A, Op. 7; 2 in F, Op. 11;* (i) *Stenka Razin* (symphonic poem), *Op. 13.*
*** ASV Dig. CDDCA 903 [id.]. (i) LSO; (ii) RPO; Yondani Butt.

ASV have reissued Yondani Butt's performance (originally offered on its own) with substantial couplings. *Stenka Razin* (never quite the popular success Glazunov intended by incorporating the *Volga boat song*) comes off well enough; there is some impressive LSO brass playing and the sinuous secondary theme is well appreciated by the LSO strings. But it is the two charming early *Serenades* that catch the ear, seductively played by the RPO. The performance of the symphony lies somewhere between the alternative Järvi (Orfeo C 157101A) and Rozhdestvensky (Olympia OCD 120) versions, and the recording is better balanced than either. One would have liked a greater sense of soaring (over the throbbing wind chords) at the opening, but the response of the LSO catches the colour and melancholy of the slow movement, and the Scherzo (easily the best movement) has sparkle. However, Järvi is more successful in the finale, which seems rather too long here and could use a shade more adrenalin. But a cultivated approach overall is never amiss with this composer.

(i) *Symphony No. 6 in C min., Op. 58; Raymonda* (ballet), *Op. 57a: suite;* (ii) *Triumphal march, Op. 40.*
*** ASV Dig. CDDCA 904 [id.]. (i) LSO; (ii) RPO; Yondani Butt.

Taken overall, Yondani Butt's is the preferred choice for Glazunov's *Sixth*, although of course couplings do come into the matter. Yet Butt's performance is marginally fresher than Järvi's, helped by the more open sound of the ASV recording, and the fine wind and brass contributions from the LSO; the brass chorale at the end of the *Variations* is effectively sonorous. The selection from *Raymonda* concentrates on the first two Acts and offers only a brief *Entr'acte* from Act III; most of the music in fact comes from Act I, some 21 minutes out of a selection lasting just over half an hour. The playing is both graceful and lively, and the recording has plenty of amplitude and warmth.

CHAMBER MUSIC

5 Novelettes, Op. 15.
(***) Testament mono SBT1061 [id.]. Hollywood Qt – BORODIN: *String quartet No. 2;*
   TCHAIKOVSKY: *String quartet No. 1.* (***)

Glazunov's *Five Novelettes,* Op. 15, were written in 1886 when the composer was coming up to twenty-one. The Hollywood Quartet's recording dates from 1955 and has not appeared in the UK before. These players bring a freshness and ardour to these charming compositions that is most persuasive. The *Novelettes* last a little under half an hour, and as a result the disc is only one second short of eighty minutes long. The sleeve warns that some CD players may have difficulty in tracking it. We have not found this to be the case, but some caution may be necessary on the part of readers with older players.

String quartets Nos. 3 in G (Slavonic), Op. 26; 5 in D min., Op. 70; The Fridays, Book 2: Kuranta; Prelude and fugue in D min.
**(*) Olympia OCD 525 [id.]. Shostakovich Qt.

Cobbett's Cyclopaedia of Chamber Music devotes a good deal of space to Glazunov's chamber music and M. D. Calvocoressi (dedicatee of Ravel's *Cinq mélodies populaire grècques*), who wrote the entry, hails the *Third Quartet (Slavonic)* of 1893 as one of 'his most brilliant and attractive works'. Glazunov's first attempt at the quartet in 1882 pre-dates his *First Symphony* and his last comes from the years of his self-imposed exile in France. The appeal of the *Third* is immediate and the thematic inspiration folk-like and of the highest level. It comes over particularly well in the persuasive and enthusiastic hands of the Shostakovich Quartet. The *Fifth Quartet* (1898) opens with a noble and expressive fugue, and on hearing it one is tempted to agree with Calvocoressi that this is the finest of the seven (though his essay was published before the last, *Hommage au passé,* was written). Good performances, though they are not the last word in polish; but they are rather too closely balanced for complete comfort.

String quartets Nos. 6 in B flat, Op. 106; 7 in C, Op. 107.
** Olympia OCD 526 [id.]. Shostakovich Qt.

The *Fifth* and *Sixth Quartets* are separated by two decades, the First World War and two revolutions. The *Sixth* was written for the eponymous Glazunov Quartet and dates from 1921, the *Seventh* (*Hommage au passé*) from 1930. The turbulence of the 1910s and '20s seems not to have cast any shadows; their invention has all the sad charm of old Russia. Glazunov – and who can blame him? – has retired into his own world and offers music that could have been composed at the beginning of his career. The Shostakovich Quartet generally play with conviction, though their performances are by no means as polished as those of Nos. 3 and 5. There is some unsatisfactory intonation in the second movement of the *Seventh* and some less than beautiful (indeed scrawny) tone. The recording is rather up-front and has some roughness on climaxes, but there is no alternative version of either work.

2 Impromptus, Op. 54; 3 Morceaux, Op. 49; 2 Poèmes-improvisations; Prelude and fugue, Op. 62; Theme and variations, Op. 72; Valse de salon, Op. 43.
*(**) Marco Polo Dig. 8.223152 [id.]. Tatjana Franová.

Glazunov is not at his most inventive or inspired in his keyboard music, though his writing for it is never less than cultivated and idiomatic. The best-known work is the *Theme and variations*, Op. 72, which Tatjana Franová plays with fluent sympathy. Generally speaking, the recital uncovers no masterpieces, though her playing could not be more persuasive. The recording, while not wholly unpleasing, does not really produce a realistic piano-sound: it is difficult to be sure where the instrument is in the aural picture. The bass is well defined but does not wholly relate to the rest of the instrument, and the overall effect is a shade synthetic.

Goldschmidt, Berthold (born 1903)

OPERA

(i) *Beatrice Cenci* (complete); (ii) *4 Lieder: Clouds; Ein Rosenzweig; Nebelweben; Time.*
*** Sony S2K 66836 (2) [id.]. (i) Simon Estes, Roberta Alexander, Della Jones, Fiona Kimm, Siegfried Lorenz, Ian Bostridge, Berlin R. Ch., Deutsches SO, Lothar Zagrosek; (ii) Iris Vermillion, composer.

Goldschmidt's earlier opera, *Der gewaltige Hahnrei* (treated to a splendid Decca recording – 440 852-2 – see our main volume), demonstrated the composer's dramatic gift, but this later opera, written in 1951 for the Festival of Britain but not performed until 1988, is in many ways even stronger. It is a direct and compact adaptation of Shelley's play, *The Cenci*, which Byron described as the finest English drama since Shakespeare but which similarly was neglected in its time. Goldschmidt's idiom is strong and forthright, individual without presenting difficulties. To a libretto by Martin Esslin the opera leads one crisply through the story of 'the virtuous murderess' who kills her father, having suffered incestuous rape by him. The first two Acts move briskly – with the second scene of Act I a colourful party scene given by Cenci – and only in the third, leading up to Beatrice's execution and a climactic monologue, does the pace grow more reflective. Even that Act is compact in scale, making this an excellent opera for disc. As in the earlier Goldschmidt opera, Lothar Zagrosek is a persuasive interpreter and the cast is a strong one. Roberta Alexander makes a moving heroine, not least in the brief, tender Arietta after the rape. She is powerfully supported by Della Jones as Beatrice's mother. Though Simon Estes does not sound evil enough for Cenci, he sings expressively with firm, noble tone. The four songs, well sung by Iris Vermillion with the nonagenarian composer accompanying, are in a balder but comparably lyrical style, making a valuable supplement. Excellent sound.

Górecki, Henryk (born 1933)

(i) *Harpsichord concerto;* (ii) *Little Requiem for a polka (Kleines Requiem für eine Polka);* (iii) *Good night (In Memoriam Michael Vyner)* for soprano, alto flute, 3 tam-tams and piano.
*** Nonesuch/Warner Dig. 7559 79362-2 [id.]. L. Sinf.; (i) David Zinman; (ii) Ezbieta Chojnacka, cond. Markus Stenz; (iii) Dawn Upshaw, Sebastian Bell, John Constable, David Hockings.

Those listeners who have encountered the *Third Symphony* and who are looking for further Górecki to explore might well start here. The *Little Requiem* (1993) opens with a single quiet bell-stroke; a piano (John Constable) then engages in a tranquil dialogue with the violins, to be rudely interrupted by a burst of bell-ringing; the reverie returns momentarily before the energetic, marcato *Allegro impetutoso* which follows. The third movement is stridently but infectiously jazzy. The piece ends with a raptly sustained elegiac *Adagio*, still dominated by the quietly assertive tolling bells. Górecki uses his basic musical material economically but with much imagination, and the performance has compelling concentration. The two-movement *Harpsichord concerto*, written a decade earlier, combines soloist and strings in a vibrant, jangly ménage: the first movement juxtaposes florid keyboard-writing over an insistent, shifting harmonic continuo from the strings; the second is more extrovert and cheerful, with the soloist and strings alternating hammered marcatos. Finally the tension resolves in a brief harpsichord flourish and a momentary rhythmic eruption from the string group. *Good night* is nocturnally serene, the composer's repetitions used to haunting effect. The work is a memorial piece for Michael Vyner who master-minded and promoted the composer's first London visit in the spring of 1989; Vyner died in the autumn of that same year. The soprano voice enters only in the third movement, with a cantilena to Shakespeare's words from *Hamlet*: 'Good night . . . and flights of angels sing thee to thy rest!' The three tam-tams poignantly add their own mystical requiem at the close. Both here and in the *Little Requiem* the very atmospheric recording brings an added dimension to the communication from performers who are obviously totally committed to the composer's cause.

VOCAL MUSIC

(i; ii; iii) *Beatus vir;* (iii) *Old Polish music;* (ii) *Totus tuus.*
*** Argo 436 835-2 [id.]; *435 835-4.* (i) Nikita Storojev; (ii) Prague Philharmonic Ch.; (iii) Czech PO,
John Nelson.

Beatus vir (for bass soloist – the eloquent Nikita Storojev – chorus and orchestra) is a strong
manifestation of the composer's Catholic faith, commissioned by the Cardinal of Cracow to mark the
900th anniversary of the Martyrdom of St Stanislaw, who was murdered while celebrating Mass. It is
the work which, alongside the *Third Symphony,* excited Michael Vyner's interest in the composer and
which in turn led to Górecki's London visit in 1989; but it is a darkly pessimistic, oppressive piece,
with little variety of feeling, which some ears find too extended for its material – for all the
commitment and intensity of the performance. *Totus tuus* for unaccompanied chorus is shorter and
more direct. *Old Polish music* is in many ways the most potent work here, using both a lullaby and
medieval organum for its source of inspiration. Performances and recording are equally impressive.

(i) *Miserere, Op. 44; Amen, Op. 35; Euntes ibant et flebant, Op. 32;* (ii) *Wuslo moja (My Vistula, grey
Vistula), Op. 46; Szeroka woda (Broad waters): choral suite of folksongs, Op. 39 (Oh, our River
Narew; Oh, when in Powistle; Oh, Johnny, Johnny; She picked wild roses; Broad waters).*
*** Nonesuch/Warner 7559 79348-2 [id.]. (i) Chicago Symphony Ch. & Lyric Op. Ch., Nelson; (ii)
Lyra Chamber Ch., Lucy Ding.

Górecki's powerful *Miserere* was prompted by the political upheaval in Poland in 1981, when a
demonstration by members of Solidarity was quelled by the militia and many workers were injured.
Górecki set a text of only five words: *Domine Deus noster, Miserere nobis*; although the work's span is
ambitious, it is sustained by profound intensity of feeling. The repetitions of the words '*Domine Deus*'
call for all the composer's resourcefulness; the poignant final cry, '*Miserere nobis*', is kept for the last
three minutes. The combined Chicago choirs maintain the sombrely atmospheric opening pianissimo
with impressive concentration, and the dynamic climax of the piece, when the combined choirs sing in
ten parts, is very compelling. The following *Amen* is powerfully concentrated, while *Euntes ibant et
flebant* (the composer's first work for unaccompanied chorus) is simpler, more serene. The five
folksong settings are also essentially expressive (even *Oh, Johnny, Johnny* is marked *Molto lento –
dolce cantabile*) and all are harmonically rich. They are beautifully sung by the smaller group. The
recording, made in the Church of St Mary of the Angels in Chicago, is admirable.

Gould, Morton (born 1913)

Spirituals for string choir and orchestra.
*** Everest/Vanguard EVC 9003 [id.]. LSO, Walter Susskind – COPLAND: *Appalachian spring* ***;
GERSHWIN: *American in Paris.* **(*)

It is unexpected to find an English performance of this essentially American piece, the more so as it
has never been bettered, not even by the composer himself. The slow movement is really moving and
A little bit of sin is wittily pungent, while the wide-ranging recording (brightly lit in a transatlantic
way) looks after the dramatic needs of *Protest* and the ambivalent exuberance of *Jubilee.* The
couplings are hardly less welcome.

Gounod, Charles (1818–93)

OPERA

Faust (complete).
(M) **(*) EMI CMS7 69983-2 (3) [Ang. CDMC 69983]. De los Angeles, Gedda, Blanc, Christoff,
Paris Nat. Op. Ch. and O, Cluytens.

In the reissued Cluytens set, the seductiveness of De los Angeles's singing is a dream and it is a pity
that the recording hardens the natural timbre slightly. Christoff is magnificently Mephistophelian.
Gedda, though showing some signs of strain, sings intelligently, and among the other soloists Ernest
Blanc has a pleasing, firm voice, which he uses to make Valentin into a sympathetic character.
Cluytens's approach is competent but somewhat workaday. The set has been attractively repackaged
and the libretto has strikingly clear print, to make a good mid-priced choice for this popular opera.
The finest modern version, conducted by Carlo Rizzi, includes Jerry Hadley, Cecilia Gasdia and
Samuel Ramey, all outstanding (Teldec 4509 90872-2).

Faust (abridged version sung in English with ballet music; introduced by Sir Thomas Beecham).
(M) *** Dutton mono 2CDAX 2001 (2) [id.] Nash, Licette, Easton, Williams, Vane, Brunskill, Carr,
   BBC Ch. & SO, LPO, Sir Thomas Beecham.

Beecham's 1929 recording, superbly transferred on the Dutton label, with full-bodied sound for voices and orchestra alike, gives a vivid and refreshing idea of British opera performance in the 1920s. The old Chorley translation is used, stilted and creaking but memorable – 'What rubbishy wine!' says Mephistopheles – and the team of top British singers of the day is at one in enunciating words with crystal clarity. Voices are firm and cleanly projected, with the bright-toned Miriam Licette as Marguerite delivering a splendid trill at the start of the *Jewel song*. Heddle Nash sings with heady tone as Faust, Harold Williams is a youthfully fresh Valentine and the distinctive flicker in Robert Easton's bass never gets in the way of clean focus in the role of Mephistopheles. Beecham himself is inspired, pointing rhythms and phrases infectiously, though, curiously, four of the 32 sides of the original 78s were conducted by Clarence Raybould. A supplement on the second CD includes a brief spoken introduction by Beecham, as well as the *Nubian dance* and *Adagio* from the ballet music – otherwise omitted, like the *Walpurgisnacht* scene.

Roméo et Juliette (complete).
(B) (**(*)) Decca Double mono 443 539-2 (2) [id.]. Jobin, Micheau, Mollet, Rialland, Rehfuss, Opéra
   Nat. Ch. & O, Erede.
(M) ** EMI CMS5 65290-2 (2) [CDMB 65290]. Corelli, Freni, Calés, Depraz, Paris Op. Ch. & O,
   Lombard.

When Gounod's free but likeable adaptation of Shakespeare has been poorly treated on record – with relatively few versions, and those quickly deleted – this 1953 Decca mono set is well worth considering. As John Culshaw describes in his autobiography, the French publishers at the last minute forced Decca to change plans from recording *Faust* to recording this much less well-known opera. Neither Culshaw as producer nor the conductor, Erede, knew the piece at all but, with a first-rate cast singing idiomatically, the result is still fresh and full of fire. It is an interesting comment that in 1953 Paris could offer a far finer team of singers than latterly, with the tenor Pierre Mollet, for example, light and airy as Mercutio, not least in the *Queen Mab aria*, and Charles Cambon a fine Capulet. The only non-French singer, Heinz Rehfuss, projects with the clearest focus as Frère Laurent, while the roles of the two lovers are taken by two vintage singers of the period, not always ideally caught on record but both warmly characterful. Janine Micheau is tenderly charming as a vulnerably girlish Juliette and, as Roméo, Raoul Jobin sings stylishly and with little of the pinched tone that too often has afflicted French tenors. The transfer is more than full-bodied enough to compensate for the slightly edgy top.

On EMI, the great pity is that the casting of this great and rich opera is basically inadequate. Neither Corelli as Romeo nor Freni as Juliet is remotely in style, even though their tones are often beautiful to the ear. Why was it not possible in a French-made recording to correct the often excruciating pronunciation of the two principals? British singers are sometimes taken to task for their poor pronunciation of French, but few if any have ever begun to approach the enormities committed here. That gets the set off to a bad start and, though Freni with her sweet tone and natural charm comes much closer to the mark than her partner, so much revolves around the lovers' four big duets. The conducting of Alain Lombard makes up some ground with its warm, idiomatic understanding; but it could all have been so much better without difficulty. The set is well presented and documented and brightly and vividly transferred, the chorus well focused yet with plenty of atmosphere overall. The break between the two CDs comes between the first and second scenes of Act III.

Grainger, Percy (1882–1961)

The Warriors (music for an imaginary ballet).
*** DG Dig. 445 860-2; *445 860-4* [id.]. Philh. O, John Eliot Gardiner – HOLST: *The Planets.* ***

Colourful and vigorous, *The Warriors* is described as 'an imaginary ballet for orchestra and three pianos', a characteristically extrovert showpiece, Grainger's largest work. With richly scored echoes of *Rosenkavalier* and *Petrushka* brought improbably together at the start, the piece throbs with energy, at one point – in a gentler interlude – involving an offstage orchestra in Ivesian superimpositions. If much of the writing, with the piano prominent in the orchestra, sounds as though it is about to turn into Grainger's *Handel in the Strand*, plus an echo or two of Eric Coates, the result is hugely enjoyable in such a fine performance as Gardiner's. It makes an unexpected and valuable coupling for his brilliant account of the favourite Holst work. Dazzling sound.

Granados, Enrique (1867–1916)

Cuentos para la juventud, Op. 1: Dedicatoria. Danzas españolas Nos. 4 & 5, Op. 37/4–5; Tonadillas al estilo antiguo: La Maja de Goya. Valses poéticos.

⊛ (BB) *** RCA Navigator Dig. 74321 17903-2. Julian Bream (guitar) – ALBENIZ: *Collection;* RODRIGO: *3 Piezas españolas.* *** ⊛

Like the Albéniz items with which these Granados pieces are coupled, these performances show Julian Bream at his most inspirational. The illusion of the guitar being in the room is especially electrifying in the middle section of the famous *Spanish dance No. 5*, when Bream achieves the most subtle pianissimo. Heard against the background silence, the effect is quite magical. But all the playing here is wonderfully spontaneous. This is one of the most impressive guitar recitals ever recorded, and for this super-bargain reissue RCA have generously added the *Tres Piezas españolas* of Rodrigo, recorded a year later and no less distinguished.

12 Danzas españolas; Goyescas.

(M) *** Ph. 442 751-2 (2) [id.]. Eduardo del Pueyo – FALLA: *Nights in the gardens of Spain.* *** ⊛

This set is justly described as 'the quintessence of Spanish pianism', for playing of this repertoire does not come any better than this. Eduardo del Pueyo, born in Aragon, made these recordings in 1956 (although the ear would hardly guess, so natural is the piano recording). His playing of the colourful *Spanish dances* has much flair and poetic delicacy – sample *No. 2 in C minor*, so beautifully articulated – and the magical pianissimo at the centre of No. 5 makes one wonder if Julian Bream listened to Del Pueyo before making his equally memorable account of this famous piece. But it is in the *Goyescas* that Del Pueyo's evocation so immediately captures the Spanish atmosphere, as in *Los requiebros* and *Coloquios en la reja* and especially in the haunting *Quejas o la maya y el ruiseñor*, while the idiomatic brilliance of *El pele* shows restraint as well as spontaneous virtuosity. The Falla coupling is perhaps even more remarkable.

Grieg, Edvard (1843–1907)

Piano concerto in A min., Op 16.

*(*) DG Dig. 439 914-2 [id.]. Jean-Marc Luisada, LSO, Tilson Thomas – SCHUMANN: *Piano concerto.* *(*)

(M) *(*) EMI Dig. CD-EMX 2195; *TC-EMX 2195* [id.]. Dmitri Alexeev, RPO, Temirkanov – SCHUMANN: *Piano concerto.* *(*)

(i) *Piano concerto in A min. Lyric pieces: Arietta; Elves' dance; Folk melody, Op. 12/1, 4 & 5; Butterfly; Little bird; To spring, Op. 43/1, 4 & 6; Notturno, Op. 54/4; Gade, Op. 57/2; Sylph; French serenade, Op. 62/1 & 3; Salon, Op. 65/4; Summer evening, Op. 71/2.*

⊛ (BB) *** Tring Dig. TRPO 24 [id.]. Ronan O'Hora, (i) with RPO, James Judd.

The Grieg *Piano concerto* is among the most elusive of works for piano and orchestra; its innocent spirit is not easily captured on record. But the young Manchester pianist, Ronan O'Hora, with a totally sympathetic partner in James Judd, now provides us with a recorded performance which is for the mid-1990s what Solomon and Clifford Curzon were for the later 1950s, Steven Kovacevich for the 1970s, and Perahia for the end of the 1980s. Indeed in imagination and delicacy of feeling, combined with natural, authoritative brilliance, this new performance is unsurpassed, and it certainly is the best recorded of all. The opening is arresting in its command, and the main theme of the first movement is introduced warmly and gracefully; but it is the melting arrival of the lovely second group which brings a moment of the utmost magic, matched by the gentle reverie of the *Adagio* and the tranquil, flute-led central episode of the finale. Yet the first-movement cadenza has seldom been played with a more flamboyant build-up of drama and tension. Throughout the pacing seems just right, and the interchange between soloist and orchestra brings a natural, spontaneous flow. The final peroration is a superb culmination and lets one understand why the last movement was so admired by Liszt. The piano is rather forwardly balanced and some listeners may find it a little bright, but in the music's gentler pages the piano's timbre is beautifully coloured. The programme is completed by a wholly delightful selection of a dozen of Grieg's most cherishable *Lyric pieces*, in which the pianist's simplicity of approach is consistently disarming. As if this were not enough, this record comes in the very lowest price-range and as such it is one of the great bargains of the catalogue.

Jean-Marc Luisada enjoys the benefit of excellent recording (the famous EMI Abbey Road Studio No. 1), which produces excellent and well-detailed sound, and Michael Tilson Thomas gives him excellent support. There are some self-conscious touches here and there (the cadenza is an example) but they would not be enough in themselves to inhibit a recommendation, were the performance of real stature or distinction.

Dmitri Alexeev's version with Yuri Temirkanov and the RPO brings pianism which is stronger on prose than poetry and, though the performance has some moments of freshness, their strengths do not outweigh much that is relatively routine.

(i) *Piano concerto in A min, Op. 16. Album Leaf, Op. 28/4; Ballade in G min., Op. 24; Lyric pieces: Op. 12/4–5; 38/1–2, 5; 43/1, 4; 47/6; 54/1, 3; 68/5.*
(M) (**) RCA mono 09026 61883-2 [id.]. Rubinstein, with (i) Phd. O, Ormandy.

This performance is discussed in greater detail in our main volume. It appeared as part of a three-CD set at the time of the 150th anniversary celebrations of Grieg's birth. Briefly, Rubinstein's account of the *Piano concerto* with the Philadelphia Orchestra under Ormandy comes from 1942; the fill-ups, including the *Ballade in G minor*, are 1953 recordings, made in Hollywood. The *Concerto* is rather stronger on brilliance than spontaneity, and the recording has more obtrusive background noise than many collectors would like. Both the *Ballade* and the *Lyric pieces* are well played but suffer from a shallow and claustrophobic acoustic.

(i) *Piano concerto in A min.;* (ii) *Peer Gynt: extended excerpts.*
(BB) **(*) EMI Seraphim CES5 68522-2 (2) [CDEB 68522]. (i) John Ogdon, New Phil. O, Berglund; (ii) Armstrong, Amb. S., Hallé O, Barbirolli – FRANCK: *Symphonic variations;* SCHUMANN: *Piano concerto.* *(*)

John Ogdon's version is disappointing. Clearly the partnership with Berglund did not work well and the end result is dull, in spite of an often bold solo contribution and fine recording from the early 1970s, most effectively remastered. Barbirolli's *Peer Gynt* selection is another matter. It dates from 1969 and was originally recorded in EMI's hi-fi-conscious Studio Two system. But the sound is ripely resonant and not very dated. If Beecham achieved greater subtlety in this music, Barbirolli (at his finest) is at least equally impressive and has memorable vocal contributions from the fresh-voiced Sheila Armstrong and the Ambrosian Singers. It is a pity that this is linked with less inspired music-making, even though the Seraphim reissue (with two discs for the cost of one medium-priced CD) is inexpensive.

Peer Gynt: suites Nos. 1, Op. 46; 2, Op. 55.
**(*) Decca Dig. 425 857-2 [id.]. San Francisco Ch. & SO, Blomstedt – NIELSEN: *Aladdin suite* etc. **(*)

Blomstedt's view of the *Peer Gynt* music is familiar from his recording of extensive parts of the complete incidental music, inclusive of dialogue. They are exchanged here for Nielsen's *Maskarade Overture* and the *Aladdin suite*. Good though the Grieg suites are, few readers will buy them in preference to Beecham (EMI CDM7 64751-2) or Karajan (DG 439 010-2).

CHAMBER MUSIC

Cello sonata in A min., Op. 36; Intermezzo in A min.
** Virgin/EMI Dig. VC5 45034-2 [id.]. Truls Mørk, Jean-Yves Thibaudet – SIBELIUS: *Malinconia* etc. **

Cello sonata in A min., Op. 36; Intermezzo in A min.; Piano sonata, Op. 7.
(BB) *** Naxos Dig. 8.550878 [id.]. Oystein Birkeland, Håvard Gimse.

The *Cello sonata* of 1882 is a stronger work than Grieg realized. The echoes of *Sigurd Jorsalfar* and the *Piano concerto* prompted him to write it off as not marking a step forward in his development. Oystein Birkeland and Håvard Gimse give the sonata an alive and sensitive account, coupled with the early and unrepresentative *Intermezzo in A minor*. They are both imaginative players and are decently recorded. Given the modest outlay involved, this has a strong advantage over its rivals, but even if it were at mid- or full-price it would be highly recommendable. Håvard Gimse's performance of the early *Piano sonata*, Op. 7, is also very good indeed. Altogether a first-rate bargain.

On Virgin the *Cello sonata* is again paired with the rather Schumannesque *Intermezzo in A minor* which Grieg composed in 1866 for his cello-playing brother. Truls Mørk plays with finesse and good poetic feeling; but Jean-Yves Thibaudet, for all his flair and sensitivity, proves somewhat overbearing. The balance favours him excessively, with the result that Truls Mørk's tone sounds very small.

String quartet No. 1 in G min., Op. 27.
(M) (***) Biddulph mono LAB 098 [id.]. Budapest Qt – SIBELIUS: *Quartet;* WOLF: *Italian serenade.* (***)

The Budapest Quartet's recording, dating from 1936, has already appeared on RCA, as part of a three-CD Historic Grieg anthology (see our main volume). There is no difference in cost between this and the Biddulph transfer, both being at mid-price, but its attractions in terms of coupling here are even stronger. The Sibelius *Voces intimae* and the Hugo Wolf *Italian serenade* are both superb performances and still remain unsurpassed. The Biddulph transfer has a slight edge on the RCA.

String quartets Nos. 1 in G min., Op. 27; 2 in F (unfinished).
(BB) *** Naxos Dig. 8.550879 [id.]. Oslo String Qt – JOHANSEN: *String quartet.* ***

As a glance at our main volume will show, the 150th anniversary of Grieg's birth in 1993 brought several modern versions: the Norwegian Quartet (Victoria), the Kontra (BIS) and the Raphael Quartet, who also included Julius Röntgen's conjectural reconstruction of the two remaining movements of the 1891 *F major Quartet* (Olympia). Rather surprisingly, the Naxos account of the quartets from the Oslo String Quartet, a relatively new group, proves the best of the lot – indeed it is the best version we have had since the Budapest. They would easily sweep the board even at full price, on account of their sensitivity, tonal finesse and blend, and the keenness of their artistic responses. They (rightly) play only the first two movements of the *F major Quartet*, leaving room for a fine quartet by Grieg's biographer, David Monrad Johansen. The recording balance, made in the Norwegian Radio studios, is excellent, neither too forward nor too recessed. Three stars – and indeed verging on a Rosette.

Violin sonatas Nos. 1 in F, Op. 8; 2 in G, Op. 13; 3 in C min., Op. 45.
*** Victoria Dig. VCD 19060 [id.]. Terje Tønnesen, Einar Henning Smebye.
*** DG Dig. 437 525-2 [id.]. Augustin Dumay, Maria João Pires.
*** Chan. Dig. CHAN 9184 [id.]. Lydia Mordkovitch, Elena Mordkovitch.
**(*) BIS Dig. CD 647 [id.]. Dong-Suk Kang, Roland Pöntinen.
* HM Dig. HMC 901492 [id.]. Olivier Charlier, Brigitte Engerer.

After a long period of neglect, violin-and-piano partnerships are turning to the three Grieg *Sonatas*, and doing so with consistent success. Like the *Piano concerto*, these works possess extraordinary resilience and survive countless repetition. They have a perennial and indestructible freshness that is quite special. Indeed among the newcomers listed above it is not easy to establish any order of priority.

Terje Tønnesen is probably better known for his work with the Norwegian Chamber Orchestra than as a soloist, and he is also one of the leaders of the Oslo Philharmonic. In each sonata he plays with much sweetness of tone and tenderness of feeling. There is a complete absence of ostentation; indeed his virtuosity is disarmingly effortless, and there is a lyric and expressive grace that is captivating. His partner, Einar Henning Smebye, is sensitive and responsive, far better than in his solo records, and the balance is ideal – not too close and not too distant. Where the Victoria label is available, this should arguably be first choice, but otherwise readers will find the Dumay–Pires (DG) and Mordkovitch (Chandos) very satisfying.

The French violinist, Augustin Dumay, and his distinguished partner, Maria João Pires, give poised, animated accounts of all three sonatas, and their CD is available both separately and as part of the six-CD Grieg Edition on DG. Their performances are exemplary in every way, and the recorded sound is also excellent in terms of both balance and realism.

Yet the same goes for Lydia and Elena Mordkovitch (*mère et fille*) on an admirably recorded Chandos CD. They, too, give splendidly fresh and well-shaped accounts of all three sonatas which give much pleasure in music-making. Affectionate yet virile performances – thoroughly recommendable.

Dong-Suk Kang produces a rich, finely focused tone, and his purity of style and intonation always inspire admiration. He is an artist of sensibility, and no one investing in the BIS recording is likely to be disappointed. Roland Pöntinen is a highly accomplished partner though a trifle too self-aware at times (the middle movement of the *C minor Sonata* is a case in point). Moreover the sound of the piano is less open and realistic than in rival versions.

Olivier Charlier and Brigitte Engerer on Harmonia Mundi give performances of some accomplishment which fall short of the distinction of their best rivals; they are not always as imaginative or sensitive. Moreover the studio in which they are recorded is a bit on the small side. Although their CD should not be written off, it is not by any manner of means a first choice.

(i) *Violin sonata No. 3 in C min., Op. 45;* (ii) *Album leaf, Op. 27/3;* (iii) *The last spring;* (iv) *String quartet in G min., Op. 27.*

(M) (***) RCA mono 09026 61826-2 [id.]. (i) Kreisler, Rachmaninov; (ii) Elman; (iii) Boston SO, Koussevitzky; (iv) Budapest String Qt.

These performances appeared as part of a historic three-CD set at the time of the 150th anniversary celebrations of Grieg's birth, and are discussed in greater detail in our main volume. The famous 1928 Kreisler–Rachmaninov set of the *Violin sonata No. 3 in C minor* is already available in RCA's ten-CD Rachmaninov retrospective and is too well known to require further discussion. The 1937 Budapest version of the *String quartet in G minor* is masterly in every way, with splendid grip but, at the same time, great lyrical warmth and freshness. An alternative and highly competitive transfer is now on offer (see above). The disc is almost worth having solely for the eloquence of the Boston Symphony Orchestra's strings in *The last spring*: their seamless phrasing under Koussevitzky still shines vibrantly down the years.

VOCAL MUSIC

Songs: *Autumn storm (Efteråsstormen); I give my song to the spring (Jeg giver mit digt til våren); I would like a waistcoat of silk (Og jeg vil ha mig en silkevest); To you (Til én) I & II.*
(M) *** Decca 440 492-2 [id.]. Kirsten Flagstad, LSO, Oiven Fjeldstad – SIBELIUS: Songs (with: Arne EGGEN: *Praise to the eternal spring of life (Aere det evige forår i livet); Eyvind ALNAES: About love (Nu brister alle de kløfter); A February morning at the Gulf (Februarmorgen ved Golfen); A hundred violins (De hundrede fioliner); Yearnings of spring (Vårlængsler);* Harald LIE: *The key (Nykelen); The letter (Skinnvengbrev)* ***).

Flagstad is in fine voice in this carefully chosen recital of Norwegian songs, hardly any of which can be really well known to the average listener. Even Grieg's songs, with the possible exception of *Autumn storm*, are almost a closed book to all but the connoisseur. Perhaps *I would like a waistcoat of silk* might ideally have had a lighter touch but, for the most part, the nobility of Flagstad's line and her concern for the words are most illuminating, and it is all the more valuable to have this repertoire in such deeply felt performances, to which the London Symphony Orchestra and Oivin Fjeldstad contribute not a little. Excellent stereo sound too, using both Kingsway Hall and Walthamstow. The reissue is part of Decca's Kirsten Flagstad Edition and is well documented.

(i) *Bergliot, Op. 42;* (ii) *Olav Trygvason, Op. 50; Funeral March for Rikard Nordraak.*
*** Virgin/EMI Dig. VC5 45051-2 [id.]. (i) Lise Fjeldstad; (ii) Solveig Kringelborn, Randi Stene, Per Vollestad, Trondheim Ch.; Trondheim SO, Ole Kristian Ruud.

The three scenes from *Olav Trygvason* are all that survives of Grieg's only operatic project. They show no great dramatic sense and, when they reached London, were greeted with particular scorn by Bernard Shaw, who dismissed them as 'a tissue of puerilities'; indeed they are more like a cantata than scenes from an opera. Neither *Olav Trygvason* nor *Bergliot*, for all their merits, are top-drawer Grieg, though the latter enjoyed great success in Grieg's lifetime and met with much acclaim at its première in Christiania (as Oslo was then known) in 1885. Strange though it may seem, *Bergliot* also enjoyed quite a vogue in France in the late 1880s. But the fashion for *mélodrame* (music as an accompaniment for declamation) has long passed and it is unlikely that *Bergliot* will return to the concert hall. Both works are included in the DG series made in Gothenburg (reviewed in our main volume), and this excellently balanced recording gives them a good run for their money. These Norwegian performances have great freshness and spirit, though the DG accounts have the greater polish and finesse. All the same, no one investing in this disc will have occasion to feel disappointed.

7 Children's songs, Op. 61; Haugtussa (song-cycle), *Op. 67; Melodies of the heart, Op. 5; 6 songs, Op. 4; 6 songs, Op. 25.*
** BIS Dig. CD 637 [id.]. Monica Groop, Love Derwinger.

The Finnish mezzo, Monica Groop, possesses beautifully focused and well-rounded tone and must be numbered among the most gifted of present-day Nordic singers. The present issue is the first in what is to be a comprehensive survey of Grieg's songs. In the greatest of Grieg's songs, the *Haugtussa* song-cycle, she proves no match in terms of imagination or character for her Swedish colleague, Ann Sofie von Otter, whose interpretation radiates life in every bar. Miss von Otter also has the advantage of the more responsive and imaginative accompanist. Everything is well sung on this BIS disc, but not so well characterized, and Love Derwinger is no match for the incomparable Rudolf Jansen (Victoria) or Bengt Forsberg (DG). Nor, for that matter, do BIS provide recorded sound that compares with their very best.

A Dream (3 versions); *Good morning; Greeting; The Mother sings; The Norse people; Solveig's cradle song; Solveig's song; With a water lily* (2 versions); *With a primrose; Eros; To Norway; I love thee* (5 versions); *A swan* (3 versions); *Bilbery slopes; At the brook; In the boat; And I shall have a true love.*
(M) (***) RCA mono/stereo 09026 61827-2 [id.]. Marsh, Melchior, Flagstad, Nilsson, Björling, Crooks, Traubel, Galli-Curci, Krogh, Schumann-Heink, Kline, Farrar, Frijsh.

The transfers here are acceptable, though not in any way superior to the specialist issues one encounters of this repertoire on the Danacord label. Still, with such celebrated singers as Björling, Farrar, Flagstad, Galli-Curci and Melchior represented, this compilation needs no further recommendation.

Haugtussa (*The Mountain maid;* song-cycle), Op. 67; Songs: *Ambition (Der ærgjerrige); Among roses (Millom rosor); At Gjaetle Brook (Ved Gjætle-Bekken); Blueberry slope (Blåbær-Li); Children's dance (A hipp og hoppe); A dream (En drøm); The encounter (Møte); Enticement (Det syng); Eros; The first meeting (Det første møte); Fra Monte Pincio (from Monte Pincio); High up in the leafy hills (I liden højt der oppe); I give my song to the spring (Jeg giver mit digt til våren); I love you (Jeg elsker Dig); In the boat (Der gynger en Båd på Bølge); The little hut (Hytten); Little Kirsten (Liten Kirsten); The little maiden (Veslemøy); Love (Elsk); Sorrowful day (Vond Dag); The water-lily (Med en vanlilje); With a primrose (Med en primulaveris).*
(M) (***) Decca mono 440 493-2 [id.]. Kirsten Flagstad, Edwin McArthur.

Alongside her Sibelius collection, this is the most valuable of the reissues included in Decca's Kirsten Flagstad Edition. It was recorded at Decca's West Hampstead studio in the spring and autumn of 1956 and, like the Brahms and Schubert Lieder which date from these same sessions, the mono recording is of the highest quality so that the ear might easily be deceived into thinking this early stereo. Flagstad is in splendid voice and this repertoire suits her admirably, for she had grown up with many of these songs. If the dark cycle about a peasant girl who falls in love and is deserted by her lover is conceived for a younger voice, Flagstad still makes it very much her own from the noble account of the very first song, 'Enticement' (*Det syng*). She is at her most compelling in the fifth (*Elsk*), about the passionate bondage of love itself, and she scales the big voice down delightfully for the light-hearted 'Children's dance'. Some of the other songs here are more familiar, none more so than *Jeg elsker dig* ('I love you') which is gloriously sung. As elsewhere in these recordings, her partner, Edwin McArthur, is wholly at one with her, much more than just an accompanist.

Haas, Pavel (1899–1944)

String quartets Nos. 2 (From the Monkey Mountains), Op. 7; 3, Op. 15.
*** Decca Dig. 440 853-2 [id.]. Hawthorne Qt – KRASA: *Quartet.* ***

Pavel Haas, like Hans Krása, was one of the many Jewish musicians who were murdered by the Nazis at the Terezín (Teresienstadt) camp. Both were born in the same year and were sent to the gas chambers on the same day. (This disc is part of the *Entartete Musik* series, which explores music that was suppressed during the years of the Third Reich.) Haas was a native of Brno and his output numbers a hundred works, including an opera, *Sarlatán* (1937). His *String quartet No. 2* dates from 1925 and its sub-title, *From the Monkey Mountains*, alludes to the Czech–Moravian highlands, which are so known in Brno. It is a highly imaginative and often beautiful score, with the strong, open-air feeling that one recognizes in Janáček. The *String quartet No. 3* (1938) comes after the lapse of a decade which had seen the rise of Nazism and the Munich treaty which led to the dismemberment and occupation of Czechoslovakia. It is a strong piece, more astringent in character than its predecessor, but it is well-argued and likeable music. The Hawthorne Quartet were members of the Boston Symphony Orchestra and have devoted themselves to composers who suffered under Nazi persecution, and they give dedicated performances. Excellent recording.

Handel, George Frideric (1685–1759)

Concerti grossi, Op. 3/1–6; Op. 6/1–12.
⊛ (M) *** Decca 444 532-2 (3) [id.]. ASMF, Marriner.

Concerti grossi, Op. 3/1–6 (including *No. 4b*); *Concerti grossi, Op. 6/1–12.*
(M) **(*) Teldec/Warner Analogue/Dig. 4509 95500-2 (4) [id.]. VCM, Harnoncourt.

Like the fine ASMF set of Bach's *Orchestral suites* (reissued on a single mid-priced CD: 430 378-2), this integral recording of the Handel *Concerti grossi* makes a permanent memorial of the partnership formed by the inspired scholarship of Thurston Dart and the interpretative skill and musicianship of (then plain Mr) Neville Marriner and his superb ensemble, at their peak in the late 1960s. Great care went into preparing the scores which are the basis of these recordings. Handel's Op. 6 had already received one outstanding recording (in the days of mono LPs), by Boyd Neel and his String Orchestra, and we hope that before too long Mike Dutton will transfer those six 10-inch LPs on to CD. But Thurston Dart's skills added an extra dimension to the Marriner enterprise and, of course, the advantages of stereo in these works with their contrasting concertino and ripieno are very obvious. Dart planned a double continuo of both organ and harpsichord, used judiciously to vary textural colour and weight. Flutes and oboes are employed (with delightful effect) where Handel suggested in Op. 3, and in Op. 6 the optional oboe parts are used in concertos 1, 2, 5 and 6. The final concerto of Op. 3 features the organ as a solo instrument, and Christopher Hogwood's more recent researches suggest that this was not what Handel originally intended (see below); but the result here very much conjures up the composer's spirit hovering in the background. Incidentally, Thurston Dart makes the point that the warm acoustic used for the recording is different from the relatively dry theatre ambience which the composer would have expected; thus the chamber organ has been balanced with discretion, for under such circumstances there is less need to add tonal body to the ripieno. The three records come at a special lower-mid price. But, alas, the superb CD transfer brings no separate cues for individual movements, only one band for each work.

The Teldec set is easily the most endearing of Harnoncourt's earlier authentic performances of baroque music. By the beginning of the 1980s, when these recordings were made (Op. 6 is digital), he was beginning to adopt less aggressive manners, yet the playing still has the characteristically vibrant rhythmic character we associate with him: tuttis have plenty of edge and lift, without being explosive. In Op. 3 tempi tend to be relaxed, but the performances are very enjoyable in their easy-going way, the ripe, fresh colouring of the baroque oboes, played expressively, is most attractive to the ear, and the string-sound is unaggressive. Tuttis are curiously dry, suggesting that the microphones were close to the violins; otherwise the sound is very good and the whole effect quite distinctive. So it is in Op. 6, where the recording is much more ample: indeed the digital sound is among the best Harnoncourt has ever received, with the most naturally refined string timbre, excellent detail and an ideal depth of acoustic. Here, as always, Harnoncourt is rhythmically gruff, and his is a performance bringing extremes of light and shade, and with the gentle playing of the solo group often lingeringly expressive. Some may find the almost brutal accents of the ripieno overdone and the dynamic contrasts too exaggerated, but Harnoncourt obviously values the music and in his hands its greatness and diversity are always obvious. There is much beautiful playing, and the jogging allegros are always nimble and polished. The famous melody of No. 12 (marked *Larghetto e piano*) is played *mezzo forte* and is fast and jaunty, utterly different from our experience of it in modern-instrument performances. But vitality is the keynote of Harnoncourt's approach and the sound of his original instruments is altogether more congenial than in Pinnock's Archiv set. Altogether a stimulating experience, to make one hear Handel's greatest orchestral work afresh. Unfortunately Op. 3 (with its extra concerto) plays for 71 minutes at Harnoncourt's chosen tempi and Teldec have spread Op. 6 uneconomically over three more CDs, playing for a total of 166 minutes, an expensive way of obtaining this music, even at mid-price. The documentation, too, is totally inadequate: merely a list of the individual movements and their cueing and timing. Even so, Harnoncourt aficionados should not hestitate: their hero is on top eccentric form here.

Concerti grossi, Op. 3/1–6.
(M) **(*) O-L Dig. 444 165-2 [id.]. Handel & Haydn Soc., Boston, Hogwood.
(M) ** Virgin Veritas/EMI Dig. VER5 61162-2 [id.]. Linde Consort, Hans-Martin Linde.

Hogwood's set with his excellent Boston players has no lack of energy and life, and a fairly high degree of polish. Intonation, too, though not always quite immaculate, is by no means a problem; although the period wind instruments bring plenty of colour to Handel's scoring, the end result is a little deadpan and lacking in geniality. However, Hogwood has taken the opportunity of checking the sources of this music throughout and has come up with a more authentic revised score for the sixth concerto, with two new movements; the original organ concerto movement has been relegated as an appendix, and is played as a separate encore.

The Linde Consort, although they are beautifully recorded in a spacious acoustic, are much less successful with Handel's Op. 3 with its sequence of jewelled movements than with the Bach *Brandenburgs*. Indeed they do not have the vitality of their finest rivals: tempi are at times so sedate that the original full-priced issue spilled over on to a second CD (although then, as now, the alternative No. 4a is included). There is some attractively woody oboe playing and other good things, of course, and at mid-price this might have been tempting; but for the most part it is *vin ordinaire*. It certainly is no match for the other original-instrument versions by Tafelmusik (Sony SK 52553) or Pinnock (DG 413 727-2), nor indeed Marriner's early Decca set using modern instruments in the same price-range (see above).

(i) *Concerti grossi, Op. 3/1–6;* (ii) *Organ concertos Nos. 1–6, Op. 4/1–6.*
(B) **(*) Ph. 442 263-2 (2) (i) ECO, Leppard; (ii) Daniel Chorzempa, Concerto Amsterdam, Schröder.

Among versions of Handel's Op. 3, Leppard's set stands high. The playing is lively and fresh, and the remastered recording sounds very good. Leppard includes oboes and bassoons and secures excellent playing all round. At times one wonders whether he isn't just a shade too elegant, but in general this reissue offers one of the best versions of Op. 3 on modern instruments. In this Duo pairing we are also offered Daniel Chorzempa's set of Handel's Op. 4 *Organ concertos,* and here we move over to period instruments. The Concerto Amsterdam, however, create a robustly substantial sound so the difference is not all that striking. They bring plenty of rhythmic buoyancy and life to the accompaniments. Chorzempa uses an appropriate Dutch organ and the balance is admirable. Regarding ornamentation, Chorzempa's approach is fairly elaborate and he interpolates a sonata movement from Op. 1 after the *Adagio* of the *Third Concerto.* The recording is again excellent, and those for whom the coupling is suitable will find this is good value.

Concerti grossi, Op. 6/1, 2, 6, 7 & 10.
**(*) HM Dig. HMC 901507 [id.]. Les Arts Florissants O, William Christie.

Vital, athletic performances from Christie, and clean, transparent recording with no lack of body and with the concertino and ripieno clearly defined. The playing in slow movements is refined and there is no lack of expressive feeling, but the result is less touching than with Marriner and, although allegros are spirited, there is more to this music than these performers discover.

(i) *Concerti grossi, Op. 6/5–6; Concerto grosso in C (Alexander's Feast);* (ii) *Music for the Royal Fireworks.*
(B) *(*) DG 439 408-2 [id.]. (i) Munich Bach O; (ii) ECO; Karl Richter.

Richter's Munich performances of the *Concerti grossi* come from the early 1970s and reflect the older German Bach tradition in Handel in their weighty expressiveness, though the contrapuntal movements are lively enough and the playing is spirited. The ECO performance of the *Royal Fireworks music* opens grandiloquently, then features strong contrasts of light and shade. The effect is not sufficiently robust to be fully in character for open-air music but is enjoyable on its own terms as a concert-hall performance because of the polished ECO response. The sound is notably more modern here than in the Op. 6 *Concerti.*

Music for the Royal Fireworks; 2 Arias for wind band; Concerti a due cori Nos. 1–3.
(M) ** O-L Analogue/Dig. 443 190-2 [id.]. AAM, Hogwood.

In the *Fireworks music* the Academy certainly make a vivid impact. The added clarity of the CD does emphasize some faults in the balance; nevertheless, Hogwood's version can be counted among the best available and has lively rhythms and keen articulation. Hogwood gives a strong impression of the score, even if no attempt is made to reproduce the forces heard in 1749. The *Concerti a due cori* are late works, probably composed in 1747/8, and were each written to be played in conjunction with a major oratorio, sharing musical material taken from familiar works (including *Messiah*). They are scored for two groups of wind instruments with an accompanying string orchestra plus continuo. Horns are strongly featured in the two *F major concertos* (Nos. 1 and 3). The present performances are lively enough, but the strings are very thin on top and there is some less than perfect intonation and ensemble. Of course there are some good things, and the resonant sound helps the aural picture (though the violins are obstinately edgy). The two *Arias for wind band* include an arrangement of an actual operatic aria (from *Teseo*) and again are rather spoilt by the inaccurate tuning of the period horns.

Music for the Royal Fireworks; Concerto grosso in C (Alexander's Feast); Overtures: Alceste; Belshazzar; Samson; Saul. Solomon: Arrival of the Queen of Sheba.
(M) *** DG Dig. 447 279-2 [id.]. E. Concert, Trevor Pinnock.

Pinnock's performance of the *Fireworks music* has tremendous zest; this is not only the safest but the best recommendation for those wanting a period-instrument version. The account of the *Alexander's Feast concerto* has both vitality and imagination and is no less recommendable. The vigorous and exhilarating performances of five *Overtures,* most of them hardly known at all but full of original ideas, even in the most highly structured pieces, make this a most interesting collection of works, and the the Queen of Sheba's arrival is always welcome. All are freshly and cleanly recorded.

Music for the Royal Fireworks: suite; Water music: suite (arr. Harty and Szell); *The Faithful shepherd: Minuet* (ed. Beecham); *Xerxes: Largo* (arr. Reinhardt).
(BB) *** Belart 450 001-2. LSO, Szell.

Many readers will, like us, have a nostalgic feeling for the Handel–Harty suites from which earlier generations got to know these two marvellous scores. George Szell and the LSO offer a highly recommendable coupling of them on a Belart super-bargain issue, with Handel's *Largo* and the *Minuet* from Beecham's *Faithful shepherd suite* thrown in for good measure. The orchestral playing throughout (from the early 1970s) is quite outstanding, and the strings are wonderfully expressive in the slower pieces. The horns excel, and the crisp new transfer seems to add to the sheer zest of the music-making. A splendid bargain.

Water music: suites 1–3 (complete).
(BB) *** ASV Dig. CDQS 6152 [id.]. ECO, George Malcolm.

This super-bargain set of the complete *Water music* on the ASV Quicksilva label from George Malcolm and the English Chamber Orchestra tends to sweep the board, except for those insisting on 'authentic instruments'. Indeed in every other sense this is a completely stylish realization of Handel's intentions, with the closing dances of the *Third Suite in G* particularly elegant, while the digital recording approaches demonstration standard. The playing is first class, articulation is deft and detail admirable. There is a sense of delight in the music which makes this version especially appealing.

Water music: suites 1–3 (complete); (i) *Organ concertos: in F (Cuckoo and the nightingale) HWV 295; in D min., HWV 304.*
(M) *(*) Teldec/Warner 4509 93668-2 [id.]. VCM, Harnoncourt; (i) with Herbert Tachezi.

Harnoncourt's use of original instruments, however admirable on most of his records, is too often aggressively unpleasant in the *Water music* – for example in the raspberry effect of trilling horns in the famous *Allegro*. Fast speeds can be very apt and effective, but here they often sound brutal and unsympathetic. The organ concertos offered as a bonus are altogether more congenial.

Complete chamber music

Volume 1: *Flute sonatas: in E min., Op. 1a/b; in G, Op. 1/5; in B min., Op. 1/9; in D (HWV 378); Halle sonatas Nos. 1–3.*
*** CRD CRD 3373; *CRDC 4073* [id.]. L'Ecole d'Orphée (Stephen Preston, Susan Sheppard, John Toll, Lucy Carolan).

Volume 2: *Oboe sonatas Nos. 1 in B flat (HWV 357); in F (HWV 363a); in C min., Op. 1/8 (HWV 366); Violin sonatas: in D min.* (original version of *Op. 1/1*), *HWV 359a; in A, Op. 1/3, HWV 361; in G min., Op. 1/6 (HWV 364a); in D, Op. 1/13 (HWV 371); Allegros for violin and continuo: in A min. (HWV 408); in C min., HWV 412.*
**(*) CRD CRD 3374; *CRDC 4074* [id.]. L'Ecole d'Orphée (David Reichenberg, John Holloway, Susan Sheppard, Lucy Carolan).

The availability of the complete CRD set of Handel's chamber music from L'Ecole d'Orphée is opportune, as the Philips set of flute sonatas on modern instruments with the estimable William Bennett, and the ASMF Chamber Ensemble series including the oboe sonatas, have both been withdrawn for the moment (hopefully to reappear in due course on Duos). The first pair of CRD CDs are very well recorded. The date is given as 1991, but they are analogue and from the early 1980s. Volume 1 contains the seven sonatas for flute (three are the so-called 'Halle' *Trio sonatas*, published in 1730 and thought to be the product of Handel's youth) as well as a sonata recently discovered in Brussels, for flute and continuo in D major (HWV 378). It was attributed to John Sigismund Weisse but has been made over to Handel as he used the striking opening theme in two other sonatas. Although no autograph survives for the 'Halle' *Sonatas*, the flute player Weidemann copied them while in London, and Handel acknowledged them as having been written while he was studying with Zachow. The question of the authenticity and provenance of some of the other music in the CRD complete set is too complicated to be gone into in these pages but is clearly set out in the insert notes. The playing itself is always spirited and intelligent, and if Stephen Preston's eighteenth-century flute timbre sounds a little watery, that is the nature of the baroque flute, and his phrasing is often beguiling. David Reichenberg's Hailperin oboe (a copy of a Paulhahn, *c.* 1720) is full of ripe colour, and the playing of both artists is immaculate. Indeed there is much to admire in these performances, in both style and execution. However, while the CDs remain available, first choice in this repertoire on original instruments remains with the Camerata Köln on Deutsche Harmonia Mundi at mid-price (GD 77152 and GD 77104 – see our main volume).

Volume 3: *Trio sonatas, Op. 2: Nos. 1 for flute, violin and continuo in B min.; 2 in G min.; 3 in B flat for 2 violins and continuo; 4 in F for recorder, violin and continuo; 5 in G min.; 6 in G min. for 2 violins and continuo.*
**(*) CRD CRD 3375; *CRDC 4075* [id.]. L'Ecole d'Orphée (John Holloway, Micaela Comberti, Stephen Preston, Philip Pickett, Susan Sheppard, Robert Wooley, John Toll).

Volume 4: *Trio sonatas, Op. 5 for 2 violins and continuo: Nos. 1 in A; 2 in D; 3 in E min.; 4 in G; 5 in G min.; 6 in F; 7 in B flat.*
**(*) CRD 3376; *CRDC 4076* [id.]. L'Ecole d'Orphée (John Holloway, Micaela Comberti, Susan Sheppard, Lucy Carolan).

Volume 5: *Sinfonia in B flat (HWV 338); Trio sonatas: in C min., Op. 2/1a; in F (HWV 392); in G min.(HWV 393); in E (HWV 394); in C (HWV 403).*
**(*) CRD 3377; *CRDC 4077* [id.]. L'Ecole d'Orphée (John Holloway, Micaela Comberti, Susan Sheppard, Lucy Carolan).

The *Trio sonatas* recorded by L'Ecole d'Orphée include the complete Op. 2 set, published by Walsh in 1732, an alternative version of another sonata of Op. 2 (namely *No. 1 in C minor*, which also appears in its B minor guise for flute, violin and continuo), the seven sonatas of Op. 5, published in 1739, and the three so-called 'Dresden' *Sonatas* (HWV 392-4), which Chrysander first published in the Händel-Gesellschaft Edition in 1879. Only one of them (in F) is totally authentic, though whoever composed the remaining two was no mean figure, and indeed a sequential passage in the opening movement of the *G minor* (HWV 383 – No. 8 in the Chrysander Edition) is echoed in the *Organ concerto*, Op. 7/5. In addition there is a very attractive *Sinfonia in B flat* (HWV 338), which is written in trio sonata form, with exuberant outer movements and a fine central *Adagio*, giving the work a bustling affinity with Bach's *Third Brandenburg concerto*. It is given a splendidly alert and sympathetic performance. There are many musical riches here and no want of accomplishment in the performances. The two violins in use by John Holloway and Micaela Comberti, one by Mariani of 1650 and another 'Anon. after Stainer', have markedly different tone-quality; and though the playing is brilliant when required, it could with advantage be more full-blooded. Readers unresponsive to the baroque violin may find their pleasure diminished by the raw, thin-edged timbre of the violins here (though this is not exaggerated by the CD remastering); but those for whom this represents no problems will find much to admire. The recording-balance tends to place the harpsichord at a disadvantage, but this does not seriously impair the production, which has excellent notes by Anthony Hicks.

As with the flute and oboe sonatas, we could wish that the Philips recordings by the ASMF Chamber Ensemble on modern instruments, which have a refreshing vigour and warmth, were available as an alternative, but perhaps they will return to the catalogue before too long as Duos. Meanwhile those who want to make a start on these wonderful works, in which Handel's invention seems inexhaustible, might begin with Volume IV of the CRD set, which includes Op. 5. Here Handel frequently borrows from himself and much of this material is also found in the overtures for the *Chandos anthems* or in the dance music for his operas. The flowing opening theme of the very first *A major Sonata* (HWV 396) has fine Handelian character while *No. 4 in G* immediately produces a whole sequence of memorable ideas, which arouses the suspicion that this highly effective grouping of movements (written between 1733 and 1735) was in fact compiled by Handel's publisher. No. 6 is also familiar, as Handel himself re-used the material of the first and fourth movements for the *Cuckoo and the Nightingale Organ concerto*. But one of the most exasperating features of these CD transfers, and one which makes them less easy to use than the original LPs, is that individual movements are uncued, only each complete work. So it is very difficult indeed to find one's way about works which often have as many as seven different movements.

Volume 6: *Recorder sonatas, Op. 1: Nos. 2 in G min. (HWV 360); 4 in A min. (HWV 362); 7 in C (HWV 365); 11 in F (HWV 369); in G (HWV 358); in B flat (HWV 377); in D min. (HWV 367a); Trio sonata in F (HWV 405).*
*** CRD 3378; *CRDC 4078* [id.]. L'Ecole d'Orphée (Philip Pickett, Rachel Beckett, Susan Sheppard, Lucy Carolan).

These CRD performances have rightly won much acclaim. There is elegant and finished playing from the two recorder players and, besides the Op.1 *Sonatas*, the programme includes a *G major Sonata*, first published in 1974, and the original D minor version of the *Flute sonata*, Op. 9/1, which has an engaging second movement based on a minor-key variant of a famous allegro in the *Water music*. The *Trio Sonata in F* for two recorders and continuo also represents a recent discovery – by Christopher Hogwood in the Library of Congress – of the second and third movements of a recorder duo and a bass line to go with all three! Excellent, intimate recording, but again with the irritating drawback that individual movements are not cued, and the *D minor Sonata* has seven of them.

Frans Brüggen Edition, Volume 9: *Recorder sonatas: in G min., HWV 360; in A min., HWV 362; in C, HWV 365; in F, HWV 369, Op. 1/2, 4, 7 & 11; in F, HWV 389, Op. 2/4. Fitzwilliam sonatas Nos. 1 in B flat, HWV 377; 3 in D min., HWV 367a.*
(M) *** Teldec/Warner 4509 97471-2 [id.]. Frans Brüggen, Alice Harnoncourt, Anner Bylsma, Nikolaus Harnoncourt, Gustav Leonhardt, Herbert Tachezi.

The four sonatas from Op. 1 are those the composer intended for the recorder; the *D minor* and the *B flat Sonatas*, HWV 367a and HVW 377, can be found in the Fitzwilliam collection. The five-movement *Sonata in F*, HVW 389, was first published in Amsterdam in about 1730 and, though it is designated a trio sonata, the recorder dominates and the violin (here Alice Harnoncourt) is very much a subordinate, shining as a solo instrument only in the third-movement *Adagio* and the following *Allegro*. All these works offer delightfully inventive music, and these performances are outstandingly successful. The spontaneity of the playing is no less striking than the way the scholarship and artistry underpin the style of the music-making. Both the cellist, Anner Bylsma, and the harpsichordist, Gustav Leonhardt, make an equal contribution to this partnership (in HWV 389 Nikolaus Harnoncourt and Herbert Tachezi provide the continuo).

Harpsichord suites Nos. 1–8, HWV 426/433; 6 Fugues or Voluntarys for organ or harpsichord, HWV 605/10; Fugues: in F; E, HWV 611/12.
*** Hyp. Dig. CDA 66931/2 [id.]. Paul Nicholson (harpsichord).

Paul Nicholson gives us Handel's major keyboard *œuvre*, not only the eight splendidly diverse suites of 1720, but also the contrapuntal *Voluntaries*, published in 1735, but probably written about 1716/17. They are simple, four-part baroque fugal pieces, varied in mood and style according to the key. As an appendix we are offered two miniature fugues, the *F major* from around 1705 and the *E major* from the time of the *Voluntaries*. Paul Nicholson's playing is quite admirable, full of life yet with a degree of intimacy that is very appealing. He has an ideal (unnamed) harpsichord, which is perfect for this repertoire and which is superbly recorded. The instrument is set back in a warm ambience, yet detail is beautifully clear. In short, one is not aware of the microphones at all, and the illusion of reality, without any suspicion of jangle, is very pleasing to the ear. Nicholson is admirably stylish, his crisp touches of ornamentation are always giving pleasure and are never fussy, and he is generous with repeats. His playing can seem to be improvisational in the preludes, fugues are crystal clear yet never stiff, and the closing *Gigues* have a joyful rhythmic lift (sample the delightful example which ends the *First suite in A major*). The most famous of the eight is, of course, No. 5 which has the variations known as '*The harmonious blacksmith*' as its finale, here ending in a blaze of bravura. But No. 3 is also very appealing and includes a masterly set of variations on a serene air which reminds the listener of the Bach *Goldberg* set. *No. 7 in G minor* has six sharply characterized movements, opening with a flamboyant *Overture*, and its finale is a superb *Chaconne* in which the harpsichord reveals the resources of its lower octaves. Highly recommended, and unlikely to be surpassed in the near future.

VOCAL MUSIC

Marian arias and cantatas: *Ah! Che troppo inequale; Donna, che in ciel; Haec est Regina;*
G. B. FERRANDINI (attrib. HANDEL): *Il pianto di Maria.*
*** DG Dig. 439 866-2 [id.]. Von Otter, Col. Mus. Ant., Goebel.

Dating from his years in Italy, these Handel works, directly linked to the worship of the Virgin Mary, inspire von Otter to give radiant performances. Ironically, the longest work, *Il pianto di Maria*, long attributed to Handel, has been found to be by G. B. Ferrandini; but it has many beauties, not least in a measured cavatina, *Se d'un Dio*. Both *Haec est Regina* and *Ah! che inequale* are strong, imaginative arias, and *Donna, che in ciel* is a superb, full-scale cantata with a fine overture and four splendid arias. Reinhard Goebel and his team give sympathetic support, though the period string-playing is on the abrasive side. Warm, immediate recording, which captures von Otter's firm mezzo superbly.

(i) *Coronation anthems (1. Zadok the Priest; 2. The King shall rejoice; 3. My heart is inditing; 4. Let Thy hand be strengthened); (ii) Concerti a due cori Nos. 2–3, HWV 333/4.*
(M) *** DG Dig. 447 280-2 [id.]. (i) Westminster Abbey Ch., Preston; (i–ii) E. Concert; (ii) Pinnock.

Those who like sparer, more 'authentic' textures will favour Preston in the *Coronation anthems* where, although the overall effect is less grand, the element of contrast is even more telling. To have the choir enter with such bite and impact underlines the freshness and immediacy. The use of original instruments gives plenty of character to the accompaniments. An exhilarating version. The new coupling of the two *Concerti a due cori* is welcome, with the performances full of rhythmic vitality.

Funeral anthem for Queen Caroline: The ways of Zion do mourn.
(M) **(*) Erato/Warner 4509 96954-2 [id.]. Norma Burrowes, Charles Brett, Martyn Hill, Stephen Varcoe, Monteverdi Ch. & O, Gardiner.

Queen Caroline – whom Handel had known earlier as a princess in Hanover – was the most cultivated of the royal family of the Georges, and when she died in 1737 he was inspired to write a superb cantata in an overture and eleven numbers including the splendid chorus, *How are the mighty fall'n*. He later used the material for the first Act of *Israel in Egypt*. Gardiner directs a stirring performance which brings out the high contrasts implicit in the music, making the piece energetic rather than elegiac. Excellent work from soloists, chorus and orchestra alike, all very well recorded in the ideal ambience of London's Henry Wood Hall, and most realistically transferred to CD. The only snag is the playing time of 44 minutes: there would have been room for another work here.

ORATORIOS

(i) *Israel in Egypt* (complete); (ii) *Chandos anthem No. 10: The Lord is my light.*
(B) *** Decca Double 443 470-2 (2) [id.]. (i) Gale, Watson, Bowman, Partridge, McDonnell, Watts, Christ Church Cathedral, Oxford, Ch., ECO, Preston; (ii) Cantelo, Partridge, King's College, Cambridge, Ch., ASMF, Willcocks.

Simon Preston, using a small choir with boy trebles and an authentically sized orchestra, directs a performance of this great dramatic oratorio which is beautifully in scale. He starts with the *Cuckoo and the nightingale organ concerto* – a procedure sanctioned by Handel himself at the first performance – and though inevitably the big plague choruses lack the weight which a larger choir gives them, the vigour and resilience are ample compensation, so that the text is illustrated with extra immediacy. Though Elizabeth Gale is not as firm a soprano as Heather Harper on Mackerras's alternative mid-priced Archiv set (DG 429 530-2 – see our main volume), the band of soloists is an impressive one and the ECO is in splendid form. The 1975 recording (originally Argo) is warmly atmospheric, more realistically balanced than the rival Archiv one, and it has been vividly transferred to CD. Moreover this Double Decca (two-for-the-price-of-one) set generously includes the tenth Chandos anthem, *The Lord is my light*, remarkable for some magnificent fugal writing and freshly performed at King's under Sir David Willcocks.

Messiah (complete).
*** HM Dig. HMC 901498.99-2 (2) [id.]. Schlick, Piau, Scholl, Padmore, Berg, Les Arts Florissants, Christie.
*(*) Ph. Dig. 434 695-2; *434 695-4* (2). McNair, Von Otter, Chance, Hadley, Lloyd, ASMF Ch., ASMF, Marriner.

William Christie and Les Arts Florissants add yet another outstanding account of *Messiah* to the current lists. More than most period performances - but like Trevor Pinnock's on DG Archiv (423 630-2), still unsurpassed - it gives the impression of a live performance caught on the wing, even though it was recorded in the studio. Christie's preference for fast, resilient speeds and light textures, not least in choruses, never prevents him from giving due emotional weight to such key numbers as *He was despised*. That is superbly sung, with touching simplicity, firm tone and flawless intonation, by the counter-tenor, Andreas Scholl. The other singers too sound fresh and young, with the two sopranos, Barbara Schlick and Sandrine Piau, delectably counterpointed, both pure and true, making light of the elaborate divisions in such a number as *Rejoice greatly*. The treble, Tommy Williams, also sings with beautiful, firm clarity in the Angel's narration, *There were shepherds abiding in the fields*. The tenor, Mark Padmore, and the bass, Nathan Berg, complete the pattern, light by old-fashioned standards but fresh and cleanly focused. Christie in his text opts for Handel's later versions of numbers, which generally tallies with what one expects. Excellent sound, though the chorus is placed a little backwardly, so that *Hallelujah* lacks something in impact, with boomy timpani.

Recorded live in Dublin on 13 April 1992, Marriner's version marked the 250th anniversary of the first performance. The line-up of soloists is impressive, but sadly the occasion falls far short of expectation, with the qualities of fire and drama lacking that one would expect at a live event. That is so even with such an outstanding singer, performing flawlessly, as Anne Sofie von Otter. Even with modern, not period, instruments there could have been more concern for idiomatic practice. The text fails to follow the original, Dublin version, as one might have expected, opting for a mixture.

Messiah (highlights).
*(*) Ph. Dig. 434 698-2; *434 698-4* [id.]. McNair, Von Otter, Chance, Hadley, Lloyd, Ch. & ASMF, Marriner.

These selections from Marriner's disappointing live performance can be recommended only to those who want a memento of a historic event.

The Occasional oratorio.
*** Hyp. Dig. CDA 66961/2 [id.]. Gritton, Milne, Bowman, Ainsley, George, New College, Oxford, Ch., King's Consort Ch. & Ens., Robert King.

Written as a rousingly patriotic celebration when the Jacobite uprising of 1745 was defeated, Handel's *Occasional oratorio* may have a slack dramatic structure but, with plentiful borrowings from such works as *Israel in Egypt*, it offers a wonderful showcase of Handel at his most inspired and vigorous. In each of the three sections or acts of roughly three-quarters of an hour short numbers predominate, the whole introduced by a grand overture in four contrasted movements. The vigorous choruses in particular, some only a few seconds long, regularly punctuate the work to heighten the effect of the arias, whether lively or beautiful, with some of the solo numbers leading directly into a related chorus with exhilarating effect. The piece culminates in an adaptation of Handel's great coronation anthem, *Zadok the priest*, with loyal cries of *God save the King* ringing out at the end. Robert King begins that last chorus with an unusually subdued account of the orchestral introduction, making the entry of the chorus all the more incandescent, and the close all the more triumphant. The whole performance is fresh and electrifying, with excellent singing from all the soloists. Susan Gritton and Lisa Milne, the clear-toned sopranos, are set against the increasingly dark counter-tenor tones of James Bowman, with John Mark Ainsley and Michael George both clear and fresh Handelian stylists. The chorus fares rather less well in a generally excellent recording for, though the ensemble is first rate, the backward balance takes some of the edge off the more dramatic choruses.

Saul (oratorio; complete).
(M) ** Teldec/Warner Dig. 4509 97504-2 (2) [id.]. Fischer-Dieskau, Rolfe Johnson, Esswood, Varady, Gale, V. State Op. Ch., VCM, Harnoncourt.

Harnoncourt's version was recorded live at the Handel tercentenary celebrations in Vienna in 1985 and, whatever the advantages of period performance, the extraneous noises of coughs and creaks, together with the odd slip of execution, seriously reduce its merits. Dietrich Fischer-Dieskau in the name-part is most characterful, but his expressive style is very heavy for Handel, particularly in the recitatives. It is still for the most part a rich and noble performance, and Julia Varady, though not quite idiomatic, is individual too, with tone cleanly focused. The English members of the cast sing stylishly, notably Anthony Rolfe Johnson as Jonathan and Paul Esswood as David. Elizabeth Gale's bright soprano is not always sweetly caught by the microphones, but it is a sympathetic performance. Harnoncourt's direction is lively but he misses much of the grandeur of the work, and some of the cuts he makes are damaging. The Vienna State Opera Concert Choir are responsive, but they never quite sound at home coping with English words. This might be worth considering at mid-price and involving only two CDs, but Gardiner's full-priced alternative is complete, offering a great deal more music, and is well worth the extra cost. Indeed it is not likely to be surpassed on disc for a long time (Philips 426 265-2 – see our main volume).

OPERA

Ariodante (complete).
(M) *** Ph. 442 096-2 (2) [id.]. J. Baker, Mathis, N. Burrowes, Bowman, Rendall, Ramey, L. Voices, ECO, Leppard.

Set improbably in medieval Scotland, Handel's *Ariodante* has a story far more direct and telling in simple emotional terms than most of his operas, even though the conflict between characters does not emerge until well into Act II. The libretto inspired Handel – who had just lost some of his finest singers to a rival opera company – to write an amazing sequence of memorable and intensely inventive arias and duets, with not a single weak link in the chain, a point superbly conveyed in this colourful, urgent performance under Raymond Leppard. The castrato role of Ariodante is a challenge for Dame Janet Baker, who responds with singing of enormous expressive range, from the dark, agonized moments of the C minor aria early in Act III to the brilliance of the most spectacular of the three display arias later in the Act. Dame Janet's duets with Edith Mathis as Princess Ginevra, destined to marry Prince Ariodante, are enchanting too, and there is not a single weak member of the cast, though James Bowman as Duke Polinesso is not as precise as usual, with words often unclear. Though this long work is given uncut, it is among the most riveting Handel opera recordings currently available, helped by the consistently resilient playing of the English Chamber Orchestra and the refined, beautifully balanced (1978) analogue recording, transferred so successfully to CD.

Hanson, Howard (1896–1981)

Symphony No. 6.
(B) ** Vox Box 116021–2 (2). Westchester SO, Landau – MACDOWELL: *Suite No. 2;* ROREM:
  Symphony No. 3; SCHUMAN: *Symphony No. 7;* THOMSON: *Louisiana Story: suite.* **

Howard Hanson's *Sixth Symphony* (1967–8) does not depart from the traditional neo-romanticism of its companions, and those who enjoy his honest, straightforward music will probably find much to delight them. However, readers will probably prefer to try and find the more modern recording from Gerard Schwarz and the Seattle Orchestra on the Delos label, which offers the *Third Symphony* as well.

Hartmann, Karl Amadeus (1905–1963)

Concerto funèbre.
*** Teldec/Warner Dig. 4509 97449–2 [id.]. Zehetmair, Deutsche Chamber Philharmonie – BERG;
  JANACEK: *Violin concertos.* ***

As one of the two couplings for his clean-cut version of the Berg *Concerto*, Zehetmair offers this strong, intense *Concerto funèbre* for violin and strings – very much reflecting in its dark moods the troubled period, 1939, when it was written. Well worth exploring.

Haydn, Josef (1732–1809)

Piano concerto in D, Hob.XVIII:11.
** DG Dig. 439 864–2 [id.]. Martha Argerich, Württemberg CO, Jörg Faerber – SHOSTAKOVICH:
  Piano concerto No. 1. **

Martha Argerich offers a weird coupling that is unlikely to make a wide appeal except among Argerich aficionados. Those wanting Haydn are more likely to turn to Ax (Sony) and those wanting Shostakovich will doubtless welcome the *First Concerto*'s companion. None will welcome the exceedingly short measure. Argerich is an artist of quality and this performance must excite admiration but, however marvellous the playing, at 40 minutes or so (and full price) this CD is uncompetitive.

Violin concertos: (i) *in C, Hob VIIa/1; in G, Hob VIIa/4;* (i; ii) *Sinfonia concertante in B flat, Hob I/ 105.*
*** Virgin/EMI Dig. VC7 59266–2 [id.].(i) Elizabeth Wallfisch; (ii) Robson, Warnock, Watkin; O of
  Age of Enlightenment.

Elizabeth Wallfisch appears here as soloist and director of all three works. The highly enjoyable result brings winningly 'authentic' alternatives to the Grumiaux versions of the *Violin concertos* (Philips 426 977-2 – see our main volume), jauntily rhythmic and, in the central *Adagio* of the C major work, appealingly reflective. The coupling (which dates from Haydn's London visit in 1792) is hardly less persuasive, with colourful and vital interplay between all the soloists but with Wallfisch firmly in command; yet the whole effect is one of relaxation, with the players conveying their enjoyment. Excellent, vivid recording, the soloists balanced forwardly within a full yet intimate ambience.

Sinfonia concertante in B flat for violin, cello, oboe, bassoon and orchestra, Hob I/105.
(BB) **(*) ASV Dig CDQS 6140 [id.]. Frieman, Pople, Anderson, Gambold, L. Festival O, Ross
  Pople – STAMITZ: *Sinfonias concertantes.* **(*)

Directing the players from the solo cello, Ross Pople draws a strong and alert rather than an elegant performance from his London Festival Orchestra, well recorded in bright, firmly focused sound. Though the solo playing is not always ideally refined, there is a winning sense of musicians acting out a drama, at speeds that are comfortable, never exaggerated. The coupling of *Sinfonias concertantes* by Stamitz is very apt and attractive.

Symphonies Nos. 22 in E flat (Philosopher); 23 in G; 24 in D; 25 in C.
*** Hyp. Dig. CDA 66536 [id.]. Hanover Band, Roy Goodman.

The Hanover Band make the grave opening march of the *Philosopher Symphony*, with its dark cor anglais colouring, sound intensely avant garde, and in the finale the horns have a high old time at Goodman's breakneck pace. Exhilarating stuff, and the horns also have a chance to shine effectively through the texture in the *G major Symphony*, which has another exuberant *Presto assai* last movement. The *Adagio* of *No. 24 in D major*, with its calm flute solo, is contrastingly spacious, as usual in Goodman's readings, and these often fiery performances are well up to the standard set in this stimulating series, with the resonant recording adding its bloom so that there is always plenty of warmth to counterbalance the bubbling high spirits.

Symphonies Nos. 22 in E flat (Philosopher); 29 in E; 60 in C (Il Distratto).
(BB) ** Naxos Dig. 8.550724 [id.]. N. CO, Nicholas Ward.

Compared with Goodman's account, the first movement of the *Philosopher* has nothing like the same darkness of colour when presented on modern instruments by the Northern Chamber Orchestra under Nicholas Ward, and the *Adagio (di Lamentatione)* is also relatively easy-going. These are warm, nicely turned performances, well recorded but somewhat undercharacterized.

Symphonies Nos. 23 in G; 24 in D; 61 in D.
(BB) *** Naxos Dig. 8.550723 [id.]. N. CO, Nicholas Ward.

The fresh, stylish approach of the Northern Chamber Orchestra seems entirely suited to these three symphonies, and here Nicholas Ward makes a persuasive case for the use of modern instruments. *Symphonies Nos. 23* and *24* were written together in 1764. These are cheerful, elegant works, full of those imaginative touches which make Haydn's earlier symphonies so stimulating. No. 24 includes a leading semi-concertante flute part (nicely managed) and the *G major* has a wistful *Andante* for strings alone, and a vital *Presto* finale, well sprinkled with strongly accented quadruplets. The opening movement of No. 61 (written a decade later, in 1776) is obviously more mature and is presented with both character and charm; its lovely *Adagio* is tenderly phrased and the hopping, skipping finale charmingly spirited, with some impressively light articulation from the violins. Excellent recording.

Symphonies Nos. 30 in C (Alleluja); 55 in E flat (Schoolmaster); 63 in C (La Roxelane).
(BB) *** Naxos Dig. 8.550757 [id.]. Northern CO, Nicholas Ward.

An entirely winning triptych of named Haydn symphonies, spanning a highly creative period from the three-movement *Alleluja* (1765), with its delightful woodwind contribution in the *Andante*, to *La Roxelane* (1780), where the *Allegretto* paints an engaging portrait of a flirtatious character in a play and the finale fizzes with energy. In between comes *The Schoolmaster*, whose Adagio brings a theme and variations of disarming simplicity. Alert and vivacious playing from all concerned; admirable pacing and first-class sound ensure a welcome for a disc that would be just as recommendable if it cost far more.

Symphonies Nos. 31 in D (Horn signal); 59 in A (Fire); 73 in D (La chasse).
*** Teldec/Warner Dig. 4509 90843-2 [id.]. VCM, Nikolaus Harnoncourt.

This is one of Harnoncourt's very best records. All three symphonies are notable for their spectacular horn parts. The playing here – using natural horns – is superb, with throatily exuberant braying at the opening of the *Horn signal*, an equally striking contribution throughout the *Fire Symphony* (where the horns are crooked in A), and more cheerful hunting-calls in the spirited finale of *La chasse*. No. 31 in D, written in 1756, is more of a sinfonia concertante (and was so designated on the title-page of the first edition). Besides the four important horn parts – the leading horn crooked in G, the other three in D) – there are extended solos for violin and cello in the outer movements: the finale is an engaging theme and variations. The playing is not only extremely vital and polished but even has an element of charm (not something one can always count on from this source). The orchestra communicate their involvement throughout. Few period records of Haydn symphonies are more invigoratingly enjoyable than this, and the recording is splendid.

Symphonies Nos. 42 in D; 45 in F sharp min. (Farewell); 46 in B.
(M) *** DG 447 281-2 [id.]. E. Concert, Pinnock.

It is good to have Trevor Pinnock's Haydn series reappearing individually at mid-price, representing his newer, easier style which, without loss of vitality, avoids excessive acerbity. The recording, too, though with detail admirably clear, has no lack of warmth. Haydn's famous *Farewell Symphony*, given a vibrant and characterful performance with a very beautiful slow movement, is coupled with two apparently straightforward but still forward-looking works, No. 42 with its memorably solemn *Andantino e cantabile* and *No. 46 in B major*. Here the ethereal 6/8 *Poco Adagio* contrasts with an invigorating scherzando finale where the high horns (crooked in B alto) produce repeated bursts of hair-raising virtuosity. And Haydn has a characteristic trick up his sleeve for, just before the end, the Minuet returns, only to be swept away by a final rally from the horns.

Symphonies Nos. 43 in E flat (Mercury); 44 in E min. (Trauer); 49 in F min. (La Passione).
(M) ** Chan. Dig. CHAN 6590 [id.]. Cantilena, Adrian Shepherd.

Two of the symphonies (44 and 49) offered by Adrian Shepherd's Cantilena come from the so-called *Sturm und Drang* set. This group captures their spirit effectively – particularly in the so-called *Trauer* or 'Mourning' *symphony* in which tempi are well judged and the textures admirably clean. *La Passione* is committed enough, though the actual playing is less accomplished than in some rivals. The *E flat Symphony* (*Mercury*) is slightly less successful and is a bit matter-of-fact. Again the sound quality is clean and pleasing and the balance generally well handled.

Symphonies Nos. 64 in A (Tempora mutantur); 84 in E flat; 90 in C.
(BB) ** Naxos Dig. 8.550770 [id.]. Nicolaus Esterházy Sinfonia, Budapest, Béla Drahos.

Well-played but in no way distinctive performances, recorded in a pleasingly warm acoustic. The account of No. 84 has nothing like the strength of characterization it finds with Bruno Weil's Tafelmusik, and the most striking performance here is of No. 90, with vigorous outer movements and a nicely paced, well-shaped *Andante*.

Symphonies Nos. 72 in D; 93 in D; 95 in C min.
(BB) *** Naxos 8.550797 [id.]. Nicolaus Esterházy Sinfonia, Béla Drahos.

These perfomances are polished, warm and spirited and, if the Naxos recording (made in the Budapest Italian Institute) is on the reverberant side, it does not cloud textures. In short this is most enjoyable, combining as it does – in spite of the number – an early symphony (probably dating from between 1763 and 1765) with two of Haydn's greatest mature works, written for Salomon's London concerts in 1791/2. Four horns are featured prominently in No. 72 and provide many bravura flourishes and virtuoso scales in the opening movement; the playing here is first class. The solo flute shares the stage with the principal violin in the concertante *Andante*, and he returns to grace the delightfully elegant variations which make up the finale. All in all, this engaging work is fully worthy to stand alongside its mature companions when played as seductively as this. The orchestral response is equally impressive in the fine slow movements of these later works, and throughout Béla Drahos's pacing is matched by the overall sense of spontaneity and style.

(Paris) Symphonies Nos. 82 in C (The Bear); 83 in G min. (The Hen); 84 in E flat.
*** Sony Dig. SK 66295 [id.]. Tafelmusik, Bruno Weil.

(Paris) Symphonies Nos. 85 in B flat (La Reine); 86 in D; 87 in A.
*** Sony Dig. SK 66296 [id.]. Tafelmusik, Bruno Weil.

Symphonies Nos. 82–87 (Paris Symphonies).
(M) ** DG Dig. 445 532-2 (2) [id.]. BPO, Karajan.

The Haydn series from Bruno Weil and Tafelmusik continues apace, and H. C. Robbins Landon (described as Musicological and Artistic Consultant) once again provides the most informative back-up documentation, well spiced with anecdotes. Notwithstanding the splendid set by the Orchestra of the Age on Enlightenment under Kuijken on Virgin, which remain very recommendable, these Sony recordings continue to set new standards in this repertoire. For the *Paris Symphonies* the size of the string group has been slightly increased (8,7,5,4,2), against which flute, and pairs of oboes, bassoons, horns and – where scored – trumpets are balanced very effectively. The texture is at once full and transparent. As before, the performances are brimful of character. How bold and strong is the first movement of *The Bear*, yet its *Allegretto* brings neatness and grace; the opening allegro of *No. 83 in G minor* has a *Sturm und Drang* quality in its incisiveness, yet the 'Hen' clucks with charming finesse. The slow movement of *No. 84 in E flat* is both subtle and imposing in its substance. Similarly, the vibrant first movement of *La Reine* (the dotted rhythms of the opening *Adagio* designed to tickle the French palate) is followed by a subtly characterized set of variations, while the remarkable *Capriccio – Largo* of No. 86 brings an improvisatory spontaneity. Minuets are rhythmically energetic, yet the pacing is not exaggerated, while finales have irrepressible spirit without being rushed. In short, if you want these symphonies performed on period instruments, this is the way to play (and record) them.

Karajan's set is big-band Haydn with a vengeance; but of course the orchestra of the *Concert de la Loge Olympique*, for which Haydn wrote these symphonies, was a large band, consisting of forty violins and no fewer than ten double-basses. It goes without saying that the quality of the orchestral playing is superb, and Karajan is meticulous in observing repeats and in his attention to detail. There is no trace of self-indulgence or mannerisms. However, these are rather heavy-handed accounts, closer to Imperial Berlin than to Paris; generally speaking, the slow movements are kept moving but the Minuets are very slow indeed, full of pomp and majesty – and, at times, too grand. In spite of the clean if slightly cool digital recordings, which have splendid presence, these performances are too charmless and wanting in grace to be wholeheartedly recommended. On CD the early-1980s digital sound, if a trifle dry, is realistically balanced and has excellent presence but sounds just a little fierce in tuttis.

Symphonies Nos. 90 in C; 91 in E flat.
** Virgin/EMI Dig. VC5 45068-2 [id.]. La Petite Bande, Sigiswald Kuijken.

Symphonies Nos. 90 in C; 91 in E flat; 92 in G (Oxford).
*** Hyp. Dig. CDA 66251 [id.]. Hanover Band, Roy Goodman.

Goodman and Kuijken are in direct rivalry over the surprisingly neglected Nos. 90 and 91, two symphonies that come between the *Paris* set and the final *London Symphonies*. On every count Goodman and the Hanover Band are preferable, with their brisker speeds and more resilient rhythms, and their disc also includes the *Oxford Symphony*. Kuijken, so masterly with the Orchestra of the Age of Enlightenment in the *Paris Symphonies*, also on Virgin, is here less lively with La Petite Bande, regularly taking *Andantes* slower than such a traditional rival as Dorati. The recording for Goodman is preferable, pleasantly atmospheric and more cleanly focused than in his earlier recordings for Nimbus.

Symphonies Nos. 93 in D; 94 in G (Surprise); 97 in C; 99 in E flat; 100 in G (Military); 101 in D (Clock) (London Symphonies).
⊛ (B) *** Ph. Duo Analogue/Dig. 442 614-2 (2) [id.]. Concg. O, Sir Colin Davis.

This Haydn series (recorded between 1975 and 1981) is one of the most distinguished sets Sir Colin Davis has given us over his long recording career, and its blend of brilliance and sensitivity, wit and humanity gives these two-for-the-price-of-one Duo reissues a special claim on the collector who has not already invested in the performances when they cost far more. There is no trace of routine in this music-making and no failure of imagination. The excellence of the playing is matched by Philips's best recording quality, whether analogue or digital. The Concertgebouw sound is resonant and at times weighty but has good definition, and the warmth and humanity of the readings are especially striking in slow movements, notably those of Nos. 93 (beautifully paced after an opening movement of comparable gravitas), 97 and 99. The *Andante* of the *Clock* is delightfully sprightly, and the *Allegretto* of the *Military Symphony* is properly grand and expansive, balanced by vital, sparkling outer movements. Excellent notes from Robin Golfding.

Symphonies Nos. 94 in G (Surprise); 100 in G (Military); Overture: La fedeltà premiata.
(BB) ** Tring Dig. TRP 021 [id.]. RPO, Stefan Sanderling.

Vigorous performances of two famous named G major symphonies with no lack of finesse in the string playing and plenty of life throughout. However, the resonant acoustic although it provides agreeable bloom prevents the kind of transparency one expects these days, and the effect is very slightly overblown. The overture is brightly done and makes a good encore.

Symphonies Nos. 95 in C min.; 96 in D (Miracle); 98 in B flat; 102 in B flat; 103 in E flat (Drum Roll); 104 in D (London) (London Symphonies).
⊛ (B) *** Ph. Duo Analogue/Dig. 442 611-2 (2). Concg. O, Sir Colin Davis.

This further Duo reissue of Sir Colin Davis's *London Symphonies* has equal stature with the first and can be recommended without reservation of any kind. The playing of the Concertgebouw Orchestra is as sensitive as it is brilliant and Davis is unfailingly penetrating. The performances continue to benefit from first-rate recorded sound, combining fullness with good clarity and definition. Overall these performances continue to top the lists for those listeners not requiring period versions. They have something of the spirit of Beecham about them, not least Nos. 95 and 96, where the solo playing is a delight. Like these two works, No. 98 has a memorably gracious slow movement and No. 102 brings an outstanding opening movement full of vitality and colour. The best-known works, Nos. 103 and 104, do not disappoint either. A bargain in every sense of the word.

Symphonies Nos. 97 in C; 98 in B flat.
(BB) ** Naxos Dig. 8.550780 [id.]. Nicolaus Esterházy Sinfonia, Budapest, Béla Drahos.

Well played and recorded, but rather straitlaced performances of two of Haydn's last masterpieces.
Fair value, but not really memorable in a competitive market.

Symphonies Nos. 99 in E flat; 100 in G (Military).
**(*) HM/BMG Dig. 05472 77328-2 [id.]. La Petite Bande, Sigiswald Kuijken.

After the success of the Petite Bande *Paris Symphonies*, this is slightly disappointing. The playing has
many virtues but tuttis are just a bit husky and the last touch of spontaneity is missing in. slow
movements, though the finales of both symphonies are full of lightness and energy. But in any case
this is one work too few for a full-priced CD: the overall playing time is only 52 minutes.

Symphonies Nos. 102 in B flat; 104 in D (London).
** Ph. Dig. 438 934-2 [id.]. VPO, André Previn.

Like his earlier Philips coupling of the *Oxford* and *Miracle Symphonies*, these are warm and often
dramatic performances (the opening of No. 104 is very imposing and the *Andante* is spacious and
beautifully played). But the full textures offered by the resonant Vienna acoustic now sound a bit
unwieldy by the side of period performances which it is surely now impossible to ignore. And to offer
only two symphonies at full price (55 minutes) is distinctly ungenerous.

CHAMBER MUSIC

Cassations (Divertimenti): in G, Hob II/1; in G, Hob II/G1; in C (Birthday), Hob II/11; in F, Hob II/
20.
(M) **(*) Virgin Veritas/EMI Dig. VER5 61163-2 [id.]. Linde Consort, Hans-Martin Linde.

Haydn's *Cassations* and *Divertimenti* have not the finesse of the best works of Mozart, but they have
plenty of imaginative touches, particularly in their instrumentation. Two of those offered here are
fairly ambitious (Hob II, Nos. G1 and 20), scored for a nonet (including a pair each of oboes and
horns); the remaining two, written around 1765, are scored for a sextet (including flute and oboe),
often used with charm and effectively demonstrating the special timbres of the early instruments
played here. Overall the performances have plenty of character, although in the hands of, say, the
ASMF they would undoubtedly be more winning still. The recording, made in a fairly reverberant
acoustic, has a quite large-scale effect, but the result is not unstylish.

(i) *Flute trios Nos. 1–4 for 2 flutes & cello (London), Hob IV/1–4;* (ii) *Flute quartets, Op. 5, Nos. 1 in*
D, Hob II/D9; 2 in G, Hob II/G4; 3 in D, Hob II/D10; 4 in G, Hob II/1; 5 in D, Hob II/D11; 6 in C,
Hob II/11.
*** Accent Dig. ACC 9283/4 (2) [id.]. (i) Bernard Kuijken, Mark Hantaï, Wieland Kuijken; (ii)
    Bernard, Siegfried & Wieland Kuijken, François Fernandez.

The *London Trios* date from 1794 during Haydn's visit to England and the first two include variations
on the song, '*Trust not too much*'. They are delightful works and receive felicitous performances from
this authentic group who make the most winning sounds. The *Flute quartets*, Op. 5, in the view of
H. C. Robbins Landon may not all be by Haydn. It seems fairly certain, however, that the first two,
also known as *Divertimenti*, are authentic, very early works from the 1750s. All the music is engaging
when played with such finesse and warmth, although this is a set to be dipped into rather than taken
in large doses. The recording is admirably fresh and realistic.

String quartets: Nos. 1 in B flat (La chasse), Op. 1/1; 32 in C, Op. 20/2; 35 in F min., Op. 20/5; 46 in
E flat, Op. 50/3; 57 in G; 58 in C; 59 in E, Op. 54/1–3; 65 in B flat; 66 in G, Op. 64/3–4; 74 in G min.
(Rider), Op. 74/3; 77 in C (Emperor), Op. 76/3; 78 in B flat (Sunrise), Op. 77/2.
(**(*)) Testament mono SBT 3055 (3) [id.]. Pro Arte Qt.

String quartets: Nos. 6 in C, Op. 1/6; 16 in B flat; 17 in F (Serenade), Op. 3/4–5 (Hoffstetter); 31 in E
flat; 34 in D, Op. 20/1 & 4; 38 in E flat (Joke); 39 in C (Bird); 42 in D (How do you do?), Op. 33/2,
3 & 6; 49 in D (Frog); 60 in A; 62 in B flat, Op. 55/1 & 3; 68 in E flat, Op. 64/6; 69 in B
flat, Op. 71/1; 72 in C; 73 in F, Op. 74/1–2; 81 in G, Op. 77/1.
(**(*)) Testament mono SBT 4056 (4) [id.]. Pro Arte Qt.

In 1931 HMV embarked on a project with the Pro Arte Quartet to record all eighty-three Haydn
Quartets. Eight large albums of seven 78-r.p.m. records were produced, each published in the Haydn
Quartet Society series, encompassing twenty-nine quartets in all. The outbreak of war put an end to
the project. Each volume offered a mixture of quartets from every period: the first, for example,

included Opp. 20/2, 33/3 and 77/1. Although Testament does not keep the exact sequence, these reissues maintain the principle of varying the contents of each of the well-filled CDs, putting the two Op. 3 quartets now known to be by Roman Hofstetter (1742–1815) on to a fourth disc in the second box. Despite their artistic excellence, none of them was reissued until EMI Référence brought out an eight-LP box in France during the mid-1980s. While LP and CD reissues have kept the name of the Busch Quartet alive, the Pro Arte (for whom, incidentally, Bartók composed his *Fourth Quartet*) is a less familiar one to modern collectors. All the players were from the Brussels Conservatoire and enjoyed international repute in the 1920s and '30s, not only for their Viennese classics but for their advocacy of contemporary music.

In their hands the Haydn *Quartets* bring us a world of delight, wisdom and sanity, and few groups are better guides. They have great purity of style and an immaculate intonation and technique, while they seem always to hit on exactly the right tempo, which in turn enables phrasing to speak naturally. The interplay between each of the musicians could hardly be more subtle in its responsiveness. However, the actual sound of these recordings calls for a little tolerance. The violin, particularly above the stave, is wanting in real bloom, and one would welcome more space between movements, which would surely not have been beyond the ingenuity of the engineers supervising these transfers, a fault which disfigured the LP versions (remastered by Keith Hardwick). Sometimes there is as little as two or three seconds. Less than perfect sound, perhaps, as might be expected from their recording dates (1931–8), but impeccable Haydn playing. The appearance on CD of these once-famous Haydn performances is a cause for celebration.

String quartets Nos. 32 in C, Op. 20/2; 44 in B flat, Op. 50/1; 76 in D min. (Fifths), Op. 76/2.
(BB) *** ASV Dig. CDQS 6144 [id.]. Lindsay Qt.

Obviously, since these are public performances, one has to accept music-making reflecting the heat of the occasion, the odd sense of roughness (the finale of Op. 76, No. 2), for these artists take risks – and this is perhaps a shade faster than it would be in a studio. There is splendid character in these performances and plenty of musical imagination. These readings have a spontaneity which is refreshing in these days of retakes! The recordings are eminently truthful and audience noise is minimal. An excellent bargain.

String quartets Nos. 35 in F min., Op. 20/5; 40 in B flat, Op. 33/4; 70 in D, Op. 71/2.
(BB) *** ASV Dig. CDQS 6146 [id.]. Lindsay Qt.

This, the third of the ASV Quicksilva reissues in the series of Haydn recordings made by the Lindsays 'live' at the Wigmore Hall during 'The Genius of Haydn' Festival in 1987 (see also above and below), is as recommendable as its predecessors. The immediacy of the playing is just as striking as before, yet at the rather serious opening of the *F minor*, Op. 20/5, the approach is appropriately sober and considered as well as spontaneous. This quartet also has a tender *Siciliano* slow movement which is played with affecting simplicity and grace. The account of the *B flat Quartet*, Op. 33/4, brings a burst of applause at the end, as well it might, with its deeply thoughtful *Largo* and scintillating finale, while the *Adagio* opening of Op. 71/2 immediately commands the listener's attention, and the work's engaging finale spontaneously gathers pace as it proceeds to its lively dénouement. Three marvellous works, recorded with striking presence.

String quartets Nos. 37–42, Op. 33/1–6; 43 in D min., Op. 42.
(B) *** HM Dig. HMA 1903002/3. Festetics Qt.

Those wanting Op. 33 on period instruments will surely be delighted with this Musique d'Abord set from the Quatuor Festetics. These Hungarians play with great spirit (the finale of the *Joke* has the requisite sense of fun), and their overall lightness of touch and the transparency of texture are very appealing. Slow movements have freshness and just the right combination of gravitas and expressive feeling: the phrasing is smoothly linear without those unattractive bulges that seem to haunt performances on original instruments. Almost every movement has the kind of sparkle and spontaneity that make one want to return to it, and the recording is most naturally balanced in the much-used Unitarian Church of Budapest. For most listeners this will be a clear first choice, for Op. 42 is also excellently played.

String quartets Nos. 37 in B min.; 38 in E flat (Joke); 41 in G, Op. 33/1–2 & 5.
(BB) **(*) Naxos 8.550788 [id.]. Kodály Qt.

String quartets Nos. 39 in C (Bird); 40 in B flat; 42 in D, Op. 33/3–4 & 6.
(BB) **(*) Naxos 8.550789 [id.]. Kodály Qt.

The Kodály Quartet play Op. 33 with an easy relaxed warmth. Their style is low-key so that the

'Joke' finale of Op. 33/2 is rather gentle and muted; on the other hand, the reason for the sobriquet of the *Bird Quartet* is affectionately conveyed and the finale is delightfully light-hearted. Slow movements are serene and quietly musical; the *Largo* of Op. 33/4 and the *Andante* of Op. 33/6 are particularly fine, and the *Allegretto* finale of this latter work also shows the group at their most lyrically relaxed. Minuets are generally full of character, with the trios nicely realized, and this applies especially to the charming middle section of the Scherzo in the *Joke Quartet*. In short these are performances which convey the players' affection for this wonderful music with no possible desire to put their own personalities between composer and listener, and some listeners may feel the approach brings at times just a hint of blandness, unusual in this series. There is much less extrovert temperament and fire than with the Lindsays, but there is room in the catalogue for both views. The Naxos recording is wholly natural with the acoustics of the Budapest Unitarian Church beautifully caught without any textural inflation.

String quartets Nos. 43 in D min., Op.42; 67 in D (Lark), Op. 64/5; 79 in D, Op. 76/5.
(BB) *** ASV Dig. CDQS 6145 [id.]. Lindsay Qt.

In many ways this is the finest of the Lindsay Haydn collections, recorded live at the Wigmore Hall in 1987. The players are given a striking presence and the spontaneity of their playing is gripping. The presto finales (particularly the moto perpetuo of *The Lark*, which overall is most strikingly done) offer fizzing bravura and the beautiful slow movement of Op. 76/5 is rapt in its quiet intensity. There are remarkably few moments of roughness of ensemble arising from the impetuosity of the playing.

String quartets Nos. 57–59 (Tost), Op. 54/1–3.
*** Hyp. Dig. CDA 66971 [id.]. Salomon Qt.

The Salomon Quartet, led by Simon Standage, play on period instruments, but there is nothing anaemic or edgy about the body of tone they command, and the pervading feeling here is of freshness, with finales spirited without being rushed off their feet. In the great *C major Quartet*, Op. 54/2, the closing helter-skelter *Presto* is articulated with appealing crispness. It is framed by a rapt *Adagio* which brings the movement to a touching close. The central slow movement is brief, but has a mood of deeply serious intensity, which the leader then embroiders almost capriciously – here with an improvisatory spontaneity. Then in the Trio of the Minuet there are extraordinary cries of despair (so uncharacteristic of Haydn), which are most tellingly played. This is one of the very best records from these excellent players and the recording is absolutely first class.

String quartets Nos. 60–62 (Tost), Op. 55/1–3.
*** ASV Dig. CDDCA 906 [id.]. Lindsay Qt.

Here the Lindsays are heard under studio conditions, but in Holy Trinity Church, Wentworth, and the results, on the second set of *Tost Quartets*, are marginally less chimerical than in their live recordings, but not less dedicated or less vital. There is of course greater polish, as the fizzing finale of Op. 55/3 readily demonstrates, while the contrapuntal second-movement *Allegro* of the famous *Razor Quartet* (Op. 55/2) brings highly disciplined ensemble. The beauty of the serene *Adagio cantabile* of the first of the set is most affecting (although one must comment that at 1 minute 44 seconds there is a curious momentary fall-off of tone which seems to be in the playing). The recording is lifelike and vivid without excessive resonance.

String quartets Nos. 67 in D (Lark), Op. 64/5; 74 in G min. (Rider), Op. 74/3; 77 in C (Emperor), Op. 76/3.
(B) *** DG 439 479-2 [id.]. Amadeus Qt.

Here is a worthwhile triptych of named quartets for those seeking to sample the Amadeus Quartet in Haydn. Their superb ensemble is immediately noticeable at the opening of the *Lark Quartet*, as is Norman Brainin's vibrato as he soars aloft, giving the Amadeus sound its special stamp. The finale brings spiccato precision that dazzles the ear. The *Largo* of the *Rider Quartet* sounds just a little deliberate but its intensity in no doubt, and the gutsy vibrancy of the playing in the finale is equally remarkable. These date from the 1970s; the *Emperor* was made a decade earlier and the recording is a trifle thinner, though the body of tone the group commands projects impressively. The performance shows these fine musicians in the best possible light. The playing is sensitive and (as always) alive, and the famous variations, which need some subtlety of treatment to avoid sounding repetitive, are memorable. The CD transfers are expertly done, and this Classikon reissue is excellent value.

String quartet No. 82 in F, Op. 77/2.
(*) Orfeo mono 361 941 [id.]. Végh Qt – BEETHOVEN: *String Quartet No.3 in D;* DEBUSSY: *Quartet.*
(*)

Admirers of the Végh Quartet may want to consider this issue, for there is always some illumination to be had from this ensemble. However, this Austrian Radio recording, made in mono at the 1961 Salzburg Festival, is less than distinguished (the sound is distinctly thin). The performance is not as polished as one would expect under studio conditions, and exposition repeats are not observed.

(i)*Symphonies Nos. 94 in G (Surprise);* (ii) *100 in G (Military); 104 in D (London)* (arr. Salomon for flute, string quartet and fortepiano).
(M) **(*) O-L Analogue/Dig. 443 194-2 [id.]. (i) Simon Preston, AAM (members), Hogwood; (ii) Lisa Beznosiuk, Salomon String Qt, Hogwood.

These engaging and ingenious arrangements were made by Salomon (long before the age of the gramophone) to enjoy Haydn's invention domestically. It is remarkable how much of the music's colour is caught in these sprightly, polished and by no means lightweight accounts. The sharp, clear and transparent sound enables detail to register consistently and the spirited music-making cannot help but give pleasure, even though the 'authentic' style is slightly astringent. However, as can be seen, two different groupings of musicians are featured here. Nos. 100 and 104 were recorded digitally in 1985 and the blend of instrumental sound is altogether smoother and more aurally pleasing; No. 94, with a slightly different ensemble, is thinner, with more edge on the violin timbre, although the 1982 analogue recording seems equally faithful.

PIANO MUSIC

Piano sonatas Nos. 1–16; 17–19 (Hob Deest) 20; 28, Hob XIV/5; 29–62, Hob XVI/1–52 & G1; XVII/ D1; The Seven last words on the Cross; Adagio in F; Capriccio in G on the song 'Acht Sauschneider müssen sein'; Fantasia in C; 7 Minuets from 'Kleine Tänz für die Jugend'; Variations in F min.; 5 Variations in D; 6 Variations in C; 12 Variations in E flat; 20 Variations in A.
(B) *** Decca 443 785-2 (12) [id.]. John McCabe.

Although Rudolph Buchbinder also made a recording of the Haydn sonatas and piano music for Telefunken on LP, his performances were accomplished and tidy but no more. It was John McCabe who, between 1974 and 1977, made the first complete survey for Argo, including also *The Seven last words on the Cross*, an arrangement not made by the composer but approved by him. It is remarkably successful here. Indeed two things shine through John McCabe's performances: their complete musicianship and their fine imagination. In these days of original instruments, some collectors might have preferred them played on the appropriate instrument, from the clavichord in the case of some of the earlier pieces through to the fortepiano. In presenting them as he does on a modern piano, McCabe makes the most of the colour and subtlety of the music, and in that respect his style is more expressive, less overtly classical than Jandó's (see below) while the (originally Argo) recording is made to sound somewhat softer-grained by the acoustic of All Saints' Church, Petersham. Given phrasing so clearly articulated and alertly phrased, and such varied, intelligently thought-out and wholly responsive presentation, this set can be recommended very enthusiastically. The recordings are of the very highest quality, truthful in timbre and firmly refined in detail, and they must be numbered among the most successful of this repertoire ever to be put on disc, for the piano is notoriously difficult to balance in eighteenth-century music. The set is most reasonably priced – admittedly not as inexpensive as the Naxos series, but more than worth the difference. McCabe uses Christa Langdon's Universal Edition texts and numbering, not the older Päsler (Haydn Society) edition, and the pianist provides his own extensive and illuminating notes. To sample the calibre of this enterprise, begin with *The Seven last words* – playing of unexaggerated expressive feeling that almost makes one believe this was a work conceived in pianistic terms.

Piano sonatas Nos. 36 in C, Hob XVI/21; 37 in E, Hob XVI/22; 38 in F, Hob XVI/23; 39 in D, Hob XVI/24; 40 in E flat, Hob XVI/25; 41 in A, Hob XVI/26.
(BB) **(*) Naxos Dig. 8.553127 [id.]. Jenö Jandó.

Piano sonatas Nos. 48 in C, Hob XVI/35; 49 in C sharp min., Hob XVI/36; 50 in D, Hob XVI/37; 51 in E flat, Hob XVI/38; 52 in G, Hob XVI/39.
(BB) *** Naxos Dig. 8.553128 [id.]. Jenö Jandó.

Jandó seems to have been very slightly below par when he recorded Volume 4 (8.553127) of his ongoing set of Haydn sonatas in May 1993. The playing is as bright and clear as before and the interpretations are well thought out, but just occasionally there is a hint of stiffness and overall there is not always the degree of spontaneity we expect from this artist.

A month later, in June of the same year, he was back on form with all the freshness that marked his earlier records in the series, as the opening of *No. 36 in C* immediately shows. The finale of *No. 37 in E major* is beautifully played, and the following two sonatas with their fine slow movements will not disappoint his admirers. Excellent piano sound, crisp but not too dry.

VOCAL MUSIC

(i) *The Creation (Die Schöpfung)*: oratorio (complete; in German); (ii) *Mass No. 6 in G (Missa Sancti Nicholai), Hob XXII/6;* (iii) *Mass No. 7 in B flat: Missa brevis Sancti Joannis de Deo (Little organ mass), Hob XXII/7.*

(B) *(*) Ph. Duo 446 175-2 (2) [id.]. (i) Giebel, Kmentt, Frick, Bav. R. Ch. & O, Jochum; (ii) Resch, Buchbauer, Ch. Viennensis; (iii) Boehm (organ); (ii; iii) Soloists from V. Boys' Ch.; V. Boys' Ch., Wiener Dom-Orchester, cond. (i) Furthmoser; (ii) Grossman.

Jochum, almost invariably inspired in romantic music, and certainly so in Bruckner, is less consistent in the music of the classical period, and here he fails to bring out either Haydn's sharp-edged drama or sparkling humour. It is a pity, too, that Gottlob Frick, normally the most consistently interesting of German basses, is well below form. The comparative dullness of the performance is not cancelled out by the remastering of the recording, which has enhanced the vividness of the sound compared with the original LPs. Two early Masses are used to frame the main work, both given respectable performances, with Grossman's account of the *Little Organ Mass* rather the more characterful (although his treble soloist from the Vienna Boys' Choir, who sings sweetly enough, is none too secure in pitch).

The Creation (Die Schöpfung).
*** Sony Vivarte SX2K 57965 (2) [id.]. Monoyios, Hering, Van der Kamp, Tölz Boys' Ch., Tafelmusik, Bruno Weil.
*** Decca 443 445-2 (2) [id.]. Ziesak, Lippert, Pape, Scharinger, Chicago Ch. & SO, Solti.
**(*) DG Dig. 427 629-2 (2) [id.]. Battle, Winbergh, Moll, Stockholm R. Ch. and Chamber Ch., BPO, Levine.
**(*) Telarc Dig. CD 80298 (2) [id.]. Upshaw, Humphrey, Cheek, Murphy, McGuire, Chamber Ch. & SO, Shaw.

Bruno Weil conducts a brisk, clean-cut reading, using the period instruments of Tafelmusik and a bright-toned chorus, augmented by the Tölz Boys' Choir. If the intimacy at times seems to reduce the scale of this masterpiece, and Weil at times is fussy over detail, the urgent exuberance of the performance is most winning, with an outstanding trio of cleanly focused soloists. The chorus is finely focused too, providing sharp, dramatic contrasts, and the orchestral sound is so clean that one can hear the fortepiano continuo even in tuttis. A good contrasting approach to Christopher Hogwood's on his large-scale period performance (Oiseau-Lyre 430 397-2).

Recorded live in the autumn of 1993, Sir Georg Solti's second recording, made (like the first) with Chicago forces, presents a striking difference. The influence of period performance means that not only does he adopt fast speeds, but his very choice of soloists reflects the new generation of light, clear singers, all excellent. Ornamentation and the use of a fortepiano continuo also give further indication of Sir Georg's new stance on this work, which results in a crisp, buoyant reading, full of dramatic contrasts, which nevertheless are not out of scale with Haydn's vision. If in such a number as the first Adam and Eve duet of Part 3 Solti's speed is excessively fast, making the result trivial, the buoyancy remains, and generally he and his team avoid breathlessness, with splendid choral singing, captured in full, bright sound. However, first choice among modern-instrument performances remains with Rattle (EMI CDS7 54159-2).

Though James Levine with his weighty forces is occasionally heavy-handed over both dynamics and rhythm, lacking rather in elegance, he conveys the joy of inspiration in this work with characteristic boldness. He is helped not just by the highly polished playing of the orchestra but by characterful singing from all three soloists and fresh, finely disciplined choral singing. The recording, made not in the Philharmonie but in the Jesus-Christus Kirche, is weighty and satisfyingly full, with ample bloom.

Robert Shaw with his keenly disciplined chamber choir conducts a strong, clean-cut performance, using an English translation modified from the traditional one. Though Shaw's generally broad speeds show little influence from period performance, his concern for clarity of texture is very different from old-style performances, and the Telarc engineers help with full, immediate sound, bringing out sharp dynamic contrasts. Dawn Upshaw adopts too romantically expressive a manner, but the solo singing is good, with Heidi Grant Murphy and James Michael McGuire brought in for the Adam and Eve numbers of Part 3.

The Creation: highlights.
(B) *** DG 439 454-2 [id.] (from recording with Janowitz, Wunderlich, Krenn, Fischer-Dieskau, Berry, V. Singverein, BPO, Karajan).

Anyone whose budget will not stretch to a complete version of Haydn's masterpiece will find that this 70-minute bargain Classikon highlights disc includes the key solos and choruses. Karajan's star-studded 1969 performance (435 077-2) remains unsurpassed.

The Seasons (*Die Jahreszeiten;* complete; in German).
(B) *** DG Double 437 940-2 (2) [id.]. Janowitz, Schreier, Talvela, V. Singverein, VSO, Karl Boehm.

Boehm's performance enters totally into the spirit of the music. The soloists are excellent and characterize the music fully; the chorus sing enthusiastically and are well recorded. But it is Boehm's set. He secures fine orchestral playing throughout, an excellent overall musical balance and real spontaneity in music that needs this above all else. The CD transfer of the 1967 recording is admirably managed; the sound overall is a little drier, but the chorus have plenty of body and there is an excellent sense of presence.

Collections

Ein Magd ein Dienerin (cantilena); *Miseri noi, misera patria!* (cantata). Interpolation arias: *Chi vive amante* (for BIANCHI: *Alessandro nell' Indie*). *La moglie quando è buona* (for CIMAROSA: *Giannina è Bernadone*). *Il meglio mio carattere* (for CIMAROSA: *L'Impresario in Augustie*). *Ah, crudel! poi chè la brami* (for GAZZANIGA: *La Vendemmia*). *Sono Alcina* (for GAZZANIGA: *Lisola di Alcina*). *Son pietosa* (for pasticcio by Naumann).
(M) *** Erato/Warner Dig. 4509 98498-2 [id.]. Teresa Berganza, Scottish CO, Leppard.

Most of the items on this delightful recital disc are 'insertion' arias which Haydn wrote for productions of other composers' operas at Esterháza in the years between 1780 and 1790. They are generally short and tuneful, boasting of the singers' constancy in love or whatever; Berganza with brilliant accompaniment sings them with delicious sparkle. The most substantial item is *Miseri noi, misera patria!*, darker and more deeply expressive: and there, too, Berganza rises superbly to the challenge. Excellent Erato recording, most successfully transferred to compact disc, where both the voice and the accompanying group sound vivid within a natural perspective. Recommended.

Henze, Hans Werner (born 1926)

Voices.
*** Berlin Classics 2180-2 BC (2) [id.]. Roswitha Trexler, Joachim Vogt, Leipzig RSO Chamber Ens., Horst Neumann.

Written for the London Sinfonietta in 1973, this massive and wide-ranging song-cycle of 22 numbers, lasting over 90 minutes, is among Henze's most inspired and characterful works. It combines the red-blooded ardour of the political pieces that he had been writing, often wild in their inspiration, with a sharpness of focus in the material and argument which has regularly marked his work, but which in his left-wing enthusiasm he for a time neglected. There is little of the delicate fantasy which has also marked much of his output, but instead he presents a vivid and striking musical response to each text in turn. So in his techniques he ranges widely, from highly sophisticated, post-serial structures to jazz, aleatory patterns and music-theatre pieces, notably in ironic songs echoing Kurt Weill, several of them setting poems by Bertolt Brecht. The wonder is that, so far from seeming too disparate a sequence, *Voices* gathers in richness as it progresses. With such specific inspirations for each piece, often with a particular dedicatee in mind, Henze readily wrote with memorable point and focus. Though until that point in his career he had written very few songs, this found him relishing a new genre all the more, varying not just the moods and themes but the forces used in each song over a very wide span, with instruments including ocarina, accordion, mouth-organ and electric guitar, as well as a large percussion section. Some of the episodes are violent (*Screams*, for example) but the work is rounded off with the most beautiful and most extended piece. Following on a swaggering, Greek-inspired number almost like a can-can, *Schluss* ('An end'), he concludes with a duet, *Blumenfest* ('Carnival of flowers'), in which mellifluous and flexible vocal lines for mezzo and tenor intertwining seem to suggest a final ray of hope, with bitterness gone. This analogue recording, made in Germany in 1980, presents a sharply focused performance, strong and dramatic, with two excellent, clean-cut soloists. It is good that at last it should be made more generally available.

Hildegard of Bingen (1098-1179)

Canticles of ecstasy.
🏵 *** HM/BMG Dig. 05472 77320-2 [id.]. Sequentia, Barbara Thornton.

Born almost exactly nine centuries ago, Abbess Hildegard of Bingen has over the last decade emerged as one of the great creative figures of medieval times, not just an inspired composer but a poet, dramatist and theologian, a correspondent with emperors and popes. Following on Gothic Voices' best-selling disc for Hyperion (CDA 66039), the fine German group, Sequentia, has under Barbara Thornton embarked on a collected recording of her works. This latest instalment is among the most moving and beautiful yet. At speeds more spacious than those of Gothic Voices, with women's voices alone, the elaborate monodic lines soar heavenwards even more sensuously, matching the imagery of Hildegard's poetry. For a meditative mood this outdoes Gregorian chant. Highly recommended.

Hindemith, Paul (1895-1963)

Piano concerto.
*** First Edition LCD 002 [id.]. Lee Luvisi, Louisville O, Leighton Smith – LAWHEAD: *Aleost* *(*); ZWILICH: *Symphony No. 2.* **

The neglect of Hindemith's beautiful *Piano concerto* (1945) is puzzling. Written for the pianist Jesús-María Sanromá and premièred at Cleveland under Georg Szell in 1957, it is a work of great lyrical feeling and fertile imagination. Its second movement begins with an evocative, slightly Bartók-like night atmosphere, with a strong sense of nature and fresh, radiant textures. It must be one of his most beautiful creations, and those who associate Hindemith with manufactured Teutonic *Gebrauchmusik* will find this music open in texture, delicate in its colourings and inspired in its material. Lee Luvisi and the Louisville Orchestra give a very good account of themselves and are more than adequately recorded. Let us hope the centenary year will bring new recordings of this piece, but in the meantime a strong recommendation for this.

(i) *Viola concerto (Der Schwanendreher);* (ii) *Nobilissima visione;* (iii) *Symphonic metamorphoses on themes by Weber.*
**(*) Berlin Classics 3041-2 [id.]. (i) Alfred Lipka, Leipzig RSO, Kegel; (ii) Dresden PO, Bongartz; (iii) Dresden State O, Suitner.

These performances come from the old East German Eterna catalogue and are of some distinction. The *Nobilissima visione* suite from the Dresden Philharmonic under Heinz Bongartz dates from 1964 and has great dignity and breadth. It is as good as any now available, including the composer's own; and the recording, though not state of the art even by the standards of its time, is still more than acceptable. A most musical performance. The *Viola concerto (Der Schwanendreher)* and the *Symphonic metamorphoses on themes by Weber* are slightly later (1970 and 1969 respectively). Alfred Lipka proves an eloquent soloist in the former and is well supported by the Leipzig Radio Orchestra under Herbert Kegel and, though theirs is not as remarkable an account as Tabea Zimmermann and the Bavarian forces (EMI CDC7 54101-2 – see our main *Guide*), it makes a good (albeit not so well recorded) alternative to Herbert Blomstedt. Otmar Suitner's account of the *Symphonic metamorphoses* may not have quite as light a touch or the sparkle of some rivals, but it is very enjoyable.

(i) *Violin concerto;* (ii) *Symphony in E flat.*
** Everest EVC 9009 [id.]. (i) Joseph Fuchs, LSO, Sir Eugene Goossens; (ii) LPO, Sir Adrian Boult;

Both performances come from 1958 and were accorded what was thought at the time to be state-of-the-art recording. Joseph Fuchs in fact provided the première recording of the *Violin concerto*, and his account can well withstand comparison with its contemporaries (Gertler and Oistrakh). In fact it is to be preferred to the former and is more richly detailed than the latter's Decca recording with Hindemith himself. That comes at mid-price on a more generously filled disc (with Kletzki's version of *Mathis der Maler* and the splendid Abbado *Symphonic metamorphosis on themes by Weber*). Sir Adrian's account of the *Symphony in E flat* has appropriate dignity and lucidity, though at full price readers are more likely to be drawn to the marvellously recorded Chandos version from the BBC Philharmonic and Yan Pascal Tortelier.

Der Dämon; (i) *Hérodiade* (two versions).
*** CPO Dig. 999 220-2 [id.]. (i) Annie Gicquel; Siegfried Mauser, Frankfurt RSO, Albert.

Der Dämon (The Demon) (1922) is an early ballet, 'a Dance Pantomime in two scenes' to a scenario of Max Krell, dating from what has been called Hindemith's 'window-breaking' modern period, and his only contribution to the genre during the 1920s. It has nothing in common with his later ballets, *Nobilissima visione* (1938) and *The Four Temperaments* (1940). At times it comes closer to the world of the *Kammermusiken*; it has much delicacy of touch and great resource in matters of colour; and it is full of imaginative, original textures. There is a prominent role for the piano, brilliantly and sensitively played by Siegfried Mauser, whose ethereal cascades afford much delight. It would make ideal listening for those who think they don't like Hindemith. *Hérodiade* dates from 1944 and derives its inspiration from Mallarmé's poem. It is an excellent idea to let us have it first with the text, then again without it, and Annie Gicquel speaks it in exemplary fashion. The recording lends it an aural halo, but this is to be preferred to too dry a sound. *Hérodiade* is a beautiful score and Werner Andreas Albert gets excellent results from his Frankfurt forces. The Hessischer Rundfunk engineers produce recordings that are a model of good balance. Strongly recommended.

Mathis der Maler (symphony); *Nobilissima visione; Symphonic metamorphosis on themes by Carl Maria von Weber*.
*** EMI Dig. CDC5 55230-2 [id.]. Phd. O, Sawallisch.
(BB) ** Naxos Dig. 8.553078 [id.]. New Zealand SO, Franz-Paul Decker.

The Philadelphia Orchestra made a celebrated 78-r.p.m. set of the *Mathis der Maler Symphony* in the days of Ormandy, and the present generation show themselves equally at home with this score. It is good to hear this great orchestra sounding itself again. Sawallisch draws a warm, rich-textured sound from them, and he also gives a performance of the *Nobilissima visione* that does justice to its breadth and dignity. Sawallisch's account of the *Symphonic metamorphosis on themes by Carl Maria von Weber* is not quite as sharp or fleet of foot as the Bernstein set, but it is still very well characterized. The *Mathis* scores over the rival Blomstedt on Decca in depth of characterization and orchestral opulence and, all things considered, should be the preferred recommendation.

The Naxos disc is certainly not to be dismissed. It is well played under a conductor who is clearly at home in this repertoire without being inspired by it, with *Nobilissima visione* the most attractive performance. Those with limited budgets will find this well-recorded super-bargain offering value for money.

Trauermusik for viola and strings.
(M) **(*) Sony SMK 48372 [id.]. Dmitri Jakubovsky, St Petersburg Camerata, Saulius Sondeckis –
     HAYDN: *Symphony No. 49;* SHOSTAKOVICH: *Chamber Symphony.* **(*)

Admirers of Hindemith are unlikely to linger longingly over the St Petersburg Camerata's hybrid programme, but those whose collections lack this particular compilation need not hesitate. It is as well played as the San Francisco version under Blomstedt, and it depends on whether you want Haydn's *La Passione* and the *Chamber Symphony*, the full string version of the *Tenth Quartet*, rather than the *Mathis der Maler Symphony* and the *Weber metamorphosis*.

String quartet No. 3, Op. 22.
⊛ (***) Testament mono SBT 1052 [id.]. Hollywood Qt – PROKOFIEV: *Quartet No. 2;* WALTON:
     Quartet in A min. (***) ⊛

Although the Hindemith quartets have not been as well served on either LP or CD as the Prokofiev, the remarkable Hollywood Quartet version of the *Third*, which first appeared on these shores in 1952, is pretty stunning. The Hollywood Quartet possessed an extraordinary virtuosity and perfection of ensemble, and it is difficult to imagine more persuasive advocacy. The transfer is excellent and, although the mono sound does not represent the state of the art these days, the performance still sweeps the board.

Mathis der Maler (opera; complete).
(M) *** EMI CDS5 55237-2 (3) [id.]. Fischer-Dieskau, Feldhof, J. King, M. Schmidt, Meven,
     Cochran, Malta, Grobe, Wagemann, Bav. R. Ch. & SO, Kubelik.

There is little doubt that the opera *Mathis der Maler* is Hindemith's masterpiece. The fine symphony which he extracted from it gives only a partial idea of its quality, for here Hindemith's theorizing went with a deep involvement with the subject. There is no mistaking that behind the characteristic gruffness of manner there is not just urgency but warmth. Fischer-Dieskau proves the ideal interpreter of the central role, the painter Mathias Grünewald, who in the troubled Germany of the sixteenth century joins the cause of the rebellious peasants – a subject with a very clear relevance to the times when the piece was written, during the rise of the Nazis. The performance includes other fine contributions from James King as the Archbishop, Donald Grobe as the Cardinal, Alexander Malta as the army commandant and Manfred Schmidt as the Cardinal's adviser. The women principals are less happily chosen; Rose Wagemann as Ursula is rather squally. But with splendid playing and singing from Bavarian Radio forces under Kubelik, this is a highly enjoyable as well as an important set. Moreover the first-class (1977) analogue recording was made in the famous Munich Herculessaal. Its warm, glowing acoustics are just as kind to the voices as to the orchestra, with the balance between soloists, chorus and orchestra very natural, as is immediately apparent in the atmospheric opening scene. The CD transfer (engineered by Simon Gibson at Abbey Road) is a model of its kind.

Holmboe, Vagn (born 1909)

Symphonies Nos. 1, Op. 4; 3 (Sinfonia rustica), Op. 25; 10, Op. 105.
*** BIS Dig. CD 605 [id.]. Aarhus SO, Arwel Hughes.

One of the first Holmboe works to reach the gramophone was his *Notturno for wind* (1940), so that this CD offers us our first glimpse of his music from the 1930s. The *First Symphony* (*Sinfonia da camera*) comes from 1935 and was actually written for the Aarhus Symphony Orchestra and its première was conducted by Thomas Jensen. Its general outlook is neo-classical and its proportions are modest (it takes about 15 minutes) but one recognizes the vital current of the later Holmboe, the lucidity of thinking and the luminous textures. The last movement has an infectious delight in life; so, too, has the exhilarating finale of the *Third* (*Sinfonia rustica*), the first of his three war-time symphonies. Holmboe has often spoken rather apologetically of his early symphonies, but it is difficult to see any objective grounds for his condescension. They are astonishingly inventive and assured for a composer still emerging from his mid-twenties. The *Tenth* (1970–71) is, of course, a piece of much greater substance, commissioned by Sixten Ehrling and the Detroit Orchestra (and recorded by him in the days of LP). It is dark, powerful and imaginative; altogether one of the Danish composer's most subtle and satisfying works. The performances and recordings are altogether first class.

Symphonies Nos 8, Op. 56 (1951); 9 (1968).
⊛ *** BIS Dig. CD 618 [id.]. Aarhus SO, Arwel Hughes.

Only three of Holmboe's symphonies were recorded in the days of vinyl (Nos. 7, 8 and 10), of which perhaps the *Eighth*, available on Turnabout (with the Royal Danish Orchestra under Jerzy Semkow), enjoyed the longest currency. This new version by the Aarhus orchestra under Owain Arwel Hughes is infinitely superior. This conductor has real feeling for the composer and not only penetrates the spirit of the score but is scrupulous in his observance of the letter. Dynamic and agogic markings are meticulously yet unobtrusively followed; one is left with the impression that this symphony has never really had its due until now. The *Ninth Symphony* is wholly unfamiliar. After its first performance in Copenhagen in 1968, which was subsequently broadcast by the BBC, it was revised and this is its première recording. A dark, powerful work, the *Ninth* is among the finest Holmboe has given us: Professor Richard Taruskin recently spoke of him in *The New York Times* as 'possibly the greatest living symphonist' and what he wrote of the *Sixth* certainly applies to the *Ninth*: 'Form and expressive content, in a word, are one. It is every symphonic composer's ideal but very few achieve it so fully.' Taruskin compared it to 'academic discourse of a thrillingly high order . . . if you have ever left a lecture hall haunted and altered, this may offer a comparable cognitive adventure.' Like the *Sixth* and *Seventh Symphonies*, this disc of the *Eighth* and *Ninth* is to be recommended with urgency. This is music which, one can feel with some certainty, future generations will want to hear. The Aarhus orchestra are equally persuasive in the *Ninth* as in the *Eighth*, and the recording is the best so far in the cycle.

Holmès, Augusta (1847–1903)

Andromeda (symphonic poem); *Ireland* (symphonic poem); (i) *Ludus pro patria: Night and love.*
Overture for a comedy; Poland (symphonic poem).
*** Marco Polo Dig. 8.223449 [id.]. Rheinland-Pfalz PO, Samuel Friedmann; (i) Patrick Davin.

Augusta Holmès was the inspiring force behind the César Franck *Piano quintet* which embodied much of that master's strong feeling for her. She was from an Anglo-Irish family that had settled in France; Alfred de Vigny was her godfather – and, some maintain, her real father. She was a person of remarkable gifts for, apart from her musical talents, she was an accomplished painter and wrote well. Unable (on account of her sex) to gain admission to the Paris Conservatoire, she received encouragement from both Liszt and Wagner before becoming a pupil of Franck. She composed some 150 songs in all but also tried her hand at larger forms, and she gained the distinction of being commissioned to write a massive work for the centenary of the French Revolution, the *Ode triomphale*, which called for no fewer than 1,200 performers and was heard at the Palais d'Industrie by an audience of 15,000! Although the *Overture for a comedy* (1876) is trite, *Andromeda* is quite striking, rather Lisztian at first and with occasional reminders of Vincent d'Indy, though some of the orchestral textures are more transparent than those of so many of the Franck circle. *Andromeda* is by far the best piece on the disc, and the best scored, though limitations in Augusta Holmès's technique (particularly her reliance on sequence, and the relatively limited development of ideas) are evident. But this is music of much interest – and its composer was obviously no mean talent. She has been well served by the Rheinland-Pfalz Philharmonic under Samuel Friedmann. The recordings too are eminently satisfactory.

Holst, Gustav (1874–1934)

Brook Green suite for string orchestra; (i) *Fugal concerto for flute and oboe. The Perfect Fool* (ballet suite), *Op. 39; St Paul's suite for string orchestra, Op. 26/2; A Somerset rhapsody, Op. 21/2.*
(M) *** EMI CD-EMX 2227; *TC-EMX 2227.* ECO, Sir Yehudi Menuhin.

There are a number of collections of Holst's shorter orchestral works currently available on CD, but none better played or recorded than this and none less expensive. It includes warmly characterized performances of both the works Holst wrote for St Paul's Girls' School, not just the *St Paul's suite* but also the *Brook Green suite*, both sounding fresh, while the rarer *Somerset rhapsody* is also very atmospherically presented. There is some delightful solo playing from Jonathan Snowden and David Theodore in the *Fugal concerto*, and many will welcome Menuhin's vivid account of *The Perfect Fool*, Holst's most familiar orchestral suite after *The Planets*. If the programme suits, you need look no further.

The Planets (suite), *Op. 32.*
*** DG Dig. 445 860-2; *445 860-4* [id.]. Monteverdi Ch. women's voices, Philh. O, Gardiner –
    GRAINGER: *The Warriors.* ***
(***) EMI mono CDC7 54837-2 [id.]. LSO, composer – ELGAR: *Enigma variations.* (***)
(M) **(*) EMI CDM5 65423-2 [id.]. R. Wagner Chorale women's voices, LAPO, Stokowski –
    RAVEL: *Alborada* **(*); STRAVINSKY: *Petrushka.* **
(M) **(*) EMI Dig. CDM7 64740-2 [id.]. Philh. O, Rattle – JANACEK: *Sinfonietta.* ***
(M) **(*) Ph. Dig. 442 408-2 [id.]. Berlin R. Ch., BPO, Sir Colin Davis.
(B) **(*) BBC Radio Classics BBCRD 9104 [id.]. BBC SO, Sargent – ELGAR: *Enigma Variations.*
    **(*)
(BB) (***) RCA Navigator 74321 17905-2 [id.]. Phd. Ch. & O, Ormandy – VAUGHAN WILLIAMS:
    Fantasias. ***
(M) ** Teldec/Warner Dig. 4509 97443-2 [id.]. New York Choral Artists, NYPO, Mehta.

Even when branching out from his usual repertory, John Eliot Gardiner has imaginative things to say in his interpretations. *The Planets* offers a performance of high voltage, with plenty of panache and an acute feeling for atmospheric colour. With speeds never exaggerated, he avoids vulgarity – perhaps having taken a lesson from Boult's classic reading – yet with his rhythmic flair he gives the pieces a new buoyancy. Outstandingly enjoyable are the two most extrovert pieces: *Jupiter, the bringer of jollity* has rarely sounded so joyful, with a hint of wildness at the start, and the dancing rhythms of *Uranus* have a scherzando sparkle, with timpani and brass stunningly caught in the full, brilliant recording. The offstage women's chorus at the end of *Neptune* has seldom been more subtly balanced. Gardiner's *Planets* stands alongside the other current highly recommendable versions, Judd on Denon (CO 75076), Dutoit on Decca (417 553-2) and Hilary Davon Wetton (Collins 1036-2) – all superb in their different ways. But none of these offers a coupling, whereas on DG the unusual Grainger coupling, typically rumbustious, pays tribute to the conductor's great-uncle, the composer Balfour Gardiner, who promoted the first performances of both works. Among bargain versions Handley remains very recommendable on Tring (TRP 007, coupled with the *St Paul's suite*).

Holst first recorded *The Planets* in 1922 in the days of acoustic engineering. There are significant differences in his later (1926) electrical recording (these were the days before Columbia, as it then was, had resolved the problem of shorter side-lengths – electric recording encompassed a wider frequency range and the number of grooves per inch was at first reduced). Hence it is arguable that under ideal conditions Holst would have taken longer in some passages (as he did in the 1922 recording of *Venus*). Be that as it may, his 1926 version is still pretty amazing – and sounds quite remarkably vivid for its day. Inhibited he may have been by the cramped conditions of the studio and the playing time but one can easily forget that, given the sheer vitality of these performances. This is an indispensable issue.

Stokowski's approach to *The Planets* is both brisk and sensuous (*Venus* very much the Goddess of Love rather than the 'bringer of peace'), with every movement except *Mercury* faster than usual. Yet such is Stokowski's magnetism that at a flowing speed *Saturn* conveys rapt stillness and the fast movements have tremendous swagger. This is very early stereo (1956) and the Capitol recording of the Los Angeles Philharmonic was made in so-called 'full-dimensional sound'. It is bright and clear but lacks the allure of RCA's 'Living stereo' of the same period. The forward balance is effective in adding pungency to *Mars*, but elsewhere – and especially in *Jupiter* and the brass opening of *Uranus* – it is a little harsh (and at 1 minute 1 second in *Jupiter* there is a tape join which snips out a fractional pause).

For Simon Rattle, EMI's digital recording provides wonderfully atmospheric sound, and the quality in *Venus* and *Mercury* is also beautiful, clear and translucent. Otherwise it is not as distinctive a version as one might have expected from this leading conductor; it is sensibly paced but neither so polished nor so bitingly committed as Karajan, Previn or Boult, and *Jupiter* is disappointing, lacking in thrust and warmth.

Sir Colin Davis's *Mars* is menacingly fast, with weighty Berlin brass and barbaric accents adding to the forcefulness. The resonant recording brings sumptuous textures to *Venus*, while even *Saturn* has a degree of opulence. *Mercury*, however, is infectiously spirited, and *Jupiter*, with a grand central tune, is bucolic in its amplitude. *Uranus* brings galumphing brass, and the closing *Neptune* is both ethereal and sensuous, an unusual combination, brought about partly by the warm reverberation. There are more subtle versions than this, but it is easy to enjoy. However, this reissue offers no coupling.

Though the label, incorrectly, suggests the Royal Festival Hall as the venue, this BBC Radio Classics account of *The Planets* was recorded, like the Elgar, in the Royal Albert Hall. One marvels that no one in the reissuing record company noticed the three-second reverbation confirming the point. Though this was a February performance, not one given at the Proms, the atmosphere is similarly electric, with the sequence of movements building warmly and atmospherically. As in the Elgar, the playing may be a degree less polished than in Sargent's studio recording, but the excitement and tension are markedly greater, and for most that is what will matter. Good, full-bodied if rather opaque sound.

Ormandy's 1975 RCA recording now reappears on RCA's super-bargain Navigator label, generously coupled with Vaughan Williams string works. It was one of the finest records he made as principal conductor of the Philadelphia Orchestra in the last few years before he retired. The playing has great electricity, and it is a pity that RCA's balancing engineers apparently sought brilliance above all else and endeavoured to make a quite artificial sonic impact. The CD transfer brings a fierce edginess in the treble (caused by placing the microphones much too close). The orchestra does not sound like this in the flesh. Even so, this is a highly compelling reading, and the sound gives added edge to the ferocity of *Mars*, balanced by an eloquently peaceful *Venus* with rapt, translucent textures. Ormandy paces the central tune of *Jupiter* slowly and deliberately. (This seems almost to be an American tradition; Ormandy's performance of Vaughan Williams's arrangement of *Greensleeves* shows a similar gravity.) The performance is at its finest in *Uranus* (with crisply vigorous brass articulation) and the restrained melancholy of *Saturn*, deeply felt and somehow personal in its communication. *Neptune* too is beautifully tapered off at the close. However, the coupled Vaughan Williams string works, recorded a few years earlier, demonstrate what a glorious body of sound the Philadelphia Orchestra could create without any artificial aid.

At the beginning of his career in the early 1970s Mehta recorded an outstanding set of *Planets* for Decca with the Los Angeles Philharmonic Orchestra, and that performance (and its superb recording – still demonstration-worthy) remains a top bargain recommendation, coupled with Boult's *Perfect Fool suite* (433 620-2). His later, Teldec version cannot compare with it for either characterization or recording, which is resonantly unrefined. The performance sounds curiously unspontaneous: there is infinitely greater life and subtlety and more vivid colouring from the orchestral playing in Los Angeles.

VOCAL MUSIC

(i) *Choral Symphony, Op. 41;* (ii) *The Hymn of Jesus, Op. 37.*

(M) *** EMI CDM5 65128-2 [id.]. (i) Felicity Palmer, LPO Ch., LPO, Boult; (ii) St Paul's Cathedral Ch., London Symphony Ch., LPO, Groves.

In the *Choral Symphony*, though the Keats poems give a faded aura to this ambitious work, Boult and his performers demonstrate the beauty and imagination of the writing. Holst even manages to set the *Ode on a Grecian Urn* without aesthetic problems and, until the finale, the writing is always taut and intensely individual. The finale is altogether looser-limbed, but Boult in this totally unsentimental performance manages to draw it together. As samplers, try the strange *Prelude* with its monotone mutterings or the seven-in-a-bar energy of the *Bacchanal*. A fine and unjustly neglected work, superbly performed. The 1974 recording remains richly atmospheric in its CD format, with the opening pianissimos of the *Prelude* and second movement enhanced by the background quiet. Many will feel that the mistiness of the sound suits the music, although the Scherzo could ideally be more sharply focused. The Groves recording of *The Hymn of Jesus* is on the whole finer than Boult's older, Decca account which has served collectors well over the years. Sir Charles Groves brings great sympathy and conviction to this beautiful and moving score whose visionary quality has never paled, and the recording has transferred very well to CD to make a highly desirable Holst coupling.

OPERA

(i) *At the Boar's Head, Op. 42* (complete); (ii) *The wandering scholar, Op. 50* (complete).
(M) *** EMI Dig. analogue CDM5 65127-2 [id.]. (i) Langridge, Palmer, Ross, Tomlinson, Wilson-Johnson, Hall, Suart, George, Royal Liverpool PO, Groves; (ii) Burrowes, Tear, Rippon, Langdon, E. Op. Group, ECO, Bedford.

Holst's formula for his Falstaff opera, *At the Boar's Head*, is an attractive one. Finding that Shakespeare's lines went naturally to dances and tunes from Playford's collection, he used that material on a libretto drawn entirely from the revelant scenes of *Henry IV, Parts I* and *II*. The result is busy-sounding in its emphasis on chattering comedy, and dramatically it is questionable. But on record the charm, colour and originality of the piece come over well, starting with an improbable drunken opening, when Bardolph begins, without accompaniment, in what for a moment sounds like sing-speech. Plainly a piece which has never been successful on stage, yet deserved a recording. With some fine singing and first-rate playing, it is admirably served here by excellent, early digital sound.

The wandering scholar, by contrast, works delightfully on stage, but on record its galumphing humour is less than sparkling. It is a very late work which the composer himself never saw produced, and the score required an amount of intelligent editing before it was given modern performances. Whatever one's response to the comedy, the musical inspiration has the sharp originality and economy one associates with Holst's last period, a fascinating score. The recording comes from the mid-1970s and was of very high quality, but the CD is something of a revelation in opening up the choral sound while still retaining the atmosphere and bloom of the analogue originals. The words of the soloists in *The wandering scholar* are also clear. An outstanding reissue in every way.

Honegger, Arthur (1892–1955)

Symphony No. 3 (Symphonie liturgique); Pacific 231; Pastorale d'été; Rugby; The Tempest: Prelude.
(i) *Le chant de Nigamon. Les Aventures du roi Pausole (opera): Overture and ballet.*
(*) Music & Arts CD 767 [id.]. O Symphonique, Honegger; (i) with Rhené-Baton.

Honegger's 1931 record of *Pastorale d'été* is available in EMI's 'Composers in Person' series, coupled with the *Cello concerto*, while *Pacific 231*, *Rugby* and the *Prelude* to *The Tempest* have been in circulation on the Pearl label together with Milhaud's *La création du monde* and the *Concertino du printemps*. The value of this disc is that it restores for the first time the Odeon 78s that Honegger made in 1930 of the *Ouverture* and *Ballet* from *Les aventures du roi Pausole* and the première recording of the *Symphonie liturgique*, made for French Decca with an unnamed orchestra, which won a *Grand Prix du Disque* in 1949. In the symphony the composer himself announces the title of each of the movements. The symphony is handicapped by obtrusively noisy surfaces and, oddly enough, is the least well recorded of the pieces here (with the exception of the dry, boxy sound of *Les aventures du roi Pausole*); moreover the orchestral playing is not as expert as later versions. It is a valuable indication of the composer's wishes, however: the middle movement is broader than either Jansons or Mravinsky. Recommended to Honegger enthusiasts rather than the wider musical public.

Hotteterre, Jacques-Martin (1674–1763)

Frans Brüggen Edition, Volume 6: *Suite No. 1 in D minor for 2 treble recorders.*

(M) *** Teldec/Warner 4509 97468-2 [id.]. Frans Brüggen, Kees Boekehardt – DIEUPART: *Suites in G min. & A.* ***

Hotteterre (known as Le Romain) came from a family famous both as composers and as instrument-makers. His suite, written for two treble recorders '*sans basse continue*', offers a charming collection of dances using a germinal idea, common to all, first heard in the opening *Gravement*. The general effect is innocuous until the ambitious five-minute finale, when the theme is developed as a *Passacaille*. The performance on original instruments is expert and pleasing.

Howells, Herbert (1892–1983)

Missa Sabrinensis.
*** Chan. Dig. CHAN 9348 [id.]. Janice Watson, Della Jones, Martyn Hill, Donald Maxwell, London Symphony Ch., LSO, Rozhdestvensky.

Following up his revelatory performance of Howells' last big choral work, the *Stabat Mater* (see below), Rozhdestvensky here conducts a passionate account of what in many ways is the most powerful of all the composer's major works. Written in 1953–4, the *Missa Sabrinensis* (the 'Mass of the Severn') is a large-scale setting – at 75 minutes almost as long as Beethoven's *Missa solemnis* – which in many ways is more revealing of Howells than either the *Stabat Mater* or the *Hymnus paradisi*, the work which set the pattern for all three. As the title implies, Howells was inspired not just by the liturgy and conventional devotional concerns, but by his deep love of the countryside round the Severn. The result is not a vaguely pastoral work, gently bringing those strands together, but one of the most full-blooded and sustained expressions of ecstasy to be found in any setting of the Mass. The work has with some justice been likened to Janáček's *Glagolitic Mass* and, though the idiom is quite different, the intensity is very similar and is sustained for far longer. There is little of the restraint that is typical of much of Howells' choral writing. Rather he exploits the lushest, most passionate elements in his richly post-impressionist style, and he hardly lets up over the whole span. You might argue that ecstasy unrestrained is in the end self-defeating but, in so urgently red-blooded a performance, few will resist. This represents a peak in Howells' creative career and, though there is some roughness in the ensemble, it would be hard to imagine a more inspired performance than Rozhdestvensky's. Over the incandescent singing of the choir, the four excellent soloists give radiant performances, with the golden-toned soprano, Janice Watson, regularly crowning the mood of ecstasy in her solos. Full, glowing, atmospheric sound to match.

Requiem; Take him, earth, for cherishing.
*** United Recordings Dig. 88033 [id.]. Sally Barber, Julia Field, Mark Johnstone, Andrew Angus, Vasari, Jeremy Backhouse – MARTIN: *Mass.* ***

The Howells *Requiem* paved the way for *Hymnus Paradisi* and is a work of considerable beauty. The Chandos version (CHAN 9019) coupled it with two fine motets with organ, *The House of the mind* and *A Sequence for St Michael*, along with some Vaughan Williams. Here, the soloists and Vasari, a choir conducted by Jeremy Backhouse, are absolutely first class and give a well-nigh exemplary performance, possibly finer than its immediate rival. Doubtless couplings will resolve the matter of choice. The present disc offers the *Requiem* in harness with another Mass from the inter-war years by Frank Martin.

Stabat Mater.
*** Chan. Dig. CHAN 9314 [id.]. Neill Archer, London Symphony Ch., LSO, Rozhdestvensky.

Completed and performed in 1965, when the composer was seventy-three, the *Stabat Mater* was Howells' last major work. This is a setting of the well-known text which outshines almost any other in its passionate involvement. Though the ecstasy is not as consistently sustained as in the earlier *Missa Sabrinensis*, with many more passages of hushed devotion, one registers with new intensity the agony of St John the Divine at the foot of the Cross, the companion of the Virgin Mary. The saint is personified in the tenor solos, here sung superbly by Neill Archer with a clear, heady tone, starting with his first thrilling entry on *O quam tristis*. As in the *Missa*, Rozhdestvensky proves the most passionate advocate, magnetically leading one through the whole rich score. Though ensemble sometimes suffers, it is a small price to pay for such thrusting, spontaneous-sounding conviction. Glowing, rich sound.

Hummel, Johann (1778–1837)

Clarinet quartet in E flat.
(M) *** O-L 444 167-2 [id.]. Alan Hacker, The Music Party – WEBER: *Clarinet quintet.* ***

A delectable work, played as beautifully as the Weber coupling. Alan Hacker uses a Goulding clarinet *circa* 1880, and this would be the sound Hummel himself would have recognized. Hacker plays allegros with plenty of character and spirit and, at times, a winning bite on the timbre, yet there is plenty of warmth in the lyrical music. The Music Party also use original instruments and their positive approach brings a matching touch of abrasiveness but no lack of feeling. Lovers of the authentic style will find this very stimulating.

Humperdinck, Engelbert (1854–1921)

The Bluebird: Prelude; Star dance. Hänsel und Gretel: Overture. Königskinder: Overture; Preludes to Acts II & III. The Sleeping Beauty: suite.
(M) **(*) Virgin/EMI Dig. CUV5 61128-2 [id.]. Bamberg SO, Karl Anton Rickenbacher.

By far the most memorable piece here is the *Hänsel und Gretel Overture*, although the Introduction to Act III of *Königskinder* is also very touching, characteristically using horns to evoke the Minstrel's last song. The *Overture* to the same opera is significant in demonstrating Humperdinck's characteristic failing – a prolixity of ideas, none of which is quite memorable enough to emerge from the ongoing energy of the writing. His post-Wagnerian orchestration can be too thick and this inhibits his festive pieces, but the lightly scored items have charm, for instance the *Star dance* from *The Bluebird* or the *Ballade* from *The Sleeping Beauty*. Rickenbacher secures warm, cultured playing from his Bambergers, and the Virgin sound is full and pleasing if lacking just a little in sparkle. Worth trying at mid-price.

Hänsel und Gretel (complete).
*** Teldec/Warner Dig.4509 94549-2 (2) [id.]. Larmore, Ziesak, Schwarz, Weikl, Behrens, Tölz Boys' Ch., Bav. RSO, Runnicles.
*** Ph. Dig. 438 013-2 (2) [id.]. Murray, Gruberová, Ludwig, Gwyneth Jones, Grundheber, Bonney, Oelze, Dresden State O, Sir Colin Davis.
(M) **(*) RCA 74321 25281-2 (2). Moffo, Donath, Fischer-Dieskau, Berthold, Ludwig, Augér, Popp, Bav. R. Ch. & RSO, Eichhorn.

The success of the Teldec version of *Hänsel und Gretel* is largely due to Donald Runnicles, who here makes a very impressive recording début in a major opera set. He has a lighter touch than his direct rivals, regularly favouring faster speeds than the others, including Tate (EMI CDS7 54022-2), whose recording was made with the same orchestra in the same venue, but is mellower, less sharply focused than this. The lightness and refinement of the playing bring transparent textures and the most delicate pianissimos. So far from reducing the impact of the performance, the lightness goes with an element of fantasy delightfully in keeping with the fairy-tale atmosphere. That approach finds a fulfilment in the waltz of triumph after the witch's death, which at a fast speed has a delicious Viennese lilt. In the *Witch's ride* Runnicles brings out a sinister snarl in the horns, and in the woodwind solos of the prelude to Act II, simulating birdsong, Runnicles adds to the fantasy by giving his soloists an extra degree of freedom, encouraging individual expressiveness. The lightness and transparency of the orchestral sound goes with a less forward balance, giving the voices extra prominence. In the casting the emphasis more than ever is on fresh, youthful voices. So it was too with Barbara Bonney and Anne Sofie von Otter in the Tate set, but here the distinction between boy and girl is if anything even more sharply drawn. Ruth Ziesak as Gretel and Jennifer Larmore as Hansel are above all natural-sounding, with little or no feeling of mature opera-singers pretending to be children, yet with no sense of strain and none of the edginess.

Fresh clarity marks the other voices too, even that of the Witch as taken by Hanna Schwarz. Though aptly she uses a croaking voice, it is no more exaggerated vocally than the funny voice she would have adopted as Octavian in the Mariandl episode of *Rosenkavalier*. Coupled with Runnicles' approach, it makes the witch sharply sinister without being too frightening. Schwarz was the Mother in the Tate set, and here Hildegard Behrens is comparably strong and characterful, with Bernd Weikl firm and dark as the Father, while young voices are chosen for the two incidental roles of Sandman and Dew Fairy. Rosemary Joshua makes a welcome recording début in opera as a bright-toned Sandman and Christine Schafer, fuller and firmer, is warmly contrasted as the Dew Fairy. On balance a first recommendation, the set brings incidentally a fascinating supplement in a brief orchestral coda, just over a minute long, which Humperdinck wrote in 1894 for a production of the opera in Dessau with Cosima Wagner as director. Ingeniously he has the Dessau national anthem set in counterpoint against various themes from the opera, with toy trumpets providing a commentary.

Sir Colin Davis has rarely conducted a more glowing opera performance on record than this. It is his inspired direction, beautifully paced, as though captured live, which above all compels attention. The performance culminates in a final reference back to the *Evening hymn* theme at the very end which in its soaring crescendo brings a genuine gulp of fulfilment, such as one experiences in a fine performance in the theatre. Though in beauty of timbre neither Edita Gruberová nor Ann Murray can quite match their principal rivals on disc, the contrast of timbre between the bright, sometimes edgy sound of Gruberová and the plainer sound of Murray is always very clearly defined, and their sharp characterization and feeling for words seals that distinction. The *Evening hymn* is raptly done at the gentlest possible pianissimo, and there is tremendous swagger in the pair's celebrations after the witch is dead. There is comparable casting for both the Mother and the Witch. Dame Gwyneth Jones could not be more positive as the Mother, singing so as to cut through all textures. And though under pressure the voice acquires a characteristic beat, the pitching is always clear and defined. Christa Ludwig gives a similarly positive and characterful performance as the Witch, putting over both the melodramatic and the comic moments with superb timing. Franz Grundheber makes a clean-toned Father, while Barbara Bonney, Gretel for Tate, here becomes the Sandman, sweetly expressive, and Christiane Oelze's light, bright soprano is most apt for the Dew Fairy. Recorded in the Lukaskirche, the sound gives plenty of bloom on voices and orchestra, though with the focus less sharp than in Runnicles' Teldec version.

There are some fine solo performances on the mid-priced 1971 RCA set, notably from Helen Donath as Gretel and Christa Ludwig as the Witch; and Kurt Eichhorn's direction is vigorous, with excellent orchestral playing and full, atmospheric recording. It is a pity that a more boyish-sounding singer than Anna Moffo could not have been chosen for the role of Hänsel but, all told, this is a colourful and enjoyable account of a unique, eternally fresh opera, well worth considering.

d'India, Sigismondo (*c.* 1582–*c.* 1630)

Il primo Libro de Madrigali (1606): *Interdette speranz'e van desio. Ottavo Libro de Madrigali: Il pastor fido,* Act IV, Scene 9: *Se tu, Silvio crudel, mi saetti* (five madrigal cycle).
⊛ (M) *** Virgin Veritas/EMI Dig. VER5 61165-2 [id.]. Chiaroscuro, L. Baroque, Nigel Rogers –
MONTEVERDI: *Madrigals.* *** ⊛

The juxtaposition of contemporaries is always fascinating, and this collection shows how much d'India and Monteverdi had in common, yet establishes clearly their individual musical personalities. The programme is described by Tim Carter, the writer of the accompanying notes, as representing the late-Renaissance 'Mannerist School', when the North Italian courts provided a haven for their recruited composers to experiment, sometimes audaciously. The opening piece, d'India's *Interdette speranz'e van desio* ('Forbidden hopes and vain desire'), is certainly freely set, and is stimulating as well as beautiful, but it is in the cycle from his Eighth Book of Madrigals, *Se tu, Silvio crudel, mi saetti,* that one experiences not only the composer's lyrical originality to the full but also his affinity with the operatic writing of his greater contemporary, Monteverdi. Here d'India exploits the full possibilities of the emotional drama of the unfortunate Silvio and his beloved Dorinda after he has wounded her in the thigh in a hunting accident. The vocal dialogue (which alternates, often subtly, solo and ensemble singing) expresses disdain and anger, love, pain and fear of death; and d'India's setting is touching and dramatic by turns, and also requires effortless vocal virtuosity. Chiaroscuro includes names like Patrizia Kwella, Wendy Burger, Charles Brett, Nigel Rogers and David Thomas; and here the quality of the performances is superlative, refined without a hint of preciosity, and always alive. The accompaniments on theorbo and harpsichord are delicately balanced, while the recording is immaculately realistic. An outstanding collection in every way.

(i) *Madrigals for 5 voices: Book No. 8* (complete); Solo madrigals and chamber duets: (ii) *Che farai, Meliseo?;* (iii) *Da l'onde del mio pianto;* (iv) *Odi quel rosignuolo;* (ii) *Qual fiera sì crudel?.* Duets: (iv; v) *Alla guerra d'amor; La mia Filli crudel; La Virtù.*
(M) *** O-L Dig. 444 168-2 [id.]. (i) Kirkby, Tubb, Nichols, Cornwell, King, Wistreich; (ii) David Thomas; (iii) Martyn Hill; (iv) Emma Kirkby; (v) Judith Nelson; Cons. of Musicke, Rooley.

Sigismondo d'India was among the vanguard of the new movement founded by Monteverdi at the beginning of the seventeenth century, and his laments show him a considerable master of expressive resource. He is highly responsive to the emotions of the poetry, and the harmonies and the unpredictable lines make this music fascinating. The performances of the complete five-part madrigals from Book 8 (1624) are authoritative, though there are moments of slightly self-conscious rubato that hold up the flow. The recording could be more spacious and warmer; despite that qualification, this is thoroughly recommendable, made the more so by the additional, earlier, solo madrigals (from 1609 and 1621) and chamber duets (1615). Those for male voices are essentially melancholy, but Emma Kirkby soon brightens things up with her sparkling, highly decorated nightingale song, and the female duets, '*My cruel Phyllis*' and '*To the war of love*', are very lively indeed. The CD transfers give an excellent natural presence.

d'Indy, Vincent (1851–1931)

(i) *Fantasy on French popular themes* (for oboe and orchestra), *Op. 31. Saugelfleurie* (Legend after a tale by Robert de Bonnières); *Tableaux de voyage, Op. 36; L'Etranger: Prelude to Act II. Fervaal: Prelude to Act I.*
** Marco Polo Dig. 8.223659 [id.]. (i) Philippe Cousu; Württemberg PO, Gilles Nopre, or (i) Jean-Marc Burfin.

The tone-poem, *Saugelfleurie*, based on a tale by Robert de Bonnières and dating from 1884, is the earliest piece on this CD and is not otherwise available at present. Not that much of this repertoire suffers from duplication: the *Tableaux de voyage* were once available on an EMI issue under Pierre Dervaux. But the last time the lovely *Prelude to Act I* of *Fervaal* was in the British catalogues was from Munch on a Decca 78-r.p.m. disc, and under Monteux. It is unaccountable that music of this quality, which also has the seeds of popularity, is so parlously neglected. New to the catalogue is the *Fantaisie sur des thèmes populaires françaises* for oboe and orchestra, which should be sought out by players: it has a fervent charm which is very winning. The performances of all these pieces are variable; they fall short of distinction but are more than routine. The recording, too, is eminently satisfactory and aficionados of French music need not hesitate.

Jour d'été à la montagne, Op. 61; (i) Symphonie sur un chant montagnard français, Op. 25.
** Erato/Warner Dig. 2292 45821-2 [id.].(i) Catherine Collard; R. France PO, Janowski.

The Erato disc is worth having for the sake of *Jour d'été à la montagne*, one of d'Indy's most inspired pieces. This version is artistically superior to the rival under Pierre Dervaux on EMI, though the late lamented Catherine Collard's version of the *Symphonie sur un chant montagnard français*, sometimes known as the *Symphonie Cévenole*, is handicapped by some unsympathetic accompanying from Janowski and a synthetic balance which does not allow the sound to expand. Good playing from the Orchestre Philharmonique de Radio France.

Symphonie sur un chant montagnard français.
(M) **(*) RCA 09026 62582-2 [id.]. Henriot-Schweitzer, Boston SO, Charles Munch – BERLIOZ: *Harold in Italy*. *(*)
(BB) **(*) Naxos 8.550754 [id.]. Thiollier, Nat. SO of Ireland, Antonio de Almeida – FAURE: *Ballade;* FRANCK: *Symphonic variations.* **(*)

The RCA is the same performance as that coupled with the Monteux version of the César Franck *Symphony* (and discussed in our main volume). Nicole Henriot-Schweitzer's playing is often exquisite – which is more than can be said of the bass-light piano, for which some allowances have to be made. Munch gets responsive support from the Boston Symphony. In any event, this is a good version which otherwise offers considerable artistic satisfaction. Late-1950s recording, but very acceptable sound.

On Naxos the French-born but American-trained François-Joël Thiollier gives an intelligent performance of the *Symphonie sur un chant montagnard*. Perfectly acceptable, perfectly well accompanied and decently recorded (though the soloist is rather forwardly placed by the engineers) and with an interesting coupling. It is worth the money, but there are finer accounts to be had, some (like Jean-Yves Thibaudet) at full-price.

Ippolitov-Ivanov, Mikhail (1859–1935)

Caucasian sketches, Op. 10.
*** Chan. Dig. CHAN 9321 [id.]. BBC PO, Fedor Glushchenko – KHACHATURIAN: *Symphony No. 3 etc.* ***

After studies in St Petersburg with Rimsky-Korsakov, Ippolitov-Ivanov became director of the Tblisi Academy of Music in Georgia when he was only twenty-four. His famous *Caucasian sketches* include folksongs from both Georgia and Armenia. In 1893 (the year of Tchaikovsky's death) he became professor of composition at the Moscow Conservatory and later its director, and he was responsible for the first performances of a number of Rimsky-Korsakov's operas, including *The Tsar's Bride* and *The Tale of Tsar Saltan*. Once a popular repertory piece, the colourful *Caucasian sketches* have fallen out of favour; only the final *Procession of the Sardar* is generously represented on CD. The present version by the BBC Philharmonic under Fedor Glushchenko is generally superior to the only other alternative on ASV (see our main volume).

Liturgy of St John Chrysostom, Op. 37; Vespers, Op. 43.
*** Sony Dig. SMK 64091 [id.]. Lege Artis Chamber Ch., Boris Analyan.

Ippolitov-Ivanov's devotional music was not only completely neglected but was forgotten even by specialists during the Soviet era, and it was not until the collapse of the USSR that it was rediscovered. These are beautiful pieces, not as profound, powerful or soulful as either Tchaikovsky's or Rachmaninov's settings, but well worth having. A useful and pleasing addition to the catalogue. The Lege Artis Chamber Choir rise excellently to the not inconsiderable demands made on them, and the recording has an appropriately warm acoustic.

Ireland, John (1879–1962)

Concertino pastorale; Downland suite (arr. composer and Geoffrey Bush); *Orchestral poem; 2 Symphonic studies* (arr. Geoffrey Bush).
*** Chan. Dig. CHAN 9376 [id.]. City of L. Sinfonia, Richard Hickox.

An outstanding disc: the finest recorded collection of Ireland's orchestral music ever. It is beautifully played and gloriously recorded. The valedictory *Threnody* of the *Concertino pastorale* and the lovely *Elegy* from the *Downland suite* show the composer at his most lyrically inspired, and the rapt playing here does them full justice: the *Threnody* is infinitely touching. The early *Orchestral poem* (1904) is a surprisingly powerful work as presented here with great passion, with splendid brass writing at its climax. There is a hint of Vaughan Williams in the quieter central section. The two *Symphonic studies* come from film music Ireland wrote for *The Overlanders*, not incorporated into the concert suites: the brass chromatics in the first have a familiar ring, the second has a wild momentum, recalling the cattle stampede in the film, but both stand up well as independent concert pieces.

PIANO MUSIC

April; The darkened valley; Green Ways (The cherry tree; Cypress; The palm and May); In those days (Daydream; Meridian); London pieces (Chelsea Reach; Ragamuffin; Soho forenoons); 3 Pastels (A Grecian lad; The boy bishop; Puck's birthday); Preludes (The undertone; Obsession; The holy boy; Fire of spring); A Sea idyll; Summer evening; The towing path.
(B) **(*) CfP Dig. CD-CFP 4674; *TC-CFP 4674*. Desmond Wright.

With full-bodied piano-sound, this very welcome disc of Ireland's piano music was recorded in Switzerland, 20 pieces in all – five groups of pieces, plus five separate ones. Though Eric Parkin has over the years recorded a far wider range of Ireland's piano music, this selection on CfP brings together most of the favourites, like *Ragamuffin* from the *London pieces* and *The holy boy*, hauntingly lyrical, the third of the four *Preludes*. *The darkened valley* and *The towing path*, too, show Ireland at his most tenderly expressive. Though Desmond Wright is not always gentle enough in his treatment, these are fresh, responsive performances which gather together some of the most appealing English piano music written this century, too long neglected.

Ives, Charles (1874–1954)

Symphony No. 3 (The camp meeting); 3 Places in New England; Set No. 1; A Set of pieces; The unanswered question.
*** DG Dig. 439 869-2 [id.]. Orpheus CO.

A good introduction to this maverick figure whose work often fascinates more than it satisfies. The Orpheus Chamber Orchestra never cease to amaze and their playing here is of their usual stunning order of accomplishment and artistry. Their account of the *Third Symphony* is as good as any in the catalogue, and the same goes for their evocative and imaginative accounts of the companion pieces.

Janáček, Leoš (1854–1928)

Violin concerto (Pilgrimage of the soul) (reconstructed Faltus & Stědrů).
*** Teldec/Warner Dig. 4509 97449-2 [id.]. Zehetmair, Philh. O, Holliger – HARTMANN: *Concerto funèbre;* BERG: *Violin concerto.* ***

In his last year Janáček worked on his opera, *From the House of the Dead*, based on Dostoevsky, the autograph score of which contains sketches for a violin concerto he had planned to call *Pilgrimage of the soul*. He used some of its ideas in the overture to the opera, but the concerto remained in fragmentary form. On his death, his pupil, Břetislav Bakala, who had seen the opera through the press, prepared a performing version of the piece. The present version, the work of Leoš Faltus and Miloš Stědrů, revived interest in the piece when it was premièred in 1988, and there are two rival accounts currently on the market (from Josef Suk on Supraphon and Christian Tetzlaff on Virgin). This is highly original music, with some delightful lyrical ideas, imaginatively scored, albeit also with moments of top-heavy orchestral writing, searing in its intensity – particularly as played here by Thomas Zehetmair and the Philharmonia under Heinz Holliger. Excellent recorded sound. This is a most rewarding triptych, well worth exploring at mid-price.

Sinfonietta.
(M) *** EMI Dig. CDM7 64740-2 [id.]. Philh. O, Rattle – HOLST: *Planets.* **(*)
(M) *** DG Dig. 445 501-2 [id.]. BPO, Abbado – BARTOK: *The Miraculous Mandarin* etc. ***
*** Sony Dig. SK 47182 [id.]. LSO, Tilson Thomas – *Glagolitic·Mass.* ***
** Decca Dig. 436 211-2 [id.]. Montreal SO, Dutoit – *Glagolitic Mass.* **

Rattle gets an altogether first-class response from the Philharmonia Orchestra and truthful yet vivid Kingsway Hall recording. His account is among the very best this work has received, but the new mid-priced Holst coupling is at a rather lower level of intensity and is less sharply defined as a recording.

Abbado's DG recording was made in 1987, some two decades after his admirable Decca version with the LSO. Now he has the advantage of digital recording and the Berlin Philharmonic Orchestra on splendid form. The Jesus-Christus Kirche provides a superbly spacious sonority for the brass. The opening of the Berlin performance brings a tautening of the pace, but the interpretation is not greatly changed and the subtleties of colour are not diminished by the more robust body of the newer version.

A strong, bold and brassy performance from Tilson Thomas, with the LSO at their virtuoso best, helped by very full recorded sound, bright as well as weighty. However, fine though this is, it would not be preferable to Rattle or to Abbado. Even more than in the *Mass* which, as with the Tilson Thomas version, comes as coupling, Dutoit is a little too civilized in his treatment of this wild music, sumptuous as the sound is.

Sinfonietta; Taras Bulba.
(M) (*) Ph. 442 660-2 [id.]. Rotterdam PO, Zinman – DVORAK: *Czech suite.* **

It is the mark of a complete lack of impact in a performance of Janáček's *Sinfonietta* when the most memorable movements are the second (*Andante*) and the fourth (*Allegretto*). The refined orchestral playing and the distanced, warmly atmospheric sound-picture take all the abrasive edge from the music, and *Taras Bulba* also projects little sense of villainy in a piece where the hero is nailed to a tree and set on fire!

Suite for string orchestra.
(BB) *** Discover Dig. DICD 920234 [id.]. Virtuosi di Praga, Vlček – SUK: *Serenade for strings* etc. ***

The expanded Virtuosi di Praga give an appropriately ardent and certainly a bravura account of Janáček's six-movement *Suite for string orchestra*, an early work (1893) yet one full of melodic diversity and individuality. The recording shows this group of seventeen players (including the leader/director, Oldřich Vlček) as possessing a vividly full sonority, yet they do not miss the work's more subtle touches, and this inexpensive disc is a welcome addition to the catalogue.

Taras Bulba.
** Ph. Dig. 432 983-2 [id.]. Leipzig GO, Masur – *Glagolitic Mass.* **

A good fill-up, warmly played, for Masur's amiable, civilized reading of the *Mass*. The mellowness of the recording undermines the bite of the music.

CHAMBER MUSIC

(i; iii) *Allegro; Dumka; Romance; Sonata* (for violin and piano); (ii; iii) *Pohádka (Fairy tale); Presto* (for cello and piano); (iii) (Piano) *In the mists; 3 Moravian dances; On an overgrown path, Series I–II; Paralipomena; Reminiscence; Piano sonata in E flat min. (I. X. 1905); Theme and variations (Zdenka's variations).*
** BIS Dig. CD 663/664 [id.]. (i) Ulf Wallin; (ii) Mats Rondin; (iii) Roland Pöntinen.

The BIS label offers an excellent collection of Janáček's music for violin, cello and – above all – piano that more than holds its own with the competition. It ranges from the earliest, the *Romance* for violin and piano from the late 1870s, to the last, the *Reminiscence* for piano, written in the last year of his life. The only alternative versions of the latter are from Firkušný on DG 429 857-2 (reviewed in our main volume) or Mikhail Rudy (EMI CDC7 54094-2). True, Pöntinen's playing, good though it is, does not possess the depth of insight of a Firkušný or, indeed, of his young Norwegian colleague, Leif Ove Andsnes. At the same time he is an unfailingly intelligent player. Ulf Wallin proves a strong yet sensitive advocate of the *Violin Sonata*, and the cellist Mats Rondin is no less admirable in the *Pohádka (Fairy tale)* and the *Presto* for cello and piano. Those wanting the set primarily for the piano music would be better served by either of the Firkušný sets or the Andsnes recital (Virgin VC7 59639-2 – see our main volume), but readers wanting the whole collection may rest assured that both playing and recording are of a generally high standard.

(i; ii) *Concertino;* (ii) *Mládi;* (i) *In the mists.*
(m) **(*) EMI CDM5 65304-2 [id.]. (i) Lamar Crowson; (ii) Melos Ens. – NIELSEN: *Wind quintet.*
***

The Melos Ensemble give a very characterful account of *Mládi* which holds up well against current alternatives. Composed in Janáček's seventieth year, *Mládi* is a remarkable evocation of youth. The analogue recording, made in the late 1960s, is very good indeed, as it is in the *Concertino* for piano, clarinet, bassoon, horn, two violins and viola, written the following year. Lamar Crowson is completely inside the idiom here and in sensitivity and imagination is second to none. Likewise *In the mists* is poetic and unfailingly perceptive and withstands comparison with both Firkušný, Andsnes and others, save for one reservation concerning the recording: the piano is not in ideal condition and there could be more space round the sound. This does not apply in the *Concertino*, which sounds suitably vibrant.

Glagolitic Mass (original version, ed. Wingfield).
*** Chan. Dig. CHAN 9310[id.]. Kiberg, Stene, Svensson, Cold, Danish Nat. R. Ch. & SO,
  Mackerras – KODALY: *Psalmus hungaricus.* ***

Though there are many fine versions of what has now become a favourite choral work, Sir Charles Mackerras's with Danish forces on Chandos has the edge over all of them. That is partly because of the text used, newly re-edited, with many amendments that reinforce the work's biting modernity. The scholar, Paul Wingfield, has managed to reconstruct Janáček's original score, before it was simplified for the first inadequate performers, and without the unauthorized amendments made in the published score after the composer's death. The added rhythmic complexities of this version, as interpreted idiomatically by Mackerras, often adopting speeds faster than usual, encourage an apt wildness which brings an exuberant, carefree quality to writing which here, more than ever, seems like the inspiration of the moment. The wildness is also reinforced by having the *Intrada* at the very beginning, before the Introduction, as well as at the end. There is no finer Janáček interpreter than Mackerras, and this is among his finest Janáček recordings. The chorus sings incisively with incandescent tone, and the tenor soloist, Peter Svensson, by far the most important of the four, has a trumpet-toned precision that makes light of the high tessitura and the stratospheric leaps that Janáček asks for. The soprano Tina Kiberg, also bright and clear rather than beautiful in tone, makes just as apt a choice. The mezzo, Randi Stene, is excellent, and only a certain unsteadiness in Ulrik Cold's relatively light bass tone prevents this from being an ideal quartet. The coupling is unexpected but very illuminating, again with the choir and tenor soloist aptly cast. Recorded sound of a weight and warmth that convey the full power of the music. Only the organ solo of the penultimate movement lacks a little in bite, thanks to a backward balance, even if it makes up in clarity.

Glagolitic Mass.
*** Sony Dig. SK 47182 [id.]. Beňačková, Palmer, Lakes, Kotcherga, Scott, London Symphony Ch.,
  LSO, Tilson Thomas – *Sinfonietta.* ***.
** Decca Dig. 436 211-2[id.]. Troitskaya, Randova, Kaludov, Leiferkus, Montreal Ch. & SO, Dutoit
  – *Sinfonietta.* **

** Ph. Dig. 432 983-2[id.]. Hruba, Lang, Mitchinson, Adam, Leipzig GO, Masur – *Taras Bulba*. **

Tilson Thomas directs a powerful, virtuoso performance of the normal published score, superbly played and sung, and helped by full, weighty recorded sound. The soprano solos are both idiomatic and beautiful as sung by Beňačková, unsurpassed by any rival; and Gary Lakes, though not quite idiomatic, uses his clean-cut, firm Heldentenor tone in the important tenor solos with no strain whatever. The London Symphony Chorus is magnificent, and the LSO plays brilliantly in every department, not least in the woodwind and brass, with the brightness of the sound adding to the impact. An excellent version if you want the *Sinfonietta* as coupling, though Rattle on EMI is in some ways more individual.

Dutoit's disc might be considered, were there not such strong competition, notably from Rattle and Tilson Thomas in this same coupling. Though the sound is sumptuous and full in the Montreal manner, the performance lacks something of the wildness and animal vigour that is essential in Janáček, sometimes even sounding Ravelian.

Masur conducts his Leipzig forces in a warm, amiable performance, matched by recorded sound – with the chorus sounding mellow – that melds textures together rather than giving them the bite that Janáček really needs. As in the Rattle version, John Mitchinson takes the important tenor solos, but here he sounds less steady and more strained. This is otherwise civilized music-making; but in such a competitive field the disc is hardly a first choice, even for anyone who specially wants this coupling.

OPERA

The excursions of Mr Brouček (complete).
*** Sup. 11 2153-2 (2) [id.]. Přibyl, Svejda, Jonášová, Czech PO Ch. & O, Jílek.
(**) Orfeo mono C 354942 (2) [id.]. Fehenberger, Wunderlich, Lipp, Bav. State Op. Ch. & O,
    Keilberth.

The appearance of František Jílek's sparkling, keenly idiomatic performance on CD fills an important gap in the catalogue. Unlike the previous Supraphon recording on LP, this one is complete, where previously, with the Neumann set, cuts were made in such passages as the religious discussion in the second part. Though Janáček seems to have intended the opera as a biting satire, this performance comes over more gently and with real charm, thanks to the understanding conducting of Jílek, but also to the characterization of the central character, the bumbling, accident-prone Mr Brouček (literally Mr Beetle). Vilém Přibyl portrays him as an amiable, much-put-upon figure as he makes his excursions, visiting the moon in the first half (signal for some effective send-ups of artists) and to Prague at the time of the Hussite Wars in the second, with any wear on the voice adding to the characterfulness. With each part just over an hour long, the opera fits neatly on to two discs, reinforcing the point that it is in many ways more effective on CD than on stage: the complicated exchanges are clearly identifiable, thanks to the libretto, while the big team of Czech singers (doubling up roles in the different parts, with Vladimir Krejčik remarkable in no fewer than seven of them) are outstanding, bringing out both the warmth and sense of fun behind the writing. The result is a delight, as sharp and distinctive as any Janáček opera. The analogue recording, made in Prague in 1980, is full and atmospheric with a fine sense of presence on CD.

Recorded live in Munich in 1959, using a German translation, the Orfeo set can be recommended only to German speakers, particularly when no libretto is provided. Though the cast includes a high proportion of star singers, notably the much-lamented Fritz Wunderlich as Mazal giving a delightful performance, Keilberth fails to capture the necessary Czech flavour, warm as his conducting is.

From the House of the Dead (complete).
** Sup. 10 2941-2 (2) [id.]. Novák, Jirglová, Přibyl, Zídek, Horaček, Souček, Czech PO Ch. & O,
    Neumann.

Recorded in 1979, a few months before the classic Decca set conducted by Mackerras, this Czech version of Janáček's last opera offers a strongly cast, idiomatic performance, with many of the same soloists generally taking different roles. For all its many qualities, for a number of reasons this is not a serious rival to the Decca set. In the central role of Goryanchikov, Richard Novák is less steady than Jedlička on Decca, and Milada Jirglová, fruity and wobbly, is even less convincing as the boy, Aljeja, than her opposite number. The Decca on two discs (430 375-2) also offers two valuable extras in *Říkadla* and *Mládí*, while providing fuller, better-focused sound. The Supraphon is too reverberant for so claustrophobic a subject. Voices tend to be set well forward of the orchestra, which tends to mask the differences in the version of the score used by Neumann, not the Kubelik edition favoured by Mackerras, which aims at re-creating Janáček's spare original scoring, but the more conventional orchestration of Chlubna and Bakala, if without Chlubna's sentimental ending.

Johansen, David Monrad (1888–1974)

String quartet, Op. 36.
(BB) *** Naxos Dig. 8.550879 [id.]. Oslo String Qt – GRIEG: *String quartets.* ***

David Monrad Johansen was an important figure in Norwegian musical life during the 1930s and his symphonic poem, *Pan* (1939), dedicated to Knut Hamsen, with its keen feeling for the Norwegian landscape, was a key work in its time. Monrad Johansen was better known, however, for his biography of Grieg and as a writer on music. (Rightly or wrongly, he came under something of a cloud after the war for his role during the Nazi occupation.) His *String quartet*, composed in 1969 when in his early eighties, is persuasively played by the Oslo String Quartet and is impeccably recorded. It is a well-crafted piece but not as distinctively personal as *Pan* or the best of his mature works.

Kabalevsky, Dmitri (1904–87)

Piano concertos Nos. (i) *2;* (ii) *3;* (iii) *4.*
* Olympia stereo/mono OCD 269 [id.]. (i) Nikolai Petrov; (ii) Emil Gilels; (iii) Yuri Popov; (i; iii) Moscow PO, (ii) Large R. & TV SO; (i) Dmitri Kitaenko, (ii–iii) composer.

The listener coming afresh to the *Piano concerto No. 2* would be forgiven for believing the composer to be a Prokofiev clone. Save for the fact that the ideas lack Prokofiev's strong profile, the work is almost wholly derivative. The main attraction here is the opportunity to hear Gilels playing the *Third Piano concerto* (1952) under the composer's own baton, only two years after its composition. But not even Gilels's magic can make anything of this trivial and insubstantial piece. Like Nikolai Petrov's performance of the *Second*, Yuri Popov's account of the *Fourth* (1979) was recorded in the early 1980s. Written for a piano competition in Prague, it aspires to – but nowhere near achieves – the character and simplicity of, say, Shostakovich's *Second Piano concerto*. The invention has facility but no substance. Shallow, brash recording.

Symphonies Nos. 1 in C sharp min., Op. 18; 2 in C min., Op. 19.
** Olympia Dig. OCD 268 [id.]. Szeged PO, Acél.

Kabalevsky was twenty-eight when he composed his two-movement *First Symphony*, and its musical language reflects something of the outlook of Miaskovsky, with whom he studied, having a well-planned sense of pace and a strong feeling for form. Its ideas unfold naturally and the musical procedures have real dignity, even if some of the material of the finale is banal. The *Second Symphony* followed two years later, in 1934, and was Kabalevsky's first major work, apart from *Colas Breugnon*, to make an impact outside the then Soviet Union. It is both more individual and tautly argued. The pianist, Murray McLachlan, who contributes an excellent note, sums up the first movement as containing 'all the features one generally associates with this composer's "harlequinesque" style . . . with lots of busy passage-work, quicksilver modulations, and a second group reminiscent of Poulenc'. Good, though not first-class, performances from the Szeged Philharmonic Orchestra under Erwin Acél (though the opening of the *Second Symphony* is nicely alert); however, the recording is handicapped by a rather cramped and constricted acoustic.

24 Preludes, Op. 38; Sonata No. 3, Op. 46; Sonatina in C, Op. 13/1.
*** Olympia Dig. OCD 266 [id.]. Murray McLachlan.

Murray McLachlan makes out a persuasive case for Kabalevsky's *24 Preludes*, Op. 38 (1943), both in his scholarly but enthusiastic liner-note and, more importantly, at the keyboard. He calls it 'a major contribution to the piano literature with immediate and popular appeal' – and almost convinces the listener that it is. There is a similarity to the Chopin *Preludes* in that the cycle contains a prelude in every key, arranged through the cycle of fifths in relative major and minor keys, but there it ends. Each of the preludes is based on a folk tune, mostly drawn from Rimsky-Korsakov's collection, and in *No. 13 in F sharp minor* we encounter the theme made famous by Stravinsky in the closing bars of *Firebird*. Closely akin to Prokofiev and Shostakovich in idiom, the set undoubtedly deserves wider recognition (this is the only recording currently available) and McLachlan does the set with great fluency and clarity of articulation. He also gives us two of Kabalevsky's best-known piano pieces, the *Sonatina* (1930) and the *Piano Sonata No. 3* (1946) with its Prokofievian middle movement, which both Horowitz and Moiseiwitsch recorded not long after the war. (Horowitz apparently played the *Preludes* as well in private recitals.) In the *Sonata*, Pizarro (see below) is the more imaginative in his handling of tone-colour and dynamic range. The piano-sound is decent but could do with greater transparency and bloom. All the same, it would be invidious to withhold a three-star grading.

Piano sonatas Nos. 1 in F, Op. 6; 2 in E flat, Op. 45; 3 in F, Op. 46; 4 Preludes, Op. 5; Recitative and Rondo, Op. 84.
*** Collins Dig. 1418-2 [id.]. Artur Pizarro.

Artur Pizarro was the 1990 Leeds Prize-winner and has already recorded a distinguished Rodrigo collection, the Scriabin *Mazurkas* and a Liszt recital on this label. On the present disc he collects the three Kabalevsky *Sonatas*, together with the early *Four Preludes*, Op. 5, and a *Recitative and Rondo* dating from 1967, the fiftieth anniversary of the October Revolution. The *Sonata No. 1 in F*, Op. 6, was composed in 1927 while Kabalevsky was still a pupil of Miaskovsky, and its opening reflects not only the latter's influence but, even more so, that of Scriabin. Pizarro makes much more of the *Third Sonata* than McLachlan and gives a highly polished account of all the pieces recorded here. Kabalevsky was an extremely facile and cultured composer, urbane and fluent rather than profound, his individuality far less developed than that of Prokofiev, Shostakovich or Miaskovsky. But nevertheless there is much here to give pleasure, particularly when it is played with such elegance. The piano-sound is truthful and reasonably fresh, though there is perhaps more resonance than some will like. Recommended.

Kalinnikov, Vasily (1866–1901)

Symphony No. 2 in A.
(*) Russian Disc mono RDCD 11155 [id.]. Leningrad PO, Yevgeni Mravinsky – GLAZUNOV: *The Seasons.* *(*)

Yevgeni Mravinsky's vital and masterly account of Kalinnikov's *Second Symphony* comes in harness with his 1953 recording of Glazunov's ballet, *The Seasons*. Though much later (1969), this recording is also mono and calls for much greater tolerance; it suffers from considerable congestion, discoloration and, as far as the strings are concerned, want of bloom above the stave. Really not recommendable at full (or any) price. Readers are referred to our main volume.

Khachaturian, Aram (1903–78)

Cello concerto in E min.; Concerto-rhapsody for cello and orchestra in D min.
**(*) Olympia Dig. OCD 539 [id.]. Marina Tarasova, Russian SO, Veronica Dudarova.

As with the case of the Miaskovsky CD which Tarasova has made with Yevgeny Samoilov and the Moscow Opera Orchestra, this issue is logically coupled and gives us both of Khachaturian's major works for the instrument. The *Cello concerto* (1946) is the last (and, to be frank, the least successful) of the three solo concertos he composed; he similarly planned three one-movement *Concerto-rhapsodies*. The present *Concerto-rhapsody for cello and orchestra in D minor* comes from 1963 and was first given by Rostropovich in London. Marina Tarasova plays with great eloquence and expressive vehemence; she has a big tone and impeccable technique. The orchestral playing is gutsy and sturdy without, perhaps, the finesse that might have toned down some of the garishness of the orchestral colours. The recording is bright and breezy – not worth a three-star grading and nor is the orchestral contribution, though Tarasova certainly is.

Piano concerto.
⊛ (M) (**(*)) RCA mono GD 60921. William Kapell, Boston SO, Koussevitzky – LISZT: *Mephisto waltz* (**(*)); PROKOFIEV: *Piano concerto No. 3.* (**(*)) ⊛
(M) **(*) Hyp. Dig. CDA 66293 [id.]. Servadei, LPO, Giunta – BRITTEN: *Piano concerto.* **(*)
(**) VAI mono VAIA IPA 1027 [id.]. William Kapell, NBC SO, Frank Black – RACHMANINOV: *Piano concerto No. 3.* (*(**))

It is difficult to imagine a better-played account of the *Piano concerto* than that by William Kapell and the Boston Symphony under Koussevitzky (though not so hard to imagine better recorded sound). This incandescent performance, which Kapell recorded in his early twenties, should persuade even those who normally find the Khachaturian concerto irredeemably cheap and tawdry. Koussevitzky gets stunning results from the orchestra and Kapell's virtuosity and delicacy are remarkable. Even if the sound calls for lots of tolerance (the recording dates from 1946), the performance soon has a mesmeric effect. One is reminded of Stravinsky's response on hearing Leonard Bernstein's *Rite of Spring*: 'Wow!'

Annette Servadei, born in South Africa of British parents and now an Italian citizen by marriage, is a pupil of (among others) Wilhelm Kempff, and the cleanness of her articulation reflects that master. In the Khachaturian concerto more than the Britten – the generous coupling for this Hyperion issue – she makes up in clarity and point for a relative lack of weight in the outer movements, which she takes at speeds marginally slower than usual. The slow movement brings hushed and intense playing, sympathetically supported by the LPO under Joseph Giunta in a digital recording that is well balanced and unaggressive and sounding good. However, ideally this work needs a stronger grip than these artists exert – the first movement in particular could do with greater thrust.

Kapell's NBC performance with Frank Black conducting comes from May 1945 (a year earlier than his Boston version), and the sound is abysmal, harsher and more cramped than with Koussevitzky. If you want the Khachaturian from this artist (and you should), then go for the Boston performance. But you should also note that the coupling on VAI, the Rachmaninov *Piano concerto No. 3*, is one of the most extraordinary and electrifying before the public. It is not a commercial recording but is an astonishing *tour de force*, second only to Horowitz and Rachmaninov himself.

Gayaneh (ballet): complete final score.
**(*) Russian Disc RDCD 11 029 (2) [id.]. USSR R. & TV Large SO, Djansug Kakhidze.

Khachaturian's original full score for *Gayaneh*, dating from 1942, is perhaps his finest extended work. Fortunately Tjeknavorian made a complete recording of it for RCA, and this is in urgent need of reissue. The composer later reworked and added to the music in order to fit a new scenario (because the earlier narrative, with its ingenuous wartime moral tone, had become embarrassing to the Soviets). The fresh inspiration of the original is expanded and often vulgarized in the later version about love and jealousy among shepherds dwelling in the mountains. But plenty of striking ideas remain. Armen, Gayaneh's lover, goes blind after a hunting accident but recovers his sight to make a happy ending, while the Griori, the villain by default, has to leave the village, taking the second female lead, Aisha, with him. This Russian recording from 1976 has great verve and energy but does not disguise the shallower invention and the inflation of the louder passages. Nevertheless the recording is vivid and, although brash, is not unacceptably so; and these performers know just how to present the folk dances.

(i) *Symphony No. 3 (Simfoniya-poema). Triumphal poem.*
*** Chan. Dig. CHAN 9321 [id.]. BBC PO, Fedor Glushchenko, (i) with Simon Lindley.
   IPPOLITOV-IVANOV: *Caucasian sketches.* ***

If the *Third Symphony* was as strong on musical substance as it is on decibels, it would be something to reckon with. But, alas, it is garish and empty; there are no fewer than eighteen trumpets in all! Analgesics and earplugs will be in brisk demand in its vicinity. The BBC Philharmonic, spurred on by their Russian conductor, play as if they believe in it, and the Chandos recording is in the demonstration category. The three stars are for the performance and the recording – not for the music!

Klami, Uuno (1900–61)

Lemminkäinen's island adventures; (i) *Song of Lake Kuujärvi; Whirls: suites Nos. 1 & 2.*
*** BIS Dig. CD 656 [id.]. (i) Esa Ruuttunen; Lahti SO, Osmo Vänskä.

While most Finnish composers of his generation succumbed to the shadow of Sibelius, Uuno Klami – like his somewhat older contemporary, Leevi Madetoja – was drawn towards French models and drank heavily the heady draughts of Ravel and Florent Schmitt. He is relatively little known and rarely if ever features in concert programmes outside his native Finland. The *Kalevala suite* (1929–33) is his best-known work (there is a recommendable Chandos recording listed in our main edition) but, like most of his music that we have heard, it remains highly derivative: Ravel, Schmitt, Falla, a dash of Sibelius and a bit of early Stravinsky are the main ingredients. Whatever else one may say, Klami was a master of orchestral colour, as one might expect from a composer who had the benefit of Ravel's criticism. *Lemminkäinen's island adventures* dates from 1934 and is actually more Sibelian than is usual with this composer. He had originally included it in the *Kalevala suite* and then published it separately, but its musical substance does not really sustain its length. The rest of the disc concentrates on the music he wrote during his last decade: the ballet, *Whirls*, begun in 1957 but never completed, and *Song of Lake Kuujärvi*, inspired by his experiences in the winter war (1939–40) and its continuation (1941–5). There is quite a lot of Prokofiev and Shostakovich in this later music and greater depth in the orchestral song. The performances are good and Esa Ruuttunen is an excellent baritone, and the recording offers wide dynamic range and natural perspective. An interesting supplement to the Chandos disc (CHAN 9268 – see our main volume) and ultimately perhaps more rewarding.

Kodály, Zoltán (1882–1967)

Dance suite.
** Everest/Vanguard EVC 9000 [id.]. LPO, Ferencsik – FALLA: *Three cornered hat.* *

Ferencsik creates a high voltage in the *Dance suite*, and the LPO playing is polished and spirited, with the gentler moments given quiet intensity. The recording is vivid but a shade harsh. But the Falla coupling is disappointing.

(i–iii; vi) *Háry Janos* (play with music): complete recording of music, with narration by Peter Ustinov; (iv) *The Peacock* (folksong for unaccompanied chorus); (ii; v–vi) *Psalmus Hungaricus;* (vi) *Variations on a Hungarian folksong (The Peacock).*
(M) **(*) Decca Double 443 488-2 (2) [id.]. (i) Olga Szönyi, Márgit László, Erszébet Komlössy, György Melis, Zsolt Bende, Láslo Palócz; (ii) Wandsworth School Boys' Ch.; (iii) Edinburgh Festival Ch.; (iv) London Symphony Ch.; (v) Lajos Kozma, Brighton Festival Ch.; (vi) LSO; all cond. Kertész.

Here we have an attempt to re-create in gramophone terms for English-speaking listeners the curious humour of the original Hungarian play. All of Kodály's music for *Háry Janos* is included, and the links are provided by Peter Ustinov in many guises. Whether the comedy stands the test of repetition is another matter, but it is good to have Kodály's full score, including a number of pieces as attractive as those in the well-known suite, and vocal versions of some that we know already. Superb recording. This Double Decca reissue also includes a much-valued performance of the *Psalmus Hungaricus*, Kodály's most vital choral work; this modern version comes as close to the ideal as one is likely to get. Kertész's energy takes one compellingly through all the straight homophonic writing, which in a lesser performance can diminish the work's stature. Here, with a chorus trained by another Hungarian musician, the results are electrifying, and the recording is outstandingly brilliant to match. The light tenor tone of Lajos Kozma is not ideal for the solo part, but again the authentic Hungarian touch helps. The *Peacock variations* make a marvellous display piece, and it was a happy idea to include the folksong itself, stirringly sung by the London Symphony Chorus. No attempt in the variations to build an intellectual structure: orchestral resource provides the mainspring, and the LSO revels in the virtuoso challenge. The CD transfers are first class throughout.

Psalmus hungaricus, Op. 13.
*** Chan. Dig. CHAN 9310 [id.]. Svensson, Copenhagen Boys' Ch., Danish Nat. R. Ch. & SO, Mackerras – JANACEK: *Glagolitic Mass.* ***
** Everest/Vanguard EVC 9008 [id.]. Raymond Nilsson, LPO Ch., LPO, Ferencsik – BARTOK: *Concerto for orchestra.* **

As the unusual but refreshing coupling for the Janáček *Mass*, the *Psalmus hungaricus* is here infected with an element of wildness that sweeps away any idea of Kodály as a bland composer. As in the Janáček, the tenor Peter Svensson is an excellent, clear-toned and incisive soloist, if here rather more backwardly balanced. The glory of the performance lies most of all in the superb choral singing, full, bright and superbly disciplined, with the hushed pianissimos as telling as the great fortissimo outbursts. It is a mark of Mackerras's understanding of the music that the many sudden changes of mood sound both dramatic and natural. Full, warm and atmospheric recording, with plenty of detail.

Ferencsik knows his Kodály, but the vibrant performance of the *Psalmus hungaricus* sung here is an English translation by Edward Dent, which is less satisfactory for a record than for a live performance. The choral singing has fervour, the soloist is more than adequate and the 1958 Walthamstow recording is spacious.

Korngold, Erich (1897–1957)

(i) *Violin concerto in D, Op. 35;* (ii) *Much Ado About Nothing* (suite), *Op. 11.*
*** DG Dig. 439 886-2 [id.]. Gil Shaham; (i) LSO, Previn; (ii) Previn (piano) – BARBER: *Violin concerto.* ***

The Korngold was written within five years of the Barber *Concerto* and makes a desirable coupling for it. Indeed the conjunction of Barber and Korngold works splendidly, when in the Barber the ripe performance brings out moments that are not too distant from the world of Hollywood music, and the Korngold then emerges as a central work in that genre. The Israeli violinist, Gil Shaham, gives a performance of effortless virtuosity and strong profile. His intonation is flawless and he plays every note as if he believes it. Shaham may not have quite the flair and panache of the dedicatee, Jascha Heifetz, in his incomparable reading, but he is warmer and more committed than Itzakh Perlman in his Pittsburgh recording for EMI (CDC7 47846-2), again with Previn conducting. There is greater freshness and conviction than in the Perlman. What consistently emerges is how electric the playing of the LSO is under Previn on the DG disc, rich and full as well as committed, echoing vintage Previn/LSO recordings of the 1970s. The recording helps, far clearer and more immediate than Perlman's EMI. It is true that in his cooler way Perlman finds an extra tenderness in such passages as the entry of the violin in the slow movement, but Shaham and Previn together consistently bring out the work's sensuous warmth without making the result soupy. It is striking how Previn as conductor, for both Shaham and Perlman, gives a rhythmic lift to the dashing *moto perpetuo* of the finale, as in the Barber finale relishing the Waltonian cross-rhythms.

The suite from Korngold's incidental music to *Much Ado About Nothing*, dating from his early, precocious period in Vienna, is for violin and piano, not the later version for orchestra with piano that was included on Ulf Hoelscher's long-deleted EMI LP of the *Concerto*. Here it provides a delightful and apt makeweight, with Previn as pianist just as understanding and imaginative an accompanist and Shaham yearningly warm without sentimentality, clean and precise in attack. The four strongly contrasted movements draw on the most open and lyrical side of the composer, again often sensuous in beauty.

Sinfonietta, Op. 5; Sursum corda, Op. 13.
*** Chan. Dig. CHAN 9317 [id.]. BBC PO, Bamert.

It was hearing a performance of Korngold's *Sinfonietta* that prompted Sibelius's remark about 'a young eagle'. Completed in 1912, it is a product of Korngold's precocious boyhood, a substantial four-movement work, a symphony in all but name, betraying a prodigious technical expertise both in the management and organization of musical ideas and in the handling of the orchestra; and not only that, the ideas themselves are of real quality and individuality. Moreover it is most skilfully scored, with Respighian pre-echoes in the Scherzo. The waltz-rhythms in the sonata-form first movement are immediately engaging, and even Korngold rarely outshone the lyrical warmth of the slow movement, while the finale brings the most extended structure of all, with more Hollywood anticipations. At 43 minutes, it is an extraordinary achievement for a fourteen-year-old and in its way is comparable (though not quite, perhaps, in quality of inspiration) only with Mendelssohn in the *Octet* and *Midsummer Night's Dream* music – an adolescent composer springing as it were fully equipped on to the musical scene. The symphonic poem *Sursum corda* comes from the post-war years, when Korngold had reached the advanced age of twenty-three! It is contemporaneous with his opera, *Die tote Stadt*. In spite of sumptuous virtuoso orchestration, it proved a flop on its first appearance in 1920, but when in 1938 its composer was working against time to write the score for the Hollywood epic with Errol Flynn, *The Adventures of Robin Hood*, he thought back to the brilliant symphonic overture he had composed 18 years earlier, *Sursum corda*. At the stroke of a pen the opening fanfare motif provided the motto theme for the hero, and he also borrowed extensively from other passages. The original virtuoso showpiece lasting 20 minutes is finer than one might expect, an extraordinarily sumptuous piece that in its wide range of moods keeps suggesting that it will turn into the *Pines of Rome*. Looking at dates, one realizes that it precedes Respighi's showpiece and deserves to be at least as well known. There are alternative versions of the *Sinfonietta*, but the present performance by the BBC Philharmonic Orchestra under Matthias Bamert is a clear front-runner and the Chandos recording is altogether superb in terms of definition and opulence. A ripely enjoyable disc of beautifully played performances, and a valuable addition to the catalogue, with the sumptuous sound-picture a little distant.

Piano trio in D, Op. 1.
*** Ph. Dig. 434 072-2. Beaux Arts Trio – ZEMLINSKY: *Piano trio.* ***

What an astonishing work for a mere child this Op. 1 *Trio* is! Although we have admired the Pacific Arts Trio on the Delos label the present version is both played and recorded better, and must supplant it. The Beaux Arts take a more leisurely and relaxed view of the piece: indeed there will be some who have become accustomed to and who will prefer the greater tautness and urgency of the Delos version. However, the Beaux Arts is now the one to have on all counts.

(i) *Piano trio in D, Op. 1; Violin sonata in G, Op. 6.*
*** EMI CDC5 55401-2 [id.]. Glenn Dicterow, Israela Margalit; (i) with Alan Stepansky.

In EMI's Anglo-American Chamber Music series, two distinguished members of the New York Philharmonic join the pianist, Israela Margalit, in more astonishing examples of the boy Korngold's precocious genius. Written when he was only twelve and dedicated to his father, Julius, the Viennese critic, the *Piano trio*, inventive and distinctive, betrays remarkably few influences, save the occasional echo of Richard Strauss, who promptly praised the boy's work. The lyricism gives promise of the future Hollywood composer, though the ripe melodies in the slow movement have a way of veering in unexpected directions. The *Violin sonata* of three years later, written for Carl Flesch and Artur Schnabel, is even more adventurous, with an extended Scherzo, the longest of the four movements, which develops from its skittish opening into darker moods. Again the slow movement, marked to be played 'with deep expressiveness', is the most richly lyrical, before the *Allegretto* finale brings an equivocal conclusion. Warmly expressive performances and full, well-balanced recording.

Krása, Hans (1899–1944)

String quartet.
*** Decca Dig. 440 853-2 [id.]. Hawthorne Qt – HAAS: *Quartets Nos. 2 & 3.* ***

Hans Krása and his compatriot, Pavel Haas, were born in the same year and sent to the gas chambers at the Terezin or Teresienstadt camp on the same day. (This disc is part of the *Entartete Musik* series which explores music that was suppressed during the years of the Third Reich.) Krása came from Prague and became a pupil of Zemlinsky, but he was influenced by French music as much as by the Viennese school. Like Haas, he was drawn to the stage; indeed his opera, *Verlobung im Traum* (1933), was a great success and was conducted by George Szell. Roland-Manuel wrote, 'his magical world is ruled over by the spirit of ironic poetry which sometimes mocks its own power to bewitch'. His *String quartet* is a remarkably mature piece for a twenty-two-year-old and, along with the occasional echoes of Janáček and the French, also burlesques a theme from Smetana's *The Bartered Bride overture*. Although there are rapidly changing moods and colours, the composer holds everything together with a keen and intelligent logic. The Hawthorne Quartet play very persuasively and are excellently recorded. A rewarding issue.

Kreisler, Fritz (1875–1962)

Violin concerto in the style of Vivaldi.
*** DG Dig. 439 933-2 [id.]. Gil Shaham, Orpheus CO – VIVALDI: *The Four Seasons.* ***

An amiable pastiche, which sounds almost totally unlike Vivaldi as we experience his music performed today – indeed the name of Boccherini could well have been substituted in the title credit and, even then, could not disguise the early-twentieth-century provenance of the work. It is warmly played and clearly enjoyed by its performers, and the sumptuousness of the sound is the more striking coming, as it does, immediately after Vivaldi's wintry winds. The brief insert notes use up nearly two and a half columns describing the history of Kreisler's concerto, leaving less than a column for Vivaldi's masterpiece.

Krommer, Franz (Kramar, František) (1759–1831)

Clarinet concerto in E flat, Op. 36; (i) *Double clarinet concertos in A flat, Opp. 35 & 91.*
(BB) ** Naxos Dig. 8.553178 [id.]. Kálmán Berkes; (i) Kaori Tsutsui; Nicolaus Esterházy Sinfonia.

Franz Krommer's clarinet concertos are renowned for their jocular character, especially in the finales, although the Op. 36 solo concerto has a slow movement which is unexpectedly dark in feeling. The *Adagios* of the two *Double concertos* are more operatic in manner; that of Op. 35 opens with a distinct atmosphere of melodrama. Both the soloists here are good players and they blend very well together; but slow movements are rather deadpan and not all the music's sense of fun comes over. Neither clarinettists nor orchestra are helped by the reverberant recording which means a forward balance for the soloists and tends to coarsen the tuttis by spreading the sound. Even so, the *Double concerto*, Op. 91, a winner if ever there was one, is very enjoyable, with the first movement swinging along merrily and the *Polacca* finale, with its jaunty duet theme introduced against orchestral pizzicatos, equally fluent.

Kuhnau, Johann (1660–1722)

Der Gerechte kommt um (motet).
(M) *** O-L 443 199-2 [id.]. Christ Church Ch., AAM, Preston – BACH: *Magnificat;* VIVALDI: *Nisi dominus* etc. ***

Kuhnau was Bach's predecessor in Leipzig. He wrote this charming motet with a Latin text; it was later arranged in a German version, and there are signs of Bach's hand in it. The piece makes an excellent makeweight coupling for the original version of Bach's *Magnificat*.

Lachner, Franz Paul (1803–90)

Symphony No. 5 in C min. (Passionata), Op. 52 (Preis-Symphonie).
**(*) Marco Polo Dig. 8.223502 [id.]. Slovak State PO (Košice), Paul Robinson.

Franz Lachner was born at Rain-am-Lech in Upper Bavaria, the son of an organist and clock-maker. His younger brother, Vinzenz, and older step-brother, Theodor, were also composers, and two sisters were organists. In 1823 Lachner moved to Vienna as organist of the Lutheran Church and became a pupil of Simon Sechter, with whom Schubert began studies and of whom Bruckner became a pupil. Lachner was soon drawn into Schubert's circle and wrote a memoir of his friend in 1881. In the 1830s he became Kapellmeister at the Mannheim Opera and then moved to a similar post in Munich, which he retained until Wagner's arrival in 1864. His *Fifth Symphony* was written the year before he went to Munich, and it won a prize offered by the *Gesellschaft der Musikfreunde* in Vienna. It is an ambitious work, lasting an hour, lyrical and well crafted. Its ideas unfold naturally and with a certain fluency; its scoring is effective and its idiom is close to the world of Schubert and Mendelssohn. It is a little conventional: phrase structures are rather four-square and predictable, and one can see why it excited Schumann's scorn (he hailed its successor as twice as good). All the same, one can see why the work enjoyed esteem in more conservative circles. It has more than mere curiosity value, and the Slovak orchestra under Paul Robinson play it with obvious enjoyment. Decent recording.

Lajtha, László (1892–1963)

Hortobágy, Op. 21; Suite No. 3, Op. 56; Symphony No. 7, Op. 63 (Revolution Symphony).
**(*) Marco Polo Dig. 8.223667 [id.]. Pécs SO, Nicolás Pasquet.

László Lajtha was one of the leading Hungarian composers and scholars to emerge after the generation of Bartók and Kodály. Indeed, as an exact contemporary of Honegger and Milhaud, he is separated from his compatriots by a mere decade. He was eminent in the field of folk-music and, in his youth, an accomplished pianist (he studied with Stavenhagen in the first decade of the century). Some of his piano music is recorded on Marco Polo, and it shows a responsiveness to the modern music of the period, above all Bartók, but also Debussy and even Schoenberg. Two of his symphonies have been recorded on Hungaraton HCD 31452 (they were welcomed in our 1992 edition, but the CD is not currently available) and the present disc brings the *Seventh* (1956), which made a strong impression on the present writer when it was programmed by the BBC in the 1950s. It is a well-wrought and eclectic score that does not quite live up to memories of the first performance but which is worth hearing. There are echoes of Bartók (the *Music for strings, percussion and celeste*), Kodály and even a reminder of Vaughan Williams. Like the latter's contemporaneous *Ninth Symphony*, Lajtha's *Seventh* makes conspicuous use of the saxophone. The scoring is effective (occasionally one is reminded of the Prokofiev-like moments in Tubin's *Sixth Symphony*) but, although it is finer than the *Fourth* or *Ninth Symphonies*, which appeared on Hungaroton, it does not possess the concentration or profile one expects of a major symphonist. The suite from *Hortobágy*, a memorable film set in the plains of Hungary, and the *Two symphonic portraits* are effectively scored but their material is insufficiently distinctive. Decent performances and recording.

Lalo, Eduard (1823–92)

Cello concerto No. 1 in D min., Op. 33.
*** Finlandia/Warner Dig. 4509 95768-2 [id.]. Arto Noras, Finnish RSO, Saraste – ELGAR: *Cello concerto.* ***

(i) *Cello concerto No. 1 in D min.;* (ii) *Namouna* (ballet): *Rhapsodies Nos.1–2; Valse de la cigarette. Rapsodie norvégien.*

(B) **(*) DG Double 437 371-2 [id.]. (i) Pierre Fournier, LOP; (ii) ORTF; Jean Martinon – BIZET: *Symphony* etc. **(*)

Arto Noras is the leading Finnish cellist of our day, and he commands impeccable technical address. Naturally any newcomer to the Elgar treads on ground hallowed by Du Pré and Barbirolli and, more recently, Sophie Rolland (ASV CDDCA 867); but Noras has no need to fear comparison with anyone, either in the Elgar or here in the Lalo *Concerto*. Yo-Yo Ma's version is not at present in currency but, even if it were, Noras could hold his own against it as well as the others listed in our main volume. He is an aristocrat among cellists in much the same way as Fournier was (and Haimowitz on DG is not). He receives very responsive support from Saraste and the Finnish Radio Orchestra, and very truthful recording.

Fournier's performance of the *Cello concerto* lends both dignity and nobility to a work whose ideas are in fact of slender substance. Martinon gets a spirited response from the Lamoureux players, but the recording is not top-drawer. There is much engaging music in *Namouna*, a ballet score much admired by Debussy and dating from 1882. The first movement opens with an unashamed Wagnerian crib from *Das Rheingold*, but elsewhere Lalo's music is more individual. He is at his finest in the gentler writing: the *Sérénade*, the *Valse de la cigarette*, and the enchanting Beechamesque lollipop, *La Sieste*. These are all memorable and nicely played within an atmospheric acoustic. The *Pas des cymbales* is admirably crisp, though in the louder sections of the score the recording is just a shade fierce. Jean Martinon is a sympathetic exponent throughout and he also gives us the attractively tuneful *Rapsodie norvégienne* in its adapted version for orchestra alone (1879). The original, composed a year earlier, featured a concertante violin.

Symphonie espagnole (for violin and orchestra), *Op. 21.*
*** Virgin/EMI Dig. VC5 45022-2 [id.]. Christian Tetzlaff, Czech PO, Pešek – DVORAK: *Violin concerto.* ***
(M) *** DG Dig. 445 549-2 [id.]. Perlman, O de Paris, Barenboim – SAINT-SAENS: *Concerto No. 3;* BERLIOZ: *Rêverie et caprice.* ***

Like his fine reading of the Dvořák *Violin concerto*, with which it is generously coupled, Tetzlaff's account of the Lalo is marked by playing of quicksilver lightness in passage-work, bringing out the element of fantasy. Equally the soloist's concentration makes for a sense of spontaneity, leading one on magnetically in this episodic work. He seems all the stronger for having a recording balance which does not spotlight the violin as sharply as in most other versions. As for Tetzlaff's accompanists – chosen no doubt specifically for the Dvořák – the Czech Philharmonic's playing under Pešek proves just as idiomatic in the Spanish dance-rhythms of Lalo as in Czech dances, with crisp ensemble and rhythms deliciously sprung. Characteristically Pešek makes orchestral textures clear, bringing out extra detail, despite the reverberant acoustic of the Dvořák Hall of the Rudolfinum in Prague, and the advantage of the resonant ambience is to give a more expansive warmth to the overall sound than in Perlman's DG version – which nevertheless remains highly recommendable at mid-price.

The 1980 DG recording of Lalo's five-movement distillation of Spanish sunshine regularly pops in and out of the catalogue and, although the lively digital sound remains a trifle dry, Perlman's performance easily maintains its place near the top of the list. Barenboim combines rhythmic buoyancy with expressive flair and the richness and colour of Perlman's tone are never more telling than in the slow movement, which opens tenderly but develops a compelling expressive ripeness. The brilliance of the Scherzo is matched by the dancing sparkle of the finale. For the reissue in the Masters series, the Berlioz *Rêverie et caprice* makes an attractive if brief bonus.

Piano trios Nos. 1 in C min., Op. 7; 2 in B min.; 3 in A min, Op. 26.
*** ASV Dig. CDDCA 899 [id.]. Barbican Piano Trio.

As always with Lalo, this is the kind of unpretentious, inventive, well-crafted and delightful music which nineteenth-century civilization seemed able to foster and their composers to produce – and of which the late twentieth is conspicuously and lamentably bare. There is little to say about the music (always a good sign) and not much more about the performances, except to note their excellence and poise. A rewarding issue, and well recorded into the bargain.

Lambert, Constant (1905–53)

(i; ii) *Concerto for piano and nine players*; (i) *Piano sonata*; (iii; i) *8 Poems of Li-Po*; (iv; i) *Mr Bear Squash-you-all-flat.*
*** Hyp. Dig. CDA 66754 [id.]. (i) Ian Brown; (ii) Nash Ens., Lionel Friend; with (iii) Philip Langridge; (iv) Nigel Hawthorne.

Constant Lambert's remarkable qualities are in excellent evidence here in the Nash Ensemble's anthology which brings two of his most powerful works, the *Concerto for piano and nine players* and the *Piano sonata*, as well as one of his most delicately wrought, the *Eight Poems of Li-Po*, in a lovely performance from Philip Langridge. The *Concerto* is already available in a very good and well-characterized version by Kathryn Stott (Argo), but Ian Brown is if anything more searching and subtle. (Forced to choose between them, though, we would part with neither!) Ian Brown proves an equally exemplary advocate in the *Piano sonata*, which is not generously represented on disc. *Mr Bear Squash-you-all-flat* is new to the catalogue: Lambert's first composition, an entertainment written at roughly the same time as Walton's *Façade*, when Lambert was still in his teens, and based on a Russian fairy story. Imaginative and accomplished but, hardly surprisingly, not top-drawer Lambert. It is not certain whether Lambert meant the text to be spoken, but Nigel Hawthorne speaks it excellently; he is somewhat reticently balanced (a fault on the right side). Nevertheless, a valuable addition to Lambert's representation on disc – speaking of which: when are Lyrita going to restore *Pomona* and *Romeo and Juliet* to circulation?

Lampe, John Frederick (1702/3–51)

(i) *Pyramus and Thisbe* (A mock opera); (ii) *Flute concerto in G (The Cuckoo)*.
*** Hyp. Dig. CDA 66759 [id.]. (i) Padmore, Bisatt, Opera Restor'd, Peter Holman; (ii) Rachel Brown.

Born in Saxony, John Frederick Lampe trained as a lawyer but soon turned to music and, around 1726, moved to London, where he played the bassoon in Handel's opera orchestra. Handel encouraged his young fellow-countryman, who also went into a short-lived opera venture with Thomas Arne. *Pyramus and Thisbe*, written in 1745, is a reworking of the entertainment given by the rude mechanicals in Shakespeare's *Midsummer Night's Dream*, with the role of the heroine, Thisbe, taken not by a man but by a soprano. The Opera Restor'd company, with Jack Edwards as stage director, here present it complete with spoken Prologue for several attendant characters. Following the overture come 16 brief numbers, with the score edited and completed by the conductor, Peter Holman. The invention is charming in a very English way, not at all reflecting Lampe's German background. Mark Padmore is outstanding as Pyramus, with Susan Bisatt a fresh-toned Thisbe. The warm, immediate recording brings out the distinctive timbre of the period instruments, notably the braying horns. As an agreeable makeweight, the disc also offers Lampe's only surviving independent orchestral work, the *G major Flute concerto*, with its three crisp movements lasting little more than 5 minutes.

Landowski, Marcel (born 1915)

(i) *Concerto for ondes martenot, strings and percussion;* (ii) *Piano concerto No. 2;* (iii) *Concerto for trumpet, strings and electro-acoustic instruments.*
*** Erato/Warner 4509 96972-2 [id.]. (i) Jeanne Loriod, O de Chambre de Musique Contemporain, Jacques Rondon; (ii) Annie d'Arco, ORTF, Jean Martinon; (iii) Maurice André, Strasbourg PO, Alain Lombard.

Marcel Landowski is little more than a name outside France, where he is much respected – and rightly so, if his symphonies are anything to go by. The new musical establishment, whose interest has centred on Messiaen and Boulez, has not paid him much attention. His musical language is firmly rooted in Honegger, whose biographer Landowski was, and to a lesser extent Roussel, and though he is perhaps not as resourceful as, say, Dutilleux, his handling of complex orchestral textures and orchestral colours is highly imaginative. Erato have published a box of some seven CDs to mark his eightieth birthday. The three concertos assembled here are all analogue recordings. Two come from the 1960s, the *Piano Concerto No. 2* was first issued in 1970, and the *Concerto for ondes martenot* in 1964. The *Concerto for ondes martenot* is the better recording in spite of its earlier provenance. In the *Piano concerto* of 1963, the balance places the soloist too prominently and the instrument itself sounds tubby. The musical invention can be compared to certain kinds of conversation, civilized and intelligent, which holds you while it goes on but which remains ultimately unmemorable. The *Concerto for ondes martenot* of 1954 is also the finer of the two works, stronger in atmosphere and invention than its companion, and its idiom is a cross between Honegger and Shostakovich. Add Bartókian *Night music* to that mix, and you have the opening of the *Trumpet concerto* (1976). As

Harry Halbreich puts it in the accompanying notes, 'the piece takes the form of an extended meditation, above all lyrical and song-like in character, which makes use of the soloist's melodic and expressive resources rather than his virtuosic agility'. Scored for small forces (no oboes, and two horns and one trombone), it also makes discreet use of magnetic tape. It is even finer than the *Concerto for ondes martenot* and its seriousness of purpose and powerful atmosphere make a strong impression. The 1978 Strasbourg recording is excellent and Maurice André plays it with total commitment. One can only hope now that younger virtuosi like Håkan Hardenberger and Sergei Nakariakov will take it up.

Symphonies Nos. (i) *1 (Jean de la peur)*; (ii) *2*; (i) *3 (Des espaces)*; *4*.
*** Erato/Warner Dig. 4509 96973-2 (2) [id.]. (i) French Nat. O; Georges Prêtre; (ii) ORTF, Jean Martinon.

The *First*, *Third* and *Fourth* of Landowski's symphonies were recorded in 1988 and have been available on a single disc (2292 45018-2), listed in our main volume. Composed over some considerable period, the *First (Jean de la peur)* comes from the immediate post-war years (1948) while the *Fourth* was a French Radio commission from 1988. To them Erato have now added an analogue (or, as the French commentator charmingly puts it, analogical) recording from 1970 of the *Second Symphony*, conducted by Jean Martinon (economically packaged in one single jewel-case). *Grove* gives its date as 1963, and it was premièred by Charles Munch two years later. Like its companions the musical language and thought processes have their roots in Honegger; the musical argument is well sustained and has a certain dignity. Even if he does not possess a strongly distinctive profile, Landowski has a powerful and fertile imagination, a resourceful sense of orchestration, and a commanding symphonic grip. He holds the listener from the first bar to the last. Martinon, whose own music inhabits a not dissimilar world, proves a wholly sympathetic interpreter and the analogue recording has no lack of warmth and space. The two-movement *Third Symphony (Des espaces)*, written in the immediate wake of the *Second* in 1965, is very atmospheric: its opening *Grave* casts a powerful spell, while the scurrying activity of the *Allegro deciso* movement is skilfully sustained. Although these are not as strong as the Honegger or Dutilleux symphonies, they are imaginative and rewarding. Prêtre gets exemplary results from the French National Orchestra. If you have the opportunity of sampling this set, try the opening minute or so of the *Fourth Symphony*, and if you respond to its world you will enjoy all these pieces. Generally excellent recorded sound.

Lang, David (born 1957)

(i) *Are you experienced?; Under Orpheus*.
(***) Chan. Dig. CHAN 9363 [id.]. (i) Composer (nar.); Netherlands Wind. Ens., Mosko – ADAMS: *Grand pianola music* etc. ***

Are you experienced? is presumably a cult work to which we would not wish to return very often, if at all. It draws its genesis from a Jimi Hendrix song and album, and the narrator/composer acts as guide through such musically illustrated experieces as 'On being hit on the head' and 'On hearing the voice of God'. It opens rather in the manner of 'Are you sitting comfortably' from the BBC's *Listen with Mother*, and very soon we were not sitting comfortably at all. To our ears, it is all pretentious and unappealing. *Under Orpheus* consists of a pair of minimalist crescendos into dissonance, the first, *Aria*, led by piano tremolandos, the second an undulating *Chorale*. Obviously the performances are very well played, and the recording is in the demonstration bracket.

Langgaard, Rued (1893–1953)

Symphonies Nos. 4 (Løvfald); 6 (Den Himmelrivande); (i) *Sfærernas Musik*.
**(*) Danacord DACOCD 340/341 [id.]. (i) Edith Guillaume, Danish R. Ch.; Danish RSO, John Frandsen.

Although this is a less comprehensive survey than those listed in our main volume, it makes for an excellent introduction to this intriguing but flawed composer. The performances are analogue and have appeared on LP during the early 1980s, though the 1973 studio performance of the *Fourth Symphony* under Frandsen has been replaced by a 1981 live performance. *Sfærernas musik (The Music of the spheres)*, written in 1918 in between the two symphonies recorded here, is an extraordinary piece of undoubted vision and originality. It has a wild-eyed intensity and a quasi-mystical quality that is unusual in the Nordic music of its time. One has the feeling that it could equally stop earlier or go on longer, but formal coherence is not Langgaard's strong suit. The performances are good and the recording eminently satisfactory without being quite in the Chandos league.

Lassus, Orlandus (c. 1530-94)

Chansons: *Bon jour mon cœur* (ensemble and solo versions); *Fleur de quinz ans; J'ayme la pierre précieuse; Margot labourez les vignes; La nuict froide et sombre; Pour courir en poste a la ville; Susanne ung jour* (with ANON.: Intablature for lute from the Wickhambrook Lute Manuscript); Motets: *Cum natus esset Jesus; In monte Oliveti; Stabat Mater.*
(M) *** Virgin Veritas/EMI Dig. VER5 61166-2 [id.]. Hilliard Ens., Paul Hillier.

One half is devoted to motets, the other to chansons; both are sung one voice to a part. The tonal blend is as perfect as is usual with this ensemble, intonation is extraordinarily accurate, and there is no vibrato. The sacred pieces, and in particular the setting of the *Stabat Mater* which opens the first half, are most impressive. In some of the chansons there is a discreet lute accompaniment to lend variety. Of the chansons, *La nuict froide et sombre* is quite magical and given with great feeling and colour. One of the other songs tells of an unscrupulous friar, in which all suggestions of virtuous behaviour bring the refrain: 'Brother Lubin can't do it'; others include a simple expression of delight in a loved one, a tale of attempted seduction based on the story of Susanna and the Elders, and a hopeful offer to a fifteen-year-old girl to '*vous faire apprendre*' (teach you how it is done!). For all these racier poems, Lassus provides the most refined setting. A useful addition to the Lassus discography and beautifully recorded.

Lawhead, Donaldson (born 1942)

Aleost.
*(*) First Edition LCD 002 [id.]. Louisville O, Zimmerman – HINDEMITH: *Piano concerto* ***; ZWILICH: *Symphony No. 2.* **

Donaldson Lawhead teaches at the University of Western Illinois and has had a career in popular music with Henry Mancini, Nelson Eddy and Bob Hope. *Aleost* derives its title from a combination of the first three letters of 'aleatory' and 'ostinato' and is a short, five-minute piece which brings together repeated patterns with chance elements. Good playing, but less than distinguished (1982) recording.

Le Flem, Paul (1881-1984)

Symphony No. 4; (i) *Le grand jardinier de France* (film music). *7 Pièces enfantines; Pour les morts (Tryptique symphonique No. 1).*
** Marco Polo Dig. 8.223655 [id.]. Rhenish PO, James Lockhart, (i) with Gilles Nopre.

Paul Le Flem is another of the French composers who is emerging from the shadows into which he has been so prematurely cast. He studied with Vincent d'Indy, who is a strong influence on his work, along with Chausson and, of course, Debussy; and he later became a pupil of Roussel. D'Indy championed his *Pour les morts*, written in memory of two of Le Flem's children, conducting its New York première in 1922. The *Fourth Symphony* brings an amazing creative vitality, when one thinks that its composer was just ninety years young at the time (1971-2). (As his dates will show at a glance, he lived to be 103.) The *Sept Pièces enfantines* is an orchestral transcription of a set of children's pieces for piano, composed in 1912, and *Le grand jardinier de France* is a film score. Both have a certain charm and would have more, had the orchestra been allowed more rehearsal. Wind intonation is not always flawless. Le Flem is not, perhaps, a major personality, but the *Fourth Symphony* is in its way quite remarkable, and had the performance greater finesse, the disc would have rated a three-star recommendation.

Lehár, Franz (1870–1948)

Friederike (complete).
(M) *** EMI CMS5 65369-2 (2). Donath, Dallapozza, Fuchs, Finke, Grabenhorst, Bav. R. Ch.,
Munich R. O, Wallberg.

The idea of Richard Tauber inspiring Lehár to write an operetta with the poet Goethe as the main
character may sound far-fetched, but that is just what *Friederike* is, more ambitious than a genuine
operetta and bringing the obvious snag for non-German speakers that there is a great deal of spoken
dialogue, the more disruptive because there is no libretto, let alone an English translation. However,
there is a track-by-track synopsis of each number, and in every other respect this is a delightful
reissue, with Helen Donath charming and sensitive in the name-part. Dallapozza has a light, heady
tenor, at times stressed by the weight of the part of Goethe but rising above all to the great Tauber
number, *O Mädchen, mein Mädchen!*, based (like other numbers) on a Goethe poem, *Mailied*. Heinz
Wallberg is a lively and persuasive director, and the 1980 recording has the bloom one associates with
German EMI productions.

Giuditta (complete).
(M) ** EMI Dig. CMS5 65378-2 (2). Edda Moser, Hirte, Gedda, Baumann, Munich Concert Ch. &
R. O, Boskovsky.

Again written as a vehicle for Richard Tauber in 1934, *Giuditta* was Lehár's own favourite among his
works. It may not have the easy tunefulness of *The Merry Widow* of a quarter-century earlier, and the
Balkan flavours may be plastered on rather thick; but with its poignant, disillusioned dénouement in
place of the usual happy ending it is both charming and distinctive. As a young man, Willi Boskovsky
played in the orchestra at its first performance; here he proves a persuasive advocate, though the
ensemble could be more polished. Gedda hardly shows his years in the Tauber role, with half-tones as
honeyed as ever. But Edda Moser is disappointing in the name-part. She may be glamorous to look
at, but the voice is consistently too hard to sound seductive, even in the song, *Mein Lippen, sie küssen
so heiss*, made so ecstatic by Schwarzkopf on her operetta record, and by Hilde Gueden on the
previous Decca set of *Giuditta* (see below). Good 1983/4 digital recording, except that the spoken
dialogue brings the performers suddenly much closer than the singing. Once again a track synopsis
takes the place of the more desirable libretto with translation.

Giuditta: highlights.
(M) **(*) Decca 436 900-2 [id.]. Gueden, Kmentt, Loose, Dickie, Czerwenka, Berry, V. State Op. Ch.
& O, Rudolf Moralt.

The Decca recording dates from 1958 and, although only highlights are offered, the 76-minute time-
span ensures that nothing of great importance is omitted. The performance is affectionately idiomatic
in a Viennese way, well sung and vividly presented. Hilde Gueden is in fresh, sparkling form and
Waldemar Kmentt makes an excellent Octavio: their duet, *Schön wie die blau Sommernacht*, makes
another attractive hit to put beside Gueden's delightful *Mein Lippen, sie küssen so heiss*. There is no
libretto but a good plot summary details individual numbers. Vivid sound ensures a welcome for this
reissue.

Der Graf von Luxemburg: highlights; *Der Zarewitsch:* highlights.
(M) *** Decca 436 896-2 [id.]. Gueden, Kmentt, V. Volksoper O, Max Schönherr.

Unlike the Decca highlights from *Giuditta* and *The Merry Widow*, these selections are not derived
from complete sets but were specially recorded together in their present format in the Sofiensaal in
1965. Although the offerings are not especially generous, with less than half an hour from each
operetta, the recording itself (produced by Christopher Raeburn) is splendid, as demonstrated by the
atmospheric opening scenes, with vivacious support from the chorus and orchestra. The two
principals are on top form so that the *Wolgalied* in *Der Zarewitsch* and the charming *Kosende Wellen*
are matched by the the the delightful waltz-duet of *Der Graf von Luxemburg, Bist du's, lachendes Glück*, a
hit if ever there was one. Brief plot summaries place each number in narrative perspective.

Das Land des Lächelns (The Land of smiles) (complete).
(M) **(*) EMI CMS5 65372-2 (2). Rothenberger, Gedda, Holm, Friedauer, Moeller, Bav. R. Ch.,
Graunke SO, Willy Mattes.

Originally issued on LP in the UK by World Record Club, this 1967 recording has on the whole
transferred well to CD. Don't be put off by the recording of the overture, which sounds thin because
of the relatively small orchestra for the opening scene, but then has plenty of theatrical presence. The
recording is atmospheric and real, not only in conveying the songs but also in the spoken dialogue,

which is well produced. The cast is strong. Gedda is in excellent form and, besides Anneliese Rothenberger, Renate Holm makes a charming contribution as Mi. The famous tunes, including '*You are my heart's delight*', are splendidly done. Yet again there is no libretto, especially desirable in the operetta; but we are offered a track-by-track synopsis of each number.

The Merry Widow (Die lustige Witwe; complete, in German).
*** DG Dig.439 911-2 [id.]. Studer, Skovhus, Bonney, Trost, Terfel, Monteverdi Ch., VPO, Gardiner.

A single-disc version of *The Merry Widow*, with full text and ample dialogue, neatly packaged with libretto, makes an attractive recommendation ahead of any rival. Anyone who marvels that the hyper-active John Eliot Gardiner has turned to Lehár should remember his similarly sparkling accounts of Messager, Chabrier and Offenbach with the Lyon Opera. Here he has the bonus of the Vienna Philharmonic very much on home ground. Amazingly, this is the first ever recording of this central Viennese operetta made by that orchestra, playing not only with a natural feeling for the idiom but with unrivalled finesse and polish. The characteristic spring which Gardiner brings to the rhythms goes with idiomatic rubato, often daringly extreme. By comparison, such a rival as Welser-Möst on EMI's 'Glyndebourne' version, recorded live, seems cautious, with recorded sound lacking the sparkle of this DG alternative. As Hanna Glawari, the widow of the title, Cheryl Studer gives her most endearing performance yet. She may not have quite the vivacity of Elisabeth Schwarzkopf in her two vintage recordings, but Studer's very first entry establishes her authority and charm, and the gentle half-tone on which she opens the soaring melody of the *Vilja-lied* is ravishing. Consistently she sings with sweeter, firmer tone than Felicity Lott on the Welser-Möst set and, though the Swedish baritone, Boje Skovhus, as Danilo cannot match the velvet of Thomas Hampson's voice for Welser-Möst, he makes an even more animated, raffish hero. The second couple, Valencienne and Camille, are delectably taken by Barbara Bonney and Rainer Trost, clear and youthful-sounding, outshining all rivals. The rest make an outstanding team, with Bryn Terfel, ripely resonant, turning Baron Mirko into more than a *buffo* character, while the choristers of Gardiner's Monteverdi Choir, obviously enjoying their Viennese outing, bring to Lehár the point and precision they have long devoted to the baroque repertory.

The Merry Widow (Die lustige Witwe): highlights.
(M) **(*) Decca 436 899-2 [id.]. Gueden, Kmentt, Grunden, Loose, Dönch, V. State Op. Ch. & O, Robert Stolz.

As with *Giuditta*, these highlights come from a complete set, recorded in Vienna in 1958 with characteristic Decca flair, already setting production values that were to establish this company's special niche in the world of opera and operetta. Here the inflated overture (arranged by the conductor for the occasion – a very mixed blessing) has been omitted and we are taken straight into the salon of the Pontevedrian Embassy, with its multitude of guests, laughter and talk, clinking cocktail glasses and rustling dresses. This extraordinary ambient effect swirls into the room in the most spectacular manner and the *Polonaise* at the beginning of Act II and the entrance of the grisettes in Act III have a similar startling presence. The recording itself is very 'live' throughout and the degree of over-brightness adds to the sparkle. Hilda Gueden gives a melting performance as the Widow and she sings the *Vilja-Lied* most seductively. Per Grunden makes Danilo a heady tenor role (it is usually sung by a baritone); Waldemar Kmentt is an appealing Camille de Rosillon and the other parts are well up to standard. We are offered more than one appearance of the famous *Waltz*, which originally appeared only briefly, towards the end of the piece. Robert Stolz, a lifelong friend of the composer, who has been closely associated with the operetta since it was written in 1905, conducts an entirely authentic performance, missing not a whit of sparkle or allure, with the Vienna State Opera Orchestra adding a characteristic lilt to the music and the chorus adding to the zest of the music-making.

'Lehar gala': Arias from: (i) *Eva;* (ii) *Friederike; Der Graf von Luxemburg; Das Land des Lächelns; Die lustige Witwe; Paganini; Schön ist die Welt; Der Zarewitsch;* (i) *Zigeunerliebe.*
(M) **(*) Decca 436 897-2 (2) [id.].(i) Pilar Lorengar, V. Op. O, Weller; (ii) Renate Holm, Werner Krenn, V. Volksoper O, Paulik.

Some 53 minutes of this hour-long compilation come from a two-LP set of operetta excerpts which Renate Holm and Werner Krenn made together in the Sofiensaal in December 1970, produced by Christopher Raeburn. They were both in splendid voice, and the opening *Merry widow waltz*, when they first sing the famous melody together and then lovingly hum it as a romantic reprise, is quite delightful. Songs like Krenn's title-number, *Schöne ist die Welt*, and Holm's *Ich bin verliebt*, from the same operetta, are splendidly done, and their charming duet from *The Land of smiles, Bei einem Tee à deux*, is matched by Krenn's heady *Dein ist mein ganzes Herz!*. The seductive *Gern hab'ich die*

Frau'n geküst from *Paganini* and the *Wolgalied* from *Der Zarewitsch* are hardly less successful, while the following duet, *Kosende Wellen*, is ravishing, as is the justly famous *Bist du's, lachendes Glück?* from *Der Graf von Luxemburg*. The only slight snag is that there is too little variety in the programme – almost all the music is relaxed and lyrical. However, to end the concert, Pilar Lorengar comes on stage and adds a Hungarian gypsy flavour with a vibrant *Hör'ich Cymbalklänge* from *Zigeunerliebe*. The recording is first class throughout.

Leigh, Walter (1905–43)

Concertino for harpsichord and string orchestra.
(B) *** BBC Radio Classics BBCRD 9119 [id.]. George Malcolm, ASMF, Marriner – FINZI: *Clarinet concerto* **(*) (with Concert ***).

Like Butterworth, whose *Banks of Green Willow* is included on this disc, Walter Leigh was killed in action before his gifts could develop fully. Inspired no doubt by the example of Poulenc and Falla, who had produced works for the medium in the early 1930s, his *Concertino for harpsichord and string orchestra*, with its heavenly slow movement, which dates from 1936, is an inventive and resourceful score, whose delights remain undimmed. It is currently unrepresented in the commercial catalogues and has surely never been played more winningly than it is here by George Malcolm. The balance with Marriner and his Academy is perfectly judged, so that the appearance of so lively a performance (from 1972), expertly engineered by the late James Burnett, usefully fills a gap. This is a highlight of a desirable bargain collection of English music, by Butterworth, Finzi, Vaughan Williams and Warlock – see our Concerts section, below.

Leoncavallo, Ruggiero (1858–1919)

I Pagliacci: highlights.
** Ph. Dig. 442 482-2 [id.] (from complete recording, with Domingo, Stratas, Pons; cond. Prêtre) – MASCAGNI: *Cavalleria rusticana:* highlights. **

This full-priced half-hour set of highlights is strictly for Domingo devotees. It is taken from the soundtrack of Zeffirelli's film of the opera, in which the great tenor, in splendid voice, heroically dominates the performance. Juan Pons sings the Prologue impressively, but the rest of the cast is far less impressive and Teresa Stratas's singing becomes very raw under pressure.

Lilburn, Douglas (born 1915)

Symphonies Nos. 1 (1949); *2* (1951); *3 in one movement* (1961).
*** Continuum Dig. 1069 [id.]. New Zealand SO, John Hopkins.

Douglas Lilburn is the doyen of New Zealand composers and, apart from his *Second Symphony*, which was briefly available on LP on the Jerusalem label, his music has enjoyed scant representation on disc – at least in the UK. The three symphonies collected here on this well-filled disc show an impressive musical mind at work. After his studies in New Zealand, Lilburn came to London and became a pupil and friend of Vaughan Williams, though he was sceptical about the then hidebound English musical establishment. There is a strong affinity with Scandinavian music, induced perhaps by the similarities of latitude and landscape, and an imposing formal coherence. The opening of the *Third Symphony in one movement* almost suggests an antipodean Holmboe. The musical invention shows a consistently high level of imagination, and the performances by the New Zealand Symphony Orchestra under John Hopkins, to whom the *Third Symphony* is dedicated, are thoroughly committed. Excellent, well-balanced recorded sound enhances the claims of this disc, and mention should be made of the unusually informative and authoritative note by John Thomson. Strongly recommended.

Liszt, Franz (1811–86)

Cziffra Edition, Volume 3: Piano concertos Nos. 1 in E flat; 2 in A.
(M) **(*) EMI CDM5 65252-2 [id.]. György Cziffra, Philh. O, André Vandernoot – TCHAIKOVSKY: *Piano concerto No. 1.* **

The two Liszt concertos suit Cziffra's bold, volatile manner very well indeed and, if there is an element of brutality in the *First Concerto*, there is also great excitement and drive, and the glittering solo playing has enormous panache. The work's lyrical side, too, is persuasively encompassed, as is the scintillating wit of the Scherzo. The *Second Concerto* is even finer. Cziffra displays a natural feeling for the often incongruous contrasts found in this work. There is much of the grand manner in his performance and he has clearly persuaded Vandernoot to back him up in his interpretation. The work's quicksilver moods bring a true feeling of spontaneity and the orchestra is with him to a man, as if together they were extemporizing it all, so that the finale brings great dash and flair. The recordings (made in 1958 and 1961) with bright primary colours and a tendency to harshness of lighting suit the music-making admirably. In spite of the use of the Kingsway Hall, the sound, though basically full, is comparatively two-dimensional. Zimerman on DG (423 571-2) or Richter on Philips (446 200-2) remain the primary recommendations for this coupling.

(i) *Piano concertos Nos. 1–2.* Symphonic poems: *Les Préludes; Mazeppa.*
**(*) Chan. Dig. CHAN 9360 [id.]. (i) Geoffrey Tozer; SRO, Järvi.

Tozer and Järvi establish a successful partnership. The Suisse Romande Orchestra, too, seems in good form. The performances are enjoyable, but alongside Cziffra they seem lightweight, although they have an attractive element of fantasy. There is nothing special, either, about the performances of the two symphonic poems, which generously increase the playing time to 71 minutes. Karajan (on DG 415 967-2 – see our main volume) is far more impressive in both, and especially in *Mazeppa*. The distant fanfare which heralds Mazeppa's triumphal return at the end of the piece, a frisson-creating moment in the Karajan performance, is here much too close.

Piano concertos Nos. (i) *1 in E flat;* (ii) *2 in A. Piano sonata in B min.*
(B) ** BBC Radio Classics BBCRD 9108 [id.]. John Ogdon, with (i) BBC Scottish SO, George Hurst; (ii) BBC SO, C. Davis.

It is good to have a memorial of so commanding a Lisztian as John Ogdon in such an enticing and generous coupling. The pity is that the performances are so variable. The *Second Concerto*, recorded at a Prom performance in 1971, is electrifying, a performance which alone makes the disc well worth buying, making one forget the vulgarity of the work, thanks to the concentration and clarity of both pianist and conductor. After that the *First Concerto*, recorded in Glasgow in 1983, is disappointingly slack, perhaps a reflection of Ogdon's periodic illness. Though the *Sonata*, recorded at the Canterbury Festival in 1987, is not as brilliant in its virtuosity as Ogdon could be at his peak, it is still a powerful and purposeful account, helped by full, immediate sound.

(i; ii) *Piano concerto No. 1 in E flat;* (i) *Piano sonata in B min.; Hungarian rhapsody No. 6;* (iii) *Années de pèlerinage: Vallée d'Obermann; Les jeux d'eau à la Villa D'Este.*
(B) **(*) DG 439 409-2 [id.]. (i) Martha Argerich; (ii) LSO, Abbado; (iii) Lazar Berman.

Argerich's approach to Liszt's flamboyant *E flat major Piano concerto* is a clear, direct, even fastidious one. She plays the *Larghetto* meltingly and there is an excellent partnership with Abbado, who seeks refinement without reducing the underlying tension. The CD remastering of the 1968 recording is very successful. The *B minor Sonata* is more characteristically impetuous. Her account has tremendous – even wilful – assurance and vigour; the bravura is breathtaking. But the work's lyrical feeling and indeed its breadth are to some extent sacrificed to the insistent forward impulse of the playing. To end the programme, Lazar Berman provides beautifully poised accounts of two favourite *Années de pèlerinage*.

A Faust Symphony.
*** EMI Dig. CDC5 55220-2 [id.]. Peter Seiffert, Ernst-Senff Ch. Male voices, Prague Philharmonic Ch., BPO, Rattle.
(M) ** Ph. Dig. 442 642-2 [id.]. Lajos Kozma, Concg. Ch. & O, Dorati.

Rattle's début recording with the Berlin Philharmonic brings an exceptionally warm and persuasive reading of the *Faust Symphony*. That it was recorded live is particularly helpful in this expansively episodic work. Rattle's spontaneity of expression, whether in pointing the main melodies or in moulding the all-important transitions, carries the ear on magnetically. He is helped by ravishing playing from the Berlin players, not least the strings, with the central movement representing the heroine, Gretchen, emerging as the high point of the performance. That the recording, made in the Philharmonie, sets the orchestra at a slight distance, notably the brass, prevents tuttis from biting as hard and as dramatically as they can. The impact of Bernstein's masterly (mid-priced) analogue version from Boston (DG 431 470-2 – see our main volume) is more powerful, but Rattle is closer to Beecham's pioneering stereo set, and on its own terms one quickly adjusts to the balances of the Berlin sound, relishing its beauty. The performance culminates in a rapt account of the choral apotheosis, with the men's chorus clearly focused and with Peter Seiffert singing radiantly, headily beautiful through the range.

The excellence of the playing of the Royal Concertgebouw Orchestra is not in question in the Philips version, recorded at public performances in 1982, but the effect in the outer movements is inclined to be melodramatic and Dorati shows little of the firmness of grip one associates with him. The slow movement is very slow indeed. The choral entry at the end makes an impressive effect within the Concertgebouw ambience, but overall this does not offer real competition to Bernstein, Muti or Beecham.

Hungarian rhapsodies Nos. 2, 6, 9, 12, 14 & 15 (arr. Peter Wolf).
(B) *** HM Dig. HMA 1903046 [id.]. Franz Liszt CO, János Rolla.

These transcriptions for strings are most enjoyable, giving the rhapsodies a chimerical lightness of texture. They are very well played indeed by this excellent orchestra, and Rolla's performances have nicely calculated rubato and plenty of spirit. Excellent, fresh recording. Not an alternative to the usual full-orchestra versions but a worthwhile bargain supplement.

SOLO PIANO MUSIC

Années de pèlerinage, 1st Year (Switzerland).
(BB) *** Naxos Dig. 8.550548 [id.]. Jenö Jandó.

Even remembering his excellent Beethoven and Haydn recordings, Jandó's performances of the Liszt *Années de pèlerinage* represent his most impressive achievement on record to date. The solemn opening of *La chapelle de Guillaume Tell* immediately shows the atmospheric feeling he can generate in this remarkable music, and its later, more grandiose rhetoric is handled with powerful conviction. *Au lac de Wallenstadt* undoubtedly sounds more delicate in Kempff's hands, but Jandó brings out the ambivalence suggested by the Byronic quotation which inspired the piece. The *Pastorale* is charmingly done, while the waters of *Au bord d'une source* trickle and dance skittishly. *Orage* rages furiously with splendid Lisztian flamboyance, yet the more subtle rhapsodical flow of *Vallée d'Obermann* is superbly controlled, contrasting with the simplicity of *Eclogue* and the nostalgia of *Le mal du pays*. Jandó then leads on naturally to a beautifully evocative performance of *Les cloches de Genève*, which again produces a thrilling climax. The recording is first class, and the feeling throughout is very much of the spontaneity of live music-making.

Années de pèlerinage, 2nd year (Italy); Supplement: Venezia e Napoli.
⊛ (BB) *** Naxos Dig. 8.550549 [id.]. Jenö Jandó.

This is Lisztian playing of the highest order, confirming the *Années de pèlerinage* as being among the supreme masterpieces of the piano. *Sposalizio* is superbly evoked, and the darker keyboard colouring of *Il penseroso* is equally compelling. The three contrasted *Petrarch Sonnets* bring the most imaginatively varied characterization, with No. 123 especially chimerical. But clearly Jandó sees the *Dante sonata* as the climactic point of the whole series. His performance has tremendous dynamism and power. One has the sense of Liszt himself hovering over the keyboard. After that, *Gondoliera* makes a wholly delightful interlude, while the closing *Tarantella* again brings astonishing impetus and bravura: Jandó's articulation is extraordinary in its lightness and clarity. Again first-class recording and the feeling of a continuous live recital. This is the disc to try first, and we have awarded it a token Rosette.

Années de pèlerinage, 3rd Year (Italy).
(BB) *** Naxos Dig. 8.550550 [id.]. Jenö Jandó.

The opening *Angelus* shows Jandó at his most imaginatively expansive and commanding, while *Les jeux d'eaux à la Villa d'Este* sparkles and glitters: this is playing of great appeal. The dark power of *Sunt lacrymae rerum* and the *Marche funèbre* bring resounding sonority from the piano's lower octaves, and then Jandó provides more expansive rhetoric for the composer's flamboyant and not entirely convincing spiritual apotheosis, *Sursum corda*. A splendid and satisfying culmination to a set of performances that can be compared with the finest from the past – including Bolet (Decca 410 160/1-2 and 411 803-2) and Berman (DG 437 206-2). The secret of Jandó's playing is that he is deeply involved in every note of Liszt's music.

Années de pèlerinage, 3rd Year: Tarantella. Harmonies poétiques et religieuses: Pensées des morts; Bénédiction de Dieu dans la solitude; Legend: St Francis of Assisi preaching to the birds. Mephisto waltz No. 1; Rhapsodie espagnole.
(M) *** Virgin Dig. CUV5 61129-2 [id.]. Stephen Hough.

Few pianists of the younger generation have quite such a magic touch as Stephen Hough, and this mid-price reissue in Virgin's new Ultraviolet series rescues one of his finest recordings. His performances of these six substantial Liszt pieces are all magnetic. With phenomenal articulation he brings sparkle and wit to the fireworks of the *Mephisto waltz* and the *Tarantella* from the third year of the *Années de pèlerinage*, and plays the extended slow movement of the *Bénédiction* with velvety warmth. The delicate tracery of the birdsong sounds in *St Francis's sermon to the birds* equally displays Hough's love of keyboard sound, beautifully caught in vivid recording. Among the most rewarding of all CDs of Liszt.

Mephisto waltz.
(M) (**(*)) RCA mono GD 60921. William Kapell – KHACHATURIAN: *Piano concerto;* PROKOFIEV:
   Piano concerto No. 3. (**(*)) ⊛

William Kapell's *Mephisto waltz*, recorded in 1945, must be one of the most dazzling ever, and it ranks alongside the likes of Horowitz, Cziffra, Richter and Pletnev. Moreover it comes with incandescent accounts of the Khachaturian *Piano concerto* (with Koussevitzky, no less), and the Prokofiev *Third Piano concerto*.

Piano sonata in B min, G. 178.
(M) **(*) EMI 09026 62590-2 [id.]. Artur Rubinstein – BACH: *Chaconne;* FRANCK: *Prelude, chorale
   and fugue.* ***

Rubinstein's performance of the *Sonata* was recorded in 1965, and there is some hardness of timbre in fortissimos. But at *piano* and *mezzo forte* levels (and there is a wider range of dynamic here than on some Rubinstein records) the tone is subtly coloured, and Rubinstein's mercurial approach to the music is wonderfully spontaneous, bringing an astonishing fire and brilliance for a pianist of his age, and considerable poetry to the more thoughtful moments.

*Cziffra Edition, Volume 1: Piano sonata in B min.; Concert paraphrase of Mendelssohn's Wedding
march from A Midsummer Night's Dream; Concert study No. 1: Waldesrauschen. Harmonies poétiques
et religieuses: Funérailles. Etudes d'éxécution transcendante d'après Paganini: La Campanella; La
Chasse.*
(M) *(**) EMI CDM5 65250-2 [id.]. György Cziffra.

Cziffra plays with extraordinary virtuosity and temperament, but his reading of the *Sonata* is exasperatingly wilful and self-aware. There are moments of exquisite poetry, but also a feeling of calculation, alternating with wild bursts of bravura. *Funérailles* is prodigiously powerful and has the widest range of mood and colour. *Waldesrauschen* brings fabulous digital dexterity, but Cziffra's impulsiveness runs away with the music's natural flow. The two *Paganini studies* show him at his most captivatingly chimerical. *La Campanella* was recorded live and its bravado brings a burst of well-deserved applause at the end; the opening of the paraphrase of the Mendelssohn *Wedding march* has a witty charm, though the grandiose central section is less appealing. The Paris studio recordings, made between 1958 and 1975, are variable, often unflatteringly hard.

*Piano sonata; 2 Légendes (St Francis of Assissi preaching to the birds; St Francis of Paolo walking on
the water); Harmonies poétiques et religieuses: Bénédiction de Dieu dans la solitude.*
(M) ** Erato/Warner Dig. 4509 97412-2 [id.]. François-René Duchable.

François-René Duchable gives a dashing account of the *B minor Sonata*; in terms of virtuosity, he is in the highest bracket. In a way, he allows his virtuosity to run away with him and dazzles rather than illuminates. Others have a greater musical impact, though this fine French pianist is often poetic, particularly in the third of the *Harmonies poétiques et religieuses*. The Erato recording is not as warm as the best of Philips (Brendel), Decca (Bolet) or HMV (Ousset).

Litolff, Henri (1818–91)

Concerto symphonique No. 4: Scherzo.
(M) *** Decca 425 082-2 [id.]. Clifford Curzon, LPO, Sir Adrian Boult – BRAHMS: *Piano concerto;*
   FRANCK: *Symphonic variations.* ***

Curzon provides all the sparkle Litolff's infectious *Scherzo* requires, and the 1958 Walthamstow Town Hall recording makes a delightful encore for the Brahms *Concerto* and the Franck *Symphonic variations* in this reissue in Decca's Classic Sound series. The fine qualities of the original sound, freshness and clarity, remain impressive.

Lloyd, George (born 1913)

Iernin (opera; complete).
*** Troy Dig. TROY 121/3 (3) [id.]. Hill Smith, Pogson, Herford, Rivers, Powell, BBC Singers &
     Concert O, composer.

George Lloyd was only twenty-one when in the early 1930s he wrote this ambitious opera, and there
is an open innocence both in the libretto (written by the composer's father in archaic opera-speak)
and in the warmly atmospheric, lyrical score. The piece was inspired by an ancient Cornish legend
about ten maidens turned into a circle of stones, one of whom, Iernin (pronounced Ee-er-nin), returns
in human form. She and the princely hero, Gerent, instantly fall in love, and though she represents
good from the faery world, with no sinister motives, she is cast out and he is cursed before the end of
Act II. The final Act sees Iernin transformed back into a stone, having sung a passionate farewell –
'*Not of your race am I*' – while Gerent returns to his faithful Cunaide, his original bride. The piece
was written for local performance in Cornwall in 1934 but, thanks to the *Times* critic seeing it and
giving it a welcoming review, it was later treated to a series of performances in London, which again
won the young composer much applause. Though this is ostensibly an old-fashioned opera, it
deserves revival, and on the recording – taken from a BBC Radio 3 presentation in 1988 – the
composer conducts a red-blooded, warmly expressive reading. Though some of the ensemble writing
is less distinguished, the offstage choruses of faery folk are most effective. As to the soloists, Marilyn
Hill Smith sings brightly in the title-role with all the agility needed, and the tenor, Geoffrey Pogson,
copes well with the hero's role, if with rather coarse tone. The most distinguished singing comes from
the rich-toned contralto, Claire Powell, as Cunaide. The third disc includes a half-hour interview with
the composer, which makes up in part for the absence of background notes in the booklet with the
libretto. Excellent, well-balanced BBC sound.

Lôbo, Duarte (c. 1565–1646)

Missa pro defunctis.
(BB) *** Naxos Dig. 8.550682 [id.]. Oxford Schola Cantorum, Jeremy Summerly – CARDOSO: *Missa*
     pro defunctis. ***

Here is another new name from the great age of Renaissance polyphony to conjure with – the
Portuguese composer, Duarte Lôbo, Mestre de Capela at Lisbon Cathedral. He was an almost exact
contemporary of Manuel Cardoso, whose music we have already discovered and who provides an
eloquent coupling for this splendid Naxos CD. As performed here, Lôbo's *Missa pro defunctis* for
double choir is a work of beautiful flowing lines (following directly on from Palestrina), bold
dramatic contrasts and ardent depth of feeling. The *Agnus Dei* is particularly beautiful. A solo treble
briefly introduces each section except the *Kyrie*, which adds to the effect of the presentation. This is
another triumph from Jeremy Summerly and his excellent Oxford group (38 singers), who catch both
the Latin fervour and the underlying serenity of a work which has a memorably individual voice.

Locatelli, Pietro Antonio (1695–1768)

Concerti grossi, Op. 1/2, 5 & 12; Il Pianto d'Arianna, Op. 7/6; Sinfonia in F min. (composta per le
esequie della sua Donna che si celebrarono in Roma).
*** Opus 111 OPS 30-104 [id.]. Europa Galante, Fabio Biondi.

Here is a most stimulating and enjoyable concert to convince any listener that Locatelli was far more
than just an accomplished also-ran pupil of Corelli. The composer himself set great store by his Opus
1 and they are remarkable works, full of individuality. The very opening of the first concerto in D
major brings a *Largo* melody of strong character, and allegros are appealingly sprightly. The last of
the set, in G minor, is one of the finest, consisting of five diverse movements, including a vivace
Sarabanda. The Sonata subtitled *Il Pianto d'Arianna*, from Opus 7, is even more ambitious, with ten
brief movements, an occasional whiff of Vivaldi, and plenty of drama. A solo violin dances like a
prima donna into the first *Adagio* and then returns, personably, into the central *Largo*, and the work
ends with a plaintively expressive slow movement. Perhaps most striking of all here is the *Sinfonia 'for
the funeral of his lady which took place in Rome'*, which opens with an accented *Lamento* of rare
intensity, in which the composer could be suggesting a heartbeat. It has to be said that this is not
certainly by Locatelli but, heard in context, it sounds like it. The performances here are full of cleanly
articulated, bouncing rhythmic vitality and are also persuasively expressive. This is another example

of the use of period instruments without any rigidity or sense of scholarly rectitude, and Fabio Biondi, who really knows his way about this repertoire, uses a triple rather than a double layout, with the concertino, a further tutti group still made up of soloists, plus the real tutti or ripieno. The organ continuo adds subtle extra colour. The recording is most vividly clear yet not too close, with plenty of natural ambience. Highly recommended.

Lotti, Antonio (c. 1667–1740)

Crucifixus.
(B) *** Decca Double 443 868-2 (2) [id.]. Palmer, Langridge, Esswood, Keyte, St John's College, Cambridge, Ch., Philomusica, Guest – BONONCINI: *Stabat Mater* ***; PERGOLESI: *Magnificat in C; Stabat Mater* **(*); D. SCARLATTI: *Stabat Mater;* A. SCARLATTI: *Domine, refugium factus es nobis; O magnum mysterium;* CALDARA: *Crucifixus.* ***

This short *Crucifixus*, which takes less than four minutes, may well have inspired the noble Caldara setting with which it frames Bononcini's beautiful *Stabat Mater* in this highly desirable collection of choral music. The Lotti setting is less elaborate in texture than Caldara's but it is hardly less noble or affecting. Performance and recording are excellent.

Ludford, Nicholas (1485–1557)

Masses; Magnificat benedicta & Motets (as listed below).
⊛ (M) *** ASV/Gaudeamus CDGAX 426 (4) [id.]. The Cardinall's Musick, Andrew Carwood.

This four-CD box gathers together the four splendid discs of Ludford's music performed by Carwood and his excellent group of singers, who are individually as impressive as in the blended whole. This is music of remarkably passionate feeling, and it brings to life a composer who spent much of his working life in St Stephen's Chapel at St Margaret's, Westminster. The cathedral records go right back to the fifteenth century (with the accounts preserved in duplicate!) and recent research has revealed fascinating personal details concerning this (until now) shadowy figure. He was an ardent Catholic and was very happily married – he paid for his wife to have her own pew and gave her an elaborate ceremonial burial. He then married again, and his second wife was instructed to prepare something more modest for his interment alongside his beloved first spouse. His music is little short of extraordinary, and we hope our Rosette will tempt collectors to explore it, either through this comprehensive box, which will retail at just short of £40, or by trying one of the individual issues.

Missa Benedicta et venerabilis; Magnificat benedicta.
*** ASV/Gaudeamus Dig. CDGAU 132 [id.]. The Cardinall's Musick, Andrew Carwood.

This was the second issue in Gaudeamus's admirable Ludford series and just missed inclusion in our last volume. Ludford uses the same plainchant for both works, but the voicing has a distinct emphasis at the lower end of the range, not only adding to the weight but also bringing a certain darkness to the sonority. The performance has the same spontaneous feeling that distinguishes this magnificent series throughout, and it confirms Ludford as one of the most emotionally communicative and original musicians of his age. The plainsong propers relate the music to the Feast of the Assumption. Excellent, full recording.

Missa Christi Virgo dilectissima; Motet: Domine Ihesu Christie.
*** ASV/Gaudeamus Dig. CDGAU 133 [id.]. The Cardinall's Musick, Andrew Carwood.

Missa Videte miraculum; Motet: Ave cuius conceptio.
*** ASV/Gaudeamus Dig. CDGAU 131 [id.]. The Cardinall's Musick, Andrew Carwood.

Nicholas Ludford is one of the least familiar of the Tudor masters; he never enjoyed the fame of his older contemporary, Fayrfax, or the much younger Tallis. Ludford was in the employ of St Stephen's Chapel, Westminster (which was destroyed by fire in 1834, three centuries after his death), and he has remained outside the repertoire of most cathedral choirs, little more than a name to those with an interest in early music. According to Dr John Bergsagel's *Grove* article, Ludford composed 11 complete Masses and three incomplete, thus making him 'the most prolific of English composers of masses'. This is music of great beauty, whose expressive eloquence and floating lines quite carry the listener away. Andrew Carwood proves an excellent advocate and the sound is also spacious and well balanced.

Missa Lapidaverunt Stephanum; Ave Maria ancilla trinitatis.
*** ASV/Gaudeamus Dig. CDGAU 140 [id.]. Cardinall's Musick, Andrew Carwood.

This fourth disc in Carwood's splendid series confirms that the Tudor composer, Nicholas Ludford, long neglected, is a polyphonic master to bracket with Taverner and Tallis. David Skinner has now extended his researches beyond Ludford's musical texts to reveal new details of his life-story and his long connection with St Stephen's, Westminster. This Mass, celebrating St Stephen the Martyr, is thought to have been written soon after he was appointed verger and organist there in 1527. In five-part polyphony the scale is formidable, culminating in a magnificent *Agnus Dei.* The performances, fresh and stylish, are punctuated by apt plainsong.

Lully, Jean-Baptiste (1632–87)

Phaëton (complete).
*** Erato/Warner Dig. 4509 91737-2 (2) [id.]. Crook, Yakar, J. Smith, Gens, Theruel, Ens. Vocale
   Sagittarius, Musiciens du Louvre, Marc Minkowski.

Mark Minkowski directs a compelling, consistently fresh and resilient reading of Lully's *tragédie en musique*, which at the time was described as 'the opera of the people'. Not only does Minkowski give the piece dramatic bite but he also brings out the colour and vigour of the many dance movements among much else. By baroque opera standards it is a compact work, 140 minutes of music squeezed on to only two CDs, and that adds to its attractions, with striking incidental movements hardly getting in the way of the story-telling. The prologue and five compact Acts have an involved plot which leads finally – as the title suggests – to the attempt of Phaeton, son of the Sun God, to drive in the chariot of the sun. This threatens to set fire to the Earth, whereupon Jupiter strikes him dead, to the apparent rejoicing of everyone. When Libye can then be partnered by her beloved Epaphus, it is hardly a tragedy at all, with their love earlier celebrated in two brief but intensely beautiful duets, punctuating the many solo airs. Any pathos is quickly swept aside in vigorous numbers, often with chorus. The solo cast is strong – with Véronique Gens most affecting as Libye, with Rachel Yakar and Jennifer Smith impressive too, and Howard Crook clean-focused and stylish in the name-part. The recording, a co-production between Erato and Radio France, is very vivid and immediate.

Lutoslawski, Witold (1916–94)

Symphonies Nos. 3–4; (i) *Les espaces du sommeil.*
*** Sony Dig. SK 66280 [id.]. LAPO, Esa-Pekka Salonen; (i) with John Shirley-Quirk.

Sony have now added a brand-new recording of the *Fourth Symphony* (completed only in 1992) to Salonen's previous coupling of No. 3 and *Les espaces du sommeil.* The format of the *Fourth,* Lutoslawski's culminating symphony, is elliptical, its broodingly atmospheric opening building through a shimmering web of orchestral colour and passages of violently energetic contrapuntal argument to an almost Waltonian lyrical cantilena and a darkly passionate climax. This slowly disintegrates into mutterings from soloists in the string section until a brief, emphatically rhythmic coda produces a sudden resolution. It is a remarkable piece, aurally fascinating as well as gripping. Salonen gives deeply committed, passionate accounts of both this and the dramatic *Third Symphony,* also built in one continuous span. Here he challenges the composer's own interpretation, and in *Les espaces du sommeil* Salonen provides a different slant from the composer himself, making it – with the help of John Shirley-Quirk as an understanding soloist – much more evocative and sensuous in full and well-balanced sound.

Lyatoshynsky, Boris (1895–1968)

Symphonies No. 1 in A min., Op. 2; Overture on 4 Ukrainian themes, Op. 20; Poem of reunification, Op. 40.
*** Russian Disc Dig. RDCD 11055 [id.]. Ukrainian State SO, Vladimir Gnedash.

Symphonies Nos. 2, Op. 26; 3 in B min., Op. 50.
*** Marco Polo Dig. 8.223540 [id.]. Ukrainian State SO, Theodore Kuchar.

Symphonies Nos. 4 in B flat min., Op. 63; 5 in C ('Slavonic'), Op. 67.
*** Marco Polo Dig. 8.223541 [id.]. Ukrainian State SO, Theodore Kuchar.

Symphony No. 4 in B flat min., Op. 63; (i) *On the banks of the Vistula, Op. 59;* (ii) *Lyric poem.*
** Russian Disc Dig. RDCD 11062 [id.]. Ukrainian State SO, Igor Blazhkov; (i) Viktor Sirenko; (ii) Fedor Glushchenko.

A new entry for the composer himself in *The Penguin CD Guide* as well as for the repertoire. Boris Lyatoshynsky was a name barely known in the West a year or so ago, though there were some Melodiya LPs of his music in circulation in the 1970s. Yet in recent months several CDs of his symphonies have appeared, including a CPO record from Cracow under Roland Bader of the *Fourth* and *Fifth Symphonies*, which has been well spoken of but which we have not yet heard. Lyatoshynsky was a pupil of Glière and, like him, much taken with the post-romanticism of Scriabin's early symphonies. His career was largely spent in Kiev, where he was regarded as the leading luminary of Ukrainian nationalism. He rates scarcely a mention in David Fanning's essay on 'The Symphony in the Soviet Union' (in *A Guide to the Symphony*, OUP, 1995) where his *Third Symphony* of 1951 is dismissed as 'feeble' (understandably, if you are comparing it with Shostakovich at his best) and the composer doesn't yet rate an entry in the *Oxford Dictionary*.

Lyatoshynsky began writing his *First Symphony* immediately after the First World War, while he was still studying with Glière in Kiev, and finished it in the early 1920s. Glière thought sufficiently well of it to conduct its première in 1923, and it is a well-crafted, confident score that inhabits the world of Russian post-nationalism, Strauss and Scriabin. It abounds in contrapuntal elaboration and abundant orchestral rhetoric. The *Second Symphony* followed in 1936, but its air of pessimism did not sit well in post-*Lady Macbeth* Russia and, like Shostakovich, Lyatoshynsky had to wait over two decades before it was first performed. Revised in 1940, it was not premièred until 1964 and was, generally speaking, still out of tune with the prevailing Soviet ideological climate. The *Third Symphony*, with which Marco Polo couple it, is a decade later and was composed in 1951, some three years after the Zhdanov affair had plunged Soviet composers into temporary paralysis. Mravinsky conducted its first performance in 1955 but, according to the conductor Theodore Kuchar's informative notes, Lyatoshynsky was still denounced during this period for his 'formalism, decadence, aggression, sadism and cacophony' – not bad going. Although the *Third Symphony* tries hard to be a good Soviet symphony, it does not wholly convince – and it does not quite ring true either as a more personal statement. (Incidentally, Mravinsky's recording of it, coupled with the Shostakovich *Festival overture*, Liadov's *Enchanted lake* and *Baba-Yaga*, is available on Russian Disc RD CD10900.)

The *Fourth Symphony* (1963) reflects something of the cultural thaw in the Soviet Union and is more directly Shostakovichian than its predecessors. It takes its inspiration from a novel by the Belgian symbolist writer, Rodenbach. Perhaps Glière, who was of Belgian descent, had drawn the composer's attention to it at some time. Its middle movement depicts what must be a mysterious, chimerical city to a Ukrainian, just as it is a source of wonder to everyone else: namely, Bruges. There is striking use of bells and celesta, and at times a suggestion of Messiaen. The *Fifth Symphony* (1966) certainly pays tribute to his master in using the Rus theme, *Il'ya Mourametz*, as well as a wide variety of Russian, Bulgarian and Serbian liturgical melodies. It aspires to explore the common roots of the Slavonic peoples; hence its title. There are many touches of colour and some token modernity, but basically this looks back to earlier masters – Glière, Rimsky-Korsakov and the Russian post-nationalists.

Those with exploratory tastes will find much to satisfy them in these symphonies, provided they are not expecting masterpieces. Whatever their failings, they are superior to the Kabalevsky symphonies and the present writer would sooner hear them than Kancheli. As far as performances are concerned, the Ukraine orchestra obviously is inside this music, and none of the playing is second rate. The Marco Polo recordings are more than marginally superior to the Russian Disc, and the performances sound much better rehearsed than is usually the case with this label, while the odd fillers on the Russian Discs are not of sufficient interest to tip the scales in their favour. Perhaps in view of the appearance of the cycle from Cracow, we had better return an interim verdict and wait until Bader's cycle is complete. In the meantime, though, no one whose interest has been aroused is likely to be disappointed with Kuchar.

MacDowell, Edward (1861–1908)

Suite No. 2 (Indian)
(B) ** Vox Box 116021–2 (2). Westphalian SO, Landau – HANSON: *Symphony No. 6;* ROREM: *Symphony No. 3;* SCHUMAN: *Symphony No. 7;* THOMSON: *Louisiana Story: suite.* **

MacDowell's generally derivative art is not generously represented in the catalogue, and this old recording is the only current version in the UK catalogue of the *Suite No. 2*, written during the first half of the 1890s, when Dvořák was staying in America. It is part of a useful but by no means top-drawer anthology of American music.

McEwen, John Blackwood (1868–1948)

A Solway Symphony; (i) *Hills o'heather; Where the wild thyme blows.*
*** Chan. Dig. CHAN 9345 [id.]. (i) Moray Welsh; LPO, Mitchell.

Sir John McEwen wrote his highly evocative *Solway Symphony* in 1911, a triptych of seascapes marked by magically transparent orchestration and crisply controlled argument. It was not performed until 1922, but then had the distinction of being the first British symphony ever to be recorded (by Vocalion in 1924). That success failed to keep it in the repertory, and this superb performance and recording is very welcome in bringing forward an outstanding work of its period. Only four years older than Vaughan Williams, McEwen was influenced by the folksong movement – notably here in *Hills o'heather* with its hints of reels – but the flavour is quite individual, with occasional echoes of Sibelius in the sparer moments. Above all, this is warm-hearted music. The first of the three movements of the symphony, *Spring tide*, is built on a striking motif, argued with clean-cut directness. The second movement, *Moonlight*, is developed, Sibelius-like, over a gently nagging ostinato, while the finale, *The sou'west wind*, opens with brassy exuberance in galloping compound time, and only later develops a stormy side, before ending darkly in F sharp minor. *Hills o'heather* is a charming movement for cello and orchestra, while *Where the wild thyme blows*, written in 1936 when McEwen retired as principal of the Royal Academy of Music, uses slow pedal points to sustain harmonically adventurous arguments. The performances, conducted by Alasdair Mitchell, who edited the scores, are outstanding, a well-deserved tribute to a neglected composer who was far more than an academic. The recording is sumptuously atmospheric.

Mackenzie, Alexander (1847–1935)

Benedictus, Op. 37/3; Burns – 2nd Scottish rhapsody, Op. 24; Coriolanus (incidental music): *suite, Op. 61; The cricket on the hearth: Overture, Op. 62; Twelfth Night* (incidental music): *Overture/suite, Op. 40.*
*** Hyp. Dig. CDA 66764 [id.]. BBC Scottish SO, Martyn Brabbins.

Sir Alexander Mackenzie became Principal of the London Royal Academy of Music and he wrote in the Stanford/Elgar/Parry tradition rather than showing any strong Scottish traits. However, in the *Burns rhapsody* he gets round the problem by using three Scottish folk tunes quite felicitously, notably 'Scots! wh hae' which is very emphatic. The second movement has charm, and indeed Mackenzie's own lyrical gift is quite striking in the jolly, at times Sullivanesque *Cricket on the hearth overture* (which also shows his deft orchestral skill), and of course the *Benedictus* with a melody typical of its time. The incidental music for *Twelfth night* is in the form of an overture, subdivided into six sections, with a Shakespeare quotation for each to identify its mood. These vignettes are attractively scored and have considerable character. The whole programme is presented with commitment and polish by the BBC Scottish Symphony Orchestra and makes a very agreeable hour and a quarter of not too demanding listening. The recording is excellent.

MacMillan, James (born 1959)

(i) *Seven last words from the Cross* (for choir and string orchestra); (ii) *Cantos sagrados* (for choir and organ).
*** RCA Catalyst Dig. 09026 68125-2 [id.]. Polyphony, with (i) LCO, composer; (ii) Christopher Bowers-Broadbent.

Following the success on RCA's Catalyst label of MacMillan's percussion concerto for Evelyn Glennie, *Veni, veni, Emmanuel*, comes this outstanding disc of two striking choral works. First seen on television in Holy Week, *Seven last words from the Cross* is a modern choral counterpart of Haydn's masterpiece. On one level it is just another of the slow-moving, easily mellifluous expressions of religious devotion that have had such spectacular success on CD. But where works by Górecki or Pärt can so readily be treated – wrongly – as aural wallpaper, MacMillan in a performance like this compels immediate and close attention. Each of these seven movements for chorus and strings intensifies each message from the Cross in dramatic contrasts and illustration. In four of them the title-words are amplified by liturgical texts in Latin or English, with the layering of musical ideas matching that of the words. Consistently they bring out the meaning so as to make one share Christ's suffering. To take the most obvious illustration, the fifth movement, *I thirst*, sparer and simpler than any, with high sustained monotones on violin harmonics, instantly has the listener translated to a parched desert.

The other work on the disc, *Cantos sagrados*, illustrates the layering device again. Written in 1989, this is a work inspired by Liberation Theology, bringing together MacMillan's left-wing views and his devout Catholicism. In each of the three movements he juxtaposes poems by Spanish-American authors (in translation) alongside traditional Latin texts, setting the violence and tragedy of political persecution against the consolations of faith. So the last and most poignant of the three, about a firing-squad, resolves on the words, ever gentler, of one of the executioners, 'Forgive me, *companero*.' This music is moving, not as wallpaper but as a vital experience. The idiom is clear and approachable, but hardly conventional. The performances, vividly recorded, are electrifying, with the players of the London Chamber Orchestra and the organist Christopher Bowers-Broadbent (in *Cantos sagrados*), as well as the fine singers of Stephen Layton's group, Polyphony, consistently inspired by the music and its composer-conductor. Characteristically, MacMillan's notes are terse, clear and helpful.

Madetoja, Leevi (1887–1947)

Symphony No. 3, Op. 55; Okon Fuoko: suite, Op. 58; Pohjolaisia suite, Op. 52.
*** Finlandia Dig. 4509-96867-2 [id.]. Finnish RSO, Saraste.

Jukka-Pekka Saraste's CD with the Finnish Radio Symphony Orchestra comes into direct competition with the Chandos issue from the Iceland Symphony Orchestra and Petri Sakari (see our main volume). For those who do not have it to hand, the *Third Symphony* was written in the mid-1920s while Madetoja was living in Houilles, just outside Paris. There are Gallic elements in this composer's music (he had hoped to study with Vincent d'Indy and, as a conductor, championed both d'Indy and Debussy, as well as such contemporaries as Szymanowski and Janáček) and, of course, Sibelius, with whom he briefly studied. But the symphony, as well as the suite from the opera *Pohjalaisia* (*The Ostrobothnians*) and the ballet-pantomime *Okon Fuoko*, shows a strong feeling for colour and atmosphere. The performances and recording are both good and there is no reason to deny them a three-star rating. All the same, Sakari gets more imaginative and sensitive performances from his Reykjavik forces, and his disc has the added and important bonus of offering the delightful *Comedy Overture* as well. Where a choice between the two is presented, do not hesitate – go for the Chandos version.

Mahler, Gustav (1860–1911)

Symphony No. 1 in D (Titan).
(M) *** EMI Dig. CD-EMX 2197; *TC-EMX 2197*. RLPO, Mackerras.
*** DG Dig. 431 769-2; *431 769-4* [id.]. BPO, Claudio Abbado.

Mackerras's Eminence version is not only one of the best-recorded of all but it offers a performance which, with crisply sprung rhythms, brings out the youthful freshness of Mahler's inspiration. The natural warmth and spontaneity of the reading have one concentrating on Mahler's arguments rather than on points of interpretation. Speeds are consistently well chosen and, though the finale is not quite so biting as the rest, the joy of the inspiration comes over winningly, so that the whole performance hangs magnetically together, making this an outstanding choice at mid-price.

Abbado's Berlin reading, like others in his Mahler series, was recorded live and, though one or two coughs intrude, the sound is fresh and full, bringing out the beauty and clarity of the Berlin strings. Though Abbado occasionally exaggerates the pointing of rhythms and speed-changes (as in the Laendler), the high voltage of the whole performance makes it most compelling, if not an obvious first choice.

Symphony No. 1 in D (with Blumine).
**(*) HM Dig. HMU 907118-2 [id.]. Florida PO, Judd.
** EMI Dig. CDC7 54647-2 [id.]. CBSO, Rattle.

James Judd demonstrates the virtuoso qualities of the Florida Philharmonic in a warm, well-pointed, spontaneous-sounding performance, slightly marred by a slow and rather heavy reading of the second-movement Laendler, which yet includes a most delicate account of the central Trio. The atmospheric recording sets the orchestra at a slight distance, which may take away some of the bite but enhances the beauty of the string-tone, not least in a dedicated performance of *Blumine*, which comes as a supplement after the symphony.

Recorded live in Symphony Hall, Birmingham, Rattle's reading with the CBSO is rather lacking in the spontaneity one expects. Speed-changes in the first movement sound self-conscious, as do the exaggerations of dotted rhythms, as in the Laendler second movement. It remains an acceptable reading, well recorded, but hardly matches Rattle's achievement in other Mahler recordings. As a preface to the main work, the *Blumine* movement, which Mahler excised from the original version of the symphony, is given with a freshness and spontaneity that rather shows up the rest.

Symphony No. 1 in D (Titan); (i) *Lieder eines fahrenden Gesellen.*
*** Teldec/Warner Dig. 9031 74868-2 [id.]. (i) Håkan Hagegård; NYPO, Masur.

Masur's live recording offers a fresh, unsentimental reading of the symphony with the generous and apt coupling of the related song-cycle, *Lieder eines fahrenden Gesellen*, all very well recorded with fine presence and atmosphere. The New York Philharmonic is in outstanding form, with crisp ensemble and clean attack. Masur underplays the irony in such characterful passages as the 'Jewish wedding' episode of the slow movement, but then allows himself a spaciously moulded account of the great melody in the finale, which contrasts with his bold, swaggering view of the main sections. Håkan Hagegård, balanced well forward, gives a clear, firm reading of the cycle, bringing word-meaning out into sharp focus. There may be even finer accounts of the symphony available, but the present coupling is still very much worth considering.

Symphony No. 2 (Resurrection).
(b) **(*) Decca Double Dig. 443 350-2 (2). Ziesak, Hellekant, San Francisco Ch. & SO, Blomstedt.
(bb) * Naxos Dig. 8.550523 (2) [id.]. Hanna Lisowska, Jadwiga Rappé, Polish Nat. RSO (Katowice), Antoni Wit.

Very well recorded in full and detailed sound and played with fine point and polish, Blomstedt's San Francisco version comes in a package of two discs at a special price – originally two for the price of one – and so makes a good bargain. The dramatic bite and rhythmic point go with keen control of tension, so that Blomstedt's slow speed for the second-movement *Andante* and fast speed for the third-movement Laendler (almost a waltz) are well sustained. In the many sections of the outer movements too, Blomstedt maintains concentration, even if at the very end of the Judgement Day scene his is an urgent and impulsive rather than a weighty reading or one with a sense of occasion. Excellent choral and solo singing.

Antoni Wit conducts a clean-cut, alert and well-pointed reading in full if slightly distanced sound. Yet, for all its fine qualities, it fails to bring out to the full the epic side of this work with its vision of Judgement Day. The impression of a relatively small-scale account is enhanced by the recorded sound, with the chorus and soloists – all first rate – set backwardly in a washy acoustic. Though the recording is refined and well detailed, other balances present problems too, for the first offstage clarion call is barely audible. Rattle's outstanding set (given a Rosette in our main volume) remains a clear first choice for this symphony (EMI CDS7 47962-8).

Symphony No. 3 in D min.
(b) (**) HM mono HMA 90501/2 [id.]. Rössl-Majdan, V. Boys' Ch., V. Konzertverein O, Charles Adler.

Harmonia Mundi on the Musique d'Abord label at budget price offers the very first recording of No. 3, made as recently as 1952. Charles Adler was one of the last surviving disciples of Mahler himself and, though ensemble is sometimes rough, as if the players were feeling their way, and the outer movements are spread very luxuriantly, dramatic tension is rarely absent. Though in this series documentation is limited, it is a pity that so little is made of the historic nature of the recording, with 1961 implied as the recording date.

(i) *Symphony No. 3. Symphony No. 10 (Adagio).*
* Sony Dig. S2K 52579 (2) [id.]. (i) Florence Quivar, Israel Kibbutz Ch. & Nat Rinat Ch.; Israel PO, Mehta.

Mehta's recording seriously lacks tension. This sounds like a run-through by performers who are not in tune with the music. It does not help that the recording is limited in range and allows the violins little bite. Mehta is best at evoking the *Wunderhorn* elements in the work, but even then ensemble is often slack. Florence Quivar is the sensitive mezzo soloist, but the recording too often brings out a marked vibrato. The fill-up of the opening *Adagio* of No. 10 is given with similar lack of commitment.

(i) *Symphony No. 3 in D min. Kindertotenlieder.*
**(*) Chan. Dig. CHAN 9117/18 [id.]. Finnie, Royal Scottish O, Järvi; (i) with R. Scottish Ch. & Junior Ch.

Järvi conducts a warmly expressive, spontaneous-sounding reading which brings out the joy behind Mahler's inspiration rather than any tragedy. This makes light of the epic qualities in this massive work, but that will please many Mahlerians. Though the ensemble of the Royal Scottish Orchestra is not as immaculate as that of some distinguished rivals, the bite of communication is always intense, helped by full, atmospheric Chandos recording. Järvi brings out the folk-like elements in the second and third movements, and Linda Finnie is a dedicated soloist in the hushed Nietzsche setting of the fourth movement, warm here rather than ominous. The bright choral singing of both women and children is a delight in the fifth movement, while the measured beauty of the finale is moulded most persuasively by Järvi, leading up inexorably to the thrust of the final climax. Not a first choice, perhaps, but quite an attractive one, particularly if you fancy *Kindertotenlieder* as a coupling. Finnie gives a felt, expressive reading, beautifully shaded in the second song. This again concentrates on warmth rather than tragedy, with the storm of the final song rather underplayed and with Finnie's tight vibrato exaggerated at times by the microphone. This does not displace Michael Tilson Thomas (Sony M2K 44553) or Bernard Haitink (Philips 432 162-2).

Symphony No. 4 in G.
*** DG Dig. 437 527-2 [id.]. Edita Gruberová, Philh. O, Sinopoli.
(BB) *** Naxos Dig. 8.550527 [id.]. Lynda Russell, Polish Nat. RSO, Antoni Wit.
(BB) **(*) RCA Navigator 74321 21286-2. Lisa Della Casa, Chicago SO, Reiner – R. STRAUSS: *Burleske.* **(*)
(M) ** Ph. 442 394-2 [id.]. Elly Ameling, Concg. O, Haitink.
** Ph. Dig. 434 123-2 [id.]. Sylvia McNair, BPO, Haitink.
*(*) Sony Dig. SK 48380 [id.]. Barbara Hendricks, LAPO, Salonen.

Sinopoli's is a positive, characterful reading which in the first movement draws an extreme contrast between the clucking opening theme – brisker than usual – and the broadly lyrical second subject – played slowly with extreme tenutos. What keeps such disparate elements together is Sinopoli's concentration, which never lets the performance fall into routine, the feeling of a run-through. The rustic elements of the second-movement Laendler, not least the bright scordatura violin, are enhanced by a delicious lilt. Though at the opening of the slow movement Sinopoli's moulding draws attention to itself, this is a rapt performance, naturally sympathetic, and Gruberová at her sweetest and freshest makes a charming soloist in the child-heaven finale, with Sinopoli jauntily exaggerating the dotted rhythms. Superb recording, as in the rest of the series.

Antoni Wit conducts a fresh, spontaneous-sounding reading, beautifully played and recorded, that can be warmly recommended at Naxos's bargain price. This is more enjoyable than many full-priced issues, with easy manners at well-chosen speeds, so that the rustic *Wunderhorn* element is sharply brought out. The flowing speed for the slow movement means that there is no suspicion of self-consciousness in the warm expressiveness. Lynda Russell is a pure-toned soprano soloist in the finale, both fresh and warm, with Wit giving a good lilt to the rhythm. Excellent sound, which gives a good bite and focus to the woodwind, so important in Mahler, though the Katowice horn favours a touch of East European tone.

Reiner's version was made – like most of his famous recordings – in Orchestra Hall, Chicago (in 1958). When it was first issued in stereo at the beginning of the 1960s we were dismissive (in an early edition of *The Stereo Record Guide*), partly on account of the recording balance and partly because of the idiosyncratic nature of the performances. The recording has been digitally remastered, with great improvement to the sound, which remains brightly lit but has attractively vivid detail, naturally glowing within the acoustic bloom of the hall. The performance is certainly wayward, but lovingly so; and everything Reiner does sounds spontaneous. There is a mercurial quality in the first movement and plenty of drama, too; the second is engagingly pointed but with a balancing warmth, the Viennese influence strong. The slow movement has striking intensity, with its rapt closing pages leading on gently to the finale in which Lisa della Casa, in ravishing voice, matches Reiner's mood. A highly individual reading, well worth its very modest price and unexpectedly but successfully coupled with the early *Burleske* of Richard Strauss, in which Reiner was joined (the previous year) by Byron Janis.

Haitink's earlier, late-1960s Concertgebouw version is predictably well played and the recording has come up very well indeed on the mid-priced CD reissue. The performance is sober, but it has an attractive simplicity, and Elly Ameling matches Haitink's approach in her serene contribution to the finale. Although it lacks drama, this is an easy version to live with, but the later, digital, Concertgebouw account with Roberta Alexander is well worth its extra cost, a most winning performance (Philips 412 119-2).

In his latest version Haitink conducts the Berlin Philharmonic in a warm, highly polished reading that can hardly be faulted, except that it rather misses the innocent freshness lying behind this of all Mahler's symphonies. In the slow movement this seems a poised rather than a rapt performance, very beautiful but not as moving as it can be. The child-heaven finale too is smoother than usual, with Sylvia McNair the light and boyish soloist. Full, well-balanced sound.

Esa-Pekka Salonen's finely detailed performance rarely conveys the freshness and magic of this work. Too often the performance sounds laboured, even when (as in the slow movement) a plain, simple approach brings the gentlest possible pianissimos. Even with Barbara Hendricks a characterful soloist, pointing the words rather heavily, the result is hardly joyful. The slightly distanced sound is on the dull side, with a heavy bass.

Symphony No. 5 in C sharp min.
(M) **(*) Virgin/EMI Dig. CUV5 61130-2 [id.]. Finnish RSO, Saraste.
** Dorian Dig. DOR 90193 [id.]. Dallas SO, Andrew Litton.
(B) HM HMA 905179 [id.]. ORTF, Hermann Scherchen.

Saraste and the Finnish Radio Orchestra offer a refined and well-paced reading, which gives a relatively light-weight view of the symphony. Mahlerian neurosis is largely missing, which might be justified in a work that ends in joy. Rhythms are beautifully sprung, and the *Adagietto* is the more tenderly moving for being a degree reticent and understated. Refined recording to match.

Soon after being appointed music director of the Dallas Symphony Orchestra, Andrew Litton made this live recording of the *Fifth*, showing not only what a fine band this is, impressive in every section, but what rapport he already had with the players. Though Litton's slow speed for the third-movement Laendler is so relaxed that the performance loses tension, the rest is compellingly alert, with crisp ensemble and well-chosen speeds. The pity is that the recording, made in the fine new Dallas hall, the Morton Meyerson Center, lacks body in the middle registers and is transferred at a low level, suggesting that (like many other successful concert halls) it is not an easy recording venue.

It is salutary to be reminded how bad Mahler performances could be as recently as 1965 in the live recording from Harmonia Mundi in the Musique d'Abord series. Hermann Scherchen was a great conductor but this is in every way a travesty of Mahler. Not only is the playing perfunctory in the allegros with Scherchen adopting impossibly fast speeds, but in the celebrated *Adagietto* he goes in the other direction with one of the slowest, most maudlin performances ever recorded. Worse still, there are savage cuts in both the third movement and the finale, so that the Scherzo, despite a sentimentally slow account of the second section, lasts a mere 5 minutes 35 seconds, where normally the timing is at least three times as long. The finale too, where the playing is scrappiest of all, brings another long cut in the middle. The sound is limited and dry, though the CD transfer gives it plenty of body. Abbado (DG 437 789-2), Mackerras (EMI CD-EMX 2164) and Barbirolli (EMI CDM7 64749-2) reign supreme in this work (see our main volume).

Symphony No. 6 in A min.
*** DG Dig. 445 835-2 [id.]. VPO, Boulez.
(B) *** Naxos Dig. 8.550529 (2) [id.]. Polish Nat. RSO (Katowice), Antoni Wit.
(B) *** Decca Double 444 871-2 (2) [id.]. Concg. O, Chailly – ZEMLINSKY: *Maeterlinck Lieder.* ***
(B) **(*) EMI CZS7 67816-2 (2). New Philh. O, Barbirolli – R. STRAUSS: *Metamorphosen.* **(*)
** Decca Dig. 436 240-2 (2) [id.]. Cleveland O, Dohnányi – SCHOENBERG: *5 Orchestral pieces.*
    WEBERN: *Im Sommerwind.* ***

Boulez in his first Mahler symphony recording for DG conducts a performance of the most enigmatic symphony which in its power and sharpness of focus transcends almost any rival. Rarely if ever has the Vienna Philharmonic been recorded with such fullness and immediacy in the Musikverein-saal as here. Boulez's control of speeds is masterful, never rushed, even though this is a performance squeezed on to a single disc, and the slow movement brings hushed, ravishingly beautiful playing of a refinement it would be hard to match. The finale is rugged and weighty, with crisp pointing of rhythms, making this an outstanding recommendation alongside Karajan (DG 415 099-2) who, on two discs, also includes Christa Ludwig's five *Rückert Lieder*. Though RL found this a performance observed rather than felt at white heat, EG was totally involved.

The excellent quality of the Katowice Orchestra of Polish Radio is impressively demonstrated in all four movements of this difficult symphony. The ensemble can hardly be faulted, hardly less polished than that of Dohnányi's Cleveland Orchestra, and the full, atmospheric recording enhances that quality with string-sound that is fresh, radiant and full of bloom, thanks in part to the helpful acoustic. Wit conducts a spacious performance, clean and well sprung, with the varying moods sharply contrasted. Above all, he conveys the tensions behind the notes, with the beauty of the slow movement warmly conveyed with easy, unexaggerated rubato and with the strings coping confidently with the occasional controlled portamento. On two full discs it becomes less of a super-bargain than some Naxos issues, but it stands comparison with any rival.

Chailly's version with the Concertgebouw offers brilliant playing and spectacular sound in a reading remarkable for the broad, rugged approach in the outer movements. There is relentlessness in the slow speed for the first movement, with expressive warmth giving way to a square purposefulness, tense and effective. The third movement brings a comparably simple, direct approach at a genuine flowing *Andante*. In its open songfulness it rouses Wunderhorn echoes. Anyone fancying the unexpected but attractive Zemlinsky coupling need not hesitate.

Barbirolli gives a characteristically expansive account of Mahler's *Sixth Symphony*, and there are many of the same fine qualities as in his version of the *Fifth*, recorded with the same orchestra a year later. But, particularly in the first movement, the slow tempo is allowed to drag a little, so that tension falls. Such wavering of concentration will not trouble everyone, but the 1967 Kingsway Hall recording has lost some of its bloom, even producing a degree of harshness in the present CD transfer. Moreover there is nothing like the same illusion of a live Barbirolli performance as there is with the *Fifth*. The coupling brings one of the most beautiful performances of Strauss's late masterpiece ever recorded; but again the sound is less full than on the original LPs.

In rich, full-bodied sound of demonstration quality Dohnányi conducts a superbly disciplined, sharply focused performance of the *Sixth*, in many ways Mahler's most problematic symphony. What is lacking is Mahlerian temperament. Strong and forthright as the performance is, it conveys nothing of uncertainty, still less of neurosis. Though the musical side could hardly be more perfectly achieved, the meaning and feelings behind the notes are conveyed only in part. What may yet swing the balance for some collectors is the coupling, superlative readings of Schoenberg's classic *Five Pieces* in their original orchestration and of the early, evocative tone-poem of Webern, *Im Sommerwind*.

Symphonies Nos. 6 in A min; 7 in E min.
**(*) EMI Dig. CDS5 55294-2 (3) [id.]. LPO, Tennstedt.

Not to be confused with Tennstedt's studio recordings of these symphonies in his Mahler cycle (EMI CMS7 64476-2 – see our main volume), the separate box from EMI offers live recordings made at the Royal Festival Hall in November 1991 and May 1993, among the last performances he conducted there before his retirement. Though they hardly replace the studio recordings, what makes them special is the extra warmth of expressiveness they offer, notably in the slow movement of No. 6 and in the two *Nachtmusik* movements of No. 7. Regularly speeds are a degree slower in both works, with Tennstedt in a live concert allowing himself greater flexibility, with more extreme tenutos, always with an expressive purpose. The downside is that ensemble is not as crisp, notably in No. 6 and in the slow introduction to the finale of No. 7. The recording of No. 6 is thin on string-tone, with too little Mahlerian bite and less detail than in the studio recording. The sound in No. 7 is good, with plenty of atmosphere as well as bite. Nevertheless, under the circumstances these reservations are of comparatively little consequence and this makes a valuable addition to the Tennstedt discography.

Symphony No. 7 in E min.
(M) *** DG Dig. 445 513-2 [id.]. Chicago SO, Abbado.
(BB) **(*) Naxos Dig. 8.550531 [id.]. Polish Nat. RSO, Michael Halász.
(*) Decca Dig. 444 446-2 (2) [id.]. Concg. O, Chailly – DIEPENBROCK: *Im grossen Schweigen*. *

Abbado's command of Mahlerian characterization has never been more tellingly displayed than in this most problematic of the symphonies; even in the loosely bound finale Abbado unerringly draws the threads together. The contrasts in all its movements are superbly brought out, with the central interludes made ideally atmospheric, as in the eeriness of the Scherzo and the haunting tenderness of the second *Nachtmusik*. The precision and polish of the Chicago orchestra go with total commitment, and the recording is one of the finest DG has made with this orchestra. A clear first choice in the mid-price range.

Very well played and treated to refined and well-balanced digital recording, the Naxos version offers excellent value on a single disc at super-bargain price. With well-chosen speeds, often brisk but unhurried, with crisp ensemble and good rhythmic point, the only snag is that, by the standards of the finest versions, it is undercharacterized, lacking both flamboyance and tragic weight. Even there one has an advantage in the haunting melody of the second *Nachtmusik*, which is the more moving for being treated in a restrained way.

With finely detailed, keenly idiomatic playing from the Royal Concertgebouw Orchestra, vividly and atmospherically recorded, Chailly conducts a reading of this most enigmatic of the Mahler symphonies which delicately brings out its vein of ironic humour as well as its gentle nostalgia. The two *Nachtmusik* movements are outstandingly well done, and so is the central Scherzo, which conveys the atmosphere of a nightmare fantasy. Chailly's approach to the outer movements is similar, lighter than usual, rather lacking the biting tensions such arguments imply. A plus point is the inclusion in the finale of the low timpani which Mengelberg had specially made for this work and which have now been restored. The rare and colourful Diepenbrock work makes a fascinating filler.

Symphony No. 7 in E min; (i) *Kindertotenlieder.*
*** DG Dig. 437 851-2 (2) [id.]. (i) Bryn Terfel; Philh. O, Sinopoli.

Sinopoli, always a very positive Mahlerian, is here at his most personal in presenting a colourful, sharply characterized reading. Even more than usual with Sinopoli it is a performance of extremes, controversial but powerful to a degree that makes the whole experience disturbing. The very opening is so gentle that the funeral march overtones are muted and one registers warmth and lyricism instead. In each section Sinopoli immediately establishes an individual approach, usually far slower than usual, sometimes much faster. The first *Nachtmusik*, shimmering and atmospheric, is as evocative as the lyrical second, in which Sinopoli at very slow speed uses extreme rubato in his careful moulding of phrase. In between, the third-movement Scherzo at high speed becomes a nightmare fantasy, while the vast finale is delivered with fine panache, at the end pushed to the verge of hysteria. The vivid recording which marks the whole series is here at its most involving, with the brass gloriously rich. Bryn Terfel's magnificent interpretation of the *Kindertotenlieder*, heartfelt and intense, crowns the issue. Soloist and conductor alike characterize each song sharply, both passionate – if in often contrasted ways – with Terfel's rich bass-baritone no less dominant for not being spotlit.

Symphonies Nos. 7 in E min.; 9 in D.
*(*) Chan. Dig. CHAN 9057/9 [id.]. Danish Nat. RSO, Segerstam.

Segerstam conducts a warm, bluff reading of the *Seventh Symphony* which makes light of its enigmatic side. He is helped by full, atmospheric recording which brings out an exceptionally ripe bloom on the brass. The two *Nachtmusik* movements are rather too heavy at slow speeds but the finale blazes to a fine conclusion. The pity is that this generally enjoyable performance is coupled with an account of the *Ninth* that is both sluggish in its speeds and lumbering in its rhythms, one of the least successful of Segerstam's Mahler series, with recording less full and ripe than most.

Symphony No. 8 (Symphony of 1000).
⊛ *** DG Dig. 435 433-2 [id.]. Studer, Blasi, Jo, Lewis, Meier, Nagai, Allen, Sotin, Southend Boys' Ch., Philh. Ch. & O, Sinopoli.
(B) *** Sony SBK 48281 [id.]. Robinson, Marshall, Heichele, Wenkel, Laurich, Walker, Stilwell, Estes, Frankfurt Kantorei, Singakademie, Limburger Boys' Ch., Op. & Museum O, Gielen.
**(*) DG Dig. 445 843-2 (2) [id.]. Studer, McNair, Rost, Von Otter, Lang, Seiffert, Terfel, Rootering, Tölz Boys' Ch., Berlin R. & Prague Philharmonic Ch., BPO, Abbado.

Giuseppe Sinopoli crowns his Mahler cycle with the Philharmonia in a ripely passionate account of this most extravagant of the series, recorded with a richness and body that outshine any digital rival. In vividness of atmosphere it is matched only by Solti's magnificent analogue version, recorded in Vienna. Sinopoli, highly analytical in his methods and flexible in his approach to speed, here conveys a warmth of expression that brings joyful exuberance to the great outburst of the opening *Veni creator spiritus*. It builds into one of the most thrilling accounts ever, helped by a superb team of soloists and incandescent choral singing, recorded with fine weight and body. In the long second movement and its setting of the closing scene of *Faust*, Sinopoli's approach is almost operatic in its dramatic flair, magnetically leading from one section to another, with each of the soloists characterizing strongly. As in the first movement, the chorus sings with fine control and incandescent tone, from the hypnotic first entry through to a thrilling final crescendo on '*Alles vergangliche*'. We accordingly transfer our Rosette from the EMI Tennstedt recording to this new one from DG.

Recorded live at the opening of the Alte Oper in Frankfurt in August 1981, Gielen's version offers a direct, fresh reading, full of atmosphere, in which brisk speeds allow ample weight. Far more than the Abbado Berlin version, it vividly conveys the atmosphere of a great event. The analogue recording is less full than some, but it is naturally balanced with plenty of presence, if with brass a little distant. The chorus sings with heartfelt intensity, and the soloists make a distinguished team, except that the ringing Heldentenor, Mallory Walker, develops a beat in the voice under stress as Dr Marianus. On a single disc at budget price in Sony's Essential Classics series, it makes an outstanding bargain.

Claudio Abbado recorded the *Symphony of a Thousand* live in the Philharmonie in Berlin in February 1994 and, from all accounts, it was a thrilling experience. Sadly – a point very clear in relation to the rival DG version from Sinopoli – the recording, keenly analytical and precisely balanced, fails to capture the very quality one would expect in a live account: a sense of atmosphere. Except in the final chorus, '*Alles vergangliche*', where the tension and slow momentum are irresistible, making a magnificent climax, this is too often a detached-sounding reading, clear and transparent rather than intense, relating the music more than usual to Mahler's *Knaben Wunderhorn* inspirations. The chorus in this live performance sings powerfully, but ensemble is not always ideally crisp. The soloists make a fine, expressive team. Cheryl Studer, who sings Magna peccatrix in the Sinopoli version, is here the Penitent Woman instead, and Sylvia McNair instead sings Magna peccatrix with fresh, light tone.

Symphony No. 8; Symphony No. 10: Adagio.
** Chan. Dig. CHAN 9305/6 (2) [id.]. Inga Nielsen, Bjerno, Bonde-Hansen, Dolberg, Gjevang,
   Sikiä, Hynninen, Stabell, Copenhagen Boys' Ch., Berlin Philharmonic Ch., Danish Nat. R. Ch. & SO, Segerstam.

The chief merit of Leif Segerstam's Danish Radio version of the *Eighth Symphony* lies in the weight and warmth of the sound, with plenty of atmosphere and the low organ sound superbly caught. After a rather perfunctory opening of the *Veni creator spiritus*, Segerstam succeeds in conveying the warmth and spontaneity of live communication, even if he hardly matches his finest rivals in intensity or refinement of detail. The result is enjoyable, with good solo and choral singing, but it fails to communicate the feeling of a great event. The first movement is preceded by a well-played, well-recorded account of the *Adagio* from the *Tenth Symphony*, which yet lacks emotional weight and tension.

Symphony No. 9 in D min.
*** DG Dig. 445 817-2 [id.]. Philh. O, Sinopoli.
(B) ** DG 437 467-2 (2) [id.]. Chicago SO, Giulini.
(BB) ** Naxos Dig. 8.550535-6 (2) [id.]. Polish Nat. RSO (Katowice), Michael Halász.

Those who want an unbuttoned, overtly emotional reading of Mahler's last completed symphony will find Sinopoli's version an excellent choice. He may occasionally nudge speeds and phrases this way and that, but always in the interests of expressive warmth; and the full, glowing sound, with radiant brass and a vivid sense of presence, adds to the impact. Few versions match this in the weight and power of the great climaxes in the massive, measured outer movements, while the crisp pointing of the middle two movements brings out their grotesquerie very vividly. Sinopoli presses so hard at the end of the third-movement Scherzo that it acquires the sort of wildness one expects in a live performance, adding to the excitement. If the slow finale is passionate rather than spiritual, Sinopoli pursues that approach to the end, with the final hushed pianissimo still retaining warmth, instead of disappearing into nothingness.

Giulini's 1977 version lacks the very quality one expects of him: dedication. He sets tempi that are a shade too measured for a sense of impetus to assert itself. The orchestral playing is of the highest quality and the Chicago recording is impressive too, though its element of glamour does not help in conveying hushed concentration. This reappears as two-discs-for-the-price-of-one as a DG Double, but Barbirolli (EMI CDM7 63115-2) manages to get the work on a single CD at mid-price, so Giulini also costs more.

Under Michael Halász the Polish Radio Orchestra of Katowice plays with the polish and finesse that also mark its Mahler recordings with Antoni Wit. But only in the long, slow finale does the performance convey the tensions of live communication, thanks largely to the heartfelt yet poised playing from the rich-toned strings. In the first movement the wind soloists are the most successful, with the chill of the flute solo in the coda beautifully set against the ripe tone of the oboe. Both there and in the middle movements Halász's rhythmic control is a little staid so that, for all the precision of the virtuoso Scherzo, it lacks excitement. Whatever the reservations, with full if slightly distanced sound, this might be considered in the lower price-range, although Karajan's mid-priced DG Double set offers a generous bonus of Lieder and is an altogether better proposition for bargain-hunters.

Symphony No. 9 in D; (i) *Kindertotenlieder; 5 Rückert Lieder.*
(B) *** DG Double 439 678-2 (2) [id.]. BPO, Karajan; (i) with Christa Ludwig.

Fine as Karajan's other Mahler recordings have been, his two accounts of the *Ninth* transcend them. It is the combination of richness and concentration in the outer movements that makes for a reading of the deepest intensity, while in the middle two movements there is point and humour as well as refinement and polish. Helped by full, spacious recording, the sudden pianissimos which mark both movements have an ear-pricking realism such as one rarely experiences on record, and the unusually broad tempi are superbly controlled. In the finale Karajan is not just noble and stoic; he finds the bite of passion as well, sharply set against stillness and repose. Yet within two years Karajan went on to record the work even more compulsively at live performances in Berlin. The major difference in that later recording is that there is a new, glowing optimism in the finale, rejecting any Mahlerian death-wish and making it a supreme achievement. That digital version remains a clear first choice (410 726-2 – see our main volume), but this earlier (1980) analogue performance makes a remarkable bargain alternative, reissued as a DG Double and costing half as much as the later, digital recording. Moreover the performances of the *Kindertotenlieder* and *Rückert Lieder* have a distinction and refinement of playing which stand out above all. Ludwig's singing is characterful too, with the poise and stillness of the songs beautifully caught. Even if the microphone conveys some unevenness in the voice, the recording is rich and mellow to match the performances.

Symphony No. 10 in F sharp (unfinished) (revised performing edition by Deryck Cooke).
(B) **(*) Decca Double Dig. 444 872-2 (2) [id.]. Berlin RSO, Chailly – SCHOENBERG: *Verklärte Nacht.* **

Reissued at bargain price on this Double Decca, Chailly's Decca version is superbly recorded and his grasp of the musical structure is keen. The Berlin Radio Orchestra is highly responsive, although the internal tension of the music-making is not as high as in some other recordings.

Kindertotenlieder; Lieder eines fahrenden Gesellen.
(M) **(*) Decca 440 491-2 [id.]. Kirsten Flagstad, VPO, Boult – WAGNER: *Wesendonck Lieder.* ***

This has been reissued as part of Decca's Kirsten Flagstad Edition which, despite any minor criticisms, remains a worthy representation of the art of one of the great singers of our time. Flagstad sings masterfully in these two most appealing of Mahler's orchestral cycles, but she is unable to relax into the deeper, more intimate expressiveness that the works really require. The voice is magnificent, the approach always firmly musical (helped by Sir Adrian's splendid accompaniment), but this recording is recommendable for the singer rather than for the way the music is presented.

Das klagende Lied (Parts I–III; complete).
** Chan. Dig. CHAN 9247 [id.]. Rodgers, Finnie, Blochwitz, Hayward, Bath Festival Ch., Waynflete Singers, Bournemouth SO, Hickox.

Richard Hickox conducts a warm, easy-going account at spacious speeds of Mahler's early essay in the macabre, bringing out its lyrical associations with his *Knaben Wunderhorn* music rather than anything more sinister. In the long first section – which Mahler himself disowned – Hickox does not quite sustain the necessary tension, not helped by the juddery baritone soloist, Robert Hayward. Hickox is most at home in the exuberantly brassy celebration music of the final wedding scene. The chorus sings warmly and idiomatically and, apart from the offstage band being too distantly off-stage in the final section, the recording is full, atmospheric and well detailed. However, Simon Rattle's EMI Birmingham version with Döse, Hodgson, Tear and Rea still remains a clear first choice (CDC7 47089-2 – see our main volume).

(i) *Des Knaben Wunderhorn;* (ii) *Lieder eines fahrenden Gesellen.*
(B) **(*) Carlton PCD 2020 [id.]. (i) Dame Janet Baker, Sir Geraint Evans, LPO; (ii) Roland Hermann, Symphonica of L.; (i; ii) Wyn Morris.

Dame Janet and Sir Geraint recorded Mahler's cycle in 1966 for Delysé, long before they both received the royal accolade. This was also Wyn Morris's first major essay in the recording studio; though he secures crisp playing from the LPO, the orchestral phrasing could ideally show more affection and be less metrical in charming songs that need some coaxing. Dame Janet in particular turns her phrases with characteristic imagination, and her flexibility is not always matched by the orchestra. Baker could hardly be more ideally cast, but Sir Geraint is more variable. He points the humour of the song about the cuckoo and the donkey with typical charm, but sometimes the voice does not sound perfectly focused. That may be attributed partly to the recording which, although vivid and warmly atmospheric, is not always cleanly detailed, as at the very opening with its resonance in the bass. However, it is good to have this recording available again at bargain price. Roland Hermann's performance of the *Lieder eines fahrenden Gesellen* is fresh, committed and intelligent, though his baritone is not always flattered by the otherwise atmospheric stereo. At times expressiveness is underlined too heavily, but better this than a lack of warmth, and there is plenty of drama. The orchestra is well caught, full and spacious. However, Szell's version of *Des Knaben Wunderhorn* with Schwarzkopf and Fischer-Dieskau remains unsurpassed (EMI CDC7 47277-2).

Das Lied von der Erde.
(B) *** BBC Radio Classics BBCRD 9120 [id.]. J. Baker, Mitchinson, BBC Northern SO, Leppard.
(B) **(*) DG 439 471-2 [id.]. Nan Merriman, Ernst Haefliger, Concg. O, Jochum. —
** EMI Dig. CDC7 54603-2 [id.]. Agnes Baltsa, Klaus König, LPO, Tennstedt.

(i) *Das Lied von der Erde;* (ii) *5 Rückert Lieder.*
(B) **(*) Sony SBK 53518 [id.]. (i) Lilli Chookasian, Richard Lewis, Philadelphia O, Ormandy; (ii) Frederika von Stade, LPO, Andrew Davis.

Taken from a performance for radio in the Free Trade Hall, Manchester, the Leppard version offers Dame Janet Baker at her very peak in 1977, giving one of the most moving and richly varied readings of the contralto songs ever. The final *Abschied* has a depth and intensity, a poignancy and, at the end, a feeling of slipping into the unconscious, that set it above even Dame Janet's earlier recording with Haitink (Philips 432 279-2). John Mitchinson may not have the most beautiful tenor, but his voice focuses ever more securely through the work, with many cleanly ringing top notes. Raymond Leppard defies any idea that he is just a baroque specialist, finding wit as well as weight and gravity. He draws fine playing from the orchestra, now renamed the BBC Philharmonic, though the body of strings is thin for Mahler. Acceptable BBC sound, with the voices naturally placed, not spotlit: with any reservations, this remains an essential purchase for admirers of Dame Janet and Mahler.

A coupling for *Das Lied* is rare enough, but so generous a one as the *Rückert Lieder* on a bargain-label issue is worth investigating. Ormandy conducts a purposeful, superbly played reading, dating from 1966, that may lack something in Mahlerian magic but which, with fine solo singing, carries you magnetically through to the final climax. Richard Lewis is by his standards sometimes a little rough in tone, but his perception is unfailing, and Lilli Chookasian's warm, weighty mezzo, with vibrato well controlled, brings poise and gravity to her songs, not least the final *Abschied*. Frederika von Stade makes a characterful soloist in the *Rückert Lieder*, sometimes colouring the voice too heavily; but, with fine bloom on the 1976 sound, she brings out ravishing tonal contrasts, helped by Andrew Davis's sympathetic accompaniment.

Generally Jochum has avoided conducting Mahler – as a Brucknerian, underlining the point that these massive masters of symphony are totally contrasted. His reading of *Das Lied*, beautiful and compelling as it is, helps to explain why, for it speaks of the radiant calm of the Bruckner temperament rather than of Mahlerian tensions. Excellent solo singing and fine, clean recording, vivid and kind to the voices: worth considering at bargain price.

It is sad that Tennstedt's recording of *Das Lied* rather fails to crown his achievement in his Mahler symphony cycle. Though his interpretative insight is never in doubt, the tension behind the performance is relatively low, not helped by the disappointing recorded sound, lacking in bass and with a relatively narrow dynamic range. The moments of hushed intensity, of which there are many, notably in the long final *Abschied*, fail to have their heart-stilling effect. In that the choice of Agnes Baltsa as mezzo soloist is in good measure to blame. Not only is the tone too often made impure with pronounced vibrato, words are so heavily inflected that the oriental detachment implied in the poems is completely missing. For all the expressive weight of the mezzo songs, the singing should be poised if the full emotion is to be conveyed. Klaus König is a clear-toned Heldentenor, strained at times at the top but always well focused, though he too misses the Mahlerian magic.

Das Lied von der Erde. (arr. Schoenberg & Riehn).
*** RCA Dig. 09026 68043-2 [id.]. Jean Rigby, Robert Tear, Premiere Ens., Mark Wigglesworth.

For the performing society he founded in Vienna, Schoenberg sparked off a whole series of chamber arrangements of works by Mahler and others. This one of *Das Lied* was left unfinished but, as completed by the scholar, Rainer Riehn, the clarification of an already transparent score brings many bonuses, not least a balance that allows the soloists to sing without stress even in the heaviest climaxes. Robert Tear's tenor tone has not sounded so free in years, and Jean Rigby movingly sustains the slowest possible speed for the long final *Abschied*, helped by the unfailing concentration of Mark Wigglesworth and the ensemble he created. In a superb instrumental team the oboe of Alison Alty is outstanding.

Malipiero, Gianfrancesco (1882–1973)

Symphonies Nos. 1 (In four tempi as The Four Seasons); 2 (Elegiaca); Sinfonia del silenzio e de la morte.
* Marco Polo Dig. 8.223603 [id.]. Moscow SO, Antonio de Almeida.

Symphonies Nos. 5 (Concertante in Eco); 6 (Degli archi); 8 (Symphonia brevis); 11 (Della Cornamuse).
* Marco Polo Dig. 8.223696 [id.]. Moscow SO, Antonio de Almeida.

Symphony No. 7 (delle canzoni); Sinfonia in one tempo; Sinfonia per Antigenida.
* Marco Polo Dig. 8.223604 [id.]. Moscow SO, Antonio de Almeida.

Symphonies Nos. 9 (dell'ahimè); 10 (Atropo); Sinfonia dello Zodiaco.
* Marco Polo Dig. 8.223967 [id.]. Moscow SO, Antonio de Almeida.

Apart from his pioneering work on his Monteverdi Edition, Malipiero was a powerful force in modern Italian music, both as a teacher and as an administrator. He played an active role in the ISCM (International Society for Contemporary Music). The *Eight string quartets* are all recorded and discussed in our main edition, where we gave a guarded welcome to the Marco Polo coupling of the *Third* and *Fourth Symphonies*. Much the same reservations apply throughout the cycle: they really need far better advocacy if they are to be remotely convincing. Some of these performances sound distinctly under-rehearsed. The *Symphony No. 6, for strings* is the only one to have been recorded before (in the days of mono LP), so any survey of this repertoire must be welcomed. But such little-known repertory deserves more persuasive performances if those who have yet to see the light are to be encouraged to pursue. The performances under Antonio de Almeida are better than rough-and-ready – but not much! The resonant acoustic serves to coarsen the texture and harshen the strings.

Martin, Frank (1890–1974)

Ballades: (i) *for cello & small orchestra;* (ii) *for flute, strings & piano;* (iii) *for piano & orchestra;* (iv) *for saxophone & small orchestra;* (v) *for viola, wind, harpsichord, timpani & percussion;* (vi) *for trombone & piano.*
*** Chan. Dig. CHAN 9380 [id.]. (i) Peter Dixon; (ii) Celia Chambers; (ii–iii; v–vi) Roderick Elms; (iv) Martin Robertson; (v) Philip Dukes, Rachel Masters; (vi) Ian Bousfield; LPO, Matthias Bamert.

The *Ballades* are among Martin's most personal utterances. Those for piano, flute and trombone come from 1939–40, the period of *Le vin herbé*; the *Ballade* for cello and small orchestra (1949) and that for viola, wind, harp, harpsichord, timpani and percussion come from 1972, the period of *Polyptyque* and the *Requiem*. Only three of the *Ballades* are otherwise currently available; there are no alternative versions of the *Saxophone ballade* or the *Ballade for cello*, except in the version with piano. The only other recording of the *Ballade for viola and wind* was by Menuhin and has long been out of circulation. So the present issue is a most valuable addition to the Martin discography, particularly in view of the excellence and commitment of the performances. Subtle, state-of-the-art recording with no false 'hi-fi' brightness, but a natural and unobtrusive presence. An indispensable disc for admirers of this subtle and rewarding master.

Symphonie concertante (arr. of *Petite symphonie concertante* for full orchestra); *Symphony; Passacaglia.*
⊕ *** Chan. Dig. CHAN 9312 [id.]. LPO, Mattias Bamert.

The *Symphony* is new to the gramophone and is a haunting and at times quite magical piece. Taking more than half an hour, it is in four movements and comes from 1936–7, so it precedes *Le vin herbé*. It was premièred by Ansermet in Lausanne the following year, but he never recorded it. Indeed it has lain neglected until now not only by the gramophone but in the concert hall. It has all the subtlety of colouring of the mature Martin and is a piece of great imaginative resource. The slow movement in particular has an other-worldly quality, suggesting some verdant, moonlit landscape, strongly related in its muted colouring to the world of Debussy's *Pelléas et Mélisande*. The two pianos are effectively used and though, as in the *Petite symphonie concertante*, lip service is paid to the twelve-note system, the overall effect is far from serial. Its main companion here is the transcription Martin made for full orchestra of the *Petite symphonie concertante* the year after its first performance, without the harp, harpsichord and piano soloists and with an ample complement of wind, brass and other instruments. Harp and piano are in fact used for colouristic effects but completely relinquish any hint of soloist ambitions. The *Passacaglia* is the only modern recording of Martin's 1962 transcription for full orchestra of his much (and rightly) admired (1944) organ piece. Sensitive playing from the LPO under Matthias Bamert and exemplary Chandos recording.

Mass.
*** United Recordings 88033 [id.]. Vasari, Jeremy Backhouse – HOWELLS: *Requiem* etc. ***

The Martin *Mass* is one of his purest and most satisfying utterances. It was written in 1922 for his own satisfaction without the thought of performance. Although there have been a number of recordings, some of quality, few remain in the catalogue for any length of time. Irrespective of competition, the present account is quite masterly in every respect and Vasari, a choir conducted by Jeremy Backhouse, get remarkably fine results. A very convincing performance, and an exemplary recording.

Martinů, Bohuslav (1890–1959)

Cello concertos Nos. 1–2.
**(*) Sup. 1110 3901-2 [id.]. Angelica May, Czech PO, Václav Neumann.

Cello concertos Nos. 1–2; Concertino in C min. for cello, wind instruments, piano & percussion.
*** Chan. Dig. CHAN 9015 [id.]. Raphael Wallfisch, Czech PO, Bělohlávek.

Neither recording is exactly new: Angelica May and the Czech Philharmonic and Václav Neumann made theirs in 1981; Raphael Wallfisch and Bělohlávek followed ten years later. The *Cello concerto No. 1* was composed in 1930 and premièred by Gaspar Cassadó the following year. Martinů revised it in 1939, expanding the orchestral forces, when the soloist was Pierre Fournier. On hearing it on French Radio in 1955 while living in Nice, the composer was struck by the inadequacy of the scoring and subjected it to a further overhaul, dropping the piano and tuba parts from the orchestra and (with the help of Fournier) revising the cadenza. It is in this third form that both artists have recorded it. The *Cello concerto No. 2*, written in New York at the turn of the year 1944–5, is the bigger of the two, some 36 minutes in all, and had to wait until Saša Večtomov performed it in 1965, six years after Martinů's death. It opens with a very characteristic and infectiously memorable B flat tune, and there is much of the luminous orchestral writing one associates with the *Fourth* and *Fifth Symphonies*. It is a warm-hearted, lyrical score with a Dvořák-like radiance.

The fine German cellist Angelica May, a Casals pupil, gives a good account of both scores and, in the absence of the Wallfisch, this is perfectly recommendable. But as both performance and recording, her version is outclassed by the Chandos, which has much greater definition and presence and also has the advantage of offering the *Concertino for cello, wind, piano and percussion* (1924). Like the *Concerto No. 2*, it languished unperformed for two decades until Ivan Večtomov (the father of Saša, who premièred the latter work) gave it in Prague in 1949.

Piano concertos Nos. 2; 3; 4 ('Incantation').
⊛ *** RCA Dig. 09026 61534 [id.]. Rudolf Firkušný, Czech PO, Libor Pešek.

In our main volume we gave a generally cool reception to Emil Leichner's recording of all five concertos with Jiří Bělohlávek and the Czech Philharmonic, very much a stopgap. The present set by Rudolf Firkušný, who premièred all three concertos and was the dedicatee of No. 3, was well worth waiting for. The finest of them is *Incantation (Piano concerto No. 4)*, which here receives a performance that is unlikely ever to be surpassed. Its exotic colourings and luminous, other-worldly landscape with its bird-like cries and extraordinary textures have never been heard to better advantage. It is a work of strong atmosphere and mystery, and Firkušný is its ideal advocate. He makes a stronger case for the *Second Piano concerto* than any previous pianist, and the brightly optimistic *Third* is hardly less persuasive. It is astonishing to think that he was over eighty when these performances were recorded. There are none of the tell-tale signs of age that distinguished many of his older contemporaries: indeed the performances radiate youthful vitality. Part of the success of these performances is the quality of the orchestral support. In the *Fourth Concerto* nothing is hurried and every phrase is allowed to breathe – and the same goes for its two companions. The recording is very good indeed.

Estampes; Overture; Les parables; Rhapsody.
**(*) Sup. Dig. 1110 4140-2 [id.]. Czech PO, Jiří Bělohlávek.

This issue concentrates on two works from the closing years of Martinů's life: both *The Parables* (1957) and the *Estampes* (1958), a highly imaginative score, are vintage Martinů and are well served here. At one point in the first movement one feels that Martinů may have been listening to Nielsen's *Fifth Symphony*. There is no alternative version of the *Estampes* currently on the market nor of *Rhapsody* or the *Overture*, a rarity, written five years earlier in Nice, which finds the composer on auto-pilot, neo-classical mode. It is by no means as imaginative or inventive as the *Estampes*, which is Martinů at his most striking. The *Rhapsody* (1928) is much more interesting but, though first championed by Koussevitzky, Ansermet and others, it has fallen out of the repertoire: it has a spikier quality and a higher norm of dissonance than usual, but its rescue is very welcome. Excellent playing from the Czech Philharmonic under Jiří Bělohlávek, decently recorded in the usual resonant acoustic of the House of Artists. Strongly recommended for the sheer interest of the repertoire.

Symphonies Nos. 1–6.
**(*) Chan. Dig. CHAN 9103/5 [id.]. Royal Scottish Nat. O, Bryden Thomson.

Symphonies Nos. 2; 6 (Fantaisies symphoniques).
**(*) Chan. Dig. CHAN 8916 [id.]. Royal Scottish Nat. O, Bryden Thomson.

Bryden Thomson's set of the Martinů symphonies appeared in the immediate wake of (and was overshadowed by) the cycle on which Bělohlávek had embarked with the Czech Philharmonic for the same label. Given the authenticity of feeling and sound which they command, and the general excellence of the BIS cycle with the Bamberg Symphony under Neeme Järvi (BIS CD 362/3), the Thomson seemed supererogatory. Yet the performances have a robust spirit and an enthusiasm which cannot be gainsaid, and they are accorded very good Chandos sound. The *Sixth Symphony* (the *Fantaisies symphoniques*) is not quite as subtle or as imaginative as the Bělohlávek on the same label, though the recording is every bit as good. The Bělohlávek series offers the *Fourth Symphony* and the *Field Mass* on CHAN 9138, and the *Sixth*, with the Janáček *Sinfonietta*, on CHAN 8897, and remains to be completed. So, for the moment, Järvi reigns supreme if you want all six symphonies.

Symphony No. 5; Les Fresques de Piero della Francesca; Memorial to Lidice; The Parables.
**(*) Supraphon mono/stereo 11 1931–2 [id.]. Czech PO, Ančerl.

Most of these are pioneering recordings (only Kubelik's recording of the *Three Frescoes* precedes Ančerl). We reported on this disc in our main volume and further hearing has prompted some modification of our review. The *Fifth Symphony* comes from 1955 and the *Memorial to Lidice* from 1957 and, although the sound is naturally constricted in range, it never detracts for one moment from the stature of these performances. They have great radiance and give enormous pleasure. The *Three Frescoes* and *The Parables* are in stereo and were made in 1959 and 1961 respectively. The *Three Frescoes* are given a marvellously glowing performance and, though it has still not been possible to remove the slight glassiness and shrillness in the string-tone above the stave, there is rather more detail and body than in the LP. *The Parables*, never released in stereo on LP in the UK, sound better, and the performances have tremendous authority, conveying that luminous quality that make the Martinů sound-world so special. An indispensable element in any Martinů collection.

(i) *Fantaisies symphoniques (Symphony No. 6); Les Fresques de Piero della Francesca; Memorial to Lidice.* (ii) *Vigilie for organ.*
**(*) Chant du Monde PR 254 050 [id.]. (i) Prague RSO, Vladimír Válek; (ii) Václav Uhlíř.

Fantaisies symphoniques (Symphony No. 6); (i) Bouquet of flowers.
(**(*)) Sup. mono 11 1932-2901 [id.]. Czech PO, Ančerl; (i) with Domaníská, Cervená, Havlak, Mráz, Kühn Children's Ch., Czech Philharmonic Ch.

Ančerl's 1960 recording of the *Fantaisies symphoniques* has an altogether special authenticity. It has greater breadth than Charles Munch's pioneering Boston account which, though it was exhilarating, was a bit over-driven. The Ančerl has now been superseded in some ways by the (relatively) recent Bělohlávek version on Chandos, but there is a visionary feel to the earlier, Supraphon account that is more easily recognized than defined. It comes with *Bouquet of flowers*, the cycle of settings of folk texts for mixed and children's chorus which charms, captivates and touches. Some allowances have to be made for the mono recording, but they are few and are more than compensated for by this inspiring music-making.

On Chant du Monde these are live Czech Radio recordings: the *Memorial to Lidice* comes from 1992, the *Sixth Symphony* from 1986 and the *Frescoes* from 1993. The sound is very resonant but there is no lack of detail; the performance of the symphony is very good indeed and, though sonically both Bělohlávek (Chandos) and Järvi (BIS) are superior, the playing has plenty of spirit and imagination. The *Memorial to Lidice* is very moving. Válek takes a broader tempo in the first two of the three *Frescoes* than Ančerl (see our main volume) and, though there is an added sense of space, some may feel a slight loss of urgency. While recognizing this, we warmed to this performance very much. The short makeweight, the *Vigilie*, is one of Martinů's last works, written only four months before his death and left unfinished. It was completed by the organist, Bedřich Janáček. A recommendable disc which is worth the money.

CHAMBER MUSIC

Cello sonatas Nos. 1 (1939); *2* (1942); *3* (1952).
*** RCA Dig. 09026 61220-2 [id.]. Janos Starker, Rudolf Firkušný.
** Sup. Dig. 11 0992-2 [id.]. Josef Chuchro, Josef Hála.

The *Cello sonatas* are well served in the catalogue. The *First* was composed in Paris in 1939; the *Second* was written three years later, while Martinů was living in America, for the Jamaican-based Czech cellist Frank Rybka; and the *Third* was composed in honour of Hans Kindler, the Dutch cellist and conductor who died in 1949. The RCA version with Starker and Firkušný is, perhaps predictably, the more impressive of the two. Firkušný's authority in this repertoire is unchallenged, and Starker has a natural eloquence though his tone is small. They are given the benefit of very good recorded sound and, at full price, are to be preferred to their Czech rivals.

Josef Chuchro and Josef Hála give admirably idiomatic performances, but their 1981 recording suffers from a less sympathetic acoustic. It is not as fresh or lively as the RCA recording and, although the Czech team play well enough, when one puts them alongside their distinguished colleagues there is no doubt as to the superiority of the latter. Starker and Firkušný can be recommended alongside (and perhaps in preference to) the Isserlis–Evans team on Hyperion.

String quartets Nos. 1–7.
**(*) Sup. 110 994-2 (3) [id.]. Panocha Qt.

While Martinů's first five symphonies were written in a relatively short space of time (1942–6) with the *Sixth* (*Fantaisies symphoniques*) following in the early 1950s, the seven *String quartets* encompass a much longer period. The *First*, originally thought to be from 1918, is probably a good bit later, and the *Seventh* (*Concerto da camera*) comes from 1947. The Panocha Quartet's recordings of the Martinů cycle were made at various times between 1979 and 1982, and comprised four LPs. The *First* of the quartets is both the longest and the most derivative. Published in 1977, long after the composer's death, it is heavily indebted to the world of Debussy and Ravel. If admirers of the composer will find little distinctive Martinů in its four movements, it still (despite some longueurs) has a certain charm. The three-movement *Second String quartet* (1925) is more of its time. The *Third* (1929) is by far the shortest (it takes barely 12 minutes) and has the nervous energy and rhythmic vitality characteristic of the mature composer. The *Fourth* (1937) and *Fifth* (1938) are close to the *Double Concerto for two string orchestras, piano and timpani*. The *Fifth* is the darkest of the quartets and in its emotional intensity is close in spirit to Janáček's *Intimate Letters*. The two post-war quartets, the *Sixth* (1946) and *Seventh* (1947), are strongly contrasted. The *Sixth* – and in particular its first movement – is a powerful and disturbing piece, and there is a sense of scale and a vision that raise it above its immediate successor, which is fluent, well crafted and nicely fashioned but wanting in the freshness and spontaneity that distinguishes, say, the *Sinfonietta giocosa*. To be frank, the quartets do not show Martinů at his most consistently inspired but are still worth investigating. The Panocha cannot match such first-rate ensembles as the Borodin, the Tokyo or the Alban Berg in terms of tonal refinement and blend, and the recordings are a bit two-dimensional. But if it is possible to imagine finer performances, in their absence this set is eminently recommendable, even though it is a bit steep to ask full price for it.

VOCAL MUSIC

The Butterfly that stamped (ballet): 5 scenes (arr. Rybár).
** Sup. Dig. 11 0380-2 [id.] Women's voices of Kühn Ch., Prague SO, Bělohlávek.

Martinů's choral ballet, *The Butterfly that stamped*, is an early work from his Paris years, written in 1926, not long after *La bagarre* and *Half-Time*, and based on one of Kipling's *Just-So* stories. Unfortunately Kipling's publisher demanded payment for the copyright, and Martinů, who was eking out a penurious existence, had to abandon the project. The five scenes have been put into a performing edition by Jaroslav Rybár. The score has a great deal of Gallic charm and does not follow the avant-garde line of *La Bagarre*. A pity that Supraphon market this slight but charming score (lasting only 41 minutes 47 seconds) at full price – without the addition of a fill-up. (One of his other works of the period could easily have been accommodated on it.) Recommended to collectors with a penchant for Martinů all the same.

The Epic of Gilgamesh (oratorio).
*** Sup. 11 1824 [id.]. Machotková, Zahradníček, Zítek, Prôša, Brousek, Czech Philh. Ch., Prague
SO, Bělohlávek.

It is good to welcome back this recording of one of Martinů's greatest works. Its merits are outlined
at some length in our main volume, but this present (1976) version can almost hold its own
artistically with the excellent Marco Polo account (8.223316), to which we accorded a Rosette. The
latter was intended to underline the inspired quality of the music itself as much as the quality of
performance and recording. This does not displace the Marco Polo but it can certainly be recommended alongside it.

Mascagni, Pietro (1863–1945)

Cavalleria rusticana: highlights.
** Ph. Dig. 442 482-2 [id.] (from complete recording, with Domingo, Obraztsova, Bruson; cond.
Prêtre) – LEONCAVALLO: *I Pagliacci:* highlights. **

Like its Leoncavallo coupling, this full-priced set of highlights (rather more than half-an-hour in
length) comes from the soundtrack of a film. It stands or falls by the listener's allegiance to Domingo,
who is undoubtedly in fine voice. His supporting cast is less impressive, with Obraztsova's somewhat
unwieldy mezzo robustly characterful rather than melting.

Massenet, Jules (1842–1912)

Le Cid: ballet suite.
(M) *** Decca Dig. 444 110-2 [id.]. Nat. PO, Bonynge – MEYERBEER: *Les Patineurs* (with DELIBES:
Naïla, LSO, Bonynge; THOMAS: *Hamlet: ballet music* ***).

Over the years, Decca have made a house speciality of recording the ballet music from *Le Cid* and
coupling it with Constant Lambert's arrangement of Meyerbeer (*Les Patineurs*). Bonynge's version is
the finest yet, with the most seductive orchestral playing, superbly recorded, with the remastering for
CD adding to the glitter and colour of Massenet's often witty scoring. For the reissue in Decca's
Ballet Gala series, Delibes' charming *Naïla Intermezzo* (a dainty little valse) and the lively, easily
melodic – if less distinctive – ballet from Act IV of Thomas's *Hamlet* have been added, played with
characteristic flair.

Hérodiade (ballet) *suite; Orchestral suites Nos. 1; 2 (Scènes hongroises); 3 (Scènes dramatiques).*
(BB) ** Naxos Dig. 8.553124 [id.]. New Zealand SO, Jean-Yves Ossonce.

The ballet suite from *Hérodiade* comes in the final scene of the opera, and the exotic nature of the
writing seems out of keeping with the strong biblical drama of the plot. Nevertheless the five
movements are nicely scored, including flutes and harp, delicate dancing strings, a luscious tune in the
middle strings, decorated by chirpy woodwind, and a vigorous dance finale. The other orchestral
suites are also well worth hearing, offering a further series of sharply memorable vignettes, demonstrating Massenet's ready store of tunes and his charmingly French orchestral palette. The opening
Pastorale of the *Suite No. 1* is attractively serene and there are some engaging variations to follow in
the second movement, while the *Nocturne* brings a strikingly operatic melody that might have been
written by Bizet, introduced by the clarinet and taken up by horn and strings. In the *Scènes
hongroises* the charming *leggiero* second movement is followed by characteristic *risoluto* brass writing.
The more histrionic *Scènes dramatiques* (with a Shakespearean inspiration) brings a touching and
very balletic central *Mélodrame*, originally entitled *Le sommeil de Desdémone*. The playing of the
New Zealand orchestra is first class, polished and vivid, and it is a pity that the microphones are
somewhat close. The wind have plenty of colour, but the string tuttis are made to sound a bit tight
and fierce.

OPERA

Esclarmonde (complete).
**(*) Koch Schwann Dig. 3-1269-2 (3) [id.]. Gavazzeni-Daviola, Sempere, Parraguin, Tréguier,
Courtis, Gabelle, Massenet Festival Ch., Budapest Liszt SO, Fournillier.

Recorded live at concert performances in October/November 1992, this is among the most successful sets to have come from the Massenet Festival in Saint-Etienne. The digital recording is full and clear, coping very well with the massed forces, giving plenty of detail, and Patrick Fournillier as a specialist interpreter of this composer persuades singers and players alike to perform with sympathy for the Massenet idiom. The Italian soprano, Denia Gavazzeni-Daviola, since her début in 1983 has concentrated on what might be called the Joan Sutherland roles, with a voice bright and clear at the top but which has fair weight down below, even though the timbre there is less sweet. Progressing from Lucia, Marie and Gilda, she tackles here the weightiest of the Massenet roles and, though she cannot match Sutherland in the warmth and weight of her singing in this music, the element of vulnerability in the princess with magic powers is more readily conveyed than with Sutherland. The Spaniard, José Sempere, sings freshly and clearly as the hero, Roland, if less ringingly and with less warmth than Giacomo Aragall, the tenor who sings opposite Sutherland on her Decca recording. Reissued on CD at mid-price, that remains the first recommendation for, quite apart from the more consistent Decca cast, the epic quality of this fairy-tale piece, as well as its sensuousness, comes out more tellingly, thanks not only to the conducting of Richard Bonynge but also to the excellent Decca analogue recording of 1975, which gives more weight to the orchestra (425 651-2 – see our main volume).

Grisélidis (complete).
*** Koch Schwann Dig. 3-1270-2 [id.]. Command, Viala, Larcher, Desnoues, Courtis, Henry,
    Treguier, Sieyès, Lyon Ch., Franz Liszt SO of Budapest, Fournillier.

Patrick Fournillier, with forces assembled for the Massenet Festival in St Etienne, here adds to the store of rare Massenet operas, offering a warm, sympathetic performance, recorded live in 1992. *Grisélidis* is a curious opera, one which, against his usual practice, took Massenet several years to complete. One reason may be that the subject – a medieval morality found in Plutarch, Boccaccio and Perrault – fits awkwardly with a broadly realistic style representing high romanticism. To suggest the medieval atmosphere and the purity of the heroine, Griselidis, Massenet exceptionally dallies with modal writing, if not very consistently, and the introduction of the Devil as a comic figure, henpecked by his wife, gets in the way of one taking the threat to Griselidis and her virtue seriously. Even so, there is much beautiful writing, representing Massenet in full maturity; and there is unlikely to be a better recording than this. Michèle Command sings warmly as the heroine and Jean-Luc Viala sings splendidly in the incidental tenor role of the shepherd, Alain, in love with Griselidis, but pushed aside by the Marquis, who sweeps her off her feet, only to prove an over-possessive husband. As the Marquis, Didier Henry is in rather gritty voice, and it is a pity that Jean-Philippe Courtis does not bring out the comedy of the Devil's role more positively, though he sings well enough. Clear, generally well-balanced recording.

Mathias, William (1934–92)

(i) *Clarinet concerto;* (ii) *Harp concerto;* (iii) *Piano concerto No. 3.*
*** Lyrita SRCD 325 [id.]. (i) Gervase de Peyer; (ii) Osian Ellis; (iii) Peter Katin; LSO or New
    Philh. O, Atherton.

This brings together three of Mathias's colourful, approachable concertos in excellent recordings, made in the 1970s by Decca and originally issued with different couplings. Helped by vividly immediate recording, the *Clarinet concerto* with its clean-cut, memorable themes sparks off an inspired performance from Gervase de Peyer, not just in the lively outer movements, but in the poignant *Lento espressivo* in the middle. The *Harp concerto* (1970) is less outward-going, but it prompts Mathias to create evocative, shimmering textures, very characteristic of him. The harp, superbly played by the dedicatee, Osian Ellis, is set alongside exotic percussion, with the finale a snappy jig that delightfully keeps tripping over its feet. In the *Piano concerto No. 3* of 1968 the outer movements bring jazzily syncopated writing, like Walton with a difference, here incisively played by Peter Katin. They frame an atmospheric central *Adagio* with echoes of Bartókian 'night music', like Bartók with a difference.

Maw, Nicholas (born 1935)

(i) *Flute quartet;* (ii) *Piano trio.*
*** ASV Dig. CDDCA 920 [id.]. Monticello Trio; with (i) Judith Pearce; (ii) Paul Coletti.

Nicholas Maw is arguably the most imaginative composer of his generation, true to himself and completely un-trendy. Commissioned by the Koussevitzky Foundation, the *Piano trio* is among his most impressive and ambitious chamber works. It was written in 1991 for the Monticello Trio, who here record it in a warmly expressive performance, fiery where necessary. Between them the two massive movements encompass the traditional four movements of classical form, with a spectral Scherzo emerging in the middle of the broadly lyrical first movement, aptly marked *un poco inquieto*. The first half of the even longer second movement, thoughtful and slow, leads to the vigorous, easily striding finale section, which finally relapses into meditation. Maw's *Flute quartet* of 1981 was written for Judith Pearce of the Nash Ensemble, who plays it most beautifully here; it is another fine example of Maw's broad romanticism, powerful and lyrical, often sensuous, approachable yet clearly contemporary. Though the central slow movement opens as a fugue, it develops emotionally to become an atmospheric nocturne, leading to a scurrying finale. Excellent performances and sound.

Maxwell Davies, Peter (born 1934)

(i) *Vesalii Icones; The Bairns of Brugh; Runes from a Holy Island*.
(M) *** Unicorn-Kanchana Analogue/Dig. UKCD 2068 [id.]. (i) Jennifer Ward Clarke, Fires of London, composer.

Maxwell Davies has the great quality of presenting strikingly memorable visions, and *Vesalii Icones* is certainly one, an extraordinary cello solo with comment from a chamber group. It was originally written to accompany a solo dancer in a fourteen-fold sequence, each dance based on one of the horrifying anatomical drawings of Vesalius (1543) and each representing one of the Stations of the Cross. Characteristically, the composer has moments not only of biting pain and tender compassion but also of deliberate shock tactics – notably when the risen Christ turns out to be Antichrist and is represented by a jaunty fox-trot. This is difficult music, but the emotional landmarks are plain from the start, and that is a good sign of enduring quality. Jennifer Ward Clarke plays superbly, and so do the Fires of London, conducted by the composer. The 1970 recording is excellent. The two shorter pieces, digitally recorded more than a decade later, make a valuable fill-up, *The Bairns of Brugh* a tender lament (viola over marimba) and *Runes* a group of brief epigrams.

(i) *Symphony No. 5;* (ii) *Chat Moss; Cross Lane Fair;* (i) *5 Klee pictures*.
*** Collins Dig. 1460-2 [id.]. (i) Philh. O; (ii) BBC PO; composer.

Maxwell Davies's *Fifth Symphony*, commissioned by the Philharmonia Orchestra and given at the 1994 Proms, marks a turning-point in his symphonic writing. Ever since he produced his first symphony in the mid-1970s Davies has grown more expansive in his symphonic style, but the *Fifth*, by contrast, is in a single movement lasting only 25 minutes, half the length of his previous symphonies. The 34 sections, some lasting several minutes and others only a few seconds, convey the tautness of a passacaglia, with groups of sections linked to produce a structure which, like Sibelius's *Seventh*, echoes the contrasted movements of a conventional symphony. Davies has sharpened his idiom too, making it more approachable and lyrical, with an underlying reliance on two plainchants from the *Liber Usualis*. Just as strikingly, his instrumental writing has a new beauty, not least in the rapt slow passages, and in the concertante passages for flute, trumpet, timpani and other instruments. A bold climax leads finally to a deeply reflective coda, confirming this as the most memorable yet of Davies's symphonies. The other works here, much lighter, all reflect in different ways the composer's preoccupation with childhood and youth. *Chat Moss*, which provided material for the symphony, evokes a childhood memory of a neighbouring heath and, more light-heartedly, *Cross Lane Fair* in 11 cleanly divided sections presents a picture of an old-fashioned fair with jugglers and roundabouts, using Northumbrian pipes set against the full orchestra, often led by brass. The *Klee portraits* were written at the beginning of Davies's career in connection with his teaching at Cirencester Grammar School, sharply establishing his distinctive tone of voice. The composer draws intense performances from both the Philharmonia (in the *Symphony*) and the BBC Philharmonic.

Collection: (i) *The Boyfriend* (film score): *Polly's dream;* (ii) *Caroline Mathilde* (ballet), *Act I: suite. St Thomas Wake (Foxtrot for orchestra on a pavan by John Bull:* excerpt; *Ojai festival overture;* (iii) *An Orkney wedding with sunrise;* (ii) *Threnody on a plainsong for Michael Vyner;* (i) *Seven in nomine* (for wind quintet, string quartet & harp): *Gloria tibi Trinitas; Canon in 6 parts;* (iv) (Piano) *Farewell to Stromness; Yesnaby ground;* (Vocal) (v) *Lullaby for Lucy;* (v–vi) *O magnum mysterium: 2 carols*.
(M) *** Collins Dig. 3003-2 [id.]. (i) Aquarius, Cleobury; (ii) BBC PO, composer; (iii) McIlwham (piper), RPO, composer; (iv) Seta Tanyel; (v) The Sixteen, Christophers; (vi) with Forbes, Trevor.

With short extracts from many Collins recordings of Maxwell Davies's music, this sampler understandably concentrates on his most approachable pieces, yet gives a good idea of his musical character and its directness of expression, often mixed with a quirky sense of humour, not least in foxtrots. The items cover the composer's whole career, ranging from the early choral work, *O magnum mysterium*, to the brief but intense *Threnody* he wrote to commemorate the death of his friend and colleague, Michael Vyner. The newcomer might start with the boisterously extrovert *An Orkney wedding with sunrise*, involving the climactic entry of bagpipes. Alternatively, the simple, haunting piano piece, *Farewell to Stromness*, makes an equally good point of entry.

OPERA

The Lighthouse (chamber opera; complete).
*** Collins Dig. 1415-2 [id.]. Mackie, Keyte, Comboy, BBC PO, composer.

The Lighthouse, one of the most successful of recent chamber operas, tells the story of three lighthouse keepers who mysteriously disappeared without explanation from a solitary lighthouse off the coast of the Outer Hebrides in 1900. The first half consists of a long Prologue involving the Court of Inquiry, where three officials are questioned wordlessly by the solo horn. The second, main section, *The Cry of the Beast*, goes back to the lighthouse itself, presenting the three keepers, taken by the same singers, who are introduced in characteristic songs, a vulgar music-hall song for Blaze, a sentimental love-ballad for Sandy, and – most significantly – a vehement revivalist song about God's revenge on the Children of Israel for Arthur, a rabble-rousing Evangelical. It is Arthur's obsession that infects all three, insisting that the Beast is coming, and the climax comes in a storm when they are all convinced that the Antichrist has arrived. The coda presents the arrival of three more keepers, the same figures transformed. It is a powerful story, simply and directly told, and though in a recording one misses the atmospheric help of a stage set, this fine performance, conducted by the composer – with the tenor, Neil Mackie, outstanding among the three soloists, undaunted by the high tessitura – brings the story home powerfully, with all its overtones, aided by the printed text.

Mayerl, Billy (1902–1959)

Aquarium suite; Autumn crocus; Bats in the belfry; Busybody; Fireside fusiliers; Four Aces suite; From a Spanish lattice; A Lily pond; Marigold; Minuet by candlelight; Parade of the sandwich-board men; Pastoral sketches; Waltz for a lonely heart.
** Marco Polo Dig. 8.223514 [id.]. Andrew Ball, Slovak RSO, Bratislava, Gary Carpenter.

Billy Mayerl was justly renowned, especially in the 1930s, for his rather stylish, sometimes gently witty, syncopated piano novelty pieces. The most famous of these, *Marigold*, gains nothing from the addition of the orchestra (especially when the tempo is so laid back), and nor do the few other examples here, such as *Bats in the belfry* and *Busybody*, with its Stravinskian allusions. Mayerl's rather watery mood-pieces are pleasant, often nicely scored (sometimes but not always by the composer – full details given here), but are instantly forgettable. They are well enough played and recorded.

Medtner, Nikolai (1880–1951)

(i) *Piano concerto No. 1 in C min., Op. 33;* (ii) *Piano quintet in C, Op. posth.*
**(*) Hyp. Dig. CDA 66744 [id.]. Dmitri Alexeev, with (i) BBC SO, Lazarev; (ii) New Budapest Qt.

The is arguably the most interesting of the three Medtner piano concertos. In his note, the soloist Dmitri Alexeev argues that the *First Piano concerto* is 'remarkable for its inspirational inner content, the beauty of its melodies and the grand scale of its structure ... and is probably his most outstanding work'. Composed during the First World War and premièred by Koussevitzky with the composer as soloist in 1918, it is a vast, one-movement sonata structure with an allegro first section leading to a theme and variations, a restatement and coda. Dmitri Alexeev plays it with virtuosity, flair and sympathy, and the BBC Symphony Orchestra under Alexander Lazarev give excellent support. The recording is very good and generally well balanced, and overall gives better results than the coupling, the late *Piano quintet in C major*, which occupied Medtner for over four decades. He began the sketches in 1903 and completed it only in 1949, regarding it as the summation of his life's work. Alexeev plays it with dedication, but the New Budapest Quartet are conscientious rather than committed or inspired partners. The two-dimensional and rather congested recording does not help. There is too little space round the five instruments, and the overall effect is a bit unrelieved.

(i) *Piano quintet in C, Op. posth.;* (ii) *Violin sonata No. 2 in G, Op. 44.*
** Russian Disc RDCD 11019 [id.]. Svetlanov, with (i) Borodin Qt; (ii) Labko.

The main work here is the *Second Violin sonata,* which Alexander Labko (about whom the liner-notes remain silent) plays with conviction and eloquence. He is generally well partnered by Yevgeni Svetlanov, who proves a sensitive pianist even if he is not perhaps the equal of the greatest virtuosi. Unfortunately the 1968 recording is not good, even for its age, and is wanting in frequency range. The *Piano quintet,* on which Medtner laboured for so long, is played with much greater variety of tone and dynamics by Svetlanov and the Borodin Quartet than in the more recent Hyperion issue. They prove far more persuasive than their modern rivals, where one is more aware of Medtner's thick textures. Again the 1968 recording calls for tolerance, but it is worth extending for the sake of some fine music-making.

Violin sonatas Nos. 1 in B min., Op. 21; 2 in G, Op. 44.
*** Chan. Dig. CHAN 9293 [id.]. Lydia Mordkovitch, Geoffrey Tozer.

The first two of Medtner's three *Violin sonatas* come on a well-recorded Chandos release. The *Sonata No. 1 in B minor* dates from 1910 and was dedicated to his sister-in-law, Anna Medtner, who later became his wife. The *Sonata No. 2 in G* was written when Medtner was living in Montmorency near Paris, though he premièred it on his 1927 visit to the Soviet Union, which he had left in the early 1920s. Lydia Mordkovitch proves a most imaginative and thoughtful advocate of the sonata. Apart from his not inconsiderable support at the keyboard, Geoffrey Tozer also contributes committed liner-notes hailing the *Second Sonata* in somewhat extravagant terms: 'It is one of Medtner's finest compositions and is one of the grandest chamber works in existence.' While Medtner does not present the strong lyrical profile or musical personality that Rachmaninov commanded, the apparently bland surface soon reveals depths that are at first hidden. As far as the *G major sonata* is concerned, the Chandos issue must remain the preferred recommendation among the three now available; Lydia Mordkovitch betrays an effortless expressive freedom, and both she and her partner are well recorded too.

Mendelssohn, Felix (1809–47)

Violin concerto in D min., Violin concerto in E min., Op. 64.
*** RCA Dig. 09026 62512-2 [id.]. Kyoko Takezawa, Bamberg SO, Claus Peter Flor.

Kyoko Takezawa gives winning accounts of both the great Mendelssohn *Violin concerto in E minor* and the youthful D minor work, resurrected over 40 years ago by Yehudi Menuhin. With a dedicated Mendelssohnian conductor, Claus Peter Flor, these are performances which consistently reflect the joy of the performers in the music. Mullova's Philips disc of the same coupling (432 077-2) offers brisker, marginally more powerful, but less affectionate readings. With a persuasive and resilient rather than a high-powered reading of the much-recorded *E minor,* Takezawa relates that mature work more closely than usual to the often Mozartian invention of the thirteen-year-old, with exceptionally neat articulation of rapid passage-work. Takezawa's reading of the *D minor* is full of fantasy, with each movement sharply characterized to make the piece seem more mature than it is. Highly recommendable as the Philips disc still is, the new RCA issue, given refined sound, must now take precedence.

Violin concerto in E min., Op. 64.
(M) *** Sony Dig. SMK 64250 [id.]. Cho-Liang Lin, Philh. O, Tilson Thomas – BRUCH: *Concerto;* VIEUXTEMPS: *Concerto No. 5.* ***
*** Denon Dig. CO 78913 [id.]. Chee-Yun, LPO, Lopez-Cóboz – VIEUXTEMPS: *Concerto No. 5.* ***
(M) *** DG Dig. 445 515-2 [id.]. Anne-Sophie Mutter, BPO, Karajan – BRAHMS: *Violin concerto.* ***
(B) *** Carlton Dig. PCD 2005 [id.]. Jaime Laredo, SCO – BRUCH: *Concerto No. 1.* ***
(***) Beulah mono 1PD 10 [id.]. Alfred Campoli, LPO, Boult – ELGAR: *Violin concerto.* (***)

Cho-Liang Lin's vibrantly lyrical account now reappears with the Bruch *G minor* plus the Vieuxtemps No. 5, to make an unbeatable mid-priced triptych. They are all three immensely rewarding and poetic performances, given excellent, modern, digital sound, and Michael Tilson Thomas proves a highly sympathetic partner in the Mendelssohn *Concerto.*

The young South Korean fiddler, Chee-Yun, joins the list of players to give inspirationally fresh accounts of Mendelssohn's lovely *Concerto*, full of sparkle and imagination. Her tone is full and sweet and the pianissimo introduction of the second subject of the opening movement is exquisite. The graceful *Andante*, played very gently at first but with a strong central climax, is capped by a vivacious finale, with Lopez-Cóboz and the LPO providing admirable support throughout; and the recording balance is excellent, the sound spacious, with just a hint of over-resonance in the bass not spoiling one's enjoyment. However, the relatively short Vieuxtemps coupling, although equally enticing, is not as generous as with Lin's competing Sony disc, which offers the Max Bruch as well.

In the Mendelssohn E minor, even more than in her Brahms coupling, the freshness of Anne-Sophie Mutter's approach communicates vividly to the listener, creating the feeling of hearing the work anew. Her gentleness and radiant simplicity in the *Andante* are very appealing, and the light, sparkling finale is a delight. Mutter is given a small-scale image, projected forward from the orchestral backcloth; the sound is both full and refined.

Laredo's version on a bargain-price CD brings an attractively direct reading, fresh and alert but avoiding mannerism, marked by consistently sweet and true tone from the soloist. The orchestral ensemble is amazingly good when you remember that the soloist himself is directing. The recording is vivid and clean.

Campoli's sweet, perfectly formed tone and polished, secure playing are just right for the Mendelssohn *Concerto*, and this is a delightful performance, notable for its charm and disarming simplicity. The 1958 recording has been impeccably transferred and, although this record is in the premium-price range, with its fine Elgar coupling it is a splendid reminder of a superb violinist.

(i) *Violin concerto in E min., Op. 64*; (ii) *Symphony No. 4 (Italian); Overtures: The Hebrides (Fingal's Cave); A Midsummer Night's Dream; Ruy Blas.*

(BB) *** EMI Seraphim CES5 68524-2 (2) [CEDB 68524]. LSO, with (i) Sir Yehudi Menuhin, cond. Rafael Frühbeck de Burgos; (ii) Previn – BRUCH: *Violin concerto No. 1.* ***

Menuhin's second stereo recording, with Rafael Frühbeck de Burgos, has its moments of roughness, but it has magic too: at the appearance of the first movement's second subject and in the slow movement, even if the timbre itself is a little spare. The recording sounds fuller than the earlier account with Kurtz, and this makes a good bargain on EMI's new Seraphim label, coupled with the Bruch *Concerto* and Previn's highly recommendable 1979 version of the *Italian Symphony*, plus the three most popular overtures. Previn, always an inspired Mendelssohnian, gives exuberant performances. In the symphony he has modified the tempo of the *Pilgrims' march* very slightly from his earlier, RCA reading, making it more clearly a slow movement, while the third movement has a cleaner culmination on the reprise. The outer movements as before are urgent, without sounding at all breathless, and are finely sprung; the essential first-movement exposition repeat is included. Recording balance has the strings a little less forward than usual, but the overall effect is agreeably full.

(i) *Violin concerto in E min.*; (ii) *A Midsummer Night's Dream: Overture, Op. 21; Scherzo; Nocturne; Wedding march. Overtures: Fingals's Cave (The Hebrides);* (iii) *Ruy Blas;* (ii) *Symphony No. 4 (Italian), Op. 90;* (iv) *Rondo capriccioso, Op. 14; Songs without words, Opp. 19/1–2; 30/4 & 6; 62/1 & 6; 67/4–6; Variations sérieuses, Op. 54.*

(B) **(*) Ph. Duo 444 302-2 (2) [id.]. (i) Accardo, LPO, Dutoit; (ii) Boston SO or BBC SO, Sir Colin Davis; (iii) New Philh. O, Sawallisch; (iv) Werner Haas.

Accardo's account of the *Violin concerto* is lithe and sparkling in the outer movements, and the slow movement, taken slower than usual, is expressive in a natural, unforced way. But some ears will find his phrasing here too restrained to capture Mendelssohn's romantic inspiration in full bloom. There are no reservations about Sir Colin Davis's coupling of an exhilarating but never breathless account of the *Italian Symphony* (complete with exposition repeat) with the four most important items from *A Midsummer Night's Dream*. Unlike so many versions of the symphony, this is not one which insists on brilliance at all costs, and the mid-1970s recording is warm and refined. One senses that the Philips engineers are working in Boston. Again there have been more delicate readings of the *Midsummer Night's Dream* pieces, but the ripeness of the Boston playing is persuasive. There is no lack of drama or evocation from the BBC Symphony Orchestra in *Fingal's Cave*, and Sawallisch opens the programme with a robust account of *Ruy Blas*. Werner Haas provides the piano interludes very musically and manages to include both the *Spring song* and *Spinning song* in his well-chosen collection of *Songs without words*. He is well recorded. But what a pity room was not found for the *Scottish Symphony*.

Symphonies Nos. 1–5.
(B) **(*) RCA 74321 20286-2 (3). Casapietra, Stolte, Schreier, Leipzig R. Ch. (in *No. 2*); Leipzig
  GO, Masur.

Symphonies Nos. 3 (Scottish); 4 (Italian), Op. 90.
(BB) ** RCA Navigator 74321 17891-2. Leipzig GO, Masur.

Recorded by Eurodisc in 1971/2, the earlier of Masur's two Mendelssohn *Symphony* cycles, reissued
in RCA's Symphony Edition, makes an excellent bargain-priced alternative to the strongly characterized later set for Teldec. The recording is warmer and more immediate, and Masur's preference for
flowing speeds in slow movements is not so marked, often with more affectionate moulding of phrase.
The performances are often more vivid and more spontaneous-sounding, notably that of No. 2, the
Hymn of Praise, where the forward focus of the voices adds to the impact of a most refreshing
reading. Sadly, the two most popular symphonies, the *Scottish* and *Italian*, are the least successful,
with generally slow speeds and slacker ensemble than in the rest. Masur here observes the exposition
repeat in the *Italian* (very important with its lead-back) but not in the *Scottish*. These are also
available separately on RCA's super-bargain Navigator label, but this is a case where Masur's mid-
priced Teldec alternative coupling of these two key works is clearly preferable. Here exposition
repeats are observed in both symphonies, the choice of speeds is more apt and the orchestral playing
is both committed and polished in ensemble. The sound may not be sharply detailed but has all the
characteristic Leipzig bloom and beauty (Teldec 45090 92148-2). The other symphonies in the RCA
set have also been issued separately at mid-price as we go to press: *Symphonies Nos. 1* and *3* (74321
20287-2); *Symphony No. 2* (74321 20288-2); *Symphonies Nos. 4* and *5* (74321 20289-2).

Symphonies Nos. 1 in C min., Op. 11; 5 in D min. (Reformation), Op. 107.
**(*) Decca Dig. 444 428-2 [id.]. Berlin RSO, Ashkenazy.

Ashkenazy conducts the former Radio Symphony Orchestra in fresh, finely moulded readings of both
symphonies, the first instalment in a projected Mendelssohn cycle. At generally spacious speeds in
slow movements, Ashkenazy phrases affectionately, with very gentle pianissimos. He brings out the
tenderness of the *Andante* of No. 1 without sentimentality and finds mystery in the slow introduction
of the *Reformation Symphony*. By contrast, allegros are taken fast, with the Minuet of No. 1
becoming almost a Scherzo, as does the second movement of the *Reformation*. There are moments in
the first movements of both symphonies when Ashkenazy comes near to sounding too hectic, but he
compensates in his springing of rhythms. As recorded, the string sound is thinner than usual with this
orchestra, but otherwise the quality is excellent.

Symphony No. 2 in B flat (Hymn of Praise), Op. 52.
**(*) EMI Dig. CDC7 49764-2 [id.]. Laki, Shirai, Seiffert, Düsseldorf Musikverein Ch., BPO,
  Sawallisch.
**(*) Chan. Dig. CHAN 8995 [id.]. Haymon, Hagley, Straka, Philh. Ch. & O, Weller.
*(*) RCA Dig. RD 60248 [60248-RC]. Popp, Kaufmann, Protschka, Bamberg Ch. & SO, Flor.

Recorded live in the Philharmonie, Berlin, Sawallisch's EMI version consistently conveys dramatic
bite. Mendelssohn's arguments, not always his most cogent, are made to seem fresh and immediate,
with warmly affectionate phrasing in slower passages never running the risk of sounding sentimental.
The sense of occasion is most telling in the choral movements, with the Düsseldorf Chorus adding
powerfully to the thrust of the performance, and with excellent solo singing. Balances are not always
ideal and there is some thinness in the strings; but this can be recommended to anyone wanting a live
account.
   The great merit of Weller's Chandos version is the warmth and weight of the recorded sound,
with a large chorus set against full-bodied, satisfyingly string-based orchestral sound. Though
Weller's speeds are sometimes dangerously slow, as in the lovely duet for the two sopranos, *Ich
harrete des Herrn*, the sense of spontaneity in the performance makes it compelling throughout, even
if ensemble is not always ideally crisp. Cynthia Haymon and Alison Hagley are warm-toned soloists,
with Peter Straka an expressive, if slightly fluttery, tenor.
   Claus Peter Flor is a sympathetic Mendelssohnian, and he has three outstanding soloists in Lucia
Popp, Julie Kaufmann and Josef Protschka, but the ill-focused, distantly balanced choral sound
effectively puts the disc out of court, robbing the performance of dramatic bite. It does not help that
the string-sound is thin. Except for those wanting original instruments, who will be well satisfied with
Christoph Spering's consistently refreshing account on Opus 111 (OPS 30-98), first choice probably
still lies with Abbado's LSO digital version (DG 423 143-2), while at mid-price Karajan remains
eminently recommendable (DG 431 471-2).

Symphony No. 3 in A min. (Scottish), Op. 56; A Midsummer Night's Dream: Overture, Op. 21 and excerpts, Op 61; Overture: The Hebrides (Fingal's Cave).
(M) **(*) Decca 443 578-2 [id.]. LSO, Peter Maag.

Under Maag, the *Scottish Symphony* is played most beautifully, and its pastoral character, occasioned by Mendelssohn's considerable use of strings throughout, is amplified by a Kingsway Hall recording of great warmth. The response of the LSO has quite remarkable freshness. But in 1960, when the record was made, the orchestra had not played this (then unfashionable) work at a concert for some years, and their pleasure in returning to such grateful music is demonstrably reflected in this highly spontaneous performance. The opening string cantilena is poised and very gracious and thus sets the mood for what is to follow. Unfortunately the first-movement exposition repeat is not observed, but to do so was not unusual in those days. One other small complaint: Maag is too ponderous in the final *Maestoso*, but there is a compensating breadth and the effect is almost Klempererian. The remastered sound is first class, with a natural balance and glowing woodwind detail. Only a degree of thinness of timbre in the violins when playing above the stave betrays the age of the original. *Fingal's Cave* is no less successful. Maag's *Overture* and excerpts from a *A Midsummer Night's Dream* derive from a more extended LP selection, dating from the earliest days of stereo (1957) and, although the items here include only the *Scherzo* (neat and nimble), *Nocturne* and *Wedding march*, together they make an attractive bonus. The fairy string music is beautifully translucent, and if Maag's treatment of the *Overture*'s forthright second subject strikes the ear as rhythmically mannered, the recording includes a strong contribution from a fruity bass wind instrument which might possibly be Mendelssohn's ophicleide but which is probably a well-played tuba. The horn soloist in the *Nocturne* is perhaps over-careful, but the tranquil mood is nicely contrasted with the short *agitato* middle section. The recording is clean and well projected; in the remastering, the luminous quality one remembers in the original has been retained. These vintage recordings, which many LP collectors will remember affectionately, are ideally suited for reissue in Decca's Classic Sound series. The collection plays for 76 minutes.

(i) Symphony No. 3 in A min. (Scottish), Op. 56; Overture: The Hebrides (Fingal's cave); (ii) Violin concerto in E min., Op. 64.
(M) **(*) Ph. 442 661-2 [id.]. (i) LPO; (ii) Concg. O, Haitink; (i) with Henryk Szeryng.

Haitink's Philips recording of the *Scottish Symphony* has beautiful sound from the late 1970s, the upper strings glowingly fresh and woodwind rich and luminous; yet the body of tone of the full orchestra does not bring clouded detail. Haitink sets a fast pace in the opening movement yet loses nothing of the music's lyrical power. There is a feeling of symphonic breadth too (helped by the resonant fullness of the recording), despite the omission of the exposition repeat. In the other three movements the warmth and glow of the Philips recording are always telling, especially at the opening of the Scherzo and for the dancing violins in the finale. The final peroration sounds magnificent. The evocation of the overture is similarly persuasive. However, Szeryng's account of the *E minor Concerto*, recorded five years earlier with the Concertgebouw Orchestra, though sensitive and lyrical has no special individual qualities, either from the soloist or in the accompaniment.

Symphonies Nos. 3 in A min. (Scottish); 4 in A (Italian).
*** Ph. Dig. 442 130-2 [id.]. ASMF, Sir Neville Marriner.
(M) **(*) DG 439 980-2 [id.]. Israel PO, Bernstein.

Symphonies Nos. 3 (Scottish); 4 (Italian), Op. 90; Overtures: Ruy Blas; Son and Stranger.
** Carlton Dig. MCD 88 [id.]. Philharmonia O, d'Avalos.

Marriner in his 1994 Philips version offers direct and sensitive readings of both symphonies, generally a fraction faster than those he recorded earlier for Decca. This time too he observes the exposition repeats in both symphonies. In the slow movements, the more flowing speeds bring a clear advantage, particularly when the Academy violins are even sweeter and purer than before, helped by recording that is a degree more refined. In the fast movements there are also many gains – as in the Scherzo of the *Scottish*, which is lighter and more transparent – but also some disadvantages, as in the first movement of the *Italian* which, though clean and clear, is rather hard-driven, not able to relax as readily as the joyful earlier reading. The coda to the finale of the *Scottish* reverses the trend, and Marriner chooses a slower speed, making the passage a fraction heavier and less buoyant, leading up to the great whoops of joy on the unison horns. All in all, an enjoyable disc, but first choice for this coupling still remains with Blomstedt and the San Francisco Symphony Orchestra, refreshingly spontaneous throughout and with sound outstandingly fine, outshining any direct rival (Decca 433 811-2). There are also splendid mid-price (Abbado: DG 427 810-2) and super-bargain (Lubbock:

ASV CDQS 6004) recommendations – see our main volume; and Masur's mid-priced Teldec coupling mentioned above should not be forgotten.

Bernstein and the Israel orchestra, recorded live in Munich in 1979, give a loving performance of the *Scottish Symphony* but their expansive tempi run the risk of overloading Mendelssohn's fresh inspiration, with the heavy expressiveness making the slow introduction and slow movement sound almost Mahlerian, as if especially for the German audience. The rhythmic lift of the Scherzo and finale makes amends, and throughout the performance a feeling of spontaneity helps one to accept the exaggerations; but it is a performance to bring out for an interesting change, rather than a version to recommend for repeated listening. The recording is well balanced and full. The sparkling account of the *Italian* was made a year earlier in the Mann Auditorium, Tel Aviv, but remains convincingly atmospheric if not ideally clear. The reading never falls into the rather exaggerated expressiveness which in places mars the coupled account of the *Scottish Symphony*. As with that work, the recordings were made at live concerts and, though speeds are often challengingly fast, they never fail to carry the exhilaration of the occasion.

Although it is recorded in exceptionally full and immediate sound, at once cleanly focused and warm, with thrilling weight of brass, the Francesco d'Avalos coupling with the Philharmonia cannot receive a clear-cut recommendation. It offers not just the two symphonies, complete with exposition repeats in both, but two of the less-played *Overtures* as well. The Philharmonia players are consistently on their toes, conveying the tensions of live performance, challenged to the limit by the conductor's very fast, often hectic speeds. There lies the shortcoming in relation to the finest of the many versions of the two symphonies. These are performances almost totally without Mendelssohnian charm, with fierceness replacing sparkle, notably in the outer movements of both. D'Avalos rarely relaxes, but the sense of spontaneity is consistently compelling and, helped by the recording, the swinging coda of the *Scottish* builds to a most satisfying conclusion, with horns braying impressively. Best of all are the two *Overtures*, fresh and bright, with *Ruy Blas* rounding off the disc in biting excitement.

Symphony No. 4 (Italian), Op. 90.
(M) *** DG Dig. 445 514-2 [id.]. Philh. O, Sinopoli – SCHUBERT: *Symphony No. 8.* *** ⊛
**(*) Decca Dig. 440 476-2 [id.]. VPO, Sir Georg Solti – SHOSTAKOVICH: *Symphony No. 5.* **(*)
(**) Sir Thomas Beecham Trust mono BEECHAM 6 [id.]. NYPO, Beecham – SIBELIUS: *Symphony No 7*; TCHAIKOVSKY: *Capriccio italien.* (**)
(*(*)) Pearl mono GEMMCD 9037 [id.]. Boston SO, Koussevitzky – SCHUBERT: *Symphony No. 8*; SCHUMANN: *Symphony No. 1.* (*(*))

Sinopoli's great gift is to illuminate almost every phrase afresh. His speeds tend to be extreme – fast in the first movement but with diamond-bright detail, and on the slow side in the remaining three. Only in the heavily inflected account of the third movement is the result at all mannered but, with superb playing from the Philharmonia and excellent Kingsway Hall recording, this rapt performance is most compelling. For refinement of detail, especially at lower dynamic levels, the CD is among the most impressive digital recordings to have come from DG.

Solti directs fresh and sympathetic, if hardly characteristic, readings of both Mendelssohn and Shostakovich. In the *Italian Symphony* you would never recognize this live performance with the Vienna Philharmonic as the work of the same conductor as Solti's earlier, Chicago recording. Though in the first movement the speed is even faster than before, if only fractionally, the lightness and resilience of the Viennese players make it seem far less tense and far more buoyant. In the finale too, the Vienna performance is lighter and more resilient, and in the middle two movements the contrasts are even more extreme, with speeds kept flowing, so avoiding the heaviness of the Chicago performance. The recording is acceptable, though it could be fuller-bodied.

Sir Thomas recorded the *Italian Symphony* only twice: once with the New York Philharmonic in 1942 and subsequently, in 1951, with the RPO. The present account does not have quite as much grace and poise as the later version; but it still has admirable freshness, and the New York orchestra play with real zest. The recording is opaque but perfectly acceptable for its period.

There is some electrifying playing from the Boston Symphony under Koussevitzky, though he does take the outer movements rather faster than most other conductors; indeed many will find them just a shade overdriven. There is some wonderful orchestral playing but the transfer does less than full justice to the Boston string-sound: it is shrill and shallow, as if the bass octave of the spectrum has been cut, and there is no body to the sonority.

Symphony No. 4 (Italian); Overtures: Fair Melusina, Op. 32; The Hebrides (Fingal's Cave), Op. 26; Son and stranger (Die Heimkehr aus der Fremde), Op. 89.
(B) *** Carlton Dig. PCD 2003 [id.]. Berne SO, Peter Maag.

Symphony No. 4 (Italian); Overture The Hebrides (Fingal's Cave); A Midsummer Night's Dream:
Overture, Op. 21; Scherzo; Nocturne; Wedding march, Op 61.
(M) **(*) Virgin/EMI CUV5 61131-2 [id.]. LSO, Barry Wordsworth.

Peter Maag, making a welcome return to the recording studio with his Berne orchestra, here offers a winningly relaxed performance of the *Italian Symphony* (including exposition repeat), plus an attractive group of overtures, which once more confirms him as a supreme Mendelssohnian. With fine ensemble from the Berne Symphony Orchestra – only marginally let down at times by the strings – the forward thrust is more compelling than with the taut, unyielding approach too often favoured today. *The Hebrides* receives a spacious reading and the two rarer overtures are a delight too, particularly *Son and stranger*, which in Maag's hands conveys radiant happiness. At bargain price, with full and brilliant recording, it is first rate.

Wordsworth combines a sparkling version of the *Italian Symphony* (with attractively light articulation in the bracing outer movements and the essential first-movement exposition repeat included), with the four most important items from *A Midsummer Night's Dream* and a very lively performance of *Fingal's Cave*. If the programme is suitable, this is certainly enjoyable and the recording is first class.

Symphony No. 4 in A (Italian); A Midsummer Night's Dream: Overture, Op. 21, & orchestral
incidental music, Op. 61.
(M) *** Virgin Veritas/EMI Dig. VER5 61183-2 [id.]. O of Age of Enlightenment, Mackerras.

Mackerras directs fresh, resilient, 'authentic'-style performances of both the *Symphony* and the *Midsummer Night's Dream* music. The middle two movements of the *Symphony* are marginally faster than usual but they gain in elegance and transparency, beautifully played here, as is the *Midsummer Night's Dream* music. It is particularly good to have an ophicleide instead of a tuba for Bottom's music in the *Overture*, and the boxwood flute in the *Scherzo* is a delight.

CHAMBER MUSIC

Cello sonatas Nos. 1 in B flat, Op. 45; 2 in D, Op. 58; Songs without words, Op. 19/1; Op. 109;
Variations concertantes, Op. 17.
*** RCA Dig. 09026 62553-2 [id.]. Steven Isserlis, Melvyn Tan.
**(*) O-L Dig. 430 245-2 [id.]. Christophe Coin, Patrick Cohen.

Steven Isserlis and Melvyn Tan convey a freshness and delight in music-making that rekindles enthusiasm for this delightful repertoire. They pace both sonatas expertly and are faithfully served by the RCA engineers. Like their colleagues, Christophe Coin and Patrick Cohen on Oiseau-Lyre, they command poetry as well as virtuosity.

Christophe Coin and Patrick Cohen use period instruments that obviously do not have the power, range or colour that modern instruments command. Coin plays a mid-eighteenth-century Milanese instrument and Cohen an 1835 fortepiano from H. Chr. Kisting, Berlin. Their playing has a vibrant quality and much poetic feeling but remains a specialist rather than a general recommendation.

Octet in E flat, Op. 20; String quintet No. 1 in A, Op. 18.
*** Virgin/EMI Veritas Dig. VC5 45168-2. Hausmusik.

Using period instruments, the British-based group, Hausmusik, gives a most refreshing performance of the *Octet* and couples it with another miraculous masterpiece of Mendelssohn's boyhood. The period performance gives extra weight to the lower lines compared with the violins, with the extra clarity intensifying the joyfulness of the inspiration. Most revealing of all is the way that the last two movements of the *Octet*, the feather-light *Scherzo* and the dashing finale, with their similar figuration, are presented in contrast, the one slower and more delicately pointed than usual, the other more exhilarating at high speed. At mid-price, a clear first choice for the *Octet*.

Piano quartets Nos. 1 in C min.; 2 in F min.; 3 in B min., Op. 1–3.
(M) *** Virgin/EMI Dig. CUV5 61203-2 [id.]. Domus.

The *Piano quartet No. 1 in C minor* was the composer's first published composition and was succeeded the following year by another, dedicated to '*Monsieur le Professeur Zelter par son élève Felix Mendelssohn-Bartholdy*', equally fluent and accomplished. However, none of the ideas of this *F minor* work are as remarkable as those of its successor in *B minor* of 1825. All three pieces have charm, vitality and musicianship, particularly in the hands of Domus, who play with the taste and discernment we have come to expect from them. Excellent recording.

String quartet No. 2 in A min., Op. 13; String quintet No. 2 in B flat, Op. 87.
(M) *** Virgin/EMI Dig. VC5 45104-2 [id.]. Hausmusik.

This makes an interesting and musically satisfying alternative to most of the current versions of this music on offer. Hausmusik is a period-instrument group – and a good one at that – who give very well-characterized readings of both the *A minor Quartet* and the much later *Second Quintet*. Phrasing is alert and articulate; they have finely blended tone and transparency of texture; above all, they communicate delight in this music. Excellent recording, too.

String quartet No. 6 in F min., Op. 80.
*** ASV Dig. CDDCA 712 [id.]. Lindsay Qt – BRAHMS: *String quartet No. 2.* ***

There is no lack of good, new recordings of the Mendelssohn quartets, whose freshness and quality of invention never fail to astonish. The Lindsays give a thoroughly involved and engaging performance of the *F minor*. No one investing in this is likely to be disappointed, either with their musicianship or with the ASV recording. Those wanting a complete set of the *String quartets* should turn to the Coull Quartet on Hyperion (CDS 44051/3) – see our main volume.

PIANO MUSIC

Preludes and fugues Nos. 1–6, Op. 35; 3 Caprices, Op. 33; Perpetuum mobile in C, Op. 33.
(BB) *** Naxos Dig. 8.550939 [id.]. Benjamin Frith.

In the first of what is obviously going to be a distinguished series, Benjamin Frith offers a highly imaginative set of the Op. 35 *Preludes and fugues*, full of diversity, from the flamboyant opening *Prelude in E minor* to the expansive *Prelude No. 6 in B flat*. The Fugues are sometimes bold, sometimes thoughtful, sometimes quite light-hearted, yet they are never made to sound trivial. The three *Caprices* are equally varied in mood and colour and are most sensitively presented, with the last one opening solemnly and then providing characteristically light-hearted Mendelssohnian dash. The *Perputuum mobile* makes a scintillating encore. Acceptably full if not remarkable piano sound, recorded in St Martin's Church, East Woodhay. But the playing promises well for what is to follow.

Songs without words, Books 1–8 (complete).
(M) ** Erato/Warner 4509 97413-2 (2) [id.]. Annie d'Arco (piano).

Annie d'Arco plays quite musically but some of the gentler evocations seem rather soft-centred, and at other times the playing does not match Barenboìm's DG performances in strength of profile. The piano recording is pleasing but a bit lacking in presence. Barenboim's DG Double is the one to go for, and it offers some additional music, too (437 470-2 – see our main volume).

Meyerbeer, Giacomo (1791–1864)

Les Patineurs (ballet suite, arr. & orch. Lambert).
(B) *** Decca Dig. 444 110-2 [id.]. Nat. PO, Bonynge – MASSENET: *Le Cid* etc. ***

Les Patineurs was arranged by Constant Lambert using excerpts from two of Meyerbeer's operas, *Le Prophète* and *L'Etoile du Nord*. Bonynge's approach is warm and comparatively easy-going but, with such polished orchestral playing, this version is extremely beguiling. The sound too is first rate.

Miaskovsky, Nikolay (1881–1950)

Cello concerto in C min., Op. 66.
⊛ (M) *** EMI CDM5 65419-2 [id.]. Rostropovich, Philh. O, Sargent – TANEYEV: *Suite de concert.*
***

(i) *Cello concerto in C min., Op. 66;* (ii) *Cello sonatas Nos. 1 in D, Op. 12; 2 in A min., Op. 81.*
*** Olympia Dig. OCD 530 [id.]. Marina Tarasova, with (i) Moscow New Op. O, Yevgeny
    Samoilov; (ii) Alexander Polezhaev.

Marina Tarasova has a strong musical personality and produces a magnificent tone. She made a great impression at various competitions during the 1980s, and deservedly so, for she plays with great warmth and eloquence – and, needless to say, flawless technical address. The Miaskovsky *Cello concerto* has an overwhelming sense of nostalgia and an elegiac atmosphere that is quite individual. Its very directness of utterance and diatonic simplicity can easily mask its depths. Although it does not encompass as wide a range as does the Elgar, it has a similarly powerful expressive impact.

Tarasova earns praise for coupling it so logically with the two *Cello sonatas*. The *Sonata in D major*, Op. 12 (1911, revised 1930), does not differ in idiom from its much later companion, *No. 2 in A minor*, Op. 81. Like Medtner or Barber, once his style was formed, Miaskovsky remained a non-developing composer, and none the worse for that. Sympathetic support from both accompanists and decent recording. However, Rostropovich's pioneering account with Sir Malcolm Sargent is still in a class of its own. It could not be played with greater eloquence and restraint, and the (1956) Abbey Road recording is amazingly full and fresh – one would never guess its age.

Sinfonietta, Op. 32/2; Theme and variations; 2 Pieces, Op. 46/1; Napeve.
*** ASV Dig. CDDCA 928 [id.]. St Petersburg CO, Roland Melia.

The *Sinfonietta for strings* comes from 1928–9 and will appeal to anyone of a nostalgic disposition. The players give an affectionate, well-prepared account of it and convey the wistful, endearing nature of the slow movement to perfection. It is certainly more sensitive than the rival account on Olympia, listed in our main volume. The *Theme and variations* (on a theme of Grieg) also has the same streak of melancholy. The first of the *Two Pieces*, Op. 46, No. 1 (1945), proved hauntingly familiar – not, as the conductor Roland Melia suggests in his note, because there are moments resembling Vaughan Williams's *Fantasia on a theme of Thomas Tallis*, which it doesn't. It is in fact a transcription and reworking for strings of the inner movements, reversing their order, of Miaskovsky's *Symphony No. 19 for military band*, composed in 1939. The St Petersburg Chamber Orchestra is an expert and responsive ensemble, and the ASV recording does them proud.

Symphony No. 6 in E flat min., Op. 23.
(**(*)) Russian Disc mono RDCD 15008 [id.]. Yurlov Russian Ch., USSR SO, Kirill Kondrashin.

Here, at long last on CD, is the première recording of the mammoth *Sixth Symphony* with choral finale, which alerted many collectors to Miaskovsky's real stature. It is Miaskovsky's most ambitious symphony and enjoyed some success in the 1920s. Its reputation was enhanced by this powerful mono recording by Kirill Kondrashin, which was only briefly available in the early 1960s on two LPs. Apart from a studio broadcast under Bernard Herrmann on the BBC, the symphony was unperformed in Britain after the war, though it was frequently programmed in the USA, most notably in Chicago, during the inter-war period. (The Chicago orchestra had a strong allegiance to Miaskovsky and commissioned the *Twenty-first Symphony*.) The *Sixth* is a seventy-minute work of considerable power and, after a long period of neglect, is available in no fewer than three recordings. The ravages and privation of the First World War and then the October Revolution, as well as private tragedies, served to make this a symphony of both tragic dimensions and dramatic vigour. There are echoes of Miaskovsky's master, Glière, and also of Scriabin but, in the trio of the Scherzo, Miaskovsky strikes that note of nostalgia and lost innocence he was to make so much his own in the *Cello concerto* (and at times in the *Violin concerto* too). It is a highly individual and often masterly score, although let down a little by its (somewhat inflated) choral finale, which employs folk and revolutionary songs, including the *Carmagnole*, which earned the symphony its nick-name, *The Revolutionary*. Neither of the versions listed in our main volume is really satisfactory and, though the present recording is not of recent provenance, this is the one to have.

String quartets Nos. 1 in A min., Op. 33/1; 4 in F min., Op. 33/4.
** Russian Disc RDCD 11013 [id.]. Taneyev Qt.

The Taneyev Quartet of Leningrad recorded all the Miaskovsky *Quartets* on LP during the course of the 1980s, and their release on CD is warmly to be welcomed. The present coupling is exactly the same as the first LP of the cycle. Although Miaskovsky composed half as many quartets as symphonies (thirteen as opposed to twenty-seven), they are hardly less important, always finely crafted and possessing moments of real depth. Like so much of Miaskovsky's music, they are conservative in idiom but their ideas are often memorable. According to Boris Schwarz in the *New Grove*, the *First Quartet* dates from 1929–30, while the unnamed author of the sleeve-notes speaks of it as a student work; in any event, few coming to it afresh would probably place it as Miaskovsky. It finds him more among the avant-garde of Russian composers than the conservative figure he became, and it has a far higher norm of dissonance than we are used to (Scriabin, Glière and even the Schoenberg of the *Second Quartet* occasionally spring to mind). It is a surprisingly fascinating and powerful score. The *Fourth, in F minor* was presented on the composer's graduation and is less challenging and more overtly lyrical and traditional in outlook. These imaginative and thought-provoking works are eminently well played, but the recording lets things down. The players are forwardly balanced, but the sound is hard and vinegary (in the *Allegretto* movement of the *Fourth*) and needs to be tamed above the stave. All the same, such is the interest of this disc that it must have a strong recommendation.

String quartets Nos. 3 in D min., Op. 33/3; 10 in F, Op..67/1; 13 in A min., Op. 86.
*** Olympia OCD 148 [id.]. Taneyev Qt.

The two-movement *Third Quartet* originally comes from 1910 but was overhauled in 1930 at the time of the *Fifteenth Symphony*. The *Tenth Quartet* also draws on the material of an earlier work, a relatively early quartet dating from 1907. During the war Miaskovsky edited a youthful quartet by Glinka for publication, and on its completion was prompted to turn to his own youthful essay. He subjected it to a radical reworking and finished the score in 1945, not long after the *Cello concerto*. It is true that the *Thirteenth Quartet*, his last (and possibly greatest) essay in the medium, could have been written in the last century – but it is more likely to be played in the next than many more self-aware and 'up-to-date' works. Despite its disarming simplicity of utterance, it is a work of great purity, lyrical warmth and a depth which at times suggests late Fauré. It is one of the few Miaskovsky quartets to have been recorded in the days of mono LP, though this performance completely supersedes it.

Milhaud, Darius (1892–1974)

Le Carnaval de Londres, Op. 172; 3 Rag-caprices; Saudades do Brasil.
*(*) Schwann Dig. 3-1138-2 [id.]. Capella Cracoviensis, Rickenbacher.

Karl Anton Rickenbacher and the Capella Cracoviensis get good results and obviously enjoy Milhaud's beguiling and lively *Saudades do Brasil* and the somewhat less successful *Le Carnaval de Londres* (1937), based on melodies from *The Beggar's Opera*. However, the recording lets things down: while it is perfectly acceptable in quieter passages, the (not unreasonably resonant) acoustic poses difficulties in balancing some of the brass, which thicken and swamp an already overcrowded texture. No match for Ron Corp's anthology on Hyperion (CDA 66594) or, in the case of the *Saudades*, Milhaud's own 1958 recording in EMI's 'Composers in Person' series (CDC7 54604-2).

La Création du monde.
(M) *** Virgin/EMI Dig. CUV5 61206-2 [id.]. Lausanne CO, Zedda – DEBUSSY: *Danse; Sarabande;* PROKOFIEV: *Sinfonietta.* ***

Milhaud's ballet, with its mixture of yearning melancholy and jazzy high spirits, comes off splendidly in Alberto Zedda's highly spontaneous account, its witty syncopations and brassy exuberance bringing an unbridled effervescence to offset the restrained blues feeling of the main lyrical theme. The performance doesn't miss the Gershwin affinities, and the very vivid recording makes a bold dynamic contrast between the work's tender and abrasive moments.

Symphonies Nos. 6, Op. 343; 7, Op. 344; Ouverture méditerranéenne.
*** DG. Dig. 439 939-2 [id.]. Toulouse Capitole O, Michel Plasson.

It is good news that the Milhaud symphonies are now receiving their due from the gramophone. The composer himself recorded the *First*, *Fourth*, *Eighth* and *Tenth*, and the present writer recalls a performance of the *Sixth* Milhaud conducted with the BBC Symphony Orchestra in the 1950s. The *Sixth* is among the most relaxed and purely beautiful of the Milhaud symphonies, and Michel Plasson and the Orchestre du Capitole de Toulouse play it with evident affection. (In fact the first movement, marked *Calme et tendre*, is just a bit too affectionate and relaxed by comparison with the composer's own reading.) The two symphonies recorded here were both composed in the spring of 1955, the *Sixth* for the 75th anniversary of the Boston Symphony Orchestra and the *Seventh* in response to a commission from the Belgian Radio. As with the glorious pastoral first movement of the *Sixth*, Plasson also lingers rather too much over the slow movement of the *Seventh* (he takes 12 minutes 27 seconds as opposed to Alun Francis' 8 minutes 52 seconds – see below). The problems posed by the exposed string writing above the stave are not helped by this tempo. The recording quality is very good, though not as finely detailed or as beautifully placed as in the earlier coupling of the *First* and *Second Symphonies* (DG 435 437-2 – discussed in our main edition) by the same artists.

Symphonies Nos. 7, Op. 344; 8 (Rhôdanienne), Op. 362; 9, Op. 380.
*** CPO Dig. CPO 999 166-2 [id.]. Basel RSO, Alun Francis.

These three symphonies were each composed two years apart. The *Seventh* and *Ninth* are both three-movement works with their centre of gravity being their slow movements. Alun Francis actually makes more sense of the slow movement of the *Seventh* than does Plasson, holding it together in an altogether more realistic tempo. It is a powerful and often searching movement, even if there is a fair amount of note-spinning in the outer movements. For that matter, so there is in the *Ninth*, though it begins splendidly with a short and lively *Modérément animé*. The *Eighth Symphony* was written for a new concert hall at the University of California in Berkeley, but its subject-matter is nearer to home. Its subtitle, *Rhôdanienne*, refers to the river Rhône, whose course the music depicts from its beginnings in the Alps down to the Camargue. If it is rich in instrumental resource and full of colour, the scoring is also open to the charge of being a bit too dense. The acoustic is drier than that of the Salle aux Grains in Toulouse, which is why the tempi are more taut and detail better defined. The Basel Radio Orchestra is a far from second-rate ensemble and in the *Seventh Symphony* hold up well against their French colleagues. Recommended.

CHAMBER MUSIC

Caprice, Op. 335a; Duo concertant, Op. 351; Petit concert, Op. 192; Le printemps, Op. 18; Violin sonata No. 2, Op. 40; Sonatine, Op. 100; Le voyager sans bagage (suite) *Op. 157b.*
** Schwann Dig. 3-1310-2 [id.]. Trio Bellerive.

Very bright, up-front recording in the suite from the music to *Le voyageur sans bagage* (1936) for clarinet, violin and piano, though it is very well played. The sound is better in the *Violin sonata No. 2* (1917) and *Le printemps* (1914), though the balance rather favours Robert Hairgrove's piano than Sandra Goldberg's violin. The performance does not have as much charm as Zimmermann and Lonquich. The pieces for clarinet and piano, the *Petit concert* (1938), the *Sonatine*, Op. 100 (1927), and the two pieces from the mid-1950s (the *Caprice*, Op. 335a, and the *Duo concertant*, Op. 351) are played with spirit, but one could imagine them being given more charm. The close, unrelieved recording is a handicap.

Violin sonata No. 2, Op. 40.
*** EMI Dig. CDC7 54541-2 [id.]. Frank Peter Zimmermann, Alexander Lonquich – AURIC: *Sonate;* FRANCAIX: *Sonatine;* POULENC: *Sonata;* SATIE: *Choses vues.* ***

Listen to Zimmermann and Lonquich play Milhaud's *Second Sonata* after hearing Sandra Goldberg and Robert Hairgrove, and it is as if one were hearing a completely different piece. There is much greater character and variety of tonal colour than in the Schwann rival, and both artists bring sparkle and charm to this piece. Beautifully present and lively recording, though the piano is slightly favoured in preference to the violin.

PIANO MUSIC

Piano sonata No. 1; L'automne; Printemps, Books 1 & 2; 4 Sketches (Esquisses); Sonatine.
(BB) ** Discover Dig. DICD 920 167 [id.]. Billi Eidi.

Milhaud was a capable pianist (he recorded his cycle, *La muse ménagère*, and *Scaramouche* with Marguerite Long). Here is a good cross-section of his output for solo piano covering four decades from the *Première Sonate* (1916) to the *Sonatine* (1956). Some of the music, such as the first book of *Printemps* (1920) or the *Quatre Esquisses* (1941), is charming; none of it makes great demands on either the pianist or the listener, and some of it is pretty inconsequential. All the same, taken in small doses, there is much that gives pleasure – and would give more if the recording were not quite so bottom-heavy or wanting in transparency. Billi Eidi's playing is fluent, sensitive and totally committed.

Millöcker, Carl (1842–99)

Der Bettelstudent (The Beggar student; complete).
(M) *** EMI CMS5 65387-2 (2). Litz, Streich, Holm, Prey, Unger, Gedda, Bav. R. Ch., Graunke SO, Franz Allers.

With a first-rate cast and excellent teamwork (the charming trio at the beginning of the third Act is a good example), this EMI reissue offers a consistently vivacious account of *Der Bettelstudent*. The plot, with its extraordinary mixture of Polish patriotism, mistaken identities and the triumph of true love, is supported by an attractively lyrical score, admirably presented here. The recording was made in two parts, six years apart (in 1967 and 1973), but the effect is consistent and displays plenty of theatrical atmosphere, and the analogue sound brings characteristic bloom. Although there is a detailed synopsis of the story-line with individual cues for each number, it is a pity that a libretto is not included.

Gasparone (complete).
(M) **(*) EMI Dig. CMS5 65363-2 (2). Rothenberger, Wewel, Brokmeier, Prey, Finke, Bav. State
   Op. Ch., Munich R. O, Heinz Wallberg.

Millöcker wrote his operetta, *Gasparone*, immediately after his most famous piece, *Der Bettelstudent*.
The former contains a fund of tunes, but this recording is not of the original work. In 1931 it was
radically recomposed by Ernst Stefan, with extra material added and with the flavour of the
nineteenth-century opera diluted in favour of the twentieth-century musical. It makes an agreeable
entertainment in a performance which draws out the expressive warmth of Millöcker's melodies to
the full. Anneliese Rothenberger is not at her sweetest as the heroine. Herman Prey sings with
bravura but could be more tender. Clear, digital recording but, as usual in this series, there is no
libretto, merely a synopsis of each individual number.

Mompou, Federico (1893–1987)

14 Cançons i dansas; Preludes Nos. 5; 6 (for the left hand); 7 (Fireworks).
⊛ *** RCA Dig. 09026 62554-2 [id.]. Alicia de Larrocha.

Alicia de Larrocha has previously recorded a group of the *Cançons i dansas* for Decca as part of a
recital of '*Musica española*'. Now she offers the whole set and is given first-class, modern, digital
recording. As we commented about the earlier Decca issue, this is gentle, reflective music which
brings peace to the listener. Its quiet, ruminative quality has something of the refinement of Debussy
with its poetic feeling, fine detail and well-calculated proportions. The sense of repose in No. 5, the
delicate loveliness of No. 7 and the wistful charm of No. 11 are characteristic of the intimacy of
feeling of this playing. The performances have much warmth and grace, and we have transferred our
Rosette from the earlier record. The present recital also includes four *Preludes*, of which No. 11 is
aptly dedicated to the pianist. Mompou could surely not hope to find a more understanding
advocate.

Montéclair, Michel de (1667–1737)

Cantatas: *Pan et Syrinx; Le Triomphe de la Constance.*
(M) *** O-L 444 169-2 [id.]. Judith Nelson, Huggett, Preston, Coin, Hogwood – François COUPERIN:
   Leçons de Ténèbres. ***

Michel Pignolet de Montéclair held no court appointment; he was a *basse de violon* player at the
Opéra and is best known as the teacher of Couperin's daughters. It is not surprising that his
instrument plays a prominent part in the accompaniment of these two classical cantatas, of which *Le
Triomphe* has a charming pastoral lyricism, while *Pan et Syrinx*, though not less appealingly melodic,
is more dramatic, with many imaginative touches in the lively accompaniment. Judith Nelson is
surely an ideal soloist, freshly appealing in the pastoral flow, and dealing with the considerable
bravura of the upper tessitura in the latter piece with captivating aplomb. She is very touching in
Pan's melancholy recitative and lament, after Syrinx has perished in the waters of the Erynmanthus;
with its flute obbligato, this brings a remarkable depth of chromatic expressive feeling. Here Stephen
Preston's contribution is most sensitive and, throughout, the stylish and lively accompaniments add
much to this most enjoyable and stimulating music.

Monteverdi, Claudio (1567–1643)

Madrigals: '*Batto', qui pianse Ergasto; Gira, il nemico insidioso amore; Hor che'l ciel e la terra; O
come sei gentile; Ogni amante è guerrir; Zefiro torna.*
⊛ (M) *** Virgin Veritas/EMI Dig. VER5 61165-2 [id.]. Chiaroscuro, L. Baroque, Nigel Rogers –
   D'INDIA: *Madrigals.* *** ⊛

A hand-picked half-dozen of Monteverdi's finest madrigals, superlatively sung, consistently bringing
out the expressive originality and the extraordinary variety of the settings, to say nothing of their
inherent vocal bravura. *Zefiro torna* is justly famous, but '*Batto', qui pianse Ergasto* is hardly less
remarkable, and the two *Madrigali guerrieri et amorosi* are very telling indeed: the darkly sustained
opening of *Hor che'l ciel e la terra e'l vento tace* ('Now that the sky, earth and wind grow silent')
sends a cold shiver down the spine and then the writing erupts into bursts of energetic feeling. The
engagingly lyrical *O come sei gentile* follows immediately after the d'India dramatized cycle from *Il*

pastor Fido and makes a fascinating comparison. Accompaniments are nicely balanced and the recording has an exceptionally real and vivid presence.

(i) *Vespro della Beata Vergine (Vespers);* (ii) Motet: *Exultent coeli.*

(B) *** Decca Double 443 482-2 (2) [id.]. (i) Gomez, Palmer, Bowman, Tear, Langridge, Shirley-Quirk, Rippon, Monteverdi Ch. & O, Salisbury Cathedral Boys' Ch., Philip Jones Brass Ens., Munrow Recorder Consort; (ii) Monteverdi Ch., Philip Jones Brass & Wind Ens.; Gardiner (with (ii) Christmas motets: G. GABRIELI: *Angelus ad pastores; Audite principes; O magnum mysterium; Quem vidistis pastores?; Salvator noster.* BASSANO: *Hodie Christus natus est* ***).

Gardiner's earlier Decca recording was made in 1974, before he had been won over entirely to the claims of the authentic school. Modern instruments are used and women's voices, but Gardiner's rhythms are so resilient that the result is exhilarating as well as grand. Singing and playing are exemplary, and the recording is one of Decca's most vividly atmospheric, with relatively large forces presented and placed against a helpful, reverberant acoustic. Now issued as a Double Decca (two CDs for the price of one), this set is well worth considering, with the addition to the *Vespers* of a collection of Christmas motets, mostly by Giovanni Gabrieli, first issued in 1972. The rich, sonorous dignity of Gabrieli's *Sonata pian'e forte* sounds resplendent, and in the choral numbers the vocal and instrumental blend is expert. The most impressive work here is Gabrieli's glorious *Quem vidistis pastores?*. Monteverdi's *Exultent caeli* is shorter, but one is again amazed by the range of expressive contrast, from the exultant opening *Let the heavens rejoice* to the magically simple setting of the phrase *O Maria*, a moment of great beauty each time it recurs. Then there is Gabrieli's fine *Salvator noster*, a motet for three five-part choirs, jubilantly rejoicing at the birth of Christ. One especially attractive feature of Gabrieli's writing is his setting of the word *Alleluia* used to close each of his pieces; the jauntiness of the style is fresh and exhilarating. The CD transfer is admirable. However, Gardiner's second recording for DG (429 565-2) is even more compellingly dramatic.

OPERA AND OPERA-BALLET

Il ballo dell'Ingrate; Il combattimento di Tancredi e Clorinda; Tirsi e Clori (opera-ballets).

⊛ *** O-L Dig. 440 637-2 [id.]. Bott, King, Ainsley, Bonner, George, New London Consort, Pickett.

The star of this outstanding Monteverdi disc is Catherine Bott, as she is of so many discs from Pickett and the New London Consort. It is both apt and attractive that for once one has all three of these inspired opera-ballets, a generous triptych. Pickett characerically presents them with a sharp clarity and concern for dramatic bite, to match and outshine any of the various rivals in each work. The voices are especially well chosen for contrast as well as for clarity. So the narration in *Tancredi*, the most substantial contribution, is taken by John Mark Ainsley with his clean-cut tenor that is yet darker and weightier than that of Andrew King, who sings Tancredi. Yet it is Catherine Bott who more than anyone brings the narrative to life, with delectably pointed and finely shaded singing, using a wider tonal range than is common in Monteverdi. Similarly in the *Ballo dell'Ingrate* she, an exceptionally animated Venus, is well contrasted with Tessa Bonner as Amore and Michael George as a sepulchral Plutone. The third work is much shorter but presents the simple dialogue of the lovers in similarly dramatic terms, with Bott partnered by Andrew King as Tirsi, joined at the end by the chorus of other soloists. First-rate, well-balanced sound.

Alfred Deller Edition: (i) *Il ballo delle ingrate;* (ii) *Lamento d'Arianna.*

(M) **(*) Van. 08.5063.71 [id.]. (i) Alfred Deller, McLoughlin, Ward, Cantelo, Amb. S., L. Chamber Players, Denis Stevens; (ii) Sheppard, Le Sage, Worthley, Todd, Deller, Bevan, Deller Consort, Deller.

Denis Stevens's pioneering stereo version of Monteverdi's *Il ballo delle ingrate* dates from 1956 and has an impressive cast, well backed up by the Ambrosian Singers and London Chamber Players. Although the orchestral sound seems rather ample to ears used to original instruments, this account rings true and there is much that is authentic, not least the decoration of the vocal line, especially by Deller himself who is most moving as Venus. Eileen McLoughlin makes a delightful Amor, and David Ward is suitably stentorian as Pluto. Readers will remember that Monteverdi wrote his early opera-ballet for performance at the wedding celebrations of Duke Francesco Gonzaga of Mantua. The Duke was to marry the young Infanta Margherita of Savoy, and the message of the opera is that she should be passionately generous in the arms of her husband-to-be. In *Il ballo* the ungrateful ladies have been confined to Hades for refusing their lovers' advances and at the end of the opera they sing a touching chorus of penitence for their unfortunate lack of ardour, followed by a plea from their leader (the sweet-voiced April Cantelo) that the noble ladies of the court should learn from their experience! It is all emotively communicated here and the recording is vivid, if rather close. In addition Deller directs a performance of the famous *Lamento d'Arianna*, sung by a vocal sextet comprising Honor Sheppard, Sally le Sage, Max Worthley, Philip Todd, Maurice Bevan and Deller himself. Here the individual voices, while having plenty of character, do not always match ideally in consort. Nevertheless a thoroughly worthwhile reissue in the Alfred Deller Edition.

L'Incoronazione di Poppea.
*** Virgin/EMI Dig. VCT5 45082-2 (3) [id.]. Arleen Augér, Della Jones, Linda Hirst, James
    Bowman, Gregory Reinhart, City of L. Bar. Sinfonia, Hickox.

The tender expressiveness of Arleen Augér in the title-role of Monteverdi's elusive masterpiece goes with a very spare accompaniment of continuo instruments, contrasting not just with the opulent score presented at Glyndebourne by Raymond Leppard, but with the previous period performance on record, that of Nikolaus Harnoncourt and the Concentus Musicus of Vienna, who has a far wider, more abrasive range of instrumental sound. Hickox overcomes the problems of that self-imposed limitation by choosing the widest possible range of speeds. The purity of Augér's soprano may make Poppea less of a scheming seducer than she should be, but it is Monteverdi's music for the heroine which makes her so sympathetic. Taking the castrato role of Nero, Della Jones sings very convincingly with full, rather boyish tone, while Gregory Reinhart is magnificent in the bass role of Seneca. James Bowman is a fine Ottone, with smaller parts taken by such excellent young singers as Catherine Denley, John Graham-Hall, Mark Tucker and Janice Watson.

Mosonyi, Mihály (1815–70)

(i) *Piano concerto in E min.;* (ii) *Symphony No. 1 in D.*
** Marco Polo Dig. 8.223539 [id.]. (i) Körmendi, Slovak State Philh. O (Košice); (ii) Slovak RSO
    (Bratislava); Stankovsky.

Mihály Mosonyi is hardly a household name in this country and his representation on disc is meagre. Originally Michael Brand and born in Bradford, he adopted Hungarian nationality and changed his name in 1859, some years after settling in Pest. Despite his origins, Mosonyi is thought of as one of the most representative nineteenth-century Hungarian composers – apart, of course, from the more obvious major figures, Liszt and Erkel. The *Symphony No. 1 in D* is an early work, composed in his late twenties and modelled on the Viennese classics in general and Beethoven in particular. The *Piano concerto in E minor*, which comes from about the same time, shows the influence of Chopin and Weber. If, like the symphony, it is not strong on individuality, it is at least well-crafted, well-bred music and well worth an occasional airing. Klára Körmendi is the fluent soloist and receives decent orchestral support from Robert Stankovsky and his Slovak forces.

Mozart, Wolfgang Amadeus (1756–91)

(i) *Clarinet concerto in A, K.622;* (ii) *Flute and harp concerto in C, K.299.*
(B) *** Carlton Dig. PCD 2011 [id.]. (i) Campbell; (ii) Davies, Masters; City of L. Sinfonia, Hickox.

David Campbell's agile and pointed performance of the clarinet work brings fastish speeds and a fresh, unmannered style in all three movements. His tonal shading is very beautiful. The earlier flute and harp work is just as freshly and sympathetically done, with a direct, unmannered style sounding entirely spontaneous.

(i) *Clarinet concerto;* (ii) *Clarinet quintet in A, K.581.*
(M) **(*) Ph. 442 390-2 [id.]. Jack Brymer, with (i) LSO, Sir Colin Davis; (ii) Allegri Qt.

Jack Brymer's earlier (1964) Philips account of the *Clarinet concerto* with Sir Colin Davis has an eloquent autumnal serenity and the reading a soft lyricism that is very appealing. However, the leisurely (1970) interpretation of the *Quintet* is more controversial. Generally the very slow tempi throughout are well sustained, although in the finale the forward flow of the music is reduced to a near-crawl. Good transfers. First choice for this coupling remains with Thea King on Hyperion (CDA 66199).

Flute concertos Nos. 1 in G, K.313; 2 in D, K.314; Andante for flute and orchestra in C, K.315.
(M) *(*) Virgin Veritas/EMI Dig. VER5 61176-2 [id.]. Hans-Martin Linde, Linde Consort.

Hans-Martin Linde conducts, as well as playing the flute. The ensemble of little more than a dozen players is expert and the textures eminently well ventilated. Listening to period flutes, one understands something of Mozart's aversion to the instrument, for the sound though at first appealing is slightly watery. Ultimately this account is let down by a want of flair and exuberance; the general approach is just a little too inhibited to be a strong recommendation. Good recorded sound and well-judged balance, but Judith Hall on Carlton/IMP remains our first recommendation.

(i) *Concerto for flute, harp & orchestra, K.299. Serenade in G (Eine kleine Nachtmusik), K.525;* (ii) *Sinfonia concertante in E flat for violin, viola & orchestra, K.364.*
*** Decca Dig. 443 175-2 [id.]. Cleveland O, Christoph von Dohnányi, with (i) Joshua Smith, Lisa Wellbaum; (ii) Daniel Majeske, Robert Vernon.

Good performances of both the *Concerto for flute, harp and orchestra* and the *Sinfonia concertante in E flat*, K.364, are not in short supply. Here are two more eminently acceptable performances, the latter coming as a memorial to Daniel Majeske, the distinguished and long-serving concert master of the Cleveland Orchestra, about whom Dohnányi writes movingly. The *Sinfonia concertante* is very well paced and completely free from any interpretative egocentricity. A musicianly, rather aristocratic performance, free from any playing to the gallery. Despite some criticism concerning multi-miking we have seen elsewhere, the recording reproduces very faithfully and freshly. The *Concerto for flute, harp and orchestra* comes off nicely and has an appropriate *joie de vivre*. Not necessarily a first choice in either work, but worth considering alongside the best, and eminently recommendable if you want this particular coupling.

Horn concertos Nos. 1–4; Concert rondo in E flat (ed. Civil).
(M) *** Ph. 442 397-2 [id.]. Alan Civil, ASMF, Marriner.
(B) **(*) Carlton Dig. PCD 2013. Richard Watkins, City of L. Sinfonia, Hickox.

Alan Civil's Philips set was made in 1973. The recording is obviously modern and the performances are highly enjoyable, with Sir Neville Marriner's polished and lively accompaniments giving pleasure in themselves. The balance has the effect of making the horn sound slightly larger than life.

Richard Watkins has the advantage of first-class modern digital recording on a bargain-priced label. He is an expert player and his seamless line in the first movement of *Concerto No. 2*, K.417, which begins his record, shows a genuine Mozartian sensibility. But this easy lyrical flow does mean that slow movements are very limpid and relaxed, and even the Rondos, articulated lightly, take wing more gently than usual. Hickox's accompaniments, on the other hand, are efficient and positive; the partnership works well in No. 3, with an attractively spontaneous interplay between horn and orchestra, the *Larghetto* slightly sombre and the finale fast and light. But generally there is a somewhat self-effacing quality to the solo performances which detracts from the music's projection, and Barry Tuckwell's Collins set has an altogether stronger profile (1153-2).

PIANO CONCERTOS

(i) *Piano concertos Nos. 1–6; 8, 9, 11–27; Concert rondos Nos. 1 in D, K.382;* (ii) *2 in A, K.386;* (iii) *Double piano concerto in E flat, K.365;* (iii; iv) *Triple piano concerto in F, K.242.*
(B) *** Decca Analogue/Dig. 443 727-2 (10) [id.]. Ashkenazy, (i) with Philh. O; (ii) LSO, Kertész; (iii) Barenboim, ECO; (iv) Fou Ts'ong.

Piano concertos Nos. 1 in F, K.37; 8 in C, K.246; 9 in E flat, K.271.
(M) **(*) Decca Dig. 425 089-2 [id.]. Vladimir Ashkenazy, Philh. O.

Piano concertos Nos. 2 in B flat, K.39; 16 in D, K.451; 17 in G, K.453.
(M) *** Decca Dig./Analogue 425 092-2 [id.]. Vladimir Ashkenazy, Philh. O.

Piano concertos Nos. 3 in D, K.40; 18 in B flat, K.456; 19 in F, K.459.
(M) *** Decca Dig./Analogue 425 093-2 [id.]. Vladimir Ashkenazy, Philh. O.

Piano concertos Nos. 4 in G, K.41; 21 in C, K.467; 23 in A, K.488.
(M) *** Decca Dig./Analogue 425 095-2 [id.]. Vladimir Ashkenazy, Philh. O.

(i) *Piano concertos Nos. 5 in D, K.175; 6 in B flat, K.238;* (ii) *Triple concerto in F, K.242.*
(M) **(*) Decca Dig./Analogue 425 088-2 [id.]. Vladimir Ashkenazy, with (i) Philh. O; (ii) Barenboim & Fou Ts'ong, ECO.

(i) *Piano concertos Nos. 11 in F, K.413; 12 in A, K.414;* (ii) *Double concerto in E flat, K.365.*
(M) **(*) Decca Dig./Analogue 425 090-2 [id.]. Vladimir Ashkenazy, with (i) Philh. O; (ii) Barenboim, ECO.

Piano concertos Nos. 13 in C, K.415; 14 in E flat, K.449; 15 in B flat, K.450.
(M) *** Decca Dig. 425 091-2 [id.]. Vladimir Ashkenazy, Philh. O.

Piano concertos Nos. 20 in D min., K.466; 22 in E flat, K.482.
(M) *** Decca Dig./Analogue 425 094-2 [id.]. Vladimir Ashkenazy, Philh. O.

Piano concertos Nos. 24 in C min., K.491; 25 in C, K.503; Rondo No. 1 in D, K.382.
(M) *** Decca Dig./Analogue 425 096-2 [id.]. Vladimir Ashkenazy, Philh. O.

(i) *Piano concertos Nos. 26 in D ('Coronation'), K.537; 27 in B flat, K.595;* (ii) *Rondo No. 2 in A, K.386.*
(M) *** Decca Dig./Analogue 425 097-2 [id.]. Vladimir Ashkenazy, with (i) Philh. O; (ii) LSO, Kertész.

Ashkenazy's set with the Philharmonia appeared over more than a decade: the early *Concertos* are the most recent (1987), while the *G major*, K.453, and the *C major*, K.467, come from 1977. The account of the *E flat Concerto*, K.365, with Barenboim and the ECO and the *Triple concerto* with Fou Ts'ong to complete the trio, is earlier still (1972). These performances have won golden opinions over the years, and the clarity of both the performances and the recordings is refreshing: indeed the fine Decca sound is one of their strongest features. With their latest remastering Decca have been able to squeeze the recordings on to ten generously full, bargain-priced CDs, which make a very attractive proposition. The CDs are also available separately at mid-price on Decca's Ovation label. If their insights do not always seem to strike quite as deeply as Perahia's, the latter's complete box on Sony, which comes on twelve mid-priced CDs (SK12K 46441), suffers from less than congenial remastering of the earlier analogue recordings, especially those made in 1976/7, where there is a loss of bloom on the orchestral strings, producing thin and even edgy sound. No such complaint can be made about the Decca transfers, which are remarkably fresh and natural. Many of these performances are among the finest available, combining refreshing spontaneity with an overall sense of proportion and balance.

Nos. *12 in A* and *13 in C* are particularly striking; with their natural, expressive feeling and sparkle, they convey real enjoyment, and the slow movement of the *A major*, K.414, is given memorable depth. These are digitally recorded and the sound is well defined and transparent, the ambience very attractive. Nos. 15 and 16 again show characteristic sensibility: both slow movements are played very beautifully yet without a trace of narcissism, and the finales sparkle. In *No. 17 in G* there is a fine sense of movement, yet nothing is hurried; *No. 19 in F* is hardly less successful, both subtle and sparkling. *No. 23 in A* – again with fine digital recording – is beautifully judged, alive, fresh and warm, while in *No. 24 in C minor* Ashkenazy has the full measure of the music's breadth and emotional power; and his playing, while showing all the elegance and poise one could desire, never detracts from the coherence of the whole. The first movement of No. 25 is on the grandest scale, and the opening movement of the *Coronation* (No. 26) is also appropriately magisterial, yet brings some exquisitely shaded playing in the *Larghetto*, while No. 27 caps the cycle impressively. The recording of these last three concertos is again digital and very lifelike: no orchestral detail is masked and the woodwind glow, while the piano timbre is most beautiful.

Piano concertos Nos. 8 in C (Lützow), K.246; 9 in E flat (Jeunehomme), K.271; Concert rondo No. 2 in A, K.386.
⊛ (M) *** Decca 443 576-2 [id.]. Ashkenazy, LSO, Kertész.

Ashkenazy's earlier, 1966 coupling with Kertész, which includes also the *A major Concert rondo*, has now been appropriately reissued in Decca's Classic Sound series and the recorded quality remains beautifully fresh and realistic. The magnificent performances originally earned the LP a Rosette and we see no reason not to carry it forward. Ashkenazy has the requisite sparkle, humanity and command of keyboard tone, and his readings can only be called inspired. He is very well supported by the LSO under Kertész, and they make an excellent case for a partnership with a sympathetic conductor, rather than having the soloist direct the proceedings from the keyboard.

Piano concertos Nos. 8 in C, K. 246; 13 in C, K. 415; 25 in C, K. 503.
(B) **(*) HM 1903022 [id.]. Kocsis, Franz Liszt CO, János Rolla.

Robust and thoroughly lively and musical accounts of Mozart's three C major concertos, a unique (75-minute) coupling. The slow movement of K.503 comes off especially well and the finale is infectious. Fine, modern, digital recording and a good balance ensure the appeal and value of the disc; even if the sound is a shade resonant, everything is clearly focused.

Piano concertos Nos. 8 in C, K.246; 23 in A, K.488; 24 in C min., K.491; 27 in B flat, K.595.
(B) *** DG Double 439 699-2 (2) [id.]. Wilhelm Kempff, Bamberg SO or BPO, Ferdinand Leitner.

Nothing Kempff recorded was without a degree of magic, and so it is here. His separate coupling of Nos. 23 and 24 with the Bamberg orchestra offered playing that was uniquely poetic and inspired, but his introvert delicacy is controversial in K.246 and K.595. Much of the playing is very dreamy and gentle (some of the detail in the piano part of K.246 is exquisite), its 'inner' quality producing a very relaxed manner, perhaps too much so in the rondo of K.595. The earlier concerto is undoubtedly livelier. For some ears – notably IM's – this is totally engrossing (especially the C major); others may respond by finding Kempff wilful to the point of eccentricity, for Leitner and the Berlin Philharmonic match his mood admirably. However, the music-making is never self-admiring and the recordings are naturally balanced. With two discs offered for the price of one, many will find this well worth trying.

Piano concertos Nos. 9 in E flat (Jeunehomme), K.271; 15 in B flat, K.450; 22 in E flat, K.282; 25 in C, K.503; 27 in B flat, K.595.

(B) *** Ph. Duo 442 571-2 (2) [id.]. Alfred Brendel, ASMF, Marriner.

A first-class follow-up to Brendel's first Duo collection of Mozart piano concertos (see our main volume). The account of the opening *Jeunehomme* is finely proportioned and cleanly articulated, with a ravishing account of the slow movement. The finale has great sparkle and finesse and the recording has exemplary clarity. Brendel is hardly less fine in K.450, and the *E flat Concerto* has both vitality and depth. Brendel's first movement has breadth and grandeur as well as sensitivity, while the *Andante* has great poetry. No. 25 (there is well-deserved applause at the close) was recorded at a live performance and has life and concentration, and a real sense of scale. Here as elsewhere the playing of the ASMF under Marriner is alert and supportive. K.595 is also among Brendel's best Mozart performances, with a beautifully poised *Larghetto* and a graceful, spirited finale. The recordings were made between 1974 and 1981 (No. 15 is digital) and offer characteristically fresh and natural sound. Highly recommended.

Piano concertos Nos. 13 in C, K.415; 24 in C min., K.491.

(M) *** Chan. Dig. CHAN 9326 [id.]. Howard Shelley, LMP.

Like Perahia before him, Howard Shelley directs from the keyboard and this, the fifth in his ongoing series, is as distinguished as its predecessors. He has immaculate keyboard manners and his strong, natural musicianship is always in evidence. An instinctive yet thoughtful Mozartian whose consummate artistry places his cycle among the very finest now on the market. Readers will note that Chandos have now made this whole series available at mid-price, and as such it is very recommendable indeed (see our main volume for previous issues).

Piano concerto No. 20 in D min., K.466.

(BB) **(*) EMI Seraphim Dig. CES5 68520-2 (2) [CDEB 68520]. Youri Egorov, Philh. O, Sawallisch
    – BEETHOVEN: *Piano concerto No. 5; Violin concerto.* **(*)

A generous coupling for an imaginative if slightly controversial account of the *Emperor* and *Violin concerto* in EMI's bargain-basement, two-disc series. The Mozart performance, though well played, is less distinctive, even though Egorov is stylish and Sawallisch finds plenty of drama in the outer movements and begins the finale, the most striking of the three, with great energy and bustle. The slow movement, too, is elegantly shaped. Good, bright (1985) EMI digital recording, made at Abbey Road.

(i) *Piano concertos Nos. 20 in D min., K.466; 21 in C, K.467.* (ii) *Serenade No. 13 in G (Eine kleine Nachtmusik), K.525.*

(BB) *** RCA Navigator 74321 17888-2. (i) Géza Anda, VSO; (ii) Bamberg SO, Jochum.

Géza Anda recorded both these concertos before for DG, but the sound on this 1973 coupling gives a fuller, warmer orchestral backing and the pianist, directing from the keyboard, ensures playing of polish and refinement. Both performances have an attractive simplicity and are admirably spontaneous, with slow movements sensitive and graciously phrased. The delicacy of the solo playing entirely avoids any suggestions of Dresden china, while the orchestral introduction to the *D minor* has plenty of atmosphere. For a bonus, Jochum provides an agreeable account of Mozart's most famous serenade. Here the full-bodied string-sound brings robustness rather than transparency, but the finale has an appropriate rhythmic lightness. Excellent value.

(i) *Piano concertos Nos. 20 in D min., K.466; 21 in C, K.467;* (ii) *22 in E flat, K.482; 23 in A, K.488.*

(BB) *** EMI Seraphim CES5 68529-2 (2) [CEDB 68529]. Annie Fischer, Philh. O; (i) Sawallisch;
    (ii) Boult.

This is one of the real bargains on EMI's Seraphim (two-for-the-price-of-one-medium-price-CD) label and well worth having, even if duplication is involved. Annie Fischer's coupling of Nos. 21–22 was very highly regarded when it first appeared in 1959 (mono only) on Columbia CX 1630. The general style of performance of Mozart concertos in recent years has tended to become more robust but, even so, Fischer's gentle, limpid touch, with its frequent use of half-tones, gives a great deal of pleasure. The slow movements of both these concertos are beautifully done, and the pianist's intimate manner is often shared by the Philharmonia's wind soloists, who offer playing of polish and delicacy. Sawallisch's contribution too is considerable, and his firm directing hand ensures that neither performance becomes effete, while the bright, clear orchestral tuttis have plenty of character. These are essentially small-scale readings and the refined approach does reduce the opportunities for displaying wit. But Fischer's silken touch is highly persuasive. In the *C major Concerto* she uses cadenzas by Busoni and in the *E flat Concerto* the first-movement cadenza is by Hummel, which adds another point of interest to this coupling.

Her coupling of the *D minor* and *A major* followed, a year later. It was obviously made in a lively and clean acoustic and the piano tone remains immediate and realistic; the instrument does not loom too large in the aural picture and the balance is most musically judged. In the *D minor Concerto* the spontaneity of the solo playing is very apparent and the phrasing invariably alive and imaginative. Boult's tempi are sensible and the orchestral playing is again felicitous, particularly from the wind. The reading perhaps misses the ultimate in breadth and dramatic fire, but it is a very good performance all the same. In K.488, Fischer plays with liveliness of feeling and refinement of touch, and the passage-work is deft. The slow movement may be in less than perfect classical style (but then, so is Barenboim's) with the main theme given a quasi-Chopinesque dressing. But the result is enticing, and in any event this is a thoroughly enjoyable and often perceptive performance. Beethoven's cadenzas are used in the *D minor Concerto*.

Piano concertos Nos. 20 in D min., K.466; 25 in C, K.503; Rondo in D, K.382.
(M) * Sony Dig. SMK 64251 [id.]. Vladar, ASMF, Marriner.

Given the abundance of competition, there is little that need detain us here. Stefan Vladar is a more than capable guide in this repertoire but not as poetic or compelling as his leading rivals. The orchestral support under Marriner is musicianly but nothing out of the ordinary. In fact nothing about these performances is out of the ordinary: the recording is bottom-heavy and opaque.

Piano concertos Nos. 21 in C, K.467; 23 in A, K.488.
(M) *** Virgin/EMI Dig. CUV5 61123-2 [id.]. Jean-Bernard Pommier, Sinfonia Varsovia.

A suprisingly rare coupling of what are now arguably the two favourite Mozart piano concertos here works very well indeed. Both performances have plenty of sparkle in outer movements – the first movement of K.467 is particularly arresting – and both slow movements are played simply and beautifully. Jean-Bernard Pommier's *Adagio* in K.488 compares favourably with Brendel's, and the string playing at the famous opening of the *Andante* of K.467 is ravishing in its transparent delicacy and gentle warmth. The finale of the same work is brisk but never sounds rushed. The sound is first class.

Piano concertos Nos. 21 in C, K.467; 24 in C min., K.491.
(B) *** Carlton Dig. PCD 2006 [id.]. Howard Shelley, City of L. Sinfonia.

Howard Shelley gives delightfully fresh and characterful readings of both the popular *C major* and the great *C minor* concertos, bringing out their strength and purposefulness as well as their poetry, never overblown or sentimental. His Carlton (formerly Pickwick) disc makes an outstanding digital bargain, with accompaniment very well played and recorded.

Piano concertos Nos. 21 in C, K.467; 27 in B flat, K.595.
(M) *(*) DG Dig. 445 516-2 [id.]. Rudolf Serkin, LSO, Abbado.

Rudolf Serkin was an artist of keen musical intellect and a fine Mozartian, as his older, CBS/Sony recordings demonstrate. But he left it rather too late in his career to begin, in his eighties, a cycle of the Mozart concertos with Abbado and the LSO. Though his thoughtfulness as an artist is often clear, his playing is at times distressingly prosaic – neither slow movement here is distinguished (the theme of the *Larghetto* of K.595 is a little sluggish, too) – with no dynamics less than mezzo forte, scrappy passage-work and uneven scales. The opening of the *B flat Concerto* is also very measured and spacious, and Serkin's contribution is wanting the grace he once commanded. There are moments of inelegance and little real sparkle in the quicker movements. Refined accompaniments from Abbado, but at times the styles clash. There are stronger and more sensitive accounts of both concertos, though few that are better recorded.

(i) *Piano concerto No. 22 in E flat, K.482. Serenade No. 13 in G (Eine kleine Nachtmusik), K.525; Symphony No. 40 in G min., K.550.*

(B) ** BBC Radio Classics BBCRD 9112 [id.]. (i) Michael Roll; BBC SO, Sir John Pritchard.

Michael Roll was the first prizewinner of the first Leeds Piano competition in 1968, and he has never enjoyed the exposure to which his gifts entitle him. He is a very musical and highly sensitive player who has more depth than flamboyance. At a time when many lesser pianists are generously represented on CD, his name is missing from the catalogue. His account of the great *E flat Concerto,* K.482, comes from a 1971 Prom and is a reading of much pianistic finesse and musical elegance. The sound is a bit thick and tubby – and there are some restive coughs. Sir John Pritchard's *G minor Symphony* is a 1981 Prom performance; it is warm and musicianly and is untouched by routine. Bigband, old-fashioned Mozart, it nevertheless has a certain style. *Eine kleine Nachtmusik* is lighter in touch, and the players appear to be enjoying themselves. The sound is a bit heavy and opaque but, for all its its sonic limitations, this is worth considering at its modest price – in particular for the sake of Michael Roll.

Piano concertos Nos. 22 in E flat, K.482; 26 in D (Coronation), K.537.

(M) *** DG Dig. 447 283-2 [id.]. Malcolm Bilson (fortepiano), E. Bar. Soloists, Gardiner.

The *Coronation concerto* is presented strongly as well as elegantly, with the authentic timpani cutting dramatically through the textures in the first movement. Full and spacious recording in a helpful acoustic. The earlier concerto is hardly less vibrant and lyrically convincing, with the contrasts of the finale particularly effective. A fine sampler for a highly stimulating and successful series. We hope more individual reissues will be made at mid-price.

Piano concertos Nos. 23 in A, K.488; 24 in C min., K.491.

(M) **(*) Ph. Dig. 442 648-2 [id.]. Mitsuko Uchida, ECO, Tate.

It a pity that for this reissue Philips abandoned the original coupling (K.482 and K.488) which made a fascinating match, presenting illuminating contrasts rather than similarities. In No. 23, Uchida's thoughtful manner, at times a little understated, is ideally set against outstanding playing from the ECO with its excellent wind soloists. In No. 24, in spite of a dramatic opening from Jeffrey Tate, her tonal refinement and delicacy are sometimes in stronger evidence than her sense of scale, and that applies especially to the reticent slow movement and finale. Of course, as one would expect from two artists of this calibre, there are many felicities, but this would not be a first choice among much competition in spite of the state-of-the-art recording balance.

Piano concertos Nos. 23 in A, K.488; 27 in B flat, K.595.

(M) *** Ph. 442 391-2 [id.]. Alfred Brendel, ASMF, Marriner.

On Philips, two of the best of Brendel's Mozart concertos. There is little to add to our comments in earlier editions. Both performances come from the early 1970s and sound wonderfully fresh in these digitally refurbished transfers. Allegiance to Gilels in K.595 remains strong. However, these performances are included in Brendel's two Duo sets of Mozart concertos (one in each) and these represent marvellous value; the present disc remains of interest to those requiring only this particular coupling.

(i) *Piano concerto No. 26 in D, K.537;* (ii) *Piano and wind quintet in E flat, K.452.*

*** Decca Dig. 443 877-2 [id.]. András Schiff, (i) Camerata Ac. Mozarteum, Salzburg, Végh; (ii) Holliger, Schmid, Thunemann, Vladkovic.

Musically the Schiff–Végh survey of the Mozart concertos, now nearing its end, has proved a great success, though the acoustic of the Grosser Saal of the Salzburg Mozarteum may be a shade too resonant for some tastes. For those to whom it is, Howard Shelley's cycle on Chandos might be the solution – and, generally speaking, where they do overlap, we prefer Shelley both artistically and as recordings. Schiff's Bösendorfer sounds a little watery in timbre (rather in the manner of a good fortepiano). Not in any doubt is the quality of his playing or the musicianship of Sándor Végh. The coupling, the *Quintet for piano and wind*, made in the Mozartsaal of the Konzerthaus, is marvellously done, though some may feel Schiff's instrument is a trifle reticently balanced in relation to the wind. Perahia and the ECO wind (Sony MK 42099) or, at mid-price, Ashkenazy with the London Wind Soloists (Decca 421 151-2), both coupled with the Beethoven *Piano and wind quintet,* Op. 16, would remain a first recommendation for those primarily wanting K.452.

VIOLIN CONCERTOS

Violin concertos Nos. 1 in B flat, K.207; 2 in D, K.211; 5 in A (Turkish), K.219.

(M) *** Virgin/EMI Dig. VC5 45010-2 [id.]. Monica Huggett, O of Age of Enlightenment.

Violin concertos Nos. 3 in G, K.216; 4 in D, K.218; Adagio in E, K.261; Rondo in B flat, K.269.
(M) *** Virgin/EMI Dig. VC5 45060-2 [id.]. Monica Huggett, O of Age of Enlightenment.

Violin concertos Nos. 1–5; Adagio in E, K.261; Rondos Nos. 1–2, K.269 & K.373.
(M) **(*) DG Dig. 445 535-2 (2) [id.]. Itzhak Perlman, VPO, Levine.
(BB) **(*) RCA Navigator 74321 21277-2 (*Nos. 1–3 & Rondo, K.373*); 74321 21278-2 (*Nos. 4–5;*
   Adagio, K.261 & Rondo K. 269). Josef Suk, Prague CO, Libor Hlaváček.

If you want performances on original instruments, this Virgin set can be strongly recommended. Monica Huggett directs from the bow and she is a superb soloist: spontaneous, vital, warm and elegant. She plays her own cadenzas, and very good they are too. Orchestral textures are fresh and transparent, ensemble is excellent, and the solo playing is without even a drop of vinegar; indeed the violin timbre, if not opulent, is firm, well focused and sparkling.

Perlman gives characteristically assured, virtuoso readings of these concertos of Mozart's youth, which, with Levine as a fresh and undistracting Mozartian, bring exceptionally satisfying co-ordination of forces. The virtuoso approach sometimes involves a tendency to hurry, and the power is emphasized by the weight and immediacy of the recording. Warmth is here rather than charm; but Perlman's individual magic makes for magnetic results all through, not least in the intimate intensity of slow movements. Those of the first two concertos are particularly graceful, but at times (and notably in the two most popular concertos, Nos. 3 and 5) he treats the works rather more as bravura showpieces than is common. However, Perlman's virtuosity is effortless and charismatic, and the orchestral playing is first class. The DG recording is well balanced, with the soloist close but not too excessively so, and the perspective is on the whole well judged.

However, the alternative set (available on two separate CDs) on RCA's super-bargain Navigator label is by no means upstaged. Josef Suk's recordings date from 1972. The solo playing has character, warmth and humanity, and its unaffected manner is especially suited to the first two concertos. The last three concertos have an agreeable simplicity and a freedom from histrionic gestures that is most welcome, and the recording, though not as vividly detailed as the DG, is agreeably smooth and natural. Hlaváček does not always make enough of the dynamic contrasts and, throughout, this music-making is dominated by Suk. This is partly a matter of the recording balance. But with any reservations noted, these are delightful performances and very good value.

Violin concertos Nos. 1–5; (i) *Sinfonia concertante in E flat for violin, viola and orchestra, K.364.*
(BB) **(*) EMI Seraphim CES5 68530-2 (2) [CDEB 68530]. Sir Yehudi Menuhin, Bath Festival O;
   (i) with Rudolph Barshai.

Menuhin's recordings of the five Mozart *Violin concertos* date from the early 1960s, a fruitful period for this fine artist, when he was closely associated with the Bath Festival. Menuhin is here both soloist and director of the orchestra, which has a genuine chamber-music sound in which every part is distinctly audible without too great a separation. Most violinists use cadenzas by Joachim, but in all but No. 3 (where he chooses those by Franco) Menuhin uses cadenzas of his own, and many may feel that they are not Mozartian. Otherwise the style is sensibly exploited, and these performances give an engaging sense of musicians making intimate music together for the joy of it. There is plenty of warmth and colour. First movements are sufficiently ebullient, without loss of dignity and grace, due to a nice choice of tempi. The solo playing is not always immaculate and, compared (say) with Grumiaux (Philips Duo 438 323-2), it is romantic, yet in slow movements Mozart's melodies are floated gracefully and effortlessly (the seraphic cantilena of the slow movement of No. 4, K.218, is very touching). One is always conscious that this is the phrasing of a master musician who can also provide the lightest touch in finales, which are alert and extrovert. In the *Sinfonia concertante* Menuhin and Barshai comprise a splendid team with happily similar views. Once again the slow movement is more romantic than in some versions, but it is impossible not to respond to its ardour. The ensemble is excellent and the cadenza ushers in some really brilliant playing. Throughout, the stereo has a bright sheen and, with the remastering, the orchestral violins are made to sound glassy above the stave, but the ear adjusts when the music-making is so distinctive and the acoustic is basically warm.

(i) *Violin concertos Nos. 3 in G, K.216; 4 in D, K.218. Serenade: Eine kleine Nachtmusik, K.525.*
(M) **(*) Sony stereo/mono SMK 64468 [id.]. (i) Zino Francescatti; Columbia SO, Walter.

Francescatti's coupling of the *Third* and *Fourth* Mozart *Concertos* is probably his best record, and in their remastered CD format these fine performances from 1958, recorded in California, are given a new lease of life. The playing is at times a little wayward, but Bruno Walter accompanies throughout with his usual warmth and insight and falls into line sympathetically with his soloist. Both slow movements are beautifully played, albeit with an intensity that barely stops short of romanticism, and the changing moods of the finale in the *G major Concerto* are admirably contrasted. In some ways the *D major* suits Francescatti's opulent style of playing best of all, and there is a warm glow about the second subject of the first movement – a sinuous and enchanting tune – that almost reminds one of Kreisler, while in both works the cadenzas are made a most attractive feature. The whole atmosphere of this music-making represents the pre-authentic approach to Mozart at its most rewarding. The sound is just right for the music, warm and full with no apologies for the ample orchestral textures. The 1954 New York recording of the *Night music* is no great asset. The playing is acceptable but the string recording is harsh and ill-focused.

Violin concerto No. 5 in A, K.219.
(M) *** DG 447 403-2 [id.]. Wolfgang Schneiderhan, BPO, Jochum – BEETHOVEN: *Violin concerto.*
*** ⊛

This was perhaps the finest of the complete set of Mozart's violin concertos which Schneiderhan recorded with the Berlin Philharmonic in the late 1960s. He plays with effortless mastery and a strong sense of classical proportion, and the Berlin orchestra support him well. The recording is realistically balanced, and this makes a generous coupling for his famous record of the Beethoven, made six years earlier.

(i) *Violin concerto No. 5 (Turkish), K.219. Divertimento for strings in D, K.136; Serenade No. 13 (Eine kleine Nachtmusik); Symphony No. 29 in A, K.201.*
(M) *(*) Virgin Dig. CUV5 61132-2 [id.]. (i) Warren-Green; LCO.

This was one of Christopher Warren-Green's rare disappointing records, made during his all-too-brief tenure leading the LCO. The playing is as polished as ever, but tempi are so brisk that the effect is at times almost perfunctory, particularly in the *Violin concerto*, which is undoubtedly played brilliantly.

Divertimenti Nos. 2 in D, K.131; 15 in B flat, K.287.
(BB) *** Naxos Dig. 8.550996 [id.]. Capella Istropolitana, Harald Nerat.

If this is the start of a new Naxos series of Mozart divertimenti from the Capella Istropolitana under Harald Nerat, then we are in for a treat. The playing is the soul of finesse, warm and cultured, and beautifully turned and polished. The string group seems just the right size, and they phrase elegantly; the sound is full and transparent, bringing the sweetest modern violin timbre, yet the effect is as refreshing as any period performance. The *D major Divertimento* is charmingly scored for flute, oboe, bassoon, four horns and strings, with woodwind adding frequent touches of colour, but it has a gracious second-movement *Adagio* cantilena of disarming simplicity for strings alone. The horns are held back for the Trios of the Minuets. They then open the finale with an eloquent quartet, and the allegro molto which follows brings a neat little theme from the strings, some joyous carolling from the woodwind and horns and dainty bravura from the flute. The *B flat Divertimento* was written five years later, in Salzburg, and is scored more simply for two horns and strings. The second-movement *Andante grazioso* and variations shows the composer at his most engaging, bringing here an exquisite response from the violins, with the horns adding a robust downward arpeggio to enliven the graceful string writing. The lovely E flat major *Adagio* has that touch of gentle pathos that is Mozart's very own, and the finale brings a recitativo from the principal violin before its lighthearted conclusion, with a feather-light response from the violins.

German dances, K.509/1–6; K.536/1–6; K.567/1–6; K.571/1–6; 12 German dances, K. 586.
*** Sony Dig. SK 46696 [id.]. Tafelmusik, Bruno Weil.

Of period-instrument ensembles, Tafelmusik must be numbered among the most persuasive. They bring the advantages of authentic instruments (clarity of texture and lightness of articulation) without the attendant aural discomfort. Bruno Weil directs light and refreshing accounts of all these pieces and is very truthfully and cleanly recorded. Readers will find most of them enjoyable and some altogether captivating.

Overtures: *La clemenza di Tito; Così fan tutte; Don Giovanni; Die Entführunbg aus dem Serail; Idomeneo; Le nozze di Figaro; Der Schauspieldirektor; Die Zauberflöte. Serenade No. 13 (Eine kleine Nachtmusik).*
*** Sony Dig. SK 46695 [id.]. Tafelmusik, Bruno Weil.

Alert and vital performances by this Canadian period-instrument group under Bruno Weil. Mozart overtures do not come much fresher than this, and the players convey pleasure and delight in what they are doing. Very clean recording quality from the Sony team of engineers.

Serenades Nos. 1 in D, K.100; 7 in D (Haffner), K.250;·9 in D (Posthorn), K.320; 13 in G (Eine kleine Nachtmusik), K.525; Serenata notturna, K.239.
(B) **(*) Decca Double 443 458-2 (2) [id.]. Vienna Mozart Ens., Willi Boskovsky.

Boskovsky and the Vienna Mozart Ensemble play with elegance and sparkle, and these performances still sound outstandingly bracing and vivid. The recordings were made in the Sofiensaal over a decade between 1968 and 1978, all by the distinguished Decca recording team of Christopher Raeburn, James Lock and Gordon Parry; yet, curiously, the remastering has altered the sound in different degrees. The account of *Eine kleine Nachtmusik*, one of the freshest and most attractive on disc and dating from 1968, now has a somewhat astringent treble, while Boskovsky's 1973 *Posthorn Serenade*, which has a natural musicality and is very well balanced, seems rather dry in the matter of string-timbre, though the bloom remains on the wind and the posthorn is tangible in its presence. Like the *Haffner serenade*, it is marvellously alive, full of the sparkle and elegance we associate with this group, with admirable phrasing and feeling for detail, yet the *Haffner* (dating from 1972) has a distinctly warmer ambience. The very engaging earliest *Serenade in D*, K.100, has the greatest glow of all, although is was recorded in 1970. Nevertheless many will count this excellent value for money in Decca's two-for-the-price-of-one series, offering 159 minutes of music on the pair of CDs.

Serenades Nos. 3 in D, K.185; 13 in G (Eine kleine Nachtmusik), K.525.
(M) **(*) O-L Dig. 443 185-2 [id.]. Schröder, AAM, Hogwood.

Mozart's first large-scale *Serenade* dates from 1773 and is sometimes given the sobriquet '*Andretter*' after the name of its commissioner, a Salzburg military official who needed music for his son's wedding. In this work Mozart established the feature of including a miniature violin concerto as part of the structure, though here its movements are interspersed with others. This presents the drawback to the present recording, for Schröder's account of the solo violin role in the *Andante* is rather too straight and direct, though he offers more charm later on when he contributes to the Trio of the Minuet. The performance overall is brimming with vitality, the finales especially neat and infectious, and those who do not object to the pervasive astringency of 'original' string timbres in a piece essentially intended to divert will find that the variety of Mozart's invention is fully characterized. In *Eine kleine Nachtmusik* Hogwood follows Thurston Dart's earlier example by adding the missing minuet to restore the original five-movement format. However – unlike Dart, who transcribed a minuet from a piano sonata – Hogwood uses a minuet which Mozart composed in collaboration with his English pupil, Thomas Attwood. All the repeats in every movement but one are observed – which is perhaps too much of a good thing, giving an overall playing time of 26 minutes! The performance is given with one instrument to a part and is sprightly and alive. The recording is first rate, although the upper string-sound is very brightly etched.

Serenades Nos. 11 in E flat, K.375; 12 in C min., K.388.
*** Decca Dig. 436 654-2 [id.]. Vienna Wind Soloists – BEETHOVEN: *Octet.* ***

Serenades Nos. 11 & 12; Adagio in B flat, K.411; Adagio in C, K.Anh94.
** Chan. Dig. CHAN 9284 [id.]. Netherlands Wind Ens.

Beautifully turned performances from the Vienna Wind Soloists come on Decca. Theirs is delightful playing, crisply articulated and intelligently phrased, fresh and natural – like the recorded sound – and a joy to listen to! What more is there to say?

To those familiar with the Netherlands Wind Ensemble's accounts of the Mozart serenades, directed by Edo de Waart (and still available in the Philips Mozart Edition 422 505-2 – see our main volume), these new versions may well disappoint – not so much on account of the recording, which is bright and lifelike, but because of the performances. They are eminently musical and well prepared, and it would be an exaggeration to call them workmanlike; they are, as one would expect, highly accomplished but not as fresh or spontaneous as the earlier set.

(i) *Sinfonia concertante in E flat for violin, viola and orchestra, K.364;* (ii) *Sinfonia concertante in E flat for oboe, clarinet, horn, bassoon and orchestra, K.297b.*
(B) *** Virgin/EMI Dig. CUV5 61205-2 [id.]. (i) Warren-Green, Chase; (ii) Hunt, Collins, Thompson, Alexander; LCO, Warren-Green.
(BB) **(*) ASV Dig. CDQS 6139 [id.]. (i) McAslan, Inque; (ii) Anderson, Hacker, Gambold, Taylor; L. Festival O, Ross Pople.

In the ideal coupling of Mozart's paired *Sinfonias concertantes*, Christopher Warren-Green is joined by Roger Chase to provide a characteristically vital account of Mozart's inspired work for violin and viola. The *Andante* is slow and warmly expressive, yet without a trace of sentimentality. This is very satisfying, with its full-timbred sound from soloists and orchestra alike. The coupling, K.297b, is even more delectable and it would be hard to imagine a more persuasive team of wind players than those here. The full-bodied recording has plenty of space and atmosphere and the soloists in both works remain real and tangible.

An attractive super-bargain coupling on ASV of two works that fit so well together on disc. The outer movements of K.364 have a fine rhythmic spring, and the *Andante* with a warm response from both soloists is touchingly expressive in a pleasingly restrained manner. Lorraine McAslan is rather near the microphone, which is not entirely flattering to her upper range in the first movement, but the viola is not too backward, and the recording projects vividly. The account of the work with wind soloists also brings a lively, alert performance with speeds relaxed enough to allow a winning lift to rhythms, making it a genial, affectionate reading which yet never falls into sentimentality. Only in the finale is the result a little heavy, but the 6/8 coda becomes all the more playful. Alan Hacker's distinctive reedy clarinet provides an extra tang, and the way the soloists appear in turn as protagonists in the variations finale is delightfully done. The sound is bright, firm and realistic.

SYMPHONIES

Symphonies Nos. 1 in E flat, K.16; 2 in B flat, K.17 (attrib. Leopold MOZART); *3 in E flat, K.18* (written by Carl ABEL); *4 in D, K.19; 5 in B flat, K.22.*
(BB) ** Naxos Dig. 8.550871 [id.]. Northern CO, Nicholas Ward.

Symphonies Nos. 6 in F, K.43; 7 in D, K.45; 8 in D, K.48; 9 in C, K.73; 10 in G, K.74.
(BB) ** Naxos Dig. 8.550872 [id.]. Northern CO, Nicholas Ward.

Naxos are here starting another complete series – of the Mozart symphonies. These first two discs cover the juvenile works, including K.17, now attributed to the composer's father, and K.18, which was Wolfgang's own copy of a work written by Carl Abel. The performances are well played, spirited and warmly recorded. Nicholas Ward brings out the solemn atmosphere of the *Andante* of the very first symphony, astonishing for an eight-year-old. Hardly less striking is the charming, serenade-like *Andante* of K.43 (1767), very vocal and Italianate in feeling. On the second disc the playing of *Molto allegro* finales is very energetic and Nicholas Ward accents strongly, to give the music as much rhythmic character as possible. The recording, made in the BBC's Manchester studio Concert Hall, is attractively warm and naturally balanced, and this is enjoyable if not distinctive music-making.

Symphonies Nos. 11 in D, K.84; 12 in G, K.110; 13 in F, K.112; 14 in A, K.114.
(BB) ** Naxos Dig. 8.550873 [id.]. Northern CO, Nicholas Ward.

Mozart completed the *D major Symphony* in Milan in July 1770 in the three-movement, Italian overture style; Nos. 12 and 13 have four movements: the *G major* was written in Salzburg in the spring of 1771, but then the Mozarts returned to Milan, where the *F major* was completed. Both are pleasing works, with courtly *Andantes* and vigorous finales. But it is K.114, another Salzburg Symphony written in December of the same year, that marks a real step forward. A major was a key that always stimulated Mozart (and the horns crooked in this key add gleaming brightness to the allegros). It has a beautiful, serene *Andante*, a Minuet with a Trio for strings alone and a dynamically exuberant finale. The performances here are warm and polished and, although in the earlier works one would have liked a bit more bite in the allegros (original instruments are an advantage in this respect), Nicholas Ward rises to the occasion in the A major work, which receives a strong and (in the slow movement) expressive response from his excellent players. Well-balanced, natural sound, except that in the finale of the A major work the horns don't pierce the texture as brightly as they might.

Symphonies Nos. 16 in C, K.128; 17 in G, K.129; 18 in F, K.130; 19 in E flat, K.132; 20 in D, K.133; 21 in A, K.134; 22 in C, K.162; 23 in D, K.181; 24 in B flat, K.182; 25 in G min., K.183; 26 in E flat, K.184; 27 in G, K.199; 28 in C, K.200; 29 in A, K.201.
*** DG Dig. 439 915-2 (4). E. Concert, Trevor Pinnock.

Trevor Pinnock and the English Concert seem for the moment to have cornered the market in performances of the Mozart symphonies on original instruments, although it will be interesting to see what Tafelmusik make of this repertoire. However, this invigorating DG box of the Salzburg Symphonies is a splendid follow-up to Pinnock's collection of the earlier juvenile works (DG 437 792-2 – see our main volume). The playing has polish and sophistication, fine intonation and spontaneity and great vitality, balanced by warm, lyrical feeling in slow movements. Indeed the account of *No. 29 in A major* is among the finest available (on either modern or original instrumnts) and the earlier A major work (No. 21) is very impressive too, as is the G minor, K.183, and the very 'operatic' *No. 23 in D major*. Another clear first choice, and not only for authenticists.

Symphonies Nos. 25 in G min., K.183; 26 in E flat, K.184; 29 in A, K.201; 32 in G, K.318.
(M) *** Dig. O-L 444 161-2 [id.]. AAM, Hogwood.

In Hogwood's view, the *G minor Symphony* (No. 25) is not a 'little G minor' after all, for with all repeats observed (even those in the minuet the second time round) it acquires extra weight; in so lively and fresh a performance as this, the extra length from repetition proves invigorating, never tedious. The *A major* – another 'big symphony' – also has an incisiveness and clarity without losing anything in rhythmic bounce. The style of the playing with its non-vibrato tang is very bright on top, and clean. Though authenticity in Mozart has moved on since these recordings were made, between 1979 and 1981 (so that the Pinnock's newest DG survey is less severe in its upper range of string-timbre and has greater polish and more precise intonation), these pioneering recordings still stimulate the ear and the recording has plenty of ambient warmth (so important in the slow movement of K.201, which is beautifully played) as well as transparency. The offering here is exceptionally generous: 76 minutes.

Symphonies Nos. 25 in G min., K.183; 29 in A, K.201; 38 in D (Prague), K.504; 40 in G min., K 550; Serenata notturna in D, K.239.
(B) *** Decca Double 444 323-2 (2) [id.]. ECO, Britten.

Benjamin Britten recorded these exhilarating performances between 1968 and 1971. In the two early symphonies it is striking that in many movements his tempi and even his approach are very close to those of Marriner on his early, Argo recordings; but it is Britten's genius, along with his crisp articulation and sprung rhythms, which offers the occasional touch of pure individual magic. Britten's slow movements provide a clear contrast, rather weightier than Marriner's, particularly in the little *G minor*, where Britten, with a slower speed and more expressive phrasing, underlines the elegiac qualities of the music. Full, well-balanced recording. In his performance of No. 40 Britten takes all the repeats – the slow movement here is longer than that of *Eroica* – but is nevertheless almost totally convincing, with the full Maltings sound to give added weight and resonance. In the *Prague*, as in No. 40, Britten conveys a real sense of occasion, from the weighty introduction through a glowing and resilient account of the *Allegro* to a full, flowing reading of the *Andante*. The addition of the *Serenata notturna*, played most engagingly, only serves to make this analogue collection more desirable, even if the CD transfers have added an extra degree of brightness on top. Well worth exploring at Double Decca price. •

Symphonies Nos. 25 in G min., K.183; 31 in D (Paris), K.297; Symphony in D (The Posthorn), after K.320; Masonic funeral music (Maurerische Trauermusik), K.477.
*** Sony Dig. SK 48385-2 [id.]. BPO, Abbado.

Claudio Abbado and the Berlin Philharmonic defy the fashion for period performance in exhilarating accounts of Mozart using modern instruments. Like his other Mozart recordings made for Sony in Berlin, this is warmly recommended to those who want to hear Mozart playing which marries sweetness and purity to crisp rhythms and dramatic bite. The third of the three symphonies on the disc is the one which Mozart adapted from the *Posthorn serenade*, selecting just the first, fifth and seventh movements. Though the three-movement symphony is so much briefer than the seven-movement *Serenade*, it seems bolder and more powerful here in a glowing performance like this. One only regrets that Mozart did not also include the sixth-movement Minuet from the *Serenade*, with posthorn in the Trio, so as to justify the same nickname. The two regular symphonies, Nos. 25 and the *Paris*, are also given fresh and alert performances. Although the string band is substantial, the purity and clarity of the playing aerates textures. Woodwind doubling is always clearly audible. The recording also captures very tellingly the lugubrious timbres of the *Masonic funeral music*, made dark with extra weight of wind set against a string section without cellos.

Symphonies Nos. 35 in D (Haffner), K.385; 36 in C (Linz), K.425; 38 in D (Prague), K.504; 39 in E flat, K.453; 40 in G min., K.550; 41 in C (Jupiter), K.551.
(B) **(*) EMI CZS5 68351-2 (2). BPO, Karajan.
(M) **(*) DG 447 416-2 (2) [id.]. BPO, Boehm.
** Decca Dig. 436 421-2 (3) [id.]. Cleveland O, Dohnányi – WEBERN: *Passacaglia* etc. ***

Karajan offers large-orchestra Mozart, the fairly reverberant acoustic giving considerable breadth and impact to the orchestra. The interpretations too have plenty of weight, notably in the *Jupiter*, although Karajan also shows poise and grace: the opening of No. 36 is especially fine. Yet in the last analysis this music-making is wanting in the final touch of spontaneity and fire and, for all the magnificent orchestral playing, the listener is sometimes left vaguely unsatisfied and not only by the lack of transparency in the orchestral textures. The recordings were made in the Berlin Jesus-Christus Kirche in 1970.

Karl Boehm's way with Mozart in the early 1960s was broader and heavier in texture than we are used to nowadays, and the exposition repeats are the exception rather than the rule; but these Berlin Philharmonic performances are warm and magnetic, with refined and strongly rhythmic playing, and there is an attractive honesty and strength about them. The *Linz*, for instance, is an example of Boehm at his finest, with an agreeable, fresh vitality; but overall there is a comfortable quality of inevitability here, perpetuating a long Mozart tradition. The recordings sound full, vivid and well-balanced in the new transfers.

To have five of the major orchestral works of Webern as the coupling for the last six Mozart symphonies may seem an odd mixture, but the idea is imaginative. Predictably, the Mozart symphonies are very well played, but these are above all beefy performances, adopting what now seem old-fashioned manners. Textures are weighty and thick – partly a question of recording quality – and equally phrasing and rhythmic control have learnt nothing from the example of period performance. Nor is there much in the way of charm or elegance in Dohnányi's approach. Taking his traditional stance, he contents himself with presenting these masterpieces relatively straight. The results are strong but not specially winning. Only in the finales of Nos. 36 and 41 is there something of the exhilaration that marks the finest readings of these much-recorded works.

(i) *Symphonies Nos. 35 in D (Haffner), K.385; 36 in C (Linz), K.425;* (ii) *Divertimento No. 1 for strings, K.136; Serenade No. 6 (Serenata notturna).*
(M) *** Virgin/EMI Dig. CUV5 61204-2 [id.]. (i) Sinfonia Varsovia; (ii) Lausanne CO, Sir Yehudi Menuhin.

As in Menuhin's winning versions of the last four Mozart symphonies, Mozart is again presented with a smile on his face. Though modern instruments are used, the scale is intimate, with textures beautifully clear. The Sinfonia Varsovia, comprising players drawn from a range of Polish orchestras, responds warmly to Menuhin as the group's chosen President. There is elegance and charm as well as energy in outer movements, and in the slow movements Menuhin moulds the phrasing with Beechamesque magic, yet never adopts excessively slow speeds or over-romantic manners. The *Serenata notturna* and the *Divertimento* (first of the so-called 'Salzburg Symphonies') make a generous coupling, both of them favourites among Mozart's shorter works. Performances are similarly fresh and elegant, though, as recorded, the strings of the Lausanne Chamber Orchestra are a degree less sweet, and the acoustic is bigger and more reverberant.

Symphony No. 40 in G min., K.550.
*** RCA Dig. 09026 68032-2 [id.]. N. German RSO, Wand – TCHAIKOVSKY: *Symphony No. 5.* ***

Unexpected as this pairing of Mozart and Tchaikovsky may be, Wand in live recordings brings them together with a radiant consistency. Though in Mozart Wand follows many of the performing manners of an earlier generation, notably with a very slow, lovingly moulded account of the second-movement *Andante*, the remarkable point is how transparent he makes the textures. Also remarkable in Wand's performance is the lightness and speed of the Minuet, a whirling one-in-a-bar to match any authenticist. The refinement of approach means that, even in the first-movement development, he seems reluctant to find menace in the music; rather he concentrates on beauty, and that without any lack of intensity. A fascinating coupling for a unique account of the Tchaikovsky, vividly recorded.

Symphonies Nos. 40 in G min., K.550; 41 in C (Jupiter), K.551.
❀ (M) *** DG Dig. 445 548-2 [id.]. VPO, Bernstein.

(i) *Symphonies Nos. 40–41;* (ii) *Serenade: Eine kleine Nachtmusik, K.525.*
(B) **(*) DG 439 472-2 [id.]. (i) BPO; (ii) VPO; Boehm.

This disc presents what are perhaps the most distinguished of all Bernstein's Mozart recordings. Both were made in the Musikverein Grosser Saal in January 1984 and were edited together from live performances. Bernstein's electrifying account of No. 40 is keenly dramatic, individual and stylish, with the finale delightfully airy and fresh. If anything, the *Jupiter* is even finer: it is exhilarating in its tensions and observes the repeats in both halves of the finale, making it almost as long as the massive first movement. Bernstein's electricity sustains that length, and one welcomes it for establishing the supreme power of the argument, the true crown in the whole of Mozart's symphonic output. Pacing cannot be faulted in any of the four movements and, considering the problems of making live recordings, the sound is first rate, lacking only the last degree of transparency in tuttis. This mid-price reissue on DG's Masters label now takes its place again at the top of the list of recommendations for this coupling.

By its side Boehm sounds mellow and cultivated but still magnetic and strong. He, of course, is much less generous in the matter of repeats, but the Berlin Philharmonic play very beautifully and the recording is agreeably warm and full, the reissue inexpensive. *Eine kleine Nachtmusik* was recorded a decade and a half later, and the VPO playing is polished and fresh, with a neat, lightly pointed finale.

CHAMBER MUSIC

(i) *Clarinet quintet in A, K.581; String quintet No. 4 in G min., K.516.*
(B) ** DG 439 460-2 [id.]. Amadeus Qt, with (i) Gervase de Peyer; (ii) Cecil Aronowitz.

It was a happy idea to pair what are perhaps Mozart's two greatest *Quintets* on this bargain Classikon reissue. Gervase de Peyer gives a warm, smiling lead in the *Clarinet quintet*, with a sunny opening movement, a gentle, expressive *Larghetto* and a delightfully genial finale. The Amadeus accompany with sensibility, and the 1975 recording is flawless. The recording of the *String quintet* (with its Elysian slow movement) was made six years earlier but the CD transfer shows its age by a degree of edginess on top which is emphasized by the accented playing at higher dynamic levels. This performance has also been admired, and there is no question about the refinement and polish of the playing, although the effect is not as fresh and pleasing as with K.581 because of the sound-quality.

Horn quintet in E flat, K.407.
(M) *** Teldec/Warner Dig. 4509 97451-2 [id.]. Radovan Vlatkovič, Berlin Soloists – BEETHOVEN: *Septet.* ***

Radovan Vlatkovič has a plumper, more resonant horn-timbre than we are used to in the UK, and he also judiciously uses a touch of vibrato in the East European manner. But he is a most musical Mozartian and his big sound is balanced with a matching sumptuous sound from the accompanying string-group. This is certainly enjoyable, with the finale as nimble as you like.

Piano quartets Nos. 1 in G min., K.478; 2 in E flat, K.493.
*** Decca Dig. 444 115-2 [id.]. András Schiff, Shiokawa, Höbarth, Perényi.

A period-instrument performance with a difference. Not only does András Schiff play Mozart's fortepiano, an Anton Walter of about 1780, but Yuuko Shiokawa plays his violin, a mid-eighteenth-century instrument from Mittenwald in Bavaria (as is Miklós Perényi's 1770 cello), while Erich Höbarth uses a viola made by Carlo Antonio Testore of Milan, also believed to have belonged to Mozart. The stringed instruments produce real warmth in the acoustic of the Wienersaal of the Salzburg Mozarteum, though the fortepiano sounds somewhat papery and wanting in timbre. Generally, these are articulate and affectionate performances which will give pleasure, though this should not be an only recommendation in this repertoire. The Beaux Arts, using modern instruments, are rather special (Philips 410 391-2), while all recordings of these two works rest in the shadow of the famous Curzon/Amadeus mono recording, coupled with the *Horn quintet* with Dennis Brain the irrepressibly spirited soloist. The transfer to CD is remarkably successful (Decca 425 960-2).

(i) *Piano trios Nos. 1 in B flat, K.254; 2 in G, K.496; 3 in B flat, K.502; 4 in E, K.542; 5 in C, K. 548; 6 in G, K.564;* (ii) *Clarinet trio (Kegelstatt) in E flat, K. 498.*
(B) *(**) Ph. Duo 446 154-2 (2) [id.]. (i) Beaux Arts Trio; (ii) Brymer, Kovacevich, Ireland.

The Beaux Arts Trio have re-recorded the *Piano trios* digitally with more modern sound, but these earlier performances, made in the late 1960s, still sound vivid and fresh. As music-making, this has almost equal artistic claims on the listener and, though the timbre of Daniel Guilet's violin is noticeably much thinner than the ear would expect in a more modern recording, if pinched it is well focused. Different ears and different reproducers will react to this with varying degrees of dissatisfaction; but Menahem Pressler's piano playing is most naturally caught. In the *Clarinet trio* the balance is such that Jack Brymer's clarinet dominates and Stephen Kovacevich's piano is slightly recessed, but the overall effect is beautiful, warmer than in the *Piano trios*. Here the later digital set is well worth the extra cost (Philips 422 079-2 – see our main volume).

String quartets Nos. 10 in C, K.170; 11 in E flat, K.171; 15 in D min., K.421.
(BB) **(*) Naxos Dig. 8.550546 [id.]. Eder Qt.

String quartets Nos. 12 in B flat, K.172; 13 in D min., K.173; 21 in D (Prussian No. 1), K.575.
(BB) **(*) Naxos Dig. 8.550545 [id.]. Eder Quartet.

String quartets Nos. 20 in D (Hoffmeister), K.499; 23 in F (Prussian No. 3), K.590; Adagio and fugue in C min., K.546.
(BB) **(*) Naxos Dig. 8.550547 [id.]. Eder Qt.

There is nothing cheap about the Naxos recordings except the asking price. The Eder Quartet are an extremely fine ensemble with an admirable sense of style and exemplary musicianship. They are handicapped by an over-resonant acoustic – but rather this than the other extreme – and the sound is undoubtedly full and truthful. They have embarked on a complete Mozart cycle of some distinction. The first two discs include five of the amazingly mature Viennese quartets of 1773, with their portents of the later Mozart, notably the touching *Un poco Adagio* of K.170 and the remarkable opening movement of the *D minor*, K.173, which also has an engagingly courtly *Andantino grazioso*.

The later *Hoffmeister* (originally published by a friend of that name), with its direct affinity with Haydn's jokiness in the finale, and the two *Prussian Quartets* show the composer at full stretch, and the performances will not disappoint. The players bring a potent intensity to the climax of the *Adagio and fugue* and, although they could perhaps have achieved more attack at the opening of the fugue, this effect is partly caused by the warm resonance. For those with limited budgets, this series is well worth considering.

String quartets Nos. 14 in G, K.387; 15 in D min., K.421; 16 in E flat, K.428; 17 in B flat (Hunt), K.458; 18 in A, K.464; 19 in C (Dissonance), K.465 (Haydn Quartets); 20 in D (Hoffmeister), K. 499; 21 in D, K.575; 22 in B flat, K.589; 23 in F, K.590 (Prussian Quartets Nos. 1–3).
(M) *** Teldec/Warner 4509 95495-2 (4). Alban Berg Qt.

These recordings were made by the Alban Berg in the latter half of the 1970s; the performances have not since been surpassed. Not all of them appeared in the UK at the time, and now they make one of the most distinguished sets of Mozart's late quartets currently available, with the additional advantage of economy. The playing is thoroughly stylish and deeply musical; it is entirely free from surface gloss and there are none of the expressive exaggerations of dynamics and phrasing that marred this group's later records of Beethoven's *Rasumovsky Quartets* for EMI. The *Haydn Quartets* are consistently successful; the *Hunt* (1979) is still possibly the finest on the market and the *Dissonance* too is first class, with a wonderfully expressive account of the slow movement. Although dynamic gradations are steep, there is no sense of exaggeration – on the contrary these are wholly excellent performances, which are recommended with enthusiasm. The account of the *First Prussian Quartet* has much style and character, and the group are at their very best in Mozart's last two quartets. Their readings have an honesty and a directness that are enhanced by polish and finesse. Ensemble cannot be faulted and, though competition is strong, their claims still rank very high. The recordings have been transferred impeccably. The sound is rather more brightly astringent in the treble than the Chilingirians on CRD (CRD 3362/4), and is obviously less modern but does not lack underlying warmth. The disc coupling K.464 and K.465 offers slightly more expansive sound than the earlier recordings.

String quartets Nos. 14 in G, K.387; 15 in D min., K.421; 16 in E flat, K.428; 17 in B flat (Hunt); 18 in A, K.464; 19 in C (Dissonance), K.465 (Haydn Quartets).
*** Denon Dig. CO 75850/2 [id.]. Kuijken Qt.

String quartets Nos. 14 in G, K.387; 15 in D min., K.421; 16 in E flat, K.428; 17 in B flat (Hunt), K.458; 18 in A, K.464; 19 in C (Dissonance), K.465; Fragment, K.464a (Haydn Quartets).
** DG Dig. 431 797-2 (3) [id.]. Emerson Qt.

String quartets Nos. 14 in G, K.387; 15 in D min., K.421.
** Decca Dig. 440 076-2 [id.]. Ysaÿe Qt.
** DG Dig. 439 861-2 [id.]. Emerson Qt.

String quartets Nos. 16 in E flat, K.428; 17 in B flat (Hunt), K.458.
**(*) Decca Dig. 440 077-2 [id.]. Ysaÿe Qt.
* Ph. Dig. 426 392-2 [id.]. Guarneri Qt.

String quartets Nos. 16 in E flat, K.428; 18 in A, K.464; Fragment (Rondo), K.464a.
**(*) DG Dig. 439 914-2 [id.]. Emerson Qt.

These are very impressive performances by the Kuijken Quartet on Denon, using original instruments. One is struck how at the opening of the *Dissonance Quartet*, which comes first on disc 1, the sparer textures add to the sense of the music's originality. Certainly slow movements sound leaner than with modern instruments, but finales dance with increased lightness. For us the Chilingirians are special in these works (CRD 3362/4), but for those wanting period performances the Kuijkens can be strongly recommended alongside the Salomon Quartet on Hyperion (CDS 44001/3 – see our main volume).

There is no question as to the power and brilliance of the Emersons' playing: the quality of their technical finish, unanimity of thought, impeccable intonation and spot-on ensemble is hardly in question. However, they do not seem fully attuned to the sensibility of the period. They play wonderfully and with great intelligence, but there is little sense of repose or relaxation in the slow movements and too much power in the outer movements. Those wanting to sample this series could try the separate CD which couples K.428, one of the most felt performances, with K.464, where the variations of the *Andante* show the players at their most articulate but less able to charm the ear. This disc also includes Mozart's projected original finale of the latter, an engaging 6/8 movement which, nevertheless, ends in mid-air where the composer abandoned it.

With the Ysaÿe Quartet the *G major*, K.387, is more closely balanced than the *D minor*, K.421, and on the second disc this also seems to apply, if to a lesser extent, when comparing K.458 with K.428. The playing in K.387 is what the French call *nerveux* and there is little sense of space in the faster movements or repose in the slow movement. In the first movement of the *D minor*, K.421, the players' feelings do not seem to be engaged, and there is a similar impression in the *Andante con moto* of K.428, although they are at their most impressive in the calm atmosphere of the *Adagio* of K.458. Although they play very well throughout these quartets, the listener is not always fully drawn into the musical argument.

Considering their eminence, the Guarneri turn in two Mozart performances that are distinctly lacking in finesse and eloquence. They are not helped by a rather closely balanced recording, surprising from Philips, whose expertise in the chamber repertoire is second to none.

String quartet No. 14 in G, K.387; (i) String quintet No. 4 in G min., K.516.
*** ASV Dig. CDDCA 923 [id.]. Lindsay Qt, (i) with Patrick Ireland.

This is what chamber-music playing is about. The Lindsays radiate a delight in their music and judge the character of each piece of music exactly. There is none of the chromium-plated perfection of the Emersons, and one has only to compare the finale of K.387, played with enormous vitality and sparkle (even with an element of risk in the virtuosity), with that of the Quatuor Ysaÿe on Decca to sense immediately that the music-making is a world apart. The slow movement of the *G minor String quintet* is very touching in its gentle intensity. These are among the very finest modern recordings of either work. They were made in All Saints', Petersham, and the fairly close microphones are in no way intrusive, capturing the players against a very attractive ambience. The disc must be recommended with enthusiasm and we hope it will be the first of a series.

String quartets Nos. 17 in B flat (Hunt), K.458; 18 in A, K.464.
*** Hyp. Dig. CDA 66234 [id.]. Salomon Qt.

We admired these performances when they appeared as part of a three-CD set, devoted to all six quartets dedicated to Haydn (CDS 44001/3 – see our main volume). Those wanting period-style performances of K.458 and K.464 will be rewarded with clarity of texture and lightness of articulation. Very good recorded sound.

String quartets Nos. 18 in A, K.464; 19 in C (Dissonance), K.465.
** Decca Dig. 440 078-2 [id.]. Ysaÿe Qt.

The *Dissonance Quartet* opens well, but the slow movement is bland and here, as in K.464, the resonant sound gives inflated textures. The playing is most enjoyable in the finale of the A major work, which is very spirited.

String quartets Nos. 21 in D, K.575; 23 in F, K.590.
**(*) Arcana Dig. A 9 [id.]. Festetics Qt.

The Hungarian Quatuor Festetics, who play '*sur instruments d'époque*', as the French so engagingly put it, have already given us a highly recommendable set of Haydn's Op. 33. But (unlike Haydn) they approach Mozart with a degree of severity that not all will take to. The opening of K.575 is superbly poised, and the *Andante* is most eloquent. But never a suspicion of a smile until the arrival of the Minuet, and even this is very purposeful. Strong accents abound, and there is something a bit spare about the finale too, vital though it is. There is some marvellous playing throughout both quartets, and the performances have much strength and gravitas, to say nothing of superb ensemble and the most careful control of light and shade. The *Andante* of the *F major Quartet*, K.590, has the strongest characterization of all – it really is a remarkably precise performance – and the vital yet clean articulation in the finale shows absolute unanimity. A record to be greatly admired, but not one to fall in love with. The recording is made in an unlikely venue, the Zögernitz Casino in Vienna, and is vividly faithful, if a bit close.

String quintets Nos. 1 in B flat, K.174 (with original version of Trio of the Minuet and Finale); in C, K.515.
(BB) **(*) Naxos Dig. 8.553103 [id.]. Eder Qt with János Fehérvári.

The augmented Eder Quartet move on to what is obviously going to be a complete set of the *String quintets*, and the first disc again displays their unexaggerated Mozartian style, a fine blend of tone and musicianship. The *Andante* of the *C major Quintet* is particularly eloquent, the finale as lively as it is graceful. The recording (again using the Budapest Unitarian Church) is full and natural, with the resonance adding ambient bloom without too much inflation. While not quite a match for the Lindsays, these performances are eminently recommendable to those with limited budgets.

Clara Haskil: The Legacy, Volume 1: Chamber music

Violin sonatas Nos. 18; 21; 24; 26; 32; 34.
(M) (***) Ph. mono 442 625-2 (5) [id.]. Arthur Grumiaux, Clara Haskil – BEETHOVEN: *Violin sonatas Nos. 1-10.* (***)

Violin sonatas Nos. 18 in C, K.301; 21 in E min., K.304; 24 in F, K.376; 26 in B flat, K.378.
(M) (***) Ph. mono 442 629-2. Arthur Grumiaux, Clara Haskil.

Violin sonatas Nos. 32 in B flat, K.454; 34 in A, K.526.
(M) (***) Ph. mono 442 630-2. Arthur Grumiaux, Clara Haskil.

These six sonatas come – coupled with the complete *Violin sonatas* of Beethoven – as Volume One of Philips's so-called 'Clara Haskil Legacy'. This was a celebrated partnership and these classic accounts, which have excited much admiration over the years (and which doubtless will continue to do so), have been excellently transferred. The original mono recordings come from the late 1950s, yet the sound is remarkably vivid and true, and background noise has been virtually vanquished. The performances represent the musical yardstick by which all later versions were judged and are highly recommendable. The discs currently are not available separately.

PIANO MUSIC

Piano sonatas Nos. 3 in B flat, K.281; 10 in C, K.330; 13 in B flat, K.333; Adagio in B min., K.540; Rondo in D, K.485.
(M) *** DG Dig. 445 517-2 [id.]. Vladimir Horowitz.

Playing of such strong personality from so great an artist is self-recommending. With Horowitz there were astonishingly few reminders of the passage of time and the artistry and magnetism remain undiminished. The recordings were made in the pianist's last vintage period, between 1985 and 1989, in either a New York studio, the pianist's home, or an Italian studio in Milan (K.333). As usual, the piano is tightly tuned and the sound is slightly shallow, though very suitable for Mozart. Remarkable playing, not always completely free from affectation; but for variety of articulation just sample the *Allegretto grazioso* finale of K.333 and, for simply expressed depth of feeling, the *Adagio*, K. 540.

VOCAL MUSIC

Concert arias: *Il burbero di buon cuore: Chi sà. Vado, ma dove, K.583. Exsultate, jubilate, K.165.*
Arias: *La clemenza di Tito: Parto, parto. Idomeneo: Ch'io mi scordi . . . Non temer, amato bene. Le nozze di Figaro: Al desio di chi t'adore; Un moto di gioia mi sento.*
(M) *** Erato/Warner Dig. 4509 98497-2 [id.]. Dame Janet Baker, Scottish CO, Leppard.

In a Mozart programme, recorded in 1984, which extends well beyond the normal mezzo-soprano repertoire, Dame Janet sings with all her usual warmth, intensity and stylishness, hardly if at all stretched by often high tessitura. The biggest challenge is the most taxing of all Mozart's concert arias, *Ch'io mi scordi di te?*, with Leppard a brilliant exponent of the difficult obbligato part. There Baker, so far from being daunted by the technical problems, uses them to intensify her detailed rendering of words. The two *Figaro* items are alternative arias for Susanna, both of them delightful. Sesto's aria from *Clemenza di Tito* presents another challenge, magnificently taken, as does the early cantata, *Exsultate, jubilate,* with its famous *Alleluia.* The other two arias were written for Louise Villeneuve – Dorabella to be – as an enrichment of her part in an opera by Soler, more delightful rarities. Excellent sound with wonderful presence, and warmly sympathetic accompaniment.

Mass No. 3 in C (Dominicus), K.66; Vesperae de Domenica, K.321.
(M) *** Teldec/Warner Dig. 2292 46469-2 [id.]. Margiono, Bonney, Von Magnus, Heilmann, Cachemaille, Arnold Schoenberg Ch., V. Hofburgkapelle Choral Scholars, VCM, Harnoncourt.

Harnoncourt is at his finest in this splendidly lively Mass which the thirteen-year-old Mozart wrote for a personal friend ten years his senior when he took holy orders. Father Dominicus was later to confirm the success of its performance at his ordination. It has sixteen brief jewels of movements, and the direct Harnoncourt style with its strong accents and positive characterization brings every one of them vividly to life. The bright tempi too are apt and the soloists equally strong. The more ambitious *Vesperae de Domenica*, written a decade later, with its plainsong introduction to each of six sections, forms a neat and joyful *Missa brevis*, here refreshingly alive and brimful of variety of invention. Again the singing of chorus and soloists alike is highly stimulating, and Harnoncourt's affection brings a committed and vivacious approach which is entirely successful. The recording is first rate.

(i; ii) *Mass No. 4 in C min. (Weisenhaus), K.139;* (i) *Exsultate jubilate, K.165.*
(M) **(*) Teldec/Warner Dig. 2292 44180-2 [id.]. (i) Barbara Bonney; (ii) Rappé, Protschka, Hagegård, Arnold Schoenberg Ch., VCM, Harnoncourt.

This lively early work responds to strong characterization and, with excellent soloists and vibrant choral singing, is another refreshing example of Harnoncourt's view of authenticity. Barbara Bonney's *Exsultate jubilate* is enjoyably bracing, though it is sung a semitone lower than in modern instrument performances. The sound is satisfactory. However, for those not insisting ·on original instruments Abbado's DG recording remains a more obvious first choice (DG 427 255-2 – see our main volume).

Mass No. 16 in C (Coronation), K.317.
(M) **(*) DG Dig. 445 543-2 (2) [id.]. Battle, Schmidt, Winbergh, Furlanetto, V. Singverein, VPO, Karajan – BEETHOVEN: *Missa solemnis.***(*)

Mass No. 16 in C (Coronation), K.317; Vesperae solennes de Confessore, K.339.
(M) ** Teldec/Warner Dig. 4509 95990-2 [id.]. Rodgers, Von Magnus, Protschka, Polgár, Arnold Schoenberg Ch., V. Hofburgkapelle Choral Scholars, VCM, Harnoncourt.

Karajan's 1985 recording of Mozart's *Coronation Mass* is certainly vibrant, with fine choral singing and good soloists. Kathleen Battle sings beautifully in the *Agnus Dei*, and the recording is bright, if not ideally expansive.

Harnoncourt is not entirely logical in using period instruments, but women rather than boy trebles in the choir. As usual, accents are strong, dynamic contrasts are exaggerated and phrasing is somewhat eccentrically moulded, although Joan Rodgers is a fine soprano soloist in both works, her line eloquent and without exaggerations. As with the *C minor Mass*, the recording has plenty of atmosphere but could be more clearly defined.

Mass No. 18 in C min., K.427.
(M) **(*) Teldec/Warner Dig. 4509 95991-2 [id.]. Láki, Dénes, Equiluz, Holl, V. State Op. Ch. Soc., VCM, Harnoncourt.

Harnoncourt's version, using period instruments, is strongly characterized, with authentic perform-ance used not to smooth away dramatic contrasts but to enhance them. The emphatic rhythmic style in both slow and fast passages will not please everyone but, with a well-chosen quartet of soloists and responsive choral singing, this will suit Harnoncourt admirers, though the reverberant recording is not always helpful to detail. Gardiner's Philips version (420 210-2) is a safer, more general recommen-dation for those wanting an 'authentic' version, and the recording, too, is clearer. For those wanting the fullness of modern instruments, Karajan's Berlin recording with the Vienna Singverein brings Handelian splendour (DG Gold 439 012-2). In the *Requiem Mass* choice lies between Gardiner again (Philips 420 197-2) and Hickox with the London Symphony Chorus (Virgin VJ7 59648-2).

Mass No. 18 in C min., K.427; Kyrie in D min., K.341.
(M) **(*) Virgin Veritas/EMI Dig. VER5 61167-2 [id.]. Barbara Schlick, Monika Frimmer, Christoph Prégardien, Klaus Mertens, Cologne Chamber Ch., Collegium Cartusianum, Neumann.

Peter Neumann's account of the *C minor Mass* has a great deal going for it: fine soloists – with Barbara Schlick always fresh and captivating in the *Laudamus te* – spacious choral singing, gloriously if somewhat backwardly recorded, and excellent playing from an authentic-sized orchestra on original instruments. The *Sanctus* is properly expansive and the overall conception warmly persuasive in its relaxed way. But in the last resort the chorus lacks the bite to make the performance really gripping. The rather solemn *Kyrie* has plenty of character with the performance darkly lyrical rather than dramatic.

OPERA

La clemenza di Tito (complete).
**(*) O-L Dig. 444 131-2 (2) [id.]. Heilman, Bartoli, Della Jones, Montague, Bonney, Ch. & AAM, Christopher Hogwood.

This provides an acceptable alternative to the superb Gardiner set on DG Archiv (421 806-2) for those who want a studio, not a live, recording and who insist of having all the recitative – which was written not by Mozart but by Süssmeyer. Both are very well cast, each bringing out the positive strengths of an opera long underestimated. Gardiner is the more persuasive advocate, helped by the natural tensions of a live occasion, with beefier instrumental sound. However, with clean, crisp manners Hogwood draws transparent textures from the players in the Academy, pointing rhythms and phrases more lightly and almost as imaginatively as Gardiner. Sesto as portrayed by the characterful Cecilia Bartoli is clearly established as the central figure in the drama, with Della Jones as Vitellia comparably positive, though neither of them produces quite such beautiful and even, cleanly focused tone as their opposite numbers for Gardiner, the magnificent Anne Sofie von Otter and Julia Varady. Diana Montague as Annio and Barbara Bonney as Servilia both weigh in favour of Hogwood, but Uwe Heilmann with his slightly fluttery tenor conveys nothing like the heroic strength of Anthony Rolfe Johnson in the title-role for Gardiner. Clean, well-balanced studio sound.

Così fan tutte (complete).

⊛ (M) *** EMI CMS7 69330-2 (3) [Ang. CDMC 69330]. Schwarzkopf, Ludwig, Steffek, Kraus, Taddei, Berry, Philh. Ch. & O, Boehm.

*** DG Dig. 437 829-2 (3) [id.]. Roocroft, Mannion, Gilfry, Trost, James, Feller, E. Bar. Soloists, Gardiner.

Boehm's classic set has been handsomely repackaged and remains a clear first choice, despite the attractions of the new Gardiner version. Its glorious solo singing is headed by the incomparable Fiordiligi of Schwarzkopf and the equally moving Dorabella of Christa Ludwig; it remains a superb memento of Walter Legge's recording genius and still bears comparison with any other recordings made before or since.

As in his earlier Mozart opera recordings, John Eliot Gardiner here chooses voices that are both fresh and well focused, with the roles of all four of the lovers taken by young singers – Amanda Roocroft, Rosa Mannion, Rainer Trost and Rodney Gilfry. For this comedy, Gardiner, more controversially, opted to get the engineers to record a live performance not in concert but on stage. Stage noises are often intrusive, with laughter and applause punctuating the performance, not always helpfully. Whatever the snags, the full flavour of *Così*, its effervescence as well as its deeper qualities, comes over the more intensely as a result and, unlike previous conductors who have adopted this course, Gardiner secures ensemble as crisp as you would expect in a studio recording. It was made in the Teatro Comunale in Ferrara, with a relatively dry acoustic giving clarity to the period instruments of the English Baroque Soloists while not undermining the bloom on the voices. Though Roocroft and Mannion do not sound quite as sweet and even as they can, few tenors on disc can rival the German, Rainer Trost, in the heady beauty of his voice, above all in Ferrando's aria, *Una aura amorosa*. The poise and technical assurance of all the singers, not least Rodney Gilfry as Guglielmo, put this among the very finest versions of *Così*, outshining many with far starrier (and older) casts. DG offers the alternative of a video version (072 436-31), also made on stage, but at the Théâtre du Châtelet in Paris instead of Ferrara, and with Claudio Nicolai instead of Carlos Feller as Alfonso. The unscripted noises are here explained in the detail of Gardiner's own (sometimes excessive) staging, but with delectably pretty scenery. The crowning achievement on both CD and video is that the dénouement in the long Act II finale has a tenderness and depth rarely matched.

Così fan tutte: highlights.

*** DG Dig. 437 994-2 [id.] (from above recording, cond. Gardiner).

The Gardiner highlights offers a generous selection (73 minutes) of key items, including the Overture. It will be especially useful to those collectors who have chosen Boehm's set and want a reminder of a splendid 'authentic' performance using original instruments.

Don Giovanni (complete).

*** DG Dig. 445 870-2 (3) [id.]. Gilfry, Orgonasova, Margiono, James, d'Arcangelo, Prégardien, Clarkson, Silvestrelli, Monteverdi Ch., E. Bar. Soloists, Gardiner.

(M) *** EMI CMS7 63841-2 (3) [Ang. CDMC 63841]. Ghiaurov, Claire Watson, Ludwig, Freni, Gedda, Berry, Montarsolo, Crass, New Philh. Ch. & O, Klemperer.

John Eliot Gardiner's set was recorded 'in connection with performances' at the Ludwigsburg Schloss Festival in 1994, mainly live but with tidying sessions afterwards. As in his *Figaro*, the result is vividly dramatic, beautifully paced and deeply expressive, with little or none of the haste associated with period practice. The performance culminates in one of the most thrilling accounts ever recorded of the final scene, when Giovanni is dragged down to hell, presented in sound of spine-tingling immediacy. Stage noises are minimally intrusive, and much is gained from having the music paced in relation to live performances. Gardiner opts for a text that is neither that of the original Prague version nor the usual amalgam of Prague and Vienna. The editor, Nicholas McNair, argues in a comprehensive note that the order adopted here is the answer truest to Mozart. It takes note not just of the extra numbers written for Vienna – Ottavio's *'Dalla sua pace'* and Elvira's *'Mi tradi'* – but also of other alterations made to accommodate them. So Leporello's *'Ah pietà'* is replaced by a recitative, which leads to a duet with Zerlina, when she ties him up. Ottavio's *'Il mio tesoro'* is then omitted, and *'Mi tradi'* follows immediately. Dramatically the result is tauter, and the numbers omitted are here included in an appendix.

The dramatic bite of the performance is established in the overture, and then initially Gardiner uses period performance for lightness and speed, as in the duet *'La ci darem'*. Sometimes lightness goes too far, as when Charlotte Margiono as Donna Elvira sings *'Ah fuggi il traditor'* in a half-tone, but increasingly Gardiner encourages his soloists, particularly Anna and Elvira, to sing expansively, bringing out the full weight of such arias as *'Mi tradi'* and Anna's *'Non mi dir'*. That last rightly becomes an emotional high point, preparing the way for exhilarating accounts of the final scene and epilogue. Fine as Margiono is, Luba Orgonasova is even more assured and characterful as Anna, and the agility of both is exemplary. Rodney Gilfry, impressive in earlier Gardiner Mozart sets, here excels himself, on one side tough and purposeful, on the other a smooth seducer, with the clean-toned voice finely shaded. Ildebrando d'Arcangelo is suitably darker-toned as Leporello, lithe and young-sounding, hardly a *buffo*. Julian Clarkson makes a crotchety Masetto, and Eirian James a warmer, tougher Zerlina than usual, aptly so for her extra scene. The Commendatore of Andrea Silvestrelli, though recessed on the recording, is magnificently dark and firm, not least in the final confrontation. A recording that sets new standards for period performance, and vies with the finest of traditional versions, of which first choice still remains with Giulini (EMI CDS7 47260-8) – see our main volume.

The lumbering tempo of Leporello's opening music will alert the listener to the predictable Klemperer approach and at that point some may dismiss his performance as 'too heavy' – but the issue is far more complex than that. Most of the slow tempi which Klemperer regularly adopts, far from flagging, add a welcome breadth to the music, for they must be set against the unusually brisk and dramatic interpretation of the recitatives between numbers. Added to that, Ghiaurov as the Don and Berry as Leporello make a marvellously characterful pair. In this version the male members of the cast are dominant and, with Klemperer's help, they make the dramatic experience a strongly masculine one. Nor is the ironic humour forgotten with Berry and Ghiaurov about, and the Klemperer spaciousness allows them extra time for pointing. Among the women, Ludwig is a strong and convincing Elvira, Freni a sweet-toned but rather unsmiling Zerlina; only Claire Watson seriously disappoints, with obvious nervousness marring the big climax of *Non mi dir*. It is a serious blemish but, with the usual reservations, for those not allergic to the Klemperer approach, this stands as a good recommendation – at the very least a commanding experience. The set now reappears at mid-price, its catalogue number unchanged, but the presentation more stylish.

Don Giovanni: highlights.
(M) **(*) DG 445 463-2 [id.] (from complete recording, with Milnes, Tomowa-Sintow, Schreier, Zylis-Gara, Mathis, Berry; cond. Boehm).

Boehm's selection is very generous (76 minutes) and is taken from live performances at Salzburg (recorded in 1977). It makes a welcome representation of a set centring round Sherrill Milnes's unusually heroic assumption of the role of the Don, and he sings with a richness and commitment to match his swaggering stage presence. The rest of the cast give stylish performances without being deeply memorable but, unlike *Così* where ensembles were less than ideally crisp, this live *Giovanni* presents strong and consistently enjoyable teamwork. The balance again favours the voices but is especially vivid in the culminating scene. For this reissue (which includes the *Overture*) an adequate cued synopsis, linked to the narrative, has been provided.

Die Entführung aus dem Serail (complete).
(B) ** DG Double 439 708-2 (2) [id.]. Köth, Schädle, Wunderlich, Lenz, Böhme, Bav. State Op. Ch. & O, Jochum.

(i) *Die Entführung aus dem Serail* (complete); (ii) Overtures: *Così fan tutte, Don Giovanni, Le nozze di Figaro, Der Schauspieldirektor, Die Zauberflöte*.
(B) (*) Decca Double mono 443 530-2 (2) [id.]. Lipp, Loose, Ludwig, Klein, Koreh, Woester, V. State Op. Ch., VPO; (ii) LSO, Josef Krips.

It is the greatest pity that the role of Constanze in Jochum's performance is taken by the shrill and shallow-sounding Erika Köth. Otherwise it would be an admirable DG Double recommendation, well recorded, with lively direction from Jochum and a wonderful contribution from the late-lamented Fritz Wunderlich. But it is worth paying the extra money for Boehm's delectable mid-priced DG set (429 868-2), with Arleen Augér ideally girlish and fresh as Constanze; for authenticists, Gardiner can be strongly recommended (DG 435 857-2 – see our main volume).

The Double Decca alternative was not just the first complete recording of *Entführung* but the first complete opera to appear on Decca LP. Under Krips's sparkling direction, with a cast drawn from the vintage post-war team at the Vienna State Opera, it is a fine if flawed performance, and it is sad that the Decca transfer deals so shabbily with a historic recording. The orchestral sound on CD completely lacks the body of the original LPs, emerging very thinly and with an impossibly fizzy top, quite different from the far fuller sound given to the overtures, recorded in London the following year. Voices are somewhat better treated. Finest among the soloists are the two tenors: both Walther Ludwig and Peter Klein sing with clear, heady tone. But Emmy Loose as Konstanze and Wilma Lipp as Blondchen are caught brightly to the point of shrillness, which tires the ear, with Loose slightly fluttery. Endre Koreh is a powerful, characterful Osmin, again with a slight flutter in the voice. Decca engineers need to listen more closely to the results they achieve from some of these early master tapes. Something obviously went wrong after the original LP issues; and this is by no means the only example of an early recording on this label which offers unacceptably 'toppy' sound in its CD transfer.

Le nozze di Figaro (complete).
(M) *** EMI CMS7 63266-2 (2) [Ang. CDMB 63266]. Schwarzkopf, Moffo, Cossotto, Taddei, Waechter, Vinco, Philh. Ch. & O, Giulini.
*** DG Dig. 439 871-2 (3) [id.]. Terfel, Hagley, Martinpelto, Gilfry, Stephen, McCulloch, Feller, Egerton, Backes, Monterverdi Ch., E. Bar. Soloists, Gardiner.
*** Teldec/Warner Dig. 4509 90861-2 (3) [id.]. Scharinger, Bonney, Margiono, Hampson, Lang, Moll, Langridge, Netherlands Op. Ch., Concg. O, Harnoncourt.
**(*) Telarc CD-80388 (3) [id.]. Miles, Focile, Vaness, Corbelli, Mentzer, Murphy, Ryland Davies, Rebecca Evans, SCO and Ch., Mackerras.

Like others in EMI's series of Mozart operas, Giulini's set has been pleasingly re-packaged and has a cleanly printed, easy-to-read libretto, giving an advantage over the competing CfP set (CD-CFPD 4724 – see our main volume). It remains a classic, with a cast assembled by Walter Legge that has rarely been matched, let alone surpassed. Taddei with his dark bass-baritone makes a provocative Figaro; opposite him, Anna Moffo is at her freshest and sweetest as Susanna. Schwarzkopf as ever is the noblest of Countesses, and it is good to hear the young Fiorenza Cossotto as a full-toned Cherubino. Eberhard Waechter is a strong and stylish Count. On only two mid-priced discs it makes a superb bargain, though – as in the other EMI two-disc version, the Gui on CfP – Marcellina's and Basilio's arias are omitted from Act IV.

Gardiner's version was recorded live in concert performances at the Queen Elizabeth Hall in London in 1993, and this brings disadvantages in occasional intrusive stage noises, but it also offers a vividly dramatic and involving experience. In one instance the effect of the moment goes too far, when Cherubino (Pamela Helen Stephen) sings '*Voi che sapete*' for the Countess in a funny, nervous voice. That is very much the exception, for Gardiner's approach is lively and often brisk, with period manners made more genial and elegant than on the rival period recording from Drottningholm on Oiseau-Lyre. One of the most consistent and characterful of modern casts is led superbly by Bryn Terfel as Figaro, already a master in this role, with the enchanting, bright-eyed Alison Hagley as Susanna. Rodney Gilfry and Hillevi Martinpelto are fresh and firm as the Count and Countess, aptly younger-sounding than usual. Carlos Feller is a characterful *buffo* Bartolo, and Francis Egerton a wickedly funny Basilio. In Act III Gardiner adopts the revised order, suggested by Robert Moberly and Christopher Raeburn, with the Countess's aria placed earlier. More controversially, in Act IV he divides the recitative for Figaro's aria so that part of it comes logically before Susanna's '*Deh vieni*'. A fine addition to Gardiner's Mozart opera series for DG Archiv.

Harnoncourt on Teldec makes the Royal Concertgebouw Orchestra produce fresh, light and transparent sounds close to period style. Speeds are relaxed, bringing out the fun and sparkle of the piece. The excellent cast has Thomas Hampson as a dominant Count, Charlotte Margiono as a tenderly sweet Countess, with Barbara Bonney a charmingly provocative Susanna and Anton Scharinger a winning Figaro, both tough and comic. Recitative at flexible speeds conveys the dramatic confrontations and complications vividly. A version that gets the best of both interpretative worlds, new and old.

The big advantage of the Telarc version is that Sir Charles Mackerras with the Scottish Chamber Orchestra provides some 34 minutes of alternative items and variants. As a Mozart scholar himself, he has done much original research on this score, and the details of his and other discoveries emerge in a conversation printed in the booklet between Sir Charles and another great Mozart scholar, H. C. Robbins Landon, who worked alongside each other some 30 years ago. It is fascinating, for example, to have two alternative versions of the Count's Act III aria, with the difficult triplets largely removed, and there is also a heavily ornamented version of Cherubino's 'Voi che sapete'. Mackerras also encourages his singers to provide ornamentation in their arias and, more than his rivals, he inserts appoggiature, avoiding 'blunt endings'.

Like Harnoncourt, Mackerras aims to get the best of both interpretative worlds, but with the balance more towards period performance, using modern instruments but in a small orchestra and with speeds generally brisker and bowing lighter. Orchestrally, this is an exceptionally characterful reading, more so than for the singing of the arias and ensembles. Alastair Miles as Figaro sings superbly with clean focus but, next to his main rivals, he is straight-faced, and similarly the Susanna of Nuccia Focile is a little lacking in charm and humour, while Carol Vaness as the Countess is not as creamy-voiced as she is in Haitink's Glyndebourne recordings for EMI, stressed perhaps by Mackerras's slow speeds (an exception) for her two big arias. The Count of Alessandro Corbelli is rather rough in tone, and Alfonso Antoniozzi is too light and unsteady as Bartolo, but Ryland Davies is a superb Basilio and Susanne Mentzer a strong Marcellina, both given their arias in Act IV, which comes complete on disc 3, along with the appendices. Conveniently, Acts I, II and III are fitted complete on the first two discs. Any reservations are made relative to only the finest rivals; with warm sound, the set can be strongly recommended, particularly to anyone who wants to hear the extra material.

Le nozze di Figaro: highlights.
**(*) DG Dig. 445 874-2 [id.] (from above complete recording, with Terfel, Hagley, Martinpelto, Gilfry; cond. Gardiner).
(M) ** O-L Dig. 443 191-2 (from complete recording, with Salòmaa, Bonney, Hagegård, Augér, Drottningholm Theatre Ch. & O, Ostman).

A selection from Gardiner's version is available, offering 69 minutes of music, including the *Overture*, but no translation, only a cued synopsis, which seems unsatisfactory for a premium-priced disc.

Ostman's was the first period-instrument performance of *Figaro*, and his ruthlessly metrical pressing forward undermines the opera's fun and dramatic point. The opera is impressively cast, with Barbara Bonney a charming Susanna and Augér singing beautifully as the Countess (in spite of the conductor's fast speeds). Håkan Hagegård is a splendid Count. The excerpts play for 66 minutes.

Die Zauberflöte (complete).
*** EMI CDS5 55173-2 (2). Janowitz, Putz, Popp, Gedda, Berry, Frick, Schwarzkopf, Ludwig, Hoffgen (3 Ladies), Philh. Ch. & O, Klemperer.
(B) ** Ph. Duo Dig. 442 568-2 (2) [id.]. Margaret Price, Serra, Schreier, Moll, Melbye, Venuti, Tear, Dresden Kreuzchor, Leipzig R. Ch., Dresden State O, Sir Colin Davis.

Klemperer's conducting of *The Magic Flute* is one of his finest achievements on record; indeed he is inspired, making the dramatic music sound more like Beethoven in its breadth and strength. But he does not miss the humour and point of the Papageno passages, and he gets the best of both worlds to a surprising degree. The cast is outstanding – look at the distinction of the Three Ladies alone – but curiously it is that generally most reliable of all the singers, Gottlob Frick as Sarastro, who comes nearest to letting the side down. Lucia Popp is in excellent form, and Gundula Janowitz sings Pamina's part with a creamy beauty that is just breathtaking. Nicolai Gedda too is a firm-voiced Tamino. The transfer to a pair of CDs, made possible by the absence of dialogue, is managed expertly. However, like Klemperer's set of Beethoven's *Fidelio*, this recording has reverted to full price and, even though it has been re-packaged, such an increase in cost seems in no way justifiable.

The last of Sir Colin Davis's recordings of Mozart's major operas, and the only one made outside Britain, is also the least successful. With speeds often slower than usual and the manner heavier, it is a performance of little sparkle or charm, one which seems intent on bringing out serious, symbolic meanings. Thus, although Margaret Price produces a glorious flow of rich, creamy tone, she conveys little of the necessary vulnerability of Pamina in her plight. Luciana Serra sings capably but at times with shrill tone and not always with complete security; while Peter Schreier is in uncharacteristically gritty voice as Tamino, and Mikael Melbye as Papageno is ill-suited to recording, when the microphone exaggerates the throatiness and unevenness of his production. The greatest vocal glory of the set is the magnificent, firm and rich singing of Kurt Moll as Sarastro. The recording is excellent. Although this Duo reissue is inexpensive, it is upstaged by the competing Halász Naxos set from Budapest (see our main volume), a very satisfying performance, well conducted and well recorded, with some very stylish solo singing (8.660030/31). At full price, first choice rests with Marriner, with the finest cast of any modern version (Philips 426 276-2).

Die Zauberflöte: highlights.
(M) **(*) DG 445 464-2 [id.] (from complete recording, with Lear, Peters, Wunderlich, Fischer-Dieskau, Crass; cond. Boehm).

The hour of excerpts from Boehm's recording is not obviously directed towards bringing out its special qualities, although there would have been room on the CD (which includes the *Overture*) for at least another quarter of an hour of music, to measure up with the companion selection from *Don Giovanni*. As with the other reissues in this series, there is now a cued synopsis of the narrative. One would have liked more of Wunderlich's Tamino, one of the great glories of the set. However, the key arias are all included and the sound is fresh and full.

RECITALS

Arias from: *La clemenza di Tito; Così fan tutte; Don Giovanni; Die Entführung aus dem Serail; Idomeneo; Le nozze di Figaro; Die Zauberflöte*.
(M) *** Ph. Dig. 442 410-2 [id.]. Cheryl Studer, ASMF, Marriner.

This is a very impressive recital indeed. Only the aria from *Idomeneo* could be considered a little under-characterized – and that is a marginal criticism; the Queen of the Night's arias from *Die Zauberflöte* are superbly done, as is the opening *Martern aller Arten* (from *Die Entführung*) and the excerpts from *Così* and *Don Giovanni* are hardly less memorable in a quite different way. Excellent accompaniments and recording, but the measure is fairly short (55 minutes).

Mussorgsky, Modest (1839–81)

Night on the bare mountain (arr. Rimsky-Korsakov); *Pictures at an exhibition* (orch. Ravel).
(M) ** Virgin/EMI Dig. CUV5 61135-2 [id.]. Royal Liverpool PO. Ch. & O, Mackerras – BORODIN: *Prince Igor: Overture and Polovtsian dances*. ***

Mackerras surprisingly comes over at a lower voltage than usual. Although his opening *Promenade* is fairly brisk, the first few pictures, though well played, are almost bland and, while *Bydlo* reaches a fairly massive climax, it is not until *Limoges* that the performance springs fully to life; then *The Hut on fowl's legs* is powerfully rhythmic, with an impressive tuba solo. *The Great Gate of Kiev* is not as consistently taut as in some versions, but it is properly expansive at the close, with the recording, always full-bodied, producing an impressive breadth of sound. Perhaps the tam-tam might ideally have been placed a fraction nearer (as it is in the famous Telarc/Cleveland recording: CD 80042). *Night on the bare mountain*, although vivid enough, lacks Satanic bite, and the closing pages fail to wring the heartstrings.

Pictures at an exhibition (orch. Ravel).
(M) *** DG 447 426-2 [id.]. BPO, Karajan – DEBUSSY: *La Mer;* RAVEL: *Boléro*. ***
⊛ (M) *** RCA 09026 61401-2 [id.]. Chicago SO, Fritz Reiner – RESPIGHI: *The Fountains of Rome; The Pines of Rome*. *** ⊛

Among the many fine versions of Mussorgsky's *Pictures* on CD, Karajan's 1966 record stands out. It is undoubtedly a great performance, tingling with electricity from the opening Promenade to the spaciously conceived finale, *The Great Gate of Kiev*, which has real splendour. Other high points are the ominously powerful climax of *Bydlo* as the Polish ox-wagon lumbers into view very weightily, and the venomously pungent bite of the brass – expansively recorded – in the sinister *Catacombs* sequence, which is given a bizarre majesty. As with many of Karajan's finest records, one has the feeling that he has rethought the score, here very much in terms of a Straussian symphonic poem, for the *Promenades*, with tempi subtly varied and sometimes slower than usual, are well integrated into the overall structure. Detail is consistently pointed with the greatest imagination, not only in the lighter moments but, for instance, in *The hut on fowl's legs*, where the tuba articulation is sharp and rhythmically buoyant. Throughout, the glorious orchestral playing, and especially the brass sonorities, ensnare the ear; even when Karajan is relatively restrained, as in the nostalgic melancholy of *The old castle*, the underlying tension remains. The remastered analogue recording still sounds marvellous, and this reissue, in DG's 'Originals' series of legendary recordings, includes a uniquely evocative performance of Debussy's *La Mer* as well as a very exciting account of Ravel's *Boléro*.

Reiner's 1957 Chicago performance is another example of vintage stereo recording at its most impressive, using simple microphone techniques to achieve a vivid yet natural sound-picture. The record was orginally issued in the UK in October 1958 (as RCA SB 2001), around the same time as Karajan's Philharmonia account. With the advantage of the rich acoustics of Symphony Hall, the RCA sound-balance is more atmospheric than the EMI recording, if less sharply focused. But Reiner's approach is evocative to match, and *The old castle*, gently nostalgic, the lumbering ox-wagon and the superb brass sonorities in the *Catacombs* sequence are all memorable. The finale climax of *The Great Gate of Kiev* is massively effective, yet the attack of the strings on their scalic passage (at 1 minute 28 seconds, band 15) shows the concentration of the playing. The remastering is fully worthy, and there is excellent documentation. Original copies of this issue had the channels reversed, but this will undoubtedly be corrected by the time we are in print.

(i) *Pictures at an exhibition* (orch. Ravel); (ii) *Pictures at an exhibition* (original piano version).
(M) **(*) Ph Dig. 442 650-2 [id.]. (i) VPO, Previn; (ii) Brendel.

Previn's Philips version was recorded during live performances in Vienna. Obviously the Philips engineers had problems with the acoustics of the Musikvereinsaal, as the bass is noticeably resonant and inner definition is far from sharp. Otherwise the balance is truthful; but the performance, though not lacking spontaneity, is not distinctive, and there is a lack of the kind of grip which makes Karajan's version so unforgettable.

Brendel's performance of the original piano score has its own imaginative touches and some fine moments: the *Ballet of the Unhatched Chicks* is delightfully articulated, and both the *Bydlo* and *Baba-Yaga* are powerful, the latter coming after a darkly evocative *Catacombs/Cum mortuis* sequence. Brendel keeps the music moving but effectively varies the style of the Promenades. The closing pages, however, need to sound more unbuttoned: Brendel is weighty, but fails to enthral the listener. The recording is faithful.

Pictures at an exhibition; St John's night on the bare mountain (original version); (i) *The destruction of Sennacherib;* (ii) *Joshua; Oedipus in Athens: Chorus of people in the temple. Salambô: Chorus of priestesses.*
*** DG Dig. 445 238-2 [id.]; *445 238-4.* BPO, Abbado; with (i) Prague Philharmonic Ch.; (ii) and Elena Zaremba.

Abbado included the four choral items on an outstanding RCA record, issued to commemorate the centenary of Mussorgsky's death in 1981. This was coupled with other short orchestral pieces besides *St John's night on the bare mountain* and is splendidly played and sung. It was also offered at mid-price (09026 61354-2) and as such received a Rosette in our main volume. This new CD offers an equally vivid account of *St John's night on the bare mountain* (or 'bald' mountain, as the Americans call it – rightly, according to Arthur Jacobs' excellent notes: the word in Russian means just that). The choral pieces are richly sung and the short cantata, *Joshua*, is particularly successful with its central solo, *The Amorite women weep*, movingly sung by Elena Zaremba. There is also much to praise in the spacious performance of the *Pictures* with its individually observed detail. It is not as electrifying as Karajan's analogue version or Sinopoli's highly recommendable digital account (DG 429 785-2), but it is notable for the refinement of its colouring and evocation, often more gently evocative than usual. One of the most telling portraits is of *Goldenberg and Schmuyle*, the one so opulently self-aware, the other obsequiously bleating; the rich Berlin brass are sonorously compelling in *Catacombs*, and *Baba-Yaga* is savagly rhythmic, while the *Great Gate of Kiev* is steadily built to a very impressive climax, with the contrasting chorale hushed, almost vocal in effect, and the tam-tam adding splendour to the final culmination.

Pictures at an exhibition (piano version).
** Decca Dig. 436 255-2 [id.]. Olli Mustonen – BALAKIREV: *Islamey* **; TCHAIKOVSKY: *Children's album.* *(*)
*(*) DG Dig. 435 616-2 [id.]. Anatol Ugorski – STRAVINSKY: *Petrushka.* *(*)

Anatol Ugorski, who gave us such an eccentric reading of Beethoven's last *Piano sonata*, Op. 111 (see our main volume), is a good deal less bizarre here, but he is up against such giants as Richter and Pletnev (the latter on Virgin VC7 59511-2 is our first choice). There is absolutely no reason for preferring him to them in terms of either personality or keyboard virtuosity.

Nor, in its different way, does the gifted Finnish pianist, Olli Mustonen, emerge at his very best in his well-recorded Decca recital. He has authority, impressive technical address and no mean command of keyboard colour. There are self-conscious touches here and there, and yet he does not bring a personal interpretative vision to bear on this familiar score.

Song-cycles: The nursery; Songs and dances of death. Songs: Darling Savishna; Forgotten; The He-Goat; The Puppet-show; Mephistopheles' Song of the flea.
🏵 *** Conifer Dig. CDCF 229 [id.]. Sergei Leiferkus, Semion Skigin.

These are impressive performances; not only does Sergei Leiferkus make a beautiful sound, but his singing has immense character and power. He can be passionate, earthy and yet aristocratic, touching and then magisterial by turn. He seems to command an unlimited range of colour and to be able to draw forth all the drama and variety of vocal timbre these songs demand. In Semion Skigin he has a pianist of commanding dramatic talent and, at the same time, exemplary restraint. This is the only Mussorgsky song-recital of recent times that can rank alongside the classic pre-war records of Kipnis or the majestic 1950s Christoff set. The Conifer recording is first class, too.

Complete songs.
** Chan. Dig. CHAN 9336–38 [id.]. Aage Haugland, Poul Rosenblom.

The Chandos survey of the complete songs, which enshrine the soul of a whole people just as completely as does *Boris Godunov* and which is arguably Mussorgsky's greatest achievement, is unbelievably the first made for CD and the first at all for nearly forty years. The last complete set was by Boris Christoff with Alexandre Labinsky and in mono (EMI CHS7 63025-2); strangely enough (unless we are much mistaken), there was no complete set made during the years of stereo LP. It must be conceded that the fine Danish bass, Aage Haugland, and his partner, Poul Rosenblom, do not banish memories of Christoff. Haugland is cultured, but the dramatic intensity, the larger-than-life characterization of the Bulgarian is simply not there. Compare, say, the first two of the *Songs and dances of death* – or, in fact, any of the songs – with Leiferkus, and you are in a totally different world. These are well recorded but much less gripping and involving.

Songs and dances of death (orch. Shostakovich).
*** EMI Dig. CDC7 55232-2 [id.]. Lloyd, Phd. O, Jansons – SHOSTAKOVICH: *Symphony No. 10.*
***

Robert Lloyd gives a commanding and sonorous account of the Shostakovich transcription of Mussorgsky's gripping *Songs and dances of death* as a fill-up to Jansons' intense and powerful reading of the Shostakovich *Tenth Symphony.*

Nepomuceno, Alberto (1864–1920)

Improviso, Op. 27/2; 2 Nocturnes; Nocturne, Op. 33; 5 Pequenas peças; Piano sonata in F min., Op. 9; Suite antiga, Op. 11.
* Marco Polo Dig. 8.223548 [id.]. Maria Inês Guimarães.

Marco Polo's enterprise is to be greatly commended, even if their choice of artists is not always beyond reproach. Nepomuceno has been spoken of as the founding father of Brazilian music: he belongs to the generation immediately before Villa-Lobos (indeed, he effected Villa-Lobos's introduction to his publisher). During studies in Europe, where he was a pupil of Guilmant among others, he met Brahms and numbered Grieg among his friends. Grieg greatly admired the *Suite antiga.* Nepomuceno was a prolific composer who tried his hand at most genres: his quartets are rewarding and well worth investigation. For the most part, his musical language tends to be Schumannesque or Brahmsian, but there are more distinctive South American touches here and there and, in the Op. 33 *Nocturne* of 1907, traces of impressionism. Maria Inês Guimarães gives workmanlike rather than imaginative performances. Although it is good to have filled in a gap in one's knowledge, it is unlikely that many collectors would return to this disc very often.

Nevin, Arthur (1871–1943)

From Edgeworth Hills.
*** Altarus Dig. AIR-CD 9024 [id.]. Donna Amato – Ethelbert NEVIN: *A Day in Venice* etc. ***

Arthur Nevin was without his older brother's melodic individuality, but he wrote spontaneously and crafted his pieces nicely. The most striking number of *From Edgeworth Hills* is the tripping *Sylphs,* very characteristic of its time, while *As the moon rose* has an agreeably sentimental tune, and the picaresque *Firefly* sparkles nicely here. *Toccatella* is rhythmically a bit awkward but is quite a showpiece, and Donna Amato plays it with real dash. Excellent recording.

Nevin, Ethelbert (1862–1901)

A Day in Venice (suite), *Op. 25; Etude in the form of a Romance; Etude in the form of a scherzo, Op. 18/1–2; May in Tuscany* (suite), *Op. 21; Napoli (En passant), Op. 30/3; Mighty lak' a rose* (after the transcription by Charles Spross); *O'er hill and dale* (suite); *The Rosary* (arr. Whelpley); *Water scenes, Op. 13.*
*** Altarus Dig. AIR-CD 9024 [id.]. Donna Amato – Arthur NEVIN: *From Edgeworth Hills.* ***

Ethelbert Nevin was born in Edgeworth, Pennsylvania (on the outskirts of Pittsburgh), in 1862. Although his father disapproved of his musical ambitions, his mother did not, and eventually he was able to study, first in Boston, then in Berlin (in the mid-1890s) and, later, in Italy. The *Water scenes* date from 1891, and with their composition Nevin scored his first great success when *Narcissus* becames a world-wide hit. In 1916 it appeared twice in a list published by Victor Records of 'ten records that should be in every Home ... which we unhesitatingly recommend to all music lovers'. Even today its melody is recognizable by most older listeners, if perhaps not so readily identified. Donna Amato, who must have found Nevin strange company after Dutilleux, Scriabin and Sorabje, grew up in the area where he was born, and she takes care not to sentimentalize these genre pieces, which can be just a little trite but also quite engaging. Perhaps she might have let herself go a little more in *Narcissus*, but elsewhere she hits the spot, notably in the closing *Barcarolle* of the *Water scenes* and in the Italian set, *A Day in Venice*, in which both *Gondolieri* and the *Venetian love song* are distinctly pleasing, while simplicity is the keynote of the final *Buona notte. Il Rusignola* (from *May in Tuscany*) is played with a nice degree of preciosity, as is the *Etude in the form of a Scherzo*, which is liltingly sub-sub-Mendelssohn. *The Rosary* was Nevin's other big hit, with the sheet music selling over a million copies in the decade following its publication in 1898. It sounds pretty ordinary now, but of course was intended to be sung. *Mighty lak' a rose* retains all its charm. The manuscript was found on the composer's desk after his death, and it makes a good epitaph – quite as memorable as MacDowell's *To a wild rose.* The recording is clear and natural in a pleasing acoustic.

Nicolai, Carl Otto (1810–49)

The Merry Wives of Windsor (Die lustigen Weiber von Windsor): complete.
(M) *** Decca 443 669-2 (2) [id.]. Ridderbusch, W. Brendel, Malta, Ahnsjö, Sramek, Donath, T. Schmidt, Sukis, Bav. R. Ch. & SO, Kubelik.

Kubelik's performance may be slightly lacking in dramatic ebullience, but its extra subtlety has perceptive results – as in the entry of Falstaff in Act I, where Kubelik conveys the tongue-in-cheek quality of Nicolai's *pomposo* writing. Ridderbusch portrays a straight and noble Falstaff. Although as an opera this may not have the brilliant insight of Verdi or all the atmosphere of Vaughan Williams, it has its own brand of effervescence which is equally endearing and is well caught here. The dialogue is crisply edited, and the recording, while fairly reverberant, is vividly atmospheric. *Faute de mieux*, it should receive a strong recommendation.

Nielsen, Carl (1865–1931)

Aladdin suite; Maskarade Overture.
**(*) Decca Dig. 425 857-2 [id.]. San Francisco Ch. & SO, Blomstedt – GRIEG: *Peer Gynt suites.*
**(*)

Blomstedt is an eminently reliable guide to this repertoire, though both Myung-Whun Chung (BIS) and Rozhdestvensky (Chandos) are more atmospheric in the *Aladdin* music, the latter in the complete score. Well played and recorded, but not quite a full three-star recommendation all the same.

(i) *Flute concerto;* (ii) *Clarinet concert, Op. 57;* (iii) *Maskarade:* excerpts.
(M) (***) Dutton Lab. mono CDLXT 2505 [id.]. (i) Holger Gilbert-Jespersen; (ii) Ib Erikson; Danish State RSO, (i; iii) Jensen; (ii) Wöldike.

Like the Jensen account of the symphonies (see below), this excellent transfer offers us a link with Nielsen's own times. Holger Gilbert-Jespersen gave the first performance of the *Flute concerto* in Paris in 1926 and was its dedicatee. This 1954 recording gives as good an indication of Nielsen's intentions as we will ever have. The *Clarinet concert* with Ib Erikson is no less masterly – and what good sound!

Hagbarth and Signe; Ebbe Skammelsen; Sankt Hansaftenspil (incidental music).
* Kontrapunkt Dig. 32188 [id.]. Henriette Bonde-Hansen, Lars Thodberg Bertelsen, Lane Lind, Nils
  Bank Mikkelsen; Funen Ac. Children's Ch., Odense Philharmonic Ch., Odense SO, Tamas Vetö.

When Nielsen's complete incidental music to Adam Oehlenschläger's *Aladdin* appeared, it came as
something of a revelation. The incidental music collected here to two more Oehlenschläger plays,
Hagbarth and Signe (1910) and *Sankt Hansaftenspil* (*St John's Eve's play*) (1913), and the music to
Harald Bergstedt's *Ebbe Skammelsen* (1925) is pretty routine stuff. All three scores were written for
productions at Dyrehavsbakken, an outdoor theatre in Klampenborg, and are for wind (in the case of
Hagbarth and Signe four bronze lurs), voices and percussion. There are altogether some forty-five
fragments, many of them simple horn-calls or short scraps of melody, few of them giving us much of
a glimpse of the real Nielsen. Good performances and recording.

Symphonies Nos. (i) *1 in G min., Op. 7;* (ii) *2 (Four Temperaments), Op. 16;* (iii) *3 (Sinfonia
espansiva), Op. 27;* (iii) *4 (Inextinguishable), Op. 29;* (i) *5, Op. 50;* (iii) *6 (Sinfonia semplice).*
*** Decca Dig. 443 117-2 (3) [id.]. San Francisco SO, Blomstedt (with Kromm, McMillan in No. 3).
(B) *** RCA Dig. 74321 20290–2. Royal Danish O, Paavo Berglund.
(**(*)) Danacord mono DACOCD 351/3 [id.]. Danish RSO; (i) Erik Tuxen; (ii) Launy Grøndahl;
  (iii) Thomas Jensen.

Blomstedt's complete Decca set appears at a modest discount – three discs for rather more than the
cost of two – and is pretty well self-recommending. Individual verdicts on the performances are to be
found in our main volume. All six are among the finest available, and the reservation concerning No.
6, where a broader tempo would have helped generate greater evocation in the opening movement, is
relatively insignificant against the overall success of this series. All Decca have now done is to
assemble the three CDs into one slipcase. To put it briefly, they remain the best all-round modern set
and can be purchased with confidence, though individual symphonies in the BIS set score very highly
– and the DG recordings with the Gothenburg orchestra are a model of what a good recording
should be. The performances are generally speaking not the equal of the Blomstedt, and the present
box holds its own.

Berglund's set with the Royal Danish Orchestra, in which Nielsen once served, was recorded
between 1987 and 1989, but until now only Nos. 1, 3, 4 and 6 have appeared separately; Nos. 2 (*The
Four Temperaments*) and 5 are new to the catalogue. The ever-fresh *First Symphony* is given a
thoroughly straightforward account and Berglund holds the architecture of the work together in a
most convincing way. Phrases are affectionately turned but never pulled out of shape. In No. 2, after
a rugged opening *Allegro collerico*, the central movements are also strongly characterized: the second
has a touch of charm as well as the composer's suggested 'hint of quiet melancholy'. The *Andante*
evolves naturally and with real depth of feeling, and the final *Allegro sangueineo* brings a spontaneous
upbeat resolution.

Berglund's account of the *Sinfonia espansiva* (No. 3) is perhaps the finest of his cycle, the best to
appear since Blomstedt's Decca version. The playing of the Royal Danish Orchestra is beautifully
prepared and full of vitality. His two soloists, though unnamed, are very good and the general
architecture of the work is well conveyed. The *Fourth* (*Inextinguishable*) is more problematic.
Generally speaking, Berglund stays close to the tempo markings but, in his desire to convey the sense
of drama and urgency, he tends to be impatient to move things on. The second movement is
beautifully done, and there is much to admire in the third, but the finale really does move and, at
such a speed, one feels rushed off one's feet, particularly in the closing paragraphs. The playing is
spirited enough, but even the Royal Danish Orchestra sounds a little out of breath at the end!

The *Fifth* (which Berglund has recorded successfully before for EMI) opens with a strong sense of
atmosphere and Berglund generates a huge climax, which then effectively subsides into desolation.
The second movement's complex structure is equally well controlled and satisfyingly resolved. Apart
from some loss of focus at the climax of the first movement, the recording encompasses the wide
dynamic range with impressive sonority and colour. In the *Sinfonia semplice* (No. 6) Berglund again
proves a perceptive guide. His performance matches Blomstedt's in integrity and insight and is
obviously the product of much thought. Here as elsewhere, the RCA engineers produce a recording
of splendid body and presence. In the event, Berglund's set can be strongly recommended alongside
(though not in preference to) Blomstedt, and it also has a distinct price advantage. As we go to press,
the three CDs have been reissued separately at mid-price: *Symphonies Nos. 1–2* (74321 20291-2);
Symphonies Nos. 3–4 (74321 20292-2); *Symphonies Nos. 5–6* (74321 20293-2).

This Danacord set of three CDs tells us more about Nielsen than almost any later performances.
Like Sibelius, Nielsen made no records of his own symphonies, but the three conductors represented
here all played under him. Thomas Jensen, who made pioneering commercial records of the *First*,

Second and *Sixth Symphonies*, is said to have had an uncanny feeling for Nielsen's own tempi. (Jensen also made the first LP version of the *Fifth*, which is strikingly akin in spirit to Tuxen's pioneering shellac set.) In any event, these mono broadcasts are the nearest we can come to Nielsen's own intentions. Only one commercial disc is included: Jensen's masterly account of the *Sixth Symphony*, better transferred than in the original Danacord LPs but still not as warm or fresh as the World Record Club LP, briefly available in the 1960s. Launy Grøndahl's version of the *Second Symphony* (*The Four Temperaments*) has tremendous fire, and Jensen's accounts of the *Third* (*Sinfonia espansiva*) and *Fourth* (*Inextinguishable*) are pretty electrifying. Danacord have replaced the 1950 Edinburgh Festival account of the *Fifth* under Tuxen with a later performance, given in Paris in 1955. There are many better recordings of these symphonies but few that come closer to their spirit; although allowances must be made for the poor quality of sound in some instances, these performances radiate an authenticity of atmosphere and love of the scores that is quite infectious.

Symphonies Nos. 1 in G min., Op. 7; 2 (The Four Temperaments), Op. 16; Bøhmisk-danske folkteone.
(M) **(*) EMI CDM5 65906-3 [id.]. Danish RSO, Blomstedt.

The EMI recordings were made in the mid-1970s and are analogue. They are very good indeed and have a warmth and clarity that challenge comparison with Blomstedt's more recent, Decca set with the San Francisco Symphony Orchestra. However, the latter has the greater fire and eloquence and is worth the extra outlay.

Symphonies Nos. (i) 1 in G min., Op. 7; (ii) 4 (Inextinguishable), Op. 29; (i) Saul and David: Prelude to Act II; (iii) The fog is lifting.
(BB) ** RCA Navigator 74321 21296-2. (i) LSO, Previn; (ii) Chicago SO, Martinon; (iii) James Galway, Sioned Williams.

Nielsen's enchanting *First Symphony* is a spontaneous, lyrical work, astonishingly fresh in impact and remarkably individual, for all its debt to Brahms and Dvořák. André Previn's account with the LSO is highly sympathetic: the playing is affectionate, fresh and alive and he is agreeably free from mannerisms. Some may feel that he takes too relaxed and lyrical a view of the slow movement; he dwells too affectionately on the oboe idea at 4 bars after A; and the third movement could undoubtedly be tauter and have a greater sense of pulse. The outer movements prompt no reservations and Previn observes repeats, which is an essential in this work. The *Prelude* is a fine piece and also well worth having. Previn is well recorded in a spacious acoustic, although the 1967 recording shows its age a little in the upper string timbre. Martinon's account of No. 4 is altogether less beguiling, the outer movements full of explosive brilliance and lacking in spontaneity. Despite superior orchestral playing, the reading is really too hard-driven to be really acceptable. The encore from James Galway with harp accompaniment is pleasing enough but hardly affects one's reservations about this uneven coupling.

(i) Symphonies Nos. 1 in G min., Op. 7; 5, Op. 50; (ii) Helios overture, Op. 17.
⊛ (M) *** Dutton Lab. mono CDLXT 2502 [id.]. Danish State RSO; (i) Thomas Jensen; (ii) Erik Tuxen.

These are exemplary transfers of the première recording of the *First Symphony* and the first LP recordings of the *Fifth* (the very first was on 78s under Tuxen) and the *Helios Overture*. Jensen and Tuxen both played under Nielsen, and their performances have a special authenticity. The quality of these Decca recordings is captured with absolute fidelity in these stunning transfers; the engineers of the day, working in the pleasingly warm yet crisp acoustic of the Danish Radio concert hall produce remarkably truthful results. An indispensable issue that belongs in every Nielsen collection.

Symphony No. 2 (The Four Temperaments), Op. 16; Amor and the poet: Overture; Snefrid.
* Kontrapunkt Dig. 32178 [id.]. Odense SO, Eduard Serov.

Eduard Serov is really inside the idiom and gives as good a reading of the symphony as any. The orchestra play with enthusiasm and commitment for him. The first movement is almost as fiery as Thomas Jensen's authoritative pioneering account. Unfortunately, the balance is unacceptably inconsistent: the first two movements are perfectly balanced, but things suddenly alter for the last two. The strings recede, there is a loss of impact and presence, and subordinate parts (the *ppp* trumpets at fig. G in the finale) loom into absurd prominence. No challenge to either Chung or either of the Blomstedt versions. *Snefrid*, composed in 1893 immediately after the *First Symphony*, was a kind of *mélodrame* by Holger Drachmann from which Nielsen made a short orchestral suite. Apart from the little overture, it is not only fully characteristic but, in *Snefrid's sleep*, quite magical. There are some obvious resonances of the *First Symphony* in the *Postlude*. The *Overture Amor and the Poet* (*Amor og*

Digteren) comes from the other end of the composer's career (1930), and is slight, not vintage Nielsen but worth hearing. It is a great pity that the symphony is so badly let down by the engineering, as the performance is so good; and *Snefrid* is something of a find.

Symphonies Nos. 2 (Four Temperaments), Op. 16; (i) 3 (Sinfonia espansiva), Op. 27.
** Chan. Dig. CHAN 9300 [id.]. (i) Kringelborn, Frederiksson; Royal Stockholm PO, Rozhdestvensky.

Much the same verdict here as for the Rozhdestvensky/Swedish coupling of Nos. 1 and 4 (CHAN 9620), reviewed in our main volume: cultured and urbane playing, very well recorded and thoroughly idiomatic in its way, but wanting in the fire and character that distinguish rival Nielsen performances. Not a first recommendation.

Symphonies Nos. 3 (Sinfonia espansiva); 4 (Inextinguishable), Op. 29.
(M) **(*) EMI CDM5 65415-2. Danish RSO, Blomstedt.

This continuation of Blomstedt's earlier EMI series from the mid-1970s is thoroughly recommendable: these performances have much of the grip and eloquence of his later, Decca set. No. 4 is excellent, with some fine woodwind playing from the Danish orchestra. The CD transfers are full and present, if not quite matching the Decca sound-quality.

Symphony No. 4 (Inextinguishable), Op. 29.
(M) *** DG Dig. 445 518-2 [id.]. BPO, Karajan – SIBELIUS: *Tapiola.* ***

One of the very finest performances of Nielsen's *Fourth* comes from Karajan. The orchestral playing is altogether incomparable and there is both vision and majesty in the reading. The strings play with passionate intensity at the opening of the third movement, and there is a thrilling sense of commitment throughout. The wind playing sounds a little over-civilized – but what exquisitely blended, subtle playing this is. It is also excellently recorded, although there is an editing error in the finale. This version is the made the more desirable in this mid-priced reissue, coupled with Karajan finest (digital) version of *Tapiola.*

Symphonies Nos. 4 (Inextinguishable), Op. 29; 5, Op. 50.
(BB) ** Naxos Dig. 8.550743 [id.]. Nat. SO of Ireland, Adrian Leaper.

There is nothing to grumble at in the Naxos coupling of these two symphonies – but nothing to get excited about either, though Leaper is a fine musician with a good feel for this repertoire. The *Fourth* is well prepared but neither highly charged nor tautly held together. Similarly, the *Fifth Symphony* is decently played but does not cast as strong a spell as the classic accounts from Jensen or Blomstedt. The recorded sound is more than acceptable. You can pay more and do worse, but it is worth paying a bit more and doing better.

Symphonies Nos. 5, Op. 50; 6 (Sinfonia semplice).
** Chan. Dig. CHAN 9367 [id.]. Stockholm PO, Rozhdestvensky.

The Stockholm Philharmonic is a refined and responsive body who play beautifully and produce a cultured sound. They are splendidly recorded and balanced, with a natural and lifelike aural perspective. Rozhdestvensky does not give us the whole picture, however, even if he comes close to it at times. He carefully displays details of the terrain without actually bringing the landscape before one's eyes. With Blomstedt and Jensen you are there, vividly experiencing the sights and sounds of Nielsen's world, but its mystery eludes Rozhdestvensky. The music is in these Swedish players' blood, but Rozhdestvensky does not have his finger on its pulse. He begins the first movement of the *Fifth* too briskly, and the *Sixth* is not the complete success that at times it promises to be.

Symphony No. 5, Op. 50; Symphonic rhapsody; Böhmisk-Dansk Folketone.
** Kontrapunkt Dig. 32171 [id.]. Odense SO, Serov.

Edward Serov has a good feeling for Nielsen, and his *Fifth Symphony* is well paced and idiomatic. The Odense orchestra plays with commitment, though they are not the equal of the Stockholm orchestra. The disc is not really good value, however, as the *Symphonic rhapsody* and the *Böhmisk-Dansk Folketone* together bring the playing time up to 52 minutes.

Wind quintet.
(M) *** EMI CDM5 65304-2 [id.]. Melos Ens. – JANACEK: *Concertino* etc. **(*)

The Melos account of the *Wind quintet* was made in the 1960s but still sounds fresh and vibrant. In its day it was a first recommendation and it still ranks among the very best. It comes, too, with a valuable Janáček coupling that includes *Mládí* and the *Concertino*. One of the most valuable and satisfying reissues of the year.

(i) *Violin sonatas Nos. 1 in A, Op. 9; 2 in G min., Op. 35. Prelude, Theme and variations, Op. 48; Preludio e presto, Op. 52.*
(*) Kontrapunkt 32200 [id.]. Søren Elbaek; (i) Morten Mogensen.

The recorded sound rules this out of court. The acoustic is cramped and claustrophobic. Søren Elbaek is a fine player and gives a good account of the solo violin pieces dating from the 1920s, but the sound is very unflattering. The two *Violin sonatas* sound as if they were recorded in a domestic living-room and are quite unenjoyable.

Nyman, Michael (born 1948)

(i) *Piano concerto;* (ii) *MGV.*
*** Argo Dig. 443 382-2; *443 382-4* [id.]. (i) Kathryn Stott, Royal Liverpool PO; (ii) Michael Nyman Band, O; composer.

Michael Nyman's *Piano concerto*, representing minimalist music at its most haunting, became a runaway hit, partly thanks to its being used on the soundtrack of Jane Campion's film, *The Piano.* As Nyman explains, the solo piano music was written first, and only later was it developed into this four-movement concerto, with movements labelled *The Beach, The Woods, The Hut* and *The Release.* It was first heard at the Lille Festival in September 1993, just when the première of *MGV* was given there. The full title is *Musique à grande vitesse,* and it was commissioned for the inauguration of the high-speed TGV train from Paris to Lille. Not surprisingly, it relies on train rhythms, with all their unexpected syncopations. With speeds and rhythms varied, it is more an evocation of trains in general than of a very fast express. The Michael Nyman Band, heavily amplified, is set as a ripieno group alongside the orchestra, giving the piece what the composer thinks of as concerto grosso associations. Powerful, forward recording. The disc comes in a double jewel-case with a sampler disc, 'Short Cuts', excerpts from Argo issues of new music by 15 composers, including Górecki, Torke, Volans, Turnage and Nyman himself.

The convertibility of lute strings; For John Cage; Self-laudatory hymn of Inanna and her omnipotence; Time will pronounce.
*** Argo Dig. 440 282-2 [id.]. James Bowman, Fretwork, Trio of London, Virginia Black, London Brass.

Under the title *Time will pronounce,* the longest work on the disc, this is a collection of the four substantial pieces for various chamber forces which Nyman wrote in the first half of 1992. Inspired by the first onslaught of the war in Bosnia, *Time will pronounce* uses a piano trio alternately to evoke the pain of war and the violence. In typical Nyman fashion it is a string of linked sections, emotionally unrelenting but with more slow music than is usual with this highly charged, self-indulgent composer. At the end the music fades inconclusively to nothing. Whatever the overstatement, the genuineness of emotion behind the writing is tellingly conveyed by the Trio of London. The *Self-laudatory hymn* is a weird but magnetic piece for the odd combination of counter-tenor and consort of viols, setting an ancient Near Eastern text with biblical overtones. It should not work, but with such performers as James Bowman and Fretwork, for whom it was written, it does. The least appealing piece is *The convertibility of lute strings,* in which Nyman exploits his aggressive vein in heavy, jangling writing for solo harpsichord. Even by his standards he has rarely written anything so relentless as the first six minutes. The slow middle section gives all too brief a respite before the relentless jangling is resumed. The only piece with jollity in it is *For John Cage,* using the ten instruments of London Brass with wit as well as colour. Originally called *Canons, chorales and waltzes,* it hints at those forms in its sectional structure rather than reproducing them, ending with a slow, chorale-like section with a crescendo at the end, leaving one hanging in mid-air. Whatever reservations have to be made about such minimalist inspirations, the individuality is undeniable, and performances and recording are vividly colourful.

Noise, sounds and sweet airs.
*** Argo Dig. 440 842-2 [id.]. Bott, Summers, Bostridge, Ensemble Instrumental de Basse-Normandie, Dominique Debart.

Rarely has Nyman's brand of minimalism been so strikingly compelling as here and, however relentless the writing over 20 linked sections, the magnetism is hard to resist. The musical material is drawn from his opera-ballet, *La princess de Milan,* with new vocal lines superimposed over the top, setting a text drawn from Shakespeare's *The Tempest,* 'very heavily and idiosyncratically edited', as

Nyman says himself. The oddest idiosyncrasy is that the three different voices keep switching roles, so that the words of Prospero, Miranda and other characters are divided among all three singers. That and the general thickness of textures makes the work less involving dramatically, but musically the overtones of medieval and oriental music married to Nyman's electronic gimmickry and minimalist motor-rhythms are most individual. The performance and recording are superb, as vivid as any Nyman on disc, giving the result a hypnotic fascination. The three soloists in particular sing magnificently, each with clear, firm, richly focused voice. Catherine Bott, always compelling, is well matched by the alto, Hilary Summers and the clear-toned young tenor, Ian Bostridge.

Nystroem, Gösta (1890–1966)

(i) *Viola concerto (Hommage à la France). Ishavet (Arctic Sea);* (ii) *Sinfonia concertante for cello and orchestra.*
*** BIS Dig. CD 682 [id.]. (i) Nobuko Imai; (ii) Niels Ullner; Malmö SO, Paavo Järvi.

Gösta Nystroem came from the western seaboard of Sweden and possessed a lifelong love of the sea, of which *Ishavet* and the *Sinfonia del mare* offer ample evidence. He was an accomplished painter and man of letters, and he was torn between these interests and music during his youthful years in Paris. It was not until the end of the 1920s that he finally opted for music. *Ishavet* (1925) is already available on Caprice, and the *Sinfonia concertante for cello and orchestra* (1944), arguably his best and most characteristic work, was long available on Swedish Society Discofil. Niels Ullner is a fine cellist with an opulent tone and eloquent phrasing and, though he does not eclipse memories of the Dane, Erling Bløndal Bengtsson, his is a thoughtful, well-integrated performance. This is not a concerto but rather a reflective exchange between soloist and orchestra, and the music has both quality and depth. The *Viola concerto* was composed after the Nazi invasion of 1940; hence its subtitle *Hommage à la France.* This is its first complete recording (the beautiful slow movement was available on a single 78-r.p.m. disc on the long-defunct Cupol label) and it has a neo-classical and eminently Gallic *joie de vivre*, as well as poignancy. Nobuko Imai plays it superbly and, throughout the whole programme, the Malmö orchestra are in excellent form under Neeme Järvi's son, Paavo. The recording is transparent and has excellent presence and definition. This now replaces the Caprice issue as a recommended introduction to Nystroem's music.

Ockeghem, Johannes (c. 1410–97)

Alma redemptoris mater; Missa Mi-Mi; Salve Regina.
*** ASV Dig. CD GAU 139 [id.]. The Clerks' Group, Edward Wickham (with motets by BUSNOIS, ISAAC and OBRECHT).

Ockeghem's *Salve Regina*, the motet *Alma Redemptoris mater* and the *Missa Mi-Mi* are contrasted here with motets by three of his contemporaries. The *Missa Mi-Mi* is so named because of the recurring descending fifth, both named 'mi' in the natural and soft hexachords. The Mass is not new to the catalogue; there is a very fine account from the Hilliards awaiting reissue, but these performances have a refreshing enthusiasm and the approach to rhythm is remarkably free. The Clerks' Group and Edward Wickham, who specialize in the music of the late Middle Ages and early Renaissance, promise us more Ockeghem, including the *Requiem* – and if the others are as good as this, readers can invest in the series with confidence.

Offenbach, Jacques (1819–80)

(i) *Gaîté parisienne* (ballet, arr. Rosenthal; complete); (ii) *Overtures and suites* from: *Orpheus in the Underworld* (1874 version, with *Pastoral ballet*); *Le voyage dans la lune* (with *Snowflakes ballet*).
(M) *** Ph. 442 403-2 [id.]. (i) Pittsburgh SO, Previn; (ii) Philh. O, Almeida.

An outstanding coupling. In *Gaîté parisienne* Previn realizes that tempi can remain relaxed and the music's natural high spirits will still bubble to the surface. The orchestral playing is both spirited and elegant, with Previn obviously relishing the score's delightful detail. This is mirrored by the Philips digital sound-balance, which has substance as well as atmosphere and brilliance. Perhaps the tuba thumping away in the bass is a shade too present, but it increases one's desire to smile through this engagingly happy music. The *Snowflakes ballet* from *Le voyage dans la lune* is a charmer, and the ballet from *Orpheus in the Underworld* is hardly less delectable. The other surprise is the *Orpheus overture*, not the one we know – which, it must be admitted, is a better-crafted piece – but a more extended work in pot-pourri style, with some good tunes. Almeida is no less high-spirited than Previn, and the Philharmonia's response is both polished and elegant. Excellent recording too.

OPERA

Les Contes d'Hoffmann (complete).
(M) ** EMI CMS7 63222-2 (2) [Ang. CDMB 63222]. Gedda, D'Angelo, Schwarzkopf, De los Angeles, Benoit, Faure, Ghiuselev, London, Sénéchal, Blanc, Chœurs René Duclos, Paris Conservatoire O, Cluytens.

Several bad mistakes in casting prevent this mid-1960s set from being the rare delight it should have been. It has some marvellous moments, and the whole of the *Barcarolle* scene with Schwarzkopf is a delight, but the very distinction of the cast-list makes one annoyed that the result is not better. André Cluytens surprisingly proved quite the wrong conductor for this sparkling music, for he has little idea of caressing the music (as Beecham did so ravishingly) and rarely fails to push on regardless. Gianna d'Angelo's Olympia is pretty but shallow, George London's Coppelius and Dr Miracle unpleasantly gruff-toned and, most disappointing of all, Victoria de los Angeles is sadly out of voice, with the upper register regularly turning sour on her. But with such artists even below their best there are characterful moments which take the listener along well enough. Cluytens in his ruthlessness has a certain demonic energy which has its dramatic side. The recording is atmospheric and the CD transer has given it added liveliness. But Bonynge's version is the one to go for, a memorable set in every way (Decca 417 363-2).

Orff, Carl (1895–1982)

Carmina Burana.
(BB) *** RCA Navigator Dig. 74321 17908-2. Hendricks, Aler, Hagegård, St Paul's Cathedral Boys' Ch., L. Symphony Ch., LSO, Mata.
*** RCA Dig. 09026 61673-2 [id.]. McNair, Aler, Hagegård, St Louis Ch. & SO, Slatkin.
** DG Dig. 439 950-2 [id.]. Bonney, Lopardo, Michaels-Moore, Arnold Schoenberg Ch., Vienna Boys' Ch., VPO, Previn.
(M) ** EMI CDM5 65207-2 [id.]. Babikan, Hager, Gardner, Houston Ch. & Youth Symphony Boys' Ch., Stokowski – STRAVINSKY: *Firebird suite*. **(*)

Mata's splendid 1980 digital recording now comes at super-bargain price and is highly recommendable on all counts. It is a joyously alive and volatile reading, not as metrical in its rhythms as most; this means that at times the London Symphony Chorus is not as clean in ensemble as it is for Previn. The choristers of St Paul's Cathedral sing with purity and enthusiasm but are perhaps not boyish enough, though the soloists are first rate (with John Aler coping splendidly, in high, refined tones, with the Roast Swan episode). There is fine warmth of atmosphere and no lack in the lower range; indeed in almost every respect the sound is superb. This is unbeatable value for those not wanting a full-priced version, where first choice remains with Blomstedt on Decca (430 509-2).

Slatkin's new RCA recording was made in St Louis in 1992 and is notable for an unbeatable trio of soloists, two of whom are featured on Mata's earlier recording. But one especially remembers Sylvia McNair's ravishing portrayal of the girl in the red tunic, whose final submission is so seductively sweet. The choral singing is enjoyably rhythmic and vigorously crisp, with the female voices charmingly flirtatious in the village green sequence, where the orchestral playing is suitably exuberant, with roistering horns. Slatkin's reading is spacious and certainly brings out the grandeur of the opening and closing sections, but in the Court of Love his trebles are very innocent; their racily knowing '*Oh, Oh, Ohs*' are without the pubescent sexual abandon of the British performances variously under Previn, Hickox (still a strong contender on Carlton PCD 855) and Mata. Incidentally, the translation given with Slatkin's CD chooses the more prudish '*I am all in bloom*' rather than '*I am bursting out all over*'. But this remains overall a very convincing performance, if not a first choice. The acoustic of St Louis Powell Symphony Hall is suitably rich and expansive but the chorus is not very sharply defined when singing softly.

Previn's newest DG record is a disappointment and no match for his earlier, EMI, analogue account (CDC7 47100-2). Only in the male Tavern chorus of Part 1 is there a reminder of the vocal swagger that makes that LSO performance so headily compulsive. Barbara Bonney, gently sensuous, is the most appealing of the three soloists, but her final submission is somewhat shrill; the tenor sounds strained when portraying the Roasted Swan. The Vienna Boys' Choir, like their counterparts in St Louis, lack the uninhibited sexual fervour of the St Clement Dane's Grammar School youngsters, who relish every innuendo in Previn's LSO version. Both the Arnold Schoenberg Choir and the VPO make impressive contributions, but overall this does not have the extra spontaneity and excitement one would expect from a live performance.

Stokowski's recording was made in 1958. His reading is essentially sensuous and atmospheric, and it is given a recessed recording to match. The rather anonymous soloists (the soprano is the finest of the group but she seems too mature for the 'Girl in the red tunic') are adequate but the choir's impact is more sonorous than biting, though it has its moments of vigour. Stokowski is genial and the music's colours glow attractively. The remastering preserves the original quality quite enjoyably, but this cannot be counted a strong recommendation and the reissue is primarily of value for the Stravinsky coupling.

Paganini, Niccolò (1782–1840)

Violin concerto No. 1 in D, Op. 6.
**(*) EMI Dig. CDC5 55026-2 [id.]; *EL 55026-4*. Sarah Chang, Phd. O, Sawallisch – SAINT-SAENS: *Havanaise; Intro & Rondo capriccioso.* **(*)

(i) *Violin concerto No. 1 in D, Op. 6. Caprices for solo violin Nos. 1, 3–4, 9–11, 14, 16–17, 24.*
(B) *** DG 439 473-2 [id.]. Salvatore Accardo; (i) LPO, Charles Dutoit.

Although Perlman's EMI version of Paganini's *First Concerto* is special (CDC7 47101-2), otherwise Accardo's account is second to none in its sense of lyrical style, finesse and easy bravura. The selection of solo *Caprices*, too, is well made, including the most famous of all, which so many other composers have used for variations of their own. Accardo presents his selection with an eloquence far beyond mere display. Excellent recording.

Sarah Chang, the *Gramophone*'s 'Young Artist of the Year', gives an astonishing display of easy violinistic fireworks in this famous bravura concerto. She made her début with it in the Avery Fisher Hall at the age of eight and now, at the relatively mature age of twelve (!), she has recorded it in Philadelphia. The slow movement is fresh and direct rather than romantic; but here, as in the famous secondary theme of the first movement, she knows how to charm the ear gently. The finale is dazzling. While Perlman remains supreme in this work, Chang can bounce her bow with aplomb and never fails to entice the ear. Sawallisch gives her admirable support, but the recording is flattering neither to soloist (balanced close) nor to orchestra, which lacks sumptousness.

Violin concerto No. 1 in D, Op. 6; I Palpiti; Perpetuela; Sonata napoleone.
(M) *** DG 439 981-2 [id.]. Accardo, LPO, Dutoit.

Accardo's classic account of the *First Concerto* is here recoupled at mid-price with attractive, shorter concertante pieces, of which the *Perpetuela* is quite dazzling and *I Palpiti* is like an operatic air with variations. The playing is elegant, polished and gleaming with easy bravura. The resonant recording makes orchestral tuttis a little bass-heavy but the solo timbre is provided with an attractive bloom.

Palestrina, Giovanni Pierluigi di (1525–94)

Ave Regina Caelorum; Lamentations of Jeremiah I–III; Gloriosi principes terrae; Missa in duplicibus minoribus II.
*** HM/BMG Dig. 05472 77317-2 [id.]. Maîtrise de Garçons de Colmar, Ens. Gilles Binchois, Cantus Figuratus, Dominique Vellard.

This ensemble produce singing of exceptional purity and quality. The Marian antiphon, *Ave Regina Caelorum*, is for two choruses, one high and one low, and was printed in 1575. The *Missa in duplicibus minoribus*, which belongs to the Mantuan repertory, was discovered in Milan as late as 1950 and is not otherwise available. All this material is sung with impressive control, a wonderfully integrated balance and great beauty of tone. Those who find Palestrina too bland should investigate this eloquent and beautifully recorded disc.

Canticum canticorum Salomonis (Song of Songs).
*** Hyp. Dig. CDA 66733 [id.]. Pro Cantione Antiqua, Bruno Turner.

The *Canticum canticorum Salomonis* is one of Palestrina's most sublime and expressive works, possibly wider in its range than anything else he composed, and certainly as deeply felt. His disclaimer in the dedication to Pope Gregory XIII, which Bruno Turner quotes at the beginning of his notes ('There are far too many poems with no other subject than love of a kind quite alien to the Christian faith'), cannot disguise the fervour which he poured into these 29 motets. The ten members of the Pro Cantione Antiqua under Bruno Turner bring an appropriate eloquence and ardour, tempered by restraint. They are accorded an excellently balanced and natural-sounding recording. This music is not generously represented on disc, but no one acquiring this is likely to be disappointed.

Canticum canticorum (Fourth Book of Motets for 5 voices from the *Song of Songs*); Madrigals for 5 voices, Book I: *8 Madrigali spirituali.*
(M) *** Virgin Veritas/EMI Dig. VED5 61168-2 (2) [id.]. Hilliard Ens., Paul Hilliard.

The 29 motets Palestrina based on the *Canticum Canticorum* (*Song of Songs*) include some of his most inspired writing; all are for five voices. Into these impassioned texts, with their strongly erotic overtones, Palestrina poured music of great feeling, remarkable beauty and finish of workmanship. *The Song of Songs* has always been regarded as a symbolic illustration of 'the happy union of Christ and His Spouse', the spouse being the Church, more especially the happiest part of it, namely perfect souls, every one of which is His beloved. The earlier LP of it by Michael Howard and the Cantores in Ecclesia (Oiseau Lyre) adopted a frankly expressive and sensuous approach, which is far removed from that of the Hilliard Ensemble. These are beautifully shaped performances, with refined tonal blend and perfect intonation, but they are more remote and ultimately rather cool in emotional temperature. The second CD includes eight Petrarch settings from the First Book of Madrigals. Excellent recording.

Missa Aeterna Christi munera; Missa Papae Marcelli.
(BB) **(*) Naxos Dig. 8.550573 [id.]. Oxford Camerata, Jeremy Summerly.

Summerly's are bold, flowing performances, lacking something in mysticism and ethereal dynamics, but sung very confidently, with textures clear and the performances alive and compelling. The Oxford Camerata consists of twelve singers, of whom a third are female, and the blend is impressive. The account of the lesser-known *Missa Aeterna Christi munera* is particularly compelling. The recording was made in Dorchester Abbey, so the ambience is flattering, although the balance is fairly close.

Missa Papae Marcelli; Alma Redemptoris mater; Magnificat 1 toni; Nunc dimittis. Stabat mater; Surge illuminare.
*** Gimell Dig. CDGIM 994 [id.]. Tallis Scholars (with ALLEGRI: *Miserere ***).

This CD is entitled 'Live in Rome'; it would be a good thing if these terminologies were discarded; it would be remarkable if they were 'Dead in Rome' but sang like this. Recorded to mark the quatercentenary of Palestrina's death, this issue has been widely trumpeted and publicized. It is nevertheless very good and deserves the numerous plaudits it has collected. The Tallis Scholars are recorded in the Basilica of Maria Maggiore in Rome, where Palestrina was a choirboy and, later, master of the choristers. The most celebrated of Palestrina's masses, *Missa Papae Marcelli*, receives as eloquent a performance as any in the catalogue. The Tallis Scholars have wonderful fluidity and the sense of movement never flags in this finely tuned, well-paced reading. Much the same goes for the remaining motets here and, of course, for the Allegri *Miserere*, which had a unique association with the Sistine Chapel until Mozart heard it and wrote it down from memory for performance elsewhere. As the recording was made before an audience, there is applause, which is quite inappropriate and very tiresome. In every other respect this is a first-class issue and can be warmly recommended. It should be noted that it is also available on videotape and laserdisc. The cameras explore the rich artistic inheritance of the Basilica and enhance the sense of atmosphere and of occasion the performances engender; in its LD form, the sound is as impressive as on CD, but the VT is remarkably firm and wide-ranging tonally. Those with suitable players may well find this an inducement which sways them in its favour; those who strongly dislike applause will doubtless turn to the many excellent rival versions.

Missa Papae Marcelli; Missa brevis.
*** Hyp. Dig. CDA 66266 [id.]. Westminster Cathedral Choir, David Hill.

David Hill and the Westminster Cathedral Choir give an imposing and eloquent *Missa Papae Marcelli* that many collectors may prefer to the new and finely sung Gimell issue from the Tallis Scholars. They, too, have the advantage of a spacious acoustic and excellent recording, and those for whom the visual element on the Tallis videotape and laserdisc offers no appeal may well prefer these fine performances.

Pandolfi Mealli, Giovanni Antonio (*fl.* 1660–69)

Violin sonatas: La cesta; La castella; La Clemente; La Sabbatina, Op. 3/2, 4, 5 & 6; La Bernabea; La Biancuccia; La vinciolina, Op. 4/1, 4 & 6; (i) Anon.: *Harpsichord suites in A, C & D.*
*** Channel Dig. CCS 5894 [id.]. Andrew Manze, (i) Richard Egarr, Fred Jacobs.

Giovanni Antonio Pandolfi Mealli's dates are unknown. *Grove* merely gives him as flourishing in the 1660s and, apart from a mention in the Innsbruck Court Archives, nothing is known of his background or career. His reputation rests on a single surviving copy of two sets of violin sonatas, six sonatas in each. Seven are recorded here, interspersed with three anonymous, French-influenced harpsichord suites, very different in style. The notes suggest the possibility that the composer was Christian Flor (1626–97). These are all rewarding and interesting scores, marvellously played by all concerned, and very well recorded too.

Pärt, Arvo (born 1935)

Collage on B-A-C-H; Cantus in memory of Benjamin Britten.
*** RCA Dig. 09026 68061-2 [id.]. Moscow Virtuosi, Vladimir Spivakov – SHOSTAKOVICH: *Chamber symphony No. 2;* DENISOV: *Variations;* SHCHEDRIN: *Stalin cocktail.* ***

These intense and very well-played performances show Pärt at his most imaginatively approachable. The three brief, neo-baroque movements (a spiccato *Toccata*, lyrical *Sarabande* – with engaging oboe solo, interrupted by saturated chords for strings and piano – and the dissonantly contrapuntal *Ricercar finale*) are like Bach seen through a distorting prism. The result is both inventive and colourful, while the Britten work uses descending scales against a tolling bell yet creates both brilliant textures and an intense climax. First-class recording and stimulating couplings.

Penderecki, Kryszstof (born 1933)

(i; iii) *Cello concerto;* (iii) *Emanationen for 2 string orchestras;* (ii–iii) *Partita for harpsichord and orchestra;* (iv) *Symphony.*
(M) *** EMI CDM5 65416-2 [id.]. (i) Siegfried Palm; (ii) Felicja Blumenthal; (iii) Polish RSO; (iv) LSO; composer.

For those who admire such athematic music, these 1972/3 recordings of Penderecki's works in authentic performances under the composer's own direction will have much to commend it. Blumenthal makes a fine contribution to the *Partita* and Palm is a superb player in the *Cello concerto*. Penderecki's music relies for its appeal on its resourceful use of sonorities, and his sound-world is undoubtedly imaginative, albeit limited. The *Symphony*, the composer's most ambitious orchestral work so far, was commissioned by a British engineering firm and first heard in Peterborough Cathedral. That setting has influenced the range of sumptuous orchestral colours devised by the composer. You may regard this as merely a sequence of brilliant effects rather than a logically argued symphony, but in this committed performance it is certainly striking and memorable. Fine recording enhances the value of this disc, and the CD transfers combine fullness with admirable presence.

Penella, Manuel (1880–1939)

El gato montes.
*** DG Dig. 435 776-2 (2) [id.]. Domingo, Villarroel, Pons, Berganza, Madrid SO, Miguel Roa.

This is a red-blooded performance of a melodramatic piece half-way between opera and zarzuela, which Plácido Domingo has a special affection for. He sings the role of the bullfighter, Rafael, in love with the heroine Soleá, who still keeps her affection for the bandit, Juanillo, *El gato montes*, 'The wildcat'. The highly coloured plot ends with the death of all three, Rafael gored to death in the ring, Soleá dying of a broken heart and *El gato montes* cornered by the police. The writing is fluent and lyrical, with scenes punctuated by attractive orchestral pieces, notably the most celebrated, a paso doble. The musical invention may not be distinguished, but in such beefy performances, with Juan Pons in the title-role a genuine rival for Domingo, it is certainly attractive. The casting of the women principals is strong too, with Veronica Villarroel fresh and bright as the heroine and Teresa Berganza as characterful as ever as the Gypsy. Full, forward sound.

Pergolesi, Giovanni (1710–36)

(i) *Magnificat in C;* (ii) *Stabat Mater.*

(B) **(*) Decca Double 443 868-2 (2) [id.]. (i) Vaughan, J. Baker, Partridge, Keyte, King's College Ch., ASMF, Willcocks; (ii) Palmer, Hodgson, St John's College, Cambridge, Ch., Argo CO, Guest – BONONCINI: *Stabat Mater;* D. SCARLATTI: *Stabat Mater;* A. SCARLATTI: *Domine, refugium factus es nobis; O magnum mysterium;* CALDARA: *Crucifixus;* LOTTI: *Crucifixus.* ***

This well-planned Double Decca collection centres on three different settings of the *Stabat Mater dolorosa.* Pergolesi's version dates from 1735 and, subsequently, settings were made by many other composers, including Vivaldi and Haydn. Pergolesi conceived a work which has secular and even theatrical overtones, and its devotional nature is unexaggerated. George Guest directs a sensible, unaffected performance, simple and expressive, with relaxed tempi, not overladen with romantic sentiment. He has very good soloists, Felicity Palmer and Alfreda Hodgson blending very well together. It is a performance that does not emphasize the music's dramatic variety, and the choral singing, though felt, is not particularly vibrant. The *Magnificat* – doubtfully attributed, like so much that goes under this composer's name – is a comparatively lightweight piece, notable for its rhythmic vitality. The King's College Choir under Willcocks gives a sensitive and vital performance, and the recording matches it in intensity of atmosphere.

(i) *Stabat Mater;* (ii) *Orfeo* (cantata).

(BB) ** Naxos Dig. 8.550766 [id.]. (i–ii) Julia Faulkner; (ii) Anna Gonda; Budapest Camerata, Michael Halász.

On Naxos, Michael Halász chooses the version of the *Stabat Mater* using just the two soloists without chorus, and the resonant ambience of the hall of Festetich Castle, Budapest, adds a spacious effect to the voices, so that the result is convincing, with the vibratos of the two singers matching quite closely. The pacing here is more lively than in the Guest account on Decca and the style of the soloists at times operatically expressive. The contribution of the soprano, Julia Faulkner, is slightly more impressive than that of the contralto, Anna Gonda, and it is the former who provides a fine performance of the *Orfeo* cantata. This encapsulates the famous story in two recitatives, each followed by an expressive aria-soliloquy from Orfeo about his predicament and his resolve to secure the return of his beloved Euridice. The Budapest Camerata accompany throughout with plenty of life and finesse. They are warmly recorded and the balance is most satisfactory.

Pfitzner, Hans (1869–1949)

(i) *Das Christ-Elflein: Overture, Op. 20. Palestrina: Preludes, Acts I, II and III.* (i; ii) *Duo for Violin, Cello and Small Orchestra, Op. 43;* (iii) Lieder: *Abbitte; Die Einsame; Der Gartner; Hast du von den Fischerkindern; Herbstgefühl; Hussens Kerker; In Danzig; Leuchtende Tage; Michaelskirchplatz; Nachts; Säerspruch; Zum Abschied meiner Tochter.*

(M) (***) EMI mono CDC5 55225-2 [id.] (i) Berlin State Opera O, composer; (ii) with Max Strub, Ludwig Hoelscher; (iii) Gerhard Hüsch; composer (piano).

Pfitzner made quite a number of records, including a memorable *Eroica* and other Beethoven symphonies, and an eloquent account of Schumann's *Second Symphony*, but he recorded relatively little of his own music: the *Das Christ-Elflein Overture*, the *Palestrina Preludes*, the *Symphony in C*, Op. 46, not to be confused with the earlier symphony, Op. 36 (a transcription of a string quartet), the *Duo for violin, cello and small orchestra*, Op. 43, the *Liebesmelodie* from the opera *Das Herz*, and some sixteen Lieder (he was a fine pianist in earlier life). The present, generously filled disc runs to 75 minutes and brings the 1931 Polydor recording of the three *Palestrina Preludes* and the 1927 *Christ-Elflein Overture*. Neither, it must be said, wears its years lightly, but all the same the former is valuable testimony of Pfitzner's intentions. The *Duo* was recorded much later, in 1938, but is a rather feeble piece; as Robin Holloway nicely puts it in the sleeve or liner-note, 'the overall impression is lacklustre, with flashes of impotent fire'. The *Lieder*, though by no means the equal of Schoeck in musical inspiration or poetic feeling, are worth having for the incomparable artistry and diction of Gerhard Hüsch. Pfitzner himself was by this time nearly seventy and given to overpedalling. (The songs were also available in a Preiser transfer, which includes the *Symphony in C* and the *Duo*, but neither of the other pieces. This CD was reviewed in our 1992 edition but is probably out of circulation by now; it was less competitively priced and offers less playing-time.)

Palestrina (opera; complete).

** Berlin Classics Dig. 0310 001 (3) [id.]. Schreier, Lang, Lorenz, Wlaschiha, Hübner, Ketelsen, Peter Jürgen Schmidt, Nossek, German Op., Berlin, Ch., Berlin State O, Suitner.

Recorded live at concert performances given in Berlin – Acts I and III in 1986, Act II in 1988 – the Berlin Classics issue of Pfitzner's epic opera is chiefly distinguished by the animated, characterful singing of Peter Schreier in the title-role. In almost every other way, even in the recorded sound, this set, worthy as it is, cannot quite match Kubelik's magnificent version recorded in Munich for DG in 1973 (427 417-2 – see our main volume). While that remains available (at mid-price) this later issue must remain second best, but Schreier's portrait of the much-troubled polyphonic master is well worth hearing, even more thoughtful and intense than that of Nicolai Gedda for Kubelik. Also distinguished among those in Suitner's cast is Ekkehard Wlaschiha, best known for his masterly singing of the role of Alberich in Wagner's *Ring* cycle, but here just as sharply focused in the relatively small role of Severolus. Siegfried Lorenz is a strong Borromeo but hardly matches Dietrich Fischer-Dieskau for Kubelik, and the rest make a good team. As for the conducting, Ottmar Suitner is efficient but rarely as imaginative as Kubelik, and the recorded sound has less body and is less atmospheric than the analogue DG. The set is a fair stop-gap, if (or when) DG's regular scything of back catalogue removes the classic Kubelik.

Pijper, Willem (1894–1947)

String quartets Nos. 1–5.
*** Olympia Dig. OCD 457 [id.]. Schönberg Qt.

Willem Pijper was a dominant force in Dutch music between the wars. This CD collects all five of his *String quartets*; the *First* (in F minor) and (at 24 minutes 8 seconds) longest is a student work, dating from 1914 and written while he was still a pupil of Johan Wagenaar. The very opening almost suggests Smetana, though the predominant influence elsewhere is Mahler. The more polytonal *Second* (1920) takes 10 minutes and shows the influence of late Debussy and Schoenberg; the *Third* (1923) is similarly short and, together with the *Fourth* (1928), shows strong Gallic sympathies (the latter is dedicated to Ravel). The post-war *Fifth Quartet* (1946) was left unfinished at his death, though two movements were completed. Pijper's music is concentrated and thoughtful, eminently civilized and predominantly gentle in outlook, even if it falls short of having that unmistakable and distinctive voice betokening a great composer. The Schönberg Quartet is one of the finest Dutch ensembles, and they are beautifully recorded. A rewarding disc, well worth investigating.

Pleyel, Ignaz (1757–1831)

(i) *Sinfonia concertante for violin, cello and strings in D. Symphony in A; Flute quartet in B.*
(BB) ** Discover Dig. DICD 920130 [id.]. (i) Bushkov, Kozodov; Moscow Concertino (members), Evgueni Bushkov.

The name of Ignaz Pleyel is famous as a French manufacturer of pianos but, around the time that Haydn was visiting London for the Salomon concerts, Pleyel was far better known as a composer and his easily tuneful, facile music was enormously popular. His writing is a bit like Boccherini without the pathos. Here the *Flute quartet* (for flute, violin, viola and cello) has surface charm and the *Symphony* is fluent, if rather too long. It has a catchy theme for its closing *Rondo*, and the *Sinfonia concertante* – easily the best work here, and half as long as the *Symphony* – is full of similarly neat invention and again brings an engaging finale. The whole programme is given persuasive advocacy by this excellent Russian group who are thoroughly within the style of the music and play with expert precision and much vitality. The snag is that they are forwardly balanced and rather dryly recorded, and the dynamic contrast of their playing is reduced by the close microphones. Even so, this inexpensive disc gives a fascinating glimpse of an interesting and distinctly talented musician.

Porter, Cole (1891–1964)

Songs: *After you; Don't look at me that way; Ev'ry time we say goodbye; I concentrate on you; I love Paris; In the still of the night; It's all right with me; I've got you under my skin; Just one of those things; Let's misbehave; Night and day; Ridin' high; So in love; True love; You'd be so nice to come home to.*
** EMI Dig. CDC5 55050-2 [id.]. Kiri Te Kanawa, New World PO, Peter Matz.

A disappointment. Kiri's rich vocal-line cannot fail to make an effect in a song like *Night and day*, and her sensuous allure is suitable for some other numbers, like *In the still of the night*. But overall the effect is blandly sensuous with not enough sparkle. Good arrangements and sumptuous sound.

Poulenc, Francis (1899-1963)

Double piano concerto in D min.
(M) *** Teldec/Warner Dig. 4509 97445-2 [id.]. Güher and Süher Pekinel, French R. PO, Janowski –
SAINT-SAENS: *Carnival of the animals.* ***

The Pekinel Duo come from mixed Spanish/Turkish parentage and their account of Poulenc's *Double concerto* is second to none. They play with great dash and sparkle, relishing the Mozartian pastiche of the *Larghetto* and the sensuous Ravelian/Satiesque nostalgia of the other lyrical ideas. Janowski provides a lively and thoroughly supportive accompaniment, and the recording balance is excellent. The only drawback is the brief time-span of this coupling (38 minutes overall), but the Saint-Saens zoological fantasy is equally enticing, so this is still a very attractive disc.

(i) *L'invitation au château (for clarinet, violin & piano);* (ii) *Mouvements perpétuels for flute, oboe, clarinet, bassoon, horn, violin, viola, cello & bass;* (iii) *Rapsodie nègre for flute, clarinet, string quartet, baritone & piano;* (iv) *Sextet for flute, oboe, clarinet, bassoon, horn & piano;* (v) *Sonata for clarinet; Sonata for clarinet & bassoon;* (vi) *Sonata for 2 clarinets;* (vii) *Sonata for flute and piano;* (viii) *Oboe sonata;* (ix) *Trio for oboe, bassoon & piano;* (x) *Villanelle for piccolo & piano.*
(B) *** Cala Dig. CACD 1018 (2) [id.]. (i–vi) James Campbell; (i–ii) Peter Carter; (i) John York; (ii–iv; vii; x) William Bennett; (ii; iv; viii; ix) Nicholas Daniel; (ii; iv–v; ix) Rachel Gough; (ii; iv) Richard Watkins; (ii) Roger Tapping; (ii) Bruno Schrecker; (ii) Chris West; (iii) Allegri Qt (Peter Carter, David Roth, Roger Tapping, Bruno Schrecker); (iii) Peter Sidhom; (iii; viii–ix) Julius Drake; (iv; vii; x) Clifford Benson; (vi) David Campbell – RAVEL: *Introduction and allegro* etc.
***

These Cala discs are a terrific bargain. The Poulenc accounts for the bulk of the two CDs (two hours' music in fact), all of it full of sparkle and freshness of invention. The discs comprise the complete chamber music for woodwind by Ravel and Poulenc, with the exception of works written primarily for the voice. The performances have great elegance and finesse. There are rarities, such as the *Rapsodie nègre* (Poulenc's Op. 2, according to the notes and Op. 1 according to the sleeve – Roger Nichols speaks of it in *New Grove* as his first published work), written when he was eighteen, and *L'invitation au château* for clarinet, violin and piano which Cala claim as a first recording. (The *Rapsodie nègre* also is not otherwise available.) Poulenc has this rare gift of being able to move from the most flippant high spirits to the deepest poignancy, as in the *Oboe sonata*, expressively played by Nicholas Daniel. His pianist, Julian Drake, is highly sensitive, though the piano is not always ideally focused in the excessively resonant acoustic. Elsewhere, in the captivating incidental music to a play by Jean Cocteau and Raymond Radiguet, *L'invitation au château*, the playing is expert, tasteful and stylish. The *Mouvements perpétuels* scored such a success in 1918 that Poulenc arranged them for flute, oboe, clarinet, bassoon, horn, violin, viola, cello and bass, in which form they delight. The *Sextet* and the various wind sonatas are beautifully played with great relish and spirit. This is a most attractive set, which deserves the widest dissemination. Had the piano been as well balanced as it is played, this would have earned a Rosette.

Cello sonata in A.
(M) ** Virgin/EMI Dig. CUV5 61198-2 [id.]. Steven Isserlis, Pascal Devoyon – DEBUSSY; FRANCK: *Cello sonatas.* **

Steven Isserlis and Pascal Devoyon play most sensitively and are inside this idiom, but the close scrutiny to which the microphone subjects them does them some disservice. Both artists show subtlety and intelligence, and their performance deserves a recommendation.

Oboe sonata; Trio for piano, oboe and bassoon.
** Claves Dig. CD 50-9020 [id.]. Goritzki, Requejo, Thuneman – SAINT-SAENS: *Sonatas.* **

Given the availability of the Cala package listed above, this is hardly an economical buy. Despite the eminence of the artists, you can buy both these pieces, together with the rest of Poulenc's output for wind instruments – and Ravel's *Introduction and Allegro* – on two Cala discs for the same outlay.

Violin sonata.
*** EMI Dig. CDC7 54541-2 [id.]. Frank Peter Zimmermann, Alexander Lonquich – AURIC: *Sonate;* FRANCAIX: *Sonatine;* MILHAUD: *Sonata;* SATIE: *Choses vues.* ***

Frank Peter Zimmermann and Alexander Lonquich give a splendidly zestful account of Poulenc's wartime *Sonata* and convey its *gamin*-like character to perfection. They have charm and vitality. The recording is beautifully present, though it slightly favours the piano.

L'Histoire de Babar, le petit éléphant.
(**) DG Dig. 439 767-2 [id.]. Jeanne Moreau, Jean-Marc Luisada – SATIE: *Collection.* (**)

Poulenc's setting of the Babar story for narration and piano is no match for *Peter and the wolf*, but it still has a distinct Gallic charm. However, although Jeanne Moreau is an impressive narrator and Jean-Marc Luisada's contribution is both vivid and atmospheric, it seems an extraordinary idea to offer the narrative in French to an English-speaking audience, even though a translation is provided. The recording is excellent, but the presentation of the Satie piano music is even more perverse.

Prokofiev, Serge (1891–1953)

Cinderella (ballet; complete), *Op. 87; Summer night: suite, Op. 123.*
⊛ *** DG Dig. 445 830-2 (2) [id.]. Russian Nat. O, Mikhail Pletnev.

Here is playing of terrific life, lightness of touch, poetic feeling and character. Quite simply the best-played, most atmospheric and affecting *Cinderella* we have ever had on disc. We found its effect tremendously exhilarating, and have had difficulty in stopping playing it! Don't hesitate – on every count this is one of the best recordings, not only of the year but the 1990s.

(i) *Piano concerto No. 3 in C, Op. 26. Symphony No.1 in D, 'Classical', Op. 25: Gavotte* (only; arr. for piano). *Piano sonata No. 4 in C min., Op. 29: Andante assai* (only). *Gavotte, Op. 32/3; Suggestion diabolique, Op. 4/4; Visions fugitives, Op. 22: excerpts: Nos. 3, Allegretto; 5, Molto giocoso; 6, Con eleganza; 9, Allegretto tranquillo; 10, Ridiculosamente; 11, Con vivacita; 16, Dolente; 17, Poetico; 18, Con una dolce lentezza.*
(***) EMI mono CDC5 55223-2 [id.]. Composer (piano); (i) LSO, Piero Coppola – GLAZUNOV: *The Seasons.* (***)

Prokofiev's pioneering account of the *Third Piano concerto* has appeared many times since the 1930s: on EMI's 'Great Recordings of the Century' on LP, and on World Records, coupled with Marguerite Long's Ravel concerto – and most recently on the Pearl CD transfer recommended in our main volume. This transfer supersedes it: not only is the sound smoother and richer, the disc offers Glazunov's remarkable recording of *The Seasons*. At 79 minutes, this is not to be missed.

Piano concertos Nos. 1 in D flat, Op. 10; 3 in C, Op. 26.
*** DG Dig. 439 898-2 [id.]. Kissin, BPO, Abbado.

Yevgeni Kissin gives a virtuosic, dashing account of both concertos and is given highly sensitive and responsive support from the Berlin Philharmonic under Abbado. It is unfailingly brilliant, aristocratic in feeling and wonderfully controlled pianism. After the big theme in the *First Piano concerto*, Kissin does not dash away in quite the same way as did Richter (in his mono recording from the late 1950s on Supraphon, which sounds pretty marvellous even as sound), and in the *Third* there is none of the wild abandon of William Kappell (see below). But this is playing of the greatest artistry and distinction; and the recording, though not as transparent as, say, Decca for Ashkenazy (there is a grainy quality about the orchestral climaxes), is still very good. It is a pity that DG did not offer a fill-up, for example one of the sonatas from Kissin, as this CD offers only 42 minutes 27 seconds of playing time. All the same, it is very highly recommendable.

Piano concerto No. 3 in C, Op. 26.
⊛ (M) (**(*)) BMG/RCA mono GD 60921 [id.]. William Kapell, Dallas SO, Dorati –
KHACHATURIAN: *Piano concerto* (**(*)) ⊛ ; LISZT: *Mephisto waltz.* (**(*))

William Kapell's account of the *Third Piano concerto* is dazzlingly brilliant, and the Dallas orchestra under Antal Dorati rise to the occasion too. Indeed this is arguably the most incandescent and vital performance of this concerto ever committed to disc. It is superior even to that of the composer himself and proceeds at a level of energy and imagination that is quite astonishing. (Some of the notes above the stave are twangy but, given the quality of the performance, one hardly notices.) It comes with an equally remarkable performance of the Khachaturian with the Boston Symphony under Koussevitzky, a powerhouse of vitality. Playing like this silences any criticism one might voice about the recorded sound, which admittedly is pretty grim. The present writer (RL) has never heard a performance to equal this.

Violin concertos Nos. 1 in D, Op. 19; 2 in G min., Op. 63.
(⊛) *** Sony SK 53969 [id.]. Cho-Liang Lin, LAPO, Esa-Pekka Salonen – STRAVINSKY: *Violin concerto.* ***
*** Denon Dig. CO-75891 [id.]. Boris Belkin, Zürich Tonhalle O, Stern.

In this generous and apt coupling, Cho-Liang Lin gives commanding performances which combine polish with concentration and deep feeling. The two Prokofiev concertos are among the composer's most richly lyrical works, and Lin brings out their romantic warmth as well as their dramatic bite. Salonen's understanding support, helped by sound more refined than this orchestra usually gets, if with weighty bass, culminates in ravishing accounts of the outer movements of No. 1 and the central slow movement of No. 2. In the Stravinsky, Salonen terraces the accompaniment dramatically, with woodwind and brass bold and full. That goes with another powerful and warmly expressive reading from Lin, confounding the composer's pronouncements on emotion in music. In this same coupling, Chung on mid-price Decca (425 003-2) offers equally compelling Prokofievian readings in excellent analogue sound, more overtly emotional if not quite so commanding.

On the Denon disc, helped by cleaner, refined sound with good presence, Belkin offers warm, strong readings with many individual insights, notably in his very measured, yearningly tender account of the slow movement of No. 2, but his disc suffers in practical terms by providing no makeweight.

Violin concerto No. 1 in D, Op. 19.
*** Sony SK 66567 [id.]. Julian Rachlin, Moscow RSO, Vladimir Fedoseyev – TCHAIKOVSKY: *Violin concerto.* ***

The yearning, hushed beauty of Rachlin's treatment of the great opening melody recalls Philip Hope-Wallace's description of Galli-Curci's singing: 'like a nightingale half asleep'. This is not only a movingly poetic performance, with the lyrical outer movements both lighter and faster-flowing than usual, but one which consistently brings out the wit and fun in the writing. It may not be everyone's first choice, but there is no more distinctive reading on disc than this, and anyone who wants this unusual coupling need not hesitate, with the Tchaikovsky also more meditative than usual.

Peter and the wolf.
(B) ** CfP CD-CFP 185; *TC-CFP 185.* Richard Baker, New Philh. O, Leppard – BRITTEN: *Young person's guide.* **

Richard Baker, balanced well forward in a different acoustic from the orchestra, provides an introductory paragraph which might become tedious on repetition. But he enters into the spirit of the story well enough and is only occasionally coy. Leppard gives an excellent account of the orchestra score, and the recording is vivid. But in the last resort, one's reaction to this record depends on how one takes to the narration, and there will be mixed views on that. First choice remains with John Gielgud's highly individual presentation on Virgin (CU5 61137-2) – see our main volume.

Romeo and Juliet (ballet), *Op. 64* (complete).
** Royal Opera House Dig. ROH 309–10 [id.]. ROHCG O, Mark Ermler.
** Chan. Dig. CHAN 9322/3 [id.]. Danish Nat. RSO, Dmitri Kitajenko.

If recording was the sole criterion, then the Royal Opera House's own recording of *Romeo and Juliet* with its fine orchestra and Mark Ermler would sweep the board. This is simply magnificent sound, with sumptuous tone and splendid body and presence. Also usually magnificent is the playing of the Opera House Orchestra, but here it is disinctly under-vitalized and wanting in zest and sparkle. Not recommended except perhaps to audio buffs who specialize in demonstration sound.

Kitajenko's account is very well recorded too, without being quite in the demonstration class of the Ermler. The performance is a very good one but without all the imaginative drive, dramatic fire or sense of atmosphere that are so essential in this wonderful score. Decca's Maazel set with the Cleveland Orchestra is still the one to go for (417 510-2 – see our main volume).

Romeo and Juliet (ballet), *Op. 64:* suites Nos. 1 & 2.
(B) **(*) Decca Double 440 630-2 (2) [id.]. SRO, Ansermet – TCHAIKOVSKY: *Swan Lake.* **(*)

Ansermet's choice of 15 key items is well made, and the performances have both atmosphere and passion (notably *Romeo with Juliet before his departure*). After the ominous introduction, the playing is rhythmically a bit sluggish. But *Juliet as a young girl* and the *Madrigal* are charming, and the love scene of *Romeo and Juliet* is genuinely touching; the *Death of Tybalt* bursts with energy, and *Masks* is nicely pointed. If the Suisse Romande Orchestra in 1961 was not one of the world's greatest ensembles, Ansermet was very persuasive and he brings everything vividly to life. The dramatically vibrant recording is well up to Decca's vintage standard of the early 1960s.

Romeo and Juliet (ballet): suites Nos. 1 & 3.
*** DG Dig. 439 870-2 [id.]. Concg. O, Myung-Whun Chung.

Myung-Whun Chung gets playing of great atmosphere, virtuosity and dramatic fire from the Royal Concertgebouw Orchestra, and DG provide a recording of great range and presence, comparable with the very best now in currency. A pity that they did not include the second suite, for which there would have been time, a self-inflicted wound which handicaps a record that should enjoy and certainly deserves the widest exposure. Those who invest in it will not be disappointed.

Sinfonietta in A, Op. 48.
(M) *** Virgin/EMI Dig. CUV5 61206-2 [id.]. Lausanne CO, Zedda – DEBUSSY: *Danse* etc.;
     MILHAUD: *Création du monde.* ***

Prokofiev could not understand why the early *Sinfonietta* failed to make an impression on the wider musical public, and neither can we. Alongside the *Classical Symphony* the *giocoso* outer movements have a more fragile geniality but they are highly delectable, as are the somewhat angular *Andante*, the brief *Intermezzo* and the witty Scherzo. The use of the orchestral palette is as subtle as it is engaging and, with Alberto Zedda's affectionately light touch and fine Lausanne playing, the piece emerges here with all colours flying. The fairly resonant sound, with the orchestra slightly recessed, adds to the feeling of warmth without blunting the orchestral articulation.

The Stone Flower (ballet): complete.
*** Russian Disc CD 11 022 (2) [id.]. Bolshoi Theatre O, Rozhdestvensky.

One might be tempted to call *The Stone Flower* the Cinderella of the Prokofiev ballets, were it not for the fact that there is one already! It is grievously (if understandably) neglected in favour of its two full-length companions, *Romeo and Juliet* and *Cinderella*. It is not as distinguished, characterful or inventive as they, but Prokofiev at second-best is still worth more than a lot of composers firing on all cylinders. There is much that is imaginative in this score, even if it is not the equal of its two companions in terms of consistency and inspiration. Rozhdestvensky's Bolshoi performance dates from 1968 and was available on three long-deleted HMV/Melodiya LPs. It still sounds pretty good on CD, but in any case has no current competitors.

Symphonies Nos. 1 in D (Classical); 5 in B flat, Op. 100.
(M) *** Ph. Dig. 442 399-2 [id.]. LAPO, André Previn.
*(*) DG Dig. 439 912-2 [id.]. Chicago SO, Levine.

Symphonies Nos. 1 in D (Classical), Op. 25; 5 in B flat, Op. 100; Romeo and Juliet: excerpts; Chout: final dance.
⊛ (M) (***) RCA mono 09026 61657-2 [id.]. Boston SO, Koussevitzky.

In the first movement of the *Fifth*, Previn's pacing seems exactly right: everything flows so naturally and speaks effectively. The Scherzo is not as high-voltage as some rivals, but Previn still brings it off well; and in the slow movement he gets playing of genuine eloquence from the Los Angeles orchestra. He also gives an excellent account of the perennially fresh *Classical Symphony*. The recording is beautifully natural, with impressive detail, range and body. Although Karajan reigns supreme in this coupling (DG 437 253-2), his analogue recording does not match this Philips competitor, and those wanting modern, digital sound will find Previn an ideal mid-priced alternative.

Koussevitzky's *Fifth Symphony* and the four movements from *Romeo and Juliet* were never issued in this country on 78-r.p.m. discs, although numbers were allotted to them, but they did appear on LP in 1977. The performances are quite simply breathtaking and have never been equalled, except perhaps by Karajan's 1969 record with the Berlin Philharmonic. Yet this has even more fire, zest and virtuosity, and the recordings, made in 1945–6, are remarkably good. The *Classical Symphony* is not to be confused with Koussevitzky's sparkling account on 78-r.p.m. records. Both the *Classical Symphony* and the *Danse finale* from *Chout* come from 1947 and were recorded when the orchestra were on a visit to Carnegie Hall, New York. Likewise these are thrilling performances on which it would be very difficult to improve and, again, few allowances have to be made for the sound-quality. An outstanding issue in every way.

The DG account of the *Fifth* from the Chicago orchestra and James Levine is pretty loud and brash. There is not much sensitivity and less subtlety, and these fine players get little chance to show their paces except in terms of technical skill. The musical rewards here are few and slender.

Symphonies Nos. 6 in E flat min., Op. 111; 7 in C sharp min., Op. 131.
** Decca Dig. 443 325-2 [id.]. Cleveland O, Ashkenazy.

Ashkenazy's account of the *Sixth Symphony* is quite easily the best recorded in the current catalogue, and the same goes for the *Seventh*. Unlike the unimpressive, two-dimensional recorded sound that DG provided for Ozawa, there is plenty of back-to-front depth as well as a natural perspective. The aural image is firmly defined and there is splendid body and presence. In his last Prokofiev CD for Decca (the *Sinfonia concertante* for cello and orchestra with Lynn Harrell) Ashkenazy was completely attuned to both the spirit and the letter of the score. In the *Sixth Symphony* he is less wholly successful. He sometimes loses the vital current that flows through its first movement, relaxing the tension a little too much. On the other hand, the *Largo* is really too fast to make the requisite contrast with the *Allegro* movement, and the opening of the finale is far too fast. The players do not sound at ease, and it is not surprising that they soon slow him down. The opening of the *Seventh Symphony* is phrased rather fussily though, further into the first movement, the music is allowed to adopt its natural flow. Generally speaking this is not quite the artistic success which one had every reason to expect. Järvi remains the most reliable guide in this repertoire (Chandos CHAN 8359 and 8442).

String quartet No. 2 in F, Op. 92.
⊛ (***) Testament mono SBT 1052 [id.]. Hollywood Qt – HINDEMITH: *Quartet No. 3;* WALTON:
   Quartet in A min. *** ⊛

There have been innumerable recordings of Prokofiev's *Second Quartet* since the pioneering Hollywood Quartet version first appeared on these shores in 1952. Not one has matched let alone surpassed this stunning performance, which has an extraordinary precision and intensity (as well as repose when this is required). The transfer sounds excellent and, although the mono sound does not represent the state of the art these days, the performance surely does. Outstanding in every way – and still after 45 years a first recommendation.

Violin sonatas Nos. 1 in F min., Op. 80; 2 in D, Op. 94 bis; 5 Mélodies, Op. 35 bis.
**(*) Decca 440 926-2 [id.]. Joshua Bell, Olli Mustonen.

Both sonatas come from the war years, and the dark *Sonata No. 1 in F minor* must be numbered among the composer's most searching works. Its companion, a transcription of the *Flute sonata*, is carefree in spirit and lyrical in feeling. Joshua Bell and Olli Mustonen give a highly intelligent reading of both pieces and the charming *Cinq Mélodies*. Their playing is worth a full three-star rating: both artists have keen and sensitive responses but they are rather let down by the recording. Although made in one of the best of venues, St George's, Brandon Hill, in Bristol, it favours the piano very much at the expense of the violin. Perlman and Ashkenazy, now restored to circulation on RCA, are to be preferred (09026 61454-2).

Piano sonata No. 2 in D min., Op. 14; Cinderella: 3 Pieces, Op. 102; Dumka; 3 Pieces, Op. 69;
Waltzes (Schubert, arr. Prokofiev).
*** Chan. Dig. CHAN 9119 [id.]. Boris Berman.

Piano sonata No. 3 in A min., Op. 28; Cinderella: 6 pieces, Op. 95; 10 Pieces, Op. 12; Thoughts, Op. 62.
*** Chan. Dig. CHAN 9069 [id.]. Boris Berman.

Piano sonatas Nos. 5 in C, Op. 38; 6 in A, Op. 82; 10 in E min., Op. 137 (fragment); *Gavotte (Classical Symphony, Op. 25); Juvenilia; Toccata, Op. 11.*
*** Chan. Dig. CHAN 9361 [id.]. Boris Berman.

As is the case with earlier records in this distinguished series, Chandos provide lifelike quality of striking presence: the recordings emanate from The Maltings, Snape, and are in the demonstration bracket. Berman always plays with tremendous concentration and control. He commands a finely articulated and vital rhythmic sense as well as a wide range of keyboard colour. The remaining volumes maintain the high standard of earlier issues (see our main volume).

In the *Second Sonata in D minor* Berman is quite magnificent and full of panache. The ebullient *Third* is coupled with the inventive but unaccountably neglected *Ten Pieces*, Op. 12, which are not otherwise available (though there are alternative versions of individual pieces). This also has the *Pensées*, Op. 62, and remains one of the most desirable of the set.

Of course with the *Sixth Sonata* Berman is traversing hotly contested ground. There is formidable competition from Yevgeni Kissin, who has recorded it twice (both times magnificently), Richter and Pogorelich (who remains current first choice: DG 413 363-2). Although Kissin's Sony recital, recorded in Tokyo, generates a level of excitement that Berman does not match, and he takes more risks, Berman's cooler and more collected reading remains eminently recommendable. Not only does he give us the original (1923) version of the *Fifth Sonata* (generally to be preferred to the revision Prokofiev made in later life) but also the minute or so that survives of a *Tenth Sonata* (otherwise only available on Murray McLachlan's Olympia disc). This takes as its starting point the *E minor Sonatina*, Op. 54, which Berman recorded earlier in his survey (coupling it with the *First Sonata* (CHAN 9017), discussed in our main volume). No reason to withhold a third star from any of these issues, which come with informative notes from David Fanning.

Piano sonatas Nos. 4 in C min., Op. 29; 5 in C, Op. 38/135; 6 in A, Op. 82; Pastoral sonatina.
** ASV Dig. CDDCA 754 [id.]. John Lill.

Good though he is, John Lill does not really match or surpass the competition here: In the *Sixth Sonata* he certainly does not command the flair and abandon of Kissin or Pogorelich, or the impressive playing of Boris Berman. Taken on its own merits, there is much that would give satisfaction, but the Lill Prokofiev cycle is not a first choice.

Piano sonata No. 7 in B flat, Op. 83.
(M) *** DG 447 431-2 [id.]. Maurizio Pollini – *Recital.* ***
** Decca Dig. 440 281-2 [id.]. Peter Jablonski – RACHMANINOV: *Piano sonata No. 2;* SCRIABIN: *Sonatas Nos. 5 & 9.* **

This is a great performance by Pollini, well in the Horowitz or Richter category. It is part of a generous CD of twentieth-century music.

Peter Jablonski is a young Swedish pianist of great gifts, who has made a considerable name for himself both in his own country and abroad. In this repertoire he faces competition from such keyboard lions as Horowitz, Richter and Pollini and Pletnev and, for all his undoubted talent, he is not in their league. The listener remains relatively unthrilled by this. Let us hope Decca will continue encouraging this artist and cast him more wisely in future repertoire.

VOCAL MUSIC

Alexander Nevsky, Op. 78.
(M) ** Decca Dig. 430 738-2 [id.]. Arkhipova, Cleveland Ch. & O, Chailly – TCHAIKOVSKY: *Francesca da Rimini.* *(*)

(i) *Alexander Nevsky, Op. 78; Lieutenant Kijé* (suite), *Op. 60.*
** Decca Dig. 430 506-2 [id.]. (i) Jard van Nes; Montreal Ch. & SO, Dutoit.

(i) *Alexander Nevsky* (cantata), *Op. 78;* (ii) *Lieutenant Kijé* (suite), *Op. 60; Scythian suite, Op. 20.*
(M) *** DG 447 419-2 [id.]. (i) Elena Obraztsova; London Symphony Ch., LSO; (ii) Chicago SO; Claudio Abbado.

Abbado's performance of *Alexander Nevsky* culminates in a deeply moving account of the tragic lament after the battle (here very beautifully sung by Obraztsova), made the more telling when the battle itself is so fine an example of orchestral virtuosity. The chorus is as incisive as the orchestra. The digital remastering of the 1980 recording has been all gain, and the sound is very impressive indeed. A fine account of *Lieutenant Kijé* and what is probably the best version of the *Scythian suite* to appear in many years make this a desirable reissue in DG's Legendary Recordings series. Abbado gets both warm and wonderfully clean playing from the Chicago orchestra and he is accorded excellent engineering. The *Scythian suite* has drive and fire: in the finale – and even in the second movement – Abbado could bring greater savagery and brilliance than he does but, given the power that the Chicago orchestra do bring to this score and the refined colouring that Abbado achieves in the atmospheric *Night* movement, there need be no real reservation in recommending this strongly.

Dutoit opens atmospherically and, with characteristically vivid St Eustache sound, Prokofiev's abrasive scoring ensures that the effect is suitably ominous. But overall Dutoit's reading lacks the necessary pungency and the *Battle on the ice* sequence fails to grip, in spite of the spectacular Decca engineering. The highlight of the performance is Jard van Nes's moving solo contribution, and the closing section produces the proper grandeur and sense of triumphant exultation. In the suite from *Lieutenant Kijé* Dutoit and his orchestra return to form, and this attractive performance combines wit and nostalgia with lustrous colour, even if the famous *Troika* could have benefited from a degree more zest.

Chailly too has the advantage of full-blooded Decca digital sound, and its richness adds to the emotional weight of the opening sections. The *Battle on the ice* is characteristically impulsive and, with Irina Arkhipova touchingly expressive in her elegiac aria, Chailly finds an effective exuberance in the work's closing pages. The recording is not always ideally clear on detail, although it is not short on spectacle and the chorus projects well, but this is not strongly competitive, for the Tchaikovsky coupling is disappointing.

Puccini, Giacomo (1858–1924)

Capriccio sinfonico; Crisantemi; Minuets Nos. 1–3; Preludio sinfonico; Edgar: Preludes, Acts I & III. Manon Lescaut: Intermezzo, Act III. Le Villi: Prelude; La Tregenda (Act II).
(M) *** Decca Dig. 444 154-2 [id.]. Berlin RSO, Ricardo Chailly.

In a highly attractive collection of Puccinian juvenilia and rarities, Chailly draws opulent and atmospheric playing from the Berlin Radio Symphony Orchestra, helped by outstandingly rich and full recording. The CD is of demonstration quality. The *Capriccio sinfonico* of 1876 brings the first characteristically Puccinian idea in what later became the opening Bohemian motif of *La Bohème*. There are other identifiable fingerprints here, even if the big melodies suggest Mascagni rather than full-blown Puccini. *Crisantemi* (with the original string quartet scoring expanded for full string orchestra) provided material for *Manon Lescaut*, as did the three little *Minuets*, pastiche eighteenth-century music.

Messa di Gloria.
(M) *** Erato/Warner Dig. 4509 96367-2 [id.]. Carreras, Prey, Amb. S., Philh. O, Scimone.

The return of Scimone's second (1983) digital recording of the Puccini *Messa di gloria* at mid-price makes this version much more competitive, even though it has no fill-up. He and a fine team are brisker and lighter than their predecessors on record, yet effectively bring out the red-bloodedness of the writing. José Carreras turns the big solo in the *Gratias* into the first genuine Puccini aria. His sweetness and imagination are not quite matched by the baritone, Hermann Prey, who is given less to do than usual, when the choral baritones take on the yearning melody of *Crucifixus*. Excellent, atmospheric sound.

OPERA

La Bohème (complete).
(M) **(*) EMI CMS7 69657-2 (2) [Ang. CDMB 69657]. Freni, Gedda, Adani, Sereni, Mazzoli, La Scala, Milan, Ch. & O, Schippers.
(B) ** Ph. 442 260-2 (2) [id.]. Ricciarelli, Carreras, Putnam, Wixell, Lloyd, ROHCG Ch. & O, Sir Colin Davis.

Freni's characterization of Mimì is so enchanting that it is worth ignoring some of the less perfect elements. The engineers placed Freni rather close to the microphone, which makes it hard for her to sound tentative in her first scene, but the beauty of the voice is what one remembers, and from there to the end her performance is conceived as a whole, leading to a supremely moving account of the Death scene. Nicolai Gedda's Rodolfo is not rounded in the traditional Italian way, but there is never any doubt about his ability to project a really grand manner of his own. Thomas Schippers' conducting starts as though this is going to be a hard-driven, unrelenting performance, but after the horseplay he quickly shows his genuinely Italianate sense of pause, giving the singers plenty of time to breathe and allowing the music to expand. The resonant, 1964 recording has transferred vividly to CD and the set has been attractively re-packaged with a excellently printed libretto.

The CD transfer in its clarity and sharp focus underlines the unidiomatic quality of Davis's reading, with un-Italianate singers like Ingvar Wixell and Ashley Putnam in key roles. As in *Tosca*, Sir Colin Davis here takes a direct view of Puccini, presenting the score very straight, with no exaggerations. The result is refreshing but rather lacking in wit and sparkle; pauses and hesitations are curtailed. Ricciarelli's is the finest performance vocally, and Davis allows her more freedom than the others. *Sì, mi chiamano Mimì* is full of fine detail and most affecting. Carreras gives a good generalized performance, wanting in detail and in intensity, and rather failing to rise to the big moments. Wixell makes an unidiomatic Marcello, rather lacking in fun, and Robert Lloyd's bass sounds lightweight as Colline. Ashley Putnam makes a charming Musetta. However, in this Duo reissue, with two CDs offered for the price of one, many will feel this is good value, although it includes a synopsis rather than a libretto. The set is well cued. First choice for this opera remains with Beecham (with De los Angeles and Bjoerling) on EMI CDS7 47235-8, or Karajan on Decca 421 049-2 (with Freni and Pavarotti).

La Fanciulla del West: highlights.

(M) *** DG 445 465-2 [id.] (from complete recording, with Neblett, Domingo, Milnes; cond. Mehta).

This is most welcome as the only current set of highlights from *Fanciulla del West*, covering the whole opera generously with 75 minutes of music. No libretto, but a good track synopsis.

Gianni Schicchi (complete).

(M) *** RCA Dig. 74321 25285-2. Panerai, Donath, Seiffert, Bavarian R. Ch., Munich R. O, Patanè.

The RCA (formerly Eurodisc) recording of *Gianni Schicchi* brings a co-production with Bavarian Radio, and the recording is vivid and well balanced. Patanè conducts a colourful and vigorous performance, very well drilled in ensembles – even when speeds are dangerously fast – and with the voices nicely spaced to allow the elaborate details of the plot to be appreciated by ear alone. Central to the performance's success is the vintage Schicchi of Rolando Panerai, still rich and firm. He confidently characterizes the Florentine trickster in every phrase, building a superb portrait, finely timed. Peter Seiffert as Rinuccio gives a dashing performance, consistently clean and firm of tone, making light of the high tessitura and rising splendidly to the challenge of the big central aria. Helen Donath would have sounded even sweeter a few years earlier, but she gives a tender, appealing portrait of Lauretta, pretty and demure in *O mio babbino caro*. Though Italian voices are in the minority, it is a confident team. In its reissued form, access to the disc has been greatly improved and there are now seven cues.

Manon Lescaut (complete).

(M) **(*) EMI CMS7 64852-2 (2) [Ang. CDMB 64852]. Caballé, Domingo, Amb. Op. Ch., New Philh. O, Bartoletti.

This EMI version, conducted by Bartoletti, is chiefly valuable for the performance of Montserrat Caballé as the heroine, one of her most affecting, with the voice alluringly beautiful. Her account of *In quelle trine morbide* is lightly flowing, while the big Act IV aria is strong and positive. Otherwise the set is disappointing, with Plácido Domingo unflattered by the close acoustic, not nearly as perceptive as in his much later, DG performance under Sinopoli. Bartoletti's conducting is also relatively coarse, with the very opening forced and breathless. The new transfer to CD, however, has improved the sound, which is now much more vivid and atmospheric; and the presentation, with a clearly printed libretto, is also attractive. Caballé admirers will not want to be without this set. Others will turn to the Levine set with Freni and Pavarotti (DG 440 200-2) which is our current first choice for this opera.

Manon Lescaut: highlights.

(M) *** DG Dig. 445 466-2 [id.] (from complete set, with Freni, Domingo, Bruson, Gambill; cond. Sinopoli).

Most of the key items are included in this well-chosen mid-price selection of highlights from the brilliant Sinopoli set which is a strong alternative recommendation for this opera (DG 413 893-2 – see our main volume). An adequate synopsis with track cues is provided in lieu of a libretto. The playing time is 66 minutes.

Tosca: highlights.

(B) *** DG 439 461-2 [id.]. Ricciarelli, Carreras, Raimondi, Ch. of German Op., BPO, Karajan.
* Sony Dig. SMK 53550 [id.]. Marton, Carreras, Pons, Hungarian State R. & TV Ch. & State O, Tilson Thomas.

Among complete sets of *Tosca*, the De Sabata version with Callas, Di Stefano and Gobbi remains unsurpassed (EMI CDS7 47175-8). However, the new bargain Classikon 70-minute selection from Karajan's powerful, closely recorded Berlin version is welcome. The breadth of Karajan's direction is well represented in the longer excerpts; there is also Tosca's *Vissi d'arte* and Carreras's two famous arias from the outer Acts. Now Scarpia's music in Act II is much better represented, essential when Raimondi is such a distinctive Scarpia with his dark, bass timbre.

This Sony Hungarian set of highlights is generous (77 minutes) but it comes from an unrecommendable complete set with Eva Marton a coarse and often unsteady Tosca and José Carreras not matching his contribution to two earlier sets for Karajan and Sir Colin Davis. Juan Pons is a lightweight Scarpia, not sinister enough.

Il Trittico: (i) *Il Tabarro;* (ii) *Suor Angelica;* (iii) *Gianni Schicchi.*
*(*) Decca Dig. 436 261-2 (3) [id.].Mirella Freni; (i) Pons, Giacomini; (ii) Souliotis; (iii) Nucci, Alagna; Maggio Musicale Fiorentino Ch. & O, Bruno Bartoletti.

It is a pity that Mirella Freni did not record *Il Trittico* earlier. It is taxing for any soprano to tackle three such contrasted roles as Giorgetta, Angelica and Lauretta, and in this 1991 recording (not issued till 1994) the only performance which sounds in character is the first of the three, with the portrait of the bargemaster's wife bright and detailed. The tenor, Giuseppe Giacomini, gives a weightier performance as Luigi than is usual, with his voice strong and baritonal. That makes Juan Pons's portrait of the cuckolded bargemaster, Michele, sound too light. The big aria, *Nulla, silenzio*, is cleanly sung, but with no bite or venom, and Bartoletti's conducting in all three operas lacks the tension needed in such colourful, atmospheric pieces. Freni's soprano too often sounds strained in the role of Angelica, spreading uncomfortably at the top under pressure and missing the beauty and poise while, characterful though she is, Elena Souliotis is vocally idiosyncratic as the Zia Principessa. The high comedy of *Gianni Schicchi* suffers most of all from Bartoletti's limpness, and Freni is not remotely young-sounding in *O mio babbino caro*. The rising tenor, Roberto Alagna, gives a clean, trumpet-toned performance as Rinuccio and, though Leo Nucci sings well enough in the title-role, he conveys nothing of the ironic humour behind this magic manipulator. The full Decca recording does little to remedy the shortcomings of the performances.

Turandot (complete).
(m) **(*) EMI CMS5 65293-2 (2) [Ang. CDMB 65293]. Caballé, Carreras, Freni, Plishka, Sénéchal, Maîtrise de la Cathédrale, Ch. of L'Opéra du Rhin, Strasbourg PO, Lombard.

Having earlier sung Liù opposite Joan Sutherland for Decca, Caballé went on to assume the more taxing role of Turandot. With Mirella Freni as Liù there is again a powerful confrontation, not between black and white but between subtler, less fixed characters. So from the very start Caballé conveys an element of mystery while Freni underlines the dramatic rather than the lyrical side of Liù's role. The pity is that the recording is unflattering to the voices – allowing Caballé less warmth and body of tone than usual, while setting Freni so close that a flutter keeps intruding. Lombard, so alert and imaginative in French music, proves a stiff and unsympathetic Puccinian so that the tenor, José Carreras, for example is prevented from expanding as he should in the big arias. Nor is the Strasbourg Philharmonic a match for the LPO on Decca. A good CD transfer and excellent back-up documentation. However, at mid-price the alternative EMI set with Birgit Nilsson as Turandot is a much better recommendation (CMS7 69327-2), but first choice rests with Sutherland and Pavarotti on Decca (414 274-2).

Purcell, Henry (1659–95)

Archiv Purcell Collection

'Purcell Edition' (complete in slipcase).
(m) **(*) DG 447 147-2 (8) [id.] (all the records are also available separately – see below).

(i) *3 Fantasias for 5 Viols; 9 Fantasias for 4 Viols; Fantasia on one note for 5 viols; In nomine for 6 viols; In nomine for 7 viols;* (ii) Duet: *How pleasant is this flowery plain;* Verse anthem: *In thee, O Lord, do I put my trust;* Song: *Oh! what a scene does entertain my sight;* Drinking song: *'Tis wine was made to rule the day;* Trio: *When the cock begins to crow.*
(m) *** DG mono 447 156-2 [id.]. (i) Schola Cantorum Basiliensis, August Wenzinger; (ii) Saltire Singers, Instrumental Ens., Hans Oppenheim.

(i) *3 Fantasias for 3 Viols; 9 Fantasias for 4 Viols; Fantasia on one note for 5 viols; In nomine for 6 viols; In nomine for 7 viols;* (ii) *Chacony in G min.*
(m) **(*) DG 447 153-2 [id.]. (i) VCM, Alice Harnoncourt; (ii) E. Concert, Pinnock.

(i) *Harpsichord suites Nos. 1–8;* (ii) *Organ voluntaries: in G; for double organ in D min.*
(m) *** DG 447 154-2 [id.]. (i) Colin Tilney (spinet); (ii) Simon Preston (organ).

Anthems: *Man that is born of woman; O God, thou has cast us out; Lord, how long wilt thou be angry?; O God, thou art my God; O Lord God of hosts; Remember not, Lord, our offences; Thou knowest, Lord, the secrets of our hearts.* Verse anthems: *My beloved spake; My heart is inditing; O sing unto the Lord; Praise the Lord, O Jerusalem; They that go down to the sea in ships. Morning Service in B flat: Benedicte omnia opera; Cantate Domino; Deus miscreatur; Magnificat; Nunc dimittis. Evening service in G min.: Magnificat; Nunc dimittis. Latin Psalm: Jehovah, quam multi sunt hostes mei. Te Deum and Jubilate in D.*
(m) *** DG 447 150-2 (2) [id.]. David Thomas, Christ Church Cathedral, Oxford, Ch., E. Concert, Simon Preston.

(i) *Ode on St Cecilia's Day (Hail! bright Cecilia);* (ii) *The Married Beau: suite for strings in D min.*

(M) **(*) DG 447 149-2 [id.]. (i) Simon Woolf, Esswood, Tatnell, Young, Rippon, Shirley-Quirk, Tiffin Ch., Amb. S., ECO, Mackerras.

Dido and Aeneas (opera; complete).

(M) **(*) DG 447 148-2 [id.]. Troyanos, McDaniel, Armstrong, Johnson, Rogers, Hamburg Monteverdi Ch., N. German R. CO, Mackerras.

'Coronation music for King James II': BLOW: *God spake sometimes in visions; Behold, O God our defender.* LAWES: *Zadok the Priest.* PURCELL: *My heart is inditing; I was glad.* CHILD: *O Lord, grant the King a long life.* TURNER: *The King shall rejoice.*

(M) **(*) DG Dig. 447 155-2 [id.]. Westminster Abbey Ch., O, Simon Preston.

This well-planned survey has the double advantage not only of showing Purcell's diverse genius but also of demonstrating the riches of DG's Archiv catalogue, ranging over nearly 50 years. The first disc here offers distinguished early recordings by the legendary Schola Cantorum Basiliensis, directed by August Wenzinger, who broke new ground in instrumental musical authenticity in the 1950s, and the talented Scottish Saltire Singers (a vocal quartet as impressive individually as in consort), who caused a sensation in Germany on their 1955 visit for a festival of British and German music. DG took the opportunity of recording their highly spontaneous accounts of a collection of Purcell's songs and a movingly intimate verse-anthem, happily adding a first-class accompanying group of German musicians.

The Purcell *Fantasias* and *In nomines* are among the most searching and profound works in all music, and the inspired performances by Wenzinger's group have never been supassed: ethereal, infinitely touching in their refined delicacy of texture. Although this first disc is mono, in no way is it technically inferior, and its natural balance and ambience almost bring an illusion of stereo. On the companion CD, the 1963 Vienna Concentus, led by Alice Harnoncourt (with Nikolaus at the time playing 'second fiddle'), provide a second (stereo) set of performances of these wonderful pieces, darkly sombre in colour, using original instruments with a minimum of vibrato, with bare but never thin textures underpinned by deeply expressive feeling. The stereo is very effective and the balance natural. Then at track 16 there is a splash of cold water in the face as Trevor Pinnock and his English Concert (recorded two decades later) demonstrate modern ideas of authenticity of style and pitch with a brightly astringent and strikingly vital account of the famous *Chacony in G minor.* This transition is not entirely comfortable, and it is better to listen to this piece as a separate item.

Colin Tilney (recorded in 1978) uses a spinet (dating from the end of the seventeenth century) which seems particularly suitable for the *Harpsichord suites.* He is in excellent form and the effect is intimate without losing the music's scale. The playing itself is extremely fine and the documentation is also of considerable interest. The instrument itself delights the ear, and the recording is most natural and uninflated. As a bonus, Simon Preston provides two organ pieces, the first piquantly registered on the instrument at Knole Chapel, Sevenoaks, and the more flamboyant *Double organ voluntary* using the organ at Lübeck Cathedral.

The admirable Christ Church two-disc collection of anthems, verse-anthems and excerpts from service settings was recorded in the London Henry Wood Hall in 1980 and lies at the very kernel of the DG-Archiv Purcell Collection. With some of the music not otherwise available, it is self-recommending. Apart from David Thomas's fine contribution (in the verse-anthems) the soloists come from the choir – and very good they are too, especially the trebles. The performances are full of character, vigorous yet with the widest range of colour and feeling, well projected in a recording which simulates a cathedral ambience yet is naturally focused and well detailed – analogue sound at its best.

A splendid all-male performance of Purcell's joyous *Ode on St Cecilia's Day* (1692) comes from Mackerras with an exceptionally incisive and vigorous choral contribution, matched by fine solo singing. Simon Woolf is ideally cast here, and the 1969 recording is excellent, although the balance between soloists and tutti does not make enough distinction in volume between the smaller and larger groups. This is supplemented by a recording of a suite for strings from *The Married Beau,* played pleasingly enough on modern instruments under Baumgartner, but in no way distinctive. The recording dates from ten years earlier but is fully acceptable.

Mackerras returns to direct a 1967 Hamburg recording of *Dido and Aeneas.* Besides being a scholarly account, it is very vital, with tempi varied more widely and more authentically than usual. There is also the question of ornamentation, and on the whole Mackerras manages more skilfully than most of his rivals. Even so, his ideas for ornamenting Dido's two big arias are marginally less convincing than Anthony Lewis on the famous Decca (originally Oiseau-Lyre) recording with Dame

Janet Baker, with many appoggiaturas and comparatively few turns and trills. He has the edge over Lewis in using Neville Boyling's edition, based on the Tatton Park manuscript, and he adds a few brief extra items from suitable Purcellian sources to fill in the unset passages of the printed libretto. As to the singing, Tatiana Troyanos makes an imposing, gorgeous-toned Dido, and Sheila Armstrong as Belinda, Barry McDaniel as Aeneas and Patricia Johnson all outshine most rival versions. Generally a fine performance; ultimately Dame Janet's Dido (Decca 425 720-2) is so moving that it more than compensates for any shortcomings, although Troyanos's account of the famous lament is undoubtedly moving. The 1967 recording is excellent.

Finally comes a collection of music by Purcell's contemporaries and successors, in refined if not always vibrant performances, with the three works of John Blow among the most impressive pieces, alongside the two Purcell contributions. Blow's extended anthem, *God spake sometime in visions*, opens the proceedings, and here one feels the music-making needs more vigour and thrust, although the choir rises to the closing '*Alleluias*'. Henry Lawes' *Zadok the Priest* is a brief (1 minute 16 seconds) but strong setting, not as memorable as Handel's famous coronation anthem, but here projecting impressively. With a single exception, all this music featured at the Coronation of King James II and, although the original order is not observed on the CD, it can easily be restored by CD programming, as the sequence is given in the accompanying note. However, William Turner's original contribution (*The King shall rejoice*) is lost and is replaced here by an elaborate symphony-anthem in praise of the king, composed some years later for St Cecilia's Day. Although it opens and closes with trumpets, it is essentially an intimate work, with plenty of fine opportunities for the choir's soloists, both individually and grouped. The principal treble, Michael Laird, sings with touching purity of line in *Thou hast giv'n him his heart's desire*, while the penultimate verse, *And why? because the King putteth his own trust, and in the mercy of the most highest he shall not miscarry*, has a beautiful, melancholy choral setting of the words '*he shall not*' that recalls the Purcell of *Dido's lament*. This piece is a real discovery and shows Turner as a composer of distinct personality. Fine, atmospheric, digital recording throughout.

Gardiner Purcell Collection

'*Gardiner Purcell Collection*'.
(M) *** Erato/Warner 4509 96371-2 (8) [id.]. Soloists, Monteverdi Ch. & O, Equale Brass Ens., E. Bar. Soloists, Gardiner.

To commemorate the tercentenary of Purcell's death, the following reissued Erato recordings, all directed with distinction by John Eliot Gardiner, are also available together in a slip-case (at a slightly reduced price); they would make splendid basis for any Purcell collection.

Come, ye sons of art away; Funeral music for Queen Mary (1695).
(M) *** Erato/Warner 4509 96553-2 [id.]. Lott, Brett, Williams, Allen, Monteverdi Ch. & O, Equale Brass Ens., Gardiner.

Come, ye Sons of Art, the most celebrated of Purcell's birthday odes for Queen Mary, is splendidly coupled here with the unforgettable funeral music he wrote on the death of the same monarch. With the Monteverdi Choir at its most incisive and understanding the performances are exemplary, and the recording, though balanced in favour of the instruments, is clear and refined. Among the soloists Thomas Allen is outstanding, while the two counter-tenors give a charming performance of the duet, *Sound the trumpet*. The *Funeral music* includes the well-known *Solemn march* for trumpets and drums, a *Canzona* and simple anthem given at the funeral, and two of Purcell's most magnificent anthems setting the *Funeral sentences*. Recording made in 1976 in Rosslyn Hill Chapel, London.

Ode on St Cecilia's day (Hail! bright Cecilia).
(M) *** Erato/Warner Dig. 4509 96554-2 [id.]. Jennifer Smith, Stafford, Gordon, Elliott, Varcoe, David Thomas, Monteverdi Ch., E. Bar. Soloists, Gardiner.

Gardiner's characteristic vigour and alertness in Purcell come out superbly in this delightful record of the 1692 *St Cecilia Ode* – not as well known as some of the other odes he wrote, but a masterpiece. Soloists and chorus are outstanding even by Gardiner's high standards, and the recording excellent. Recording made in 1982 in the Barbican Concert Hall, London.

Dioclesian; Timothy of Athens.
(M) *** Erato/Warner Dig. 4509 96556-2 (2) [id.]. Dawson, Fisher, Covey-Crump, Elliott, George, Varcoe, Monteverdi Ch., E. Bar. Soloists, Gardiner.

The martial music, shining with trumpets, is what stands out in *Dioclesian*, adapted from a Jacobean play first given in 1622. Gardiner is such a lively conductor, regularly drawing out the effervescence in Purcell's inspiration, that the result is delightfully refreshing, helped by an outstanding team of soloists. The incidental music for *Timon of Athens* offers more buried treasure, including such enchanting inventions as *Hark! how the songsters of the grove*, with its 'Symphony of pipes imitating the chirping of birds', and a fine *Masque for Cupid and Bacchus*, beautifully sung by Lynne Dawson, Gillian Fisher and Stephen Varcoe. Excellent Erato sound. Recordings made in Rosslyn Hill Chapel, London, in 1987.

The Indian Queen (incidental music; complete).
(M) *** Erato/Warner 4509 96551-2 [id.]. Hardy, Fisher, Harris, Smith, Stafford, Hill, Elwes, Varcoe, Thomas, Monteverdi Ch., E. Bar. Soloists, Gardiner.

The reissued Erato version is fully cast and uses an authentic accompanying baroque instrumental group. The choral singing is especially fine, with the close of the work movingly expressive. John Eliot Gardiner's choice of tempi is apt and the soloists are all good, although the men are more strongly characterful than the ladies; nevertheless the lyrical music comes off well. The recording is spacious and well balanced. Recording made in 1979 in Henry Wood Hall, London.

King Arthur (complete).
(M) *** Erato/Warner Dig. 4509 96552-2 (2) [id.]. Jennifer Smith, Gillian Fischer, Priday, Ross, Stafford, Elliot, Varcoe, Monteverdi Ch., E. Bar. Soloists, Gardiner.

Gardiner's solutions to the textual problems carry complete conviction, as for example his placing of the superb *Chaconne in F* at the end instead of the start. Solo singing for the most part is excellent, with Stephen Varcoe outstanding among the men. *Fairest isle* is treated very gently, with Gill Ross, boyish of tone, reserved just for that number. Throughout, the chorus is characteristically fresh and vigorous, and the instrumentalists beautifully marry authentic technique to pure, unabrasive sounds. Digital recording, made in 1983 in St Giles, Cripplegate, London.

The Tempest (incidental music).
(M) *** Erato/Warner 4509 96555-2 [id.]. Jennifer Smith, Hardy, Hall, Elwes, Varcoe, David Thomas, Earle, Monteverdi Ch. & O, Gardiner.

Whether or not Purcell himself wrote this music for Shakespeare's last play (the scholarly arguments are still unresolved), Gardiner demonstrates how delightful it is, a masterly collection, in performances both polished and stylish and with excellent solo and choral singing. At least the overture is clearly Purcell's, and that sets a pattern for a very varied collection of numbers, including three *da capo* arias and a full-length masque celebrating Neptune for Act V. The 1979 recording, made in London's Henry Wood Hall, is full and atmospheric; the words are beautifully clear, and the transfer to CD is admirably natural.

INSTRUMENTAL MUSIC

3 Fantasias for 5 viols; 9 Fantasias for 4 viols; Fantasia on one note for 5 viols; In nomine for 6 viols; In nomine for 7 viols.
(M) *** Virgin Veritas/EMI Dig. VC5 45062-2 [id.]. Fretwork.

It is astonishing that some of the greatest music ever written by an English composer, breathing the same rarefied air as late Beethoven, remained totally unknown for over two centuries. Purcell wrote these *Fantasias* in 1680 at the time of his twenty-first birthday, consciously adopting what was then considered an archaic style, but displaying not only an astonishing contrapuntal skill but also a harmonic and structural adventurousness which leaps the centuries, sounding to us amazingly modern still in its daring chromaticisms. Purcell never had the *Fantasias* published, but by happy chance they survived in manuscript, coming latterly to be regarded as even more revealing examples of the composer's genius than his more fashionable instrumental music. The players of Fretwork use viols with a concern for matching, tuning and balance which is quite exceptional, and their natural expressiveness matches the deeper implications of these masterpieces in microcosm. This makes a superb modern successor to the earlier recordings by Wenzinger and his Schola Cantorum Basiliensis and by Harnoncourt, both included in DG's Archiv Purcell Collection, above.

Pavans 1–4; Beati omnes qui timent Dominum; In guilty night (Saul and the Witch of Endor); Jehova, quam multi sunt hostes mei; My beloved spake; Te Deum & Jubilate (for St Cecilia's Day, 1694); Te Deum; When on my sick bed I languish.
*** Virgin/EMI Dig. VC5 45061-2 [id.]. Taverner Ch., Consort & Players, Andrew Parrott.

Starting with an exceptionally brisk and compelling account of the *Te Deum and Jubilate*, Parrott and his team provide a refreshing and illuminating survey of Purcell's vocal music, punctuated by four of the adventurous, intense *Pavans* which Purcell wrote in his youth, at about the same time as the great sequence of string *Fantasias*. In the relatively brief span of 70 minutes Parrott ranges wide, with the elaborately contrapuntal Latin anthem, *Jehova, quam multi sunt*, one of Purcell's finest, made the more moving, if less grand, with one voice per part, and with the scena about the Witch of Endor, *In guilty night*, thrillingly dramatic. Well-matched singing and playing, atmospherically recorded.

Sonatas of 3 Parts Nos. 1–12, Z.790/801; Sonatas of 4 Parts Nos. 1–10, Z.802/810; Chacony in G min., Z.730; Pavans, Z.438/52; Three parts upon a ground in D, Z.731.
*** Chan. Dig. CHAN 0572/3 [id.]. Purcell Qt.

These authoritative and thoroughly enjoyable accounts of Purcell's *Sonatas* have now been gathered together on two CDs without the miscellaneous items which filled out a third (see our main volume). Whichever format is chosen, this set can be thoroughly recommended.

KEYBOARD MUSIC

Harpsichord suites Nos. 1–8, Z.660/663; 666–9; Ground in G min., Z.221; A new Ground in E min., Z.682; Hornpipe, Z.685.
**(*) HM Dig. HMC 901496 [id.]. Kenneth Gilbert (harpsichord).

Not surprisingly, Kenneth Gilbert gives authoritative, stylish and completely spontaneous accounts of these fine suites. He plays a Couchet-Taskin of 1671. The snag is the reverberant recording, which spreads the harpsichord sound so that it tends to become aurally tiring after a while. The Chandos anthology (CHAN 0571) below gives a splendid example of how pleasingly a harpsichord can sound in this repertoire if the acoustic is more intimate.

'The Purcell Manuscript': *Suites: in A min. & C; Prelude; 3 Minuets; 3 Airs; Thus happy and free; Trumpet minuet; Minuet; 3 Hornpipes.*
*** Virgin/EMI Dig. VC5 45166-2 [id.]. Davitt Moroney (virginals or harpsichord) (with Giovanni DRAGHI: *Suites: in A; C min.; G; G min.;* GIBBONS: *Prelude in G* ***).

This charming disc presents the complete contents of a keyboard lesson-book, discovered in London towards the end of 1993, one of only 15 or 16 Purcell manuscripts to have survived. In his own hand he copied out pieces evidently for a pupil to play. Of the 20 Purcell pieces here, mostly miscellaneous but including *Suites in A minor* and *C major*, five were previously unknown, and six more are arrangements of theatre-pieces unique to this book. Tiny as they are, between them they significantly amplify the picture we have of Purcell's keyboard music. The manuscript also includes a favourite keyboard piece of Orlando Gibbons, the *Prelude in G*, and four suites by Purcell's contemporary, Giovanni Batista Draghi (*c.* 1640–1708), a rival teacher who may well have taken over the pupil's lessons after Purcell's early death. Crisp and bright, Davitt Moroney uses a virginals for the Purcell and two different harpsichords for the more elaborate Draghi pieces.

VOCAL MUSIC

Anthems & Verse anthems: (i) *Behold, I bring you glad tidings; In Thee, O Lord do I put my trust;* (ii) *Jehova, quam multi sunt hostes mei; Lord, how long wilt thou be angry; My beloved spake;* (ii) *O sing unto the Lord a new song; They that go down to the sea in ships; Who hath believed our report.*
(M) *** Decca 444 525-2 [id.]. Soloists, St John's College, Cambridge, Ch., George Guest; (i) with John Scott (organ) (ii) ASMF.

This selection of eight superb ceremonial pieces, intended for Charles II's Chapel Royal, comes from two Argo LPs, recorded a decade apart but with the sound remarkably consistent. On the first occasion the late Inia te Wiata was outstanding, showing his sense of style in *They that go down to the sea in ships*, especially when he combines in duet with Charles Brett; on the second (of which only two out of five anthems are included) it was Paul Esswood and Ian Partridge who stood out.

Alfred Deller Edition: (i) *Come ye sons of art (Ode on the birthday of Queen Mary, 1694);* Anthems: (ii) *My beloved spake;* (iii) *Rejoice in the Lord alway (Bell anthem);* (iv) *Welcome to all the pleasures (Ode on St Cecilia's Day, 1683).*
(M) **(*) Van. 08.5060 71 [id.]. Alfred Deller, Deller Consort; (i) Mark Deller, Mary Thomas, Bevan, Oriana Concert Ch. & O; (ii) Cantelo, English, Bevan; (iii; iv) Kalmar O; (iii) Thomas, Sheppard, Tear, Worthley; Oriana Concert O; (iv) Cantelo, McLoughlin, English, Grundy, Bevan.

An enjoyable anthology, now reissued as part of the Alfred Deller Edition, showing Deller at his finest. The other soloists are good too, especially the tenor, Gerald English. The two anthems make a fine centrepiece, responding to the demand of Charles II for composers 'not to be too solemn' and to 'add symphonies, etc., with instruments' to their sacred vocal music. The *Bell anthem* is so called because of the repeated descending scales in the introduction. The warm, expressively played accompaniments are rather different from the effect one would achieve today with original instruments. The recording is closely balanced; although made at either Walthamstow or Cricklewood Church, the effect is not quite as spacious as one would expect, though pleasingly full.

Come, ye sons of art away; Ode on St Cecilia's day: Welcome to all pleasures. Funeral music for Queen Mary; Funeral sentences.
(M) **(*) Virgin/EMI Veritas Dig. VC5 45159-2 [id.]. Taverner Consort, Ch. & Players, Parrott.

Though Parrott cannot quite match his rival, Trevor Pinnock, in the *St Cecilia* and *Queen Mary* odes, with speeds generally slower and rhythms rather less alert, his are still very fine performances, sounding more intimate as recorded. Parrott takes the view that Purcell would have used a high tenor and not a second counter-tenor in *Sound the trumpet*, and it works well, with John Mark Ainsley joining the counter-tenor, Timothy Wilson. The coupling is not generous but is apt and well contrasted. In his pursuit of authenticity Parrott has eliminated the timpani part from the well-known solemn march for slide trumpets (performed here on sackbutts) in the *Queen Mary Funeral music* – a pity when it becomes far less effective. The central anthem is beautifully done, and it is good also to have the three *Funeral sentence anthems*, written a few years earlier.

Funeral music for Queen Mary: March, Anthem and Canzona; 3 Funeral sentences; 2 Elegies; 2 Coronation anthems; Anthem for Queen Mary's birthday, 1688: Now does the glorious day appear.
*** Sony Dig. SK 66243 [id.]. Kirkby, Tubb, Chance, Bostridge, Richardson, Birchall, Westminster Abbey Ch., New London Consort, Martin Neary (with music by TOLLETT; PAISIBLE; MORLEY; BLOW).

In the ample acoustic of Westminster Abbey, where the music was first performed in 1695, Martin Neary, Purcell's latterday successor as master of music there, gives the same sequence of funeral music as Harry Christophers on his excellent Collins disc, plus an even more generous collection of other works inspired by Queen Mary. The result is less polished, less clear, with the sound of traffic murmuring in from outside, but undeniably more atmospheric, conveying a weightier devotional intensity. One has a genuine sense of a great ceremonial, not just in the funeral music but in the other works too, including the glorious 1688 Birthday ode, *Now does the glorious day appear*, the first that Purcell composed for the new Queen. Preference between this and the Collins disc might be left to a choice between fresh soprano voices, as used in The Sixteen's disc, and the boy trebles of the Abbey Choir, more authentic and beautifully tuned but not quite so precise. The soloists are outstanding, notably the counter-tenor, Michael Chance, and the tenor, Ian Bostridge.

Funeral music for Queen Mary: March, Anthem and Canzona; 3 Funeral sentences; 2 Elegies; Anthem for Queen Mary's birthday, 1692: Love's goddess sure was blind.
*** Collins Dig. 1425-2 [id.]. The Sixteen, Harry Christophers (with MORLEY: *Funeral sentences;* TOLLETT; PAISIBLE: *Marches*).

With the help of the scholar, Bruce Wood, Harry Christophers was here the first on disc to restore the original sequence of musical numbers given at the funeral of Queen Mary in 1695. The well-known *March* and *Canzona*, as well as the beautiful anthem, *Thou know'st, Lord, the secrets of our hearts*, are presented along with the settings of the remaining funeral sentences by Thomas Morley, equally inspired, as well as marches by James Paisible and Thomas Tollett. Authentic military drums are used on their own, so that the marches are less atmospheric than usual, but, with superb, crisply precise singing from the Sixteen in the choral numbers, the whole programme is electric in its intensity. Not least of the delights is the performance of the 1692 Birthday ode, *Love's goddess sure was blind*, given in Bruce Wood's authentically revised text with tenor replacing soprano, as well as two magnificent elegiac anthems to Latin words. Excellent sound, both atmospheric and clear.

Ode on St Cecilia's Day (Hail! bright Cecilia).
(M) *** Virgin/EMI Dig. VC5 45160-2 [id.]. Kirkby, Chance, Kevin Smith, Covey-Crump, Elliott, Grant, George, Thomas, Taverner Ch. & Players, Parrott.

Though Parrott's Virgin/EMI version lacks the exuberance of Gardiner's outstanding Erato issue (see above), in a more reticent way it brings a performance full of incidental delights, particularly vocal ones from a brilliant array of no fewer than twelve solo singers, notably five excellent tenors. With pitch lower than usual, some numbers that normally require counter-tenors can be sung by tenors. Interestingly, Parrott includes the *Voluntary in D minor* for organ before the wonderful aria celebrating that instrument and St Cecilia's sponsorship of it, *O wondrous machine*. It holds up the flow, but at least on CD it can readily be omitted.

Collections

(i) *Abdelazar: suite;* (i; ii) *Cibell for trumpet and strings;* (i) *Dioclesian: Dances from the Masque; Overtures: in D min.; G min.;* (i; ii) *Sonata for trumpet and strings;* (i) *Staircase overture; Suite in G, Z.770; Timon of Athens: Curtain tune;* (Keyboard): (iii) *New Irish tune; New Scotch tune; Sefauchi's farewell; Suite No. 6 in D;* Songs: (iv; i) *Hark how all things; If Love's sweet passion;* (iv; iii) *If music be the food of love; Lord what is man (Divine hymn);* (iv; i) *See even night is here; Thus the ever grateful Spring.*
*** Chan. CHAN 0571 [id.]. (i) Purcell Qt; (ii) Mark Bennett; (iii) Robert Woolley; (iv) Catherine Bott.

Catherine Bott opens this 72-minute concert with a glorious account of one of Purcell's most famous Shakespearean settings, most artfully decorated: *If music be the food of love*; if anything, the later song, *See, even Night herself is here*, is even more ravishing, given an ethereal introduction by the string group. The instrumental items are most rewarding, notably the attractive unpublished suite of dances in G, while the three Overtures are full of plangent character. Robert Woolley's harpsichord contribution is most infectious (the *New Irish tune*, incidentally, is 'Lilliburlero') and he is beautifully recorded, the harpsichord set back in an intimate acoustic and perfectly in scale. There are few better Purcell anthologies than this, and overall the CD gives an ideal introduction to the music of one of the very greatest English composers. The Chandos recording is first class, well up to the standards of the house.

'Pocket Purcell': *Fantasia VIII; Three parts upon a ground;* Anthem: *Rejoice in the Lord, alway.* Funeral sentences: *Man that is born of woman; In the midst of life; Thou knowest Lord.* (Keyboard) *Ground in Gamut; Organ voluntary in D min.* Songs: *Close thine eyes; If music be the food of love;* Duets: *Close thine eyes; Of all the instruments. Suite of theatre music.*
**(*) Virgin/EMI VC5 45116-2 [id.]. Taverner Consort Ch. & Players, Andrew Parrott.

This attempt at an authentic 'Pocket Purcell' nearly comes off. If perhaps it tries to do too many different things in the space of one 66-minute CD, it certainly shows the composer's breadth and variety of achievement. Opening with a four-movement *Suite of theatre music* brightly played (and including the inevitable *Rondeau* from *Abdelazar* which Britten borrowed for his *Young person's guide*). There is also a touching *Fantasia for viols*, a delightful set of keyboard divisions on a *Ground in Gamut*, admirably played by John Toll, and an equally engaging joke-duet for two tenors, *Of all the instruments that are*. The single famous solo song is a welcome inclusion, but Emily Van Evera, for all her agility, does not display quite the charm of Emma Kirkby; the anthem, however, is very fresh in the refined Taverner manner, and the *Funeral sentences* have genuine atmosphere. But the highlight of the collection is the closing item, the *Masque of the Four Seasons* from *The Fairy Queen*, showing Purcell not only at his most exuberant but also at his most melancholy and darkly imaginative, with Jeremy White's splendidly sonorous performance of the great bass aria, *Next, winter comes slowly*. Fine, vivid recording; but this would be far more attractive at mid-price.

Anthems: *Blow up the trumpet in Zion; Hear my prayer, O Lord; I will sing unto the Lord as long as I live; Lord, how long wilt thou be angry?; O God, the King of glory; O God, thou art my God; O God, thou hast cast me out; Remember not, Lord, our offences. Funeral music for Queen Mary (March; Canzone; Funeral sentences: Man that is born of woman; In the midst of life; Thou knowest Lord; March; Queen's Epicideum; Thou Knowest, Lord, the secrets of our hearts; March). Organ voluntaries: in C; D min.; G.*
(BB) ** Naxos Dig. 8.553129 [id.]. Oxford Camerata, Jeremy Summerly; Laurence Cummings.

A worthy attempt to provide a single, budget-priced CD for the tercentenary, celebrating Purcell's church music but also including his *Funeral music for Queen Mary*. In the latter work, a modest brass group appears for the *Marches*, but otherwise the vocal music is organ-accompanied by Laurence Cummings, who also provides acceptable accounts of three solo voluntaries. Although the anthems are sung with warmth and eloquence, the most impressive performance here is the Latin motet, *Jehova, quam multi sunt hostes mei*, with excellent solo contributions from Andrew Carwood and Michael McCarthy. Similarly, it is a soloist who stands out at the centre of the *Funeral music*, with the girl treble Carys-Anne Lane's touching account of *Incassum Lesbia* (the *Queen's Epicedium*). Translations are provided for both works. Pleasing, spacious recording in the Chapel of Hertford College, Oxford. Good value, but this is not in the same class as the two-disc Christ Church collection, above, or indeed the excellent St John's collection of anthems on Decca (444 525-2 – see above).

Songs of welcome and farewell: *O dive custos Auriacae domus (Elegy on the death of Queen Mary); Incassum, Lesbia rogas (The Queen's Epicedium); Raise, raise the voice (Ode for St Cecilia's day); Welcome, vicegerent of the mighty king (Welcome song for Charles II); Why, why are all the Muses mute? (Elegy on the death of Thomas Farmer); Young Thirsis' fate, ye hills and groves, deplore (Elegy on the death of Thomas Farmer); The Fairy Queen: O let me ever, ever weep.*
*** Teldec/Warner Dig. 4509 95068-2 [id.]. Suzie le Blanc, Barbara Borden, Steve Dugardin, Douglas Nasrawi, Harry van der Kamp, Simon Grant, Tragicomedia, Stephen Stubbs & Erin Headley.

Tragicomedia here involves eight talented singers from America and Europe who, with clean, firm voices, sharp attack and precise ensemble, give refreshing performances of a well-varied selection of seven of Purcell's occasional pieces. Those who resist the idea of following Robert King's outstanding series for Hyperion (see our main volume) might opt for this disc, very well recorded. As well as well-known items like the two magnificent *Elegies* for Queen Mary's Funeral, it includes several rarities to cherish. Clean, forward sound to match.

THEATRE MUSIC

Instrumental suites from: *Dioclesian; The Fairy Queen; The Indian Queen; King Arthur*.
**(*) Sony Dig. SK 66169 [id.]. Tafelmusik, Jean Lamon.

Although Purcell's standard of invention is high and these period performances are vital and alive, if not always strong on expressive charm, it seems perverse to offer 71 minutes of mostly instrumental snippets from essentially vocal works. When the trumpets enter, there is an element of grandeur, certainly, but this is not a disc to play all at once. The bright recording has great immediacy.

Dido and Aeneas.
*** Erato/Warner Dig. 4509-98477-2 [id.]. Gens, Berg, Marin-Degor, Brua, Fouchécourt, Les Arts Florissants, William Christie.
**(*) O-L Dig. 436 992-2 [id.]. Bott, Ainsley, Kirkby, Chance, AAM, Hogwood.

On Erato instead of Harmonia Mundi, William Christie and Les Arts Florissants continue their outstanding series of Purcell recordings. The scale is intimate, with one instrument per part, and one voice per part in choruses, yet the emotions conveyed are the opposite of miniature. With his long experience of staging this and other Purcell works, Christie cunningly varies the pace to intensify the drama. Though speeds are generally fast, with tripping rhythms and light textures, bringing out the joy of so many numbers, Christie points an extreme contrast in Dido's two big arias, giving them full expressiveness at measured speeds. In the final exchanges between Dido and Aeneas the hastening speed of the recitative directly reflects the mounting tensions. What then sets this above other period performances is the tragic depth conveyed by Veronique Gens in Dido's great *Lament*, taken very slowly, with the voice drained and agonized in a way that Janet Baker supremely achieved (Decca 425 720-2).

Though not all the other French singers match Gens in her fine English pronunciation, this is an exceptionally strong and well contrasted team of singers with cleanly focused voices. The young Canadian baritone, Nathan Berg, dark and heroic of tone, is outstanding as Aeneas, making this thinly drawn character for once more than a wimp. Textually this version is interesting for supplying two very brief extra numbers to fill in the music missing from the end of Act II, as indicated in the suriviving libretto. Pointing out that, as usually performed, the Act ends in the wrong key (A minor), Bruce Wood supplies a *Chorus of triumph* for the witches - a capable pastiche of Purcell to fit Nahum Tate's text - plus a *Grove's dance*, taken from the *Magicians' dance* written for the play, *Circe*. Together they last less than 90 seconds.

Hogwood's version, using a full complement of period strings instead of the very spare forces of other recent recordings, offers a well-paced, strongly drawn reading featuring an outstanding Dido in Catherine Bott. As in her many recordings with Philip Pickett and the New London Consort, she commandingly exploits her distinctive mezzo, firm and clear in period style but used with subtle degrees of coloration. If in the final Lament she fails to convey as much agony of emotion as such a rival as Véronique Gens (in the William Christie Erato version issued simultaneously with this), that is partly due to Hogwood's faster, less hushed approach to this supreme moment. Otherwise the consistent thoughtfulness of Bott's singing shines out, and the Belinda of Emma Kirkby – herself a pioneer as a period-performance Dido – provides a bright, striking contrast. The tenor Aeneas of

John Mark Ainsley is sensitive and detailed but not always involved-sounding. What for some may be a drawback is the idiosyncratic casting of both the Sorceress as a baritone and of the Sailor as a boy-treble. Such novelties may be refreshing at a first hearing but rarely survive repeated hearings on disc. By contrast, what is particularly successful is having the counter-tenor, Michael Chance, singing the brief role of the Spirit. The recording is full and well balanced, though with the voices slightly distanced, making the central characters a degree less involving.

The Fairy Queen.
(BB) *** Naxos Dig. 8.550660-1 (2) [id.]. Diane Atherton, Kym Amps, Angus Davidson & Soloists, The Scholars Bar. Ens., led by David van Asch.
**(*) EMI Dig. CDS5 55234-2 (2). Bickley, Hunt, Pierard, Crook, Padmore, Wilson-Johnson, Wistreich, L. Schütz Ch., L. Classical Players, Norrington.
**(*) Erato/Warner Dig. 4509 98507-2 (2) [id.]. Bott, Thomas, Schopper, Amsterdam Bar. Ch. & O, Koopman.

For Naxos at bargain price the Scholars Baroque Ensemble offer an outstanding version of Purcell's semi-opera, not always quite as beautifully sung as the finest rivals, but stylishly presented with a refreshing vigour in its scholarly approach. The recording too is exceptionally bright and immediate, regularly giving the illusion of a dramatic entertainment on stage. Logically this version, unlike previous ones, presents the purely instrumental numbers designed as interludes for *A Midsummer Night's Dream* as an appendix, rather than including them during the course of the musical entertainment of five separate masques. So the performance starts with the very brief Overture instead of the First Musick Prelude, and the variety of expression throughout is well caught and contrasted. The humour of the Scene of the Drunken Poet is touched in delightfully without exaggeration, thanks to David van Asch, as is the Dialogue between Corydon and Mopsa, though the counter-tenor, Angus Davidson, has a flutter in the voice that the recording exaggerates. One or two of the others are not always quite steady either. Outstanding among the sopranos are Diane Atherton, singing most beautifully in the Night solo of Act II, and Kym Amps, not only bright and agile in *Hark! the ech'ing air* but making the plaint, *O ever let me weep*, of Act V into the emotional high-point of the whole performance. In the edition specially prepared for the Ensemble it is made the more affecting with lamenting oboe obbligato. Instrumental playing on period instruments is first rate, and the chorus sings consistently with bright, incisive attack. However, those willing to stretch to a full-price set will find Gardiner's recording finer still, with outstanding soloists (DG 419 221-2).

Roger Norrington recorded *The Fairy Queen* following a 'Purcell Experience' weekend, culminating in a concert performance of this inspired but disjointed semi-opera. There is a refinement and polish about the solo singing and the ensemble which reflects that intensive preparation. Where William Christie's earthier reading with Les Arts Florissants reflects experience of stage production, bold, jolly and intense, Norrington's wears its polished manners in a crisp, lightly rhythmic way, helped by the finely honed playing of the London Classical Players. Speeds are often brisk, with rhythms lightly sprung, and the impressive line-up of soloists brings distinctive characterization from such singers as David Wilson-Johnson as the Drunken Poet, Mark Padmore in the tenor songs of Act IV and Lorraine Hunt in *Hark! The ech'ing air*, taken very fast and lightly. There is less fun and less dramatic bite here than in Christie's or Gardiner's versions but, recorded in a spacious acoustic, Norrington's light, clean approach never diminishes Purcell's bubbling inspiration.

Ton Koopman's version is generally rather mellower than its period-performance rivals, starting with a very spacious account of the opening of the overture. Koopman's approach to each successive number is strongly characterized, at times idiosyncratic, but always convincing, and he offers some fine solo singing from the three billed soloists, notably from Catherine Bott whose accounts of *Ye gentle spirits*, taken very slowly, and of *Hark! The ech'ing air* have an unsurpassed richness and intensity. The soloists billed in small print are less consistent, but Koopman's understanding of this enigmatic Purcell masterpiece is never in doubt, including its humour, as in his bluff account of the dialogue of Corydon and Mopsa. He is helped by excellent singing and playing from the Amsterdam Choir and Orchestra.

King Arthur.
⊛ *** Erato/Warner Dig. 4509 98535-2 (2) [id.]. Gens, McFadden, Padmore, Best, Salomaa, Les Arts Florissants, William Christie.

Recorded at sessions immediately after Christie's spectacular production of *King Arthur* in Paris in February 1995 – complete with the Dryden play – this recording of the musical numbers consistently reflects stage experience. Some may not like the crowd noises in the more rollicking numbers but, more than his rivals, Christie brings out the jollity behind much of the piece. Even the pomposo manner of some of the Act Tunes (or interludes) has fun in it, with the panoply of the ceremonial music swaggering along genially. Few will resist the jollity of *Your hay it is mow'd* when the chorus even includes 'gentlemen of the orchestra' in the last verse. Unlike the Gardiner version (also Erato), this one does not in that character number have the bass soloist (Petteri Salomaa) singing in a broad Mummerset dialect, but it is still earthy enough. Christie's soloists are generally warmer and weightier than Gardiner's, notably Véronique Gens as Venus, sustaining Christie's exceptionally slow speed for *Fairest isle*. Otherwise speeds are generally on the fast side, with *Shepherd, shepherd, cease decoying* deliciously light and brisk. The vigour of Purcell's inspiration in this semi-opera has never been more winningly conveyed in a period performance on disc, with full-bodied instrumental sound set against a helpful but relatively dry acoustic, giving immediacy to the drama.

Rachmaninov, Sergei (1873–1943)

Piano concertos Nos. 1 in F sharp min., Op. 1; 4 in G min., Op. 40.
** EMI Dig. CDC5 55188-2 [id.]. Mikhail Rudy, St Petersburg PO, Jansons.

These are cultured rather than high-voltage performances from Mikhail Rudy and the St Petersburg Philharmonic under Mariss Jansons, with some beautiful orchestral playing and pianism of elegance and finesse. Ultimately, however, these are just a bit too laid-back and insufficiently involving to make the pulse quicken. Fine recording, but no challenge to such masters as the composer himself or, nearer our own times, Pletnev in No. 1 and Michelangeli in No. 4.

Piano concertos Nos. 1 in F sharp min., Op. 1; 4 in G min., Op. 40; Rhapsody on a theme of Paganini, Op. 43.
(M) *** Chan. CHAN 6605 [id.]. Earl Wild, RPO, Horenstein.

The Earl Wild set with Horenstein originally derived from RCA. It was produced by Charles Gerhardt and was recorded at the Kingsway Hall in 1965, to be issued subsequently in a subscription series through *Reader's Digest* magazine. The choice of soloist and conductor seemed controversial: Horenstein had a good reputation in the German classics and his musicianship was in no doubt, but to couple him to a young American virtuoso without a background of European music-making was risky. In the event, however, they worked marvellously together, with Horenstein producing an unexpected degree of romantic ardour from the orchestra and both artists finding the natural feeling for the ebb and flow of phrases, so readily demonstrated in the composer's own performances, and which has now become a hallmark of Rachmaninovian interpretation. Earl Wild's technique is prodigious and sometimes (as in the first movement of the *Fourth Concerto*) he almost lets it run away with him. This is not to suggest that the bravura is exhibitionistic for its own sake, and Wild's impetuosity is very involving. What is surprising is how closely the interpretations here seem to be modelled on the composer's own versions – not slavishly, but in broad conception. This applies strikingly to the *First Concerto* and the *Rhapsody*. In the former Ormandy brings rather more romantic subtlety than Horenstein to the gentle secondary theme of the first movement and in the memorably lyrical idea of the finale (with his indulgent but irresistible nudge); in the eighteenth variation of the *Rhapsody*, Horenstein does not quite match Stokowski's flair, although in both instances his rather straighter approach is still idiomatically sensitive and helped by the rich body given to the strings by the Kingsway ambience. All in all, this is a first-class and very rewarding set, and the sumptuousness of the sound belies the age of the recording; its sheer amplitude means that the tapes have had to be transferred at modest level and have a middle and bass emphasis, but the CDs are very believable indeed, and the richness is exactly right for the music. The digital remastering is very successful, the overall balance is convincing, and the sound is full and brilliant. The companion CD including the *Second* and *Third Concertos* (CHAN 6507) is discussed in our main volume.

Piano concerto No. 2 in C min., Op. 18.
(M) *** 447 420-2 [id.]. Sviatoslav Richter, Warsaw PO, Stanislaw Wislocki – TCHAIKOVSKY: *Piano concerto No. 1*. (**)

(i) *Piano concerto No. 2 in C min, Op. 18. Preludes: in B flat; in D min.; in D; in G min.; in E flat; in C min., Op. 23/2–7; in C sharp min., Op. 3/2.*
** RCA Dig. 09026 61679-2 [id.]. Barry Douglas, (i) LSO, Tilson Thomas.

With Richter the long opening melody of the first movement is taken abnormally slowly, and it is only the sense of mastery that he conveys in every note which prevents one from complaining. The slow movement too is spacious – with complete justification this time – and the opening of the finale lets the floodgates open the other way, for Richter chooses a hair-raisingly fast allegro. He does not, however, let himself be rushed in the great secondary melody, so this is a reading of vivid contrasts. The sound is very good. It's a great pity that the performance chosen as the new coupling for DG's series of Legendary Recording performances should be Tchaikovsky's *First Concerto*, with Karajan and the Berlin Philharmonic. The Rachmaninov readily fits this description, but the Tchaikovsky certainly does not, except as an example of a performance where two great artists pull simultaneously in different directions.

Barry Douglas's performance with the LSO and Michael Tilson Thomas does not quite take off: it would be an exaggeration to call it prosaic, but it is less imaginative or tonally refined than one would expect from a Tchaikovsky Competition winner. The set of *Preludes* is more involving. Good recording.

Piano concertos Nos. 2 in C min., Op. 18; 3 in D min., Op. 30.
** Sony Dig. SK 47183 [id.]. Bronfman, Philh. O, Salonen.

Yefim Bronfman with Esa-Pekka Salonen and the Philharmonia Orchestra gives very cultured performances, well prepared and musicianly. But if you have just been listening to the *Third* from William Kapell (see below) or Horowitz and Rachmaninov, this will seem wanting in zest and abandon. Bronfman is an astonishing pianist, but he takes all too few risks here. No quarrels with the excellent orchestral playing or the fine recorded sound.

Piano concerto No. 3 in D min., Op. 30.
(*(**)) VAI mono VAIA IPA 1027 [id.]. William Kapell, Toronto SO, Sir Ernest MacMillan –
    KHACHATURIAN: *Piano concerto.* (**)

During his short life William Kapell was closely identified with this concerto, and this performance was recorded in Toronto at a public concert in 1948 when he would have been in his mid-twenties. It is obvious that he knew Rachmaninov's own recording, and equally obvious that he is also very much his own man. He is one of the very few pianists who can be compared to Horowitz and Rachmaninov himself. He plays the same cadenza as they did. The sound is very poor indeed, but the playing is absolutely electrifying. If only some of the more recent performances the companies have been offering had a tenth its level of energy, sheer abandon and poetic ardour.

Piano concerto No. 3; Rhapsody on a theme of Paganini.
** EMI Dig. CDC7 54880-2 [id.]. Mikhail Rudy, St Petersburg PO, Mariss Jansons.

As in the case of his companion disc, coupling Nos. 1 and 4, the EMI engineers get a magnificent, richly detailed sound and Mariss Jansons draws splendid playing from the St Petersburg Philharmonic. Mikhail Rudy does not play with the electrifying abandon that the composer himself commanded; like Evgeny Kissin (on RCA – see our main volume), his approach is more judicious; but his younger compatriot produces the more subtle and cultured pianism. For all its qualities, this *Third Piano concerto* does not set the pulse racing; and the *Rhapsody on a theme of Paganini* does not begin to match Pletnev's masterly recording with Pešek on Virgin.

(i) *Piano concerto No. 3 in D min., Op. 30. Preludes: Op. 23/2 in B flat; 5 in G min.; 6 in E flat; 9 in E flat min.; 10 in G flat.*
** Teldec/Warner Dig. 9031 73797-2 [id.]. Boris Berezovsky; (i) Philh. O, Inbal.

Boris Berezovsky made a strong impression at the 1990 Leeds Competition with a powerfully wrought and classically pure Beethoven *G major Concerto*, and he went on to win the Tchaikovsky Competition the following year. The high hopes one had for his *Third Piano concerto* are not fully realized; he is a fine Rachmaninov stylist, as his various *Preludes* show, and his technique is more than equal to the cruel demands this concerto makes. He plays the big second cadenza, as do most of the younger keyboard lions, though Rachmaninov was right to prefer the first when he recorded the work himself, as the second is at times quite ugly. But like Kissin, Berezovsky's performance is restrained and cultured: he does not let rip or generate the kind of excitement essential for this concerto's success.

Piano concerto No. 3 in D min., Op. 30; Piano sonata No. 2 in B flat min., Op. 36 (original version).
** Nimbus Dig. NI 5348 [id.]. John Lill, BBC Nat. O of Wales, Tadaaki Otaka.

John Lill couples his account of the Rachmaninov *Third Concerto* with the original version of the *Sonata No. 2 in B flat minor*, the same coupling as favoured by Cécile Ousset in her now-deleted EMI account. Needless to say, Lill's playing commands admiration, but the concerto's fires do not burn fiercely enough. He takes a spacious, almost severe view of the score, which some might find undercharacterized. Like Berezovsky, Bronfman and indeed most pianists nowadays, he plays the second, more big-boned and powerful of the two cadenzas. The BBC National Orchestra of Wales under Tadaaki Otaka give excellent support, and the Nimbus engineers produce eminently respectable results.

Symphonic dances, Op. 45.
*** Everest/Vanguard EVC 9002 [id.]. LSO, Sir Eugene Goossens – STRAVINSKY: *Rite of spring* **

Sir Eugene Goossens conducts a particularly attractive performance of the three *Symphonic dances*. The lyrical secondary theme of the first movement, introduced by the saxophone, is hauntingly nostalgic and the same bitter-sweet lyricism is felt in the '*valse triste*' of the second movement. The burst of passionate feeling and the underlying hint of foreboding are convincingly resolved in the finale. The LSO playing is first class; there is ardour and exuberance, yet ensemble holds crisply together. The recording from the late 1950s is one of the finest of those which Everest made at Walthamstow: full-bodied, clear and with just the right degree of brilliance. But at full price this reissue is uncompetitive.

Symphonic dances, Op. 45; (i) *Vocalise, Op. 34/14.*
(M) *** Sony SMK 57660 [id.]. Novosibirsk PO, Arnold Kaz; (i) with Nelly Lee – STRAVINSKY: *Jeu de cartes.* **(*)

Arnold Kaz is not a household name and Novosibirsk is not on the common tourist trail, but there is nothing offbeat about this performance. Indeed the *Symphonic dances* get a more than respectable performance; the playing of the Novosibirsk Philharmonic is warm and musical, and Arnold Kaz draws imaginative and sensitive phrasing from his players. A far more enjoyable performance than many from better-known orchestras and glossier maestros – and very well recorded. Without disrespect to Nelly Lee, who trained (and now teaches) at St Petersburg, it would have been better to have had the purely instrumental version of *Vocalise*.

Symphony No. 1 in D min., Op. 13; Etudes-tableaux, Op. 39/2, 6, 7 & 9 (orch. Respighi).
*** Nimbus Dig. NI 5311 [id.]. BBC Welsh SO, Tadaaki Otaka.

As we mentioned in our main volume, the BBC Welsh Symphony Orchestra is a totally different body from the one that older listeners may recall from the 1960s and '70s and, under its fine Japanese conductor, Tadaaki Otaka, produces a much more finely focused and warmer sonority. In this characterful and excellently shaped reading of the *First Symphony* they give an excellent account of themselves. The recording, too, is very acceptable, though detail is not as well defined or as cleanly laid out as in some other three-star versions, thanks no doubt to the resonance of the acoustic. Respighi's masterly transcriptions of the four *Etudes-tableaux* comprise an appealing makeweight and may sway many collectors. There is only one alternative listed in our main volume, by Gennady Rozhdestvensky and the LSO (Collins), coupled with the rather overrated Schoenberg transcription of the Brahms *G minor Piano quartet*. This Nimbus disc is not a first choice but still merits three stars. Those wanting a complete set of the three Rachmaninov *Symphonies* can choose between Litton (Virgin VMT7 59279-2) and Previn (EMI CMS7 64530-2), while Ashkenazy's fine Decca series is available on separate discs: 436 479-2, 436 480-2 and 436 481-2 – see our main volume.

Symphony No. 2 in E min., Op. 27.
(M) **(*) Chan. Dig. CHAN 6606 [id.]. SNO, Sir Alexander Gibson.

Gibson and the Scottish National Orchestra have the advantage of an excellent digital recording, made in the Henry Wood Hall in Glasgow. The brass sounds are thrilling, but the slightly recessed balance of the strings is a drawback and there is not the body of tone demonstrated by both the Decca and Pickwick (now Carlton) versions recommended in our main volume. But this is a freshly spontaneous performance and overall the sound is admirably natural, even if it includes some strangely unrhythmic thuds at climaxes (apparently the conductor in his excitement stamping on the podium).

Cello sonata in G min., Op. 19.
** RCA RD 60598 [09026 60598-2]. Janos Starker, Shigeo Neriki – BRAHMS: *Sonata;* SCHUMANN: *Fantasiestücke.* **

The piano part dominates in the Rachmaninov sonata but, even allowing for this, Shigeo Neriki swamps his distinguished partner in their 1990 recording. In any event, the recording is bright and realistic but places us rather too close, with resultant aural fatigue. Its artistic excellence is not in question: Starker is a wonderfully aristocratic player and those who are undeterred by the prospect of sitting in the first row, as it were, might consider this.

Trios élégiaques Nos. 1 in G min., Op. posth.; 2 in D min., Op. 9.
** Chan. Dig. CHAN 9329 [id.]. Bekova Trio.

The Bekova Trio are three sisters. Their well-recorded accounts of these eloquent Rachmaninov scores are musicianly and well shaped without being in any way distinguished or memorable. In short, they serve *vin ordinaire* as opposed to the fine vintage offered by the Beaux Arts in this coupling.

PIANO MUSIC

Elégie, Op. 3/1; Etudes-tableaux, Op. 39/3 & 5; Moments musicaux, Op. 16/3–6; Preludes, Op. 23/1, 2, 5 & 6; Op. 32/12.
(M) *** EMI CD-EMX 2237. Andrei Gavrilov – SCRIABIN: *Preludes.* ***

There is some pretty remarkable playing here, especially in the stormy *B flat major Prelude*, while the *G sharp minor* from Op. 32 has a proper sense of fantasy. More prodigious bravura provides real excitement in the *F sharp minor Etude-tableau*, Op. 39/3, and in the *E minor Moment musical*, while Gavrilov relaxes winningly in the *Andante cantabile* of Op. 16/3 and the *Elégie*. Sometimes his impetuosity almost carries him away, and the piano is placed rather near the listener so that we are nearly taken with him, but there is no doubt about the quality of this recital.

24 Preludes (complete); Piano sonata No. 2 in B flat min., Op. 36.
(BB) *** Decca Double 443 841-2 [id.]. Vladimir Ashkenazy.

Considering his popularity and their quality, it is odd that Rachmaninov's *Preludes* have not been recorded complete more often. Ashkenazy's were the first to appear on CD, with the excellent recording further enhanced. There is superb flair and panache about this playing. Perhaps the stormy *B flat major Prelude*, Op. 23/2, is even more hair-raising in Sviatoslav Richter's hands but, as the *G minor Prelude* demonstrates, Ashkenazy's poetic feeling is second to none. At Double Decca price this sweeps the board. As a bonus, the compact discs offer the *Second Piano sonata*, with Ashkenazy generally following the 1913 original score but with some variants. He plays with great virtuosity and feeling, and the result is a *tour de force*.

Piano sonata No. 2 in B flat min., Op. 35.
** Decca Dig. 440 281-2 [id.]. Peter Jablonski – PROKOFIEV: *Piano sonata No. 7;* SCRIABIN: *Piano sonatas Nos. 5 & 9.* **

Peter Jablonski is a young Swedish pianist of great gifts who has made a considerable name for himself both in his own country and abroad. In this repertoire he faces competition from such keyboard lions as Horowitz, Richter and Pollini, Ashkenazy and Pletnev; and, for all his undoubted talent, he is not in their league. The listener remains relatively unthrilled by this. Let us hope Decca will continue encouraging this artist and cast him more wisely in future repertoire.

Songs: *Child, you are beautiful like a flower; How I languish; Morning; Spring waters.*
** Ph. Dig. 442 536-2 [id.]. Dmitri Hvorostovsky, Mikhail Arkadiev – (with BORODIN) – RIMSKY-KORSAKOV and TCHAIKOVSKY: *Songs.* **

Dmitri Hvorostovsky has captured a wide public following since he won the 'Cardiff Singer of the World Competition', some years back, and he undoubtedly makes a glorious sound. His admirers will want this disc, though the recital as a whole falls short at times in terms of characterization. Good recording.

Raff, Joachim (1822–82)

Symphony No. 1 in D (An das Vaterland), Op. 96.
** Marco Polo Dig. 8.223165 [id.]. Rhenish PO, Friedman.

Symphony No. 2 in C, Op. 140; Overtures: Macbeth; Romeo and Juliet.
** Marco Polo Dig. 8.223630 [id.]. Slovak State PO (Košice), Urs Schneider.

Symphonies Nos. 3 in F, Op. 153 (Im Walde); 10 in F min. (Zur Herbstzeit), Op. 213.
** Marco Polo Dig. 8.223321 [id.]. Slovak State PO (Košice), Urs Schneider.

Symphonies Nos. 3 in F (Im Walde), Op. 153; 4 in G min., Op. 167.
**(*) Hyp. Dig. CDA 66638 [id.]. Milton Keynes CO, Hilary Davan Wetton.

Symphonies Nos. 4 in G min., Op. 167; 11 in A min. (Der Winter), Op. 214.
*(*) Marco Polo Dig. 8.223529 [id.]. Slovak State PO (Košice), Urs Schneider.

Symphony No. 5 in E (Lenore), Op. 177; Overture, Ein feste Burg ist unser Gott, Op. 127.
*(*) Marco Polo Dig. 8.223455 [id.]. Slovak State PO (Košice), Urs Schneider.

Raff was Liszt's assistant at Weimar during the early 1850s and helped prepare his orchestral scores. He enjoyed enormous standing during his lifetime: Ebenezer Prout was not alone in ranking him alongside Wagner and Brahms. His stock fell after his lifetime and he is best remembered for a handful of salon pieces. However, he composed no fewer than eleven symphonies between 1864 and 1883, some of which have excited extravagant praise. (The composer-conductor Bernard Herrman called No. 5, which he recorded for Unicorn, 'one of the finest examples of the Romantic Programme school – it deserves a place alongside the *Symphonie fantastique* of Berlioz, the *Faust Symphony* of Liszt and the *Manfred Symphony* of Tchaikovsky'.) Yet generally speaking Raff's music is pretty bland, though far from unambitious. The *First Symphony (An das Vaterland)*, takes itself very seriously and runs to over 70 minutes. To be frank, it places some strain on the listener's concentration, and many will not stay the course. Though it won a prize during the composer's lifetime, it can seem hard work from a modern perspective! Although the well-played and -recorded *Symphony No. 2 in C* has a certain charm, it is predominantly Mendelssohnian and, although outwardly attractive, it remains pretty insubstantial. Sampling the performances listed above, one is left in no doubt that they are conscientious in approach but are recommendable to the initiate rather than to the unconverted.

Of the eleven symphonies it is the *Fifth (Lenore)* which has captured the imagination of many. No doubt this may be accounted for by the somewhat macabre programme that inspired its finale (the eponymous heroine gallops on horseback with the ghost of her dead lover and is herself abandoned in an open grave). Although the symphony itself is more inspired than some of its companions (it has a particularly eloquent slow movement), it does need rather better advocacy than it receives from the Slovak Philharmonic under Urs Schneider. The Unicorn-Kanchana version by the LPO under Bernard Herrmann (UKCD 2031), made over a quarter of a century ago (and listed in our main volume), has greater polish and allure, and the recording holds up well against this digital newcomer. The Overture, *Ein feste Burg ist unser Gott*, is hardly sufficient to tip the scales in its favour.

The *Eleventh Symphony in A minor* was left incomplete on Raff's death in 1882 and is not otherwise available; the *Fourth* of 1871, available on the Hyperion version under Hilary Davan Wetton, is not sufficiently persuasive. This music has moments of charm but is essentially second-rate and it must have the most expert advocacy and opulent recorded sound if it is to be persuasive; neither of these two versions is really first class. One needs a Beecham to work his magic on these scores. In these performances they are merely amiable, if insignificant.

Rameau, Jean Philippe (1683–1764)

Les Indes galantes: suites for orchestra.
**(*) Ph. Dig. 438 946-2 [id.]. O of 18th Century, Frans Brüggen.

Brüggen and his 'authentic' group have already given us orchestral suites from Rameau's *Les Boréades* and *Dardanus* (Philips 420 240-2), and his performance of the Prologue and four suites from *Les Indes galantes* is equally alive and responsive. The playing can be both pleasingly robust and engagingly delicate (as in the charming *Air pour l'adoration du soleil* from the third suite, *Les Incas du Pérou*). However, the total playing time of this CD is barely 44 minutes, and a comparable selection from Herreweghe and his Chapelle Royale Orchestra on Harmonia Mundi is offered at bargain price (HMA 901130 – see our main volume).

Naïs: orchestral suite. Le Temple de la Gloire: orchestral suite.
*** HM Dig. HMU 907121 [id.]. Philharmonia Bar. O, Nicholas McGegan.

The scurrying opening of the *Overture* to *Naïs* is unexpected, but the trumpets soon enter grandly enough. There is much delightful music here, not least the *Rigaudons* (with tambourines, which reappear later in their own featured number) or the more imposing *Entrée des Lutteurs* and *Air de Triomphe*, with the trumpets returning (they are also used in the later *Minuets*), while the quirky *Chaconne* is lighthearted, too, and is beautifully scored for strings and woodwind. The delicate *Musette* evokes a period French painting, and the brief pair of *Pas de deux* put the violins on points. The *Overture* for *Le Temple de la Gloire* is appropriately imposing, yet with most of the instruments then indulging in blithe trills to set the happy, Arcadian pastoral scene. The following *Air tendre pour les Muses*, with its delicate flute solo, is enchanting and the *Musette* is as evocatively graceful as anything in French ballet music. The *Gigue un peu gaie* is charmingly self-descriptive, but later the trumpets re-enter and the writing becomes more robust. However, yet again the *Pasacaille* is lightened with flutes, although the final movement in this form brings a touch of gentle dignity. The playing by the Philharmonia Baroque Orchestra has ravishing finesse, showing original instruments at their most persuasively delicate, textures always transparent; the ear is continually beguiled by this warm and polished playing, beautifully recorded. A quite lovely disc, and at 71 minutes not a morsel too long.

OPERA-BALLET AND OPERA

Castor et Pollux (complete).
(M) **(*) Erato/Warner Dig. 4509 95311-2 (2) [id.]. Jeffes, Huttenlocher, Jennifer Smith, Buchan,
    Wallington, Parsons, Rees, E. Bach Festival Singers & Bar. O, Charles Farncombe.

Farncombe – with a cast which gave this tragédie lyrique at Covent Garden and in Paris – uses the revised edition of 1754. The allegorical Prologue is eliminated and the rest made tauter and less expansive. The result is certainly dramatic enough and though Farncombe – after a brisk and refreshing account of the Overture – fails to spring rhythms brightly enough, this is an admirable mid-priced set, marked by an agreeably authentic orchestral contribution and some stylish singing, notably from Huttenlocher as Pollux, who was not in the stage performances. Excellently clear, 1982 digital recording with a most attractive ambience, made at All Saints', Tooting. The documentation, too, is admirable.

Castor et Pollux: highlights.
*** HM Dig. HMC 901501 [id.] (from above recording, with Les Arts Florissants, cond. William
    Christie).

It is good to have a one-disc selection from this opera (69 minutes), which should surely tempt those not able to manage Christie's complete set.

Dardanus (complete).
(M) **(*) Erato/Warner 4509 95313-2 (2) [id.]. Gautier, Eda-Pierre, Von Stade, Devlin, Teucer,
    Soyer, Van Dam, Paris Op. Ch. & O, Rayond Leppard.

For the production at the Paris National Opéra, Leppard prepared a satisfying conflation of the very different versions of this important work (which Rameau revised): not just the 1739 score but the score for the 1744 revival, which involved radical rewriting of the last two Acts. Though the French chorus and orchestra (using modern instruments) here fail to perform with quite the rhythmic resilience that Leppard usually achieves on record, the results are refreshing and illuminating, helped by generally fine solo singing and naturally balanced (if not brilliant) 1980 analogue recording, smoothly transferred to CD, with the choral sound quite vivid. José van Dam as Ismenor copes superbly with the high tessitura, and Christiane Eda-Pierre is a radiant Venus. The story may be improbable (as usual), but Rameau was here inspired to some of his most compelling and imaginative writing. Well documented and well worth exploring.

Les Indes galantes (complete).
(M) *** Erato/Warner 4509 95310-2 (3) [id.]. Jennifer Smith, Hartman, Elwes, Devos, Huttenlocher,
    Ens. Vocale à Cœur Joie de Valence, Paillard O, Valence, Paillard.

We have had various selections, suites and transcriptions from Rameau's *ballet héroïque*; now at last comes a splendid complete recording of the whole work, nearly three and a half hours of richly inventive music with hardly a routine bar. When first performed in 1735, the piece comprised the Prologue and three Acts; the third, *Les Fleurs*, was already being revised by the ninth performance, and in 1736 the last Act, *Les Sauvages*, was added and, in its final form, the work met with great success. The plot is complicated but brings opportunities for a splendid tempest and sailors' chorus in Act I, which is set in Turkey. Act II moves to Peru, with a Sun Festival and a volcano erupting (admittedly not as spectacular as the tempest), and Act III with its floral festival is appropriately pastoral and picturesque. Finally we are taken to an Amazonian forest, where the two principal European characters are courting an Indian girl, Zima. She chooses one of her own tribe instead, but a pipe of peace ensures a final reconciliation; there are spectacular trumpets and a triumphant aria from the heroine before the closing ballet. The work is full of lyrical inspiration, and Jennifer Smith sings ravishingly in the roles of Phani, Fatime and Zima, while John Elwes as Tacmas and Adario brings a headily beautiful light-tenor response. Gerda Hartman as Hébé, Emilie and Zaire is charmingly lightweight, if not always quite as secure as Smith, and Philippe Huttenlocher sings all his roles with distinction. The duets and ensembles are often inspired, and the quartet, *Tendre amour*, in

Scene 7, which comes before the ballet divertissement of Act III, is fully worthy of Mozart. Paillard directs the proceedings with much flair and warmth, and the 1974 recording is vividly atmospheric. With first-class documentation and a full translation, this is a set to cherish.

Naïs (complete).
(M) *** Erato/Warner 4509 98532-2 (2) [id.]. Russell, Caley, Caddy, Tomlinson, Jackson, Parsons, Ransome, E. Bach Festival Ch. and Bar. O, McGegan.

Rameau's opera *Naïs* was commissioned by the Opéra to commemorate the Treaty of Aix-la-Chapelle and first appeared in 1749. It tells of Neptune's courtship of the water-nymph Naïs and is full of bold invention. The overture has some astonishing dissonances and syncopations, and the opening battle scenes in which the Heavens are stormed by the Titans and Giants are quite striking. The melodic invention later in the work is not perhaps as elevated or inspired as the very finest Rameau, but it is still of fair quality and at times is very beautiful indeed. The performance, based on the 1980 English Bach Festival production, is full of spirit and uses authentic period instruments to good effect. The work is not long, and the rewards of the music are such as to counterbalance any reservations one might have as to imperfections in ensemble or the like. Admirers of Rameau will need no prompting to acquire this attractive reissue. The unconverted should sample the opening, which will surely delight and surprise. The sound of this 1980 recording (made at Abbey Road) was always excellent; it is strikingly well balanced, but on CD it sounds even more vivid and present, without any loss of ambience or naturalness. Highly recommended.

Rautavaara, Einojuhani (born 1928)

Symphony No. 6 (Vincentiana); (i) Cello concerto; Op. 41.
*** Ondine Dig. ODE 819-2 [id.]. (i) Marko Ylönen; Helsinki PO, Max Pommer.

The *Sixth Symphony* comes from 1992 and is a large-scale work of over 42 minutes. Like Hindemith's *Mathis der Maler Symphony* or Norman Dello Joio's *Triumph of St Joan*, it draws on material from the opera, *Vincent* (1985–7), based, as its title implies, on the life of van Gogh. There is, appropriately enough, no lack of colour, though the score tends to be both eclectic and amorphous. The orchestral scoring itself is quite sumptuous and there is no lack of incident. However, the invention is hardly symphonic and the canvas does not fully sustain interest. It comes with a much earlier and more cogently argued piece, the *Cello concerto* of 1968, which is expertly played by Marko Ylönen. The recording is very impressive, well detailed and present, and is in the demonstration bracket.

Ravel, Maurice (1875–1937)

Alborada del gracioso.
(M) **(*) EMI CDM5 65423-2 [id.]. French Nat. R. O, Stokowski – HOLST: *The Planets* **(*); STRAVINSKY: *Petrushka.* **

Stokowski's idiomatic account from the French National Orchestra dances infectiously and the 1958 recording sounds fuller than the coupled *Planets*; but the fortissimos remain rather harsh, if extremely vivid.

Alborada del gracioso; Boléro; Rapsodie espagnole; Le tombeau de Couperin; La valse.
(BB) *** RCA Navigator 74321 17902-2. Dallas SO, Eduardo Mata.

The late Eduardo Mata was a first-class Ravellian and his Dallas orchestra was in fine shape when these recordings were made, between 1980 and 1984. The performances are both vivid and subtle; *Le tombeau de Couperin* has no want of elegance and the expansive climaxes of *Boléro* and *La valse* are very compelling. The recording has the most spectacular dynamic range; indeed it is in the demonstration class for its period, especially for those who like glittering percussion, while the Dallas hall provides plenty of atmosphere. The *Alborada* flashes, the *Rapsodie* shimmers and there is a balmy underlying patina of sensuous colour. At super-bargain price, this is highly recommendable.

Boléro.
(M) *** DG 447 426-2 [id.]. BPO, Karajan – DEBUSSY: *La Mer;* MUSSORGSKY: *Pictures.* ***

Karajan's 1964 *Boléro* is a marvellously controlled, hypnotically gripping performance, with the Berlin Philharmonic at the top of its form. The reissue is outstanding among DG's Legendary Recordings series of 'Originals', and the couplings both show Karajan at his very finest.

Boléro; Daphnis et Chloé: suite No. 2; Pavane pour une infante défunte; Rapsodie espagnole; La valse.
*(*) Ph. Dig. 438 209-2 [id.]. O de Paris, Semyon Bychkov.

Sumptuous, three-star Philips recording for this anthology, but in every other respect this falls short of excellence. The playing has little real intensity or atmosphere, and the overall results are curiously monochrome. Put this *Rapsodie espagnole* alongside Reiner (RCA GD 60179) or Karajan (DG Gold 439 013-2) or Mata on RCA's super-bargain label (see above), and you are in a totally different world. This is not really competitive at full (or any other) price.

Piano concerto in G; Piano concerto for the left hand in D.
(B) **(*) DG Double 439 666-2 (2) [id.]. Monique Haas, ORTF O, Paul Paray – BARTOK: *Piano concerto No. 3* etc. (**); DEBUSSY: *Préludes, Books I and II.* **(*)

Monique Haas's performances are neat and nicely turned. The *Concerto in G* lacks sparkle in the finale, perhaps, but the *Left hand concerto* has plenty of atmosphere, even if not as dynamic as some. Nevertheless both concertos are more than serviceable and are welcome accounts. They have the advantage of good (1965) recording, and their merits cannot be denied. As a bargain double, with its (mono) Bartók and (stereo) Debussy couplings, this is quite an attractive offering.

(i–ii) *Piano concerto in G; Piano concerto for the left hand;* (ii) *La valse;* (Piano) (i) *Valses nobles et sentimentales.*
(B) *** CfP CD-CFP 4667; TC-CFP 4667. (i) Philip Fowke; (ii) LPO, Baudo.

The performances of the *Concertos* by Philip Fowke with Baudo and the LPO are particularly attractive in the way they bring out the jazzy side of Ravel's inspiration, treating the misplaced accents and syncopations less strictly than some, but with winning results. In the slow movement of the *G major Concerto* the Spanish overtones also come out strongly, and Fowke's solo playing in the *Valses nobles et sentimentales* is clean, bright and rhythmic in a muscular way, without ever becoming brutal or unfeeling; nor does he lack poetry. Baudo and the orchestra also give a strongly characterized reading of *La valse*, brisker than some, with waltz rhythms powerfully inflected. Excellent 1988 recording, made in St Augustine's, Kilburn, vivid and attractively atmospheric; this disc and tape are irresistible at bargain price.

(i; ii) *Piano concerto in G;* (iii) *Ma Mère l'Oye* (suite); (i) *Gaspard de la nuit.*
(B) **(*) DG 439 450-2 [id.]. (i) Martha Argerich; (ii) BPO, Abbado; (iii) Alfons and Aloys Kontarsky.

Argerich's half-tones and clear fingerwork give the *G major Concerto* unusual delicacy, but its urgent virility – with jazz an important element – comes over the more forcefully by contrast. The compromise between coolness and expressiveness in the slow minuet of the middle movement is tantalizingly sensual. Her *Gaspard de la nuit* abounds in character and colour. The *Concerto* balance is very successful. The performance of *Ma Mère l'Oye* from the Kontarsky duo is a useful bonus, although the sound is rather dry and unflattering.

(i) *Daphnis et Chloé* (complete ballet); *Alborada del gracioso; Boléro.*
(M) **(*) DG Dig. 445 519-2 [id.]. LSO, Abbado; (i) with L. Symphony Ch.

The brilliant playing of the LSO under Abbado is a tribute both to his training of the orchestra over his years as music director, and of the players' devotion. The clarity is phenomenal, helped by an exceptionally analytical DG recording which has the widest possible dynamic range – so much so that the pianissimo at the very opening is barely audible for almost thirty seconds. For all its refinement and virtuosity, this is a performance to admire rather than love, lacking the atmospheric warmth that marks, say, the Dutoit version (Decca 400 055-2 – still first choice). There is a lack of mystery in the scene-setting, and in *Daybreak* the flute and piccolo comments fail to suggest bird-song. Yet with an abundance of cueing facilities – 24 tracks plus 58 more index-points – coupled with a very detailed scenario, enjoyment is greatly enhanced.

Ma Mère l'Oye.
(M) *** Mercury 434 343-2 [id.]. Detroit SO, Paray – DEBUSSY: *Ibéria* etc. ***

Paray's gently evocative *Ma Mère l'Oye* is most beautifully played and recorded. The score's calm innocence with its undercurrent of quiet ecstasy is caught perfectly and the translucence of the sound, recorded in Detroit's Ford Auditorium, offers rather more transparency than with the hardly less fine Debussy couplings. *Laidonerette, Empress of the Pagodas* with its impressive stroke on the tam tam is thoroughly exotic, and the closing portrayal of the *Fairy garden* is exquisite. So lustrous is the sound that it is almost impossible to believe the early recording date: 1957.

Rapsodie espagnole.
(B) **(*) BBC Radio Classics BBCRD 9107 [id.]. New Philh. O, Stokowski (with Concert) –
  BRAHMS: *Symphony No. 4*; VAUGHAN WILLIAMS: *Tallis Fantasia.* **(*)

This Stokowski performance, from an Albert Hall concert in May 1974, comes with a Brahms *Fourth* of the highest voltage. The *Rapsodie espagnole* would no doubt cast a spell under concert conditions, but it is by no means as magical or as atmospheric as Reiner's recording of the previous decade, and is by no means as well recorded. The sound has warmth but is wanting in transparency. All the same, this is a disc well worth considering for the sake of a thrilling Brahms *Fourth.*

CHAMBER MUSIC

Introduction and allegro for flute, clarinet, strings and harp.
(***) Testament mono SBT 1053 [id.]. Gleghorn, Lurie, Stockton, Hollywood Qt – CRESTON:
  Quartet; DEBUSSY: *Danse sacrée* etc. TURINA: *La Oración del torero;* VILLA-LOBOS: *Quartet No. 6.* (***)

The Hollywood Quartet's version of the *Introduction and allegro* gives us an example of the exquisite flute playing of Arthur Gleghorn as well as the artistry of Mitchell Lurie and Ann Mason Stockton. A fine performance, sounding remarkably fresh for a 1951 recording. It comes as part of an outstanding anthology of Hollywood Quartet recordings, including their pioneering accounts of Villa-Lobos's *Sixth Quartet* and Creston's *Quartet,* Op. 8.

(i) *Introduction and allegro;* (ii) *Pièce en forme de habanera.*
(B) *** Cala Dig. CACD 1018 (2) [id.]. James Campbell; (i) William Bennett, Ieuan Jones, Allegri
  Qt; (ii) John York – POULENC: *L'invitation au château* etc. ***

These performances are recommendable in their own right, but they come in a particularly valuable two-CD set for the price of one, which includes over two hours of music for wind instruments by Poulenc. It is sheer delight from start to finish and cannot be too strongly recommended.

Introduction and allegro; Pièce en forme de habanera; Pavane pour une Infante défunte.
** EMI Dig. CDC7 54884-2 [id.]. Klinko, Soloists from Paris-Bastille Op. O – DEBUSSY: *Danses
  sacrée et profane* etc. **

Markus Klinko and his colleagues from the Orchestre de l'Opéra de Paris Bastille give one of the most satisfying accounts of Ravel's *Introduction and allegro* to have appeared in recent years. It is beautifully balanced and is done with impeccable taste. The other two pieces, the *Pavane pour une Infante défunte* and the *Pièce en forme de habanera,* are heard in arrangements for flute and harp and violin (less agreeably played by Frédéric Laroque) and for harp alone and are not in the same league.

Ma Mère l'Oye; Rapsodie espagnole (arr. Peter Sadlo).
*** DG Dig. 439 867-2 [id.]. Martha Argerich, Nelson Freire, Peter Sadlo, Edgar Guggeis –
  BARTOK: *Sonata for 2 pianos & percussion.* ***

This is not Ravel's own transcription of *Rapsodie espagnole* or his original *Ma Mère l'Oye* but an arrangement for two pianos and two percussion players to match up with their account of the Bartók *Sonata for two pianos and percussion.* After saying that, it must be added that the additional parts are done with eminently good taste, restraint and musical imagination (they are drawn and adapted from Ravel's own orchestral version) – but, all the same, is there a need for them at all? A disc which it is more interesting to hear once or twice than to repeat.

Piano trio in A min.
** RCA Dig. 09026 68062-2 [id.]. Previn, Rosenfeld, Hoffman – DEBUSSY: *Piano trio.* **
* Erato/Warner Dig. 2292 44937-2 [id.]. Trio Fontenay – FAURE: *Piano trio* **; DEBUSSY: *Piano
  trio.* *
(*) Dorian Dig. DOR 90187 [id.]. Rembrandt Trio – CHAMINADE: *Piano trio No. 1;* SAINT-SAENS:
  Piano trio No. 1. (*)

Older collectors will recall that André Previn made a most distinguished LP recording of the Ravel *Piano trio* with Yong Uck Kim and Ralph Kirschbaum in 1974, coupling it with Shostakovich. RCA would have been better advised to have insisted on a more substantial coupling than the early Debussy *G major Trio,* offered here, which is slight and uncharacteristic of the master. However, fine as this is – and its quality is not in doubt – it is handicapped by the coupling and the fact that the playing time is only 48 minutes. One can do better than this at premium price, notably with the Beaux Arts Trio (Philips 411 141-2).

The Trio Fontenay have made a strong impression in other repertoire, but the magic of Ravel's *Piano trio* eludes them. Part of the problem is the close balance and over-lit aural image, which does not enhance the atmosphere. This represents no serious challenge to the recommendations listed in our main volume.

In the Rembrandt Trio, the pianist Valerie Tryon is the dominant partner. Gérard Kantarjian and Coenraad Bloemendal are pale and colourless by her side. The recording is perfectly acceptable without being distinguished, but artistically the performance is not really competitive.

(i) *Pièce en forme de habanera;* (ii) *Sonata for violin and cello;* (iii) *Sonate posthume;* (iv) *Tzigane;* (v) *Violin sonata.*
** HM/Praga PR 254016 [id.]. (i–iii) Josef Suk; (i; iii) Josef Hála; (ii) André Navarra; (iv–v) David Oistrakh; (iv) Vladimir Yampolsky; (v) Frida Bauer.

The studio performances come from Czech Radio broadcasts, and the others from public concerts. In the lovely, posthumously published *Sonata* (1897), Josef Suk and Josef Hála are not wholly well served by the 1979 recording, which does not accurately reflect Suk's beauty of tone. Moreover Hála is not the most sensitive partner. The *Sonata for violin and cello* is persuasively played by Suk and Navarra, but the 1967 sound, though not scrawny, is wanting in bloom. By far the best thing on this disc is a 1966 performance of the *Violin sonata* by Oistrakh and Frida Bauer whose pianism has all the imagination and sensitivity that are missing in the Suk–Hála partnership. It is far better tonally, though it is not superior to the Philips recording Oistrakh and Bauer made at much the same time. The 1959 mono recording of *Tzigane* with Vladimir Yampolsky as pianist has magnificent authority and virtuosity. Where the Oistrakh–Bauer CD on Philips is still in circulation, that is the one to have, but this is an acceptable alternative.

String quartet in F.
** Erato/Warner Dig. 4509 96361-2 [id.]. Keller Qt – DEBUSSY: *Quartet.* **
(M) ** DG Dig. 445 509-2 [id.]. Emerson Qt – DEBUSSY: *Quartet.* **

String quartet in F; (i) Introduction and allegro for harp, flute, clarinet & string quartet.
**(*) BMG/RCA Dig. 09026 62552-2 [id.]. (i) Galway, Stolzman, Lehwalder; Tokyo Qt – DEBUSSY: *Quartet.* **(*)

The Keller Quartet are a youngish Hungarian group who came to international attention when they won a number of prizes in 1990, including the Evian competition. They offer the usual coupling, the Debussy quartet without any bonus. It is tauter and more dramatic than some of its rivals but, for all its merits, it does not match those rivals in terms of subtlety and tonal finesse.

The Tokyo Quartet are another matter and, although their performance is not entirely free from some self-regarding touches, its tonal finesse is a joy in itself. In the *Introduction and allegro*, the balance tends to favour Galway, to put it mildly, and there is at times a danger of it becoming a flute concerto!

The Emerson have stunning ensemble, precision of attack and body of sound on DG – and are determined not to let us forget it. But their performance, though less affected than that of the Borodin for example, is just too chromium-plated and jet-powered, hardly in tune with Ravel's sensibility. First choice rests with the Carmina Quartet (Denon CO 75164).

PIANO MUSIC

A la manière de Borodine; A la manière de Chabrier; Gaspard de la nuit; Habanera; Jeux d'eaux; Menuet antique; Menuet sur le nom de Haydn; Miroirs; Pavane pour une enfant défunte; Prélude; Sonatine; Le tombeau de Couperin; Valses nobles et sentimentales; (i) Ma Mère l'Oye.
(B) ** Sony SB2K 53528 (2). Philippe Entremont; (i) with Dennis Lee.

Entremont is not insensitive but he sets greater store by clarity of detail than atmosphere. The recording is closely balanced and at times shallow, but sounds much better on CD than on its original LP issue. There are some good things here, but also some less effective moments: at the opening of the second CD *Ondine* seems prosaic by the side of the finest performances. Pascal Rogé offers this repertoire on a Double Decca set (two discs for the price of one) and, though he is at times a little cool, he is better recorded (in 1973/4) and his playing is generally to be preferred (440 836-2).

A la manière de Borodine; A la manière de Chabrier; Gaspard de la nuit; Jeux d'eau; Menuet antique; Menuet sur le nom de Haydn; Miroirs; Pavane pour une enfante défunte; Prélude; Sérénade grotesque; Sonatine; Le tombeau de Couperin; La valse; Valses nobles et sentimentales.
(M) *** Chan. Dig. CHAN 7004/5 [id.]. Louis Lortie.

Chandos have now put Louis Lortie's two Ravel discs together. The first, including *Le tombeau de Couperin, Jeux d'eau, La valse* and the *Valses nobles et sentimentales*, was warmly welcomed in our 1992 edition and we found his *Gaspard de la nuit* with its chilling and atmospheric account of *Le gibet* particularly impressive. Now that these are repackaged at mid-price, let us hope that they will gain the wider dissemination to which their merits entitle them. The Chandos sound, which emanates from The Maltings, Snape, is very realistic and truthful.

A la manière de Borodine; A la manière de Chabrier; Jeux d'eau; Menuet antique; Menuet sur le nom de Haydn; Miroirs; La parade; Pavane pour une infante défunte; Prélude; Sérénade grotesque; Sonatine.
(BB) * Naxos Dig. 8.550683 [id.]. Thiollier.

Whatever, you may ask, is *La parade?* The note suggests that this sequence of dances, some in fragmentary form, derives from the improvisations Ravel made in 1898 for Isadora Duncan's classes, which would place it alongside the *Pavane pour une infante défunte* in date. It certainly does not have the elegance or finish of the *Pavane* or of any of the other pieces on this record, and its presence should not sway the collector in the disc's favour. François-Joël Thiollier's playing falls short of real distinction: he is no match for Lortie, Thibaudet, Crossley or Rogé, and nor is the recorded sound.

Gaspard de la nuit; Sonatine; Valses nobles et sentimentales; La Valse.
** Teldec/Warner Dig. 4509 94539-2 [id.]. Boris Berezowsky.

Boris Berezowksy is a Tchaikovsky Piano Competition prizewinner and an artist of stature. But his Ravel is stronger on temperament than on *tendresse.* In his *Gaspard de la nuit,* the opening of *Ondine* is far from soft enough (it is marked *pianopianissimo* but barely sounds *piano*) and softer dynamics are inconsistent. The middle section of *Le gibet,* marked *pp,* is softer than some other passages marked *ppp,* and his playing is generally very masculine and masterful, as if he is at times trying to eschew the gentle pastel colours and impressionistic mists favoured by some artists. Generally speaking, though it is strongly characterized and has lots of atmosphere, his *Gaspard* is no match for Gavrilov's EMI performance from 1974 or Pogorelich on DG – to look no further than the Slavonic pianists. All the same, there is a lot to admire here and there is no lack of sensibility and feeling. The Teldec recording is very present, bright and well detailed.

Jeux d'eau; Miroirs; Sonatine.
** DG Dig. 439 927-2 [id.]. Lilya Zilberstein – DEBUSSY: *Estampes* etc. **

Lilya Zilberstein is an impressive player and is blessed with formidable technical address and keen sensitivity. In these Ravel pieces, however, she does not always convince. Her *pianissimo* at the beginning of *Jeux d'eau* is a case in point, and she shows little feeling for the tonal subtleties of *Miroirs.* Part of the problem is the recording, which is overlit and close.

VOCAL MUSIC

3 Chansons.
*** Ph. Dig. 438 149-2 [id.]. Monteverdi Ch., O Révolutionnaire et Romantique, Gardiner – FAURE: *Requiem;* DEBUSSY; SAINT-SAENS: *Choral songs.* ***

With his superb choir, Gardiner lightly and crisply touches in the wit and humour behind the two outer songs with their sixteenth-century overtones, and he draws out the lyrical beauty of the central one. A welcome addition to the fascinating group of works chosen by Gardiner as coupling for his expressive reading of the Fauré Requiem.

(i) *Chansons madécasses;* (ii) *Don Quichotte à Dulcinée; 5 mélodies populaires grêcques;* (iii) *3 poèmes de Stéphane Mallarmé.*
(M) *** Sony SMK 64107 [id.]. (i) Norman, Ens. InterContemporain; (ii) José van Dam; (iii) Jill Gomez; BBC SO, Boulez – ROUSSEL: *Symphony No. 3.* **(*)

With three characterful and strongly contrasted soloists, Boulez's collection of Ravel songs with orchestra (including arrangements) makes a delightful mid-priced collection and is especially valuable as the *Don Quichotte* and the *Greek popular songs* are rarely heard in this orchestral form. Van Dam may not be as relaxed here as he was with piano accompaniment (on the HMV recording with Dalton Baldwin which is currently withdrawn), but the dark, firm voice is just as impressive Excellent sound, full and atmospheric, with translations provided; the addition of Boulez's impressive (1975) version of Roussel's *Third Symphony* makes this reissue all the more desirable.

OPERA

L'enfant et les sortilèges (complete).

⊛ (***) Testament mono SBT 1044 [id.]. Nadine Sautereau, André Vessières, Solange Michel, Denise Scharley, Yvon Le Marc'Hadour, Joseph Peyron, Martha Angelici, French Nat. R. Ch. and O, Ernest Bour.

(M) *** EMI Dig. CD-EMX 2241 [id.]. Wyner, Augér, Berbié, Langridge, Bastin, Amb. S., LSO, Previn.

With special access to vintage EMI material, Testament here offer a superlative transfer of the unsurpassed first recording of Ravel's charming one-Acter under Ernest Bour. There is a magic about this performance that completely captivates the listener. Those coming to it with nostalgic feelings for the original 78s (it was never transferred to LP in this country, though it appeared briefly in France) will find their memories have not deceived them. Each part, from Nadine Sautereau's Child, Yvon Le Marc'Hadour's Tom-Cat and Clock and Solange Michel's touching squirrel, to Denise Scharley as the Dragonfly and the Mother, could not be improved upon in character, subtlety and style. The singing and playing of the French Radio forces are vital and imaginative. Ravel's exquisite score is heard to best advantage in this extraordinary transfer, in which every detail in the recording comes across to perfection. Though the 1947 mono sound is short on mystery, the sharpness of focus, with voices firm and immediate, heightens the authentic Frenchness of the reading, both jewelled and purposeful. So far from being vague in an impressionistic way, Ravel's inspiration is revealed in crisp precision, not a dream but a clear, intimate vision of childhood. With no stars but with no weak link, the singers make an outstanding team, helped by sound which, with background hiss eliminated, has astonishing presence. No other version casts quite such a strong spell.

Previn's dramatic and highly spontaneous reading of *L'Enfant* certainly brings out the refreshing charm of this still neglected masterpiece. Helped by a strong and stylish team of soloists, this makes superb entertainment. On CD, the precision and sense of presence of the digital recordings come out the more vividly, with subtle textures clarified and voices – including the odd shout – precisely placed. That precision goes well with Previn's performance, crisply rhythmic rather than atmospherically poetic. Those wanting a modern, digital recording should be well satisfied with this at mid-price, for a full libretto with translation is included.

L'heure espagnole (complete).

(M) (***) EMI mono CDM5 65269-2 [id.]. Duval, Giraudeau, Vieuille, Herent, Clavensy, O. du Théâtre Nat. de l'Opéra-Comique, André Cluytens.

This recording, with Denise Duval as Concepcion and Jean Giraudeau as Gonzalve, was recorded at the Théâtre des Champs-Elysées in 1952 and makes its first appearance in Britain. (There was an excellent Vox LP of the opera with Janine Linda as Concepcion and René Leibowitz conducting, and Ansermet's Decca account appeared not long afterwards; this may have militated against the issue of this disc – the market was less accustomed to duplication then than it is now.) It could not have been withheld on artistic grounds, for this version is every bit as good as Cluytens' account of Stravinsky's *Le rossignol*, made at much the same period. Denise Duval is altogether superb, as is the rest of the cast for that matter. Apart from the quality of the singing, the artists of this period understood the importance of diction and acting. The sound comes up very well indeed, and the set should give much pleasure.

Reinecke, Carl (1824–1910)

Fantasiestücke, Op. 43.

*** EMI Dig. CDC5 55166-2 [id.]. Caussé, Duchable – BEETHOVEN: *Notturno* ***; SCHUBERT: *Arpeggione sonata.* **

Reinecke was among the most prolific of nineteenth-century composers: he had nearly reached Op. 300 by the time of his death in 1910. He succeeded Mendelssohn and Gade as conductor of the Gewandhaus Orchestra and became director of the Leipzig Conservatoire in 1897. His musical language is Schumannesque and the *Fantasiestücke*, Op. 43, which come from 1854–59, the period when Reinecke was musical director at Barmen (now part of Wuppertal), owe an obvious debt to Schumann's *Märchenbilder*. They are very slight, but Caussé and Duchable make out the best possible case for them.

Respighi, Ottorino (1879–1936)

Ancient airs and dances: suites 1 & 3; The Birds (Gli uccelli); 3 Botticelli pictures (Trittico Botticelliano).
🕸 *** DG Dig. 437 533-2 [id.]. Orpheus CO.

These pieces are stunningly played by this remarkable, conductorless ensemble. Their ensemble is terrific, rhythms wonderfully articulate and the music has a sense of joy and vitality. Sensitive accounts of the *Trittico Botticelliano* and an exhilarating, songful one of *The Birds*. Very fine recording, too.

Belfagor overture; 3 Corali; (i) Fantasia slava for piano and orchestra; Toccata for piano and orchestra.
*** Chan. Dig. CHAN 9311 [id.]. (i) Geoffrey Tozer; BBC PO, Downes.

It does not seem so very long ago that Respighi's representation in the catalogue was confined to the three sets of *Ancient airs and dances*, the Roman trilogy, the Botticelli triptych and the *Brazilian impressions*. Now, in no small measure due to the enterprise of Chandos, the situation is completely changed. Hot on the heels of their *Concerto gregoriano*, *Sinfonia drammatica* and the two piano concertos come other rarities. The best thing here is the *Toccata for piano and orchestra*, in which Respighi himself was soloist at its New York première in 1928. Like much else from this composer, it failed to gain a foothold in the repertoire. It is better argued and structured, more inventive and novel, as well as more musically rewarding, than either of the piano concertos, and its appearance on disc cannot be too warmly welcomed. Tozer plays with considerable bravura and panache and the BBC Philharmonic under Sir Edward Downes are admirably supportive. The *Fantasia slava* is shorter and less interesting, and the same goes for the three chorale arrangements. The *Belfagor overture* is the second of the two works Respighi wrote under that name, a re-composition based on themes from his opera, and not the curtain-raiser heard in the theatre. Excellent in every way, and with recording of first-class quality.

Piano concerto in A min.; Concerto in modo misolidio.
** Chan. Dig. CHAN 9285 [id.]. Geoffrey Tozer, BBC PO, Downes.

Respighi wrote his *Piano concerto in A minor* in 1902, just after graduating. At the time he was helping to eke out a living playing the viola in the Russian Imperial Orchestra in St Petersburg, with the result that the influence of Rachmaninov and other Russians is strong. Grieg is echoed in the scherzando writing for the piano, with the very key of the work hinting at the influence of Schumann too. In three movements, lasting 24 minutes, it makes a welcome addition to the catalogue. It is aptly coupled with a much later and more ambitious concertante work with piano, the *Concerto in modo misolidio* ('in the mixolydian mode'), which, like Respighi's *Concerto gregoriano* (with violin), reflects Respighi's fascination with early Church music. Though the slow movement has echoes of Vaughan Williams's *Tallis fantasia*, and the Passacaglia finale brings some much-needed tautness, it remains too diffuse a work, too extended for its material. The impact of Geoffrey Tozer's playing in both works is undermined by the backward balance of the piano, with only the A minor work taking fire.

The Fountains of Rome; The Pines of Rome.
🕸 (M) *** RCA 09026 61401-2 [id.]. Chicago SO, Fritz Reiner – MUSSORGSKY: *Pictures at an exhibition.* *** 🕸
🕸 (M) *** RCA 0926 68079-2 [id.]. Chicago SO, Fritz Reiner – DEBUSSY: *La Mer.* ***

Reiner's legendary recordings of *The Pines* and *Fountains of Rome* were made in Symphony Hall, Chicago, on 24 October 1959, and the insert notes with this CD re-create those remarkable sessions, which followed live performances of Respighi's two finest symphonic poems earlier that same week. The extraordinarily atmospheric performances have never been surpassed since. The opening of the *Fountain of Valle Giulia at dawn* captures a sultry Italian warmth on what was a bleak autumn morning in Chicago, and the slightly recessed orchestral image in the glowing hall acoustics adds to the magic, both here and in *The pines of the Janiculum*, where there is exquisitely rapturous response from the strings. The turning on of the Triton fountain brings an unforced cascade of orchestral brilliance, while the triumphal procession of Neptune's chariot across the heavens which forms the powerful centrepiece of the Trevi portrait has an overwhelmingly spacious grandeur. Similarly the climax of *The pines of the Appian Way* is prepared with subtle control, and when the big moment comes it is electrifying. The marvellous orchestral playing is matched by the skill of RCA's technical team, led by Dick Mohr, and indeed by the new generation of transfer engineers, who have put it all on CD with complete fidelity. Reiner's performances are available with two alternative couplings, Debussy's *La Mer* and his equally riveting (1957) recording of the Mussorgsky/Ravel *Pictures at an exhibition*.

VOCAL MUSIC

La Primavera; (i) *4 Liriche su poesie popolari armene (1921)* (arr. Adriano).
**(*) Marco Polo Dig. 8.223595 [id.]. Henrietta Lednárová, Jana Valásková, Beata Geriová, Miroslav Dvorský, Richard Haan, Vladimir Kubovčic, Slovak Ph. Ch., Slovak RSO (Bratilava); (i) Denisa Slepkovská, Ens., Adriano.

La Primavera is an ambitious cantata for six soloists, chorus and orchestra dating from 1922, the year of the *Concerto gregoriano* (1922). Like the concerto, it was a failure at its first performance and, although Respighi himself attributed this to the limitations of the performance, others, notably Gianandrea Gavazzeni who had been at the première under Bernardino Molinaro, blamed the poet. Constant Zarian was much influenced by Armenian folk poetry, and both works on this CD are settings of his verse. In his memoir of Respighi he speaks of Zarian's text as 'empty, pseudo-poetical banalities ... a sequence of saccharine nonsense'. Whether or not Respighi met Zarian during his years in Russia is unclear but he decided on setting some of his *Voci di Chiesa* in 1917, by which time the poet was living in Istanbul. *La Primavera* takes 45 minutes and is not vintage Respighi. But, although it has moments of bombast and periodically finds his muse on automatic pilot, it has some music of real quality and in particular the sixth of the seven movements; there are evocative and opulently scored orchestral interludes. The *Quattro liriche su poesie popolari armene*, which Respighi wrote for his wife (she was also an authoritative exponent of *La Sensitiva* and *Il Tramonto*, and recorded two of the songs on 78-r.p.m. discs), are simple and affecting. They are given here in Adriano's arrangement for flute, oboe, clarinet, bass clarinet, bassoon, trombone and harp. The performances throughout are more than adequate and are acceptably recorded.

Rimsky-Korsakov, Nikolay (1844–1908)

Antar (Symphony No. 2), Op. 9; Capriccio espagnol, Op. 34; Le Coq d'or (suite); *May night overture; Russian Easter festival overture; Sadko* (musical picture), *Op. 5;* (i) *The Snow Maiden* (suite); *The Tale of Tsar Saltan* (suite).
(B) ** Ph. Duo 442 605-2 (2) [id.]. Rotterdam PO, David Zinman; (i) with Roberta Alexander & Women's Ch.

This is an exceptionally generous and attractive compilation, including most of Rimsky's short orchestral works, plus *Antar*. The Rotterdam orchestra plays with appealing freshness and the recording is pleasingly rich and atmospheric. Zinman secures quite lustrous playing in the *Capriccio*, and he finds plenty of atmosphere and colour in *Sadko* and the *May night overture*, with its languorous opening horn solo. *Antar* again brings beauty and warmth in the orchestral playing, with the central movements appealingly done. But here, as in the *Russian Easter festival overture*, more zest would have been welcome, and in the famous Spanish caprice the adrenalin begins to run only at the end. In the *Snow Maiden suite* the *Dance des oiseaux* brings an effective vocal contribution, but the *Tumblers* are not very boisterous fellows. The sinuously sentient qualities of *Le Coq d'or* are somewhat over-refined, and in *Tsar Saltan* the bumble-bee buzzes gently. Generally there is a lack of charisma here, not helped by recording which, though full and rich, lacks sparkle.

(i) *Scheherazade, Op. 35; May night overture; Christmas Eve (suite); Dubinushka, Op. 62; Russian Easter Festival overture, Op. 36; Sadko (musical picture), Op. 5;* (i) *The Snow Maiden (suite). Tsar Saltan (suite), Op. 57; Tsar Saltan* (opera): *The Flight of the bumblebee.*
(B) **(*) Decca Double 443 464-2 (2) [id.]. SRO, Ansermet, (i) with Geneva Motet Ch.

This is all repertoire for which Ansermet was famous in the early stereo era, and *Scheherazade* must be counted a historic recording. It dates from 1960, and the sound is very impressive for its period, the sonorous rasp of the brass at the start and the weighty spectacle of the shipwreck sequence in the finale, with its splashing tam tam, offers quality regarded as of demonstration standard in its day and not very far short of it now in this newly remastered CD transfer which has a greatly improved focus. The balance of the solo violin (Lorand Fenyves a seductive Scheherazade) is nicely judged and the percussive condiment adds to the brilliance. As to the interpretation, Ansermet's skill as a ballet conductor comes out persuasively. The outer movements with their undoubted sparkle are the finest: the first is dramatic and the last is built steadily to a climax of considerable impact. The music's sinuous qualities are not missed and every bar of the score is alive. *May Night* was recorded a year earlier and the strings have far less lustre; but the *Tsar Saltan suite*, also made in 1959, shows Ansermet and the Decca engineers in glittering form, especially in the recording of brass and woodwind and, if again the upper strings are rather thin, the third movement is certainly vibrant in its colourful detail. The *Flight of the bumblebee* is rather leisurely, but perhaps we are too used to this piece being used as a virtuoso show-off.

The second disc opens with a characteristic (1959) account of the *Russian Easter Festival overture*. The opening has translucent vividness and the whole performance is warmly coloured rather than specially vital, although it is by no means dull. Ansermet is at his finest in the *Christmas Eve suite*, dating from 1958 but only occasionally sounding its age. Rimsky's scenario is particularly delightful with its imagery of a broomstick ride in the snow, a ballet of stars and comets, and a snowstorm of falling stars. Thence to a witches' sabbath, and on to the Imperial Palace and a grand polonaise. Finally, as we draw near home, Christmas day is dawning and we hear the church bell and horns softly intoning a Christmas hymn. This is most enjoyable music and it is played with much affection and that mixture of spontaneity and remarkably graphic orchestral palette which made Ansermet's performances special. It is a great pity that the separate movements of this 24-minute suite are not separately cued. *Dubinushka* is a piece with a revolutionary connection (all the composer's music was banned for a while in consequence of his writing it). It is an engaging if repetitive arrangement of the radical song, *The little oak stick*, treated in polonaise style, and it has some typical brass fanfare writing. Ansermet is (again in 1958) well served here by the engineers, as he is in *Sadko*, an exotic fairy-tale, opening atmospherically but with a colourful storm as its climax, handled with characterisic aplomb. The earliest recording offered here is *The Snow Maiden suite* (1957) and if the best item turns out to be our old friend, the *Dance of the tumblers*, the choral *Dance of the birds* is also an attractive trifle (although the choral singing could be more refined). Once again the sound is remarkably warm and richly coloured, and once again Decca omit to provide cues for individual movements. Yet even allowing for such reservations, this set can certainly be recommended at Double Decca price: the performances and recordings have far more character than David Zinman's Rotterdam compilation on Philips, discussed above.

Scheherazade, Op. 35.
**(*) Decca Dig. 443 703-2 [id.]. Concg. O, Chailly (with STRAVINSKY: *Scherzo fantastique*).

(i) *Scheherazade, Op. 35;* (ii) *Capriccio espagnol, Op. 34.*
**(*) EMI Dig. CDC7 55227-2 [id.]. LPO, Jansons.

(B) **(*) DG Analogue/Dig. 439 443-2 [id.]. (i) Boston SO, Ozawa; (ii) Gothenburg SO, Neeme Järvi.

(BB) ** RCA Navigator 74321 17899-2. (i) Phd. O, Ormandy; (ii) RCA Victor SO, Kondrashin.

(i–ii) *Scheherazade, Op. 35;* (iii–iv) *Capriccio espagnol, Op. 34;* (i; iv) *Russian Easter festival overture, Op. 36.*
(M) *** Ph. 442 643-2 [id.]. (i) Concg. O; (ii) Kondrashin; (iii) LSO; (iv) Markevitch.

Kondrashin's version of *Scheherazade* with the Concertgebouw Orchestra has the advantage of splendid (1980) analogue recorded sound, combining richness and sparkle within exactly the right degree of resonance. Here the personality of Hermann Krebbers (the orchestra's concert-master) very much enters the picture, and his gently seductive portrayal of Scheherazade's narrative creates a strong influence on the overall interpretation. His exquisite playing, especially at the opening and close of the work, is cleverly used by Kondrashin to provide a foil for the expansively vibrant contribution of the orchestra as a whole. The first movement, after Krebbers' tranquil introduction, develops a striking architectural sweep; the second is vivid with colour, the third beguilingly gracious; while in the finale, without taking unusually fast tempi, Kondrashin creates an irresistible forward impulse, leading to a huge climax at the moment of the shipwreck. On CD one notices that inner detail is marginally less sharp than it would be with a digital recording, but the analogue glow and naturalness more than compensate, and the richness of texture is just right for the music. While Mackerras on Telarc (CD 80208) reigns supreme at premium price, Kondrashin becomes a strong first recommendation in the mid-price range, particularly as the couplings are generous, giving an overall playing time of 74 minutes. Markevitch gives an excellent account of the *Russian Easter festival overture* with the same orchestra, with fine orchestral playing to bring out the score's glowing colours in the Amsterdam acoustic. The *Capriccio espagnol*, too, is brilliantly played by the LSO, and here the sound also has considerable allure, with the present CD transfer much more vivid than the original LP.

On EMI Jansons gives us a very well-played and warmly distinctive version of Rimsky-Korsakov's *Scheherazade* with much to recommend it. Good characterization and dramatic feeling; perhaps the slow movement has one or two mannerisms, but these are convincing enough in context. After the big brassy opening, Jansons keeps power in reserve, building up more slowly than usual. What then comes out in all four movements is the way he points rhythms, lilting, bouncy and affectionate, to distinguish this from most other versions. This is a *Scheherazade* that dances winningly, less earnest than usual, often suggesting a smile on the face. Jansons' control of structure leads to a most satisfying resolution at the great climax towards the end of the finale, as the main theme returns *fortissimo*. This is far more than a virtuoso exercise, brilliant as the playing is, with Joakim Svenheden a warmly expressive soloist. The *Capriccio espagnol* brings a similar combination of expressive warmth and exuberance, with the brilliant *Alborada* at the beginning played with such springy rhythms that it is made to sound relaxed, jolly rather than fierce. Not that there is any shortage of biting excitement in either work. The balance between the solo violin and the orchestra could not be judged better, and there is no lack of detail. But the recorded sound has less bloom and transparency than others made in Abbey Road Studio No. 1; climaxes are tight and do not open out enough. It is a bit lacking in front-to-back depth. Tonally, Kondrashin with the Concertgebouw, made in 1980, and Beecham with the RPO, made two decades earlier, sound infinitely richer and fresher. And the Philips mid-priced Kondrashin reissue offers also an extra work.

Chailly's new Decca *Scheherazade* has sound out of Decca's top drawer, with all the glowing lustre one expects from the Concertgebouw acoustics. Jaap van Zweden's assumption of the role of voluptuous storyteller, though sweetly sinuous, does not have a strong enough profile to dominate the narrative, especially at the opening and close of the work. Chailly's reading is spacious rather than electrifying, although the climaxes of the outer movements still readily engulf the listener when the orchestral playing is committed and the orchestral sound has this degree of amplitude and bite. But it is in the sensuous grace of the two central movements, with their translucent detail, that the performance is at its most appealing. The brief Stravinsky encore is beautifully played and has never been recorded more richly.

Ozawa's earlier (1977) *Scheherazade* is an attractive performance, richly recorded. The first movement is strikingly spacious, building to a fine climax; if the last degree of vitality is missing from the central movements, the orchestral playing is warmly vivid. The finale is lively enough, if not earth-shaking in its excitement; the reading as a whole has plenty of colour and atmosphere, however, and is certainly enjoyable. Moreover Järvi's digital *Capriccio espagnol* is a distinctive and worthwhile bonus, brilliantly recorded.

Ormandy's version dates from 1973 and offers some characteristically brilliant playing from the Philadelphia Orchestra: the wind solos in the central movements are superb, especially the principal bassoon and clarinet. The leader, too, is a suitably sinuous storyteller. Ormandy's is a spacious reading, lacking the last degree of drive in the finale, in spite of the bravura orchestral response. But the close-miked recording, though clean and clear, is simply not sumptuous enough to add the necessary glamour to this score, although it must be admitted that at the opening of *The young prince and the young princess* the voluptuous body of Philadelphia string-tone is quite overwhelming and triumphs over the unflattering acoustic. When one turns to the coupled *Capriccio espagnol* one enters a different sound-world; even though that recording was made in 1958 – fourteen years before the main work – its natural resonance ensures bloom on the orchestra and it is still impressive on all counts. As for the performance, it remains among the finest ever put on disc. Kondrashin generates great flair and excitement, with glittering colour and detail in the variations and the *Scene e canto gitano*. In the closing section the ensemble occasionally slips momentarily with Kondrashin's breathless onward thrust, but the excitement is very tangible.

Tsar Saltan, Op. 57: March.
(M) *** Telarc Dig. CD 82015 [id.]. RPO, André Previn – TCHAIKOVSKY: *Symphony No. 5.* ***

The crisp, stylized *March* from *Tsar Saltan*, a fairy-tale piece, makes a delightful bonne-bouche, a welcome if ungenerous fill-up to Previn's outstanding account of the Tchaikovsky *Fifth Symphony*, equally well played and recorded.

Songs: *The clouds begin to scatter; The Octave; The Wave breaks into spray.*
** Ph. Dig. 442 536-2 [id.]. Dmitri Hvorostovsky, Mikhail Arkadiev – (with BORODIN) –
   RACHMANINOV; TCHAIKOVSKY: *Songs.* **

Rimsky-Korsakov wrote over 80 songs, but they are seldom to be heard in the concert hall. Dmitri Hvorostovsky has captivated the public with his glamorous profile and good looks, and he makes a glorious sound in the three songs on his new anthology called '*My restless soul*'. His admirers will want this disc, but the Tchaikovsky and Rachmaninov songs, strong on beauty of sound though they are, are short on characterization. Good recording.

OPERA

Sadko (complete).
*** Ph. Dig. 442 138-2 (3) [id.]. Galusin, Tsidipova, Tarassova, Minjelkiev, Gergalov, Grigorian, Alexashin, Diadkova, Boitsov, Bezzubenkov, Ognovenko, Gassiev, Putilin, Kirov Op. Ch. & O, Gergiev.

Rimsky-Korsakov, a harsh self-critic, thought highly of *Sadko* and even went so far as to say (in 1902, six years before his death), '. . . all my operas (after *Sadko*) have, I think, only temporary interest; then they will completely and finally disappear from the stage and only *The Snow Maiden* will remain associated with my name'. (Admittedly he had yet to compose *The Legend of the Invisible City of Kitezh* and *Le coq d'or* when he passed that judgement.) Despite the absence of dramatic characterization, *Sadko* deserves his approbation, for it is full of melodic inspiration and atmosphere. Rimsky called it an *opera bïlina* and was at pains to stress that it was not so much drama as a sequence of epic scenes. The *bïliny* are epic tales of folk origin dealing with half-legendary heroes, not dissimilar in fact to the *Kalevala*. Indeed there is something of the feeling of a pageant about it: there are seven tableaux, unfolding a simple story in a series of set numbers, scenes and dances. The plot is simple: Sadko is a humble minstrel who competes with the wealthy merchants of Novgorod and attains wealth and happiness by enchanting the Sea King and marrying his daughter.

Whatever its dramatic weaknesses, the score is full of glorious musical invention, sumptuously orchestrated, which puts the listener completely under its spell. There are even one or two reminders of Wagner (Rimsky had heard *The Ring* in St Petersburg in 1889, some six years before its completion), and one realizes how much Debussy and Dukas owed him. The Sadko of Vladimir Galusin is very good, though his handling of dynamic nuance is not always subtle; and the vibrato to which one is long accustomed in Russian sopranos is not worrying in Valentina Tsidipova's portrayal of the Sea Princess, Volkhova. Indeed most of the roles are well sung, with the possible exception of Gegam Grigorian's rather tight-throated Hindu merchant. The conducting of Valery Gergiev is one of the highlights of the performance: he brings great warmth and feeling for colour to the opera. The recording is very good, though there are some stage noises, inevitable in stage performances. There is an excellent video (070 439-1 for the laserdisc; 070 439-3 for the VHS cassette), well directed for the cameras by Brian Large; both sound and vision are particularly impressive on Laserdisc. Thoroughly recommended.

Rodrigo, Joaquín (born 1902)

Concierto de Aranjuez.
(B) ** DG 439 458-2 [id.].Narciso Yepes, Spanish R. & TV O, Alonso – FALLA: *El amor brujo; Nights in the gardens of Spain.* **(*)

Yepes' late-1960s version of the *Concierto* is not very imaginatively conducted by Alonso, who is rhythmically rather stiff in the finale. Yepes is at his finest in the *Adagio*, but the studio recording is dry and unflattering. First choice remains with Bonell and Dutoit on Decca, also coupled with de Falla (430 703-2).

SOLO GUITAR MUSIC

Tres Piezas españolas.
⊛ (BB) *** RCA Navigator Dig. 74321 17903-2. Julian Bream (guitar) – ALBENIZ: *Collection;* GRANADOS: *Collection.* *** ⊛

Rodrigo's *Three Spanish pieces* are characteristically inventive, the central *Passacaglia* quite masterly and the closing *Zapateado* attractively chimerical in Julian Bream's nimble figers. This 1983 recording has been added to what was already one of the finest of all recorded guitar recitals of Spanish music. An outstanding bargain in every way.

PIANO MUSIC

A l'ombre de Torre Bermeja; 2 Berceuses; 4 Estampas Andaluzas; 3 Evocaciones (Homenaje a Joaquin Turina); 4 Piezas; 5 Piezas del Siglo XVI (Diferencias sobre Antonio de Cabezón's Canto del Caballero; 2 Pavans of Muis de Milan; Pavan of Enríquez de Valderrábano; Fantasia que contrahace la harpa de Ludovico of Alonso Mudarra).
*** Collins Dig. 1434-2 [id.]. Artur Pizarro.

It is good to have a highly recommendable single-CD representation of Rodrigo's evocative and sharply characterized piano music, opening with five pieces in which the composer draws on earlier Spanish musicians of the sixteenth century – after the fashion of Ravel's *Le tombeau de Couperin*. Of the two gentle *Berceuses*, the *Berceuse d'Automne*, with its sombre, tolling-bell-like figure, is particularly haunting, while the *Turina Evocations* and the even more overtly Spanish *Estampas Andaluzas* glitteringly demonstrate a wide palette of pianistic colour, especially the brilliant closing *Barquitos de Cádiz*. Artur Pizarro (1990 Leeds prize-winner) is thoroughly at home in this repertoire and plays with panache, demonstrating a striking Spanish sensibility and feeling for dynamic nuance. His account of the last piece on this disc, *A l'ombre de Torre Bermeja* is a *tour de force* of spontaneous pianistic flair. He is splendidly recorded.

Roger-Ducasse, Jean-Jules (1873–1954)

Au jardin de Marguérite: Interlude; Epithalame; Prélude d'un ballet; Suite française.
*** Marco Polo Dig. 8.223641 [id.]. Rheinland-Pfalz Philh. O, Segerstam.

Le joli jeu de furet: Scherzo; Marche française; Nocturne de printemps; Orphée: 3 fragments symphoniques; Petite suite.
*** Marco Polo Dig. 8.223501 [id.]. Rheinland-Pfalz Philh. O, Segerstam.

Those who wish that Ravel and Roussel had been more prolific should investigate these releases. Not that the music of Roger-Ducasse matches Ravel in sheer perfection or strength of personality, or Roussel in terms of inventive vitality or imagination; but he has an elegance and feeling for atmosphere that distinguish Gallic *petits-maîtres*. Roger-Ducasse was a pupil of Fauré and pursued a distinguished career as an inspector of schools alongside his creative activities. BBC listeners will recall his name from odd broadcasts, but he was neglected on record until the French label Cybella issued some of this material, including the wonderfully evocative *Nocturne de printemps*. This and the fragmentary but imaginative *Prélude d'un ballet* show a post-impressionist, Debussy-like figure with a refined feeling for the orchestra; elsewhere, in *Orphée* for example, the influence of d'Indy can be discerned. There are touches of Ravel and in the *Epithalame* something of the high spirits of Les Six. None of this is great music but much of it is rewarding and, in the case of the *Nocturne de printemps*, haunting. It is better crafted than Aubert and more interesting than many other of the lesser French composers of the period. Segerstam has a good feeling for this repertoire and gets atmospheric and sensitive performances from his Baden-Baden forces and good, serviceable recordings from the Marco Polo and radio engineers.

Rorem, Ned (born 1923)

Symphony No. 3.
(B) ** Vox Box 116021–2 (2). Utah SO, Abravanel – HANSON: *Symphony No. 6;* MACDOWELL: *Suite No. 2 (Indian);* SCHUMAN: *Symphony No. 7;* THOMSON: *Louisiana Story: suite.* **

Ned Rorem enjoys something of a cult status on certain American campuses. He is best known for his writing for the voice, and for a memoir, *The Secret Diaries of Ned Rorem*, which enjoyed a *succès de scandale* in the 1960s. It is obvious from this 1960s recording of the *Third Symphony* that he has a good feeling for colour and that his inclination is towards the lyrical phrase rather than the symphonic span. He is not the master of the long-breathed lines or powerfully argued paragraphs in the manner of Piston, Schuman or Diamond. The Utah orchestra under the late Maurice Abravanel give well-prepared performances and are decently recorded.

Rossini, Gioacchino (1792–1868)

Ballet music from: *Mosè; Otello; Le siège de Corinthe; William Tell.*
(B) **(*) Ph. Duo 442 553-2 (2) [id.]. Monte Carlo Op. O, Antonio de Almeida – DONIZETTI: *Ballet music.* ***

The Paris tradition of demanding ballet music in an opera may be irritating for the modern opera-goer (when he or she gets a chance to see a complete performance of these operas); but Rossini's sparkling invention is always worth hearing. Not all of these items are lightweight, and Almeida draws positive and vigorous performances from the Monte Carlo orchestra. The strings often play with finesse, notably in the famous *William Tell ballet*, but the orchestra cannot quite provide the colour and degree of zestful brilliance which makes the Philharmonia Donizetti coupling so attractive.

The sound in Monte Carlo, although agreeable, is less vivid than in London. Even so, this is very enjoyable.

La Boutique fantasque (ballet, arr. Respighi).
(B) *** Decca Dig. 444 109-2 [id.]. Nat. PO, Bonynge – BRITTEN: *Matinées musicales; Soirées musicales.* ***

Bonynge goes for sparkle and momentum above all in Respighi's brilliant arrangement of Rossini. The Decca recording has great brilliance and the orchestral colours glitter within the Kingsway Hall ambience. This account is not as atmospheric at the opening as some versions have been, but it remains infectiously enjoyable and is appropriately part of Decca's Ballet Gala series.

String sonatas Nos. 1–6 (complete).
(BB) *** Decca Double 443 838-2 (2) [id.]. ASMF, Marriner (with CHERUBINI: *Etude No. 2 for French horn and strings* (with Barry Tuckwell); BELLINI: *Oboe concerto in E flat* (with Roger Lord) ***) – DONIZETTI: *String quartet.* ***

We have a very soft spot for the sparkle, elegance and wit of these ASMF performances of the Rossini *String sonatas*, amazingly accomplished products for a twelve-year-old. The parts were only discovered in the Library of Congress just after the Second World War. The music corresponds with previously known works for wind quartet and early string quartets, but there is no doubt that the orignal scoring was for two violins, cello and double-bass which takes a genuine solo role in the *Third Sonata*. Marriner offers them on full orchestral strings but with such finesse and precision of ensemble that the result is all gain. The 1966 recording still sounds remarkably full and natural, and the current CD transfer adds to the feeling of presence. The overall playing time of just over 80 minutes means that the six sonatas will not comfortably fit on a single CD, so the new Double Decca two-for-the-price-of-one format is ideal, with other music added. Apart from the Donizetti *Quartet*, which has an appropriately Rossinian flavour, the two minor concertante works are well worth having, with both Barry Tuckwell (in what is in essence a three-movement horn concertino) and Roger Lord in excellent form.

PIANO MUSIC

Sins of old age (Péchés de Vieillesse): Album de Château: Nos. 2–3; Album pour les enfants adolescents: Nos. 1 & 9; Compositions diverses et esquisses: No. 5. Quelques riens pour album Nos. 3, 5, 12, 16 & 24. Book 9 (Untitled), Nos. 2–3, 5 & 7 (Marche et réminiscences pour mon dernier voyage).
** ASV Dig. CDDCA 901 [id.]. Alberto Portugheis.

Rossini wrote his '*Sins of old age*' (there are more than 150 of them) during the last decade of his life and he favoured bizarre titles after the manner of Satie half a century later, although the writing itself is not usually quirky. The pieces are pleasing enough and some of the best ideas have been borrowed by others (notably the third of the *Riens – Danse sibérienne*, which Respighi used in *La boutique fantasque*). The most ambitious included here is the final item of the programme (*Marche et réminiscences pour mon dernier voyage*), which is a kind of witty pastiche of a funeral march, quoting from eight of Rossini's best-known operas. Alberto Portugheis plays simply and musically but in a deadpan manner, and one feels the need for more sparkle and a sense of whimsy, particularly in the operatic interpolations (the arrival of the *William Tell* galop should surely bring a smile). The recording is of good quality.

Stabat Mater.
(B) (***) DG Double mono 439 684-2 (2) [id.]. Stader, Radev, Haefliger, Borg, Berlin RIAS Chamber Ch., St Edwidge's Cathedral Ch., Berlin RIAS SO, Fricsay – VERDI: *Requiem.* (***)

It is the vitality and drama that come over most strongly in Fricsay's strong and spontaneous account of a work that can easily sound lightweight. Even the tenor's *Cujus animam*, jaunty as the rhythm may be, has a warm, lyrical resilience, and the fervour of the choral singing is matched by the soloists. The effect is very much of compellingly live music-making; and this makes a worthy coupling for Fricsay's electrifying account of the Verdi *Requiem*. The mono recording from the mid-1950s has astonishing vividness and the conveyed atmosphere means that no apologies whatever need be made for the sound.

OPERA

Overtures: *Il barbiere di Siviglia; La cambiale di matrimonio; La gazza ladra; L'Italiana in Algeri;*

Otello; La scala di seta; Semiramide; Le siège de Corinthe; Il signor Bruschino; Tancredi; Torvaldo e Dorliska; Il Turco in Italia; Il viaggio a Reims; William Tell.
(B) *** Decca Double 443 850-2 (2) [id.]. Nat. PO, Riccardo Chailly.

In 1981 Chailly and the National Philharmonic made the first compact disc of Rossini overtures (in the Kingsway Hall), and this was was among the finest of the first generation of Decca recordings in this medium, even if the treble is very brightly lit. These performances are now combined with their further compilation, recorded at Walthamstow Assembly Hall in 1984, to make a desirable bargain double, with each collection presented on a separate disc. The balance of the recordings is truthful, with the orchestral layout very believable. Each of the solo woodwind is naturally placed within the overall perspective, and the violins have a clean focus, with pianissimo detail given striking presence. At times on the first disc there is a degree of digital edge on tuttis, but the bustle from the cellos is particularly engaging. The solo playing is fully worthy of such clear presentation: the cellos at the opening of *William Tell* and the principal oboe and horn in *The Italian girl* and *Il Turco in Italia* respectively all demonstrate that this is an orchestra of London's finest musicians. The wind articulation in *La scala di seta* is admirably clean, although the bow-tapping at the opening of *Il signor Bruschino* is rather lazy. Just occasionally elsewhere the ensemble slips when Chailly lets the exhilaration of the moment triumph over absolute discipline and poise. But if you want precision and virtuosity alone, go to Karajan (DG 439 415-2); under Chailly, the spirit of the music-making conveys spontaneous enjoyment too, especially in *The thieving magpie* and the nicely paced account of *William Tell*. Incidentally, *Il viaggio a Reims* had no overture at its first performance, but one was cobbled together later, drawing on the ballet music from *Le siège de Corinthe*.

The second collection shows a distinct improvement in offering cleaner ensemble and more polished detail while retaining the high spirits and geniality of the first. The novelties, *Otello* – played with great dash – and *Torvaldo e Dorliska*, with its witty interchanges between woodwind and strings, are among the highlights. *Semiramide* is also elegantly played and *The Barber* is nicely elegant. As before, detail is wonderfully clear in the music's gentler sections, yet the sound is noticeably fuller, approaching demonstration standard, with the vivid tuttis bringing only a touch of aggressiveness on the fortissimo strings. However, this can be tamed, and the performances are undoubtedly as infectious as they are stylish. Other, even finer collections of the key overtures are listed in our main volume, for instance Reiner (RCA GD 60387) with his Rosette, but the Double Decca set is certainly worth considering.

Overtures: *Il barbiere di Siviglia; La Cenerentola; La gazza ladra; L'Italiana in Algeri; La scala di seta; Il Signor Bruschino.*
(M) (*) Mercury 434 345-2 [id.]. Minneapolis SO, Antal Dorati – VERDI: Overtures. **

This is one of Mercury's and Dorati's rare failures. The dead acoustics of the Northrop Auditorium are entirely unsuitable for Rossini's warmth and wit and, although the orchestral playing is lively and quite polished, Dorati's deadpan performances compensate little.

Armida (complete).
**(*) Sony Dig. S3K 58968 (3) [id.]. Fleming, Kunde, Francis, Kaasch, Bosi, Zennaro, Fowler,
    D'Arcangelo, Zadvorny, Teatro di Bologna Ch. & O, Gatti.

Recorded live in Bologna in upfront sound with a noisy audience, this Sony set presents an enjoyable account of a curiosity written in the year following *The Barber of Seville*. Just as in *Cenerentola* Rossini eliminated the supernatural from the Cinderella story, so here he demystifies Tasso's legend of the sorceress, Armida. Memorable among the many ensembles are the often-sensuous duets between Armida and her beloved, Ramiro. Under Daniele Gatti the performance is lusty rather than subtle, but Renée Fleming (the much-admired Countess in 1974's *Figaro* at Glyndebourne) sings commandingly in the title-role, with the voice both golden and flexible, extending down to a ripe chest-register. As in other Rossini *opere serie*, four tenors are required – with three of them singing a splendid trio in Act III, a generally stylish team strongly led by Gregory Kunde as Rinaldo. However, first choice for this opera rests with the Koch Europa set with Cecilia Gasdia, Chris Merritt, William Matteuzzi and Bruce Ford, conducted by Scimone (350211 – see our main volume).

Il barbiere di Siviglia (complete).
*** Ph. Dig. 446 448-2 (2) [id.]. Baltsa, Allen, Araiza, Trimarchi, Lloyd, Amb. Op. Ch., ASMF,
    Marriner.
(M) *** EMI CMS7 64162-2 (2) [id.]; (B) CfP *TC-CFPD 4704*. De los Angeles, Alva, Cava,
    Wallace, Bruscantini, Glyndebourne Festival Ch., RPO, Gui.

(B) (**) Decca Double mono 443 536-2 (2) [id.]. Simionato, Misciano, Bastianini, Corena, Siepi, Maggio Musicale Fiorentino Ch. & O, Erede.

Il Barbiere was Sir Neville's first opera recording and he finds a rare sense of fun in Rossini's witty score. His characteristic polish and refinement – beautifully caught in the clear, finely balanced recording – never get in the way of urgent spontaneity, the sparkle of the moment. Thomas Allen as Figaro – far more than a *buffo* figure – and Agnes Baltsa as Rosina – tough and biting too – manage to characterize strongly, even when coping with florid divisions, and though Araiza allows himself too many intrusive aitches he easily outshines latterday rivals, sounding heroic, not at all the small-scale tenorino, but never coarse either. Fine singing too from Robert Lloyd as Basilio.

Victoria de los Angeles is as charming a Rosina as you will ever find: no viper this one, as she claims in *Una voce poco fa*, and that matches the gently rib-nudging humour of what is otherwise a 1962 recording of the Glyndebourne production. It does not fizz as much as other Glyndebourne Rossini on record but, with a characterful line-up of soloists, it is an endearing performance which in its line is unmatched. The recording still sounds well. Tape collectors should be very well satisfied with the CfP equivalent, issued at bargain price on two cassettes in a chunky box, with synopsis instead of libretto. The CDs have been handsomely re-packaged and the documentation is freshly printed.

Recorded in 1956, the Double Decca mono set of *Il barbiere*, well transferred, is well worth hearing for the characterful portrayals of the principal characters, all from vintage Italian singers at their peak. As Rosina, Simionato may not be ideally flexible in her ornamentation, but her rich, robust mezzo could not be more firmly distinctive, and Bastianini offers a comparably strong, purposeful and clean-cut Figaro. Fernando Corena as Bartolo and Cesare Siepi as Basilio make a classic pair of *buffo* basses, even if Siepi's massive *La calunnia* is astonishingly slow. Alvinio Misciano, the least well-known of the principals, is a clear-toned *tenore di grazia*, only occasionally ungainly as Almaviva. Erede conducts a warmly idiomatic reading. However, the top recommendation for this opera is the Decca version with Cecilia Bartoli, who even outshines the memorable Agnes Baltsa on the reissued Marriner set. Like the conductor, Patanè, she brings out all the opera's fun (425 520-2).

Il barbiere di Siviglia: highlights.
*** Teldec/Warner Dig. 4509 93693-2 [id.] (from complete recording, with Hagegård, Larmore, Giménez; cond. López-Cobos).
(M) *(*) Sony Dig. SMK 53501 [id.]. Marilyn Horne, Nucci, Ramey, Dara, Barbacini, La Scala, Milan, Ch. & O, Chailly.

Teldec offers a generous and comprehensive 76-minute selection from a performance which is outstanding in every way. Jennifer Larmore is an enchanting Rosina; the dry-toned Figaro, Håkan Hagegård, brings out the opera's humour, and Raúl Giménez makes a stylishly attractive hero. López-Cobos directs zestfully and the ensembles are as infectious as they are spirited.

Chailly's 1982 set is generally coarse and disappointing, not helped by indifferent playing by the Orchestra of La Scala. This highlights CD is mainly of interest for those wanting to hear Marilyn Horne's formidable Rosina, the voice still agile if not as cleanly focused as it once was. The others do not match her. The selection offers 74 minutes, including the Overture.

La Cenerentola (complete).
*** Teldec/Warner Dig. 4909 94553-2 (2). Larmore, Giménez, Quilico, Corbelli, Scarabelli, ROHOCG Ch. & O, Rizzi.

Cenerentola has been a lucky opera on disc, and Carlo Rizzi's Teldec version with Covent Garden forces is a keen contender with the finest, an obvious first choice for many. Jennifer Larmore makes an enchanting heroine, with her creamily beautiful mezzo both tenderly expressive in cantilena and flawlessly controlled through the most elaborate coloratura passages. She may not be the fire-eating Cenerentola the vibrant Cecilia Bartoli is on Chailly's outstanding Decca version (the clear rival for first choice – 436 902-2), but this is a more smiling character, not least in the final exuberant rondo, *Non più mesta*, which sparkles deliciously, more relaxed than with Bartoli. As Ramiro, Raúl Giménez sings with a commanding sense of style, less youthful but more assured than his rival, while Alessandro Corbelli is far more aptly cast here as Don Magnifico than as Dandini in the Decca set. Here the Dandini of Gino Quilico is youthful and debonair, and Alastair Miles is a magnificent Alidoro. Though the Covent Garden forces cannot quite match the close-knit Bologna team in underlining the comedy as in a live performance, as directed by Carlo Rizzi they are consistently more refined, with more light and shade, bringing out the musical sparkle all the more. Excellent, well-balanced sound.

La Cenerentola: highlights.
(M) ** Sony SMK 53502 [id.]. Terrani, Araiza, Trimarchi, Dara, Ravaglia, W. German R. (male)
      Ch., Cappella Coloniensis, Ferro.

Ferro's *La Cenerentola* lacks that essential ingredient of Rossini: fizzing high spirits. Even the
heroine's brilliant final aria hangs fire, in spite of a generally fine, stylish contribution from Lucia
Valentini Terrani. The cast overall is strong and the selection here runs to 76 minutes. But overall this
is disappointing.

La Donna del lago (complete).
*(*) Ph. Dig. 438 211-2 (2) [id.]. Anderson, Merritt, Dupuy, Blake, La Scala, Milan, Ch. & O, Muti.

Recorded live at La Scala, Milan, in June 1992, the Philips version of this opera, freely adapted from
Scott's novel, *The Lady of the Lake*, is no match for the earlier, Sony version with the Chamber
Orchestra of Europe under Maurizio Pollini (M2K 39311 – see our main volume). Muti here may be
a more forceful conductor but the ensemble work of both chorus and orchestra is rough by
comparison with the Sony performance, recorded after Pesaro Festival performances. The dry Scala
sound is also unkind to the solo voices, exaggerating any unevenness. Rockwell Blake as Umberto
(King James V) is made to sound strangulated as well as wobbly, and Chris Merritt in the other tenor
role of Rodrigo (Roderick di Dhu) is powerful but coarse next to his Sony rival. With sweetness
undermined by uneven production, June Anderson is no match for Katia Ricciarelli at her finest;
Giorgio Surjan pales next to Samuel Ramey, with none of the Scala soloists outshining their
predecessors. Limited sound completes the disappointment.

La gazza ladra: highlights.
(M) * Sony Dig. SMK 53503 [id.]. Ricciarelli, Matteuzzi, Ramey, Di Nissa, D'Intino, Furlanetto,
      Prague Philharmonic Ch., Tyurin RAI SO, Gelmetti.

Here are 74 minutes of music from a recording made at the Rossini Festival in Pesaro in 1989. Alas,
the results are too rough and unstylish to give much pleasure. The cast is strong, with four excellent
singers in the principal roles, but ensemble is slipshod and the recording unflatteringly dry. Of
curiosity value only.

L'Italiana in Algeri: highlights.
(M) *** Sony SMK 53504 [id.] (from complete recording with Terrani, Araiza, Dara, Ganzarolli;
      cond. Ferro).

A first-rate set of highlights (72 minutes) from a first-rate version, with Lucia Valentini Terrani
seductively leading a consistently strong cast. However, first choice for the complete opera remains
with Abbado's brilliant Vienna set with Baltsa, Raimondi and Dara (DG 437 331-2).

Mosè in Egitto (complete).
(M) * Ph. 442 100-2 (2) [id.]. Rossi-Lemeni, Lazzari, Taddei, Filippeschi, De Palma, Danieli,
      Mancini, Ch. & O of Teatro di San Carlo di Napoli, Serafin.

This early (1956) Serafin set first appeared in highlights form on a bargain LP. The recording now
sounds immensely more vivid in its CD format and Serafin's direction is undoubtedly lively. The
ensembles are more impressive than the solo numbers. Rossi-Lemeni as Moses is woolly-sounding,
and Filippeschi, the tenor, is coarse and unimaginative. This costs the same as Scimone's later set on
the same label (Philips 420 109-2 – see our main volume) which is superior in every way.

Il Signor Bruschino (complete).
*** DG Dig. 435 865-2 [id.]. Battle, Ramey, Lopardo, Desderi, Larmore, ECO, Ion Marin.

You could hardly devise a starrier cast for this 'comic farce in one act' than that assembled by DG,
with even the tiny role of the maid, Marianna, taken by Jennifer Larmore. Ion Marin springs
rhythms very persuasively, with the first Cavatina of Gaudenzio, the tutor, so delectably pointed in
the introduction that one registers the character even before Samuel Ramey enters. Kathleen Battle
makes a provocative heroine and the tenor, Frank Lopardo, sings sweetly and freshly as Sofia's lover,
Florville. He is delightfully agile in his patter duet with Filiberto, the innkeeper, taken by Michele
Pertusi. Excellent, well-balanced sound. The single disc (76 minutes) comes complete with libretto,
translation and notes in a double-disc jewel-case.

Tancredi (complete).
(B) *** Naxos Dig. 8.660037/8 [id.]. Podles, Jo, Olsen, Spagnoli, Di Micco, Lendi, Capella Brugensis,
      Brugense Coll. Instrumentale, Alberto Zedda.

The enterprise of Naxos in recording one of the rarer operas of Rossini is triumphantly rewarded, for this set completely displaces the only rival version from Sony (S3K 39073). That came on three full-priced discs against the two here, and the eminent Rossini scholar and conductor, Alberto Zedda, proves a far more resilient, generally brisker and lighter Rossini interpreter than his counterpart. The main glory of the Sony version, recorded live, was the singing of Lella Cuberli as the heroine, Amenaide, but Sumi Jo completely outshines her in dazzlingly clear coloratura, as well as imaginative pointing of phrase, rhythm and words. The mezzo, Ewa Podles, is less characterful, but the voice is firm and rich as well as flexible; but it is the tenor, Stanford Olsen, previously heard as Belmonte on John Eliot Gardiner's recording of *Entführung*, who offers some of the freshest, most stylish and sweetly tuned singing from a Rossini tenor in recent years. The voice is not only agile but evenly produced over its whole range, with no strain on top. The recording is a little lacking in body, but that partly reflects the use of a small orchestra, and the voices come over well. Having a studio rather than a live recording (like the Sony) means that ensembles are crisper and better focused. An Italian libretto is provided but no translation. Instead, a helpful synopsis is geared to the different tracks on the discs; had there been a libretto, this could well have received a Rosette.

Il Turco in Italia: highlights.
(M) **(*) Sony Dig. SMK 53505 [id.]. Ramey, Caballé, Dara, Palacio, Berbié, Amb. Op. Ch., Nat. PO, Chailly.

Chailly's recording is very well conducted, with a good feeling for theatrical timing. His cast is strong. Montserrat Caballé as Fiorilla is less girlish than she might be, and Samuel Ramey is a rather straight-laced Selim, but his singing is splendid; and this makes an enjoyable selection, brightly recorded. Hoever, for the complete opera on turns even more readily to Marriner's Philips version with Sumi Jo, Simone Alaimo and Enrico Fissore (434 129-2).

Arias from *L'assedio di Corinto; Bianca e Faliero; Elisabetta, Regina d'Inghilterra; Guglielmo Tell; Otello; Semiramide; Tancredi.*
(M) **(*) Virgin/EMI CUV5 61139-2 [id.]. Katia Ricciarelli, Lyon Op. Ch. & O, Ferro.

Admirers of this artist will surely want this recital, even if Ricciarelli was past her peak when it was recorded in 1989. There is rare material here, sung with much character and at times (as the opening excerpt from *L'assedio di Corinto* and the *Romanza* from *William Tell* readily show) her line is beautifully spun. But elsewhere, when under stress, she sounds less comfortable, although her vigorous sense of dramatic style often carries the day. Ferro conducts sympathetically and the Lyon Opera Chorus gives good support. The recording is vivid, too.

Roussel, Albert (1869–1937)

Symphony No. 3 in G min., Op. 42.
(M) **(*) DG Dig. 445 512-2 [id.]. O Nat. de France, Bernstein – FRANCK: *Symphony.* **(*)
(M) **(*) Sony SMK 64107 [id.]. NYPO, Boulez – RAVEL: *Chansons.* ***

This is a much less comfortable symphony than the Franck, with which it is coupled, and Bernstein compulsively brings out all its energy and pungent dissonance, and yet he lightens the mood attractively for the high-spirited finale. The 'live' recording is extremely vivid but a shade harsh.

Boulez's first movement is surprisingly slow (it is still pungent but has less electricity and brilliance than Bernstein's CBS disc, just reissued). The slow movement, however, has great warmth and humanity. Unfortunately, the recording, made in the Manhattan Center in 1975, is not as first rate as the performance: the acoustic is reverberant and there is plenty of body, but the upper strings are rather shrill. Nevertheless the CD sounds much better than the LP did, with more weight to balance the bright upper range; with the splendid Ravel couplings, this makes an alternative mid-priced recommendation.

Symphonies Nos. 3 in G min., Op. 42; 4 in A, Op. 53; Bacchus et Ariane, Op. 43: suite No. 2; Sinfonietta for string orchestra, Op. 52.
**(*) Chan. Dig. CHAN 7007 [id.]. Detroit SO, Neeme Järvi.

A more logical coupling of previously available material coupled with other French masters. Not absolutely ideal performances, perhaps, but very much better than most of the alternatives, and certainly very recommendable, given the good sound and Järvi's obvious enthusiasm for this repertoire.

Rubbra, Edmund (1901–86)

(i) *Viola concerto, Op. 75;* (ii) *Violin concerto, Op. 101.*
*** Conifer Dig. CDCF225 [id.]. (i) Rivka Golani; (ii) Tasmin Little; RPO, Vernon Handley.

With the exception of his *Sinfonia concertante* for piano and orchestra, all the Rubbra concertos come from the 1950s. The *Viola concerto* was written for William Primrose in 1952, and the *Violin concerto* for Endré Wolf in 1959. (The *Piano concerto in G major* is now in urgent need of a modern recording, though until that comes along Testament should reissue the 1957 Denis Matthews–Malcolm Sargent account.) The *Viola concerto* is a work of euphony and depth; and Rivka Golani's account is a first recording. Tasmin Little's version of the *Violin concerto* has an effortless and masterly virtuosity; she is well recorded and the RPO under Vernon Handley give excellent support. This now displaces Carl Pini on Unicorn.

Rubinstein, Anton (1829–94)

Piano concertos Nos. 1 in E, Op. 25; 2 in F, Op. 35.
** Marco Polo Dig. 8.223456 [id.]. Joseph Banowetz, Czech State PO, Alfred Walter.

Piano concerto No. 5 in E flat, Op. 94; Caprice russe, Op. 102.
**(*) Marco Polo Dig. 8.223489 [id.]. Joseph Banowetz, Slovak RSO (Bratislava), Stankovsky.

Rubinstein was the first composer of concertos in Russia and was enormously prolific. His *First Piano concerto in E major*, dating from 1850, is greatly indebted to Mendelssohn though it is more prolix. As David Brown puts it, Rubinstein's 'enormous facility was unhindered by originality, and he was unashamedly eclectic and conservative'. The *Third Piano concerto in G* (1853–4) is more concentrated, and there is a recording of the *Fourth in D minor* (1864) by his pupil, Josef Hofmann (see Recitals, below); no later pianist has equalled that. By the mid-1860s Rubinstein's perspective had broadened (rather than deepened), and the *Fifth Piano concerto in E flat* (1874) is an ambitious piece, longer than the *Emperor* and almost as long as the Brahms *D minor*. No less a pianist than Joseph Levinne championed it during the early years of the century and no doubt its prodigious technical demands (it was not dedicated to Alkan for nothing) have stood in the way of its wider dissemination. It has all the fluent lyricism one expects of Rubinstein, though most of its ideas, attractive enough in themselves, overstay their welcome.

Joseph Banowetz has now recorded all the concertos for Marco Polo and, although the orchestral support and the recording do not rise much above routine, there is nothing ordinary about Banowetz's pianism. The *Fifth*, at least, is worth investigating (for the *Fourth*, one should turn to Hofmann.) The *Caprice russe* was written four years after the concerto, but the fires were obviously blazing less fiercely. All the same, this is an issue of some interest, and the solo playing has conviction.

Symphony No. 1 (Ivan the Terrible).
* Marco Polo Dig. 8.223277 [id.]. CSS PO, Stankovsky.

Symphony No. 2 in C (Ocean), Op. 42.
* Marco Polo Dig. 8.223449 [id.]. Slovak PO, Gunzenhauser.

Symphony No. 3 in A, Op. 56; Eroica fantasia, Op. 110.
* Marco Polo Dig. 8.223576 [id.]. Slovak RSO (Bratislava), Robert Stankovsky.

Symphony No. 4 in E flat (Dramatic).
* Marco Polo Dig. 8.223319 [id.]. CSS PO, Stankovsky.

Symphony No. 5 in G min., Op. 107; Overture, Dmitri Donskoi; Faust, Op. 68.
* Marco Polo Dig. 8.223320 [id.]. Georges Enescu State PO, Andreescu.

Symphony No. 6 in A min., Op. 111.
** Marco Polo Dig. 8.220489 [id.]. Philh. Hungarica O, Varga.

In the words of David Brown, our leading authority on Russian music, 'no one could pretend [Rubinstein's] symphonies merit even a modest toehold in our regular concert repertoire ... Insofar as a Rubinstein style can be identified, it is a compound of Mendelssohn and Schumann, the more radical of mid-century composers like Liszt and Berlioz being firmly excluded.' The symphonies are certainly of lesser interest than the piano concertos, and readers who don't know the Balakirev, Kalinnikov or Arensky symphonies should explore those first. The *Ocean Symphony*, written in 1851 in four movements, revised twice in 1863 when two further movements were added, and again in 1880, was popular in its day and in its final form runs to seven movements. Professor Brown calls it 'a watery Mendelssohnian piece' and it is not easy to sustain unwavering attention over the course of its 72 + minutes. The Slovak Philharmonic Orchestra of Bratislava under Stephen Gunzenhauser do their best, and the 1986 recording is more than adequate.

Music of lesser stature calls for interpreters of quality and flair if it is to have a chance of convincing the listener. The *Third Symphony* is not endowed with ideas of interest or even with personality and, although it is not entirely without merit, it is mostly predictable stuff. The playing by the Bratislava Radio Symphony Orchestra is fairly routine and Robert Stankovsky brings few insights to the score. The *Eroica Fantasia*, as its high opus number suggests, is a later and, if anything, even less inspired work.

The *Fourth Symphony*, the *Dramatic*, of 1874 runs to some 65 minutes and is not a strong work. Its thematic substance is pretty thin and, despite its epic pretensions, there is little sense of sweep or consistency of inspiration. The *Fifth* of 1880 sprawls less; it lasts under 40 minutes and its ideas, some of them folk-inspired, are held together better. The playing of the Georges Enescu Philharmonic Orchestra of Bucharest under Horia Andreescu is more persuasive than that of its companions. The *Symphony No. 6 in A minor*, composed in 1886, has much stronger material but, despite a relatively strong first movement, the work disintegrates towards the end. However, of the six symphonies this is the one to investigate. The performance and recording are not earth-shattering but are perfectly acceptable.

Sæverud, Harald (1897–1993)

5 Capricci, Op. 1; Easy Pieces for piano, Opp. 14 & 18; Siljuslåtten, Op. 17.
**(*) Victoria Dig. VCD 19084 [id.]. Smebye.

Sæverud's piano music is little known outside Norway and it deserves better. It has a fresh, naïve directness which is touching and, like so much else by Sæverud, is full of character. Pieces like the *Silkesokk-slåtten* (*Silk-sock dance*), composed on the birth of the composer's son, Ketil Hvoslef, and the *Småfuglsvals* (*Little bird's waltz*) are quite captivating. Nielsen is said to have admired Sæverud's early music, and readers with a taste for the Danish master will enjoy this admittedly limited but engaging repertoire. The pianist Einar Henning Smebye plays with intelligence and subtlety, though the recording is too close to be ideal.

Songs and dances from Siljustøl (Slåtter og stev fra Siljustøl), Opp. 21–22, 24 & 25.
**(*) Victoria Dig. VCD 19085 [id.]. Smebye.

Siljustøl was the name of Sæverud's home outside Bergen, and he composed these simple sets of *Slåtter og stev fra Siljustøl* (*Songs and dances from Siljustøl*) during the 1940s (save for Op. 25, which was written during the following decade). All these pieces are short and most are delightful, but they are best dipped into, rather than heard straight off. Smebye plays with style and relish and, apart from the rather close balance (one hears him stamping the pedals at one point), the recording is very clear and clean.

Saint-Saëns, Camille (1835–1921)

(i) *Carnival of the animals;* (ii) *Le Cygne; Piano concertos Nos.* (iii) *2 in G min., Op. 22;* (iv) *4 in C min., Op. 44;* (v) *Violin concerto No. 3 in B min., Op. 61;* (vi) *Danse macabre, Op. 40;* (v) *Introduction and Rondo capriccioso, Op. 28;* (vii) *Symphony No. 3 in C min. (Organ), Op. 78.*
(B) **(*) Ph. Duo 442 608-2 (2) [id.]. (i) Villa, Jennings, Pittsburgh SO, Previn; (ii) Gendron, Gallion; (iii) Davidovich, Concg. O, Järvi; (iv) Campanella, Monte Carlo Op. O, Ceccato; (v) Szeryng, Monte Carlo Op. O, Remoortel; (vi) Concg. O, Haitink; (vii) Chorzempa, Rotterdam PO, Edo de Waart.

This inexpensive Duo collection is described as 'The Best of Saint-Saëns' and indeed it does include good and sometimes fine performances of many of the composer's most attractive orchestral and concertante works. Notable here is Previn's (1980) digital recording of the *Carnival of the animals*, as fine as almost any available. The music is played with infectious rhythmic spring and great refinement. It is a mark of the finesse of this performance – as well as its polish – that the memorable cello solo of *Le Cygne* is so naturally presented, with the engineers refusing to spotlight the soloist. The shading of half-tones in Anne Martindale Williams's exquisitely beautiful playing is made all the more tenderly affecting. And, to please everyone, Philips have also included a second performance by the inestimable Maurice Gendron, when this famous piece is treated to a more assertively romantic but no less elegant presentation. Bella Davidovich then gives a most sympathetic account of the *G minor Piano concerto* and she draws pleasing tone-quality from the instrument, even if she lacks the last degree of brilliance and flair, notably in the Scherzo. Yet she has the advantage of excellent orchestral support from the Concertgebouw Orchestra (who also give a lively account of the *Danse macabre* under Haitink) and again natural digital recording. In the *C minor Concerto* (which is analogue) the effect is harder, partly because Michele Campanella is a more boldly extrovert soloist; but this account has undoubted vitality and no lack of *espressivo*. Henryk Szeryng gives clean, immaculate performances of the *B minor Violin concerto* and the *Introduction and Rondo capriccioso*. His approach is aristocratic rather than seductive, though in the encore the bravura and sense of style make for impressive results. The contribution of the Monte Carlo orchestra is adequate but is not helped by a somewhat dated 1969 recording which spotlights the violin and does nothing for the rather pale colours provided by the woodwind soloists. De Waart's 1976 recording of the famous *Organ Symphony* cannot be said to be among the most exciting versions available but, with polished orchestral playing and refined Philips sound, it is certainly enjoyable, with a warm *Poco adagio*, and the organ glories at the end of the symphony are given plenty of breadth and impact by the recording.

Carnival of the animals.
(M) *** Teldec/Warner Dig. 4509 97445-2 [id.]. Güher & Süher Pekinel, French R. PO, Janowski –
   POULENC: *Double piano concerto.* ***

The piano duo, Güher and Süher Pekinel – of mixed Turkish/Spanish parentage – make a sparklingly spontaneous contribution to Saint-Saëns's zoological fantasy, readily dominating the performance with their scintillating pianism. Janowski and the French Radio Orchestra provide admirable support, and Saint-Saëns's portrait gallery comes vividly and wittily to life, from the unhurried *Tortoises* and the neatly focused Offenbachian *Elephant* to the fragile, fluttering *Aviary* and the very self-assured *Pianists*. The gentle dignity of Eric Levionnais's *Le Cygne* makes a touching highlight, leading on to an exhilarating finale. The performance is beautifully recorded and naturally balanced within an attractively warm ambience; although the playing time (38 minutes) is short, this mid-priced CD remains highly recommendable, alongside the Virgin recording by Anton Nel and Keith Snell, with the Academy of London conducted by Richard Stamp, which is coupled with Sir John Gielgud's unforgettable narration of *Peter and the wolf* (CUV7 61137-2).

(i) *Cello concerto No. 1, Op. 33;* (ii) *The swan;* (iii) *Allegro appassionato, Op. 43; Cello sonata No. 1, Op. 32; Chant saphique, Op. 91; Gavotte, Op. posth.; Romances Nos. 1 in F, Op. 36; 2 in D, Op. 51;* (iv) *Prière* (for cello & organ).
*** RCA Dig. 09026 61678-2 [id.]. Steven Isserlis; (i) LSO, Tilson Thomas; (ii) Tilson Thomas,
   Dudley Moore; (iii) Pascal Devoyon; (iv) Stephen Grier.

Steven Isserlis's record of the *Cello concerto in A minor* was part of the Channel 4 'Concerto' series with Dudley Moore, which also included Kyoko Takezawa's remarkable account of the Bartók *Violin concerto* and Barry Douglas's performance of Rachmaninov's *Second Piano concerto*. But the present issue has a completely separate life and RCA have made some valuable additions to the concerto. Of particular interest is the *Cello sonata No. 1 in C minor*, composed in the same year (it immediately precedes the concerto in Saint-Saëns's opus list), in which he is accompanied with elegance and finesse by Pascal Devoyon. Isserlis himself plays with the musicianship and virtuosity one has come to expect from him. Most of the remaining pieces are both worthwhile and entertaining, particularly the *Allegro appassionato*. The *Prière*, Op. 159, for cello and organ was written as late as 1919 and is a small but affecting addition to the composer's representation on CD. The recorded sound is very good indeed and the disc is thoroughly recommendable on all counts.

Piano concertos Nos. 1–5.
(B) *** Decca Double 443 865-2 [id.]. Pascal Rogé, Philh. O, RPO or LPO, Charles Dutoit.

Played as they are here, these concertos can exert a strong appeal: Pascal Rogé brings delicacy, virtuosity and sparkle to the piano part and he receives expert support from the various London orchestras under Dutoit. Altogether delicious playing and excellent piano-sound from Decca, who secure a most realistic balance. In every respect this set outclasses Aldo Ciccolini's survey of the early 1970s, good though that was. On CD the five *Concertos* are successfully accommodated on two discs and the digital remastering is wholly successful, retaining the bloom of the analogue originals, yet producing firmer detail and splendid piano-sound. Now reissued as a Double Decca set (two-records-for-the-price-of-one) the value is obvious.

Violin concerto No. 3 in B min., Op. 61.

(M) *** DG Dig. 445 549-2 [id.]. Perlman, O de Paris, Barenboim – LALO: *Symphonie espagnole;* BERLIOZ: *Rêverie et caprice.* ***

On DG, Perlman achieves a fine partnership with his friend, Barenboim, in a performance that is both tender and strong, while Perlman's verve and dash in the finale are dazzling. The forward balance is understandable in this work, but orchestral detail could at times be sharper. The Berlioz *Rêverie et caprice* has been added for this reissue.

Havanaise, Op. 83; Introduction & Rondo capriccioso, Op. 28.

**(*) EMI Dig. CDC5 55026-2 [id.]; *EL5 55026-4.* Sarah Chang, Phd. O, Sawallisch – PAGANINI: *Violin concerto No. 1.* **(*)

Although she misses some of the sultry seductiveness in the *Havanaise,* the twelve-year-old Sarah Chang still captures the gleaming Spanish sunshine, both here and in the dashing *Rondo capriccioso.* She is well supported by Sawallisch, but is not flattered by the close recording-balance; the orchestra, too, lacks opulence. However, first choice still rests with Perlman (EMI CDC7 47725-2).

(i) *Morceau de concert* (for violin & orchestra) *in A, Op. 20;* (i; ii) *La muse et le poète* (duo for violin, cello & orchestra), *Op. 132;* (iii) *Odelette for flute and orchestra in D, Op. 162; Romance for flute and orchestra in D flat, Op. 37. Suite for orchestra in D, Op. 49;* (iii; iv) *Tarantelle for flute, clarinet & orchestra in A min., Op. 6. Une nuit à Lisbonne (barcarolle), Op. 63.*

**(*) EMI Dig. CDC7 54913-2 [id.]. (i) Fontanarosa; (ii) Hoffman; (iii) Novakova; (iv) Vieille; Ens. O de Paris, Kantorow.

Morceaux de concert were Saint-Saëns's speciality, and the violin piece here of that name is nearly as attractive as the more famous *Havanaise,* if not quite as memorable. Like the duo, *La muse et le poète,* the solo playing is of high quality but is let down by the close microphones, which too often seem to impair recordings made in the Paris Salle Wagram and which here add a certain edginess to the violin timbre and adversely affect the balance with the cello. The works for flute are equally pleasingly played, and this time the forward sound is very acceptable. But the highlight here is the *Tarantelle,* a chattering, conversational piece between flute and clarinet, begining seductively and, with its swirls and glissandos, becoming increasingly infectious. Two flutes take a solo role in the engaging central *Gavotte* of the neo-baroque orchestral *Suite,* while the closing lollipop celebrating *A night in Lisbon* is a charming barcarolle with harp. A highly agreeable 71-minute collection of musical morsels, generally well recorded, except for the artificial treble emphasis on the pieces with violin.

Symphony No. 3 in C min., Op. 78.

(B) *** Carlton Dig. PCD 2010 [id.]. Chorzempa, Berne SO, Maag.

Maag's extremely well-recorded Berne performance has a Mendelssohnian freshness and the sprightly playing in the Scherzo draws an obvious affinity with that composer. The closing pages have a convincing feeling of apotheosis and, although this is not the weightiest reading available, it is an uncommonly enjoyable one in which the sound is bright, full and suitably resonant. However, Munch's Boston recording still leads the field for this much-recorded symphony (and it also includes *La Mer* and Ibert's *Escales*). The recording is magnificent (RCA 09026 61500-2).

CHAMBER MUSIC

Bassoon sonata, Op. 168; Clarinet sonata, Op. 167; Caprice on Danish and Russian airs for flute, oboe, clarinet and piano, Op. 79; Feuillet d'album, Op. 81 (arr Taffanel); *Oboe sonata, Op. 166; Odelette for flute and piano, Op. 162; Romance in D flat for flute and piano, Op. 37; Tarantelle for flute, clarinet and piano, Op. 6.*

(B) *** Cala Dig. CACD 1017 (2) [id.]. William Bennett, Nicholas Daniel, James Campbell, Rachael Gough, & Ens. – DEBUSSY: *Chamber music.* ***

Saint-Saëns possessed enormous fertility, and the music collected here is unfailingly inventive and civilized. The *Sonatas for clarinet, for oboe* and *for bassoon,* Opp. 166–168, are all late works, composed when he was eighty-six and living in his favourite winter haunt, the Hôtel de l'Oasis in Algiers. (He planned a Sonata for cor anglais and piano, too.) They are elegantly finished but surprising pieces, with an unaccustomed depth of feeling. The *Caprice* is a diverting kind of pot-pourri, inspired by the composer's visit to Russia in 1876, when he met Tchaikovsky and returned to Paris with the score of *Boris Godunov,* thus kindling the flame of interest in Mussorgsky that burned so brightly in later years. Paul Taffanel's arrangement of the *Feuillet d'album,* Op. 81, for flute, oboe and two each of clarinets, bassoons and horns, is a first recording and, like almost everything on this record, refreshing and elegant. That goes for the performances too, which are well recorded though the piano is occasionally overpowering. Strongly recommended – and outstanding value, considering that one gets two CDs for the price of one, economically packaged and liberally annotated.

Bassoon sonata in G, Op. 168; Oboe sonata in D, Op. 166.
** Claves Dig. CD 50-9020 [id.]. Thuneman, Requejo, Goritzki – POULENC: *Sonata; Trio.* **

This is not an economical buy. Despite the eminence of the artists, you can buy both these late sonatas, together with the rest of Saint-Saëns's output for wind instruments – and in addition the complete wind output of Debussy – on two Cala discs for the same outlay – see above.

Piano trio No. 1 in F, Op. 18.
(*) Ara. Dig. Z 6643 [id.]. Golub–Kaplan–Carr Trio – DEBUSSY; FAURE: *Trios.* *
(*) Dorian Dig. DOR 90187 [id.]. Rembrandt Trio – RAVEL: *Piano trio;* CHAMINADE: *Piano trio No. 1.* (*)

David Golub, Mark Kaplan and Colin Carr give a very good account of themselves in the *Piano trio in F major*. They are intelligent and imaginative, though in the variation movement Kaplan is not as commanding or full-bodied tonally as his opposite number in the Beaux Arts Trio (see our main volume). The piano dominates in the right way, and David Golub makes a particularly strong and vital impression. They are very well recorded too.

In the Rembrandt Trio, the pianist Valerie Tryon dominates the proceedings and neither of her partners, Gérard Kantarjian and Coenraad Bloemendal, matches her in terms of musical personality. In fact they are rather colourless players and, though the recording is perfectly acceptable, the performance is not really competitive.

VOCAL MUSIC

Choral songs: Calme des nuits; Des pas dans l'allée; Les fleurs et les arbres.
*** Ph. Dig. 438 149-2 [id.]. Monteverdi Ch., O Révolutionnaire et Romantique, Gardiner – FAURE: *Requiem;* DEBUSSY; RAVEL: *Choral works.* ***

Three charming examples of Saint-Saens's skill and finesse in drawing inspiration from early sources in a way remarkable at the time he was writing. Gardiner and his team give ideal performances, adding to the valuable list of rarities which he provides as coupling for the Fauré *Requiem*.

Salieri, Antonio (1750–1825)

Fortepiano concertos: in B flat and C.
*** Teldec/Warner Dig. 4509 94569-2 [id.]. Andreas Staier, Concerto Köln – STEFFAN: *Fortepiano concerto.* ***

Although Salieri certainly was not responsible for Mozart's death, after the film *Amadeus* it has been only too easy for his music to be written off as a very pale imitation of that master. Yet these two attractive works show him as quite a dab hand at a keyboard concerto with a distinct personality of his own. They were written in 1778 'for two ladies', who must have been skilled keyboard players, for they are both technically demanding. The rising arpeggio opening of the *C major Concerto* is a bit square, but its ideas are deftly handled and it has a charming minor-key serenade for its *Larghetto* that reminds one a little (at first) of the slow movement of the Mozart *A major*, K.488, but then later produces an unusual and effective pizzicato accompaniment; the spirited finale is in contrast to its sad little coda. The *B flat Concerto* opens strongly and has most agreeable secondary material; the *Adagio* brings the more conventional device of an Alberti bass (which works rather well on the fortepiano), and then closes with a winningly cheerful Minuet, almost a lollipop, with simple but effective variations, giving Staier plenty of opportunities to show the fortepiano's paces. Moreover he convinces us that this is music which is more effective on a period instrument, contributing his own creative cadenzas which the concertos clearly need. Overall, the performances here could hardly be more persuasive, with the bold, slightly abrasive tuttis from the Concerto Köln adding to the strength of characterization. The recording is first class.

Sallinen, Aulis (born 1935)

Symphonies Nos. 2 (Symphonic dialogue for solo percussion player and orchestra), Op. 29; 6 (From a New Zealand Diary), Op. 65; Sunrise Serenade, Op. 63.
*** BIS Dig. CD 511 [id.]. Malmö SO, Okko Kamu.

The *Second Symphony* dates from 1972 and, like the *First*, is a one-movement affair lasting a quarter of an hour. Its sub-title, *Symphonic dialogue for solo percussion player and orchestra*, gives an accurate idea of its character, pitting the fine soloist, Gerd Mortensen, against the remaining orchestral forces. The main work is the ambitious *Sixth Symphony* (1989–90), composed in response to a commission from the New Zealand Symphony Orchestra. Like the *Third Symphony*, it is powerfully evocative of natural landscape; indeed it is one of the strongest and most imaginative of all Sallinen's symphonies. Okko Kamu gets very responsive playing from the Malmö Symphony Orchestra in both symphonies and in the slight but effective *Sunrise Serenade* (1989). The recording is in the highest traditions of the house.

Symphonies Nos. 4, Op. 49; 5 (Washington mosaics), Op. 57; Shadows (Prelude for orchestra), Op. 52.
*** BIS Dig. CD 607 [id.]. Malmö SO, James De Preist.

We list Okko Kamu's recording of the *Fourth Symphony* coupled with the *Cello concerto* and *Shadows* in our main volume (FACD 346), while the *Fifth* (*Washington mosaics*), also well played and recorded by Helsinki forces under Kamu, is coupled on another Finlandia disc (FACD 370) with the feeble and unappealing *Nocturnal dances of Don Juanquixote*. Suffice it to say that these new performances by the Malmö Symphony Orchestra under James De Preist are every bit as good as the Helsinki rivals and, if anything, the recording has more impressive range and definition.

Satie, Erik (1866–1925)

Choses vues à droit et à gauche (sans lunettes).
*** EMI Dig. CDC7 54541-2 [id.]. Frank Peter Zimmermann, Alexander Lonquich – AURIC: *Sonate;* FRANCAIX: *Sonatine;* MILHAUD: *Sonata No. 2;* POULENC: *Sonata.* ***

Satie's only piece for violin and piano, the *Choses vues à droit et à gauche (sans lunettes)* bears charming titles: (1) *Choral hypocrite* ('*My chorales are like those of Bach's, with the difference that they are fewer in number and less pretentious*'); (2) *Fugue a tâtons;* and (3) *Fantaisie musculaire.* They are only moderately amusing but are played with splendid elegance by these two artists.

Avant-dernières pensées; Gnossiennes Nos. 1–3; Gymnopédie No 1; Sports et divertissments; Pièces froides: Airs à faire fuir; Vexations.
(**) DG Dig. 439 767-2 [id.]. Moreau, Luisada – POULENC: *L'Histoire de Babar.* (**)

Jean-Marc Luisada plays this repertoire with real sensitivity and is particularly impressive in creating the atmosphere of the *Pièces froides.* He is also well recorded. However, Jeanne Moreau's *sotto voce* recitations of the composer's thoughts about the music's descriptive content are intrusive, and in our view these vocal comments would be useful only if the listener could programme them out at will. The narrative of the *Babar* coupling is also presented in French.

Scarlatti, Alessandro (1660–1725)

Motets: De tenebroso lacu; Infirmata, vulnerata; (i) Salve Regina. Totus amore languens.
(M) *** Virgin Veritas/ EMI VC5 45103-2 [id.]. Gérard Lesne; (i) Véronique Gens; Il Seminario Musicale.

The remarkably gifted alto, Gérard Lesne, together with the refreshingly stylish instrumental group, Il Seminario Musicale, are rediscovering baroque repertoire that has been virtually forgotten for two centuries. Lesne has already given as an outstanding collection of motets of Baldassare Galuppi (VC5 54030-2 – see our main volume); now he turns to Alessandro Scarlatti, who wrote about a hundred such works. Often strikingly original, in many ways they are like vocal concerti grossi, contrasting slow and fast movements to suit the text; at the same time they combine an Italianate expressive melodic cantilena with an operatic feeling for drama. *De tenebro lacu* evokes a vision of souls in hell and the highly imaginative string introduction (a simple but spiky falling arpeggio) creates the mood for the opening words, 'From the depths of the dark lake'. The profound melancholy of *Infirma, vulnerata* is revealed with touching eloquence. Lesne is right inside the music's expressive world and it is difficult to imagine this being better (or more authentically) sung. In the setting of *Salve Regine* he is joined by the fresh-voiced (and, when necessary, spirited) Véronique Gens, and their voices blend admirably. Perhaps most moving of all is the solemnly tragic *Totus amore languens*, whose mood then lifts joyfully in the final section: 'What could be more delectable than this heavenly ardour?' Throughout, the accompaniments are creative, vital and warmly supportive – stimulating and beautiful in their own right. This is period-instrument performance at its most revealing. The recording is vivid, yet has just the right degree of warmth and spaciousness. Full translations are provided.

Motets: *Domine, refugium factus es nobis; O magnum mysterium.*
(B) *** Decca Double 443 868-2 (2) [id.]. Schütz Ch. of L., Roger Norrington – BONONCINI: *Stabat Mater ***; PERGOLESI: *Magnificat in C; Stabat Mater ***(*); D. SCARLATTI: *Stabat Mater;* CALDARA: *Crucifixus;* LOTTI: *Crucifixus.* ***

These two motets are fine pieces that show how enduring the Palestrina tradition was in seventeenth-century Italy. They are noble in conception and are beautifully performed here and, given first-class sound, make a fine bonus for this enterprising Double Decca collection of Italian baroque choral music.

Scarlatti, Domenico (1685–1757)

Keyboard sonatas, Kk. 9, 27, 33, 69, 87, 96, 159, 193, 247, 427, 492, 531; Fugue in G min., K.30.
(M) *** Erato/Warner 4509 96960-2 [id.]. Anne Queffélec (piano).

Anne Queffélec employs a modern Steinway with great character and apomb. She immediately captures the listener in the dashing opening of the *D major Sonata*, Kk. 96, with its lively fanfares and, in the gentler *B minor*, Kk. 27, her rippling passage-work is Bach-like in its simplicity. She alternates reflective works with those sonatas calling for sparkling bravura and her choice is unerringly effective, so that Kk. 159 in C with more hunting-calls follows the more introvert *D minor*, Kk. 9, and leads on to the thoughtful but not doleful *F minor*, Kk. 69. Only in the vibrant *D major*, Kk. 33, is there a hint of the harpsichord in her tone production, but this keen articulation is altogether apt. The recital closes with a *Fugue* which unfolds with calm inevitability. The 1970 recording is first class; the piano is naturally focused and has plenty of space, without any resonant blurring.

Keyboard sonatas, Kk. 25, 33, 39, 52, 54, 96, 146, 162, 197–198, 201, 303, 466, 474, 481, 491, 525, 547.
**(*) Sony SK 53460 [id.]. Vladimir Horowitz (piano).

Provided you are prepared to accept sometimes less than flattering and often rather dry recorded sound, this is marvellous playing which sweeps away any purist notions about Scarlatti having to be played on the harpsichord; it has one marvelling at the richness, not merely of the musical argument, but of the often orchestra-sounding piano texture. Ralph Kirkpatrick has told us that Scarlatti sometimes had string or brass tone in mind. The eighteen sonatas were chosen by Horowitz after he had recorded nearly twice as many throughout 1964. The very opening, staccato *D major*, Kk. 33, is made to sound very brittle by the close balance, but in the following *A minor*, Kk. 54, the pianist's gentle colouring is fully revealed. Here, as in the two slow *F minor sonatas*, Kk. 466 and Kk. 481, the music is particularly beautiful in a way not expected of Scarlatti. The playing time has been extended to 72 minutes by the addition of six more sonatas to the content of the original CD.

Stabat Mater.
(B) **(*) Decca Double 443 868-2 (2) [id.]. Schütz Ch. of L., Roger Norrington – BONONCINI: *Stabat Mater ***; PERGOLESI: *Magnificat in C; Stabat Mater ***(*); A. SCARLATTI: *Domine, refugium factus es nobis; O magnum mysterium;* CALDARA: *Crucifixus;* LOTTI: *Crucifixus.* ***

Scarlatti's *Stabat Mater* is an early work, written during the composer's sojourn in Rome (1714–19) when he was *maestro di capella* at S. Giulia, and it shows him to be a considerable master of polyphony. It is extended in scale (32 minutes) and taxing to the performers. The performance here is admirable, though not always impeccable in matters of tonal balance; and the recording is very good. Overall this well-designed Double Decca set combines three fine *Stabat Mater* settings with other comparable baroque choral music, all well performed and impressively recorded.

Schmelzer, Johann (c. 1620–80)

Sonata natalitia a 3 chori; Sonata II a 8 chori; 3 Sonatas a 3; Sonata a 4; Sonata a 5; Sonata IV a 6; Sonata I a 8.

(M) ** Teldec/Warner 4509 95989-2 (2) [id.]. VCM, Harnoncourt – FUX: *Concentus musico instrumentis.* ***

Like Fux, with whose music this programme of sonatas is coupled, Schmelzer was Kapellmeister at the Hapsburg court; but on the evidence of this disc his output was more limited in appeal and his scoring relatively clumsy. While the *Sonata natalitia*, using recorders, piffari (early oboes), trombones and strings, certainly creates aurally fascinating and intricate textures, some of the other works, especially those for brass (where the clarinos produce a curious throttled tone), are less successful. It is when we come to the *Sonata IV a 6* (for two violins, three viols and continuo), the *Sonata a 3* (for violin, viola (violetta), viol and continuo), and the *Sonata a 3* (for three violins and continuo) that the composer begins really to stimulate the listener properly, and it is a pity that these were not added on to the Fux programme to make a single CD instead of giving Schmelzer a 48-minute disc to himself. No complaints about the recording, which is excellent.

Schmitt, Florent (1870–1958)

Symphony No. 2, Op. 37; La danse d'Abisag, Op. 75; (i) Habeyssée (suite for violin and orchestra), Op. 110. Rêves, Op. 65.

*** Marco Polo Dig. 8.223689 [id.].(i) Hannele Segerstam; Rheinland-Pfalz PO, Leif Segerstam.

At last there seems to be a resurgence of interest in Schmitt who was for so long a one-work composer – and that a rarely played one. Now that *La tragédie de Salomé* is available, not only in the composer's pioneering 1930 recording but in its complete (1907) form, attention seems to be turning to his other music. The present issue brings *La danse d'Abisag*; like the much earlier *Tragédie de Salomé*, this has a biblical theme: unlike Salome, Abisag, despite her erotic dancing, fails to arouse the ageing monarch (King David). The *Symphony No. 2*, Op. 137, so numbered to distinguish it from the *Symphonie concertante for piano and orchestra*, was a work of Schmitt's advanced age – and no mean achievement for a composer in his eighty-eighth year! In terms of orchestral expertise and flair, it is second to none, and the opulence of its palette and imaginative vitality is remarkable. *Rêves* is an early piece, inspired by a poem by Léon-Paul Fargue and appropriately atmospheric; and *Habeyssée*, said to be inspired by an Islamic legend, is a three-movement suite for violin and orchestra whose title could also possibly represent the French pronunciation of the first three letters of the alphabet! Whether or not this is the case, this is a rewarding issue which offers some good playing from the Rheinland-Pfalz Orchestra under Segerstam, who excels in this repertoire. Good recording too.

Schnittke, Alfred (born 1934)

Concerto grosso No. 1; Quasi una sonata; Moz-Art à la Haydn; A Paganini.

(M) *** DG Dig. 445 520-2 [id.]. Kremer, Smirnov, Grindenko, COE, Schiff.

The *Concerto grosso* is already available at bargain price on Classikon in this very performance, coupled with Lutoslawski and Ligeti (DG 439 452-2 – see our main volume). If, however, you want to jump in at the deep end of the Schnittke repertoire, the present collection offers the formidable, at times even ferocious, *Quasi una sonata* with its extraordinary scratchings and abrasions, the pastiche *Moz-Art à la Haydn*, which is almost humorous, and the virtuoso solo violin piece, *A Paganini*. The performances here are expert, very committed and brilliantly recorded.

Piano sonata.

*** Chan. Dig. CHAN 8962 [id.]. Boris Berman – STRAVINSKY: *Serenade* etc. ***

Berman gives as persuasive an account of Schnittke's *Piano sonata* as it is possible to imagine. He is very well recorded, too, and the three Stravinsky pieces with which it comes are also given with great pianistic elegance.

Schoeck, Othmar (1886–1957)

Der Sänger (The Singer), Op. 57.
** Koch Schwann Dig. 310921 [id.]. Frieder Lang, Ruth Lang-Oester.

The exploration of Schoeck's enormous output for the voice proceeds apace. *Der Sänger* was written in 1944–5, the closing year of the Second World War, and is a setting of twenty-six poems by the nineteenth-century Swiss poet, Heinrich Leuthold, to whose work Schoeck's friend, Hermann Hesse, had introduced him. Apart from *Der Sänger*, he provided the inspiration for another set, *Spielmanns-weisen*. Its sentiment harmonized with Schoeck's own feelings of melancholia and the feeling that he had been denied the recognition to which his talents entitled him. Like the other late song-cycles *Unter Sternen (Under the stars)* and *Das stille Leuchten (The silent light)* it contains songs of great beauty.

OPERA

Penthesilea, Op. 39.
*** Orfeo C 364942 B [id.]. Helga Dernesch, Jane Marsh, Mechthild Gesendorf, Marjana Lipovšek, Theo Adam, ORF SO, Albrecht.

Penthesilea is arguably Schoeck's masterpiece. It is a highly concentrated and powerfully atmospheric piece whose fall-out remains long after the performance is over. Like Strauss's *Elektra*, it is set in the Ancient World, is in one Act and has a high norm of dissonance – hardly surprising, given the action of the opera. The libretto is shaped by Schoeck himself and is based on the last part of Kleist's play of the same name. Penthesilea is the leader of the Amazons, female warriors each of whom may give herself to a man only if he has first been vanquished in battle. Penthesilea believes that she has conquered Achilles in combat and, struck by her beauty, he permits her to do so. They fall in love, but when the truth emerges Penthesilea is horror-struck. Achilles challenges her to another combat and, as token of his love, comes to battle unarmed. He is wounded by an arrow and torn to pieces by Penthesilea's dogs. Appalled at these developments, Penthesilea takes her own life.

So gripping is Schoeck's opera, so masterly its sense of pace and dramatic contrast, that one is on the edge of one's seat throughout. Despite its kinship with Strauss's expressionism, its sound-world is quite distinctive. The score is punctuated with offstage war cries and dissonant trumpet-calls (Ronald Crichton speaks of its language 'as surpassing *Elektra* in ferocity'. Its scoring is quite unusual: four violins only; a huge wind section, including ten clarinets at various pitches; brass and two pianos. At times the writing almost looks forward to Britten. The present production was recorded by Oesterreich-ischer Rundfunk (ORF) at the 1982 Salzburg Festival and has performances of thrilling intensity from Helga Dernesch in the title-role and Theo Adam as Achilles, as well as Jane Marsh (Prothoe) and Marjana Lipovšek (the High Priestess). It completely supersedes the earlier, two-LP set under Zdenec Macal, made in 1974. The recording has ample detail and presence and is in every way satisfactory.

Venus (complete).
*** MGB Musikszene Schweiz CD 6112 (2) [id.]. Lang, Popp, O'Neal, Fassbender, Skovhus, Alföldi, Heidelberg Kammer Ch., Basle Boys' Ch., Swiss Youth PO, Venzago.

Venus was written in 1919–21 and is based on a libretto by Schoeck's school-friend, Armin Rüeger; since its first performance in Zurich in 1922 it has suffered almost complete neglect. Rüeger drew on two sources for his text: Prosper Mérimée's *La Vénus d'Ille* and a short story by Eichendorff called *Das Marmorbild*. The basic argument is simple and comes from Ovid, though Rüeger sets the action in a country castle in the south of France. The amateur archaeologist Peyrehorade has unearthed a bronze statue of Venus. The son of the house is playing a ball game just before his wedding and, finding his wedding-ring an encumbrance, puts it on the finger of the statue of Venus, only to discover that the finger bends. The statue interposes itself between him and his bride, and the opera ends with his death. The tenor role is particularly demanding and may have hampered the work reaching the international stage; and, according to Mario Venzago's footnote in the booklet, there are innumerable textual problems to sort out. The only extant score is at times difficult to decipher and is full of clef and transposition errors; there are also irreconcilable differences between the piano reduction and the full score. Be that as it may, Venzago's conducting radiates total dedication, and so does the playing of the young Swiss orchestra. The opening scene almost prompts one's thoughts to turn to the Strauss of *Ariadne*, but as the opera unfolds Venzago's view of the work as partly 'an enormous orchestral poem (exposition, development, Scherzo and recapitulation) with obbligato voices' seems more and more valid. The sheer quality of the invention is notable amd many of the ideas, particularly the Venus motive, have great tenderness and delicacy. Schoeck's scoring is superb, and those who know *Penthesilea* or *Massimila Doni* should lose no time in acquiring this glorious score. The performance may not be absolutely ideal vocally, but it is worth putting up with that for the sake of such a beautiful work. Good and atmospheric recording.

Schoenberg, Arnold (1874–1951)

Chamber Symphony No. 1, Op. 9; 5 Orchestral pieces, Op. 16.
*** Decca Dig. 436 467-2 [id.]. Concg. O, Chailly – WEBERN: *Passacaglia* etc. ***

These Schoenberg pieces (like the coupled Webern) were originally used as fill-ups for Chailly's rather less recommendable performances of the Brahms symphonies. Here more appropriately paired with Webern, these strongly committed and full-blooded performances can be given a cordial welcome. Though in the *Chamber Symphony* the solo violins emerge a little edgily, the recording is generally full and vivid.

(i) *Chamber Symphony No. 1, Op. 9;* (ii; iii) *Erwartung;* (iii) *Variations for orchestra, Op. 31.*
*** EMI Dig. CDC5 55212-2 [id.]. (i) Birmingham Contemporary Music Group; (ii) Bryn-Julson;
(iii) CBSO; Sir Simon Rattle.

With Rattle consistently warm and persuasive in three key works, this is the perfect disc for anyone wanting to explode the idea of Schoenberg as bogeyman. The longest piece here is the early monodrama, *Erwartung* ('Anticipation'), a work that can easily repel with its very subject, a woman's self-tortured search by moonlight for her lover, whose dead body she horrifically stumbles over at the climax of this half-hour sequence. Equally in Schoenberg's taxing atonal vocal lines, the singing of the soprano soloist can repel. But here, like Jessye Norman in her Philips recording, Phyllis Bryn-Julson sings with a clarity and definition to coax the ear instead of assaulting it. She may not be as dominant or powerful as Norman but, bright and clear, she gives a more vulnerable portrait, tender and compelling, with Rattle more urgent than James Levine for Norman. By contrast, Rattle is daringly expansive in the *Variations* of 1928, even more so than Karajan in his classic recording with the Berlin Philharmonic. The Birmingham players may not always be quite so refined as the Berliners, but they play with even greater emotional thrust and with a keener sense of mystery, while heightened dynamic contrasts add to the dramatic bite. With Rattle there is no question of missing the heart behind the composer's severe intellectual argument. In the *Chamber Symphony No. 1* Rattle, with fifteen players from the Birmingham Contemporary Music Group, springs rhythms infectiously, relaxedly bringing out the thrust of argument. The playing may not be as bitingly crisp as in some rival versions but it has far more character, thanks to both conductor and players. Superb sound.

Chamber Symphony No. 2; Music to a motion-picture scene; Verklaerte Nacht.
*** Teldec/Warner Dig. 9031 77314-2 [id.]. COE, Holliger.

Holliger and the Chamber Orchestra of Europe give one of the most passionate performances of Schoenberg's *Verklaerte Nacht* on disc, reflecting 'the glow of inmost warmth' in the Richard Dehmel poem which inspired it. It is imaginatively coupled with representative works from later periods, the atmospheric *Incidental music to a motion-picture scene* of 1930 and the *Chamber Symphony No. 2*, which he worked on at various times over more than 30 years between 1906 and 1939. Holliger and the COE are more expansive, as well as more committed, than the Orpheus Chamber Orchestra on their DG disc coupling both concertos with *Verklaerte Nacht*, bringing out a lilting Viennese quality in the second of the two movements of the *Chamber Symphony No. 2*. First-rate sound.

5 Orchestral pieces, Op. 16.
*** Decca Dig. 436 240-2 (2) [id.]. Cleveland O, Dohnányi – MAHLER: *Symphony No. 6* **; WEBERN:
Im Sommerwind. ***

Dohnányi and the Cleveland Orchestra seem more at home in the music of the Second Viennese School than in Mahler. In many ways outshining the strong, direct reading of the main Mahler work, Dohnányi's reading of Schoenberg's seminal *Five Pieces* is both powerful and moving. The perfection of ensemble goes with a depth of feeling that is largely missing in the Mahler, and the recording, full, rich and weighty, is of demonstration quality.

Pelleas und Melisande, Op. 5; Verklaerte Nacht, Op. 4.
*** DG Dig. 439 942-2 [id.]. Philh. O, Sinopoli.

Sinopoli's is a unique and generous coupling for a single CD, bringing together the two most ambitious works that Schoenberg completed before launching into his experiments in pure atonality. Sinopoli's view of both is unusually broad and expansive, taking no less than six minutes longer over *Pelleas* than Boulez in his Erato version. In that vast symphonic poem Sinopoli cannot quite match the biting passion and sharp characterization of Karajan in his superb Berlin performance (currently available only as part of a mid-priced three-disc collection of music of the Second Viennese School: 427 424-2 – see our main volume); but he finds an impressionistic beauty to this richly varied score which for once relates it to the Debussy masterpiece on the same subject. In *Verklaerte Nacht* Sinopoli does not draw such weight of sound from the Philharmonia strings as do some other versions which use the 1943 string orchestra score, but in his refinement he relates it more clearly to the chamber scale of the original sextet. Glowing sound to match.

Verklaerte Nacht, Op. 4.
(B) ** Decca Double Dig. 444 872-2 (2) [id.]. Berlin RSO, Chailly – MAHLER: *Symphony No. 10.*
 **(*)

Chailly's version of Schoenberg's work is very well played and recorded, but it is in no way distinctive.

(i) *Verklaerte Nacht, Op. 4; 5 Orchestral pieces, Op. 16;* (ii) (Piano): *3 Pieces, Op. 11; 6 Little Pieces, Op. 19.* arr. BUSONI: *Piece, Op. 11/2 (Konzertmässige interpretation).*
*** Teldec/Warner Dig. 4509 98256-2 [id.]. (i) Chicago SO, Barenboim; (ii) Barenboim (piano).

Barenboim's Teldec disc makes a fascinating coupling, exploiting his gifts as both conductor and pianist. His reading of *Verklaerte Nacht* in the 1943 string orchestra version is weighty and passionate, with the Chicago strings playing superbly, while the *Five Orchestral pieces* are comparably purposeful and sharply characterized. They lead naturally to the miniatures for piano, which Barenboim interprets with persuasive warmth, treating them rather like Brahms 'with the wrong notes'. He concludes with a fascinating rarity, an elaborate rearrangement of the second of the Op.11 *Pieces* which Busoni made in 1909, turning it into something close to late Liszt. Not surprisingly, Schoenberg did not approve, but it is undeniably far more pianistic than the original, a point well brought out by Barenboim. The notes are excellent, with copious musical illustrations. Warm sound, if not ideally detailed in the orchestral works.

Chamber symphony No. 1 (arr. Anton Webern, for piano quintet).
** DG Dig. 437 804-2 [id.]. Paul Gulda, Hagen Qt – BRAHMS: *Piano quintet.* **

Schoenberg's admiration for Brahms is well known, so that this coupling has a certain logic. However, Webern's arrangement of the *Chamber Symphony*, Op. 9, was made when this music was inaccessible to the wider musical public; performances of the original were few and far between, the gramophone was in its infancy, and an arrangement for chamber forces was a sensible way to enable music-lovers to get to know the piece. To revive it now seems an act of misplaced piety, when Schoenberg's piece can easily be heard in its original form. It is well enough played and recorded, but it is coupled with a rather self-conscious account of the Brahms *F minor Quintet.*

Gurrelieder.
*** DG Dig. 439 944-2 (2) [id.]. Sweet, Jerusalem, Lipovšek, Wekler, Langridge, Sukowa, Vienna
    State Op. Ch., Schoenberg Ch., Slovak Phil Ch., BPO, Abbado.
** Sony Dig. S2K 48077 (2) [id.]. Marton, Quivar, Hotter, Lakes, Garrison, NY Choral Artists,
    NYPO, Mehta.

Recorded live in the Philharmonie, Berlin, Abbado's version begins magnetically with the most delicate tracery of sound, immediately capturing both atmosphere and dramatic intensity. From then on, the live experience comes over vividly, with an outstanding line-up of soloists to match those of any other rival set. Though Siegfried Jerusalem as Waldemar is not quite as firmly focused as he was on Riccardo Chailly's Decca set (also recorded in Berlin, but in the studio), he conveys more passion, and regularly Abbado's reading is freer and more volatile than Chailly's, with a sense of wonder enhanced by the very atmosphere of a concert. Susan Dunn as Tove in Chailly's version is firmer and truer than Abbado's Sharon Sweet, whose tight vibrato is often intrusive, but this is a strong, characterful reading, and Marjana Lipovšek is deeply moving as the Wood-Dove, with the hushed tension behind her big solo tellingly conveyed. Philip Langridge is outstanding as Klaus-Knarr and Hartmut Welker makes a bluff if slightly unsteady Peasant. The only soloist who is controversial is the woman speaker, Barbara Sukowa, whose use of sliding *Sprech-Stimme*, chattering in the style of *Pierrot Lunaire*, comes near to being comic. With the Berlin Philharmonic's playing richly and atmospherically caught, this must now stand as a first choice among live recordings, though the extra weight and detail of the sound in Chailly's studio version will for many make that still preferable (Decca 430 321-2 – see our main volume).

Mehta's version has many merits but, quite apart from a flawed cast, it seems literal and lacking in magic next to the finest versions. The backward balance of the orchestra also adds to a lack of dramatic bite. Though Gary Lakes is a cleanly focused Waldemar, the voice is edgy rather than sweet, and Eva Marton's heavy vibrato prevents her dramatic singing as Tove from sounding anything but ugly even in gentler moments. Among the others, Florence Quivar is excellent as the Wood-Dove.

Schreker, Franz (1878–1934)

Die Gezeichneten (opera): complete.
*** Decca Dig. 444 442-2 (3) [id.]. Kruse, Connell, Pederson, Muff, Berlin R. Ch. & O, Zagrosek.
*(*) Marco Polo Dig. 8.223328/30 [id.]. Soloists, Dutch R. & TV Ch. & O, De Waart.

Franz Schreker's career was an extraordinary one. He established his reputation early in the century, not only as a composer but also as a conductor. It was he who defied formidable problems to give a triumphant first performance of Schoenberg's massive Gurrelieder. Soon after that he himself had great success with his operas, not least Die Gezeichneten (literally 'The branded' or 'stigmatized'), and they were performed more widely in Germany in the 1920s than any other contemporary operas. Yet their vogue was short-lived. The Nazis condemned them as decadent, and by the time Schreker died in 1934 they were already being dropped from the repertory. The opening prelude of this opera with its magic, shimmering sounds, using the most exotic orchestration, establishes the hothouse atmosphere of a story which in its melodrama can indeed be regarded as decadent, if hardly more so than Strauss's Salome. What Zagrosek's gloriously recorded version demonstrates even more strikingly than De Waart's live recording is the range of atmospheric beauty in the score. Ripe echoes of composers from Scriabin to Puccini intensify the story of a dying woman painter, Carlotta, who deserts her faithful, ugly lover, Alviano, in favour of the physical love of Tamare, finally giving herself to him with fatal consequences. The Decca cast has no weak link, with Heinz Kruse fresh and clear-toned in the taxing tenor role of Alviano and Elizabeth Connell conveying with sharp clarity the positive yet vulnerable character of the heroine. Monte Pederson in cleanly focused singing conveys the animal quality of Tamare, while Alfred Muff is well contrasted as the older figure of Duke Adorno. Zagrosek draws dedicated playing and singing from the massive ensemble, and the beautifully balanced sound is of demonstration quality.

Though De Waart's version on Marco Polo also offers a fine performance, it hardly competes when substantial cuts are made in Act III of a very long opera.

Schubert, Franz (1797–1828)

Symphonies Nos. 1 in D, D.82; 4 in C (Tragic), D.417; Overture in the Italian style in C, D.591.
*** Teldec/Warner Dig. 4509 97509-2 [id.]. Concg. O, Harnoncourt.

Symphonies Nos. 3 in D, D.200; 5 in B flat, D.485; 8 in B min. (Unfinished).
*** Teldec/Warner Dig. 4509 97511-2 [id.]. Concg. O, Harnoncourt.

Symphonies Nos. 2 in B flat, D.125; 6 in C, D.589.
** Teldec/Warner Dig. 4509 97510-2 [id.]. Concg. O, Harnoncourt.

Symphony No. 9 in C (Great), D.944.
**(*) Teldec/Warner Dig. 4509 97512-2 [id.]. Concg. O, Harnoncourt.

It is a pity that Harnoncourt in his Schubert cycle did not turn to the Chamber Orchestra of Europe instead of to the Concertgebouw. His Beethoven cycle with that young orchestra has a freshness and intensity not quite matched in these weightier, bigger-scale performances. Had he done so, it would have been even more fascinating to compare Harnoncourt's Schubert with Abbado's, also featuring the COE. As it is, Harnoncourt takes a relatively severe view, and significantly he is at his finest in the darkness of the Tragic Symphony. There is little of Schubertian charm here, with his eccentrically slow tempo for the finale of No. 6 in its lumbering gait missing the pure sunlight of the piece. Echoing period practice, Harnoncourt's preference for short phrasing also tends to make slow movements less songful, though equally it adds to the bite and intensity of other movements, notably Scherzos with their sharp cross-rhythms. Not that any reservations detract seriously from a most refreshing cycle, direct and unmannered. Though the reverberance of the Amsterdam Concertgebouw hall obscures detail in tuttis, as well as reinforcing the weight of sound, the recording is warm and otherwise helpful. Harnoncourt, like Abbado, has used specially prepared texts, but they avoid the radical changes that spice the Abbado set, which remains a clear first choice in this repertoire (DG

423 651-2 – see our main volume). The two discs to go for are the pairing of the *Tragic* with No. 1 and the generous triptych of Nos. 3, 5 and the *Unfinished*.

No. 1 is given a very strong performance and sounds more mature than usual, though the *Andante* has no lack of grace, and the same comment might be applied to Nos. 3 and 5. The *Allegretto* of the *D major Symphony* is not pointed as wittily as with Beecham, but it still has charm. The *Unfinished* brings evocative atmosphere combined with high drama, and all these works show Harnoncourt at his most characterful; moreover Harnoncourt and his players obviously relish the Rossinian touches in the *Italian overture* which comes as an encore to the superb account of the *Tragic Symphony*. Like the *Fifth Symphony*, the overture sounds relatively weighty but has plenty of zest and a brilliant close.

Symphonies Nos. 1 in D, D.82; 2 in B flat, D.125.
(BB) **(*) Naxos Dig. 8.553093 [id.]. Failoni O of Budapest, Michael Halász.

Michael Halász and the Failoni Orchestra are affectionately easy-going rather than overtly dramatic, but they play both these works most winningly, finding all the delicacy of Schubert's inspiration. The recording too is full and naturally balanced, and one's only reservation is that the resonance of the Italian Institute in Budapest makes the tuttis spread and lose some of the sharpness of focus. But this is a most enjoyable disc nevertheless and well worth its modest cost. Abbado's sparkling DG disc, however, is worth the extra outlay (423 652-2).

Symphonies Nos. 3 in D, D.200; 6 in C, D.589.
(BB) *** Naxos Dig. 8.553094 [id.]. Failoni O of Budapest, Michael Halász.

These are entirely delightful performances, fully capturing the innocent charm of these youthful symphonies. The Failoni strings play with airy grace and the woodwind bring a similarly delicacy of colour to their solos and gentle chording, as in the first movement of No. 6, while in the finale of the same work the dancing violins have the lightest rhythmic touch. Michael Halász is most sensitive and in the *Allegretto* second movement of No. 3 – Schubert at his most endearingly ingenuous – the conductor's style is Beechamesque in its affectionate elegance. The economy of Schubert's scoring means that the resonant acoustic affects the clarity of the tuttis only marginally and it certainly lends an attractive bloom to the proceedings.

Symphonies Nos. 4 in C min. (Tragic), D.417; 8 in B min. (Unfinished).
(BB) ** Discovery Dig. DICD 920213 [id.]. Helsingborg SO, Avi Ostrowsky.

Ostrowsky finds more drama in the outer movements of the *Tragic Symphony* than Michael Halász, but the latter is the more imaginative and Ostrowsky's slower tempo for the *Andante* is not necessarily an advantage. In the *Unfinished*, he is very dramatic indeed with the wide dynamic range, emphasizing the conductor's bold contrasts. The orchestra plays sympathetically throughout and the Helsingborg Concert Hall provides a very suitable acoustic. But despite very good recording, this is not memorable. Abbado's splendid version of the *Tragic* is coupled with an equally fine account of No. 3 (DG 423 653-2).

Symphonies Nos. 4 in C min. (Tragic), D.417; Grand duo in C, D.812 (orch. Joachim).
(BB) **(*) Naxos 8.553095 [id.]. Failoni O of Budapest, Michael Halász.

Halász presents the *Tragic Symphony* – Schubert himself gave the work its title – sympathetically and, though this is not a strongly dramatic reading, the resonant acoustic adds a certain weight, and the *Andante* is warmly and expressively played. This inexpensive disc is valuable for its coupling, the orchestration of the large-scale *Grand Duo* for piano duet, written in 1824 and orchestrated by the violinist Josef Joachim. The result sounds surprisingly 'symphonic', with the first two movements both much darker in feeling than the early symphonies, although a lighter mood arrives in the extended, jaunty finale. The work is convincingly played, with gravitas and freshness nicely balanced. The warm resonancy of the Budapest Italian Institute suits this work very well.

Symphony No. 5 in B flat, D.485.
(M) *** RCA 09026 61793-2 [id.]. Chicago SO, Fritz Reiner (with MENDELSSOHN: *Hebrides overture* ***) – BRAHMS: *Symphony No. 3.* ***

Reiner's is a most attractive performance, brightly and clearly recorded, yet with a glowing ambience. This reading of No. 5, essentially sunny and with an easy-going *Andante*, brings a strongly vigorous finale, following a third movement where Reiner indulges the trio with an affectionate rallentando. Mendelssohn's famous Hebridean overture comes as an exciting encore: its storm has seldom sounded more dramatic, yet the lyrical warmth is not missed. Again, fresh sound.

Symphonies Nos. 5 in B flat, D.485; 6 in C, D.589; 8 in B min. (Unfinished).
(M) (***) Dutton Lab. mono CDLX 7014 [id.]. LPO, Sir Thomas Beecham.

Here are more miraculous Dutton transfers – of Sir Thomas Beecham's legendary earlier Schubert recordings, made in 1937 (the *Unfinished*), 1939 (No. 5) and 1944 (No. 5), with the LPO. Nos. 5 and 6 were later re-recorded by Beecham with the RPO in stereo (EMI CDM7 69750-2), but it is fascinating to hear these earlier versions so faithfully reproduced. No. 5 was always greatly admired; No. 6, recorded when Beecham returned to England from America, apparently brought ensemble problems and a number of re-takes, but the results in the end were well up to form. The *Unfinished*, as dramatic as it is seamless, is surely among the greatest of all recordings of this much-recorded symphony. The ear is astonished by the breadth of dynamic range possible in the 78-r.p.m. era and the warmth of the sound overall, recorded at Abbey Road or Kingsway Hall (No. 5). The documentation observes in No. 5: 'second movement swish as on original master', but the surface background generally is so diminished by the CEDAR process that it ceases to be a consideration. For the younger listener it will be a revelation to discover how realistic those old 78s could sound and how wonderful were these performances.

Symphony No. 8 (Unfinished).
⊛ (M) *** DG Dig. 445 514-2 [id.]. Philh. O, Sinopoli – MENDELSSOHN: *Symphony No. 4 (Italian).*
***

*** DG Dig. 439 862-2 [id.]. NY Met. O, Levine – BEETHOVEN: *Symphony No.3.* ***
(*(*)) Pearl GEMMCD 9037 [id.]. Boston SO, Koussevitzky – MENDELSSOHN: *Symphony No. 4;*
    SCHUMANN: *Symphony No. 1.* (*(*))
(BB) ** Tring Dig. TRP 022 [id.].RPO, Claire Gibault – BEETHOVEN: *Symphony No. 5.* **(*)

Sinopoli secures the most ravishingly refined and beautiful playing; the orchestral blend, particularly of the woodwind and horns, is magical. It is a deeply concentrated reading of the *Unfinished*, bringing out much unexpected detail, with every phrase freshly turned in seamless spontaneity. The contrast, as Sinopoli sees it, is between the dark – yet never histrionic – tragedy of the first movement, relieved only partially by the lovely second subject, and the sunlight of the closing movement, giving an unforgettable, gentle radiance. The exposition repeat is observed, adding weight and substance. This takes its place among the recorded classics. The warmly atmospheric recording, made in Kingsway Hall, is very impressive.

Levine in his strong, dramatic reading demonstrates the prowess of his own opera orchestra in the regular orchestral repertory. After the sombre opening motif, the brightness of the first subject leads on to a performance full of bold contrasts, with the crescendo at the beginning of the development bringing a frisson of excitement, as a live performance would. Full-bodied sound, set against greater reverberance than you normally find in Manhattan Center recordings. A good recommendation for anyone wanting this in the attractive and generous but unusual coupling with Beethoven's *Eroica.*

Koussevitzky's 1936 account of the *Unfinished* has dignity and eloquence. It is beautifully played, but the present transfer robs it of sonority. The recording is top-heavy and it sounds as if there is an octave missing in the bass. An unpleasant sound, but a wonderful performance.

Claire Gibault is both dramatic and sensitive to the work's powerful romantic feeling. Her reading has a striking momentum, but for many listeners her tempi for the second movement will seem fractionally too fast.

Symphonies Nos. 8 in B min. (Unfinished); 9 in C (Great).
** DG Dig. 437 689-2 [id.]. Dresden State O, Sinopoli.

Sinopoli recorded the *Unfinished* before, with the Philharmonia, in an exceptionally spacious, intense reading (see above). The 1992 Dresden recording is not only markedly faster, the speeds are more flexible and Sinopoli's observance of dynamic markings is also freer. Nevertheless the radiant playing of the Dresden orchestra helps to make it convincing, but in the *Great C major* the instability of tempo is more damaging to overall cohesiveness. The result lacks the strength and purposefulness of the finest readings.

Symphony No. 9 in C (Great), D.944.
(BB) *(*) Naxos Dig. 8.553096 [id.]. Failoni O of Budapest, Michael Halász.

The *Ninth* is the one disappointment of the Halász cycle. His control of tempo in the first movement is not always convincing, and the *Andante* does not avoid a suspicion of routine. The Scherzo goes well, but the conductor's grip on the finale is not always taut enough, and the listener is made conscious of its length. First choice for the *Great C Major* rests jointly with Abbado (DG 423 656-2) and, for those preferring period instruments, Mackerras (Virgin VER5 61245-2).

CHAMBER MUSIC

Arpeggione sonata in A min., D. 821.
**(*) EMI Dig. CDC5 55166-2 [id.]. Caussé, Duchable – BEETHOVEN: *Notturno;* REINECKE:
    Fantasiestücke. ***
** DG Dig. 419 787-2 [id.]. Haimovitz, Levine – SCHUMANN: *Adagio & allegro* etc. **

Gérard Caussé gives a refined account of the *Arpeggione sonata* with François-René Duchable. His
viola sounds closer to the original instrument than does the modern cello. Though he is the opposite
of insensitive, Duchable is not always the most imaginative partner. Readers should turn to Maisky
and Argerich, also coupled with music of Schumann (Philips 412 230-2).

   Matt Haimovitz is far less restrained or refined than Caussé and he tends to gush. This is upfront
recording in the current DG manner.

Arpeggione sonata, D.821 (arr. for cello).
(M) **(*). Decca 443 575-2 [id.]. Rostropovich, Britten – BRIDGE: *Cello sonata.* ***

Rostropovich gives a curiously self-indulgent interpretation of Schubert's slight but amiable *Arpeggione sonata.* The playing of both artists is eloquent and it is beautifully recorded, but it will not be to
all tastes. However, the 1968 recording is particularly valuable for its coupling of the Bridge *Sonata.*
The reissue is part of Decca's Classic Sound series.

(i) *Fantasy in C, D.934;* (i; ii) *Piano trio No. 2 in E flat, D.929;* (iii) *String quartets Nos. 8 in B flat,
D.112 (Op. 168); 14 in D min. (Death and the Maiden), D.810; 15 in G, D.887 (Op. 161).*
(***) Pearl mono GEMMCDS 9141 (2) [id.]. (i) Adolf Busch, Rudolf Serkin; (iii) with Hermann
    Busch; (iii) Busch Qt.

Some have spoken of the Busch Quartet's Schubert as the greatest ever committed to disc. Certainly
the *G major Quartet* has never had so searching and powerful a reading, and the early *B flat Quartet,*
which used to be known as Op. 168, sounds every bit as captivating as one remembers it from the
days of shellac. The *E flat Trio* and the *C major Fantasy* are also in the highest class, and the Pearl
transfers are very good indeed. These two CDs, packed economically in one jewel-case, encompass
three LPs and are really excellent value for money. A lovely set.

Octet in F, D.803.
(M) *** O-L Dig. 444 160-2 [id.]. AAM Chamber Ens.

The Academy's Chamber Ensemble, using period instruments, brings out the open joyfulness of
Schubert's inspiration, with excellent matching and vivid recording. The reading is not at all stiff or
pedantic, but personal and relaxed, with the clarinettist, Antony Pay, the obvious leader, playing his
solos with yearning beauty, notably in the second-movement *Andante,* which has heavenly gentleness
and repose. Lightness is the keynote, with speeds never eccentrically fast. However, first choice (as
with Mendelssohn's *Octet*) rests with Hausmusik, and their version was awarded a Rosette in our
main volume (EMI CDC7 54118-2).

Piano quintet in A (Trout), D. 667; Adagio and Rondo concertante in F, D.487.
(M) ** Virgin/EMI Dig. VC5 61140-2 [id.]. Domus (with Chi-chi Nwanoku).

The Domus recording on Virgin with Chi-chi Nwanoku as double-bass offers some splendid and
intelligent playing, in particular from the pianist, Susan Tomes. They would enjoy a higher star-rating
were the recording better balanced and the piano better focused. They offer the appealing *Adagio and
Rondo concertante in F major* as a fill-up, to which they add a double-bass part, but the recording
again poses problems. The Decca *Trout* with András Schiff and the Hagen Quartet is still the one to
go for (411 975-2).

String quartet No. 8 in B flat, D.112.
(M) (***) EMI mono CHS5 65308-2 (4) [id.]. Busch Qt (with MENDELSSOHN: *Capriccio in E min.*) –
    BEETHOVEN: *String quartets.* *** ⊛

The excellence and lightness of spirit the Busch communicate in this quartet is exhilarating. There is
an alternative transfer available on Pearl (see above).

*String quartets Nos. 12 in C min. (Quartettsatz), D.703; 13 in A min., D.804; 14 in D min. (Death and
the Maiden); 15 in G, D.887.*
⊛ (B) *** Ph. Duo 446 163-2 (2) [id.]. Italian Qt.

The Italian Quartet's 1965 coupling of the *Quartettsatz* and the *Death and the Maiden quartet* was
counted the finest available in its day, with the famous variations played with great imagination and
showing a notable grip in the closing pages. Technically the playing throughout is remarkable. There

is just a hint of edge on the sound at times, but the original recording was very well balanced, and the CD adds to the immediacy. These players' understanding of Schubert is equally reflected in their performance of the *A minor Quartet*, recorded a decade later. Originally the long exposition repeat was omitted to get the work on a single LP side; now it has been restored. The familiar '*Rosamunde*' slow movement is (to our ears) beautifully paced – though some may find it a bit slow – and again has an impressive command of feeling. The 1976 sound, too, is first class. The *G major Quartet* is, if anything, even finer. The conception is bold, the playing is distinguished by the highest standards of ensemble, intonation and blend, and the recording is extremely vivid. The Italians take an extremely broad view of the first movement and they shape the strong contrasts of tempo and mood into an impressively integrated whole. The playing is no less deeply felt elsewhere in the work, making this – even after nearly two decades – one of the most thought-provoking accounts of the *Quartet* now before the public. The 1977 recording still sounds remarkably real and present. The CD transfers throughout this set are a great credit to the Philips engineers.

String quintet in C, D.956.
*** Channel Classics Dig. CCS 6794 [id.]. Orpheus Qt, Peter Wispelwey.
*** Teldec/Warner Dig. 4509 94564-2 [id.]. Borodin Qt, Misha Milman.
(***) Biddulph mono LAB 093 [id.]. Pro Arte Qt with Anthony Pini – BRAHMS: *String sextet No. 1.*
  (***)

Two outstanding new versions of the Schubert *Quintet* that reinforce its claims to be among the very greatest of all chamber works. Neither quite matches our two primary recommendations in depth of intensity – the Lindsays (ASV CDDCA 537) with their sense in the *Adagio* of appearing motionless, suspended as it were between reality and dream, or the Aeolian Quartet on Saga (EC 3368) who daringly adopt the slowest possible tempo and create hushed pianissimos of the most extraordinary concentration. But the Orpheus Quintet still offer a performance of communicated warmth and feeling, both in the slow movement and in the remarkable *Andante* central section of the Scherzo. The playing is fresh and feels alive, and the recording has striking body and realism.

On Teldec, the augmented Borodin Quartet command the listener's rapt attention throughout a performance which demonstrates both their emotional involvement and their almost unique unanimity of ensemble. Indeed the sustained D flat major central episode of the Scherzo brings a quite extraordinary matching of tone and ensemble, with the group seemingly speaking with a single hushed voice, whereas in the Orpheus account the listener is more aware of the presence of individual players. In the first movement the more romantic feeling of the secondary theme is at one with the atmosphere of the finale, which liltingly brings a reminder that Schubert also composed the *Rosamunde* ballet music. The *Adagio* is beautifully played, but its special, almost unearthly intensity is not experienced to the full, as the players strive – with great success – to create the most beautifully blended sound. The recording is superbly balanced, and it is impossible for the listener not to respond to music-making of this calibre.

The Pro Arte Quartet's 1935 account of the Schubert *Quintet*, with Anthony Pini as second cello, dominated the pre-war catalogues. Its humanity and warmth still tell and, though it was to give way after the war to the superb Hollywood account, newly restored on Testament (SABT 1031 – see our main volume) and the version by Casals on Philips, it still casts a spell, particularly in the slow movement. It comes with a fine account of the Brahms *B flat Sextet*, made in the same year. Needless to say, some allowance has to be made for the recording, eminently well transferred though it is.

PIANO MUSIC

Piano duet

Divertissement à la hongroise, D.818; Lebensstürme, D.947; 2 Marches caractéristiques, D.886.
(BB) ** Naxos Dig. 8.550555 [id.]. Jenö Jandó, Ilona Prunyi.

No complaints about Jandó and Prunyi, but they are nowhere near in the same league as Tal and Groethuysen on Sony (S2K 58955 – see our main volume). Although this is at full price and we are as keen on economy as the next person, it really is worth paying extra for playing of such vibrant personality and imagination.

Fantasia in F min., D.940.
*** Chan. Dig. CHAN 9162 [id.]. Lortie, Mercier – MOZART: *Andante with variations* etc. ***

We commented on the Mozart *Sonata in A major*, K.448, and the *Andante and variations* in our main volume (page 764), but the Schubert slipped through the net. Suffice it to say that the Louis Lortie–Hélène Mercier partnership is as impressive here as it is elsewhere. The Schubert holds its own even against such illustrious competition as the Lupu–Perahia recording on Sony, also coupled with Mozart's K.448. Very good recording.

Solo piano music
Allegretto in C min., D.915; 3 Klavierstücke (Impromptus), D.946.
(B) ** Carlton Dig. PCD 1002 [id.]. Joeres – VOŘÍŠEK: *Impromptus.* **

It was an intelligent idea to couple these Schubert *Impromptus* with the Voříšek pieces that inspired them (and indeed the whole genre). The German pianist, Dirk Joeres, is a sensitive and imaginative player, and his playing will give pleasure, though his recording is just a shade bass-heavy.

Impromptus 1–4, D.899; Moments musicaux 1–6, D.780; 6 German dances, D.820; Grazer Galopp, D.925; Hungarian melody in B min., D.817.
*** Decca Dig. 430 425-2 [id.]. András Schiff.

Impromptus Nos. 5–8, D.935; 3 Klavierstücke, D.946; Allegretto in C min., D.915; 12 Ländler, D.790.
*** Decca Dig. 425 638-2 [id.]. András Schiff.

It was with this pair of 1990 discs that András Schiff laid the foundations for his Schubertian odyssey. The playing is idiomatic, intelligent and humane, and the recording more than acceptable. It is impossible to recommend his *Impromptus* over and above those of Perahia, Gavrilov, Brendel or Lupu, but no one who has found satisfaction in his current survey of the sonatas will be disappointed with them. We had hoped the arrangement of repertoire would have been reordered by Decca so that (as with major competitors) the eight *Impromptus* would have been placed on a single CD, but that has not yet happened.

Impromptu No. 1, D.899; Klavierstück in E flat min., D.946/1 (original versions); 3 Klavierstücke, D.946; 6 Moments musicaux, D.780.
*** EMI/Virgin Dig. VC7 59 288-2 [id.]. Orkis (fortepiano).

As we said of his set of *Impromptus* in our main volume, those who think they are allergic to the fortepiano should try listening to Lambert Orkis. He has a refreshing vitality and is fully attuned to the Schubertian sensibility. Those who enjoyed the *Impromptus* will need no further prompting, but others should try this disc. We have here playing of imagination and artistry, and very well recorded too. The disc is of particular interest in that it affords an opportunity to hear the shorter, original version of the first *Impromptu* of the D.899 group, and the pencilled draft of the first *Klavierstücke* with the additional episode which Schubert later excised. A fascinating and rewarding disc.

Moments musicaux Nos. 1–6, D.780; 3 Klavierstücke, D. 946.
(M) *** Virgin Veritas/EMI Dig. VER5 61161-2 [id.]. Melvyn Tan (fortepiano) – BEETHOVEN: *Allegretto in C min.* etc. ***

These pieces sound very effective indeed on Melvyn Tan's fortepiano (a modern instrument by Derek Adlam, modelled on an 1814 Viennese instrument). Tan finds a remarkable range of colour and, though the effect is less mellow than with a modern instrument, one's ears adjust almost immediately, so strongly does his playing project. Indeed, with textures clear but by no means bare, the music's inner emotional feeling is conveyed the more readily, while the perky *No. 3 in F minor* has a most engaging character when articulated with such precison.

Piano sonatas Nos. 2 in C, D.279; 11 in F min., D.625; 21 in B flat, D.960.
*** Decca Dig. 440 310-2 [id.]. András Schiff.

Piano sonatas Nos. 4 in A min., D.537; 20 in A, D.959.
*** Decca Dig. 440 309-2 [id.]. András Schiff.

Piano sonatas Nos. 7 in E flat, D.568; 19 in C min., D.958.
*** Decca Dig. 440 308-2 [id.]. András Schiff.

We discussed the first three volumes in András Schiff's projected seven-CD survey of the Schubert sonatas for Decca. In his note, Schiff calls them 'among the most sublime compositions written for the instrument' – and he plays them as if they are, too. There is formidable competition, particularly in the *A major* and great *B flat Sonata* from Kempff and Kovacevich (see below), but those who have started collecting this new cycle can be reassured that the finesse and insight that distinguished the earlier issues are present in these newcomers.

Piano sonatas Nos. 13 in A, D.664; 14 in A min., D.784; Hungarian melody, D.817; 12 Waltzes, D.145.
⊛ (M) *** Decca 443 579-2 [id.]. Ashkenazy.

A magnificent record in every respect. Ashkenazy is a great Schubertian who can realize the touching humanity of this giant's vision as well as his strength. There is an astonishing directness about these performances and a virility tempered by tenderness. This matches Ashkenazy's own high standards, and Decca have risen remarkably to the occasion. The 1966 analogue recording, reissued in Decca's Classic Sound series, has splendid range and fidelity. We gave the original LP a Rosette and see no reason to withhold it now.

Piano sonatas Nos. 13 in A, D.664; 21 in B flat, D.960.
*** Decca Dig. 440 295-2 [id.]. Radu Lupu.

Notwithstanding their ongoing series of Schubert *Sonatas* from András Schiff, Decca have celebrated Radu Lupu's first return to the studios in over a decade with new recordings of two Schubert *Sonatas*. It is one of the most searching of all new Schubert recordings and finds this masterly pianist at his most eloquent and thoughtful. Not as well recorded as Schiff – but don't let that worry you. This is rather special playing.

Piano sonata No. 17 in D, D.850; Impromptus in A flat; in G flat, D.819/3–4; Moments musicaux Nos. 1–6, D. 780.
(M) *** Decca 443 570-2 [id.]. Clifford Curzon.

The passage to savour first in the *Sonata* is the beginning of the last movement, an example of the Curzon magic at its most intense, for with a comparatively slow speed he gives the rhythm a gentle 'lift' which is most captivating. Some who know more forceful interpretations (Richter did a marvellous one) may find this too wayward, but Schubert surely thrives on some degree of coaxing. Curzon could hardly be more convincing – the spontaneous feeling of a live performance captured better than in many earlier discs. Curzon also gives superb performances of the *Moments musicaux*. These readings are among the most poetic in the catalogue, and the recording throughout is exemplary. The *Impromptus* make an attractive bonus (the *G flat major* particularly magical) in this reissue in Decca's Classic Sound series, and they too are beautifully played. The recording remains of Decca's finest analogue quality.

Piano sonata No. 21 in B flat, D.960; Allegretto in C min., D.915; 12 Ländler, D.790.
⊛ *** EMI Dig. CDC5 55359-2 [id.]. Kovacevich.

Stephen Kovacevich made a memorable recording of the great *B flat major Sonata* for Hyperion which (in our 1988 edition) we called 'one of the most eloquent accounts on record of this sublime sonata and one which is completely free of expressive point-making. It is an account which totally reconciles the demands of truth and the attainment of beauty.' One could well say the same of the present version, though, if anything, it explores an even deeper vein of feeling than its predecessor. Indeed it is the most searching and penetrating account of the work to have appeared in recent years and, given the excellence and truthfulness of the recording, must carry the strongest and most enthusiastic recommendation.

Piano sonata No. 21 in B flat, D.960; Impromptus: in G flat; in E flat, D.899/2 & 3; in B flat, D.935/3; Moments musicaux: in A flat; in F min., D.780/2 & 5.
⊛ (B) *** DG 439 462-2 [id.]. Wilhelm Kempff.

It is a tribute to Kempff's inspirational artistry that with the most relaxed tempi he conveys such consistent, compelling intensity in Schubert's greatest sonata. So completely spontaneous is the effect that he is seemingly playing the work in front of the listener here and now rather than in 1967 when this miraculously realistic and beautiful recording was made. Kempff's long-breathed expressiveness is hypnotic, so that here quite as much as in the *Great C major Symphony* one is bound by the spell of the heavenly length. Rightly, Kempff repeats the first-movement exposition repeat with the important nine bars of lead-back and, though the overall manner is less obviously dramatic than is common, the range of tone-colour is magical, with sharp terracing of dynamics to plot the geography of each movement. This remarkable performance belongs to a tradition of pianism that has almost disappeared, and we must be eternally grateful that its expression has been so glowingly captured. After the sonata we are offered an attractively diverse mini-recital of *Moments musicaux* and *Impromptus*, opening with the treasurable *G flat Impromptu*, D.899/2. This is perhaps the very finest of all the distinguished reissues on DG's Classikon bargain label so far.

VOCAL MUSIC

Lieder, Vol. XXI: Songs from 1817–18: *Die abgeblühte Linde; Abschied von einem Freunde; An die Musik; An eine Quelle; Erlafsee; Blondel zu Marien; Blumenbrief; Evangelium Johannes; Der Flug der Zeit; Die Forelle; Grablied für die Mutter; Häbflings Liebeswerbung; Impromptu; Die Liebe; Liebhaber in allen Gestalten; Lied eines Kind; Das Lied vom Reifen; Lob der Tränen; Der Schäfer und der Reiter; Schlaflied; Schweizerlied; Sehnsucht; Trost; Vom Mitleiden Mariä.*
*** Hyp. Dig. CDJ 33021 [id.]. Edith Mathis, Graham Johnson.

Instead of adopting a particular theme for this sequence, sung with characteristic sweetness by the Swiss soprano, Edith Mathis, Graham Johnson has devised a delectable group of 24 songs written in 1817–18, including a high proportion of charmers. Two of them are among the best known of all Schubert's songs, *Die Forelle* ('The trout') and *An die Musik*, here sung with disarming freshness and given extra point through Johnson's inspired playing. The songs in swinging compound or triple time are particularly delightful, as are the often elaborately decorative accompaniments which Johnson points with winning delicacy. As always, his notes make one ever eager to listen with new ears. How fascinating to find that Goethe's attempts to imitate Swiss dialect in the *Schweizerlied* are far from perfect. The song remains a delight.

Lieder, Vol. XXII: *'Schubertiad II': Der Abend; Das Abendroth; An die Sonne; An Rosa I & II; An Sie; Das Bild; Cora an die Sonne; Cronnan; Die drei Sänger; Die Erscheinung; Furcht der Geliebten; Gebet wahrend der Schlacht; Genugsamkeit; Das Grab; Hermann und Thusnelda; Das Leben ist ein Traum; Lob des Tokayers; Lorma; Das Mädchen aus der Fremde; Morgenlied; Punschlied; Scholie; Selma und Selmar; Die Sterne; Trinklied; Vaterlandslied.*
*** Hyp. Dig. CDJ 33022 [id.]. Lorna Anderson, Catherine Wyn-Rogers, Jamie MacDougall, Simon Keenlyside; Graham Johnson.

The year 1815 was an *annus mirabilis* for Schubert, and Graham Johnson here, from the wealth of songs written in those twelve months, devises a sequence such as the composer might have performed with friends in an intimate Schubertiad. So the solo items are punctuated by three male-voice quartets and one trio for female voices in which the main soloists, listed above, are joined by four other distinguished singers: Patricia Rozario, Catherine Denley, John Mark Ainsley and Michael George. Though most of the 28 items are brief, they include one more-extended song, *Die drei Sänger* ('The three minstrels'), in which Schubert adventurously illustrates the narrative in an almost operatic way. The final page is missing from the manuscript, which has meant that for 150 years the piece has been almost totally neglected. Though, as Johnson suggests, Schubert's experimenting is only partially successful, no song-lover will reject such a rarity, here sensitively completed by Reinhard von Hoorickx.

Lieder, Volume XXIII: Songs from 1816: *Abendlied; Abschied von der Harfe; Am ersten Maimorgen; An Chloen; Bei dem Grabe meines Vater; Edone; Der Entfernten; Freude der Kinderjahre; Die frühe Liebe; Geist der Liebe; Gesänger des Harfners aus 'Wilhelm Meister' (Wer sich der Einsamkeit ergibt; Wer nie sein Brot mit Tränen ass; An die Türen will ich schleichen); Das Grab; Der Hirt; Julius an Theone; Der Jüngling an der Quelle; Klage; Die Knabenzeit; Der Leidende (2 versions); Die Liebesgötter; Mailied; Pflügerlied; Romanze; Skolie; Stimme der Liebe; Der Tod Oscars; Zufriedenheit.*
*** Hyp. Dig. CDJ 33023 [id.]. Christoph Prégardien, Graham Johnson.

The German lyric tenor, Christoph Prégardien, uses his lovely voice with its honeyed tone-colours through a wide, expressive range in a very varied selection of songs from 1816. It is his artistry as well as Johnson's that makes the opening item so riveting, a long narrative song to words by Ossian in translation, which could easily seem boring in less sensitive hands but which Prégardien's feeling for word-meaning helps to bring to life. Even Fischer-Dieskau ignored such songs in his big survey for DG, but Johnson and his singers consistently demonstrate their fine qualities. That is followed by a brief chorus, *Der Grab*, sung by the London Schubert Chorale, which Johnson intends as a comment on that narrative. The poet is Johann von Salis-Seewis, who is also represented by four solo songs, including the ravishing *Der Jungling an der Quelle*, one of the most haunting that Schubert ever composed. In that year Schubert was expanding the range of poets he chose to set, including Johann Mayrhofer for the first time, here represented by the little-known *Der Hirt* ('The shepherd'). The selection of 19 items is rumbustiously rounded off by a drinking-song, *Skolie*.

Lieder: *Erlkönig; Erster Verlust; Fischerweise; Die Forelle; Ganymed; Gesang des Harfners I (Wer sich der Einsamkeit ergibt); Ihr Bild; Der Jungling und der Tod; Liebesbotschaft; Nacht und Träume; Der Schiffer; Seligkeit; Der Wanderer an den Mond.*
(M) (***) Decca mono 440 065-2 [id.]. Souzay, Bonneau – SCHUMANN: *Dichterliebe.* (***)

Gérard Souzay recorded the majority of these songs in 1956, though three of them, *Gesang des Harfners, Erlkönig* and *Fischerweise*, were recorded in 1950 at the outset of his international career. Souzay was the first French singer to have mastered German song; more often than not, Schubert and Schumann were sung by such masters as Georges Thill, Vanni-Marcoux and Panzéra in French. The voice possesses a wonderful freshness and poignancy; and 'the beauty of timbre and evenness of production' to which John Steane alludes in his authoritative notes is strikingly in evidence. Souzay's command of legato is matched by an ability to characterize that is second to none and which he must have learnt from his teachers, Croiza and Bernac. There is all too little of his German Lieder on disc at present though Philips did briefly restore his *Winterreise* and *Die schöne Müllerin* to circulation some time ago. The early Schubert discs he made for Decca are to be cherished, and their reissue could not be more timely or welcome. Readers are also referred to the four-CD Philips set of his French repertoire listed under the Recitals section of this volume.

Lieder: *An die Laute; An die Leier; An die Musik; An Silvia; Auf der Bruck; Du bist die Ruh';
Erlkönig; Das Fischermädchen; Die Forelle; Ganymed; Gruppe aus dem Tartarus; Heidenröslein;
Lachen und Weinen; Litanei auf das Fest; Meeres Stille; Der Musensohn; Rastlose Liebe; Schäfers
Klagelied; Ständchen; Die Taubenpost; Der Tod und das Mädchen; Der Wanderer; Wandrers
Nachtlied.*
*** DG Dig. 445 294-2 [id.]. Bryn Terfel, Malcolm Martineau.

Bryn Terfel's DG disc of Schubert appeared at the period when he was scoring sensational success in début recitals both at the Salzburg Festival and in New York. It confirms how this young Welsh bass-baritone has an exceptional gift to project his magnetic personality with comparable intensity, whether in opera or in Lieder, whether live or on disc. Terfel's achievement emerges the more tellingly when the disc appeared simultaneously with another excellent issue in which another British singer, Simon Keenlyside, is also accompanied by Malcolm Martineau. Terfel emerges from the comparison as an even more positive artist, giving strikingly individual and imaginative readings of these 23 favourite songs.

As you immediately realize in the three songs common to both collections – *Heidenröslein, An Silvia* and *Du bist die Ruh'* – Terfel is far more daring in confronting you face to face, very much as the young Fischer-Dieskau did, using the widest range of dynamic and tone. You might argue that Terfel's characterization of the different characters in *Erlkönig* is too extreme, but it is a measure of his magnetism that the result is so dramatically compelling. Full, firm sound.

Lieder: *An die Musik; An Sylvia; Auf dem Wasser zu singen; Ave Maria; Du bist die Ruh'; Die
Forelle; Ganymed; Gretchen am Spinnrade; Heidenröslein; Im Frühling; Die junge Nonne; Litanei;
Mignon und der Harfner; Der Musensohn; Nacht und Träume; Sei mir gegrüsst; Seligkeit.*
(B) *** Carlton Dig. PCD 2016 [id.]. Felicity Lott, Graham Johnson.

At bargain price, Felicity Lott's collection brings an ideal choice of songs for the general collector. With Graham Johnson the most imaginative accompanist, even the best-known songs emerge fresh and new, and gentle songs like *Litanei* are raptly beautiful.

Lieder: *An Sylvia; Auf der Bruck; Bei dir allein; Du bist die Ruh'; Der Einsame; Freiwilliges
Versinken; Gondelfahrer; Die Götter Greichenlands; Gruppe aus dem Tartarus; Heidenröslein;
Himmelsfunken; Im Haine; Der Jüngling an der Quelle; Lied eines Schiffers; Nachtviolen; Prometheus;
Ständchen; Die Sterne; Waldesnacht; Der Wanderer an den Mond.*
(M) *** EMI Dig. CD-EMX 2224; *TC-EMX 2224.* Simon Keenlyside, Malcolm Martineau.

The velvety beauty of Keenlyside's cleanly focused baritone goes with fresh, thoughtful readings of 20 favourite songs, perfectly judged, with ever-sensitive accompaniment from Martineau. At mid-price it makes another outstanding recommendation for a Schubert disc which includes one or two unusual songs among many favourites.

(i) *Lazarus* (cantata); (ii) *Mass in G, D.167.*
(M) *** Erato/Warner 4509 98533-2 (2) [id.].(i) Armstrong, Welting; (i–ii) Chamonin, Rolfe Johnson;
(i) Hill; (i–ii) Egel, Ch. and New French R. PO, Guschlbauer.

Lazarus is a rarity both in the concert hall and as recorded music. Schubert put the score on one side in February 1820 and never returned to it; perhaps he realized that it was too wanting in contrast and variety. About 80 minutes or so survive, and then the work comes to an abrupt end in the middle of a soprano solo! Yet, for all its uniformity of mood and pace, *Lazarus* is well worth having on record. Some of it is as touching as the finest Schubert, and other sections are little short of inspired; there are some thoroughly characteristic harmonic colourings and some powerful writing for the trombones. Much of it is very fine indeed, though it would be idle to pretend that its inspiration is even or sustained. Nevertheless no Schubertian would want to be without it, for the best of it is quite lovely. The singers and the French Radio forces are thoroughly persuasive, and it would be difficult to fault Theodore Guschlbauer's direction or the warm quality of the sound achieved by the engineers. The *G major Mass*, an earlier piece written when Schubert was only eighteen, has less depth and subtlety than the best of *Lazarus*; but there are some endearing moments and the *Agnus Dei* is poignant. Again the performance and recording here are excellent.

Magnificat, D.486; Offertorium, D.963; Stabat Mater, D.383.
(M) *** Erato/Warner 4509 96961-2 [id.]. Armstrong, Schaer, Ramirez, Huttenlocher, Goy, Lausanne Vocal Ens. & CO, Corbóz.

Schubert's strikingly fresh setting of the *Stabat Mater* (in Klopstock's German translation) dates from the composer's nineteenth year, yet it shows him at the height of his early powers and has many anticipations of later music, especially in the Terzetto for soprano, tenor, bass and chorus (No. 11) and the fine chorus, *Wer wird Zähren sanften Mitleids* (No. 5), with its superb horn-writing. There is a lovely, Bach-like tenor aria, with oboe obbligato, in which Alejandro Ramirez is very stylish; and the bass aria, *Sohn des Vaters*, recalls the Mozart of *Die Zauberflöte*. Here Philippe Huttenlocher may not be quite dark enough but his pure-sounding baritone remains very appealing. The chorus is incisive, both in counterpoint in Schubert's lively if somewhat pedagogic fugues, and in the simple chordal writing. The other, lesser pieces make a good coupling, also persuasively directed by Corboz, and the recording, although not crystal clear, has transferred vividly.

Die schöne Müllerin (song-cycle), *D. 795.*
(M) *** CfP CD-CFP 4672; *TC-CFP 4672* [id.]. Ian and Jennifer Partridge.
**(*) Decca Dig. 440 354-2 [id.]. Uwe Heilmann, James Levine.

Dietrich Fischer-Dieskau's classic 1972 version with Gerald Moore on DG remains among the finest ever recorded (415 186-2), and this is also available within his huge, all-embracing box of Lieder – see Vocal Recitals, below. However, Ian Partridge's is an exceptionally fresh and urgent account. Rarely if ever on record has the dynamic quality of the cycle of Schubert songs been so effectively conveyed, rising to an emotional climax at the end of the first half with the song *Mein!*, expressing the poet's ill-found joy welling up infectiously. Partridge's subtle and beautiful range of tone is a constant delight, and he is most imaginatively accompanied by his sister, Jennifer. The balance of the 1973 recording is forward and present: this is an outstanding bargain reissue and should win many new friends for Lieder.

With James Levine a sensitive accompanist, the tenor, Uwe Heilmann, gives a deeply felt reading, often headily beautiful but at times too heavily pointed both in detail of word-meaning and in musical phrase. The last two songs about the brook are finely sustained at spacious speeds, giving a foretaste of the darkness of *Die Winterreise*. The recording – made in the Margrave's opera house in Bayreuth in August 1992 – captures the distinctive voice well but, with lightness in the bass, makes the piano too clattery.

Winterreise (song-cycle), D.911.
(M) *** DG 447 421-2 [id.]. Dietrich Fischer-Dieskau, Joerg Demus.
*** Virgin/EMI Dig. VC5 45070-2 [id.]. Thomas Allen, Roger Vignoles.
(M) **(*) DG Dig. 445 521-2 [id.]. Christa Ludwig, James Levine.

There are those who regard Fischer-Dieskau's third recording of *Winterreise* as the finest of all, such is the peak of beauty and tonal expressiveness that the voice had achieved in the mid-1960s, and the poetic restraint of Demus' accompaniment. The recording still sounds well, and as a mid-price reissue in DG's Legendary Recordings series it certainly makes an excellent recommendation.

Thomas Allen, understandingly supported by Roger Vignoles, tackles this Everest of the Lieder repertory with a beauty of tone and line that sets his reading apart. Allen's concentration on purely musical qualities, far from watering down word-meaning, is used to intensify the tragic emotions of the wandering lover. Allen uses a wider dynamic range than most of his direct rivals, shading the voice down to a half-tone for intimate revelations, then expanding dramatically, using the art of the opera-singer. In the two final songs, *Die Nebensonnen* and *Der Leiermann*, he is very restrained, keeping them hushed instead of underlining expressiveness. The poignancy of Schubert's inspiration is allowed to speak for itself.

With James Levine a concentrated and often dramatic accompanist, consistently adding to the sense of spontaneous and immediate communication, Christa Ludwig gives a warmly satisfying performance, making use of the mature richness of the voice rather than bringing any striking new insights. Though the different sections of *Frühlingstraum*, for example, are beautifully contrasted, it is the extra darkness of the piano in low keys that adds most to the tragedy. Full, natural recording.

Schuman, William (1910–1992)

Symphony No. 7.

(B) ** Vox Box 116021–2 (2). Utah SO, Abravanel – HANSON: *Symphony No. 6;* MACDOWELL: *Suite No. 2 (Indian);* ROREM: *Symphony No. 3;* THOMSON: *Louisiana Story: suite.* **

William Schuman's *Seventh Symphony* dates from 1961 – the same year as Walter Piston's *Seventh*. It is by no means equal in inspiration to Nos. 3–6, all of them highly individual masterpieces in different ways, which should be represented in the catalogue in numerous recordings. Why have Sony not released Bernstein's superb accounts of the *Third* and *Fifth* (and, more impressive than the present work, its successor, No. 8), which he recorded during his spell with the New York Philharmonic in the 1960s? The *Seventh* is frankly arid and manufactured; having known this in its LP form for many years, we have never learnt to love it. The late-lamented Maurice Abravanel, who did so much for modern American music, does all he can for this piece. Decent recording.

Symphony No. 10 (American Muse); American Festival overture; New England triptych. IVES, arr. SCHUMAN: *Variations on America.*

*** RCA Dig. 09026 61282-2 [id.]. St Louis SO, Slatkin.

It is difficult to escape the impression that Schuman's symphonic muse slumbered a little after the *Sixth*, which Ormandy recorded so eloquently in the 1950s. All (save Nos. 1 and 2, which he suppressed) have been recorded, though not all are currently available. His *Tenth Symphony* was composed in 1975 for the United States Bicentennial; it is a three-movement piece whose centre of gravity resides in its big, contemplative middle movement with the usual polytonal choral harmonies. But splendid though much of it is, Schuman's inspiration is touched a little by routine, the gestures sound just a little too much like self-imitation when put alongside the more spontaneous eloquence of symphonies 3–6. There is plenty of excitement in the outer movements and the St Louis orchestra play with enormous conviction. Their performance of the *American Festival overture* is pretty dazzling, too, and yields little to Bernstein's DG account. Both the *New England triptych* and the Ives transcription, *Variations on America*, fare equally well. Those who have been bitten by the Schuman bug will be grateful for this excellent première recording, but for those coming to his music afresh, the *Third* and *Fifth Symphonies* make a better entry point into his world.

Schumann, Robert (1810–56)

Cello concerto in A min., Op. 129.

*** BIS Dig. CD 486 [id.]. Torleif Thedéen, Malmö SO, Markiz – ELGAR: *Concerto.* ***

After listening to Gidon Kremer's account of Schumann's own arrangement of the concerto (see below), it is a relief to return to the original. The young Swedish virtuoso, Torleif Thedéen, is splendidly recorded on BIS, and the Malmö orchestra give him sympathetic support. He plays with a refreshing ardour, tempered by nobility and a reticence that is strongly appealing. He couples it with an account of the Elgar that is every bit as attuned to the latter's sensibility as any in the catalogue. Strongly recommended.

Piano concerto in A min., Op. 54.

(BB) *(*) EMI Seraphim CES5 68522-2 (2) [CDEB 68522]. John Ogdon, New Philh. O, Berglund – GRIEG: *Concerto* *(*); *Peer Gynt* ***; FRANCK: *Symphonic variations for piano and orchestra.* *(*)

*(*) DG Dig. 439 914-2 [id.]. Jean-Marc Luisada, LSO, Tilson Thomas – GRIEG: *Concerto.* *(*)

*(*) EMI Dig. CDM7 64451-2 [id.]. Dmitri Alexeev, RPO, Yuri Temirkanov – GRIEG: *Concerto.* *(*)

* Sony Dig. SK 52567 [id.]. Kissin, VPO, Giulini (with GRIEG: *Carnival scene, Op. 19/3; I love you, Op. 41/3;* LISZT: *Concert paraphrases of Schubert's Erlkönig; Die Forelle; Soirées de Vienne; Valse caprice No. 6* ***).

(M) (*) Decca mono 425 968-2 [id.]. Lipatti, SRO, Ansermet (with BEETHOVEN: *Concerto No. 4* (*)).

(i) *Piano concerto in A min., Op. 54; Arabeske, Op. 18; Etudes symphoniques, Op. 13.*

(M) **(*) DG Dig. 445 522-2 [id.]. Pollini; (i) BPO, Abbado.

(i) *Piano concerto in A min., Op. 54; Carnaval, Op. 9; Kinderszenen (Scenes from childhood), Op. 15.*

(B) **(*) DG 439 476-2 [id.]. Wilhelm Kempff; (i) Bav. RSO, Kubelik.

Kempff, after a rather positive account of the opening chords of the *Piano concerto*, proceeds characteristically to produce an unending stream of poetry. The dialogue of the *Intermezzo* is like an intimate conversation overheard. Tempi are generally leisurely, notably so in the finale where, with fine support from the Bavarian Radio Orchestra under Kubelik, the main theme has an engaging lilt.

Good early-1970s recording. Of the solo recordings neither is among Kempff's more compelling Schumann performances. The comparatively extrovert style of *Carnaval* does not seem to suit him too well and there is no special degree of illumination such as we expect from this artist either here or in the *Scenes from childhood*. Good rather than outstanding piano recording, made in the same period as the concerto.

Pollini's account of the concerto is not without tenderness and poetry (witness the slow movement), but he is at times rather business-like and wanting in freshness. He is handicapped by rather unventilated recording and an inconsistent balance. (The piano seems much further back in the slow movement by comparison with the first.) The coupled piano pieces, however, are in every way successful. His account of the *Symphonic studies* has a symphonic gravitas and concentration; it also has the benefit of excellent recorded quality. Pollini includes the five additional variations that Schumann omitted from both the editions published during his lifetime, placing them as a group between the fifth and sixth variations.

John Ogdon, as in the other works on this well-transferred CD, is unexpectedly below form in what should be one of the most poetic of piano concertos. Clearly the partnership with Berglund did not work well. The interchanges with the orchestral wind soloists in the first movement are lacklustre and the performance overall refuses to catch fire.

DG's digital account with Jean-Marc Luisada and the LSO under Michael Tilson Thomas was made at the EMI Abbey Road No. 1 Studio and offers present and well-detailed sound. Some self-conscious touches apart, there is little out of the ordinary here and the pianism, though accomplished, falls short of real distinction.

Like its Grieg coupling, the performance by Alexeev and Temirkanov is stronger on prose than poetry, though – as with Luisada on DG – the recording is very good.

Evgeny Kissin sounds inhibited and ill at ease in his recording with Giulini and the Vienna Philharmonic. Although he can produce a wide range of pianissimo colour, we do not hear it. Come to think of it, we hear hardly any dynamic shading much below mezzo forte, so closely are we placed. Giulini's soggy accompaniment does not help either. Instead of the normal Grieg coupling, we have a couple of miniatures, the *Carnival scene*, Op. 19/3, and a transcription of his most famous song, *Jeg elsker Dig*, as well as some Liszt paraphrases, including Schubert's *Erlkönig* and *Die Forelle*. All these are played with a spontaneity and poetry that are so elusive in the concerto and need recoupling.

Lipatti's broadcast with the Suisse Romande Orchestra under Ansermet does not show the great pianist at his best. The Karajan Philharmonia version is the one to have (EMI CDH7 69792-2). The Suisse Romande oboe is particularly sour, and the accompaniment generally is prosaic and the recording very indifferent. The Beethoven coupling is no incentive either. Among modern recordings, Kovacevich and Sir Colin Davis stand supreme (Philips 412 923-2).

(i) *Piano concerto in A min., Op. 54;* (ii) *Violin concerto in D min.*
*(**) Teldec/Warner Dig. 4509 90696-2 [id.]. (i) Argerich; (ii) Kremer; COE, Harnoncourt.

In her live recording of the *Piano concerto*, Martha Argerich gives a vividly compelling, characteristically volatile reading, at once poetic and full of fancy, powerful and often wildly individual. The performance, recorded in the Stefaniensaal, Graz, in July 1992 culminates in an account of the finale so daring one wants to cheer at the end, so freely does the adrenalin flow. Though the orchestra is hard-pressed to keep up with her at her fast basic speed, there is a splendid swing to the rhythm and no sense of haste. The central *Andantino grazioso* too brings fantasy and flair, a freely spontaneous reading; but, earlier, the first movement takes some time to settle down. Argerich plays with her usual concentration, but her wilfulness seems to unsettle the players, and the woodwind ensemble at the start is surprisingly rough, not at all typical of this superb orchestra. Kremer's performance of the still-neglected *Violin concerto* is disappointing in comparison with the warmth and bravura of his earlier version, recorded for EMI with Riccardo Muti and the Philharmonia Orchestra. Not only is the speed of the first movement slower, Kremer sounds heavy and over-emphatic to the point of self-consciousness. The slow movement then lacks the magic it had before, the hushed tenderness that made one listen intently, beautiful as Kremer's playing still is. When it comes to the finale, the choice of speed is wildly eccentric, a half-speed such as you would use for a rehearsal, dull and plodding despite the efforts of the orchestra. In neither concerto is the recorded sound ideally warm or full-bodied, with tuttis rather muddy in texture.

Violin concerto in A min., Op. 129 (arr. from *Cello concerto* by the composer and orch. Shostakovich).
**(*) DG Dig. 439 890-2 [id.]. Kremer; Boston SO, Ozawa – SHOSTAKOVICH: *Violin concerto No. 2.*
**(*)

Gidon Kremer's coupling is ingeniously conceived: both the Shostakovich and Schumann concertos are Op. 129. But hang on, you will say, isn't that the opus number of the *Cello concerto in A minor*? Indeed it is – but Schumann himself made an arrangement of the solo part for solo violin; this performance combines that with the orchestral version of the *Cello concerto* which Shostakovich made, aiming to improve on Schumann's own orchestration. Shostakovich's aim in renovating the orchestration – with changes predominantly in the tuttis – was to improve the work for his protégé, Rostropovich. This is the first time Schumann's violin version of his *Cello concerto* has been put on disc. As Kremer demonstrates, there is much to be said for the solution of using the Shostakovich scoring as an accompaniment for the violin version, when the main result of Shostakovich's tinkerings is to give more edge to the orchestral part, making the tuttis cleaner and bolder. The result is a concerto that is not just lighter than the cello version, but lacking the brilliance one usually asks for in a violin concerto, for Schumann's rewriting of the solo line is remarkably discreet, hardly exploiting the potential of the instrument. Nevertheless, Kremer in this live recording performs the piece with his usual flair and imagination, adopting speeds rather faster than those usual in the cello version, and the orchestra sounds fuller-bodied than in the genuine Shostakovich *Concerto*, which comes as coupling.

Symphonies Nos. 1–4.
(B) *** RCA 74321 20294-2 (2). Phd. O, James Levine.
(M) ** Teldec/Warner Dig. 4509 95501-2 (2) [id.]. LPO, Kurt Masur.

The RCA bargain 'Symphony Edition' has already proved a resounding success with Wand's Beethoven and Brahms sets (especially the former) and Berglund's Nielsen. Now comes a splendid set of Schumann to cap the series. Recorded in a glowingly warm acoustic, the Philadelphia Orchestra has seldom sounded so rich-textured over recent years. The strings expand gloriously in the *Adagio* of No. 2; the brass produce the most expansive sonorities in the *Rhenish*. The performances are as vital as they are warm, and Levine usually produces accelerandos at the ends of outer movements to increase the excitement. The series is capped with a superb version of No. 4, where the powerful link into the finale brings brass playing to remind one not only of Wagner but of the *Ring*, and the very flexible account of the finale itself is not only thrilling but in its control of tempo shows that Levine has listened to the famous Furtwängler interpretation, absorbed its detail and made it his own. As we go to press, the two discs have been issued separately at mid-price: *Symphonies Nos. 1* and *3* (74321 20295-2) and *Symphonies Nos. 2* and *4* (74321 20296-2).

Against this, the Masur set, well played as it is and given full-blooded digital sound, is less convincing. The performances have boldness and strength, but slow movements do not match Levine's in romantic expansiveness and the second movement of the *Rhenish* is comparatively brusque. In the *Fourth Symphony* Masur uses the original (1841) Leipzig version of the score favoured by Brahms, where the differences are most marked in the finale.

Symphonies Nos. 1 in B flat (Spring); 2 in C; 3 (Rhenish); 4 in D min. (original Leipzig version); *Overture, scherzo and finale, Op. 52.*
🏵 *** RCA Dig. 09026 61931–2 (2) [id.]. Hanover Band, Goodman.

Roy Goodman's versions on period instruments are a revelation, not just an academic exercise. Few period performances of nineteenth-century works can match these refreshing accounts, either for the vigour and electricity of the playing or for the new perceptions given. Convincingly Goodman shows how these works are far more cohesive in their often volatile inspiration than many used to think. Textures are clarified, but never to reduce the impact of the music, rather to give them exceptionally clean-cut terracing of sound, thanks also to the satisfyingly beefy recording. Most thrilling are the antiphonal contrasts of the brass choirs, setting the braying timbre of period horns (two of the four natural valveless instruments in Nos. 1 and 4, as the composer wanted) against the brightness of the trumpets. The sharp accenting of woodwind comment, often syncopated, is also enhanced, with Goodman securing superb ensemble. The strings are naturally thinner, with violins and cellos unable to expand over the wide dynamic range of modern instruments, but Goodman compensates in encouraging a warmly espressivo style in slow movements, with *Andantes* flowing easily, never trivialized. The first disc contains the three works dating from 1841, not just the *Spring Symphony* (No. 1) and the *Overture, scherzo and finale* but the original Leipzig version of the *Symphony No. 4*, usually heard in the revision of ten years later. Not only is the scoring lighter, the slow transitions into the Allegros of the outer movements are both more compact, with each sequence made very convincing by Goodman, particularly the big crescendo into the finale. Brahms preferred this earlier version, and here one registers why.

Symphony No. 1 in B flat (Spring), Op. 38.
(M) *** DG 447 408-2 [id.]. BPO, Karajan – BRAHMS: *Symphony No. 1.* ***
(*(*)) Pearl GEMMCD9037 [id.] Boston SO, Koussevitzky – MENDELSSOHN: *Symphony No. 4;*
   SCHUBERT: *Symphony No. 8.* (*(*))

Karajan is totally attuned to Schumann's sensibility and he provides a strong yet beautifully shaped performance of the *Spring Symphony*. The very opening is electrifying with the Berlin Philharmonic giving of their finest, and this unsurpassed reading makes a highly appropriate coupling with Brahms in DG's Legendary Performances series of 'Originals'. The sound is an obvious improvement on previous CD incarnations of this well-balanced analogue recording from the early 1970s, adding body and weight to the clear, fresh detail.

   Koussevitzky's account of the *Spring Symphony* opens majestically and is marvellously played, but the present transfer robs it of sonority. It has too much treble and the upper strings sound acidulated. The lower strings of the Boston Symphony never sounded like this on 78s. An unpleasant sound, but a magnificent performance.

Symphony No. 3 in E flat (Rhenish), Op.97.
(M) *** DG Dig. 445 502-2 [id.]. LAPO, Giulini – BEETHOVEN: *Symphony No. 5.* ***

Despite the aristocratic qualities that distinguish his performances and the spirituality that is in evidence, Giulini can often obtrude by the very intensity of his search for perfection; as a result, while the sound he produces is of great beauty, he does not always allow the music to unfold effortlessly. This *Rhenish* is, however, completely free of interpretative exaggeration and its sheer musical vitality and nobility of spirit are beautifully conveyed. The Los Angeles players produce a very well-blended, warm and cultured sound that is a joy to listen to in itself. The 1980 recording is also extremely fine and, with its superb Beethoven coupling, this is very highly recommendable.

CHAMBER MUSIC

Adagio and allegro, Op. 70.
** RCA Dig. 09026 61562-2 [id.]. Janos Starker, Rudolf Buchbinder – BRAHMS: *Cello sonatas.* **

Janos Starker's account of the *Adagio and allegro*, Op. 70, has impressive artistic credentials but suffers from an overlit recording. The piano is too dominant and the listener is consistently close, with resulting aural fatigue. As anyone who has heard him in the flesh knows, Starker produces a small tone and, though he plays with impeccable taste and musicianship, it is a pity that Buchbinder does not scale down his tone to match.

Adagio & allegro, Op. 70; Fantasiestücke, Op. 73; 5 Stücke im Volkston, Op. 102.
** DG Dig. 429 787-2 [id.]. Haimovitz, Levine – SCHUBERT: *Arpeggione sonata.* **

Matt Haimovitz and James Levine give what can best be described as tonally over-nourished accounts of these pieces. Haimowitz, though a player of great natural gifts, is a little too prone to overemphasize, and too many phrases are in expressive italics.

Clarinet sonatas (arr. of *Violin sonatas*) *Nos. 1 in A min., Op. 105; 2 in D min., Op. 121; 3 Romanzen, Op. 94.*
** Sony SK Dig. 48035 [id.]. Neidich, Hokanson.

Charles Neidich won the 1985 Walter Naumburg Competition for the clarinet and plays the two violin sonatas in a transcription for his instrument along with the *Three Romances*, Op. 94, originally written for the oboe. The sonatas do not really work in this medium (the clarinet sonority at the top of the register is shrill and insufficiently sustained), though Neidich is a sensitive enough player and Leonard Hokanson a wonderful partner. His piano is not ideally balanced (there is too much resonance and the instrument is not in perfect condition).

Fantasiestücke, Op. 73.
*** Decca Dig. 430 149-2 [id.]. Cohen, Ashkenazy – BRAHMS: *Clarinet sonatas.* ***
** RCA RD 60598 [09026 60598-2]. Starker, Neriki – BRAHMS; RACHMANINOV: *Sonatas.* **

A thoroughly recommendable account by Franklin Cohen and Vladimir Ashkenazy of these lovely pieces; if you want them on clarinet, this version is as good as any. It is well recorded, too. In the cello version, Starker's playing is warm and lyrical, but all too often Shigeo Neriki swamps his distinguished partner. The sound is vivid and realistic but places us rather too close, with resultant aural fatigue. Starker is a wonderfully aristocratic player and, again, those who are undeterred by the prospect of sitting in the first row, as it were, need not hesitate.

Piano quintet in E flat, Op. 44.
* Sony Dig. SK 58954 [id.]. Artis Qt with Stefan Vladar – BRAHMS: *Piano quintet.* *

Sony's recording with Stefan Vladar and the Artis Quartet is unfortunately a non-starter. The balance favours the piano at the expense of the strings, though not perhaps as much as it does in the Brahms coupling. But even apart from the larger-than-life, bottom-heavy piano-sound, the performance – for all its strength – is no match for existing recommendations. First choice rests with the augmented Beaux Arts Trio (Philips 420 791-2), coupled with the Op. 47 *Piano quartet*; while at super-bargain price Jenö Jandó and the Kodály Quartet offer strong characterization and very good sound. They are coupled with the Brahms *Piano quintet* (Naxos 8.550406).

Piano trios Nos. 1–3; Fantasiestücke, Op. 88.
*** Ph. Dig. 432 165-2 (2) [id.]. Beaux Arts Trio.

The Beaux Arts are probably the safest bet in this repertoire, an instance of the most obvious recommendation being the best. Not that competition is exactly legion, but none that we have heard can outclass the Beaux Arts in terms of musicianship and finesse. Cultured playing, matched by truthful and present recording.

Piano trios Nos. 2 in F, Op. 80; 3 in G min., Op. 110; Fantasiestücke, Op. 88.
** CRD Dig. CRD 3458 [id.].Israel Piano Trio.

We reviewed the first volume of the *Trios* in our main edition. This is much the same: lively, articulate playing with a sometimes too forceful pianist. Not in the same class as the Beaux Arts.

String quartet No. 1 in A min., Op. 41/1.
*** RCA Dig. 09026 61438-2 [id.].Vogler Qt – BRAHMS: *String quartet No. 3.* ***

String quartet No. 3 in A, Op. 41/3.
*** RCA Dig. 09026 61866-2 [id.]. Vogler Qt – BRAHMS: *String quartet No. 2.* ***

Fine accounts of both *Quartets* from the Vogler, an extremely fine quartet who have recently recorded the quartets of both Brahms and Schumann. If the coupling meets your particular needs, it would really be difficult to improve on them. They have the advantage of a rich and beautifully blended sonority and refined musicianship. Moreover the RCA recording is very good indeed. If the *F major Quartet*, Op. 41/2, when it arrives, is their equal, this is likely to be a first recommendation for some years to come.

Violin sonatas Nos. 1 in A min., Op. 105; 2 in D min., Op. 121; Phantasiestücke, Op. 73; Märchenbilder, Op. 113; 3 Romanzen, Op. 94.
(*) RCA 09026 68052-2 (2) [id.]. Pinchas Zukerman, Marc Neikrug.

The Schumann *Violin sonatas* are not all that generously represented in the catalogue, and on the face of it this issue, offering as it does the *Phantasiestücke*, Op. 73, the *Drei Romanzen* and the *Märchenbilder*, which Zukerman plays on the viola, is a useful addition. Neikrug could learn a thing or two about sensitivity from Leonard Hokanson or Martha Argerich (see our main volume) and Zukerman plays with the detached efficiency of a machine-tool-maker. This issue is for those who like industrial rather than human Schumann. Kremer and Argerich remain first choice for the two *Violin sonatas* (DG 419 235-2).

PIANO MUSIC

Arabeske in C, Op. 18; Bunte Blätter, Op. 99; Carnaval, Op. 9; Kreisleriana, Op. 16; 2 Novelettes, Op. 21/1 & 8; Toccata in C, Op. 7.
(BB) *** EMI CMS7 64301-2 (2) [id.]. Youri Egorov.

Two CDs for the same outlay as one mid-price disc represents a great bargain, particularly when the playing is as full of personality as it is here. Like so many Russian pianists, Youri Egorov had a great natural feeling for Schumann and his account of the *Kreisleriana*, made in the 1970s not long after he settled in the West, was particularly successful. The whole programme is very well recorded in good analogue sound. Egorov's early death was a great loss and we are glad to note that EMI have reissued his *Emperor concerto* coupled with the *D minor Concerto*, K.466, of Mozart in their new Seraphim duo series at the same price (see above).

Arabeske, Op. 18; 3 Romanzen; Faschingsschwank aus Wien; Waldszenen.
**(*) DG Dig. 437 538-2 [id.]. Maria João Pires.

Maria João Pires is an artist of insight and temperament. Her Schumann recital, though not in the same league as Lupu's, is well worth hearing. She is a musician of intuition who is thoroughly inside Schumann's world and though in none of these pieces would her version be a first choice, it is still deserving of recommendation.

Carnaval, Op. 9; Kreisleriana, Op. 16.
** Ph. Dig. 442 777-2 [id.]. Mitsuko Uchida.

Mitsuko Uchida, entering an area with which we do not normally associate her, gives pianistically impressive performances and enjoys the advantage of first-class Philips recording. However, she seems all too anxious to make points and unwilling to allow the invention to flow naturally. This does not represent a challenge to the rival accounts listed in our main edition, especially Barenboim, whose bargain coupling of *Carnaval, Faschingsschwank aus Wien* and the *Kinderszenen* is particularly recommendable (DG 431 167-2).

Davidsbündertänze, Op. 6; Fantasiestücke, Op. 12.
(BB) *(*) Naxos Dig. 8.550493 [id.]. Benjamin Frith.

Benjamin Frith, who is also undertaking a Mendelssohn survey for Naxos, is an impressive if rather impulsive interpreter of Schumann. Yet he can be touchingly poetic, as in the opening *Des Abends, Warum?* and *Fabel* from the *Fantasiestücke.* However, Naxos had not, in 1991, solved their studio problem for recording the piano, and the results here in the Clara Wieck Auditorium, Heidelberg, fail to bring enough depth of sonority for this repertoire.

Humoreske, Op. 20; Kinderszenen, Op. 15; Kreisleriana, Op. 16.
*** Decca Dig. 409 496-2 [id.]. Radu Lupu.

This is Schumann playing of quite exceptional insight and naturalness. Lupu is one of the few Schumann interpreters whose understanding of the composer can be measured alongside that of Murray Perahia. His account of the *Humoreske,* Op. 20, is the most poetic and spontaneous since the famous Richter version (issued over here in the 1950s on Parlophone), and the *Kreisleriana* are hardly less magical. This is playing of great poetry and authority. The recording is excellent, albeit resonant, and although there are odd occasions where twangy notes disturb they are of small moment in playing of such distinction. The Schumann piano disc of the year.

VOCAL MUSIC

Dichterliebe (song-cycle).
(M) (***) Decca mono 440 065-2 [id.]. Souzay, Bonneau – SCHUBERT: *Lieder.* ***

This is one of the song records of the year. There have been many recordings of *Dichterliebe* by numerous artists, including such distinguished names as Gerhard Hüsch, Fischer-Dieskau, Hermann Prey and many others, but two of them are very special: the post-war set made in the 1940s by Aksel Schiötz and Gerald Moore, and the present set from Gérard Souzay and Jacqueline Bonneau, recorded in 1953 at the beginning of his international career. Souzay's voice possesses a wonderful freshness and poignancy; and 'the beauty of timbre and evenness of production' to which John Steane alludes in his authoritative notes is strikingly in evidence. The command of legato is matched by an ability to characterize that is second to none. Readers are also referred to the four-CD Philips set of his French repertoire, listed under the Recitals section of this volume.

Frauenliebe und Leben (song-cycle), *Op. 42.*
⊛ (M) *** Saga EC 3361-2 [id.]. Dame Janet Baker, Martin Isepp (with Lieder recital ***).

Janet Baker's range of expression in her earlier, Saga recording of the Schumann cycle runs the whole gamut from a joyful golden tone-colour in the exhilaration of *Ich kann's nicht fassen* through an ecstatic half-tone in *Süsser Freund* (the fulfilment of the line *Du geliebter Mann* wonderfully conveyed) to the dead, vibrato-less tone of agony at the bereavement in the final song. Martin Isepp proves a highly sensitive and supportive partner, and the recording balance – originally curiously artificial – has been immeasurably improved by the CD transfer.

Das Paradies und die Peri, Op. 50.
*** RCA/Eurodisc Dig. RD 69105 [69105-2-RC] (2). Büchner, Schiml, Kaufmann, Planté, Schopper, Sweet, Schmiege, Bamberg Ch. & SO, Kuhn.

Though Clara Schumann described this secular oratorio as the most beautiful work that her husband had yet written, it cannot in lyrical invention match the songs that he was writing at the same time in the early 1840s. Even so, this morality on the theme of salvation has many beauties, and Gustav Kuhn, also responsible for an inspired account of the later, more crisply inspired cantata, *Der Rose*

Pilgerfahrt, conducts his Bamberg forces with freshness and sympathy. This Eurodisc set offers a finer team of soloists and brighter, better-balanced recording than the rival issue on Erato under Armin Jordan, which suffers from indifferent soloists and dim recording of the chorus. The two most important soloists are both clearly preferable in this Eurodisc version: Sharon Sweet powerful if not always ideally firm as the Peri and Eberhard Buchner clear, fresh and keenly idiomatic as the first tenor.

Der Rose Pilgerfahrt, Op. 112.
*** Chan. Dig. CHAN 9350 [id.]. Inga Nielsen, Deon van der Walt, Annemarie Møller, Guido Paevatalu, Danish Nat. R. Ch. and SO, Gustav Kuhn.

Schumann wrote his cantata, *Der Rose Pilgerfahrt* ('The Pilgrimage of the rose'), in 1851 towards the end of his career, inspired by a fairy-tale in verse sent to him by a young poet, then unknown, Moritz Horn. Originally he composed it with piano accompaniment and it was given privately in that form, a sequence of twenty-four varied numbers, some of them linked in subtle, evocative ways. Later he orchestrated the sequence; and the pity is that such a charming, fresh inspiration is so little known, for it defies the usual verdict that Schumann's later music lacks the spark which fired him earlier. The very opening has the lyrical openness of Schubert, its freshness enhanced by the interplay of solo voices and women's chorus. The idiom, as well as recalling Schubert, often suggests the folk-based writing of Humperdinck in *Hänsel und Gretel*, similarly innocent-seeming, but in fact subtle. Gustav Kuhn conducts an aptly bright and atmospheric performance, very well recorded, with the warm-toned Inga Nielsen and the clear-toned tenor, Deon van der Walt, in the two principal roles of the heroine, Rosa, and the tenor narrator. The chorus and orchestra are first rate, with colourful genre numbers including a chorus of elves and a drinking song. The recording, sponsored by Danish Radio, is full-bodied and atmospheric. A valuable rarity. Sadly, the booklet contains no translation alongside the German text, though Richard Wigmore's note and summary are very helpful.

Scenes from Goethe's Faust.
**(*) Sony Dig. SK 66308 (2) [id.]. Terfel, Mattila, Rootering, Bonney, Wottrich, Vermillion, Poschner-Klebel, Graham, Blochwitz, Peeters, BPO, Abbado.
(M) **(*) EMI Dig. CMS7 69450-2 (2) [id.]. Fischer-Dieskau, Mathis, Berry, Gedda, Daniels, Lövas, Schwarz, Sharp, Gramatzki, Stamm, Düsseldorf Music Soc. Ch., Tölz Boys' Ch., Düsseldorf SO, Klee.

Anticipating Berlioz a few years later, Schumann selected random scenes from *Faust* to make a highly individual cantata, dramatically inconsistent but with many fine passages. Abbado's recording was taken live from concert performances in June 1994, using a cast, headed by Bryn Terfel in the title-role and with Karita Mattila as Gretchen, that could hardly be bettered at the time. Abbado's direction is strong and sympathetic, and the singing good; but one has only to go back to Benjamin Britten's inspired Decca recording of 1972 (reissued on CD at mid-price: 425 705-2) to find even keener imagination, not just in the conducting but in the singing too. Bryn Terfel is thoughtful and expressive as Faust, but Fischer-Dieskau was far more illuminating and detailed, while Elizabeth Harwood as Gretchen sang even more radiantly than Mattila here, bringing out the heroine's tenderness and vulnerability. Equally, Jan-Hendrik Rootering as Mephistopheles here is not as characterful as John Shirley-Quirk. The analogue 1972 sound is also rather cleaner than the 1994 digital, but, were the Decca set to become unavailable, this Sony will always provide a most enjoyable recording of an all-too-rare work.

Klee takes a sharply dramatic view of Schumann's strange collection of Goethe portraits and with bright, atmospheric, digital recording the score is made to seem less wayward than it can. The cast of singers is strong, but Fischer-Dieskau is here not as steady as he was in Britten's recording of ten years earlier. Nor – particularly in the final scene – does Klee have the imaginative insights that gave that recording such compelling magic and earned it a Rosette in our main edition (Decca 425 705-2).

Schütz, Heinrich (1585–1672)

Sinfoniae sacrae, Op. 66/2–13, 15, 17–19 (SWV 258–269, 271, 273–5).
(M) *** Erato/Warner Dig. 4509 96964-2 [id.]. Dietschy, Bellamy, Laurens, Zaepfel, Elwes, De Mey, Fabre-Garrus, Les Saqueboutiers de Toulouse.

Schütz's twenty *Sinfoniae sacrae* of 1629, of which sixteen are included here, are the result of the Dresden composer's second visit to Italy in 1628, when he was strongly influenced by Monteverdi and the Italian concertato style. These pieces fascinatingly combine voices and instruments in a single texture, usually with an interweaving interplay, and rarely with the instruments acting just as an obbligato. Here the collection is framed by the lively opening *Buccinate in neomenia tuba* (No. 19), which is complex and colourful, with its paired tenors, cornet, bass-trumpet and bassoon, and the equally joyful *Veni dilecte mi* (No. 18), where the voices of two sopranos and two tenors intermingle with a pair of sackbutts. The latter dialogue of a Shulamite and her lover, together with Nos. 9–10 (where tenor and bass are joined by two violins), are expressive settings from the *Song of Songs.* Several numbers are more lightweight, and the engaging *Exultate cor meum in Domino* (No. 2) brings a charming soprano solo, agreeably answered by a pair of overlapping cornets, while one of the most unexpected and effective combinations is No. 6, *Jubilate Deo omnis terra*, where a solo bass (here the excellent Bernard Fabre-Garrus) is joined by two flutes. Perhaps the most famous is the tragic *Fili mi, Absalon* (No. 13), David's lament, in which the eloquent bass-line is amplified by magnificent interludes for four sackbutts, which are here gloriously sonorous and the effect very moving. The performances are eminently stylish and freshly spontaneous, and the instrumentalists are expert – and, moreover, play in tune. The balance is beautifully judged, with voices and instruments within the same perspective, and the digital recording is wholly realistic.

Scriabin, Alexander (1872–1915)

Symphonies Nos. (i) 1 in E, Op. 26; 2 in C min., Op. 29; 3 in C min. (Le divin poème); 4 (Poème de l'extase), Op. 54; (ii) 5 (Prometheus), Op. 60; (iii) Piano concerto in F sharp min., Op. 20. Rêverie.
(B) ** RCA 74321 20297-2 (3). Frankfurt RSO, Kitajenko, with (i) Siniawskaia, Fedin; (ii) Figuralchor, Krainev; (iii) Oppitz.

Older collectors will recall that Frankfurt Radio forces recorded the Scriabin symphonies for Philips in the days of LP. This re-make is in its way no less desirable, though it would be idle to pretend that it offers a serious challenge to Riccardo Muti's set with the Philadelphia Orchestra on EMI. That however does not offer the early, Chopinesque *Piano concerto in F sharp minor* as part of the package; nor does it come at so competitive a price. Be warned, however, that Dmitri Kitajenko does not shrink from adding to the percussion and adding cymbal clashes at will. Not content with that, he goes even further and adds a chorus at the closing section of *Poème de l'extase.* One does not have to be a purist to find this unacceptable in the absence of any supporting documentary evidence as to Scriabin's own wishes. If the *Poème de l'extase* cannot be recommended, the *Prometheus* has much in its favour, including some impressive pianism from Vladimir Krainev. It is not however to be preferred to the Ashkenazy–Maazel version on Decca nor is Gerhard Oppitz's account of the concerto as subtle or imaginative as the Ashkenazy. However, the discs can be purchased separately, and the first three symphonies are certainly recommendable at the price. Not only are the performances thoroughly idiomatic but the recorded sound has much going in its favour too; it is rich in detail and has plenty of air round the aural image. For the record, the *First Symphony* is coupled with *Le poème de l'extase* on the first disc (74321 20298-2); the *Second* with the *Piano concerto* (74321 20299-2) and the *Third* with *Prometheus* and the *Rêverie* (74321 20300-2). The third disc carries the strongest recommendation. All the same, even here the Muti remains far superior.

Le Poème de l'extase, Op. 54.
(M) *** Sony SM2K 64100 (2) [id.]. NYPO, Boulez – BARTOK: *Wooden Prince* etc. **(*)

Boulez's electrifying account of *Le Poème de l'extase* (not previously released) is surely unsurpassed on record for its ardour and the way Boulez controls the overall shaping of its climaxes and balances the orchestra so that the all-important trumpet part emerges from within a texture that is inherently voluptuous, even if the sound-quality itself could be more alluring. The recording, made in the Avery Fisher Hall, is, however, full and atmospheric and the work's final orgasmic culmination is almost overwhelming, with superb playing from the NYPO. This needs to be recoupled more appropriately on a single CD.

12 Etudes, Op. 8; 2 Nocturnes, Op. 5; Piano sonatas Nos. 2 in G sharp min. (Sonata fantasy), Op. 19; 3 in F sharp min., Op. 23.
** ASV Dig. CDDCA 882 [id.]. Gordon Fergus-Thompson.

Preludes: in B, Op. 2/2; C sharp min., Op. 9/1; 24 Preludes, Op. 11; 6 Preludes, Op. 13; 5 Preludes, Op. 15; 5 Preludes, Op. 16; 7 Preludes, Op. 17.
** ASV Dig. CDDCA 919 [id.]. Gordon Fergus-Thompson.

Although Gordon Fergus-Thompson is almost totally inside the Scriabin world, one crucial ingredient eludes him: a sense of manic possession. Naturally there is always a fear that finesse and polish will suffer if too many risks are taken, but without demonic fire and rapt absorption something essential is lost. Fergus-Thompson's account of the massive *Third Sonata* does not really surpass the earlier version he made in the late 1980s, nor does it eclipse memories of broadcast performances he has given. The smaller-scale *Etudes*, Op. 8, are generally very much better – but, as we said in our main volume of Piers Lane's Hyperion survey of the complete *Etudes* (CDA 66607), one misses the nervous intensity, the imaginative flair and feverish emotional temperature that a Scriabin interpreter must command even in the early, Chopinesque pieces. A greater range of keyboard colour and subtlety in the handling of dynamic nuance shadings is needed at times even on the second disc, devoted to the *Preludes*. On the whole there are better things here, and playing of considerable atmosphere and refinement – though he pulls some of the *Preludes*, Op. 11, hopelessly out of shape. The recordings are generally lifelike and present, but neither of these CDs does this fine artist as much justice as his earlier set of the *Sonatas Nos. 4, 5, 9* and *10*.

Preludes, Op. 11, Nos. 2, 4–6, 8–14, 16, 18, 20, 22 & 24.
(M) *** EMI CD-EMX 2237. Andrei Gavrilov – RACHMANINOV: *Elégie* etc. ***

Gavrilov's selection from Opus 11 is arbitrary. At times his approach is impetuous, and dynamics can be exaggerated; but playing of this order is still pretty remarkable. The balance is not too close, yet the CD brings a tangible presence and the piano timbre is well caught.

Piano sonatas Nos. 5, Op. 53; 9 (Black Mass), Op. 68.
** Decca Dig. 440 281-2 [id.]. Jablonski – PROKOFIEV: *Piano sonata No. 7;* RACHMANINOV: *Piano sonata No. 2.* **

Despite his Polish name, Peter Jablonski is Swedish, and he is very gifted. For all his youth he has made a considerable name for himself, but these two Scriabin *Sonatas* are something of a disappointment. They are played well enough but are not strongly characterized, and in an area in which such keyboard tigers as Richter and Horowitz freely roam they need greater character to justify a place in any recommended list.

Sculthorpe, Peter (born 1929)

(i) *Nourlangie* (for solo guitar, strings and percussion). *From Kakadu; Into the dreaming.*
*** Sony Dig. SK 53361 [id.]. John Williams; (i) Australian CO, Richard Hickox – WESTLAKE: *Antartica suite.*

Peter Sculthorpe, born in Tasmania, finds much of his inspiration in the physical nature of the Australian landscape. *Nourlangie* is an extraordinarily imaginative and evocative piece, inspired by the composer's first sight of the enormous monolithic rock of that name in the Kakadu National Park. The music fuses evocation (the opening, with sounding gongs, is very compelling) and local dance song, which are effectively and naturally integrated into the texture to give a strong underlying melodic vein. The central climax brings a great burst of 'birdsong' and later bird-calls decorate the closing section. The piece has moments of serenity yet demonstrates the power of nature to send the spirit soaring. The performance here is superb, with John Williams's guitar heard in a concertante role, admirably balanced within the overall sound-picture. The other two pieces are for solo guitar. *From Kakadu* is an intimate, improvisatory piece, somewhat minimalist in conception, in four changing sections, *Grave, Comodo, Misterioso* and *Cantando*, which sustains its ten-minute length admirably. *Into the dreaming* was inspired by a quiet solitary walk in the Valley of Winds at Katajuta in Uluru National Park. It opens mystically but generates much energy in its central section before returning to the restrained mood of the opening. John Williams plays both pieces with total spontaneity and complete improvisational freedom. He is most naturally, if forwardly, recorded. With its stimulating coupling, this whole concert is highly recommendable.

Shchedrin, Rodion (born 1932)

Stalin cocktail.
*** RCA 09026 68061-2 [id.]. Moscow Virtuosi, Vladimir Spivakov – SHOSTAKOVICH: *Chamber symphony No. 2;* PÄRT: *Collage on B-A-C-H* etc.; DENISOV: *Variations.* ***

Shchedrin's *Stalin cocktail* was written as a celebratory encore piece for Spivakov and his excellent chamber group. A nightmare-like presentation of a very famous Russian folksong cocks a snook at

Stalin for whom the tune was once adapted with sycophantic lyrics. The cocktail is dashed to the ground at the close with a piercing vocal splash from all members of the orchestra.

Shostakovich, Dmitri (1906–75)

Ballet suites Nos. 1–5; Festive overture, Op. 96; Katerina Ismailova: suite.
*** Chan. Dig. CHAN 7000/1 [id.]. RSNO, Järvi.

This highly entertaining set generally represents Shostakovich in light-hearted, often ironic mood, throwing out bonnes-bouches like fireworks and with a sparkling vividness of orchestral colour. The *Ballet suites* were the composer's way of satirically but anonymously re-using material from earlier works which lay unperformed for political reasons. The first four suites were put together between 1949 and 1953, and the offbeat writing offers a wide range of styles, from rather scrumptious and not entirely elegant waltzes to raucous circus effects bursting with irreverent high spirits. There are plenty of good tunes (witness the touching cello solo in the slow movement of the *Second suite*, the very engaging *Elegy* from the *Third*, and the enticing if sombre Introduction to No. 4, which also has a bouncy *Waltz* and a jolly *Scherzo tarantella*). The *Fifth suite* draws entirely on music from a 1931 ballet, *The Bolt* (see below), set in a factory where a worker tries to sabotage a lathe by the insertion of a bolt into the machine's driving mechanism. Not surprisingly, the piece was not welcomed by the Soviet authorities and the graphic orchestral writing, which pokes fun at all and everything, was acceptable only when the music was no longer associated with its original scenario. This is the most extended of the five suites, offering nearly half an hour of music, full of wry, quirky ideas, typical of the young Shostakovich. The *Suite* from *Katerina Ismailova* (*Lady Macbeth of Mtsensk*) consists of entr'actes from between the scenes which effectively act as emotional links, and the writing is both illuminating and characterful. Järvi is entirely at home in all this music and clearly relishes its dry humour. The playing is equally perceptive and full of flair. The recording is spectacular and resonantly wide-ranging in the Chandos manner.

The Bolt (ballet; complete recording).
*** Chan. Dig. CHAN 9343/4 (2) [id.]. Royal Stockholm PO, Stockholm Transport Band,
    Rozhdestvensky.

Dating from 1931, *The Bolt* is a massive ballet-score that in its original form sank without trace, largely thanks to the feeble, cumbersome propagandist libretto. This was the period building up to the time when Soviet artists were controlled with a new rigour; with its element of sharp irony this was not a work that, for all its propaganda element – with important dances for choruses of technicians and workers, a blacksmith and members of the Young Communist League – was ever going to qualify for revival. Yet the dances are so sharp and colourful in their inspiration that over the years suites of movements have been heard, and now Rozhdestvensky in this vivid, full-blooded recording resurrects the complete score of 43 movements, lasting two and a half hours. The music readily demonstrates how dazzlingly inventive the young Shostakovich was, even when faced with an indifferent subject. What other composer would write such a sharp little piece entitled *The Naval disarmament conference*, with Spanish rhythms making it sound almost like an earthier version of Walton's *Façade*? Rozhdestvensky plainly believes passionately in this score, and he draws an electrifying performance from the Swedish orchestra of which he is music director. In demonstration sound, it makes a most attractive box of delights, even if it is hardly a masterpiece.

Chamber symphony No. 2.
*** RCA Dig. 09026 68061-2 [id.]. Moscow Virtuosi, Vladimir Spivakov – DENISOV: *Variations*.
    PART: *Collage on B-A-C-H* etc. SHCHEDRIN: *Stalin cocktail*. ***

Vladimir Milman's arrangement of the *Third String quartet* as the *Chamber symphony No. 2* is every bit as effective as No. 1, transcribed by Barshai from the *Eighth*. The F major Quartet ranges enigmatically wide in mood, opening skittishly in folksong style and with a strongly rhythmic Scherzo. At its heart is a powerful *Adagio* passacaglia which is to return to cap the passionate climax of the finale, which then moves towards a final *piano-pianissimo* of bleak oblivion. The piece is played marvellously here, and the bright yet spacious recording seems just right for the music.

(i) *Cello concerto No. 2, Op. 126. Symphony No. 5 in D min., Op.47.*
(B) ** DG 439 481-2 [id.]. (i) Rostropovich, Boston SO, Ozawa; (ii) Nat. SO of Washington,
    Rostropovich.

Rostropovich's outstanding mid-1970s recording of the *Second Cello concerto* is also available as part of a highly recommendable DG Double compendium of concertante cello works, including music by Tchaikovsky, Boccherini, Vivaldi and others (437 952-2 – see our main volume). That is far more recommendable than this vibrant but highly idiosyncratic account of the *Fifth Symphony*. Although the finale is intense and exciting, there is also a hectoring quality which is distinctly unappealing.

Piano concertos Nos. (i) *1 in C min., Op. 35;* (ii) *2, Op. 102;* (iii) *Cello sonata in D min., Op. 40.*
(**) Russian Disc mono RDCD 15005 [id.]. Composer, with (i) Moscow PO, Samosud; (ii) Moscow RSO, Gauk; (iii) Rostropovich.

Shostakovich himself recorded the two concertos in Paris in 1958 with the French Radio Orchestra and André Cluytens. The present versions were also made in the 1950s, though the Paris recordings found the composer, perhaps, in slightly better pianistic form. In his youth Shostakovich had been a gifted player and even entered the very first Warsaw Competition in 1925, in which he reached the final round. The attraction of the Russian Disc version is the presence of the *Cello sonata* with the young Rostropovich as his partner. It goes without saying that the disc is a valuable historical document, useful as an indication of the composer's intentions. However, in neither case could these performances be more than a supplementary recommendation. The EMI 'Composers in Person' coupling, reviewed in our main volume, offers the youthful, derivative but delightful *Fantastic Dances*, Op. 5, and five of the *Preludes and Fugues*, Op. 87, as a fill-up.

Piano concerto No. 1 in C min., for piano, trumpet and strings, Op. 35.
** DG Dig. 439 864-2 [id.]. Martha Argerich, Guy Touvron, Württemberg CO, Jörg Faeber –
HAYDN: *Piano concerto.* **

Martha Argerich is brilliant, virtuosic, marvellous – and infuriating. The finale is completely rushed off its feet, and there are other personal touches which prompt more admiration than pleasure. Anyway, whatever the quality of the playing, at 41 minutes and at full price this is unlikely to gain wide currency except among Argerich aficionados. The Classics for Pleasure disc of the two *Piano concertos* by Alexeev, Philip Jones (trumpet) and the ECO under Maksymiuk remains a clear first choice for this coupling (CD-CFP 4547).

Violin concerto No. 2 in C sharp min., Op. 129.
** DG Dig. 439 890-2 [id.]. Gidon Kremer, Boston SO, Ozawa – SCHUMANN: *Violin concerto* (arr.
of *Cello concerto*). **

Gidon Kremer's DG account of the Op. 129 concerto with Ozawa and the Boston Symphony is played with his customary aplomb and mastery. As usual, he likes to be provocative and he couples it, not with the *First concerto* of Shostakovich, but with Schumann's *Cello concerto*, but in Shostakovich's orchestration, which was made for Rostropovich. The present account is well played, though the recording is not really in the demonstration bracket. Both as a performance and as a recording this would have to have something very special to offer to displace the more logical coupling of the two Shostakovich concertos. The alternative accounts by Dmitri Sitkovestsky and the BBC Symphony (Virgin VC7 59601-2) or Mordkovitch and Järvi (Chandos CHAN 8820) are much to be preferred.

The Gadfly (suite), *Op. 97a; Hamlet* (film incidental music), *Op. 116:* excerpts; *King Lear* (suite), *Op. 58a.*
**(*) Koch Dig. 3-7274-2. [id.]. Korean Broadcasting System SO, Vakhtang Jordania.

The Gadfly (suite), *Op. 97a; Hamlet* (suite), *Op. 116.*
** Cap. Dig. 10 298 [id.]. Berlin RSO, Leonid Grin.

The Korean Radio forces offer *The Gadfly* and *King Lear* suites and the first, third and fourth movements of the *Hamlet* music, while the Capriccio disc opts for all eight movements of the latter. Neither offers short change in that both discs run to nearly 80 minutes. *The Gadfly* is not great Shostakovich; nor is it new to the catalogue. The Koch disc is to be preferred for the greater intensity and discipline of the orchestral response, and the three movements from *Hamlet* are keenly felt. Both are eminently recommendable discs.

Symphonies Nos. 1–15; (i; ii) *From Jewish folk poetry;* (ii) *6 Poems of Marina Tsvetaeva.*
(B) *** Decca Dig./Analogue 444 430-2 (11) [id.]. Varady, Fischer-Dieskau, Rintzler; (i) Söderström, Karczykowski; (ii) Wenkel; Ch. of LPO or Concg. O; LPO or Concg. O, Haitink.

No one artist or set of performances holds all the insights into this remarkable symphonic canon, but what can be said of Haitink's set is that the playing of both the London Philharmonic and the Concertgebouw orchestras is of the highest calibre and is very responsive; moreover the Decca recordings, whether analogue or digital, are consistently of this company's highest standard, outstandingly brilliant and full. If without the temperament of a Mravinsky, Haitink proves a reliable guide to this repertoire, often much more than that, and sometimes inspired. No. 1 may lack something in youthful high spirits, but Nos. 2 and 3 are admirably committed and readily demonstrate the realistic balance and presence of the Decca sound. No 4 is unexpectedly refined and the demonic quality which can make this work so compelling is underplayed. But No. 5 is very impressive, with the Concertgebouw Orchestra in splendid form and the contribution of the Decca engineers beyond praise. There could perhaps be more passionate feeling in the slow movement, and this comment could also apply to the *Seventh*. But in its opening movement Haitink is eminently direct in a work now revealed as having quite different implications from those suggested by the Soviet propaganda machine and, without wearing his heart on his sleeve, he finds deep seriousness in the rest of this underrated symphony. No. 6 is characteristically refined and powerful, and Haitink presents a strongly architectural reading of the *Eighth*, providing an unusually satisfying solution to the problems inherent in its apparently lightweight finale. No. 9 is superb, one of the finest in the cycle, while in No. 10 Haitink really has the measure of both the first movement and the malignant Scherzo, even if later in the work the concentration is less powerfully sustained. In No. 11 (*The Year 1905*) the overall structural control is most impressive, yet again the last degree of tension is not consistently present throughout. No. 12, with its evocation of the revolutionary *Year 1917*, does not always show the composer at his most inspired, but the slow movement is marvellously atmospheric and the fine Concertgebouw playing almost carries the day. In No. 13 (*Babi-Yar*) Haitink's directness and strength of purpose work well, particularly in the long *Adagio* first movement. Marius Rintzler proves to be a magnificent bass soloist, and the resolution of the finale is highly successful. Haitink is also in his element in sustaining the sombre darkness of No. 14, with its various settings of poems on the theme of death, each sung in the original language. Again he has fine soloists in Varady and Fischer-Dieskau, and here the *Six Poems of Marina Tsvetaeva* prove a considerable makeweight, splendidly sung by Ortrun Wenkel. No. 15 caps the cycle, bringing a uniquely successful performance of a work of quirky unpredictability which Haitink manages to make sound both genuinely symphonic and bitingly urgent, helped by superb playing from the LPO. The bonus here is the song-cycle, *From Jewish folk poetry*, in which Ryszard Karczykowski, vibrantly Slavonic, stands out among the three soloists. All in all, a considerable achievement. The eleven discs are now offered together at bargain price, but they also remain available separately at mid-price – see our main volume.

Symphonies Nos. 1 in E min., Op. 10; 12 in D min. (The Year 1917), Op. 112.
(M) ** BMG/Melodiya 74321 19848-2 [id.]. Moscow PO, Kondrashin.

Symphonies Nos. (i) 2 in B (October Revolution), Op. 14; (ii) 14 in G min., Op. 135.
(M) *** BMG/Melodiya 74321 19844-2 [id.]. (i) Russian Republic Ch.; (ii) Tselovalnik, Nestorenko;
    Moscow PO, Kondrashin.

Symphonies Nos. (i) 3 in E flat (The First of May), Op. 20; 5 in D min., Op. 47.
(M) ** BMG/Melodiya 7432 119845-2 [id.]. (i) Russian Republic Ch.; Moscow PO, Kondrashin.

Symphony No. 4 in C min., Op. 43.
(M) *** BMG/Melodiya 74321 19840-2 [id.]. Moscow PO, Kondrashin.

Symphonies Nos. 6 in B min., Op. 54; 10 in E min., Op. 93.
(M) *(*) BMG/Melodiya 74321 19847-2 [id.]. Moscow PO, Kondrashin.

Symphony No. 7 in C (Leningrad), Op. 60.
(M) ** BMG/Melodiya 74321 19839-2 [id.]. Moscow PO, Kondrashin.

Symphony No. 8 in C min., Op. 65.
(M) *(*) BMG/Melodiya 74321 19841-2 [id.]. Moscow PO, Kondrashin.

Symphonies Nos. 9, Op. 70; 15 in A, Op. 103.
(M) **(*) BMG/Melodiya 74321 19846-2 [id.]. Moscow PO, Kondrashin.

Symphony No. 11 (The Year 1905), Op. 103.
(M) ** BMG/Melodiya 74321 19843-2 [id.]. Moscow PO, Kondrashin.

Symphony No. 13 in B flat min. (Babi Yar), Op. 113.
(M) *** BMG/Melodiya 74321 19842-2 [id.]. Eisen, Russian Republic Ch., Moscow PO,
    Kondrashin.

Kirill Kondrashin's cycle was made over a long period of time: the *Fourth Symphony* dates from 1962, not long after its first performance at the end of the previous year, while the last to appear (in the mid-1970s) were Nos. 7 (*Leningrad*), 14 and 15. We have discussed them all in past editions of the *Penguin Guide* (and its predecessor, the *Stereo Record Guide*) over the years. The set is of importance in that Shostakovich himself expressed confidence in this conductor, and it is clear that in many instances he comes closer than most to the spirit of this music. The cycle appeared as a twelve-LP box in the mid-1980s, and readers who possess that (but who want to have some or all of these works on CD) will doubtless welcome guidance. They were also in currency with specialist dealers on the Chant du Monde label, not separately but variously packaged in double-CD packs.

Not all the performances struck us then (nor do they now) as *sans pareil*. In none of them is the playing of the Moscow Philharmonic as distinguished or as finely disciplined as in many rival accounts: think of the New York Philharmonic for Mitropoulos in the *Tenth* (Sony MPK 45968) – not to mention the Berlin Philharmonic for Karajan (DG 413 361-2) or the Philadelphia for Ormandy in Nos. 13–15, which RCA should restore to the catalogue without delay. Nor, to be fair, are Kondrashin's insights deeper than those of Mravinsky or (in the case of Nos. 5, 6, 7 and 11) Stokowski. It is rare to find one cycle that fulfils the aspirations with which it embarks and, although Haitink and the Concertgebouw have strong merits, there is no single survey that is absolutely ideal in every respect.

As is so often the case, those performances closer to the work's birthpangs, such as Nos. 4, 13 and 14, make the strongest impression in Kondrashin's hands. Despite the sonic limitations inevitable over the course of over 30 years, the *Fourth* is almost indispensable. It has that sense of discovery, raw intensity and sheer eloquence which silence criticism – or should do. And although the 1967 account of the *Thirteenth* is not as chilling or compelling as the very first performance that he gave in 1962 with Vitaly Gramadsky and which circulated in the West on an LP made from tapes smuggled out of the Soviet Union, this still has an authentic feel to it that makes its claims on the collector strong. Both the *Fourteenth*, song-cycle-cum-symphony, and the enigmatic *Fifteenth Symphony* have much to recommend them.

Elsewhere the cycle is less even. The brisk tempi Kondrashin adopts for the first movement of both the *Sixth* and *Eighth* symphonies diminish their intensity of feeling and directness of effect. The latter is something of a disappointment and, though he makes out a stronger case for the *Third* than some rivals, he is no match for Mravinsky in the *Twelfth*. Generally speaking, although we have not heard every symphony alongside the 1985 EMI Melodiya LPs, the BMG/RCA transfers do not always enjoy an automatic superiority in an A/B comparison. The Moscow Philharmonic strings are by no means as sumptuous as those of the USSR State Academic Symphony (or the 'USSR Symphony' as it was known at one time), nor as responsive as those in Pletnev's Russian National Orchestra; and they do not sound quite as warm or smooth as on the LP. It is difficult to generalize, but the bass is sometimes firmer and definition is keener. There are roughnesses on the originals that are not quite smoothed out. If your LPs are in good condition in those symphonies to which you need to return, there is little need to make the change.

Symphonies Nos. 1 in F min., Op. 10; 5 in D min., Op. 47.
**(*) Sup. 11 1951-2 [id.]. Czech PO, Karel Ančerl.

Both performances are good and the *Fifth* is excellent. In their day they were highly recommendable (the *First* dates from 1964 and the *Fifth* from 1961). The sound has less body and presence than in more modern recordings but Ančerl shapes the slow movement of the *Fifth* with a powerful eloquence. It is to be preferred to many modern, glossier performances with brightly lit, state-of-the-art recording.

Symphonies Nos. 2 in B (October Revolution), Op. 14; 3 in E flat (The First of May), Op. 20.
*** Teldec/Warner Dig. 4509 90853-2 [id.]. London Voices, LSO, Rostropovich.

Although Rostropovich is often prone to excessive expressive vehemence and tends on occasion to italicize and point-make, these two performances, like his accounts of the *First* and *Ninth*, have a natural eloquence that is very persuasive. The LSO respond to his playing with real fervour; everything is well prepared and well thought out, and he has the advantage of very well-engineered sound. Perhaps it could be objected that the two symphonies do not offer enough playing-time for a premium-priced disc, but the quality of this issue is not in doubt. Recommended.

Symphony No. 5 in D min., Op. 47.
**(*) Decca Dig. 440 476-2 [id.]. VPO, Solti – MENDELSSOHN: *Symphony No. 4.* **(*)

(i) *Symphony No. 5 in D min., Op. 47;* (ii) *Hamlet* (film incidental music), *suite, Op. 116.*
(BB) *** RCA Navigator 74321 24212-2 [id.]. (i) LSO, Previn; (ii) Belgian RSO, José Serebrier.

Previn's RCA version, dating from early in his recording career (1965), remains at the top of the list of bargain recommendations. This is one of the most concentrated and intense readings ever, superbly played by the LSO at its peak. What has always marked out Previn's reading is the spaciousness of the first and third movements, held together masterfully. In the third movement he sustains a slower speed than anyone else, making it deeply meditative in its dark intensity; and the purity and beauty of the Previn version have never been surpassed, notably in the long-legged second subject, while his build-up in the central development section brings playing of white heat. The bite and urgency of the second and fourth movements are also irresistible. Only in the hint of analogue tape-hiss and a slight lack of opulence in the violins does the sound fall short of the finest modern digital recordings – and it is more vividly immediate than most. The new coupling is appropriate. *Hamlet* obviously generated powerful resonances in Shostakovich's psyche and produced vivid incidental music: the opening Ball scene is highly reminiscent of *Romeo and Juliet*. The playing of the Belgian Radio Orchestra under Serebrier is eminently serviceable without being really distinguished, but with atmospheric recording this 28-minute suite makes a considerable bonus.

In Shostakovich's *Fifth Symphony* Solti, no doubt encouraged by the Vienna Philharmonic, adopts a more espressivo style than in his previous Shostakovich recordings, with the *Largo* slow movement beautifully moulded at a flowing speed, conveying warmth in a movement which is often treated with emotional reserve. The great soaring second-subject theme of the first movement too is given the warmth of the Vienna strings, and in both the Scherzo and finale Solti brings out Shostakovich's wry humour rather than his more brutal qualities. Throughout, the players are obviously enjoying their outing with Solti. When the live recording, made in the Musikverein, is not very full-bodied, this is hardly a first choice, but both the Mendelssohn and the Shostakovich provide a welcome slant on the works themselves and on the conductor.

(i) *Symphonies Nos. 6 in B min., Op. 54;* (ii) *9 in E flat, Op. 70.*
**(*) Everest EVC 9005 [id.]. (i) LPO, Boult; (ii) LSO, Sargent.

Boult secures very good playing from the LPO and the late-1950s Walthamstow recording is excellent. But he is not as intense as he might be and this inevitably detracts from the sense of symphonic architecture. Sargent's account of the *Ninth* is lyrical and attractive, with infectious vitality in the odd-numbered of the five movements. One is at times reminded of Prokofiev's *Classical Symphony*, which Sargent also did well. Again the recording is very good indeed, approaching the demonstration class. This is undoubtedly an enjoyable coupling. However, these accounts are upstaged by Previn's *Sixth* (on EMI CDM7 69564-2) and Haitink's *Ninth* (Decca 425 066-2) – both differently coupled.

Symphony No. 8 in C min, Op. 64.
(M) *** EMI CDM5 65417 [id.]. LSO, Previn.

Previn's EMI version of the *Eighth Symphony* remains fully recommendable, with more charisma than gravitas, but with plenty of emotional commitment. The LSO is prompted by Previn to playing that is both intense and brilliant, while the recording is outstandingly full and vivid.

Symphony No. 10 in E min., Op. 93.
*** EMI Dig. CDC5 55232-2 [id.]. Phd. O, Jansons – MUSSORGSKY: *Songs and dances of death.* ***

Symphony No. 10 in E min.; Festival overture, Op. 96.
(M) ** Virgin/EMI Dig. CUV5 61134-2 [id.]. LPO, Andrew Litton.

Mariss Jansons' account of the *Tenth Symphony* is one of the best we have had for some time. He draws a splendid response from the Philadelphia Orchestra and has tremendous fervour. There are some tempo transitions that will not convince all listeners and some over-emphatic accentuation at times in the first movement. The very opening seems a shade too deliberate and the ensuing section (fig. 5 marked crotchet 108) sounds too fast and does not seem to grow naturally from it. But it is obvious that this performance is the result of real feeling and much thought. Jansons applies the brakes at the poignant woodwind cry (clarinets and oboes at fig. 188), which is a pity. The recording is very present and climaxes have plenty of impact: if one is being very pernickety, there is not quite enough transparency (air round the individual instruments) or front-to-back depth. These are small reservations and do not affect a three-star verdict on all counts. Karajan's DG version (413 361-2) remains pre-eminent, but offers no coupling.

Andrew Litton draws refined playing from the LPO in both the symphony and the brassy overture which precedes it, matched by refined, slightly distanced, recorded sound. Unfortunately these are two Shostakovich works which demand more rugged treatment. Not only does the overture miss something in extrovert panache, a sense of daring, the great span of the first movement of the symphony fails to build to the necessary climax when tension is kept low, however beautiful the incidental detail. The Scherzo is more biting but is not demonic as it should be; and the last two movements, with such relaxed and refined treatment, become elegant, where they should convey bluff, rugged strength.

Symphony No. 13 in B flat min. (Babi Yar), Op. 113.
** Denon Dig. CO 75887 [id.]. Robert Holl, Viennensis Ch., VSO, Eliahu Inbal.

Inbal's account of *Babi Yar* is a curiously un-Russian affair and is no match for the best modern versions or the authoritative Kondrashin version which lays bare the soul of this underrated oratorio-cum-symphony. Robert Holl is an impressive singer, but the whole spirit of the performance, recorded at a concert performance at the Vienna Konzerthaus, sounds alien – like hearing Proust in German or Hölderlin in French. Here and there details are beautifully fashioned, and there is no lack of feeling. Kondrashin (see above) or Haitink (available separately on Decca 425 073-2) are clearly preferable.

Piano quintet in G min., Op. 57.
** Audivis Valois Dig. V 4702 [id.]. Monte Carlo Pro Arte Quintet – BORODIN: *Piano quintet.* **

The Monte Carlo Pro Arte group give a faithful and intelligent account of the *Piano quintet* and they command a wide expressive and dynamic range. The balance is more successfully managed than in the coupling, and there is slightly greater depth here. If the performance is a fine one, it does not displace such distinguished rivals as Richter and the Borodin Quartet (EMI CDC7 47507-2) or Ashkenazy and the Fitzwilliam (currently withdrawn). All the same, these players on Valois give us a rarity in Borodin's *Piano quintet in C minor*, an early, uncharacteristic but enjoyable work of which there is no current alternative.

String quartets Nos. 1 in C, Op. 49; 2 in A, Op. 68; 3 in F, Op. 73.
** Koch Schwann Dig. 310 128 [id.]. Manhattan Qt.

String quartets Nos. 9 in E flat, Op. 117; 10 in A flat, Op. 118.
** Koch Schwann Dig. 310 166 [id.]. Manhattan Qt.

String quartets Nos. 14, Op. 142; 15, Op. 144.
** Koch Schwann Dig. 3-1071-2 [id.]. Manhattan Qt.

There are few reservations here, artistically, save for the fact that the playing, though very good, is by no means superior to that of the Borodin (EMI) or Fitzwilliam Quartets. The main reservation (and this applies to all three CDs here) concerns the acoustic, which is dryish and wanting in bloom.

String quartets Nos. 1 in C, Op. 49; 2 in A, Op. 68; 4 in D, Op. 83.
*** Koch/Consonance 81-3005 [id.]. Beethoven Qt.

String quartets Nos. 3 in F, Op. 73; 6 in G, Op. 101.
*** Koch/Consonance 81-3007 [id.]. Beethoven Qt.

String quartets Nos. 7 in F sharp min., Op. 108; 8 in C min., Op. 110; 15 in E flat min., Op. 144.
*** Koch/Consonance 81-3006 [id.]. Beethoven Qt.

The Beethoven Quartet recorded the Shostakovich *Piano quintet* with the composer in the days of mono LP, and their members were the dedicatees of many of the string quartets, and gave their premiere performances. They worked in close collaboration with Shostakovich himself; their records, made not long after the ink had dried on the works themselves, have a special intensity as well as authority. Indeed they make more sense of some of the later quartets than even such illustrious competitiors as the Borodins and the Fitzwilliam (see our main volume). But not only are they artistic documents, they are vital, sensitive performances that can be enjoyed without making any allowances for the sound. This cycle, which will presumably be completed during the lifetime of the book, is to be strongly recommended to all who care about this extraordinary repertoire.

String quartets Nos. 1 in C, Op. 49; 8 in C min., Op. 110; 9 in E flat, Op. 117.
(BB) ** Naxos Dig. 8.550973 [id.]. Eder Qt.

The Eder Quartet turn from Mozart to Shostakovich with equal commitment, and these performances are strong and intense. But the forward balance and the resonant Budapest Unitarian Church acoustic create an inflated effect and the bleak opening *Largo* of Shostakovich's best-known *C minor Quartet*, which comes first on the CD, immediately seems too close and orchestral in texture. But there is no doubt that this is playing of much character, and the grotesquely plangent character of the *Ninth Quartet* is powerfully conveyed.

PIANO MUSIC

24 Preludes and fugues, Op. 87.
🏵 (M) *** BMG/Melodiya 74321 19849-2 (3) [id.]. Tatiana Nikolayeva.

Preludes and fugues Nos. 1–12, Op. 87.
*(*) Kingdom Dig. KCLCD 2023 [id.]. Marios Papadopoulos.

Preludes and fugues Nos. 13–24, Op. 87.
*(*) Kingdom Dig. KCLCD 2024/5 [id.]. Marios Papadopoulos.

Tatiana Nikolayeva's 1990 Hyperion recording of the *Twenty-four Preludes and fugues* (CDA 66441/
3) inevitably makes special claims on the collector. It was greeted with great acclaim when it appeared
in 1991, and it rightly collected several awards, including a Rosette in our 1992 edition. It is hardly
necessary to remind collectors that it was Nikolayeva's Bach playing that inspired Shostakovich to
compose his own set, and she brings to this music a special authority as well as a lifetime's love of the
music. Although her Hyperion recording prompted 'no complaints', the fact remains that this
Melodiya set, made in 1987 (and which RL purchased in Moscow some years ago), is if anything
cleaner and better focused (if a bit dry), and the Rosette should perhaps now be transferred to it. In
neither reading will readers be disappointed. Perhaps now that RCA have acquired the Western
rights of the Melodiya catalogue, they will consider restoring Nikolayeva's first, 1961 recording, if
this proves practicable.

   No disrespect to Marios Papadopoulos that his survey of the *24 Preludes and fugues* has to take
second place to Nikolayeva. He is far from negligible in this repertoire but his insights inevitably do
not match hers. Nor does the recording quality.

Sibelius, Jean (1865–1957)

Violin concerto in D min., Op. 47.
(M) *** Decca 425 080-2 [id.]. Kyung-Wha Chung, LSO, Previn – TCHAIKOVSKY: *Violin concerto.*
***

** Sony Dig. SK 58967 [id.]. Midori, Israel PO, Mehta – BRUCH: *Scottish fantasy.* **

While Cho-Liang Lin's performance on Sony (MK 44548) with the Philharmonia Orchestra under
Salonen is very special and was given a Rosette in our main volume, that is coupled with the Nielsen
Concerto. Anyone preferring a coupling with the Tchaikovsky and looking for a mid-priced recommendation will find that Kyung Wha Chung has inimitable style and an astonishing technique, and her
feeling for the Sibelius *Concerto* is second to none. André Previn's accompanying cannot be praised
too highly: it is poetic when required, restrained, full of controlled vitality and well-defined detail.
The 1970 Kingsway Hall recording is superbly balanced and produces an unforced, truthful sound.
This is a most beautiful account, poetic, brilliant and thoroughly idiomatic, and must be numbered
among the finest versions of the work available; the coupling with Tchaikovsky is very appropriate
for reissue in Decca's Classic Sound series.

   Recorded live, Midori gives commanding performances of both works, at once pure in tone and
warmly expressive, defying the acoustic of the Mann Auditorium in Tel Aviv. The sound is opaque
and wanting in freshness and orchestral climaxes do not open out sufficiently. It is a tribute to
Midori's mastery that despite this handicap her playing has all the precision one would expect in the
studio, exceptionally clean and precise, not least above the stave. There is then the gain in tension one
would expect in live performances, with the main lyrical themes of the first two movements of the
Sibelius given rapt intensity, and with a thrilling coda to the first movement. The finale is remarkable
for the clean precision of her playing, with detail sharply defined even in the heaviest bravura
passages. Midori receives decent support from Mehta and the Israel orchestra but, faced with such
rival recordings as Cho-Liang Lin and Chung, this is not by any manner of means a strongly
competitive contender.

(i) *Violin concerto in D; Symphony No. 2 in D, Op. 43.*
(BB) **(*) RCA Navigator Dig./Analogue 74321 17904-2. (i) Dylana Jenson; Phd. O, Ormandy.

Dylana Jenson is a young American violinist, born in 1961, who has the full measure of this concerto.
She hardly puts a foot wrong anywhere and her account has all the sense of space, nobility and
warmth that one could want. The virtuosity she commands seems quite effortless and is completely at
the service of the music. Her tone is fine-spun and vibrant, and she communicates the sense of
atmosphere and mystery in the opening to splendid effect. Originally on LP she was let down by

opaque sound, but the CD transfer has transformed the quality of the 1980 digital recording, which is now clarified yet retains plenty of ambience. The violin is forwardly placed but naturally caught and the result is most satisfying. Ormandy's 1972 account of the *Second Symphony* was originally issued as a quadraphonic LP, and the sound is undoubtedly spacious, although the violin timbre (as so often in American records of that time) lacks something in refinement because of the close microphones. But they play marvellously and the superbly disciplined response of the whole orchestra cannot fail to hold the listener. Although Ormandy's reading rarely sheds new light on this wonderful score, there is no doubt that the rich sweep of the Philadelphia strings in the big tune of the finale – underpinned by the power and sonority of the brass – is compulsive in its intensity.

Symphonies Nos. 1–7.
(M) * Finlandia Dig. 4509 99963-2 (3) [id.]. Finnish RSO, Saraste.

Symphonies Nos. 1 in E min., Op. 39; 2 in D, Op. 43; 4 in A min., Op. 63; 5 in E flat, Op. 82.
(B) *** Ph. Duo 446 157-2 (2) [id.]. Boston SO, Sir Colin Davis.

Symphonies Nos. 3 in C, Op. 52; 6 in D min., Op. 104; 7 in C, Op. 105; (i) *Violin concerto in D min., Op. 47. Finlandia, Op. 26; Legends: The swan of Tuonela, Op. 22/2; Tapiola, Op. 112.*
(B) *** Ph. Duo 446 160-2 (2) [id.]. (i) Salvatore Accardo; Boston SO, Sir Colin Davis.

Sir Colin Davis's set of the symphonies, recorded during the second half of the 1970s, is undoubtedly among the finest of the collected editions, and now it is not only the least expensive (offered for the cost of two premium-price CDs) but three tone-poems and an estimable account of the *Violin concerto* are thrown in for good measure. Indeed Accardo's performance of the latter is very high on the recommended list. There is no playing to the gallery, and in the slow movement there is a sense of repose and nobility. The finale is exhilarating, and there is an aristocratic feeling to the whole that is just right. *Tapiola*, too, is atmospheric and superbly played. In terms of sheer mystery and power it stands among the best. Davis's feeling for Sibelius is usually matched by the orchestral response. Nos. 1, 2, 5 and 7 were the first to be recorded, in 1975/6. The idiomatic playing Davis secures from the Boston orchestra is immediately apparent in the *First Symphony*. Tempi are well judged and there is a genuine sense of commitment and power. The recording, however, is not quite as fine as Ashkenazy's at mid-price on Decca (436 473-2) and the string-tone could be fresher at the top. The brass is in danger of overwhelming the violins. However, the remastering has undoubtedly improved the overall depth of acoustic, and in the great tune of the finale there is little to cavil at. Davis's account of No. 2 is again dignified and well-proportioned, free from any excesses or mannerisms. Although it does not displace Ashkenazy's newest Decca account, also made in Boston (436 566-2), it has sensitivity and freshness in its favour and can hold its head high, even in a field where competition is so strong. Again the remastering has opened out the recording; the strings now sound fresher at the top and the bass is firmer. Davis's accounts of the *Third, Fourth* and *Sixth Symphonies* are among the finest on disc and they are excellently recorded. In the *Third* Davis judges the tempi in all three movements to perfection; no conductor has captured the elusive spirit of the slow movement or the power of the finale more effectively. In this respect he surpasses even the authoritative Kajanus set of pre-war days. The *Fourth* is arguably the finest of the cycle; there is a powerful sense of mystery, and the slow movement in particular conveys the feeling of communication with nature that lies at the heart of its inspiration. Tempi relate beautifully and Davis has the courage to take the slow movement really slowly. The *Fifth* is a little lacking in atmosphere; it is no match for Karajan (whose outstanding 1964 performance is available on DG's bargain Classikon label – 439 418-2). Davis is idiomatic and unfussy, like the *Seventh*. Moreover the recording of these two works is again slightly two-dimensional, although this is much less noticeable now than it was on LP. The *Sixth* is altogether more impressive and much more vivid as sound.

Ashkenazy's Decca set is still available on four mid-priced discs (421 069-2). It is a rich, consistently enjoyable cycle and many of the recordings are of demonstration quality. Davis's cycle can be recommended with equal confidence alongside it. Even if the Philips engineers are less evenly successful in dealing with the recalcitrant acoustics in Boston, the rich hall ambience still makes an impressive contribution to the fullness and spaciousness of the sound.

Jukka-Pekka Saraste has only just finished recording the symphonies with this orchestra for RCA. Someone must think that he brings exceptional insights to record them all over again – admittedly in the heady atmosphere of St Petersburg's white nights. The performances, with the exception of No. 3, which is a bit rushed, are sound rather than special. The recordings are decent but not out of the ordinary. No challenge to existing recommendations.

Symphonies Nos. 1 in E min., Op. 38; 3 in C, Op. 52.
(***) Testament mono SBT 1049 [id.]. Philh. O, Kletzki.

EMI included Kletzki's account of the *Second Symphony* in one of their recent *Artist Profiles*. The *First Symphony* has never been reissued since it was issued on mono LP in 1954, while the *Third Symphony* has never appeared before in the UK. Why Walter Legge never issued it remains a mystery. It was briefly published in the USA in harness with David Oistrakh's 1954 version of the *Violin concerto* with the Stockholm Festival Orchestra under Sixten Ehrling. It is very different in approach from the Anthony Collins LP (see our main volume), which takes a somewhat racy view of both the first and second movements. Indeed Collins took only 24 minutes 41 seconds over the whole piece as opposed to Kletzki's 27 minutes 20 seconds and Colin Davis's 30 minutes 25 seconds – and their respective timings give a clue as to their approach. Kletzki is tauter than the traditional Kajanus school yet far less headlong (or headstrong) than Collins. In both scores he and the Philharmonia Orchestra strike the right balance between the romantic legacy of the nineteenth century and the more severe climate of the twentieth. The recordings are beautifully balanced and have great warmth, and they come up splendidly in these transfers. A valuable addition to the Sibelius compact discography and strongly recommended.

Symphonies Nos. 3 in C, Op. 52; 5 in E flat, Op. 82.
*** RCA Dig. 09026 61963-2 [id.]. LSO, Sir Colin Davis.

Sir Colin Davis's Sibelius cycle with the LSO at the Barbican's 1992 Scandinavian Festival was widely (and rightly) acclaimed. Andrew Porter spoke of it in *The Observer* newspaper as comparable with Furtwängler's post-war cycle of Beethoven symphonies. The present recordings were made at Walthamstow during the course of that cycle. Davis's account of the *Third Symphony* has a majesty and power that have few rivals. We suspect, too, that his *Fifth* will be to the 1990s what Kajanus and Koussevitzky were to the war years, and Karajan (DG) and Bernstein (Sony) were to the 1960s – and, nearer home, what the Rattle Philharmonia account was to the early 1980s. There is tremendous grandeur here as well as a feeling for the natural symphonic current that flows in these wonderful works. The recording has a splendour worthy of the music and the players. Both performances (and especially the *Fifth*) offer a marked advance on Davis's earlier, Boston versions – see above.

Symphony No. 5 in E flat, Op. 82; Finlandia, Op. 26; Tapiola, Op. 112; Valse triste, Op. 44/1.
(B) ** Carlton Dig. PCD 1114 [id.]. RPO, Enrique Bátiz.

The *Fifth Symphony* from Enrique Bátiz and the RPO is imposing and has the benefit of generally first-class recording. The second half of the first movement is a shade too fast, but the performance has spaciousness and grandeur. *Tapiola*, on the other hand, does not fare so well; it is too fast and also wanting in mystery. The vividness and presence of the recording are a plus but, in so keenly contested a field, this is not a challenge.

Symphonies Nos. 5 in E flat, Op. 82; 6 in D min., Op. 104; Legend: The Swan of Tuonela, Op. 22/3.
(M) *** DG 439 982-2 [id.]. BPO, Karajan.

Karajan's 1965 *Fifth* is indisputably the finest of the four he made. It is already available on DG's Classikon bargain label (DG 439 418-2), coupled with short orchestral pieces. The new mid-priced reissue is obviously even more attractive, coupled with his glorious 1967 account of the *Sixth*, which remains almost unsurpassed by more recent accounts. The brooding *Swan of Tuonela* is placed between the two symphonies and is played just as admirably by the Berlin Philharmonic on their finest form. The CD transfers are miraculously managed so that the recordings show little sign of their age.

(i) *Symphony No. 7 in C, Op. 105; Pelléas et Mélisande (suite): Mélisande;* (ii) *A Spring in the Park, Entr'acte, Death of Mélisande. The Tempest: Prelude; suites 1 & 2 (excerpts); Scènes historiques: Festivo, Op. 25/4; In memoriam, Op. 59; Legend: Lemminkäinen's Homeward Journey, Op. 22/4.*
(M) (***) Dutton Lab. mono CDAX 8013 [id.]. (i) NYPO (ii) LPO; Sir Thomas Beecham.

Beecham's 1942 performance of the *Seventh Symphony* with the New York Philharmonic has greater power and tautness, and its fires burn more intensely, than either of his two other performances on CD (Helsinki, 1954, on Ondine and RPO, 1957, on EMI). Beecham was not satisfied with it (probably the acoustic of the Liederkranz Hall in New York displeased him), and he sued Columbia for issuing it on 78-r.p.m. records without his clearance – and lost! In any event, it makes its first appearance on this side of the Atlantic. It is magisterial and splendid, and sounds magnificent in this transfer. The *Pelléas* and *Tempest* excerpts come from the pre-war Sibelius Society issues, made with the London Philharmonic Orchestra in 1937–9. The *Prelude* to *The Tempest* (also available on EMI) has never been surpassed in atmosphere and menace; nor have the *Oak-tree* and the *Intrada and Berceuse* been realized with greater poetry. These are new to the CD catalogue, as is *Festivo*, issued on a Columbia blue-label 78, a performance of great elegance and style. Whether Beecham's account of *In memoriam* has been equalled is a moot point, but what is incontrovertible is that his *Lemminkäinen's Homeward Journey* has not only never been surpassed but never equalled in its hell-for-leather abandon. These transfers succeed in making them sound more vivid and alive than they have ever done before.

Symphony No. 7 in C, Op. 105; Pelléas et Mélisande: Mélisande. Op. 46/2.
(**) Sir Thomas Beecham Trust mono BEECHAM 6 [id.]. NYPO, Beecham. – MENDELSSOHN:
 Symphony No. 4; TCHAIKOVSKY: *Capriccio italien.* (**)

This is the same recording as that included on the Dutton Laboratory reissue listed above. Sibelians will want to give priority to the former, as it contains material that has not been available since the days of 78-r.p.m. records. It is moreover by far the better transfer. The other two performances, of the *Italian Symphony* and the *Capriccio italien*, are both from 1942 and are of considerable but not necessarily compelling interest. The Tchaikovsky is certainly worth hearing. The recording is opaque but perfectly acceptable for its period.

Tapiola, Op. 112.
(M) *** DG Dig. 445 518-2 [id.]. BPO, Karajan – NIELSEN: *Symphony No. 4.* ***

This is Karajan's fourth and undoubtedly greatest account of *Tapiola*, for he has the full measure of its vision and power. Never has it sounded more mysterious or its dreams more savage; nor has the build-up to the storm ever struck such a chilling note of terror: an awesomely impressive musical landscape; while the wood-sprites, weaving their magic secrets, come vividly to life.

CHAMBER MUSIC

(i) *Piano quartet in C min.* (for piano, two violins and cello); (ii) *String trio in G min.; Suite in A for string trio;* (iii) *Violin sonata in F.*
*** Ondine Dig. ODE 826-2 [id.]. (i) Novikov, Quarta, Miori, Rousi; (ii) Söderblom, Angervo, Gustafsson; (iii) Kovacic, Lagerspetz;

These are all early and uncharacteristic works, which Sibelians have read about in John Rosas's study and the first volume of Erik Tawaststjerna's biography, but which they have never actually heard, since until recently the manuscripts were not in the public domain. The *Violin sonata in F major* (1889) shows him still under the spell of Grieg. Only three movements of the *Suite in A major* for string trio (1888) survive (these artists give us what remains of the fourth movement, a *Gigue*); and its companion, the *String trio in G minor*, is also unfinished. Sibelius himself gave its date of composition as 1885 but in his authoritative notes Dr Kari Kilpeläinen quotes it as much later – 1893 or 1894, that is, after the *Kullervo Symphony*. Only the *Lento* survives intact, though the disc also gives a realization of what remains of the sketches of two other movements. The *Quartet in C minor* for piano, two violins and cello is a set of variations from the composer's Vienna year, 1891. All this is largely uncharacteristic and, save for the opening of the *A major Suite*, offers few glimpses of the mature Sibelius. The performances are dedicated and beautifully recorded.

String quartet in D min., 'Voces intimae', Op. 56.
(***) Biddulph mono LAB 098 [id.]. Budapest Qt – GRIEG: *Quartet;* WOLF: *Italian serenade.* (***)

A welcome transfer – the first on CD – of the 1933 pioneering *Voces intimae*, still unbeaten. It briefly appeared on LP (on the World Record label) and is newly (and well) transferred here by Ward Marston. Sibelians will need no reminders of its excellence – and the same goes for the couplings.

MUSIC FOR VIOLIN AND PIANO

Malinconia, Op. 20; 2 Pieces, Op. 77; 4 Pieces, Op. 78.
** Virgin/EMI Dig. VC5 45034-2 [id.]. Mørk, Thibaudet – GRIEG: *Sonata* etc. **

Like Grieg, Sibelius also had a cello-playing brother, which is probably why the Opp. 77 and 78 pieces for violin and piano are marked as playable by the cello. *Malinconia* was written for the cellist and conductor, Georg Schnéevoigt, and his wife Sigrid and is emphatically not top-drawer Sibelius. Truls Mørk and Jean-Yves Thibaudet play these pieces well enough, but the balance is unsatisfactory and favours the pianist excessively, with the result that Mørk's tone sounds very small.

5 Danses champêtres, Op. 106; Novellette, Op. 102; 5 Pieces, Op. 81; 4 Pieces, Op. 115; 3 Pieces, Op. 116.
*** BIS Dig. CD 625 [id.]. Nils-Erik Sparf, Bengt Forsberg.

In his youth Sibelius had visions of becoming a violinist and, though his ambitions were (fortunately for us) thwarted, his feeling for the instrument shines through even the slightest of the pieces recorded here. Many of them, such as the delightful *Rondino* from Op. 81, are little more than salon music, but some of the others are rewarding pieces. Indeed the first of the *Danses champêtres* almost suggests the music to *The Tempest*, written at much the same time. Both the Opp. 115 and 116 pieces contain music of quality. As in the companion disc, Nils-Erik Sparf and Bengt Forsberg prove as imaginative as they are accomplished, and the only marginal criticism concerns the balance, which tends to favour the piano whose tone sounds a little thick at the bass end of the aural spectrum. However, this is not worrying enough to justify qualifying a full three-star recommendation.

2 Pieces, Op. 2 (2 versions); Scaramouche: Scène d'amour. 2 Serious melodies, Op. 77; 4 Pieces, Op. 78; 6 Pieces, Op. 79; Sonatina in E, Op. 80.
*** BIS Dig. CD 525 [id.]. Nils-Erik Sparf, Bengt Forsberg.

This CD offers the first recording of the 1888 versions of the *Grave* and the *Perpetuum mobile*, the two pieces which Sibelius assigned to Opus 2, together with the 1911 versions, in which the former was revised as *Romance in B minor* and the latter overhauled as *Epilogue*. The former bears a certain affinity to the slow movement of the *Violin concerto* and the prevalence of the tritone in the latter acts as a reminder that it was reworked in the wake of the *Fourth Symphony*. Exemplary performances of the later pieces, including *Laetare anima mea* and the 1915 *Sonatina*, Op. 80. As in the companion disc, Nils-Erik Sparf and Bengt Forsberg prove imaginative and intelligent interpreters of this repertoire, and the only marginal criticism is the sound-quality. Again it favours the piano, whose tone sounds a little thick at the bottom end of the spectrum.

PIANO MUSIC

Autrefois, Op. 96b; 5 Esquisses, Op. 114; Finlandia, Op. 26; 8 Pieces, Op. 99; 5 Pieces, Op. 101; 5 Pieces, Op. 103; Valse chevaleresque, Op. 96c; Valse lyrique, Op. 96a.
*** Continuum CCD 1071 [id.]. Annette Servadei.

6 Bagatelles, Op. 97; Melody for the Bells of Berghäll Church, Op. 65b; 5 Pieces, Op. 75; 13 Pieces, Op. 76; 5 Pieces, Op. 85; 6 Pieces, Op. 94.
*** Continuum Dig. CCD 1070 [id.]. Annette Servadei.

We welcomed the earlier issues in Annette Servadei's survey of the piano music, even if it is the medium in which Sibelius was least at home. By the exalted standards he set elsewhere, Sibelius's contribution to the keyboard seems limited in inventive resource. The *Melody* he wrote for the bells of Berghäll Church, first heard at its inauguration in 1912, is slight but charming. Sibelius actually begrudged every minute he spent on the wartime sets, Opp. 75, 76 and 85, and the violin and piano pieces he wrote at that time, for they held up his work on the *Fifth Symphony*. Few of them are worthy of him. There are some echoes of the *First Sonatina* in *Aquileja*, and pieces like *När rönnen blommar* ('When the rowan blossoms') from the Op. 75 set, and *Berger et bergerette* have a certain charm. *Finlandia*, the *Valse lyrique*, *Autrefois* and *Valse chevaleresque* are all transcriptions of orchestral pieces. These were, of course, made when the piano arrangement served to give this music wider currency, a function long overtaken by the gramophone. No pianist, however imaginative and sensitive, could possibly convey the charm of *Autrefois*. Some of the later nature pieces are effective. Annette Servadei plays with sympathy and delicacy throughout and, generally speaking, the recording is very natural.

SONGS

Songs: *Arioso; Autumn evening (Höstkväll); Black roses (Svarta rosor); But my bird is nowhere to be seen (Men min fågel märks dock icke); Come away, death (Komm nu hit, död!); The diamond in the March snow (Diamanten på Marssnön) ; Did I dream? (Var det en dröm); The first kiss (Den första kyssne); The girl returned from meeting her lover (Flickan kom ifrån sin älsklings möte); On a veranda by the sea (På verandan vit havet); Sigh, rushes, sigh (Säv, säv, susa); Since then I have stopped asking (Se'n har jag ej frågat mera); Spring fleets fast (Våren flyktar hastigt); To the night (Til kvällen).*
(M) *** Decca 440 492-2 [id.]. Kirsten Flagstad, LSO, Oiven Fjeldstad – GRIEG: *Songs* (with: Arne
    EGGEN: *Praise to the eternal spring of life (Aere det evige forår i livet);* Eyvind ALNAES: *About*

love (Nu brister alle de kløfter); A February morning at the Gulf (Februarmorgen ved Golfen); A hundred violins (De hundrede fioliner); Yearnings of spring (Vålængsler); Harald LIE: *The key (Nykelen); The letter (Skinnvengbrev)* ***).

Some of the Sibelius songs here were orchestrated by the composer, but seven of them remained in their original form (voice and piano) until transformed, usually with great skill, by such arrangers as Jalas, Pingoud, Fougsted and Hellman. This recording, made in the early days of stereo, still sounds astonishingly good, and Sibelius-singing does not come like this any more! These classic performances, now reissued in Decca's Kirsten Flagstad Edition, give a magnificent impression of Sibelius's not inconsiderable range as a song-composer, and the addition of the songs by Grieg and other Norwegian composers will perhaps tempt the listener to explore further in this repertoire. The CD transfers are first class.

Diamanten på Marssnön (The diamond in the March snow), Op. 36/6; Drömmen (The dream), Op. 13/5; Flickan kom ifrån sin älsklings möte (The tryst), Op. 37/5; Höstkväll (Autumn evening), Op. 38/1; Kyssens hopp (The kiss's hope), Op. 13/2; Längtan heter min arvedel (Longing is my heritage), Op. 86/2; Lastu lainehilla (Driftwood), Op. 17/7; Näcken (The water-sprite), Op. 57/8; Narciss (Narcissus); Norden (The north), Op. 90/1; På verandan vid havet (On a balcony by the sea), Op. 38/ 2; Sången om korspindeln (Song of the spider), Op. 27/4; Souda, souda, sinisorsa (Paddle, paddle, little duckling); Svarta rosor (Black roses), Op. 36/1; Teodora (Theodora), Op. 35/2; Var det en dröm (Was it a dream); Våren flyktar hastigt (Spring flies), Op. 13/4; Vilse (Astray), Op. 17/4.
** Finlandia Dig. 4509-96871-2 [id.]. Tom Krause, Gustav Djupsjöbacka.

Tom Krause recorded two Sibelius song-recitals in his prime and, together with Elisabeth Söderström, included them all on five LPs in the late 1970s. The present CD, which contains two dozen songs, should not be confused with them. Krause was almost sixty when he made this disc and though, as one would expect from so intelligent an artist, his voice is in generally good shape, it does not have the freshness or the tonal bloom which distinguished his earlier recordings, and his vibrato is now wider at climaxes. He understands this repertoire as few others do, and his insights are as deep – as in the remarkably expressionistic *Teodora.* He is well supported by Gustav Djupsjöbacka, and the recording is truthfully balanced. It is to be hoped that Decca will restore their complete set within the lifetime of this book.

Simpson, Robert (born 1921)

Symphonies Nos. 3 (1961); *5* (1971).
*** Hyp. Dig. CDA 66728 [id.]. RPO, Handley.

Hyperion put us much in their debt by their championship of this extraordinary composer (though their enterprise has, of course, had the support of the Robert Simpson Society). In the early 1950s EMI recorded the *First Symphony* with the LPO under Sir Adrian Boult but, for all their much-publicized advocacy of British music, did nothing subsequently. Horenstein's account of the *Third* with the LSO has done long service and is of particular value in being coupled with the *Clarinet quintet* (Unicorn UKCD 2028 – see our main volume). Vernon Handley's new disc brings us the première recording of the *Fifth Symphony*, a work of striking power and range. It is combative and intense and enjoys at times an almost unbridled ferocity that enhances the admittedly few moments of repose. No admirer of the composer – and no one who cares about twentieth-century music in general – should pass these performances by, for it is music of a vital and forceful eloquence. Fine playing by the RPO under Handley, and exemplary recording.

Quartet for horn, violin, cello and piano; Horn trio (for horn, violin and piano).
*** Hyp. Dig. CDA 66695 [id.]. Richard Watkins, Pauline Lowbury, Christopher Green Armytage, Caroline Dearnley.

The *Quartet for horn, violin, cello and piano* of 1976 is a remarkable work. Originally intended as a one-movement piece, the composer added to its long first movement, *moto crescente*, a theme and variations. The invention is of unfailing quality and imagination, and its development magnificently sustained. The composer's command of large-scale musical thinking is much in evidence – but so, too, is his feeling for sonority. He draws some extraordinary sounds from these four instruments. In some ways this is one of his most deeply original and compelling works. The later *Horn trio*, written for Anthony Halstead, Frank Lloyd and Carol Slater, immediately pre-dates the *Ninth Symphony*. These are most impressive pieces, and the performances are completely dedicated and highly imaginative. Excellent recording too.

Sirmen, Maddalena Lombardini (1745–1818)

String quartets Nos. 1 in E flat; 2 in B flat; 3 in G min.; 4 in B flat; 5 in F min.; 6 in E.
*** Cala Dig. CACD 1019 [id.]. Allegri Qt.

Maddelena Lombardini was born in Venice and (with the aid of a scholarship) became a student at one of the *Mendicanti ospedale* (orphanages), the Italian ancestors of our present academies of music. They were originally intended for orphans but were later extended to fee-paying children with identifiable parents. She proved so talented that the governors sent her to continue her studies with Tartini and it was primarily as a violinist, in his view 'absolutely without equal', that she first made her reputation, although she also trained as a singer. Her contractual bondage to the ospedali was such that she could be freed from her obligations to pursue an independent career only by becoming a nun or by marrying. Tartini did his best to find her a suitable match, but it was by her own resourcefulness that she eventually found the necessary husband, one Lodovico Sirmen (also a violinist); as she produced a daughter very soon after she was married, her method is not a mystery. She received a dowry from the Mendicanti and back-pay, but this considerable accrual of funds was paid to her husband and passed to her only on his death, some 45 years later! Meanwhile Madame Sirman travelled through Europe as a successful virtuoso, and by 1771 she was in London playing at the concerts organized by Abel and J. C. Bach. Around this time her husband returned to Italy and apparently took up with a countess. However, his wife had a Venetian priest as a permanent part of her travelling entourage, and perhaps the consolation he offered her was more than spiritual. When her style of fiddling became outmoded (as speed came to be considered more desirable than polish and elegance), she turned to singing and secured a well-paid five-year appointment at the Dresden Opera, then moving on to St Petersburg, where her husband temporarily rejoined her as leader of the orchestra. Finally Madame Sirmen returned home to Italy, where she spent the last 30 years of her life as teacher rather than performer.

Her *String quartets* (plus a similar batch of string trios and six violin concertos) date from her years at the orphanage and were published in Paris in 1769 by another enterprising woman, Madame Berault. Feminists will note that the title-page attributes the works jointly to her husband and herself, with his name first(!), whereas he almost certainly had no hand in their composition. The string quartet medium was at that time in its infancy (the present contribution is approximately contemporary with Haydn's Opus 9 set) and thus her easy skill in handling the medium is the more remarkable. The works are not always dominated by the first violin, and their formal design is hardly Haydn-derived. There are two movements to each quartet, but the structure often subdivides into sections using different tempi. The second movement of No. 3, for instance, alternates major and minor (fast–slow–fast–slow), with a brief animated coda; *No. 6 in E major* frames a spirited *Con brio* with a gracious minuet and, most striking of all, *No. 5 in E minor* introduces a touching *Larghetto* which (within a span of eight minutes) returns after the central allegro. The collection here opens with No. 4 which in its extended first movement (marked *Cantabile*, though it is not slow) uses a typical, simple sonata form format, with two basic musical ideas. But *No. 1 in E flat* is thematically and structurally a more interesting work, and it has a particularly striking second-movement *Allegretto* which is worthy of the young Mozart. The vivacious finale of the *Second Quartet*, which is used to end the disc, is comparable with Haydn.

The Allegri Quartet obviously lived with this music for some time before this record was made, and they play it with much style and conviction, conveying their own pleasure in part-writing which is obviously enjoyable to play. The leader, Peter Carter, contributes a brief appreciation of the quality of the music as a part of very comprehensive notes. With excellent recording, admirably present but naturally balanced, this is very much worth exploring.

Smetana, Bedřich (1824–84)

Má vlast (complete).
(BB) *** Naxos Dig. 8.550931 [id.]. Polish Nat. RSO (Katowice), Antoni Wit.
*** Chan. Dig. CHAN 9366 [id.]. Detroit SO, Neeme Järvi.
(M) *** Ph. Dig. 442 641-2 [id.]. Concg. O, Antal Dorati.
(M) *** Virgin/EMI Dig. CUV5 61223-2 [id.]. RLPO, Pešek.
**(*) Sony Dig. SK 58944 [id.]. Israel PO, Mehta.

Antoni Wit and his excellent Polish National Radio Orchestra have already provided an outstanding Mahler *Fourth* that stands high in the current list of recommendations. Now, in a hardly less competitive area, they give us a superbly played and consistently imaginative account of Smetana's

Má Vlast, a work whose patriotic aspirations can so readily turn into rhetoric. Not here, however. The spacious opening of *Vyšehrad*, marginally slower than usual, glows with romantic evocation, and its lovely harp theme is developed with an expansive, radiant beauty, with magically soft horn-calls and gentle woodwind when it is reprised in the closing pages. Equally the flutes, trickling down from the sources of the *Vltava*, captivate the ear and the famous string-tune is unusually gracious and relaxed. The wedding scene on the river becomes delightfully folksy rather than forcefully rhythmic, then the moonlight glitters on the waters of the lake with a phosphorescent radiance. Again the horns softly intone their fanfares and the swirling woodwind prepares for the expansive return of the great string-melody. This idyll is dramatically interrupted by the appearance of the St John's rapids, and there is a superb climax, with thundering (but not exaggerated) timpani, and the main theme gathers pace for the triumphant climax. The opening of *Šárka* brings tingling melodrama, with the neurosis then subsiding naturally for the jaunty theme which follows, leading to the passionately rhapsodic central section and some glorious string-playing. *From Bohemia's woods and fields* opens with opulent expansiveness, and later the ethereal high string entry is exquisitely made, while the folk-dance episode brings a whiff of Dvořák in its flowing lyricism. The opening horn-call of *Tábor* emerges atmospherically from the mists of the past and the music develops great weight and gravitas, although it has plenty of impetus too, with the woodwind chorale providing contrasting repose. *Blaník* follows on naturally, with the charming pastoral sequence offering more lovely playing from the Polish wind (and horn) soloists. Both the two final symphonic poems are full of incident, but they are extended and use the same basic material; the performance of them needs to sustain a high level of intensity to hold the listener throughout. Wit and his players are clearly involved in every bar, and each episode of the narrative is resourcefully presented, not least the charming (almost Tchaikovskian) 'marche miniature' which achieves magnificent grandiloquence, being finally joined – in a satisfyingly broad climax – by the great *Vyšehrad* theme, and the piece closes to joyous fanfares. The warm resonance of the Concert Hall of Polish Radio in Katowice seems right for this very individual reading, full of fantasy, which goes automatically to the top of the list alongside Kubelik's distinguished and justly renowned, 1990 Czech Philharmonic version on Supraphon, which is rather special (11 1208-2 – see our main volume).

Järvi's, too, is an enjoyably vivid performance, and he has the double advantage of first-class playing from the highly committed Detroit orchestra and the splendid acoustics of Symphony Hall. Typically expert Chandos balancing brings a sound-picture approaching demonstration standard, warm and atmospheric but with more sharply defined detail than in Katowice. The romantic *Vyšehrad* is fresh and immediate, and the mountain streams of *Vltava* gleam brightly in the sunlight before the string-tune arrives and moves on with plenty of lyrical impetus. The jaunty village wedding is followed by an evocation of lovely, ethereal moonlight (matched by the high strings in *From Bohemia's woods and fields*) and the rapids bring high drama. *Šárka* is very dramatic indeed, with great melodramatic gusto and a heartfelt response from the strings. The opening of *Tábor* is tellingly ominous, and the weight of the Detroit brass makes a powerful contribution to both of the final two sections of the score. Throughout the whole performance Järvi's pacing is tauter than Wit's and he has no difficulty in maintaining tension. If the pastoral section of *Blaník* has not quite the rustic charm of the Polish Radio account, the zest of the Detroit music-making is always compelling, and the culminating climax is thrilling rather than expansively grandiloquent.

Dorati's is an extremely fine account of Smetana's cycle, avoiding most of the pitfalls with a reading which brings both vivid drama and orchestral playing of the finest quality. The music-making has a high adrenalin level throughout, yet points of detail are not missed. The accents of *Vyšehrad* may seem too highly stressed to ears used to a more mellow approach to this highly romantic opening piece, and *Vltava* similarly moves forward strongly. In the closing *Blaník*, Dorati finds dignity rather than bombast and the pastoral episode is delightfully relaxed, with a fine rhythmic bounce to the march theme which then leads to the final peroration. The Philips sound is splendid, with a wide amplitude and a thrilling concert-hall presence, and this reissue on the Philips Solo label makes an obvious recommendation in the mid-price range.

Pešek's reading does not miss the music's epic patriotic feeling, yet never becomes bombastic. There is plenty of evocation, from the richly romantic opening of *Vyšehrad* to the more mysterious scene-setting in *Tábor*, while the climax of *Šárka*, with its potent anticipatory horn-call, is a gripping piece of melodrama. The two main sections of the work, *Vltava* and *From Bohemia's woods and fields*, are especially enjoyable for their vivid characterization, while at the very end of *Blaník* Pešek draws together the two key themes – the *Vyšehrad* motif and the Hussite chorale – very satisfyingly.

After all this excellence it would be easy to undervalue Mehta's Israel performance, but he clearly enjoys the music and so do the Israeli players; the recording, though much less warmly expansive than Wit's or Dorati's – and certainly not in the Chandos bracket – is fuller and somewhat more atmospheric than we often experience in Tel Aviv, although it is at times unrefined and string detail is husky. Mehta's tempi are close to Järvi's in the first three symphonic poems, rather more expansive in the second triptych. *Vyšehrad* comes off quite effectively. But after an attractively delicate opening, the great string-tune of *Vltava* fails really to take off, and the climax needs a more expansive acoustic. The opening of *Tábor* isn't very arresting either, and both here and in *Blaník*, although the adrenalin runs freely, there is an element of bombast (the comparatively dry acoustic does not help) and Mehta seldom displays the imaginative flair of his competitors.

(i) *Má Vlast: Vyšehrad; Vltava; From Bohemia's woods and fields;* (ii) *The Bartered Bride: 3 Dances.*
(B) ** DG 439 451-2 [id.]. (i) Boston SO, Kubelik; (ii) BPO, Karajan.

These excerpts, which offer what many would regard as the three finest of the six tone-poems making up *Má Vlast*, come from Kubelik's second (1970) stereo recording with the Boston Symphony Orchestra which, though perceptive and very well played, suffered from close microphones, thus robbing the orchestra of a good deal of the natural sumptuousness afforded by the acoustics of Symphony Hall, Boston. The warm basic ambience remains but, as remastered, in *Vyšehrad* and in the great string-theme of *Vltava* the massed violins could ideally be richer. However, the ear adjusts and these are otherwise excellent performances. The *Polka, Furiant* and *Entry of the Comedians* from *The Bartered Bride* offer no such problems and are played with much panache by the Berlin Philharmonic under Karajan. But this Classikon bargain disc is not very full at 54 minutes: there would have been room for the overture, too.

Má Vlast: Vltava.
(M) (**) Sony mono SMK 64467 [id.]. NYPO, Bruno Walter – BRAHMS: *Hungarian dances Nos. 1, 3, 10 & 17;* J. STRAUSS: *Overtures; Waltzes.* (***)

Although the opening has fine delicacy and the moonlight sequence is highly atmospheric, the restricted dynamic range and studio-ish sound prevent Walter's 1941 mono recording from expanding at climaxes.

OPERA

The Bartered Bride: overture.
(M) *** RCA 09026 62587-2 [id.]. Chicago SO, Fritz Reiner – DVORAK: *Symphony No. 9* etc.;
   WEINBERGER: *Schwanda: polka and fugue.* ***

The easy, bustling virtuosity of the Chicago strings makes this vivacious performance of Smetana's famous overture hard to beat when the recording, too, is full yet has clear inner detail.

The Bartered Bride: highlights.
(M) **(*) Sup. 112251-2 [id.] (from complete recording, with Beňačková, Dvorský, Prague Ch., CPO, cond. Kosler).

A well-made if not strikingly generous set of highlights from the sparkling complete set (103511-2) praised in our main volume. But the documentation includes only a list of excerpts unrelated to any synopsis, and there is no translation.

The Brandenburgers in Bohemia (complete).
**(*) Sup. 11 1804-2 (2) [id.]. Zídek, Otava, Subrtová, Kalaš, Joran, Vich, Prague Nat. Theatre soloists, Ch. & O, Jan Hus Tichý.

Smetana was forty before he wrote this, his first opera, understandably a mixture of strong, confident musical gestures and dramatic ineffectiveness. The plot is based on an episode of thirteenth-century Czech history, when the country was occupied by Brandenburg forces, and it is likely to confuse anyone but a history specialist. Though much of the dramatic interest centres on the fate of the heroine, Liduše, abducted by a Prague burgher with the mercenary Germanic name of Tausendmark, the love interest which must sustain any romantic opera is sketched in only cursorily. The main duet between Liduše and her beloved, Junoš, is charming and jolly rather than heartfelt, an opportunity missed. Nevertheless there is much to enjoy in a performance as lively as this, with stirring patriotic choruses sung with a will, even if their melodic invention is hardly distinguished. The recording was made as long ago as 1963, but it sounds well in the CD transfer, with the three Acts squeezed on to two very well-filled discs. Milada Subrtová sings with appealingly sweet, firm tone as Liduše, and the young Ivo Zídek makes a fresh-voiced hero, strained only a little on top. Tausendmark is sung by a stalwart veteran, Zdeněk Otava, making up in bite what he lacks in vocal quality. A collector's item.

Dalibor (complete).

*** Sup. 11 2185-2 (2) [id.]. Přibyl, Kniplová, Jindrák, Svorc, Horáček, Prague Nat. Theatre Ch. &
   O, Jaroslav Krombholc.

Smetana was at the peak of his creative powers when he wrote *Dalibor*, conceiving it while he was still
writing *The Bartered Bride*. The contrast of mood and subject is extreme between that peasant
comedy and this Gothic historical tragedy about a knight, Dalibor, and a vengeful heroine, Milada,
who all too quickly capitulates into love and devotion for the man she once hated. Yet in the
development of the plot, when the imprisoned hero's lover is disguised as the gaoler's assistant,
Dalibor readily evokes associations with *Fidelio* and the subject prompted Smetana to write some of
his most inspired music. Where in his first opera, *The Brandenburgers in Bohemia*, the patriotic
choruses are conventional, here the opening chorus brings a stirring and measured number in triple
time and a minor key. The confrontations between hero and heroine also inspire Smetana to some
glorious writing, richly lyrical, most notably the love duet in the prison scene of Act II. This vintage
set of 1967, sounding more vivid and fuller-blooded than many more recent recordings, features in
those roles two of the most distinguished Czech singers of their time, both in their prime, the tenor
Vílém Přibyl and the dramatic soprano, Nadezda Kniplová. The other principals are not so
consistent, but Krombholc proves a most persuasive advocate, consistently bringing out the red-
blooded fervour of the writing. Highly recommended to anyone who wants to investigate beyond *The
Bartered Bride*. A full translation is provided.

The Two Widows (complete).

** Sup.11 2122-2 (2) [id.]. Sormová, Machotková, Zahradníček, Horáček, Prague Nat. Theatre Ch.
   & O, Jílek.

** Praga/Chant du Monde PR 250 022/3 (2) [id.]. Jonášová, Machotková, Svejda, Jedlička, Prague
   RSO, Krombholc.

Starting with a jolly chorus, *The Two Widows* gives promise of rivalling in brightness Smetana's
earlier comic masterpiece, *The Bartered Bride*. Though so Czech in its flavour, it was in fact drawn
from a French source, and amid the rustic amosphere there is something of Gallic sparkle. But this is
a tale of country life in the big house rather than among the peasantry, with the plot centring on two
cousins, both widows, and inconsequential confusions over which of them is going to marry the hero,
Ladislav. It all gets sorted out happily in the end but it takes a long time, with not very much
happening. That said, Smetana offers much delightful music and, if one regrets having choral
contributions only at the very beginning and at the ends of each of the two Acts, there are some
charming numbers in between, not least an aria for the hero, '*When Maytime arrives*', at the
beginning of Act II. Jiří Zahradníček is at his best there, singing lustily, though in gentler moments
Slavonic unsteadiness develops. Jaroslav Horáček is effective in the *buffo* bass role of Mumlal but,
sadly, the casting of the two widows, both sopranos, involves the major role of Karolina going to the
shrill and wobbly Naďa Sormová, while Marcela Machotková, who is altogether sweeter and firmer,
with a mezzo-ish quality, is consigned to the role of Anežka with far less to sing, even though it is she
who gets the hero. Recorded in 1975, this lively performance under Frantisek Jílek is on the whole
well transferred to CD, though in a dry-ish acoustic the Prague Theatre violins sound undernourished.
The libretto includes a very necessary translation.

   Recorded in 1974, only eighteen months earlier than the Supraphon version, the Praga set, as
transferred to CD by Chant du Monde, offers a more genial performance, a degree more expansive
but in sound that is rougher and edgier, with less sense of presence. In the role of Ladislav, Miroslav
Svejda has a more pleasing lyric tenor than his opposite number and is far more headily beautiful in
the hero's aria. Jana Jonášová as Karolina is steadier than Sormová but, if anything, even shriller,
not so warmly expressive in her Act II monologue. Again Machotková is excellent as Anežka, and
Dalibor Jedlička is a first-rate *buffo* bass. Two balancing points against the Praga set are that Act II
starts on the first disc, where Supraphon has one disc per Act, and that Praga offers only an English
translation with no Czech text.

Smyth, Ethel (1858–1944)

(i) *Double concerto* (trio) *in A for violin, horn & piano* (arr. composer); (ii; iii) *4 Songs: Odelette; La
danse; Chrysilla; Ode Anacréonique* (for mezzo soprano and chamber ensemble); (ii; iv) *3 Songs: The
clown; Possession; On the road* (for mezzo soprano and piano).

** Trouba Dig. TRO-CD 1405 [id.]. (i) Renate Eggebrecht-Kupsa, Franz Draxinger, Céline Dutilly;
   (ii) Melinda Paulsen; (iii) Ens. Schmeller; (iv) Angela Gassenhuber.

The *Horn trio* was originally a *Double concerto* (first performed in the Queen's Hall in 1927 by Jelly d'Arányi and Aubrey Brain with its dedicatee, Sir Henry Wood, conducting) and was arranged by the composer herself, and very effectively so. Occasionally casting a nod at the Brahms *Horn trio* (mostly in the jolly, dancing finale), it remains very much Dame Ethel's own piece and at times sounds quite modern – in the best sense. Highly inventive and tuneful, it obviously makes considerable demands on its players. After a memorably serene opening by the violinist, it is despatched here with much feeling and some aplomb, with fine horn playing, even if it has a few rough moments elsewhere. Well worth having on disc. The *Four songs* (1907) are French settings, the first three to texts by Henri d'Régnier and the third, a wild drinking song, a French translation from the Greek. The scoring is for flute, string trio, harp and percussion. With flute obbligati, Ravelian influences are strong, but all four are very successful, often exotic and always melodically strong. The three English songs (1913) are set to poems by Maurice Baring (*The clown*) and Ethel Carnie, and also show Dame Ethel's fine feeling for words. The performances are strong, but Melinda Paulsen is too often inclined to let fly on fortissimos for the vocal line to be always entirely comfortable. The pianist, Angela Gassenhuber, is most supportive. Good recording. Translations are provided, but the notes are a bit sparse. However, they do include a eulogy from Sir Thomas Beecham, reprinted from *The Musical Times* of 1958, describing Dame Ethel as 'a composer of originality, spirit, vigour, with a talent for emphasis ... Nothing could tame her and when I think of her, I think of her as a grand person, a great character.' This certainly comes out in her music.

(i; ii) *Cello sonata in A min., Op. 5;* (iii) *String quartet in C min;* (iii; iv) *String quintet in E, Op. 1;* (v; ii) *Violin sonata in A min., Op. 7.*
** Trouba Dig. TRO-CD 03 (2) [id.]. (i) Friedemann Kupsa; (ii) Céline Dutilly; (iii) Fanny
    Mendelssohn Qt; (iv) with Johanna Varner; (v) Renata Eggebrecht-Kupsa.

This music is very eclectic indeed, but Dame Ethel knows how to construct a movement with the strongest musical impulse in the traditional late-nineteenth-century style; moreover there is no shortage of good tunes here, even if the *Cello sonata* and, particularly, the *Violin sonata* (both early works dating from 1887) sound as if Brahms had written them. (The secondary theme of the opening movement of the latter work and the main theme of the lovely *Romanze* are particularly endearing.) In the *String quintet* (1883) the influences are distinctly Slavonic, with a strong flavour of Dvořák. The *Adagio* is heart-warming; the Scherzo and the ingenuously folksy finale are very lively in their ready flow of ideas. All these performances here, if not immaculate, are warmly persuasive and they project the music admirably. The *String quartet*, written between 1902 and 1912, is a different matter, a much more complex work, by no means backward-looking, with a remarkable slow movement which has something of the searching spirit of Schubert. The *Quartet* is obviously very difficult, for the playing here, though very committed, is rough and ready, with moments of insecure intonation. It is a pity that the discs are not available separately, for the coupling of the *Violin sonata* and *String quintet* is very recommendable. The recording is fully acceptable if not refined.

The Wreckers (opera) complete.
**(*) Conifer Dig. CDCF 250/1 (2) [id.]. Sidhom, Owens, Lavender, Wilson-Johnson, Bannatyne-
    Scott, Roden, Sand, Huddersfield Ch. Soc., BBC PO, Odaline de la Martinez.

Recorded live at the 1994 Proms in a concert performance at the Royal Albert Hall, the Conifer set of *The Wreckers* fills an important gap in the catalogue, even if this is hardly as striking as some other Smyth works such as the *Mass in D*. The colourful overture has remained reasonably well known, but in melodic invention the rest of the opera hardly lives up to that opening. The plot is strong and sharply conceived, set in Cornwall and culminating in the drowning of the hero and heroine, trapped in a cave by vengeful villagers. That close, which brings some of the most powerful writing in the opera, has been described fairly enough as 'Aida-on-sea', but the close of that death scene is triumphant rather than suffocated. Too often earlier in the opera, Smyth's dramatic timing is faulty, undermining powerful moments with trivial filling material.

Nevertheless, with Odaline de la Martinez directing a committed performance, this high-romantic melodrama makes an enjoyable piece, for all the lack of hummable tunes. One problem of the casting is that the role of the heroine is given to a mezzo soprano, and Anne-Marie Owens copes valiantly with the extreme range required. Justin Lavender makes a clear-toned hero, ostensibly too light for the role but sounding well on record. The others are stronger – David Wilson-Johnson characterful as the lighthouse keeper, Judith Howarth sweet-toned as the hero's jilted girlfriend and Peter Sidhom most powerful of all as the minister, suggesting that voices of Wagnerian strength might make a difference. Sadly, here the chorus is too backwardly balanced.

Stamitz, Karl (1745–1801)

Sinfonias concertantes: (i) *in C for 2 violins and orchestra;* (ii) *in D for violin, viola and orchestra.*
(BB) **(*) ASV Dig. CDQS 6140 [id.]. Richard Friedman, L. Festival O, Ross Pople; with (i) Steven
    Smith; (ii) Roger Best – HAYDN: *Sinfonia concertante.* **(*)

Two fine examples of Karl Stamitz's virile music-making make this an attractive coupling for Haydn
and worth considering in the lowest price-range. Stamitz may not match Mozart but he is a
personality in his own right and such a work as the *Sinfonia concertante in C for two violins*, here
projected with fine spontaneity, brings a slow movement where one of the two soloists, playing alone,
presents a 'singing' cantilena almost worthy of his greater contemporary. This *Andante* is also
felicitously scored, with effective writing for the horns. The first movement has some good ideas too,
and it is only the *Minuet* finale that lapses into conventionality; even so, like the first movement, the
writing for the two soloists is inventively conceived. The companion *Sinfonia concertante for violin
and viola*, if not quite so interesting in its material, has a historic link with Mozart's work for the
same combination; as such, it makes fascinating listening. However, although the two soloists here
play freshly and stylishly, they lack individuality of profile and, while Ross Pople directs the orchestra
strongly, with tender feeling in the central *Romance*, one remembers that an earlier CBS/Sony
account of this work by Stern and Zukerman (with the ECO under Barenboim) had far more
personality.

Stanford, Charles (1852–1924)

(i) *Concert piece for organ and orchestra;* (ii) *Clarinet concerto in A min., Op. 80; Irish rhapsodies Nos.
1 in D min., Op. 78; 2 in F min. (Lament for the Son of Ossian), Op. 84;* (iii) *3 for cello and orchestra,
Op. 137; 4 in A min. (The fisherman of Loch Neagh and what he saw); 5 in G min., Op. 147;* (iv) *6 for
violin and orchestra, Op. 191; Oedipus Rex prelude, Op. 29.*
*** Chan. Dig. CHAN 7002/3 [id.]. (i) Gillian Weir; (ii) Janet Hilton; (iii) Raphael Wallfisch; (iv)
    Lydia Mordkovitch; Ulster O, Vernon Handley.

Stanford's set of *Irish rhapsodies* (two of them concertante pieces with highly responsive soloists) are
the more impressive when heard as a set. They originally appeared coupled with the symphonies but
sometimes seemed stronger and more concentrated than these more ambitious works. They are
splendidly played and recorded. Gillian Weir makes a first-class soloist in the *Concert piece for organ
and orchestra* and Janet Hilton is hardly less appealing in the work for clarinet. An essential
supplement for those who have already invested in the four-CD box of the symphonies (CHAN
9279/81 – see our main volume).

Songs of the Fleet, Op. 117; Songs of the sea, Op. 91.
(M) **(*) EMI CDM5 65113-2 [id.]. Benjamin Luxon, Bournemouth SO Ch. & O, Del Mar –
    DELIUS: *Sea drift.* **

This is a very welcome coupling of Stanford at his most uninhibitedly vigorous. The four *Songs of the
sea* are more immediately memorable in their boisterous way, with *The Old Superb* a real hit; but the
Songs of the Fleet (also setting Newbolt poems, but with SATB chorus) make a pleasant sequel.
Luxon's voice is quite well caught by the microphones, but the resonance takes some of the bite from
the words of the chorus. Yet Del Mar's understanding of the idiom makes for lively and enjoyable
results.

Steffan, Joseph Anton (Stěpán) (1726–97)

Fortepiano concerto in B flat.
*** Teldec/Warner Dig. 4509 94569-2 [id.]. Andreas Staier, Concerto Köln – SALIERI: *Fortepiano
    concerto.* ***

The Bohemian-born Stěpán was forced by the invading Prussian armies to leave home and make for
Vienna, where as a pupil of Georg Wagenseil (Who is he, you may well ask!) he became Steffan,
before taking over court duties; alas, he began to go blind in the 1770s, although he continued
composing; and this work dates from a decade later. It is a fluent and inventive, if slightly overlong
piece, with a rather fine slow movement; the concerto also opens with an extended and quite touching
Adagio in D minor. Staier's performance is highly persuasive and he is given alert and sympathetic
support by the excellent Concerto Köln.

Stenhammar, Wilhelm (1871–1927)

(i) *Symphonies Nos. 1 in F; 2 in G min., Op. 34; Serenade for orchestra, Op. 31* (with *Reverenza* movement); *Excelsior Overture, Op. 13; The Song (Sången): Interlude, Op. 44; Lodolezzi sings (Lodolezzi sjunger): suite;* (ii) *Piano concertos Nos. 1 in B flat min., Op. 1;* (iii) *2 in D min., Op. 23;* (iv) *Ballad: Florez och Blanzeflor;* (v) *2 Sentimental Romances;* (vi) *Midwinter, Op. 24; Snöfrid, Op. 5.*

(M) *** BIS Dig. BIS CD 714/716 [id.]. (i) Gothenburg SO, Neeme Järvi; (ii) Love Derwinger; (iii) Cristina Ortiz; (iv) Peter Matthei; (v) Ulf Wallin; (vi) Gothenburg Ch.; (ii–v) Malmö SO, Paavo Järvi.

All these performances have been reviewed individually in our main edition. They are now repackaged at a distinctly advantageous price, presumably to meet the claims of the DG package listed below comprising Stenhammar's purely orchestral works. Special points to note are: first, that this is the only version of the *Serenade for orchestra* to include the *Reverenza* movement which Stenhammar subsequently withdrew; secondly, that the *First Piano concerto* makes use of Atterberg's original orchestration, which came to light only recently in America; and, thirdly, this is the most comprehensive compilation of Stenhammar's orchestral music now on the market. All the performances and recordings are of high quality, and the only serious criticism to make affects the first movement of the *Second Symphony*, which Järvi takes rather too briskly. The dazzling performance of the *Second Piano concerto* by Janos Solyom (recently reissued on EMI) has a slight edge over the Ortiz, but hers is a good account, full of sparkle. All the recordings are digital save for that of the *First Symphony*, which comes from a 1982 concert performance and has great warmth and transparency. Apart from the DG, that is its only recording, and many other works (*Midwinter, Lodolezzi sings* and the *Excelsior overture*) are not otherwise available. Recommended with enthusiasm.

Symphonies Nos. 1 in F (1902–3); 2 in G min., Op. 34; Serenade in F for orchestra, Op. 31; Overture, Excelsior!
*** DG Dig. 445 857-2 [id.]. Gothenburg SO, Neeme Järvi.

As a glance at the above will show, the DG set is less comprehensive but it contains Stenhammar's orchestral masterpieces, the *Serenade* and the *Second Symphony*, the former without the *Reverenza* movement which the composer excised when he revised the work and transposed the outer movement from E major to F. It is good to see these works appearing on an international label. Neeme Järvi and the Gothenburg Symphony Orchestra record them with the same team and in the same venue as they did for BIS. The *Second Symphony* is a distinct improvement on the earlier recording – the first movement is more measured and dignified, and the steadier tempo allows detail to register more effectively. Only in the fugal section of the finale does Järvi rush things a bit. There is very little to choose between the two versions of the *First Symphony*; perhaps the earlier, analogue recording has the greater warmth and spontaneity. The Gothenburg orchestra plays with real enthusiasm both here and in the *Excelsior! overture*. The *Serenade* comes off well, except for the glorious *Notturno*, which is faster and less atmospheric than before. Despite these provisos, the set is thoroughly recommendable and should do much for Stenhammar's cause in those areas where BIS records are not strongly stocked.

7 Songs from Thoughts of Solitude, Op. 7; 5 Songs to texts of Runeberg, Op. 8; 5 Swedish songs, Op. 16; 5 Songs of Bo Bergman, Op. 20; Songs and Moods, Op. 26; Late Harvest.
**(*) BIS Dig. CD 654 [id.]. Mattei, Lundin.

Only two of the three-dozen Stenhammar songs on this disc last longer than four minutes: *Jungfru Blond och Jungfru Brunett* ('Miss Blonde and Miss Brunette') and *Prins Aladin av Lampan* ('Prince Aladdin of the Lamp'), both of which are to be found on the set of 30 songs recorded by Anne Sofie von Otter and Håkan Hagegård on the Caprice Musica Svecicae label (MSCD 623 – see our main volume). As a song composer Stenhammar was often inspired and never routine in his responses to his poets (he shared Sibelius's taste for Fröding and Runeberg), his craftsmanship is always fastidious and in the posthumously published *Efterskörd* ('Late Harvest') and the *Thoughts of Solitude, Op. 7*, brings to light some songs of great eloquence and beauty that are not readily available outside Sweden. Peter Mattei is an intelligent singer, well endowed vocally; the voice is beautiful, but he has a tendency to colour the voice on the flat side of the note, and on occasion (in *Prins Aladin*, for example) is flat. Bengt-Ake Lundin deserves special mention for the sensitivity and responsiveness of his accompanying, and the recording is excellent.

Strauss, Johann, Jnr

Johann Strauss Jnr: The Complete Edition

Volume 37: *Triumph-Marsch* (orch. Fischer). Polkas: *Das Comitat geht in die Höh!; Sonnnenblume; Tanz mit dem Besenstiel!* (all arr. Pollack); (i) *Romance No. 2 in G min. for cello and orchestra, Op. 35* (arr.Schönherr); Quadrilles: *Die Königin von Leon* (arr. Pollack); *Spitzentuch. Neue Steierische Tänze* (orch. Pollak); *Traumbild II;* Waltzes: *Jugend-Träume* (orch. Pollack); *Schwungräder.*
*** Marco Polo Dig. 8.223237 [id.]. Slovak State PO (Košice), Christian Pollack; (i) with Regina Jauslin.

This is among the most interesting and worthwhile issues from the huge output of Marco Polo's Complete Edition so far. Moreover it includes the waltz with which the nineteen-year-old Johann Junior created his first sensation at Zum Sperlbauer in Vienna. He had taken over the orchestra's direction in February 1845, and during a summer's night festival in August of that same year *Jugend-Träume* was introduced. It received five encores! The waltz is entirely characteristic, opening with a lilting theme on the strings and moving from one idea to another with the easy facility that distinguishes his more famous waltzes. The original performing material for the piece has not survived, and the conductor has convincingly refashioned the piece from a later, truncated edition, with reduced orchestration. Christian Pollack is a Strauss scholar, and in almost every case here he has worked from piano scores or incomplete scoring. Particularly delectable is the set of *New Styrian dances*, seductively written in the Ländler style of Lanner's *Steyrische Tänze.* Here an almost complete piano version was available, while the orchestral parts end with the third dance; Pollack has therefore scored the fourth dance (very convincingly) in the style of the other three. The *Tanze mit dem Besenstiel!* ('Dance with the broomstick!') derives from material in Strauss's none too popular opera, *Jabuka* (a work prompted by the success of Smetana's *Bartered Bride*). The orchestral *pot-pourri* was made by a publisher's hack, Louis Roth; the composer thought it 'hopelessly bad' and tried to improve the draft manuscript where he could, without reworking the whole piece. He asked that Roth's name be stated clearly on the printed work as being responsible for its format and instrumentation, but the request was ignored by his publishers. While the *Romance for cello and orchestra* is agreeably slight, the other striking novelty here is *Traumbild II*, a late domestic work in two sections, the first of which is a gentle and charming 'dream-picture' of Strauss's wife, Adèle; the second shows the other side of her nature – more volatile and capricious. Both are in waltz time. Christian Pollack is not just a scholar but an excellent performing musician, and the playing here is polished, relaxed and spontaneous in an agreeably authentic way. With good recording and superb documentation (often revealing complete details of the source material), this is recommended even to those not collecting the complete Strauss Edition.

Volume 38: *Wiener Garnison-Marsch* (orch. Babinsky); *Ninetta-Galopp;* Polkas: *Damenspende; Lagerlust; Maskenzug* (2nd version); *Nimm sie hinn!; Zehner* (2nd version); Quadrilles: *Eine Nacht in Venedig; Serben* (orch. Babinski); Waltzes: *An der Elbe; Faschings-Lieder* (orch. Kulling); *Leitartikel.*
**(*) Marco Polo Dig. 8.223238 [id.]. Slovak State PO (Košice), Alfred Walter.

Leitartikel opens very agreeably, but *An der Elbe* is a real find among the waltzes, a charming melodic sequence with a striking introduction. But the *Ninetta-Galopp* with its perky main theme and swirling woodwind answer has the potential to become a Strauss lollipop, while the more sedate *Maskenzug-Polka française* closes the programme engagingly. This is one of Alfred Walter's better programmes, nicely played and well recorded.

Volume 39: *Ninetta-Marsch.* Polkas: *I Tipferl; Sylphen; Unparteiische Kritiken;* Quadrilles: *Jabuka; Slaven-Ball* (both orch. Pollack); Quodlibet: *Klänge aus der Raimundzeit;* Waltzes: *Abschied; Irenen* (orch. Babinski); *Hell und voll.*
**(*) Marco Polo Dig. 8.223239 [id.]. Slovak State PO (Košice), Christian Pollack.

The two most interesting items here both date from Johann's last years, the *Abschieds* (Farewell) *waltz* and the *Klänge aus der Raimundzeit* (1898), an affectionate *pot-pourri* including tunes by Johann Senior and Lanner. Johann originally called this good-humoured quodlibet 'Reminiscenz. Aus der guter alten Zeit' ('From the good old days'). The score of the waltz is written in the composer's own handwriting; his widow, Adèle, offered it to be performed posthumously in 1900. The composer left it unfinished and it is not known who completed it for its début. It opens with a romantic horn-call, introducing the main tune, which then becomes more nostalgic. The *I Tipferl-Polka français* is based on a popular comic song from Strauss's *Prinz Methusalem*, and the couplet: 'The man forgot – the little dot, the dot upon the i!' is wittily pointed in the music, while the jolly, tuneful *Jabuka-Quadrille* derives from another not too successful operetta (see Volume 37). It has been piquantly scored by Christian Pollack, who directs excellent performances of all the music here which, although of varying quality, is never dull.

Volume 40: *Hochzeits-Praeludium;* Polkas: *Herzenskönigin; Liebe und Ehe; Wildfeuer;* Quadrilles: *Ninetta; Wilhelminen* (orch. Babinski); Waltzes: *Heimats-Kinder* (orch. Babinski); *The Herald* (orch. Schönherr); *Irrlichter; Jubilee* (orch. Cohen).
*(*) Marco Polo Dig. 8.223240 [id.]. Slovak RSO (Bratislava), Bauer-Theussl.

Volume 41: March: *Wo uns're Fahne weht;* Polkas: *Newa; Shawl;* Quadrilles: *Martha; Vivat!;* Waltzes: *Burschen-Lieder; Gedankenflug; Lagunen. Traumbild* (symphonic poem). *Aschenbrödel (Cinderella): Prelude to Act III.*
** Marco Polo Dig. 8.223241 [id.]. Slovak RSO (Bratislava), Michael Dittrich.

Volume 42: *Hommage au public russe;* March: *Piccolo;* Polkas: *An der Moldau; Auroraball; Grüss aus Osterreich; Sängerlust; Soldatespiel;* Waltzes: *Gartenlaube; Hirtenspiele; Sentenzen.*
**(*) Marco Polo Dig. 8.223242 [id.]. Slovak State PO (Košice), Christian Pollack.

For volumes 40 to 42 Christian Pollack returns, but we also meet two new conductors, Franz Bauer-Theussl and Michael Dittrich. As it turns out, the music-making in Volume 40 under Bauer-Theussl immediately proves heavy-handed in the opening waltz, and the feeling throughout is that he is conducting for the commercial ballroom rather than the concert hall. As Pollack demonstrates in Volume 42, much more can be made of relatively strict tempo versions than Bauer-Theussl does with the *Irrlichter* and *Herald* waltzes. He also takes the polkas and quadrilles in a leisurely fashion, although the polka-mazurka, *Liebe und Ehe*, with its charming flutes at the opening, is still engaging. The *Jubilee Waltz* was written for the Strausses' American visit in 1872, when in Boston he conducted its première, played by a 'Grand Orchestra' of 809 players, including 200 first violins! With this kind of spectacle it is not surprising that he chose to end a not particularly memorable piece by including a few bars of the American national anthem in the coda. The other novelty here is the *Wedding* (*Hochzeits*) *prelude* which Strauss wrote for his stepdaughter's marriage. It includes solo parts for organ (harmonium), violin and harp, but is otherwise undistinguished.

Without being exactly a live wire, Michael Dittrich makes a good deal more of Volume 41. He is able to relax and at the same time coax the orchestra into phrasing with less of a feeling of routine, as in the *Shawl-Polka*, which lilts rather nicely, and the comparatively sprightly *Vivat!*. There are some winning flutes at the opening of *Burschen-Lieder waltz*, and both this and *Gedankenflug*, which also begins enticingly, bring some promise that even more could be made of them, given really imaginative presentation. The *Martha-Quadrille*, not surprisingly, quotes *M'appari*, among other themes from Flotow's opera, which took Vienna by storm in 1847. Dittrich fails to make a great deal of the one relatively well-known waltz here, *Lagunen*, but he manages the *Aschenbrödel Prelude* colourfully and does very well indeed by the *Traumbild I* ('Dream picture No. 1'), a warmly relaxed and lyrical evocation, quite beautifully scored. It was written towards the end of the composer's life, for his own pleasure. The orchestra obviously respond to the conductor's sympathetic direction and play beautifully, catching the work's nostalgia very nicely, while the resonant recording suits the music's gentle mood: the coda is really quite exquisite.

But when we come to Volume 42. so striking is the added vivacity that it is difficult to believe that this is the same orchestra playing. The opening *Piccolo-Marsch* and the *Auroraball polka français* are rhythmically light-hearted, as are all the other polkas in the programme, and if the *Hirtenspiele* (or 'Pastoral play') *waltz* is not a masterpiece, it is still freshly enjoyable in Pollack's hands, despite the demands of a ballroom tempo. The *Sentenzen Walzer* was written for a Vienna Law Students' faculty ball and is a most attractive piece, with a string of good ideas. Pollack plays it straightforwardly but still manages to give it a nice lilt. The *Hommage au Public Russe* uses themes by Glinka and the listener is suddenly surprised by the rushing strings from the *Overture Ruslan and Ludmilla*. There are other good tunes too, and it is nicely scored. The *Gartenlaube-Walzer* is a real find; it has a charming introduction with a neat little flute solo, then the opening tune, lightly scored, is very engaging indeed and, when it arrives, the string melody is one of Strauss's more memorable. It is a great pity that Marco Polo did not hire the services of Christian Pollack much earlier in the series. Even the recording sounds better-focused here.

'1995 New Year's Day concert': *An der schönen blauen Donau; Mephistos Höllenrufe; Morgenblätter; Perpetuum mobile; Process; Reitermarsch; Russische Marsche-Phantasie; Schützen;* Josef STRAUSS: *Arm in Arm; Auf Ferienreisen; Mein Lebenslauf ist Lieb' und Lust; Thalia.* Eduard STRAUSS: *Electrisch polka;* Johann STRAUSS Snr: *Alice polka; Radetzky march.*
*** Sony SK 66860; *ST 66860* [id.]. VPO, Zubin Mehta (with LANNER: *Favorit-Polka*).

Even more than usual, the 1995 New Year Concert reflected the personality of its conductor, Zubin Mehta, a bluff and jolly master of ceremonies, as he was also in the 'Three Tenors' concerts both in Rome and in Los Angeles. In the programme there is a high proportion of rarities, including two total novelties, buried for a century in some archive in Coburg. The slinky and lyrical Mazurka polka, *Thalia*, by Josef Strauss is particularly delightful, and Eduard Strauss's *Electrisch polka* is as breezily energetic as one would expect. Other rare charmers include the *Alice polka* with Czech overtones, by Johann Strauss the elder, dedicated to Princess Alice, daughter of Queen Victoria, and the *Russian March-fantasy* by Johann Strauss the younger, even more Slavonic in flavour. Lanner's *Favorit polka* includes an authentic Rossini crescendo, and even in this context the swinging waltz, *Mephistos Höllenrufe* (*Mephisto's calls from Hell*), might win a prize for oddity of title. *Morgenblätter* (*Morning Papers*), remains well known, but it is odd, when its main tune is so haunting, that Josef Strauss's waltz, *Mein Lebenslauf ist Lieb' und Lust*, once translated as 'Live, love and laugh', is not played much more. If Mehta's traditional rounding off for the *Perpetuum mobile* polka ('Und so weiter', and so on) comes in a little too quickly, and the audience starts clapping in the *Radetzky march* too soon (remember the way Karajan controlled them!), that plainly reflects the exuberance of the occasion, well caught on a very well-filled disc.

Waltzes: *Accelerationen; An der schönen blauen Donau (Blue Danube); Du und Du; Frühlingsstimmen (Voices of spring); Geschichten aus dem Wiener Wald (Tales from the Vienna Woods); Kaiser (Emperor); Künsterleben (Artist's life); Liebeslieder; Morgenblätter (Morning papers); Rosen aus dem Süden (Roses from the South); 1001 Nacht; Wein, Weib und Gesang (Wine, women and song); Wiener Blut (Vienna blood); Wiener Bonbons; Wo die Zitronen blühn (Where the lemon trees bloom)*. Josef STRAUSS: *Dorfschwalben aus Osterreich; Sphären-klange (Music of the spheres)*.
(B) *** Decca Double 443 473-2 (2) [id.]. VPO, Willi Boskovsky.

These recordings span Willi Boskovsky's long recording career with the VPO for Decca, stretching over two decades, when his records dominated the LP discography in the Strauss family repertoire. The first group to be recorded (*Liebeslieder*, ending disc 1, *Wiener Blut*, *Wiener Bonbons* and *Artist's life*, which open disc 2) are particularly 'live' and fresh, dating from 1958; and the last, a charmingly lilting performance of Josef Strauss's *Village swallows*, comes from 1976. One might think that such a succession of Strauss waltzes spread over two discs might produce a degree of listening fatigue, but that is never the case here, such is Johann's resource in the matter of melody and freshness of orchestration. The playing is reliably idiomatic in a coaxing, Viennese way and has striking spontaneity and life. Indeed there are some splendid performances and, if the opening item on disc 1, the *Blue Danube* (a little mannered), and the *Emperor* (lacking regality but with a beautiful coda) have been recorded elsewhere with greater memorability, *Tales from the Vienna Woods* is splendid, with a deliciously authentic zither solo; and both *Roses from the South* and *1001 Nights* are superb. *Wo die Zitronen blühn* with unashamed rubato comes off most winningly, and *Wine, women and song* with its four-and-a-half-minute introduction is another success; Josef's *Music of the spheres* is hardly less beguiling. The earliest recordings show their age a bit in the violin tone, but Decca set high technical standards from the beginning, and from the 1960s onwards the strings are tonally more expansive, while the glorious Viennese ambient glow is consistent throughout. Indeed on CD it is remarkable just how well these vintage recordings sound. With 145 minutes of music offered on a Double Decca reissue (two discs for the price of one), this is excellent value.

OPERA

Overtures: *Die Fledermaus; Der Zigeunerbaron*. Waltzes: *An der schönen blauen Donau; Geschichten aus dem Wiener Wald; Kaiser; Wiener Blut*.
(M) (***) Bruno Walter Edition: Sony mono SMK 64467 [id.]. Columbia SO, Bruno Walter –
BRAHMS: *Hungarian dances Nos. 1, 3, 10 & 17* (***); SMETANA: *Vltava*. (**)

It is good to have a reminder of Bruno Walter's way with Johann Strauss, full of vivacity, and with *Wiener Blut* obviously the conductor's favourite among the waltzes here, as he coaxes the opening beguilingly and then draws some ravishing playing from the violins. The two overtures are bright and volatile. No apologies whatsover about the 1956 mono recording, which is warm and spacious and sounds almost like early stereo.

Die Fledermaus (complete).
(M) *** EMI CMS 7 69534-2 (2). Rothenberger, Holm, Gedda, Dallapozza, Fischer-Dieskau, Fassbaender, Berry, V. State Op. Ch., VSO, Boskovsky.

A bargain version of Johann Strauss's scintillating operetta, well recorded in digital sound and complete with substantial dialogue, clearly has a place; but the singing lets this Naxos set down. After a promising account of the overture, crisp and bright if not quite Viennese, the entry of Alfred signals the worst. It would be hard to imagine the would-be Italian tenor's role sung more lumpishly, with coarse Germanic tone. When Adele arrives, her combination of flutter in the voice and shrillness is equally hard to take, particularly as her confident overacting involves shrieks that are comic in a way she plainly does not intend. The sonic production here is fine, well recorded with just enough crowd-noises in the party scene of Act II and with dialogue – more than usual on disc – trippingly spoken by singers obviously well drilled, but the voices regularly sound too old, almost all of them unsteady in ways that the microphone exposes. Even Gabriele Fontana, who sings Rosalinde, is deeply disappointing, for the voice has plainly deteriorated since she sang Mozart at Glyndebourne. Johannes Wildner is an efficient director, but drilling the Bratislava chorus involves military-style rhythms rather than the graciousness and sparkle of Strauss's Vienna.

Fortunately EMI have just restored the mid-priced Boskovsky set to the catalogue. Though he sometimes fails to lean into the seductive rhythms as much as he might, his is a refreshing account of a magic score. Rothenberger is a sweet, domestic-sounding Rosalinde, relaxed and sparkling if edgy at times, while, among an excellent supporting cast, the Orlovsky of Brigitte Fassbaender must be singled out as the finest on record, tough and firm. The entertainment has been excellently produced for records, with German dialogue inserted, though the ripe recording sometimes makes the voices jump between singing and speaking. The remastering is admirably vivid. At full price Previn's enjoyably idiomatic Philips set (432 157-2) with Kiri te Kanawa, and with Brigitte Fassbaender a dominant Prince Orlovsky, remains a clear first choice.

Die Fledermaus: highlights.
(M) **(*) Decca 421 898-2 [id.]. Janowitz, Holm, Kmentt, Kunz, Waechter, Windgassen, V. State Op. Ch., VPO, Karl Boehm.

It is good to have a generous (76 minutes) set of highlights from Karl Boehm's 1971 recording of *Fledermaus*, which has not yet been issued on CD. Boehm conducts with great warmth and affection, and the recording was made without dialogue, which many will prefer. The stars of the performance are undoubtedly Gundula Janowitz, in rich voice as Rosalinde, and Renate Holm as Adèle. The male principals are rather less impressive and the use of a male Orlovsky has less dramatic point on record than it would on stage. Windgassen, who assumes this role, is vocally here much inferior to, say, Brigitte Fassbaender. But (with fairly good documentation, though with no translation) there is much to enjoy, and the vintage Decca recording was made in the Sofiensaal.

Der Zigeunerbaron (arr. Harnoncourt; Linke: complete).
*(**) Teldec/Warner Dig. 4509 94555-2 (2) [id.]. Coburn, Lippert, Schasching, Hamari, Holzmair, Oelze, Von Magnus, Lazar, Arnold Schoenberg Ch., VSO, Harnoncourt.

When *Zigeunerbaron*, second only to *Fledermaus* among Strauss operettas, has been so neglected on disc, this new Teldec set, offering a more expanded text than ever before, fills an important gap. Harnoncourt, as a Viennese and with a Viennese orchestra, ensures that the Strauss lilt is winningly and authentically observed from the *pot-pourri* overture onwards, and Harnoncourt's concern (as a period specialist) for clarity of texture gives the whole performance a sparkling freshness. Sadly, the casting is seriously flawed, when the central character of the gypsy princess, Saffi, is taken by a soprano, Pamela Coburn, who, as recorded, sounds strained and unsteady. She projects little of the glamour needed, the quality that Elisabeth Schwarzkopf so radiantly displayed on the classic EMI mono set of 1954 (which has currently reappeared in the EMI catalogue: CHS7 69526-2). The others are better, with Rudolf Schasching catching the fun behind the comic role of the pig-breeder, Zsupán, authentically but without exaggeration, and the light tenor, Herbert Lippert, is charming as the hero, Barinkay. Among the rest, the mezzo, Elisabeth von Magnus, sings in cabaret style in the supporting role of Mirabella, given a major point-number here, often omitted. Christiane Oelze as Arsena, the girl who does not get the hero, sings far more sweetly than Coburn, and Julia Hamari as Saffi's foster-mother, Czipra, sounds younger than her daughter. The recording is full and vivid, but many will feel that there is too much German dialogue – largely accounting for the extended length of two and a half hours.

Strauss, Josef (1827–70)

Josef Strauss: The Complete Edition

Volume 1: Polkas: *Angelica; Bauern; Eislauf; Etiquette; Moulinet; Thalia.* March: *Galenz. Kakadu-quadrille.* Waltzes: *Fantasiebilder; Marien-Klänge; Wiegenlieder.*
** Marco Polo Dig. 8.223561 [id.]. Budapest Strauss SO, Alfred Walter.

It is good to see Marco Polo now exploring the output of Josef Strauss, of which we know remarkably little. Indeed almost all the items in this first volume are completely unfamiliar. The opening quadrille, *Kakadu* (*Cockatoo*) was Josef's last and is based on themes from Offenbach's equally unfamiliar operetta. When first heard in 1870, it was designed as a promotional exercise for the stage work. Alfred Walter gives it an affectionate performance; his easy-going style permeates the whole programme, and most of the polkas are left badly needing a more vital pacing. The waltzes are lilting in a lazy way: Walter shapes the evocative opening of *Fantasiebilder* rather beautifully, helped by polished and sympathetic playing from a group of Hungarian players 'dedicated to the rediscovery and performance of music by the celebrated Strauss family'. *Wiegenlieder* (*Cradle songs*) is another waltz which opens very enticingly and ought to be better known: it has a charming main theme and is nicely scored. The closing *Eislauf polka*, so very like the writing of Johann Junior, ends the concert spiritedly, and this well-recorded disc has great documentary interest, while the back-up notes are equally praiseworthy.

Strauss, Richard (1864–1949)

Also sprach Zarathustra, Op. 30; Death and transfiguration, Op. 24; Don Juan, Op. 20; Ein Heldenleben, Op. 40; Till Eulenspiegel; Der Rosenkavalier: Waltz sequence. Salome: Salome's dance of the seven veils.
(B) *** EMI CZS5 68110-2 (2) [id.]. Dresden State O, Rudolf Kempe.

Kempe's 1974 *Also sprach Zarathustra*, though powerful in its emotional thrust, is completely free of the sensationalism that marks so many newer performances. It is admirably paced and, while the Dresden orchestra may yield in virtuosity – though not much – to the Berlin Philharmonic under Karajan, whose version was made in the same year, the EMI digital remastering retains the opulence of the Dresden acoustic and the orchestral sound has both body and bloom. Kempe's *Death and transfiguration* and *Till Eulenspiegel* are also marvellously characterized, and the Dresden Staatskapelle is hardly less refined an instrument than the Berlin Philharmonic. The rather mellow portrayal of *Till* is particularly attractive. *Don Juan* is also comparable with Karajan's reading and certainly does not come off second best. *Ein Heldenleben* glows with life under one of the most distinguished Straussians of our time and the closing pages have a special kind of rapt intensity. The richness of string-tone in *Salome's dance*, a sinuously sensuous performance, and in the *Rosenkavalier Waltz sequence* has been superbly caught in the excellent CD transfer. With two discs offered for the price of one, this is a top bargain in the Strauss discography.

Burleske for piano and orchestra.
(BB) **(*) RCA Navigator 74321 21286-2. Byron anis, Chicago SO, Reiner – MAHLER: *Symphony No. 4* **(*).

The *Burleske* was a product of the composer's later twenties, when his brilliance almost outshone his inventiveness. The brilliance is brought out well by Byron Janis, who also does not miss the music's witty or lyrical side. The recording gives a brilliantly sparkling, somewhat dry piano-image and the orchestra too is brought forward by the comparatively close microphones (although there is no lack of ambience), but this helps to ensure that Strauss's youthful writing does not sound too sweet.

(i) *Horn concertos Nos. 1 in E flat, Op. 11; 2 in E flat;* (ii) *Duet concertino for clarinet and bassoon. Wind serenade in E flat, Op. 11.*
(M) *** EMI Dig. CD-EMX 2238; *TC-EMX 2238* [id.]. (i) David Pyatt; (ii) Joy Farrall, Julie Andrews; Britten Sinfonia, Nicholas Cleobury.

David Pyatt gives a ripely exuberant performance of the first of Strauss's two *Horn concertos*, which is very much in the spontaneous style of the Mozart concertos. The more elusive first movement of the *Second Concerto* is shaped – often quite subtly – in an attractively rhapsodical style; the ecstatic solo line of the *Andante*, gently introduced by the oboe, is beautifully played while the finale brings heady, lightly tongued bravura. The outer movements of the gently rapturous *Duet concertino* (a late masterpiece, written the year before the *Vier letzte Lieder*) are presented with enticing delicacy of texture, and the slow movement again brings a most touchingly doleful opening solo, this time from the bassoonist, Julie Andrews. Cleobury and the Britten Sinfonia give sensitive support throughout, and the early *Serenade* is also made the more attractive by the lightness of touch of the wind blending, its sonorities always fresh, never congealing, helped by the naturally balanced recording, made in the Henry Wood Hall, Southwark. For those who want a change from the Dennis Brain Philharmonia accounts of the *Horn concertos* from the 1950s, this would be a distinct contender.

Death and transfiguration, Op. 24; Don Juan, Op. 20.

(M) (**(*)) Bruno Walter Edition: Sony mono SMK 64466 [id.]. NYPO, Bruno Walter (with DVORAK: *Slavonic dance, Op. 46/1*) – BARBER: *Symphony No. 1.* (**)

Death and transfiguration, Op. 24; Don Juan, Op. 20; Till Eulenspiegel, Op. 28.

(M) (***) EMI mono CDH5 65197-2 [id.]. VPO, Furtwängler (with SMETANA: *Má Vlast: Vltava* ***).

Death and transfiguration; Don Juan; Till Eulenspiegel; Der Rosenkavalier: suite.

(M) ** Mercury 434 348-2 [id.]. Minneapolis SO, Antal Dorati.

Furtwängler's are wonderfully rich and humane performances, with that glowing sound the great conductor made so much his own. All these recordings are mono and were produced by Walter Legge or Laurance Collingwood, with Anthony Griffith and Robert Beckett as engineers. They wear their years very lightly indeed. The performances themselves have a tremendous fall-out and resonate in the mind long after they are over. Strongly recommended.

Walter recorded these tone-poems in the studio in 1952; the sound, though not well balanced, is reasonably expansive for its period, a bit empty-studio-ish but much better than the coupled Barber *Symphony*. The performances are both warmly romantic and high in adrenalin; indeed the playing of the NYPO is at times quite wild in *Don Juan*. Precision of string ensemble is less impressive, but Walter finds a very special atmosphere for the opening and closing pages of *Death and transfiguration.*

Dorati was to record these three symphonic poems again, digitally, in Detroit for Decca with greatly improved sound, but his interpretations remained much on the same lines. *Till Eulenspiegel* suits him best, and the racy impetus of the string (and horn) playing communicates excitingly in spite of the spiky Minneapolis sound. Detail is vividly characterized, notably the moment when Till scorns his betters and goes off whistling down the street, while the final climax is like Judgement Day itself. The suite from *Der Rosenkavalier* bursts with rhythmic vigour and displays much orchestral virtuosity at climaxes, but elsewhere the recording is a bit lean in its colouring. *Death and transfiguration*, too, needs a more sumptuous acoustic although no one could say that Dorati is not dramatic; *Don Juan* is heroic in the pulsing energy and vigorous determination of the chase, but the sensuality again is not helped by the rather dead acoustic of the Northrop Auditorium.

Death and transfiguration; Metamorphosen for 23 solo strings; (i) Vier letzte Lieder (4 Last songs).

(M) **(*) DG 447 422-2 [id.]. BPO, Karajan, (i) with Gundula Janowitz.

(i) *Death and transfiguration;* (ii; iii) *Vier letzte Lieder;* (ii; iv) *Capriccio: closing scene.*

(B) ** DG 439 467-2 [id.]. (i) Dresden State O, Boehm; (ii) Gundula Janowitz; (iii) BPO, Karajan; (iv) Bav. RSO, Boehm.

Karajan surpassed his analogue recordings of both *Death and transfiguration* and the *Metamorphosen* when he re-recorded them digitally, but the earlier versions offered here are still powerful and convincing In the *Four last songs*, Janowitz produces a beautiful flow of creamy tone while leaving the music's deeper and subtler emotions under-exposed. The transfers are very impressive, and *Death and transfigration* can still be regarded as a showpiece among Karajan's earlier Berlin recordings.

Boehm's *Death and transfiguration* was recorded live (there is a cough near the opening to prove it) at the 1972 Salzburg Festival. It is a performance of great excitement and strong tensions, but the recording is slightly overweighted at the top. The same Janowitz coupling of the *Vier letzte Lieder* was a curious choice (as Karajan provided the accompaniment), but Boehm returns for the final scene of *Capriccio*, where Janowitz is at her best (though, as in the songs, no match for Schwarzkopf).

Don Juan; Till Eulenspiegel; Salome: Dance of the seven veils.

*** Everest/Vanguard EVC 9004 [id.]. NY Stadium SO, Stokowski – CANNING: *Fantasy on a hymn tune.* ***

A justly famous Stokowski triptych from the late 1950s, with the spacious recording now cleaned up and sounding very well indeed. Not surprisingly with the old magician in charge, Salome is made to languish more voluptuously than ever before, and even *Till* in his posthumous epilogue has a languishing mood on him. *Don Juan* indulges himself with rich sensuality, yet leaps off into the fray with undiminished vitality, while the great unison horn-call is held back with a compellingly broadened thrust. As ever, Stokowski is nothing if not convincing, and those looking for really ripe versions of these pieces need not hesitate. The Canning coupling is also worth having.

Metamorphosen for 23 solo strings.
(B) **(*) EMI CZS7 67816-2 (2) [id.]. New Philh. O, Barbirolli – MAHLER: *Symphony No. 6.* **(*)

Barbirolli's version of the *Metamorphosen* is a fine one, with a warm glow and an intense, valedictory feeling, and the playing of the NPO strings is most eloquent. The 1967 Abbey Road recording still sounds well; however, although it still has weight, the present CD transfer has lost some of its original bloom and opulence. This performance has a powerful ambience but, as in the earlier issue, it is coupled to Mahler's *Sixth symphony*, and those who don't care for Sir John's reading of that work will presumably think twice before committing themselves. However, in this two-for-the-price-of-one reissue it is still worth considering.

Sinfonia domestica, Op. 53; Festliches Praeludium; Till Eulenspiegel, Op. 28.
*** EMI Dig. CDC5 55185-2 [id.]. Phd. O, Sawallisch.

Wolfgang Sawallisch belongs to the great tradition of German musician-conductors as opposed to the shallow, glossy showmen cultivated by the media. His *Sinfonia domestica* is *echt*-Strauss, unexaggerated and civilized. He draws excellent playing from the Philadelphia Orchestra and gives a performance that reveals this score for what it is: one of the finest of Strauss's works. Clemens Kraus and Fritz Reiner both made classic accounts of such excellence as to intimidate other contenders. This is easily the best *Sinfonia domestica* since the Karajan version of the 1970s, and it is accorded refined and well-detailed sound.

Sinfonia domestica; Suite in B flat for 13 wind instruments, Op. 4.
(M) ** Virgin/EMI Dig. CUV5 61142 [id.]. Minnesota O, Edo de Waart.

Anyone who feels that Strauss's domestic revelations need tempering with a little discretion will enjo Edo de Waart's Minnesota performance, which is very well played and does not miss the ardour of the Adagio love scene between Strauss and his wife. The *Suite in B flat* is beautifully played and comparably refined. Both are naturally recorded.

Capriccio, Op. 85: String sextet.
*** Hyp. Dig. CDA 66704 [id.]. Raphael Ens. – BRUCKNER: *String quintet.* ***

The opening sextet from Strauss's last opera, *Capriccio*, makes an excellent fill-up to the Bruckner *String quintet*. Obviously readers are unlikely to buy the Bruckner for the sake of such a short work, even though it is of great beauty, but those who do will be rewarded by some fine music-making and recording.

Piano quartet in C min., Op. 13.
*(*) Koch Schwann Dig. 3-1127-2 [id.]. Berlin Philharmonic Qt – SUK: *Piano quartet.* *(*)

The Strauss *Piano quartet in C minor* is an early and uncharacteristic piece, dating from 1883–4, when the composer was in his late teens. Michael Kennedy calls it 'a massive act of homage to Brahms'; although it is not great music, it is eminently well crafted. The Berlin Philharmonic Quartet give a conscientious and well-played account, though they suffer from a very studio-like recording acoustic, with not enough air round the sound.

Lieder: *Ach, weh mir undglückhaftem Mann; All meine Gedanken; Breit' über mein Haupt; Freundliche Vision; Heimliche Aufforderung; Ich liebe dich; Mein Auge; Morgen; Die Nacht; Nachtgang; Nichts; Ruhe, meine Seele; Ständchen; Traume durch die Dämmerung; Wie solten wir geheim sie halten; Wozu noch, Mädchen; Zueignung.*
(M) *** Ph. 442 744-2 (2) [id.]. Gérard Souzay, Dalton Baldwin – WOLF: *Italienisches Liederbuch.* ***

Souzay seldom disappoints, and this is a wonderful recital, unquestionably one of the finest Strauss Lieder collections available. In subtlety of phrasing and beauty of line Souzay is here at his finest, and songs like *Ich liebe dich* or the delightful *Serenade* sound freshly minted. There is also a superb lightness of touch when called for. The accompaniments are characteristically sensitive and perceptive, and the recording is well balanced. But why did this have to come in harness with the *Italian Lieder Book* (as part of the Philips Early Years series), rather than be available separately?

OPERA

Vienna State Opera: Volume V (1933–43): (i) *Die Aegyptische Helena:* excerpts; (ii) *Daphne:* excerpts;
(iii) *Die Frau ohne Schatten:* excerpts.
(M) (***) Koch Schwann mono 3-1455-2 (2) [id.]. V. State Op. O, with (i) Viorica Ursuleac, Franz
   Völker, Margit Bokor, Alfred Jerger, Helge Roswaenge, cond. Clemens Krauss; (ii) Maria
   Reining, Alf Rauch, Anton Dermota, cond. Rudolf Moralt; (iii) Torsten Ralf, Hilde Konetzni,
   Elisabeth Höngen, Josef Herrmann, Else Schulz, Herbert Alsen, Emmy Loose, Wenko Wenkoff;
   cond. Karl Boehm.

These excerpts from *Die Aegyptische Helena* from 1933 are conducted by Clemens Krauss, with
Franz Volker superb but with Viorica Ursuleac rather raw in the title-role. The *Daphne* excerpts
under Rudolf Moralt date from 1942, with Maria Reining below her best but with two excellent
tenors, Alf Rauch as Apollo and the lyrical Anton Dermota as Leukippos. Central to this volume is
the selection from *Die Frau ohne Schatten* under Karl Boehm, almost an hour and a half of excerpts
with Torsten Ralf as the Emperor and Hilde Konetzni as the Empress, though Boehm went on to
make two complete recordings of this opera with infinitely better sound. A fascinating pair of discs,
just the same, in spite of the very primitive sound.

Arabella (complete).
(M) (***) DG mono 445 342-2 (3) [id.]. Reining, Hotter, Della Casa, Taubmann, VPO, Boehm.

Recorded live in August 1947 at the Salzburg Festival, the Boehm recording was issued in 1994 to
celebrate the centenary of his birth, a radiant account with an outstanding cast. It is the more
valuable when Boehm never tackled the opera again and, from his warmth and understanding here,
one wonders why. Maria Reining, best known on record for her Marschallin for Erich Kleiber, is
here in far firmer, truer voice, conveying not just the dignity of the heroine but the depth of feeling
behind her often imperious manner. Boehm's slow speeds tax her occasionally (as in the lovely
opening solo of *Aber der Richtige*), but it is a small price to pay when, thanks to full-bodied mono
sound, the voice conveys such presence. Hans Hotter too in his early maturity is in splendid voice, a
superb Mandryka, characterful and well focused. Lisa della Casa, destined to make the role of
Arabella a speciality, is here a charming Zdenka, fresh and girlish; and the rest of the cast includes
many Viennese stalwarts of the period. Despite the limitations of the orchestral sound and some very
rough playing, it is a most cherishable set. Interestingly, Acts II and III are linked together, with the
Fiakermilli's brief final solo omitted, so that Mandryka's last line moves straight into the Act III
Prelude.

'Vienna State Opera Live': Volume 15: (i) *Arabella:* excerpts; (ii) *Friedenstag:* complete; (iii) *Ariadne
auf Naxos:* excerpts
(M) (**) Koch Schwann mono 3-1465-2 (2) [id.]. (i) Viorica Ursuleac, Margit Bokor, Alfred Jerger,
   Adele Kern, Gertrude Rünger, Richard Mayr; (ii) Hans Hotter, Ursuleac, Herbert Alsen, Josef
   Wit, Hermann Wiederman, Mela Bugarinovic; V. State Op. O; both cond. Clemens Krauss; (iii)
   Anny Konetzni, Sev Svanholm, Kern, Else Schulz, Jerger, Alexander Pichler, Alfred Muzzarelli;
   V. State Op. O, Rudolf Moralt.

Strauss's one-Act opera, *Friedenstag*, was first heard in 1938, barely a year before the outbreak of the
Second World War. The plea for peace which forms the basis of the plot may have been timely but, in
the context of the Nazi regime under which the composer was working, it might have been counted a
cynical choice of subject, had the composer been politically more aware. It ends in a triumphalist
final ensemble which plainly roused the audience, and could well do the same in a modern
performance. This is one of only two complete operas in the May Archive of Vienna State Opera
recordings, and in one brief patch of 30 seconds the sound is totally submerged beneath the
background noise, which remains heavy throughout. Happily, the voices generally come over well.
Clemens Krauss, to whom the opera was dedicated, is a warmly responsive interpreter, drawing out
the rich lyricism of this score, not least when his wife, the principal soprano, Viorica Ursuleac, is
singing. Her monologues, as well as the duets with the heroine's husband, the Commandant of a
besieged fortress, are the high points of a score which represents Strauss returning to his ripest, most
forthright vein. It may not be a subtle work but it is a highly enjoyable one, even with such a scrubby
recording.

It is also fascinating on the first disc to have also four extracts from the first Vienna production of
Arabella, given only four months after the Dresden première, with the same principals and conductor,
Krauss again. In 1933 Ursuleac is even warmer and firmer than in 1939, though the sound is even
more seriously obscured by background noise. The *Ariadne* excerpts, recorded in 1941, are also
valuable but even more frustrating, with the extracts fading in and out of big numbers at awkward

moments. The casting too is flawed, with Anny Konetzni a fruity and none too steady Ariadne, Else Schulz shrill on top as the Composer, while the brilliant contribution of the Zerbinetta, Adele Kern, is undermined by suddenly distant recording.

Ariadne auf Naxos (complete).
(M) (*(**)) DG 445 332-2 (2) [id.]. Della Casa, Gueden, Seefried, Schock, Schöffler, VPO, Boehm.
(M) *(*) Decca 443 675-2 (2) [id.]. Leonie Rysanek, Jurinac, Peters, Peerce, Berry, Dickie, Preger, VPO, Leinsdorf.

Boehm had a natural affinity with this opera. It was the last one he conducted, at the Salzburg Festival in 1980, and here, 26 years earlier, his affection for this elegant, touching score similarly glows through the whole performance. Lisa della Casa is a poised, tender Ariadne, totally rapt in the final duet with Bacchus. Even though her later studio recordings of the *Lament* are more assured than this, the passion of the climax of that key solo is most involving. As in Karajan's studio recording, Irmgard Seefried as the Composer and Rudolf Schock as Bacchus have few equals; but what crowns the whole performance is the charming Zerbinetta of Hilde Gueden, not just warmly characterful but fuller-toned than almost any. The snag is the recording, fizzy in the orchestral sound, with even the voices rather thinly recorded. The Vienna State Opera recording of 1944, available on Koch, has more vivid, fuller-bodied sound.

Although one has reservations about Leinsdorf's contribution, this Decca reissue is a well-produced medium-priced version of an enchanting opera. Rysanek's rather fruity voice is not ideally cast in the part of Ariadne. Sena Jurinac, as the Composer, in the Prologue is very effective; her singing has character, and there is good support from the rest of the cast, but the performance is not strong on charm. The early (1958) recording, made in the Sofiensaal, sounds well on this new CD transfer but, with all the current competition, remains uncompetitive. Even leaving aside the classic mono account with Schwarzkopf (EMI CMS7 69296-2), those looking for a mid-priced stereo version would do far better with Solti's London version with Leontyne Price and Tatiana Troyanos as the Composer (Decca 430 384-2).

'Vienna State Opera live': Volume 23: *Ariadne auf Naxos* (complete).
(M) (***) Koch 3-1473-2 (2). Reining, Seefried, Noni, Lorenz, Schoeffler, Vienna State Op. O, Boehm – WAGNER: *Meistersinger:* excerpts. (**)

Recorded live in June 1944, not long before the Vienna State Opera was bombed, this is a glowing account of *Ariadne*, given in honour of the eightieth birthday of the composer. With an outstanding cast, it is here presented in sound that is astonishingly full-bodied for the period. The sense of presence on the voices is most compelling, and it is fascinating to hear Seefried in the first of her three magnificent recorded performances, singing with, if anything, even more passion than later, in full, firm sound. Maria Reining makes a warm, touching Ariadne, and Max Lorenz as Bacchus has rarely been matched in subsequent recordings, sweeter and less strenuous than most Heldentenoren. Alda Noni makes a bright, mercurial Zerbinetta, not always note-perfect in her coloratura but with plenty of sparkle, and Paul Schoeffler is warm and wise as the Music-master. With 40 minutes of *Meistersinger* excerpts as filler, it is a historic set for non-specialists to consider.

Capriccio (complete).
(M) **(*) DG 445 347-2 (2) [id.]. Janowitz, Troyanos, Schreier, Fischer-Dieskau, Prey, Ridderbusch, Bav. RSO, Karl Boehm.

In this elusive opera it is impossible to avoid comparison with Sawallisch's classic mono version with Schwarzkopf and Fischer-Dieskau (EMI CDS7 49014-8). Gundula Janowitz is not as characterful and pointful a Countess as one really needs (and no match for Schwarzkopf), but Boehm lovingly directs a most beautiful performance of a radiant score, very consistently cast, beautifully sung and very well recorded for its period (1971). There is full documentation, including translation.

Daphne (complete).
(M) *** DG 445 322-2 (2) [id.]. Gueden, Wunderlich, King, Schöffler, VSO, Karl Boehm.

The DG set is a live recording, made during the 1964 Vienna Festival, and it provides an enticing reissue. It could hardly be better cast, with the tenors James King as Apollo and Fritz Wunderlich as Leukippos both magnificent. Hilde Gueden makes a delectable Daphne and gives one of her finest performances on record, while Karl Boehm, the opera's dedicatee, brings out the work's mellowness without any loss of vitality.

Elektra (complete).
(M) ** DG 445 329-2 (2) [id.]. Borkh, Schech, Madeira, Fischer-Dieskau, Dresden State O, Karl Boehm.

The voices in the 1960 DG recording of Boehm, made in the helpful acoustic of the Lukaskirche in Dresden, have warmth and immediacy, underlining the power of Inge Borkh, tough in the title-role with an apt touch of rawness, of Jean Madeira as Klytemnestra, firm and positive, and of Dietrich Fischer-Dieskau, incomparable as Orestes. Their contributions are very vivid; but the distancing of the orchestra, and with it the relative thinness of the strings, means that a vital element in this violent opera is underplayed. The clarity of CD with its full body of sound brings an improvement on the original LPs, but Karl Boehm's masterly timing in this opera deserves to have a more substantial showing. The only weakness to note in the cast is the Chrysothemis of Marianna Schech, thin and unsteady and with touches of shrillness. First choice remains with the Solti set with Birgit Nilsson (Decca 417 345-2 – see our main volume).

Der Rosenkavalier (complete).
(M) **(*) Ph. 442 086-2 (3) [id.]. Lear, Von Stade, Welting, Bastin, Hammond Stroud, Netherlands
    Op. Ch., Rotterdam PO, Edo de Waart.
(M) ** DG 445 338-2 (3) [id.]. Ludwig, Troyanos, Mathis, Adam, Wiener, VPO, Boehm.

The glory of the 1976 set conducted by Edo de Waart is the singing of Frederica von Stade as Octavian, a fresh, youthful performance, full of imagination. Next to her the others are generally pleasing but rarely a match for the finest performances on other sets, though it is good to have Derek Hammond Stroud's Faninal. Evelyn Lear produces her creamiest, most beautiful tone but spreads uncomfortably in the Act III Trio. Jules Bastin gives a virile performance as Ochs; the disappointment is the Sophie of Ruth Welting, often shallow of tone. The Rotterdam orchestra plays very well for its principal conductor of the 1970s and is beautifully recorded. The transfer is first class, refined in details, giving a fresh presence to the voices. The libretto is admirably clear and the layout has an Act to each of the three CDs.

Issued in 1994 as one of the Strauss opera series celebrating the centenary of Boehm's birth, the DG set was recorded live at the 1969 Salzburg Festival, very valuable when this most distinguished Strauss advocate never recorded Strauss's most popular opera in the studio. Inevitably it is a flawed document, not just because of loud stage-noises but because the stereo recording is thinner, with less body, than earlier mono recordings in the series – also from Austrian Radio sources. Nevertheless the voices have fair presence, and it is good to hear Christa Ludwig as the Marschallin, here more emphatic than in her studio recording for Bernstein, and again bringing echoes of Schwarzkopf, the Marschallin with whom she sang Octavian. Tatiana Troyanos makes a warm, animated Octavian and Edith Mathis a bright, characterful Sophie, just occasionally forced into shrillness. The snag is the gritty Ochs of Theo Adam, not at all jovial even when he blusters in sing-speech. Boehm is above all a genial interpreter, relishing the waltz-rhythms, but the emotions of a live event lead him at climaxes to draw out the music exaggeratedly in a way uncharacteristic of him. However, a primary recommendation remains with Karajan's great (1956) version with Schwarzkopf (EMI CDS7 49354-8) or, for those preferring a modern, digital set, Haitink's Dresden recording with Anne Sofie von Otter an ideal Octavian and Dame Kiri te Kanawa as the Marschallin (EMI CDS7 54259-2).

Salome (complete).
*** Decca Dig. 444 178-2 (2) [id.]. Malfitano, Terfel, Riegel, Schwarz, Begley, VPO, Chrisoph von
    Dohnányi.
(M) **(*) DG 445 319-2 (2) [id.]. Gwyneth Jones, Fischer-Dieskau, Dunn, Cassilly, Hamburg State
    Op. O, Boehm.
** Ph. Dig. 432 153-2 (2) [id.]. Norman, Morris, Raffeiner, Witt, Leech, Dresden State O, Seiji
    Ozawa.

Dohnányi's recording closely reflects the stage experience which he and his principals, as well as the orchestra, had in the production first seen at the Salzburg Festival. It is a clear, sharply focused reading, in full-ranging sound more refined than any, a product of the new Decca studios in the Konzerthaus in Vienna. With the orchestra set further behind the voices than usual in Decca opera recordings, the violence is to a degree underplayed and the chamber quality of the score (intended by Strauss) enhanced. Older versions provide serious competition, notably Solti's fiercely dramatic Decca set with Birgit Nilsson (414 414-2), and Sinopoli's sensuous one with Cheryl Studer (DG 431 810-2). Like Studer, Catherine Malfitano brings out the girlish element in Salome, while also bringing out her malevolence. The beat in her voice can be distracting, occasionally turning into a wobble, but she rises superbly to the final scene, with full power and precision, a thrilling climax. As Jokanaan, Bryn Terfel is even finer than he was for Sinopoli, rich and firm, with the voice of the prophet from the cisterns clearly focused. Kenneth Riegel as a neurotic Herod, Hanna Schwarz as a powerful, sharply dramatic Herodias and Kim Begley as a ringing Narraboth are all outstanding.

Unlike the Salzburg Festival performances in the Boehm centenary series, this live recording of *Salome* was made by DG engineers, suffering none of the limitations of radio recording. The occasion was the première of the Hamburg State Opera production in November 1970. In this violent opera Boehm conducts a powerful, purposeful performance which in its rhythmic drive and spontaneity is most compelling, not least in *Salome's dance*, which seems a necessary component rather than an inserted showpiece. Gwyneth Jones, though squally at times, is here at her most incisive, and her account of the final scene is chilling, above all when she drains her voice for the moment of pianissimo triumph, having kissed the dead lips of Jokanaan. Fischer-Dieskau characteristically gives a searchingly detailed, totally authoritative performance as John the Baptist: one believes in him as a prophet possessed. With Richard Cassily as a powerful Herod, the rest of the cast is strong, making this a fair contender among live recordings.

Jessye Norman has made some outstanding Strauss recordings, but she is miscast as Salome. Though her word-pointing is as detailed and as sensitive as ever, with her massive, rich voice she conveys little that is girlish about the character, let alone anything sinister or depraved. This is a noble Salome, with the evil underplayed. That impression is intensified by Ozawa's smooth, even bland conducting. The playing of the orchestra is beautiful, with many superb woodwind solos, but even Salome's dance lacks the bite and violence that must accompany its sensuousness. The Jokanaan of James Morris is gruff, and only the Narraboth of Richard Leech shines out distinctively.

Die schweigsame Frau (complete).
(M) (***) DG mono 445 335-2 (2) [id.]. Gueden, Wunderlich, Prey, Hotter, VPO, Boehm.

With a cast that could hardly be bettered, Boehm masterfully relishes the high spirits as well as the classical elegance of this late Strauss opera, the first performance of which he conducted in 1936. Issued to celebrate the centenary of the conductor's birth, this historic recording was made in mono by Austrian Radio at the 1959 Salzburg Festival and, though the acoustic is dry and stage noises are often fearsomely intrusive, the sense of presence on the voices makes it consistently involving. Based on Ben Jonson's *Epicoene* but updated to 1780 by the librettist, Stefan Zweig, this comic opera about an old bachelor who hates noise is above all centred on lively, sharply pointed ensembles, and the starry cast is here splendidly drilled to bring out the humour. Hans Hotter in his prime makes a wonderfully bluff curmudgeon, pointing every word characterfully. Hilde Gueden – greeted with wild applause on her first entry along with Fritz Wunderlich – is a deliciously minx-ish heroine, using her distinctive golden tone, while the young Wunderlich gives a glorious performance. The duet for hero and heroine at the end of Act II, much more lyrical than the rest of the opera, is a high spot. As the barber who aids the conspiratorial young couple against the old man, Hermann Prey has rarely sounded stronger or more beautiful on disc. With this issue available, the continuing absence of the EMI stereo version under Marek Janowski is far less serious.

Stravinsky, Igor (1882–1971)

Agon; Jeu de cartes; Orpheus.
**(*) Decca Dig. 443 772-2 [id.]. Deutsches SO, Berlin, Vladimir Ashkenazy.

An intelligently planned disc comprising three of Stravinsky's most exhilarating ballets. Ashkenazy and the Deutsches Symphonie Orkester give us very well-played accounts of all three, and they are accorded more than decent Decca recording. There are slight reservations about the third star because there are rivals which have even greater zest and character.

Apollo (*Apollon musagète;* complete ballet); (i) *Capriccio for piano and orchestra. Pulcinella* (ballet): *suite.*
(M) *** Decca 443 577-2 [id.]. (i) John Ogdon; ASMF, Marriner.

This newly remastered recording in Decca's Classic Sound series, with the sound aptly vividly lit, was one of the first on which the St Martin's Academy, known for many years as an outstanding recording team in baroque music, spread its wings in the music of the twentieth century. The results are superb. It remains a demonstration disc of its period (the two ballets recorded in the Kingsway Hall in 1967), particularly in the *Pulcinella* suite, where the sharp separation of instruments (for example, double-basses against trombones in the *Vivo*) makes for wonderful stereo, with the precision of the playing outshining that of almost all rival versions. The ethereal string-tones of *Apollo* (Stravinsky finally came to prefer the English to the French title) make an ideal coupling, with the elegantly polished response of the Academy players comparing impressively with the outstanding Karajan version. Again, thanks both to the fine recording, made at The Maltings in 1970, and to the pointed playing of the Academy, the neo-classical quality of the *Capriccio*, a charming work, is beautifully underlined, while the soloist, John Ogdon, provides the contrasting elment of sinewy toughness. An outstanding disc in every way.

(i) *Apollo (Apollon Musagète)* (ballet): complete; *Circus polka;* (ii) *Petrushka* (ballet: 1911 score): complete.
(B) *** DG 439 463-2 [id.]. (i) BPO, Karajan; LSO, Dutoit.

Apollo is a work in which Karajan's moulding of phrase and care for richness of string texture make for wonderful results, especially in the glorious *Pas de deux*. Throughout, the writing is consistently enhanced by the magnificent playing of the Berlin Philharmonic. The recording, made in the Jesus-Christus Kirche in 1972, is of DG's highest quality and in no way sounds its age. The *Circus polka* is played with comparable panache. The coupling is Charles Dutoit's first recorded *Petrushka*, made for DG in the Henry Wood Hall in 1975/6, before he had become a star conductor on the Decca roster. Interestingly, it was made almost impromptu: a planned opera recording fell through, and sessions were hastily reallocated with little advance planning. The result is triumphantly spontaneous in its own right, with rhythms that are incisive yet beautifully buoyant, and a degree of expressiveness in the orchestral playing that subtly underlines the dramatic atmosphere and is especially magical in the Third Tableau. The final section too is strongly coloured, so that the gentle closing pages make a touching contrast to the gaiety of the early part of the scene. The remastered recording is atmospheric and vivid, though not as smooth on top as the Karajan couplings. However, the only fault of balance is the prominence of the concertante piano soloist, Támas Vásáry, in the *Danse russe*. Both ballets are generously cued, and altogether this bargain Classikon coupling is very good value.

(i) *Apollo (Apollon musagète); Circus polka; 4 Norwegian moods; Suites Nos. 1–2;* (ii) *The Soldier's tale (L'histoire du soldat);* (iii) *Symphony of Psalms.*
(M) *** Ph. 438 973-2 (2) [id.]. (i) LSO; (ii) Cocteau, Ustinov, Fertey, Tonietti, Parikian & Instrumental Ens.; (iii) Russian State Ac. Ch. & O; Markevitch.

Igor Markevitch was one of Cortot's proteges and during the late 1920s enjoyed the patronage of Diaghilev, thus exciting the jealousy and hostility of Stravinsky. After the war he became more active as a conductor than composer, and relations between 'the two Igors' became cordial. Markevitch made a celebrated recording for HMV of *The Rite of spring* with the Philharmonia in the 1950s and went on to record *Apollon musagète* with the LSO in 1963, a beautifully lucid and idiomatic performance with great balletic feeling. The shorter pieces, the *Norwegian moods* and the two *Suites for small orchestra*, are done with great personality. His account of *L'histoire du soldat* was mounted in Vevey (next to Montreux) in 1962 to mark his fiftieth birthday, for which he persuaded a less than youthful Jean Cocteau to appear as the narrator and Peter Ustinov as the Devil. The *Symphony of Psalms* was recorded on his visit to the USSR in the same year, and has wonderfully characterful (but not always dead-in-tune) singing. *L'histoire du soldat* is a drier recording than either its London or Moscow companions, but it says much for the skills of the engineers of the 1960s that the sound is so beautifully transparent and the string-tone silky. An altogether admirable and rewarding set.

Apollo (Apollon musagète) (ballet; complete); *Concerto in D for strings; Danses concertantes; Dumbarton Oaks concerto.*
*** Decca Dig. 440 327-2 [id.]. Montreal Sinf., Charles Dutoit.

Dutoit adds to his anthology of Stravinsky recordings with this exceptionally generous and well-planned coupling, one which firmly keeps *Apollo* in its original chamber scale, for the orchestra is not the Montreal Symphony but the Sinfonietta. If inevitably in *Apollo* one lacks the ripe opulence of Karajan and the Berlin Philharmonic (DG), there is a clarity of focus and immediacy that the composer would have approved of, set in glowing sound. Dutoit is adept in bringing out the Stravinskian wit and point that in many numbers is set against the smooth string-lines of this lovely work. This great classical ballet is not just beautiful or statuesque, but has fun in it too. The other three works are very well matched and given strongly characterized performances, with variety of expression defying the old idea that this is drily neo-classical Stravinsky. Though Dutoit could give more lightness to the *Brandenburg*-like textures of the *Dumbarton Oaks concerto*, it would be hard to imagine a more genial version of the *Concerto in D*, full of light and shade, or a more exuberant one of the *Danses concertantes* of 1944.

Capriccio for piano and orchestra; Concerto for piano and wind instruments; Movements for piano and orchestra; Symphonies of wind instruments.
*** Sony Dig. SK 45797 [id.]. Paul Crossley, L. Sinf., Salonen.

This is the sort of repertoire in which Esa-Pekka Salonen excels and in which Paul Crossley is also expert. All three performances can hold their own with the best, as indeed can the *Symphonies of wind instruments*. It is good to make the acquaintance of this CD, which can be confidently recommended to all lovers of the composer. Excellent digital recording too.

(i) *Le chant du rossignol; 4 Etudes for orchestra;* (ii; iii) *L'Histoire du soldat;* (iii; iv) *Pulcinella* (ballet): complete; (v) *3 Pieces for string quartet;* (vi) *Madrid* (étude for pianola); (vii) *4 Russian peasant songs;* (viii) *Le rossignol* (opera; complete).
(M) **(*) Erato/Warner Analogue/Dig. 4509 98955-2 (3) [id.]. (i) O Nat. de France; (ii) Roger Planchon, Patrice Chéreau, Antoine Vitez; (iii) Ens. InterContemporain; (iv) with Murray, Rolfe Johnson, Estes; (v) InterContemporain Qt; (vi) Rex Lawson (pianola); (vii) Cantin, Melleret, Gantiez, R. France Ch.; (viii) Bryn-Julson, Caley, Laurence, Palmer, George, Howlett, Tomlinson, BBC Singers, BBC SO; Boulez.

An interesting collection which includes a first-class performance of Stravinsky's early opera, *Le rossignol*. Boulez's account of this exotic work, with strong influences from Rimsky-Korsakov as well as music anticipating the early Stravinsky ballets, is as evocative as it is dramatic. It is sung in Russian and is provided with an excellent translation in the fairly well-cued libretto. Phyllis Bryn-Julson is impressively accurate in the Nightingale's complex upper tessitura and sings affectingly in her exchanges with Death, where Elizabeth Laurence's dark mezzo is well contrasted. Ian Caley makes an appealing Fisherman (who introduces and closes the opera). The recording is a bit close but does not lack ambience. However, *L'Histoire du soldat* is presented in French, with the narrator sounding rather verbose in a lengthy text which will not attract most English-speaking listeners as there is no accompanying translation. The performance, too, could be more atmospherically colourful. In both the symphonic poem, *Le Chant du rossignol*, which the composer arranged from his operatic score, and in *Pulcinella* detail is captured vividly and the playing is often masterly. Boulez's singers in the latter work are splendid in every way; here the pacing is more extreme than Marriner's account (see above), with contrasts between movements almost overcharacterized. The (otherwise good) 1980 recording has more edge than the Decca and the strings have a tendency to thinness. Of the shorter pieces, the four succinct *Russian peasant songs* are given an almost medieval character by their bare harmonies, while the three terse, spare pieces for string quartet are all superbly played and sharply etched. Stravinsky wrote *Madrid* as a result of a commission from the Aeolian pianola manufacturing company and produced a concentrated 'tribute' to Spanish dance music heard through a distorting lens. We hear this piece again as the orchestrated fourth *Etude*, while the *Petrushka*-like second *Etude* was dubbed *Eccentric* by the composer; it evokes a memory of the stage performance of Little Tich, a great London clown whom Stravinsky saw perform in 1914, just before he wrote the string quartet pieces from which the first three *Etudes* are transcribed. Generally recommended, but it would be ideal to have the second disc, with the opera and the shorter works, available separately.

Concerto in E flat (Dumbarton Oaks); 8 Instrumental miniatures; (i) *Ebony concerto.*
(M) *** DG 447 405-2 [id.]. (i) Michel Arrignon; Ens. InterContemporain, Pierre Boulez – BERG: *Chamber concerto.* ***

A highly suitable coupling for the Berg in DG's 'Originals' series. The close sound almost reminds one of the effect of some early Columbia records which Stravinsky himself made before the war: the dry, spiky, black-and-white images of the early cinema. Yet the effect on DG is never two-dimensional and lacking in ambient colour. The playing of the Ensemble InterContemporain is very brilliant indeed. There is much to enjoy in these performances, which are spiced with the right kind of wit and keenness of edge, and even those who do not normally respond to Boulez's conducting will be pleasantly surprised with the results he obtains here.

Concerto in E flat for chamber orchestra (Dumbarton Oaks); Pulcinella (suite).
(M) *** DG Dig. 445 541 [id.]. Orpheus CO – BARTOK: *Divertimento for strings* etc. **(*)

Remarkably fine playing from this conductorless group. Their ensemble in the *Pulcinella suite* is better than that of most conducted orchestras, and the overall impression they convey is one of freshness and spontaneity. Much the same must be said of *Dumbarton Oaks*, which has great zest and brilliance. The DG recording is clean and lifelike and the perspective very natural. While this disc does not eclipse memories of all rivals, it can more than hold its own with most competition, past and present.

Violin concerto.
*** Sony Dig. SK 53969 [id.]. Cho-Liang Lin, LAPO, Esa-Pekka Salonen – PROKOFIEV: *Violin concertos Nos. 1 & 2.* *** ⊛

As in the two Prokofiev concertos, so in the Stravinsky Lin plays with power and warmth, while Salonen terraces the accompaniment dramatically, with woodwind and brass bold and full. In this same coupling Chung on mid-priced Decca (425 003-2) offers equally compelling readings in excellent analogue sound, with more wit brought out in this Stravinsky work. But in the Prokofiev the balance of advantage goes marginally to Lin.

(i) *Violin concerto;* (ii; iii) *Ebony Concerto;* (iv) *Symphony in C; Symphony in three movements;* (iii) *Symphonies for wind instruments;* (v) *Symphony of Psalms.*
(B) **(*) Ph. Duo 442 583-2 (2) [id.]. (i) Grumiaux, Concg. O, Bour; (ii) Pieterson; (iii) Netherlands Wind Ens., Edo de Waart; (iv) LSO, C. Davis; (v) Russian State Ac. Ch. & SO, Markevitch.

A lithe, refined account of the *Violin concerto* from Grumiaux and the Concertgebouw Orchestra. It is enormously vital, but its energy is controlled and the tone never becomes unduly aggressive. The 1967 recording is just a little dated but preserves a good balance between soloist and orchestra. George Pieterson's version of the *Ebony concerto* with the Netherlands Wind Ensemble is not as overtly jazzy as some but it does not lack rhythmic bite, and its dry, sardonic wit and the dark sonorities of the finale make it individual. The *Symphonies for wind instruments* also show the controlled blend of colour for which this Dutch wind group are famous. Sir Colin Davis's account of the *Symphony in C* is splendidly alert, well played and stimulating. The performance of the *Symphony in three movements* is also lively, but compared with Stravinsky's own it is over-tense. By taking very fast tempi which barely allow any lift to the rhythm, Davis ends by overplaying the music. The sound from the mid-1960s is a little sparse in texture in the CD transfer, but this suits the style of the performances. Markevitch's 1964 Russian performance of the *Symphony of Psalms* is as vibrantly Slavonic as one could wish, yet the closing 'Alleluias' still bring a frisson in their raptly gentle expressive feeling. The sound is brightly vivid but not harsh.

Complete ballets: *The Firebird;* (i) *Les Noces; Petrushka* (original 1911 score); *The Rite of spring.*
(B) ** Decca 443 467-2 (2) [id.]. SRO, Ansermet; (i) with Retchitzka, Devallier, Cuénod, Rehfuss, Homeffer, Peter, Rossiaud, Aubert, Geneva Motet Ch.

In their day these were much-admired performances and recordings of the three major early ballets. *The Firebird* is very early stereo indeed (1955); *Petrushka* and *The Rite* come from 1957, and *Les Noces* is later (and sounds it: 1961). At this distance of time the shortcomings of the SRO, which in the late 1950s was not the fine body it had been in the immediate post-war period, are evident, and the transfers tend to exaggerate the weakness of timbre in the upper strings by making it seem thin, ill-focused and shrill. *Petrushka* suffers most, and one feels that Ansermet's lively reading could be made to sound better than this. *The Firebird* is much smoother and has plenty of ambience. Detail is exceptionally clear, filled in like vivid embroidery on fine gauze. But the massed strings still sound emaciated. On balance one is prepared to put up with the defects in the orchestra for the sake of Ansermet's view of the *Rite of spring*, which has integrity, besides generating considerable rhythmic excitement and often striking melancholy of atmosphere. Here the sound is better too. *Les Noces* is altogether disappointing. Ansermet fails to capture the essential bite of Stravinsky's sharply etched portrayal of a peasant wedding. The hammering rhythms must sound ruthless, and here they are merely tame.

The Firebird (ballet): complete (with rehearsal).
(M) *** Decca 443 572-2 [id.]. New Philh. O, Ernest Ansermet.

The Firebird (complete ballet); *Le chant du rossignol.*
** Chan. Dig. CHAN 8967 [id.]. Danish Nat. RSO, Kitajenko.

Ansermet came to London in November 1968 to re-record the complete *Firebird* in the Kingsway Hall, only a few months before he died. He was in great spirits, fiery and not easily pleased, a fact which comes out in the 49-minute rehearsal sequence which is included on a second (free) CD. It is not one of the most illuminating rehearsal records we have heard, being far too closely concerned with details of the score (almost essential to have a copy before the references are plain), but overall the character of the man comes out vividly, and there are one or two moments which are inimitable, as when he recognizes one of the New Philharmonia percussion players and says warmly: 'I'm glad to see you since long time,' only to resume his manner of irritation at once: 'Then do it as you did in the old times.' This London version, though not immaculate in ensemble in *Kastchei's dance*, has more polished playing than that which Ansermet recorded earlier with his own Suisse Romande Orchestra, but generally the interpretations are amazingly consistent. At times one suspects the new version is a degree slower, but on checking you find that the difference lies in the extra flexibility and polish of the London players. The recording was a demonstration disc in its day and is reissued in Decca's

Classic Sound series, well documented by current CD standards. The first-class transfer readily demonstrates the atmosphere and vividly dramatic detail for which this conductor's records were justly famous.

The Firebird in its complete form is generously represented in the current catalogue, and the Danish Radio performance under Dmitri Kitajenko, though far from negligible, is not a front-runner either as a performance or as a recording. It is quite atmospheric and the orchestral playing is as expert as one would expect from this fine ensemble, and neither it nor *Le chant du rossignol* will disappoint greatly. All the same, one can do better; and in *The Firebird* Dorati's electrifying 1960 Mercury version is still an obvious first choice (432 012-2).

Firebird suite (1919).
(M) *** DG 447 414-2 [id.]. (i) Grace Bumbry; Berlin RSO, Maazel – FALLA: *El amor brujo* etc. **
(M) **(*) EMI CDM5 65207-2 [id.]. BPO, Stokowski – ORFF: *Carmina Burana*. **

There has never been a finer recorded account of the 1919 version of the *Firebird suite* than Maazel's. It was recorded in 1958 and the stereo is magically atmospheric. The orchestral playing has great éclat: its colours are wonderfully subtle. In the gentler music the effect is exquisite, with the oboe soloist in the *Dance of the Princesses* and the bassoon in the *Berceuse* playing with the utmost delicacy. The ferocity of the *Infernal dance* breaks the spell momentarily, and Maazel omits the few bars included by Stravinsky to bridge the violent change of mood. But then comes the luminous climax of the finale, with the Berlin violins quite luscious in thirds, even though here the actual sound slightly betrays the age of the recording. This is truly a Legendary Performance, fully worthy of inclusion in DG's set of 'Originals'; but it is a great pity that the equally memorable original coupling of *Le chant du rossignol* was abandoned in favour of the Falla, which by comparison is second rate.

The 1957 EMI recording preserves one of the rare occasions when Stokowski conducted the Berlin Philharmonic. He obviously revels in the lustrous solo woodwind playing and the refined string ensemble, and readily creates the radiant 'drenched' violin sound in the finale for which he was famous. The performance is essentially sensuous, but its magic is in no doubt. The recorded quality is remarkably full, with an attractive ambient glow.

Jeu de cartes.
(M) **(*) Sony SMK 57660 [id.]. Novosibirsk PO, Arnold Kaz – RACHMANINOV: *Symphonic dances*.
***

Arnold Kaz's version of *Jeu de cartes* comes in Sony's competitively priced 'St Petersburg Classics' series. Kaz is not a celebrated conductor though he produces more musical results than many who are, and the Novosibirsk orchestra is not a virtuoso ensemble, but it is a very good one. There are more brilliant and harder-etched accounts of this score around, but this is very enjoyable indeed – very fresh, far better than routine without quite being touched by real distinction. It comes with a Rachmaninov *Symphonic dances* that is very well worth having. The same goes for the Stravinsky: it is a far more enjoyable performance than some we have from better-known orchestras and glossier maestros, and the recording is eminently satisfactory. Good value for money.

(i) *Petrushka* (ballet; 1911 version); (ii) *Ragtime; The Soldier's tale (suite); Octet for wind*.
** Chan. Dig. CHAN 9291 [id.]. (i) SRO; (ii) SNO (members); Järvi.

The five-CD collection of which this forms part is reviewed in our main volume. Neeme Järvi's account of *Petrushka* is decently played, though in terms of polish and virtuosity the Suisse Romande Orchestra do not match their rivals in this widely recorded repertoire. The other pieces are well done – the *Octet for wind* is very lively – though they would not necessarily be first choices. The very good Chandos recording is a plus.

(i) *Petrushka* (complete 1911 score); (ii) *The Rite of spring*.
(M) **(*) Sony SMK 64109 [id.]. (i) NYPO; (ii) Cleveland O; Pierre Boulez.
(M) ** Decca 440 064-2 [id.]. (i) Julius Katchen; Paris Conservatoire O, Pierre Monteux.

There is a controlled intensity about Boulez's 1971 New York performance of *Petrushka* which in the original version of the score puts the ballet closer than usual to the barbaric work which followed. In this process of clarification and intensification – often using tempi that are slower than usual – Boulez may miss some of the wit, but it is undoubtedly a compelling performance and it is a pity that the 1971 recording, made in the Avery Fisher Hall, becomes fierce at higher dynamic levels. Similarly in the *Rite of spring*, recorded two years earlier in Severance Hall, Cleveland, tempi are generally measured. Boulez developed his reading over the preceding years so that he finally came to a view of the work approaching that of Stravinsky himself in his own final recorded version. Boulez is less lyrical than the composer but compensates with relentless rhythmic urgency. After Stravinsky's own version, which is not only uniquely authoritative but also uniquely compelling, Boulez's is among the most completely recommendable accounts. The massive vividness of sound matches the monolithic quality of the interpretation. The CD transfer is bright, but the effect is often thrilling, particularly at such moments as the brass contrasts in *Jeux des cités rivales*.

Monteux's recordings date from the early days of stereo, *The Rite* from 1956 and *Petrushka*, with Julius Katchen recruited to play the solo piano role, a year later. As Monteux conducted the first performance of the former ballet, it is valuable to have his account return to the catalogue. But in neither work is the French orchestral playing anything to write home about. The woodwind in *Petrushka* is at times less than pleasing and the overall ensemble in *The Rite* is not ideally assured. The sound is atmospheric but thin in the upper range.

Petrushka (1947 score); *Circus polka; Fireworks, Op. 4.*
(M) ** Carlton Dig. IMGCD 1610 [id.]. RPO, Bátiz – BORODIN: *Polovtsian dances.* **

With bright, forward, well-detailed recording, the Bátiz issue brings a performance of comparatively little sparkle or charm, more emphatic than usual, but therefore looking forward illuminatingly to the *Rite of spring*. The crispness of ensemble, the resilence of rhythms and the distinction of much of the solo work (notably the first flute) lightens what could have been too heavy, with some speeds slower than usual. The two lightweight fill-ups are certainly too heavily done, but are worth having as makeweights.

Petrushka: suite.
(M) ** EMI CDM5 65423-2 [id.]. BPO, Stokowski – HOLST: *The Planets;* RAVEL: *Alborada.* **(*)

The Berlin Philharmonic seems not completely happy in the *Petrushka* suite, a 16-minute selection from the complete ballet that starts with the *Russian dance*. The Berlin strings sound too saturated in tone for this music, brilliant as the wind playing is, and the 1957 recording is not particularly distinguished.

The Rite of spring.
(*) Everest EVC 9002 [id.]. LSO, Sir Eugene Goossens – RACHMANINOV: *Symphonic dances.* *

Sir Eugene Goossens seems an unexpected conductor in Stravinsky, yet he gave the first performance of *The Rite of spring* in England. His approach is circumspect and the performance moves forward with a remorseless steadiness, notably so in Part 1, while there is a total absence of romanticism in the long lyrical section which opens Part 2. The playing of the LSO is well disciplined and the recording is very spectacular, a reverberant acoustic (Walthamstow) not clouding the detail but certainly adding sonic excitement, notably in Goossens' bold, dramatic strokes, like the big horn tune towards the end.

PIANO MUSIC

3 movements from Petrushka.
(M) *** DG 447 431-2 [id.]. Maurizio Pollini – *Recital.* ***
*(*) DG Dig. 435 616-2 [id.]. Ugorski – MUSSORGSKY: *Pictures at an exhibition.* *(*)

Staggering, electrifying playing from Pollini, creating the highest degree of excitement. This is part of an outstandingly generous recital of twentieth-century piano music.

There are well over a dozen versions now on the market, so Anatol Ugorski is up against stiff competition, not least from Maurizio Pollini on the same label (now repackaged at mid-price in DG's 'Originals' series). Although he generates some excitement, Ugorski's playing is simply not in that league.

Piano sonata; Piano-rag music; Serenade in A.
*** Chan. Dig. CHAN 8962 [id.]. Boris Berman – SCHNITTKE: *Sonata.* ***

Boris Berman is an artist of powerful intelligence who gives vivid and alertly characterized accounts of all these pieces. Excellent piano sound, too, from the Chandos engineers. Strongly recommended.

Suk, Josef (1874–1935)

Serenade for strings in E flat, Op.6.
(M) **(*) Virgin/EMI Dig. CUV5 61144-2 [id.]. LCO, Christopher Warren-Green – DVORAK: *Serenade.* **(*)

Serenade for strings in E flat, Op. 6; Meditation on an old Czech hymn (St Wenceslas), Op. 35a.
(BB) **(*) Discover Dig. DICD 920234 [id.]. Virtuosi di Praga, Oldřich Vlček – JANACEK: *Suite.* ***

Warren-Green and his LCO give a wonderfully persuasive account of Suk's *Serenade*, making obvious that its inspiration is every bit as vivid as in the comparable work of Dvořák. One readily feels the added intensity which this group's leader and conductor believes comes from performing (even in the recording studio) standing up. The gleaming radiance of tone in the opening *Andante* is matched by the sparkle of the following *Allegro ma non troppo e grazioso* which has much charm, the haunting nostalgia of the *Adagio* and the spirited joy of the closing *Allegro giocoso*. The recording, made in All Saints', Petersham, is well up to the standard of previous records from this group, fresh, full and natural without blurring from the ecclesiastical acoustic. However, the original CD also included the Tchaikovsky *Serenade*, which is now missing, so even at mid-price this is not such a bargain as it looks, with only 52 minutes' playing time.

Judging by the photo-insert, the Prague Virtuosi have been somewhat expanded from the eleven soloists who made up the original group, to sixteen plus the leader/conductor, Oldřich Vlček. Certainly they create a richly full-bodied sonority here and play this music idiomatically and with ardent, expressive feeling. Some might feel that the *Serenade* benefits from a slightly more subtle and less extrovert approach, but the passionately gripping account of the *Wenceslas meditation* brings an entirely appropriate emotional intensity. Splendidly vivid recording,

Piano quartet in A min., Op. 1.
*(*) Koch Schwann Dig. 3-1127-2 [id.]. Berlin Philharmonic Qt – R. STRAUSS: *Piano quartet.* *(*)

The *Piano quartet in A minor* comes from 1891 and is a student work, written when Suk was seventeen and very much under the shadow of Dvořák, whose son-in-law he was later to become. It is a highly accomplished piece and well worth investigating. The Berlin Philharmonic Quartet give a conscientious and workmanlike account, though they suffer from a very studio-like recording acoustic, with not enough air round the sound.

Sullivan, Arthur (1842–1900)

Symphony in E (Irish); Imperial march; Overture in C (In Memoriam); Victoria and Merrie England suite.
** CPO Dig. CPO 999171-2 [id.]. BBC Concert O, Owain Arwel Hughes.

A well-planned and acceptably recorded but, in the last resort, disappointing collection. The first movement of the *Symphony* obstinately refuses to take off and, as Hughes observes the exposition repeat, its 16 minutes' length seems like a lifetime. The other movements are rather more successful, and Linden Harris plays the oboe theme of the *Allegretto* nicely enough. But in almost every way this performances is upstaged by the excellent EMI/Groves version with the Royal Liverpool Philharmonic Orchestra, an unlikely coupling for the HMV/Sargent complete recording of *Patience*, which is also a great success. If you want the symphony, that's the place to go for it (CMS7 64406-2 – see our main volume). The other items here pass muster, with the ballet suite easily the most enjoyable item, especially the finale, *May Day festivities*, which might well have been an undiscovered interlude from *The Yeomen of the Guard*.

HMS Pinafore.
⊛ *** Telarc Dig. CD 80374 [id.]. Suart, Allen, Evans, Schade, Palmer, Adams, Ch. & O of Welsh Opera, Mackerras.

Following up the success of his two previous Telarc recordings of G & S (*The Mikado* CD 80284 and *Pirates of Penzance* CD 80353) Sir Charles Mackerras here gives an exuberant reading of the first operetta of the cycle. The lyricism and transparency of Sullivan's inspiration shine out with winning freshness. One keeps relishing how, in seeming simplicity over transparent textures, Sullivan displays his gift for fitting totally contrasted themes together in close counterpoint. The casting is not just starry but inspired. So in such a number as Captain Corcoran's *Fair moon to thee I sing* one relishes the pure beauty of the melody as sung by Thomas Allen, sharpened by innocent send-up in Gilbert's verses. Even such a jaunty number as the 'encore' trio, *Never mind the why and wherefore*, gains in point when so well sung and played as here, with Allen joined by Rebecca Evans as an appealing Josephine and Richard Suart as a dry Sir Joseph Porter. Michael Schade is heady-toned as the hero, Ralph Rackstraw, while among character roles Felicity Palmer is a marvellously fruity Little Buttercup, with Richard van Allan as Bill Bobstay and the veteran, Donald Adams, a lugubrious Dick Deadeye. As with the previous CDs of *Mikado* and *Pirates of Penzance*, Telarc squeezes the whole score on to a single CD, vividly recorded.

Suppé, Franz von (1819–95)

Complete overtures

Volume 1: Overtures: *Carnival; Die Frau Meisterin; Irrfahrt um's Glück (Fortune's Labyrinth); The Jolly Robbers (Banditenstreiche); Pique Dame; Poet and Peasant; Des Wanderers Ziel (The Goal of the Wanderers). Boccaccio: Minuet & Tarantella. Donna Juanita: Juanita march.*
** Marco Polo Dig. 8.223647 [id.]. Slovak State PO (Košice), Alfred Walter.

Volume 2: Overtures: *Beautiful Galatea (Die schöne Galatea); Boccaccio; Donna Juanita; Isabella; Der Krämer und sein Kommis (The Shopkeeper and his Assistant); Das Modell (The Model); Paragraph 3; Tantalusqualen. Fatinitza march.*
** Marco Polo Dig. 8.223648 [id.]. Slovak State PO (Košice), Alfred Walter.

Volume 3: Overtures: *Fatinitza; Franz Schubert; Die Heimkehr von der Hochzeit (Homecoming from the wedding); Light Cavalry; Trioche and Cacolet; Triumph. Boccaccio: March. Herzenseintracht polka; Humorous variations on 'Was kommt dort von der Höh'; Titania waltz.*
** Marco Polo Dig. 8.223683 [id.]. Slovak State PO (Košice), Alfred Walter.

Alfred Walter and Marco Polo, already well on the way towards completing their Johann Strauss Edition, now turn their attention to another composer who made a successful career in Vienna. Yet, in spite of his very German name, Franz von Suppé had a Belgian father and grandfather – though his mother was Viennese born. As a youth, Suppé's musical talents were obvious to the local bandmaster and he was also encouraged by the choirmaster of Spalato Cathedral to write an early Mass. So when his father sent him off to study law in Padua, the budding composer took the opportunity to visit the opera house in Milan, where he became thoroughly immersed in the works of Rossini, Donizetti and Verdi, all of whom he met. In 1840 he finally took up a professional career, making his début as an 'honorary' conductor in the Josefstadt Theatre; his first successful stage work dates from a year later. But it was not until 1860 that he began writing his inconsequential Viennese operettas, and most of his famous overtures (all that have survived of this output outside Vienna) date from the 1860s, notably *Beautiful Galatea* (1865) and *Light Cavalry* (1866), although *Boccaccio*, Suppé's greatest stage success, is a late work (1879). The overture most popular of all, *Poet and Peasant* (of which countless arrangements were made), predates the others and was written well before 1846, when the comedy with songs, to which it was finally appended, first appeared.

Walter's performances here are unsubtle, but they have a rumbustious vigour that is endearing and, with enthusiastic playing from the Slovak Orchestra who are obviously enjoying themselves, the effect is never less than spirited. Many of the finest of the lesser-known pieces are already available in more imaginative versions from Marriner (EMI CDC7 54056-2) or played with greater polish and a certain gravitas by the RPO under Gustav Kuhn (RCA RD 69037 and RD 69226) – see our main volume. But Walter has uncovered some attractive novelties, as well as some pleasing if inconsequential interludes and dances. On Volume I, *Carnival* (nothing like Dvořák's piece), opens rather solemnly, then introduces a string of ideas, including a polka, a waltz and a galop. *Die Frau Meisterin* also produces an engaging little waltz. *Des Wanderers Ziel* begins very energetically and, after brief harp roulades, produces a rather solemn cello solo and brass choir; later there is an attractive lyrical melody, but there are plenty of histrionics too, and the dancing ending brings distinctly Rossinian influences.

In Volume II *Isabella* is introduced as a sprightly Spanish lady, but Viennese influences still keep popping up, while *Paragraph 3* summons the listener with a brief horn-call and then has another striking lyrical theme, before gaiety takes over. *Das Krämer und sein Kommis* proves to be an early version (the ear notices a slight difference at the dramatic opening) of an old friend, *Morning, noon and night in Vienna*. *Donna Juanita* brings a violin solo of some temperament; then, after some agreeably chattering woodwind, comes a grand march.

On the third CD, *Tricoche and Cacolet* immediately introduces a skipping tune of great charm and, after another of Suppé's appealing lyrical themes, ends with much rhythmic vigour. The biographical operetta about *Schubert* opens with an atmospheric, half-sinister reference to the *Erlkönig* and follows with further quotations, prettily scored; however, the writing coarsens somewhat vulgarly at the end. Not surprisingly, *Triumph*, with characteristic brass writing, is both rhetorical and repetitive, but still produces one good slow tune and yet another galop. But the prize item here is a set of extremely ingenuous variations (Germanically humorous, and complete with a piccolo solo) on a local folksong, which translates as *What comes there from on high?*. It seems like a cross between '*A hunting we will go*' and '*The Grand old Duke of York*'.

Syberg, Franz (1904–55)

(i) *Allegro sonatissimo;* (ii) *Scherzando;* (iii) *String trio.*
* Kontrapunkt Dig. 32197 [id.]. (i–ii) Morten Mogensen; (ii) Toke Lund Christiansen; Ebbe Monrad Møller; (i; iii) Søren Elbæk; (iii) Piotr Zelazny; (ii–iii) Troels Svane Hermansen.

The Danish composer Franz Syberg was the son of the painter Frits Syberg and studied with Karg-Elert in Leipzig in the 1920s. He was a provincial organist for most of his life. The bulk of his music comes from the 1920s and early 1930s: he gave up composing in the early 1940s to devote himself to farming. The *Allegro sonatissimo* (1926) for violin and piano, written in his early twenties, is a bit Regeresque. The two companion works, a *Scherzando* for flute, oboe, piano and cello and a *String trio*, both date from 1934. The *Scherzando* is vaguely Hindemithian; and the *String trio*, which runs to almost half an hour, is more individual but no less unmemorable. Unfortunately the value of this enterprise is diminished by a dry and claustrophobic recording; the players are too close. The *String trio* is well crafted but essentially arid; even so, it deserved better recording.

Syrewicz, Stanislas (20th century)

The Choir (incidental music for BBC TV dramatization).
*** Decca Dig. 448 152-2 [id.]. Anthony Way, Gloucester Cathedral Ch., Warsaw Philh. O, Davis Briggs (also includes: BRITTEN: *Jubilate Deo;* STANFORD: *Magnificat in G;* TAVENER: *Hymn to the Mother of God;* FRANCK: *Panis angelicus;* MENDELSSOHN: *Oh for the wings of a dove;* WESLEY: *Blessed be the God and Father: Love one another* (with James Hopkins). TALLIS: *Salvator mundi;* BRAHMS: *Cradle song;* HANDEL: *Zadok the Priest* (King's College Ch., ECO, Willocks); *Messiah: Hallelujah Chorus* (ASMF Ch., Marriner); MOZART: *Così fan tutte: Trio: O soave si il vento* (Lucia Popp, Brigitte Fassbaender, Tom Krause)).

The Choir: introductory theme. FRANCK: *Panis angelicus;* MENDELSSOHN: *Oh for the wings of a dove.*
*** Decca Dig. Single 448 164-2 [id.].

Many readers will have enjoyed BBC TV's dramatization of Joanna Trollope's *The Choir*, depicting the conflicting passions and turbulent, even sinister, political machinations going on within the close of an English cathedral. For the filming, Gloucester Cathedral was used and the choir (threatened with redundancy in the plot) spiced the narrative with much splendid church music. The telling background score was written by the Polish-born Stanislas Syrewicz, hence the use of the Warsaw Philharmonia to provide orchestral support. His various atmospheric interludes (often effectively menacing) are in effect a set of variations on the simple but potent chordal theme heard at the opening. In the story, the cathedral choir is saved by a hit single, provided by its leading chorister, and the eleven-year-old Anthony Way (who was borrowed from St Paul's Cathedral Choir for the series), besides showing himself to be a natural actor, turned fiction into fact by producing his own hit single for Decca. His voice, while not without the essential purity, is warmer, more sensuous than that of Master Ernest Lough, and Franck's *Panis angelicus* (resplendently dressed up by Syrewicz) makes the strongest appeal. *Oh for the wings of a dove* is less precise in pitch than Lough's famous version but is still touching. He is then joined by an able young colleague in a duet by Samuel Wesley. The Gloucester Cathedral Choir give a ravishing account of John Tavener's *Hymn to the Mother of God* (the cathedral ambience adding much to their eloquence) and, with help from the Decca archives, the Choirs of the ASMF and King's College are on hand for fine performances of the two Handel showpieces. The only disappointment is the Tallis motet, *Salvator mundi*, which is lacking in intensity and grip. With first-rate Decca sound, this is a surprisingly entertaining mix – even including Mozart's heavenly Trio from *Così fan tutte*.

Szymanowski, Karol (1882–1937)

Violin concertos Nos. 1, Op. 35; 2, Op. 31.
(M) **(*) EMI CDM5 65418-2 [id.]. Kulka, Polish RSO, Maksymiuk (with GORECKI: *3 Pieces in the old style* ***) – BAIRD: *Colas Breugnon suite.* ***

These marvellous concertos have not been as well served on record as the Bartók or Prokofiev. The performances here are committed and highly finished; they convey much of the ecstasy, longing and sensuousness of these luminous scores. Both works are rich in atmosphere, full of the exotic colours and the sense of rapture that permeate Symanowski's very finest scores. The acoustic is reverberant, and that adds to the overheated impression conveyed in the *Second*, which is played powerfully, though it is not quite as refined in character here as in Szeryng's version, made in the early 1970s. Kulka and Maksymiuk could perhaps have brought greater poignancy and longing to the *First Concerto*. The multi-mike balance produces vivid sound, but the perspective is not entirely natural and the overall effect is one of glare. However,both these performances are persuasive enough to be recommendable, and the Baird and the well-known Górecki suites make a good bonus.

(i) *Symphony No. 3 (Song of the night), Op. 27;* (ii) *Litania do Marii Pany, Op. 59;* (iii) *Stabat Mater, Op. 53.*
*** EMI Dig. CDC5 55121-2 [id.]. (i) Jon Garrison; (ii–iii) Elzbieta Szmytka; (iii) Florence Quivar, John Connell; CBSO Ch., CBSO, Rattle.

Given his sympathetic feeling for Janáček and Nielsen, it was only a matter of time before Simon Rattle turned to another composer with a keen feeling for nature and for the earth. Szymanowski also has that fastidious ear for texture and heightened sense of vision that distinguish mystics, and nowhere is atmosphere more potent than in the *Third Symphony*, the *Song of the night*. Sir Simon is equally committed and persuasive in the *Stabat Mater*, these days a standard coupling, and one of the unequivocally great choral works of the century. These are very good performances and the sumptuous and finely detailed recording is absolutely state-of-the-art.

(i) *Symphony No. 4 (Symphonie concertante), Op. 60;* (ii) *Harnasie* (ballet pantomime), *Op. 55.*
(M) **(*) EMI CDM5 65307-2 [id.]. (i) Piotr Paleczny, Polish Nat. RSO, Jerzy Semkow; (ii) Bachleda, Kwasny, Krakow Polish R. Ch. & SO, Antoni Wit.

Piotr Paleczny is no mean artist and he has all the finesse and imagination as well as the requisite command of colour that the *Symphonie concertante* calls for; Wit provides him with admirable support. On the whole this makes an even stronger impression than the alternative performance on Marco Polo (8.223290 – see our main volume), which anyway is differently coupled. *Harnasie* is also very successful: it reflects Szymanowski's discovery of the folk music of the Tatras which surfaced first in the Op. 50 *Mazurkas* for piano. It calls for large forces, including a solo violinist as well as a tenor and full chorus, and poses obvious practical production problems. The story tells how the heroine is rescued from a forced wedding to a rich old farmer by the brigand, Harnas, and his followers (the Harnasie); she has misgivings about her new situation, and her new husband wonders if his bride will take to him and imagines their mutual ecstasy if she does. As always with this composer, there is the sense of rapture, the soaring, ecstatic lines and the intoxicating exoticism that distinguish the mature Szymanowski, and it comes across most tellingly here. The only snag is that the sound, though spaciously wide-ranging, is made a bit fierce on top by the CD remastering.

String quartets Nos. 1 in C, Op. 37; 2, Op. 56.
**(*) ASV Dig. CDDCA 908 [id.]. Maggini Qt – BACEWICZ: *String quartet No. 4.* **

The Szymanowski *Quartets* have an intoxicating and hypnotic quality and have attracted several recordings in the last few years, most notably by the Carmina Quartet on Delos (CO 79462) and the Varsovia on Olympia. (The Carmina deservedly won various awards, including one from Britain's *Gramophone* magazine, and was accorded a Rosette in our main edition.) Either is to be preferred to this newcomer, which is not to say that the Maggini do not evince commitment. They are an accomplished ensemble and play with great feeling for Szymanowski, but they are outclassed by the Carmina in sheer tonal finesse.

Fantasia in C, Op. 14; 9 Preludes, Op. 1; Prelude and fugue in C sharp min.; Piano sonatas Nos. 1 in C min., Op. 8; in A, Op. 21; 4 Studies, Op. 4; Variations in B flat min., Op. 3; Variations on a Polish folk-theme in B min., Op. 10.
*(*) Nimbus Dig. NI 5405/6 [id.]. Martin Jones.

Martin Jones championed Szymanowski way back in the 1960s when he recorded the *Masques* and other pieces for the Argo label. Although his skill, sympathies and artistry are not in question, his chronological sweep of the piano music is badly handicapped by Nimbus's over-reverberant and badly balanced recording. Dennis Lee on Hyperion remains the finest and best recorded of Szymanowski interpreters and will soon hopefully follow up his impressive set of the Op. 4 *Etudes, Masques* and *Métopes*.

(i) *King Roger* (opera; complete); (ii) *Harnasie (The Highland Robbers)* (ballet pantomime), *Op. 55.*
*** Olympia OCD 303A/B [id.]. (i) Hiolski, Rumowska, Nikodem, Pustelak, Dabrowski, Malewicz-Madey, Polish Pathfinders' Union Children's Ch.; (ii) Bachleda; (i–ii) Warsaw Nat. Op. House Ch. & O; (i) Mierzejewski; (ii) Wodiczko.

(i) *King Roger* (opera; complete); (ii) *Prince Potemkin: incidental music to Act V.*

*(*) Marco Polo Dig. 8.223339/40 [id.]. Hiolski, Ochman, Zagórzanka, Grychnik, Mróz, Malewicz-Madey, Cracow Philh. Boys' Ch., Polish State Philh. Ch. & O (Katowice), Karol Stryja; (ii) Polish Nat. RSO (Katowice), Antoni Wit.

These two Olympia CDs accommodate Szymanowski's masterpiece, the opera *King Roger*, and his last stage-work, the ballet *Harnasie*. Both recordings date from the mid-1960s; they first appeared here, on the Muza label, in very inferior LPs which sounded as if they were made from dog biscuits. The present transfer has made a magnificent job of the originals, which sound strikingly detailed and rich. *King Roger* is the product of Szymanowski's fascination with eastern mysticism and Arab culture. It is set in twelfth-century Sicily and its opening scene, at Mass in the Cathedral of Palermo, is music of awesome beauty. The sense of ecstasy he evokes is intoxicating, and the complex textures and unparalleled wealth of colour he has at his command are impressive by any standards. The Dionysiac atmosphere will be familiar to those who know *The Song of the night* and the *First Violin concerto*. Andrzej Hiolski is a more than adequate Roger and Hanna Rumowska an excellent Roxana. The whole cast is dedicated and the extensive forces involved, including a children's choir and a large orchestra and chorus, respond to the direction of Mieczyslaw Mierzejewski with fervour. It is a pity that Rowicki's later account of *Harnasie*, made in the mid-1970s, could not have been chosen in preference to this earlier version, which runs to about 25 minutes, whereas the whole ballet takes about 34. Not that there are any serious inadequacies here, for the playing and singing are totally committed and do justice to its hedonistic nationalism. An indispensable set for all lovers of this composer.

King Roger has one of the most inspired and awe-inspiring openings in all twentieth-century opera and in Roxana's aria one of the most captivating and haunting of musical ideas. Its first Act, still composed in the exotic, heavily scented and heady atmosphere of the *First Violin concerto* and the *Song of the night*, is at variance with the sparer textures of his later folk-inflected idiom, which surfaces in the last part of the opera. There is some good singing from the Roxana of Barbara Zagórzanka and the Shepherd of Wieslaw Ochman, though it must be conceded that Andrzej Hiolski in the title-role is no longer as fresh-timbred or well-focused vocally as he was in Muza's pioneering LP version from the 1960s. But all this is academic, since the *sine qua non* of any *King Roger* is atmosphere – and this Marco Polo alternative has all too little.

Tallis, Thomas (c. 1505–85)

Alfred Deller Edition: *Lamentations of Jeremiah the Prophet.* 5 hymns: *Deus tuorum militum; Jam Christus astra ascenderat; Jesu Salvator Saeculi; O nata lux de lumine; Salvator mundi Domine.*

(M) ** Van. 08.5062 71 [id.]. Deller Consort (with Wilfred Brown, Gerald English, Eileen McLoughlin (in hymns), Maurice Bevan, Deller.

Alfred Deller pioneered so much repertoire on LP, and even today Tallis's settings of the *Lamentations of Jeremiah* are not generously represented on disc. They are here given poised, expressive performances and the motets are presented with their alternating plainsong. However, there is comparatively little difference in dynamic range between the plainsong and the hymns, and the closely balanced recording robs the *Lamentations* of much of their atmosphere, while no real pianissimos are possible. The sound itself is full and truthful, but this cannot compare with the Gimell recording of the complete *Lamentations* plus eight motets and a rare Marian antiphon (CDGIM 025; *1385T-25* – see our main volume).

Taneyev, Sergei (1856–1915)

Suite de concert (for violin and orchestra), *Op. 28.*

(M) *** EMI CDM5 65419-2 [id.]. David Oistrakh, Philh. O, Malko – MIASKOVSKY: *Cello concerto.* *** ⊕

David Oistrakh's superb account of Taneyev's attractively diverse *Suite*, ranging from rhapsodic ardour in the first (of five movements) to sparkling virtuosity in the *Tarantella* finale, has been available only rarely, even on LP. The early (1956) stereo is of high quality and few would guess the age of the recording from the present CD transfer, which is full-bodied and admirable.

Tchaikovsky, Peter (1840–93)

Andante cantabile, Op. 11; Nocturne, Op. 19/4 (both arr. for cello & orchestra); *Pezzo capriccioso, Op. 62; Variations on a rococo theme, Op. 33* (original versions).
(M) **(*) Virgin/EMI Dig. CUV5 61225-2 [id.]. Isserlis, COE, Gardiner (with GLAZUNOV: *2 Pieces, Op. 20; Chant du ménestrel, Op. 71;* RIMSKY-KORSAKOV: *Serenade, Op. 37;* CUI: *2 Morceaux, Op. 36 ***).

The composer himself arranged the *Andante cantabile* for cello and orchestra from his *D major String quartet*, transposing it from B flat to B major, but it was not published until after his death. The published score of the *Rococo variations* (as presented so unforgettably by Rostropovich and Karajan as one of DG's Legendary performances on DG 447 413-2), omits the short scherzando, Variation No. 8, and alters the order of the others. There is evidence that the composer accepted the revision without exactly approving it and, while the differences are not fundamental, most collectors will want to hear the composer's original intentions; indeed, one hopes that the original version will eventually become standard. Isserlis's playing has slight reserve but also an elegant delicacy which is appealing, although it suits Glazunov and Cui rather better than it does Tchaikovsky's *Andante cantabile*. John Eliot Gardiner provides gracefully lightweight accompaniments and the Virgin recording is faithfully balanced, fresh in texture and warm in ambience. Some listeners may find this music-making lacking in extrovert feeling; others may feel that its lightness of touch makes a special appeal.

Capriccio italien, Op. 45.
(**) Sir Thomas Beecham Trust mono BEECHAM 6 [id.]. NYPO, Beecham – MENDELSSOHN: *Symphony No. 4;* SIBELIUS: *Symphony No. 7 etc.* (**)

Sir Thomas recorded the *Capriccio italien* only twice and on both occasions with American orchestras. This account with the New York Philharmonic comes from 1942, the same year as his now celebrated Sibelius *Seventh*, which is also on this disc. It is a thrilling account which finds the New York orchestra and their British guest on excellent musical terms. The recording is somewhat opaque but perfectly acceptable for its period.

Capriccio italien; Francesca da Rimini; 1812 Overture; Romeo and Juliet.
(M) ** DG Dig. 445 523-2 [id.]. Chicago SO, Barenboim.
(M) ** DG Dig./Analogue 439 983-2 [id.]. Israel PO, Bernstein.

Barenboim is too ready to let the tension relax to be entirely convincing throughout this programme, although his affection for the music is never in doubt. He is slinkily persuasive in the *Capriccio*, but by the finest Chicago standards *1812* is much less impressively played, though not without excitement. The recording could expand more and the violin sound has a distinct digital edge. The *Capriccio* is more agreeable overall. In *Romeo and Juliet* Barenboim conveys a sensuous quality in the love theme but the ardour of the performance is sporadic, though there is a burst of excitement in the feud music. The middle section of *Francesca da Rimini* yields some fine solo wind playing, notably from the clarinet; but the full nervous tension of the outer sections is partly subdued by the conductor's partiality for breadth, although the coda is exciting enough. The sound is always vivid.

Bernstein's approach to *Francesca* certainly conveys the passion of the story, but the Israel Philharmonic does not play the central section as idyllically as one might hope; moreover Bernstein's pacing is idiosyncratic and unconvincing here. *Romeo and Juliet* is only moderately exciting, in spite of a brilliant sound-balance. The Tel Aviv acoustic is too dry for music which needs a warmly expansive resonance. With the extra presence and definition in the digitally recorded works (the *Capriccio* and *1812*), the ear can accept – though not revel in – the chosen ambience. At the end of *1812* the cannon make a spectacular effect, though the sudden peal of bells near the end seems contrived. Overall, this cannot be recommended with any great enthusiasm, and readers are referred to alternative compilations listed in our main book, notably Ashkenazy's fine programme with the RPO which includes the *Capriccio, Francesca da Rimini* and *Romeo and Juliet*, plus the *Elégie for strings* (Decca 421 715-2). Those wanting *1812* could choose Sian Edwards's excellent mid-priced alternative on EMI (CD-EMX 2152), which also offers *Francesca, Marche slave* and *Romeo*.

Piano concerto No. 1 in B flat min., Op. 23.
(M) ** Cziffra Edition, Volume 3: EMI CDM5 65252-2 [id.]. György Cziffra, Philh. O, André Vandernoot – LISZT: *Piano concertos Nos. 1 & 2.* **(*)
(M) (**) DG 447 420-2 [id.]. Sviatoslav Richter, VSO, Karajan – RACHMANINOV: *Piano concerto No. 2.* ***

Piano concerto No. 1; Dumka, Op. 59.

(BB) *(*) Discover Dig. DICD 920118 [id.]. David Lively, Slovak R, New PO, Rahbahri (with BALAKIREV: *Islamey* *).

(i) *Piano concerto No. 1. The Seasons, Op. 37: January; February; April; May; August; October; November; December.*

(B) *** Tring. Dig. TRP 023 [id.]. Ronan O'Hora, (i) with RPO, James Judd.

Having already given us an outstanding version of the Grieg *Concerto*, Ronan O'Hora and James Judd repeat their success with a memorably fresh, new look at Tchaikovsky's *B flat minor Concerto*. The very opening is gloriously arresting, and then O'Hora sets off with a crisp, sparkling duplet rhythm for the main theme of the allegro, pulling back naturally and poetically for his gentle introduction of the lovely secondary group, which surely reminds us of the moonlight sequence from Tchaikovsky's *Romeo and Juliet*. There is a definite pause before the development but the tension does not drop, and the movement proceeds compulsively, with the orchestra responding with a fine romantic sweep to O'Hora's flamboyant octaves. Judd builds a really powerful introduction for the cadenza which is in every way a highlight of the performance. The *Andante semplice* brings contrasting delicacy, and in the central section O'Hora's chimerical lightness is like a will-o'-the-wisp. Then the finale makes a fitting culmination, with the joyful spirit of Russian dance paramount, rather than any barnstorming; but the exciting final reprise of the big tune is capped with a stormy bravura flourish from the soloist. The whole performance has the spontaneous feel of a live occasion, and the recording balance (by Dick Lewzey and David Richardson, who also worked on the companion Grieg issue) is just about ideal, with a bold, natural piano-image set against a richly spacious orchestral tapestry. As with his Grieg record, the pianist chooses a coupling of solo pieces, in this case eight out of the twelve 'months' which make up *The Seasons*. They are presented with an agreeable, impulsive charm and plenty of colour. *May night*, the November *Troika* and the warmly lyrical October *Autumn song* are particularly successful.

Surprisingly, the Cziffra Tchaikovsky *B flat minor* comes off much less successfully than its Liszt couplings. Cziffra, as always, displays a prodigious technique but the symbiosis he found with Vandernoot and the Philharmonia in Liszt is not sustained here. After a crude opening, during the first movement conductor and soloist seem not wholly agreed on the degree of forward thrust the music needs; sometimes one presses on, sometimes the other. The *Andante* offers nothing special, and the finale is very much a Russian dance and lacks the barnstorming one would expect; the reprise of the big tune is pulled right back very spaciously indeed, almost losing the music's impetus, and only the pianist's final burst of energy saves the day. Despite the use of the Kingsway Hall, the 1958 recording, with its bright primary colours and tendency to harshness of lighting, is comparatively two-dimensional and the strings tend to shrillness.

The element of struggle for which this work is famous is all too clear in the Richter/Karajan performance; not surprisingly, these two musical giants do not always agree: each chooses a different tempo for the second subject of the finale and maintains it, despite the other. However, in both the dramatic opening and the closing pages of the work they are agreed in a hugely mannered, bland stylization which is not easy to enjoy. Elsewhere, in the first movement both conductor and pianist play havoc with any sense of forward tempo (although they both produce some real bursts of excitement here and there), and Richter's excessive rubato in the lyrical second-subject group is unspontaneous. Clearly two major artists are at work, but it is difficult to praise the end-product as a convincing reading. The recording is full-blooded, with a firm piano image. The reissue in DG's Legendary Recordings series is coupled with an outstanding recording of Rachmaninov's *Second Piano concerto* with Stanislaw Wislocki and the Warsaw Philharmonic.

Although agreeable enough and unexceptionally recorded, the David Lively/Rahbari performance of the Tchaikovsky concerto on Discover emphasizes its lyrical nature at the expense of exuberance and dash: the rhetoric is played down even in the grand finale, where the final statement of the tune is broad rather than arresting. The Balakirev coupling is quite well played but not distinctive, and the piano timbre here is shallow.

(i) *Piano concerto No. 1 in B flat min.;* (ii) *Violin concerto in D.*

(BB) *** RCA Navigator 74321 17900-2 [id.]. (i) John Browning; (ii) Erick Friedman; LSO, Ozawa.

Browning's mid-1960s interpretation of the solo role in the *Piano concerto* is remarkable, not only for power and bravura but for wit and point in the many *scherzando* passages, and in the finale he adopts a fast and furious tempo to compare with Horowitz. Erick Friedman, Heifetz's pupil, is a thoughtful violinist who gives a keenly intelligent performance of the companion work, imbued with a glowing lyricism and with a particularly poetic and beautiful account of the slow movement. There is plenty of dash and fire in the finale, and Ozawa gives first-rate support to both soloists. The recording is excellent. Two performances to match those of almost any rival; moreover this disc is in the lowest price-range.

Violin concerto in D, Op. 35.
*** Sony Dig. SK 66567 [id.]. Julian Rachlin, Moscow RSO, Vladimir Fedoseyev – PROKOFIEV: *Violin concerto No. 1.* ***
(M) *** Decca 425 080-2 [id.]. Kyung-Wha Chung, LSO, Previn – SIBELIUS: *Violin concerto.* ***

While Kyung-Wha Chung's reissued Decca version, coupled with the Sibelius at mid-price, might seem a more obvious first choice among recent arrivals, this new RCA recording, coupled with Prokofiev, brings a refreshing new look at a much-loved concerto. As in the Prokofiev, Julian Rachlin gives an exceptionally characterful and distinctive reading, not conventionally high-powered but thoughtful and hushed in intensity, rare qualities in this concerto. He is helped by a natural balance for the solo instrument in these live recordings, made in the Moscow Conservatoire in February 1994. Some may feel that Rachlin's determination to observe every pianissimo marking detracts from the power of his reading, but with magnetic concentration he makes such bravura passages as the big cadenza sound like spontaneous expression, volatile and mercurial, not just a display vehicle. Rachlin uses echo effects – not always marked in the score – in the lyrical episodes of both the central *Canzonetta* and the finale, where he not only plays with yearning beauty but also gives sparkle to the main theme rather than thrusting on with sheer power. The volatile quality of this live recording sets problems for the orchestra, which is not always crisp in its ensemble, but the soloist's performance is what matters.

Chung's earlier recording of the Tchaikovsky *Concerto* with Previn conducting has remained one of the strongest recommendations for a much-recorded work ever since it was made, right at the beginning of her career. Although she recorded it later with Dutoit, anyone should be well satisfied with Chung's 1970 version with its Sibelius coupling. Her technique is impeccable and her musicianship of the highest order, and Previn's accompanying is highly sympathetic and responsive. This has warmth, spontaneity and discipline, every detail is beautifully shaped and turned without a trace of sentimentality. The recording is well balanced and detail is clean, though the acoustic is warm. This is a very distinguished record, very suitable for reissue in Decca's Classic Sound series.

(i) *1812 Overture;* (ii) *Romeo and Juliet* (fantasy overture); (iii) *Serenade for strings in C, Op. 48.*
(M) **(*) DG Dig. 439 468-2 [id.]. (i) Gothenburg SO, Järvi; (ii) Philh. O, Sinopoli; (iii) Orpheus CO.

Järvi's *1812* is exciting – and not just for the added Gothenburg brass and artillery or for the fervour of the orchestra at the opening. Järvi clearly knows how to structure the piece, and he obviously enjoys the histrionics, and so do we. Sinopoli's reading of *Romeo and Juliet*, however, is not so spontaneous-sounding, with a hint of self-consciousness at the first entry of the big love theme; however, there is plenty of uninhibited passion on the later repeats. In the *Serenade for strings* no one could accuse the Orpheus Chamber Orchestra of lack of energy in the outer movements; indeed the finale has tremendous bustle and vigour, the sheer nervous energy communicating in exhilarating fashion. Overall it is an impressive performance, even if the problems of rubato without a conductor are not always easily solved. The *Waltz* is nicely relaxed, but the sudden slowing at its coda is not quite convincing, nor is a spurt of accelerando towards the end of the *Elégie*. At the end of the first movement, when the great striding opening tune is reprised, it is heavily accented for no apparent reason. Yet there is much that is fresh here, and one cannot but admire the precision of ensemble. The sound is first class, with the acoustics of the Performing Arts Center at New York State University providing plenty of warmth as well as clarity and a full, firm bass-line, very important in this work.

(i) *Fatum* (symphonic poem), *Op. 77;* (ii; iii) *Francesca da Rimini* (fantasy after Dante), *Op. 32;* (ii; iii) *Hamlet* (fantasy overture), *Op 67a;* (iv; v) *Romeo and Juliet* (fantasy overture); (i) *The Storm, Op. 76; The Tempest, Op. 18; The Voyevoda, Op. 78* (symphonic poems);(iv; iii) *Overture 1812, Op. 49.*
(B) **(*) Ph. Duo 442 586-2 (2) [id.]. (i) Frankfurt RSO, Eliahu Inbal; (ii) New Philh. O; (iii) Igor Markevitch; (iv) Concg. O; (v) Bernard Haitink.

A most important reissue in that it gathers together on a two-for-the-price-of-one Duo set finely committed performances of four of Tchaikovsky's little-known symphonic poems in excellent recordings from the mid-1970s with the right kind of sonority and ambience. The most remarkable piece (which is superbly performed by Inbal and the Frankfurt orchestra) is *The Storm*, a surprisingly coherent structure in sonata form which suddenly appeared in 1864 as Tchaikovsky's first fully fledged orchestral composition (after various student efforts). It has all the fingerprints of the later masterpieces: individual and attractive melodic and harmonic content and an astonishing orchestral flair. Yet the composer never published it. The work is based on Ostrovsky's play, *Katya Kabanová*, which also formed the basis for Janáček's opera, and any Tchaikovskian who is not familiar with it is in for a surprise. In his splendid biography of the composer, David Brown comments: 'Much of *The Storm* has the familiar and individual sound of Tchaikovsky's own mature orchestration. Already he is showing that natural facility of conceiving his ideas directly in terms of orchestral textures and colour. The entire exposition, the dark opening which ushers in the piece, and the little interlude by the Volga are beautifully characteristic conceptions, skilfully realized, while the whole work is lucidly designed and free from overstatement and structural prolixity.' *The Voyevoda* is a very late work which is unconnected with the opera of the same name (they are based on different subjects). If not entirely successful, it has some good ideas and characteristic orchestration. But it so dissatisfied its composer – though not the press and public – at its first performance that he tore up the score in anger and despair. Fortunately the orchestral parts survived. *Fatum*, written four years after *The Storm*, is a much less successful and less assured piece and rests completely in the shade of the composer's first great masterpiece, *Romeo and Juliet*, which followed in 1869 (although it was revised twice, in 1870 and 1880). *The Tempest* arrived in 1873 and is a highly imaginative piece, if flawed. It is notable for its memorably passionate love theme and the atmospheric opening and close depicting Prospero's island and the sea. Here the performance is very ardent, but the reverberant acoustic makes Tchaikovsky's climaxes a bit noisy. Markevitch's accounts of *Francesca da Rimini* and *Hamlet* have characteristic intensity and drive, but are weaker in dealing with the lyrical passages, although there are no complaints about the orchestral playing. Haitink's *Romeo and Juliet* is full of atmosphere and is spaciously conceived, although it builds up a full head of passion rather slowly. *1812* makes a lively bonus, rather individual in its pacing, but not unconvincingly so. But it is for the four novelties that this set is worthwhile.

Francesca da Rimini.
(M) ** Virgin/EMI Dig. CUV5 61124-2 [id.]. Houston SO, Christoph Eschenbach – DVORAK: *Symphony No. 9.* **
(M) *(*) Decca Dig. 430 738-2 [id.]. Cleveland Ch. & O, Chailly – PROKOFIEV: *Alexander Nevsky.* **

Eschenbach's performance of *Francesca da Rimini* has similar qualities to those in the Dvořák symphony with which it is coupled. With clean textures and ensemble, with rhythms crisply resilient and with the brass section gloriously ripe, it is a refreshing performance which yet lacks Tchaikovskian passion. It makes a generous and unusual fill-up for the *New World Symphony*.

Chailly is superbly recorded in Decca's most spectacular manner and he secures excellent playing from the Cleveland Orchestra, especially in the work's middle section. But there is not enough adrenalin and drive here, and the outer climaxes, depicting Dante's inferno, are underpowered.

(i) *The Nutcracker* (ballet): complete; (ii) *Sleeping Beauty* (ballet): highlights.
(B) *** Ph. Duo 444 562-2 (2) [id.]. (i) Concg. O, with boys' Ch., Dorati; (ii) LSO, Fistoulari.

Dorati's 1975 complete *Nutcracker* with the Concertgebouw Orchestra was given a Rosette by us when it first appeared on LP, and it now makes a clear first choice in the bargain category, more particularly as it is coupled with Fistoulari's equally outstanding 1962 set of highlights from the *Sleeping Beauty*. In the former the playing of the Concertgebouw Orchestra is immensely refined yet often very dramatic. Dorati's conception is both vivid and strong. Its vitality is noticeable from the *Miniature overture* onwards with an engaging rhythmic spring and no forcing of accents. The Pine forest journey has seldom sounded more ardent and is built to a tremendous climax. Then the *Waltz of the Snowflakes* produces the most delightfully fresh choral quality from the Boys' Choir of St Bravo Cathedral, Haarlem. Dorati's attention to detail is affectionate, and in the dances which make up Act II his characterization is sure, although the *Waltz of the Flowers* could ideally have more lilt. The CD transfer brings less sumptuous sound than on the old LPs, but the Concertgebouw ambience ensures body as well as vividness. Fistoulari's greatness as a ballet conductor is well celebrated by the *Sleeping Beauty* selection, which was extremely well recorded in its day and has transferred to CD with striking amplitude and brilliance. He conducted Tchaikovsky without hysteria yet generated great excitement, as the breadth and power of the *Rose adagio* immediately demonstrates, while the delightful *Panorama* is admirably relaxed and glowing. The selection is well made and satisfying, with plenty of charm and sparkling colours from the LSO wind players.

Nutcracker suite; Sleeping Beauty: suite; Swan Lake: suite.
** DG Dig. 437 806-2 [id.]. VPO, James Levine.

Nutcracker suite; Sleeping Beauty: excerpts; Swan Lake: suite.
*** Decca Dig. 443 555-2 [id.]. Montreal SO, Dutoit.

Dutoit's complete Decca recordings of *The Nutcracker* (440 477-2) and *Swan Lake* (436 212-2) are highly recommended in our main volume and the two suites derived from these sets are elegantly and vividly played, and recorded in Decca's best manner. Readers will note that this means that in the *Nutcracker suite* the *Dance of the Sugar Plum Fairy* has the extended ballet ending, rather than the concert coda. Listening to Dutoit's approach to *Swan Lake* immediately after Sawallisch (see below), one finds the latter more dramatically vital, though the Decca sound is much smoother and richer. The *Sleeping Beauty* excerpts are taken from Dutoit's recording of *Aurora's Wedding* (a bonus with *The Nutcraker*), which is Diaghilev's truncated version of the ballet, including the *Introduction* and then drawing entirely on Act III. Thus the present 22-minute set of excerpts taken from that source misses out some key items, notably the *Panorama*, which is perhaps the composer's finest inspiration in the whole score.

Levine's triptych is comparably generous (72 minutes). His three suites are all new recordings and, indeed, the *Panorama* is presented here very gracefully. But overall these are well-played, polished selections with some nice touches, but they are in no way distinctive, and DG's so-called 4D recording, while brilliant and full, is just a little short on hall ambience. Collectors will do far better with Rostropovich's superb Berlin Philharmonic performances of the three suites, which are in a different category altogther. Indeed they are enchanting and have the benefit of beautiful analogue recording, given entirely beneficial digital remastering. There is only 69 minutes of music here, but every one of them offers sheer joy. This should have been included in DG's 'Originals' series of Legendary Recordings. However, we gave it a Rosette in our main volume (429 097-2).

Serenade for strings in C, Op. 48.
(M) **(*) Ph. Dig. 442 402-2 [id.]. Bav. RSO, Sir Colin Davis – DVORAK: *Serenade.* **(*)

Like the Dvořák coupling, Sir Colin Davis's performance is on the heavy side, with rich timbres from the Bavarian Radio strings and a resonant bass amplifying the breadth and warmth of the reading. While rhythms are resilient, and this is warmly attractive in its way, at times a lighter touch would have been welcome.

The Sleeping beauty (ballet; complete).
(B) ** Ph. Duo 446 166-2 (2) [id.]. Concg. O, Dorati.

Dorati's complete *Sleeping Beauty* was recorded over a period between May 1979 and January 1981. It is a consistently vibrant and dramatic account, supported by firm, rich recording and splendid orchestral playing (especially in the last Act, which gives the orchestral wind soloists many chances to shine). Yet this is a score that – for all its melodic inspiration – can momentarily disengage the listener's attention; and here, in spite of the drama, this does happen. Everything is well characterized, but at times there is a lack of magic. Those looking for a bargain version of this splendid score should turn to Andrew Mogrelia and the Slovak State Philharmonic Orchestra on Naxos, which presents an ideal combination of warmth, grace and vitality. Indeed, this remains a clear first choice among all available versions, irrespective of cost (8.550490/2).

Swan Lake (ballet; complete), *Op. 20.*
**(*) EMI Dig. CDS5 55277-2 (2). Phd. O, Sawallisch.

Sawallisch is clearly the right man to make a new recording of Tchaikovsky's greatest ballet score, for he approaches it with appealing freshness as if it had been written yesterday, and the Philadelphia Orchestra play superbly. But, as so often, they are let down by the choice of venue for the recording: in this instance, the Memorial Hall, Fairmount Park, whose apparently intractable acoustics have brought unnaturally close microphone placing. There is no lack of atmosphere, as the very opening demonstrates, with its enticing oboe solo and warm lower strings (although immediately one notices that the violins could be richer in timbre). But soon it is apparent that fortissimos are unrefined, with fierce cymbals, grainy violins, even an element of harshness. The Philadelphia strings don't sound like this at a live concert. But there is also much to enjoy, and splendid vigour, as in the *Allegro giusto* which immediately follows. The first and most famous *Waltz* (gorgeously played) lilts attractively, as again does the later example (track 11 – very affectionate) and the briefer piece which comes in the *Danses des cygnes* at the end of Act II (track 22). How engaging are the cygnets, tripping in very precisely and with irresistible style (track 25), while in the famous *pas de deux* of Odette and the Prince (track 26) the violin and cello duet brings ravishingly serene yet voluptuous solo playing, with the two instruments in absolute symbiosis. There are so many instances of Sawallisch's nicely judged pacing and the responsive solo playing: the elegantly tripping clarinet in the *Intrada* of Act III (track 9), followed by the chirping flute and piccolo, and the delicate interplay of harp, oboe and flute in the wistful fifth variation of the *Pas de six* are just two examples, while in the interpolated *Danse russe* the concert master, Norman Carol, brings a passionate zigeuner verve to his violin solo. Above all, Sawallisch's direction combines a flowing spontaneity with an overall feeling for Tchaikovsky's structure. The thrilling final climax (with gorgeously full horn-tone at the restatement of the famous *idée fixe*), makes an overwhelming apotheosis, even if the shrillness added to the violins, who are playing with enormous fervour and weight of sonority, is not a plus factor. A splendidly stimulating set, nevertheless. But why can't EMI find a hall worthy of this great orchestra? First choice remains with Dutoit (Decca 436 212-2).

Swan Lake (ballet), *Op. 20* (slightly abridged recording of the European score).
(B) **(*) Decca Double 440 630-2 (2) [id.]. SRO, Ansermet – PROKOFIEV: *Romeo and Juliet.* **

Returning to Ansermet's 1959 recording of *Swan Lake*, one is amazed by the vigour of the playing and the excellence of the recording. The Drigo version of the score, which Ansermet uses, dates from 1895; Drigo added orchestrations of his own, taken from Tchaikovsky's piano music (Op. 72), yet he left out some 1,600 bars of the original score. Ansermet offers the Act I introduction and Nos. 1–2, 4, 7 and 8; Act II, Nos. 10–13; Act III, Nos. 15, 17–18 and 20–23, with No. 5 (the *Pas de deux)* then interpolated before Nos. 28 and 29 from Act IV. Despite the obvious gaps, most of the familiar favourites are included here, and the music-making has such zest and colour that one cannot but revel in every bar. The solo wind playing is not always as sweet-timbred as in some other versions, but the violin and cello solos are well done, and there is not a dull moment throughout. The transfer is well managed, full-blooded and bright, and there is not too much wrong with the timbre of the upper strings. It was a happy idea to couple this on its Double Decca reissue with a selection of 15 items from the two suites from Prokofiev's *Romeo and Juliet* ballet, even if the orchestral playing is less impressive.

(i) *Symphonies Nos. 1 in G min. (Winter daydreams); 2 in C min. (Little Russian); 3 in D (Polish);*
(ii) *Francesca da Rimini.*
(B) *** Ph. Duo 446 148-2 (2) [id.]. (i) LSO; (ii) New Philh. O; Markevitch.

This Philips Duo offers an inexpensive way of collecting thoroughly recommendable performances of the first three Tchaikovsky symphonies, recorded in the mid-1960s and offering warmly atmospheric, resonant and full-bodied sound. Markevitch is a genuine Tchaikovskian and his readings have fine momentum and plenty of ardour. In the *First Symphony* he finds the Mendelssohnian lightness in his fast pacing of the opening movement, while there is real evocation in the *Adagio* and a sense of desolation at the reprise of the *Andante lugubre*, before the final rousing peroration. In the *Little Russian Symphony* the opening horn solo is full of character and the allegro tautly rhythmic. The *marziale* marking of the *Andantino* is taken literally, but its precise rhythmic beat is well lifted. The finale is striking for its bustling energy rather than its charm. The *Polish Symphony* has a comparably dynamic first movement, but the central movements are expansively warm, and the ballet-music associations not missed. The finale is strongly full-blooded. *Francesca da Rimini* is very exciting too, and there is some lovely wind playing from the New Philharmonia in the central section.

Symphonies Nos. (i) *2 in C min. (Little Russian);* (ii) *5 in E min., Op. 64.*
(**) Beulah mono 1PD11 [id.]. (i) Cincinnati SO, Goossens; (ii) National SO, Sydney Beer.

Goossens' Cincinnati recording of the *Little Russian Symphony* was one of two which appeared in the early 1940s, a work previously neglected by the record companies. In the Beulah transfer, Goossens' brisk and dramatic reading comes over with splendid bite. Throughout the performance – with a relatively fast second-movement *Andantino marziale* – Goossens' springing of rhythm is most persuasive. If the tempo for the Scherzo is on the cautious side, Goossens' rhythmic resilience and the crisp precision of the playing prevent it from dragging. The Beulah CD is commendably clean and full, capturing a fine sense of presence, with the pitch of the timpani at the start of the second movement remarkably well caught.

By contrast, the pioneer Decca *ffrr* recording of Tchaikovsky's *Fifth* is disappointing, not nearly as good as the Dutton transfer of other NSO recordings from 1944 (see Concerts, below). The swishy surface is very distracting in quiet passages, and the lack of body in the sound is unfair to a system which – as the Dutton disc demonstrates – produced astonishing sound-quality for the time. Though hardly a great conductor, Sidney Beer was highly regarded by the many musicians he worked with, generously spending his wealth on bringing together in the National Symphony Orchestra a remarkable body of players including Dennis Brain, Leon Goossens, Gareth Morris, Reginald Kell and Bernard Walton. As his fresh and direct reading of Tchaikovsky's *Fifth* demonstrates (sadly marred by a 'traditional' 100-bar cut of a key passage in the finale), he was able to inspire them on record to produce electrifying results. There may be the occasional muddle in the strings, but a compelling thrust is there. Readers should be reminded of Abbado's DG coupling of the *Second* and *Fourth Symphonies* (429 527-2) which is one of the best Tchaikovsky bargains in the catalogue.

Symphonies Nos. 4 in F min., Op. 36; 5 in E min., Op. 64; 6 in B min. (Pathétique).
(M) *** DG mono 447 423-2 (2) [id.]. Leningrad PO, Evgeny Mravinsky.
(M) *(*) Teldec/Warner Dig. 4509 95981-2 (2) [id.]. Leipzig GO, Kurt Masur.

Mravinsky re-recorded the three last symphonies of Tchaikovsky with his Leningrad orchestra for DG in stereo, but these legendary earlier, mono performances from the mid-1950s were even more satisfying and they sound marvellously vivid. Indeed on this remastered set the sound is so full and spacious that at times one could almost believe it to be stereo. The earlier readings, without loss of concentration, were less exaggeratedly histrionic, and Mravinsky's speeds for the finale of the *Fourth Symphony* particularly, but also for the *Fifth*, were not as frenetic as in the stereo versions. In the first movement of the *F minor Symphony* the build-up of tension over the rocking string figure brings a very Russian espressivo from the violins, and the climax of the *Andantino* really takes wing. After the balalaika pizzicatos, the centrepiece of the Scherzo is full of personality, with a witty piccolo solo. The opening of the *Fifth* again brings an added dimension of Russian melancholy, and Mravinsky sustains a lyrical intensity throughout the symphony characteristic of all his Tchaikovsky readings. The composer's marking for the slow movement 'con alcuna licenza' is taken very literally: this is a performance of great dramatic extremes, with quite arbitrary changes of tempo, which are seemingly spontaneous, the only drawback for Western ears being the solo horn with his undeniable wobble. The finale has great zest, with blazing perorations from the brass. The emotional power of Mravinsky's *Pathétique* has been equalled elsewhere but never surpassed. The climax of the first movement has tremendous passion, the Scherzo/march is brilliantly pointed yet has plenty of weight, and the finale is deeply eloquent, genuinely touching rather than hysterical. The special rasp of the Russian trombones, which the composer would have recognized, is very telling here, as elsewhere.

Masur's readings are rich and refined, very much reflecting the German symphonic tradition rather than anything Russian. Looking at Tchaikovsky without a hint of hysteria underlines the symphonic strength, as it did with both Klemperer and Boehm; unlike those Germanic predecessors, Masur is warm and smooth rather than rugged. Speeds are spacious and the orchestral sound, somewhat distanced, is well blended with woodwind behind the strings. A major snag in the *Fifth Symphony* is the ponderousness of the slow introductions to the outer movements, while the *Pathétique* has a very low level of tension in spite of consistently fine playing from the Leipzig orchestra. The recording throughout is full and natural but does not really provide the necessary brilliance for this music.

Symphony No. 5 in E min., Op. 64.
*** RCA Dig. 09026 68032-2 [id.]. N. German RSO, Wand – MOZART: *Symphony No. 40.* ***
(M) *** Telarc Dig. CD 82015 [id.]. RPO, Previn – RIMSKY-KORSAKOV: *Tsar Saltan: March.* ***

Symphony No. 5 in E min., Op. 64; 1812 Overture, Op. 49.
* DG Dig. 429 751-2 [id.]. BPO, Ozawa.

Unexpectedly and generously coupled with Mozart's *G minor Symphony*, Wand's live recording brings a unique reading of Tchaikovsky's *Fifth*, one which might be described as the vision of a great Brucknerian, not in any way dull or boring but rapt, refreshing and intense. Wand may almost totally ignore the neurotic side of the composer, with no menace in the slow introduction; but from first to last he clarifies textures and lifts rhythms to have one hearing the music as though spring-cleaned. His own delight shines out as each fresh idea appears. The rapt account of the slow movement then starts with a most beautiful, hushed account of the opening horn solo, and continues from there in an almost devotional manner. The degree of restraint, with pianissimos of breathcatching delicacy, makes the results the more moving, while the climaxes brought by the purified second theme glow even more intensely than usual, with only the second intrusion of the motto theme at all menacing. The waltz lilts easily and delicately, and then the finale brings at last a sense of release. Fate motif and all, this becomes a triumphant work, brilliant and exciting, with the slow march of the coda flowing more easily than usual. In all this Wand owes much to the players of the North German Radio Orchestra, helped by the engineers, so that many details which are normally obscured are brought out with distinctive timbres – notably of the horns – set against a glowing acoustic.

Previn's version brought his first recording with the RPO, the orchestra of which he was already the musical director designate (in 1984), and the quality of the playing is a tribute to a fast-blossoming relationship. Previn's fine concern for detail is well illustrated by the way that the great horn melody in the slow movement (superbly played by Jeff Bryant with firmly focused tone and immaculate control of phrasing) contains the implication of a quaver rest before each three-quarter group, where normally it sounds like a straight triplet. In the first movement rhythms are light and well sprung, and the third movement is sweet and lyrical yet with no hint of mannerism, for Previn adopts a naturally expressive style within speeds generally kept steady, even in the great climax of the slow movement which then subsides into a coda of breathtaking delicacy. Not that Previn misses any of the drama or excitement; and the finale, taken very fast indeed, crowns an outstandingly satisfying reading. The Telarc recording is spectacularly full and wide-ranging, with a rich string patina and superbly tangible brass; it is otherwise naturally balanced within an ideally resonant concert-hall acoustic. Previn has made few finer records than this.

Ozawa's DG account of the *Fifth Symphony* is really rather ordinary. The Berlin Philharmonic seem to have lost the distinctive sound they once commanded, and Ozawa has no really individual interpretative viewpoint. All rather routine, though the recording is good. First choice for the *Fifth* remains with Sian Edwards and the LPO (EMI CD-EMX 2187 – see our main volume).

Symphony No. 6 in B min. (Pathétique), Op. 74; Marche slave, Op. 31.
(BB) ** Tring Dig. TRP 011 [id.]. RPO, Sir Yehudi Menuhin.

(i) *Symphony No. 6 (Pathétique);* (ii) *Swan Lake* (ballet suite).
(B) *** DG 439 456-2 [id.]. (i) Leningrad PO, Mravinsky; (ii) BPO, Karajan.

Mravinsky's very Russian (stereo) account of the *Pathétique* is justly renowned. It is deeply passionate, yet the second subject of the first movement is introduced with much tenderness. The last two movements are very fine indeed; the Scherzo/march is brilliantly pointed, yet has plenty of weight, and the finale is very moving without ever letting the control slip. The first movement could be more richly textured, but its eloquence and power are in no doubt. The present transfer reveals that the 1960 recording was made in Wembley Town Hall, which explains the agreeable ambience, even if at times the Russian brass comes over raucously at climaxes. Karajan's *Swan Lake suite* has characteristic charisma and excitement, with polished BPO playing seemingly aiming for brilliance, and the recording, made a decade after the symphony, has somewhat less allure in the matter of string sonority. But no one could complain of lack of vividness.

Menuhin's performance has its moments of excitement but in the last resort does not leave a very deep impression. In passionate feeling it cannot compare with Mravinsky on DG. The central movements go best, the third more Scherzo than march. Throughout, ensemble could be crisper and, although the very end of the finale is moving, with an eloquent contribution from the RPO brass, the movement's earlier climax is slightly mannered. There is a proper pause before *Marche slave* and this sparklingly alive and spontaneous performance, despite somewhat over-brilliant sound, demonstrates what is missing in the symphony. Recording good, but artificially balanced and rather two-dimensional. Pletnev's Virgin Classics recording with the Russian National Orchestra remains in a class of its own (VC7 59661-2) and was given a Rosette in our main volume.

(i) *Symphony No. 6 (Pathétique); Romeo and Juliet (fantasy overture);* (ii) *The Nutcracker; Sleeping Beauty; Swan Lake:* excerpts.
(BB) *** EMI Seraphim CES5 68537-2 (2) [CDEB 68537]. Philh. O, with (i) Carlo Maria Giulini; (ii) Erfrem Kurtz; with Y. Menuhin.

A splendid super-bargain compilation on Seraphim. Giulini's EMI performance of the *Pathétique* (which has far more individuality and imagination than his later, Los Angeles, digital version for DG) was recorded with the Philharmonia at its peak in 1959, and this reissue still sounds excellent in the CD transfer. Giulini takes a spacious view of the *Pathétique*. There is a degree of restraint in the way he interprets the big melodies of the first and last movements, which are given an almost Elgarian nobility. Yet passionate intensity is conveyed by the purity and concentration of the playing, which equally builds up electric tension and excitement without hysteria. It now comes coupled with his equally fine performance of *Romeo and Juliet*, recorded two years later, a not dissimilar reading and equally superbly played. Giulini's restraint at the opening does not mean any lack of tension, and his spacious arching of the great love theme – whether tenderly gentle and full of moonlight, or ardently soaring – never loses its dignity. The work's climax is dramatically very powerful. The second of the two CDs in this inexpensive package also shows the Philharmonia Orchestra at its absolute peak. The early (late 1950s) stereo sounds astonishingly full, and the performances combine elegance and finesse with sparkle and colour. Here all of the *Nutcracker suite* is included except the *Chinese dance*, an inexplicable omission that would have nicely fitted on, as the programme plays for 77 minutes 39 seconds.

Variations on a Rococo theme (for cello and orchestra), Op. 33.
⊛ (M) *** DG 447 413-2 [id.]. Rostropovich, BPO, Karajan – DVORAK: *Cello concerto.* *** ⊛
(BB) *** EMI Seraphim CES5 68521-2 (2) [CEDB 68521]. (i) Paul Tortelier, N. Sinfonia, Yan
    Pascal Tortelier – DVORAK: *Cello concerto etc.* ***

Rostropovich uses the published score rather than the original version which more accurately reflects
the composer's intentions. But this account, with Karajan's glowing support, is so superbly structured
in its control of emotional light and shade that one is readily convinced that this is the work
Tchaikovsky conceived. Its variations form (at which he was unsurpassed) shows the composer at his
most masterly, with the spontaneous melodic development continually seducing the ear when the
playing is so eloquently elegant. The recording (made in the Jesus-Christus Kirche) is beautifully
balanced and is surely one of the most perfect examples of DG's analogue techniques. It sounds
remarkably real and present in this superb remastering and well deserves its place at the head of
DG's 'Legendary Recordings series'.

A finely wrought account from Tortelier *père*, accompanied by the Northern Sinfonia under
Tortelier *fils*. This is very enjoyable, if perhaps not quite so distinguished as Rostropovich on DG.
Well worth considering when the Dvořák couplings are so generous.

CHAMBER MUSIC

Piano trio in A min., Op. 50.
**(*) Sony Dig. SK 53269 [id.]. Yefim Bronfman, Cho-Liang Lin, Gary Hoffman – ARENSKY: *Piano
    trio No. 1.* **(*)

In some ways the new Sony account from Yefim Bronfman, Cho-Liang Lin and Gary Hoffman is a
clear front-runner. Theirs is a keenly lyrical and expressive performance of this work, which suffers
from a less than ideally balanced recording. Yefim Bronfman is allowed to swamp the texture when
the dynamic level rises, even though, as in the Arensky with which it is coupled, it is obvious that he
is playing with delicacy. Both Cho-Liang Lin and Gary Hoffman are marvellous players whose
refinement and purity give unfailing delight. If you can make allowances for the bias towards the
piano, this will be your preferred choice. Artistically this is an instance of a less than 3-star
recommendation taking precedence over its rivals on purely musical grounds.

String quartet No. 1 in D, Op. 11.
(***) Testament mono SBT 1061 [id.]. Hollywood Qt – GLAZUNOV: *5 Novelettes;* BORODIN: *String
    quartet No. 2 in D.* (***)
(M) *(*) DG Dig. 445 551-2 [id.]. Emerson Qt – BORODIN: *String quartet No. 2* *(*); DVORAK: *String
    quartet No. 12 (American).* **

At the time when the Hollywood Quartet's LP first appeared, in 1953, there were complaints
concerning both the Tchaikovsky and the Borodin, that the sound was a bit steely. Although, for
once, it is possible to speak of later recordings, most notably by the Borodin Quartet (BMG/
Melodiya 74321 18290-2, which at mid-price contains all three *Quartets* plus the *Souvenir de
Florence*), as matching – and even surpassing – the Hollywood group, this present account is still a
performance of real fervour that has a persuasive eloquence which still puts one under its spell. The
sound has been improved, and the addition of the Glazunov, which is new to the catalogue, enhances
its value. The disc runs to one second short of 80 minutes, and the sleeve warns that some CD players
may have difficulty in tracking it. We have not found this to be the case, but some caution may be
necessary on the part of readers with older players.

The Emerson Quartet are immaculate in terms of technical address, but they do not allow the
music to speak for itself. We are rarely unaware of their virtuosity. The DG recording is very clean
and present.

PIANO MUSIC

Children's album, Op. 35.
*(*) Decca Dig. 436 255-2 [id.]. Mustonen – BALAKIREV: *Islamey* **; MUSSORGSKY: *Pictures.* **

The Finnish pianist Olli Mustonen is well recorded by Decca, and the works here are very well
played, too. But in terms of subtlety of keyboard colouring and sheer simplicity of utterance he is no
match for a Pletnev or a Richter. Mustonen's playing is not free from artifice, and there must be a
childlike simplicity blended with the wisdom of maturity if these pieces are to make the right impact.

The seasons, Op. 37b.
** Chan. Dig. CHAN 9309 [id.]. Luba Edlina – BORODIN: *Petite Suite.* **

The seasons, Op. 37b; 6 Pieces, Op. 21.
*** Virgin/EMI Dig. VC5 45042-2 [id.]. Mikhail Pletnev.

Mikhail Pletnev has exceptional feeling for Tchaikovsky and finds more in this music than any other pianist. His insights reveal depths that are hidden to most interpreters and he grips one here from first note to last, not only in *The seasons* but also in the charming and touching *Six morceaux*, Op. 21. This is the best account of both to have reached the gramophone, and it surpasses memories of Lev Oborin's account of the former. Fresh and natural recorded sound.

Luba Edlina's performance of *The seasons* had the misfortune to appear in the immediate wake of Pletnev on Virgin, and is another instance of the better being the enemy of the good. She plays intelligently (and often sensitively) and is well recorded, but Pletnev plays with infinitely more sensitivity and imagination.

VOCAL MUSIC

The Snow Maiden (Snegourotchka): complete incidental music.
*** Chan. Dig. CHAN 9324 [id.]. Irina Mishura-Lekhtman, Vladimir Grishko, Michigan University Musical Soc., Detroit SO, Järvi.

Alexander Ostrovsky's play, *The Snow Maiden*, based on a Russian folk-tale, is best known in the West through Rimsky-Korsakov's opera, but Tchaikovsky, well before his colleague, wrote this incidental music for a stage production of the play at the Bolshoi in 1873, using and adapting folk themes. It remained a favourite work of his and, until Rimsky stole a march on him, he intended to turn it into an opera. The consistent freshness and charm of invention comes out in Järvi's reading of the 19 numbers, lasting just under 80 minutes. It makes a delightful, undemanding cantata, very well played and sung, and vividly recorded. It is instructive of Tchaikovsky's mastery to compare the alternative versions of a single song for the shepherd, Lel, equally effective but one lighter than the other. This now replaces the earlier Chant du Monde version.

SONGS

Ah, if only you could for one moment; Amid the din of the ball; I bless you, forests; I should like in a single word; It happened in the early spring; The love of a dead man; My protector, my angel, my friend; On the golden cornfield; Not a word, O Beloved; We sat together; Whether the day reigns.
** Ph. Dig. 442 536-2 [id.]. Dmitri Hvorostovsky, Mikhail Arkadiev – (with BORODIN); RIMSKY-KORSAKOV; RACHMANINOV: *Songs.* **

Dmitri Hvorostovsky captivated the public at the 'Cardiff Singer of the World' competition, some years ago, but he has not quite lived up to his initial promise. The eleven songs recorded here with Mikhail Arkadiev are not generously enough represented in the catalogue for us to look askance at 'My restless soul', which is what Philips call this CD. Hvorostovsky makes a glorious sound but, while he looks after the sounds, the sense does not always take care of itself. The lack of characterization of which some have complained is well to the fore here. After a while one song sounds all too much like the next. Very good recording.

OPERA

Eugene Onegin: highlights.
(M) **(*) DG Dig. 445 467-2 [id.] (from complete set, with Allen, Freni, Von Otter, Shicoff, Burchuladze; cond. Levine).

Even though the Levine set is not our first choice for the complete opera (which still resides with the Decca Solti version: 417 413-2), this 75-minute selection brings out the superb qualities of the singing. It includes the Letter scene (with Freni a freshly charming Tatyana), the Waltz and Polonaise scenes (with the excellent Leipzig Radio Chorus), also the Act II Duel scene and other key arias, all strongly characterized, and the entire closing scene (11 minutes). The recording, made in the Dresden Lukaskirche, is too closely balanced and unatmospheric; but as a sampler this is clearly valuable.

Mazeppa (complete).
*** DG Dig. 439 906-2 (3) [id.]. Leiferkus, Gorchakova, Larin, Kotscherga, Dyadkova, Stockholm Royal Op. Ch., Gothenburg SO, Neeme Järvi.

Full of magnificent music, *Mazeppa* - dating from 1884, five years after *Eugene Onegin* - has been sadly neglected on disc. Apart from a Russian set, briefly available, this is the first complete recording of the opera, and it satisfyingly fills an important gap with a performance thrillingly sung and vividly conducted. In Britain the opera was not helped by a notorious production at the Coliseum in London involving a chain-saw massacre, and appreciation may well have been discouraged too by the very plot, involving an anti-hero in Mazeppa who is far from being a noble Ukrainian freedom-fighter, whether in the opera or in the Pushkin poem on which it is based. Here Sergei Leiferkus sings the role superbly, with his very Russian-sounding tone a little grainy and tight in the throat, and entirely apt for the character. There is no flaw either among the other principals. Sergei Larin, in what might seem the token tenor part of Andrey, sings with such rich, heroic tone and keen intensity that the character springs to life. Equally, the magnificent, firm-toned bass, Anatoly Kotscherga, father of the heroine, Maria, confirms the high impressions he created in his Boris recording with Abbado. As Maria, Galina Gorchakova also emerges as one of the latter-day stars among Russian singers, with her rich mezzo gloriously caught, even if the final lullaby for her dead lover, Andrei, could be more poignant. Järvi draws electric playing from the Gothenburg orchestra, not least in the fierce battle music which opens Act III. The only disappointment is that the opportunity was not taken of also recording the conventional finale to the opera which Tchaikovsky originally wrote.

Pique Dame (complete).
(M) ** BMG/Melodia 74321 17091-2 (3) [id.]. Atlantov, Milashkina, Levko, Fedosseiev, Borisova, Valaitis, Bolshoi Theatre Soloists, Ch. & O, Mark Ermler.

This was recorded at the Bolshoi in 1974 and now passes from the Philips label to RCA. The sense of presence and atmosphere makes up for shortcomings in the singing, with Vladimir Atlantov as Herman too taut and strained, singing consistently loudly, and with Tamara Milashkina producing curdled tone at the top, not at all girlish. Both those singers, for all their faults, are archetypally Russian, and so – in a much more controlled way – is Valentina Levko, a magnificent Countess, firm and sinister.

Telemann, Georg Philipp (1681–1767)

Oboe concertos: in D min.; E min.; F min.
(M) *** Virgin Veritas/EMI Dig. VER5 61152-2 [id.]. Hans de Vries, Alma Musica Amsterdam, Bob van Asperen – ALBINONI: *Concertos from Op. 9.* ***

Hans de Vries is a very fine player and he produces an attractively full yet refined timbre from his baroque oboe (which dates from 1735). Apart from the stylishness of his phrasing, there are absolutely no intonation problems and the bravura articulation in the moto perpetuo *Allegro molto* second movement of the *E minor Concerto* is astonishingly clean. The authentic accompaniments are alert and stylish and not in the least vinegary. The solo balance seems excessively forward, but that may be partly the result of the acoustic, and the accompanying strings remain well in the picture.

The Frans Brüggen Edition, Volume 10: *Concertos: in C; à 6 in F; Suite (Overture) in A min., TWV 55:a2*
(M) *** Teldec/Warner 4509 97472-2 [id.]. Frans Brüggen, VCM, Harnoncourt.

The *Suite in A minor* is Telemann's equivalent of Bach's *Orchestral Suite No. 2 in B minor*. It is one of his finest works, with some movements given enticing sobriquets: *Les Plaisirs, Air à l'Italien* and *Rejouissance*. The couplings here also show the composer on top form. The *Concerto a flauto dolce* (recorder) *in C* has an opening *Allegretto* melody worthy of Handel, then produces a most effective pizzicato accompaniment. The central movements are hardly less inventive, then the finale is a fast minuet in which Brüggen has chance for nimble bravura. The bassoonist, Otto Fleischmann, is very much the co-star of the ambitious four-movement *Concerto à 6* (for recorder, bassoon and string quartet). This also opens graciously, with a solemn bassoon contribution, and it is the bassoon which leads the dialogue of the following *Vivace*. The part-writing in the finale is particularly felicitous. With superb solo playing and lively but not too abrasive accompaniments from Harnoncourt's VCM, this can be cordially recommended. Excellent 1960s recording, admirably transferred.

Recorder concerto in G min.; Double concerto in E min. for recorder, transverse flute & strings; Double concerto in A min. for recorder, viola da gamba & strings; Double concerto in A for 2 violins in scordatura; Concertos for 4 violins: in C and D.
(B) ** DG Analogue/Dig. 439 444-2 [id.]. Soloists, Col. Mus. Ant., Goebel.

These are chamber concertos rather than solo concertos such as we associate with Bach and Vivaldi. They are diverting and inventive without at any point touching great depths; like so much Telemann, they are pleasing without being memorable. They are eminently well served by these artists, except that the transfer of these analogue recordings from 1979 has produced a string ripieno with an unpleasant edge, which is difficult for the ear to accept. The final *Double concerto* on the disc (for recorder, transverse flute and strings) was recorded digitally in 1986 and the quality here is smoother. But this reissue, for all the obvious vitality of the playing, is strictly for authenticists.

Tafelmusik (Productions 1–3) complete.
(M) *** Teldec/Warner 4509 95519-2 (4) [id.]. Concerto Amsterdam, Frans Brüggen.

Brüggen's Teldec set was made in the mid-1960s. The playing is very good indeed, and the recorded quality, like so many of these Das Alte Werk reissues, is first rate, with the usual proviso that the balance is forward, reducing the range of dynamic. The solo playing is expert (Hermann Baumann and Adriaan van Woudenberg are the impressive horn players in the *Double concerto* in the Third Book). The performances have vitality throughout, the sound is full yet has a spicing of astringency, and this mid-priced reissue compares very favourably with the premium-priced sets listed in our main volume.

CHAMBER MUSIC

Essercizii musicale: Trio sonata in C min. for recorder, oboe and continuo, TWV 42:c2. Der getreue Musik-Meister: Sonata for recorder and violino piccolo, TWV 40:111. Quartets: in A min. for recorder, oboe, violin and continuo, TWV 43:a3; in G for recorder, oboe, violin and continuo, TWV 43:g6; in G min. for recorder, two violins and continuo, TWV 43:g3; in G min. for recorder, violin, viola and continuo, TWV 43:g4; Trio Sonatas: in A min. for recorder, violin and continuo, TWV 42:a1; in A min. for recorder, violin and continuo, TWV 42:a4; in A min. for recorder, oboe and continuo, TWV 42:a6; in C for recorder, pardessus de viole and continuo, TWV 42:c2; in C min. for recorder, oboe and continuo, TWV 42:c7; in D min. for recorder, pardessus de viole and continuo, TWV 42:d7; in D min. for recorder, violin and continuo, TWV 42:d10; in E min. for recorder, oboe and continuo, TWV 42:e6; in F for recorder, pardessus de viole and continuo, TGWV 42:f6; in F for recorder, violin and continuo, TWV 42:f8; in F for recorder, oboe & continuo, TWV 42:f9; in F for recorder, oboe and continuo, TWV 42:f15; in F min. for recorder, violin and continuo, TWV 42:f2; in G min. for recorder, pardessus de viole and continuo, TWV 42:g9.
(M) *** Teldec/Warner 4509 97455-2 (3) [id.]. Kees Boeke, Walter van Hauwe, Hans de Vries, Alice Harnoncourt, Anita Mitterer, Woulter Möller, Bob van Asperen.

There is a great deal of music here, lasting for nearly three hours, but Telemann admirers will find nearly all of it aurally fascinating. The works are cunningly selected from a great range of works of a similar nature, often showing the composer at his most inventive. As can be seen, there is considerable variety of texture, and within there is a fair variety of style. Performances are expressive and lively and there is much unostentatious virtuosity; in this case, scholarship and authenticity do not intimidate the music-making and it communicates readily. As with most Das Alte Werk reissues from the 1970s, the sound is closely balanced, which reduces the range of dynamic, although the playing itself is expert and has plenty of light and shade. This is not music to be played all at once: the listener must make his own choice. But on the second disc, for instance, there is an aurally intriguing *Sonata for recorder and violino piccolo* (from *Der getreue Musik-Meister*) and the ·*Trio sonata* (for recorder, oboe and continuo) and two *Quartets* which follow all show the composer on top form.

The Frans Brüggen Edition, Volume 1: *Essercizii musici: Sonata in C, TWV 41:C5; in D min., TWV 41:d4. Fantasias: in C, TWV 40:2; in D min., TWV 40:4; in F, TWV 40:8; in G min., TWV 40:9; in A min., TWV 40:11; in B flat, TWV 40:12. Der getreue Music-Meister: Canonic sonata in B flat, TWV 41:B3; Sonatas in C, TWV 41:C2; in F, TWV 41:F2; in F min., TWV 41:f1.*
(M) *** 4509 93688-2 [id.]. Frans Brüggen, Anner Bylsma, Gustav Leonhardt.

In this single-disc anthology of Telemann's chamber music Brüggen plays with his usual mastery and, as one would expect from Gustav Leonhardt's ensemble, the performances have polish and authority, and they are excellently recorded. The music itself is highly inventive and entertaining.

(i) *6 Paris quartets (Nouveaux quatuors en six suites)* (1738): *Nos. 1 in D min.; 2 in A min.; 3 in G; 4 in B min.; 5 in A; 6 in E min.;* (ii) (Orchestral) *Suites: in E flat (La Lyra) for strings;* (iii) *in F for solo violin, 2 flutes, 2 oboes, 2 horns, strings & timpani.*
(M) *** Teldec/Warner 4509 92177-2 (2) [id.]. (i) Quadro Amsterdam (Frans Brüggen, Jaap Schröder, Anner Bylsma, Gustav Leonhardt); (ii) Concerto Amsterdam, Frans Brüggen; (i) with Schröder.

In 1730 Telemann published a set of six quartets for violin, flauto traverso, viola da gamba and bass continuo, and these were sufficiently popular to be pirated by the French publishing house, Le Clerk, and reprinted in 1736 – without the composer's permission. Telemann learned by this experience. During a long and fruitful visit to Paris in 1737/8, by virtue of a *Privilège du Roi*, he was able himself to publish a new and even finer set. These are most inventive works, altogether delightful, and the level of inspiration is extraordinarily even. Needless to say, they were an enormous success in Paris, after being first performed by a group consisting of Herr Blavet (flute), Guignon (violin), and the Forcroys, father and son (cello and viola da gamba respectively). Telemann was ecstatic about their music-making: 'If only words were enough to describe the wonderful way in which the quartets were played!' he commented in his memoir of the visit. He would surely have been equally pleased by these performances by the Amsterdam Quartet, impeccably recorded in 1964, 250 years later. When these records first appeared, we commented: 'The performances are of such a high order of virtuosity that they silence criticism, and Frans Brüggen in particular dazzles the listener.' Moreover the recording is of the very first class, beautifully balanced and tremendously alive (like the performances themselves), and the CD transfer, as is invariably the case with these Das Alte Werk reissues, is immaculate. To fill out the space on the second CD, we are offered a pair of orchestral suites. The *Suite in F* is the more ambitious and probably dates from the beginning of the 1730s; the autograph score was found in Dresden, and this was almost certainly one of the works *'per molti strumenti'* written (and not only by Telemann), for the local orchestra, so famous at the time. The concertante scoring makes considerable demands on the various soloists, especially the solo violin, and the horns. The *La Lyra Suite in E flat major* is much earlier, but its invention is hardly less resourceful and in the third movement, *La Vielle*, Telemann gives a more than passable imitation of a hurdy-gurdy.

Paris quartets Nos. 1 in D; 5 in A; Hamburg quartets (1730): Sonata No. 2 in G min.; Suite No. 2 in B min.
(M) *** Virgin/EMI VC5 45045-2 [id.]. Wilbert Hazelzet, Trio Sonnerie.

Hazelzet and the Trio Sommerie, in what is clearly going to be an ongoing series, offer us two of the most attractive *Paris quartets*, plus a pair of the slightly less ambitious earlier quartets, which turn out to be of a higher quality than their reputation led one to expect. The *Air* in the *Second Suite* shows Telemann at his finest in its expressive interplay between flute and violin. The performances are of a high calibre and are representative of modern practice, using original instruments, bringing lighter textures and greater delicacy of style. Thus they have a different kind of charm. Tempi with the Trio Sonnerie are almost always brisker, with both losses and gains; for instance, the *Tendrement* second movement of the *Paris Quartet No. 1* is just that bit more seductive in Amsterdam, while in the *Gai* second movement of *No. 5 in A* Hazelzet probably wins on points. The Trio Sonnerie are led by the expert Monica Huggett, and their timbre is cleaner, more transparent than Brüggen's group; but who can say which is the more authentic? Certainly the results on Virgin Veritas are refreshingly different, while the sound is truthful and again very well balanced.

Thomson, Virgil (1896–1989)

Louisiana Story: suite.
(B) ** Vox Box 116021–2 (2). Westphalian SO, Landau – HANSON: *Symphony No. 6;* MACDOWELL: *Suite No. 2 (Indian);* ROREM: *Symphony No. 3;* SCHUMAN: *Symphony No. 7.* **

Virgil Thomson's score for Robert Flaherty's film, *Louisiana Story*, is probably his best-known work and certainly his most recorded. This serviceable account comes in a useful compilation of American works, though it must be conceded that few are really first rate or representative of the composers at their best. This piece is probably the only exception.

Ticheli, Frank (born 1958)

Postcard; Radiant voices.
*** Koch Dig. 3-7250-2 [id.]. Pacific SO, Carl St Clair - CORIGLIANO: *Piano concerto.* ***

Frank Ticheli, composer-in-residence to this Pacific orchestra largely made up of musicians from film studios, here offers two warm, unproblematic works, ingeniously and wittily argued, full of engaging echoes of composers from Bartók and Copland to John Adams, with a flavouring of Walton in the jazz rhythms. First-rate performances and sound. An attractive coupling for the ambitious, similarly communicative *Piano concerto* of John Corigliano.

Tippett, Michael (born 1905)

Symphony No. 1; (i) *Piano concerto.*
*** Chan. Dig. CHAN 9333 [id.]. (i) Howard Shelley; Bournemouth SO, Richard Hickox.

Those who thought that Sir Colin Davis's pioneering recordings of the first three Tippett symphonies were definitive (latterly issued with Solti's reading of No. 4 in a three-disc box – Decca 425 646-2) will find fresh revelation in Richard Hickox's readings, not least in the *First Symphony*. Hickox may be less biting, but he gives an extra spring to the chattering motor rhythms at the start, and from then on the Bournemouth performance is regularly warmer and more expressive, as in the distinctive trumpet melody in the slow movement. In the last two movements too, Hickox finds more fun and jollity in Tippett's wild inspirations. The *Piano concerto*, with Howard Shelley a superb soloist, brings another revelatory performance, warm and affectionate but purposeful too, rebutting any idea that with their fluttering piano figurations these are meandering arguments. Warm, full, atmospheric sound, with the piano balanced within the orchestra instead of in front of it. This must now be a first recommendation, and it certainly displaces the Ogdon.

Symphony No. 2; New Year (opera): *suite.*
*** Chan. Dig. CHAN 9299 [id.]. Bournemouth SO, Richard Hickox.

As in the *First Symphony*, Hickox with extra lift in the rhythms brings out the joy behind Tippett's inspirations without ever losing a sense of purpose. This may be a less biting performance than Sir Colin Davis's on Decca, but it is consistently warmer, with extra fun and wit in the third-movement Scherzo. The coupling is also valuable, when Tippett's own suite from his last opera, *New Year*, brings out the colour and wild energy of this inspiration of his mid-eighties. If anything, the music seems the more telling for being shorn of the composer's own problematic libretto. The obbligato instruments – saxophones, electric guitars and kit drums – are most evocatively balanced in the warm, atmospheric recording.

(i) *Symphony No. 3. Praeludium for brass, bells and percussion.*
*** Chan. Dig. CHAN 9276 [id.]. Bournemouth SO, Richard Hickox; (i) with Faye Robinson.

In two long movements, each lasting nearly half an hour, the *Third Symphony* is not easy to hold together and, though Richard Hickox and the Bournemouth orchestra cannot match the original performers, Sir Colin Davis and the LSO, in sheer power, they find more light and shade over the long span. Hickox gives wit to the Stravinskian syncopations in the first section and then dedicatedly carries concentration through the pauses of the slow second half of the movement. Hickox brings fun to the galumphing introduction to the second movement – 'Like a juggler with five different objects in the air at once,' said Tippett – leading to the sequence of blues sections with soprano soloist. Though Faye Robinson's voice is not as warm or firm as Heather Harper's was, she is more closely in tune with the blues idiom, helping to build the sequence to a purposeful conclusion in the long final scena. The recording is full and warm to match. The *Praeludium for brass, bells and percussion* was written in 1962 for the 40th anniversary of the BBC, a gruff, angular piece hardly suggesting celebration, but none the less welcome in a well-played performance.

Symphony No. 4; Fantasia concertante on a theme of Corelli; (i) *Fantasia on a theme of Handel* (for piano and orchestra).
*** Chan. Dig. CHAN 9233 [id.]. (i) Howard Shelley; Bournemouth SO, Hickox.

Tippett wrote his *Fourth Symphony* in 1976–7 for Sir George Solti and the Chicago Symphony Orchestra, a brilliant virtuoso piece in a single movement of sharply defined sections, broadly representing a life-cycle from birth to death. Richard Hickox and the Bournemouth Symphony are less weighty than those originators, but they are generally warmer and more atmospheric. In place of Solti's fiery brilliance, Hickox brings an element of wildness to the fast sections and he also finds a vein of tenderness in the meditative sections. The well-known *Corelli Variations* have never sounded quite as sumptuous and resonant as here, and the disc is generously rounded off with a welcome rarity: the early *Handel Fantasia for piano and orchestra*, conceived between the *Concerto for double string orchestra* and the oratorio, *A Child of our Time*. Howard Shelley is most convincing in the weighty piano-writing, like his accompanists giving the music warmth. Full-blooded sound to match. Solti's own brilliant Chicago recording of the *Symphony* (coupled with the exotic *Byzantium*) is still available (Decca 433 668-2).

(i) *A Child of our Time* (oratorio); (ii) *The Knot Garden* (opera; complete).
*** Ph. 446 331-2 (2) [id.]. (i) Norman, J. Baker, Cassily, Shirkey-Quirk, BBC Singers, BBC Ch. Soc. & SO; (ii) Herinx, Minton, Gomez, Barstow, Carey, Tear, Hemsley, ROHCG O; C. Davis.

We have had to wait a long time for Sir Colin Davis's superb recorded performance of *The Knot Garden* to appear on CD; but now it arrives, aptly coupled with Davis's 1975 recording of the oratorio, *A Child of our Time*, on a pair of well-filled CDs, but at full price. As Tippett has grown older, so his music has grown wilder, and those accustomed to the ripe qualities of *The Midsummer Marriage* may be disconcerted by the relative astringency of the later opera, a garden conversation-piece to a libretto by the composer, very much in the style of a T. S. Eliot play. The result, characteristically, is a mixture, with the mandarin occasionally putting on a funny hat, as in the jazz and blues passages for the male lovers, Dov and Mel. The brief central Act, called *Labyrinth*, has characters thrown together two at a time in a revolving maze, a stylized effect which contributes effectively to Tippett's process of psychiatric nerve-prodding. But the whole thing projects splendidly here when recorded so vividly, even if the sound itself is a little dry. The recording of *A Child of our Time* is also cleanly defined, here suiting Davis's performance, more sharply focused than most. Speeds are on the fast side, both in the spirituals, which here take the place that Bach gave to chorales, and in the other numbers. Consistently Davis allows himself far less expressive freedom than the composer in his outstanding Collins version (1339-2) and he misses the tenderness which can make the setting of *Steal away* at the end of Part 1 so moving. He seems determined that there shall be no suspicion of sentimentality in this commentary on a news story of the late 1930s. With Davis the 'Time' of the title is not just the 'Thirties or any period of comfortable nostalgia, but now. He has a superb quartet of soloists; and their fine contribution, together with that of the chorus, matches this approach. The result makes a refreshing alternative to the composer's own account.

Tomlinson, Ernest (born 1924)

Aladdin: 3 dances (Birdcage dance; Cushion dance; Belly dance); Comedy overture; Cumberland Square; English folk-dance suite No. 1; Light music suite; Passepied; (i) *Rhapsody and rondo for horn and orchestra; Rigadoon; Shenandoah* (arrangement).
*** Marco Polo Dig. 8.223513 [id.]. (i) Richard Watkins; Slovak RSO (Bratislava), composer.

This second collection of the light music of Ernest Tomlinson is every bit as enjoyable as the first. The opening *Comedy overture* is racily vivacious, and there are many charming vignettes here, delectably tuneful and neatly scored, the oboe often used very felicitously. *Dick's maggot* from the suite of English folk-dances is very catchy and the pastiche dance movements are nicely elegant. The *Pizzicato humoresque* (from the *Light music suite*) is every bit as winning as other, more famous pizzicato movements, and in the *Rhapsody and rondo* for horn Tomlinson quotes wittily from both Mozart and Britten. The composer finally lets his hair down in the rather vulgar *Belly dance*, but the concert returns to grace for the charming closing *Georgian miniature*. As before, the playing is elegant and polished, its scale perfectly judged, and the recording is first class.

Truscott, Harold (1914–1992)

Symphony in E; Elegy for string orchestra; Suite in G.
*** Marco Polo 8.223674 [id.]. Nat. SO of Ireland, Gary Brain.

Here is another British symphonic name to conjure with. Harold Truscott was Principal Lecturer of Music at Huddersfield Polytechnic until 1979. In the 1950s he broadcast as a pianist for the BBC, specializing in Schubert. Two of his own piano sonatas were heard on the radio in 1969, played by John Ogdon. But in general his music was a casualty (like the work of so many other 'traditional' composers) of the William Glock regime in the 1960s. This record suggests that his writing, for all its eclectic influences, has genuine individuality and power. The moving *Elegy* for strings, elliptical in structure, is little short of a masterpiece, and the three-movement *Symphony* (premièred as a complete work on this record), which dates from the end of the 1940s, is a powerfully argued piece. It has an outstandingly cogent *Molto Adagio* finale (almost as long as the two other movements put together) which creates a commanding sense of apotheosis. The *Suite in G* shows Truscott's vivid orchestral sense, with the brass opening the piece dramatically and then making a piercing interjection into the melancholy woodwind *Fughetta* which follows. The *Molto Andante* confirms the intensity of feeling the composer could create with string textures. Gary Brain seems to have an instinctive feel for all these works and holds together the turbulent moods of the first movement of the *Symphony* coherently, while the Dublin orchestra rise to the occasion and play with much conviction throughout. The recording is full-bodied, with the resonance at the service of the music but without clouding textures. Well worth exploring. Start with the very touching *Elegy*, but the *Symphony* will repay repeated listening, too.

Turina, Joaquin (1882–1949)

La Oración del torero, Op. 34.
(***) Testament mono SBT 1053 [id.]. Hollywood Qt – CRESTON: *Quartet;* DEBUSSY: *Danses sacrées;* RAVEL: *Intro and allegro;* VILLA-LOBOS: *Quartet No. 6.* (***)

When this first performance appeared in the early 1950s, one critic hailed it as making Turina's famous piece sound better than it really was. Certainly it is difficult to imagine it being played with greater expressive eloquence or more perfect ensemble. It comes as part of a valuable and beautifully transferred anthology devoted to the incomparable Hollywood Quartet.

Ullmann, Viktor (1898–c. 1944)

(i) *Der Kaiser von Atlantis* (opera; complete); (ii) *Hölderlin Lieder: Abendphantasie; Der Frühling; Wo bist du?*
*** Decca Dig. 440 854-2 [id.].(i) Kraus, Berry, Vermillion, Lippert, Mazura, Leipzig GO, Lothar Zagrosek; (ii) Vermillion, Alder.

In Decca's *Entartete Musik* series, *Der Kaiser von Atlantis* ('The Emperor of Atlantis') stands out as a work actually written in a Nazi concentration camp. Like thousands of other Jews, Viktor Ullmann was imprisoned in Terezin (or Theresienstadt), the camp which the Nazis cynically presented to the world as 'a model ghetto' but which in fact was a transit camp for Auschwitz. It was a closed community of intellectuals, which ironically enabled Ullmann – hardly successful as a composer before the war – to fulfil himself in his music, most strikingly in this opera for seven voices and thirteen instruments, lasting just under an hour. With the central character, Kaiser Overall, a caricature of Hitler, introduced by a parody of the German national anthem, it is not surprising that the SS banned the planned performance of the piece in the camp, but happily the score has survived. Sharp, Weill-like writing, with the chance availability of such instruments as organ and banjo heightening the flavour, is tempered by echoes of Zemlinsky and Berg. The result is a strongly drawn sequence involving not just Overall but the key figure of Death, Harlequin, a Drummer-girl and two soldiers, one of them, Bubikopf, sung by a soprano. The death theme from Suk's *Asrael Symphony* is the centre of a complex web of references intended for the Terezin audience, a cultural elite. The mixture of satire with an element of poignancy is undoubtedly moving, not least in the use of Luther's hymn, *Ein feste Burg*, in the finale. Zagrosek conducts an outstanding performance with a characterful, well-cast team of soloists, led superbly by the baritone, Michael Kraus, as Overall. The three settings of Hölderlin, written in the same year, are mellower in style, with Ullmann's admiration of Berg flowering in warmly romantic, tonal writing. They are beautifully sung by Iris Vermillion, accompanied at the piano by Jonathan Alder. Excellent recording. The single CD comes in a box with libretto, text and translations, plus copious notes.

Vainberg, Moishei (born 1919)

The Golden Key (ballet), *Op. 55: suites Nos. 1–3; suite 4:* excerpts.
*** Olympia OCD 473 [id.]. Bolshoi Theatre O, Mark Ermler.

The Golden Key is a full-length ballet dating from 1955, based on a story by Alexis Tolstoy. The scenario concerns a troupe of puppets with a Petrushka or Pierrot-like figure at the centre. This generous selection (not far short of 80 minutes) gives a good idea of the quality of Vainberg's invention and his skill in making telling character-studies. One does not necessarily want to play all 26 of the movements at one go, without the benefit of stage action, but there is some arresting music here and it is well performed by Bolshoi forces under Mark Ermler, and decently recorded.

Symphonies Nos. (i) 6 in A min.; (ii) 10 in A min.
** Olympia stereo/mono OCD 471 [id.]. (i) Moscow Ch. School Boys' Ch., Moscow PO, Kondrashin; (ii) Moscow CO, Barshai.

Moishei (since 1985 Mieczyslaw) Vainberg is enormously prolific and has some 22 symphonies to his credit. In *A Guide to the Symphony* (Oxford, 1995), David Fanning speaks of 'a steady flow of expressive, inventive and expertly controlled music, much indebted to, but never wholly overshadowed by Shostakovich'. In the days of LP the only symphony of his briefly in circulation on EMI/ Melodiya was the *Fourth*, which also showed the influence of Hindemith and Honegger, coupled with a very Shostakovichian *Violin concerto*. The *Sixth Symphony* is a dark and powerful work, once available on a Melodiya LP, and ultimately more satisfying than the *Tenth* for strings, whose invention does not fully sustain its length. Both works are nevertheless worth exploring and, though the recordings are analogue (and, in the case of the *Sixth*, only in mono), they are, if not three-star, more than acceptable. The performances under Kirill Kondrashin and Rudolf Barshai are persuasive and authoritative.

Vaughan Williams, Ralph (1872–1958)

English folksong suite; Fantasia on a theme by Thomas Tallis; Fantasia on Greensleeves; (i) *The lark ascending. The Wasps: Overture; Entr'acte No. 1; March of Kitchen Utensils.*
(BB) ** Tring Dig. TRP 031 [id.]. (i) Jonathan Carney; RPO, Christopher Seaman.

The highlight here is a rapt account of the idyllic *Lark ascending*, with Jonathan Carney the highly sensitive soloist often sustaining a haunting pianissimo solo line. The *Tallis fantasia* is also a fine performance, both ethereal and passionate; but this, like the whole programme, is affected by too close microphones in a reverberant acoustic. The dynamic range of the recording is realistically wide, but fortissimos inevitably bring fierceness, even though the basic ambience is spacious.

Fantasia on Greensleeves; Fantasia on a theme of Thomas Tallis.
(BB) *** RCA Navigator 74321 17905-2. Phd. Ch. & O, Ormandy – HOLST: *The Planets.* (***)

Gloriously ripe performances of both works from Ormandy and the Philadelphia strings, recorded in 1970 and 1972 respectively. Subtlety is not the strong point and the second orchestra in the *Tallis fantasia* is made to seem too close; but the warm intensity of the playing confounds such criticism and there is a gravity in the way Ormandy presents the famous *Greensleeves* melody that is very endearing. There are few recordings that in their resonant opulence show the body of tone the Philadelphia strings could command at this time.

Fantasia on Greensleeves; (i) *The lark ascending.*
(B) *** DG 439 464-2 [id.]. (i) Zukerman; ECO, Barenboim – BRITTEN: *Serenade*; DELIUS: *On hearing the first cuckoo in spring* etc. ***

This DG Classikon bargain CD makes a most attractive anthology. Zukerman's account of *The lark ascending* has a uniquely rapturous pastoralism and it is beautifully played and recorded.

Fantasia on a theme of Thomas Tallis.
(BB) **(*) BBC Radio Classics BBCRD 9107 [id.]. New Philh. O, Stokowski (with Concert) –
    BRAHMS: *Symphony No. 4;* RAVEL: *Rapsodie espagnole.* **(*)
(BB) ** BBC Radio Classics BBCRD 9119 [id.]. New Philh. O, Sir Adrian Boult (with Concert) –
    LEIGH: *Harpsichord concertino;* FINZI: *Clarinet concerto* etc. **(*)

The Stokowski performance comes from an Albert Hall concert in May 1974 and is scrupulously prepared. Stokowski recorded the piece commercially in 1952, and this later reading is marginally more expansive. There is a characteristic sophistication of texture and a strong sense of atmosphere, while dynamic shadings and nuances are meticulous. But the BBC sound, though warm, is not transparent; the close microphones restrict full dynamic expansion of climaxes. All the same, this is an inexpensive disc, well worth investigating, not least for the sake of the Brahms *Symphony*.

Sir Adrian's performance with the New Philharmonia comes from a Cheltenham Festival concert of 1972. Strong, atmospheric and firmly focused, rather bottom-heavy recording. Not superior to any of Boult's commercial recordings either artistically or technically, but again this is part of an attractive bargain concert which includes attractive concertante works by Finzi and Walter Leigh. However, first choice in this repertoire still rests with Christopher Warren-Green, whose mid-priced Virgin disc with the London Chamber Orchestra offers both the *Tallis Fantasia* and *Greensleeves*, plus a radiant *Lark ascending* and more string music by Elgar – see our main volume (CUV5 61126-2).

Fantasia on a theme by Thomas Tallis; Five variants of Dives and Lazarus; In the Fen country; Norfolk Rhapsody No. 1 in E min.; Variations for orchestra (orch. Jacob); *The Wasps: Overture.*
**(*) Ph. Dig. 442 427-2 [id.]. ASMF, Marriner.

Opening with a bright and brisk account of *The Wasps overture*, this collection is valuable in including the rare *Variations*, written as a brass band test-piece in 1957 and skilfully orchestrated by

Gordon Jacob. Not a masterpiece, but worth having on disc. The other works are very well played; but *Tallis*, though beautiful, lacks the last degree of ethereal intensity. Marriner makes up with the climax of *Dives and Lazarus* which is richly expansive, and he and the ASMF are at their finest in the gentle, evocative opening and closing sections of the *First Norfolk rhapsody*. *In the Fen country* brings more fine playing; and overall this is an enjoyable programme, if not showing these artists at their very finest. The recording too, though spacious, is good rather than outstanding.

Job (A masque for dancing); The Wasps overture.
*(**) Everest/Vanguard EVC 9006 [id.]. LPO, Boult (with ARNOLD: *4 Scottish dances*: cond. composer **(*)).

The Everest performance of *Job* under the work's dedicatee was in fact Boult's second LP of Vaughan Williams's ballet (which was refused by Diaghilev as being 'too English and too old-fashioned') since Boult had recorded it previously in mono for Decca. The Everest version is sensitive and spontaneous but, unusually for this label, the recording, although basically spacious, is made aggressive at climaxes because of the close microphoning of the brass, which sound strident, while the massed strings are somewhat tight. Now we discover that the recording venue was the Royal Albert Hall, and obviously the engineers could not cope with the hall's notorious resonance. *The Wasps overture* was done at Walthamstow and sounds full and unconfined. What an outstanding performance, too, with plenty of sparkle but with a very broad tempo for the beautiful secondary theme, both when it first appears on the strings and when reprised later on the brass and wind. Its timing is 10 minutes 26 seconds, whereas Sargent used to take it at a spanking pace in order to fit it on two 78-r.p.m. sides (at about two minutes less). Malcolm Arnold conducts his own *Scottish dances* with élan and is especially persuasive in the third with its glorious picture of the Highland scenery, which produced one of loveliest tunes the composer ever wrote. This is properly expansive; otherwise the brightly vivid sound is not quite as smooth as the best Everest reissues. There are much more satisfying versions of *Job* on CD, notably from Barry Wordsworth (Collins 1124-2) and Hickox (EMI CDC7 54421-2) – see our main volume.

Symphonies Nos. 1–9; (i) *Flos campi; Serenade to music.*
(M) *** EMI Dig./Analogue CD-BOXVW 1 (6) [id.]. Soloists, Liverpool Philharmonic Ch., Royal Liverpool PO, Vernon Handley; (i) with Christopher Balmer.

Handley's set consists of the six individual CDs in a handsome blue slipcase, and it will especially suit those wanting modern, digital sound; only the *Sinfonia Antartica* is analogue – and that is still a fine modern recording, offering also the orchestral version of the *Serenade to music* as a fill-up. In all his Vaughan Williams recordings Handley shows a natural feeling for expressive rubato and is totally sympathetic. Many of his performances are first or near-first choices, and No. 5 is outstanding in every way, receiving a Rosette in our main volume. This disc also includes a very successful account of *Flos campi*.

A London Symphony (No. 2); Partita for double string orchestra.
(BB) *** Belart mono/stereo 461 008-2 [id.]. LPO Sir Adrian Boult.

Boult's 1952 recording of the *London Symphony* has great atmosphere and intensity. His later, EMI performance is warmer, but the voltage of this first LP version is very compelling, bringing the feeling of a live performance. The mono sound is spacious and basically full, but the violins sound very thin above the stave, and the remastering has not improved matters, especially in the glorious slow movement. But such is the magnetism of the music-making that the ear readily adjusts. The *Partita* was recorded in the earliest days of stereo in 1956. It is not one of the composer's most remarkable works (it was originally a double string trio) and it does not inspire Boult as does the symphony; but it is well played and the string sound here is more agreeable, if not outstanding.

Symphonies Nos. 2 (A London Symphony); 8 in D min.
*(*) Teldec/Warner 4509 90858 [id.]. BBC SO, Andrew Davis.

The Teldec recording has magnificent presence and definition. This would be a front runner if the performances had been of equal quality. Of course there are good things – in particular the Scherzo of the *London Symphony*. There is impressive atmosphere at the very beginning of the symphony, but as a whole this is no match in terms of grip or concentration for the best rivals – and certainly not for Barbirolli's remarkable EMI (originally Pye) version, also coupled with No. 8. Though omitted from our main volume, as it is currently unavailable, we hope it will soon be restored to circulation.

Symphonies Nos. 3 (Pastoral); 6 in E min.
(BB) **(*) Naxos Dig. 8.550733 [id.]. Bournemouth SO, Kees Bakels.

Kees Bakels' serenely expressive account of the *Pastoral* has moments of drama to heighten its quiet intensity of atmosphere. There is much lovely orchestral playing, with the soloists in the Bournemouth Symphony Orchestra (notably the oboe, violin and trumpet) very sympathetic to the music's subtle, lyrical resonance. The account of the *Sixth* does not catch the degree of underlying menace in the *Lento* second movement that seemed so prophetic at the symphony's broadcast première (under Boult) but the performance overall has plenty of life and vigour, and Bakels sustains the epilogue with an ethereal, glowing pianissimo. First-rate Naxos recording in both works. However, Previn on RCA remains first choice for the *Pastoral Symphony* (GD 90503), while in the *Sixth* Andrew Davis's Telarc CD is also highly recommendable (9031 73127-2).

Symphony No. 4 in F min.; Fantasia on Greensleeves; Fantasia on a theme of Thomas Tallis;
(i) *Serenade to music.*
(M) *** Sony SMK 47638 [id.]. NYPO, Bernstein; (i) with Addison, Amara, Farrell, Chookasian,
Tourel, Verrett-Carter, Bressler, Tucker, Vickers, London, Flagello, Bell.

This is one of the most rewarding of the reissues in the Bernstein Edition. The account of the *Fourth Symphony* is strangely impressive. Bernstein's first movement is slower than usual but powerful and very well controlled; he captures the flavour and intensity of the score as well as the brooding intensity of the slow movement. The New York orchestra play very well indeed, particularly in the extremely characterful Scherzo. This is a thoroughly competitive reading, freshly thought out and with a compelling integrity to commend it. The 1965 Avery Fisher recording, though not first class, is very well transferred. The *Tallis fantasia*, spacious and essentially serene, is just short of being romantic but retains its elegiac atmosphere. Here the venue is the more resonant Manhattan Center, and the 1976 sound is full and rich-textured. The *Greensleeves fantasia*, also taken expansively, uses a solo violin in its central section. The performance of the *Serenade* features a star-studded cast and, though they are rather forwardly balanced, the ambience has agreeable warmth and the performance catches the work's radiance, with Adele Addison singing Portia's closing solo (*Soft stillness and the night*) quite beautifully.

Symphonies Nos. (i) *4 in F min.;* (ii) *5 in D.*
(M) (***) Dutton Lab. mono CDAX 8011 [id.]. (i) BBC SO, composer; (ii) Hallé O, Barbirolli.
** Teldec/Warner Dig. 4509 90844-2 [id.]. BBC SO, Andrew Davis.

Vaughan Williams may not have been a great conductor, but when in 1937 he recorded his violent *Fourth Symphony* with the BBC Symphony Orchestra, then at its pre-war peak, he proved a bitingly urgent inspirer. This historic recording has been transferred to CD by Michael Dutton in astonishingly full-bodied sound, bringing out the high voltage of the playing, never quite matched since on record. Aiming to shock, RVW said he wasn't sure he liked the piece, but it was what he meant. After that, the *Fifth Symphony*, inspired by Bunyan, held no shocks; but, more than anyone, Sir John Barbirolli in this première recording of 1944, made in the year following its first performance, brings out a rare passion behind the seamless pastoral idiom. The great climaxes in the first and third movements are more red-blooded than in any recordings since. Though the string-playing of the wartime Hallé may not be as immaculate as one would expect today, this inspired performance, vividly transferred, has one consistently magnetized.

Though Andrew Davis draws beautiful, refined playing from the BBC orchestra in both symphonies, there is a lack of dramatic tension, which – particularly in the violent No. 4 – prevents the performance from catching fire. One can pick out many passages which, with the help of superb recorded sound, are as beautiful as any ever recorded, but the parts do not add up to a satisfying whole.

Symphony No. 9 in E min.
**(*) Everest/Vanguard EVC 9001 [id.]. LPO, Boult – ARNOLD: *Symphony No. 3.* **(*)

Boult's first stereo record of the *Sixth* on Everest is prefaced on CD by a brief speech from the conductor, regretting the composer's death seven months before the recording was undertaken. The sound was very good for its day with a wide dynamic range, and it sounds even better now, although the actual tonal quality has not the warmth and lustre of more recent versions of the work. Boult's interpretation changed very little over the years; this early version seems tauter than the later remake for EMI (CDM7 64021-2), but this may be partly the effect of the less expansive sound. Slatkin and the Philharmonia remain a first recommendation for a coupling of the *Eighth* and *Ninth Symphonies* (RCA 09026 61196-2).

Alfred Deller Edition: Arrangements of folksongs (with Deller Consort, Desmond Dupré, lute): *An acre of land; Bushes and briars; Ca' the yowes; The cuckoo and the nightingale; The dark eyed sailor;*

Down by the riverside; A Farmer's son so sweet; Greensleeves; John Dory; Just as the tide was flowing; The jolly ploughboy; Loch Lomond; The lover's ghost; My boy Billy; The painful plough; The spring time of the year; The turtle dove; Ward the Pirate; Wassail song.
(M) ** Van. 08.5073.71 [id.].

These highly artistic folksong settings can be effectively performed either by choir or by soloists. Although basically Deller allocates one voice to each part, there are some doublings where – for example – the two voices do not blend well. The spirit in which these settings are performed is, however, admirable. Deller himself sings *Down by the riverside* as a solo, with lute accompaniment, and this is effectively followed by the gentle choral version of *Bushes and briars*. Similarly, Deller's *My boy Billy* is followed by the atmospheric *The spring time of the year*, and the solo *The cuckoo and the nightigale* by the choral *Loch Lomond*, one of the most enjoyable arrangements here. The recording is a little dry, but the stereo adds to the sense of atmosphere.

Veracini, Francesco Maria (1690–1768)

Overtures (Suites) Nos. 1 in B flat; 2 in F; 3 in B flat; 4 in F; 6 in B flat.
*** DG Dig. 439 937-2 [id.]. Col. Mus. Ant., Goebel.

The flamboyant and eccentric Florentine composer, who spent almost the entire middle period of his life working away from home, successfully penetrated and then established himself at the Dresden court (something Vivaldi never managed to do) and moved on only after (apparently) throwing himself from an upstairs window in 1722. A further catastrophe awaited him two decades later when, after a final visit to London, his ship was wrecked in the Channel on his journey home to Italy, and he lost his two treasured Stainer violins, which he had nicknamed St Peter and St Paul. He spent the last years of his life in charge of the music in two churches in Florence, where he died in 1768. Dresden represented the peak of his career, and these concertos were composed for the Dresden court orchestra, probably around 1716. Their character brings a curious amalgam of Italian volatility and German weight, and they have something in common with the orchestral suites of Telemann. Yet Telemann loved instrumental light and shade, whereas Veracini favoured tutti scoring and, although oboes and bassoons are included, they are used to reinforce and colour the texture rather than provide solo instrumental contrast. There is of course the interplay of counterpoint, but Veracini seemed to relish the favourite Dresden device of the time, a unison minuet, with the fullness of orchestral sonority paramount. The music is strong in personality and there is no shortage of ideas, but energy is more important than expressive lyricism, with usually a single brief sarabande to provide contrast as the centrepiece of up to half-a-dozen dance movements. *No. 4 in F* is entirely rhythmic and a good example of what Veracini can do within this framework; but *No. 3 in B flat* is the most appealing and varied, with its contrapuntal central *Allegro* a comparative lollipop, with its engaging imitative interplay coming just before the customary vibrant *Sarabande*. The Musica Antiqua Cologne, with their pungent tuttis, seem custom-made for this repertoire, playing with consistent vitality and obviously enjoying the music's Germanic flavour. The recording is first class, within a spacious acoustic.

12 Sonate accademiche, Op. 2.
*** Hyp. Dig. CDA 66871/3 (3). Locatelli Trio.

Alongside his fame as a composer, Veracini was renowned as a master of the violin, and he knew it, boasting that there 'was but one God and one Veracini', so that even Tartini was initimidated by his prowess. The twelve *Sonate accademiche* date from 1744. They are much more Italianate than the overtures, though German influence remains strong. The writing has a rhapsodic exuberance and drive, in common with the orchestral works and, like the overtures, the format is heavily laced with dance movements. But there are touching lyrical interludes and some really lovely slow movements. The *Siciliana* which opens *No. 5 in G minor* is a fine example, and this same work includes both an *Andante* and a searching *Largo*. Sonata *No. 9 in A* even includes a *Scozzesse*, introducing the air, *Tweedside*, with reel-like variations. The *Tempo giusto* opening of *No. 11 in E* anticipates a Mozart piano concerto, and then, after a striking *Largo e nobile,* we are reminded of Boccherini in the *affettuoso* Minuet. But the last *Sonata* is quite masterly, opening with a descending minor scalic theme, which is first used for a *Passacaglia*, then for a *Capriccio cromatico*, and finally provides the basis for an ambitious closing *Ciaccona* (nearly six minutes long) which ends the piece more cheerfully, with much opportunity for bravura. In short, these are fascinatingly inventive works, showing their little-known composer as a great deal more than a historical figure. The Locatelli Trio, led by Elizabeth Wallfisch, are a first-class group and their authentic style, strongly etched, is full of joy in the music's vitality, while the composer's lyrical side is most persuasively revealed. Paul Nicholson's continuo is very much a part of the picture, especially in the works using an organ – which is very pleasingly balanced. The recording is vividly real and immediate.

Verdi, Giuseppe (1813–1901)

Overtures and Preludes: *Aida* (Prelude); *Alzira; Aroldo* (Overtures); *Attila; Un ballo in maschera* (Preludes); *La battaglia di Legnano; Il Corsaro* (Sinfonias); *Ernani* (Prelude); *La forza del destino; Un giorno di regno; Giovanna d'Arco* (Sinfonias); *Luisa Miller* (Overture); *Macbeth; I Masnadieri* (Preludes); *Nabucco* (Overture); *Oberto, Conte di San Bonifacio* (Sinfonia); *Rigoletto; La Traviata* (Preludes); *I vespri siciliani* (Overture).
(M) *** DG 439 972-2 (2) [id.]. BPO, Karajan.

It is good to have Karajan's complete set of Overtures and Preludes back in the catalogue. The 1975 recording was one of the very best made in the Philharmonie: the sound combines vividness with a natural balance and an attractive ambience. As we have commented before, the performances have an electricity, refinement and authority that sweep all before them. The little-known overtures, *Alzira, Aroldo* and *La battaglia de Legnano* are all given with tremendous panache and virtuosity. Every bar of this music is alive and, with all the exuberance, Karajan skirts any suggestion of vulgarity. Try the splendid *Nabucco*, or the surprisingly extended (8-minute) *Giovanna d'Arco* to discover the colour and spirit of this music-making, with every bar spontaneously alive, while there is not the faintest suggestion of routine in the more familiar items.

Overtures: *La forza del destino; Nabucco; I vespri siciliani. La Traviata: Preludes, Acts I & III.*
(M) ** Mercury 434 345-2 [id.]. LSO, Antal Dorati – ROSSINI: *Overtures.* (*)

Dorati is an unexpected conductor in Verdi, and these performances are red-blooded as well as fresh and clear, if not distinctive. The LSO playing is good and the dramatic passages in the earlier overtures have both power and brilliance. The *Traviata Preludes*, however, are somewhat lacking in tension and Italianate warmth. The 1957 recording, made at Watford Town Hall, is far superior to the lustreless Rossini coupling with which these performances are saddled.

Requiem Mass.
🏵 (B) (***) DG Double mono 439 684-2 (2) [id.]. Stader, Dominguez, Carelli, Sardi, St Edwidge's Cathedral Ch., Berlin RIAS SO, Fricsay – ROSSINI: *Stabat Mater.* (***)
(M) (***) Dutton Lab. mono CDLX 7010 [id.]. Caniglia, Gigli, Stignani, Pinza, Rome Opera Ch. & O, Serafin.
** Erato/Warner Dig. 4509 96357-2 (2) [id.]. Marc, Meier, Domingo, Furlanetto, Chicago Ch. & SO, Barenboim.
*(*) RCA Dig. 09026 60902-2 (2). Vaness, Quivar, O'Neill, Colombara, Bav. R. Ch. & SO, Sir Colin Davis.
(M) *(*) EMI Dig. CD-EMXD 2503 (2); *TC-EMXD 2503.* Connell, Gunson, Barham, Tomlinson, Brighton Festival Ch., Royal Choral Soc., RPO, Arwel Hughes.

(i) *Requiem;* (ii) *4 Sacred pieces.*
*** Ph. Dig. 442 142-2 (2) [id.]. (i) Orgonosova, Von Otter, Canonici, Miles; (ii) Donna Brown; Monteverdi Ch., ORR, Gardiner.

Gardiner, in this first recording of the Verdi *Requiem* using period forces, is unlikely to be matched for a very long time. This is a magnificent version, searingly dramatic and superbly recorded, with fine detail, necessary weight and atmospheric bloom. It can be recommended as a first choice among modern digital recordings even to collectors not drawn to period performance. Period instruments add to the freshness of the reading, whether in the hushed, meditative sequences or in the great dramatic outbursts, notably in the *Dies irae*, where the bite and clarity of the textures, both choral and orchestral, intensify Gardiner's thrusting sense of drama. With a choir of 70, all of them keenly disciplined professionals, Gardiner has the best of both worlds: as recorded, there is ample weight and power as well as a rare refinement in the singing. The soloists make a characterful quartet, with the vibrant Orgonosova set against the rock-steady von Otter, and with Canonici bringing welcome Italianate colourings to the tenor role. Alistair Miles is a strong bass, not quite ideally dark but untroubled by the tessitura. The *Four Sacred pieces* are equally revealing, completely shedding any sanctimonious overtones in their new freshness. The longest and most complex of the pieces, the final *Te Deum*, is the most successful of all, marked by thrillingly dramatic contrasts, as in the fortissimo cries of '*Sanctus*'.

Fricsay's electrifying mono recording of Verdi's *Requiem* caused a sensation when it first appeared on LP in the mid-1950s. In tingling drama it has never since been surpassed, especially in the *Dies irae*; yet there is glorious lyrical singing from the fine team of soloists too, the tenor Gabor Carelli's *Ingemisco* is ravishing, while the *Sanctus* is wonderfully light and joyful. The closing *Lux aeterna* is raptly beautiful, for Fricsay's concentration never falters. The CD transfer enhances the bite of the choral projection without losing the atmospheric warmth of a recording that even today can startle by its immediacy and impact.

The Dutton Sound transfer of Serafin's historic recording of 1939 restores to the catalogue a pioneering 78-r.p.m. set which, with all-Italian forces, relates the work to the Verdian operatic tradition more closely than most latterday versions. The beefy, Italianate sound of the chorus is what Verdi himself no doubt had in mind, and the team of soloists is characterfully representative of the finest Italian singing at that period. The recording was built round the tenor then supreme in Italy, Beniamino Gigli, singing with his most golden tone. Though his tendency to aspirate the vocal line and to bring his half-tone down to a gentle croon may upset the purists, few performances are as winning as his, and both Ebe Stignani and Ezio Pinza are at their supreme best, rarely matched since. The soprano, Maria Caniglia, is more variable but, always dramatic, she rises splendidly to the challenge of the final *Libera me*. Whether because of co-ordination problems between such distinguished soloists, a brief *a capella* passage of 11 bars for mezzo, tenor and bass soloists is omitted towards the end of the *Lux aeterna*. With Serafin adopting faster speeds than have become normal, the complete work fits easily on a single CD. Well worth having as a supplement to modern versions.

Daniel Barenboim conducts a warm, powerful performance which is not helped by a lack of weight in the recording, made in Orchestra Hall, Chicago. With the chorus less well focused than it should be, the glory of the set lies in the solo singing from an exceptionally starry quartet, all individually characterful yet well matched as a team. Ensemble is often less crisp than one would expect from this source. At full price and with no fill-up, this can be recommended only to those who specially fancy the soloists.

Sir Colin Davis conducts his Bavarian forces in a mellow, relaxed reading which underplays the drama of this masterpiece, conveying too little of its tensions. The recessed recording of the chorus intensifies that impression. With a good but not outstanding quartet of soloists, and with no fill-up on two full-priced discs, this is uncompetitive.

Recorded live at St Paul's Cathedral, the Eminence version from Owain Arwel Hughes is very atmospheric, with hushed pianissimos to have you catching the breath, and with more detail conveyed than you would expect in such a reverberant acoustic. Yet the choral sound is mushy, and the soloists are very variable, with the magnificent bass of John Tomlinson here sounding unsteady.

OPERA

Aida (complete).
(M) *** EMI CMS7 69300-2 (3) [Ang. CDMC 69300]. Freni, Carreras, Baltsa, Cappuccilli, Raimondi, Van Dam, V. State Op. Ch., VPO, Karajan.

On EMI, Karajan's is a performance of *Aida* that carries splendour and pageantry to the point of exaltation. Yet Karajan's fundamental approach is lyrical. On record at least, there can be little question of Freni lacking power in a role normally given to a larger voice, and there is ample gain in the tender beauty of her singing. Carreras makes a fresh, sensitive Radames, Raimondi a darkly intense Ramphis and Van Dam a cleanly focused King, his relative lightness no drawback. Cappuccilli here gives a more detailed performance than he did for Muti on EMI, while Baltsa as Amneris crowns the whole performance with her fine, incisive singing. Despite some over-brightness on cymbals and trumpet, the Berlin sound for Karajan, as transferred to CD, is richly and involvingly atmospheric, both in the intimate scenes and, most strikingly, in the scenes of pageant, which have rarely been presented on record in greater splendour. The set has been attractively re-packaged and remains first choice for the opera, irrespective of price.

Aida: highlights.
(B) **(*) DG Dig. 439 482-2 [id.] (from complete recording, with Ricciarelli, Obraztsova, Domingo, Nucci, Ghiaurov; cond. Abbado).
(M) *(*) Sony Dig. SMK 53506 [id.] (from complete recording, with Millo, Domingo, Zajick, Morris, Ramey, Met Op. Ch & O; cond. Levine).

In Abbado's 1981 La Scala *Aida*, it is the men who stand out, Domingo a superb Radames, Ghiaurov as Ramphis, Nucci a dramatic Amonasro, and Raimondi as the King. Ricciarelli is an appealing Aida, but her legato line is at times impure above the stave, and Elena Obraztsova produces too much curdled tone as Amneris. The recording is bright and fresh, but not ideally expansive in the ceremonial scenes. As is usual with DG's bargain Classikon series, the documentation is good, though without translations. The selection offers 64 minutes of music.

Levine's 1990 recording of *Aida*, made with Met. forces in the limited acoustic of the Manhattan Center, is hardly among the most successful versions of this much-recorded opera. Both Aprile Millo in the title-role and Dolora Zajick as Amneris are disappointing in the unevenness of their vocal production and, though Plácido Domingo again makes a commanding Radames and the selection is more generous than its DG competitor (75 minutes), the recording is again not expansive enough to do full justice to the grand spectacle of Verdi's score.

Un ballo in maschera: highlights.
(M) *** DG Dig. 445 468-2 [id.] (from complete set, with Ricciarelli, Domingo, Bruson, Gruberová, Raimondi; cond. Abbado).

The 68-minute selection from the Abbado version, which includes the *Prelude* and opens brightly with *S'avanza il conte*, makes a good mid-priced choice, with a cued synopsis of the narrative for the listener to follow the action. The excerpts are well chosen to represent Domingo, but Ricciarelli's splendid contribution is not neglected. The CD transfer faithfully reflects the qualities of the complete set. First choice for a complete recording of *Un ballo* remains with Solti (with Margaret Price and Pavarotti) – Decca 410 210-2.

Don Carlos (complete).
(M) *** EMI CMS7 69304-2 (3) [Ang. CDMC 69304]. Carreras, Freni, Ghiaurov, Baltsa, Cappuccilli, Raimondi, German Op. Ch., Berlin, BPO, Karajan.

Karajan opts firmly for the later, four-Act version of the opera, merely opening out the cuts he adopted on stage. The *Auto da fé* scene is here superb, while Karajan's characteristic choice of singers for refinement of voice rather than sheer size consistently pays off. Both Carreras and Freni are most moving, even if *Tu che le vanità* has its raw moments. Baltsa is a superlative Eboli and Cappuccilli an affecting Rodrigo, though neither Carreras nor Cappuccilli is at his finest in the famous oath duet. Raimondi and Ghiaurov as the Grand Inquisitor and Philip II provide the most powerful confrontation. The sound is both rich and atmospheric and is made to seem even firmer and more vivid in its current remastering, giving great power to Karajan's uniquely taut account of the four-Act version. The set's presentation has also been attractively redesigned, and this set remains at the top of the recommended list.

Don Carlos: highlights.
(M) **(*) Sony Dig. SMK 53507 [id.] (from complete recording, with Furlanatto, Millo, Zajick, Sylvester, Chernov; cond. Levine).

Although, like Levine's *Aida*, this Met. *Don Carlos* highlights was recorded in the Mahattan Center, the sound is comparatively full and vivid, and the performance has a dramatic thrust that reflects opera-house experience. Michael Sylvester (as Don Carlos) and April Millo (as Elisabetta) are both well cast and, if the rest of the team are more uneven and Ferruccio Furlanetto is a less than ideal King Philip, this 74-minute selection makes a more than acceptable mid-priced sampler.

Falstaff (complete).
** Sony Dig. S2K 58961 (2) [id.]. Pons, Frontali, Vargas, Dessì, O'Flynn, Manca di Nissa, Gavazzi, Barbacini, Roni, Ziegler, La Scala, Milan, Ch. & O, Muti.

Recorded live at La Scala, Milan, in June 1993, Riccardo Muti's version of *Falstaff* suffers from dull, sodden orchestral sound that prevents the brightness and energy of the performance from having anything like its full impact. The voices too are heard as though through a gauze – which is a great pity when the cast is first rate. Relative newcomers like Maureen O'Flynn, Bernadette Manca di Nissa, Ramon Vargas and Roberto Frontali are all very impressive indeed, firm and clear of focus, matching the more established singers. Daniela Dessì makes a warm, positive Alice, and only Juan Pons in the title-role is disappointing, not because of any vocal shortcoming, but because his is not a voice that readily conveys comedy, and his characterization is too plain to suggest the Shakespearean strength and variety of the fat knight. Giulini's DG set still makes a clear first choice in this opera (410 503-2).

Luisa Miller: highlights.
(M) *** Sony Dig. SMK 53508 [id.] (from complete recording, with Domingo, Millo, Chernov, Rootering, Quivar, Plishka; cond. Levine).

This is easily the finest of the current Sony series of Verdi highlights recorded at the Met. under

James Levine. The 75-minute selection is well chosen and, with Chernov (as Miller) and Domingo (as Rodolfo) both on top form, this can be strongly recommended, as can the complete set from which it comes (Sony S2K 48073).

Otello (complete).
*** DG Dig. 439 805-2 (2) [id.]. Domingo, Studer, Leiferkus, Ch. & O of Bastille Opera, Myung-Whun Chung.

Plácido Domingo's third recording of *Otello* proves to be his finest yet, more freely expressive, even more involved than his previous ones. In the earliest, with James Levine conducting (RCA), the voice may be more ringingly heroic, but the baritonal quality of his tenor now brings new darkness, with the final solo, *Niun mi tema*, poignantly tender. Cheryl Studer gives one of her finest performances as Desdemona, the tone both full and pure, while Sergei Leiferkus makes a chillingly evil Iago, the more so when his voice is the opposite of Italianate, verging on the gritty, which not everyone will like. With plenty of light and shade, Myung-Whun Chung is an urgent Verdian, adopting free-flowing speeds yet allowing Domingo full expansiveness in the death scene. The Chorus and Orchestra of the Bastille Opera excel themselves, setting new standards for an opera recording from Paris, and the sound is first rate, though transferred at a slightly low level. This now makes a pretty clear first choice for this much-recorded opera.

Otello: highlights.
**(*) Decca Dig. 440 843-2 [id.] (from complete set, with Pavarotti, Te Kanawa, Nucci; cond. Solti).

Those preferring a complete set with Domingo as Otello may be glad to try the Pavarotti/Te Kanawa/Nucci alternative in highlights form, even if the selection is not very generous for a full-priced CD (59 minutes). Dame Kiri's *Willow song* is glorious and Pavarotti's contribution is also memorable, heightened by his golden tone and his detailed feeling for words. Solti conducts vividly, adopting faster speeds than usual, while the contribution from the Chicago Chorus adds much to the impact of a set where the digital sound is fuller and more present than on almost any rival version.

Otello (complete; in English).
(B) **(*) CfP CFPD 4736 (2) [id.]. Craig, Plowright, Howlett, Bottone, ENO Ch. & O, Mark Elder.

Recorded live at the Coliseum in London, the ENO version of *Otello* is inevitably flawed in the sound; but those who seek records of opera in English need not hesitate, for almost every word of Andrew Porter's translation is audible, despite the very variable balances inevitable in recording a live stage production. Less acceptable is the level of stage noise, with the thud and blunder of wandering feet all the more noticeable on CD. The performance itself is most enjoyable, with dramatic tension building up compellingly. Charles Craig's Otello is most moving, the character's inner pain brought out vividly, though top notes are fallible. Neil Howlett as Iago may not have the most distinctive baritone, but finely controlled vocal colouring adds to a deeply perceptive performance. Rosalind Plowright makes a superb Desdemona, singing with rich, dramatic weight but also with poise and purity. The Death scene reveals her at her finest, radiant of tone, with flawless attack.

Rigoletto (complete).
(B) ** Decca Double 443 853-2 (2) [id.]. MacNeil, Sutherland, Cioni, Siepi, Malagu, Acadamy of Santa Cecilia, Rome, Ch. & O, Sanzogno.

The earlier Sutherland recording came a decade before her triumphant partnership with Pavarotti and with Milnes making a formidable assumption of the title-role (Decca 414 269-2). By comparison, in 1961, Cornell MacNeil was a resonant but uncharacterful Rigoletto, although Cioni, if conventional, sings well enough as the Duke of Mantova. Sutherland's own performance epitomizes her soft-grained style at its most extreme. The result is often intensely beautiful, particularly in *Caro nome*, but as a dramatic experience it cannot compare with the later Decca set. Nino Sanzogno jogs through everything very neatly, but it is the fine technical quality of the recording and the reliability of the singing that engage the attention, rather than the drama. The reissue is very reasonably priced, but it is worth paying a bit more for the far more dramatic RCA mid-priced Solti set, with Robert Merrill dark and firm as Rigoletto, Anna Moffo an engaging Gilda and Alfredo Kraus a stylish Duke (GD 86506 – see our main volume). However, first choice remains with Sinopoli, whose cast includes Bruson, Gruberová and Shicoff (DG 412 592-2).

Simon Boccanegra.
(B) **(*) Discover Dig. DICD 920225/6 [id.]. Tumagian, Gauci, Aragall, Mikulas, Sardinero, BRTN Philharmonic Ch. and O, Alexander Rahbari.

On the Discover bargain label this well-paced reading is newly recorded in good digital sound with strong casting. Excellent East European principals are joined by the long-established Spanish tenor, Giacomo Aragall, and the baritone, Vincente Sardinero. Miriam Gauci is a vibrant, sympathetic Amelia, and though Eduard Tumagian is not the most characterful Boccanegra and Peter Mikulas could be darker-toned in the bass role of Fiesco, their voices are clear and well-focused, despite backward balance. Libretto in Italian only. Good value, but this does not upstage the Abbado version with Cappuccilli, Freni and Ghiaurov, which was given a Rosette in our main volume (DG 415 692-2).

La Traviata (complete).
❀ *** Decca Dig. 448 119-2 (2) [id.]. Gheorghiu, Lopardo, Nucci, ROHCG Ch. & O, Solti.

Defying the problems of recording opera live at Covent Garden, the Decca engineers here offer one of the most vivid and involving versions ever of *La Traviata*, full and immediate in sound and with fair bloom on the voices. By record company standards this was a last-minute project when Solti insisted that his first ever version in the theatre of this central Verdi opera should be recorded live. He realized that his inspired choice for the heroine, the young Romanian soprano, Angela Gheorghiu, was already emerging as one of the great Violettas of our time, and he wanted her performance, as well as his, caught on the wing. In a magnetic reading he treats the piece, not with his old fierceness, but with refinement and tenderness as well as emotional weight from the ravishingly hushed opening of the Prelude onwards. The intensity of a live occasion comes over consistently, with little or no intrusion from stage or audience noises, merely an enhancement of the event. As on stage, Gheorghiu brings heartfelt revelations, using her rich and vibrant, finely shaded soprano with consistent subtlety. Youthfully vivacious in the first Act, dazzling in her coloratura, she already reveals the depths of feeling which compel her later self-sacrifice. In Act II she finds ample power for the great outburst of '*Amami, Alfredo*', and in Act III almost uniquely uses the second stanza of *Addio del passato* (often omitted) to heighten the intensity of the heroine's emotions. Frank Lopardo, better known as a Rossini tenor, here emerges as a fresh, lyrical Alfredo with a distinctive timbre, passionate and youthful-sounding too. The gentle cadenza in duet at the end of '*Parigi o cara*' on the reunion of hero and heroine in Act III has a poise and hushed beauty rarely matched. Leo Nucci, a favourite baritone with Solti, provides a sharp contrast as a stolid but convincing Germont. This is now a leading contender among all the many rival sets and for many it will be a first choice. A video version – taken from a single performance, not (like the CDs) an edited compendium of a series – is also offered (VHS 071 431-3; Laserdisc 071 428-1), letting one appreciate how Gheorghiu's physical beauty matches her voice, and how elegant and atmospheric Richard Eyre's Covent Garden production is, with sets by Bob Crowley.

Il Trovatore (complete).
(M) **(*) EMI CMS7 69311-2 (2) [CDMB 69311].Price, Bonisolli, Cappucilli, Obraztsova,
     Raimondi, German Op. Ch., Berlin Ch., BPO, Karajan.
**(*) Decca Dig. 444 442-2 (2) [id.]. Pavarotti, Banaudi, Verrett, Nucci, Maggio Musicale Fiorentino
     Ch. & O, Mehta.
(B) ** Ph. Duo Dig. 446 151-2 [id.]. Carreras, Ricciarelli, Mazurok, Toczyska, Lloyd, ROHCG Ch.
     & O, C. Davis.

The later Karajan set with Leontyne Price promised much but proved disappointing, largely because of the thickness and strange balances of the recording, the product of multi-channel techniques exploited over-enthusiastically. So the introduction to Manrico's aria, *Di quella pira*, provides full-blooded orchestral sound, but then the orchestra fades down for the entry of the tenor, who in any case is in coarse voice. In other places he sings more sensitively, but at no point does this version match that of Mehta on RCA (RD 86194). CD clarifies the sound but makes the flaws in the original recording all the more evident.

Recorded in 1990 but not issued for almost five years, the Decca set made in Florence is designedly a vehicle for the superstar, Pavarotti, and he responds with a bravura performance. Some 14 years after he had made his first recording for Decca (opposite Joan Sutherland in 1976) his voice is as heroic and golden as ever, and with superstardom has come a greater freedom and flair, with crystal-clear words delivered as characterfully as ever. Yet the later performance is marred by mannerisms that on disc more than in live performance grow irritating, notably a throaty roaring in moments of climax and the ending of phrases on little effortful grunts. Mehta's speeds are consistently faster than Bonynge's on the earlier set so that, for all its exhilaration, the speed of *Di quella pira* at the end of Act III makes it sound a little perfunctory next to the earlier account. Pavarotti devotees will hardly worry, and the other three principals make a strong, reliable team. Antonella Banaudi – who was Leonora opposite Pavarotti in the live Florence production – sings cleanly and firmly, with a mezzo-ish tinge in the tone, fine flexibility and a precise trill. Yet there is little charm or tenderness so that, next to Pavarotti, her reading seems undercharacterized. Shirley Verrett makes as firm an Azucena as ever, and in the fine, subtle shading of her legato lines she seems in such a duet as *Ai nostri monti* to show up the relative coarseness of Pavarotti, whose *Riposa, o madre* in response is delivered fortissimo. Leo Nucci is strong and reliable as the Count but not very imaginative. Mehta is vital as well as brisk in an opera which brings out the best in him, but this cannot match his classic reading for RCA with Leontyne Price and the young Domingo. The Florence orchestra is lively but sometimes coarse, with the immediate, full recording setting the instruments behind the singers, who – Pavarotti most of all – confront you eyeball to eyeball.

Sir Colin Davis offers a fresh and direct, slightly understated reading. The refinement of the digital recording makes for a wide, clean separation but, with the backward placing of the orchestra, the result does not have the dramatic impact of the Mehta RCA version. The *Anvil chorus* sounds rather clinical and other important numbers lack the necessary swagger. Ricciarelli's Leonora is most moving, conveying an element of vulnerability in the character, but Carreras lacks the full confidence of a natural Manrico. He is less effective in the big, extrovert moments, best in such inward-looking numbers as *Ah si ben mio*. Toczyska's voice is presented rather grittily in the role of Azucena. Mazurok similarly is not flattered by the microphones but, with clean, refined ensemble, this emerges as the opposite of a hackneyed opera. The mid-priced RCA Mehta set with Domingo, Leontyne Price, Milnes and Cossotto is the one to have (RD 86194 – see our main volume).

Vieuxtemps, Henri (1820–81)

Violin concerto No. 5 in A min., Op. 37.
(M) *** Sony Dig. SMK 64250 [id.]. Cho-Liang Lin, Minnesota O, Marriner – BRUCH; MENDELSSOHN: *Concertos.* ***
*** Denon Dig. CO 78913 [id.]. Chee-Yun, LPO, Lopez-Cóboz – MENDELSSOHN: *Concerto No. 5.* ***

Cho-Liang Lin plays with flair and zest and is well supported by Sir Neville Marriner and the Minnesota Orchestra. The recording is first class, and the couplings of the more famous concertos of Bruch and Mendelssohn could not be more appropriate.

The young South Korean violinist, Chee-Yun, made her début with the Vieuxtemps No. 5 at the tender age of thirteen in the 1980s, with the NYPO; and her performance shows how well she understands the piece in its attractive combination of affection and maturity. The plaintive *Andante* is touching and the brief finale given with comparable dash and sparkle. She is well recorded, but this Denon record is short measure by comparison with Lin's Sony CD, which also has a price advantage.

Villa-Lobos, Heitor (1887–1959)

Bachianas Brasileiras No. 2: The little train of the Caipira.
(*) Everest/Vanguard EVC 9007 [id.]. LSO, Sir Eugene Goossens – ANTILL: *Corroboree* **(*); GINASTERA: *Estancia; Panambi.* *

It is good to have a recommendable mid-priced version of Villa-Lobos's engaging tone-picture of a little country train in São Paulo, Brazil, which the composer experienced in 1931. It is a counterpart to Lumbye's *Copenhagen Steam Railway galop* and, if not quite as indelible as this, still gives a realistic impression, strong on local colour. The composer uses Brazilian percussion instruments to suggest train noises over which there is a soaring theme in the strings. The performance is excellent and the recording vivid. It is slightly over-resonant, which implies close microphones, and a slight edge to the violins. But the resulting sound-picture is strongly projected.

Bachianas Brasileiras Nos. 2 (The little train of the Caipira); 4; (i) 5 for soprano and 8 cellos; (ii) Chorus No. 10: Rasga o Coraçâo; (iii) Miniaturas Nos. 2 (Viola); 3, Cantilena; (iv) Momoprecoce (Fantasy for piano and orchestra).
(***) EMI stereo/mono CDC5 55224-2 [id.]. (i) French Nat. RO, composer; (i) with Victoria de los Angeles; (ii) Ch. des Jeunesses Musicales de France; (iii) Feredrick Fuller; (iv) Magda Tagliaferro.

No one has been more persuasive than the composer in *The little train of the Caipira*, and the recording certainly has plenty of local colour with its exotic percussive effects. Victoria de Los Angeles' golden voice sounds ravishing in the famous *Bachianas Brasileras No. 5*, even if the recording is not entirely flattering; and the other, rarer works, notably the *Fantasy for piano and orchestra*, are welcome in this reissue in EMI's Composer in Person series, which now take the two most familiar items into the premium-price bracket.

String quartet No. 6.
(***) Testament mono SBT 1053 [id.]. Hollywood Qt – CRESTON: *Quartet;* DEBUSSY: *Danses sacrées;* RAVEL: *Intro and allegro;* TURINA: *La Oración.* (***)

The *Sixth Quartet* was composed in 1940 and this superb performance recorded in 1949. It is a slight but amiable score, ultimately facile but pleasing and well crafted. The Hollywood Quartet invariably consulted composers, and Tully Potter's excellent sleeve-note tells how composer and quartet met with no common language to help them but with a large bottle of whisky, which seemed to secure complete rapport. It would be hard to imagine a finer performance than this.

Vivaldi, Antonio (1675–1741)

L'estro armonico (12 concertos), *Op. 3* (complete).
(B) **(*) Ph. Duo 446 169-2 (2) [id.]. Garatti, Altobelli, Colandrea, Cotogni, Gallozzi, Michelucci, Vicari, I Musici.

L'estro armonico, Op. 3; (i) *Bassoon concerto in A min., RV 498;* (ii) *Flute concerto in C min., RV 441;* (iii) *Oboe concerto in F, RV 456;* (i; iii; iv) *Concerto in F for 2 oboes, bassoon, 2 horns and violin, RV 574.*
(B) *** Decca Double 443 476-2 (2) [id.]. ASMF, Marriner; with (i) Martin Gatt; (ii) William Bennett; (iii) Neil Black; (iv) Celia Nicklin, Timothy Brown, Robin Davis, Iona Brown.

Those who have not been won over to the more abrasive sound of original instruments will find Marriner's set no less stylish. As so often, he directs the Academy in radiant and imaginative performances of baroque music and yet observes scholarly good manners. The delightful use of continuo – lute and organ as well as harpsichord – the sharing of solo honours and the consistently resilient string playing of the ensemble make for compelling listening. The 1972 recording, made in St John's, Smith Square, is immaculately transferred, and as a bonus we are offered four of Vivaldi's most inventive concertos which occupied a whole LP to themselves when first issued in 1977. Each work has its own individuality and its own special effects. The *A minor Bassoon concerto* has a delightful sense of humour and in RV 441 the flute chortles like a bird. The work for oboes and horns is agreeably robust but has an imaginatively scored slow movement. The recording is a model of clarity and definition and has plenty of warmth and atmosphere.

The competing Philips Duo offers fresh and lovely performances; melodies are finely drawn and there is little hint of the routine which occasionally surfaces in I Musici – and, for that matter, in Vivaldi himself. However, in making comparisons this group often yields to St Martin-in-the-Fields, who have crisper textures and convey greater enthusiasm. Even so, I Musici are a good choice and are certainly recommendable. However, whereas the Decca Marriner set (at the same cost) offers extra works as a bonus, this Philips reissue, with its overall playing time of just two hours, offers none.

The Trial between harmony and invention: The Four Seasons, Op. 8/1–4; Violin concertos: in E flat (La tempesta di mare), RV 253; in C (Il Piacare), RV 108; in B flat (La Caccia), RV 362; in D, RV 210, Op. 8/5–6, 10–11.
(M) *** Virgin Veritas/EMI Dig. VER5 61172-2 [id.]. Monica Huggett, Raglan Bar. Players, Nicholas Kraemer.

Vivaldi's *Four Seasons* certainly suits the astringency and athleticism of 'authentic' performance style; and Monica Huggett's stimulating Virgin Veritas CD makes a fine mid-priced alternative to the premium version by Jean Lamon and Tafelmusik (Sony SK 48251), which is highly recommended in our main volume, even if Huggett does not quite match it in sheer exuberance of pictorialism. The shepherd's dog on Virgin is in a mellower mood, but the light texture and dancing tempo of the finale of *Spring* is matched by the sense of fantasy in the central movement of *Summer*, while the sheer rumbustious energy of the latter's last movement is gloriously invigorating. The *Adagio* of *Autumn* has a delicate, sensuous somnambulance, and only the opening of *Winter* is relatively conventional, although certainly not lacking character. Four other concertos from Op. 8 are also included, all played in fine style; like the *Seasons*, none brings any of the uncomfortable exaggerations of phrasing that used to haunt early-instrument performances. Indeed the supple solo line is a constant pleasure, as is Monica Huggett's easy, exhilarating bravura, well matched by Raglan's zestful accompaniments.

The recording is splendidly present and clean, and the whole effect freshly spontaneous.

The Four Seasons, Op. 8/1–4.
*** DG Dig. 439 933-2 [id.]. Gil Shaham, Orpheus CO – KREISLER: *Violin concerto in the style of Vivaldi.* ***
(B) **(*) Carlton Dig. PCD 2000 [id.]. Jaime Laredo, SCO.

The Four Seasons, Op. 8/1–4; Quadruple violin concerto in B min., Op. 3/10; Violin concerto in E flat (La tempesta di mare), Op. 8/5; Flute concerto in G min., Op. 10/3.
(M) ** EMI CDM5 65338-2 [id.]. Virtuosi di Roma, Renato Fasano.

(i) *The Four Seasons, Op. 8/1–4;* (ii) *Violin concertos: in E flat (La tempesta di mare), Op. 8/5, RV 253; in E (L'amoroso), RV 271.*
(BB) ** RCA Navigator 74321 17884-2. (i) Salvatore Accardo, O de Camera Italiana; (ii) Patrice Fontanarosa, I Nuovi Virtuosi di Roma.

(i; ii) *The Four Seasons, Op. 8/1–4;* (i; iii) *Violin concerto in E flat (La tempesta di mare), Op. 8/5, RV 253;* (iv) *Triple concerto in F for flute, oboe and bassoon, RV 570; Double concerto in G min. for flute and bassoon (La Notte), RV. 104.*
(BB) *** ASV Dig. CDQS 6148 [id.]. (i) José-Luis Garcia; (ii) ECO; (iii) Fort Worth CO, Giordano; (iv) William Bennett, Neil Black, Robin O'Neill, ECO, Malcolm.

(i) *The Four Seasons, Op. 8/1–4; Quadruple violin concerto in B flat, RV 553. Concerto for strings in G (alla rustica), RV 151; Sinfonia in G, RV 146.*
(M) *** Virgin/EMI VC5 45117-2 [id.]. (i) Chiara Banchini, Alison Bury, John Holloway, Elizabeth Wallfisch; Taverner Players, Andrew Parrott.

Gil Shaham and the excellent, conductorless Orpheus Chamber Orchestra combine to present a strongly characterized, eminently musical set of *Seasons* which, orchestrally at least, seeks in some ways to emulate period-instrument performances with bright, bracingly athletic string-textures – sample the opening movement of *Autumn* – and gutsy virility when called for, as in the summer storms (tracks 5–6). Gil Shaham plays beautifully and with freshness, but in the last resort this performance has nothing really new to say about this much-recorded work. It is given first-rate sound with plenty of presence. The main claim to fame of this CD is the coupling (Kreisler's charming pastiche concerto which sounds more like Boccherini than Vivaldi); and this is recognized in the accompanying notes, which devote most of the available space to the former, rather than to the latter. They do tell us, however, that *The Four Seasons*, forgotten for two centuries, except in France (where *Spring* inspired at least one cantata) was revived in the late 1920s by the conductor Bernadino Molinari in comparatively large-scale performances. However, the writer omits to tell us that, in more recent times, it was Hermann Scherchen who pioneered the first 78-r.p.m. recording in the 1940s, and Karl Münchinger with the Stuttgart Chamber Orchestra whose famous first mono LP for Decca, in the early 1950s, stimulated the beginning of the steady, then spectacular rise in public awareness that eventually made it the most popular classical work of all time.

The Taverner Players offer yet another authentic version which stimulates the ear without acerbity. They are not the first group to use a different soloist for each of Vivaldi's *Four Seasons*, and this works well, with plenty of tingling vitality overall and a good deal of imaginative freedom from each in turn, with Chiara Banchini setting the style in her duets with the leader in her volatile account of *Spring*. In the *Adagio* of *Summer*, Alison Bury's timbre is pure with a minimum of vibrato, yet the playing is appealingly expressive. There is no lack of sensuous lustre in the hazy evocation of the slow movement of *Autumn* (the brooding harpsichord continuo particularly effective) and Elizabeth Wallfisch's contribution to the outer movements gleams with bravura. John Holloway's upper tessitura in *Winter* is suitably mercurial. The four players join together for the *Concerto for four violins in B flat*, offered as the principal bonus; it is an interesting work, if not quite as memorable as its more familiar companion in B minor, but it demands and receives much virtuosity from its soloists. The *Sinfonia* and *Concerto alla rustica* bring much energy and tonal bite from the orchestral strings, and the recording is suitably vivid throughout.

The ASV version of *The Four Seasons*, with José-Luis Garcia as soloist and musical director, was chosen on BBC Radio 3 as ideal for 'Building a Record Library' (in its original, full-priced format). That was before many of the current versions made their appearance, but one can understand the reasons for its choice. The recording acoustic (All Hallows Church, London) is particularly pleasing, with the violins of the accompanying group sweetly fresh and the soloist nicely balanced. The overall pacing is beautifully judged, and each movement takes its place naturally and spontaneously in relation to its companions. The effects are well made, but there are no histrionics and, although the continuo does not always come through strongly, the unnamed player makes a useful contribution to a performance that is very easy to live with. The one drawback to this issue is that there is only one track for each of the *Four Seasons*. The new couplings add two versions of *La tempesta del mare*, both the one with solo violin (from Op. 8) and the even more engaging triple concerto arrangement for flute, oboe and bassoon. The equally attractive flute/bassoon version of *La Notte* completes the listener's pleasure. The wind soloists are illustrious and George Malcolm's accompaniments are a model of baroque style.

Jaime Laredo's performance has great spontaneity and vitality, emphasized by the forward balance which is nevertheless admirably truthful. The bright upper range is balanced by a firm, resonant bass. Laredo plays with bravura and directs polished, strongly characterized accompaniments. Pacing tends to be on the fast side; although the reading is extrovert and the lyrical music – played responsively – is made to offer a series of interludes to the vigour of the allegros, the effect is exhilarating rather than aggressive. However, there is no extra music.

Not unexpectedly, Accardo on his earlier, RCA Navigator version makes an accomplished and appealing soloist and the Orchestra de Camera Italiana offer full, bright supporting textures. The programmatic drama is conveyed well, but musical values are paramount and this is enjoyable in its fresh, direct manner, if not especially memorable. The sound is vivid, and this might be considered at bargain price, especially as the two couplings are brightly and vigorously done and digitally recorded; but there are many other more striking versions.

The version by the Virtuosi di Roma features only two different soloists (Luigi Ferro and Guido Mozzato). Renato Fasano directs a straightforward but in no way distinctive set of performances, and the early (1959) recording has lost some of its allure in the transfer to CD. The familiar *Quadruple Violin concerto* from *L'Estro armonico* is lively enough, but the sound here is a little edgy, and each of the other concertos, which are well enough played, brings a noticeable change of ambience and acoustic.

Complete cello concertos

Volume 1: *Cello concertos: in C, RV 398; in C, RV 399; in D, RV 404; in D min., RV. 406; in F, RV 410; in F, RV 412; in A min., RV 419.*
(BB) *** Naxos Dig. 8.550907 [id.]. Raphael Wallfisch, City of L. Sinfonia, Nicholas Kraemer.

Volume 2: *Cello concertos: in C, RV 400; in C min., RV 401; in E flat, RV 408; in G, RV 413; in A min., RV 422;* (i) *Double cello concerto in G min., RV 531.*
(BB) *** Naxos Dig. 8.550908 [id.]. Raphael Wallfisch, (i) with Keith Harvey; City of L. Sinfonia, Nicholas Kraemer.

Volume 3: *Cello concertos: in C min., RV 402; in D, RV 403; in D min., RV 407;* (i) *in E min., RV 409; in A min., RV 418; in B flat, RV 423; in B min., RV 424.*
⊛ (BB) *** Naxos Dig. 8.550909 [id.]. Raphael Wallfisch, (i) with Johanna Graham; City of L. Sinfonia, Nicholas Kraemer.

Volume 4: *Cello concertos: in D min., RV 405; in F, RV 411; in G, RV 414; in G min., RV 416 & RV 417; in A min., RV 420 & RV 421.*
(BB) *** Naxos Dig. 8. 550910 [id.]. Raphael Wallfisch, City of L. Sinfonia, Nicholas Kraemer.

Vivaldi liked to write for instruments playing in the middle to lower register, and he left 27 solo concertos for the cello, all of which are here. This Naxos series is part of an overall survey, with plans eventually to record every one of the Vivaldi concertos! Certainly the company has begun admirably and the choice of Raphael Wallfisch as soloist could hardly have been bettered. He forms an admirable partnership with the City of London Sinfonia, directed from the harpsichord or chamber organ by Nicholas Kraemer. The first concerto of Volume 1, the fine *F major*, RV 412, sets off with great energy and produces a characteristically atmospheric central *Larghetto*. Wallfisch plays with restrained use of vibrato and a nicely judged expressive feeling. In the *A minor* work which follows (RV 419), Kraemer effectively uses an organ continuo to enliven the opening tutti and underpin the singing cello line in the *Andante*. The alert, resilient orchestral string-playing in the allegros is a pleasure in itself. The *C major Concerto*, RV 398, with its deeply eloquent *Largo* is particularly impressive, and the *F major*, RV 410, which ends the first CD with great flourishes of solo bravura, is also a most enjoyable work.

Besides several very striking solo works, Volume 2 of the Naxos series includes Vivaldi's only *Double cello concerto*, with much bustling interchange in the outer movements and the soloists answering each other eloquently in the *Largo*. In the *G major* solo *Concerto*, RV 413, there is a brilliantly articulated *moto perpetuo* semiquaver theme which alternates between soloist and orchestra; then follows a thoughtful slow movement, somewhat improvisatory in feeling, in which Wallfisch is in his element, suspended over Kraemer's gentle organ continuo. Bravura passage-work returns in the finale. The *C minor Concerto*, RV. 401, has a highly expressive imitative opening from the strings, which the cello then embroiders with increasing complexity. The *Adagio* brings a sense of sombre melancholy, dispelled by the more positive (and characteristic) finale. By contrast, the last work on the disc, in C major, is essentially extrovert. Throughout these performances one admires the soloist's subtle use of light and shade and his partnership with the accompanying group and Nicholas Kraemer's continuo.

Volume 3 is a particularly fine collection and as good a place to start as any. The soloist's bravura staccato playing at the opening on the *B flat major*, RV 423, commands the listener's attention at the very beginning of the disc, and this work has a matching good-humoured finale. The finale of the *A minor*, RV 418, has enormous zest, and the first movement of the *D major*, RV 403, with its strong dotted rhythms, is equally vibrant. The pensive *Largo* of the *B minor*, RV 424, is beautifully shaped, with another vociferous finale to follow. The *Concerto in D minor*, RV 407, is one of Vivaldi's very best, and its central *Largo e sempre piano* again brings a touching solo response. Vivaldi is never predictable, and perhaps the most striking work of all here is the *E minor Concerto*, RV 409, where the cello is joined by a subservient and somewhat doleful solo bassoon. In the *Adagio – Allegro molto* opening movement, the two soloists wind their way through a melancholy *recitativo*, regularly interrupted by modest bursts of energy from the string tutti, reminding one of *The Four Seasons*; then in the much briefer *Allegro – Adagio* slow movement the procedure is reversed: the orchestral strings are gently sustained and the soloists busy. The finale is more conventional in manner, but the presence of the bassoon ensures that the effect is still aurally intriguing.

Volume 4 brings a further batch of concertos notable for their vitality and the vigorous bravura demanded from the soloist. The thoughtful *Adagio* of the *D minor*, RV 405, is enhanced by a subtle organ continuo, and in the finale the bite of the cello bow on the strings is very invigorating. But it is the *A minor Concerto*, RV 420, which stands out here. Its *Andante* opening (again with organ continuo) is very engaging, while in the central *Adagio* the positive dotted rhythms of the tutti contrast tellingly with a more lyrical solo response; then in the galloping finale the cello gets his chance to let off steam, with boisterous accents in the bustling solo line. The serenely nostalgic *Largo* of the *G major*, RV 414, is again followed by a finale which demands much virtuosity from the cello, while the *Andante* central movement of the *G minor Concerto*, RV 417, brings an entirely one-sided conversation, as the soloist provides an extended, aria-like soliloquy, with only a continuo accompaniment.

Throughout these four discs there is never a hint of routine. Wallfisch's playing has extraordinary precision, and both he and the accompanying group continually communicate their enthusiasm for this endlessly inventive music. The recording is vividly realistic and the balance seems very well judged indeed within the warm but never clouding ambience of All Saints' Church or Conway Hall, London. A remarkable achievement, standing very high indeed in the Vivaldi discography. We award a token Rosette to Volume 3, but the final volume is hardly less stimulating, and our accolade could surely apply to either of the other two.

6 Flute concertos, Op. 10.
(M) *** O-L 444 163-2 [id.]. Stephen Preston, AAM, Hogwood.

Stephen Preston plays a period instrument, a Schuchart, and the Academy of Ancient Music likewise play old instruments. Their playing is eminently stylish, but also spirited and expressive, and they are admirably recorded, with the analogue sound enhanced further in the CD format. At medium price this makes a clear first choice among period performances. However, Patrick Gallois and the Orpheus Chamber Orchestra are particularly attractive for those preferring modern instruments, and this disc is well worth its extra cost (DG 437 839-2).

Guitar concertos in C, RV 82; in D, RV 93.
(M) *** DG 439 984-2 [id.]. Siegfried Behrend, I Musici – CARULLI: *Concerto in A;* GIULIANI: *Concerto in A, Op. 30.* ***

Both these concertos are transcriptions of chamber works intended for the lute. They work well enough on guitar and are most elegantly played here. Although – as the opening of the *D major* shows – there is no lack of life in the performances, their predominating characteristic is of smooth elegance, and a more robust and sinewy effect can be more telling in this repertoire.

(i) *Oboe concertos: in C, RV 540; in D min., RV 454; in F, RV 457;* (i–ii) *Double oboe concerto in D min., RV 535;* (i; iii) *Double concerto for oboe, bassoon and orchestra in G, RV 545;* (i–iii) *Concerto for 2 oboes, 2 violins, bassoon and orchestra, RV 557;* (i) *Recorder concerto in F, RV 442.*

(B) *** HM Dig. HMA 1903018 [id.]. (i) Marie Wolf (oboe or recorder); (ii) Márton Brandisz; (iii) Paul Tognon; Capella Savaria, Pál Németh.

While two of the solo oboe concertos here were conceived for bassoon, Marie Wolf with her warm phrasing and clean tonguing makes them all sound custom-made for her principal instrument. Indeed she creates robust yet creamy tone on her baroque oboe, especially in the *Largo* of RV 454, while the chromatic 'slides' in the work's first movement are most seductively managed. In the double concertos the other wind soloists produce equally characterful timbres: the two oboes blend well together, yet have individuality, while the combination of oboe and the chortling, woody bassoon must surely make the listener smile at the genial exchanges. Then Marie Wolf turns to her recorder and charms us yet again. The delightful slow movement of RV 442 is made the more fragile by the use of muted strings in the orchestra and the accompaniments have finesse and transparency. Indeed there are few more appealing bargain collections of Vivaldi wind concertos played on original instruments than this. The recording is beautifully balanced and truthful.

Frans Brüggen Edition, Volume 8: *Chamber concertos in C, RV 87; in D, RV 92 & RV 94; in G min., RV 105; in A min., RV 108; in C min., RV 441; in F, RV 442.*

(M) *** Teldec/Warner 4509 97470-2 [id.]. Frans Brüggen, Jürg Schaeflein, Otto Fleischmann, Alice Harnoncourt, Walter Pfeiffer, Nikolaus Harnoncourt, Gustav Leonhardt; VCM, Harnoncourt; Concerto Amsterdam, Schröder.

Vivaldi's *Chamber concertos* are among his most aurally stimulating with period instrumental combinations of recorder, oboe, violin and bassoon. The *G minor Concerto*, RV 105, offers all four, with the most piquant interplay. However, the opening *Concerto in D*, RV 94, catches the ear since for its *Largo* Vivaldi borrows a movement from *The Four Seasons*. All the small-scale works here use soloists from Harnoncourt's group, with Alice's violin notable for its abrasive edge, while in the *C minor Concerto*, RV. 441, the Vienna Concentus Musicus bring characteristically bright, thin string-timbre. But its clean profile sets off Bruggen's virtuosity, and he provides some astonishing roulades in the closing *Presto*. The Concerto Amsterdam provide the backing for the final work on the disc, the strings (still period instruments, although muted) much warmer and sweeter. This is one of Vivaldi's most imaginative concertos. In the first movement there is some delicious interplay between the recorder and the solo violin (Jaap Schröder), then, after a lovely central *Siciliano*, the recorder and violin have more lively imitative dialogue. No complaints about the excellent Das Alte Werk sound, vividly transferred.

Concertos for strings and continuo: in C, RV 114; in C min., RV 118; in C min., RV 120; in D min., RV 128; in E min., RV 133; in F min., RV 143; in G (Alla Rustica), RV 151; in G min., RV 152; in G min., RV 157; in A, RV 158; in B flat (Conca), RV 163; in B flat, RV 167. Sinfonias for strings and continuo: in C, RV 116; in E, RV 132; in E min., RV 134; in F, RV 137; in F, RV 140; in G, RV 146; in B min., RV 168.

(M) *** Erato/Warner Analogue/Dig. 4509 96382-2 (2) [id.]. Sol. Ven., Claudio Scimone.

As can be seen from the collection below, Vivaldi wrote three-part Italian overtures, which he called sinfonias, for his operas, but some sixty other similar works have survived which are independent of any stage connections. They were never as popular as the concertos and only one was printed in the composer's lifetime. For Vivaldi the terms sinfonia and concerto for strings seem to be interchangeable; indeed RV 134, which has a fugal opening movement, was first called a concerto, and the composer added the description 'sinfonia' later to the manuscript. The finales of RV 120 and RV 152, both called concertos, are also contrapuntal and these fugues show an attractive, extrovert vitality. But Vivaldi is never predictable, and many of the individual movements here show his imagination at full stretch. The *Sinfonia in G*, RV 146, opens the first disc with typically arresting flourishes, followed by a wistful *Andante*, with the melody floating over gentle pizzicatos like a song with mandolin, while the *Concerto in C*, RV 114, has a highly inventive *Chaconne* for the finale. It is a fast movement and so within its 3 minutes 25 seconds a great deal happens. We all know the *Alla rustica Concerto*, but RV 163 (curiously subtitled *Conca*) is another short but masterly piece, its three movements all springing from the opening phrase. The central *Andante* is for all the world like an operatic aria without the vocal line. Indeed many of the slow movements here are very touching, not least the restless *Andante molto* of RV 152, the lyrical A minor cantilena of RV 158, the solemn *Largo* of RV 120 and, perhaps most strikingly of all, the *Sinfonia in F*, RV 137, where the 'singing' *Andante*, with its touch of chromatic melancholy, contrasts so well with the very positive outer movements. This makes a fine close to a fascinating programme, revealing a little-known side of a great composer. The performances (using modern instruments) are vital and expressively penetrating, and the recording, whether analogue or digital (as with RV 116, 118, 137 and 143), is fresh and naturally balanced.

(i) *Violin concertos: in C min. (Il Sospetto), RV 199;* (ii) *in D (Grosso Mogul), RV 208; in D (L'inquietudine), RV 234;* (i) *in E (Il Ripososo), RV 270; in E (L'Amoroso), RV 271; in B flat (O sia il corneto da posta), RV 363;* (i; iii) *Quadruple violin concerto in B flat, RV 553.*
(M) ** Erato/Warner Analogue/Dig. 4509 97415-2 [id.]. (i) Piero Toso; (ii) Marco Fornaciari; (iii) with Sasaki, Bartagnin, Scalabrin; Sol. Ven., Scimone.

Piero Toso is a first-rate Vivaldi soloist and his playing in the lovely *Cantabile* of *L'Amoroso*, the *Andante* of *Il Sospetto* and the *Largo* of the *Posthorn concerto* is ravishing in tone and phrase. Incidentally, the nickname of the latter comes from the dotted rhythms and fanfare effects (with double-stopping) in the first movement. Marco Fornaciari is also a fine player, and he makes a good deal of the *Grave-Recitativo* of the *Grosso Mongol concerto* (another puzzling Vivaldi sobriquet), even if he is a bit romantic in his lyrical style. The snag is that, while Scimone's accompaniments are lively and stylish, the resonant acoustic combined with the CD remastering coarsens the string tuttis. The quality is cleaner in the digital *L'Inquietudine* and *Quadruple violin concerto*, which latter work comes off here with more charm than in the authentic performance by the Taverner players (see above).

Miscellaneous Concerto Collections

Cello concerto in B min., RV 424; Oboe concerto in A min., RV 461; Double concerto in C min. for oboe and violin, RV Anh. 17; Violin concerto in D (Il grosso mogul), RV 208; Sinfonia in B min. (Al Santo Sepolcro), RV 169; Sonata a 4 in E flat (Al Santo Sepolcro) for 2 violins, viola and continuo, RV 130.
(M) ** Teldec/Warner 4509 97454-2 [id.]. Schröder, Möller, Piguet, Concerto Amsterdam, Schröder.

There is an element of too great a rectitude here, and the forward balance characteristic of the Das Alte Werk series seems to emphasize the somewhat stiff approach, although allegros are alert and the players manage a tellingly austere atmosphere for the remarkable opening of the *Sinfonia al Santo Sepolcro*. The recording readily captures the robust and somewhat pungent timbres, and those who favour Vivaldi played on period baroque instruments will certainly find the late-1970s analogue sound faithful and transferred immaculately to CD.

Double concertos: for 2 cellos in G min., RV 531; 2 flutes in C, RV 533; 2 trumpets in C, RV 537; Concerto for Flautino (sopranino recorder) in C, RV 443; Concertos for strings: in D min. (Madrigalesco), RV 129; in G (Alla rustica), RV 151; in G min., RV 153; Quadruple concerto for 2 violins & 2 cellos in D, RV 564; L'Estro armonico: Quadruple violin concerto in B min., Op. 3/10, RV 580.
(M) *** O-L 443 198-2 [id.]. Soloists, AAM, Hogwood.

This concert duplicates some of the programme offered below by Kraemer and soloists from the City of London Sinfonia, and it is instructive in comparing the two CDs to discover from the Naxos disc how much current performers on modern instruments have learned from the authenticists. But the colouring and tang of the Academy of Ancient Music playing remains enticing in its own way. Not everything in this issue is of equal substance: the invention in the *Double trumpet concerto*, for example, is not particularly strong; but for the most part it is a rewarding and varied programme. It is especially appealing in that authenticity is allied to musical spontaneity. The *Concerto for two flutes* has great charm and is dispatched with vigour and aplomb. Performances and recording alike are first rate. For the reissue, three extra works have been added (giving an overall playing time of 70 minutes), most notably the famous *Quadruple violin concerto* from *L'Estro armonico*, taken from the Academy's splendid complete set, with John Holloway, Monica Huggett, Catherine Mackintosh and Elizabeth Wilcock the excellent soloists.

Double cello concerto in G min., RV 531; Double concerto for violin & cello in F, RV 544; Triple concerto for violin & two cellos in C, RV 561; Quadruple concerto for 2 violins & 2 cellos in D, RV . 564; Double violin concerto for violin & violin per eco lontano in A, RV 552; Triple violin concerto in F, RV 551.
**(*) Teldec/Warner Dig. 4509 94552-2 [id.]. Christophe Coin, Il Giardino Armonico, Milan, Giovanni Antonini.

Easily the most striking of the six concertos here, all performed on original instruments, is the *Concerto in A*, RV 552, for violin and 'violino per eco lontano', where the echo effects are most engagingly managed. Christophe Coin is the only soloist listed on the frontispiece – and that is perhaps appropriate, as the *Double cello concerto* is a memorably fine performance, especially the melancholy interplay of the *Largo* and the bustling bravura of the finale. Coin's excellent partner is Paolo Beschi. The other concertos are all lively enough, but the overall effect is a little anonymous. The tuttis have plenty of life, helped by the bright, slightly astringent upper range. The recording itself is agreeably spacious, but there are more attractive groupings of Vivaldi concertos which cost less than this.

Double concertos: for 2 flutes in C, RV 533; for 2 horns in F, RV 538 & RV 539; for 2 trumpets in C,
RV 537; for oboe and bassoon in G, RV 545; Concerto (Sinfonia in D) for strings, RV 122;
Quadruple concerto for 2 oboes and 2 clarinets, RV 560.
(BB) *** Naxos Dig. 8.553204 [id.]. Soloists, City of L. Sinfonia, Nicholas Kraemer.

An enjoyably lively clutch of concertos, very well recorded in All Saints' Church, East Finchley. The opening double concertos for two horns, RV 539, two flutes, RV 533, and two trumpets, RV 537, all go well enough and offer expert solo contributions, but then at the arrival of the *Quadruple concerto for two oboes and two clarinets* the playing suddenly sparks into extra exuberance, and one senses the musicians' enjoyment of one of Vivaldi's most imaginatively scored multiple works. The *Concerto for two horns* which follows (RV 538) has a similar (bold) ebullience, and the concert is rounded off by a captivating account of RV 545, where both the oboe and bassoon clearly relish every bar of their engaging dialogue. Throughout, Kraemer's accompaniments are polished and spirited.

OVERTURES

Opera overtures: *Armida al campo d'Egitto; Arsilda, Regina di Ponto (Orlando Furioso); Bajazet (Tamerlano); Dorilla in Tempe; Farnace; Giustino; Griselda; L'Incoronazione di Dario; L'Olimpiade; Ottone in Villa; La vertità in cimento.*
(M) *** Erato/Warner 4509 96381-2 [id.]. Sol. Ven., Scimone.

Orchestrally we usually hear Vivaldi in concertante music and so to have him writing sinfonias for strings alone is something of a novelty. Although the concerto grosso element with its bold dynamic contrasts remains strong, the inclusion of a courtly minuet section in nearly all of these overtures adds to their appeal. The first piece here, *Dorilla in Tempe*, brings a familiar Vivaldi tune, drawing on *Spring* from *The Four Seasons*, ready for the opera's opening chorus, which has the same theme. *Ottone in Villa* reverts unashamedly to concerto grosso style by featuring a concertino of two violins and two oboes. *Griselda* is rhythmically a very characterful piece but it too includes a stately central dance, and in *La vertità in cimento* the rather beautiful flowing central tune is heard against a pizzicato accompaniment, a device repeated in *Arsilda, Regina di Ponto*. Both end with a sprightly dance. *Bajazet*, unexpectedly, includes horns to fill out the sonority in the outer sections. The performances here are full of life and colour, and the excellent 1978 analogue recording projects the music vividly. Not a CD to be played all at one go, but offering plenty of colourful ideas.

CHORAL MUSIC

Motets: *Canto in prato, RV 623; In furore giustissimae irae, RV 626; Longa mala umbrae tertores, RV 640; Vos aurae per montes (per la solennita di S. Antonio), RV 634.*
(M) *** Erato/Warner Dig. 4509 96966-2 [id.]. Cecilia Gasdia, Sol. Ven., Scimone.

Though the booklet for this collection of Vivaldi rarities fails to provide texts for these four solo motets, they make a delightful collection, also displaying the formidable talent of a rising star among Italian sopranos, Cecilia Gasdia. Vivaldi's solo motets might be described structurally as concertos for voice, but generally with a recitative between first movement and slow movement. *Canto in prato* is the exception, with three jolly, rustic allegros in succession. Lively performances and well-balanced recording.

(i) *Gloria in D, RV 588; Gloria in D, RV 589;* (ii; iii) *Beatus vir in C, RV 597; Dixit dominus in D, RV 594;* (iv; iii) *Magnificat in G min., RV 610.*
(B) *** Decca Double Dig./Analogue 443 455-2 (2) [id.]. (i) Russell, Kwella, Wilkens, Bowen, St
    John's College, Cambridge, Ch., Wren O, Guest; (ii) Jennifer Smith, Buchanan, Watts, Partridge,
    Shirley-Quirk, ECO, Cleobury; (iii) King's College, Cambridge, Ch.; (iv) Castle, Cockerham,
    King, ASMF, Ledger.

The two settings of the *Gloria* make an apt and illuminating pairing. Both in D major, they have many points in common, presenting fascinating comparisons, when RV 588 is as inspired as its better-known companion. Guest directs strong and well-paced readings, with RV 588 the more lively. Good, warm recording to match the performances. *Dixit dominus* cannot fail to attract those who have enjoyed the better-known *Gloria*. Both works are powerfully inspired and are here given vigorous and sparkling performances with King's College Choir in excellent form under its latest choirmaster. The soloists are a fine team, fresh, stylish and nimble, nicely projected in the CD format. But what caps this outstanding Vivaldi compilation is the earlier King's account of the inspired *Magnificat in G minor*. Ledger uses the small-scale setting and opts for boys' voices in the solos such as the beautiful duet (*Esurientes*) which is most winning. The performance overall is very compelling and moving, and the singing has all the accustomed beauty of the King's records. The transfer of an outstanding (1976) analogue recording to CD is admirable, even richer than its digital companions.

(i) *Nisi dominus (Psalm 126), RV 608;* (ii) *Nulla in mundo pax sincera, RV 630.*
(M) *** O-L 443 199-2 [id.]. (i) James Bowman; (ii) Emma Kirkby; AAM, Preston – BACH: *Magnificat;* KUHNAU: *Der Gerechte kommt um.* ***

The solo motet, *Nulla in mundo pax sincera,* has Emma Kirkby as soloist coping splendidly with the bravura writing for soprano. James Bowman is also a persuasive soloist in the more extended, operatic-styled setting of Psalm 127. But since Vivaldi probably wrote *Nisi Dominus* for the Pietà, a Venetian orphanage for girls, readers might prefer a soprano voice.

Vives, Amadeo (1871–1932)

Dona Francisquita.
**(*) Sony Dig. S2K 66563 (2) [id.]. Domingo, Arteta, Mirabal, Del Portal, Cordoba Theatre Ch., Sevilla SO, Roa.

Even among the hundred and more zarzuelas written by this composer, *Dona Francisquita,* a light-hearted love story, is by far the most popular: no fewer than 5,000 performances were given in Spain over the twenty years after its first performance in 1923. It is full of charming ideas, skilfully presented. This version stands out from previous complete recordings through the strength of Plácido Domingo in the role of the hero, Fernando. Domingo's love of the genre shines out in every note he sings, with his diction immaculately clear. Even if vocally he is hardly matched by Ainhoa Arteta in the title-role, her light, bright, agile soprano is well suited to the part of an ingénue. Linda Mirabel, a warm-toned mezzo, sings Aurora, the actress, though the second tenor, Enrique del Portal, as the hero's friend, Cardona, is very thin-toned. At least there is no confusion with Domingo. Enrique Roa, who earlier conducted an electrifying account of Penella's *El gato montes* for DG, also with Domingo as the hero, understands the idiom perfectly, but here with an indifferent orchestra and the sound a little backward the impact of the performance is less, for all the brightness and energy.

Voříšek, Jan Vaclav (1791–1825)

Impromptus Nos. 1–6, Op. 7.
(B) ** Carlton Dig. PCD 1002 [id.]. Dirk Joeres – SCHUBERT: *Impromptus* etc. **

It was an intelligent idea to couple these *Impromptus,* which inspired the whole genre, with Schubert's better-known and more searching pieces. The German pianist, Dirk Joeres, is a sensitive and imaginative player, and his playing will give pleasure, though his recording is just a shade bass-heavy. (These performances do not displace Radoslav Kvapil's recital on Unicorn, listed in our main volume – DKPCD 9145 – but the Carlton disc is inexpensive and worth trying.)

Wagner, Richard (1813–83)

Der Ring des Nibelungen: an introduction to *The Ring* by Deryck Cooke, with 193 music examples.
(M) *** Decca 443 581-2 (2) [id.]. VPO, Solti.

The reissue in Decca's Classic Sound series of Deryck Cooke's fascinating and scholarly lecture is most welcome. Even though the CD reissue omits the printed text, the principal musical motives are all printed out in the accompanying booklet and they demonstrate just how the many leading ideas in *The Ring* develop from one another, springing from an original germ. The discourse is riveting, though even dedicated Wagnerians may not want to hear it many times over. The music examples, many of them specially prepared, are not always inserted with the skill one is accustomed to on BBC Radio 3, but this is still a thoroughly worthwhile acquisition for those who already have recordings of the operas.

Siegfried idyll.
(M) *** DG 439 969-2 (2) [id.]. BPO, Karajan – BRUCKNER: *Symphony No. 8 in C min.* ***

Karajan's account is unsurpassed. The string section of the Berlin Philharmonic produces radiant tone and the 1977 recording is full and truthful.

(i) *Overture: Der fliegende Holländer.* (ii) *Lohengrin: Prelude to Act I. Die Meistersinger: Overture.*
(iii) *Parsifal: Prelude and Good Friday music.* (iv) *Tannhäuser: Overture.*
(B) **(*) DG 439 445-2 [id.]. (i) Bayreuth (1971) Festival O, Boehm; (ii) BPO, Kubelik; (iii) Bav.
   RSO, Jochum; (iv) German Op. O, Berlin, Otto Gerdes.

Most of these performances are duplicated in a particularly attractive DG Double set of Wagner's orchestral excerpts mentioned in our main volume, but this shorter, Classikon bargain collection includes Jochum's superb account of the *Parsifal* excerpts and is quite worthwhile in its own right.

Lohengrin: Preludes to Acts I & III; Die Meistersinger: Prelude. Parsifal: Good Friday music.
Tannhauser: Overture and Venusberg music. Tristan und Isolde: Prelude & Liebestod.
(M) ** Mercury 434 342-2 [id.]. LSO, Dorati.

These are vibrantly direct performances, and no one could deny the moments of excitement or the competence of the LSO playing. But there is no incandescence in the *Parsifal* music or the *Lohengrin Prelude to Act I.* Like other Mercury recordings made in London (in this case, at Wembley or Watford Town Halls) at this period (1959/6), the sound is very immediate and for its time faithful, but the acoustic is not really ideal for the music.

Wesendonck Lieder.
(M) *** Decca 440 491-2 [id.]. Kirsten Flagstad, VPO, Boult – MAHLER: *Kindertotenlieder* etc. **(*)

Now, like the operatic reissues below, part of Decca's Kirsten Flagstad Edition, this performance remains treasurable. Flagstad's glorious voice is perfectly suited to the rich inspiration of the *Wesendonk Lieder. Im Treibhaus* is particularly beautiful. Fine accompaniment, with the 1956 recording sounding remarkable for its vintage, and skilfully remastered.

OPERA

Der fliegende Holländer (complete).
** EMI CDS5 55179-2 (3). Adam, Silja, Talvela, Kozub, Burmeister, Unger, BBC Ch., New Philh.
   O, Klemperer.
(M) * Ph. 442 103-2 (2) [id.]. Crass, Silja, Greindl, Uhl, Bayreuth (1961) Festival Ch. & O, Sawallisch.

Predictably, Klemperer's reading is spacious in its tempi – involving a third disc in its CD reissue – and the drama hardly grips you by the throat. But the underlying intensity is irresistible. This could hardly be recommended as a first choice, but any committed admirer of the conductor should try to hear it. It is a pity that Anja Silja was chosen as Senta, even though she is not as squally in tone here as she can be. Otherwise a strong vocal cast, much beautiful playing (particularly from the wind soloists) and a lively if not particularly atmospheric recording, made to sound drier still in its CD format. The set has been vividly remastered and sounds better than it ever did, but EMI's repackaged reissue is on three full-priced CDs, which is totally uncompetitive, especially when compared with the splendid Naxos set on two bargain-priced CDs, which is also to be preferred on artistic grounds (8.660025/6).

The 1961 Philips 'live' Bayreuth set is also not a serious competitor. Even Fritz Uhl, the Tristan of Solti's set, is disappointing. On the Bayreuth stage the size of his voice seems to diminish. Franz Crass has an attractive enough voice but is not exactly imaginative. Anja Silja generally sings in tune (surprisingly rare for Sentas), but it is not a very sweet sound. *Senta's ballad* is sung at the original pitch, but unhappily this puts too much of a strain on Mme Silja. Neither the conducting nor the orchestral playing is especially distinguished, and the shufflings on the stage are not an advantage.

Götterdämmerung (complete).
*** Teldec/Warner Dig. 4509 94194-2 (4) [id.]. Jerusalem, Anne Evans, Kang, Von Kannen,
   Bundschuh, Meier, Turner, Bayreuth (1991) Festival Ch. & O, Barenboim.
*** DG Dig. 439 385-2 (4) [id.]. Goldberg, Behrens, Salminen, Wlaschiha, Studer, Weikl, Schwarz,
   NY Met. Op. Ch. & O, Levine.

Recorded at the 1991 Bayreuth Festival, a year earlier than *Siegfried*, Barenboim's live recording is not quite the culmination one had hoped for in his cycle for Teldec. That is partly because the recording does not capture the acoustic of the Festspielhaus as faithfully as the 1992 *Siegfried*, with the orchestra rather drier and the stage voices inconsistently set in a rather more reverberant acoustic. The weighty reproduction of timpani also tends to cloud textures in moments of climax. There is also the problem in this opera, more than the rest of the *Ring*, of stage noises, particularly in the Harry Kupfer production which uses the chorus actively even at the end of the Immolation scene, rather undermining its rapt intensity, when the fulfilment motif enters at last. Anne Evans sweetly and purely rises to the challenge of that radiant close of the tetralogy, compensating for any lack of power in the clarity of focus and expressive intensity of her singing, making Brünnhilde a very human figure to excite the deepest sympathy. Whatever reservations have to be made about the recording, it is satisfyingly weighty and has more presence than its direct digital rivals, recorded in the studio under Haitink (EMI) and Levine (DG). On balance, it stands as the most recommendable of latterday versions of this final opera, thanks not only to the beauty as well as the imagination of Evans's singing, more satisfying than that of her squally rivals, but also to the superb singing of Siegfried Jerusalem. As in *Siegfried*, his live Bayreuth recording outshines his already outstanding achievement in the same role in the Haitink version, even if the stresses of a long evening begin to show by the end. Eva-Maria Bundschuh makes a fresh, bright Gutrune and Waltraud Meier a powerful Waltraute, giving an animated account of her Act I narration. Bodo Brinkmann is an old-sounding, rather uneven Gunther, Philip Kang a powerful but gritty Hagen and Gunter von Kannen an unsinister Alberich. Any disappointment there is small compared to the keen tension and excitement of this live recording under Barenboim, consistently gripping in a way studio recordings tend to be. As a performance it may not outshine either Solti's pioneering version or Karl Boehm's live account from Bayreuth – both of which still sound splendid – but it satisfyingly completes the finest of modern *Ring* cycles on disc.

Levine's hardly less compelling reading of *Götterdämmerung* stands out from the other three operas in his *Ring* cycle, with the sound rather more ample than in the earlier operas. The cast is a powerful one, with even the Norns cast from strength. Cheryl Studer as Gutrune, Matti Salminen as Hagen and Ekkehard Wlaschiha as Alberich have few equals, even if the contributions of both Hildegard Behrens as Brünnhilde and Rainer Goldberg as Siegfried are flawed, the one too edgy to convey beauty of line, whatever her power, the other growing gritty under pressure even in this, one of his finest recordings. For those wanting to sample the Levine *Ring*, this is the opera to go for.

Götterdämmerung: scenes (sung in German): *Dawn; Brünnhilde and Siegfried's entrance; Siegfried's Rhine journey; Siegfried's funeral march; Brünnhilde's immolation.*
(M) *** CfP CD-CFP 4670; *TC-CFP 4670* [id.]. Rita Hunter, Alberto Remedios, LPO, Mackerras.

This Classics for Pleasure disc of highlights was made in 1972, six years before the classic complete set in English by the same artists. Vocally what stands out in Hunter's performance is the pinging precision of even the most formidable exposed notes. Here she revealed herself to be a natural competitor in the international league, and her simple, fresh manner in the most intense moment of the *Immolation*, the hushed farewell of *Ruhe, du Gott*, is caught most affectingly. Remedios is also in splendid form, and Mackerras draws dedicated and dramatic playing from the LPO. The recording still sounds very impressive indeed, full-blooded and present, with the closing scene magnificently vivid. An outstanding bargain.

Lohengrin (complete).
*** DG Dig. 437 808-2 (3) [id.]. Jerusalem, Studer, Meier, Welker, Moll, Schmidt, V. State Op. Ch., VPO, Claudio Abbado.

Lohengrin has been a lucky opera on disc, and Claudio Abbado adds another magnificent reading to set alongside such classic performances as Kempe's (EMI CDS7 49017-2) and Solti's (with Jessye Norman and Plácido Domingo on Decca 421 052-2). It is no accident that all three feature the Vienna Philharmonic, playing with incandescent tone and rare subtleties of dynamic shading. But where Solti takes a very measured view, Abbado keeps Wagner's square rhythms flowing more freely, allowing himself a greater measure of rubato. That in turn reflects his experience with these same performers at the Vienna State Opera, and throughout the set one registers that, though this has all the benefits of a studio performance in precision, it consistently reflects stage experience, never more so than in the final dénouement and Lohengrin's departure. That Abbado's speeds are generally faster than Solti's (with the Act III *Prelude* a notable exception, where Abbado's compound time is more springy) means that the complete opera is squeezed on to three instead of four discs, giving it the clearest advantage. For the general collector this will now be first choice. The DG engineers have done wonders in getting a big, warm, spacious sound in the Vienna Musikvereinsaal, not always the easiest acoustic for a big-scale recording, though in clarity and natural focus the Decca recording for Solti is marginally finer still. As Elsa, matching her earlier, Bayreuth performance on Philips, Cheryl Studer is at her sweetest and purest, bringing out the heroine's naïvety more touchingly than Jessye Norman, whose weighty, mezzo-ish tone is thrillingly rich but is more suited to portraying other Wagner heroines than this. Though there are signs that Siegfried Jerusalem's voice is not as fresh as it once was, he sings commandingly, conveying both beauty and a true Heldentenor quality. Where Plácido Domingo, producing even more beautiful tone, tends to use a full voice for such intimate solos as *In fernem Land* and *Mein lieber Schwann*, Jerusalem sings there with tender restraint and gentler tone. Among the others, Waltraud Meier as Ortrud and Kurt Moll as King Heinrich are both superb, as fine as any predecessor, and though in the role of Telramund Hartmut Welker's baritone is not ideally steady, that tends to underline the weakness of the character next to the positive Ortrud. Though Kempe's vintage set boasts a cast overall still unsurpassed, Abbado's now matches it in its combination of high drama, rapt intensity and warmth of expression, enhanced by full-bodied, modern recording. A magnificent achievement.

Die Meistersinger (complete).
*** EMI CDS5 55142-2 (4) [id.]. Weikl, Heppner, Studer, Moll, Lorenz, Van der Walt, Kallisch, Bav. State Op. Ch., Bav. State O, Sawallisch.
(M) (*(**)) Decca mono 440 057-2 (4) [id.]. Schoeffler, Gueden, Treptow, Edelmann, Dönch, Poell, Dermota, Schürhoff, V. State Op. Ch., VPO, Knappertsbusch.

Sawallisch's fine set was the first studio recording of *Meistersinger* to be made in digital sound, and Wagner's great ensembles have never been heard on disc with such glorious warmth and fullness. Sawallisch also paces the work in reflection of his long experience of performing it in the opera house with the same musicians. Add to that the most radiant and free-toned Walther on disc, the Canadian, Ben Heppner, and you have a superb set, one that for many will be a clear first choice. In sheer beauty Heppner even outshines Plácido Domingo on Jochum's DG set, as he does in variety of expression and feeling. The *Prize Song* in Act III brings a heartfelt climax, with the following ensemble rounded off exquisitely with a perfectly even trill from Cheryl Studer as Eva. Her contribution is hardly less remarkable than Heppner's, at once powerful and girlishly tender, with the voice kept pure. If she is less affecting than she might be in the poignant duet with Sachs in Act II and in the great *Quintet* of Act III, that has something to do with a limitation in Sawallisch's reading, fine as it is. It rarely brings a gulp to the throat, rarely finds the poetic magic that this of all Wagner's operas can convey, and Act II, with the opening prelude too soft-grained for this buoyant music, rather lacks freshness. Though the cast is more consistent vocally than any rival team, the characterization could be more searching. Bernd Weikl makes a splendid Sachs, firm and true of voice, but something of the nobility of the master-shoemaker is missing. There is compensation in his virility, but you would hardly think of this character as a wise, benevolent adviser. His monologues are all impressive musically. He is far more satisfying than many a woolly wobbler of a Sachs, but less so emotionally. Deon van der Walt is a strong David, clear-cut and fresh, with Cornelia Kallisch making a traditionally fruity yet firm Magdalene. Siegfried Lorenz is a well-focused Beckmesser who refuses to caricature the much-mocked Town Clerk, and Kurt Moll is a magnificent Pogner. The chorus (balanced a little backwardly) and orchestra play with the warmth and radiance associated with recordings made in the Herkulessaal in Munich.

In 1950 Decca promoted a recording of Act II of *Meistersinger* - the first ever - as one of its initial opera projects on LP. The success of that was so great that, the following year, the rest of the opera was recorded with the same cast, and that is what reappears here at last on CD. Knappertsbusch takes a characteristically spacious view, but one which brings out the comedy as well as the poignancy of the piece. Maybe in reflection of the order of recording, Act II stands out as one of the most moving on disc, matched since but not surpassed. Paul Schoeffler with his dark, slightly metallic tone makes a searching Hans Sachs, wise and benevolent but unsentimental. Hilde Gueden is an enchanting Eva, with her unmistakable golden tone making the heroine provocative, even minxish. Her duet with Sachs is a high point, touching rare depths of emotion when Sachs remembers the wife and family who died, while then selflessly refusing to push himself forward as Eva's partner. The rest of the cast, though not so characterful, is still very strong, notably Anton Dermota as David and Karl Dönch as Beckmesser, with Günther Treptow not too strenuous as Walther. Sadly, the Decca transfer is edgy, with string-tone far more acid-sounding than on the original LP, even if voices come over well. Except for those attracted to Sawallisch's new digital set above, first choice for this opera remains with Jochum on DG, with the memorable and highly individual portrayal of Hans Sachs by Fischer-Dieskau (415 278-2).

'Vienna State Opera live': Volume 23: *Die Meistersinger*: excerpts: *Fliedermonolog* and Sachs–Eva duet; Sachs–Beckmesser duet; Act III: Quintet, Sachs's final monologue.

(M) (**) Koch-Schwann mono 3-1473-2 (2) [id.]. Herrmann, Kunz, Lorenz, Reining, Klein, Vienna State Op. O, Boehm – R. STRAUSS: *Ariade auf Naxos*. (***)

This 40-minute selection of excerpts from a Vienna State Opera performance of *Meistersinger* in 1943, conducted by Karl Boehm (Vol. 23 of the Vienna State Opera series), comes as a supplement to Boehm's historic recording of Strauss's *Ariadne auf Naxos*. The funereally slow account of Sachs's *Fliedermonolog* from Josef Herrmann leads on to charming performances of the duets with Eva and with Beckmesser. The sound is dim, and the recordings of Walther's *Prize song*, superbly sung by Max Lorenz, and of Sachs's final monologue are unceremoniously cut off; but the sense of occasion is most compelling, making this a valuable document.

Die Meistersinger: highlights.

(M) *** DG 445 470-2 [id.] (from complete recording, with Fischer-Dieskau, Domingo, Ligendza, Hermann, Laubenthal, Ludwig; cond. Jochum).

(M) (***) EMI mono CD-EMX 2228 [id.] (from complete recording, with Frantz, Schock, Grümmer, Frick, Kusche, Unger, Höffgen; cond. Kempe).

Jochum's is a performance that, more than any on record, captures the light and shade of Wagner's most warmly approachable score, its humour and tenderness as well as its strength; and for those who opt for another complete version these DG excerpts are especially valuable for giving fair samples of the two most individual performances: Fischer-Dieskau as a sharply incisive Sachs, his every nuance of mood clearly interpreted, and Domingo a golden-toned if hardly idiomatic Walther. Needless to say, the 76-minute selection, opening with the *Overture*, includes the Act III Quintet, also the opera's closing scene. The recording, made in March 1976 in the Berlin Jesus-Christus Kirche with the voices placed rather closely, matches the fine quality of the complete set.

The 72-minute selection from Kempe's classic EMI mono set is not dissimilar, this time demonstrating Ferdinand Frantz's comparatively weighty, dark-toned Sachs, while Rudolph Schock, with his distinctive timbre between lyrical and heroic, is ideally suited to the role of Walther. Elisabeth Grümmer is a meltingly beautiful Eva, particularly so in the great Act III Quintet. Again voices are closely balanced and there is striking clarity of focus so that, although the orchestra sounds relatively thin, one soon adjusts when the singing is so fine and there is good ambience.

Parsifal (complete).

**(*) DG Dig. 437 501-2 (4) [id.]. Domingo, Norman, Moll, Morris, Wlaschiha, Rootering, Met. Op. Ch. & O, James Levine.

(M) (***) Decca mono 425 976-2 (4) [id.]. Windgassen, Mödl, Weber, London, Uhde, Van Mill, Bayreuth (1951) Festival Ch. & O, Knappertsbusch.

James Levine's DG set is his second recording of Wagner's last opera, his first being done for Philips in 1985 during the Bayreuth Festival. In each his speeds outstrip almost anyone in slowness, but curiously it was easier to accept such expansiveness in a live account, recorded in the mellow acoustic of the Festspielhaus. The New York studio performance at times seems to hang fire - as in the Transformation scene of Act I - even though overall it takes almost ten minutes less. Many will find it a small price to pay for a performance, vividly recorded, involving a cast as starry as any that could be assembled. Whatever determined scoffers may say, the two superstars involved, Jessye Norman as Kundry and Plácido Domingo in the title-role, give performances that in every way live up to their reputations, not just exploiting beauty of sound (how rare in either role!) but backing it with keen characterization and concern for word-meaning. If Domingo has been criticized for his German pronunciation, it is something which only native German-speakers need worry about. Kurt Moll as Gurnemanz and Ekkehard Wlaschiha as Klingsor are both magnificent, firm and characterful, while James Morris as Amfortas gives a powerful performance, with slightly gritty tone adding to the character's sense of pain. Jan-Henrik Rootering's bass as Titurel is atmospherically enhanced by an echo-chamber, pointing the relative lack of reverberation in the main, firmly focused recording, one of the most vivid yet made in the Manhattan Center. If Levine's slow speeds will prevent this from being a first choice with most Wagnerians, this version brings many compensations.

Recorded at the Bayreuth Festival in 1951 with John Culshaw in charge of a Decca recording team, but with Teldec (then Decca's associate company) organizing the project, this very first version of *Parsifal* here comes in a good alternative pressing to that offered on the Teldec label. Hans Knappertsbusch was the inspired choice of conductor made by Wagner's grandsons for the first revivals of *Parsifal* after the war. The cast is very fine, with Wolfgang Windgassen making other Heldentenors seem rough by comparison, singing with warmth as well as power. Ludwig Weber is magnificently dark-toned as Gurnemanz, much more an understanding human being and less a conventionally noble figure. Martha Mödl is both wild and abrasive in her first scenes and sensuously seductive in the long Act II duet with Parsifal; Hermann Uhde is bitingly firm as Klingsor. Though the limited mono sound is not nearly as immediate or atmospheric as later stereo versions, with much thinner orchestral texture, the voices come over well, and the chorus is well caught. Karajan remains first choice among modern versions and was given a Rosette in our main volume (DG 413 347-2).

Das Rheingold (complete).
** DG Dig. 445 295-2 (2) [id.]. Morris, Wlaschiha, Ludwig, Häggander, Svendén, Jerusalem, Lorenz, Mark Baker, Zednik, Moll, Rootering, Hong, Kesling, Parsons, Met. Op. O, James Levine.

Originally issued on three CDs, Levine's version has sensibly been re-transferred on to two, making it more competitive with other latterday versions. The casting is strong, based on the live production at the Met. in New York, but, with little sense of presence in the recording, the voices lose some of their bloom. James Morris here sounds rougher than for Haitink on his EMI set, but Ekkehard Wlaschiha is a magnificent Alberich, with Heinz Zednik a well-focused Mime, Siegfried Jerusalem a powerful if undercharacterized Loge and Christa Ludwig a characterful Fricka. Yet neither in sound nor in pacing does the performance capture the sense of a live occasion very vividly, and this set will appeal mainly to those who have had experience of the opera-house performances. Otherwise Solti on Decca still heads the list of recommendations (414 101-2).

The Ring (complete).
(B) *** Ph. 446 057-2 (14) [id.]. Nilsson, Windgassen, Neidlinger, Adam, Rysanek, King, Nienstedt, Esser, Talvela, Böhme, Silja, Dernesch, Stewart, Hoeffgen, Bayreuth Festival (1967) Ch. & O, Boehm.
(M) ** DG Dig. 445 354-2 (14) [id.]. Behrens, Goldberg, Morris, Norman, Ludwig, Moll, Met. Op. O, Levine.

Anyone who prefers the idea of a live recording of the *Ring* cycle can be warmly recommended to Boehm's fine set, more immediately involving than any. Recorded at the 1967 Bayreuth Festival, it captures the unique atmosphere and acoustic of the Festspielhaus very vividly. Birgit Nilsson as Brünnhilde and Wolfgang Windgassen as Siegfried are both a degree more volatile and passionate than they were in the Solti cycle (at mid-price on Decca 414 100-2, given a Rosette in our main volume). Gustav Neidlinger as Alberich is also superb, as he was too in the Solti set; and the only major reservation concerns the Wotan of Theo Adam, in a performance searchingly intense and finely detailed but often unsteady of tone even at that period. The sound, only occasionally constricted, has been vividly transferred. Philips are currently offering this version of the *Ring* in a 14-disc limited edition (which means in effect for a limited time) at bargain price. Waverers should snap this up while it is still around, even if they already have the incomparable Solti set (Decca 414 100-2).

DG have sensibly repackaged Levine's New York *Ring* cycle on 14 discs at a special mid-price, and some listeners will welcome so strongly cast a recording in up-front studio sound, even though aggressively digital and not always kind to voices. The glory of the cycle is the conclusion, Levine's powerful reading of *Götterdämmerung*, with the sound rather fuller than in the earlier operas. Yet overall this is a set with too many flaws and disappointments, best recommended to those who have enjoyed Levine's spacious reading at the Met. or relayed on television.

Siegfried (complete).
*** Teldec/Warner Dig. 4509 94193-2 (4) [id.]. Jerusalem, Anne Evans, Tomlinson, Clark, Von Kannen, Philip King, Svendén, Leidland, Bayreuth (1992) Festival Ch. & O, Barenboim.

Barenboim's live recording of *Siegfried*, made at the Bayreuth Festival in 1992, is the finest of latterday digitally recorded versions, whether in the full-ranging, immediate sound, the exceptionally strong casting or the dramatic tensions of the reading which vividly bring out the emotions of a stage performance. There is no finer interpreter of the role of Mime today than Graham Clark, as his performance in the 1995 Covent Garden production has confirmed. On disc the characterization may sometimes sound extreme, but here is a powerful, clean-cut tenor voice that makes the dwarf into an intensely compelling character. Four other key principals are also the same as at Covent Garden. In the title-role Siegfried Jerusalem completely outshines his already fine performance on Haitink's studio recording for EMI. His voice has grown fuller and more powerful without losing any beauty, and the recording helps to give it more weight. Few Siegfrieds since Wolfgang Windgassen begin to match him, and John Tomlinson is the firmest, most darkly projected Wanderer among current rivals. You may argue that the older Wotan should not sound so virile, but Tomlinson's superb singing goes with keen musical imagination and concern for word-meaning. As for Anne Evans as Brünnhilde, she too brings out the beauty of Wagner's lines, focusing cleanly and purely, with some thrilling top notes and not a suspicion of a wobble. If in the theatre this is not the loudest Brünnhilde, it is one which has you responding the more intensely for its freshness and clarity. The fifth principal from the Covent Garden cast is the splendid Erda of Brigitta Svendén, with other roles cast well, if not outstandingly. But what confirms this, recorded last in the series, as the high point in Barenboim's Bayreuth cycle is the incandescence of his conducting, given extra impact by the vivid sound and consistantly reflecting his experience of working with these musicians.

Tristan und Isolde (complete).

(M) *** EMI CMS7 69319-2 (4) [Ang. CDMD 69319]. Vickers, Dernesch, Ludwig, Berry, Ridderbusch, German Op. Ch., Berlin, BPO, Karajan.

*** Teldec/Warner Dig. 4509 94568-2 (4) [id.]. Meier, Jerusalem, Lipovšek, Salminen, Struckmann, Berlin State Op. Ch., BPO, Barenboim.

(M) *** Decca 443 682-2 (4) [id.]. Mitchinson, Gray, Howell, Joll, Wilkens, Folwell, Welsh Nat. Op. Ch. & O, Goodall.

Karajan's is a sensual performance of Wagner's masterpiece, caressingly beautiful and with superbly refined playing from the Berlin Philharmonic. Dernesch as Isolde is seductively feminine, not as noble as Flagstad, not as tough and unflinching as Nilsson; but the human quality makes this account if anything more moving still, helped by glorious tone-colour through every range. Jon Vickers matches her in what is arguably his finest performance on record, allowing himself true pianissimo shading. The rest of the cast is excellent too. The recording has been remastered again for the present reissue and the 1972 sound has plenty of body, making this an excellent first choice, with inspired conducting and the most satisfactory cast of all. The set has also been attractively repackaged with cleanly printed documentation.

Daniel Barenboim follows up his live recording of the *Ring* cycle, made at Bayreuth (on balance the most successful of the modern digital sets), with this glowing account of *Tristan*, recorded in opulent sound under studio conditions in the Philharmonie. As a Furtwängler devotee, Barenboim has learnt much from that master's classic recording, and Act I is comparably spacious. After that the urgency of the drama prompts speeds that move forward more readily than Furtwangler's. One resulting merit of this Teldec issue is that, though it stretches to four discs, like most other versions, Acts II and III are each complete on a single disc, with the only break between discs at an unobtrusive point in Act I. the cast is an exceptionally strong one, with Waltraud Meier as Isolde graduating from mezzo soprano to full soprano, breasting the top Cs easily, showing no sign of strain, and bringing a weight and intensity to the role that reflect her earlier experience. The vibrato sometimes grows obtrusive, and even in the final *Liebestod* there is a touch of rawness under pressure; but the feeling for line is masterly, always with words vividly expressed. Siegfried Jerusalem, with a more beautiful voice than most latterday Heldentenoren, makes a predictably fine Tristan, not quite as smooth of tone as he once was and conveying the poignancy of the hero's plight in Act III rather than his suffering. Few could match him today. Marjana Lipovšek is among the most characterful of Branganes, strong and vehement, while Matti Salminen is a resonant, moving King Mark. Only the gritty tones of Falk Struckmann as Kurwenal fall short, a particular blemish in Act III. With weighty, full-ranging and well-balanced sound, this is a first-rate recommendation for a modern digital set.

Based on the much-praised production of the Welsh National Opera company, Goodall's recording of *Tristan* was made in 1980/81, not on stage but at Brangwyn Hall, Swansea, just when the cast was steamed up for stage performances. With long takes, the result is an extremely fresh-sounding performance, vivid and immediate, more intimate than rival versions yet bitingly powerful. Typically from Goodall, it is measured and steady, but the speeds are not all exceptionally slow and, with rhythms sharply defined and textures made transparent, he keeps the momentum going. So with the frenzied lovers' greetings in Act II Goodall's tread is inexorable at his measured speed and the result is compelling. The WNO orchestra is not sumptuous, but the playing is well-tuned and responsive. Neither Linda Esther Gray nor John Mitchinson is as sweet on the ear as the finest rivals, for the microphone exaggerates vibrato in both. But Mitchinson never barks, Heldentenor-style, and Gray in her first major recording provides a formidable combination of qualities: feminine vulnerability alongside commanding power. Gwynne Howell is arguably the finest King Mark on record, making his monologue at the end of Act II, so often an anti-climax, into one of the noblest passages of all. This may not have the smoothness of the best international sets but, with its vivid digital sound, it is certainly compelling, and a libretto in three languages is an additional bonus.

Tristan und Isolde: highlights.
(B) *** DG 439 469-2 [id.] (from complete (1966) Bayreuth recording, with Windgassen, Nilsson, Waechter, Ludwig; cond. Boehm).

With a playing time of 77 minutes, this well-documented bargain set of highlights, taken from Boehm's gripping 1966 Bayreuth Festival set, can be cordially welcomed. Each excerpt is related to the narrative and the opera is strongly cast, with Birgit Nilsson's closing *Liebestod* richly ecstatic.

Die Walküre: Act I (complete).
(M) *** Ph. 442 640-2 [id.]. Leonie Rysanek, James King, Gerd Nienstedt, (1967) Bayreuth Festival O, Boehm.

It seems not unusual to have Act I of *Die Walküre* offered alone on disc, and indeed the sequence of events between Siegmund, Sieglinde and Hunding make a miniature opera in their own right. Boehm's is our preferred complete set of this opera (for readers able to accept the inevitable noises of a live performance at Bayreuth), so collectors who have the Solti *Ring* will welcome this well-transferred CD as a sampler of a highly involving performance from 1967. The complete Boehm set remains available (Philips 412 478-2 – see our main volume).

OPERA RECITALS

(i) *Götterdämmerung: Starke Scheite schichtet mir dort (Immolation scene); (ii) Lohengrin: Einsam in trüben Tagen. Parsifal: Ich sah das Kind. Die Walküre, Act I: Der Männer Sippe; Du bist der Lenz;* (iii) Act II: *Siegmund! Sieh' auf mich! (Todesverkündigung).*
(M) **(*) Decca stereo/mono 440 495-2 [id.]. Kirsten Flagstad; (i) Oslo PO or Norwegian State R. O, Fjeldstad; (ii) VPO, Knappertsbusch; (iii) VPO, Solti.

Kirsten Flagstad's 1956 Wagner recordings with Knappertsbusch were uneven. Sieglinde's solo (*Der Männer Sippe*) is magnificent, but the scale of the voice makes *Elsa's dream* from *Lohengrin* seem a little unwieldy; and, fine as it is vocally, Kundry's *Herzeleide* (*Parsifal*) sounds rather staid for a seductress. However, to redress the balance Decca have added the 1957 *Death announcement scene* from the partial recording of Act II of *Die Walküre*, with Set Svanholm as Siegmund. He sings intelligently, if not always with grateful tone-colour, but it is Solti's conducting that prevents any slight blemishes from mattering here. The recording, too, is remarkably vivid. The collection ends with Flagstad's mono recording of the *Immolation scene* from *Götterdämmerung*, with Fjeldstad providing passionate support. She was over sixty when this was made, in the studio of Norwegian Radio in 1956, but the result is vocally thrilling and, despite the degree of hardness of the mono recording and the two-dimensional orchestra, it is the highlight of the disc.

Walton, William (1902–83)

'Walton edition': (i; ii) *Viola concerto;* (i; iii) *Violin concerto;* (iv) *Coronation marches: Crown imperial; Orb and sceptre; Façade (suites Nos. 1–2); Hamlet: Funeral march. Henry V (scenes from the film with Sir Laurence Olivier & chorus; suite, arr. Mathieson); Johannesburg festival overture; Partita for orchestra; Portsmouth Point overture; Richard III: Prelude & suite. Spitfire prelude and fugue; Symphony No. 1 in B flat min.;* (v) *The Wise Virgins (ballet suite)* & (iv) *Sheep may safely graze;* (iv; vi) *Belshazzar's Feast.*
(M) *** EMI stereo/mono CHS5 65003-2 (4) [CDHD 65003]. (i) Sir Yehudi Menuhin; (ii) New Philh. O; (iii) LSO; (iv) Philh. O; (v) Sadler's Wells O; (vi) with Donald Bell, Philh. Ch.; all cond. composer.

EMI follows up its revelatory Elgar Edition with this handsome Walton Edition, bringing together the composer's own EMI recordings not previously available on CD, with some of the most important dating from the mono interregnum before stereo arrived. The big revelation is Walton's own recording of the *First Symphony*, made in mono in October 1951, and here presented with far more bite and body than ever it had on the long-deleted LP. It emerges as among the most exciting versions ever, consistently displaying the Walton characteristic – faithfully observed later by such devotees as Previn – of treating the persistent syncopated rhythms with a jazzy freedom. The passion behind the performance is intense, most of all in the slow movement, which gains from superb woodwind playing from the Philharmonia soloists. Comparing Walton's 1959 stereo version of *Belshazzar's Feast* here with his earlier one of 1943 is fascinating, with speeds consistently more spacious, but with tensions just as keen and ensemble consistently crisper, though with less mystery conveyed. The one snag is the soloist, Donald Bell, clean of attack but uncharacterful.

Belshazzar and the *Symphony* make up the first disc, very generous measure, and all four discs are very well filled indeed. The second disc, entirely stereo, couples Menuhin's recordings of the *Violin* and *Viola concertos* with his version of the *Partita*, made in 1959. The new transfer of that last, fuller than before, reveals what extra fun Walton himself finds, bouncing the rhythms. Though Menuhin's account of the *Viola concerto* is a little effortful, not always flowing as it should, his viola sound is gloriously rich and true, and when it comes to the *Violin concerto*, recorded in July 1969, this is a vintage Menuhin performance, marked by his very distinctive tone and poignantly tender phrasing.

The third disc, mono except for Walton's scintillating account of the *Johannesburg Festival overture* and the *Hamlet Funeral march*, brings together the shorter pieces. This 1955 account of the *Façade suites* lacks the tautness of Walton's consistently brisker pre-war versions, not helped by less immediate recording. The *Coronation marches* and *Portsmouth Point*, recorded in 1953 to celebrate the Queen's coronation, have a beefy strength, with Walton as conductor bringing out not just the swagger but also the full-throated emotion behind the marches. The 1953 sessions also produced a new version of the Bach arrangement, *Sheep may safely graze*, warmer and more refined than the one in the original (1940) recording of *The Wise Virgins*. That was made with the Sadler's Wells Orchestra in July 1940, bright and vigorous, even if the ensemble is not of the crispest.

The final disc contains the film music – the *Spitfire Prelude and fugue*, the *Richard III Prelude* and *Suite* and the *Henry V Suite*, all made in 1963 as a package. Most important is the belated restoration of the complete Henry V sequence with Laurence Olivier, recorded in 1946 on four 78-r.p.m. records, but reissued on LP by RCA with seven minutes of cuts from the opening and closing scenes. The transfer is again first rate, with the atmospheric quality of the writing vividly caught, even if the mono sound lacks a little in body. The sound of arrows at the climax of the Agincourt charge has never been matched on subsequent recordings. What consistently comes out throughout the set is that in his seemingly reticent way Walton was just as inspired a conductor of his own music as Elgar was of his.

Coronation marches: Crown Imperial; Orb and Sceptre.
(M) *** EMI CDM5 65584-2 [id.]. LPO, Boult – ELGAR: *Collection.* ***

Walton's two *Coronation marches* make a reasonably appropriate coupling for Boult's collection of Elgar miniatures. It was Boult who first conducted them in Westminster Abbey (in 1937 and 1953 respectively) and he brings plenty of flamboyance to them. The (1977) Kingsway Hall recording is rich in amplitude, though lacking the last degree of brilliance by modern digital standards.

Façade (original version; complete).
(BB) ** Belart 450 136-2 [id.]. Dame Peggy Ashcroft, Paul Schofield, L. Sinf., composer.

Façade (absolutely complete).
(BB) *** Discover Dig. DICD 920125 [id.]. Hunter, Melologos Ens., Van den Broeck.

Enterprisingly the Discover International label at bargain price offers the most complete version of Walton's Entertainment yet, using a group of Belgian instrumentalists, the Melologos Ensemble, under Silveer van den Broeck. With a natural feeling for the young composer's tongue-in-cheek parodies, they point rhythms deliciously in a clean-cut way. When the reciter, Pamela Hunter, has made a speciality of reciting these Edith Sitwell poems, not exactly imitating Dame Edith herself but observing the strictly stylized, rhythmically crisp manner originally laid down, it makes a welcome and delightful disc. Five items appear here for the first time, adding to those resurrected by Walton himself in *Façade 2*. What one registers here, even more than with *Façade 2* alone, is that the early settings are more experimental and less sharply parodistic than the later, well-known ones, though in the accompaniment to one of them, *Aubade* ('Jane, Jane, tall as a crane'), there is a clear tongue-in-cheek reference to Stravinsky's *Rite of spring*. The recording is cleanly focused, balanced with the voice in front of the players yet obviously in the same acoustic, not superimposed; and the clarity and point of the solo playing, notably from the flute and clarinet, are splendid. Pamela Hunter is excellent too, happily characterizing with a minimum of 'funny voices'. At the price, a disc to recommend to all.

Walton's own stereo version from the early 1970s makes a fascinating supplement. Peggy Ashcroft is aptly characterful. She often lags behind the beat, but this adds to the sense of magnetic idiosyncrasy, and she is recorded so close that her breath is constantly in one's ear. Paul Schofield is the slowest and least rhythmic of reciters, but the composer keeps the music going as a subtle, quiet commentary in the background, and the effect is unique. The stereo is both atmospheric and immediate, and you can hear every word. Not a first choice, but an interesting bargain supplement to the essential Discover version.

Film music: *As you like it: suite. The Battle of Britain: suite. Henry V: suite. History of the English speaking peoples: March. Troilus and Cressida* (opera): *Interlude*.
(B) *** EMI Dig. CDM5 65585-2 [id.]. LPO Ch. & O, Carl Davis.

No composer has followed on the Elgar ceremonial tradition with such brilliance and panache as Walton. Here, with many items never recorded before, is a heart-warming celebration of that side of his work, helped by red-blooded performances from the LPO under the tireless advocate, Carl Davis. *The Battle of Britain suite* presents the music that (for trumpery reasons) was rejected for the original film, including a Wagnerian send-up and a splendid final march. Another vintage Walton march here was written for a television series based on Churchill's history, but again was never used. It is a pity that the *Henry V suite* does not include the Agincourt charge, but it is good to have the choral contributions to the opening and closing sequences. Best of all, perhaps, is the long-buried music for the 1926 Paul Czinner film of *As You Like It*. Walton, having just had great success with his *First Symphony*, here exuberantly does some joyful cribbing from Respighi, Ravel and others, but remains gloriously himself, making one regret that as a serious composer he was self-critical to the point of inhibition. If only he had allowed himself to throw off music like this rather more often, we would all have gained by it. Warm, opulent recording.

Symphony No. 1 in B flat min.; Coronation marches: Crown Imperial; Orb and Sceptre.
(M) **(*) Telarc Dig. CD 82016 [id.]. RPO, André Previn.

Symphony No. 1; Portsmouth Point overture.
(M) **(*) Virgin/EMI Dig. CUV5 61146-2 [id.]. LPO, Slatkin.

Previn's view of Walton's electrifying *First Symphony* has grown broader and less biting with the years. The sumptuous Telarc recording also makes for warmth rather than incisiveness. Those who know Previn's incomparable earlier reading for RCA (GD 87830) may well be disappointed; however, with fine playing from the RPO and with the slow movement more richly luxuriant than before, this is still a most enjoyable reading. The two *Coronation marches* make a colourful and welcome fill-up. *Crown Imperial* sounds especially expansive, with full-bodied Telarc sound, and altogether this is well worth acquiring as a more mature alternative to the indispensable RCA version of the symphony. However, the finest modern digital recording is Simon Rattle's, coupled with the *Cello concerto* (EMI CDC7 54572-2 – see our main volume).

The brilliance, bite and clarity of sound in Slatkin's version of the *First Symphony* reinforce the tautness of the performance, nagging the mind with repetitive rhythms and tension piled on tension. Slatkin does not have quite the rhythmic mastery in giving a jazzy lift to syncopations or in moulding Waltonian melody that you find in both Previn's versions, and the Scherzo is almost breathlessly fast. But the finale is magnificent, bringing thrust and power, and culminating superbly in the uninhibited triple timpani passage near the end. Slatkin takes an equally electric view of the *Overture*, again played brilliantly by the LPO.

CHAMBER MUSIC

(i) *5 Bagatelles for solo guitar;* (ii; iii) *Duets for children;* (iv; ii) *2 Pieces for violin and piano; Toccata for violin and piano;* (ii) (Piano) *Façade: Valse;* (v; i) *Anon in love* (for tenor & guitar); (v; ii) *2 Songs for tenor: The Winds, The Tritons.*
*** Chan. Dig. CHAN 9292 [id.]. (i) Carlos Bonell; (ii) Hamish Milne; (iii) Gretel Dowdeswell; (iv) Kenneth Sillito; (v) John Mark Ainsley.

The important newcomer here is the *Toccata for violin and piano*, which Walton wrote between 1922 and 1923, a curious mixture of cadenza and rhapsody of 15 minutes in a disconcertingly un-Waltonian style. Two songs for tenor are fascinating early works too, with a rushing accompaniment for *The Winds*, while *The Tritons* is chaconne-like, with a melody quite untypical of Walton. Milne and Dowdeswell bring out what charming, sharply focused ideas are contained in the ten *Duets for children*. For one who was no child-lover – see Susana Walton's *Behind the Façade* – Walton shows a remarkable gift for capturing a child's imagination, as in *Ghosts*. His own piano arrangement of the *Valse* from *Façade* is so thorny that even Hamish Milne has to go cautiously. The two violin pieces – using French troubadour songs – are spin-offs from the *Henry V* incidental music and, in the second, *Scherzetto*, reflect what their composer had learnt, writing for Heifetz. The two works with guitar are well known in Julian Bream's performances and recordings. Bonell is lighter and more delicate than Bream (see under Concerts, below), both in the *Bagatelles* and in *Anon in Love*, but is no less persuasive. Similarly, John Mark Ainsley lacks some of the punch of Peter Pears, for whom the cycle was written, but in a gentler way taps the wit and point of these Elizabethan conceits. A delightful collection, full of revealing insights into the composer's complex character.

String quartet in A min.

⊛ *** Testament mono SBT 1052 [id.]. Hollywood Qt – HINDEMITH: *Quartet No. 3*; PROKOFIEV: *Quartet No. 2.* (***) ⊛

*** Hyp. Dig. CDA 66718 [id.]. Coull Qt – BRIDGE: *3 Idylls;* *** ELGAR: *Quartet.* **(*)

Walton's only quartet has been decently represented in the catalogue over the years, but the pioneering account by the Hollywood Quartet, made in 1950, has still not been surpassed. It first appeared on a Capitol LP in harness with the Villa-Lobos *Sixth Quartet.* The sound comes up very well, though it is not, of course, state of the art. Moreover it comes with equally strong couplings and cannot be too strongly recommended.

The Elgar and Walton *Quartets* make an apt and attractive coupling, and here the Coulls, unlike their direct rivals, offer as bonus a fine example of Frank Bridge's quartet-writing. In the Walton, the reading captures movingly the spirit of Waltonian melancholy, bringing out the elegiac intensity of the extended *Lento* slow movement, taken at a very measured pace. The Coulls are splendid too in capturing the element of fun in Walton's scherzando ideas. The Brittens on Collins (1280-2), also offering the Elgar, are more bitingly powerful, but they find less fantasy.

OPERA

Troilus and Cressida (complete).

⊛ *** Chan. Dig. CHAN 9370/1 (2) [id.]. Arthur Davies, Howarth, Howard, Robson, Opie, Bayley, Thornton, Owen-Lewis, Opera North Ch., English N. Philh. O, Richard Hickox.

(M) **(*) EMI CMS5 65550-2 (2) [id.]. Cassilly, J. Baker, Bainbridge, English, Luxon, Van Allan, Rivers, Lloyd, ROHCG Ch. and O, Lawrence Foster.

Few operas since Puccini have such a rich store of memorable tunes as *Troilus and Cressida.* As Chandos's magnificent recording shows, based on Opera North's 1995 production – using Walton's tautened score of 1976 but with the original soprano register restored for Cressida – this red-bloodedly romantic opera on a big classical subject deserves to enter the regular repertory. Rounding off Chandos's complete Walton Edition, the recording was made in between the live theatre performances. Judith Howarth portrays the heroine as girlishly vulnerable, rising superbly to the big challenges of the love duets and final death scene. Arthur Davies is an aptly Italianate Troilus, an ardent lover, and there is not a weak link in the rest of the characterful cast, with Nigel Robson a finely pointed Pandarus, comic but not camp, avoiding any echoes of Peter Pears, the originator. As Evadne, Cressida's maid, Yvonne Howard produces firm, rich mezzo tone, and the role of Calkas, Cressida's father, is magnificently sung by Clive Bayley. The role of Diomede, Cressida's Greek suitor, can seem one-dimensional but Alan Opie, in one of his finest performances on record, sharpens the focus, making him a genuine threat, a noble enemy. Richard Hickox draws magnetic performances from chorus and orchestra alike, bringing out the many parallels with the early Walton of *Belshazzar's Feast* and the *Symphony No. 1.* More clearly than ever with this recording we can see that this, Walton's only full-length opera, acted as a watershed in his career, at once the last of the electrically intense, passionately romantic works which marked the first half of his career, and the first of the refined, more reflective works of the post-war period. As for the recorded sound, the bloom of the Leeds Town Hall acoustic allows the fullest detail from the orchestra, enhancing the Mediterranean warmth of the score, helped by the wide dynamic range. The many atmospheric effects, often offstage, are clearly and precisely focused, and the placing of voices on the stereo stage is also unusually precise.

The great glory of EMI's live recording, made at Covent Garden during the 1976 revival, is the singing of Dame Janet Baker in the role of Cressida. Though the dry acoustic takes some of the bloom away from the voice, the glorious variety of her tonal colourings still gives a superb idea of Dame Janet's masterly singing in opera at the very peak of her career. Walton recast the role for a mezzo specially so that Dame Janet could sing it and, though the voice and personality speak always of total fidelity – not exactly consistent with the heroine's character even in this Chaucer-based version of the story – the weight, beauty and heartfelt expressiveness are wonderfully telling, giving a distinctive slant to the whole opera. It is good to have this historic document on CD, even if in face of the magnificent Chandos recording, based on the Opera North production, it inevitably remains second best, not helped by intrusive audience noises. The one compensation of the very dry Covent Garden sound, both for the singers on stage and for the orchestra in the pit, is that the dramatic bite is often enhanced, as in the grinding brass dissonances at the start of Cressida's final solo. Otherwise the beauty of Walton's writing, for voices and orchestra alike, is minimized and, though the singers make a characterful team with no weak link, the voices are never flattered. Richard Cassilly as Troilus uses his powerful Heldentenor tone intelligently, but the lower register is often gritty. Whatever the limitations of the orchestral sound, the bite and purposefulness of Lawrence Foster's conducting – with speeds regularly faster than Hickox's – comes over well, even if he fails to match Hickox in expressive warmth or natural feeling for the Walton idiom.

Ward, John (1571–1638)

Cor mio, deh non languire; Cruel unkind; Down in a dale; Fantasias a 6: Nos. 1 in A min.; 2 in F; 3 in A min.; 4 in G min.; 7 in C min. If Heaven's just wrath; In nomine a 6: No. 2 in C min. My breast I'll set upon a silver stream; No object dearer; Well-sounding pipes.
*** Musica Oscura Dig. 070981 [id.]. Consort of Musicke, Anthony Rooley.

Down caitive wretch/ Prayer is an endless chain; Have mercy upon me; How long wilt thou forget me; I will praise the Lord; Let God arise; O let me tread in the right path; O Lord consider my great moans; Praise the Lord, O my soul (2 versions); This is a joyful, happy, holy day.
*** Musica Oscura Dig. 070982 [id.]. Consort of Musicke, Anthony Rooley.

As Anthony Rooley and the Consort of Musicke have shown in previous recordings, John Ward was one of the greatest madrigalists of the Jacobean period. On this showing his church music was just as inspired in its dark intensity, a model for Purcell's finest. All but one of these ten Psalm-settings and anthems are in the minor mode, with grinding suspensions regularly bringing astonishingly adventurous chromatic harmonies in complex polyphony. Emma Kirkby leads the team of soloists, sensitively accompanied by the viols of Rooley's Consort.

Warlock, Peter (1894–1930)

Capriol suite.
(BB) ** BBC Radio Classics BBCRD 9104 [id.]. Hirsch Chamber Players, Leonard Hirsch (with Concert) – FINZI: *Clarinet concerto* etc.; LEIGH: *Harpsichord concertino;* VAUGHAN WILLIAMS: *Tallis fantasia.* **(*)

This is a very decent, lively and well-articulated performance of the *Capriol suite* that comes from 1965. Although it is well played, it is not very special – and the *Capriol suite* is not a rarity. The sound is very good for its date, better in fact than some of the other material in this first BBC release.

(i) *Capriol suite;* (ii) *The Curlew* (song-cycle); *5 Nursery jingles. The Birds; Chopcherry; Fairest May; Mourn no moe; My gostly fader; Sleep; The water lilly.*
(BB) **(*) ASV CDQS 6143 [id.]. (i) RPO, Barlow; (ii) James Griffett, Haffner Qt; Mary Murdoch, Mary Ryan.

Though this performance of *The Curlew* is not so beautiful or so imaginative as Ian Partridge's (on EMI CDM5 65101-2 – see our main volume), it is good to have a whole record of songs by a composer with a strikingly distinctive feeling for English verse. Each one of these songs is a miniature of fine sensitivity, and James Griffett sings them with keen insight, pointing the words admirably. The instrumental playing is most sensitive, and the recording, made in Christ Church, Chelsea, is warmly atmospheric yet clear. The performance of the *Capriol suite* is also a very good one, and the digital recording is first rate. This CD is well worth its modest cost.

Weber, Carl Maria von (1786–1826)

Symphonies Nos. 1 in C; 2 in C, J.50/51. Die Drei Pintos: Entr'acte. Silvana: Dance of the young nobles; Torch dance. Turandot: Overture; Act II: March; Act V: Funeral march.
⊛ (BB) *** Naxos Dig. 8.550928 [id.]. Queensland PO, John Georgiadis.

Symphonies Nos. 1 in C; 2 in C; (i) Konzertstück, Op. 79.
*** EMI Dig. CDC5 55348-2 [id.]. L. Classical Players, Roger Norrington; (i) with Melvyn Tan.

Weber wrote his two symphonies in the same year (1807) and, though both are in C major, each has its own individuality. The witty orchestration and operatic character of the writing are splendidly caught in these sparkling Queensland performances, while in the slow movements the orchestral soloists (notably the languishing viola in the *Adagio* of No. 2) relish their solos, for all the world like vocal cantilenas. Weber's scoring is often adventurous and he finds plentiful opportunities for the horns to shine, especially in the playful main theme of the *Presto* finale of No. 1. Weber's writing is often unpredictable, not least in the surprising closing bars of No. 2; and Georgiadis and his players present both works with striking freshness and spontaneity. The Naxos recording is in the demonstration class, and the disc is made the more attractive for the inclusion of orchestral excerpts from two little-known operas and incidental music from *Turandot*. The *Entr'acte* from the incomplete *Die Drei Pintos* was put together by Mahler from Weber's sketches.

If you want period performances, Roger Norrington's with the London Classical Players meet the bill admirably and the symphonies come up with striking freshness. They are as refreshing as Melvyn Tan's account of the *Konzertstück* is dashing and dazzling. Compared with the sound of modern instruments, the effect is undoubtedly gruffer, but there is also rather more gravitas and the drama is heightened, with the spirit of Beethoven not far away, although neither of the symphonies is a weighty work in a Beethovenian sense. Here, in contrast with his Beethoven interpretations, Norrington favours relatively relaxed allegros, yet rhythms are so well sprung that there is no hint of sluggishness. The quirkiness of some of the writing is reinforced, notably in the unexpected pauses which punctuate the argument, as in the first movement of No. 1 and the brief finale of No. 2. The bite is greater with period instruments, with contrasts of light and shade emphasized. The wit of the finale of No. 1 is caught spiritedly, with the braying of the hand horns adding to the movement's character. However, though the textures are refined, the recording sometimes clouds big tuttis in a way one does not expect with simulated authenticity. Particularly beautiful are the oboe solos from Anthony Robson and the long cello solo in the *Adagio* of No. 2, originally written for the celebrated London cellist, Piatti, and here gloriously played by Jennifer Ward-Clarke: one is reminded of a slow movement of Haydn. The brief Minuet is vibrant (as indeed it is with Georgiadis) and the *Scherzo presto* finale, alert and crisply enunciated, gives the feeling of great vigour, whereas in fact the Australian performance is fractionally faster. As his bonus, Norrington offers the *Konzertstück*, with Melvyn Tan playing a Derek Adlam copy of an appropriate Streich instrument of 1815. He makes an impressive case for using an authentic fortepiano with its rather dry treble response, although the piece is made to seem more lightweight than usual. Personal taste will decide whether this relatively romantic work sounds better on a modern concert grand, as played, say, by Alfred Brendel. Here it remains a display piece, not because of conventional keyboard bravura but through the diamond clarity of the rapid figuration as delivered by Tan, even if the result is to suggest an occasional banality of argument.

Clarinet quintet in B flat, Op. 34.

(M) *** O-L 444 167-2 [id.]. Alan Hacker, The Music Party – HUMMEL: *Clarinet quartet.* ***

If you want to hear how Weber's *Clarinet quintet* must have sounded during his lifetime, Alan Hacker and the Music Party will probably be your first choice. The Gerock clarinet Hacker uses is from 1804, eleven years before the first complete performance of the *Quintet*. It is not of course the smooth, mellifluous instrument Gervase de Peyer uses in his version (Decca 430 297-2), and the strings do not sound as blended as one would expect in a modern quartet. Hacker plays with his customary artistry and sensitivity, and with lots of bite and sparkle in the bravura passages. The recording is clear and vivid. Antony Pay's alternative authentic version (also on Oiseau-Lyre: 433 044-2 – see our main volume) is also highly recommendable, but Hacker has a price advantage and an ideal coupling.

PIANO MUSIC

Piano sonata No. 1 in C, Op. 24 (J.138); Invitation to the dance, Op. 65 (J.260); 6 Variations on an original theme, Op. 40 (J.7); 9 Variations on a Russian theme: 'Schöne Minka', Op. 40 (J.179).

(BB) ** Naxos Dig. 8.550988 [id.]. Alexander Paley.

Piano sonata No. 2 in A flat, Op. 39 (J.199); Grande Polonaise, Op. 21 (J.59); 6 Variations on Naga's aria: 'Woher mag dies wohl kommen?' from Vogler's opera, Samori, Op. 6 (J.43); 7 Variations on a gypsy song, Op. 55 (J.219).

(BB) ** Naxos Dig. 8.550989 [id.]. Alexander Paley.

Piano sonata No. 3 in D min., Op. 49 (J.206); Momento capriccioso, Op. 12 (J.56); 7 Variations on an original theme, Op. 9 (J.55); 7 Variations on Binchi's air: 'Vien quà, Dorina bella', Op. 7 (J.53); 8 Variations on the Air de ballet from Castore e Polluce by Abbé Vogler, Op. 5 (J.40).

(BB) ** Naxos Dig. 550990 [id.]. Alexander Paley.

Piano sonata No. 4 in E min., Op.70 (J.287); Les Adieux, Op. 81 posth.; Polacca brillante (L'hilarité), Op. 72 (J.268); Rondo brillante (La gaité), Op. 62 (J.252); 7 Variations on a theme from Méhul's opera, Joseph, Op. 28 (J.141).
(BB) **(*) Naxos Dig. 8.553006 [id.]. Alexander Paley.

Alexander Paley's survey of Weber's piano output is certainly comprehensive. His playing has finesse and polish and is often thoughtful, but it tends to reveal relatively little below the surface of the music. The result is generally pleasing, although at times Paley's rubato in Weber's secondary lyrical ideas is a little fussy and in the sets of variations, after announcing each theme characterfully, the playing seems to slip back into routine as if Paley were not really involved with Weber's invention. What does fire him is the bravura writing, and the Mendelssohnian *Momento capriccioso* on the third disc is vivaciously done. For some reason, the *Fourth E minor Sonata* also excites a strong response and this is easily the most compelling performance of the four. Then the closing *Rondo* and *Polacca* are thrown off infectiously. So disc four is the place to start if you are tempted by these inexpensive discs, which are all well recorded. But the sonata performances by Hamish Milne (on CRD) and Martin Jones (on Pianissimo), discussed in our main volume, are well worth their extra cost.

Der Freischütz (opera; complete).
**(*) RCA Dig. 09026 62538-2 (2) [id.]. Sweet, Ziesak, Seiffert, Rydl, Scharinger, Berlin R. Ch., German Opera, Berlin, O, Janowski.
(M) ** Decca 443 672-2 (2) [id.]. Behrens, Donath, Meven, Kollo, Moll, Brendel, Grumbach, Bav. R. Ch. & SO, Kubelik.

In full-bodied, if not always refined, sound, with voices well forward, Marek Janowski conducts a strong, generally enjoyable performance that does not replace earlier versions such as Carlos Kleiber's on DG (415 432-2), or indeed Keilberth – see below. Outstanding in the cast are Ruth Ziesak as Aennchen, light and sparkling, and Peter Seiffert who, as Max, produces unstrained, heroic tone. As Kaspar, Kurt Rydl suffers from the closeness of the recording, which exaggerates an unevenness of production, though the characterization is strong. The key figure is that of the heroine, Agathe, with Sharon Sweet generally controlling her weighty soprano well in the lovely legato lines of her two big arias, but sounding too lusty, rarely producing a true pianissimo. This hardly matches the finest performances in this difficult role. As for the big dramatic moments, the forward sound adds to their power, atmospheric subtlety is lacking, even in the Wolf's Glen scene. While it is still available, first choice for this opera remains with Keilberth's early EMI set with Elisabeth Grümmer singing exquisitely as Agathe. What makes this still our favourite recommendation is the superbly atmospheric realization of the famous Wolf's Glen scene; moreover this set is offered at mid-price (CMS7 69342-2).

   Kubelik takes a direct view of Weber's high romanticism. The result has freshness but lacks something in dramatic bite and atmosphere. There is far less tension than in the finest earlier versions, not least in the Wolf's Glen Scene, which in spite of full-ranging, brilliant recording seems rather tame. The singing is generally good – René Kollo as Max giving one of his best performances on record – but Hildegard Behrens, superbly dramatic in later German operas, here as Agathe seems clumsy in music that often requires a pure lyrical line. The sound has been succesfully remastered; but this cannot compare with Keilberth's early EMI set, a warm, exciting account of an opera that must be played and sung for all it is worth.

Der Freischütz: highlights.
(B) *** DG 439 440-2 [id.] (from complete recording, with Janowitz, Mathis, Schreier, Adam, Vogel, Crass, Leipzig R. Ch., Dresden State O, Carlos Kleiber).

Anyone looking for a set of highlights from *Der Freischütz* cannot better this bargain Classikon disc, taken from a compelling performance which is consistently well sung and dramatically conducted by Carlos Kleiber. The 73-minute selection includes the full Wolf's Glen scene at the end of Act II, and the 1973 recording still sounds very well indeed.

Webern, Anton (1883–1945)

Passacaglia, Op. 1; 6 Pieces, Op. 6a; 5 Pieces, Op. 10; Symphony, Op. 21; Variations, Op. 30.
*** Decca Dig. 436 421-2 (3) [id.]. Cleveland O, Dohnányi – MOZART: *Symphonies Nos. 35–36; 38–41.* **

These five major works of Webern come as the unexpected but refreshing coupling for the last six Mozart symphonies in Dohnányi's weightily traditional, very well-played performances. But it is in Webern rather than Mozart that Dohnányi and the Cleveland Orchestra find themselves completely at home. These are not just refined but warmly expressive performances, such as one ideally wants if Webern's cryptic, purposeful writing is to be fully appreciated. Sensibly, the Webern items are presented in chronological order, so that on the first disc after the *Haffner* and *Linz Symphonies* the openly romantic *Passacaglia*, Op. 1, leads naturally to the *Six Pieces*, Op. 6, in their original, unrevised scoring. The sound is full and rich in the Cleveland manner, which suits the spare Webernian textures far better than Mozartian tuttis.

Passacaglia; Im Sommerwind.
*** Decca Dig. 436 467-2 [id.]. Concg. O, Chailly – SCHOENBERG: *Chamber symphony No. 1 etc.* ***

Both the Webern and the Schoenberg items on this disc were originally used as fill-ups for Chailly's recordings of the four Brahms symphonies. But those who want a more conventional coupling can be safely recommended to these finely moulded, superbly recorded versions.

Im Sommerwind.
*** Decca Dig. 436 240-2 (2) [id.]. Cleveland O, Dohnányi – MAHLER: *Symphony No. 6* **(*);
  SCHOENBERG: *5 Orchestral pieces.* ***

Dohnányi as a Mahlerian may be short on temperament, but his reading of Webern's early tone-poem, *Im Sommerwind*, could not be more radiant, with the subtle changes of mood most delicately conveyed to bring out the full, impressionistic beauty of this evocative piece from 1904. Superb, full and well-balanced sound.

Weinberger, Jaromír (1896–1967)

Schwanda the Bagpiper: Polka and fugue.
(M) *** RCA 09026 62587-2 [id.]. Chicago SO, Fritz Reiner – DVORAK: *Symphony No. 9 etc.*;
  SMETANA: *Bartered Bride: overture.* ***

This infectious orchestral display-piece was better known in the days of 78s. Reiner and his fine orchestra give a bravura performance, building to a huge climax. The Chicago recording is excellent and this CD overall is most attractive.

Weir, Judith (born 1954)

OPERA

Blond Eckbert (complete).
*** Collins Dig. 1461-2 [id.]. Nerys Jones, Owens, Ventris, Folwell, ENO Ch. & O, Sian Edwards.

Recorded live at the Coliseum in London as a by-product of Channel Four's television relay, this gives a vivid idea of a fascinating opera, stylized and allusive, that, in a way typical of this adventurous composer, presents a curious, even sinister, German folk-tale with symbolic overtones. Not everyone will respond to the bald style of the libretto, with characters on entry tending to sing monologues about their life-stories rather than joining in conversation. Yet the bright clarity and fresh invention of Weir's writing follows on the style she has adopted with such success in previous operas and mini-operas. The original English National Opera staging was over-elaborate for so basically simple a piece, which makes this disc welcome in letting one appreciate the musical qualities without distraction. The singing is clean-cut and generally fresh, with Christopher Ventris excellent in multiple tenor roles, but with Nicholas Folwell gruff-sounding in the title-role. Excellent sound.

(i) *The Consolations of scholarship;* (ii) *Missa del Cid;* (iii) *King Harald's Saga.*
*** United Dig. 88040 CD [id.]. (i) Linda Hirst, Lontano, Odaline de la Martinez; (ii) Herrett,
  Combattimento, Mason; (iii) Jane Manning.

Starting with *King Harald's Saga* in 1979, Judith Weir has developed a genre that might be described as the mini-opera. With pin-point brevity the results are sharply stylized in a way that points forward to Weir's full-length operas. *King Harald's Saga* is a 13-minute sequence in three Acts, based on the Norwegian invasion of Britain under Harald Hardradi in 1066. With Jane Manning the magnetic soloist, it has the singer unaccompanied in a virtuoso performance. In the other two operas on this disc, Weir again uses spoken dialogue freely, with the solitary singer in each freely ringing the changes, but the chamber accompaniments expand the range of expression. *The Consolations of scholarship* – written in 1985, two years before Weir produced her much-praised *Night at the Chinese Opera* – has a libretto reflecting the style of Yuan drama, the oldest form of Chinese play. The mixture of speech, declamation and aria was suggested by the original text, involving a surprisingly elaborate story about a boy thwarting a wicked general's plot against the Emperor. The *Missa del Cid* of 1988, also lasting 20 minutes, is simpler in outline though again involving an elaborate story, with the exploits of El Cid told by an Evangelist in a sequence built on the six sections of the Latin Mass. The idiom in each opera is distinctive and new, but not hard to take in, with the story element more clearly established than in many far longer operas. Performances and recording are excellent, with Linda Hirst joined by Odaline de la Martinez in *Consolations* and Nick Herrett with Combattimento under David Mason in the *Missa*.

Wert, Giaches de (1535–96)

Il settimo libro de madrigali.
(M) *** Virgin Veritas/EMI Dig. VER5 61177-2 [id.]. Consort of Musicke, Anthony Rooley.

Giaches de Wert was Monteverdi's predecessor in Mantua at the court of Count Alfonso Gonzaga. He was fairly prolific: this is the seventh of twelve books of madrigals, published in 1581 to celebrate the nuptials of the Duke's son, Vincenzo, and the final dialogue madrigal, *In qual parte sì ratto* ('Where are his swift pinions'), cleverly embroiders the elements of the bridegroom's family (an eagle) and those of his bride (the hyacinth: 'A flawless white pearl'). The opening madrigal is celebratory: *Sorgi e rischiara* ('Arise, light up the sky with thy approach, Holy Mother of love, lead in the day'), but many of the other varied settings are concerned with the trials and disappointments of love, with references to the 'sad heart', while – even more extraordinarily – the tenth suggests *Voi volete ch'io muoi* ('You wish that I were dead'). De Wert certainly emerges here as a composer of expressive depth and personality and with a fine feeling for words; his individuality is notable in *Solo e pensoso* ('Alone and bowed') with its very striking melodic contour. He is not another Monteverdi but his art is well worth knowing, and the singing here is persuasive, expressively responsive and beautifully blended, even if it does not always make the music project irresistibly. The recording is well up to the high standard of this stimulating Veritas series.

Westlake, Nigel (born 1958)

Antartica (suite for guitar and orchestra).
*** Sony Dig. SK 53361 [id.]. John Williams, LSO, Paul Daniel – SCULTHORPE: *Nourlangie* etc.

Nigel Westlake was born in Perth, Australia, and his music makes a fine coupling for the works by his older contemporary, Peter Sculthorpe. *Antartica* is a film-score written to accompany an Imax large-screen documentary about the frozen continent. Westlake's music is highly imaginative and inventive and stands up memorably on its own. The guitar is used both with the orchestra and to play haunting, improvisatory-styled interludes. The opening section, *The last place on earth*, dramatically accompanies an aerial shot of the icecap, taken at midnight, yet in the full daylight of the midnight sun; *Wooden ships*, opening mysteriously, brings the first explorers and a really haunting tune, which is developed orchestrally from the opening guitar solo. *Penguin ballet*, subtly scored, has both charm and piquant liveliness, while the finale, *The ice core*, is connected with the discovery of the hole in the ozone layer and the consequent changes to the earth's atmosphere. It opens ethereally but gathers energy and momentum for an optimistic, dance-like, but by no means complacent ending. The suite is consistently compelling, and the scoring and writing for the solo instrument are very resourceful indeed. John Williams clearly relishes the considerable demands of the solo part, and Paul Daniel shapes the music spontaneously and skilfully. The recording is in the demonstration bracket, though the solo guitar is very forwardly balanced. Well worth exploring: there is no barbed wire here.

Weyse, Christoph Ernst Friedrich (1774–1842)

Symphonies Nos. 1 in G min., DF117; 2 in C, DF118; 3 in D, DF119.
** Marco Polo/Da Capo 8.224012 [id.]. Royal Danish O, Schønwandt.

Admirers of the great Danish baritone, Aksel Schiøtz, will have encountered Weyse's songs; indeed he is known exclusively outside Denmark for his output of solo song. Born in north Germany, Weyse settled in Denmark in the year of the French Revolution. His seven symphonies all date from the early part of his career (1795–9) and the three recorded here were all composed in 1795, when he was twenty-one. They were subsequently revised in 1805, 1797 and 1800 respectively. Weyse also re-used them in other contexts; as late as 1832, the *First Symphony* was used as incidental music for Ewald's *Death of Baldur*, and the finale of the *Second* was pressed into service as the overture to his opera, *The sleeping draught*. As one might expect, the example of Haydn affected Weyse strongly, and the minor-key symphonies in particular are reminiscent of Haydn's *Sturm und Drang* symphonies. Michael Schønwandt gives vital yet sensitive accounts of all three symphonies and is well served by the engineers. This lively music is worth investigating.

Widor, Charles-Marie (1844–1937)

Organ symphonies: No. 5 in F min., Op. 42/1 (complete); 6 in B, Op. 42/2: 1st movt; 8 in B, Op. 42/4: 4th movt (Prelude).
(M) *** Saga EC 3361-2 [id.]. David Sanger (organ of St Peter's Church, Clerkenwell, London).

David Sanger's account of the Widor *Symphony No. 5* is first class in every respect and is recorded with fine bloom and clarity. His restraint in registering the central movements prevents Widor's cosy melodic inspiration from sounding sentimental, and the finale is exciting without being overblown. The other symphonic movements are well done but serve to confirm the conclusion that the famous *Toccata* from No. 5 was Widor's masterpiece. The Clerkenwell organ has a pleasingly wide palette of colour, perhaps surprisingly well suited to this repertoire.

Wieniawski, Henryk (1835–80)

Capriccio-waltz, Op. 7; Gigue in E min., Op. 27; Kujawiak in A min.; Légende, Op. 17; Mazurka in G min., Op. 12/2; 2 Mazurkas, Op. 19; Polonaise No. 1 in D, Op. 4; Russian carnival, Op. 11; Saltarello (arr. Lenehan); Scherzo-tarantelle in G min., Op. 16; Souvenir de Moscou, Op. 6; Variations on an original theme, Op. 15.
(BB) **(*) Naxos Dig. 8.550744 [id.]. Marat Bisengaliev, John Lenehan.

Brilliant playing from this remarkable Russian fiddler, born in Kazakhstan, who studied at the Tchaikovsky Conservatoire, and so is immediately at home in the opening *Souvenir de Moscou*, played (like the rest of this programme) with all the requisite flair and virtuosity. All the dazzling violin fireworks are ready to bow here, from left-hand pizzicatos in the *Russian carnival* to multiple stopping (and some lovely, warm lyricism) in the *Variations on an original theme*, plus all the dash you could ask for in the closing *Scherzo-tarantelle*. The four *Mazurkas* have plenty of animated folk feeling and local colour, while the beautiful *Légende* (which Wieniawski dedicated to his wife as a nuptial gift) is both touchingly gentle and passionately brilliant. Marat Bisengaliev is without the larger-than-life personality of a Perlman, but he is a remarkably fine player and a stylist, as well as being able to produce a sparkling moto perpetuo at will, as in the Neapolitan *Saltarello*, arranged by the pianist, John Lenehan, who provides his partner with admirable support throughout. The snag is the very reverberant acoustic of the Rosslyn Hill Chapel, Hampstead – so obviously empty. One adjusts to this (with some reluctance); otherwise the sound and balance are natural enough.

Wirén, Dag (1905–86)

Serenade for strings in G, Op. 11.
*** BMG/RCA Dig. RD 60439 [60439-2-RC] [id.]. Guildhall String Ens., Robert Salter – *Concert*. ***

(BB) *** Naxos Dig. 8.553106 [id.]. Bournemouth Sinf., Richard Studt – Concert: *Scandinavian string music*. ***

The engaging *String serenade* is Dag Wirén's one claim to international fame, and it is superbly played by the Guildhall String Ensemble under Robert Salter within a first-class collection of comparable pieces, given state-of-the-art sound.

It is good also to welcome an outstanding super-bargain version of Dag Wirén's deservedly popular *Serenade*. The natural impetus and lyrical charm of the first movement is most winning and the Scherzo brings fizzing bravura, while the colour and mood of the *Andante* is aptly caught. The finale certainly earns its hit status, full of spontaneous, lilting energy. First-rate recording within an entirely recommendable concert of Scandinavian string music, not all of it familiar.

Wolf, Hugo (1860–1903)

Italian serenade.
(***) Biddulph mono LAB 098 [id.]. Budapest Qt – GRIEG; SIBELIUS: *Quartets.* ***

A welcome transfer – the first on CD – of the 1933 pioneering *Italian serenade.* It has a spring in its step and a lightness of touch that are almost unique, and it is well transferred here by Ward Marston. The couplings also show how special this ensemble was in the 1930s.

Italienisches Liederbuch (complete).
*** Hyp. Dig. CDA 66760 [id.]. Felicity Lott, Peter Schreier, Graham Johnson.
(M) *** Ph. 442 744-2 (2) [id.]. Elly Ameling, Gérard Souzay, Dalton Baldwin – R. STRAUSS: *Lieder.*
***
*** Teldec/Warner Dig. 9031 72301 [id.]. Barbara Bonney, Håkan Hagegård, Geoffrey Parsons.

No accompanist, not even Gerald Moore himself, has revealed quite so profound an understanding of this cycle as Graham Johnson, and with two of his favourite Lieder-singers on Hyperion he conjures up a performance full of magic, compelling from first to last. You might describe him here as an interventionist partner, for in so many of these songs his free expressiveness establishes the character of the particular piece, whether charming, comic, tough or tragic, even before the singer begins. Yet, so far from being intrusive in his playing, he consistently heightens the experience, drawing out from Felicity Lott one of her most intense and detailed performances on record, totally individual, with few echoes of the inevitable model, Schwarzkopf. Peter Schreier, one of the supreme masters of Lieder today, responds to his characterful accompanist, as he has also done in his discs of Schubert with András Schiff, eager to accept the challenge and to intensify his expression of word-meaning, his shading of tone-colours. If, under pressure, his voice shows signs of wear, it is a small price to pay, and having a tenor instead of the usual baritone brings many benefits in this sharply pointed sequence. The triumph of this issue is crowned by the substantial booklet provided in the package, containing Johnson's uniquely perceptive commentary on each song – alone worth the price of the disc. Excellent sound.

Elly Ameling, delicately sweet and precise, contrasts well with Souzay, with his fine-drawn sense of line. The charm and point of these brief but intensely imaginative songs are well presented, with perceptive accompaniment from Dalton Baldwin. The coupled Richard Strauss recital also shows Souzay at his most perceptive. It is not clear whether the unforgettable 1969 version with Schwarzkopf and Fischer-Dieskau (CDM7 63732-2) is currently available, as it seems to pop in and out of the EMI catalogue quite arbitrarily; that has the advantage of being offered uncoupled, on a single, mid-priced CD.

Recorded in Berlin, the Teldec CD presents a fresh, direct and intensely satisfying reading of this characterful sequence of 46 songs. Barbara Bonney uses her bright, clear soprano with keen imagination, often with echoes of Schwarzkopf, but with many individual insights. Håkan Hagegård is less individual but still gives a strong, firm reading, even if his baritone has often sounded more beautiful on disc. Geoffrey Parsons is the keenly responsive accompanist, sharply reflecting his singers' approach to each poem. First-rate sound.

(i; ii) *Italienisches Liederbuch* (complete). (ii) Eichendorf Lieder: *Erwartung; Der Freund; Der Glücksritter; Heimweh; Lieber Alles; Liebesglück; Der Musikant; Die Nacht; Nachtzauber; Der Schreckenberger; Der Scholar; Seemanns Abschied; Der Soldat I & II; Das Ständchen; Unfall; Verschwiegene Liebe; Der verzweifelte Liebhaber. In der Fremde I, II & IV; Nachruf; Rückkehr.* Michelangelo Lieder: *Alles endet, was entstehet; Fühlt meine Seele das ersehnte Licht; Wohl denk'ich oft an mein vergangnes Leben.*
(M) *** DG 439 975-2 (2) (i) Christa Ludwig; (ii) Dietrich Fischer-Dieskau; Daniel Barenboim.

Fischer-Dieskau is superb in these varied items from the *Italian Song Book*, always underlining the word-meanings with the inflexion of a born actor, helped by the understanding accompaniment of Barenboim. In the women's songs, Christa Ludwig is less uninhibited and, after Schwarzkopf's accounts of such jewels as *Wer rief dich denn*, these may seem undercharacterized, with the voice not always perfectly steady; but Ludwig too has natural compulsion in her singing and responds splendidly to the pointed playing of Barenboim. The *Eichendorf* and *Michelangelo Lieder* make a splendid supplement for the CD issue, and the mid-1970s recording gives an entirely natural effect.

Spanisches Liederbuch (complete).
*** EMI CDS5 55325-2 (2) [id.]. Anne Sophie von Otter, Olaf Bär, Geoffrey Parsons.

Completed barely six months before Geoffrey Parsons' untimely death, the EMI set of the *Spanish Songbook* makes a superb memorial to that great accompanist, here working with two of the most searching and stylish Lieder singers of the present generation. After experience of performing the complete cycle in concert, they opt for an order of the songs quite different from the original published order, seeking to find 'a dramatic shape that worked in the atmosphere of a concert'. The re-ordering in the ten sacred songs – which, as usual, come first – is not drastic, but in the 34 secular songs there is a radical shuffling, even if the concluding *Geh, geliebter*, spaciously and delicately done, remains in place. Quite apart from Parsons' superb contribution, rapt and dark in the sacred songs, volatile and sparklingly articulated in the secular, the performances of both soloists vie with those on the classic DG set with Elisabeth Schwarzkopf and Dietrich Fischer-Dieskau, accompanied by Gerald Moore (423 934-2). Generally in the new set the manner is more intimate, often more subdued, with speeds generally broader, making a seven-minute difference overall. For the lighter songs von Otter uses a much brighter tonal range than elsewhere, though in such a song as *In dem Schatten meiner Locken* she remains more intimate than Schwarzkopf, pointing the words and phrases with comparable character. Generally the pointing of words is even more vivid in the earlier set but, helped by the extra sparkle of Parsons' playing, this provides a superb alternative, very well recorded.

Zemlinsky, Alexander von (1871–1942)

Piano trio in D min., Op. 3.
*** Ph. Dig. 434 072-2. Beaux Arts Trio – KORNGOLD: *Piano trio.* ***

This is a transcription of the *Trio for clarinet, piano and cello* which Zemlinsky himself made, and which in some ways is to be preferred to the original. The textures are better balanced and more transparent. The Beaux Arts play this early work with great spirit and just the right blend of vitality and sensitivity. The recording is exemplary.

6 Maeterlinck Lieder, Op. 3.
(B) *** Decca Double 444 871-2 (2) [id.]. Concg. O, Chailly – MAHLER: *Symphony No. 6.* ***

Beautifully sung by Jard van Nes in her finest recording to date, these ripely romantic settings of Maeterlinck make an unusual but valuable fill-up for Chailly's rugged and purposeful reading of the Mahler *Symphony*. This is very much the world of medieval chivalry which inspired *Pelléas et Mélisande*, and Zemlinsky responds wholeheartedly. The rich, vivid recording captures van Nes's full-throated singing with new firmness.

Zwilich, Ellen (born 1939)

Symphony No. 2.
** First Edition LCD 002 [id.]. Louisville O, Leighton Smith – HINDEMITH: *Piano concerto* ***;
   LAWHEAD: *Aleost.* *(*)

Ellen Taaffe Zwillich was a pupil of Dohnányi in Florida and then of Roger Sessions and Elliott Carter, though she is not a disciple of either. She is an accomplished musician and, apart from playing the piano and trumpet, studied the violin with the famous Galamian, playing in the American Symphony Orchestra under Stokowski. Her *First Symphony* (1982) won a Pulitzer Prize and prompted the San Francisco Orchestra to commission the *Second Symphony* in 1985. The work is called a 'cello symphony', since the cellos play a dominant role in the musical argument. The invention is solid and well argued, rather than inspired; it is music that commands respect though it is not easy to discern a voice of strong individuality. Good playing and decent recording.

Collections

'The Originals: Legendary performances from the DG Catalogue'

'The Originals' (complete)
(M) **(*) DG 447 398-2 (29 CDs for the cost of 26) [id.].

BARTOK: *Piano concertos Nos. 1–3.*
Géza Anda, Berlin RSO, Ferenc Fricsay (447 399-2).

BEETHOVEN: *Symphonies Nos. 5 in C min., Op. 76; 7 in A, Op. 92.*
VPO, Carlos Kleiber (447 400-2).

BEETHOVEN: *Symphony No. 9 (Choral); Overture Coriolan.*
Janowitz, Rössel-Majdan, Kmentt, Berry, V. Singverein, BPO Karajan (447 401-2).

BEETHOVEN: *Piano concertos Nos. 4 in G; 5 in E flat (Emperor).*
Wilhelm Kempff, BPO, Karajan (447 402-2).

(i) BEETHOVEN: *Violin concerto in D.* MOZART: *Violin concerto No. 5 (Turkish), K.219.*
Wolfgang Schneiderhan, BPO; (i) cond. Eugen Jochum (447 403-2).

BEETHOVEN: *Piano sonatas Nos. 8 in C min. (Pathétique), Op. 13; 14 in C sharp min. (Moonlight),*
Op. 27/2; 21 in C (Waldstein), Op. 53; 23 in F min. (Appassionata).
Wilhelm Kempff (447 404-2).

(i) BERG: *Chamber concerto for piano, violin and 13 wind instruments.* STRAVINSKY: *Dumbarton Oaks*
concerto; 8 Instrumental miniatures; (ii) *Ebony concerto.*
(i) Barenboim, Zukerman; (ii) Michel Arrignon; Ens. InterContemporain, Pierre Boulez (447 405-2)

BERLIOZ: *Symphonie fantastique, Op. 14.* CHERUBINI: *Anacréon overture.* AUBER: *La Muette de*
Portici overture.
LOP, Igor Markevitch (447 406-2).

BRAHMS: (i) *Piano quartet No. 1 in G min., Op. 25. 4 Ballades, Op. 10.*
Gilels, (i) with Amadeus Qt (447 407-2).

BRAHMS: *Symphony No. 1 in C min., Op. 68.* SCHUMANN: *Symphony No. 1 in B flat (Spring).*
BPO, Karajan (447 408-2).

BRUCKNER: *Masses Nos. 1 in D min.; 2 in E min.; 3 in F min.*
Soloists, Bav. R. Ch. & O, Eugen Jochum (447 409-2 (2)).

DVORAK: *Symphonies Nos. 8 in G, Op. 88; 9 in E min. (From the New World), Op. 95.*
BPO, Rafael Kubelik (447 412-2).

DVORAK: *Cello concerto in B min., Op. 104.* TCHAIKOVSKY: *Variations on a Rococo theme, Op. 33.*
Mstislav Rostropovich, BPO, Karajan (447 413).

(i) FALLA: *El amor brujo (ballet); 4 Dances from The Three-cornered hat: Dance of the Miller's wife*
(Fandango); Dance of the neighbours (Seguidilla); Dance of the Miller (Farruca); Final dance
(Jota). STRAVINSKY: *Firebird suite (1919 version).*
(i) Grace Bumbry; Berlin RSO, Lorin Maazel (447 414-2).

LISZT: *Les Préludes; Mazeppa; Hungarian rhapsody No. 4.* SMETANA: *Má Vlast: Vyšehrad; Vltava.*
BPO, Karajan (447 415-2).

MOZART: *Symphonies Nos. 35 in D (Haffner), K.385; 36 in C (Linz), K.425; 38 in D (Prague),*
K.504; 39 in E flat, K.543; 40 in G min., K.550; 41 in C (Jupiter), K.551.
BPO, Karl Boehm (447 416-2 (2)).

PROKOFIEV: (i) *Alexander Nevsky* (cantata), *Op. 78;* (ii) *Lieutenant Kijé (suite)*, *Op. 60; Scythian suite, Op. 20*.
(i) Elena Obraztsova; London Symphony Chorus, LSO; (ii) Chicago SO; Abbado (447 419-2).

(i) RACHMANINOV: *Piano concerto No. 2 in C min., Op. 18.* (ii) TCHAIKOVSKY: *Piano concerto No. 1 in B flat min., Op. 23.*
Sviatoslav Richter; (i) Warsaw PO, Stanislaw Wislocki; (ii) VSO, Karajan (447 420-2).

SCHUBERT: *Winterreise* (song-cycle), *D.911.*
Dietrich Fischer-Dieskau, Joerg Demus (447 421-2).

Richard STRAUSS: *Death and transfiguration, Op. 24; Metamorphosen for 23 solo strings;* (i) *Vier letzte Lieder (4 Last songs)*.
BPO, Karajan; (i) with Gundula Janowitz (447 422-2).

TCHAIKOVSKY: *Symphonies Nos. 4 in F min., Op. 36; 5 in E min., Op. 64; 6 in B min. (Pathétique), Op. 74.*
Leningrad PO, Evgeny Mravinsky (447 423-2 (2)).

Collections

DEBUSSY: *La Mer.* MUSSORGSKY: *Pictures at an exhibition* (orch. Ravel). RAVEL: *Boléro.*
BPO, Karajan (447 426-2).

(i) BACH: *Violin concertos Nos. 1 in A min., BWV 1041; 2 in E, BWV 1042;* (ii; iii) *Double violin concerto in D min., BWV 1043.* (iii) BEETHOVEN: *Romances for violin and orchestra Nos. 1 in G; 2 in F, Opp. 40; 50.* (iv) BRAHMS: *Violin concerto in D, Op. 77.* TCHAIKOVSKY: *Violin concerto in D, Op. 35.*
David Oistrakh (with (i) VSO; (ii) Igor Oistrakh; (iii) RPO, Sir Eugene Goossens; (iv) Dresden State
O, Franz Konwitschny (mono) (stereo/mono 447 427-2 (2)).

CHOPIN: *Scherzo No. 3 in C sharp min., Op. 39; Barcarolle in F sharp min., Op. 60.* BRAHMS: *2 Rhapsodies, Op. 79.* PROKOFIEV: *Toccata, Op. 11.* RAVEL: *Jeux d'eau.* LISZT: *Hungarian rhapsody No. 6; Piano sonata in B min.*
Martha Argerich (447 430-2).

STRAVINSKY: *3 movements from Petrushka.* PROKOFIEV: *Piano sonata No. 7 in B flat, Op. 83.*
WEBERN: *Variations for piano, Op. 27.* BOULEZ: *Piano sonata No. 2.*
Maurizio Pollini (447 431-2).

DG's set of 29 Originals come simply packaged in a cardboard box. Rather engagingly, each individual CD looks like a miniature reproduction of the original vinyl LP, with its yellow label and the light 'reflected on the surface'; but of course the music is engraved underneath as a digital formula, and the technology is entirely different. In almost every case the transfers show a distinct improvement over previous incarnations of these recordings on CD: the remastering more naturally reflects the ambient warmth and fullness of the analogue LP pressings, though the focus is firmer. In certain cases – Kempff's Beethoven *Piano sonatas*, the glorious Jochum versions of the Bruckner *Masses,* Karajan's *Pictures at an exhibition,* with its superbly sonorous Berlin brass – the improvement is quite remarkable. The great majority of these CDs are worthy of a place in any collection, but a few of the choices (perhaps understandably) are just a little misguided for such a prestigious box. If you buy them all, three are thrown in for nothing, but in fact there are about half a dozen which, in a crowded marketplace, would be far from a first choice for the repertoire concerned. Markevitch's *Symphony fantastique*, for all its merits, is hardly a great interpretation, and the Auber and Cherubini overtures, thrown in as makeweights, sound distinctly brash. Boehm's Mozart *Symphonies*, too, warmly enjoyable as they are, have been left behind by current performance practice and would have been better reissued as a bargain-price DG Double. Maazel's gorgeous Berlin account of Stravinsky's *Firebird suite*, dating from the late 1950s, was one of the half-dozen finest recordings he ever made, but it was a pity that DG did not retain the original coupling, an equally lustrous account of *Le chant du rossignol*, as the Falla replacement is no substitute. The Richter/Karajan performance of the Tchaikovsky *B flat minor Piano concerto* is the exact opposite of an artistic symbiosis; it is 'legendary' only as an example of a rare concerto recording in which conductor and pianist are simultaneously pulling in two different directions. Finally, Martha Argerich's 1961 début recital (see below) offers a distressing example of a fabulous technique being applied to achieve musically unacceptable results, making charismatic display an overriding priority, with the playing often perversely idiosyncratic in its flashy dynamism. All these CDs are discussed separately above under their respective composer entries.

Concerts of Orchestral and Concertante Music

Academy of Ancient Music, Christopher Hogwood

PACHELBEL: *Canon & Gigue.* HANDEL: *Water music: Air. Berenice: Overture; Minuet; Gigue.* VIVALDI: *Flute concerto in G min. (La notte), Op. 10/2.* BACH: *Christmas oratorio, BWV 248: Sinfonia. Quadruple harpsichord concerto in A min., BWV 1065.* CORELLI: *Concerto grosso (Christmas concerto), Op. 6/8.* A. MARCELLO: *Oboe concerto in D min.*
(M) **(*) O-L Analogue/Dig. 443 201-2 [id.].

It seems a curious idea to play popular baroque repertoire in a severe manner. Pachelbel's *Canon* here sounds rather abrasive and lacking in charm. But those who combine a taste for these pieces with a desire for authenticity should be satisfied. The selection for this reissue has been expanded and altered. Handel's Queen of Sheba no longer arrives – and she is not missed (for she was much more seductive in Beecham's hands) – and the highlight of the original, full-priced compilation (a pair of Gluck dances) is no longer present! Instead, we get several new items taken from another Academy of Ancient Music compilation of baroque music associated with Christmas, notably Corelli's splendid Op. 6/8, in which the playing has a suitably light touch, and Vivaldi's engaging *La notte Flute concerto*, while Bach's *Quadruple harpsichord concerto* substitutes for the famous Vivaldi work for four violins (Op. 3/10). On the whole an enjoyable mix. The new playing time is 67 minutes.

Academy of St Martin-in-the-Fields, Sir Neville Marriner

'Academy Favourites': HANDEL: *Solomon: Arrival of the Queen of Sheba. Berenice: Minuet. Water music: suite.* VIVALDI: *Concerto for 4 violins, Op. 3/10* (with Alan Loveday, Carmel Kaine, Iona Brown, Roy Gillard). BACH: *Suite No.3 in D, BWV 1069.* MOZART: *Serenade: Eine kleine Nachtmusik.*
(M) *** Decca 436 999-2 [id.].

Here is an archetypal programme of baroque favourites: repertoire in which Marriner and his Academy made their name. Every performance here is fresh, and the recordings (made between 1964 and 1974) are smoothly transferred and still sound first class.

C. P. E. Bach Chamber Orchestra, Hartmut Haenchen

C. P. E. BACH: *Berlin sinfonia in D, Wq. 176.* MOZART: *Serenade in G (Eine kleine Nachtmusik), K.525.* J. S. BACH: *Brandenburg concerto No. 3, BWV 1048.* BRITTEN: *Simple symphony* (for strings), Op. 4. HANDEL: *Water music: Suite No. 2.*
*(*) Sony Dig. SK 48062 [id.].

The orchestra obviously includes good players and they are very well recorded indeed. However, the conductor is unimaginative and *kapellmeisterish*.

Baroque music

Baroque music: *'The Splendour of the Baroque'* (with (i) I Musici, with Ayo, Michelucci & others; (ii) Grumiaux; (iii) ECO, or New Philh. O, Leppard; (iv) ASM, Marriner; (v) German Bar. Soloists; (vi) Rouen Chamber O; (vii) Dresden State O, Negri; (viii) Antiqua Musica O, Jacques Roussel): (i) BACH: *Brandenburg concertos Nos. 1–6.* (ii; iii) *Violin concertos Nos. 1–2.* (iii) HANDEL: *Water music (suites 1–3).* (iv) BONONCINI: *Sinfonia.* TELEMANN: *Concertos for trumpet;* (i) *for viola.* (i) BONPORTI: *Concerti a quattro.* PACHELBEL: *Canon.* A. SCARLATTI: *Il giardino di rose overture.* LOCATELLI: *L'Arte del violino; Concerto grosso.* VIVALDI: (i) *Four Seasons; Concertos for violin;* (vii) *for orchestra.* ALBINONI: (i) *Adagio* (arr. Giazotto); *Concertos for oboe; 2 oboes; violin.* (iii) BOYCE:

Cambridge installation ode. PERGOLESI: *L'Olimpiade overture.* (i) MANFREDINI; TORELLI; CORELLI; GEMINIANI; (iv) JACCHINI; (v) DE FESCH; ZELENKA; (vi) CAPUZZI; LEO; LECLAIR; GAVINIES; (viii) QUANTZ: *Concertos; Concerti grossi.*
(B) ** Ph. 438 921-2 [id.].

This impressively wide-ranging baroque collection offers a good standard of performance and generally good (though variable) standards of recording. There is much of interest here, particularly the Locatelli *L'Arte del violino* and the Bonporti *Concerti a quattro* (both beautifully played, with Roberto Michelucci as soloist). But to include these perfectly respectable but not particularly recent accounts of Bach's *Brandenburgs*, Vivaldi's *Four Seasons*, Pachelbel's *Canon* and Handel's *Water music* means that this collection will be of interest only to the beginner or to those willing to duplicate.

BBC Philharmonic Orchestra, Matthias Bamert

Stokowski Encores: HANDEL: *Overture in D min.* GABRIELI: *Sonata piano e forte.* CLARKE: *Trumpet Prelude.* MATTHESON: *Air.* MOZART: *Rondo alla turca.* BEETHOVEN: *Adagio* from *Moonlight sonata.* SCHUBERT: *Serenade.* FRANCK: *Panis Angelicus.* CHOPIN: *Funeral march.* DEBUSSY: *The Girl with the flaxen hair.* IPPOLITOV-IVANOV: *In the manger.* SHOSTAKOVICH: *United Nations march.* TCHAIKOVSKY: *Andante cantabile.* ALBENIZ: *Festival in Seville.* SOUSA: *The Stars and Stripes for ever.* (all arr. Leopold Stokowski).
*** Chan. Dig. CHAN 9349 [id.].

Matthias Bamert and the BBC Philharmonic follow up their disc of Stokowski's opulent Bach arrangements with this mixed bag of 15 items, six of them new to disc, again showing what a master of sound-quality the cunning old maestro was. However outrageous it may seem to take a tiny harpsichord piece by a contemporary of Bach and Handel, Johann Mattheson, and inflate it on full strings, the result caresses the ear, and the Chandos engineers come up with recording to match. Amazingly, Mozart's *Rondo Alla Turca* becomes a sparkling moto perpetuo, Paganini-like, with Stokowski following Mozart himself in using 'Turkish' percussion, *Entführung*-style. The opening *Adagio* of Beethoven's *Moonlight sonata* with lush orchestration then echoes Rachmaninov's *Isle of the Dead*, with menace in the music. Stokowski's arrangement of the Handel *Overture in D minor* (taken from the *Chandos anthem No. 2*) is quite different from Elgar's transcription of the same piece, opulent in a different way, with timbres antiphonally contrasted. If Bamert cannot match the panache of Stokowski in the final Sousa march, *The Stars and Stripes for ever*, that is in part due to the recording balance, which fails to bring out the percussion, including xylophone. The least attractive item is Schubert's *Serenade*, given full Hollywood treatment not just with soupy strings but with quadruple woodwind trilling above. Hollywood treatment of a different kind comes in the *United Nations march* of Shostakovich, in 1942 used as the victory finale of an MGM wartime musical, *Thousands Cheer.* Stokowski promptly cashed in with his own non-vocal arrangement. A disc for anyone who likes to wallow in opulent sound.

BBC Symphony Orchestra, Sir Adrian Boult

English music: WALTON: *Portsmouth Point overture; Crown imperial.* VAUGHAN WILLIAMS: *Fantasia on a theme by Thomas Tallis.* BLISS: *Music for strings.* ELGAR: *Introduction and allegro for strings; Dream of Gerontius: Prelude. Imperial march, Op. 32. Sospiri, Op. 70. Enigma variations, Op. 36.* BUTTERWORTH: *A Shropshire lad* (rhapsody) (with Hallé O).
(**) VAI Audio mono VAIA 1067-2 (2) [id.].

Boult's zestfully briny first recording of *Portsmouth Point* has all the vitality we remember from the 78-r.p.m. disc (a double-sided 10-inch which just accommodated Boult's 5 minutes 14 seconds) and the acerbity of the treble suits this piece. For the rest, although transfers are clean, the dry, studio-ish sound is too clean-cut on top to be quite natural and lacks supporting body and weight. This cannot compare with the Dutton Lab transfers of the 1938 LSO/Bruno Walter recordings – see below. Here Bliss's *Music for strings* makes tiring listening and Elgar's *Introduction and allegro* is too bracing by half. Shrillness sets in for *Enigma* and, especially, the climaxes of *Crown imperial*. Easily the most satisfactory transfer is of the Butterworth *Rhapsody* featuring the Hallé Orchestra, where the quieter pages are quite luminous. The performances throughout show Boult as a young conductor in the 1930s, often using faster speeds in *Enigma* than he did later. The documentation is unacceptably sparse for a full-priced set and the recording venues are not given. Still of interest, but disappointing. Dutton Laboratories need to turn their attention to this repertoire.

BBC Symphony Orchestra, Andrew Davis

'The Last Night of the Proms (100th Season), 1994' (with (i) Bryn Terfel; (ii) BBC Singers, BBC Symphony Ch.; (iii) Evelyn Glennie; (iv) Michael Davis): BACH: *Toccata and fugue in D min.* (orch. Sir Henry Wood). (i; ii) WALTON: *Belshazzar's Feast.* (iii) MIKI: *Marimba spiritual.* (ii; iv) MASSENET: *Thaïs: Méditation.* ELGAR: *Pomp and circumstance march No. 1.* WOOD: *Fantasia on British sea songs.* (i; ii) ARNE, arr. Sargent: *Rule Britannia! PARRY: Jerusalem.* TRAD.: *Auld Lang Syne* (audience).
(***) Teldec/Warner Dig. 4509 97868-2 [id.].

The last night of the 1994 Promenade Concert season aptly celebrated the 100th season, when Andrew Davis opened the proceedings with a brilliantly colourful account of Sir Henry Wood's audacious and marvellously effective orchestration of Bach's *D minor Toccata and fugue.* Wood, having suffered from adverse criticism in the past, attributed the scoring to a Paul Klenovsky – a Russian pupil of Glazunov, who had recently died – and only after it had been well received did he reveal that the arrangement was his own work – no doubt with some satisfaction. The recording is perhaps the best ever made in the Royal Albert Hall, a richly resonant yet never clouded sound-picture, the upper range brilliant with a sonorously resounding bass. When we move on to Andrew Davis's dramatically eloquent account of *Belshazzar's Feast* the glorious choral contribution demonstrates how perfectly suited Walton's masterly oratorio is to the hall's famous and sometimes intractable acoustics. From the powerful trombone opening and the riveting 'Thus spake Isaiah' from the BBC Singers and Symphony Chorus, the listener is held under the music's spell, and Bryn Terfel's resonant 'If I forget thee' is as compelling as his cry 'Babylon is a great city', while the choral responses to 'Praise ye' are as thrilling as the 'writing hand' sequence is creepily sinister. Evelyn Glennie's bravura marimba display and the sensuously romantic Massenet *Méditation*, with the chorus softly sustained behind Michael Davis's languorous violin solo, together make an attractive interlude. But then we come to Elgar's *Pomp and circumstance* and the younger element of the audience becomes intrusively vulgar in their crude humour, making a real nuisance of themselves with intrusive bangs and cracks. Then, just before the entry of the great melody, there is a ripple of laughter in the audience (the joke unexplained to the unknowing listener) and, though the melody itself produces heartfelt singing, one simply would not want to return to such an intrusion on a record. However, much worse is to come in the *Sea songs Fantasia*, where the end of the elegantly played cello solo, *Tom Bowling*, is utterly ruined by a squeaker from a member of the audience; and there is a further and even more unpleasant bleat at the close of *Home, sweet home.* Sir Henry welcomed audience participation with clapping in the *Sailor's hornpipe* and encouraged the singing of *Rule Britannia!*, but he would have been horrified by the absence of audience discipline here, with the hornpipe punctuated with further grating sound-effects. The addition of further clapping and whistling to *See, the conqu'ring hero comes!* is hardly more agreeable. *Rule Britannia!* again introduces the resounding Bryn Terfel (yet brings another joke in the middle), and together with *Jerusalem* cannot fail to make an impact, with such vocal commitment from the audience and the gloriously expansive sound. But the promenaders' intrusiveness goes far beyond the bounds of youthful high spirits, and this CD must be approached with extreme caution.

BBC Symphony Orchestra, Sir Charles Groves

English music: ELGAR: *Cello concerto* (with Zara Nelsova, cello). VAUGHAN WILLIAMS: *In the fen country.* PURCELL: *Abdelazar: suite* (with Royal Liverpool PO, Sir Malcolm Sargent): BRITTEN: *Young person's guide to the orchestra (Variations on a theme of Purcell).*
(B) **(*) BBC Radio Classics BBCRD 9111 [id.].

Outstanding among these Proms performances, recorded by the BBC between 1969 and 1977, is Zara Nelsova's warm and intense reading of the Elgar *Cello concerto*, with Sir Charles Groves adding to the electricity. This is a performance of touching simplicity by a fine soloist who has been too little recorded. Groves is similarly purposeful in the Britten *Variations*, where the biting tension in the statement of the Purcell theme contrasts with the easy-going manners in the same theme, as heard in the last movement of the Purcell suite from which it derives, as conducted by Sir Malcolm Sargent. The rare Vaughan Williams piece, a 'symphonic impression' first heard in 1909, makes a warmly attractive fill-up. Atmospheric if not very clearly defined sound. A 71-minute collection that is more than the sum of its parts.

Belgian Radio & TV Philharmonic Orchestra, Brussels, Alexander Rahbari

Romantic symphonic music from Antwerp: MORTELMANS: *Spring idyll.* ALPAERTS: *Pallieter: Wedding feast.* VAN HOOF: *1st Symphonic suite.* BLOCKX: *Milenka: Flemish Fair.* STERNFIELD: *Song and dance at the court of Mary from Burgundy.*
(BB) ** Discover Dig. DICD 920100 [id.].

Flemish rhapsodies: BRUSSELMANS: *Flemish rhapsody.* SCHOEMAKER: *Flemish rhapsody.* DE JONG: *Flemish rhapsody.* ABSILL: *Flemish rhapsody.* ROUSSEL: *Flemish rhapsody.* DE BOECK: *Flemish rhapsody.*
(BB) **(*) Discover DICD 920101 [id.].

This is all unknown repertoire – easy-going late nineteenth-or twentieth-century music from Belgium. On the first CD, Mortelmans' *Spring idyll* is lyrically appealing but perhaps a shade extended for its thematic content, the Jef Van Hoof and Jan Blockx suites agreeably inventive but innocuous. By far the most attractive music comes in the suite of *Song and dance from Burgundy*, nicely scored and piquantly harmonized dances by Susato and his sixteenth-century contemporaries, somewhat comparable with Respighi's *Ancient airs and dances*.

The Flemish rhapsodies all use folk material very effectively, although Brusselmans employs themes of his own invention, written in folk style. All these works are colourfully orchestrated and make agreeable listening, using jolly tunes which in flavour are often like Christmas carols. By far the most striking is the work by the Frenchman, Albert Roussel, which has a characteristic touch of harmonic astringency to tickle the ear. The playing of the Brussels orchestra under Rahbari is enthusiastic yet does not lack finesse, and the recording has an attractive concert-hall ambience and balance. It is not always too sharply defined in some of the more elaborately scored climaxes of the rhapsodies, but the effect is natural. The documentation is excellent.

Bell, Joshua (violin), RPO, Litton

SAINT-SAENS: *Introduction and rondo capriccioso, Op. 28.* MASSENET: *Thaïs: Méditation.* SARASATE: *Zigeunerweisen, Op. 20.* CHAUSSON: *Poème.* YSAYE: *Caprice d'après l'étude en forme de valse de Saint-Saëns.* RAVEL: *Tzigane.*
*** Decca Dig. 433 519-2 [id.].

A splendid showcase for a first-rate American virtuoso and musician of the younger generation who has not yet established his personality as an artist in Britain as firmly as on the other side of the Atlantic. Whether in Sarasate, Saint-Saëns or Ysaÿe the easy, sparkling brilliance of bow on string (with dashes of pizzicato) is balanced with a warm melodic line that can be sultry or chimerical by turns. He plays with style and an impressive range of colour. While the Chausson *Poème* has much delicacy of feeling, the Ravel *Tzigane* brings a gusty, almost malevolent, incandescent energy. Litton accompanies with characteristic polish and feeling for detail, and Decca produce vividly realistic projection for their soloist.

Berlin Philharmonic Orchestra, Herbert von Karajan

'Meditation' (Overtures and Intermezzi): Johann STRAUSS Jnr: *Der Zigeunerbaron overture.*
MASSENET: *Thaïs: Méditation* (with Anne-Sophie Mutter). CHERUBINI: *Anacréon overture.* WEBER: *Der Freischütz overture.* SCHMIDT: *Notre Dame: Intermezzo.* PUCCINI: *Intermezzi: Suor Angelica; Manon Lescaut.* MASCAGNI: *L'amico Fritz: Intermezzo.* HUMPERDINCK: *Hansel and Gretel overture.*
MENDELSSOHN: *Hebrides overture (Fingal's Cave), Op. 26.*
(M) *(*) EMI Dig./analogue CDM7 64629-2 [id.].

A curiously planned if generous (78 minutes) programme, deriving from three different sources. It opens with a rather weighty analogue account of Strauss's *Zigeunerbaron overture*, then moves on to the digital items, first the *Méditation* from *Thaïs* (with Anne-Sophie Mutter a gently restrained soloist), immediately followed by the *Anacréon overture*, with textures reminiscent of plum pudding.

CONCERTS OF ORCHESTRAL AND CONCERTANTE MUSIC

The Weber and Humperdinck overtures, too, are disappointing, the first lacking electricity, the second charm. The *Intermezzi* are much more successful, played very passionately and sumptuously, with the ample recording providing somewhat over-nourished string-textures with a touch of grit in the treble. The best piece by far is the closing *Hebrides overture*, recorded much earlier (in 1960) and beautifully managed.

'The Art of Herbert von Karajan': MOZART: *Symphony No. 41 (Jupiter)*. HAYDN: *Symphony No. 104 (London)*. SCHUBERT: *Symphony No. 8 (Unfinished)*. J.STRAUSS Jnr: *Die Fledermaus* (overture). WEBER: *Der Freischütz* (overture). BRAHMS: *Tragic overture, Op. 81*. SIBELIUS: *Symphony No. 5; Valse triste*. BEETHOVEN: *Fidelio* (overture). WAGNER: *Der fliegende Holländer* (overture). SMETANA: *Má Vlast: Vltava*. DVORAK: *Symphony No. 9 (From the New World)*. RAVEL: *Boléro*. CHABRIER: *España*. BIZET: *L'Arlésienne*. DEBUSSY: *Prélude à l'après-midi d'un faune; La Mer*.
(M) ** EMI CMS7 64563-2 (4) [id.].

While the playing of the Berlin Philharmonic is always a joy Karajan made few of his finest recordings of key repertoire during his second period with EMI (between 1970 and 1980), and though the sound is richer than with some of his DG records of the 1960s it is often less refined and the effect heavier. Thus Mozart's *Jupiter* does not have the spontaneity even of his first stereo version for Decca while the account of Haydn's *London Symphony* is distinctly ponderous. With Dvořák's *New World* it is more a case of swings and roundabouts; while the earlier DG in some ways sounds fresher, the EMI of 1977 is also very successful, as is Schubert's *Unfinished* (1975), rapt and concentrated; however with the Sibelius *Fifth* again the preference remains with the 1964 DG version, indisputably the finest of the four recordings he made of this symphony. The key Debussy repertoire brings a similar clear preference for DG and while many of the shorter pieces here are impressive, this set as a whole is primarily for Karajan admirers who want to hear everything he did for the gramophone.

LISZT: *Les Préludes, G.97*. SIBELIUS: *Finlandia, Op. 26; Pélleas et Mélisande: suite*. SMETANA: *Má vlast: Vltava*.
(M) *** DG Dig. 445 550-2 [id.].

This is an outstanding concert, showing Karajan at his most charismatic; and the orchestral playing is certainly in a class of its own. In the performance of *Pelléas et Mélisande* we have a version of Sibelius's subtle and atmospheric score that can compare with the classic Beecham version, originally dating from 1957. Indeed in certain movements, *By spring in the park* and the *Pastorale*, it not only matches Sir Thomas but almost surpasses him. The *Pastorale* is altogether magical, and there is plenty of mystery in the third movement, *At the seashore*, omitted from the Beecham version. Some may find the opening movement, *At the castle gate*, a little too imposing, but the fervour and eloquence of the playing should win over most listeners. The recording is very striking, with great clarity and presence. Karajan is also at his finest in this performance of *Vltava*, and there is some radiant playing from the Berlin orchestra in the moonlit stillness before the river approaches the St John's Rapids. *Les Préludes* is vibrant but a little brash. *Finlandia* reinforces the feeling that this Berlin Philharmonic/Karajan partnership has never been equalled, not even by Toscanini and the NBC Symphony Orchestra.

(i) Berlin Philharmonic Orchestra; (ii) Berlin RIAS Symphony Orchestra; (iii) Berlin Radio Symphony Orchestra; (iv) Vienna Philharmonic Orchestra; (v) South German Radio Symphony Orchestra, Ferenc Fricsay

'Ferenc Fricsay Portrait': (i) BEETHOVEN: *Symphony No. 9* (with Irmgard Seefried, Maureen Forrester, Ernst Haefliger, Dietrich Fischer-Dieskau, St Hedwig's Cathedral Ch.)(stereo; 445 401-2).

BARTOK: *Violin concerto No. 2* (with Tibor Varga); (ii) *Dance suite; Cantata profana* (with Helmut Krebs, Dietrich Fischer-Dieskau, RIAS Chamber Ch., St Hedwig's Cathedral Ch.) (mono; 445 402-2).

(ii) R. STRAUSS: *Don Juan, Op. 20; Duet-Concertino for clarinet, bassoon, strings and harp* (with Heinrich Geuser, Willi Fugmann); *Burleske, Op. 11* (with Margrit Weber); (i) *Till Eulenspiegel, Op. 28* (mono; 445 403-2).

(ii) LIEBERMANN: *Furioso*. BLACHER: *Paganini variations, Op. 26*. EGK: *French suite*. (iii) VON EINEM: *Piano concerto, Op. 20* (with Gerty Herzog); *Ballade for orchestra, Op. 23* (mono/stereo; 445 404-2).

STRAVINSKY: (ii) *The Rite of spring; Petrushka* (1947 version); (iii) *Movements for piano and orchestra* (with Margrit Weber) (mono/stereo; 445 405-2).

(ii) ROSSINI: *Overtures: Il barbiere di Siviglia; Tancredi; Il Signor Bruschino; La gazza ladra; Semiramide.* VERDI: *Overtures: Nabucco; La traviata* (Preludes to Acts I & III); *La forza del destino; Aida; I vespri siciliani* (mono; 445 406-2).

BRAHMS: (iv) *Symphony No. 2 in D, Op. 73;* (iii) *Variations on a theme of Haydn, Op. 56a; Alto rhapsody, Op. 53* (with Maureen Forrester, RIAS Chamber Ch.) (mono; 445 407-2).

MOZART: (ii) *Requiem Mass No. 19 in D min., K.626* (with Elisabeth Grümmer, Gertrude Pitzinger, Helmut Krebs, Hans Hotter, RIAS Chamber Ch., St Hedwig's Cathedral Ch.); (iii) *Adagio and fugue in C min., K.546* (mono/stereo; 445 408-2).

TCHAIKOVSKY: (i) *Symphony No. 6 (Pathétique);* (ii) *Violin concerto in D, Op. 35* (with Yehudi Menuhin) (mono; 445 409-2).

KODALY: (ii) *Dances of Marosszék;* (iii) *Symphony; Psalmus hungaricus, Op. 13* (with Ernst Haefliger, St Hedwig's Cathedral Ch.) (mono/stereo 445 410-2).

Bonus CD: (v) SMETANA: *Má Vlast* (extracts): *Vltava* (rehearsal and concert performance) (mono; 445 411-2).
⊛ (M) *** DG mono/stereo 445 400-2 (10) [id.] (records available separately).

Although many younger collectors know their Furtwängler, Beecham and Monteux, the Hungarian conductor, Ferenc Fricsay, never enjoyed cult status. The appearance of this ten-CD box offers an excellent opportunity to evaluate him, and DG deserve congratulations on its planning and presentation – and on making each disc separately available as well, thus bringing it within the grasp of any serious collector. To many, we are sure, it will come as something of a revelation: indeed, although we admired and respected Fricsay in the 1950s and '60s, coming back to these performances (or, in some cases, hearing them for the first time) serves afresh to reaffirm his stature.

One striking feature of the collection is the sheer quality of the sound produced by the DG engineers of the 1950s. One thing is quite self-evident: that the original mono pressings did scant justice to their achievement. The original LPs did not reproduce such vivid detail, such presence or body. Among the riches that are assembled here, one of the surprises is *The Rite of spring* (445 405-2), far removed from any vestige of the current view of the work as some kind of sanitized orchestral showpiece. This brings this score alive with a freshness and ferocity that remind one of the first encounter with this extraordinary score. *The Rite* is far more savage and powerful than Markevitch's celebrated account with the Philharmonia that came out at the same time. This is a must.

Naturally the contemporary music with which Fricsay was specially associated must have first claim. The DG Dokumente version of the Bartók *Divertimento* and *Music for strings, percussion and celeste* (see our main volume) does not prepare you for the excellence of the Bartók disc here (445 402-2). His *Dance suite* is one of the best ever committed to disc, wonderfully idiomatic, vital and yet relaxed; the *Cantata profana* too is excellent, though Tibor Varga's account of the *Violin concerto* does not displace Menuhin. Of particular value is the disc coupling Rolf Liebermann's *Furioso*, Werner Egk's *French suite*, two von Einem works, and Boris Blacher's *Paganini variations* (445 404-2). The Blacher was almost a popular warhorse in the 1950s, so frequently did it appear; it is a resourceful and diverting piece which, like his engaging *Concertante musik*, should be a popular repertory piece. Apart from these and the Kodály (445 410-2), which are effortlessly idiomatic and thrillingly alive, Fricsay is no less impressive in the mainstream repertoire.

In Richard Strauss he is hardly less persuasive, and the disc devoted to that master is to be particularly recommended for a delightful performance of the *Duet-Concertino for clarinet, bassoon, strings and harp.* We remember what an enormous impact his splendid Tchaikovsky *Pathétique* made on collectors when it first appeared: it remains one of the most vital and intense of all recorded performances and still carries an enthusiastic recommendation. The Brahms *Second Symphony*, one of his later recordings (1961), which has not appeared before in Britain, has a rich, lyrical warmth and a sense of forward movement worthy of Bruno Walter. Needless to say, the box is not comprehensive: there are Mozart symphonies and operas, now in currency separately, and the three Bartók *Piano concertos* with Géza Anda reappear among DG's 'Originals'. Those buying the ten CDs as a package get a bonus disc, which includes a 1960 performance of Smetana's *Vltava*, made with the orchestra of Süddeutsches Rundfunk, with an hour-long rehearsal in their Stuttgart studios. It is easy to follow but there is a précis of his remarks in both English and French. We do not normally give rosettes for this kind of compilation, but this should certainly have one in recognition of the care lavished on it, and the artistic and technical excellence of these performances.

Berlin Philharmonic Orchestra, Paris Conservatoire Orchestra or Belgian Radio & TV Orchestra, André Cluytens

'Artist profile': BEETHOVEN: *Symphony No. 6 in F (Pastoral), Op. 68.* BERLIOZ: *L'enfance du Christ: La fuite en Egypte: Overture; Shepherds' farewell* (with René Duclos Ch.). DEBUSSY: *Jeux.* FRANCK: *Le chasseur maudit.* PIERNE: *Concertstück, Op. 39, for harp and orchestra* (with Annie Challan). ROUSSEL: *Bacchus et Ariane, Op. 43: suite No. 2; Sinfonietta, Op. 52; Le festin de l'araignée (fragments symphoniques), Op. 17.*
⊛ (B) *** EMI CZS5 68220-2 (2) [id.].

There is something special about this compilation. André Cluytens was a much-underrated conductor and, though his account of the *Pastoral Symphony* with the Berlin Philharmonic was highly acclaimed on its first appearance, he was generally taken for granted during his lifetime. His 1957 recording of the *Pastoral* with the same orchestra was in mono, and some would say it was even more inspired. In any event it made a sufficient impression to encourage EMI to re-record it in 1960 and then to go on to do a complete cycle. The stereo version (offered here) is radiant and glowing – as good as any made during the 1960s, and better than many that followed. His account of *Jeux* with the Orchestre de la Société des Concerts du Conservatoire was vastly more atmospheric than the Boulez account with the Philharmonia (CBS) that came out at much the same period, though some of the subtlety, delicacy and the slight haze of the old LPs have been lost in the transfer. (The original opens out and has much greater range, but the present disc is still very good and reproduces smoothly on most machines.) The Pierné rarity is also beautifully done and makes a welcome addition to the catalogue. The second *Bacchus et Ariane* suite is both exhilarating and atmospheric, and never has Roussel's spider feasted so sumptuously and in such an exotic ambience as it does here. Let us hope that EMI will restore Cluytens' account of Debussy's *Images* and the Roussel *Third* and *Fourth Symphonies*. At full price these two discs would be well worth having, but for so modest an outlay they represents an altogether outstanding bargain. One of the most rewarding issues of the year.

Boston Pops Orchestra, Arthur Fiedler

'Hi-Fi Arthur Fiedler': RIMSKY-KORSAKOV: *Le coq d'or suite.* ROSSINI: *William Tell overture.* TCHAIKOVSKY: *Marche slave.* CHABRIER: *España.* LISZT: *Hungarian rhapsody No. 2; Rákóczy march.*
(M) ** BMG/RCA 09026 61497-2.

After the excellence of the Boston and Chicago reissues in BMG/RCA's 'Living Stereo series' (complete with original sleeves and LP logo) this is a disappointment. The opening *Coq d'or suite*, although atmospheric, creates a low level of tension and there is distortion at the climax of the March. The other pot-boilers are vivid enough, but there is nothing here in any way individual, although the orchestral playing is consistently alert.

Bournemouth Sinfonietta, Richard Studt

Scandinavian string music: GRIEG: *Holberg suite.* Dag WIREN: *Serenade, Op. 11.* SVENDSEN: *2 Icelandic melodies; Norwegian folksong; 2 Swedish folksongs, Op. 27.* NIELSEN: *Little suite in A min., Op. 1.*
(BB) *** Naxos Dig. 8.553106 [id.].

The liltingly spontaneous account of the Dag Wirén *Serenade* ensures a welcome for this enjoyable collection of Scandinavian music. The performance of Grieg's perennially fresh *Holberg suite* is hardly less successful in its combination of energy and polish, folksy charm and touching serenity in the famous *Air*. Nielsen's *Little suite* also has plenty of style and impetus, the changing moods of the finale neatly encompassed. The Svedsen folksong arrangements belong to the 1870s. The two *Icelandic melodies* are melodically robust but the *Norwegian folksong* is gentler and quite lovely. Yet it is the second of the two *Swedish folksongs* that most reminds the listener of Grieg. All are played with a natural expressive feeling, and the recording, made in the Winter Gardens, Bournemouth, has a fine, full sonority to balance its natural brilliance.

English string music: BRITTEN: *Variations on a theme of Frank Bridge, Op. 10.* HOLST: *St Paul's suite, Op. 29/1.* DELIUS: *2 Aquarelles.* VAUGHAN WILLIAMS: *5 Variants of Dives and Lazarus.* WARLOCK: *Capriol suite.*
(BB) *** Naxos Dig. 8.550823 [id.].

This is the finest of three concerts of string music, recorded for Naxos by Richard Studt and the excellent Bournemouth Sinfonietta. The Britten *Frank Bridge variations* is particularly memorable, showing easy virtuosity yet often achieving the lightest touch, so that the *Vienna waltz* movement sparkles in its delicacy. The *Funeral march* may not be so desperately intense as Karajan's famous mono version with the Philharmonia, but it is still very touching; and the following *Chant* is ethereal in its bleakly refined atmosphere. The sprightly Holst *St Paul's suite* and Warlock's *Capriol,* agreeably robust, could hardly be better played, while Vaughan Williams's *Dives and Lazarus* is especially fresh and conveys the famous biblical story of the rich man and the beggar most evocatively, especially in the very beautiful closing section, when Lazarus finds himself in heaven. The recording, made in St Peter's Church, Parkestone, is full-bodied, immediate and real – very much in the demonstration bracket.

20th-Century string music: BARTOK: *Divertimento.*
BRITTEN: *Simple symphony, Op. 4.* WALTON: *2 Pieces from Henry V: Death of Falstaff (Passacaglia); Touch her soft lips and part.* STRAVINSKY: *Concerto in D.*
(BB) ** Naxos Dig. 8.550979 [id.].

This is the least successful of the three concerts of string music recorded by Naxos in Bournemouth. The Sinfonietta players do not sound completely at ease in the shifting moods of the Bartók *Divertimento* and their ensemble could be crisper in the Stravinsky *Concerto.* The *Simple Symphony* comes off brightly, with a gently nostalgic *Sentimental sarabande* and a brisk, alert finale, but the *Playful pizzicato* could be more exuberant, especially in its famous trio which the composer did so joyously. The two Walton pieces are warmly atmospheric, and there are no complaints about the sound.

Bournemouth Sinfonietta or Symphony Orchestra, Norman Del Mar

English music: HOLST: *Brook Green suite; A Somerset rhapsody.* DELIUS: *Air and dance.* VAUGHAN WILLIAMS: *Concerto grosso; Aristophanic suite: The Wasps.* ELGAR: *Serenade for strings.*
(M) *** EMI CDM5 65130-2 [id.].

This CD generously combines the contents of two previously issued LPs of English music, substituting Elgar's *Serenade* for Warlock's (which now appears in an attractive anthology centring entirely on that composer's music – see above). Holst's *Brook Green suite* was originally written for the St Paul's School for Girls, where Holst was in charge of music. It emerged as far more than an exercise for students, as Del Mar's dedicated performance demonstrates, most strikingly in the vigorous final dance. The *Concerto grosso* of Vaughan Williams on the other hand was written for a jamboree at the Royal Albert Hall with hundreds of string players of the Rural Music Schools Association. Here (in its début recording) it is given as a straight work for double string orchestra. The enchanting Delius miniatures and the evocative Holst *Somerset rhapsody* make an excellent contrast, while the *Wasps* overture – here dashingly performed – and the other items in the suite are delightful, too. Del Mar brings out the wit in the *March of the kitchen utensils* with his mock pomposity. The recording throughout is splendid.

(i) Brymer, Jack (clarinet), Vienna State Opera Orchestra, Felix Prohaska; (ii) David Glazer (clarinet), Würtemberg CO, Faerber; (iii) Joza Ostrack (clarinet), Mozart Festival Orchestra, Lizzio

Clarinet concertos: (i) KROMMER: *Concerto in E flat.* WAGNER (BAERMANN): *Adagio for clarinet and strings.* DEBUSSY: *Première rapsodie.* (ii) WEBER: *Clarinet concerto No. 1 in F min.; Clarinet concertino, Op. 26;* STAMITZ: *Concerto No. 3.* (iii) MOZART: *Concerto in A, K.622.*
(M) *** Van. 08.9176.72 (2)

Jack Brymer's performance of the Krommer *Concerto* with its melting *Adagio* and delightful, chortling finale is a joy, while the Baermann *Adagio* (once attributed to Wagner) and the Debussy *Rapsodie* are also superbly poised. David Glazer's Weber (the *First concerto* and the engaging *Concertino*) is most elegant, with the slow movement of the concerto beautifully phrased and both finales winningly jocular – the close of the *Concertino* chirrups just as it should. The Stamitz is plainer but still very agreeable. Joza Ostrack's performance of the greatest work of all, by Mozart, agreeably combines warmth and finesse; so altogether this makes a worthwhile anthology. Accompaniments are well managed and the recordings are all fully acceptable, if not absolutely refined; but the interest of the repertoire – so conveniently gathered together – more than compensates. No recording dates are given.

Cantelli, Guido: *'Artist profile'* – see under Philharmonia Orchestra etc.

Casals, Pablo (cellist, conductor)

Casals Edition

(with (i) Paul Baumgartner; (ii) John Wummer, Bernard Goldberg, Prades Festival O) BACH: (i) *Viola da gamba sonatas Nos. 1–3, BWV 1027–9;* (ii) *Brandenburg concerto No. 4 in G, BWV 1049.* (M) ** Sony mono SMK 66572 [id.].

(with (i) Dame Myra Hess, Joseph Szigeti; (ii) Mieczyslaw Horszowski, Alexander Schneider): (i) BRAHMS: *Piano trio in C, Op. 87.* (ii) MENDELSSOHN: *Piano trio in D min., Op. 49.* (M) ** Sony mono/stereo SMK 66571 [id.].

(cond. Perpignan Festival O; with (i) Yvonne Lefebure; (ii) Rudolf Serkin) MOZART: *Piano concertos Nos. (i) 20 in D min., K.466; (ii) 22 in E flat, K.482.* (M) ** Sony mono SMK 66570 [id.].

(cond. Perpignan Festival O; with (i) Marcel Tabuteau, Alexander Schneider) MOZART: *Symphony No. 29 in A, K201; Eine kleine Nachtmusik; (i) Divertimento No. 11 in D, K251.* (M) ** Sony mono SMK 66569 [id.].

Casals was a great musician, so that nothing he touched is without interest to musicians or music-lovers alike. These four discs give a glimpse of the breadth and depth of his musicianship – not that all of them are likely to win (or necessarily deserve) universal favour. CBS documented all these Prades and Perpignan performances in a handsome LP set, some of whose contents are reproduced here. The Bach sonatas with Paul Baumgartner as pianist were recorded in 1950 at the inaugural Prades Festival and, flawed though they may be in some respects (grunts and other extraneous noises), they are performances of great humanity, as indeed was the *Fourth Brandenburg* with two fine flautists, John Wummer and Bernard Goldberg, with the Prades Festival Orchestra. Needless to say, the orchestral forces are fairly large, and the continuo is a piano (as was common at this time) – think of the Boston set under Koussevitzky with its wonderfully light accents – but good style is related to musical truth and sensitive phrasing more than it is to the correct size or composition of ensembles. The 1950 recordings naturally call for some tolerance but are still more than just acceptable.

The Brahms *C major Trio*, Op. 87, with Joseph Szigeti and Myra Hess, comes from 1952 and has appeared previously, in harness with the Szigeti and Ormandy account of the *Violin concerto*, with the Philadelphia Orchestra, when we described it as perhaps low on 'fi' but high on musicianship and humanity: 'a richly rewarding account that soon rises above the inevitable sonic limitations, Szigeti's moments of rough tone and Casals's groans'. The Mendelssohn *Trio*, recorded in 1961 (with Alexander Schneider and Mieczyslaw Horszowski) in the White House, at the request of President Kennedy, is in stereo and finds Casals inspired but not in the fullest command of his instrument. The ghost of the celebrated 1929 recording with Thibaud and Cortot is not wholly exorcized.

The Mozart concertos also come from the 1952 Perpignan Festival and are again mono. The *D minor*, K.466, with Yvonne Lefebure, has not appeared before, and it shows elegance and taste, though Serkin's *E flat*, K.482, has the greater character. Neither is a 'library' choice, but there are lessons to be learnt from both performances. Serkin is still the responsive and sensitive artist he was in pre-war days, before the mannerisms that disfigured his Mozart playing in the 1960s afflicted him. The *Symphony No. 29 in A* and the remaining pieces on the same disc also derive from Perpignan in 1952 and have that vitality and dedication we associate with Casals as a great musician. The *Divertimento* also affords an opportunity to hear the legendary Marcel Tabuteau, a player of unfailing eloquence and artistry.

Chicago Symphony Orchestra, Fritz Reiner

'The Reiner sound': RAVEL: *Rapsodie espagnole; Pavane pour une enfante défunte.* LISZT: *Totentanz* (with Byron Janis). WEBER/BERLIOZ: *Invitation to the dance.* RACHMANINOV: *The Isle of the dead, Op. 29.*
(M) *** BMG/RCA 09026 61250-2.

'The Reiner sound', a combination of marvellous orchestral playing and the glorious acoustics of Chicago's Orchestra Hall, recorded with the simplest stereo microphone techniques, is heard at its finest and most distinctive in the superb Ravel items, which are also available separately, coupled with an equally magical Debussy *Ibéria* (GD 60179 [60179-2-RG]). But the present 68-minute collection (dating from between 1956 and 1959) is worth anyone's money. The Liszt *Totentanz* brings an exciting bravura contribution from Janis, and the Weber is agreeably polished and spirited. The microphone balance in *The Isle of the dead* is a shade close, but this, too, is one of the finest of Reiner's Chicago recordings.

'Russian showpieces': MUSSORGSKY: *Pictures at an exhibition* (orch. Ravel); *Night on a bare mountain* (arr. Rimsky-Korsakov). TCHAIKOVSKY: *Marche slave; Suite No. 1: march miniature.* BORODIN: *Polovtsian march.* KABALEVSKY: *Colas Breugnon overture.* GLINKA: *Ruslan and Ludmilla overture.*
(M) *** BMG/RCA 09026 61958-2 [id.].

Reiner's famous (1957) recording of the *Pictures* (discussed in the composer section) is linked with a powerful *Night on the bare mountain* within a 1959 concert of shorter Russian pieces, all brilliantly played and spectacularly recorded. Reiner's account of the *Russlan and Ludmilla overture* is not quite as taut as Solti's famous LSO version, but its racy geniality is very attractive. *Colas Breugnon* with its syncopated cross-rhythms has plenty of gusto; the *Polovtsian march* is robustly rhythmic and Tchaikovsky's *Marche slave* suitably sombre, yet with an exciting coda.

Cincinnati Pops Orchestra, Erich Kunzel

'Favourite overtures': SUPPE: *Light cavalry; Poet and peasant.* AUBER: *Fra Diavolo.* HEROLD: *Zampa.* REZNICEK: *Donna Diana.* OFFENBACH: *Orpheus in the Underworld.* ROSSINI: *William Tell.*
*** Telarc Dig. CD 80116 [id.].

We are indebted to a reader for drawing our attention to the omission from previous editions of this spectacularly recorded (1985) collection of favourite bandstand overtures. The playing has fine exuberance and gusto (only the galop from *William Tell* could perhaps have had greater impetus) and the resonant ambience of Cincinnati's Music Hall lends itself to Telarc's wide-ranging engineering, with the bass drum nicely caught. Perhaps the opening of *Fra Diavolo* would have benefited from a more transparent sound, but for the most part the opulence suits the vigorous style of the music-making, with *Zampa* and the Suppé overtures particularly successful.

Cluytens, André: *'Artist profile'* – see under Berlin Philharmonic Orchestra etc.

Columbia Symphony Orchestra, Bruno Walter

Bruno Walter Edition (complete)
(M) **(*) Sony stereo/mono SX10K 66247 (10) [id.].

BEETHOVEN: *Symphonies Nos. 1 in C, Op. 21; 2 in D, Op. 36; Coriolan Overture* (SMK 64460).
BEETHOVEN: *Symphonies Nos. 3 in E flat (Eroica), Op. 55; 8 in F* (SMK 64461).
BEETHOVEN: *Symphonies Nos. 4 in B flat, Op. 60; 6 in F (Pastoral), Op. 68* (SMK 64462).
BEETHOVEN: *Symphonies Nos. 5 in C min., Op. 67; 7 in A, Op. 92* (SMK 64463).
BEETHOVEN: *Symphony No. 9 in D min., Op. 125* (with Cundari, Rankin, Da Costa, Wilderman, Westminster Ch. (SMK 64464)).

BEETHOVEN: *Symphonies Nos. 4, 5, 7 & 9* (rehearsals) (SMK 64465).
BARBER: *Symphony No. 1, Op. 9.* Richard STRAUSS: *Don Juan; Death and transfiguration.* DVORAK: *Slavonic Dance, Op. 46/1* ((mono) SMK 64466).

Johann STRAUSS Jnr: Waltzes: *An der schönen blauen Donau; Geschichten aus dem Wiener Wald;*

Kaiser Weiner Blut; Overtures: *Die Fledermaus; Der Zigeunerbaron.* BRAHMS: *Hungarian dances Nos. 1, 3, 10 & 17.* SMETANA: *Vltava* (both with NYPO) ((mono) SMK 64467).

MOZART: (i) *Violin concertos Nos. 3 in G, K.216; 4 in D, K.218; Serenade No, 13 (Eine kleine Nachtmusik), K.525* ((i) with Zino Francescatti (SMK 64468)).

BRAHMS: (i) *German Requiem;* (ii) *Alto rhapsody, Op. 53* (with (i) Seefried, London, Westminster Ch., NYPO; (ii) Mildred Miller, Occidental College Concert Ch., Columbia SO ((mono/stereo) SMK 64469)).

Although he enjoyed a position of pre-eminence in the 1930s, Bruno Walter was never invited to record a Beethoven cycle. Duplication was less frequent then than it is now, and Weingartner and Toscanini dominated the field. (Walter's glorious pre-war records of the *Pastoral Symphony* with the Vienna Philharmonic give some idea of how good it might have been.) After he settled in the United States he recorded all nine symphonies with the New York Philharmonic and Philadelphia orchestras, but the set offered here is with the Columbia Symphony, made in California in 1958/9, not long before he died, and by general consent the finer of the two by a considerable margin. These performances embody the humane, songful approach which characterized his finest work, their warmth standing out in contrast against the gaunt, often matter-of-fact approach of Klemperer. Tempi are not exaggerated and, although Walter may not have had the electricity and fiery qualities that distinguish Toscanini's NBC Beethoven, there is no lack of either rhythmic vitality or lyrical intensity. There is also a rehearsal disc (available as part of the set) which shows his courteous, gentle, yet firm approach to music-making in the slow movement of the *Fourth,* the first movements of the *Fifth* and *Seventh* and the Scherzo of the *Ninth.* All these recordings are discussed more fully under their individual entries, as they are all available separately. Of particular interest in the present set is the 1945 version of Barber's *First Symphony,* which makes its first appearance since the two blue-label 78-r.p.m. discs were withdrawn in the early 1950s. Not only is this the only *American* symphony, it is the only *contemporary* symphony Walter recorded: his repertoire never embraced much modern music (though he did conduct Wellesz's *Prospero's spell*). Like the two Strauss tone-poems with which it is coupled, it is a mono disc and, though the resulting transfer produces cleaner and better-focused sound than the originals, it still calls for some tolerance. Walter's Mozart was particularly notable for its humane qualities, and he gives admirable support to Francescatti, his soloist in the two best-known violin concertos, who is at times over-tense – what the French would call *nerveux.* The Brahms *Requiem* with the youthful Irmgard Seefried and George London comes from 1954 and is also in mono. Its companion, the *Alto Rhapsody,* with Mildred Miller comes from 1962, the year of his death, and is less successful. However, this is a collection which serious collectors will want to have.

Concertgebouw Orchestra

'Early years' (cond. (i) Eduard van Beinum; (ii) Kiril Kondrashin; (iii) Karl Boehm; (iv) George Szell; (v) Paul van Kempen; (vi) Pierre Monteux): (i) BEETHOVEN: *Symphony No. 2 in D;* (ii) *Symphony No. 3 in E flat (Eroica).* (iii) R. STRAUSS: *Death and transfiguration.* MOZART: *Symphony No. 26 in E flat, K.184;* (iv) *Symphony No. 34 in C, K.388.* (v) TCHAIKOVSKY: *Symphony No. 6 in B min. (Pathétique).* (vi) SCHUBERT: *Symphony No. 8 (Unfinished).*
(M) *** Ph. mono 438 524-2 (3) [id.].

This is one of the most successful sets in Philips's *'Early years'* series. Some of the performances here come close to greatness and nearly all are touched by distinction. They represent quite a time-span: Paul van Kempen's *Pathétique,* made in 1951, is very impressive indeed, and so for that matter is the Kondrashin *Eroica* from 1979. Eduard van Beinum was always respected, but this account of Beethoven's *Second Symphony* prompts one to feel that he is actually underrated. A useful and worthwhile compilation, despite variable sound-quality.

(i) Concertgebouw Orchestra; (ii) LSO, Pierre Monteux

(i) BEETHOVEN: *Symphony No. 3 in E flat (Eroica).* SCHUBERT: *Symphony No. 8 (Unfinished).* (ii) TCHAIKOVSKY: *Swan Lake* (ballet): *highlights.* BRAHMS: *Symphony No. 2 in D, Op. 73; Tragic overture, Op. 81; Academic festival overture, Op. 80.* RAVEL: *Boléro; La valse; Ma Mère l'Oye.* DEBUSSY: *Images; Le martyre de Saint Sébastien.*
(M) ** Ph. 442 544-2 (5) [id.].

This Philips box, celebrating Monteux's recordings in London and Amsterdam during the early 1960s, is rather a mixed offering. Monteux's 1962 Concertgebouw *Eroica* is better played (though not better recorded) than his Vienna Philharmonic version for Decca of five years earlier (see above, under its composer entry). But in any case that Vienna performance is much more satisfying interpretatively; the Philips version is let down by the absence of real weight in the *Funeral march*. Monteux's *Unfinished* is also disappointing. In the first movement there is an unashamed speed-change between the first and second subjects, while Monteux believes in treating the second movement in leisurely fashion and obtaining the maximum contrast. This is not among his more alert performances, although the recording is full and well balanced. The Concertgebouw Orchestra seemed to inspire him less than the LSO. However, much the same comments must be made about his London account of Brahms's *Second Symphony*, which offers relaxed idiomatic playing and an eminently sound reading; yet the performance fails to resound in the memory in quite the way of his earlier Decca records of the Beethoven symphonies. Incidentally, the *Tragic overture*, recorded at the same time, which has rather more drama, has not been issued before.

Monteux's complete 1964 version of Ravel's *Ma Mère l'Oye* is a poetic, unforced reading given characteristically refined and naturally balanced sound by the Philips engineers, though the effect is not as translucent as Paray's Mercury version (see under the composer). *La Valse* goes well too, but *Boléro* brings a slight quickening of tempo in the closing pages.

The 59-minute selection from Tchaikovsky's *Swan Lake*, often reissued in the days of LP, was one of Monteux's Philips successes. The spacious acoustic means that the 1962 recording hardly sounds dated, and it suits the conductor's approach to the finale, which he takes slowly – some might feel too slowly – and grandly, supported by rich-toned brass. Throughout, the LSO playing is beautifully turned. Hugh Maguire is the only individual to be named (for his violin solo in the Dance of Odette and the Prince), but the comparably fine contribution of the principal oboe is also worth noting.

Undoubtedly the best of the five discs included here is the classic Monteux coupling of *Images* and the orchestral version of *Le martyre de Saint Sébastien*, and this needs restoring to the catalogue as an individual issue. Monteux's performance of *Images* was notable for its freshness and impetus (although this is achieved by the concentration of the playing rather than by fast tempi). The 1963 recording is another tribute to the Philips engineering of the time, for there is a fine sheen of warmth and sensuousness to the strings (especially in *Les parfums de la nuit*), while the woodwind is delicately hued. This vivid yet refined feeling for colour is carried through into the orchestral sections from *Le martyre*. The fragility of texture of Debussy's exquisite scoring is marvellously balanced by Monteux, and he never lets the music become static.

Concertgebouw Orchestra, Georg Szell

'The Concertgebouw recordings': SCHUBERT: *Rosamunde: Overture; Ballet music No. 2; Entr'actes Nos. 1 & 3.* MENDELSSOHN: *A Midsummer Night's Dream: Overture; Scherzo; Nocturne; Wedding march.* MOZART: *Symphony No. 34 in C, K.388.* BEETHOVEN: *Symphony No. 5 in C min., Op. 67.* SIBELIUS: *Symphony No. 2 in D, Op. 43.*
(M) *** Ph. 442 727-2 (2) [id.].

George Szell was musical director of the Cleveland Orchestra from 1946 until his death in 1970, and he turned his players into an ensemble of the most remarkable virtuosity. But he also occasionally guest-conducted other orchestras with great success, and the present anthology spans the decade from 1957 to 1966. Probably the most striking performance here is the Sibelius *D major Symphony*. Szell's reading is marvellously taut and well held together, and its merits are well known: great tension and power. The remastered sound is a great improvement on the earlier CD reissue. Beethoven's *Fifth* is hardly less thrilling; if not quite as intense as his Cleveland version, that is not necessarily a drawback, with such fine playing. The Schubert and Mendelssohn incidental music is hardly less impressive. The *Rosamunde overture* has a strikingly resilient spring and the *Ballet music* and *Entr'actes* match polish and charm. Particularly attractive is the way Szell quickens the pace of the middle section of the *B flat Entr'acte* so that the effect of the reprise of the famous principal melody is heightened. The lightness and clean, sweet articulation of the violins in the Mendelssohn *Midsummer Night's Dream overture* are a delight: the wonderfully nimble wind-playing in the *Scherzo* is no less engaging, and there is a fine horn solo in the *Nocturne*. Szell, as usual, offers big-band Mozart, but the playing in the *Andante* has refinement as well as warmth, and the finale brings a bustle achieved from articulation of great precision.

Czech Philharmonic Orchestra, Gerd Albrecht

HAAS: *Studies for string orchestra.* SCHULHOF: *Symphony No. 2.* ULLMAN: *Symphony No. 2.* KLEIN: *Partita for strings.*
*** Orfeo Dig. C 337941 A [id.].

Like the issues in Decca's *Entartete Musik* series, this Orfeo disc features music dismissed by the Nazis as decadent, all here by Jewish composers from Czechoslovakia slaughtered in the Holocaust. Pavel Haas, often counted as Janáček's most important pupil, wrote his *Studies* in Theresienstadt, the prison camp where the Nazis assembled Jewish intellectuals, later to be killed in death camps. Tautly argued in four sections lasting eight minutes, it was given its first performance in the camp under one of the then inmates who happily managed to survive, Karel Ančerl, later the conductor of the Czech Philharmonic. Albrecht and today's Czech Philharmonic bring out the vitality of the writing, with no hint in it of self-indulgence or self-pity. This is a composer writing in sight of death simply because he has to, relishing a last opportunity. The *Symphony No. 2* of Erwin Schulhof was written in 1932, long before the Nazis invaded Czechoslovakia, a work very much of its period with a charming *Scherzo alla Jazz* influenced by Stravinsky's *Soldier's tale*. The *Symphony No. 2* of Viktor Ullmann, also in four crisp movements, was one of no fewer than 25 works that he wrote in Theresienstadt, including the opera, *The Emperor of Atlantis*, also on disc. Though he was a pupil of Schoenberg, he here returned to tonality, communicating directly. The youngest of the four, Gideon Klein from Moravia, more specifically drew inspiration from folk roots, very much in the way that Bartók did in Hungary. His *Partita for strings*, like the Pavel Haas *Studies*, has darkness in it, notably in the central variation movement, but here too the piece culminates in a mood of energetic optimism, a heart-warming expression of defiance. Very well played and recorded, the four works are the more moving for giving only momentary hints of what the composers were going through. First-rate sound.

Cziffra, Georges (piano)

Cziffra Edition, Volume 2: CHOPIN: *Piano concerto No. 1 in E min., Op. 11* (with O de Paris, György Cziffra, Jr). *Ballade No. 4 in F min., Op. 52; Etudes: in E; in A flat, Op. 10/3 & 10; in A flat & F min., Op. 25/1–2; Impromptu No. 1 in A flat, Op. 29; Nocturne No. 2 in E flat, Op. 9/2; Polonaise in A (Military), Op. 40/1.*
(M) ** EMI CDM5 65251-2 [id.].

The Cziffra Edition comes from EMI France and was prompted by the pianist's death in 1994. He was a pianist of prodigious technical gifts and a wide stylistic range. His playing always has great personality, but its impulse is at times exasperatingly wayward. When he kept his emotional responses in check (as in early French keyboard music), his performances could be very impressive and, if you accept the unrestricted flamboyance, his Liszt could also be pretty staggering. Cziffra's account of the Chopin *E minor Concerto* has plenty of life, helped by a robust orchestral contribution from his son, who yet opens the central *Romance* very persuasively. There are moments of genuine poetry but the reading as a whole is characteristically extrovert. The solo performances are less attractive and too often sound calculated. Fair recording, using the Paris Salle Wagram. The concerto dates from 1968 and the rest from over the next decade.

Cziffra Edition, Volume 3 (with Philh. O, André Vandernoot): LISZT: *Piano concertos Nos. 1 in E flat; 2 in A.* TCHAIKOVSKY: *Piano concerto No. 1 in B flat min., Op. 23.*
(M) **(*) EMI CDM5 65252-2 [id.].

The two Liszt concertos suit Cziffra's bold, volatile manner very well indeed and the glittering solo playing has enormous panache, while there is no lack of lyrical warmth. The *Second Concerto* is even finer than the *First*. There is much of the grand manner in his performance and he has clearly persuaded Vandernoot to back him up in his interpretation. The work's quicksilver moods bring a true feeling of spontaneity. Surprisingly, the Tchaikovsky *B flat minor* comes off very much less successfully. Cziffra, as always, displays a prodigious technique but, during the first movement, conductor and soloist seem not wholly agreed on the degree of forward thrust the music needs. In spite of the use of the Kingsway Hall, the recordings (made in 1958 and 1961) are comparatively two-dimensional and the strings tend to shrillness in the Tchaikovsky.

Detroit Symphony Orchestra, Neeme Järvi

'Encore!': CHABRIER: *Fête polonaise.* GLINKA: *Kamarinskaya; Valse fantaisie.* SIBELIUS: *Andante festivo for strings.* BOLZONI: *Minuet.* DVORAK: *Humoresque.* DARZINS: *Valse mélancholique.* ELLINGTON: *Solitude* (trans. for strings). SHOSTAKOVICH: *The Gadfly: Romance.* MUSSORGSKY: *Gopak.* DEBUSSY: *Suite bergamasque: Clair de lune.* SCHUMANN: *Abendlied, Op. 107/6.* MEDINS: *Aria.* GERSHWIN: *Promenade: walking the dog.* SOUSA: *The Stars and Stripes forever.*
**(*) Chan. Dig. CHAN 9227 [id.].

The acoustics of Detroit's Orchestra Hall, made famous by the Mercury engineers at the end of the 1950s, remain impressive and the Detroit orchestra is flattered here by opulently glowing sound, which especially suits the Glinka pieces and the lovely Sibelius *Andante festivo.* The rest of the programme is rather slight, consisting entirely of lollipops, some well-known, plus a few engaging novelties. All are presented with Järvi's customary flair and are very well played. If you enjoy this kind of concert, there is no need to hesitate for the programme is generous: 73 minutes.

Eastman Wind Ensemble, Frederick Fennell

American wind band music: Morton GOULD: *West Point (Symphony for band).* GIANNINI: *Symphony No. 3.* HOVHANESS: *Symphony No. 4, Op. 165* (cond. A.Clyde Roller).
(M) ** Mercury 434 320-2 [id.].

Fine playing, but the music here is often too inflated to give pleasure on repetition. Gould's *West Point Symphony* is in two movements, *Epitaphs* (which at 11 minutes 55 seconds is far too long) and *Marches.* The *Symphony No. 3* of Vittorio Giannini improves as it proceeds: the Scherzo and finale are the most interesting movements and the most attractively scored. Best by far is the Hovhaness *Symphony No. 4* (admirably directed by A.Clyde Roller) with its bold, rich, brass sonorities in the slower outer movements contrasting with marimba, vibraphone and other tuned percussion instruments in the central *Allegro.* Splendid sound, too.

Music from ballet and opera: SULLIVAN/MACKERRAS: *Pineapple Poll: suite* (arr. Duthoit). ROSSINI/ RESPIGHI: *La boutique fantasque: suite* (arr. Dan Godfrey). GOUNOD: *Faust: ballet suite* (arr. Winterbottom). WAGNER: *Lohengrin: Prelude to Act III; Bridal chorus* (arr. Winterbottom); *Elsa's procession* (arr. Cailliet). *Das Rheingold* (arr. Dan Godfrey).
(M) ** Mercury 434 322-2 [id.].

Although played with characteristic Eastman verve, this is essentially a programme for admirers of wind band transcriptions – here mostly traditional scorings by prominent British military band arrangers. Little of this music gains from its loss of string textures, and the famous Respighi/Rossini *Boutique fantasque* lacks sumptuousness. All this would be entertaining on the bandstand, but at home the ear craves the full orchestra.

English music

English music ((i) LPO; (ii) New Philh. O; (iii) Sir Adrian Boult; (iv) ASMF, Marriner; (v) Hirsch Chamber Players, Leonard Hirsch; (vi) BBC Northern SO, Bryden Thomson): BUTTERWORTH: (i; iii) *The Banks of green willow.* VAUGHAN WILLIAMS: (ii; iii) *Fantasia on a theme of Thomas Tallis.* (iv) LEIGH: *Harpsichord concertino* (with George Malcolm). (v) WARLOCK: *Capriol suite.* FINZI: (vi) *Clarinet concerto* (with Janet Hilton); (i; iii) *Introit for violin and orchestra* (with Gerald Jarvis).
(B) **(*) BBC Radio Classics BBCRD 9119 [id.].

This mixed bag of BBC recordings from various sources offers a delightful collection. The charming Walter Leigh *Concertino* in three compact movements – including a heavenly central *Andante* – has never been recorded so ravishingly as by George Malcolm. It is also good to have a Finzi novelty in the beautiful *Introit* (with another memorable main theme), though the soloist, Gerald Jarvis, could be sweeter. Janet Hilton is an agile soloist in the Finzi *Clarinet concerto*, though the transfer gives her instrument a flutter in the finale. Boult as ever is most persuasive in all he conducts, and it is good to have a vintage artist like Leonard Hirsch conducting his own orchestra in the Warlock, even if the performance itself is a little bland. The sound is good throughout and this 77-minute concert is well worth its modest cost.

English Northern Philharmonia, David Lloyd-Jones

'Victorian concert overtures': MACFARREN: Chevy Chase. PIERSON: Romeo and Juliet, Op. 86.
SULLIVAN: Macbeth. CORDER: Prospero. ELGAR: Froissart, Op. 19. PARRY: Overture to an unwritten
tragedy. MACKENZIE: Britannia, a nautical overture, Op. 52.
*** Hyp. Dig. CDA 66515 [id.].

Sir George (Alexander) Macfarrren (1813–87) was an English composer of Scottish descent who
taught at and eventually became Principal of the Royal Academy of Music. His music was very
successful in its day; he was a distinguished early editor of Purcell's *Dido and Aeneas* and of major
stage works of Handel; many of his own operas were produced in London, including one based on
the story of Robin Hood. A CD showing us a wider range of his music is overdue; meanwhile he
makes a strong contribution to this collection of Victorian concert overtures with *Chevy Chase*, a
spirited, tuneful piece that was admired by Mendelssohn. Pierson's *Romeo and Juliet* hardly explores
its theme with any substance but Frederick Corder's *Prospero* has a certain flamboyant gravitas.
Mackenzie's *Britannia* is a pot-boiler featuring a borrowed tune now famous at the Proms. Against
all this and more, Elgar's *Froissart* stands out as the early masterpiece it was. The whole concert is
persuasively performed by the excellent Northern Sinfonia under the versatile David Lloyd-Jones.
Not an indispensable disc, but a fascinating glimpse of music that was heard at the spa and by end-
of-the-pier orchestras which flourished in Victorian and Edwardian England and which established a
tradition whereby British orchestral players had to sight-read new pieces 'at the show'. Excellent
recording.

English Sinfonia, Sir Charles Groves

'Entente cordiale': FAURE: Masques et bergamasques, Op. 112; Pavane, Op. 50. ELGAR: Chanson de
nuit; Chanson de matin, Op. 15/1–2. DELIUS: On hearing the first cuckoo in spring. RAVEL: Pavane
pour une infante défunte. WARLOCK: Capriol suite. BUTTERWORTH: The Banks of green willow.
SATIE: Gymnopédies Nos. 1 & 3 (orch. Debussy).
(B) *** Carlton Dig. PCD 2017.

Having given us some attractive Haydn recordings with the English Sinfonia, Sir Charles Groves then
offered a happy juxtaposition of French and British music. He opens with a performance of Fauré's
Masques et bergamasques which is sheer delight in its airy grace, and later he finds passion as well as
delicacy in the Butterworth rhapsody, very effectively followed by Debussy's languorous orchestrations of the Satie *Gymnopédies*. Groves's approach to Warlock's *Capriol* dances is essentially genial
(Marriner's version has more zest); but all this music-making is easy to enjoy. The playing is polished
and spontaneous and the recording, made at Abbey Road, quite splendid.

Ensemble Wien

'Lanner and Strauss Waltzes, Polkas, Galops': LANNER: Jubel waltz; Eisens und Katinkens Vereinigung
galop; Die Werber waltz; Hans Jörgel polka; Abendsterne waltz; Vermählungs waltz. Johann STRAUSS
Snr: Tivoli-Rutsch waltz; Eisle- und Beisele-Sprünge polka; Cachucha galop; Kettenbrücke Waltz;
Gitana galop. Josef STRAUSS: Die guten, alten Zeiten waltz.
**(*) Sony Dig. SK 52485 [id.].

It is good to have a modern, digital collection of this early Viennese dance repertoire, even if the
recording is too immediate and unglamorous and the playing, though immaculate, too often a bit stiff
and unsmiling. Much of Lanner's music is instantly forgettable and needs a coaxing charm of the
kind Boskovsky could so easily manage. Paul Guggenberger, the leader, understands the Viennese lilt
and often plays rather nicely (as in *Die Werber* and the *Abendsterne waltz* which charmingly recalls a
famous folk-tune); but almost all the pieces seem to open rather gruffly, partly the effect of the close
microphones. Once we reach the group of four pieces by Johann Strauss Senior at the end of the
programme, the players seem to relax more, and the Josef Strauss waltz which comes at their centre is
the highlight of the programme. But even here the rhythm seems too calculated.

Fleisher, Leon (piano), Boston Symphony Orchestra, Seiji Ozawa

Left-hand Piano concertos: BRITTEN: *Diversions for piano and orchestra.* PROKOFIEV: *Piano Concerto No. 4.* RAVEL: *Piano concerto in D for the left hand.*
*** Sony Dig. SK 47188 [id.].

These superb concertante works, originally written for the one-armed Austrian pianist, Paul Wittgenstein, but rejected by him, make the perfect vehicle for one of the finest of all American pianists, Leon Fleisher. Unable to play with his right hand any longer, Fleisher here shows that his power and artistry are undiminished from the days when he was the favourite recording pianist of George Szell, with the vintage Cleveland orchestra. Though the Ravel and Prokofiev concertos have been recorded many times, these accounts are a match for any of them, while Britten's highly original set of variations is a rarity on disc, very welcome indeed in Fleisher's masterly performance.

Folkwang Horn Ensemble, Hermann Baumann

'St Hubert Mass' (Hunting music): ZWIERZINA: *3 Trios.* SCHNEIDER: *3 Trios.* CORRETTE: *Concerto for 4 horns & organ ('La Choisy').* CHALMEL: *Marche solonnele.* TYNDARE: *La Rally-Paper.* BELLECROIX: *La Chabot.* SOMBRUN: *Souvenir de Bretagne.* ROSSINI, arr. Baumann: *La Grande Fanfare.* PONT: *Fanfare des bois.*
*** Ph. Dig. 426 301-2 [id.].

The German horn-player, Hermann Baumann, with a team of well-matched colleagues gives a brilliant, ripe-toned display of festive hunting music drawn from traditional sources and made into a sequence, the *St Hubert Mass.* Also – with Wolfgang Glasener at the organ – he and his partners play a glorious *Concerto in C* by the eighteenth-century French composer, Michel Corrette, as well as shorter pieces by Zwierzina, Schneider, Chalmel, Sombrun and Rossini. Ripe recording to match.

(i) French National Radio Orchestra; (ii) London Symphony Orchestra, Leopold Stokowski

DEBUSSY: (i) *Images:* (ii) *Ibéria. Nocturnes* (with BBC Women's Chorus). RAVEL: *Rapsodie espagnole.* (i) IBERT: *Escales.*
(M) *** EMI CDM5 65422-2 [id.].

This brings together two separate LPs, with the *Nocturnes* and the Ravel *Rapsodie*, brilliantly done by the LSO, representing one of the very finest of Stokowski's Capitol records, made at Abbey Road in 1957. Here is 'full dimensional sound' with the microphones less close than in most of the American recordings on this label, and there is atmosphere as well as brilliance. The second of the *Nocturnes*, *Fêtes*, is taken fast, giving it electric intensity. *Sirènes* is then sensuously evocative, leading on to the thrillingly high-powered reading of the Ravel. In the French recordings, made in the Salle Wagram in 1958, the sound is brightly lit, but there is still plenty of ambience. The playing of the French National Radio Orchestra is warmly persuasive but with ensemble less crisp. Stokowski's panache and his feeling for colour are consistently persuasive, with the opening evocation of *Palermo* in *Escales* bringing some unforgettably languorous playing from the strings, while the combination of Mediterranean warmth and passion in *Valencia* is even more highly charged. Though the 1957/8 recordings do not convey a true pianissimo, the dynamic range is still impressive and the sound is wonderfully vivid and immediate.

Fricsay, Ferenc: 'Portrait' – see under Berlin Philharmonic Orchestra etc.

Gallois, Patrick (flute)

'Une flûte à l'opéra' (with L. Festival O, Ross Pople): Opera arias for flute and orchestra from VERDI: *La Traviata* (arr. Genin; orch. Guiot); *Un ballo in maschera* (arr. Genin; orch. Pierre). ROSSINI: *William Tell* (arr. Demersseman/Berthelemy; orch. Gallois). GODARD: *Berceuse de Jocelyn.* MASSE: *Les noces de Jeanette: Air du rossignol* (both arr. & orch. Pierre). MASSENET: *Thaïs: Méditation* (arr. Prezman). BIZET: *Carmen fantasia* (arr. Borne; orch. Pierre).
*** DG Dig. 445 822-2 [id.].

Patrick Gallois is clearly a new international star in the flautists' firmament. His tone is uniquely recognizable and beautiful, his playing naturally stylish, his musicianship impeccable and, as this light-hearted and entertaining collection demonstrates, his technique is dazzling. Unlike James Galway, he plays a modern wooden flute which he suggests is particularly suitable for the present repertoire as it has 'more colour and juster intonation than a traditional wooden flute ... and its timbre is closer to that of the human voice than a metal instrument'. He certainly makes it tell in the scintillating coloratura with which he surrounds the selection from Verdi's *La Traviata* and the excerpts from *William Tell*, which feature a brief but witty morsel of the famous *Galop* with the most engaging additional embroidery. Ross Pople opens the famous *Berceuse de Jocelyn* with lovely, gentle playing from the orchestral strings, and the charm of the flute solo here is very seductive, while in the equally popular *Méditation* from *Thaïs* the melodic line is richly expressive without any feeling of sentimentality. Finally we are offered all those hits from *Carmen* which Sarasate arranged so effectively for the violin. Gallois' claim as to the vocal possibilities of his instrument is readily apparent here in the quite beautiful performance of the *Flower song*; he is hardly less bewitching in the 'Habañera' and then decorates it with great panache, finally frolicking nimbly through the *Danse bohème* and genially introducing the *Toreador song* as a surprise just before a breathtaking final burst of bravura.

'Flute concertos from Sans-Souci' (with C. P. E. Bach CO, Peter Schreier): C. P. E. BACH: *Concerto in G, Wq. 169.* BENDA: *Concerto in E min.* FREDERICK THE GREAT: *Concerto No. 3 in C.* QUANTZ: *Concerto in G.*
*** DG Dig. 439 895-2 [id.].

C. P. E. Bach (fairly briefly), Benda and Quantz were all musicians in the employ of Frederick the Great, whose own *Flute concerto* included here is rather impressive, notably its *Grave* slow movement. The Bach concerto is well known and the chamber orchestra carrying his name makes the very most of its sprightly outer movements while Gallois' contribution throughout the programme is impeccably stylish and elegant and his decoration always imaginative. The *Adagio un poco Andante* of the Benda *Concerto* shows his luminous line, as does the rather lovely *Arioso* which is the centrepoint of the Quantz work; it is played most delectably, followed by a lively moto perpetuo finale of equal charm. Here the neat string articulation and the soloist's finesse mirror each other equitably, as they do in the catchy last movement of the Benda work. Fresh, clean recording and a bright string-sound demonstrate that modern instruments can present this repertoire with the same lightness and transparency as original intruments. There are few collections of baroque flute concertos in this bracket and none more generous (77 minutes) – but this is not a concert to be played all at once.

Galway, James (flute)

'Greatest hits', Vol. 2 (with various artists): ASHMAN/MENCKEN: *Beauty and the Beast.* TRAD. (arr. Galway) *Zui Zui Zukkorobashi. Irish medley. Crowley's reel.* arr. The Chieftains: *Full of joy* (both with The Chieftains). arr. Dankworth: *The fluter's ball* (with Cleo Laine). NORTH/ZARET: *Unchained melody.* MANCINI: *Two for the Road; Viewer mail theme; Something for the Leprechaun* (with Nat. PO, composer). BACH: *Jesu, joy of man's desiring* (with Munich RSO, Georgiadis). DEBUSSY: *Petite suite: Ballet.* GORDON: *Unforgettable.* FLEMING/MORGAN: *Dreams.* JOHN/OSBORNE: *Blue eyes.* UTA: *Song of the seashore.* DE VORZON-BOTKIN: *Nàdia's theme.* GRAINGER: *Molly on the shore.* MARAIS: *Le Basque.*
(M) ** BMG/RCA 09026 61178-2.

Although there is some attractive folk material, from China and Japan as well as from Ireland – very much Galway's speciality – the selection here is a little diluted by pop material. No doubt the very winning *Le Basque* of Marais was also a popular hit in its day, but it is a good deal more enduring than the theme from Disney's *Beauty and the Beast*, which is pleasant enough but not distinctive. But Galway's sheer charisma can almost make a silk purse out of less than top-grade material, and this is enjoyable enough as wallpaper music. The sound is always agreeable.

Gieseking, Walter (piano), Berlin Opera Orchestra, Hans Rosbaud

'First concerto recordings': BEETHOVEN: *Piano concerto No. 1 in C, Op. 15.* MOZART: *Piano concerto No. 9 in E flat (Jeunehomme), K.271. Piano sonata No. 17 in B flat, K.570.*
(**) APR mono APR 5511 [id.].

The frontispiece of the CD reads *'Walter Gieseking – His first concerto recordings',* but in fact the Mozart *E flat concerto*, K.271, was also *its* first recording and, but for Schnabel, the Beethoven would have been a first also. Both the concertos were recorded in Berlin in 1936–7 and originally appeared on Columbia light-blue-label 78s. The acoustic is on the dryish side, particularly in the Mozart, and the balance close. (There is not a great deal of air round the instruments.) Nevertheless the sound is perfectly acceptable, and the Beethoven is a performance of brilliance and power, though not the equal (if memory does not deceive) of Gieseking's *Fourth in G major.* Although there are many felicitous touches in the *Jeunehomme concerto,* he recorded Mozart concertos later on to greater poetic effect. In the *B flat Sonata,* K.570, on the other hand, his playing is far finer than in the later, LP version he recorded in the mid-1950s, shortly before his death.

Gould, Glenn (piano)

Glenn Gould Edition

BACH: *Harpsichord concertos Nos. 1–5; 7, BWV 1052/6 & BWV 1058* (with Columbia SO, Bernstein (No. 1) or Golschmann).
(M) (**) Sony mono (No. 1)/stereo SM2K 52591 (2) [id.].

BACH: *Fugues, BWV 953 & BWV 961; Fughettas, BWV 961 & BWV 902; 6 Little Preludes, BWV 933/938; 6 Partitas, BWV 825/830; Preludes, BWV 902 & 902/1a; Prelude and fugue, BWV 895; 2 Preludes & fughettas, BWV 899/900.*
(M) (**) Sony SM2K 52597 (2) [id.].

BACH: *Goldberg variations, BWV 988; Three-part Inventions, BWV 788/801.*
(M) (**) Sony SMK 52685 [id.] (live recordings from Salzburg and Moscow).

BACH: *Goldberg variations, BWV 988; Well-tempered Clavier: Fugues in E, BWV 878; F sharp min., BWV 883.*
(M) (**(*)) Sony mono SMK 52594 [id.] (1955 recording).
(M) (**) Sony Dig. SMK 52619 [id.] (*Variations* only).

BACH: *15 Two-part Inventions; 15 Three-part Inventions, BWV 772/801.*
(M) (**) Sony SMK 52596 [id.].

BACH: *Well-tempered Clavier, Book I, Preludes and fugues Nos. 1–24, BWV 858/869.*
(M) (**) Sony SM2K 52600 (2) [id.].

BACH: *Well-tempered Clavier, Book II, Preludes and Fugues Nos. 25–48, BWV 882/893.*
(M) (**) Sony SM2K 52603 (2) [id.].

BACH: *Well-tempered Clavier: Preludes and fugues: in E, BWV 878; in F sharp min., BWV 883.*
HANDEL: *Harpsichord suites Nos. 1–4, HWV 426/9.*
(M) (**) Sony mono/stereo SMK 52590 [id.].

BACH: *Sonata for violin and harpsichord No. 4 in C min. BWV 1017.* BEETHOVEN: *Violin sonata No. 10 in G, Op. 96.* SCHOENBERG: *Phantasy for violin and piano, Op. 47* (all with Yehudi Menuhin).
(M) (**) Sony mono SMK 52688 [id.].

BEETHOVEN: *Piano concertos Nos. 1–5* (with Columbia SO, Golschmann (No.1); Columbia SO, Bernstein (Nos. 2–3); NYPO, Bernstein (No. 4); America SO, Stokowski (No. 5)).
(M) (***) Sony SM3K 52632 (3) [id.].

BEETHOVEN: *7 Bagatelles, Op. 33; 6 Bagatelles, Op. 126; 6 Variations in F, Op. 34; 15 Variations with fugue in E flat (Eroica), Op. 35; 32 Variations on an original theme in C min., WoO 80.*
(M) (**) Sony SM2K 52646 (2) [id.]. .

BEETHOVEN: *Piano sonatas Nos. 24 in F sharp, Op. 78; 29 in B flat (Hammerklavier).*
(M) (**) Sony SMK 52645 [id.].

BIZET: *Nocturne No. 1 in F; Variations chromatiques.* GRIEG: *Piano sonata in E min., Op. 7.* SIBELIUS: *Kyllikki (3 Lyric pieces), Op. 41; Sonatines Nos. 1–3, Op. 67/1–3.*
(M) (**(*)) Sony SM2K 52654 (2) [id.].

BRAHMS: (i) *Piano quintet in F min., Op. 34.* SCHUMANN: (i) *Piano quartet in E flat, Op. 47* (with (i) Montreal Qt; (ii) Juilliard Qt (members).
(M) (**) Sony SMK 52684 [id.].

BRAHMS: *4 Ballades, Op. 10; Intermezzi, Op. 76/6–7; Op. 116/4; Op. 117/1–3; Op. 118/1, 2 & 6; Op. 119/1; 2 Rhapsodies, Op. 79.*
(M) (**) Sony Analogue/Dig. SM2K 52651 (2) [id.].

HAYDN: *Piano sonata in E flat, Hob XVI:49.* MOZART: *Piano concerto No. 24 in C min., K.491* (with CBC SO, Walter Süsskind); *Fantasia (Prelude) and fugue in C, K.394; Sonata in C, K.330.*
(M) (**) Sony SMK 52626 [id.].

HINDEMITH: (i) *Alto horn sonata in E flat;* (ii) *Bass tuba sonata;* (i) *Horn sonata;* (iii) *Trombone sonata;* (iv) *Trumpet sonata* (with: (i) Mason Jones; (ii) Abe Torchinsky; (iii) Henry Charles Smith; (iv) Gilbert Johnson).
(M) (**) Sony SM2K 52671 (2) [id.].

HINDEMITH: *Piano sonatas Nos. 1–3.*
(M) (**(*)) Sony SMK 52670 [id.].

LISZT: *Concert paraphrases* of Beethoven's *Symphonies Nos. 5 in C min.; 6 in F (Pastoral): 1st movt.*
(M) (**) Sony SMK 52636 [id.].

LISZT: *Concert paraphrase* of Beethoven's *Symphony No. 6 in F (Pastoral).*
(M) (*) Sony SMK 52637 [id.].

Richard STRAUSS: *Piano sonata in B min., Op. 5; Enoch Arden, Op. 38; 5 Pieces, Op. 3;* (i) *Ophelia Lieder, Op. 67* (with Elisabeth Schwarzkopf).
(M) (**(*)) Sony Dig./Analogue SM2K 52657 (2) [id.].

Contemporary music: MORAWETZ: *Fantasy in D min.* ANHALT: *Fantasia.* HETU: *Variations, Op. 8.* PENTLAND: *Ombres.* VALEN: *Piano sonata No. 2.*
(M) (**) Sony SMK 52677 [id.].

Consort music: BYRD: *1st Pavane & Galliard.* GIBBONS: *Fantasy in C min.; Allemande; Lord Salisbury's pavane & galliard.* BYRD: *Hugh Ashton's ground; 6th Pavane & galliard; A Voluntary; Selliger's round.* SWEELINCK: *Fantasia in D (Fantasia cromatica).*
(M) (**) Sony stereo/mono SMK 52589 [id.].

GOULD: *Lieberson madrigal; So you want to write a fugue* (McFadden, Keller, Fouchécourt, Van Kamp, Naoumoff, Ens., Rivvenq); *String quartet No. 1* (Monsaingeon, Apap, Caussé, Meunier); *2 Pieces for piano; Piano sonata* (unfinished) (Naoumoff); *Sonata for bassoon and piano* (Marchese, Naoumoff).
(M) (**) Sony Dig. SMK 47814 [id.].

As the above listing shows, Sony have done Glenn Gould proud in assembling so comprehensive a discography. We have commented separately on some of these issues earlier in these pages or in our main volume – though, to be frank, Gould is an artist who excites such strong passions that guidance is almost superfluous. For his host of admirers these discs are self-recommending; those who do not respond to his pianism will not be greatly interested in this edition. For long he enjoyed cult status, enhanced rather than diminished by his absence from the concert hall. There is too much that is wilful and eccentric in these performances for any of them to rank as a sole first recommendation. Yet if for his devotees virtually all his recordings are indispensable, for the unconverted a judicious approach is called for.

Generally speaking, his earlier recordings are to be recommended to those who are sceptical as to his gifts. There is nothing eccentric about the early recordings. His 1957 performances of the Beethoven *Second Piano concerto* with Ladislav Slovák in Leningrad and Bernstein in New York are first rate in every respect. He leaves everything to his fingers rather than his head, and his performance is eminently sensitive. We have commented on these individually and on the set of Beethoven concertos, made with Golschmann, Bernstein and Stokowski. (The *C major Concerto*, with Vladimir Golschmann, is particularly exhilarating, and both this and the *C minor* with Bernstein command admiration.) There is no questioning Gould's keyboard wizardry or his miraculous control of part-writing in Bach, for which he had much intuitive feeling. The majority of his Bach discs evince strong personality and commitment throughout, even though the tiresome vocalise (which became an increasing source of frustration, particularly later in his recording career) is a strain. The famous 1955 38-minute repeatless mono recording of the *Goldberg* sounds more of a curiosity nowadays, but it is nothing if not a remarkable feat of digital prestidigitation.

Gould possessed a fine and inquiring mind and both a sharp and an original intellect, as readers of the strongly recommended collection of his writings on music, *The Glenn Gould Reader*, will know.

(Judging from the sampler Sony CD, widely available also on videocassette and laserdisc and containing *So you want to write a fugue* and some of his CBC television appearances, his sense of humour was less sophisticated, in fact pretty cringe-making.) His enterprise and intellectual curiosity, however, inspire respect. Everthing he does is the result of artistic conviction, whether it is championing Bizet's *Nocturne* and *Variations chromatiques* ('a giddy mix of Chopin and Chabrier') or Schoenberg. He had great feeling for Hindemith and championed this complser at a time when he had become comparatively unfashionable, and likewise *Kyllikki* and the three *Sonatinas* of Sibelius. In fact his tastes are always unpredictable: Strauss's *Enoch Arden*, Grieg's early *Sonata*, and the *Second Piano sonata* of the Norwegian 12-note master, Fartein Valen. And who, nowadays, would dare to play Byrd and Gibbons on the piano? On some of these we have commented individually, either here or in our main volume.

Sony deserve congratulations on this formidable enterprise, and collectors will note that the sound-quality of the originals has in the main been much improved – as 'indeed it needed to be. However, the sound generally has insufficient freshness and bloom, and the eccentricity (some might say egocentricity) of some of Gould's readings and the accompanying vocalise are often quite insupportable.

Guildhall String Ensemble, Robert Salter

Scandinavian suite: NIELSEN: *Little suite, Op. 1.* GRIEG: *Holberg suite, Op. 40; 2 Elegiac melodies, Op. 34; 2 Melodies, Op. 53.* SIBELIUS: *Romance in C, Op. 42.* Dag WIREN: *Serenade, Op. 11.*
*** RCA Dig. RD 60439 [60439-2-RC] [id.].

A programme of popular favourites for strings by Grieg, Nielsen and Sibelius, not forgetting the perennially fresh *Serenade* by Dag Wirén. The playing is very good indeed, and no one wanting this repertoire is likely to find anything significantly superior to this splendidly recorded and alertly played collection.

Gutman, Michael (violin), Royal Philharmonic Orchestra, José Serebrier

'Four seasons': MILHAUD: *Spring concertino.* RODRIGO: *Concierto d'estio (Summer concerto).* CHAMINADE (orch. Paul Ut): *Autumn.* SEREBRIER: *Winter concerto.*
**(*) ASV Dig. CDDCA 855 [id.].

This is a well-conceived anthology that went a bit awry. Milhaud's *Spring concertino* is a fresh one-movement piece with a whiff of jazz *à la français*, and Rodrigo's *Concierto de estio*, conceived in the manner of Vivaldi, is the composer's own favourite among his many concertos; the central movement is an engaging *Sicilienne* with variations. Chaminade's *Autumn* is the composer's arrangement for violin and piano of her most successful lollipop, which another hand has subsequently orchestrated. The snag is that the conductor here, José Serebrier, has produced an undistinguished and rather wild concerto for *Winter*, even quoting themes associated with that season from Haydn, Glazunov and Tchaikovsky: the result is a bit of a hotch-potch. Performances and recording do not let the side down, but ASV need to reissue this with a further winter appendix – there is plenty of room, for the CD plays for only around 54 minutes.

Hall, Nicola (guitar), London Mozart Players, Andrew Litton

PAGANINI: *Violin concerto No. 2 in B min., Op. 7* (trans. Hall). SARASATE: *Zigeunerweisen* (trans. Hall). CASTELNUOVO-TEDESCO: *Guitar concerto.*
*(*) Decca Dig. 440 293-2 [id.].

This is a singularly misguided issue. There is no denying Nicola Hall's virtuosity, but her transcriptions of these two famous violin showpieces are completely ineffective. The solo guitar is but a pale imitation of a violin, and Andrew Litton spends most of his time trying to scale down his accompaniment to avoid drowning the modest sound of his soloist. The Castelnuovo-Tedesco *Concerto* immediately demonstrates that Hall can play with great charm in a work suited to her instrument, and here the partnership is fruitful in every way. But the rest is a fiasco.

Hallé Orchestra, Sir John Barbirolli

French music: DEBUSSY: *Prélude à l'après-midi d'un faune.* FAURE: *Pelléas et Mélisande – suite.*
IBERT: *Divertissement.* SAINT-SAENS: *Carnival of the animals* (with Rawicz & Landauer). BIZET:
L'Arlésienne: excerpts: *Prélude; Adagietto; Farandole.*
(M) (***) Dutton Lab. mono CDSJB 1002 [id.].

Dating from between 1950 and 1954, these heart-warming recordings not only show off Barbirolli's
Hallé at a vintage period, but consistently demonstrate what natural sympathy he had for this
French repertory. Regularly he brings out the red-blooded qualities of French music, alongside
the subtle evocation of atmosphere. Equally his sense of humour and fun bubbles over in the riotous
'Italian Straw Hat' music of Ibert's *Divertissement.* Michael Kennedy in his illuminating note
points out how irritated Barbirolli would be if audiences in such music failed to laugh out loud.
Thanks to the Barbirolli Society, these recordings come in transfers by Dutton Sound, using
CEDAR-based techniques on more recent material than that company had tackled previously.
The absence of surface hiss is particularly welcome in such a piece as the Debussy, an easily
flowing reading presented with a vivid sense of presence and weight of sound. For the Saint-Saëns
Carnival of the animals EMI brought in the most popular piano duo of the day, Rawicz and
Landauer, offering energy and brilliance to match Barbirolli's own. Again the fun of the piece is
brought out, though it is a pity that *The Swan* is given to the full cellos, hardly a match for a cello
section today.

Haskil, Clara (piano).

Clara Haskil: The Legacy: Volume II: Concertos (for Volumes I & III, see below, under Instrumental
recitals)

BEETHOVEN: *Piano concerto No. 3 in C min., Op. 37.* CHOPIN: *Piano concerto No. 2 in F min., Op. 21.*
FALLA: *Nights in the gardens of Spain* (all with LOP, Markevitch). MOZART: *Piano concertos Nos. 9
in E flat (Jeunehomme), K.271; 23 in A, K.488; Concert rondo in A, K.386* (with VSO, Sacher or
Paumgartner); *20 in D min., K.466* (two versions, with VSO, Paumgartner or LOP, Markevitch); *24
in C min., K.491* (with LOP, Markevitch). SCHUMANN: *Piano concerto in A min., Op. 54* (with Hague
PO, van Otterloo).
(M) **(*) Ph. mono/stereo 442 631-2 (4) [id.].

This second box of recordings, issued in the Philips 12-disc 'Clara Haskil Legacy', is of concertante
works. The earliest of Haskil's concerto records is the Schumann (1951) and is not quite as poetic as
that of her compatriot, Lipatti (Haskil was born in Bucharest), though there are some wonderful
things, such as the reposeful development section of the first movement and the slow movement. The
Hague orchestra's oboe has a surprisingly wide vibrato. Haskil's refinement and grace are to be heard
at their best in the Mozart concertos, (K.466 and K.491 were recorded in the month before her death)
and her fire and temperament, albeit beautifully controlled in the Falla *Nights in the gardens of Spain.*
Her family had originally come from Spain. One snag about the set is that the Beethoven is split over
two CDs.

Harty, Sir Hamilton – see under London Philharmonic Orchestra

Hofmann, Josef (piano)

'The Complete Josef Hofmann', Vol. 2 (with Curtis Institute Student O, cond. Reiner or Hilsberg):
BRAHMS: *Academic festival overture.* RUBINSTEIN: *Piano concerto No. 4 in D min.* CHOPIN: *Ballade
No. 1 in G min., Op. 23; Nocturne in E flat, Op. 9/2; Waltz in A flat, Op. 42; Andante spianato e
Grande Polonaise brillante in E flat, Op. 22* (2 versions); *Nocturne in F sharp, Op. 15/2; Waltz in D
flat, Op. 64/1; Etude in G flat, Op. 25/9; Berceuse in B flat, Op. 57; Nocturne in C min., Op. 48/1;
Mazurka in C, Op. 33/3; Waltz in A flat, Op. 34/1.* HOFMANN: *Chromaticon for piano & orchestra* (2
versions). MENDELSSOHN: *Spinning song in C, Op. 67/4.* RACHMANINOV: *Prelude in G min., Op. 23/5.*
BEETHOVEN–RUBINSTEIN: *Turkish march.* MOSZKOWSKI: *Caprice espagnole, Op. 37.*
⊛ (***) Vai Audio mono VAIA/IPA 1020 (2) [id.].

Josef Hofmann's amazing 1937 performance of Rubinstein's *Fourth Piano concerto* has long been a much-sought-after item in its LP format, and those who possess it have treasured it. The performance was attended by practically every pianist around, including Rachmaninov and Godowsky. (It was the latter who once said to a youngster who had mentioned a fingerslip in one of Hofmann's recitals, 'Why look for the spots on the sun!') In no other pianist's hands has this music made such sense: Hofmann plays his master's best-known concerto with a delicacy and poetic imagination that are altogether peerless. Olin Downes spoke of his 'power and delicacy, lightning virtuosity and the capacity to make the keyboard sing, the richness of tone colouring and incorruptible taste'. The 1937 concert included the Brahms overture, a speech by Walter Damrosch, the incomparable performance of the Rubinstein concerto and, after the interval, a Chopin group. One is tempted to say that the *G minor Ballade* has never been surpassed. The second CD includes four later items, recorded in 1945. Once again – and it can't be said too often – the Rubinstein is phenomenal.

(Philip) Jones Brass Ensemble

'Great marches': VERDI: *Aida: Grand march.* GANNE: *Marche Lorraine.* TURLET: *Ambre et Meuse.* TEIKE: *Old comrades.* TRAD., arr. Miller: *Marching through Georgia.* DAN: *Shukuten march.* ALFORD: *Colonel Bogey.* COATES: *Dam Busters.* FUCIK: *Entry of the gladiators.* J.F. WAGNER: *Under the Double Eagle.* TRAD., arr. Alford: *Lillibulero.* Johann STRAUSS Snr: *Radetzky march.* ELGAR: *Pomp and circumstance march No. 1.* MENDELSSOHN: *Midsummer Night's Dream: Wedding march.* SCHUBERT: *Marche militaire.* MEYERBEER: *Le Prophète: Coronation march.* WAGNER: *Tannhäuser: Grand march.* SOUSA: *Washington Post; The Stars and Stripes forever.*
(M) *** Decca Dig. 430 754-2; *430 754-4* [id.].

With a programme covering the widest geographical range and even including an item from Japan (by Ikuma Dan), this is as diverse a collection of 'marching' and concert marches as you are likely to find anywhere. Nearly 76 minutes of lively music, played with remarkable precision and fine tonal balance. Philip Jones readily finds the different rhythmic feeling and character of the pieces from France, Germany and Britain and, if perhaps an American group would bring even more pep to the Sousa items, there is certainly no lack of spirit here. The sound is first class.

Kirov Theatre Orchestra, Valery Gergiev

Russian music: GLINKA: *Russlan and Ludmilla: Overture.* KHACHATURIAN: *Gayaneh: Sabre dance. Spartacus: Adagio.* BORODIN: *Prince Igor: Polovtsian dances* (with Kirov Theatre Ch.); *Polovtsian march.* LIADOV: *Baba-Yaga, Op. 56. Kikimora, Op. 63.* TCHAIKOVSKY: *Overture 1812, Op. 49* (with Royal Dutch Marine Band).
** Ph. Dig. 442 011-2; *442 011-4* [id.].

A good, colourful but not distinctive concert of Russian music. Gergiev takes the opening *Russlan and Ludmilla* at an exhilarating pace, but the effect is of helter-skelter dash rather than the bravura excitement that comes from crisp articulation and precise ensemble in the strings. The Khachaturian items are suitably vivid, pressed forward ardently, and the *Polovtsian march* has a strong, Slavic character. The *Polovtsian dances* (minus the percussion-led *Dance of the Polovtsi Maidens*) produce an exciting climax, although the spacious romanticism of the chorus at the opening is a shade bland. The Liadov pieces have atmosphere and character but are not sharply etched. Best is *1812*, an enjoyably expansive performance with jaunty woodwind, flowing strings and plenty of amplitude for a spectacular close, with a convincing cannonade.

Kubelik, Rafael: '*Artist profile*' – see under Royal Philharmonic Orchestra

Kurtz, Efrem: '*Artist profile*' – see under Philharmonia Orchestra

Leningrad Philharmonic Orchestra, Yevgeni Mravinsky

The Mravinsky Edition (complete)
(M) **(*) RCA 74321 25189-2 (10) [id.].

Volume 1: BRAHMS: *Symphony No. 2 in D, Op. 73.* SCHUBERT: *Symphony No. 8 in B min. (Unfinished), D.759.* WEBER: *Oberon: Overture.*
(M) **(*) RCA 74321 25190-2 [id.].

Volume 2: MOZART: *Overture: The Marriage of Figaro; Symphony No. 39 in E flat, K.543.*
MUSSORGSKY: *Khovanshchina: Prelude to Act I.* SIBELIUS: *Legend: The Swan of Tuonela, Op. 22/2; Symphony No. 7 in C, Op. 105.*
(M) **(*) RCA 74321 25191-2 [id.].

Volume 3: STRAVINSKY: *Agon* (complete). SHOSTAKOVICH: *Symphony No. 15 in A, Op. 141.*
(M) **(*) RCA 74321 25192-2 [id.].

Volume 4: BRUCKNER: *Symphony No. 9 in D. min.*
(M) ** RCA 74321 25193-2 [id.].

Volume 5: TCHAIKOVSKY: *The Nutcracker:* excerpts. PROKOFIEV: *Romeo and Juliet: suite No. 2.*
(M) *** RCA 74321 25194-2 [id.].

Volume 6: HINDEMITH: *Symphony, Die Harmonie der Welt.* HONEGGER: *Symphony No. 3 (Symphonie liturgique).*
(M) *** RCA 74321 25195-2 [id.].

Volume 7: BEETHOVEN: *Symphony No. 4 in B flat, Op. 60.* TCHAIKOVSKY: *Symphony No. 5 in E min.*
(M) **(*) RCA 74321 25196-2 [id.].

Volume 8: BARTOK: *Music for strings, percussion and celeste.* DEBUSSY: *Prélude à l'après-midi d'un faune.* STRAVINSKY: *Apollo* (ballet; complete).
(M) **(*) RCA 74321 25197-2 [id.].

Volume 9: SHOSTAKOVICH: *Symphonies Nos. 6 in B min., Op. 54; 10 in E min., Op. 93.*
(M) **(*) RCA 74321 25198-2 [id.].

Volume 10: WAGNER: *Götterdämmerung: Siegfried's Funeral march. Lohengrin: Preludes to Acts I & III. Die Meistersinger: Overture. Tannhäuser: Overture. Tristan und Isolde: Prelude & Liebestod. Die Walküre: Ride of the Valkyries.*
(M) **(*) RCA 74321 25199-2 [id.].

Always admired by the well-informed enthusiast, Yevgeni Mravinsky's stature has gained increasing recognition among the wider musical public outside his native country since his death in 1988. Olympia has managed to keep a fair number of these classic performances available and many will be familiar to regular readers. Mravinsky did not make many commercial records: the derisory terms offered to the Leningrad orchestra during the days of the Soviet Union were not conducive to recording. Moreover Mravinsky did not like recording under studio conditions, and so the bulk of his legacy derives from the concert hall. The discs are available both separately and as a ten-CD set.

(Volume 1: 74321 25190-2) Mravinsky's accounts of the Brahms *Second Symphony* and the Schubert *Unfinished Symphony*, together with the Weber *Oberon Overture*, come from concerts given at the end of April 1978. They should not be confused with the performances he gave at the Vienna *Festwochen* later that summer (for which they were obviously preparation) and which appeared briefly on a four-LP EMI/Melodiya set in the early 1980s, including also the *Fifth Symphonies* of Tchaikovsky and Shostakovich. (Then the Vienna *Oberon*, at under 9 minutes, occupied a whole LP side!) Generally speaking these performances are, if anything, finer, with a moving *Unfinished* and a lyrical but vital Brahms.

(Volume 2: 74321 25191-2) The Mozart pieces, the *Figaro overture* and the *Symphony No. 39 in E flat*, come from the same 1965 concert as the the two Sibelius works, *The Swan of Tuonela* and the *Seventh Symphony*. The Mussorgsky *Dawn on the Moscow river*, the evocative *Prelude* to the first Act of *Khovanshchina*, was given two days earlier. Mravinsky often programmed the *Seventh* (as well as, apparently, the *Third Symphony*). It first appeared on an HMV/Melodiya LP in 1972, coupled with a powerfully eloquent 1965 performance of the Shostakovich *Sixth Symphony*. It is a performance of stature. Even if Mravinsky rushes the very opening ascent in the cellos and the trombone does have a wide vibrato, it has that intensity this score must have. Although the characterful account of the *Figaro overture* has been available before on Olympia, the Mozart symphony has not; it is a performance of the old school, with great power and again much lyrical intensity. There is a slight drop in pitch at 5 minutes 15 seconds into the slow movement.

(Volume 3: 74321 25192-2) That same intensity is to be found in the 1965 performance of Stravinsky's *Agon*, even if it is evident that the players are not completely inside this particular score; some of the jewelled, hard-edged sound-world Stravinsky evokes is missing. The sound is perfectly acceptable without being in the first flight. Although he did not conduct its première (that honour fell to the composer's son, Maxim), Mravinsky conducted Shostakovich's *Fifteenth Symphony* in 1972 (recorded in mono on Melodiya), but the present version comes from May 1976 and was previously issued in Japan on Victor and subsequently released here on Olympia (also coupled with *Agon*). As we said of that issue, 'authenticity of feeling and dramatic power compensate for imperfections of execution – and generally rough recording [and] the darkness and intensity of the slow movement come over superbly in [Mravinsky's] hands'. There is no doubting the special insights he brings to the work. Judging from the passages we compared in the Olympia and RCA transfers, the differences between them are marginal. The new transfer has perhaps a fractionally sharper image.

(Volume 4: 74321 25193-2) Bruckner's *Ninth Symphony* comes from a public performance in 1980, though, for all the skill of the RCA team, the sound still remains fairly coarse and rough-grained. The performance has tremendous grip and strong personality, though Mravinsky moves things on sometimes where greater breadth might be better, and there are some idiosyncratic touches (excessive slowness at letter R in the Novak Edition, track 1, 15 minutes 50 seconds), but sonic limitations do inhibit a strong recommendation.

(Volume 5: 74321 25194-2) The excerpts from Tchaikovsky's *Nutcracker* and the *Second suite* from Prokofiev's *Romeo and Juliet* are identical with the performance that previously appeared on Philips in 1988. Mravinsky's excerpt starts with a sequence from the first Act: the departure of the guests and the children, the return of Clara, the coming to life of the Dolls, the Gingerbread Soldiers and the Battle of the Mice, through to the journey to the Kingdom of the Sweets and the *Waltz of the snowflakes*. Then come two excerpts from Act II, the *Pas de deux* between the Sugar Plum Fairy and Prince Charming and the final *Waltz and apotheosis*. It is all quite magical, possessing all the warmth and enchantment one could wish for, and the sound is every bit as good as the Philips transfer. The Prokofiev, too, is music-making of real stature. As we said first time round, 'phrases breathe and textures glow; detail stands in the proper relation to the whole. There is drama and poetry, and wonderfully rapt *pianissimi*.' However, the fourth movement, the *Dance* in the printed score, is omitted from this recording. There is no need to withhold a third star from this – surely one of the classic recordings of this repertoire, and one of the finest things in this Mravinsky Edition.

(Volume 6: 74321 25195-2) Both the Hindemith *Symphony, Die Harmonie der Welt*, and Honegger's masterly *Symphonie liturgique* come from 1965 and were available on HMV/Melodiya in the 1970s, the former uncoupled, the latter in harness with the Bartók *Music for strings, percussion and celeste*. Both are performances of stature and few allowances need to be made for the sonic limitations of either work. Sonically this is infinitely superior to the 1980 Bruckner *Ninth* or the 1976 Shostakovich *Tenth*. In fact the CD is among the most desirable of the present set. Mravinsky maintains a tremendous grip on the Hindemith and, although his *Liturgique* does not command the subtlety of colour and refinement of texture found by both Karajan and Jansons, it is still a very distinguished and imaginative performance. Given the decent sound, there is no need to withhold a third star.

(Volume 7: 74321 25196-2) The Beethoven *Fourth Symphony* dates from 29 April 1973, and is the same version that appeared on Olympia, coupled with the *Symphony No. 4 in B minor* by Vadim Salmanov (1912–78). It is a performance that calls only the most exalted comparisons to mind – Weingartner, Toscanini's pre-war BBC performances. The Tchaikovsky *Fifth Symphony* comes from the same concert (in its previous incarnation it was coupled with some Liadov and Mussorgsky) – and what a concert it must have been! It excited enthusiasm first time round; we spoke of it as 'even more electrifying than either of the earlier DG versions', though noting that climaxes were 'still somewhat rough'. RCA's advanced technology has managed to tame them a little, and this account can certainly be recommended alongside the DG versions – and the coupling certainly makes it highly recommendable.

(Volume 8: 74321 25197-2) The performance of Bartók's *Music for strings, percussion and celeste*, the Debussy *Prélude à l'après-midi d'un faune* and Stravinsky's *Apollo* all come from 1965, which would seem to be a good vintage for Leningrad recordings and, in the Bartók at least, an unbronchial time for audiences. Even the pianissimo introduction to the Bartók is relatively (though not completely) undisturbed. The Stravinsky, which is new to UK catalogues, finds the Leningrad strings in splendid form, although Mravinsky rather favours a more heavily accented articulation and less seductive tone-quality than we find in Markevitch's 1963 LSO recording. The balance is closer than in the Bartók. There are some extraneous audience noises here, too, which will irritate some listeners.

(Volume 9: 74321 25198-2) Mravinsky conducted the premières of many Shostakovich symphonies, including the *Fifth*, *Sixth* and *Tenth*, and he was the dedicatee of the *Eighth*. His account of the *Sixth* comes from 1972 (and is not the same as the one previously coupled with the Sibelius *Seventh*). Though its first movement is not in fact slower than his 1965, it is not quite as intense in feeling. The *Tenth Symphony* was among the symphonies Mravinsky conducted in 1976 to mark what would have been the composer's seventieth birthday. The opening bars suffer from an intrusively restive audience (and the microphones do not capture the very first note). The performance (31 March 1976) is tremendously intense and of great documentary interest. It is the same as that published in Japan on Victor and is (according to Derek Hulme's authoritative *Catalogue, Bibliography and Discography*) in mono; though this is not stated on the disc, it certainly sounds as if it is. Generally speaking, the recording is not as good as its 1972 companion.

(Volume 10: 74321 25199-2) It goes without saying that, though he made headway in Russia before the Nazi invasion in 1941, Wagner's music struck unpleasing resonances in the post-war years. Mravinsky's Wagner is of stature and breadth, and the anthology of pieces collected here ranges from 1965 to 1982, the year of his retirement. Variable quality but invariably fine playing from the Leningrad orchestra, and decent transfers. Incidentally, the complete set comes in a very flimsy cardboard slipcase – ours came unstuck within the first few minutes' use!

Linhares, Dagoberto (guitar), Camerata Cassovia

'Guitar concertos': VIVALDI: *Concertos: in A for guitar, violin, viola & cello, RV 82; in D for 2 violins & lute, RV 93; Double guitar concerto in G, RV 532* (with Raymond Migy). GIULIANI: *Concerto, Op. 30*. TORROBA: *Sonatina*.
(BB) *(*) Naxos Dig. 8.550483 [id.].

There is some attractive music here (74 minutes of it) but the acoustic of the House of Arts, Košice, offers problems in making the textures seem fresh. Vivaldi's RV 82 was originally a *Trio for violin, lute and continuo*; here textures are thick and only the guitar comes through; one longs for the transparency possible with original instruments. RV 93 comes off better and, though the two violins are given a back seat, the *Largo* shows the composer at his finest, as does the well-known and lovely *Andante* which is the centrepiece of RV 532, intended for mandolins. The Giuliani *Concerto*, with its innocently dotted first-movement theme, wistful *Siciliana* and lively *Alla polacca*, is quite well done, though the recording still sounds opaque and Johannes Wildner fails to make things really sparkle. The find is the charming Torroba *Sonatina*, full of local colour and warmth, but even if the Spanish dance rhythms of the finale need a brighter projection this is still very agreeable.

Liverpool Philharmonic Orchestra, Sir Malcolm Sargent

English and Irish music (with (i) Webster Booth; (ii) Huddersfield Choral Soc.; (iii) David Wise): IRELAND: *A London overture.* HARTY: *A John Field suite.* COLERIDGE TAYLOR: (i) *Hiawatha's Wedding feast: On away awake beloved.* BALFOUR GARDINER: *Shepherd Fennell's dance.* VAUGHAN WILLIAMS: (iii) *The Lark ascending.* HOLST: (ii) *The Hymn of Jesus.*
(M) (***) Dutton mono CDAX 8012 [id.].

This centenary tribute to Sir Malcolm Sargent concentrates on his remarkable wartime work with the Liverpool Philharmonic, an orchestra which had him as chief conductor from the time in 1942 that it became a permanent body. Sargent quickly put the orchestra on the map, not least as a recording band. As the recordings here confirm (all but *The Lark ascending* dating from wartime, 1943–4), the woodwind team was outstanding, with the *Nocturne* in Harty's *John Field suite* offering a magical clarinet solo from Reginald Kell. Far rougher was the string ensemble, and the Harty in particular, involving only a small body of players, sounds seedy, for all the rhythmic verve. Consistently Sargent's rhythmic control, from the vivid account of the Ireland overture onwards, amply compensates for string shortcomings. CD transfers are first rate, with the satisfyingly full-bodied sound one expects from the Dutton use of the CEDAR process. The Coleridge-Taylor – with Webster Booth producing shiningly clear tenor tone – has a higher surface hiss, and the Holst is a degree mistier than the rest – apt enough for such evocative choral writing. The performance has a thrust and dramatic intensity unsurpassed since. *The Lark ascending* dates from 1977, offering marginally clearer sound, with David Wise a tenderly responsive, totally unmannered soloist. A heartwarming centenary tribute, representing Sargent at his finest.

Lloyd Webber, Julian (cello)

'*English idyll*' (with ASMF, Neville Marriner): VAUGHAN WILLIAMS: *Romanza*. ELGAR: *Romance in D min., Op. 62; Une idylle, Op. 4/1*. DELIUS: *2 Pieces for cello and chamber orchestra*. GRAINGER: *Youthful rapture. Brigg Fair* (arrangement). DYSON: *Fantasy*. IRELAND: *The holy boy*. WALFORD DAVIES: *Solemn melody*. HOLST: *Invocation, Op. 19/2*. Cyril SCOTT: *Pastoral and reel*.
**(*) Ph. 442 530-2 [id.].

The highlights of Julian Lloyd Webber's programme of English concertante miniatures are the Holst *Invocation*, with its nocturnal mood sensitively caught, and George Dyson's *Fantasy*, where the playing readily captures Christopher Palmer's description: 'exquisitely summery and sunny – its chattering moto perpetuo evokes images of bees and butterflies'. Grainger's passionate *Youthful rapture* is given just the right degree of ardent espressivo, as are Delius's warmly flowing *Caprice* and *Elegy*, written (during the composer's last Fenby period) for Beatrice Harrison. The two transcriptions, Vaughan Williams's *Romanza* (originally part of the *Tuba concerto*) and the Elgar *Romance*, conceived with bassoon in mind, were both arranged for cello by their respective composers and are effective enough in their string formats, although by no means superseding the originals. However, Lloyd Webber gives the full romantic treatment both to John Ireland's simple tone-picture, *The holy boy*, and to Grainger's arrangement of *Brigg Fair*, to which not all will respond; for the closing Cyril Scott *Pastoral and reel* (with its telling drone effect) he returns to a more direct style, with pleasing results. Sympathetic accompaniments and warm, atmospheric recording.

'*The Julian Lloyd Webber collection*' (with ECO or RPO, (i) Barry Wordsworth; (ii) Nicholas Cleobury): Andrew LLOYD WEBBER: *Theme and Variations 1–4*. (i) *Aspects of Love: Love changes everything. Phantom of the Opera: Music of the night*. (ii) SAINT-SAENS: *The Swan*. MOZART: *Rondo alla Turca*. DEBUSSY: *Clair de lune*. BACH/GOUNOD: *Ave Maria*. VANGELIS: *Un après-midi* (with Vangelis & synthesizers). LENNON/MCCARTNEY: *When I'm sixty-four*. TRAD.: *Skye boat song; Londonderry air*. ALBINONI: *Adagio* (arr. Giazotto). BERNSTEIN: *West Side Story: Somewhere*. BACH: *Jesu, joy of man's desiring*. LEHAR: *You are my heart's delight*. RIMSKY-KORSAKOV: *Flight of the bumble-bee*. Johann & Josef STRAUSS: *Pizzicato polka*. SCHUMANN: *Träumerei*. ELGAR: *Cello concerto:* 1st movt (cond. Y. Menuhin).
** Ph. Dig.446 050-2 [id.].

Seventy-five minutes of cello lollipops may be too much of a good thing for some tastes. J. L. W. describes the content as being 'drawn – with one important exception – from [his] less "serious" recordings', and the programme establishes its popular credentials by opening with the Andrew Lloyd Webber *Paganini variations*, used as signature tune for ITV's South Bank Show. There are many good tunes here, but mostly romantic ones; a few more bumble-bees would have been advantageous. However, this fine British cellist knows how to shape a good tune: Schumann's *Träumerei*, for instance, is presented very persuasively. The 'exception' ends the programme: the first movement of Elgar's *Cello concerto*, tempting enough, but ending rather abruptly: the slow movement would surely have been a better choice. Pleasant recording.

London Philharmonic Orchestra, Sir Hamilton Harty

'The art of Sir Hamilton Harty' (recordings from 1933 and 1935): BAX: *Overture to a picaresque comedy*. BERLIOZ: *Roméo et Juliet, Op. 7: Romeo's reverie and Feast of the Capulets. Funeral march for the last scene of Hamlet, Op. 18/3*. HANDEL, arr. HARTY: *Royal Fireworks music: suite; Water music: suite*. SCHUBERT: *Marche militaire*. SIBELIUS: *Valse triste*. SMETANA: *Overture: The Bartered Bride*.
(M) (***) Dutton Lab. mono CDLX 7016 [id.].

These early recordings Sir Hamilton Harty made for Columbia come up sounding better than ever. No later recording has come anywhere near Harty's pioneering account of Bax's *Overture to a picaresque comedy*, which has great character and sparkle. It is a marvellous piece, and this alone would be worth the price of the record. But Harty's Berlioz was unsurpassed in its day. His *Romeo's reverie and Feast of the Capulets*, which featured in Percy Scholes's 'Columbia History of Music' on two 10-inch 78s (which RL still treasures) combines atmosphere and magic, and not even Colin Davis's *Funeral march for the last scene of Hamlet* erases the memory of this 1937 version. All the other items give unalloyed pleasure, and the Dutton transfers are of the highest quality.

London Symphony Orchestra, Ataulfo Argenta

'España': CHABRIER: *España*. RIMSKY-KORSAKOV: *Capriccio espagnol, Op. 34.* GRANADOS: *Spanish dance No. 5 (Andaluza), Op. 37.* MOSZKOWSKI: *5 Spanish dances, Book I, Op. 12.* DEBUSSY: *Images.*
(M) *** Decca 443 580-2 [id.].

Ataulfo Argenta (about whom the documentation of this reissue in Decca's 'Classic Sound' series says nothing) was one of the more promising stars on the Decca roster in the late 1950s, but sadly he died before the promise could fully be realized. Nevertheless this brightly recorded mixture of Spanishry, mostly from the pens of non-Spaniards, readily displays his flair, not least in the sparkling account of Chabrier's title-piece. The slight but endearingly dated Moszkowski dances (once introduced by their composer at a Henry Wood Promenade Concert) are beautifully played, and the last three are especially successful. But the highlight of the disc is Rimsky's *Capriccio* which (alongside Maazel's DG Berlin Philharmonic version from the same period) has never been surpassed for its brilliance and Mediterranean colour, with superb virtuosity from the LSO. The 1957 Kingsway Hall recording with its glittering percussion is dazzling in this CD transfer and only a slight tightness in the upper range of the violins prevents the highest technical accolade. The fullness and range are astonishing for their time, and the Decca recording team can well be proud of the early stereo. The Debussy *Images* (recorded in Victoria Hall, Geneva, the same year) show the conductor's fine ear for intricate detail, so well etched by the recording, but the response of the Suisse Romande Orchestra (used to playing this work under Ansermet) has less allure and body of tone than that produced by the LSO. A fascinating collector's CD, just the same.

London Symphony Orchestra, Richard Bonynge

'Ballet gala, I – The art of the prima ballerina': MINKUS: *La Bayadère.* DRIGO: *Pas de trois.* ADAM: *Giselle:* excerpts. LOVENSKJOLD: *La Sylphide.* TCHAIKOVSKY: *Swan Lake: Black Swan Pas de deux.* TRAD.: *Boléro 1830* (arr. James O'Turner). PUGNI: *Pas de quatre.*
(M) **(*) Decca 433 861-2 [id.].

Although the music is not arranged in historical order, this series has the effect of showing the background history against which the great nineteenth-century ballet scores were written. With the original LPs came a lavishly illustrated booklet; the 73-minute CD offers more austere presentation with barely adequate documentation. However, Bonynge knows what this music is all about and, while the ten-minute excerpt from *Giselle* seems superfluous (and the performance a shade below par), the curiosities are certainly vivacious, if a little anonymous. The recording is bright and immediate, but the CD transfer has lost some of the analogue glamour.

'Ballet gala, II – Pas de deux': *Pas de deux* from MINKUS: *Don Quixote; Paquita.* TCHAIKOVSKY: *Sleeping Beauty; The Nutcracker.* DRIGO: *La Esmerelda; Le Corsaire.* HELSTED: *Flower Festival in Genzano.* AUBER: *Pas classique.*
(M) *** Decca 433 862-2 [id.].

None of this is great music but much of it is winningly tuneful. This indeed was the writing that created the classic dance format which inspired Tchaikovsky, Delibes and Prokofiev. With nicely pointed orchestral playing and loving arches of string phrasing, Richard Bonynge makes this relatively slight music sound highly romantic. The *Pas de deux* from *Paquita* has a tune for the middle strings; the Auber *Pas classique* a typical horn theme, and the Drigo and Helsted items have those flowing string melodies which anticipate *Giselle*. The recording still sounds full but is not as glowingly warm as the original LP, to which the Tchaikovsky excerpts have been added.

'Ballet gala, III – Homage to Pavlova': SAINT-SAENS: *The Swan.* TCHAIKOVSKY: *The Seasons: December; Melody (Souvenir d'un lieu cher), Op. 42/3.* RUBINSTEIN: *Feramors: Danses des fiancées de Cachemir.* CZIBULKA: *Love's dream after the ball.* KREISLER: *The Dragonfly (Schön Rosmarin).* ASAFYEV: *Papillons.* LINCKE: *Gavotte Pavlova (Glow worm idyll).* DELIBES: *Naïla: Intermezzo.* CATALANI: *Danza delle Ondine.* KRUPINSKI: *Polish wedding: Mazurka.* DRIGO: *Le réveil de flore* (Parts I & II).
(M) *** Decca 433 863-2 [id.].

This is quite the most rewarding of the four reissues in Decca's '*Ballet gala*' series. It contains the greater part (76 minutes) of the music included on a pair of LPs which originated in 1969, celebrating the artistry of Pavlova by presenting a concert of pieces to which she regularly danced. As with the companion '*Art of the prima ballerina*' a lavish booklet has here been replaced by sparse notes. But the music itself is beautifully played and recorded, and the CD transfer retains the allure of the

Kingsway Hall recording. The programme gathers together a number of works normally heard (if at all) in cheap salon orchestra arrangements and here shows their charm when played so affectionately and with such polish by a full orchestra. Lincke's *Glow worm idyll*, a once hackneyed piece, was intended to sound like this and, like Czibulka's *Love's dream after the ball* and Catalani's engaging *Danza delle Ondine*, brings some lovely, transluscent string sounds, as does the more familiar Delibes *Intermezzo*. The longest piece is Drigo's *Le réveil de flore*, attractive sub-*Nutcracker*; but almost all the items are valuable in providing outstanding performances, splendidly recorded, of true light music.

'Ballet gala, IV – Invitation to the waltz': WEBER/BERLIOZ: *Invitation to the dance*. CHOPIN: *Les Sylphides* (orch. Roy Douglas). Johann & Josef STRAUSS: *Bal de Vienne* (*Die Fledermaus* ballet suite). LUIGINI: *Ballet Egyptien, Op. 12*.
(M) **(*) Decca 433 864-2; *433 864-4* [id.].

The highlight here is a fine modern recording of Luigini's *Ballet Egyptien*, an attractively tuneful piece. To older readers the opening will recall Richard Murdoch on BBC Radio at a vintage period reciting nonsense words: 'My aunt's name is Ella Wheeler Waterbutton, she lives down in Burton-on-Trent; when she goes out shopping on a bicycle, she always gets her handlebars bent.' Bonynge's *Les Sylphides* is well played, if no match for Karajan in suave elegance, but the rest of the programme is lively enough. The Weber/Berlioz and Chopin items are digital, the rest high-quality analogue transfers from the 1970s.

'Ballet Gala: Ballet music from opera' ((i) with Nat. PO): from ROSSINI: *William Tell*. DONIZETTI: *La Favorita*. GOUNOD: *Faust; La Reine de Saba*. MASSENET: *Le Roi de Lahore*. (i) *Ariane*. BERLIOZ: (i) *Les Troyens*. SAINT-SAENS: *Henry VIII*.
(M) ** Decca 444 108-2 [id.].

Although all this music is brightly played and vividly recorded, this is not one of the more enticing collections in Decca's Ballet Gala series. Composers were obliged to write a ballet for any work performed at the Paris Opéra and, while they usually came up with amiable and colourful music, it seldom showed them at their best. Donizetti's suite from *La Favorita* and Gounod's *Faust ballet* make the strongest impression here, while the two excerpts from Massenet's *Le Roi de Lahore* are agreeable enough. The latter two are taken from complete sets; the rest of the programme was recorded independently. For some reason, Bonynge's *William Tell ballet*, though lively enough, is a little below par (perhaps because he uses stage tempi), and even he cannot make Gounod's *Waltz* from Act II of *La Reine de Saba* sound more than a milk-and-water version of the more famous waltz from *Faust*.

London Symphony Orchestra, Albert Coates

'Russian favourites': GLINKA: *Russlan and Ludmilla: Overture; Kamarinskaya*. BORODIN: *In the Steppes of Central Asia; Prince Igor: Polovtsian march*. LIADOV: *8 Russian folksongs, Op. 58*. MUSSORGSKY: *Sorochinsky Fair: Gopak*. TCHAIKOVSKY: *Marche slave*. RIMSKY-KORSAKOV: *May night: Overture. Dubinushka; Maid of Pskov: Storm music; Mlada: Procession of the Nobles; Snow Maiden: Danse des bouffons*. STRAVINSKY: *The Firebird: The princesses' game; Infernal dance*.
(***) Koch mono 37700-2 [id.].

On the Koch Historic label comes a collection of Coates's recordings with the LSO of Russian lollipops, vividly transferred by H. Ward Marston. Made between 1928 and 1930, they sound astonishingly fresh, with brass bright and forward. The *Procession of the Nobles* from Rimsky-Korsakov's *Mlada* has never been recorded with such flair and excitement, and consistently these performances reflect the natural understanding of a musician of British parentage born in Russia. As well as four other Rimsky items, the disc also has nine favourite pieces by Glinka, Borodin (a famous version of *In the Steppes of Central Asia*), Liadov, Mussorgsky, Tchaikovsky and Stravinsky.

London Symphony Orchestra, Antal Dorati

ENESCU: *Rumanian rhapsody No. 2*. BRAHMS: *Hungarian dances Nos. 1–7; 10–12; 15; 17–21; Variations on a theme of Haydn, Op. 56a*.
(M) ** Mercury 434 326-2 [id.].

Dorati is completely at home in the Enescu *Second Rhapsody* (played passionately – but, as music, not nearly as memorable as No. 1) and the Brahms *Hungarian dances*, where he captures a true Hungarian spirit. When he takes a piece faster than expected, one does not feel he is being wilful or intent on showing off, but simply that he and his players are enjoying themselves. If the delicious rubato in No. 7 does not spell enjoyment, one would be very surprised. The recording, made at either Watford or Wembley, sounds firmer and cleaner than on LP. The *Variations* are enjoyable but not distinctive.

Marsalis, Wynton (trumpet), ECO, Leppard

'The London concert': HAYDN: *Concerto in E flat.* L. MOZART: *Concerto in D.* FASCH: *Concerto in D.* HUMMEL: *Concerto in E.*
*** Sony Dig. SK 57497 [id.].

The title of this collection suggests a live occasion, but in fact these four concertos were recorded over a period of a week in 1993, at St Giles's Church, Cripplegate. The playing is as expert and stylish as we have come to expect from this remarkable American player. His approach, as we have noticed before, is just a little cool but none the worse for that for there is also admirable poise, and in the finale of the Hummel he lets himself go with the most infectious bravura. Incidentally there is no improvising in cadenzas: 'I don't feel comfortable enough to improvise in music of this period,' Marsalis tells us candidly in the notes. The recording gives him a striking but not exaggerated presence in relation to the orchestra.

Minneapolis Symphony Orchestra, Antal Dorati

Concert: GERSHWIN: *An American in Paris.* COPLAND: *Rodeo (4 Dance episodes).* SCHULLER: *7 Studies on themes of Paul Klee.* BLOCH: *Sinfonia breve.*
(M) ** Mercury 434 329-2 [id.].

This is a disappointing collection, a rare occurrence for this label, but you can't win them all! Dorati's *Rodeo* lacks the incandescent vitality of Bernstein's electrifying New York version, and Gershwin's *American in Paris* doesn't suit the Hungarian conductor too well either (try the big blues tune at its trumpet entry). The almost over-detailed recording does not help, either here or in Bloch's rather dry *Sinfonia breve*, which needs richer string textures. It is highly suitable for Schuller's sharply etched *Seven studies on themes of Paul Klee* but, brilliantly though this is played, the music itself does not live up to the promise of titles like *The twittering machine* and *Little blue devil*.

Mravinsky, Yevgeni: *'The Mravinsky Edition'* – see under Leningrad Philharmonic Orchestra

'Musica española'

'Musica española' (played by: (i) SRO, Ansermet; (ii) New Philh. O, Fruühbeck de Burgos; (iii) De Larrocha, LPO, Fruühbeck de Burgos; (iv) LSO, Argenta; (v) Ricci, LSO, Gamba; (vi) SRO, López-Cobos): (i) ALBENIZ: *Iberia* (suite; orch. Arbós); *Navarra.* (ii) *Suite española* (orch. Fruühbeck de Burgos); (iii) *Rapsodia española.* (iv) GRANADOS: *Goyescas: Intermezzo; Danza española No. 5.* (v) SARASATE: *Aires gitanos (Zigeunerweisen).* (iii) TURINA: *Rapsodia sinfónica.* (vi) *La oración del torero; Danzas fantásticas.*
(M) **(*) Decca Analogue/Dig. 433 905-2 (2) [id.].

Generous measure, colourful music and vivid Decca sound, though the digital Turina recordings at the close of Disc 2 are obviously more modern than the (admittedly impressive) Ansermet offerings from 1960 which open the concert. Highlights include Alicia de Larrocha's brilliant concertante performances of two virtually unknown works, and Ricci's *Aires gitanos* (better known by its German name as it was published by Sarasate in Leipzig) and full of gutsy gypsy temperament. Fruühbeck de Burgos's apt orchestrations of the *Suite española* are particularly enjoyable.

'Musica española' II (Music by non-Spanish composers, played by: (i) SRO; (ii) Ansermet; (iii) LSO; (iv) Argenta; (v) with Ricci): (i; ii) GLINKA: *Jota aragonesa (Spanish overture No. 1).* (iii; iv) RIMSKY-KORSAKOV: *Capriccio espagnol.* MOSZKOWSKI: *Spanish dances Nos. 1–5.* (i; ii; v) LALO: *Symphonie espagnole.* (iii; iv) CHABRIER: *España.* (i; iv) DEBUSSY: *Images: Iberia.* (i; ii) RAVEL: *Rapsodie espagnole; Pavane pour une infante défunte; Alborada del gracioso; Boléro.*
(M) ** Decca 433 911-2 (2) [id.].

Ansermet and Argenta are both at home in this repertoire and the early Decca stereo (1957–63) emerges with impressive colour and range. Ricci gives a vibrant account of the *Symphonie espagnole*, full of gypsy flair, although some might not like his bold, febrile timbre. The engaging but very lightweight Moszkowski *Spanish dances* belong to a past era and are not otherwise available. Overall this is enjoyable without being distinctive.

Mutter, Anne-Sophie (violin)

'*Modern*': STRAVINSKY: *Violin concerto in D* (with Philh. O, Sacher). LUTOSLAWSKI: *Partita for Anne-Sophie Mutter* (with Philip Moll, piano); *Chain II* (with BBC SO, composer). BARTOK: *Violin concerto No. 2*. MORET: *En rêve* (with Boston SO, Ozawa). BERG: *Violin concerto*. RIHM: *Time chant* (with Chicago SO, Levine).
(B) *** DG Dig. 445 487-2 (3) [id.].

Here is an unexpected portrait of an outstanding young artist linked with the attractions of inexpensively cutting one's teeth on twentieth-century violin repertoire, offered in brilliant, modern, digital recordings. The Stravinsky *Concerto* makes a splendid opener: there is no more recommendable version, with wit and feeling nicely balanced and excellent, sharply defined sound. The Berg is hardly less successful. Mutter opens with the most delicate pianissimo and her reading is intensely passionate. Her Bartók is more controversial, played with stunning virtuosity and brilliance but at times overcharacterized, even glossy in its brilliance, and in the scherzando section of the second movement she is much faster than the metronome marking; indeed the performance tends to sensationalize the concerto, although the playing is not unfelt and the bravura is astonishing. The Lutoslawski pieces are among the best of his recent compositions and evoke a powerful response from their dedicatee. The Moret is a slight but enticing piece with plenty of shimmering sonorities and a dazzling solo part. The finale erupts suddenly but the introspective musing of the earlier writing returns with sporadic bursts of energy from the soloist which bring the piece to a lively conclusion. The Rihm concerto is a rhapsodical, meditative piece, its effect heightened by the orchestral backing. It is played with superb concentration.

Nakariakov, Sergei (trumpet), Lausanne Chamber Orchestra, López-Cobos

JOLIVET: *Concertino for trumpet, piano and strings* (with Alexander Markovich, piano). HUMMEL, TOMASI, HAYDN: *Trumpet concertos*.
*** Teldec/Warner Dig. 4509 90846-2 [id.].

The very gifted teenage Russian trumpeter makes a brilliant contribution to the Jolivet *Double concerto*. His partner, the pianist Alexander Markovich, plays very well too, but the balance is less than ideal, with the piano set rather backwardly and not emerging strongly until the very animated finale. Yet, at under ten minutes, the work does not outstay its welcome and it has a catchy, angular main theme. The Tomasi solo concerto is more kaleidoscopic, with lyrical and rhythmic elements alternating and a whiff of jazz in the melodic style. The cadenza has side-drum interjections. The central *Nocturne* brings a nostalgic muted solo from Nakariakov and the blithe finale demands bravura from all concerned. In the Haydn and Hummel *Concertos* Nakariakov does not quite match the famous Hardenberger performances, and the orchestral playing in Lausanne is serviceable rather than outstanding. Nakariakov plays the Hummel in the key of E flat, rather than the brighter E major favoured by Hardenberger, but both this and the Haydn bring a superb solo contribution from the young Russian virtuoso, and the lovely *Andante* of the latter work is memorably warm and graceful before a sparkling finale which matches that of the Hummel in high spirits.

National Symphony Orchestra

'*This is full frequency range recording*' (cond. (i) Sydney Beer; (ii) Anatole Fistoulari; (iii) Boyd Neel; (iv) Victor Olof):(i) BIZET: *L'Arlésienne: suite No. 1*. (ii) BERLIOZ: *Damnation de Faust: Hungarian march*. GLIERE: *The Red Poppy: Russian sailors' dance*. TCHAIKOVSKY: *Marche slave; The Oprichnik: Overture*. (i) WAGNER: *Götterdämmerung: Siegfried's Rhine Journey*. (iii) SAINT-SAENS: *Danse macabre*. WOLF-FERRARI: *The Jewels of the Madonna: Intermezzos, Acts I and II*. (i) DELIUS: *Irmelin prelude*. (iv) CHABRIER: *España*.
(M) (***) Dutton mono CDK 1200 [id.].

The Dutton Laboratory transfers are wonderfully full-bodied, cleaned of surface hiss in an outstandingly successful application of the CEDAR process. Made by the National Symphony Orchestra between June and November 1944, these recordings represented the full emergence of Decca's newly developed recording process with an extended range. The founder of the orchestra, using his wealth benevolently, was Sidney Beer, who persuaded many star players to join him. Particularly impressive are his readings of the Bizet suite and the Wagner, with wind and brass superbly caught. Boyd Neel steps away from his usual image as a chamber conductor in a crisp, flamboyant account of *Danse macabre* with Leonard Hirsch, the NSO leader, a prominent and firm soloist. The Wolf-Ferrari interludes are less successful, with higher hiss and violins less sweet. Fistoulari was a totally underrated conductor of Russian music, and his bright, rhythmically alert contributions inspire recordings of such vividness one can hardly believe they are over 50 years old; the rare *Oprichnik Overture* is specially welcome. Most spectacular of all is the final item, Chabrier's *España*, with Victor Olof, best known as recording producer for both EMI and Decca, here whizzing the players thrillingly through the showpiece. The occasion prompted his engineering colleague, Arthur Haddy, to produce sound that is so vivid, with a remarkably wide dynamic range, one could almost swear it is in stereo. (But then, as Haddy has told us, even in those early days he understood fully the acoustic nature of stereo, and he placed his mono microphones to capture the hall ambience as well as the direct sound from the orchestral instruments.) Malcolm Walker provides a model note, not just outlining the background of *ffrr* but giving an impressively detailed history of the Decca company from 1929 onwards.

New London Consort, Philip Pickett

'The Feast of Fools': 1st Vespers; Music from the Office; The drinking bout in the cathedral porch; Mass of the asses, drunkards and gamblers; 2nd Vespers; Ceremony of the Baculus; The banquet; Processional.
*** O-L Dig. 433 194-2 [id.].

Philip Pickett and the New London Consort, inspired in their treatment of early music, present an invigorating, ear-catching sequence drawn from the roistering parodies of church practice that in medieval times were celebrated between Christmas and Epiphany. In modern terms the jokes may be heavy-handed, whether involving vestry humour, drunken cavortings or animal-imitations (as in the *Kyrie* of the *Asses, 'Hinhan Eleison'*), but the wildness of much of the music is infectious, performed here with uninhibited joy. Carl Orff's *Carmina Burana* (inspired from similar Latin sources) hardly outshines these originals.

New Philharmonia Orchestra, Leopold Stokowski

BRAHMS: *Symphony No. 4 in E min., Op. 98.* KLEMPERER: *Merry waltz.* RAVEL: *Rapsodie espagnole.* VAUGHAN WILLIAMS: *Fantasia on theme of Thomas Tallis.*
(B) **(*) BBC Radio Classics BBCRD 9107 [id.].

This BBC recording of May 1974 makes a fascinating document, allowing us to witness one of the very last live concerts that Leopold Stokowski conducted. The pity is that in the reverberant acoustic of the Royal Albert Hall the sound takes away from the bite which marked Stokowski's last appearances, and the close microphones are unflattering to the violins. The expansive account of the Vaughan Williams works best, warm and atmospheric rather than intense, although the dynamic range is reduced; and the Ravel too gains from atmospheric sound, even if the excitement of the final *Feria* is dampened a little – the performance itself short of electrifying. Klemperer's *Merry waltz* is a charming tribute from one veteran conductor to another who had died the previous July. The Brahms suffers most from the recording and cannot compare with some of the superb studio recordings Stokowski made in the months and years after this concert. Speeds are on the brisk side, especially in the outer movements, and Stokowski's control of tension is masterly; though ensemble is slacker than would have been accepted in the studio, this remains highly compelling music-making, and the CD is well worth its modest cost.

Oistrakh, David (violin)

'The Originals' (with (i) VSO; (ii) Igor Oistrakh; (iii) RPO, Goossens; (iv) Dresden State O, Konwitschny):(i) BACH: (i) *Violin concertos Nos. 1 in E; 2 in A min;* (ii; iii) *Double violin concerto in*

D min., BWV 1041/3. BEETHOVEN: (iii) *Romances Nos. 1 in G, 2 in F, Opp. 40 & 50.* BRAHMS: (ii)
Violin concerto, Op. 77. TCHAIKOVSKY: *Violin concerto, Op. 35.*
(M) (***) DG stereo/mono 447 427-2 (2) [id.].

In 'The Originals' series at mid-price, DG here offers reissues of classic Oistrakh recordings
unavailable for years in any format. Rarest are the 1954 mono recordings of the Brahms and
Tchaikovsky *Concertos*, more relaxed, more volatile readings than those Oistrakh recorded later in
stereo. Oistrakh moves effortlessly from dashing bravura to the sweetest lyricism, the complete
master. The Bach and Beethoven offerings are hardly less welcome. Allowing for the practice of the
time, these Bach performances are all strong and resilient, consistently bringing out the sweetness and
purity of Oistrakh's playing, not least in the rapt accounts of the slow movements. Directing the
Vienna Symphoniker from the violin, Oistrakh may make the tuttis in the two Bach solo concertos
rather heavy, but he then transforms everything the moment he starts playing. The Bach *Double
concerto* with Oistrakh father and son, accompanied by Goossens and the RPO, is more magnetic
still, and they accompany him no less sympathetically in the warm, poised readings of the two
Beethoven *Romances.*

Jean-François Paillard Chamber Orchestra, Paillard

'Baroque melodies': ALBINONI: *Adagio* (arr. Giazotto). PACHELBEL: *Canon.* BACH: *Suite No. 2, BWV
1067: Minuet and Badinerie. Cantata No. 140: Wachet auf. Cantata No. 147: Jesus bleibet meine
Freude. Suite No. 3, BWV 1068.* HANDEL: *Concerti grossi* (excerpts): *Op. 6/6: Musette. Op. 6/10:
Gavotte.* VIVALDI: *Piccolo concerto in A min, P. 83: Larghetto.* MARCELLO: *Oboe concerto in C min.:
Adagio.* CORELLI: *Badinerie & Gigue.* VIVALDI: *Violin concerto in A min., Op. 3/6: Allegro.* ZIPOLI:
Adagio for oboe, cello and strings. RAMEAU: *Tambourins.* MOLTER: *Trumpet concerto in D: Andante
for strings.* CLARKE: *Trumpet voluntary.*
(M) **(*) BMG/RCA Dig. 09026 65468-2 [id.].

There seems to be an unlimited market for baroque collections including the Albinoni *Adagio* and
Pachelbel *Canon,* and this one is as good as most. The various individual concertante movements are
well chosen and expertly played on modern instruments by soloists of the calibre of Christian Larde
(flute/piccolo) and Pierre Pierlot (oboe). The orchestral playing does not lack warmth and style, and
the recording is excellent, but this group sounds blander than the Academy of St-Martin-in-the-Fields
in this repertoire. Nevertheless, with 73 minutes' music, this is a very agreeable late-evening
collection.

Parkening, Christopher (guitar), ASMF, Iona Brown

Concertante works for guitar: WARLOCK: *Capriol suite* (arr. Russ). VIVALDI: *Concertos in D & C,
RV 93 and RV 425; Trio in C, RV 82* (with Lionel Hardy, John Constable). PRAETORIUS:
Terpsichore: Suite in D.
** EMI Dig. CDC5 55052-2 [id.].

This recital is disappointingly lacking in vitality, and the Vivaldi performances sound too much like a
routine run-through (RV 93 has nothing like the life and colour invested in it by John Williams in his
much more spontaneous Seville concert – see our main volume). Easily the best item is Patrick Russ's
ingenious arrangement of Warlock's *Capriol suite,* where the central sections are both tender and
piquant – although even here the accompaniments lack real zest in the outer movements.

Perlman, Itzhak (violin)

BACH: *Partita No. 2, BWV. 1004: Chaconne. Concertos: in E, BWV 1042; in G min., BWV 1056;* (i)
Double violin concerto in D min., BWV 1043 ((i) with Zukerman; ECO, Barenboim); *Double concerto
for violin & oboe, BWV 1060* (with Ray Still, Israel PO). VIVALDI: *Four seasons* (with Israel PO).
BEETHOVEN: *Concerto, Op. 61.* TCHAIKOVSKY: *Concerto, Op. 35; Sérénade mélancholique, Op. 26*
(all with Phd. O, Ormandy). MENDELSSOHN: *Concerto, Op. 64.* BRUCH: *Concerto No. 1, Op. 26* (both
with Concg. O, Haitink). *Concerto No. 2, Op. 44; Scottish fantasy, Op. 46.* GLAZUNOV: *Concerto,
Op. 82.* CASTELNUOVO-TEDESCO: *Concerto No. 2 (I Profeti).* KHACHATURIAN: *Concerto.*
SHOSTAKOVICH: *Concerto No. 1, Op. 99.* TCHAIKOVSKY: *Meditation, Op. 42/1* (all with Israel PO,
Mehta). SIBELIUS: *Concerto, Op. 47.* KORNGOLD: *Concerto, Op. 35.* CONUS: *Concerto.* SINDING:

Suite, Op. 10 (all with Pittsburgh SO, Previn). BRAHMS: *Concerto, Op. 77* (with Chicago SO, Giulini). DVORAK: *Concerto, Op. 53* (with LPO, Barenboim). VIEUXTEMPS: *Concertos Nos. 4–5* (with O de Paris, Barenboim). RAVEL: *Tzigane*. SAINT-SAENS: *Havanaise, Op. 83* (with O de Paris, Martinon). WIENIAWSKI: *Concertos Nos. 1–2* (with LPO Ozawa); plus encores for violin & piano (with Sanders). PROKOFIEV: *Violin concerto No.1* (with BBC SO, Rozhdestvensky). BARTOK: *Concertos Nos. 1–2* (with LSO, Previn). PAGANINI: *24 Caprices, Op. 1*. KREISLER: *Caprice Viennoise, Op. 2; La Chasse (Caprice in the style of Cartier); Liebesfreud; Liebeslied; Preghiera in the style of Martini; Romance, Op. 4; Schön Rosmarin; Tempo di minuetto in the style of Pugnani*. Arrangements: DVORAK: *Slavonic dance No. 2 in E min., Op. 46/2; Songs my mother taught me, Op. 55/4;* PAGANINI: *Moto perpetuo, Op. 11*. TARTINI: *Fugue in A*. RACHMANINOV: *Marguerite (Daisies), Op. 38/3*. GLUCK: *Mélodie*. GARTNER: *Viennese melody*. CHOPIN: *Mazurka in A min., Op. 67/4*.

Chamber music: BEETHOVEN: *Piano trio No. 7 (Archduke)*. TCHAIKOVSKY: *Piano trio, Op. 50* (both with Ashkenazy, Harrell). MOZART: *Oboe quartet* (with Still, Zukerman, Harrell). SPOHR: *Duo concertante, Op. 67/2* (with Zukerman). STRAVINSKY: *Divertimento; Duo concertante; Suite italien*; also works by TCHAIKOVSKY & RACHMANINOV (with Samuel Sanders).

Encores I: by NOVACEK, BEN HAIM, DEBUSSY, SARASATE, PONCE, MOSZKOWSKI, CHOPIN, POULENC, SAINT-SAENS, PARADIES, ELGAR, FOSTER, VIEUXTEMPS (with Sanders).

Encores II: by PREVIN, TOSELLI, PONCE, MASSENET, TOSTI, TCHAIKOVSKY, JOPLIN (with various artists).

(B) *** EMI Analogue/Dig. CZS4 83177-2 (20).

Over the fullest repertory, this 20-disc set, designed to celebrate Perlman's fiftieth birthday in 1994, provides a formidable survey of his work. The dozens of concertos, together with many shorter works, consistently bring home the richness of his playing, both tonally and expressively, his peerless virtuosity and the strength of his artistic personality. One great merit of most of these discs is that they provide generous and well-planned couplings, different from the original issues. So Perlman's dazzling versions of the two Wieniawski concertos with Ozawa and the LPO, dating from 1973, here have five Wieniawski lollipops as supplement; while another attractive coupling brings together not just the Bruch *Concerto No. 2* and the *Scottish fantasy* (as originally linked) but the Bruch *First Concerto*, with Haitink, making a disc lasting almost 80 minutes. Perlman's studio recording of the Brahms *Concerto* with Giulini and the Chicago orchestra has been preferred to his later, more magnetic Berlin version with Barenboim, and the Korngold *Concerto* is an odd coupling. By contrast, the Beethoven, coupled with the Mendelssohn, is here offered not in the studio version with Giulini but in the live Berlin account with Barenboim, even more compelling. One classic Perlman recording with Previn and the LSO which here arrives belatedly on CD is of the Bartók *Concerto No. 2*. As a performance it has never been surpassed, helped by full-bodied, analogue recording; but the coupling is another odd one, the Conus *Violin concerto*, that Heifetz made his own, and the Sinding *Suite*. Perlman's lively, traditional account of Vivaldi's *Four seasons* is well supplemented by his reading of the great *Chaconne* from Bach's solo *Violin partita No. 2*, and the Bach *Violin concertos* disc contains four works, all given weighty performances with unashamedly romantic, expansive slow movements. Discs of chamber music include Perlman's very spacious accounts of the three Brahms *Violin sonatas* with Ashkenazy and the Tchaikovsky *Piano trio* with Harrell as well as Ashkenazy, though here the piano is thinly recorded. That last is intelligently supplemented by Tchaikovsky's two shorter concertante works for violin: the *Meditation* and the *Sérénade mélancolique*. The last three discs are of lollipops, one of them centring on Kreisler, another on Heifetz, with the third containing some of Perlman's collaborations with André Previn, both on jazz pieces and on Scott Joplin rags. The 20 discs contain among them an almost inexhaustible store of superb playing. There are some discrepancies between the recordings but, whatever their vintage, Perlman's violin is consistently caught in all its fullness and warmth, with the instrument always balanced close, as this artist always demands in the studio. The cost of this set is likely to be about around £125 (with a reasonable discount).

Philadelphia Orchestra, Leopold Stokowski

'Philadelphia rarities' (1928–1937): arr. Stokowski: *2 Ancient liturgical melodies: Veni, Creator Spiritus; Veni, Emmanuel*. FALLA: *La vida breve: Spanish dance*. TURINA: *Gypsy dance, Op. 55/5*. DUBENSKY: *Edgar Allan Poe's 'The Raven'* (narr. Benjamin de Loache). arr. Konoye: *Etenraku: Ceremonial Japanese prelude*. MCDONALD: *The legend of the Arkansas traveller; The Festival of the workers (suite): Dance of the workers. Double piano concerto* (with Jeanne Behrend & Alexander

Kelberine). EICHHEIM: *Oriental impressions: Japanese nocturne. Symphonic variations: Bali.* SOUSA: *Manhattan Beach; El Capitan.*
(M) (***) Cala mono CACD 0501 [id.].

In many ways this is the most fascinating CD (if not the most musically satisfying) among the spate of recent Stokowski reissues. All these recordings (except two, Turina's *Gypsy dance* and Sousa's *Manhattan Beach*, which apparently never saw the light of day) come from previously issued RCA Victor 78-r.p.m. masters, and the transfers are not only remarkably good in themselves (if perhaps not quite up to the Dutton standard) but show what splendid recorded sound Stokowski was achieving in Philadelphia as early as 1929. The opening Stokowski liturgical arrangements show how that master of orchestral sonority could make liturgical chants his very own, with a discreet tolling bell to indicate their source. Falla's *Spanish dance* shows him at his most sparklingly chimerical. Dubensky's music does not add a great deal to Edgar Allan Poe, but the narrator, Benjamin de Loache, certainly does, presenting the narrative with the essentially genial, melodramatic lubricity of Vincent Price. A collector's item! Hidemaro Konoye and Stokowski and his players conspire between them to provide an extraordinarily authentic Japanese sound in *Etenraku*, and then in *The Legend of the Arkansas Traveller* we have a complete change of local colour for Alexander Hilsberg's folksy, sub-country-and-western violin solo. Alas, the *Dance of the workers* is pretty thin stuff and the *Symphonic rhumba* isn't much better. Henry Eichheim's Japanese and Balinese impressions are suitably exotic, but not music one would wish to return to. As for Harl McDonald's *Double piano concerto*, the estimable Edward Johnson, who provides the characteristically thorough notes, sums it up aptly as 'Rachmaninov dabbling in South American dance music', and the second-movement theme and variations momentarily (perhaps intentionally) recalls the *Rhapsody on a theme of Paganini*. Much of the piano writing is splashy and the finale, 'in which the hair of all concerned is well and truly let down' (Johnson again), is spectacularly based on the *Juarezca*, a jazzy Mexican dance. The two soloists provide convincing, extrovert dash, and Stokowski obviously revels in what Noël Coward might have described as 'potent cheap music' if with nothing like the melodic appeal of Coward's own work. The two Sousa marches have both poise and élan, but here the sound is barely adequate – not the fault of the CD transfer. The programme lasts for 78 minutes and Stokowksi aficionados need not hesitate.

(i) **Philharmonia Orchestra,** (ii) **Berlin Philharmonic Orchestra, Herbert von Karajan**

'Herbert von Karajan conducts': RESPIGHI: (i) *The Pines of Rome.* SMETANA: (ii) *Má Vlast: Vltava.* SIBELIUS: (i) *Finlandia.* BERLIOZ: *Overture: Le Carnaval romain; Les Troyens: Royal hunt and storm.* BIZET: *Carmen: Suite No. 1.*
(M) *** EMI CD-EMX 2222; *TC-EMX 2222* [id.].

This is a shrewdly chosen concert to show Karajan mainly at his very finest during his first period with EMI, when Walter Legge was managing his recordings. The Philharmonia Orchestra – which plays in all but one of the items here – were at their peak, as is very obvious in the thrillingly tangible virtuosity of the *Pines of Rome* and the *Carnaval romain overture.* The *Carmen suite* shows a lighter touch than in Karajan's later, Berlin Philharmonic recording, and Berlioz's *Royal hunt and storm*, if without quite the panache of Beecham or Munch, is still pretty exciting. All these recordings were made in the Kingsway Hall and their spacious vividness belies the early recording date (1958/9). The central movement of the *Pines of Rome* is memorably evocative and *I pini della via Appia* opens with a compellingly sinister tread.

Philharmonia Orchestra, Otto Klemperer

HANDEL: *Concerto grosso in A min., Op.6/4.* MOZART: *Serenade No. 6 (Serenata notturna), K.239.* BRAHMS: *Variations on a theme of Haydn, Op. 56a.* J. STRAUSS Jnr: *Kaiser (Emperor) Waltz.* R. STRAUSS: *Till Eulenspiegel.*
(M) **(*) EMI CDM7 64146-2 [id.].

A curiously devised collection, as the Mozart and Brahms items are mono, though they sound extremely well and the performances show Klemperer at his finest. He brings his own special magisterial qualities to the *Emperor Waltz* and his portrayal of *Till.* But the highlight of the collection is the Handel *Concerto grosso*, a great performance in the German tradition with unashamedly spacious tempi revealing the work's full, lyrical grandeur. Walter Legge's 1956 stereo was of demonstration standard in its day.

Philharmonia Orchestra or NBC Symphony Orchestra, Guido Cantelli

'Artist profile': MOZART: *A musical joke, K.522; Symphony No. 29 in A, K.201*. BEETHOVEN: *Symphony No. 7 in A, Op. 92*. SCHUBERT: *Symphony No. 8 in B min. (Unfinished)*. FRANCK: *Symphony in D min.*
(B) *** EMI CZS5 68217-2 (2) [id.].

Cantelli's major recordings should be permanently available at prices accessible to all. Not only do these classic accounts have the authority of a master-conductor, they also have a perfect sense of proportion, phrasing that is alive and supple, and a natural elegance. The Mozart *A major Symphony*, K.201, blends style and an expressive freedom which seems totally spontaneous yet which is beautifully shaped and controlled. This is music-making of an order of which period-instrument groups should be envious. The Beethoven *Seventh Symphony* is well held together without being in the least overdriven, and the Schubert *Unfinished* is also a selfless reading, free of idiosyncrasy and all the more full of character for being so. The Franck *Symphony*, recorded with the NBC Symphony for which he was being groomed after Toscanini, is also a performance of some stature. The recordings wear their years lightly: they are now 40 years old and are still going strong.

Philharmonia Orchestra or Royal Philharmonic Orchestra, Efrem Kurtz

'Artist profile': RIMSKY-KORSAKOV: *The snow maiden: suite. Le Coq d'or: suite; Dubinushka, Op. 62*. LIADOV: *Kikimora, Op. 63; Baba-Yaga, Op. 56; The enchanted lake, Op. 62; A musical snuffbox, Op. 32*. SHOSTAKOVICH: *Symphony No. 1 in F, Op. 10*. KHACHATURIAN: *Masquerade: Waltz; Galop*. GLINKA: *A life for the Tsar* (ballet music). KABALEVSKY: *The Comedians: suite, Op. 26*. PROKOFIEV: *Symphony No. 1 in D (Classical), Op. 25*.
(B) *** EMI CZS7 67729-2 (2) [id.].

These Kurtz recordings were made between 1957 and 1963, but the sound has dated hardly at all and on CD sounds both colourful and lustrous. The playing of the Philharmonia in the Prokofiev and Shostakovich symphonies is superbly polished and responsive and the performances combine wit and high spirits with much character; the Rimsky-Korsakov suites and Liadov tone-poems (with the RPO playing in the latter) bring comparable finesse and plenty of atmosphere. The effect in *Le Coq d'or* is vividly refined rather than sultry, but *The snow maiden* sparkles, and the Kabalevsky *Comedians suite* has ebullience without vulgarity. Glinka's attractive dances from *A life for the Tsar* show why he was regarded as the 'father' of Russian orchestral music. It is good to have Kurtz's distinguished contribution to the early EMI stereo catalogue properly represented in what is one of the very best of EMI's 'Artist profile' series: this is well worth its modest cost.

Pittsburgh Symphony Orchestra, William Steinberg

'Orchestral masterworks': RAVEL: *Boléro; La Valse*. TCHAIKOVSKY: *Capriccio italien*. BORODIN: *Polovtsian dances*. GLINKA: *Kamarinskaya*. MUSSORGSKY: *Night on the bare mountain*.
(M) ** EMI CDM5 65204-2 [id.].

It is good to have a programme from Steinberg, who is otherwise represented only by his charismatic DG version of Holst's *Planets*. Here his account of Tchaikovsky's *Capriccio italien* is even more individual. The introduction of the famous echo theme is very slow indeed, and it is to his credit that he can sustain the orchestral tension at this pace. He shows this same skill in Ravel's *Boléro*, and *Night on the bare mountain* does not lack excitement. But easily the most attractive performance here is the sparkling *Kamarinskaya* of Glinka. This is very early stereo, from the Capitol label, but the effect is spacious, if not comparable with the sound the RCA engineers were achieving in Chicago at the same period.

'Q the Classics'

'*Q the Classics* (A modern guide to contemporary classics)': John TAVENER: *The Protecting veil:* opening section (Isserlis, LSO, Rozhdestvensky). BARBER: *Adagio for strings* (City of L. Sinf., Hickox). GLASS: *Façades* (John Harle and Simon Haram, soprano saxophones). REICH: *8 Lines*. VAUGHAN WILLIAMS: *Fantasia on a theme by Thomas Tallis* (London Chamber O, Christopher Warren-Green). BRITTEN: *Peter Grimes: Sea interlude No. 3: Moonlight* (RLPO, Pešek).
*** Virgin/EMI Dig. VC5 45021-2 [id.].

It's a pity that this excellent anthology is not offered at mid-price, particularly as it is essentially a sampler. Yet it effectively covers contemporary trends in non-barbed-wire minimalist writing and, by including the atmospheric Britten evocation and Vaughan Williams's string masterpiece (in a superlative performance), it establishes the traditional twentieth-century background. Opening with the intensely felt and immediately communicative introduction to Tavener's *Protecting veil* (which will surely tempt anyone), it includes characteristic examples from three other minimalist composers, with only Reich's *Eight Lines* failing to convince. Here 18 minutes of repetitive writing, sounding as if the pick-up is stuck in the groove, long outlasts its welcome.

Radio Television Eireann Concert Orchestra, Dublin, Ernest Tomlinson

'*British light music – Miniatures*': Anthony COLLINS: *Vanity Fair*. Mark LUBBOCK: *Polka dots*. Armstrong GIBBS: *Dusk*. Benjamin FRANKEL: *Carriage and pair*. Vivian ELLIS: *Coronation Scot*. Arthur BENJAMIN: *Jamaican song; Jamaican rumba*. Robert DOCKER: *Tabarinage*. ELGAR: *Beau Brummel*. Harry DEXTER: *Siciliano*. Ken WARNER: *Scrub, brothers scrub!* Gordon JACOB: *Cradle song*. Thomas ARNE, arr. TOMLINSON: *Georgian suite: Gavotte*. Gilbert VINTER: *Portuguese party*. Geoffrey TOYE: *The Haunted ballroom* (concert waltz). Edward WHITE: *Puffin' Billy*. George MELACHRINO: *Starlight Roof waltz*. Clive RICHARDSON: *Beachcomber*.
**(*) Marco Polo Dig. 8.223522 [id.].

The fine Sibelius conductor, Anthony Collins, was once asked in a BBC interview what he valued most among his achievements, and his (perhaps surprising) reply was, 'Vanity Fair'; and he explained that this little novelty piece had gained such popularity that he knew it would give pleasure 'long after my conducting has been forgotten'. Although his recordings have certainly not been forgotten, he was right to be proud of this delightful vignette, for its theme is indelible, and it comes up very freshly here in a programme of unassuming orchestral lollipops, including many items with almost equally catchy musical ideas, even a *Gavotte* by Thomas Arne, arranged by the conductor to sound just a little like a caricature. The tunes are usually pithy and short, like Harry Dexter's daintily wispy *Siciliano*, but sometimes the writing is gently evocative, like the two romantic waltzes, *Dusk* of Armstrong Gibbs, and Geoffrey Toye's *Haunted ballroom*, and Gordon Jacob's delicate *Cradle song*. Novelties like Benjamin Frankel's clip-clopping *Carriage and pair*, Edward White's *Puffin' Billy*, and Ken Warner's moto perpetuo, *Scrub, brothers scrub!* readily evoke the world of Leroy Anderson, while Clive Richardson's quirky *Beachcomber* makes one want to smile. The conductor, Ernest Tomlinson, who has already provided a highly recommendable Marco Polo disc of his own music (8.223413), understands that their very slightness is part of the charm of nearly all these pieces, and he presents them with a simplicity that is wholly endearing. The only relative disappointment is Vivian Ellis's wittily evoked *Coronation Scot*, which needs much more verve than it receives here. Good playing and good recording, although the acoustic effect noticeably becomes more brash for the second item, Mark Lubbock's breezy *Polka dots*.

Rampal, Jeanne-Pierre (flute)

'*20th century flute masterpieces*' (with (i) LOP, Froment; (ii) O de l'ORTF, Martinon; (iii) LOP, Jolivet; (iv) Robert Veyron-Lacroix): (i) IBERT: *Concerto*. (ii) KHACHATURIAN: *Concerto* (arr. from *Violin concerto*). (ii) JOLIVET: *Concerto*. (iii) MARTINU: *Sonata*. HINDEMITH: *Sonata*. PROKOFIEV: *Sonata in D*. POULENC: *Sonata*.
(M) **(*) Erato/Warner 2292 45839-2 [id.].

The concertos on the first CD have less than perfectly focused orchestral strings, and the Khachaturian arrangement is dispensable. But the Ibert *Concerto* is winning and the more plagent Jolivet not inconsiderable. The highlights of the collection are all on the second disc, three out of four of them inspired works delightfully written for the instrument and marvellously played. Only the first movement of the Hindemith is a bit below par in its utilitarian austerity; the cool slow movement and more vigorous finale have something approaching charm. The Prokofiev *Sonata* (also heard in a version for violin – but the flute is the original) is a masterpiece, and Rampal makes the very most of it. Then comes the delightful Poulenc piece with its disarmingly easy-flowing opening, delicious central cantilena and scintillating finale with hints of *Les Biches*. The recording of the sonatas, made in 1978, is vividly firm and realistic. If this set is reissued later on a Bonsai Duo, it will be well worth seeking out.

(i) RCA Victor Symphony Orchestra (ii) Symphony of the Air, Leopold Stokowski

'Rhapsodies': (i) LISZT: *Hungarian rhapsody No. 2*. ENESCU: *Rumanian rhapsody No. 1*. SMETANA: *Má Vlast: Vltava. The Bartered Bride overture.* (ii) WAGNER: *Tannhäuser: Overture and Venusberg music* (with chorus). *Tristan und Isolde: Prelude to Act III*.
(M) *** BMG/RCA 09026 61503-2 [id.].

Recorded in 1960 and 1961, this collection shows the great orchestral magician at his most uninhibitedly voluptuous. The opening tutti of the Liszt *Hungarian rhapsody* with full-throated horns and richly sonorous double basses makes a huge impact, and the Enescu is comparably sumptuous in its glowing colours. *Vltava* is romanticized, with an expansive treatment of the main lyrical theme, but *The Bartered Bride Overture* is bursting with energy, with the stereo clearly defining the emphatic string entries of the opening fugato. The *Overture and Venusberg music* from *Tannhäuser* combines sensuousness with frenetic excitement, and then a sentient relaxation appears in the *Tristan Prelude* to Act III. This is over-the-top Stokowski at his most compulsive, but is not for musical puritans. The CD transfers encompass the breadth of amplitude of the forwardly balanced recordings without problems.

Rostropovich, Mstislav (cello)

'Masterpieces for cello' (with various orchestras and conductors): BERNSTEIN: *3 Meditations for cello and orchestra* (from *Mass*). BOCCHERINI: *Cello concerto No. 2*. GLAZUNOV: *Chant du Ménestrel*. SHOSTAKOVICH: *Cello concerto No. 2*. TARTINI: *Cello concerto*. TCHAIKOVSKY: *Andante cantabile; Variations on a rococo theme*. VIVALDI: *Cello concertos, RV 398 and RV 413*.
(B) *** DG Double 437 952-2 (2) [id.].

A self-recommending set, with two CDs for the price of one. Each of the works included is discussed under its composer entry. The only drawback is the inadequate documentation.

'Rostropovich live' (with Moscow PO or USSR R. & TV O, Rozhdestvensky): ELGAR: *Cello concerto in E min., Op. 68*. RESPIGHI: *Adagio with variations for cello and orchestra*. MILHAUD: *Cello concerto No. 1, Op. 136*.
*(**) Russian Disc RDCD 11 104 [id.].

A larger-than-life account of the Elgar *Concerto* from Rostropovich, a performance of contrasts with great dash in the Scherzo, yet an *Adagio* of deep inner feeling and a gentle, heart-touching reprise at the close of the finale. The Respighi *Variations* are beautifully played and made almost to seem as inspired as the Tchaikovsky *Rococo* set, while the diverse moods of the Milhaud concerto – *Nonchalant, Grave and Joyeux* – are winningly characterized. The 1964 analogue recording is fully acceptable, not as flattering to Rostropovich's tone as Western recordings and with the orchestra noticeably thin in the tuttis of the Milhaud. With only 52 minutes' playing time, this CD, for all its attractions, is overpriced.

(i) Royal Philharmonic Orchestra; (ii) Vienna Philharmonic Orchestra, Rafael Kubelik

'Artist profile': (i) BRAHMS: *Hungarian dances Nos. 17–21*. (ii) BORODIN: *Symphony No. 2 in B min*. TCHAIKOVSKY: *Symphony No. 4 in F min., Op. 36*. MARTINU: *Les fresques de Piero della Francesca*. JANACEK: *Taras Bulba*. BARTOK: *Concerto for orchestra*.
(B) *** EMI CZS5 68223-2 (2) [id.].

Kubelik's concert opens well. In the Brahms *Hungarian dances* he sounds as if he is enjoying himself, and the RPO responds with good-humoured virtuosity. However, the originally rich and sonorous (1957) Kingsway Hall sound has lost some of its allure in the attempt of the engineers to achieve greater transparency: now the bright upper range sounds somewhat artificial. Elsewhere the transfers are wholly praiseworthy, and when we move to the Sofiensaal for the 1960 Borodin *Second* there is an agreeable warmth. The Scherzo glows, even if it is easy-going, and the *Andante* is wonderfully romantic from its opening horn solo to when the big tune returns opulently on the massed strings. Kubelik sustains the tension less readily in the first movement, and its lack of tautness means that the changes of tempo for the main theme are not entirely convincing. The finale, however, bursts with colour and makes a satisfying culmination.

Kubelik's Tchaikovsky *Fourth* is a fine and often brilliant reading. If not electrifying, it has very real qualities of understanding and sympathy for the composer's intentions, plus a remarkable freedom from idiosyncrasies, notably in the first movement which offers both drama and excitement in a way that makes it a fine performance to live with. Elsewhere the felicities are many, not least in a most beautifully played and shaped *Andantino*, which has grace and warmth in the outer sections, while the central climax is ardently conveyed and the coda shaped with care. The Scherzo goes well, and the playing makes us more conscious than usual of the composer's apt contrasting of the three orchestral sonorities: plucked strings, woodwind (dominated by the brilliance of the piccolo) and the crisp richness of the brass. The finale is splendid, not rushed but with plenty of adrenalin, the well-prepared coda among the most exciting on record, helped by a 1960 recording of substantial weight as well as brilliance. In short this is remarkably successful and is preferable to many more spectacular and perhaps idiosyncratic versions.

The Bartók *Concerto for orchestra* (1958) was one of the first successful versions in stereo, and it remains fresh and highly enjoyable. It offers first-rate playing and apt tempi, and the vigour of the intepretation reflects the music's inherent virtuosity, especially in the outer movements, without going over the top. The opening is particularly atmospheric and the RPO strings bring lots of bite to their first entry. The central movements have plenty of colour and the fourth-movement *Intermezzo* is particularly characterful. Kubelik never forces his own personality over the voice of the composer, which is allowed to speak for itself. Here the 1958 Kingsway Hall recording sounds hardly dated at all. One could say the same for *Taras Bulba*, recorded at the same time. Indeed it is difficult to credit the recording date, so vivid and full-blooded is the quality. Kubelik's later version, made for DG with the Bavarian Radio Orchestra, is a little more refined but not less vital.

No less persuasive is the pioneering stereo account of the *Frescoes of Piero della Francesca*, inspired by the fifteenth-century frescoes by the Umbrian painter of that name in the church of San Francesco at Arezzo in Italy, depicting 'The History of the True Cross'. Kubelik conducted its première only two years before making this recording, which is vivid and full of intensity, if without the last degree of opulence. The two discs (offered for the price of one) play for 157 minutes and quite admirably represent Kubelik's earlier recording period with EMI, before he moved on to DG.

Saint Louis Symphony Orchestra, Leonard Slatkin

Russian music: GLINKA: *Ruslan and Ludmilla overture.* BORODIN: *In the Steppes of Central Asia.* TCHAIKOVSKY: *Marche slave.* RIMSKY-KORSAKOV: *Russian Easter festival overture.* GLIERE: *The Red Poppy; Russian sailors' dance.*
(M) ** Telarc CD 82013 [id.].

There seems no reason why Telarc should have provided such short measure for this reissue. The performances are good if not perhaps distinctive, except that the close of *Marche slave* brings a spectacular splash of percussion (bass drum and cymbals) and in the languorous interweaving of the sinuously beautiful themes of Borodin's *In the Steppes of central Asia* the warm resonance of the recording is very appealing. The accelerando of Glière's *Russian sailors' dance* is vividly managed, and it is a pity that the overall playing time is unacceptably short: 41 minutes.

Sargent, Sir Malcolm

'*Sir Malcolm Sargent conducts British music*' (with (i) LPO; (ii) LSO; (iii) Mary Lewis; Tudor Davies & O.; (iv) Royal Choral Soc.; (v) New SO): (i) HOLST: *Perfect fool: suite.* (ii) BRITTEN: *Young person's guide to the orchestra.* (iii) VAUGHAN WILLIAMS: *Hugh the Drover: Love duet.* ELGAR: (iv) *I sing the birth;* (ii) *Pomp & Circumstance Marches Nos. 1 & 4.* (v) COLERIDGE-TAYLOR: *Othello: suite.* (ii) BAX: *Coronation march.*
(***) Beulah mono 1PD13 [id.].

The impact of the trombones at the start of Holst's *Perfect fool* music, the first item here, is astonishing, bringing it home what vivid sound the early Decca *ffrr* system produced. Despite high surface hiss, the clarity and presence are most impressive. Sargent was at his finest in this repertory, and it is very welcome to have his personal electricity so vividly conveyed throughout the disc, and most of all in the recording, taken from the sound-track of the original COI film, of Britten's *Young person's guide*. The optical transfer by Martin Sawyer produces far more vivid and satisfyingly weighty results than one would ever expect. The *Love duet* from *Hugh the Drover* was recorded in 1924 in limited pre-electric sound, but the Elgar part-song, recorded live at the Royal Albert Hall in 1928, also soon after the first performance, is vividly atmospheric. The *Othello suite* of Coleridge-Taylor, another première recording, is a sequence of brief genre pieces, with recording more than lively and colourful enough to make one forget the high surface-hiss. The three marches at the end were recorded for the Queen's coronation in 1953, with Sargent taking an uninhibitedly broad view of the great tunes in both the Elgar favourites, and with Bax doing a fair imitation of Walton.

Scottish Chamber Orchestra, Laredo

'String masterpieces': ALBINONI: *Adagio in G min.* (arr. Giazotto). HANDEL: *Berenice: Overture. Solomon: Arrival of the Queen of Sheba.* BACH: *Suite No. 3, BWV 1068: Air. Violin concerto No. 1 in A min., BWV 1041: Finale.* PACHELBEL: *Canon.* PURCELL: *Abdelazer: Rondo. Chacony in G min.*
(B) *** Carlton Dig. PCD 2001.

An excellent issue. The playing is alive, alert, stylish and committed without being overly expressive, yet the Bach *Air* has warmth and Pachelbel's *Canon* is fresh and unconventional in approach. The sound is first class, especially spacious and convincing on CD, well detailed without any clinical feeling. The Purcell *Rondo* is the tune made familiar by Britten's orchestral guide; the *Chaconne* is played with telling simplicity.

Serenades: 'Favourite Serenades'

'Favourite Serenades' (played by (i) Netherlands CO, Zinman; (ii) ECO, Leppard; (iii) I Musici; (iv) ASMF, Marriner; (v) Accardo, Leipzig GO, Masur; (vi) Netherlands Wind Ens., Edo de Waart; (vii) Catherine Michel, Monte Carlo Op. O, Almeida): (i) TCHAIKOVSKY: *String serenade, Op. 48.* (ii) DVORAK: *Serenade for strings, Op. 22.* (iii) MOZART: *Eine kleine Nachtmusik.* (iv) HOFFSTETTER/HAYDN: *Serenade from String quartet in F, Op. 3/5.* (v) BRUCH: *Serenade for violin and orchestra, Op. 75.* (iii) WOLF: *Italian serenade in G.* (vi) R. STRAUSS: *Serenade for wind, Op. 7.* (vii) RODRIGO: *Concierti serenade for harp and orchestra.*
(B) **(*) Ph. 438 748-2 (2) [id.].

A generous 156-minute anthology about which there are few reservations. Zinman's account of the Tchaikovsky *Serenade* has not the very strongest profile, but it is polished and warmly recorded. I Musici play Wolf's infectiously gay little masterpiece extremely well, even if perhaps they do not do full justice to its effervescent spirit and sheer *joie de vivre*. Everything else here will certainly give pleasure, especially the rare Max Bruch concertante serenade, so enticingly tuneful with Accardo in ravishing form. Catherine Michel's account of Rodrigo's *Serenade concerto* for harp is not quite as enticing as Zabaleta's famous DG version, but the spicy harmonies are made to catch the ear with piquant abrasiveness. Excellent sound (mostly from the 1970s) and smooth remastering ensure aural pleasure throughout.

Serenata of London, Barry Wilde

SIBELIUS: *Suite champêtre, Op. 98b; Canzonetta, Op. 62a.* TCHAIKOVSKY: *Elegy in G.* DVORAK: *2 Waltzes, Op. 54/1-2; Nocturne in B, Op. 40; Humoresque in G flat, Op. 101.* ELGAR: *Salut d'amour, Op. 12; Sospiri, Op. 70.* GRIEG: *2 Melodies, Op. 53; Nordic melodies, Op. 63; 2 Elegiac pieces, Op. 34.*
(B) *** Carlton Dig. PCD 1108 [id.].

The Serenata of London under Barry Wilde here provides a very well-balanced concert of comparatively lightweight repertoire, played with such agreeable finesse and warmth that it makes a highly enjoyable hour-long entertainment. Whether in little-known Sibelius, the lovely Tchaikovsky *Elegy*, the delectable Dvořák *Waltzes* or the Grieg *Melodies*, the spontaneity of the playing brings the music to life, and the size of the orchestra seems just right when they are so well recorded.

Silvestri, Constantin

'Artist profile' (with (i) Philh. O; (ii) VPO; (iii) Bournemouth SO; (iv) LPO; (v) Paris Conservatoire O): (i) RIMSKY-KORSAKOV: *May night overture.* (ii) RAVEL: *Rapsodie espagnole.* (iii) ELGAR: *Overture: In the South (Alassio), Op. 50.* (iv) DVORAK: *Symphony No. 8 in G, Op. 88.* (v) GLINKA: *Overture Ruslan and Ludmilla.* (i) BORODIN: *Prince Igor: Overture; Polovtsian dances.* TCHAIKOVSKY: *Symphony No. 5 in E min., Op.64.*
(B) **(*) EMI CZS5 68229-2 (2) [id.].

The generous collection here (155 minutes) certainly provides an accurate profile of a brilliantly talented Romanian musician who moved from Budapest to Paris and on to London in 1957, to spend the last decade of his life making music in Britain. Undoubtedly the highlight of this concert is the electrifying account of Elgar's *In the South overture*, recorded with the Bournemouth Symphony Orchestra in 1967, only two years before Silvestri's death, a performance which has never been surpassed in its ongoing intensity. Silvestri knits the structure together more convincingly than one would have believed possible, and the strong forward thrust does not prevent the Italian sunshine (as seen through English eyes) bringing a Mediterranean glow to the score's atmospheric central interlude. But it is the virile opening and closing sections which Silvestri makes so compelling; at the same time he draws a parallel with the music of Richard Strauss. The Bournemouth orchestra (of which Silvestri had been musical director since the beginning of the 1960s) is highly committed and provides playing of a virtuoso order.

The introspective temperament of Tchaikovsky's *Fifth Symphony* also suits Silvestri and, in spite of the characteristic eccentricities of rubato (which are not always quite spontaneous), he builds up the climaxes in the first two movements with great excitement. The hushed opening of the *Andante cantabile* with its sombre lower strings is very telling, and the horn solo is quite lovely; the waltz, too, is given real elegance. The finale opens with dignity and then the *Allegro vivace* goes with the wind, with brilliant Philharmonia virtuosity carrying the day. Here the early-1957 Kingsway Hall recording, though full-bodied, has a degree of harshness. The Borodin *Prince Igor overture* generates similar romantic feeling (with another superb horn solo) and thrust, and the *Polovtsian dances* glow with colour and sweep to their close with explosive energy.

Silvestri's LPO recording of Dvorak's *Eighth* is also enjoyable: at times wilful, at others warm and genial, full of verve, but never eccentric. The orchestral playing is appealingly affectionate in the central movements, and the (1957) Kingsway Hall recording is remarkably good. Each of the two discs opens with a Russian overture in which Silvestri, the Romanian, readily shows his volatile Slavonic temperament. Rimsky-Korsakov's *May night* has a particularly enticing blend of rich colours and vivid detail while the Glinka *Ruslan and Ludmilla* generates exciting bravura from the Philharmonia strings, without being pressed too hard. The glitteringly extrovert account by the VPO of Ravel's *Rapsodie espagnole*, if not particularly subtle, brings plenty of excitement.

Slovak State Philharmonic Orchestra (Košice), Mika Eichenholz

'Locomotive music (A musical train ride)' Vol. 1: LANNER: *Ankunfts Waltz.* Johann STRAUSS Snr: *Reise Galop; Souvenir de Carneval 1847 (quadrille); Eisenbahn-Lust (waltz).* HOYER: *Jernban galop.* Johann STRAUSS Jnr: *Reiseabenteuer waltz.* MEYER: *Jernvägs galop.* Eduard STRAUSS: *Glockensignale waltz; Mit Dampf polka; Lustfahrten waltz; Tour und Retour polka.* Josef STRAUSS: *Gruss an München polka.* GRAHL: *Sveas helsning till Nore waltz.* LUMBYE: *Copenhagen Steam Railway galop.*
**(*) Marco Polo Dig. 8.223470 [id.].

'Locomotive music' Vol. 2: LANNER: *Dampf Waltz.* FAHRBACH: *Locomotiv galop.* Johann STRAUSS Jnr: *Wilde Rosen waltz; Vergnügungszug polka; Spiralen waltz; Accelerationen waltz.* GUNGL: *Eisenbahn-Dampf galop.* Eduard STRAUSS: *Polkas: Reiselust; Ohne Aufenthalt; Treuliebchen; Ohne Bremse; Von Land zu Land; Bahn frei; Feuerfunken waltz.* ZIEHRER: *Nachtschwalbe polka.*
**(*) Marco Polo Dig. 8.223471 [id.].

This seems a happy idea on which to base a two-CD collection of Viennese-style dance music, but in the event the only piece which celebrates the effect of a train journey really successfully is the *Copenhagen Steam Railway galop*, which begins with the passengers gathering in elegant anticipation at the station and follows with the train starting off, merrily rattling along and finally coming to a halt. The Slovak performance has rather a good whistle but seems more concerned with rhythm than with charm and cannot compare with the account included in the splendid Unicorn collection of Lumbye's dance music so beautifully played by the Odense Symphony Orchestra under Peter Guth, which carries a Rosette. The first Marco Polo disc opens with Lanner's *Ankunfts* ('Arrival') *waltz*, which ironically dates from before the railway had even arrived in Vienna. It is enjoyable for itself; the other highlights are more descriptive. Frans Hoyer's *Jernban-Galop* makes a fair shot of a train starting up and has a rather engaging main theme, while Jean Meyer's *Jernvägs-Galop* follows Lumbye's pattern of an elegant opening and a whistle start, with the side-drum snares giving a modest railway simulation. This too is attractive melodically, but the coda is too abrupt. Eduard Strauss's *Mit Dampf* has a rather half-hearted whistle but plenty of energy, and his *Lustfahrten waltz* is lyrically appealing.

The second disc opens with Lanner again, but the *Dampf* refers to the steam of a coffee house! It is followed by Fahrbach's jolly *Locomotiv-Galop*, where the effects are minimal and primitive. However, Joseph Gungl does better, with an opening whistle which returns on a regular basis against supporting bass-drum beats. Johann Strauss's *Vergnügungszug polka* concentrates on the exhilaration of a day out on an excursion train, but Eduard Strauss's *Bahn frei*, comparably zestful, manages a cleverly brief introductory train imitation, and *Ohne Aufenthalt* has a gentle bell to set off. If most of this repertoire is unadventurous in terms of evocation, it is all tuneful and brightly presented; the playing is not without finesse and has plenty of zest, and the orchestra is very well recorded – and not in a train shed either. But these are full-priced CDs and one is plainly not travelling in a first-class carriage with the VPO.

Stokowski, Leopold – see under French National Radio Orchestra, Philadelphia Orchestra and Symphony of the Air

Symphony of the Air, Leopold Stokowski

RESPIGHI: *The Pines of Rome.* KHACHATURIAN: *Symphony No. 2 (The Bell).* SHOSTAKOVICH: *Symphony No. 1 in F min., Op. 10; Prelude in E flat* (orch. Stokowski); *Lady Macbeth of Mtsensk: Entr'acte.* BLOCH: *Schelomo (Hebrew rhapsody)* (with Georg Neikrug, cello). FRESCOBALDI: *Gagliarda.* PALESTRINA: *Adoramus te.* CESTI: *Tu mancavi a tormentarmi, crudelussima speranza* (all 3 orch. Stokowski). GABRIELI: *Sonata pian' e forte.*
(M) *** EMI ZDMB5 65427-2 (2) [id.].

This brings together a varied group of recordings made by Stokowski with the Symphony of the Air (formerly NBC Symphony Orchestra) on the United Artists label. Nearly all were made at Carnegie Hall in 1958/9 and, if the playing is variable, Stokowski's readings are all characterful and compelling. He conducts the Respighi with characteristic flair and intensity so that, quite apart from the panache of the outer movements, the clarinet solo in the third movement leading up to the nightingale-sounds has rarely been more evocative. He plays the bombastic Khachaturian symphony, inspired by the Second World War, for all it is worth and a lot more besides. In these two works the sound is less full and open than on the Capitol recordings that Stokowski made in London and Paris during the same period. But the Shostakovich *First Symphony* has a convincing concert-hall balance and is pointedly done, an outstanding performance even if the first movement is relatively relaxed, slacker than the rest. *Schelomo* (forwardly but not too dryly recorded in the Manhattan Towers Hotel, New York City) has Neikrug as a satisfyingly firm and expressive cello soloist, even if he hardly matches Feuermann on Stokowski's classic Philadelphia recording. The maestro's own arrangements of sixteenth- and seventeenth-century Italian pieces may be as unauthentic as could be, but the performances are magnetic, especially the accounts of the richly scored Palestrina piece and the infinitely touching *Aria* of Pietro Cesti, played most beautifully. The brass in the solemn Gabrieli *Sonata* is thrilling, with the Carnegie Hall acoustic adding to the sonority.

Virtuosi di Praga, Oldřich Vlček

Music for strings: GRIEG: *Holberg suite.* RESPIGHI: *Ancient airs and dances: Suite No. 3.* ELGAR: *Serenade in E min., Op. 20.* ROUSSEL: *Sinfonietta, Op. 52.*
(BB) **(*) Discover Dig. DICD 920236 [id.].

The Prague Virtuosi are an expert body of soloists who command an impressive sonority in spite of their modest size (here eleven players). Some ears might feel that the Elgar *Serenade* lacks ripeness of Elgarian feeling, yet the *Larghetto* is tenderly affecting. Equally, the Respighi suite of *Ancient airs* sounds fresher, less anachronistically voluptuous than usual. The chamber scale suits the *Holberg suite* admirably, with plenty of energy and bite. But undoubtedly the most effective performance here is the Roussel *Sinfonietta*, bracingly astringent and grippingly vital.

Walter, Bruno: *'Bruno Walter Edition'* – see under Columbia Symphony Orchestra

Instrumental Recitals

Argerich, Martha (piano)

CHOPIN: *Scherzo No. 3 in C sharp min., Op. 39; Barcarolle in F sharp min., Op. 60.* BRAHMS: *2 Rhapsodies, Op. 79.* PROKOFIEV: *Toccata, Op. 11.* RAVEL: *Jeux d'eau.* LISZT: *Hungarian rhapsody No. 6; Piano sonata in B min.*
(M) (**) DG 447 430-2 [id.].

This particular 'Legendary Recording' in DG's series of 'Originals' presents Argerich's remarkable début LP recital, recorded for DG in 1961. The phenomenal technique (she was twenty-one at the time) is as astonishing as the performances are musically exasperating. This artist's charismatic impulsiveness is well known, but in presenting the opening Chopin *Scherzo* she seems not to want to show any musical control whatsoever and is carried away by her own glittering roulades; the *Barcarolle* is also very volatile, but here she does not ride roughshod over the lyrical flow. The Brahms *First Rhapsody* is explosively fast; then suddenly she puts the brakes on and provides most poetic playing in the central section. Such a barnstorming approach is more readily at home in the Prokofiev *Toccata*, and she goes over the top in the Liszt *Hungarian rhapsody* with a certain panache. *Jeux d'eau* brings a certain Ravelian magic. The Liszt *Sonata* has been added on; it dates from a decade later and yet again, although the bravura is breathtaking and there is no lack of spontaneity, the work's lyrical feeling and indeed its breadth are to some extent sacrificed to the insistent forward impulse of the playing. Good but not exceptional recording, a bit hard in the Liszt, though that may well reflect faithfully the percussive attack of Argerich's powerful hands.

Arrau, Claudio (piano)

Recital: LISZT: *Liebestraume No. 3 in A flat; Etudes d'exécution transcendante: Harmonies du soir.* CHOPIN: *Nocturnes Nos. 17 in B; 18 in E, Op. 62/1–2.* BRAHMS: *Scherzo in E flat min., Op. 4.* BEETHOVEN: *Rondo in G, Op. 51/2.* SCHUBERT: *Impromptu in G flat, D.899.* SCHUMANN: *Waldszenen: Vogel als Prophet. Romance in F sharp., Op. 28/2; Arabeske in C, Op. 18.* DEBUSSY: *Estampes: Soirée dans Grenade. Images, Book II: Poissons d'or.*
(M) **(*) Ph. 438 305-2 [id.].

Claudio Arrau is heard here at his very finest in the glorious account of Schubert's *G flat Impromptu* and in the music of Schumann and Debussy. If in Liszt's *Liebestraume* and the Chopin *Nocturnes* his gentle fluctuations of rubato may not seem entirely spontaneous to some ears, this is still masterly playing and the Philips analogue recording is superbly full in timbre and admirably present.

Ashkenazy, Vladimir (piano)

'Piano favourites': BEETHOVEN: *Für Elise; Piano sonata No. 14 (Moonlight), Op.; 27/2.* SCHUMANN: *Kinderszenen: Träumerei. Arabeske.* CHOPIN: *Mazurka in B flat, Op. 7/1; Nocturnes: in E flat, Op. 9/ 2; in B, Op. 32/1; Waltzes: in E flat (Grand valse brillante), Op. 18; in B min., Op. 69/2; Polonaise in A flat, Op. 53.* LIADOV: *Musical snuffbox, Op. 32.* MUSSORGSKY: *Pictures: The hut on hen's legs; The great gate of Kiev.* RAVEL: *Pavane pour une infante défunte.*
(M) **(*) Decca Dig. 430 759-2 [id.].

A well-selected and generous (71 minutes) recital. All the recordings are digital – but, even so, there are slight differences in piano timbre (and level) between items, most noticeable when Chopin's *Mazurka in B flat* closely follows the mellower (and rather deliberate) account of Schumann's *Träumerei*. It might have been better to end with the Mussorgsky *Great gate of Kiev* but, as it is, the fine performance of Beethoven's *Moonlight sonata* is far from an anticlimax.

Bashmet, Yuri (viola), Mikhail Muntian (piano)

GLINKA: *Viola sonata in D min.* ROSLAVETS: *Viola sonata.* SHOSTAKOVICH: *Viola sonata, Op. 147.*
**(*) BMG/RCA Dig. 09026 61273 [id.].

Bashmet makes a powerful response to Shostakovich's bleak, desperately felt *Viola sonata*; he balances it with Glinka's guilelessly youthful piece and another work by Nikolai Roslavets which not all listeners will welcome with open arms, its apparent emotional force seeming something of an illusion if one returns to it very often.

Beaux Arts Trio

'*A Celebration (1955–1995)*': RAVEL: *Piano trio in A min.* HAYDN: *Piano trio in G, Hob XV/25.*
FAURE: *Piano trio in D min., Op. 120.* BEETHOVEN: *Piano trio No.7 (Archduke).* SCHUMANN: *Piano trio No. 2 in F, Op. 80.* MENDELSSOHN: *Piano trio No. 1 in D min., Op. 49.* HAYDN: *Piano trio in F sharp min., Hob XV/26.* SCHUBERT: *Piano quintet in A (Trout), D.667* (with Samuel Rhodes & Georg Hörtnagel); *Piano trio No. 1 in B flat, D.898.* BRAHMS: *Piano trio No. 1 in B, Op. 8.*
TCHAIKOVSKY: *Piano trio in A min., Op. 50.* ROREM: *Spring music.*
(M) *** Ph. Analogue/Dig. 446 360-2 (4 + 1) [id.].

As can be seen, the present set celebrates the fiftieth anniversary of the Beaux Arts Trio, and even if over the years there have been changes in personnel the character of their playing (with its immaculate ensemble and spontaneity of feeling) has been stimulated and masterminded throughout by the unostentatious dominance of the pianist, Menahem Pressler, always sharply imaginative, who remains as influential as ever. The first group – in which Pressler was partnered by Daniel Guilet and Bernard Greenhouse – won a *Grand Prix du Disque* with Dvořák's *Dumky Trio* (a surprise omission here) and survived intact until 1968 when Guilet retired, to be replaced by Isidore Cohen. Then in 1987 ill health forced Greenhouse to follow him, and Peter Wiley took over the cello role. In 1992 Cohen retired and the newest member of the group (heard here only in the Rorem *Spring music*) is the violinist, Ida Kavafian. The earliest recordings here (the Ravel, Haydn *G major Trio*, Hob XV/25, and the Fauré) are offered on a separate bonus disc which comes in a separate cardboard sleeve, inside the slipcase. For some reason, in the accompanying booklet Philips are very coy about recording dates, merely saying that 'the repertoire on the bonus CD stems from older sources and is therefore not always of optimum sound quality' (Daniel Guilet's violin is somewhat meagre in timbre, especially in the Ravel and Fauré, but the cello and piano are naturally focused). Some recording dates for the other works are not stated at all, with only a series of unlinked overall publication dates given for the complete set. However, identification of the individual publication dates for each performance is given on each disc, and we have listed the works in approximate order of recording. Rightly, the earlier (1965) account of the *Archduke Trio* is included; it has more spontaneity than the later version, and the overall feeling is of lightness and grace. The Scherzo is a delight, and elsewhere there is an attractive pervading lyricism, so typical of the Beaux Arts style. Some of the other works have been re-recorded digitally with even greater success, notably the Ravel (where originally we noted a lack of charm on the part of Daniel Guilet). But the earlier versions remain thoroughly worthwhile. The playing in the Mendelssohn *D minor Trio* is thoroughly alive and musical, and the Schubert *Trout* is delightfully fresh. Every phrase is splendidly alive, there is no want of vitality and sensitivity; the *B flat Piano trio*, however, is the later, digital version from the mid-1980s, and the performance, though enjoyable, is not quite as spontaneous as the earlier, analogue version. The Brahms, also digital, shows the later group (including Cohen) at its finest, the playing always vital and sensitive, as does the Tchaikovsky *Trio*. This is a another case where the later version is distinctly superior to the earlier, analogue account. The fugue (originally omitted) is now restored, although there is still a sizeable cut in the final coda. But this remains a fine reading, and the recording is very vivid and present.

Berman, Lazar (piano)

Live recital – 27th June 1992: SCHUBERT: *Piano sonata No. 21 in B flat, D960.* LISZT: *Concert paraphrases of Schubert Lieder: Der Leiermann; Täuschung; Gretchen am Spinnrade; Die junge Nonne; Ave Maria; Erlkönig. Mephisto waltz; Années de pèlerinage, 1st Year: Chapelle de Guillaume Tell.* BEETHOVEN/RACHMANINOV: *Extract from The Ruins of Athens.*
(BB) ** Discovery DICD 920164/5 (2) [id.].

Berman's 1992 recital is uncommonly well recorded for a live occasion and the presence of the artist is in no doubt; indeed we have to wait a full half-minute for him to start after the introductory applause. His account of Schubert's last, greatest sonata is obviously both felt and considered. It is certainly dramatic but also wayward, and not all will respond to Berman's agogic distortions of the flow, particularly in the first movement. The Liszt items provide repertoire for which he is famous and the *Mephisto waltz* shows him at his most commanding. Some of the Schubert song transcriptions may be felt to be over-dramatized, though no one could complain about the *Erl-King*. The Beethoven/Rachmaninov encore is properly piquant.

Bowyer, Kevin (organ)

Blackburn Cathedral organ: *'A feast of organ exuberance'*: WOLF–G. LEIDEL: *Toccata Delectatione, Op. 5/35.* SWAYNE: *Riff-Raff.* BERVEILLER: *Suite; Cadence.*
(M) *** Priory Dig. 001 [id.].

This is an auspicious start for a new, reasonably priced, Priory series, given superb digital recording. The spectacular sound made by the magnificent 1969 Walker organ in Blackburn Cathedral is well demonstrated by this first-rate recital. Leidel is from the former East Germany, and his acknowledged influences from Messiaen and Scriabin are well absorbed into his own style. The *Toccata for pleasure* is titillating in its colouring and certainly exuberant in its extravagant treatment of its basic idea, which goes far beyond the minimalism achieved by many of his contemporaries. Giles Swayne is Liverpool-born and his quirky *Riff-Raff*, in the words of the performer, suggest 'isolated flashes of light of varying intensity'. Berveiller comes from the traditional French school of Dupré. His *Suite* is eminently approachable music, with a whimsical second-movement *Intermezzo* to remain in the memory, and a smoothly rich *Adagio*, before the Widorian finale. His *Cadence* provides a lightweight but by no means trivial encore. What one remembers most of all from this concert is the magnificent sonority of the organ, beautifully captured within its natural ambience, and that in itself shows how well composers and performer have combined their talents.

Bream, Julian (guitar)

Julian Bream Edition, Vol. 14: *'Dedication'*: BENNETT: *5 Impromptus.* WALTON: *5 Bagatelles.*
MAXWELL DAVIES: *Hill runes.* HENZE: *Royal winter music.*
(M) *** RCA 09026 61597-2 [id.].

Julian Bream recorded these four (out of many) works, of which he is a dedicatee, in 1981 and 1982. For most listeners the engaging Walton *Bagatelles* will prove the most rewarding music, although Henze's extensive atonal suite of miniature portrayals of Shakespearean characters (some 31 minutes overall) is texturally highly imaginative. Maxwell Davies's *Hill runes* are often hauntingly atmospheric, and the Bennett *Impromptus* ingenious in construction. The recording is most real, and this makes another welcome addition to the Julian Bream Edition.

Sonatas: Antonio JOSE: *Sonata* (ed. Bream). PAGANINI: *Grand sonata, Op. 9* (ed. Bream).
CASTELNUOVO-TEDESCO: *Sonata (Omaggio a Boccherini), Op. 77.*
*** EMI Dig. CDC5 55362-2 [id.].

In his continuing series of digital recordings for EMI, Julian Bream here offers three major sonatas. The most striking movement of the work by Antonio José is the vibrant finale, but the pensive *Pavana triste* is also quite haunting. Bream comments: 'You can tell José's sonata was written by someone who played the piano, not the guitar,' but, as edited here, the result is totally convincing. Paganini's *Grand Sonata* was written as an unequal duo with violin, but Bream has effectively incorporated the relatively flimsy violin part into the guitar texture. It is an amiable work with a delicate second-movement *Romance* in siciliano style and a set of variations on an agreeably innocent theme for its finale, which demands and receives considerable unostentatious bravura. Castelnuovo-Tedesco's *Sonata* has bright outer movements framing another siciliano slow movement (*dolce malinconico*) and an elegant *grazioso* Minuet. The performances could hardly be more persuasive, subtle in nuance and colour. The recording, too, is naturally present without being over-projected.

Brüggen, Frans (recorder)
'The Frans Brüggen Edition'

Complete Frans Brüggen Edition
(M) *** Teldec/Warner 4509 97475-2 (12) [id.].

Volume 1: TELEMANN (with Anner Bylsma, Gustav Leonhardt): *Essercizii musici: Sonata in C, TWV 41:C5; in D min, TWV 41:d4. Fantasias: in C, TWV 40:2; in D min., TWV 40:4; in F, TWV 40:8; in G min., TWV 40:9; in A min., TWV 40:11; in B flat, TWV 40:12. Der getreue Music-Meister: Canonic sonata in B flat, TWV 41:B3; Sonatas in C, TWV 41:C2; in F, TWV 41:F2; in F min., TWV 41:f1* (4509 93688-2).

Volume 2: *Italian recorder sonatas* (with Anner Bylsma, Gustav Leonhardt): CORELLI: *Sonatas: in F, Op. 5/4; La Follia (Variations in G min.), Op. 5/12.* BARSANTI: *Sonata in C.* VERACINI: *Sonatas in G; in A min.* (1716). BIGAGLIA: *Sonata in A min.* CHEDEVILLE: *Sonata in G min., Op. 13/6.* MARCELLO: *Sonata in D min., Op. 2/11* (4509 93669-2).

Volume 3: *English ensemble music* (with Kees Boeke, Walter van Hauwe, Anner Bylsma, Gustav Leonhardt, Brüggen Consort): HOLBORNE: *Dances and airs.* TAVERNER: *In nomine.* TYE: *In nomine (Crye).* BYRD: *In nomine; The leaves be green.* Thomas SIMPSON: *Bonny sweet Robin.* MORLEY: *La Girandola; Il Lamento; La Caccia.* JEFFREYS: *Fantasia.* PARCHAM: *Solo in G.* Robert CARR: *Divisions upon an Italian ground.* William BABELL: *Concerto in D.* PEPUSCH: *Sonata in F.* PURCELL: *Chaconne in F* (4509 97465-2).

Volume 4: *Early baroque recorder music* (with Kees Boeke, Walter van Hauwe, Anner Bylsma, Wouter Möller, Bob van Asperen, Gustav Leonhardt): Jacob VAN EYCK: *Batali; Doen Daphne d'over schoonne Maeght; Pavane Lachryme; Engels Nachtegaeltje.* FRESCOBALDI: *Canzon: La Bernadina.* Giovani Paolo CIMA: *Sonatas in D & G.* Giovanni Battista RICCIO: *Canzon in A; Canzon in A (La Rosignola).* SCHEIDT: *Paduan a 4 in D.* ANON.: *Sonata in G* (4509 97566-2).

Volume 5: *Late baroque recorder music* (with Jeanette van Wingerden, Kees Boeke, Walter van Hauwe, Franz Vester, Joost Tromp, Brian Pollard, Anner Bylsma, Wouter Möller, Gustav Leonhardt, Bob van Asperen): TELEMANN: *Quartet in D min., TWV 43:d1.* FASCH: *Quartet in G.* LOEILLET: *Quintet in B min.* QUANTZ: *Trio sonata in C.* Alessandro SCARLATTI: *Sonata in F.* Johann MATTHESON: *Sonata No. 4 in G min.* (4509 97467-2).

Volume 6: *French recorder suites* (with Kees Boeke, Nikolaus Harnoncourt, Anner Bylsma, Gustav Leonhardt): Charles DIEUPART: *Suites in G min. & A.* HOTTETERRE: *Suite No. 1* (4509 97468-2).

Volume 7: *French recorder sonatas* (with Kees Boeke, Walter van Hauwe, Anner Bylsma, Gustav Leonhardt): Philibert DE LAVIGNE: *Sonata in C (La Barssan).* BOISMORTIER: *Sonata in F.* PHILIDOR: *Sonata in D min.* Louis-Antoine DORNEL: *Sonata (a 3 Dessus) in B flat.* François COUPERIN: *Le rossignol-en-amour* (4509 97469-2).

Volume 8: VIVALDI: *Chamber concertos* (with Jürg Schaefleit, Otto Fleischmann, Alice Harnoncourt, Walter Pfeiffer, Nikolaus Harnoncourt, Gustav Leonhardt): *in C, RV 87; in D, RV 92 & RV 94; in G min., RV 105; in A min., RV 108; in C min., RV 441; in F, RV 442* (4509 97470-2).

Volume 9: HANDEL: *Recorder sonatas* (with Alice Harnoncourt, Anner Bylsma, Nikolaus Harnoncourt, Gustav Leonhardt, Herbert Tachezi): *in G min., HWV 360; in A min., HWV 362; in C, HWV 365; in F, HWV 369, Op. 1/2, 4, 7 & 11; in F, HWV 389, Op. 2/4. Fitzwilliam sonatas Nos. 1 in B flat, HWV 377; 3 in D min., HWV 367a* (4509 97471-2).

Volume 10: TELEMANN: *Concertos and orchestral music* (with VCM, Harnoncourt): *Concertos: in C; à 6 in F; Suite (Overture) in A min., TWV 55:a2* (4509 97472-2).

Volume 11: J. S. BACH: *Chamber and orchestral music* (with Jeanette van Wingerden, Leopold Stastny, Marie Leonhardt, Nikolaus Harnoncourt, Gustav Leonhardt, Herbert Tachezi): *Concertos: in A min., BWV 1044; in F, BWV 1057; Sonata concerto from Cantata No. 182; Sonatina from Cantata No. 106; Trio sonata in G, BWV 1039* (4509 97473-2).

Volume 12: *Recorder sonatas and concertos* (with Frans Vester, Alice Harnoncourt, Nikolaus Harnoncourt, Anner Bylsma, Gustav Leonhardt, Herbert Tachezi, VCM; Amsterdam CO): LOEILLET: *Sonata in C min.; Sonata in G.* SAMMARTINI: *Concerto in F.* HANDEL: *Trio sonata in B min.* NAUDOT: *Concerto in G.* TELEMANN: *Double concerto in E min.* (4509 97474-2).

Frans Brüggen is perhaps the greatest master of the recorder of the post-war era. In his hands phrases are turned with the utmost sophistication, intonation is unbelievably accurate and matters of style exact. There is spontaneity too and, with such superb musicianship and the high standard of recording we have come to expect from the Teldec Das Alte Werk series, these reissues in Brüggen's own special edition can almost all be recommended without reservation. He is equally at home in early or late baroque music. Throughout the collection, Frans Brüggen and his estimable colleagues demonstrate various period instruments; Anner Bylsma, Gustav Leonhardt and Bob van Asperen are present to provide a distinguished continuo, while Harnoncourt and the Vienna Concentus Musicus and Schröder's Amsterdam Chamber Orchestra are available for authentic concerto accompaniments.

Volume 1 is a single-disc anthology of Telemann's chamber music. Brüggen plays with his usual mastery and, as one would expect from Gustav Leonhardt's ensemble, the performances have polish and authority, and they are excellently recorded.

Volume 2 with its collection of Italian recorder sonatas is surely a perfect sampler for the whole edition, for it gives the opportunity for this king of recorder players to demonstrate his expertise and musicianship to maximum effect, admirably partnered by Anner Bylsma and Gustav Leonhardt. Perhaps the Corelli *Variations* need the violin to be fully in character, though the recorder version is authentic and aurally most engaging. Corelli puts the famous 'Follia' melody through all possible hoops and Brüggen obliges with nimble virtuosity. Alongside the other work by Corelli (written with the violin in mind) is the fine sonata of Marcello with its memorable slow movement. The Veracini works are also primarily for violin, though the recorder is an optional alternative for the *G major Sonata*. All this music is played with exemplary skill, and no recorder enthusiast will want to be without this splendid example of Brüggen's art; even if some of the music by the minor composers has limited appeal, there is plenty to stimulate te ear in this 73-minute programme, which is recorded with remarkable realism and immaculately transferred to CD.

The collection of English ensemble music which constitutes Volume 3 is particularly diverting, opening with Holborne's *Suite of dances and airs* which alternates recorder and viols. The several *In nomines* are all differently scored and are very different in character too, while the folksong arrangements by Byrd and Simpson are touching. The *Solo* (Suite) by Andrew Parcham, the *Divisions* of Robert Carr and Pepusch's *Sonata* are all engaging and are played with characteristic skill and musicianship so that only occasionally does the ear detect the limitations of early instruments.

Volume 4 introduces works by Jacob Van Eyck, which are unaccompanied but are aurally titillating, particularly the primitive *Batali* with its 'bugle' calls, while the florid upper tessitura of *Engels Nachtegaeltje* really takes wing. The Frescobaldi *Canzon* and the works by Cima and Riccio use an organ and cello continuo, and the delightful *La Rosignola* is for recorder trio with cello and harpsichord.

Later baroque chamber music is represented on Volume 5, with works by Alessandro Scarlatti, Telemann and Johann Mattheson standing out, while Volume 6 brings entertainingly elegant and tuneful *Suites* by Dieupart (a French-born musician who taught in London around 1700 and whose harpsichord music influenced Bach) and Hotteterre (known as Le Romain). These suites are very much cast in the style favoured by Telemann, with an *Overture* and a collection of dances. Of these Johann Mattheson (whose own sonata is included in Volume 5), described the allemande as 'a serious and elaborately worked out piece, whose broken harmonies bear the imprint of a contented or satisfied mind that delights in order and calm', while the *courante* suggests 'Sweet hope', the *sarabande* 'immoderate ambition' and the *gavotte* 'triumphant joy'.

Volume 7 concentrates on French recorder sonatas and brings another vivid nightingale evocation – *Le rossignol-en-amour*, by François Couperin.

Volumes 8–10 are composer collections of music by Vivaldi, Handel and more Telemann, all discussed in detail under their composer entries, above. Volume 11, offering a Bach collection, is the only relative disappointment. Two of the major works here are transcribed, and BWV 1044 comes off more effectively than BWV 1057. Best is the *Trio sonata in G*, BWV 1039, although the two cantata excerpts are pleasing.

A final excellent sampler is provided by the collection of *Recorder sonatas* and *concertos* which makes up Volume 12, featuring a chamber ensemble and both the Amsterdam Chamber Orchestra and the Vienna Concentus Musicus. The Telemann *Double concerto in E minor for recorder and flute* is a particularly fine one, and the dulcet duet in the slow movement begins rather like Handel's *Where'er you walk*. The Sammartini *Concerto* has a unexpectedly solemn *Siciliano* for its slow movement. The Handel *Trio sonata* is a splendid work, and the two Loeillet *Sonatas* are light and airy and full of charm, while even the less striking Naudot piece emerges as music of character. All these performances are outstandingly successful.

The recordings were nearly all made during the 1960s, with a few dating from the following decade, and they are of the highest quality, as are the vivid CD transfers. Documentation is very good, and all the discs are available separately. You could start almost anywhere – and you will surely come back for more. The complete set offers a small saving on the cost of the dozen individual CDs.

Chorzempa, Daniel (organ of the Cadets' Chapel, West Point, New Jersey, USA)

WAGNER (arr. Lemare): *Tannhäuser: Pilgrims' Chorus. Die Walküre: Ride of the Valkyries. Die Meistersinger: Overture.* RHEINBERGER: *Sonata No. 11 in D min., Op. 148: Cantilena.* GIGOUT: *Grand chœur dialogué.* VIERNE: *Pièces en style libre Nos. 14, Scherzetto; 19, Berceuse.* BOELLMAN: *Suite gothique.*
(M) *(*) Ph. Dig. 438 309-2 [id.].

The West Point instrument is a spectacularly large one with 18,000 pipes comprising 286 ranks. Perhaps understandably, Daniel Chorzempa turns to Wagner transcriptions to show its resources of colour and its wide range of dynamic. However, his account of the *Ride of the Valkyries* is rhythmically awkward and unexciting, and *Die Meistersinger overture* is much too spacious, with the music nearly coming to a halt in the middle section (it takes 13 minutes, far longer than an average orchestral performance. Chorzempa is clearly at home in the simplistic but effective Boëllmann *Suite gothique*, but Gigout's *Grand chœur dialogué* is too heavy and deliberate. The highlights of the programme are the two Vierne *Pièces en style libre*, well played and nicely contrasted. The sound is impressively clear and spacious.

Composers at the piano

Famous composers playing their own works on the Welte Mignon piano (1905–6): Richard STRAUSS: *Salome: Salome's dance. Feuersnot: Love scene. Rêverie, Op. 9/4; Ein Heldenleben: Liebesszene.* SAINT-SAENS: *Samson et Dalila: Dance of the Priestesses of Dagon; Delilah's air.* D'ALBERT: *Tiefland: Pedro's arrival at the Mill; Nuri's song; Spanish dancing song.* HUMPERDINCK: *Hänsel und Gretel: Pantomime.* KIENZL: *Der Evangeligmann: Selig sind, die Verflogung leiden.* LEONCAVALLO: *Pagliacci: Intermezzo. Romance in A min.* GRIEG: *Pictures from life in the country: The bridal procession passes, Op. 19/2.* MAHLER: *Ich ging mit Lust durch einen grünen Wald. Lieder eines fahrenden Gesellen; Symphony No. 4: 4th movement.*
(M) ** Teldec/Warner 4509 95354-2 [id.].

We are convinced that the Welte Mignon system, whereby the player cuts a piano roll direct from the keyboard, can be uncannily accurate, and the best example of this early method of recording lies with Rachmaninov's recordings of his own repertoire. But here the results, if fascinating, are also very disappointing. With one exception, none of these composers seems able to project his own music and usually demonstrates clumsy technique. The exception is Edvard Grieg, and his fresh presentation of a simple country scene has remarkable presence and charm. The sound itself is very good, as the Welte Mignon playbacks were recorded in excellent stereo in 1969/70.

Cziffra, György (piano)

Cziffra Edition, Volume 1: LISZT: *Piano sonata in B min.; Concert paraphrase of Mendelsssohn's Wedding march from A Midsummer Night's Dream; Concert study No. 1: Waldesrauschen. Harmonies poétiques et religieuses: Funérailles. Etudes d'éxécution transcendante d'après Paganini: La Campanella; La Chasse*
(M) *(**) EMI CDM5 65250-2 [id.].

Cziffra plays with extraordinary virtuosity and temperament, but he can also be exasperatingly wilful and self-aware. There are moments of exquisite poetry but also a feeling of calculation, alternating with wild bursts of bravura. The two *Paganini studies* show him at his most spontaneously volatile. The Paris studio recordings, made over a period between 1958 and 1975, are variable, and often unflatteringly hard.

Cziffra Edition, Volume 4: DAQUIN: *Le coucou; L'hirondelle.* LULLY: *Gavotte & Rondeau.* RAMEAU: *Le rappel des oiseaux; Tambourin; L'Egyptien; La Poule; Dardanus: Rigaudon.* F. COUPERIN: *Les Papillons; Les Moissonneurs; Les Folies françaises ou les Dominos; Les Barricades mystérieuses; L'Anguille; La Bandoline; Les petits moulins à vent; Le Tic-toc ou les maillotins.* RAVEL: *Le tombeau de Couperin: Toccata. Sonatine; Jeux d'eau.*
(M) **(*) EMI CDM5 65253-2 [id.].

Cziffra liked to play seventeenth- and eighteenth-century keyboard music, and his carefully developed and very individual articulation – crisp, bold and strong (but never ugly) – bears in mind the fact that this was music designed for a harpsichord; yet there is no possible doubt that his piano uses hammers on its strings. Lully's *Gavotte and Rondo* and Rameau's *Tambourin* are most strongly characterized and *L'Egyptien* is quite as immediate as *La Poule*, which clucks very positively indeed. It is, however, the Couperin group which is the most successful of all, with the divisions of *Les Folies françaises ou les Dominos* full of charm and character, and *Les Moissonneurs* very rhythmic and positive. *L'Anguille* is delightful and in *Les petits moulins à vent* one can sense the gusting of the wind. *Le Tic-toc ou les maillotins* is hardly less engaging. The Ravel performances are of the very highest calibre, showing profound delicacy of feeling. The account of the *Sonata* is quite incandescent, abounding in character and colour; and *Jeux d'eau* glitters iridescently and is technically a *tour de force*. Recordings are forwardly balanced but reasonably faithful, again using the Paris Salle Wagram, mostly in 1980/81, but with the Ravel dating from over a decade earlier. It is important not to reproduce the earlier music too loudly.

Cziffra Edition, Volume 5: MOZART: *Piano sonata No. 8 in A min., K.310.* BEETHOVEN: *Piano sonata No. 22 in F, Op. 54.* SCHUMANN: *Etudes symphoniques, Op. 13; Novelette in F sharp min., Op. 21.*
(M) **(*) EMI mono/stereo CDM5 65254-2 [id.].

In Mozart, Cziffra assumes a much less flamboyant keyboard personality. His playing is alive, precisely articulated and, with its own kind of reserve, quite stylish. The thoughtful presentation of the *Andante cantabile* is unashamedly expressive in pianistic terms and most engagingly so, and he varies the keyboard colour with subtle shadings. The finale ripples along with the lightest touch, yet with never a suspicion of Dresden figurines, while the ear again notes the changes of colour between left and right hand, achieved with the finest sensibility. Cziffra's choice of a Beethoven sonata is not an obvious one and his reading is strong and penetrating, the varying moods of the *Tempo di Minuet* spontaneously compelling, while the *Allegretto* again shows his great variety of touch throughout its unforceful *moto perpetuo*. The simplicity of presentation here in some ways reminds one of Kempff. The Schumann *Etudes symphoniques* open gravely, then the first variation sets off with an impulse which is never to flag throughout. This is playing of ready virtuosity and considerable variety from a keyboard lion whose impulsiveness bursts out in the bravura studies but which can be reined back poetically in an instant and hold the listener by its very poise. The finale with its strong chordal flourishes combines spontaneous feeling with fire. The *Novelette* is even more chimerical in its wide-ranging mood and dynamic. The recordings were made in the Salle Wagram, Paris, between 1957 (the Mozart is mono, and acoustically rather dead, although otherwise faithful) and 1968, and the sound is satisfactory; only in the bolder Schumann studies (1960) does the upper dynamic level harden.

Cziffra Edition, Volume 6: Encores and Arrangements: BACH/BUSONI: *Chorales: Wachet auf, BWV 645; In dir ist Freude, BWV 615; Erschienen ist der herrliche Tag, BWV 629.* Domenico SCARLATTI: *Sonatas: in C, Kk 159; in A, Kk 113; in D, Kk 96.* François COUPERIN: *Les Moissonneurs.* LULLY: *Gavotte in D min.* RAMEAU: *Dardanus: Rigaudon.* MOZART: *Sonata, K.331: Alla turca.* MENDELSSOHN: *A Midsummer Night's Dream: Scherzo.* BIZET: *L'Arlésienne: Minuet* (both arr. Rachmaninov). FRANCK: *Prélude, choral et fugue.* DEBUSSY: *Le plus que lente.* DOHNANYI: *Capriccio, Op. 28.* KHACHATURIAN: *Gayaneh: Sabre dance* (arr. Cziffra).
(M) *** EMI CDM5 65255-2 [id.].

If you want a single disc to remember the sheer individuality and character of Cziffa's playing – and indeed his fabulous digital dexterity – this collection of encores and transcriptions is the one to go for. The opening Bach/Busoni arrangements are most impressive. *Wachet auf* is gentle yet very clear and positive, and the staccato articulation in the third (*Erschienen ist der herrliche Tag*), against which the chorale is purposefully projected, brings masterly pianism, as does the gracefully light presentation of the first of the three Scarlatti *Sonatas* (Kk 159) while the second (Kk 113) brings some astonishing runs. The Couperin, Lully and Rameau encores are also included in Volume 4, but here they have even more charm, while the famous Mozart *Alla turca* is bracingly clear, almost suggesting a fortepiano. Like the elaborate paraphrase of Bizet's engaging *Minuet* from *L'Arlésienne*, Rachmaninov's famous arrangement of the Mendelssohn *Scherzo* from *A Midsummer Night's Dream* is just a little mannered, and the César Franck *Prélude, chorale and fugue* is very romantic indeed, but Debussy's *La plus que lente* is appealingly rhapsodic. The Dohnányi *Capriccio* brings almost unbelievable, quicksilver brilliance, and the exhilarating *Sabre dance* is even more breathtaking in its glittering profusion of notes. The recordings cover two decades of Cziffra's performing career, the earliest in 1956, the last in 1975, and generally the sound is very believable and present.

Duo Reine Elisabeth (Wolfgang Manz and Rolf Plagge)

Russian music for two pianos: STRAVINSKY: *Petrushka.* SCRIABIN: *Romance in A min.*
SHOSTAKOVICH: *Concertino, Op. 94.* RACHMANINOV: *6 Morceaux, Op. 11.*
(BB) *** Discover Dig. DICD 920150 [id.].

Petrushka has plenty of colour and a surprising degree of charm; the finale swings along infectiously.
The melodically lavish, early Scriabin *Romance* then contrasts aptly with the wittily audacious
Shostakovich *Concertino*, which has the temerity to open with an echo of the slow movement of
Beethoven's *G major Piano concerto*. The six Rachmaninov *Morceaux* are strongly and colourfully
characterized, and their diversity gives much pleasure. In short, Wolfgang Manz and Rolf Plagge
create an impressive artistic symbiosis, playing with spontaneity as well as commanding impressive
technical resource. Very good recording too – not too reverberant. A bargain.

Feinberg, Alan (piano)

'The American virtuoso': MACDOWELL: *Concert étude; Hexentanx.* FAURE (arr. Grainger): *Après un
rêve; Nell.* GOTTSCHALK: *Manchega; The Union; Home sweet home; Souvenir de Porto Rico.* BEACH:
Scottish legend; Tyrolean valse-fantaisie; Fireflies; A Hermit thrush at eve. DOWLAND (arr. Grainger):
Now, o now, I needs must part. CARRENO: *Corbeille de fleurs.* GRAINGER: *Irish tune from County
Derry.* GERSHWIN: *The Man I love* (arr. Grainger); *Clap yo' hands* (trans. Wodehouse).
**(*) Argo Dig. 436 121-2 [id.].

Feinberg's recital is most notable for the delightful tone-pictures of Amy Beach: *Scottish legend*,
Fireflies and *A Hermit thrush at eve* are all charmingly evocative, without being cosy. The Gottschalk
pieces have dash and leaven the programme, but more Mrs Beach would have been welcome. The
Grainger arrangements, too, are enticing. But perhaps overall this well-recorded 74-minute recital
needed a bit of ballast; so much of this is very lightweight.

Freeman-Attwood, Jonathan (trumpet), Iain Simcock (organ)

Sonatas for trumpet and organ: ALBINONI: *Sonatas in A, Op. 1/3 & Op. 6/11; in C.* FRESCOBALDI:
Canzona seconda detta la Bernardina; Canzona terza detta la Lucchesina. FASCH: *Concerto in D for
clarino.* MUFFAT: *Suite in F from Indissolubilis Amicitia.* VIVIANI: *Sonata No. 1 in C.* TELEMANN:
Concerto in C min. MOURET: *Symphonies de Fanfares.*
*** Proudsound Dig. PROUCD 135 [id.].

The combination of trumpet and organ has recently become fashionable as a way of playing baroque
music, and the present collection is justified by the sheer excellence of the trumpet playing and the
appealing musicianship of Jonathan Freeman-Attwood, who essays a wide dynamic and expressive
range. He is tastefully accompanied on the organ of Bromley Parish Church by Iain Simcock. The
recording, too, is first class, well balanced and pleasingly set back so that the trumpet has a gleaming
presence without overwhelming the listener. Virtually the entire programme consists of arrangements
(and how effective are the two Frescobaldi *Canzonas*). One piece actually conceived for trumpet with
'organo o gravicembalo' is the five-movement *Sonata* of Viviani, a pleasingly simple work, while in
the third movement (*Les Gendarmes*) from Muffat's engaging suite from *Indissolubilis Amicitia*, the
trumpeter is required to stamp his foot vehemently to imitate pistol-shots. All the music here is
agreeable, but this is strictly a record to be dipped into rather than played throughout: 66 minutes of
trumpet and organ can be too much of a good thing.

Green, Gareth (organ of Chesterfield Parish Church)

English organ music: LANG: *Tuba tune, Op. 15.* HOWELLS: *3 Psalm preludes, Op. 32.* ELGAR: *Sonata
No. 1, Op. 28.* VAUGHAN WILLIAMS: *Rhosymedre (Hymn prelude).* WHITLOCK: *Hymn Preludes: on
Darwell's 148th; on Song 13.* COCKER: *Tuba tune.*
(BB) *(*) Naxos Dig. 8.550582 [id.].

The organ as recorded here has no clarity of profile, and even the two characterful *Tuba tunes* fail to
make their full effect. The sound in the *Hymn* and *Psalm Preludes* is washy and indistinct. Gareth
Green obviously plays the early Elgar *Sonata* very well but it makes an impact only in its more

powerful moments, and it is difficult to find a volume level which reveals the unfocused, quieter detail while not having the climaxes too loud.

Hall, Nicola (guitar)

'The art of the guitar': WALTON: 5 Bagatelles. BACH: (Unaccompanied) Violin sonata No. 2 in A min., BWV 1003 (arr. Hall). TORROBA: Sonatina. RODRIGO: Invocación y danza (Hommage à Manuel de Falla). MERTZ: Hungarian fantasy, Op. 65/1.
**(*) Decca Dig. 440 678-2 [id.].

Nicola Hall, a pupil of John Williams, gives an astonishing display of her virtually flawless technique in a well-chosen programme in which the highlight is the set of Five Bagatelles of Walton, played with warmth, some subtlety and considerable panache. She is disappointing in her Bach transcription, however, far too literal and studied: the third-movement Andante plods along heavily. But the Torroba Sonatina sparkles with Spanish sunshine and the opening of the Rodrigo Invocación is quite haunting. The Mertz Hungarian fantasia, not in itself an especially inspired piece, brings a chance for glittering virtuosity and a very exciting coda. The recording has a vivid yet natural presence and enough – but not too much – resonance, so that the guitar sounds real and life-sized.

Hamelin, Marc-André (piano)

'Live at Wigmore Hall': BEETHOVEN (arr. Alkan): Piano concerto No. 3: first movt. CHOPIN (arr. Balakirev): Piano concerto No. 1: Romanza. ALKAN: Trois grandes études. BUSONI: Sonatina No. 6 (Chamber Fantasy on Carmen). MEDTNER: Danza festiva, Op. 38, No. 3.
⊛ *** Hyp. Dig. CDA 66765.

This is among the most spectacular piano issues of the decade. It captures live one of the programmes given in June 1994 at Wigmore Hall by the French-Canadian pianist, Marc-André Hamelin, in a series called 'Virtuoso Romantics'. Bizarre as the mixture is, it works magnificently, thanks not only to Hamelin's breathtaking virtuosity, finger-perfect, but to his magnetism. As well as the Three Grandes Etudes of Alkan, he plays Alkan's arrangement of the first movement of Beethoven's Third Piano concerto. Thanks to his sharp clarity, one marvels afresh at the purposefulness of the writing, and he revels in Alkan's manic six-minute cadenza, which in dotty inspiration even quotes the finale of Beethoven's Fifth Symphony. Balakirev's arrangement of the Romanza from Chopin's First Piano concerto then offers yearning poetry, with two flamboyant display-pieces as encores: Busoni's Carmen fantasy and Medtner's Danza festiva.

Haskil, Clara (piano)

Clara Haskil: The Legacy: Volume 1: Chamber music (with Arthur Grumiaux)

BEETHOVEN: Violin sonatas Nos. 1–10. MOZART: Violin sonatas Nos. 18; 21; 24; 26; 32; 34.
(M) (***) Ph. mono 442 625-2 (5) [id.].

BEETHOVEN: Violin sonatas Nos. 1 in D; 2 in A; 3 in E flat, Op. 12/1–3; 4 in A min., Op. 23.
(M) (***) Ph. mono 442 626-2.

Violin sonatas Nos. 5 in F (Spring), Op. 24; 6 in A, Op. 30/1; 7 in C min., Op. 30/2.
(M) (***) Ph. mono 442 627-2.

Violin sonatas Nos. 8 in G, Op. 30/3; 9 in A (Kreutzer), Op. 47; 10 in G, Op. 96.
(M) (***) Ph. mono 442 628-2.

MOZART: Violin sonatas in C, K.301; E min., K.304; F, K.376; B flat, K.378.
(M) (***) Ph. mono 442 629-2.

Violin sonatas in B flat, K.454; A, K.526.
(M) (***) Ph. mono 442 630-2.

Volume 3: Solo piano music
BEETHOVEN: Sonatas Nos. 17 in D min. (Tempest), Op. 31/2; 18 in E flat Op. 31/3 (two versions).
MOZART: Sonata in C, K.330; 9 Variations on a minuet by Jean-Pierre Duport, K.573. RAVEL: Sonatine. Domenico SCARLATTI: Sonatas in E flat, Kk.193; B min., Kk.87; F min., Kk.386. SCHUBERT:

Sonata No. 21 in B flat, D.960. SCHUMANN: *Abegg variations, Op. 1; Bunte Blätter, Op. 99;*
Kinderszenen, Op. 15; Waldszenen, Op. 82.
(M) **(*) Ph. mono/stereo 442 635-2 (3) [id.].

Clara Haskil is a much-venerated pianist, as the very appearance of this 12-CD set shows. Hailed by
the German critic, Joachim Kaiser, in his *Grosse Pianisten in unserer Zeit* as 'almost a saint of the
piano', she has long enjoyed cult status and an aura of reverence that may have put some collectors
off. This set affords an admirable opportunity for 'putting the record straight'; each of the three
volumes is available separately but single discs from the collection are not. The first volume (five
CDs) is devoted to the Beethoven and Mozart sonatas with her long-standing partner, Arthur
Grumiaux; the second (four CDs) is devoted to her various concerto recordings, including two of the
Mozart *D minor,* K.466, one with the Wiener Symfoniker and Paul Sacher in mono (1954), the
second with the Lamoureux Orchestra and Markevitch (1960); the third volume (three CDs) collects
her solo repertoire, including two different accounts of the Beethoven sonatas (1955 and 1960).

The earliest recordings, the three Scarlatti sonatas, Ravel's *Sonatine* and the Schumann *Abegg*
variations and the *Piano concerto in A minor* (with Willem van Otterloo conducting the Hague
Orchestra) come from 1951, and the last, the Mozart *Piano concertos in D minor,* K.466, and *C minor,*
K.491, and the Beethoven *C minor concerto,* from 1960, the year of her death. Although it is
doubtless a truism, her playing is more private than public; hers is a reflective, inward-looking
sensibility with nothing of the virtuoso or showman. Her musical dedication is total. Her Schumann
is particularly searching and penetrating. She is, to quote one London critic (Hilary Finch in *The*
Times), 'one of those rare artists who seem to be able to reinhabit the dreamlike consciouness of a
child still undivided from the sentient world of plant and animal life'. And there is an innocence
about her Mozart which makes it wonderfully fresh and immediate.

She had begun life as a mathematical prodigy, and she took up the violin before going on to make
the piano her instrument. Perhaps part of the success of her partnership with Arthur Grumiaux in the
cycle of Beethoven and Mozart sonatas may spring from the understanding she gained of the violin as
well as the experience of her earlier partnerships with Enescu, Szigeti and Francescatti. Both the
Mozart and Beethoven sonatas were reissued on bargain label in LP format, and subsequently on
CD. (The Beethoven appeared in a three-CD set, coupled exactly as it is here.) Philips are reticent in
disclosing whether they are mono or stereo: they are in fact mono. Notwithstanding, the sound is
very pleasing indeed and the playing is beautifully natural yet innately aristocratic.

The solo recordings are equally self-recommending and her Schumann in particular is of exceptional insight. The set is accompanied by very perceptive notes by Max Harrison.

Horowitz, Vladimir (piano)

'The Private Collection': BACH: *Toccata and fugue in C min., BWV 911.* CHOPIN: *Fantaisie in F min.,*
Op. 49; Polonaise in C sharp min., Op. 26/1; Mazurka in B min., Op. 30/2. CLEMENTI: *Sonatas: Op.*
36/1; Op. 24/2: Allegro con brio; Op. 34/1: Un poco andante. MENDELSSOHN: *Song without words in B*
flat, Op. 67/3. LISZT: *Consolations Nos. 4 & 5.* RACHMANINOV: *Etude-tableau in C min., Op. 39/7.*
(***) RCA mono 09026 62643-2 [id.].

This is the first of two discs that emanate from Carnegie Hall concerts Horowitz gave during 1945–50
and which were recorded for his own use and stored in his New York home. Not long before his
death he gave the collection to Yale University Library. His friend and producer, Thomas Frost,
discovered among them some two hours of repertoire that Horowitz had never committed to disc,
and they make their appearance now. The playing is in every way quite remarkable, whether it is the
energy generated in the Clementi or the feather-like delicacy the great pianist can harness when he so
desires. The Rachmaninov is tremendously intense and imbued with a hypnotic atmosphere that is
quite individual. Never mind the surface imperfections inevitable in acetates, this playing makes one
realize why people still speak of these concerts with awe.

Hunt, Donald (organ of Worcester Cathedral)

English organ music 2: ELGAR: *Sonata No. 2, Op. 87a; Cantique, Op. 3.* PARRY: *Choral fantasia on an*
old English tune. HOWELLS: *Siciliano for a High Ceremony.* WHITLOCK: *Plymouth suite.* VAUGHAN
WILLIAMS: *3 Preludes on Welsh hymn tunes.* SUMSION: *Intermezzo; Ceremonial march.*
(BB) * Naxos Dig. 8.550773 [id.].

The organ loft of Worcester Cathedral would seem in principle to be the right place to record Elgar, but the Naxos engineers seem to have been unable to control the resonance and everything here is unattractively diffuse in outline. The amiable miniatures which make up the Whitlock *Plymouth suite* come off best, notably the *Chanty*, but the Howells and Vaughan Williams pieces are very misty. Donald Hunt's account of the Elgar *Sonata* is flabby and the memorable tune with its associations with the *Severn suite* lacks any kind of swinging exuberance.

John, Keith (organ)

Organ of St Mary's, Woodford: *'Toccata!':* BACH/BUSONI: *Partita No. 2 in D min., BWV 1004: Chaconne* (trans. K. John). BACH/RACHMANINOV: *Partita No. 3 in E, BWV 1006: suite* (trans. K. John). GUILLOU: *Sinfonietta.* HEILLER: *Tanz-Toccata.*
(M) *** Priory Dig. PRCD 002 [id.].

It was a most imaginative idea to use Busoni's arrangement of Bach's famous *D minor Partita for unaccompanied violin* as a basis for an organ transcription, and the result is like nothing you have ever heard before – especially when Keith John gets cracking on the pedals. The three excerpts from the *E major Partita* (as originally transcribed by Rachmaninov) are hardly less successful: how well the opening *Prelude* sounds on the organ, and one can forgive Keith John's affectionately mannered touch on the famous *Gavotte*. We then have a dramatic, almost bizarre change of mood and colour from Jean Guillou's 'neoclassical' (more 'neo' than 'classical') *Sinfonietta*. Even though it opens with a Bachian flourish, its colouring and atmosphere are highly exotic, the austere central *Allegretto* leading to a somewhat jazzy but naggingly insistent, partly contrapuntal and plangent *Gigue*. Heiller's *Tanz-Toccata*, with its complex rhythms and chimerical changes of time-signature, finally brings a positive link with Stravinsky's *Rite of spring* during the insistent motoric final pages. After his remarkable Bach performances, Keith John's kaleidoscopic registration here shows how adaptable and versatile is the modern (1972) organ at St Mary's, Woodford.

Kayath, Marcelo (guitar)

'Guitar classics from Latin America': PONCE: *Valse.* PIAZZOLA: *La muerte del angel.* BARRIOS: *Vals, Op. 8/3; Choro de saudade; Julia florida.* LAURO: *Vals venezolanos No. 2; El negrito; El marabino.* BROUWER: *Canción de cuna; Ojos brujos.* PERNAMBUCO: *Sons de carrilhões; Interrogando; Sono de maghia.* REIS: *Si ela perguntar.* VILLA-LOBOS: *5 Preludes.*
(B) *** Carlton Dig. PCD 2012 [id.].

Marcelo Kayath's inspirational accounts of the Villa-Lobos *Preludes* can stand comparison with the finest performances on record. He plays everything here with consummate technical ease and the most appealing spontaneity. His rubato in the Barrios *Vals* is particularly effective, and he is a fine advocate too of the engaging Lauro pieces and the picaresque writing of João Pernambuco, a friend of Villa-Lobos. The recording, made in a warm but not too resonant acoustic, is first class.

Kocsis, Zoltán (piano)

'Children's corner': MOZART: *Piano sonata No. 15 in C, K.545.* BEETHOVEN: *Sonatinas in F & G.* SCHUMANN: *Kinderszenen, Op. 15.* DEBUSSY: *Children's corner.* BARTOK: *Microcosmos Nos. 58, 77, 94, 97, 100, 116, 120, 126, 129–132 & 137.*
(B) HM Dig. HMA 190 3006 [id.].

A well-planned and potentially attractive recital is spoiled here by Kocsis's propensity for fast tempi. He dashes off the first movement of Mozart's famous *C major Sonata* at the speed of a stage coach being pursued by highwaymen, and he is similarly unrelenting in his approach to the Beethoven *Sonatinas*. When the charming opening movement, *Von fremden Ländern und Menschen*, of Schumann's *Kinderszenen* is so lacking in affectionate poise, one's patience evaporates. Not recommended.

Kudo, Shigenori (flute), Rachel Talitman (harp)

BOIELDIEU: *Sonata.* RAVEL: *Pavane pour une infante défunte.* BIZET: *Carmen: Intermezzo.* FRANCAIX: *Cinque piccoli duetti.* DAMASE: *Sonata.*
(BB) ** Discovery Dig. DICD 920141 [id.].

This recital fails to get off to a good start. The harp is balanced forwardly and the resonant sound robs the ingenuous Boieldieu *Sonata* of freshness, while the famous Bizet *Intermezzo* sounds clumsy when the robust harp accompaniment outbalances the flute. However, things improve in the five *Piccoli duetti* of Jean Françaix, delightful *morceaux* of much individuality, and in Jean-Michel Damase's much more ambitious *Sonata*, which yet has comparable subtlety alongside its direct melodic appeal. These artists are thoroughly at home here, and even the recording sounds more effective.

Lawson, Peter and Alan MacLean (piano duet)

English music for piano duet: BERNERS: V*alses bourgeoises; Fantasie espagnole; 3 Morceaux.* Constant LAMBERT: *Overture* (ed. Lane); *3 Pièces nègres pour les touches blanches.* RAWSTHORNE: *The Creel.* WALTON: *Duets for children.* Philip LANE: *Badinages.*
*** Troy Dig. TROY 142 [id.].

We know the Troy label best as the purveyor of the music of George Lloyd, but here it turns to other English composers, and those in whom wit was a most important condiment. The collection centres on Lord Berners, who had a recurring twinkle in the eye and loved to parody; moreover his inspiration regularly casts a glance in the direction of Satie and Poulenc, as the *Trois morceaux* readily demonstrate. Both Walton and Constant Lambert were his friends, admired his individuality and came under his influence. Lambert's *Trois pièces nègres* have a Satiesque title, yet they are all the composer's own work: the *Siesta* is quite haunting and the catchy *Nocturne* brings sparkling Latin-American rhythmic connotations, far removed from Chopin. The four engaging Rawsthorne miniatures, inspired by Izaak Walton's *Compleat Angler*, fit equally well into the programme. The Walton *Duets for children* have a disarming simplicity and often a nursery rhythm bounce, *Hop scotch* is particularly delightful, and vignettes like *The silent lake* and *Ghosts* will surely communicate very directly to young performers. Walton's final *Galop* was arranged by Philip Lane, who also provides four of his own pieces to close the concert with a strongly Gallic atmosphere. Performances by Peter Lawson and Alan MacLean are strong on style yet also convey affection. They have panache, too, so necessary in this lighthearted repertoire if it is not to sound brittle. The result is very enjoyable. Excellent recording in a nicely resonant but not muddy acoustic.

'Liebestraüme'

'Liebestraüme' (Romantic piano music played by (i) Bolet; (ii) Ashkenazy; (iii) De Larrocha; (iv) Lupu): (i) LISZT: *Liebestraüme No. 3; Etude de concert No. 3 (Un sospiro).* (ii) RACHMANINOV: *Prelude in C sharp min., Op. 3/2.* CHOPIN: *Nocturne in F min., Op. 55/1; Etude in E (Tristesse), Op. 10/3.* BEETHOVEN: *Piano sonata No. 14 (Moonlight), Op. 27/2.* (iii) CHOPIN: *Prelude No. 15 in D flat (Raindrop).* SCHUBERT: *Impromptu in A flat, D.899/4.* SCHUMANN: *Romance, Op. 28/2.* (iv) BRAHMS: *Rhapsody in G min., Op. 79/2.*
(M) *** Decca 425 085-2 [id.].

Jorge Bolet's warmly romantic account of Liszt gives this specially assembled (63-minute) CD its title and is also the only true digital recording included in the programme. But the sound is generally excellent and the digital remastering, if producing a rather forward image, offers truthful quality throughout. The performances are distinguished and there is passionate contrast in Ashkenazy's Rachmaninov. Lupu's Brahms is rather less extrovert in feeling; generally, the recital has a nicely relaxed atmosphere.

Little, Tasmin (violin), Piers Lane (piano)

'Virtuoso violin': KREISLER: *Prelude and allegro in the style of Pugnani; Caprice viennoise.* BRAHMS: *Hungarian dance Nos. 1 & 5.* SHOSTAKOVICH: *The Gadfly: Romance.* DRIGO: *Valse bluette.* FIBICH: *Poème.* FALLA: *La vida breve: Spanish dance.* WIENIAWSKI: *Légende, Op. 17.* SARASATE: *Introduction and Tarantelle, Op. 43.* BLOCH: *Baal Sheem: Nigum.* DEBUSSY: *Beau soir.* RIMSKY-KORSAKOV: *Flight of the bumble bee* (both arr. Heifetz). DELIUS: *Hassan: Serenade* (arr. Tertis). KROLL: *Banjo and fiddle.* RAVEL: *Tzigane.*
(B) *** CfP Dig. CD-CFP 4675; *TC-CFP 4675* [id.].

A pretty dazzling display of violin fireworks from a brilliant young fiddler who conveys her delight in her own easy virtuosity The opening Kreisler pastiche, *Prelude and allegro*, is presented with real style, and later the *Caprice viennoise* has comparable panache and relaxed charm. The schmaltzy daintiness of Drigo's *Valse bluette* is followed by an unexaggerated but full-timbred warmth in Fibich's *Poème*. The gypsy temperament of the Falla and the ready sparkle of Sarasate's *Taranatella* and Kroll's *Banjo and fiddle* are offset by the lyrical appeal of the more atmospheric piece. The violin is very present – perhaps the microphones are a fraction too close, but the balance with the piano is satisfactory and there is not the exaggerated spotlight here which virtually ruins Perlman's comparable 1994 collection with Samuel Sanders called '*Bits and Pieces*' (EMI CDC7 54882-2), where immediately in the opening Corelli Op. 5 *La Folia* chaconne, as arranged by Kreisler, the violin-timbre is made to sound aggressive, even harsh.

Ma, Yo-Yo (cello), Lynn Chang, Ronan Lefkowitz (violins), Jeffrey Kahane, Gilbert Kalish (pianos)

IVES: *Trio for violin, clarinet and piano*. BERNSTEIN: *Clarinet sonata* (arr. Ma). KIRCHNER: *Triptych*. GERSHWIN: *3 Preludes* (arr. Heifetz/Ma).
*** Sony Dig. SK 53126 [id.].

An unexpectedly rewarding and beguiling mix which is more than the sum of its component parts. The whole 65-minute recital is just the thing for late-evening stimulation. The early Bernstein sonata transcription is full of that ready melodic and rhythmic appeal which makes the composer's concert music so individual, and the Gershwin encore, equally felicitously transcribed, is hardly less appealing. The meat of the programme is in the Kirchner *Triptych,* while jokesy Ives provides a *Trio* (quoting corny 'folk' tunes with relish), bringing the usual audacious 'remembering', this time picturing '*Sunday evening on the campus*', thus concluding the entertainment with much spirit and aplomb.

Malinkova Sisters (piano duo)

'*Memories of the Bolshoi*': TCHAIKOVSKY: *Nutcracker suite*. PROKOFIEV: *Romeo and Juliet: 5 Pieces*. KHACHATURIAN: *Spartacus: suite*.
** Koch Dig. 3-7172-2 [id.].

Although they play brilliantly and very musically, and are most realistically recorded, only in the Prokofiev do the Malinkova sisters convince us that this is music which is equally valid in pianistic terms. There is plenty of energy and colour in the other works, but the *Nutcracker suite* sounds like merely an orchestral imitation and Khachaturian's *Spartacus* badly needs its orchestral dress, particularly the violins in the famous *Adagio of Spartacus and Phrygia*.

Munrow, David (recorder, flageolet)

The Amorous Flute (with Oliver Brookes, bass viol & cello; Robert Spencer, theorbo or guitar; Christopher Hogwood, harpsichord): ANON.: *Faronells ground; 6 Tunes for the instruction of singing-birds; Sonata in G*. DIEUPART: *Sarabande, gavotte, menuet en rondeau*. Daniel PURCELL: *Sonata in D min*. Nicola MATTEIS: *Ground after the Scotch humour*. PARCHAM: *Sonata in G*. HANDEL: *Sonata in F, Op. 1/11*. PEPUSCH: *4 Unaccompanied preludes*.
(M) *** Decca 440 079-2 [id.].

With a whole Brüggen Edition included, it would be unthinkable not to include also a collection from the late David Munrow who, apart from being a supremely expert player of the recorder, the flageolet, and any other possible pipe with holes in it, did so much to propagate early music in the LP era. The title of this collection comes from Nicholas Brady's poem, 'Hail! Bright Cecilia', which Purcell set for his familiar *Ode for St Cecilia's Day* in 1694: 'In vain the am'rous flute and soft guitar, jointly labour to inspire, ardent love and loose desire'. With Munrow directing the proceedings, one might possibly remove the first two words from the quotation. Certainly all the music here springs vividly to life, from the engaging, opening, anonymous divisions on the famous ground, *La Folia*, through to the jolly *Sonata* by Andrew Parcham, with its ready fund of tunes, to Handel's fine Op 1/11. Munrow takes up his flageolet to present the *Six tunes for the instruction of singing-birds*, which should surely tempt the most recalcitrant pet songbird to burst into imitative voice. There are plenty of other opportunities for bravura, not least in the opening Pepusch *Prelude*, while the charming little anonymous Italian sonata makes a diverting coda. Two small complaints: the recording is balanced very closely indeed, and there are too few cues – none for individual sonata movements. But the effect is most vivid.

'Musica española'

'Musica española' (music for guitar, I, played by: (i) William Gómez; (ii) Timothy Walker; (iii) John Williams; (iv) Eduardo Fernández; (v) Carlos Bonell): ANON.: (i) *Jeux interdits (Romance).* (ii) MUDARRA: *Fantasia X.* SOR: (i) *Minuetos Nos. 9 & 25;* (iii) *Variations on a theme of Mozart;* (iv) *Gran Solo, Op. 14; Sonata in D min., Op. 25; Sonata in D, Op. 15/2: Allegro moderato. 6 Estudios; Les adieux; Fantasia elegíaca.* TARREGA: *Recuerdos de la Alhambra; Estudio brillante; 5 Preludios; Minuetto; 3 Mazurcas;* (ii) *Lágrima; La alborada;* (v) *Introduction and fantasia on themes from La Traviata.* CHAPI: *Serenata morisca.* GRANADOS: (iii) *La maja de Goya;* (iv) *Danzas españolas Nos. 5 & 10.*
(M) ** Decca Analogue/Dig. 433 932-2 (2) [id.].

'Musica española' (music for guitar, II, played by: (i) Eduardo Fernández; (ii) John Williams; (iii) Carlos Bonell; (iv) William Gómez; (v) S. & E. Abreu; (vi) E. Abreu; (vii) Timothy Walker; (viii) Montreal SO, Dutoit): ALBENIZ: (i; ii) *5 Piezas.* VALVERDE: (iii) *Clavelitos.* LLOBET: *Scherzo-vals;* (i) *6 Canciones catalanas.* FALLA: *Homenaje a Debussy.* TURINA: *4 Piezas.* (iv) DE LA MAZA: *Habanera.* (i; iii; v) SEGOVIA: *5 Piezas.* (vi; iv) TORROBA: *2 Piezas.* (i) *Sonatina.* (iv; vii) RUIZ-PIPO: *2 Piezas.* RODRIGO: (i) *3 Piezas españolas;* (iii; viii) *Concierto de Aranjuez; Fantasia para un gentilhombre.*
(M) ** Decca Dig./Analogue 433 935-2 (2) [id.].

These two boxes of guitar music cover a wide range of repertoire and the considerable contribution of Eduardo Fernández to each is highly distinguished. Moreover he is digitally recorded. However, the other items come from a variety of sources and, although the playing is always good, the sound does not always match in dynamic level and, occasionally, pitch. Dipped into, there is much to give pleasure and stimulation here, but played continuously there are some awkward joins.

'Musica española' (music for violin and harp, played by (i) Alfredo Campoli, Daphne Ibbott; (ii) with Belinda Bunt; (iii) Ruggiero Ricci; (iv) Ernest Lush; (v) Louis Persinger; (vi) Marisa Robles; (vii) Philh. O, Dutoit): SARASATE: (i) *8 Danzas españolas;* (iii; iv) *Jota aragonesa;* (iii; v) *Capricho vasco; Introducción y tarantela;* (i; ii) *Navarra* (for 2 violins). (vi) NARVAEZ: *Variaciones populares sobre Guárdame las vacas.* CABAZON: *Pavana y variaciones.* SANZ: *La Serenissima.* Mateo ALBENIZ: *Sonata in D.* Isaac ALBENIZ: *Torre Bermeja.* FALLA: *Three cornered hat: Miller's dance.* GURIDI: *7 Piezas* (for harp). GOMBAU: *Apunte bético.* ALFONSO: *Cadenza.* FRANCO: *Canción y danza.* RODRIGO: (vi; vii) *Concierto de Aranjuez* (arr. for harp).
(M) **(*) Decca Analogue/Dig. 433 938-2 (2) [id.].

Campoli, in excellent form, opens this recital and, with art that disguises art, he makes the first four books of Sarasate's *Spanish dances* and the *Navarra* (in which he is joined by Belinda Bunt) sound effortless yet brilliant. He is most truthfully recorded (in 1977). Then Ricci provides three more pieces, displaying even greater fire and temperament, though he is less consistently caught by the engineers (the *Capricho vasco* is fierce). Marisa Robles then provides an attractive programme of transcriptions and works written for harp (of which the engagingly diverse seven pieces of Guridi are a highlight) and closes the programme with a most enjoyable transcription of the famous Rodrigo *Concierto de Aranjuez*, which is digitally recorded.

Nakariakov, Sergei (trumpet), Alexander Markovich (piano)

ARBAN: *Variations on a theme from Bellini's 'Norma'; Variations on a Tyrolean song.* BIZET, arr. Waxman: *Carmen fantasy.* BRANDT: *Concert piece No. 2.* FALLA: *Spanish dance.* FAURE: *Le réveil.* PAGANINI: *Caprice, Op. 1/17; Moto perpetuo, Op. 11.* SARASATE: *Zigeunerweisen, Op. 20/1.* SAINT-SAENS: *Le cygne.*
**(*) Teldec/Warner Dig. 4509 94554-2 [id.].

The young Russian trumpeter, Sergei Nakariakov, exhibits some stunning technique in his Teldec recital, coupling various trifles including Franz Waxman's *Carmen fantasy* and Paganini's *Moto perpetuo*, as well as the remainder of his programme. He was only seventeen when this recording was made and, although not many will want to hear more than a few of these pieces at a time, there is much to enjoy. He is a veritable Russian Håkan Hardenberger, save for the fact that, on the evidence of this disc, he does not always command the latter's extraordinary variety of tonal colour or his impeccable taste.

Oslo Wind Ensemble

Scandinavian wind quintets: FERNSTROM: *Wind quintet, Op. 59.* KVANDAL: *Wind quintet, Op. 34; 3 Sacred Folktunes.* NIELSEN: *Wind quintet, Op. 43.*
(BB) *** Naxos Dig. 8.553050 [id.].

A super-bargain account of the Nielsen *Quintet*, more relaxed in its tempi and measured in approach than the account by the Scandinavian Quintet on Marco Polo – see below. Very decently recorded, too. The Swedish musician, John Fernström, was a prolific composer whose output runs to twelve symphonies and much else besides. (He was for years solely represented in the catalogue by a *Concertino for flute, women's choir and small orchestra*). This *Wind quintet* is not quite so charming, but is well worth hearing – as, for that matter, is the *Wind quintet* by the Norwegian, Johan Kvandal, a thoughtful figure who is a composer of imagination and substance.

Pollini, Maurzio (piano)

STRAVINSKY: *3 movements from Petrushka.* PROKOFIEV: *Piano sonata No. 7 in B flat, Op. 83.* WEBERN: *Variations for piano, Op. 27.* BOULEZ: *Piano sonata No. 2.*
(M) *** DG 447 431-2 [id.].

The Prokofiev is a great performance, one of the finest ever committed to disc; and the Stravinsky *Petrushka* is electrifying. Not all those responding to this music will do so quite so readily to the Boulez, fine though the playing is; but the Webern also makes a very strong impression. This is the equivalent of two LPs and is outstanding value. It is a natural candidate for reissue in DG's set of 'Originals' of legendary performances.

Rachmaninov, Sergei (piano)

'The Ampico piano-roll recordings 1919–33': BACH: *Partita No. 4: Sarabande.* BEETHOVEN: *Ruins of Athens: Turkish march.* GLUCK, arr. Sgambasti: *Melodie d'Orfeo.* MENDELSSOHN: *Song without words (Spinning song), Op. 67/4.* HENSELT: *Si oiseau j'étais, Op. 2/6.* LISZT: *Concert paraphrases on: Schubert's Das Wandern; Mädchens Wunsch of Chopin, Op. 74/1.* SCHUBERT: *Impromptu No. 4 in A flat, Op. 90.* CHOPIN: *Scherzo in B flat min., Op. 31; Nocturne in F, Op. 15/1; Waltzes: in E flat, Op. 18; in F, Op. 34/1.* BIZET arr. Rachmaninov: *L'Arlésienne: Minuet.* PADEREWSKI: *Minuet in G, Op. 14/1.* RUBINSTEIN: *Barcarolle.* TCHAIKOVSKY: *Troika in E, Op. 37/11; Valse in A flat, Op. 40/8.*
(M) ** Decca 440 066-2 [id.].

After Rachmaninov's Ampico-roll recordings of his own music (Decca 425 964-2 – see our main volume) this is curiously disappointing. The playing often seems unrelaxed, even stiff (the Bach, for instance, or Liszt's paraphrase of Schubert's *Das Wandern*). The Chopin pieces seem to come off best (although the effect is not entirely spontaneous) and, while this is very accomplished and often characterful music-making (as in the closing Tchaikovsky items), the great pianist seems at times to be inhibited by the recording conditions. The actual sound (the player-piano was reproduced in Kingsway Hall in 1978/9) is real and vivid, if a trifle hard-edged.

Reykjavik Wind Quintet

Jean-Michel DAMASE: *17 Variations.* DEBUSSY (arr. Bozza): *Le petit nègre.* FAURE (arr. Williams): *Dolly suite: Berceuse, Op. 56/1.* FRANCAIX: *Quintet No. 1.* IBERT: *3 Pièces brèves.* MILHAUD: *La cheminée du roi René, Op. 205.* PIERNE: *Pastorale, Op. 14/1.* POULENC (arr. Emerson): *Novelette No. 1.*
*** Chan. Dig. CHAN 9362 [id.].

A delightful recital for late-night listening. Elegant, crisp playing from this accomplished Icelandic ensemble. The Damase *Variations* are delightful, as indeed are the Françaix and Milhaud pieces, and the Chandos recording is in the best traditions of the house.

Richter, Sviatoslav (piano)

BEETHOVEN: *Piano sonatas Nos. 3 in C, Op. 2/3; 4 in E flat, Op. 7; 27 in E min., Op. 90.*
**(*) Olympia OCD 336 [id.].

SCHUBERT: *Piano sonatas Nos. 19 in C min., D.958; 21 in B flat, D.960.*
**(*) Olympia Dig. OCD 335 [id.].

RACHMANINOV: *Etudes-tableaux, Opp. 33 & 39; 6 Preludes, Op. 23/1–2, 4–5, 7–8; 7 Preludes, Op. 32/ 1–2, 6–7, 9–10, 12.*
**(*) Olympia Dig./Analogue OCD 337 [id.].

Most of these recordings have been available in Germany on Ariola or Eurodisc: few have been readily obtainable in this country. Sonically they leave a good deal to be desired: in most instances the balance is fairly close and the acoustic on the dry side, without being unacceptably so. They call for tolerance, but this is well worth extending for the sake of this music-making. The early Beethoven sonatas are from 1975 and the *E minor*, Op. 90, comes from 1971. The *C major Sonata*, Op. 2, No. 3, is far more powerful than one is used to encountering, particularly in the intensity of the slow movement; Richter's view of the *E flat*, Op. 7, familiar from an earlier recording Philips issued in the 1960s, is further deepened. There is a marvellously inward feeling and a sense of profound euphony in the *E minor*, Op. 90.

The Schubert sonatas were recorded in the early 1970s; the *C minor Sonata*, D.958, in 1973, the *B flat*, D.960, in the previous year; neither has been in currency in the UK. Richter's way with Schubert is well known and his view of the *B flat* well known from an EMI version. Some listeners have difficulty in coming to terms with the sheer scale of his first movement: it seems almost timeless, just as the almost static inwardness of the slow movement is not for those in a hurry. As in Bruckner, the listener has to adjust his sense of space and time. Richter's Schubert probably goes deeper than almost any other pianist now before the public (except perhaps Perahia, who has yet to record the *B flat*).

Some of the Rachmaninov *Etudes-tableaux* have been available before, but again most are new to this country. The majority of the pieces were recorded in 1971 but others are later. The playing is of a rare order of mastery and leaves strong and powerful resonances. Richter's conception goes far beyond the abundant virtuosity this music calls for, and the characterization of this music is strong and searching. If you invest in no other of these Olympia CDs, this is the one that is unique – which makes the poor sound-quality particularly regrettable.

'The Philips Richter Authorised Edition'
**(*) Ph. 438 612-2 (21) (includes book: Sviatoslav Richter Portraits).

BACH: *Concerto in the Italian style, BWV 971; 4 Duets, BWV 802–5; English suites Nos. 3 in G min., BWV 808; 4 in F, BWV 809; 6 in D min., BWV 811; Fantasy in C min., BWV 906; French suites Nos. 2 in C min., BWV 813; 4 in E flat, BWV 815a; 6 in E, BWV 817; Overture (Partita) in the French style, BWV 831; Toccatas: in D min., BWV 913; in G, BWV 916.*
**(*) Ph. 438 613-2 (3) [id.].

BEETHOVEN: *Piano sonatas Nos. 19 in G min.; 20 in G, Op. 49/1–2; 22 in F, Op. 54; 23 in F min. (Appasssionata), Op. 57; 30 in E, Op. 109; 31 in A flat, Op. 110; 32 in C min., Op. 111.*
**(*) Ph. Dig. 438 486-2 (2) [id.].

BEETHOVEN (with (i) Moraguès Qt; (ii) members of the Borodin Qt): (i) *Piano quintet in E flat, Op. 16;* (ii) *Piano trio in B flat, Op. 97. Rondos: in C; in G, Op. 51/1–2; Piano sonatas Nos. 18 in E flat, Op. 31/3; 28 in A, Op. 101.*
**(*) Ph. Dig. 438 624-2 (2) [id.]. .

BRAHMS: *Ballade in G min., Op. 118/3; Capriccio in C, Op. 76/8; Intermezzo in E min., Op. 116/5; Rhapsody in E flat, Op. 119/4; Piano sonatas Nos. 1 in C, Op. 1; 2 in F sharp min., Op. 2; Variations on a theme by Paganini, Op. 35.* SCHUMANN: *Blumenstück, Op. 19; 3 Concert Etudes on Caprices by Paganini, Op. 10/4–6; Fantasy in C, Op. 17; March in G min., Op. 76/2; 4 Nachtstücke, Op. 23; Novelette in F, Op. 21/1.*
**(*) Ph. Dig. 438 477-2 (3) [id.].

HAYDN: *Piano sonatas Nos. 39 in D, Hob XVI/24; 62 in E flat, Hob XVI/52.* WEBER: *Piano sonata No. 3 in D min., Op. 49.* BEETHOVEN: *Piano sonatas Nos. 9 in E, Op. 14/1; 11 in B flat, Op. 22; 12 in A flat, Op. 26; 27 in E min., Op. 90.*
**(*) Ph. Analogue/Dig. 438 617-2 (2) [id.].

MOZART: *Piano sonatas Nos. 2 in F, K.280; 5 in G, K.283; 13 in B flat, K.333; 14 in C min., K.457; Sonata in F: Andante and allegro, K.533; Rondo, K.494; Fantasia in C min., K.475.*
**(*) Ph. Dig. 438 480-2 (2) [id.].

SCHUBERT: *Piano sonatas Nos. 9 in B, D.575; 15 in C (Relique), D.840; 18 in G, D.894.*
*** Ph. 438 483-2 (2) [id.].

CHOPIN: *Barcarolle in F sharp, Op. 60; Etudes, Op. 10/1–5, 10–12; Etudes, Op. 25/5–8, 11–12; Nocturne in F, Op. 15/1; Polonaises: in C sharp min., Op. 26/1; in C min., Op. 40/2; Polonaise-Fantaisie in A flat, Op. 61; Preludes, Op. 28/6–11, 17, 19, 23–24.* LISZT: *Consolation No. 6; Etudes d'exécution transcendante, Nos. 1–3, 5, 7–8, 10–11; Etudes de concert: 'Un sospiro'; 'Gnomenreigen'; Hungarian rhapsody No. 17; Klavierstück in F sharp; Mephisto-Polka; Polonaise No. 2 in E; Piano sonata in B min.; Scherzo in G min.; Trübe Wolken.*
**(*) Ph. Dig. 438 620-2 (3) [id.].

SCRIABIN: *2 Dances: 'Guirlandes'; 'Flammes sombres', Op. 73; Fantasie in B min., Op. 28; Poème-Nocturne; Vers la flamme, Op. 72.* PROKOFIEV: *Cinderella: excerpts, Op. 87; Danza and waltz, Op. 32/1 & 4; Légende, Op. 26/6; Piano sonatas: Nos. 4 in C min., Op. 29; 6 in A, Op. 82; Visions fugitives, Op. 22/3–6, 8–9, 11, 14–15; 18.* SHOSTAKOVICH: *Preludes and fugues, Op. 87/4, 12, 14–15, 17, 23.*
*** Ph. 438 627-2 (2) [id.].

We list the details of these recordings which Philips announced in the autumn of 1994 as the 'Authorised Richter Edition'. If they are good enough for Richter, they ought to be good enough for us. However, unusually for Philips, the documentation concerning the date and provenance of these records is meagre or non-existent. So this is in the nature of an interim report, noting their presence and availability. To start with, although many of the recordings appear to be digital, the quality of the sound is extremely variable. As those who know some of his Ariola discs will testify, Richter has not always enjoyed the benefit of outstanding recording venues or perhaps been tolerant of the needs of recording engineers. Even more than most artists, he is primarily concerned with matters of interpretation and artistic truth, and the actual quality of sound would not be a primary concern to the eminent octogenarian. But, generally speaking, these are self-recommending performances which admirers of this pianist will want to have anyway. In Beethoven, Richter's voice is uniquely authoritative, in Schubert his profoundly spacious readings, recorded live, have extraordinary concentration. The indispensable compilation of Prokofiev, Scriabin and Shostakovich is a combination of studio recordings and live recitals; the Mozart collection brings dryness of timbre to match a very positive, classical style. The Liszt playing is little short of inspired, especially the *Sonata*, but the recordings are again confined. The Schumann performances, too, inhabit an area of repertoire in which Richter has something very special to say, and the playing triumphs over any sonic limitations; the Brahms sonatas, on the other hand, are made to sound hard at higher dynamic levels. All the Bach performances, aristocratic and masterly, were recorded live, and these superbly controlled interpretations, unashamedly pianistic, are often surprisingly generous with repeats. The recordings are scheduled to be released in rather more digestible instalments during the coming months and we shall hope to return to them in our next edition.

Recital: PROKOFIEV: *Sonata No. 2 in D min., Op. 14.* STRAVINSKY: *Piano rag music.* SHOSTAKOVICH: *Preludes & fugues, Op. 87.* WEBERN: *Variations.* BARTOK: *3 Burlesques, Op. 80.* SZYMANOWSKI: *Métopes: L'île des sirènes; Calypso.* HINDEMITH: *1922 Suite for piano, Op. 26.*
(*) Decca Dig. 436 456-2 [id.].

It is difficult to understand why Richter passed these records, made in 1989, when the others (of Brahms, Haydn and Schumann), issued at the same time, are so successful. The Viennese recital – a temptingly wide-ranging group of twentieth-century piano works – could hardly be more promising, but sadly the performances too often lack the necessary rhythmic bite, and the piano sound from the Yamaha Centre in Vienna is hopelessly twangy and unrealistic.

Romantic piano sonatas

'Great Romantic piano sonatas': CHOPIN: *Sonata No. 2 in B flat min. (Funeral march), Op. 35.* LISZT: *Sonata in B min.* (Rafael Orozo); *Années de pèlerinages: Sonetto 104 del Petrarca* (Claudio Arrau). SCHUMANN: *Sonata No. 2 in G min., Op. 22* (Dinorah Varsi). SCHUBERT: *Sonata No. 21 in B flat,*

D.960 (Ingrid Haebler). TCHAIKOVSKY: *Sonata in G, Op. 37* (Paul Crossley). SCRIABIN: *Sonata No. 4, Op. 30* (Jean Louis Steuerman).
(B) ** Ph. Duo 442 617-2 (2).

Philips do not always field their first team for this admittedly generous 151 minutes of Romantic piano music. Ingrid Haebler gives a relatively intimate reading of Schubert's greatest piano work; but if the scale is small the playing is appealing and she makes the finale very much her own. Dinorah Varsi gives a good account of herself in Schumann, but this performance does not really take pride of place in the catalogue. Rafael Orozo is direct and musical in Chopin, but this performance becomes really special only in the central section of the slow movement. His Liszt sonata is another matter: bold, ambitious in scale and very commanding indeed, and strikingly well recorded. Arrau follows with the *Petrarch Sonnet*, which has a finely calculated atmosphere and is remarkably gripping. But he is no more arresting than Orozo. Paul Crossley does not quite catch the grand manner of the Tchaikovsky, but he plays the work spontaneously and musically, with a finely shaped slow movement. Steuermann opens Scriabin's Op. 30 impressively, but the *Prestissimo volando* is less firmly controlled, not helped by a very resonant recording.

Romero, Pepe (guitar)

Spanish music (with (i) Celín Romero): ANON.: *Jeux interdits.* ALBENIZ: *Suite española, Op. 47: Sevilla; Granada. Recuerdos de viaje, Op. 71: Rumores de la caleta. Mallorca* (barcarolle), *Op. 202. España (6 hojas de álbum), Op. 165: Asturias;* (i) *Tango.* GRANADOS: (i) *Danzas españolas, Op. 37: Andaluza; Goyescas: Intermezzo.* Celedonio ROMERO: *Malagueña; Romantico.* TARREGA: *Capricho arabe; Pavana.* SOR: *Introduction & variations on a theme by Mozart, Op. 9.*
(M) **(*) Ph. Dig. 434 727-2 [id.].

A thoroughly professional and immaculately played collection of favourites. The effect is intimate, pleasing rather than electrifying – the virtuoso showing his paces in familiar pieces. The flamenco-based pieces by the performer's father, Celedonio, bring a sudden hint of fire. For the reissue Celín Romero joins his brother for three duets, and this brings added spontaneity, although the intimate mood remains – witness the Granados *Spanish dance* which does not have the electricity of Julian Bream's solo version. The recording is very natural, but no information is provided about the music (except titles).

Los Romeros

Spanish guitar favourites (with Pepe Romero, Celín Romero, Celedonio Romero, Celino Romero): GIMENEZ: *La boda de Luis Alonso: Malagueña – Zapateado; El baile de Luis Alonso: Intermedio.* BOCCHERINI: *Guitar quintet No. 4 in D, G.448: Grave – Fandango.* Celedonio ROMERO: *Fantasia Cubana; Malagueñas.* FALLA: *El amor brujo: Ritual fire dance.* SOR: *L'encouragement, Op. 34.* PRAETORIUS: *Bransle de la torche; Ballet; Volta.* TARREGA: *Capricho árabe.* TURINA: *La oración del torero.* TORROBA: *Estampas.*
⊛ *** Ph. Dig. 442 781-2 [id.].

The famous Los Romeros guitar quartet (father Celedonio and three sons, led by Pepe) have never sounded quite like this before on record. The playing throughout is both vibrant and seemingly totally spontaneous, although the group were in fact recorded under studio conditions in the San Luis Rey Mission in California. Opening with a compelling *Malagueña – Zapateado* of Jerónimo Giménez and closing with an engaging and lighter *Intermedio* encore by the same composer, both from zarzuelas, this 74-minute collection of mainly Spanish music grips and entertains the listener as at a live concert. Celedonio contributes two pieces of his own, a charming solo lightweight *Fantasia Cubana*, and the others join him for his glittering flamenco *Malagueñas*, which has an improvisatory central section before the dashing coda with castanets. Among the more famous pieces arranged for the four players are the very effective Falla *Ritual fire dance* and Turina's *La oración del torero* (full of evocation), while Sor's *L'encouragement*, with its ingenuous lilting *Cantabile*, a simple but artful *Theme and variations* and elegant closing *Valse*, is played as a duet by Pepe and Celino. Tárrega's haunting *Capricho árabe* is exquisitely phrased by Celino. The arrangement of the three Praetorius dances, with an added condiment of percussion, is colourfully in period. The title of Torroba's collection of *Estampas* recalls the little Japanese prints which also inspired Debussy, and these eight sharply etched vignettes bring a highly imaginative response from the group, making this a highlight of the concert. The recording gives the guitars splendid presence against the attractively warm ambience, which in no way blurs the sharpness or focus of the players' attack.

Russian Piano School

Russian Piano School: '*The great pianists*' Volumes 1–10.

RCA/Melodiya are currently offering eleven CDs that survey the Russian piano tradition from the generation of Goldenweiser and Neuheus, whose pianistic pedigree goes back to the nineteenth-century masters, through to such younger virtuosi as Pletnev and Kissin. All of them have been digitally remastered with great care with 20-bit technology and NoNoise processing and, though the results are inevitably variable (particularly in the earlier recordings), the series affords an invaluable opportunity to steep oneself in the Russian pianistic tradition. Although the set is available in a slipcase, with a small saving in cost (74321 25172-2), the discs are also available separately at mid-price.

Goldenweiser, Alexander Borisovich

Volume 1: ARENSKY: *Forgotten rhythms: Sari, Op. 28/4.* BORODIN: *Petite suite: Mazurka.* GOLDENWEISER: *Song and dance.* MEDTNER: *Novella in C min., Op. 17/2.* RACHMANINOV: *Morceaux de salon: Barcarolle in G min., Op. 10/3. Suite No. 2, Op. 17* (with Grigori Ginsburg). TCHAIKOVSKY: *Dialogue in B, Op. 72/8; Meditation, Op. 72/5; Romance in F, Op. 51/5; Valse sentimentale in F min., Op 51/6.*
(M) (***) RCA mono 74321 25173-2 [id.].

Alexander Goldenweiser (1875–1961) was a pupil of Siloti, Rachmaninov's cousin and himself a pupil of Liszt, and his class-mates at the Moscow Conservatoire included Scriabin, Rachmaninov and Medtner. His composition studies were with Arensky, Ippolitov-Ivanov and Taneyev, all pupils of Tchaikovsky. He lived to be eighty-six and recorded these pieces between 1946 and 1955, when he would have been in his seventies. His own pupils included Tatiana Nikolayeva, Lazar Berman, Dmitri Bashkirov and the composer Kabalevsky. Of particular interest is his powerful 1948 recording of the Rachmaninov *Second Suite* (with Grigori Ginsburg as the second pianist), since the composer dedicated the piece to him. He wears his virtuosity lightly and, like all the greatest pianists, his lightness of touch leaves one unaware of hammers. The Tchaikovsky pieces of Op. 72 have a particularly touching quality. The recordings come up surprisingly well, given their age.

Neuheus, Heinrich

Volume 2: MOZART: *Rondo in A min., K.511; Sonata in D for two pianos, K.448* (with Stanislav Neuhaus). DEBUSSY: *Préludes, Books I & II: Danseuses de Delphes; La sérénade interrompue; La puerta del vino; Des pas sur la neige; Les sons et les parfums tournent dans l'air du soir; Les collines d'Anacapri; Bruyères; Minstrels.* PROKOFIEV: *Visions fugitives, Op. 22.*
(M) (***) RCA mono 74321 25174-2 [id.].

Heinrich Neuheus (1888–1964) is one of the most legendary figures among Russian pianists, the teacher of Richter and Gilels among others, a cousin of Szymanowski, much spoken of but scarcely glimpsed on a record label. He studied with Tausig and Godowsky before going on to become an influential teacher, as was his son, Stanislav (1927–80), with whom he recorded the Mozart *Sonata in D major*, K.488, in 1950. The eight Debussy *Préludes*, recorded in 1946 and 1948, have a powerful atmosphere and a refined sense of colour. Acceptable sound, though with not a great deal of top. It is difficult to imagine the *Visions fugitives*, recorded in 1956 when Neuheus was in his late sixties, being played with greater character.

Feinberg, Samuil

Volume 3: BACH, trans. Feinberg: *Sonata No. 5 in C, BWV 529: Largo. Chorale preludes: Allein Gott in der Höh sei Ehr, BWV 711; Allein Gott in der Höh sei Ehr, BWV 662* (two versions); *Wer nur den lieben Gott lässt walten, BWV 647; Allein Gott in der Höh sei Ehr, BWV 663.* MOZART: *Piano sonatas Nos. 4 in E flat, K.282; 18 in D, K.576; Fantasia and fugue in C, K.394; 12 Variations on an allegretto in B flat, K.500.*
(M) (***) RCA mono/stereo 74321 25175-2 [id.].

Samuil Yevgenyevich Feinberg (1890–1972) was a pupil of Goldenweiser and will be one of the discoveries of this collection for many non-specialist collectors. So wide a range of colour and sonority does he command that one is at times tempted to believe that there is more than one pianist playing. His style has a melting lyricism, a limpid tone-quality and a miraculous *pianissimo*; his sonority is of exceptional richness and finesse. He is the opposite of the modern jet-setting virtuoso, and both the transcriptions of Bach organ works and the Mozart are of altogether exceptional beauty. The recordings date from 1951–3, with the exception of four of his Bach transcriptions, which date from 1962. The recordings are very acceptable indeed: playing of this artistry deserves the widest dissemination.

Yudina, Maria

Volume 4: BARTOK: *Mikrokosmos, Books 5 & 6:* excerpts. BERG: *Sonata, Op. 1.* HINDEMITH: *Sonata No. 3.* KRENEK: *Sonata No. 2, Op. 59.* STRAVINSKY: *Serenade in A.*
(M) (***) RCA mono/stereo 74321 25176-2 [id.].

Maria Yudina (1899–1970) studied at first with the legendary Essipova, herself a Leschetizky pupil, and, after her death, was a fellow-student at Leningrad with Sofronitsky; Glazunov appointed her to a teaching post on the spot during her graduation recital. Her openness to modern developments in the West is well illustrated by the recordings assembled here. She carried on a long correspondence with Stravinsky, with whom she is pictured (in the sleeve-note) on his visit to Russia in 1962. These are impressive records: she makes Hindemith's *Sonata No. 3* sound more compelling than almost any other artist who has recorded it, and she succeeds in making Krenek's *Second Sonata* sound like music – no mean achievement! The recordings date from 1960–64 and are of eminently acceptable quality.

Sofronitsky, Vladimir

Volume 5: CHOPIN: *Nocturnes in F & F sharp, Op. 15/1–2; Scherzo No. 1 in B min., Op. 20.* MOZART: *Fantasia in C min., K.475.* PROKOFIEV: *Grandmother's Tales, Op. 31; Pieces for piano, Op. 12/2, 3 & 6–9; Sarcasm, Op. 17/3; Vision fugitive, Op. 22/7.* RACHMANINOV: *Moments musicaux, Op. 16/2 & 5.* SCHUBERT: *Impromptus, D.899/3 & 4.* SCHUMANN: *Sonata No. 1 in F sharp min., Op. 11.* SCRIABIN: *Sonata No. 4 in F sharp, Op. 30; Poème tragique, Op. 34; Valse in A flat, Op. 38; Etude in B flat min., Op. 8/11.*
(M) (**(*)) RCA mono 74321 25177-2 (2) [id.].

Vladimir Sofronitsky (1901–61) is best remembered as a Scriabin interpreter (he married the composer's daughter and was hailed by Tatiana Schloezer, Scriabin's widow, as the finest interpreter of her husband's music). He studied in Warsaw and had attracted the attention of Glazunov, who sent him to study with Alexander Michalowski. In the late 1920s he spent some time in Warsaw and Paris, where he earned the admiration of Prokofiev, whose friendship he enjoyed after his return to the Soviet Union. Sofronitsky was never cultivated by the Soviet regime and rarely appeared in the West, eventually succumbing to drink and drugs. All except the Prokofiev pieces come from a recital at the Small Hall of the Tchaikovsky Conservatoire in the year before his death. The Prokofiev Op. 31 comes from 1946 and the remainder of the group from 1953, recorded in the Scriabin Museum. In the fullness of time RCA will doubtless get round to reissuing all his Scriabin. In the meantime the *Fourth Sonata* gives a good idea why he is so much admired in this composer.

Richter, Sviatoslav

Volume 6: BACH: *Concerto in F in the Italian style, BWV 971.* BEETHOVEN: *Sonata No. 12 in A flat, Op. 26.* CHOPIN: *Ballades Nos. 1 in G min., Op. 23; 2 in F, Op. 38.* HAYDN: *Sonata No. 50 in C, Hob. XVI:50.*
(M) (*(*)) RCA mono 74321 25178-2 [id.].

The Bach *Italian concerto* was recorded in 1948, though it is difficult to credit it, given the excellence of its sound and the relative indifference (to put it mildly) of the later recordings offered here. It is much superior to the 1960 Haydn or Beethoven. Like most of the repertoire on this disc, it is given a performance of much distinction. The Haydn, Beethoven and Chopin items were recorded at recitals in 1960–63, but if the sound is shallow and poor in quality the playing is not. Richter recorded these pieces in the West, and older readers will doubtless recall the various CBS, RCA and EMI LP issues. Perhaps the first movement of the Haydn is too fast for comfort – but still, what playing! The Beethoven sounds very papery in tone and, though the playing is magisterial, the unpleasing sound makes its claims less pressing than many of the other discs in this collection.

Gilels, Emil

Volume 7: BACH: *Prelude and fugue in D, BWV 532.* BEETHOVEN: *32 Variations on an original theme, WoO 80.* LISZT: *Rapsodie espagnole.* PROKOFIEV: *Visions fugitives, Op. 22/1, 3, 5 & 11.* WEBER: *Sonata No. 2 in A flat, Op. 39.*
(M) (**(*)) RCA mono 74321 25179-2 [id.].

Gilels is represented by a recital given in the Grand Hall of the Philharmonic in Leningrad in January 1968. Such is the quality of his pianism that the (very much less than state-of-the-art) recording does not make this anything other than a highly recommendable issue. There are some smudges (as was often the case with Gilels in the concert hall) but they are of little account, given the musical insights and the beauty of sound he produced. The Liszt *Rapsodie espagnole* is pretty breathtaking and the Weber *Sonata No. 2 in A flat* is played with elegance and finesse. Despite the fact that it was January in Leningrad, the audience is very quiet, warmed no doubt by the white-hot, risk-taking pianism which confronted them.

Berman, Lazar

Volume 8: LISZT: *Etudes d'exécution transcendante; Hungarian Rhapsody No. 9 in E flat.*
(M) (**(*)) RCA mono 74321 25180-2 [id.].

The recordings of the *Etudes d'exécution transcendante* were made in the early part of 1959 and the *Hungarian rhapsody* (*Pesther Carneval*) two years later – and they leave something to be desired in terms of presence. However, the sound is vastly superior to the Richter CD reviewed above. As with the latter, no quarrels with the playing, which is absolutely stunning. Effortlessly virtuosic and brilliant, yet poetic and tender when required, and obviously with an immense dynamic range, only partly captured by the engineers. Pianistically this is without question a three-star recommendation.

Pletnev, Mikhail

Volume 9: MOZART: *Sonata No. 16 in B flat, K.570.* PROKOFIEV: *Sonata No. 7 in B flat, Op. 83.* SHCHEDRIN, arr. Pletnev: *Prologue and Horse-racing from Anna Karenina.* TCHAIKOVSKY, arr. Pletnev: *Nutcracker suite.*
⊛ (M) *** RCA Analogue/Dig. 74321 25181-2 [id.].

We have long been urging the reissue of Mikhail Pletnev's astonishing transcription of the *Nutcracker suite* which he recorded when he was twenty-one. (EMI originally issued this, but they never promoted it with vigour and, as a result, it disappeared within a couple of years.) Pletnev produces a wider range of colour from the keyboard than most orchestras command, and in the Shchedrin *Anna Karenina* an extraordinarily wide dynamic range. Small wonder that he has become so effective a conductor. Like the Prokofiev *Seventh Sonata*, these were all recorded after he won the Tchaikovsky Competition in 1978. The Mozart is later (1984) and completes a recital which is pre-eminent even in this remarkable series.

Kissin, Yevgeni

Volume 10: PROKOFIEV: *Visions fugitives, Op. 22/10, 11, 16 & 17; Dance in F sharp min., Op. 32/1.* RACHMANINOV: *Etudes-Tableaux, Op. 39/1–6, 9; Preludes: in G flat, Op. 23/10; A min., Op. 32/8. Lilacs, Op. 21/5* (trans. Kissin). SCRIABIN: *Preludes, Opp. 27/1–2; 37/1–4; Etude in C sharp min., Op. 42/5; 4 Pieces, Op. 51.* KISSIN: *2 Inventions.*
(M) *** RCA 74321 25182-2 [id.].

These recordings were made at recitals given at the Grand Hall of Moscow Conservatoire in 1984 and 1986 when Kissin was twelve and fourteen respectively. (He had, after all, played both the Chopin *Concertos* when he was thirteen!) What is there left to say about this remarkable youngster, save that the playing has extraordinary assurance, dazzling technical address and splendid taste. This listener was left spellbound by the sheer passion and brilliance of the playing. The acoustic is a bit reverberant but, given this youth's poetic insight and artistry, technical reservations are of minimal importance.

Scandinavian Wind Quintet

Danish concert: NIELSEN: *Wind quintet, Op. 43.* HOLMBOE: *Notturno, Op. 19.* NORGARD: *Whirl's world.* ABRAHAMSEN: *Walden.*
*** Marco Polo Dacapo Dig. 8.224001 [id.].

A worthwhile issue of all-Danish repertory that deserves wide currency. The Scandinavian Wind Quintet give an eminently acceptable account of the Nielsen which can stand up to most of the competition. The Holmboe *Notturno* is a beautiful piece from 1940 whose language blends the freshness of Nielsen with the neo-classicism of Hindemith yet remains totally distinctive. The Nørgård is less substantial but is not otherwise available; Hans Abrahamsen's *Walden* is thin but atmospheric. Very present and lifelike recording.

Steele-Perkins, Crispian (trumpet) Stephen Cleobury (organ)

'The King's trumpeter': MATHIAS: *Processional.* L. MOZART: *Concerto in E flat.* BOYCE: *Voluntaries in D.* ANON.: *3 16th Century dances.* TELEMANN: *Concerto da caccia in D.* GOUNOD: *Meditation: Ave Maria.* STEEL: *6 Pieces, Op. 33.*
**(*) Priory Dig. PRCD 189 [id.].

Crispian Steele-Perkins is here given a chance to show his paces on a modern trumpet. The programme opens with Mathias's distinctly catchy *Processional* and covers a fairly wide range of repertoire, ending with the six characterful pieces by Christopher Steele. The disc is relatively short measure (53 minutes), but the playing is first class and the balance most convincing.

Thurston Clarinet Quartet

'Clarinet masquerade': FARKAS: *Ancient Hungarian dances from the 17th century.* MOZART (arr. Whewell): *Divertimento No. 2.* TOMASI: *3 Divertissements.* GARNER (arr. Bland): *Misty.* JOBIM (arr. Bland): *The Girl from Ipanema.* DESPORTAS: *French suite.* ALBINONI (arr. Thilde): *Sonata in G min.* STARK: *Serenade.* GERSHWIN (arr. Bland): *Rhapsody: Summertime.* PHILLIPS (arr. Harvey): *Cadenza;* (arr. Fernandez): *Muskrat Sousa.*
(M) *** ASV Dig. CDWHL 2076 [id.].

A light-hearted concert, but an entertaining one which will especially appeal to those who like the clarinet's sonority, reedier than the flute's and with more character. The opening suite of Hungarian folk dances (with the chirps and cheeps in the finale very engaging) leads on to a Mozart *Divertimento* for basset horns. The other pieces, the insouciant Tomasi and the Desportes suite (full of Ravelian elegance) are all amiable, and the arrangement of Gershwin's *Summertime* has the famous opening swerve of *Rhapsody in blue* as its introduction. Finally there is the exuberant *Muskrat Sousa* which features a combination of *12th Street Rag* and *South Rampart Street Parade.* The recording is immaculately vivid.

Tureck, Rosalyn (piano)

'Live at the Teatro Colón': BACH: *Adagio in G, BWV 968; Chromatic fantasia and fugue, BWV 903; Partita No. 1, BWV 825: Gigue. Goldberg variation No. 29, BWV 988; Clavierbüchlein for Anna Magdelena Bach: Musette in D.* MENDELSSOHN: *Songs without words, Op. 19/1.* SCHUBERT: *Moments musicaux Nos. 2 in A flat; 3 in F min.* BACH/BUSONI: *Chaconne (from BWV 1004).* BRAHMS: *Variations and fugue on a theme by Handel, Op. 24.*
**(*) VAI Audio Dig. VIAI 1024-2 (2) [id.].

Rosalyn Tureck has lost none of her magic, as this Buenos Aires (1992) live recital demonstrates, and it is good to find her so sympathetic in Schubert and Mendelssohn, as well as in Bach. Her articulation in the Brahms *Handel variations* suggests she is thinking as much of Handel as of Brahms, but that is a comment, not a criticism. The Bach/Busoni *Chaconne* is splendid. Excellent recording, but there are two snags: the almost hysterical applause which bursts in as soon as a piece has ended and the fact that this recital would almost have fitted on one CD. These two play for just 83 minutes 31 seconds.

Wagler, Dietrich (organ)

'Great European organs, No. 24': Freiberg Dom, Silbermann organ: SCHEIDT: *Magnificat noni toni.*
CLERAMBAULT: *Suite de premier ton.* BUXTEHUDE: *Prelude and fugue in D min.* KREBS: *Choral preludes: Mein Gott, das Herze bring ich dir; Herr Jesus Christ, dich zu uns wend; Herzlich tut mich verlangen; O Ewigkeit du Donnerwort.* J. S. BACH: *Fantasie in G; Prelude and fugue in C.*
**(*) Priory Dig. PRCD 332 [id.].

The organ, rather than the player, is the star of this record; the latter's performances are sound but very much in the traditional German style. But he knows his instrument and the opening *Magnificat Noni toni* of Scheidt sounds resplendent, with the following Clerambault *Suite* also very effectively registered. A well-balanced programme, lacking only the last degree of flair in presentation.

Wells, Colin (organ of Lincoln Cathedral)

English organ music: JACOB: *Festal flourish.* ALCOCK: *Introduction and passacaglia.* HOWELLS: *Master Tallis's Testament.* MACPHERSON: *Andante in G.* HARRIS: *Flourish for an occasion; Prelude in E flat; Reverie.* George BENNETT: *Elegiac prelude.* BLISS: *Sovereign's fanfare; Fanfare for the bride; Wedding fanfare.* PARRY: *Choral prelude on Melcombe.* STANFORD: *Postlude on a theme of Gibbons; Fantasia and Toccata in D min.*
* Priory Dig. PRCD 379 [id.].

A remarkably dull record, notable mainly for the truthful recording of the organ, a mellow-sounding instrument which Colin Wells plays without seeming to generate any intensity or momentum. He makes Alcock's *Introduction and Passacaglia* sound very flabby indeed, and the Stanford *Fantasia and toccata* seems endless. The fanfares and flourishes come off best, for the organ can imitate brass rather agreeably.

Yates, Sophie (virginals)

English virginals music: BYRD: *Praeludium – Fantasia; The barley breake; The Tennthe pavan (Sir William Petre); Galliard to the Tennthe pavan; The woods so wild; Hugh Aston's ground; The Bells.*
DOWLAND: *Lachrymae pavan* (arr. Byrd). James HARDING: *Galliard* (arr. Byrd). GIBBONS: *Fantasia.*
ANON.: *My Lady Careys dompe.* TOMKINS: *Barafostus's dreame.* Hugh ASTON: *Hornepype.* BULL: *In nomine.*
** Chan. Dig. CHAN 0574 [id.].

Sophie Yates is a thoughtful and accomplished player and she uses a modern copy by Peter Bavington of an Italian instrument made at the very beginning of the seventeenth century. Her programme is well thought out and, even though it is dominated by the music of Byrd, it is musically well balanced. The snag is the resonant recording, which gives a larger-than-life impression of the instrument which even the lowering of the volume control does not entirely diminish.

Zimmermann, Frank Peter (violin), Alexander Lonquich (piano)

AURIC: *Sonata in G.* FRANCAIX: *Sonatine.* SATIE: *Choses vues à droite et à gauche (sans lunettes).*
MILHAUD: *Sonata No. 2, Op. 40.* POULENC: *Sonata.*
** EMI Dig. CDC7 54541-2 [id.].

Frank Peter Zimmermann and Alexander Lonquich offer a French programme of unusual interest. Their programme is discussed under the individual composers but, taken by and large, it is rather let down by the balance, which enables the pianist to dominate the aural picture too much.

Vocal Recitals and Choral Collections

Academy of Ancient Music, Christopher Hogwood

'Venice Preserv'd' (with Emma Kirkby, Judith Nelson, Nigel Rogers): MONTEVERDI: Laudate Dominum; Sancta Maria; Salve Regina; Salve, O Regina; Exulta filia Sion. MARINI: Sonata a tre. A. GABRIELI: Intonatione del primo tono. G. GABRIELI: Fuga del nono tono; Sonata con tre violini; Intonatione del primo tono. LEGRENZI: La pezzoli. CIMA: Canzona, la novella. CAVALLI: Canzon a tre. **(*) O-L 425 891-2 [id.].

Venice is very much in the Early Music News at the moment – see below – and this is an attractive if comparatively lightweight Venetian programme. Emma Kirkby and Judith Nelson's voices match delightfully in Monteverdi duets, and Nigel Rogers' solo performances are equally distinguished and enjoyable. Hogwood and his Academy provide instrumental interludes, including a Sonata by Marini (Who's he, you may well ask) and music by both the Gabrielis. A rather good mix but not a specially generous one (52 minutes) – so why a reissue at full price of a record made over a decade ago?

Anonymous Four

'Love's illusion': Music from the Montpellier Codex.
*** HM Dig. HMU 907109 [id.].

The Anonymous Four (Ruth Cunningham, Marsha Genensky, Susan Hellauer and Johanna Rose) are an American vocal quartet whose voices merge into a particularly pleasing blend. Recorded warmly and atmospherically, the sound they make has a rich, soaring beauty, often tinged with a plangent nostalgia. The programme here is of French motets from the Montpellier Codex (collected in France around 1400), which means that the richer harmonies are often spiced with the barer organum. The songs are about submission, grief, the pleasures of spring – both pastoral and personal – and, of course, the joy of love itself, and indeed the desire to love. The style of performance of this music is essentially conjectural, but the results here are convincing and beautiful. The group tell us that they have occasionally added vocal drones and doublings, but mainly the music is presented without idiosyncrasy. However, some of the briefer pieces are performed more than once, in order to highlight one particular voice part or to allow the whole work to make the fullest impression upon listeners.

Augér, Arleen (soprano)

'Grandi Voci': Arias from: MOZART: Le nozze di Figaro; Don Giovanni (with Drottningholm Court Theatre O, Ostman). Mass No. 18 in C min. (Great), K.427: Et incarnatus est (with AAM, Hogwood). HAYDN: Scena di Berenice: Berenice, che fai? La Circe: Son pietosa, son bonina. Arianna a Naxos; Il canzoniere: Solo e pensoso. Miseri noi, misera patria (with Handel & Haydn Society, Hogwood).
(M) *** Decca Dig. 440 414-2 [id.].

Arleen Augér is a pure-toned Countess in Ostman's period-instrument performance of Le nozze di Figaro and a radiant Donna Anna in his rather more successful Drottningholm Don Giovanni. Neither of these complete recordings could be counted a first choice (or anything like it), so to preserve the key arias is very worth while, while Hogwood's recording of Mozart's Mass in C minor includes a filled-out orchestration for Et incarnatus est, which suites Augér's voice to perfection. However, the main interest of this fine recital is the series of arias and cantatas by Haydn (lasting nearly an hour) which she recorded with the Handel and Haydn Society of Boston in 1988. She personifies the lamenting Ariadne and Berenice to perfection and is equally touching in Son pietosa, son bonina, which the composer himself extracted from his opera, La Circe, for concert performance. Perhaps finest of all is the lovely Miseri moi, misera patria, only recently rediscovered, a lament for a desecrated city pillaged by marauding troops, which certainly has something to say to our own generation.

Baillie, Dame Isobel (soprano)

'The unforgettable Isobel Baillie': HANDEL: *Samson: Let the bright Seraphim. Rodelinda: Art thou troubled. Messiah: I know that my Redeemer liveth; If God be with us. Theodora: Angels ever bright and fair. Joshua: Oh! Had I Jubal's lyre.* BACH: *Cantata No. 68: My heart ever faithful; Cantata No. 201: Ah yes, just so* (arr. Mottl). MOZART: *La finta giardiniera: A maiden's is an evil plight. The marriage of Figaro: O come, do not delay.* HAYDN: *The Creation: With verdure clad.* MENDELSSOHN: *Elijah: Hear ye, Israel.* OFFENBACH: *Tales of Hoffmann: Doll's song.* SCHUBERT: *The shepherd on the rock* (with Charles Draper, clarinet); *To music.* ARNE: *Where the bee sucks.*
⊛ (M) *** Dutton Lab. mono CDLX 7013 [id.].

It must be unique for a soprano's recording career to span over half a century, yet over all that time Isobel Baillie rarely if ever let down her maxim which provided the title of her autobiography: 'Never sing louder than lovely'. Indeed it is difficult to think of another collection of soprano arias (and this one plays for 75 minutes) which is entirely without vocal blemish and which offers such consistently ravishing sound. The present writer met the singer on a lecture tour, after she had retired from the concert platform, and she confessed that she found it just a little difficult to come to terms with how much money she had earned from Handel's *I know that my Redeemer liveth*. And this was certainly her most popular record during the war years. Alan Blyth describes this famous 1941 performance in the accompanying insert leaflet: 'Notes are hit fully and truly in the middle, and they are joined together in a seamless line. At the same time Baillie was able to swell and diminish her tone with total ease.' Like the rest of the programme, it is flawlessly transferred by the miraculous Dutton / CEDAR process, and one can enjoy Leslie Heward's warm Hallé accompaniment alongside the voice. In her duet with the trumpet (Arthur Lockwood) which opens the disc, *Let the bright Seraphim*, her bright, gleaming tone wins out every time, and elsewhere there are dazzling displays of agility (as in the 1930 *Doll's song* and the delightful Arne *Where the bee sucks* from 1943) as well as purity and loveliness (as in the 1941 *Art thou troubled* or Susanna's aria from *The marriage of Figaro*, recorded in 1927). Her simplicity of style was just right for Schubert, and her account of *The Shepherd on the rock*, recorded a year later, shows the bright, fresh timbre, which was uniquely hers, under perfect control. The timbre of Charles Draper, the distinguished clarinettist who plays the obbligato, by comparison seems dry and lustreless. But this in itself is of interest in demonstrating how the style of clarinet playing has changed in the intervening years, to become warmer, more succulent and with freer use of vibrato. A record to treasure on all counts.

Baker, Dame Janet (mezzo-soprano)

Mélodies, English song and German Lieder: FAURE: *Automne; Prison; Soir; Fleur jetée; En sourdine; Notre amour; Mai; Chanson du pêcheur (Lamento); Clair de lune (Menuet).* STANFORD: *La Belle dame sans merci.* PARRY: *Proud Maisie; O mistress mine.* BUSCH: *Rest.* WARLOCK: *Pretty ring time.* VAUGHAN WILLIAMS: *Linden Lea.* GURNEY: *The fields are full.* BRITTEN: *Corpus Christi carol.* IRELAND: *The Sally Gardens.* QUILTER: *Love's philosophy.* SCHUBERT: *Am Grabe Anselmos; Abendstern; Die Vögel; Strophe aus Die Götter Griechenlands; Gondelfahrer; Auflösung.* R. STRAUSS: *Morgen!; Befreit.*
(M) *** EMI CDM5 65009-2 [id.].

This admirable and generous collection draws on three LP recitals from the late 1960s. Dame Janet is one of those rare British singers who feel naturally for French *mélodie*, not only the musical style and idiom but the pronunciation and illumination of words, as this lovely group of Fauré settings so readily demonstrates. She is hardly less impressive in German Lied, so that after the chattering gaiety of Schubert's *Birds* we have the wonderfully lyrical and expressive *Die Götter Griechenlands* ('Lovely world, where are you'), followed by the *Song of the Gondolier* and the rapturous *Auflösung*. The English songs cover a very wide range. The richness of those by Stanford and Parry, for example, will surprise many, and besides the rarities there are such established favourites as Vaughan Williams's *Linden Lea* and the sparkling *Love's philosophy* of Quilter. In Richard Strauss the two artists again combine to create remarkable atmosphere, with a marvellous contribution from Gerald Moore at the introduction to *Morgen!*, which is ravishingly sung. The recording is most naturally balanced, and the CD transfer gives a vivid presence, with only a touch of over-brightness on vocal peaks. Highly recommendable and the playing time is very generous: 75 minutes.

Lieder (with Martin Isepp, piano): SCHUMANN: *Frauenliebe und Leben* (song-cycle), *Op. 42* *** ⊛ .
SCHUBERT: *Heimliches Lieben; Minnelied; Die Abgeblühte Linde. Der Musensohn.* BRAHMS: *Die
Mainacht; Das Mädchen spricht; Nachtigall; Von ewiger Liebe.*
(M)*** Saga EC 3361-2 [id.].

Janet Baker's inspirational account of *Frauenliebe und Leben*, part of this early Lieder recital for
Saga, has never been surpassed. The Schubert songs are not quite on this level (*Der Musensohn* a little
jerky), but the Brahms are beyond praise. This is singing of a quality that you find only once or twice
in a generation and – whatever the price – this CD is a collector's piece. The stereo on the original
LP was curiously balanced, with voice and piano unnaturally separated, but the CD transfer
transforms the sound, with oddities ironed out. Set in a dryish acoustic, the quality is now full-
bodied, with a vivid sense of presence to make the transcendental performances even more involving.

'Grandi voci': RAVEL: *3 Poèmes de Stéphane Mallarmé; Chansons madécasses.* CHAUSSON: *Chanson
perpétuelle, Op. 37.* DELAGE: *4 Poèmes hindous* (with the Melos Ensemble). Arias from: PURCELL:
Dido and Aeneas. RAMEAU: *Hippolyte et Aricie* (with ECO, Lewis). BACH: *Cantata, BWV 170* (with
ASMF, Marriner). CAVALLI: *La Calisto* (with LPO, Leppard).
⊛ (M) *** Decca 440 413-2 [id.].

The performances of French mélodies included on this record are very beautiful indeed. Chausson's
extended cantilena about a deserted lover has a direct communication which Dame Janet contrasts
with the subtler beauties of the Ravel songs. She shows great depth of feeling for the poetry here and
an equally evocative sensitivity to the songs about India, written in 1912 by Ravel's pupil, Maurice
Delage, which are by no means inferior to the songs by his more famous contemporaries. With
superb, atmospheric playing by the Melos group and an outstanding 1966 (originally Oiseau-Lyre)
recording, this ravishing collection must be placed among Dame Janet's most outstanding recordings.
For the current reissue, more remarkable examples of her art have been generously added, not least
the lovely Bach aria, *Vergnügte Ruh'*, the dramatic excerpt from Cavalli's *La Calisto* in Raymond
Leppard's imaginative realization, and, of course, her heartrending account of Dido's lament, *When I
am laid in earth.*

(i) **Baker, Dame Janet** (mezzo-soprano); (ii) **John Shirley-Quirk** (baritone); (iii) **John Carol Case** (baritone); with **Martin Isepp, Daphne Ibott** or **Viola Tunnard** (piano); (iv) **Bournemouth SO, Sir Charles Groves**

'Music of England' (ii) BUTTERWORTH: *A Shopshire Lad: Loveliest of trees.* (iv) DELIUS: *On hearing
the first cuckoo in spring.* (i) GURNEY: *I will go with my father a-ploughing.* (iv) HOLST: *Somerset
rhapsody.* (iii) ELGAR: *Shepherd's song;* (iv) *Introduction and allegro for strings, Op. 47.* (ii) VAUGHAN
WILLIAMS: *Linden Lea.*
(M) *(*) Saga EC 3353-2 [id.].

A disappointing sampler to remind us that Saga have some splendid recordings of English songs in
their vaults still awaiting reissue, recorded by artists of the calibre of Dame Janet Baker and John
Shirley-Quirk, both at the beginning of their careers. The measure here is meagre (40 minutes) and
the orchestral performances, although sympathetically played under Sir Charles Groves, bring stereo
of limited range.

Baltsa, Agnes (soprano)

'Great voice': Arias and excerpts (with various other artists) from: MOZART: *Don Giovanni.* BIZET:
Carmen. VERDI: *La forza del destino.* WAGNER: *Tannhäuser.* R. STRAUSS: *Der Rosenkavalier.*
(B) **(*) DG Dig. 431 101-2 [id.].

This was the first of eight recitals assembled by DG featuring their leading contracted vocal artists
under the generic title 'Grosse Stimmen'. The content here is fairly generous (64 minutes), but the
recital (like the rest of the series) is issued without documentation of any kind, except a list of
contents: titles, artists and recording dates. The excerpts here come from various complete sets and
Baltsa's vibrant personality is at its most compelling in three excerpts from *Carmen*, supported by
Carreras, with Karajan at the helm. She is a strong Donna Elvira in *Don Giovanni* (although the
microphones do not always flatter her) and impressively brilliant as Preziosilla in the *Rataplan*
number from *Forza del destino*, although charm is not her strong suit. She has plenty of character as

Octavian in *Der Rosenkavalier*, blending well with Janet Perry's Sophie in the Silver rose presentation scene. But in her seduction of Domingo's noble *Tannhäuser* her tone is rather unyielding. It is a fair portrait, nevertheless, if not exactly an endearing one, for her stage personality comes over as rather hard, although the programme is undoubtedly aptly chosen and this is fair value at bargain price.

Battle, Kathleen (soprano)

'*Kathleen Battle in concert*' (with James Levine, piano): PURCELL: *Come all ye songsters; Music for a while; Sweeter than roses.* HANDEL: *O had I Jubal's lyre.* MENDELSSOHN: *Bei der Wiege; Neue Liebe.* R. STRAUSS: *Schlagende Herzen; Ich wollt'ein Sträusslein binden; Säusle, liebe Myrte.* MOZART: *Ridente la calma; Das Veilchen; Un moto di gioia.* FAURE: *Mandoline; Les roses d'Ispahan; En prière; Notre amour.* Spirituals: *Honour, honour; His name so sweet; Witness; He's got the whole world in his hands.*
(M) *** DG Dig. 445 542-2 [id.].

Kathleen Battle is at her most characterful and provocative in this recital with Levine, recorded live in the Mozarteum in Salzburg as part of the 1984 Festival. Her singing of Susanna's little alternative aria from *Figaro, Un moto di gioia*, is a particular delight, and Levine – from Ohio, like Battle herself – proves a splendidly pointed and understanding accompanist. Helpfully atmospheric recording.

Battle Kathleen (soprano) and Plácido Domingo (tenor)

'*Battle and Domingo Live*' (with Metropolitan Opera O, Levine): Arias & duets from: VERDI: *La traviata.* DONIZETTI: *Don Pasquale; Lucia di Lammermoor; L'elisir d'amore.* GOUNOD: *Roméo et Juliette.* MOZART: *Don Giovanni.* LEHAR: *Die lustige Witwe.* Overtures to: VERDI: *La forza del destino.* ROSSINI: *L'Italiana in Algeri.*
(M) *** DG Dig. 445 552-2 [id.].

These gala occasions can often be very stimulating for the audience, but only very occasionally do they produce an outstanding record. The present recital is surely the exception that proves the rule. From Levine's vibrant *La forza del destino overture* onwards, the 'live' communication of these performances comes across readily. The *La Traviata* duet has great charm, with Domingo obviously matching his voice to the smaller but lovely sound which Battle naturally commands. The lesser-known duet from *Romeo and Juliet* is hardly less delightful, and *Là ci darem la mano* is engagingly relaxed and elegant: who wouldn't be seduced by this Don? No complaints about the solo arias either, but the unforgettable charmer is the final ravishing Waltz duet from *The Merry widow* which is (quite rightly) sung in English. The ringing final cadence is breathtaking. Few hours of operatic excepts are as magical as this one, and the recording is splendid.

Berganza, Teresa (mezzo-soprano)

'*Great voice*': Excerpts from: BIZET: *Carmen.* ROSSINI: *Il barbiere di Siviglia; La Cenerentola; Stabat Mater.* MOZART: *La clemenza di Tito.* FALLA: *El amor brujo.*
(B) **(*) DG 431 102-2 [id.].

Berganza's fresh-voiced mezzo, agile and secure and not without charm, is attractively bright-sounding in Rossini and crisply stylish in Mozart, but her Carmen is lacking in red-blooded projection. The darker side of the voice and its ready Spanish inflexion come over splendidly in the four excerpts from Falla's *El amor brujo*, although the flamenco style has a cultured veneer: it is strong without being earthily uninhibited. The voice records well and overall this is an enjoyable 63 minutes. But there is no documentation except for a list of titles and recording dates.

Bergonzi, Carlo (tenor)

'*Grandi voci*' (arias from): VERDI: *Aida; Luisa Miller; La forza del destino; Il trovatore; Un ballo in maschera; Don Carlo; La Traviata.* MEYERBEER: *L'africana.* GIORDANO: *Andrea Chénier.* CILEA: *Adriana Lecouvreur.* PUCCINI: *Tosca; Manon Lescaut; La Bohème.* PONCHIELLI: *La Gioconda.*
(M) **(*) Decca 440 417-2 [id.].

This recital, consisting mainly of Bergonzi's early stereo recordings, a dozen arias recorded with the

Orchestra of the Santa Cecilia Academy, Rome, under Gavazenni in 1957, shows him on consistently peak form. He does not attempt the rare pianissimo at the end of *Celeste Aida*; but here among Italian tenors is a thinking musical artist who never resorts to vulgarity. The lovely account of *Che gelida manina* (with Serafin) comes from two years later. The early stereo has transferred well and retains a bloom on the voice. The other recordings also derive from sets: *La Traviata* (1962), *Un ballo* (1960–61), *Don Carlo* (1965), both with Solti, while the stirring *Cielo e mar* from *La Gioconda* (1967) shows that Bergonzi's tone retained its quality. These added items help to make up a generous playing time of 71 minutes, besides adding variety to what was originally essentially a collection of favourites. Everything sounds fresh.

Bjoerling, Jussi (tenor)

Operatic recital: Arias from: PONCHIELLI: *La Gioconda*. PUCCINI: *La Fanciulla del West; Manon Lescaut*. GIORDANO: *Fedora*. CILEA: *L'Arlesiana*. VERDI: *Un ballo in maschera; Requiem*. MASCAGNI: *Cavalleria Rusticana* (with Tebaldi). LEHAR: *Das Land des Lächelns*.
(M) *** Decca 443 930-2.

Jussi Bjoerling provides here a flow of headily beautiful, finely focused tenor tone. These may not be the most characterful renderings of each aria, but they are all among the most compellingly musical. The recordings are excellent for their period (1959–60). The Lehár was the last solo recording he made before he died in 1960. The transfers to CD are admirably lively and present.

Caballé, Montserrat (soprano)

'Rossini, Donizetti and Verdi rarities' (with RCA Italiana Ch. & O, (i) Cillario; (ii) Guadagno; (iii) Amb. Op. Ch., LSO Cillario): Arias & excerpts from: (i) ROSSINI: *La Donna del lago; Otello; Stabat Mater; Armida; Tancredi; L'assedio di Corinto*. (ii) DONIZETTI: *Belisario; Parisina d'este* (with M. Elkins, T. McDonnnell). *Torquato Tasso; Gemma di Vergy*. (iii) VERDI: *Un giorno di regno; I Lombardi; I due Foscari* (with M. Sunara); *Alzira; Attila; Il Corsaro; Aroldo* (with. L. Kozma).
(M) *** BMG/RCA GD 60941 (2).

Between 1968 and 1970 Montserrat Caballé made three separate LP collections of rare arias by Rossini, Donizetti and Verdi and, although not everything included is as rare today, novelties still remain, especially in the Donizetti section. This was the last to be recorded, and here Caballé's conviction as well as her technical assurance make for highly dramatic results in scenas that not many years ago would have been laughed out of court. The placing of the voice in the *Belisario* item is superbly assured from the very start, and the control of tone is immaculate, with never a hint of forcing even in the most exposed fortissimo. It makes these rarities more attractively convincing that the arias are presented with surrounding detail from a group of well-chosen supporting artists. The Rossini selection is no less rewarding, though the aria from the *Stabat Mater* hardly qualifies as a rarity. The Verdi arias, taken from operas of the early years when the composer was working 'in the galleys', make a further commandingly brilliant recital when sung with such assurance. Caballé is again at her finest, challenged by the technical difficulties as well as by the need to convey the drama. She makes one forget that between the big, memorable tunes there are often less-than-inspired passages. Fine accompaniments throughout and splendidly smooth and vivid CD transfers ensure the success of these two discs, between them offering 144 minutes of music.

Operatic excerpts (with Pavarotti, Milnes, Baltsa) from VERDI: *Luisa Miller*. BELLINI: *Norma*. BOITO: *Mefistofele*. PUCCINI: *Turandot*. GIORDANO: *Andrea Chénier*. PONCHIELLI: *La Gioconda*.
(M) *** Decca 443 928-2 [id.].

This is another of those outstanding Decca anthologies which adds up to more than the sum of its parts. There are 76 minutes of vibrant and often beautiful singing. Although the disc centres on Caballé and is described as 'Operatic arias', there are in fact plenty of duets, and ensembles too. All the excerpts come from highly recommended complete sets, and Pavarotti figures often and strongly. In Bellini, Giordano or Boito, and especially as Liù in *Turandot*, Caballé is often vocally ravishing and she finds plenty of drama and power for Verdi and Ponchielli. There are at least two and sometimes three or four items from each opera, admirably chosen to make consistently involving entertainment. Alas, the back-up notes are inadequate, concentrating on Caballé's association with each of the operas included. Nevertheless this rewarding collection can be recommended to novices as well as to experienced collectors.

'Great voice': excerpts from: GOUNOD: *Faust; Roméo et Juliette.* MEYERBEER: *Les Huguenots.*
CHARPENTIER: *Louise.* BIZET: *Carmen.* PUCCINI: *Manon Lescaut* (with Domingo). R. STRAUSS:
Salome (Closing scene).
(B) ** DG 431 103-2 [id.].

Most of the content of Caballé's contribution to DG's *'Grosse Stimmen'* series is drawn from a 1971
recital of French arias. Although the quality of the voice is in no doubt, this was not in fact one of
this artist's more distinctive recitals. The vocal line is sometimes not perfectly judged (her earlier,
RCA recording of Charpentier's *Depuis le jour* was finer; here the aria's key moments are managed
confidently but the performance as a whole is simply less beautiful). In the Gounod numbers the style
is not fined down enough: the voice seems a trifle unwieldy. The Meyerbeer item is the most
convincing. DG's recording is warm, with a resonant acoustic, kind to both the voice and the superb
orchestral playing from the New Philharmonia under Reynald Giovaninetti. The duet from *Manon
Lescaut (Tu, tu amore?)* with Domingo is vibrantly exciting, but the recording, made at a live
performance, is somewhat less flattering. (It is included also on Domingo's recital in this series.) The
highlight here is the final scene from *Salome*, recorded with Leonard Bernstein in 1978, although the
orchestral sound could ideally be more sumptuous. But the performance is imaginatively full of
contrasts, the sweet innocent girl still observable next to the bloodthirsty fiend. The disc is poorly
presented, with nothing about music or artist, only titles and recording dates.

Callas, Maria (soprano)

'Favourite operatic arias' from: PUCCINI: *La Bohème; Tosca.* BELLINI: *Norma.* DONIZETTI: *Lucia di
Lammermoor.* VERDI: *Ernani; Aida.* PONCHIELLI: *La Gioconda.* GLUCK: *Orphée et Eurydice.*
GOUNOD: *Roméo et Juliette.* THOMAS: *Mignon.* BIZET: *Carmen.* SAINT-SAENS: *Samson et Dalila.*
MASSENET: *Le Cid.*
(M) *** EMI CDM7 67797-2 [id.].

Callas is not a predictable choice for Mimi, but her characterization is strong. Many of these items
are taken from complete operas and recitals recorded in the 1960s. Callas's later sets of *Lucia* and
Norma are both well represented here, but even finer is the *Suicidio!* from her second version of
Ponchielli's *La Gioconda*, among her finest achievements. The *Carmen* items, taken from the complete
set, are more questionable in their fierceness but are totally individual – as indeed, flawed or not, is
the last-recorded item here, Aida's *Ritorna vincitor*, made in 1972. The transfers capture the voice
well.

'La Divina 2': Arias from: GLUCK: *Alceste; Orphée et Eurydice.* BIZET: *Carmen.* VERDI: *Ernani;
Aida; I vespri siciliani; La Traviata; Don Carlo.* PUCCINI: *Manon Lescaut; La Bohème.* CHARPENTIER:
Louise. THOMAS: *Mignon.* SAINT-SAENS: *Samson et Dalila.* BELLINI: *La Sonnambula.* CILEA: *Adriana
Lecouvreur.* DONIZETTI: *Lucia di Lammermoor.*
*** EMI CDC7 55016-2 [id.].

So generously representative a selection (76 minutes) from the recordings of Maria Callas must
inevitably bring up much exciting material, and this well-chosen recital consistently shows her either
at her finest or near it. The recordings cover a decade from 1954 to 1964 and include much that is
arrestingly dramatic (Gluck and Verdi) and ravishing (Puccini and Cilea), while everything shows
that special degree of imagination which Callas brought to almost everything she did. The *Mignon
Polonaise* is not ideally elegant but it has a distinctive character and charm, and it is almost irrelevant
to criticize Callas on detail when her sense of presence is so powerful. The excerpt from *La Traviata*
was recorded live in Lisbon in 1958 and even the audience noises cannot detract from its magnetism.

Cambridge Singers, John Rutter

'The Cambridge Singers Collection' (with Wayne Marshall, City of L. Sinf.): DEBUSSY: *3 Chansons
d'Orleans.* Folksongs (arr. Rutter): *The Keel row; The Willow tree.* Gregorian Chant: *Regina caeli
laetare.* BRUCKNER: *Ave Maria.* VERDI: *Laudi alla Vergine Maria.* STANFORD: *Magnificat in D; Te
Deum in C.* PURCELL: *Remember not, Lord, our offences.* TAVERNER: *Christe Jesu, pastor bone.*
PHILIPS: *O Beatum et sacrosanctum diem.* PEARSALL: *Lay a garland.* RUTTER: *Riddle song; Waltz;
Magnificat* (1st movement); *The Wind in the willows* (excerpt, with The King's Singers, Richard
Baker, Richard Hickox). TRAD. (arr. Rutter): *Sing a song of sixpence.*
(M) **(*) Coll. Dig. CSCD 501 [id.].

Here is an attractively chosen, 64-minute sampler, including a wide range of tempting repertoire from arrangements of folksongs to Stanford and Verdi. The Taverner and Philips items are particularly welcome. Rutter includes a fair proportion of his own music, but the opening (only) from his setting of *The Wind in the Willows* will not be something one would want to return to very often.

Caruso, Enrico (tenor)

'Verismo arias (1906–1916)' from PUCCINI: *La Bohème* (with Melba, Farrar, Viafora, Scotti); *Tosca; Madama Butterfly* (with Farrar, Scotti). PONCHIELLI: *La Gioconda*. MASCAGNI: *Cavalleria rusticana*. LEONCAVALLO: *La Bohème; Pagliacci*. FRANCETTI: *Germania*. GIORDANO: *Andrea Chénier*. PUCCINI: *Manon Lescaut*.
(M) *** BMG/RCA 09026 61243-2.

French opera (1906–1916): Highlights from GOUNOD: *Faust* (with Farrar, Scotti, Journet). Arias from: MASSENET: *Le Cid; Manon*. BIZET: *Carmen; Les pêcheurs de perles*. SAINT-SAENS: *Samson et Dalila*. HALEVY: *La juive*.
(M) *** BMG/RCA 09026 61244-2.

These two discs, alongside a Verdi collection (see our main volume), are phenomenally well transferred with the aid of special digital techniques that seek to eliminate the unwanted resonances of the acoustic horn used in the original recording process. This restoration was achieved in the early 1980s using a Soundstream programme, master-minded by Thomas Stockham. The results are uncannily successful: the voice emerges with remarkable freshness and purity (sample the *Flower song* from *Carmen*) and only the accompaniments, heavily laden with wind and brass, give the game away; otherwise one might think the recordings much more modern. The two selections include many famous records, covering the decade of 1906–16, and it is good to hear such singers as Melba, who joins Caruso in the duet, *O soave fanciulla*, and Farrar, Viafora and Scotti in the Act III *Bohème Quartet*. Farrar, Journet and Scotti are also present in the seven items from *Faust* included on the French recital. There are obviously more issues to come; they will be most welcome.

Cerquetti, Anita (soprano)

'Grandi voci' (arias from): VERDI: *Aida; I vespri siciliani; Nabucco; Ernani; La forza del destino*. BELLINI: *Norma*. SPONTINI: *Agnes von Hohenstaufen*. PUCCINI: *Tosca*. PONCHIELLI: *La Gioconda* (with Giulietta Simionato, Mario del Monaco, Ettore Bastianini, Florence Festival Ch. & O, Gianandrea Gavazzeni).
(M) ** Decca 449 411-2 [id.].

This recital sports a really fearsome portrait of Madame Cerquetti with rasberry lips pouting furiously – a Casta diva indeed! In the aria of that name, Cerquetti's entrance is rather marred by an unforgivably flat flute obbligato. Cerquetti's half-tone at the beginning of the aria is most ingratiating (if not entirely free of squelching in toothpaste bursts), but the voice hardens when pressed. With such a big voice the degree of flexibility is credible, but ideally Bellini requires even greater sense of style. The rare aria, *O re dei cieli*, from Spontini's *Agnes von Hohenstaufen* also brings shrill fortissimo attack, but the *Nabucco* excerpt shows up Cerquetti's voice more impressively, with a fine sense of attack in the dramatic recitative, and her richly spun *Vissi d'arte* suggests she was a formidable Tosca. The most impressive items here come from her 1957 complete set of *La Gioconda*; they are rather fine and certainly powerful. The recording is spacious and free without being markedly brilliant. In 1961 Cerquetti withdrew from the operatic stage (temporarily, as she thought) but her attempts to return were thwarted by the pre-eminence of Callas and Tebaldi.

Christofellis, Aris (sopraniste)

'Farinelli et son temps' (with Ensemble Seicentonovecento, Flavio Colusso): arias from: DUNI: *Demofoonte*. GIACOMELLI: *Merope*. METASTASIO: *La Partenza*. HANDEL: *Ariodante; Serse*. BROSCHI: *Artaserse*. HASSE: *Artaserse; Orfeo*. ARIOSTI: *Artaserse*. PERGOLESI: *Adriano in Siria*.
*** EMI Dig. CDC5 55250-2 [id.].

What did operatic castratos sound like in the eighteenth century? The only recording of a genuine castrato, made at the turn of the century, is a travesty, merely the squawking of an old man. By any reckoning, here is a much closer answer, a finely trained high falsettist who, in the beauty and evenness of the sound, with a minimum of ugly hooting, suggests that this may well approximate to the sound of a castrato. A recording may exaggerate the size of Christofellis's voice – by report the singing of the great castratos was exceptionally powerful – but he is artist enough, with a formidable technique, to make a splendid show in this dazzling series of arias originally written for the great castrato, Farinelli. Some of his cadenzas are breathtaking. One brief song is by Farinelli's greatest friend, the librettist Metastasio, and Farinelli's own setting of the same words is also included. The items from Handel's *Ariodante* and *Serse*, better known than the rest, come in performances which stand up well against those we have had from female singers, and Christofellis in his note pays tribute to the pioneering work of Marilyn Horne. The performances are all lively and alert, and the recording of the voice is full and vivid, though the instrumental accompaniment is backwardly placed.

Concentus Musicus Vocal Ensemble, Galliard Brass Ensemble

'*A Christmas celebration*' (with Harvard Glee Club; Western Wind; New York Harp Ens.) Vol. 1: SCHEIDT: *In dulci jubilo*. DAVISON: *Bring a torch, Jeanette Isabella!*. ANON.: *Greensleeves to a ground; Nowell sing we both all and sum; Expression*. Spiritual: *I believe this is Jesus*. TRAD. arr. Price: *Joy to the world; Ding dong merrily on high; O come, O come Emmanuel; It came upon the midnight clear; Gloucester wassail; I saw three ships*. HANDEL: *Messiah: Pastoral symphony*. PRAETORIUS: *Psallite; Lo, how a rose e'er blooming*. HANDEL: *O Magnum mysterium*. BILLINGS: *Boston and Judea*. VALENTINI: *Christmas symphony*. HOLST: *Personent hodie*. BACH: *Jesu, joy of man's desiring. Keyboard concerto in F min., BWV 1056: Largo*. ARAUJO: *Los cofla desde la estleya*. LASSUS: *Virginis aeternum*.

Vol. 2: TRAD., arr. Price: *Carol of the bells; Angels we have heard on high; O come all ye faithful; Rejoice and be merry; Deck the hall; The first Noel; Wexford carol*. BIEBL: *Ave Maria*. XIMENO: *Ay ay Galeguiños*. TORELLI: *Christmas concerto: Largo & Vivace*. ANON.: *Gaudete; Star in the East; Tantum ergo; In dulci jubilo*. Spiritual: *He is King of Kings*. BELCHER; READ; BILLINGS: *While shepherds watched* (3 settings). BACH: *Well-tempered Klavier, Book I, Prelude in E flat min., BWV 853*. IVES: *Christmas carol*. GUERRERO: *Hoy, José, se os da en el Suelo*. NARDINI: *Adagio*. WEELKES: *Hosanna to the Son of David*. GRUBER: *Silent night*.
** MusicMasters Dig. 01612-67077-2 (2) [id.].

As can be seen above, the range of music on this pair of Christmas CDs is very wide indeed, and it is all very well recorded. But this is very much a transatlantic offering which will not appeal to all British tastes. Most of the traditional carols are arranged for the Galliard Brass Ensemble (a quintet) by Richard Price and are played very robustly, and the same approach is applied to Bach's chorale, *Jesu, joy of man's desiring*, which is very unsubtle. The same composer's famous *Largo* from the *F minor Keyboard concerto* is played on the harp, as is the excerpt from the *Well-tempered Clavier* in Volume II, and the effect, as in the other baroque instrumental items, is very romantic. The vocal performances on the other hand are often curiously laid-back, especially when the music is early. Of course there are many good things here, but the effect of alternating different ensembles makes the programme seem very bitty.

Crespin, Régine (soprano)

'*Portrait*': Arias from VERDI: *Il trovatore; Otello; Un ballo in maschera; Macbeth; Don Carlo; Aida*. ROSSINI: *Guillaume Tell*. BERLIOZ: *La damnation de Faust*. WAGNER: *Tannhäuser; Lohengrin; Die Walküre; Parsifal. Wesendonck Lieder*. Arias from: BERLIOZ: *Les Troyens*. Excerpts from: MASSENET: *Hérodiade*. PUCCINI: *Tosca*. Songs: SCHUMANN: *Liederkreis, Op. 39*. DUPARC: *L'invitation au voyage; Testament; Chanson triste; Le manoir de Rosemonde; Elégie; Phidylé*. FAURE: *Soir; Le secret; Au bord de l'eau. Après un rêve; Clair de lune*. CANTELOUBE: *Chants d'Auvergne: Lo fiolairé; Lou coucut*. ROUSSEL: *Cœur en péril*. SAUGET: *Berceuse créole*.
(M) ** EMI stereo/mono CDM7 64434-2 (4) [id.].

No longer can any one company provide a complete portrait of a singer; it is a pity that, in a recital of this kind, the major labels cannot make a deal and exchange masters, when surely EMI would have borrowed Crespin's famous Decca recordings of Berlioz and Ravel song-cycles (with Ansermet) and other items as well. What we are offered is a rather mixed bag. She is impressive (and in fine voice) in Verdi and often splendid in Wagner, but her Puccini (in French!) is less inviting and the Lieder and mélodies are more uneven. On the whole, this is a recital essentially for admirers of this artist rather than for the general collector. The recordings were made over more than a decade, from the late 1950s to the early 1970s. Good transfers.

'Grandi voci' (with Ch. of the Grand Théâtre, Suisse Romande O, Alain Lombard, or Vienna Volksoper O, Georges Sebastian): Arias from: GLUCK: Iphigénie en Tauride. BERLIOZ: La Damnation de Faust. GOUNOD: Sapho. BIZET: Carmen. OFFENBACH: La Grande Duchesse de Gérolstein; La belle Hélène; La Périchole. HAHN: Ciboulette. CHRISTINE: Phi-Phi. MESSAGER: J'ai deux amants. O. STRAUSS: Les Trois valses.
(M) *** Decca 440 416-2 [id.].

More than any other of her many recordings, this presents the complete Crespin, a commanding personality with a ringing, vibrant voice, but also an artist with a keen sense of fun. Marvellous as the opera rarities are, ranging wide, the operetta items are what most listeners will remember with most affection – the duchess reviewing her troops, the heroine tipsy in La Périchole – vulgarity skirted by the naughtiest and most tantalizing of margins. Fine 1970/71 recording, and this reissue now has an overall timing of 73 minutes. Not to be missed.

Danish National Radio Choir, Stefan Parkman

'Scandinavian contemporary a cappella': TORMIS: Raua needmine. NORGARD: And time shall be no more. RAUTAVAARA: Suite de Lorca, Op. 72. SANDSTROM: A cradle song. JERSILD: 3 Romantike korsange.
*** Chan. Dig. CHAN 9264 [id.].

Tormis is an honorary Scandinavian: he hails from Estonia. Jørgen Jersild and Per Nørgård are both Danish, Sven-David Sandström Swedish (and mightily overrated in his homeland), and Einojuhani Rautavaara comes from Finland. Stefan Parkman has brought the Danish National Radio Choir to considerable heights and now it almost (but not quite) rivals the Swedish Radio Choir in its heyday under Eric Ericsson. None of the music is quite good enough to enter the permanent repertory in the way that the sublime motets of Holmboe's Liber canticorum should and doubtless will. By their side, this is all pretty small beer, but the Jersild and Rautavaara are worth investigating.

Deller, Alfred (counter-tenor)

HMV recordings 1949–54 (with (i) Wenzinger Viol Trio; Desmond Dupré, (ii) guitar or (iii) lute; (iv) Walter Bergmann, harpsichord; (v) Basil Lam, harpsichord, Terence Weil, cello; (vi) string orchestra; (vii) Geraint Jones, organ): (i) CICONIA: O rosa bella. BEDYNGHAM: O rosa bella. (ii) DOWLAND: Fine knacks for ladies; In darkness le me dwell; (iii) Flow my ears; Sorrow, sorrow stay. CAMPION: It fell on a summer's day. ROSSETER: What then is love but mourning? MORLEY: It was a lover and his lass; O Mistress mine. WILSON: Take, O take those lips away. JOHNSON: Where the bee sucks; Full fathom five. ANON.: Sing, willow; Peg-a-Ramsay; Caleno custure me!; Greensleeves. PURCELL: (iv) Epithalamium; Sweeter than roses; Music for a a while; If music be the food of love; (v) Retired from any mortal's sight; Thus to a ripe consenting maid; (v; vi) Hark, how all things; (vii) An evening - hymn.
(M) (**(*)) EMI mono CDH5 65501-2 [id.].

This generous EMI collection (77 minutes) arrives opportunely to make a preface for Deller's later, stereo repertoire, reissued in the Vanguard Deller Edition. The recordings date from early in his career when, almost single-handedly, he changed attitudes to the counter-tenor timbre, presenting it as a beautiful and not an odd phenomenon. In the accompanying notes Lionel Salter relates how intially his voice 'caused perplexity, even downright hostility among some musicians and audiences', but he overcame such prejudice by 'his profound intuitive musicianship', beauty of line and subtle control of dynamic nuance and colour. In these HMV recordings his special sound is beautifully captured at its freshest (even if the accompaniments at times seem more primitive) and the programme readily shows his special feeling for Elizabethan repertoire, notably the sad-eyed songs of Dowland and the simple, lyrical beauty of Purcell. Music for a while, his very first 78-r.p.m. record, was recorded in 1949 and justly became one his first 'hits'. His son, Mark, recalls that when the test pressing arrived, the family did not have a record player on which to sample it. In some ways the closing Evening hymn is even more gently ravishing. However, although Lionel Salter's accompanying essay about the artist and his music is admirable, no texts are included, as they are with all the Vanguard discs below.

Alfred Deller Edition

'Western wind and other English folksongs and ballads' (with Desmond Dupré, lute & guitar, John Southcott, recorder): *Western wind; Early one morning; Black is the colour; All the pretty little horses; Lowlands; The Sally gardens; Bendemeer's Stream; Annie Laurie; The Miller of the Dee; Cockles and mussels; Drink to me only; The foggy, foggy dew; The frog went a-courtin'; The turtle dove; Pretty Polly Oliver; The carrion crow; The wife of Usher's Well; Henry Martin; I am a poor wayfaring stranger; Cold blows the wind; Skye boat song; Every night the sun go's down; Song of a wedding.*
(M) *** Van. 08.5032.71 [id.].

Vanguard's Deller Edition could hardly open more propitiously than with this ravishing collection of folksongs, recorded in 1958 when the great counter-tenor was at the very peak of his form. The early stereo gives a lovely bloom to his voice, and here, as throughout this fine series, the CD transfers are of a high calibre. The opening *Western wind* is justly another of Deller's 'hits', but *Lowlands* is hardly less beautiful, and many other items here show the magic of his tonal nuancing and his natural, spontaneous musicianship. *Annie Laurie* is wonderfully fresh and brings a frisson as he soars up to the top of his range, while the irrepressible *Miller of Dee*, the petite *Pretty Polly Oliver*, and jaunty *Foggy dew* show him well able to lighten his presentation in the most sparkling manner. *Every night when the sun goes in* brings an almost Gershwinesque, bluesy feeling. In the charming *All the pretty little horses*, *The Frog went a'courtin'* and the *Skye boat song*, John Southcott touches in discreet obbligati on the recorder, and throughout Desmond Dupré provides persuasive lute accompaniments. The last four songs listed appear on record for the very first time in any format.

Tavern songs: *'Catches, glees and other diverse entertainments'* (with the Deller Consort): PURCELL: *Man is for woman made; Sir Walter; To thee and to the maid; Chiding catch; Once, twice, thrice; When the cock begins to crow; Epitaph, Under this stone; An ape, a lion, a fox, and an ass; True Englishmen; Young Collin; If all be true.* Earl of MORNINGTON: *'Twas you, sir.* SAVILE: *Had she not care enough.* TURNER: *Young Anthony.* TRAD.: *Amo amas, I love a lass.* CORNYSHE: *Ah, Robin; Hoyda, jolly Rutherkin.* LAWES: *Bess Black; Sing fair Clorinda; The captive lover.* ANON.: *I am athirst; Troll the bowl; We be soldiers three; He that will an alehouse keep; Inigo Jones; Summer is icumen in.* ECCLES: *Wine does wonders.* TRAVERS: *Fair and ugly, false and true.* BENNET: *Lure, falconers lure.* ROGERS: *In the merry month of May.* SPOFFORTH: *L'ape e la serpe.* HILTON: *Call George again.* ATTERBURY: *As t'other day.* ARNE: *The street intrigue; Which is the properest way to drink.* BLOW: *Bartholomew Fair; The self banished; Galloping Joan.* BOYCE: *John Cooper.* BARNABY: *Sweet and low.*
(M) **(*) Van. 08.5039.71 [id.].

In this extraordinarily generous 78-minute collection from 1956, 40 items in all, the Deller Consort consisted of Gerald English, Wilfred Brown, Maurice Bevan, Edgar Fleet and Owen Grundy, and they sing, unaccompanied, various catches and glees, part-songs, rounds (of which *Summer is icumen in* is a prime example) and semi- madrigals from both Elizabethan and Restoration England, right up to the pre-Victorian period. A catch was essentially a round, written in three or more voices, so that each succeeding singer had to 'catch' his first entry with the melody; the term 'glee' is less precise but eventually came to mean a part-song in harmony, as distinct from the polyphonic catch. The opening 'Choice collection of the most diverting catches', attributed to Purcell, are mainly bawdy, explicitly about the joys of love-making in an age of frankness. The Elizabethan romantic lute-songs had an essential finesse and delicacy of feeling, so the more robust dialogue pieces acted as a healthy counterbalance. The popular ballads could also be restrained, and this opening group ends with a touching glee, *Under this stone*, about the late-lamented Gabriel John. There are many other part-songs intended to charm with their vivacity, and *Young Anthony peeping through the keyhole*, by William Turner (1651–1740) becomes more complex as its hero eagerly joins the two ladies he has overheard discussing their probity. Another catch by John Cooper brings an engaging *double entendre* about *John Cooper*, who is finding difficulty boring a great piece of timber; his wife brings his breakfast 'and cry'd here's a morsel for me and for thee'. *Ah, Robin*, a lovely glee by William Cornyshe, is better known today, slightly altered in rhythm, as *Sing we Nowell*, while the music for the glee/ madrigal *Amo, amas, I love a lass*, with its naughty Latin parody text, could have come straight out of *HMS Pinafore*. Purcell's 'patter' trio, *True Englishman*, also shows how much Sullivan borrowed from this fertile source. *We be soldiers three* even quotes doggerel French in the way of British soldiers who, in this instance, have returned from the Flemish wars, while *L'ape e la serpe*, a late-eighteenth-century glee by Reginald Spofforth, is sung in Italian. The performances are suitably direct, never prissy, and this especially applies to the robust drinking songs, although occasionally one would have welcomed a more spontaneous earthy bite. Among other highlights are the simple setting of *Fair and ugly* of John Travers (1703–58) and the lovely *Sing fair Clorinda* of Henry Lawes, in which Deller leads the group to ravishing effect; this is followed by the Restoration pastoral *In the merry month of May* of Benjamin Rogers. Some of the songs are descriptive and give us period detail of English life, such as John Blow's *Bartholomew Fair* or Thomas Arne's *The street intrigue*, both very robustly done; but Blow is shown at his most touching in *The self banished*. The recording is clear and immediate, the ambience dry but pleasing.

PURCELL (with the Deller Consort, (i) Oriana Concert Choir & O; (ii) L. Kalmar O, Walter Bermann, harpsichord)): (i) *Come ye sons of art (Ode on Queen Mary's birthday, 1694); Rejoice in the Lord alway (Bell anthem);* (ii) *My beloved spake; Welcome to all pleasures (Ode on St Cecilia's Day, 1683).*
(M) **(*) Van. 08.5060.71 [id.].

These Purcell performances convey much joy in the music-making, even if for some ears the warmly upholstered (and tonally beautiful) overtures may sound slightly anachronistic. It is good to hear Deller in the famous solos, notably *Strike the viol*, with its intertwining flute obbligato (in *Come ye sons of art*), and *Here the Deities approve* in *Welcome to all the Pleasures*, while in the former he is joined by his son, Mark – who sounds more like a treble – for the 'counter-tenor' duet, *Sound the trumpet*. The Deller Consort almost turns *My beloved spake* into a series of madrigals. Pleasingly full sound from 1962.

'Madrigal masterpieces': The Renaissance in France, Italy and England (with Eileen Pouler, Mary Thomas, Wilfred Brown, Gerald English, Maurice Bevan, Geoffrey Coleby, Deller Consort): JANNEQUIN: *Ce moys de may; La bataille de Marignan; Au joly boys.* LASSUS: *Mon cœur se recommande à vous; Matona mia cara.* MARENZIA: *Scaldava il sol.* MONTEVERDI: *Baci, soavi, e cari; Ecco mormorar l'onde; A'un giro sol bell'occhi; Non piu guerra!; Sfogava con le stelle.* BYRD: *My sweet little baby* (lullaby). MORLEY: *Now is the month of maying.* GESUALDO: *Ecco moriro dunque / Hai gia mi disco loro.* TOMKINS: *When David heard that Absolom was slain.*
(M) ** Van. 08.5061.71 [id.].

We have moved on in the style of performance of Italian madrigals since this collection was (excellently, if closely) recorded in 1959. The Deller Consort are entirely happy in the English repertoire. Morley's *Now is the month of maying* almost explodes with spring-like vitality, and the Byrd and Tomkins items are beautiful. The Lassus *Mon cœur se recommande à vous* is touchingly serene in the same way, and *Matona mia cara* is freshly presented, but the Jannequin and Monteverdi items are less successful, although *Baci, soavi, e cari* has an appealing simplicty.

TALLIS (with Wilfred Brown, Gerald English, Eileen McLoughlin, Maurice Bevan, Deller Consort): *Lamentations of Jeremiah the Prophet.* 5 hymns alternating plainchant and polyphony: *Deus tuorum militum; Jam Christus astra ascenderat; Jesu Salvator Saeculi; O nata lux de lumine; Salvator mundi Domine.*
(M) ** Van. 08.5062.71 [id.].

Alfred Deller pioneered so much repertoire on LP, and even today Tallis's settings of the *Lamentations of Jeremiah* are not generously represented on disc. They are given poised, expressive performances and the motets are presented with their alternating plainsong, but the close recording robs the music-making of atmosphere and the dynamic range is very limited.

MONTEVERDI: *Il ballo delle Ingrate* (with Eileen McLoughlin, David Ward, April Cantelo, Amb. S., L. Chamber Players, Dennis Stevens); *Lamento d'Arianna* (with Honour Sheppard, Sally le Sage, Max Worthley, Philip Todd, Maurice Bevan, Deller Consort).
(M)**(*) Van. 08.5063.71 [id.].

Deller's pioneering 1956 stereo recording of Monteverdi's *Il ballo delle Ingrate* would not, perhaps, be a first choice today, but at the time he had the advantage of Dennis Steven's scholarly assistance, and the performance has remarkable authenticity as well as considerable dramatic life. The famous *Lamento d'Arianna* is slightly less successful – see our fuller review in the main composer index, above.

'The three ravens': Elizabethan folk and minstrel songs (with Desmond Dupré, guitar & lute): *The three ravens; Cuckoo; How should I your true love know; Sweet nightingale; I will give my love an apple; The oak and the ash;* (Lute) *Go from my window; King Henry; Coventry carol; Barbara Allen; Heigh ho, the wind and the rain; Waly, waly; Down in yon forest; Matthew, Mark, Luke and John;*

(Lute) *A Toye; The Tailor and the mouse; Greensleeves; The Wraggle Taggle Gipsies; Lord Rendall; Sweet Jane; The frog and the mouse; The seeds of love; Near London town; Who's going to shoe your pretty little foot?; Blow away the morning dew; Searching for lambs; Sweet England; Dabbling in the dew; Just as the tide was flowing.*
(M) **(*) Van. 08.5064.71 [id.].

Opening charismatically with *The three ravens*, this very early (1956) recital contains some outstanding performances, notably of *Barbara Allen*, the delightful *Tailor and the mouse*, *The frog and the mouse*, and the captivating *Who's going to shoe your pretty little foot?*. *Searching for lambs* brings another favourite melody, and Deller's inimitable *Greensleeves* is certainly memorable. As before, Desmond Dupré provides highly sympathetic accompaniments, and here he also has a couple of solo opportunities in which to shine. But although the mono recording is admirably truthful, this collection is not quite so spontaneously appealing as the stereo recital listed above, even if it is comparably generous (73 minutes).

'The holly and the ivy': Christmas carols of old England (with April Cantelo, Gerald English, Maurice Bevan, Deller Consort, Stanley Taylor, recorder, Desmond Dupré, lute): *Patapan; We three kings of orient are; I saw three ships; The Coventry carol; It came upon the midnight clear; Good King Wenceslas; Once in Royal David's city; Rocking; The first nowell; God rest you merry gentlemen; Wither's Rocking hymn; Silent night; Wassail song; Dormi Jesus; Boar's head carol; Past three o'clock; Lullay my liking; Adam lay ybounden; Herrick's carol; Angelus ad Virginem; The holly and the ivy; O little one sweet; Song of the Nuns of Chester; Winter-Rose; In dulci jubilo.*
(M) **(*) Van. 08.5065.71 [id.].

Opening vivaciously with *Patapan*, this Christmas collection, simulating a visit from a village group of waits, often has a pleasing simplicity, although at times its madrigalesque style may strike some ears as lacking robustness. The Consort is heard at its best in *I saw three ships*, *Good King Wenceslas* and *The holly and the ivy*. But the highlights are all from Deller himself, and he is in magical form in the *Angelus ad Virginem*, *Winter-Rose* (with a delicate recorder obbligato from Stanley Taylor) and *O little one sweet*, more robust in *Adam lay ybounden*, but again displaying his unique nuancing of colour and dynamic. His serene account of the *Coventry carol* is heard here on disc for the first time.

François COUPERIN: *Leçons des ténèbres I–III* (excerpts) (with Wifred Brown, Desmond Dupré, viola da gamba, Harry Gabb, organ).
(M) *(*) Van. 08.5066.71 [id.].

Although there is some remarkable singing here, Deller cannot compare with Gérard Lesne in this repertoire – his manner is curiously histrionic and self-aware, unusually so for this artist. Harry Gabb's discreet organ accompaniment is to be commended, but Dupré's viola da gamba is too backwardly balanced.

'Duets for counter-tenors' (with Mark Deller & Bar. Ens.): MORLEY: *Sweet nymph, come to thy lover; Miraculous love's wounding; I go before my darling.* PURCELL: *Sweetness of nature.* SCHUTZ: *Erhöre mich wenn ich; Der Herr ist gross.* JONES: *Sweet Kate.* ANON.: *Ah, my dear son.* MONTEVERDI: *Currite populi; Angelus ad pastores ait; Fugge, fugge, anima mea; Salve Regina.* BLOW: *If my Celia could persuade; Ah, heaven, what is't I hear.* DEERING: *O bone Jesu; In coelis.*
(M) *(*) Van. 08.5067.71 [id.].

Deller's style needs no advocacy, and he has trained his son well to follow faithfully in his footsteps. But although Mark has a fine (treble rather than alto) voice, he does not have his father's subtle instinct for light and shade. So in this case a succession of duets for counter-tenors proves far from ideal planning for a whole recital. Moreover the voices are placed very forwardly, somewhat edgily recorded, and robbed of a convincing dynamic range; there are no possibilities for pianissimo singing here.

William BYRD: *'Byrd and his age'* (with Wenzinger Consort of Viols of Schola Cantorum Basiliensis, August Wenzinger): *My sweet little darling; Lullaby, my sweet little baby* (both arr. Fellowes); *Fantasia for viols in G min.; Ye sacred muses (Elegy on the death of Thomas Tallis); Come pretty babe* (arr. Peter le Huray & Thurston Dart). ANON.: *Guishardo; Ah, silly poor Joas; O Death, rock me asleep.* WHYTHORNE: *Buy new broom.* Richard NICHOLSON: *In a merry May morn.* Robert PARSONS: *Pandolpho* (all six arr. Peter Warlock). William CORKINE: *What booteth love?* (arr. Thurston Dart). FERRABOSCO: *Fantasias for viols: in F & G.*
(M) ** Van. 08.5068.71 [id.].

The advantage of accompaniments from the excellent Schola Cantorum Basiliensis under Wenzinger is reduced by the rather forward balance of the voice in relation to the string group, and when the viols play alone the effect is rather dry. It is on the whole a melancholy programme, although *Buy new brooms* comes centrally as a bright diversion. But it is *Ah, silly poor Joas*, the Byrd *Lullaby*, and especially the very touching *Pandolpho* that are memorable, while the closing *O Death, rock me asleep* shows Deller at his most moving.

BACH and HANDEL: BACH: *Cantata No. 170: Vergnügte Ruh', beliebte Seelenlust* (with Leonhardt Bar. Ens.); *Cantata No. 54: Widerstehe doch: Aria: Widerstehe doch; Recitative: Die Art verruchter Sünden; Aria: Wer Sünde tut, der ust vom Teufel. Mass in B min.: Agnus Dei.* HANDEL: Arias: *Orlando: Ah! stigie larve* (Mad scene). *Jepthe: Tis heav'ns all ruling power. Theodora: Kind heaven; Sweet rose and lily.*
(M) ** Van. 08.5069.71 [id.].

These are among Deller's earliest recordings for Vanguard, dating from 1954. In the Bach cantatas Leonhardt provides dull, plodding accompaniments, and his ensemble of original instruments is uninspiringly meagre. The interest of this collection then centres on Deller himself, and he rises to the occasion, especially in the *Agnus Dei* from the *Mass in B minor*, which is most beautifully sung. The Handel accompaniments are more robust and it is good to hear Deller in these operatic excerpts, especially in Orlando's mad scene, but he is also at his finest in both the excerpts from *Theodora*.

'The Cries of London and English Ballads and folksongs': The Cries of London (with April Cantelo, Wilfred Brown, Amb. S., Deller Consort, L. Chamber Players): John COBB: *These are the cries of London.* RAVENSCROFT: *New oysters; Bellman's song; The painter's song; Brooms for old shoes.* DERING: *The cries of London* (all ed. Stevens); *Country cries* (ed. Revell). ANON.: *A quart a penny; I can mend your tubs and pails.* NELHAM: *Have you any work for the tinker?* (all ed. Stevens). WEELKES: *The cries of London* (ed. Noble). English ballads and folksongs (with Deller Consort; Desmond Dupré, lute): *When cockleshells turn silver bells; An Eriskay love lilt; Peggy Ramsay* (arr. Gerard Williams); *Bushes and briars; Brigg Fair; The cruel mother; A sweet country life* (arr. Imogen Holst); *The bitter withy; Lang a growing; The lover's ghost; Lovely Joan; She moved through the fair; A brisk young lad he courted me* (arr. Norman Stone); *Geordie.*
(M) **(*) Van. 08.5072.71 [id.].

Though they have now virtually died out in a noisy age, the traditional cries of London's street-vendors date back unaltered in the annals of time. In the seventeenth century they tempted many composers to set them in the form of robust catches and rounds which have little more than novelty value, although Deller here makes *The bellman's song* seem quite lyrical. Richard Dering's *Fantasia* is altogether more sophisticated and creates a continuous ten-minute musical kaleidoscope, ingeniously linking the airs in a seemingly natural sequence, ending with a melodious apotheosis on the words 'and so good night'. Weelkes's selection is little more than half as long, using one soloist, here the fresh-voiced April Cantelo. Even so, she gets through a great many lyrical exhortations to buy, ending with a gentle *Alleluia*. The second half of the recital brings Deller back (in 1959) to the world of ballads and folksongs, opening with a bewitchingly gentle account of *When cockleshells turn silver bells*. Both *The lover's ghost* and the *Eriskay love lilt* take him soaringly upwards, rapturously comparable with *Annie Laurie* on an earlier recital. He is effectively joined by the Consort in *Peggy Ramsay* and they bring variety to the collection with characteristic accounts of *A sweet country life* and *A brisk young lad*. Dupré and his lute set the scene for the lovely *Bushes and briars*. The *cruel mother*, which tells a dreadful story of infanticide, also shows him imaginatively stretched, while *Lang a-growing* with its neat Scottish snap is most effectively done.

VAUGHAN WILLIAMS: Arrangements of folksongs (with Deller Consort, Desmond Dupré, lute): *An acre of land; Bushes and briars; Ca' the yowes; The cuckoo and the nightingale; The dark-eyed sailor; Down by the riverside; A farmer's son so sweet; Greensleeves; John Dory; Just as the tide was flowing; The jolly ploughboy; Loch Lomond; The lover's ghost; My boy Billy; The painful plough; The spring time of the year; The turtle dove; Ward the Pirate; Wassail song.*
(M) ** Van. 08.5073.71 [id.].

These highly artistic folksong settings can be effectively performed either by choir or by soloists, and here Deller often alternates his own estimable solo contributions with choral versions. The recording is a little dry, but the stereo adds to the sense of atmosphere. An enjoyable collection, but not one of the finest of the series. It is discussed more fully under its composer listing, above.

Domingo, Plácido (tenor)

Operatic scenes from: OFFENBACH: *Contes d'Hoffmann* (with Sutherland, Tourangeau). BIZET: *Carmen* (with Troyanos, Te Kanawa). WAGNER: *Lohengrin* (with Randová, Norman, Sotin).
(M) *** Decca 421 890-2 [id.].

Here are extended excerpts from three of Domingo's most rewarding Decca opera sets, 21 minutes and five arias from his first, most successful *Tales of Hoffmann*, nearly half an hour from *Carmen*, and two key arias from his superb *Lohengrin*, with Solti – the line and colour of *In fernem Land* make this performance truly memorable. But this is essentially for Domingo admirers who prefer recitals to complete sets, or even highlights.

'Great voice': Excerpts from: BIZET: *Carmen* (with Berganza). PUCCINI: *Manon Lescaut* (with Caballé); *Fanciulla del West.* VERDI: *La Traviata* (with Cotrubas); *Macbeth.* WAGNER: *Tannhäuser.* Songs: CATARI: *Core'ngrato.* LARA: *Granada.* LEONCAVALLO: *Mattinata.* FREIRE: *Ay, ay, ay.* CURTIS: *Non ti scordar di me.*
(B) **(*) DG 431 104-2 [id.].

Certainly the collection assembled for DG's *'Grosse Stimmen'* series shows Domingo in his best light. Opening with the *Flower song* from *Carmen* (noble in line rather than melting), it includes also the vibrant 'live' *Manon Lescaut* duet which is also featured on the companion Caballé recital (only this time, curiously, the applause is cut off at the end). Stylish in Verdi and warmly moving in Walther's *Prize song* from *Die Meistersinger*, with resonant choral backing, the disc ends with a few top Italian pops, over-recorded but certainly making an impact. But the selection (59 minutes) is not as generous as other CDs in this series and, as usual, there is no documentation other than titles. At bargain price, however, many will be tempted.

'Domingo sings Càruso': Arias from LEONCAVALLO: *La Bohème; Pagliacci.* DONIZETTI: *L'elisir d'amore.* MASSENET: *Manon; Le Cid.* CILEA: *L'Arlesiana.* FLOTOW: *Martha.* PUCCINI: *La Fanciulla del West; La Bohème.* VERDI: *Rigoletto; Aida.* MEYERBEER: *L'Africana.* GOUNOD: *Faust.* HALEVY: *La juive.* MASCAGNI: *Cavalleria rusticana.*
(M) **(*) BMG/RCA 09026 61356-2 [id.].

This rather perversely named reissue is based on the contents of an LP originally called, more pertinently, 'The art of Plácido Domingo', recorded in 1971 with the LSO under Santi. Four more items have been added, but all are from the same period and, like the others, show the strong, resonant voice and the scope of Domingo's artistry at that stage in his career. With clear, direct sound, the heroic stage presence comes over well, the ringing tone able to impress in a lyrical phrase, even though more fining down of the tone and a willingness to sing really softly more often would enhance the listener's pleasure. But in the theatre this is obviously a voice to thrill, and the engineers have captured it directly and realistically, from the sobbing verismo of *Pagliacci* to the crisp aristocracy in *Rigoletto*. The selection is an interesting one – the opening aria from Leoncavallo's *Bohème* suggests that this opera is worth reviving.

'Grandi voci' (arias from): BIZET: *Carmen.* WAGNER: *Lohengrin.* R. STRAUSS: *Die Frau ohne Schatten* (with LPO or VPO, Solti). OFFENBACH: *Les Contes d'Hoffmann* (with SRO, Bonynge). MEYERBEER: *L'Africaine.*
(M) *** Decca Analogue/Dig. 440 410-2 [id.].

All but one of these recordings come from distinguished complete sets in which Domingo played a major part in ensuring their excellence. Whether as a superb Lohengrin or as the Emperor in Solti's more recent *Die Frau ohne Schatten,* there is no mistaking the nobility of this singing, and the great tenor readily shows his range in the excerpts from *Carmen* and the sparkling *Legend of Kleinzach* from *Contes d'Hoffmann*, all given vintage Decca sound. *O paradis* was recorded live in Rome in 1990.

'Domingo favourites'; Arias from: DONIZETTI: *L'elisir d'amore.* VERDI: *Ernani; Il trovatore; Aida; Nabucco; Don Carlos.* HALEVY: *La Juive.* MEYERBEER: *L'Africaine.* BIZET: *Les Pêcheurs de perles; Carmen.* PUCCINI: *Tosca; Manon Lescaut.*
(M) *** DG Dig. 445 525-2 [id.].

The greater part of this collection is taken from a 1980 digital recital, recorded in connection with yet another gala in San Francisco. The result is as noble and resplendent a tenor recital as you will find. Domingo improves in detail even on the fine versions of some of these arias he had recorded earlier, and the finesse of the whole gains greatly from the sensitive direction of Giulini. Though the orchestra is a little backward, the honeyed beauty of the voice is given the greatest immediacy. The other items are taken from Domingo's complete sets of *Don Carlos* (with Abbado), *Nabucco*, *Manon Lescaut* and *Tosca* (with Sinopoli), and are well up to the high standards this great tenor consistently sets for himself.

East London Chorus, Locke Brass Consort, Michael Kibblewhite

'*Essentially Christmas*' (with Jane Lister, harp): BLISS: *Royal fanfares I–II*. Arr. Edwards: *Wassail! (Sussex carol; Lute-book lullaby; Gloucestershire wassail)*. WALTON: *Coronation Te Deum* (arr. Palmer). KELLY: *6 Abingdon carols (King Herod and the cock; Dark the night; The carnal and the crane; Jesu, son most sweet and dear; Spanish carol; Sweet dreams, form a shade)*. RUTTER: *Te Deum*. VAUGHAN WILLIAMS: *Blessed Son of God; O clap your hands*. ARNELL: *Ceremonial and Flourish*. GRAINGER: *English Gothic music: Angelus ad virginem; Puellare gremium; The matchless maiden*. GREGSON: *Make a joyful noise*.
*** Koch Dig. 3-7202-2 [id.].

In fact this collection is hardly 'essentially Christmas', for the programme includes regal fanfares and various spectacular pieces for other occasions, all in highly effective arrangements so that the accompaniments can be given over to brass. Apart from the Walton and Rutter works, and Vaughan Williams's splendid *O clap your hands* (all otherwise available), there is also Edward Gregson's appropriately named *Make a joyful noise*, which receives its cheerful première recording here. Bryan Kelly's *Abingdon carols* are essentially austere, often with a certain medieval flavour, so they make a good foil, as does Percy Grainger's *English Gothic music*, also recorded here for the first time. These eccentric arrangements with their 'elastic scoring' seem determinedly inauthentic and all the more enjoyable for that. With excellent support from the Locke Brass Consort, Michael Kibblewhite and his East London Singers give vigorous yet finished performances in which exuberance often erupts, though they catch the darker mood of the six *Abingdon carols* equally impressively. The expansive digital recording has plenty of brilliance and breadth of sonority to make this a Christmas record that can be used at other times during the year. The CD was sponsored by Tate & Lyle. Good for them!

Fischer-Dieskau, Dietrich (baritone)

'*Fischer Dieskau Lieder Edition*' (complete).
⊛ (BB) ******* DG 447 500-2 (44) [id.].

To celebrate the seventieth birthday of the great German baritone, DG have published a justifiably extravagant Lieder Edition, summing up the astonishing achievement of the greatest male Lieder singer of our time – although, in making such a claim, one must not forget Gérard Souzay's inestimable contribution in the area of French art-song. The set is offered at budget price, with two discs thrown in for good measure (44 CDs for the price of 42).

Each individual composer grouping is also available separately, still very competitively priced. With consistent artistry from all concerned and with first-class transfers, these CDs are self-recommending. We have discussed the Schubert in previous volumes, and much else, too, in individual issues. Fischer-Dieskau's mastery never ceases to amaze. Sample this set at almost any point and the same virtues emerge: characteristic beauty of vocal tone and an extraordinarily vivid power of characterization and vocal colouring. No less remarkable are his accompanists, including the incomparable Gerald Moore and Daniel Barenboim, whose sensitivity and command of keyboard colour make for consistently memorable results. The Liszt collection is especially valuable. As in a number of other fields, Liszt has been severely under-appreciated as a song composer. This collection of 43 songs plus an accompanied declamation should do much to right the balance. The sheer originality of thought and the ease of the lyricism are a regular delight. Fischer-Dieskau's concentration and inspiration never seem to falter, especially in the most famous of the songs, the *Petrarch Sonnets*, and Barenboim's accompaniments could hardly be more understanding.

SCHUBERT: Lieder (with Gerald Moore, piano): Volume 1 (1811–17); Volume 2 (1817–28). Song-cycles: *Die schöne Müllerin; Schwanengesang; Die Winterreise*.
(B) ******* DG 437 214-2 (21) [id.].

Lieder, Volume I (1811–17): *Ein Leichenfantasie; Der Vatermörder* (1811); *Der Jüngling am Bache* (1812); *Totengräberlied; Die Schatten; Sehnsucht; Verklärung; Pensa, che questo istante* (1813); *Der Taucher* (1813–15); *Andenken; Geisternähe; Erinnerung; Trost, An Elisa; Die Betende; Lied aus der Ferne; Der Abend; Lied der Liebe; Erinnerungen; Adelaide; An Emma; Romanze: Ein Fräulein klagt'*

im finstern Turm; An Laura, als sie Klopstocks Auferstehungslied sang; Der Geistertanz; Das Mädchen aus der Fremde; Nachtgesang; Trost in Tränen; Schäfers Klagelied; Sehnsucht; Am See (1814); *Auf einen Kirchhof; Als ich sie erröten sah; Das Bild; Der Mondabend* (1815); *Lodas Gespenst* (1816); *Der Sänger* (1815); *Die Erwartung* (1816); *Am Flusse; An Mignon; Nähe des Geliebten; Sängers Morgenlied; Amphiaraos; Das war ich; Die Sterne; Vergebliche Liebe; Liebesrausch; Sehnsucht der Liebe; Die erste Liebe; Trinklied; Stimme der Liebe; Naturgenuss; An die Freude; Der Jüngling am Bache; An den Mond; Die Mainacht; An die Nachtigall; An die Apfelbäume; Seufzer; Liebeständelei; Der Liebende; Der Traum; Die Laube; Meeres Stille; Grablied; Das Finden; Wandrers Nachtlied; Der Fischer; Erster Verlust; Die Erscheinung; Die Täuschung; Der Abend; Geist der Liebe; Tischlied; Der Liedler; Ballade; Abends unter der Linde; Die Mondnacht; Huldigung; Alles um Liebe; Das Geheimnis; An den Frühling; Die Bürgschaft; Der Rattenfänger; Der Schatzgräber; Heidenröslein; Bundeslied; An den Mond; Wonne der Wehmut; Wer kauft Liebesgötter?* (1815); *Der Goldschmiedsgesell* (1817); *Der Morgenkuss; Abendständchen: An Lina; Morgenlied: Willkommen, rotes Morgenlicht; Der Weiberfreund; An die Sonne; Tischlerlied; Totenkranz für ein Kind; Abendlied; Die Fröhlichkeit; Lob des Tokayers; Furcht der Geliebten; Das Rosenband; An Sie; Die Sommernacht; Die frühen Gräber; Dem Unendlichen; Ossians Lied nach dem Falle Nathos; Das Mädchen von Inistore; Labetrank der Liebe; An die Geliebte; Mein Gruss an den Mai; Skolie – Lasst im Morgenstrahl des Mai'n; Die Sternenwelten; Die Macht der Liebe; Das gestörte Glück; Die Sterne; Nachtgesang; An Rosa I: Warum bist du nicht hier?; An Rosa II: Rosa, denkst du an mich?; Schwanengesang; Der Zufriedene; Liane; Augenlied; Geistes-Gruss; Hoffnung; An den Mond; Rastlose Liebe; Erlkönig* (1815); *Der Schmetterling; Die Berge* (1819); *Genügsamkeit; An die Natur* (1815); *Klage; Morgenlied; Abendlied; Der Flüchtling; Laura am Klavier; Entzückung an Laura; Die vier Weltalter; Pflügerlied; Die Einsiedelei; An die Harmonie; Die Herbstnacht; Lied: Ins stille Land; Der Herbstabend; Der Entfernten; Fischerlied; Sprache der Liebe; Abschied von der Harfe; Stimme der Liebe; Entzückung; Geist der Liebe; Klage: Der Sonne steigt; Julius an Theone; Klage: Dein Silber schien durch Eichengrün; Frühlingslied; Auf den Tod einer Nachtigall; Die Knabenzeit; Winterlied; Minnelied; Die frühe Liebe; Blumenlied; Der Leidende; Seligkeit; Erntelied; Das grosse Halleluja; Die Gestirne; Die Liebesgötter; An den Schlaf; Gott im Frühling; Der gute Hirt; Die Nacht; Fragment aus dem Aeschylus* (1816); *An die untergehende Sonne* (1816/17); *An mein Klavier; Freude der Kinderjahre; Das Heimweh; An den Mond; An Chloen; Hochzeitlied; In der Mitternacht; Trauer der Liebe; Die Perle; Liedesend; Orpheus; Abschied; Rückweg; Alte Liebe rostet nie; Gesänge des Harfners aus Goethes Wilhelm Meister: Harfenspieler I: Wer sich der Einsamkeit ergibt; Harfenspieler II: An die Türen will ich schleichen; Harfenspieler III: Wer nie sein Brot mit Tränen ass. Der König in Thule; Jägers Abendlied; An Schwager Kronos; Der Sänger am Felsen; Lied: Ferne von der grossen Stadt; Der Wanderer; Der Hirt; Lied eines Schiffers an die Dioskuren; Geheimnis; Zum Punsche; Am Bach im Frühling* (1816); *An eine Quelle* (1817); *Bei dem Grabe, meines Vaters; Am Grabe Anselmos; Abendlied; Zufriedenheit; Herbstlied; Skolie: Mädchen entsiegelten; Lebenslied; Lieden der Trennung* (1816); *Alinde; An die Laute* (1827); *Frohsinn; Die Liebe; Trost; Der Schäfer und der Reiter* (1817); *Lob der Tränen* (1821); *Der Alpenjäger; Wie Ulfru fischt; Fahrt zum Hades; Schlaflied; Die Blumensprache; Die abgeblühte Linde; Der Flug der Zeit; Der Tod und das Mädchen; Das Lied vom Reifen; Täglich zu singen; Am Strome; Philoktet; Memnon; Auf dem See; Ganymed; Der Jüngling und der Tod; Trost im Liede* (1817).
(b) *** DG 437 215-2 (9) [id.].

Lieder, Volume II (1817–28): *An die Musik; Pax vobiscum; Hänflings Liebeswerbung; Auf der Donau; Der Schiffer; Nach einem Gewitter; Fischerlied; Das Grab; Der Strom; An den Tod; Abschied; Die Forelle; Gruppe aus dem Tartarus; Elysium; Atys; Erlafsee; Der Alpenjäger; Der Kampf; Der Knabe in der Wiege* (1817); *Auf der Riesenkoppe; An den Mond in einer Herbstnacht; Grablied für die Mutter; Einsamkeit; Der Blumenbrief; Das Marienbild* (1818); *Litänei auf das Fest Allerseelen* (1816); *Blondel zu Marien; Das Abendrot; Sonett I: Apollo, lebet noch dein Hold verlangen; Sonett II: Allein, nachdenken wie gelähmt vom Krampfe; Sonett III: Nunmehr, da Himmel, Erde schweigt; Vom Mitleiden Mariä* (1818) ; *Die Gebüsche; Der Wanderer; Abendbilder; Himmelsfunken; An die Freunde; Sehnsucht; Hoffnung; Der Jüngling am Bache; Hymne I: Wenige wissen das Geheimnis der Liebe; Hymne II: Wenn ich ihn nur hab; Hymne III: Wenn alle untreu werden; Hymne IV: Ich sag es jedem; Marie; Beim Winde; Die Sternennächte; Trost; Nachtstück; Prometheus; Strophe aus Die Götter Griechenlands* (1819); *Nachthymne; Die Vögel; Der Knabe; Der Fluss; Abendröte; Der Schiffer; Die Sterne; Morgenlied* (1820); *Frühlingsglaube* (1822); *Des Fräuleins Liebeslauschen* (1820); *Orest auf Tauris* (1817); *Der entsühnte Orest; Freiwilliges Versinken; Der Jüngling auf dem Hügel* (1820); *Sehnsucht* (1817); *Der zürnenden Diana; Im Walde* (1820); *Die gefangenen Sänger; Der Unglückliche; Versunken; Geheimes; Grenzen der Menschheit* (1821); *Der Jüngling an der Quelle* (1815); *Der Blumen Schmerz* (1821); *Sei mir gegrüsst; Herr Josef Spaun, Assessor in Linz; Der Wachtelschlag Ihr Grab;*

Nachtviolen; Heliopolis I: Im kalten, rauhen Norden; Heliopolis II: Fels auf Felsen hingewälzt; Selige Welt; Schwanengesang: Wie klage'ich's aus; Du liebst mich nicht; Die Liebe hat gelogen; Todesmusik; Schatzgräbers Begehr; An die Leier; Im Haine; Der Musensohn; An die Entfernte; Am Flusse; Willkommen und Abschied (1822); *Wandrers Nachtlied: Ein Gleiches; Der zürnende Barde* (1823); *Am See* (1822/3); *Viola; Drang in die Ferne; Der Zwerg; Wehmut; Lied: Die Mutter Erde; Auf dem Wasser zu singen; Pilgerweise; Das Geheimnis; Der Pilgrim; Dass sie hier gewesen; Du bist die Ruh; Lachen und Weinen; Greisengesang* (1823); *Dithyrambe; Der Sieg; Abendstern; Auflösung; Gondelfahrer* (1824); *Glaube, Hoffnung und Liebe* (1828); *Im Abendrot; Der Einsame* (1824); *Des Sängers Habe; Totengräbers Heimwehe; Der blinde Knabe; Nacht und Träume; Normans Gesang; Lied des gefangenen Jägers; Im Walde; Auf der Bruck; Das Heimweh; Die Allmacht; Fülle der Liebe; Wiedersehn; Abendlied für die Entfernte; Szene I aus dem Schauspiel Lacrimas; Am mein Herz; Der liebliche Stern* (1825); *Im Jänner 1817 (Tiefes Leid); Am Fenster; Sehnsucht; Im Freien; Fischerweise; Totengräberweise; Im Frühling; Lebensmut; Um Mitternacht; Über Wildemann* (1826); *Romanze des Richard Löwenherz* (1827); *Trinklied; Ständchen; Hippolits Lied; Gesang (An Silvia); Der Wanderer an den Mond; Das Zügenglöcklein; Bei dir allein; Irdisches Glück; Wiegenlied* (1826); *Der Vater mit dem Kind; Jägers Liebeslied; Schiffers Scheidelied; L'incanto degli occhi; Il traditor deluso; Il modo di prender moglie; Das Lied im Grünen; Das Weinen; Vor meiner Wiege; Der Wallensteiner Lanznecht beim Trunk; Der Kreuzzug; Das Fischers Liebesglück* (1827); *Der Winterabend; Die Sterne; Herbst; Widerschein* (1828); *Abschied von der Erde* (1825/6).
(B) *** DG 437 225-2 (9) [id.].

Lieder, Volume III: Song-cycles: *Die Schöne Müllerin; Schwanengesang; Die Winterreise.*
(B) *** DG 437 235-2 (3) [id.].

SCHUMANN: Lieder (with Christoph Eschenbach, piano): *Myrten, Op. 25/1–3; 5–8; 13; 15–19; 21–2; 25–6. Lieder und Gesänge, Op. 27/1–5; Op. 51/4; Op. 77/1 & 5; Op. 96/1–3; Op. 98/2, 4, 6 & 8; Op. 127/2–3. Gedichte, Op. 30/1–3; Op. 119/2. Gesänge, Op. 31/1 & 3; Op. 83/1 & 3; Op. 89/1–5; Op. 95/ 2; Op. 107/3 & 6; Op. 142/1, 2 & 4; Schön Hedwig, Op. 106. 6 Gedichte aus dem Liederbuch eines Malers, Op. 36. 12 Gedichte aus Rückerts Liebesfrühling, Op. 37. Liederkreis, Op. 39. 5 Lieder, Op. 40. Romanzen und Balladen, Op. 45/1–3; Op. 49/1–2; Op. 53/1–3; Op. 64/3; Belsatzar, Op. 57. Liederkreis, Op.24. 12 Gedichte, Op. 35. Dichterliebe, Op. 48. Spanisches Liederspiel, Op. 74/6, 7 & 10. Liederalbum für die Jugend, Op. 79; Der Handschuh, Op. 87. 6 Gedichte von Nikolaus Lenau und Requiem (Anhang, No. 7), Op. 90. Minnnespiel, Op. 101. 4 Husarenlieder, Op. 117. Heitere Gesänge, Op. 125/1–3. Spanische Liebeslieder, Op. 138/2, 3, 5 & 7. Balladen, Op. 122/1–2. Sechs frühe Lieder, Op. posth. (WoO 21).*
(B) *** DG 445 660-2 (6) [id.].

BRAHMS: Lieder (with Daniel Barenboim, piano): *Gesänge, Op. 3/2–6; Op. 6/2–6; Mondnacht, Op. 7/ 1–4 & 6; Op. 43/1–4; Op. 46/1–4; Op. 70/1–4; Op. 71/1–5; Op. 72/2–5. Lieder und Romanzen, Op. 14/ 1–8; Gedichte, Op. 19/1–2, 3 & 5; Lieder und Gesänge, Op. 32/1–9; Op. 57/2–8; Op. 58/1–8; Op. 59/ 1–4, 6–7; Op. 63/1–9; Romanzen, Op. 33/1–15; Lieder, Op. 47/1–4; Op. 48/1, 2, 5–7; Op. 49/1–5; Op. 85/1–2, 4–6; Op. 86/2–5; Op. 94/1–3 & 5; Op. 95/2, 3 & 7; Op. 96/1–4; Op. 97/1–3, 5–6; Op. 105/4–5; Op. 106/1–5; Op. 107/1–2 & 4. Neuen Gesänge, Op. 69/3, 5 & 7. Vier ernste Gesänge, Op. 121.*
(B) *** DG 447 501-2 (6) [id.].

LISZT: Lieder (with Daniel Barenboim, piano): *Der Alpenjäger; Anfangs wollt' ich fast verzagen; Angiolin dal biondo crin; Blume und Duft; Comment, disaient-ils; Die drei Zigeuner; Du bist wie eine Blume; Der du von dem Himmel bist; Enfant, si j'étais roi; Eine Fichtenbaum steht einsam; Es muss ein Wunderbares sein; Es rauschen die Winde; Der Fischerknabe; Gastibelza; Gestorben war ich; Der Hirt; Hohe Liebe; Ich möchte hingehn; Ihr Glocken von Marling; Im Rhein, im schönen Strome; In Liebeslust; J'ai perdu ma force et ma vie; Klinge leise, mein Lied; Lasst mich ruhen; Die Lorelei; Morgens steh' ich auf und frage; Oh! quand je dors; O Lieb, so lang du lieben kannst; Petrarch sonnets Nos. 1–3; Schwebe, schwebe blaues Auge; S'il est un charmant gazon; Die stille Wasserrose; Des Tages laute Stimmen schweigen; La tombe et la rose; Der traurige Mönch; Uber allen Gipfeln ist Ruh; Die Vätergruft; Vergiftet sind meine Lieder; Le vieux vagabond; Wer nie sein Brot mit Tränen ass; Wieder möcht' ich dir Begegnen; Wie singt die Lerche schön.*
(B) *** DG 447 508-2 (3) [id.].

Richard STRAUSS: Lieder (with Wolfgang Sawallisch, piano): *5 kleine Lieder, Op. 69; Lieder, Op. 10/ 2–7; Op. 15/2 & 5; Op. 17/2; Op. 19/1–6; Op. 26/1–2; Op. 27/1, 3 & 4; Op. 29/1 & 3; Op. 31/4; Op. 32/1–5; Op. 36/1 & 4; Op. 37/1–2, 5–6; Op. 49/6; Op. 56/1 & 3; Op. 67/6. Schlichte Weisen, Op. 21; Vier Gesang, Op. 87.*
(B) *** DG 447 512-2 (2) [id.].

WOLF: Lieder (with Daniel Barenboim, piano): *23 Eichendorf Lieder; 42 Goethe Lieder; 7 Heine Lieder; 4 Lenau Lieder; 3 Gedichte von Michelangelo; Mörike Lieder* (complete); *6 Reinick Lieder; 4 Gedichte von Robert Reinick. 3 Gedichte nach Shakespeare und Lord Byron.* Miscellaneous Lieder by Peitl; Von Matthisson; Körner; Herloßsohn; Hebbel; Von Fallersleben; Sturm; Von Scheffel.
(B) *** DG 447 515-2 (6) [id.].

Other Recordings

'*Great voice*': Arias from: MOZART: *Die Zauberflöte; Don Giovanni; Le nozze di Figaro.* WAGNER: *Die Meistersinger.* Lieder: MAHLER: *Lieder eines fahrenden Gesellen: Ging heut morgen übers Feld. Ich atmet' einen linden Duft.* BEETHOVEN: *Zärtliche Liebe; Es war einmal ein König.* BRAHMS: *Heimweh II.* SCHUBERT: *Die schöne Müllerin: Das Wandern. Winterreise: Der Lindenbaum. Der Musensohn.* SCHUMANN: *Dichterliebe, Op. 48: Im wunderschönen Monat Mai. Liederkreis, Op. 39: Mondnacht.* WOLF: *Der Feuerreiter.* R. STRAUSS: *Heimliche Aufforderung.*
(B) *** DG 431 105-2 [id.].

This is one of the most enjoyable and rewarding of DG's '*Grosse Stimmen*' series, although the lack of translations is particularly serious in the case of the Lieder. Fischer-Dieskau is always a joy in Mozart and particularly so as Papageno in *Die Zauberflöte*, a role he never assumed on stage. As Hans Sachs in *Meistersinger* he is wonderfully warm in the *Fliedermonolog* and, after the second, more spectacular choral excerpt from Wagner's opera (*Ehrt eure deutschen Meister*), the Mahler songs which follow make a tender contrast. Indeed Fischer-Dieskau's Lieder singing can stand any amount of aural scrutiny and the rest of the programme is delightfully chosen, especially the lovely Schumann songs, followed by the lively Wolf *Der Feuerreiter*. The recordings range over three decades of his recording career from 1958 (an engaging account of Beethoven's *Es war einmal ein König*) to 1984, and the final song, Richard Strauss's *Heimliche Aufforderung*, has much subtlety of word-colouring.

'*Grandi voci*': Arias and excerpts from: MOZART: *Le nozze di Figaro.* HAYDN: *Acide e Galatea.* VERDI: *Macbeth; La Traviata; Don Carlo.* PUCCINI: *Tosca.* WAGNER: *Götterdämmerung; Parsifal.* MOZART: *Mentre ti lascio, K.513.* MAHLER: *Das Lied von der Erde: Der Einsame im Herbst.* SCHUMANN: *Scenes from Goethe's Faust: Ein Sumpf zieht am Gebirg'hin; Hier ist die Aussicht frei.*
(M) *** Decca 440 409-2 [id.].

This generous (74-minute) collection provides further evidence of the enormous span of Fischer-Dieskau's artistry, including as it does unexpected corners of the repertory. His keenly intelligent, stylish command, whether as the Count in *Figaro*, as Macbeth, as Scarpia, or in the Britten recording of Schumann's *Faust scenes*, is extraordinary. First-rate transfers.

Flagstad, Kirsten (soprano)

Kirsten Flagstad Edition

Kirsten Flagstad Edition (complete).
(M) **(*) Decca stereo/mono 440 490-2 (5) [id.].

MAHLER: *Kindertotenlieder; Lieder eines fahrenden Gesellen* (with VPO, Boult). WAGNER: *Wesendonck Lieder* (with VPO, Knappertsbusch) (440 491-2).

SIBELIUS: Songs: *Arioso; Autumn evening (Höstkväll); Black roses (Svata rosor); But my bird is nowhere to be seen (Men min fågel märks dock icke); Come away, death (Komm nu hit, död!); The diamond on the March snow (Diamanten på Marssnön); Did I dream? (Var det en dröm); The first kiss (Den första kyssne); The girl returned from meeting her lover (Flickan kom ifrån sin älsklings möte); On a veranda by the sea (På verandan vit havet); Sigh, rushes, sigh (Säv, säv, susa); Since then I have stopped asking (Se'n har jag ej frågat mera); Spring fleets fast (Våren flyktar hastigt); To the night (Til kvällen).* GRIEG: *Autumn storms (Efteråsstormen); I give my song to the spring (Jeg giver mit digt til våren); I would like a waistcoat of silk (Og jeg vil ha mig en silkevest); To you (Til én) I & II.* Arne EGGEN: *Praise to the eternal spring of life (Aere det evige forår i livet).* Eyvind ALNAES: *About love (Nu brister alle de kløfter); A February morning at the Gulf (Februarmorgen ved Golfen); A hundred violins (De hundrede fioliner); Yearnings of spring (Vårlængsler).* Harald LIE: *The key (Nykelen); The letter (Skinnvengbrev)* (with LSO, Oivin Fjeldstad) (440 492-2).

GRIEG: Haugtussa (*The Mountain maid*; song-cycle), *Op. 67*; Songs: *Ambition (Der ærgjerrige); Among roses (Millom rosor); At Gjaetle Brook (Ved Gjætle-Bekken); Blueberry slope (Blåbær-Li); Children's dance (A hipp og hoppe); A dream (En drøm); The encounter (Møte); Enticement (Det syng); Eros; The first meeting (Det første møte); Fra Monte Pincio (from Monte Pincio); High up in the leafy hills (I liden højt der oppe); I give my song to the spring (Jeg giver mit digt til våren); I love you (Jeg elsker Dig); In the boat (Der gynger en Båd på Bølge); The little hut (Hytten); Little Kirsten (Liten Kirsten); The little maiden (Veslemøy); Love (Elsk); Sorrowful day (Vond Dag); The water-lily (Med en vanlilje); With a primrose (Med en primulaveris)* (with Edwin McArthur) (mono 440 493-2).

BRAHMS: *Vier ernste Gesänage (4 Serious songs);* Lieder: *Alte Liebe; Am dem Kirchhofe; Am Sonntag Morgen; Bei dir sind meine Gedanken; Dein blaues Auge; Treue Liebe; Wie Melodien zieht es mir; Wir waldelten.* SCHUBERT: *Am Grabe Anselmos; An Der Erlkönig; Ave Maria; Das Mächens Klage; Dem Unendlichen* (with Edwin McArthur) (mono 440 494-2).

WAGNER: (with (i) Oslo PO or Norwegian State RO, Fjeldstad; (ii) VPO, Knappertsbusch; (iii) VPO, Solti): (i) *Götterdämmerung: Starke Scheite schichtet mir dort (Immolation scene).* (ii) *Lohengrin: Einsam in trüben Tagen. Parsifal: Ich sah das Kind. Die Walküre, Act I: Der Männer Sippe; Du bist der Lenz;* (iii) *Act II: Siegmund! Sieh' auf mich! (Todesverkündigung)* (stereo/mono 440 495-2).

The Decca producer John Culshaw was (understandably) a great admirer of the art of Kirsten Flagstad and it was he who persuaded her to come out of retirement in the mid-1950s. Not only did she contribute to Solti's great *Ring* cycle, singing the part of Fricka (for the first time) in *Das Rheingold*, but other recordings were planned, and most of them are here. She had recorded some of this repertoire earlier for EMI when she was in her prime in the mid-1940s, notably the Grieg and Norwegian songs. Yet the later, Decca recordings, which have more faithful sound, demonstrate again her masterly sense of pacing and of vocal colour and her command of evocation. These and the equally fine Sibelius songs are discussed more fully under their composer entries.

In Lieder, Flagstad may not have the evenness of line or bring the perception of word-meanings of the greatest German Lieder singers, but her voice is admirably suited to the *Four Serious songs* of Brahms, of which the third, *O Tod, O Tod, wie bitter bist du*, is most deeply felt, while among the other Brahms songs *Am Sonntag Morgen* brings wonderfully radiant tone and *Dein blaues Auge* is very touching. In Schubert, although the voice at times seems less than wieldy, the operatic drama of *Der Erlkönig* is as memorable as the gently ravishing cantilena of *Am Grabe Anselmos* and the hardly less sympathetic *Alte Liebe*. Here, as elsewhere, Edwin McArthur's accompaniments are a model of support for the great voice and make a sensitive and imaginative impression in their own right. The mono recordings, made at Decca's West Hampstead studios in the spring and late autumn of 1956, are naturally atmospheric, and the ear would hardly guess the sound was not early stereo. The stereo Wagner recordings with Knappertsbusch are uneven, although Flagstad was a superb Sieglinde, and her glorious voice is perfectly suited to the rich inspiration of the *Wesendonk Lieder*. Moreover the excerpt from Solti's partial recording of Act II of *Die Walküre* and the earlier (mono) Immolation scene from Fjeldstad's 1956 *Götterdammerung* provide an outstanding reminder of one of the finest Brünnhildes of our time. Throughout this set (which presents the the five individual CDs in a slipcase) the transfers are consistently vivid, and the documentation is good, with translations provided thoughout.

Freni, Mirella (soprano)

'Verismo arias' (with O del Teatro La Fenice, Robert Abbado) from: CILEA: *L'Arlesiana; Adriana Lecouvreur.* GIORDANO: *Andrea Chénier.* CATALANI: *La Wally; Loreley.* ALFANO: *Risurrezione.* MASCAGNI: *Cavalleria Rusticana; Lodoletta; Iris.* ZANDONAI: *Francesca da Rimini.* PUCCINI: *Gianni Schicchi.*

(M) ** Decca Dig. 433 316-2 [id.].

An interesting and enterprising collection, recorded in 1990. But Freni should have tackled this very demanding programme earlier in her long career. This is singing which would readily pass muster in the opera house and which is potentially beautiful and always characterful. But, even with the very experienced Christopher Raeburn producing the sessions, the voice is not flattered by the microphones and, too often under stress, the singing is strained and approaching squalliness. Otherwise the recording is first class, and the accompaniments are very sympathetic.

'Grandi voci' (arias from): PUCCINI: *La Bohème; Tosca; Madama Butterfly.* ROSSINI: *Guglielmo Tell.*
VERDI: *Falstaff.* LEONCAVALLO: *Pagliacci.* BOITO: *Mefistofele.* BELLINI: *Bianca e Fernando.*
Folksongs, arr. BALILA PRATELLA: *Ninnananna di Modigliana; Ninnananna romagnola.*
(M) *** Decca Analogue/Dig. 440 412-2 [id.].

Since making most of these recordings – many of them taken from complete Decca sets made
between 1963 and 1980, including her superb Mimi and Butterfly with Karajan – Freni has expanded
to even more dramatic roles, but her purity, clarity and sweetness in these mainly lyric roles are a
constant delight, nicely varied. The recital ends with two delightful lullabies, essentially folksongs,
arranged by Francesco Balila Pratella. The sound is consistently fresh.

Fretwork

'The English Viol' (with Catherine Bott, soprano, Jeremy Budd, treble, Michael Chance, counter-
tenor and (i) Red Byrd): ANON.: *The dark is my delight; Allemande and Galliard* (from *Lumley
Books*); *In paradise.* FERRABOSCO I: *In Nomine a 5.* HOLBORNE: *Pavan and Galliard.* BYRD: *Christe
redemptor a 4; In nomine a 5 No. 4; Ah silly soul.* DOWLAND: *Lachrimae gementes; Semper Dowland
semper dolens; M. Bucton his Galiard.* FERRABOSCO II: *Pavan and Alman.* GIBBONS: *Fantasia a 6 No.
2; Fantasia a 3 for the 'Great dooble bass'; The silver swan; Fantasia a 2. The cry of London, Part II.*
LAWES: *Fantazy a 5 on the playnesong in G min.; Gather ye rosebuds; Aire`a 6 in G min.* LOCKE:
Consort of 4 parts in F. PURCELL: *Fantasia a 4 in B flat No. 5; In nomine a 6.*
❀ (M) *** Virgin Veritas/EMI Dig. VER5 61173-2 [id.].

Fretwork was one of the really outstanding groups of artists which Virgin Records promoted from
their inception and they offer viol playing which is in a class of its own. This superb 77-minute
anthology draws on recordings made between 1988 and 1994: the excellence is unvarying: these
players catch perfectly the spirit of the later-Tudor and early-Stuart periods. The playing itself has
immaculate ensemble and intonation, restrained feeling and great freshness. Much of the music is
relatively austere but the effect on the listener is hypnotic. The special character of Elizabethan
romantic melancholy is well caught by Dowland (especially in his autobiographical *Semper Dowland,
semper dolens*), but there is lively part-writing too, notably from Lawes and Locke. Lawes's *Fantasy a
5 'on the playnesong'* is touchingly expressive, the music's sonority coloured subtly by an (uncredited)
chamber organ continuo, while the two pieces by Purcell are also quietly moving. The instrumental
music is sprinkled with brief, cheerful, vocal items, delightfully sung, and the selection includes an
excerpt from *The Cry of London*, where the vocal group, Red Byrd, offer every conceiveable
commodity for sale, from a pair of oars and a good sausage to bread and meat 'for the prisoners of
the Marshalsea'. Altogether an ideal introduction to a period in English history which was musically
very productive. The recording could hardly be bettered.

Ghiaurov, Nicolai (bass)

'Russian songs' (with (i) Zlatina Ghiaurov (piano), or (ii) Kaval Ch. & O): (i) TCHAIKOVSKY: *None
but the lonely heart; Not a word, O my love; Don Juan's serenade; It was in the early spring; Mid the
noisy stir of the ball; I bless you, woods.* BORODIN: *For the shores of your far-off native land.* GLINKA:
Midnight review. RUBINSTEIN: *Melody.* DARGOMIZHSKY: *The worm; Nocturnal breeze; The old
corporal.* (ii) Folksongs: *The cliff; the Volga boatmen; The little oak cudgel; Bandura; Stenka Razin;
Along Petersburg Street; In the dark forest; Dark eyes; Dear little night; The Twelve brigands;
Farewell, joy.*
(B) *** Decca Double 443 024-2 (2) [id.].

One of the problems of producing a record of Russian songs is the inherent danger of monotony of
dark colouring and Slavic melancholy. This difficulty is not entirely avoided in Ghiaurov's 1971
recital, as the Tchaikovsky songs have (understandably) been grouped together and have a recognizably similar idiom. Even so, there is some splendid music, and *It was in early spring* and *I bless you,
woods* are particularly memorable for their characteristically yearning melodic lines. With the
appearance of Glinka's colourful *Midnight review* the mood lightens (even though this is a descriptive
piece about old soldiers rising from their graves for a ghostly parade). The three Dargomizhsky songs
are notably fine, the third a masterpiece worthy of Mahler in its control of atmosphere. *The old
corporal* is being marched to his death at the hands of the firing squad. He has been rude to an officer
('too young to insult old soldiers') and is to be shot as an example. He accepts his fate philosophically
and bears no grudge against his companions who are to dispatch him to the next world; instead he

thinks back over his long and varied military life. It is a touching finish to a finely sung and accompanied recital.

For the reissue, the solo recital has been paired with a vibrantly authentic collection of folksongs with the Kaval Chorus and Orchestra – plentifully spiced with balalaikas. Favourite items like the *Volga Boatmen* and *Dubinushka* ('The little oak cudgel'), *Dark eyes* ('Ochi chorni') cannot fail when sung so vividly and presented so atmospherically – the recording was made in the warm acoustics of the Vienna Sofiensaal in 1973. But most effective of all is the closing *Farewell, joy* with its characteristically Slavonic yearning. The choir open *pianissimo* and make an impressive backing for the eloquent solo line, sung with Slavonic flair and unashamed temperament.

'Gramophone Greats'

'20 Gramophone All-time Greats' (original mono recordings from 1907–1935): LEONCAVALLO: *Pagliacci: Vesti la giubba* (Caruso); *Mattinata* (Gigli). BISHOP: *Lo here the gentle lark* (Galli-Curci with flute obbligato by Manuel Beringuer). PURCELL: *Nymphs and shepherds* (Manchester Schools Children's Choir (Choir Mistress: Gertrude Riall), Hallé O, Harty). MENDELSSOHN: *Hear my prayer – O for the wings of a dove* (Ernest Lough, Temple Church Ch., Thalben Ball). MARSHALL: *I hear you calling me* (John McCormack). ELGAR: *Salut d'amour* (New SO, composer). J. STRAUSS: *Casanova: Nuns' Chorus* (Ch. & O of Grossen Schauspielhauses, Berlin, Ernst Hauke). RACHMANINOV: *Prelude in C sharp min. Op. 3/2* (composer). TRAD.: *Song of the Volga Boatmen* (Chaliapin). KREISLER: *Liebesfreud* (composer, Carl Lamson). MOSS: *The floral dance* (Peter Dawson, Gerald Moore). BACH: *Chorale: Jesu, joy of man's desiring* (arr. & played Dame Myra Hess). HANDEL: *Messiah: Come unto Him* (Dora Labette, O, Beecham). SAINT-SAENS: *Samson and Delilah: Softly awakes my heart* (Marian Anderson). BIZET: *Fair Maid of Perth: Serenade* (Heddle Nash). CHOPIN: *Waltz in C sharp min., Op. 64/2* (Cortot). LEHAR: *Land of Smiles: You are my heart's delight* (Richard Tauber). KERN: *Showboat: Ol' man river* (Paul Robeson). SULLIVAN: *The lost chord* (Dame Clara Butt).

(M) (***) ASV mono CDAJA 5112 [id.].

It seems strange and somewhat sad that this marvellous collection of classical 78-r.p.m. hit records, covering a period of three decades, should be coming from ASV rather than HMV (EMI), who are responsible for so many of the actual recordings. Their amazing technical excellence means that they can be enjoyed today as they were then, with occasional clicks and generally not too intrusive background 'surface' noise to create the right ambience. Caruso still projects vividly from a 1907 acoustic master and Amelita Galli-Curci's soprano is as clear and sweet as the day it was made (1919). Other highlights (for us) include the Manchester School Children's choir of 250 voices, electrically recorded in Manchester's Free Trade Hall in 1929. The story goes that, just before the record was made, Sir Hamilton Harty bought cream buns and pop for every child, and that accounts for the warm smile in the singing. Master Ernest Lough's *O for the wings of a dove* is another miracle of perfection from a young boy treble, and Peter Dawson's exuberant *Floral dance* has astonishing diction – you can hear every word – and here Gerald Moore's bravura accompaniment is a key part of the sheer pleasure this performance still gives. Finally, Dame Clara Butt with her deep masculine contralto, clanging like a bell in its lowest register, delivers the sacred piece so beloved by Victorians: Sullivan's *Lost chord*. The transfers are all good (except perhaps for Dame Myra Hess's *Jesu, joy of man's desiring*, where the background surely could have been cut back a bit more).

Gruberová, Edita (soprano)

'French and Italian opera arias' (with Munich R. O, Kuhn): DELIBES: *Lakmé: Bell song*. MEYERBEER: *Les Huguenots: Nobles seigneurs, salut! GOUNOD: Roméo et Juliette: Waltz song*. THOMAS: *Hamlet: Mad scene*. DONIZETTI: *Lucia di Lammermoor: Mad scene*. ROSSINI: *Semiramide: Bel raggio lusinghier. Il barbiere di Siviglia: Una voce poco fa.*

(M) *** EMI Dig. CD-EMX 2234 [CDM5 65557-2].

Gruberová, for long type-cast in the roles of Queen of the Night and Zerbinetta, here formidably extends her range of repertory in a dazzling display of coloratura, impressive not only in the Italian repertory but in the French too, notably the *Hamlet* mad scene. The agility is astonishing, but the tone as recorded often hardens on top, although the CD provides extra fullness and clarity.

Hagegård, Håkan (baritone), Thomas Schuback (piano)

'Dedication': BRAHMS: An die Nachtigall; An ein Veilchen; An die Mond. FOERSTER: An die Laute. GOUNOD: A toi mon cœur. HAHN: A Chloris. MOZART: An Chloë, K.524; Ich würd' auf meinem Pfad (An die Hoffnung), K.390. SCHUBERT: An Mignon; An den Tod; An den Mond; An den Leier; An die Musik; Am mein Herz. STRAUSS: Zueignung. WOLF: An eine Aeolsharfe.
**(*) BIS CD 54 [id.].

This recital is called 'Dedication' and it begins with the Strauss song of that name. The collection first appeared in LP form in 1976 but was in circulation only intermittently in this country. The record was made at the outset of the distinguished Swedish baritone's career when he was in his mid-twenties and in wonderfully fresh voice. He sounds very much like a youthful Fischer-Dieskau but is at times a trace too studied, colouring the voice rather too expressively and adopting rather self-consciously deliberate tempi. There are times when one longs for him to be a little more unbuttoned. However, there is far more to admire and relish than to criticize, in particular the gloriously fresh vocal tone, and the sensitive playing of Thomas Schuback. Admirers of this artist will probably have this on LP; others need not hesitate.

Hespèrion XX

'Llibre Vermell de Montserrat' (A fourteenth-century pilgrimage): O Virgo splendens; Stella splendens in monte; Laudemus Virginem Mater est; Los set goyts recomptarem; Splendens ceptigera; Polorum regina omnium nostra; Cincti simus concanentes: Ave Maria; Mariam Matrem Virginem; Imperayritz de la ciutat joyosa; Ad mortem festinamus; O Virgo splendens hic in monte celso.
(M) *** Virgin Veritas/EMI VER5 61174-2 [id.].

In the Middle Ages the Spanish monastery of Montserrat was an important place of pilgrimage and, although a great deal of the music held in the library there was lost in a fire at the beginning of the nineteenth century, one early manuscript, the Llibre Vermell (Red Book), has survived to remind us of the music of that period. It dates from 1400 and is especially fascinating in including ten anonymous choral songs for the use of the pilgrims 'while holding night vigil' who may 'sometimes desire to sing and dance in the Church Square (where only respectable and pious songs may be sung)'. The music is extraordinarily jolly and robust, often written in the style of the French virelai (featuring alternating musical lines, with the first framing a central repeated tune). Canonic devices are also used and the effect is often quite sophisticated. There is no better example of this spirited music than Los set goyts, an infectious round dance complete with refrain. Various instrumental groupings add lively colour and support to the vocal line; the performances are full of joy, though at times emotionally respectful too. The analogue recording was made in France, but the resonant acoustic seems perfectly judged. This is a life-enhancing collection to cheer one up, and it shows that life in the Middle Ages was not always grim.

Holm, Renate (soprano), Werner Krenn (tenor), Vienna Volksoper Orchestra, Walter Weller

'Operetta gala' (with (i) Pilar Lorengar): Arias and duets from J. STRAUSS Jr: (i) Der Zigeunerbaron; Eine Nach in Venedig. MILLOCKER: Der Bettelstudent. SUPPE: Boccaccio. KALMAN: Die Zirkusprinzessin. DOSTAL: Clivia; Die ungarische Hochzeit; Die Csárdásfürstin. KUNNEKE: Der Vetter aus Dingsda. KATTNIGG: Bel Ami; Mädels vom Rhein. ZELLER: Der Vogelhändler. CZERNIK: Chi sa?.
(M) **(*) Decca 436 898-2 [id.].

This recital is taken from a two-LP collection, recorded in the Sofiensaal in 1970. The Lehár items have been reissued separately (see above under the composer) and, to make up the playing time, Pilar Lorengar contributes three additional numbers. Renate Holm and Werner Krenn have very fresh and pleasing voices, and their lyrical singing is most beguiling. The programme opens delectably with the number made famous by Hollywood as 'One day when we were young', and there are plenty of other attractive contributions from both these artists, not least Werner Krenn's Ich bin nur ein armer Wandergesell' (more familiar as 'Good night, pretty maiden, good night') from Künneke's Cousin from nowhere and the charming duet, Bel ami, of Kattnigg. Pilar Lorengar's contributions offer more fluttery and forceful soprano tone, but she sings her Hungarian-styled numbers with much character. The real snag is that overall there is too much lyrical music of a similar style. What a pity Decca did not add a chorus and have more lively numbers to offer contrast. No complaints about Walter Weller's stylish accompaniments, and the vintage Decca recording is first rate.

Horne, Marilyn (mezzo-soprano)

Arias from: ROSSINI: *Il barbiere di Siviglia; Semiramide; L'italiana in Algeri; La Cenerentola.* BELLINI: *I Capuletti e i Montecchi.* DONIZETTI: *Lucrezia Borgia; La figlia del reggimento.*
(M) *** Decca 421 891-2 [id.].

Apart from Orsini's vivacious *Il segreto per esser felice* – a winner if ever there was one – which comes from the 1963 complete set of *Lucrezia Borgia*, all these items are drawn from two recitals which Marilyn Horne made for Decca in 1964/5, conducted by her husband, Henry Lewis. It is the Rossini items for which she is rightly famous, but in the excerpt from *La figlia del reggimento* she is in equally striking form, and her singing continually delights and astonishes with its remarkable range – virtuosity exploited with red-blooded fervour. Excellent recording, with the voice sounding very fresh.

'Grandi voci' Arias from: HANDEL: *Semele; Rodelinda.* MOZART: *La clemenza di Tito.* GLUCK: *Alceste.* BIZET: *Carmen.* SAINT-SAENS: *Samson et Dalila.* GOUNOD: *Sapho.* ROSSINI: *L'Italiana in Algeri; La donna del lago.* Song: ARDITI: *Boléro.*
(M) *** Decca Analogue/Dig. 440 415-2 [id.].

The dramatic opening aria, *Iris hence away*, from Handel's *Semele*, sets the scene on this as a recital from an artist who surely personifies the generic title of this fine Decca series. Most of the other items come from a trio of LP recitals which Marilyn Horne made with her husband, Henry Lewis (who had guided her career), between 1964 and 1967. Her performance of Handel's *Dove sei* is as powerful as it is moving, and these widely varied excerpts show her as having a really big, firm mezzo voice, yet finding no difficulty whatever in coping with the most tricky florid passages. The range is astounding, and the vibrancy of the *Carmen* excerpts make a foil for the Delilah characterization. The famous *Mon cœur s'ouvre à ta voix* is taken in a long-breathed, spacious manner to bring out the music's richly sensuous potential. When every single item brings wonderment, it is impossible to single out one above the rest. The 76-minute collection ends with a live recording of *Mura felici* from *La Donna del lago*, made much later, in 1981, but the vocal flexibility is as amazing as ever and the chest register still seemingly as powerful.

Huddersfield Choral Society, Brian Kay; Phillip McCann; Simon Lindley

'A Christmas celebration' (with Sellers Engineering Band): TRAD.: *Ding dong merrily on high; Kwmbaya; Joys seven; Away in a manger; Deck the hall; O Christmas tree (Tannenbaum); Coventry carol.* JAMES: *An Australian Christmas.* GRUBER: *Silent night.* BACH: *Cantata No. 140: Zion hears the watchmen's voices.* GARDNER: *The holly and the ivy.* arr. Richards: *A merry little Christmas.* HOLST: *In the bleak mid-winter.* arr. Willcocks: *Tomorrow shall be my dancing day.* BRAHMS: *Lullaby.* arr. Smith: *Santa Claus-Trophobia.* MATHIAS: *Sir Christèmas.* LANGFORD: *A Christmas fantasy.*
(M) *** Chan. Dig. CHAN 4530.

Sumptuously recorded in the generous acoustic of Huddersfield Town Hall, opening with a spectacular arrangement of *Ding dong merrily* and closing with Gordon Langford's colourful pot-pourri *Fantasy*, this CD offers rich choral tone, well laced with opulent brass. There are simple choral arrangements too, beautifully sung by the Huddersfield choir, like Stephen Cleobury's *Joys seven*, Langford's *Deck the hall* and David Willcocks's slightly more elaborate *Tomorrow shall be my dancing day*, while Grüber's *Silent night* remains the loveliest of all serene carols. In other favourites the brass is nicely intertwined, as in *Away in a manger* and the *Coventry carol*, or it provides a sonorous introduction, as in Holst's *In the bleak mid-winter*. Mathias's rhythmically energetic *Sir Christèmas* provides a little spice. The brass are given their head in a solo spot, an effective novelty number, *Santa Claus-Trophobia*, arranged by Sandy Smith, which brings an impressive contribution from the solo tuba. Undoubtedly the brass contribution adds much to the entertainment value of this superbly recorded and well-presented 70-minute concert.

Italian Opera: 'Favourite Italian opera'

'Favourite Italian opera' (sung by: (i) Amb. S., LSO, Abbado; (ii) Bergonzi; (iii) Pavarotti; (iv) Di Stefano (v) Cossotto; (vi) Tebaldi; (vii) Corelli; (viii) St Cecilia, Rome, Ch. & O, Serafin; (ix) Freni; (x) Anita Cerquetti; (xi) Bastianini; (xii) Simionato; (xiii) Bruno Previdi; (xiv) Del Monaco; (xv) Maria Chiara): excerpts from: VERDI: (i) *Nabucco;* (ii) *Aida;* (iii) *Rigoletto.* DONIZETTI: (iv) *L'Elisir d'amore;* (v) *La Favorita.* PUCCINI: (vi) *Gianni Schicchi; La Rondine;* (vii) *Tosca;* (viii) *Madama Butterfly;* (ix; iii) *La Bohème;* (iii) *Turandot.* BELLINI: (x) *Norma.* ROSSINI: (xi) *Il barbiere di Siviglia;* (xii) *La Cenerentola.* (xiii) GIORDANO: *Fedora.* LEONCAVALLO: *Pagliacci.* CATALANI: *La Wally.* (M) ** Decca 421 895-2.

A perfectly good but not distinctive collection, generous in playing time (75 minutes) and offering consistently vivid (if occasionally slightly dated) sound. Highlights include Pavarotti in *La donna è mobile* from *Rigoletto* and *Nessun dorma* from *Turandot* (which ends the recital), and he is joined by Freni for *Sì, mi chiamano Mimì* from *Bohème.* Di Stefano, Tebaldi, Bergonzi and Simionato all make sterling contributions, but other performances, though rousing, are more routine.

Jo, Sumi (soprano)

Virtuoso arias (with Monte Carlo PO, Olmi) from: ROSSINI: *Il barbiere di Siviglia.* BELLINI: *La sonnambula.* DONIZETTI: *Lucia di Lammermoor.* DELIBES: *Lakmé.* R. STRAUSS: *Ariadne auf Naxos.* VERDI: *Rigoletto.* MEYERBEER: *Dinorah.* BERNSTEIN: *Candide.* MOZART: *Die Zauberflöte* (with O de Paris Ens., Jordan). YOUNG-HA HOON: Song: *Boribat.*
*** Erato/Warner Dig. 4509 97239-2 [id.].

This is among the most brilliant and commanding recitals of coloratura arias made in the 1990s. Though the recording brings out a slight flutter in Sumi Jo's lovely voice, the sweetness and tenderness of her singing, so different from the hardness of many coloratura sopranos, is formidably established over the widest range of arias. Sumi Jo's clarity, with no hint of stridency, coupled with a dreamy quality in the delivery, reminds one of the remark of an opera critic many years ago, that Galli-Curci sounded like 'a nightingale half-asleep'. Not that there is anything sleepy in Sumi Jo's singing, which is beautifully controlled. That is so both in firework arias like Rosina's *Una voce poco fa* from Rossini's *Barber* and over the sustained spans of the big aria in Bellini's *La sonnambula* (full recitative leading to *Ah non credea mirarti* and *Ah! non giunge*) and the Mad scene from Donizetti's *Lucia di Lammermoor.* Though *Glitter and be gay* from Bernstein's *Candide* lacks a little in fun, Delibes' *Bell song* from *Lakmé* is aptly sensuous and Zerbinetta's aria from *Ariadne auf Naxos* aptly extrovert, while the reading of the Queen of the Night's second aria from Mozart's *Zauberflöte* is lighter and even faster than with Solti in his Decca set. With tenderness and poise a regular ingredient alongside brilliance, not least in the honeyed sounds of the final Korean song, all ten arias are to be cherished. The voice is well caught, though the orchestral accompaniment has less presence.

'Carnaval!' (with ECO, Richard Bonynge): French coloratura arias from: OFFENBACH: *Un mari à la porte.* MASSENET: *Don César de Bazan.* Félicien DAVID: *La Perle du Brésil.* GRETRY: *L'Amant jaloux.* BALFE: *Le puits d'amour.* MESSAGER: *Madame Chrysanthème.* THOMAS: *Le songe d'une nuit d'été.* ADAM: *Les pantins de Violette; Si j'étais roi.* HEROLD: *Le pré aux clercs.* DELIBES: *Le roi l'a dit.* BOIELDIEU: *La fête du village voisin.* MASSE: *La Reine Topaze: Carnaval de Venise.*
🏵 *** Decca Dig. 440 679-2 [id.].

If anything, this singing is even more astonishing than Sumi Jo's Erato recital, above. The music may be more frivolous, but what delectable freshness and vocal sparkle there is in every number, and this repertoire is far rarer. After the frothy Offenbach introduction, the nightingale lightness and precision in Massenet's *Sevillana* from *Don César de Bazan* is matched by the vocal poise in the *Couplets du Mysoli* from David's *La Perle du Brésil,* with William Bennett playing the flute solo. Equally, Jo trills along seductively in Adam's *Chanson du canari,* in which the song's pensive quality is also nicely caught. This is Galli-Curci territory, and Sumi Jo doesn't come second best; moreover her voice is fuller and warmer. The softness and delicious ease of her pianissimo top notes also recall Rita Streich at her finest, in both Adam and Thomas, and in the Grétry *Je romps la chaîne qui m'engage.* Her ravishingly easy legato in Balfe's *Rêves d'amour* is a joy, while Hérold's *Jours de mon enfance* brings a duet with a solo violin (the excellent Anthony Marwood), and here one is reminded of the young Sutherland. Delibes' *Waltz song* from *Le roi l'a dit* is bewitching, and the recital ends with a sparkling *Boléro* of Boieldieu and an unforgettable interpolation of the *Carnival of Venice* into an aria by Victor Massé, with astonishingly free divisions. Throughout, Bonynge provides stylish and beautifully pointed accompaniments, as he has done for Sutherland in the past, and the Decca recording could hardly be bettered.

Lontano, Odaline de la Martinez

'*British women composers, Vol. 1*': WALLEN: *It all depends on you.* COOPER: *The Road is wider than long.* MACONCHY: *My dark heart.* LEFANU: *The Old woman of Beare.*
**(*) Lorelt Dig. LNT 101 [id.].

This *avant-garde* music will perhaps suit some tastes; little that happens here is predictable. *It all depends on you* brings a rather curious setting of poems by Philip Larkin, presented in a very colloquial style by Fiona Baines with instrumental support. There are moments of jazz, and the last song is an almost unaccompanied setting of *Lift through the breaking day*. Then comes a much more popularly styled work, *The Road is wider than long*, in no way difficult and quite ear-catching. Elizabeth Maconchy provides a more complex setting of Synge poems, *My dark heart*, which is certainly imaginative in its instrumentation. Jane Manning is the confident soloist here and also in a partly sung, partly spoken, version of an Irish poem by Nicola LeFanu. Excellent recording, but this record is not for general consumption.

'*British women composers, Vol. 2*': DE LA MARTINEZ: *Canciones.* WEIR: *Airs from another planet.* MAXWELL: *Pibroch.* TANN: *Winter sun, summer rain.* ALBERGA: *Dancing with the shadow* (suite). **(*) Lorelt Dig. LNT 103 [id.].

The programme here is more tangible than on Volume 1, and also rather more accessible. The most striking works are Judith Weir's *Airs from another planet* for piano and wind quintet, where four Scottish dances are heard through a musical distorting prism. The last is a bagpipe air, and that prepares the way for Melinda Maxwell's *Pibroch*, evoked rather hauntingly on oboe and cello. The programme opens with four vibrant and very free Lorca settings by Odaline de la Martinez, accompanied by percussion, except for the third, a love song, in which the piano adds to the atmosphere. Hilary Tann's *Winter sun, summer rain*, where the closing section pictures 'that very special light which illuminates the Welsh countryside in the aftermath of a rainfall', is a piece for viola, cello, flute, clarinet and celeste. Finally *Dancing with the shadow* by Eleanor Alberga is a not too thorny three-movement piece for flute, clarinet, violin, cello and percussion, with a very lively finale. Fine performances and clear recording, but only for the adventurous.

Luxon, Benjamin (baritone), David Willison (piano)

'*The world of favourite ballads*': HARRISON: *Give me a ticket to heaven.* TOSTI: *Parted.* HUHN: *Invictus.* SANDERSON: *Friend o'mine.* QUILTER: *Now sleeps the crimson petal.* MOSS: *The floral dance.* MURRAY: *I'll walk beside you.* STERNDALE-BENNETT: *The carol singers.* RASBACH: *Trees.* WATSON: *Anchored.* ANON., arr. KAYE: *Mr Shadowman.* TOURS: *Mother o' mine.* ADAMS: *The holy city.* JACOBS/BOND: *A perfect day.* GLOVER: *Rose of Tralee.* LAMB: *The volunteer organist.* MASCAGNI: *Ave Maria.* CLARKE: *The blind ploughman.* BRAHE: *Bless this house.* DAVIS: *God will watch over you.* (M) *** Decca 443 391-2; *443 391-4* [id.].

Here Benjamin Luxon provides a solo collection of some 20 ballads, recorded in 1975. The bluff hints of characterization never step into the area of outright send-up, although just occasionally he goes over the top. A touch more restraint in *The floral dance*, where the final verse is very histrionic, would have been welcome, although David Willison's piano accompaniment conjures up the 'fiddle, cello, big bass drum, cornet, flute and euphonium' rather effectively. Yet Peter Dawson showed how a more direct manner could be so telling in this famous number (see above, in '*Gramophone Greats*'). The sentimental ballads like *I'll walk beside you*, *A perfect day* and the *Rose of Tralee* are very pleasingly done, while Roger Quilter's *Now sleeps the crimson petal* is sung beautifully. But it is the dialogue songs that come off especially well, notably *Mr Shadowman*, which is most engaging, and, best of all, the opening number, '*Give me a ticket to heaven please, before the last train is gone*', which is a real show-stopper. David Willison accompanies most sympathetically and the recording is suitably vivid. However, there are a few strenuous fortissimos where the voice seems to catch the microphone and the tone is harshened.

Luxon, Benjamin (baritone), Robert Tear (tenor), André Previn (piano)

'Victorian ballads': SULLIVAN: *The Dickey bird and the Owl*. DIX: *The Trumpeter*. LESLIE: *Anabelle Lee*. HAINES: *Cigarette*. DIBDIN: *Tom Bowling*. MARCHANT: *The moon has raised her lamp above*. BALFE: *Excelsior; Come into the garden Maude*. BLOCKLEY: *The Arab's farewell to his favourite steed*. HATTON: *The lark now leaves his wat'ry nest*. BRAHAM: *The death of Nelson*. OFFENBACH: *Gendarmes duet*. SERJEANT: *Watchman, what of the night*. BISHOP: *Home! Sweet home!*. arr. Moffat: *My snowy-breasted pearl; The wee cooper o' Fife*. CLAY: *I'll sing thee songs of Araby*.
(M) *** EMI CDM7 67808-2 [id.].

At the time this record was made, in the early 1970s, Benjamin Luxon had made something of a speciality of singing Edwardian ballads, often together with Robert Tear. The direct style is in the best tradition of Peter Dawson (whose record of Dix's *The Trumpeter* was famous in 78-r.p.m. days – as much as anything for its clear delivery and crystal-clear diction). The present recital opens engagingly with Sullivan's humorous duet, *The Dicky bird and the Owl*, with its reminders of *Cox and Box*, and includes many favourites, from *Come into the garden Maude*, which is managed without a hint of send-up, to *The Arab's farewell to his favourite steed*, complete with spoken introduction describing the sentimental situation of the song. *The Death of Nelson* is as dramatic as anyone could want, and the duets, serious and lyrical – *Watchman what of the night* (one of the finest things on the disc), and the humorous gendarmes ('We run them in') – bring enthusiastic participation from both artists. Robert Tear's feelings about the programme are well expressed in the accompanying note: 'These songs are not just amusing museum relics, but living music full of lovely melody and the grand sentiment, as pertinent to their age as Dowland's and Monteverdi's were to theirs.' The collection is generous (73 minutes) and given vivid recording, but it is a pity that the documentation is so sparse: even the titles are minuscule.

Moscow Liturgic Choir, Father Amvrosy

'Kiev Christmas liturgy – the celebration of the Nativity': *Christmas Eve hymns and prayers. Grand Compline: God is with us. Matins (Short Litany); Two songs; Glory to Christmas; Proclamation and Reading of the Gospel according to St Matthew; Three chants; Selected hymns; The Canon: 9th Ode (selected verses); Two songs (The Dismissal).*
** Erato/Warner Dig. 2292 45961-2 [id.].

To Western ears this collection will not sound very Christmassy. The fourteen-strong choir are very accomplished and their voices blend with a fine sonority, but the style of the music itself has a limited range. The programme begins with excerpts from the original hymns, used by the Orthodox Church at Christmas, but becomes really animated to reach some kind of climax only at the *Proclamation of the Gospel according to St Matthew*. The closing section is also quite poignant, but this well-recorded CD would have been more useful with adequate documentation to explain the significance of each of the nine tracks.

Nash, Heddle (tenor)

'The incomparable Heddle Nash': PUCCINI: *La Bohème, Act IV* (complete; with Lisa Perli, Brownlee, Alva, Andreva, LPO, Beecham). Arias from: MOZART: *Così fan tutte* (with Ina Souez); *Don Giovanni* (all in Italian). ROSSINI: *The Barber of Seville*. VERDI: *Rigoletto*. BIZET: *The Fair Maid of Perth*. Johann STRAUSS Jr: *Die Fledermaus* (with Denis Noble) (all in English).
(M) (***) Dutton Lab. mono CDLX 7012 [id.].

Once again Dutton Laboratories provide incomparable transfers from 78s – of such quality that Beecham's extraordinarily theatrical (1935) Act IV of *La Bohème*, sung in Italian, communicates like a modern recording. Heddle Nash sings ardently, but Lisa Perli (Dora Labette) as Mimi is equally touching and, if the rest of the cast are less distinctive, Beecham's direction carries the day. Nash's four Mozart recordings (also sung in Italian) are included, notably the 1929 *Il mio tesoro*. Most cherishable of all is the *Serenade* from *The Fair Maid of Perth* from 1932, but there is some very striking Verdi in English, full of flair (in spite of awkward words) and a sparkling Johann Strauss duet with Dennis Noble. It seems carping to criticize that, with only 69 minutes, there would have been room for more. But what there is is technically state of the art.

Nilsson, Birgit (soprano)

'Great voice': Arias from MOZART: *Don Giovanni.* WEBER: *Oberon.* WAGNER: *Tannhäuser; Tristan und Isolde.* R. STRAUSS: *Salome.* BEETHOVEN: *Ah! Perfido, Op. 65.*
(B) **(*) DG 431 107-2 [id.].

Birgit Nilsson's representation in DG's *'Grosse Stimmen'* series certainly demonstrates the forcefulness of her vocal personality. She is a formidable Donna Anna, breathing fire in *Or sai chi l'onore* (though her coloratura in *Non mi dir* is uncomfortably strained) and equally arresting in Rezia's famous *Ozean du Ungeheuer* from Weber's *Oberon*. She can be tender, too, as Elisabeth in *Tannhäuser*; although the key scene from Strauss's *Salome* (recorded live in 1972) shows her full vocal power, it is – not surprisingly – Isolde's *Liebestod*, taken from the 1966 Bayreuth recording and passionately conducted by Karl Boehm, which shows her at her peak, radiant of tone and completely in control to the last note. Alas, like the other CDs in this series, there is no information provided about either the singer or the music, except for titles and recording dates. But at bargain price it is otherwise well worth considering.

Oberlin, Russell (counter-tenor), Seymour Barab (piano)

Troubadour and trouvère songs, Volume 1: BRULE: *Cil qui d'amor me conseille.* DE BORNEIL: *Reis glorios, verais lums e clartatz.* DANIEL: *Chanson do – Ih mot son plan e prim.* D'EPINAL: *Commensmens de dolce saison bele.* RIQUIER: *Ples de tristor, marritz e doloires*; DE VENTADOUR: *Can vei la lauzeta mover.*
*** Lyrichord LEMS 8001 [id.].

It is good to see the legendary Russell Oberlin return to the catalogue. Older readers will recall his Covent Garden appearance as Oberon in Britten's *Midsummer Night's Dream*. Unfortunately his concert career was cut short and he has since pursued a distinguished career as a scholar. This 1958 recital of *Troubadour and trouvère songs* first appeared on the Experiences Anonymes label and, like so many of his all-too-few recordings (including an incredible Handel aria disc), has long been sought after. This voice was quite unique, a *real* counter-tenor of exquisite quality and, above all, artistry. The disc is expertly annotated and is of quite exceptional interest. LEMS stands for Lyrichord Early Music Series, and the discs we have so far heard (and on which we will report in the next edition) are artistically impressive.

Opera: 'Essential Opera'

'Essential opera I': BIZET: *Carmen: Prelude* (LPO, Solti); *Flower song* (Domingo). PUCCINI: *Tosca: Vissi d'arte* (Kiri Te Kanawa). *La Bohème: Che gelida manina. Turandot: Nessun dorma* (both Pavarotti); *Non piangere Liù . . . Ah! per l'ultima volta!* (Pavarotti, Montserrat Caballé, Nicolai Ghiaurov, Tom Krause). *Gianni Schicchi: O mio babbino caro* (Tebaldi). *Madama Butterfly: Un bel dì vedremo* (Mirella Freni). VERDI: *Il Trovatore: Anvil chorus. Nabucco: Va pensiero (Chorus of Hebrew slaves)* (Chicago Symphony Ch. & O, Solti). *Rigoletto:* Quartet: *Bella figlia dell'amore* (Sutherland, Tourangeau, Pavarotti, Milnes). *Aida: Grand march and ballet* (La Scala, Milan, Ch. & O, Maazel). MOZART: *Nozze di Figaro: Voi che sapete* (Frederica von Stade). *Don Giovanni: Finch'han dal vino* (Bernd Weikl). CATALANI: *La Wally: Ebben? Ne andrò lontana* (Tebaldi). ROSSINI: *Il barbiere di Siviglia: Largo al factotum* (Leo Nucci). OFFENBACH: *Barcarolle: Belle nuit, o nuit d'amour* (Sutherland and Huguette Tourangeau). MASCAGNI: *Cavalleria rusticana: Intermezzo* (Nat. PO, Gavazzeni).
**(*) Decca Analogue/Dig. 433 822-2 [id.].

'Essential opera II': WAGNER: *Die Walküre: The ride of the Valkyries* (VPO, Solti). BIZET: *Carmen: Habanera* (Tatiana Troyanos). MOZART: *Le nozze di Figaro: Non più andrai* (Samuel Ramey); *Dove sono* (Kiri Te Kanawa). *Così fan tutte:* Trio: *Soave sia il vento* (Lucia Popp, Brigitte Fassbaender; Tom Krause). *Don Giovanni:* Duet: *Là ci darem la mano* (Popp; Krause). *Die Zauberflöte: Der Vogelfänger bin ich ja* (Michael Kraus). PUCCINI: *Madama Butterfly: Humming chorus* (Vienna State Op. Ch., Karajan). *Turandot: Signore ascolta!* (Montserrat Caballé). *Tosca: E lucevan le stelle* (Domingo). *La Bohème: Sì, mi chiamano Mimì; O soave fanciulla* (Freni; Pavarotti). VERDI: *La Traviata: Un dì felice* (Joan Sutherland; Luciano Pavarotti). *Rigoletto: La donna è mobile* (Pavarotti). LEONCAVALLO: *Pagliacci: Vesti la giubba* (Pavarotti). ROSSINI: *Il barbiere di Siviglia: Una voce poco fa* (Cecilia Bartoli). BIZET: *Les pêcheurs de perles:* Duet: *Au fond du temple saint* (Gregory Cross;

Gino Quilico). CILEA: *L'Arlesiana: Lamento di Federico* (José Carreras). DELIBES: *Lakmé:* Duet: *Dôme épais le jasmin* (Sutherland; Jane Berbié). GOUNOD: *Faust: Soldiers' chorus* (Ambrosian Opera Ch., LSO, Bonynge).
**(*) Decca Analogue/Dig. 440 947-2 [id.].

With a great deal of hype, Decca's first (full-priced) 'Essential opera' compilation became a chart-topper and sold in large quantities. It includes many favourites, offering 77 minutes of music and some obvious star performances, mostly from Pavarotti and Freni, and Domingo's *Flower song* from *Carmen*. Although generally the excerpts are vividly presented, Solti opens the programme with a *Carmen Prélude* that offers less brilliant sound than usual from Decca. The Tebaldi excerpt from Catalani's *La Wally* is most welcome, but is it 'essential opera'? Not everything is quite on this artist's level and it is easy to find similar and, in certain cases, preferable selections from the same source, costing less.

The second selection (78 minutes) follows a similar formula. Solti again opens the proceedings with an exciting *Ride of the Valkyries* (though, curiously, an orchestral version without the vocal parts) and there is plenty to enjoy. But one of the most memorable excerpts, the great love scene from Act I of *La Bohème* (*Sì, mi chiamano Mimì . . . O soave fanciulla*) with Freni and Pavarotti, is also available on other, less expensive anthologies.

Operatic Duets: 'Great love duets'

'Great love duets' (sung by Sutherland, Freni, Pavarotti, Tebaldi, Corelli, M. Price, Cossutta): PUCCINI: *Madama Butterfly; La Bohème; Tosca; Manon Lescaut.* VERDI: *Otello; La Traviata.*
(M) *** Decca 433 439-2 [id.].

This collection in Decca's mid-price Opera Gala series is very well chosen, starting and ending with duets from two of Karajan's outstanding Puccini recordings for Decca, *Madama Butterfly* and *La Bohème*, both with Freni and Pavarotti. The *Bohème* item includes not only the duet, *O soave fanciulla*, but also the two favourite arias which precede it, *Che gelida manina* and *Sì, mi chiamano Mimì*. Sutherland joins Pavarotti for a very moving account of the lovers' final meeting on Violetta's death bed in the last Act of *La Traviata*, with *Un dì felice* and the gentle *Parigi o cara* meltingly sung. Tebaldi is well represented as Manon Lescaut, and Margaret Price is a ravishing Desdemona, singing *Già nella notte densa*, taken from Solti's complete *Otello*.

Oxford Pro Musica Singers, Michael Smedley

'Follow that star' (with Timothy Bennett). *Carols in close harmony:* BLANE: *Have yourself a merry little Christmas.* BERNARD: *Winter wonderland.* GRITTON: *Follow that star; On olde rhyme; Deck the hall.* COOT: *Santa Claus is coming to town.* HAIRSTON: *Mary's boy child.* BARRATT: *Just another star.* WELLS: *The Christmas song.* TRAD.: *Ding dong merrily on high; The angel Gabriel; Gaudete; Riu, riu chiu!; Coventry carol; In dulci jubilo.* GRUBER: *Silent night.* HOWELLS: *A spotless rose.* arr. Rutter: *I wonder as I wander.* TAVENER: *The Lamb; Nativity; Today the Virgin.* CORNELIUS: *Three Kings.* arr. David Blackwell: *The Virgin Mary had a baby boy; Mary had a baby; Jingle bells.*
**(*) Proudsound Dig. PROUCD 134 [id.].

The first nine carols here are arranged by Peter Gritton in the American close-harmony style – and, provided you can enjoy the sentimentality of Judy Garland's number from *Meet Me in St Louis*, *Have yourself a merry little Christmas*, and the even more famous *Winter wonderland*, you can ignore the brackets round the third star. The excellent Oxford Pro Musica Singers seem as much at home here as they are in David Blackwell's arrangements of *The Virgin Mary had a baby boy* and *Mary had a baby* in the rhythmic style of spirituals, and the somewhat over-elaborate but effective *Jingle bells*. In between come some splendid traditional carols, including the folksy *Riu, riu chiu!*, all beautifully sung, and – perhaps the highlight of the concert – three glorious modern carols by John Tavener. The digital recording is first class.

Patti, Adelina (soprano)

'The Era of Adelina Patti' ((i) Adelina Patti, (ii) Victor Maurel; (iii) Pol Plançon; (iv) Mattia Battistini; (v) Mario Ancona; (vi) Lucien Fugère; (vii) Francisco Vignas; (viii) Emma Calvé; (ix) Maurice Renaud; (x) Fernando de Lucia; (xi) Francesco Tamagno; (xii) Nellie Melba; (xiii) Félia Litvinne; (xiv) Wilhelm Hesch; (xv) Lillian Nordica; (xvi) Mario Ancona; (xvii) Edouard de Reszke;

(xviii) Marcella Sembrich; (xix) Francesco Marconi; (xx) Mattia Battistini; (xxi) Lilli Lehmann; (xxii) Sir Charles Santley) Arias from: VERDI: (ii) *Falstaff;* (i, iii,) *Don Carlos;* (iv, xx) *Ernani;* (v, xiv) *Otello.* ADAM: (iii) *Le Chalet.* GLUCK: (vi) *Les Pèlerins de la Mecque.* MOZART: (i, ii, xx) *Don Giovanni;* (i, vii, xxi) *Le nozze di Figaro.* MEYERBEER: (vii) *Le Prophète.* BIZET: (viii) *Carmen.* MASSENET: (ix, xi) *Hérodiade;* (x) *Manon.* THOMAS: (xii) *Hamlet.* WAGNER: (xiii) *Lohengrin;* (xiv) *Die Meistersinger von Nürnberg.* ERKEL: (xv) *Hunyadi László.* DONIZETTI: (xvi) *La favorita;* (xix) *Lucrezia Borgia;* (xii) *Lucia.* BELLINI: (i) *La Sonnambula;* (xviii) *I Puritani.* FLOTOW: (xvii) *Martha.* ROSSINI: (x) *Il barbiere di Siviglia.* GOMES: (xx) *Il Guarany.* Songs by TOSTI; (vi) RAMEAU; (i, vi) YRADIER; (i) HOOK; (i) BISHOP; (ix) GOUNOD; (xv) R. STRAUSS; (xxii) HATTON.
(M) (***) Nimbus mono NI 7840/41 [id.].

The very first item on this wide-ranging collection of historic recordings has one sitting up at once. The voice ringing out from the loudspeakers prompts cheering from the singer's little audience. The clear-toned baritone is singing *Quand'ero paggio* from Verdi's *Falstaff* and, encouraged, he repeats it. More cheering and a third performance, this time in French, to cap the occasion. The singer is Victor Maurel, the baritone whom Verdi chose as his first Falstaff in 1893 and, before that, his first Iago in *Otello.* The recording dates from 1907, and many lovers of historic vocal issues will remember it well. Yet hearing it on the Nimbus transfer to CD brings a sense of presence as never before.

That company's controversial technique of playing an ancient 78 disc with a thorn needle on the best possible acoustic horn gramophone is at its most effective here, with exceptionally vivid results on these acoustic recordings. They not only convey astonishing presence but also a sense of how beautiful the voices were, getting behind the tinny and squawky sounds often heard on old 78s. This is an ideal set for anyone not already committed to historic vocals who simply wants to investigate how great singing could be 90 years ago, providing such an unexpected mix of well-known items and rarities, to delight specialists and newcomers alike.

The first of the two discs offers recordings that Nimbus regards as technically the finest of their day, including Patti in 1906, not just singing but shouting enthusiastically in a Spanish folksong, *La Calesera*, '*Vivan los españoles!*' Recorded much later in 1928 comes the French baritone, Lucien Fugère, eighty at the time but singing with a firm focus that you might not find today in a baritone in his twenties.

The second of the two discs has just as fascinating a mixture, but the recordings 'have not survived the decades so well'. Even so, it is thrilling to hear Sir Charles Santley, born in 1834, the year after Brahms, singing *Simon the Cellarer* with tremendous flair at the age of seventy-nine, and the coloratura, Marcella Sembrich, sounding even sweeter in Bellini than on previous transfers.

Pavarotti, Luciano (tenor)

'*King of the high Cs*': Arias from: DONIZETTI: *La fille du régiment; La Favorita.* VERDI: *Il Trovatore.* R. STRAUSS: *Der Rosenkavalier.* ROSSINI: *Guglielmo Tell.* BELLINI: *I Puritani.* PUCCINI: *La Bohème.*
(M) *** Decca 433 437-2 [id.].

A superb display of Pavarotti's vocal command as well as his projection of personality. Though the selections come from various sources, the recording quality is remarkably consistent, the voice vibrant and clear; the accompanying detail and the contributions of the chorus are also well managed. The Donizetti and Puccini items are particularly attractive. The opening number – Tonio's aria from the Act I finale of *La fille du régiment* – ending with a whole series of 'pinging' top Cs, is thrillingly hair-raising. The recordings were made between 1967 and 1972 when the voice was at its freshest.

'*Grandi voici*' (with Nat. PO, Chailly or Fabrittis): GIORDANO: *Fedora: Amor ti vieta. Andrea Chénier: Colpito qui m'avete ... Un di all'azzuro spazio; Come un bel dì di maggio; Si, fui soldata.* BOITO: *Mefistofele: Dai campi, dai prati; Ogni mortal ... Giunto sul passo estremo.* CILEA: *Adriana Lecouvreur: La dolcissima effigie; L'anima ho stanca.* MASCAGNI: *Iris: Apri la tua finestra!* MEYERBEER: *L'Africana: Mi batti il cor ... O Paradiso.* MASSENET: *Werther: Pourquoi me réveiller.* PUCCINI: *La Fanciulla del West: Ch'ella mi creda. Manon Lescaut: Tra voi belle; Donna non vidi mai; Ah! non v'avvicinate! ... No! No! pazzo son!* (with Howlett).
(M) **(*) Decca Dig. 440 400-2 [id.].

This first digital recital record from Pavarotti had the voice more resplendent than ever. The passion with which he tackles Des Grieux's Act III plea from *Manon Lescaut* is devastating, and the big breast-beating numbers are all splendid, imaginative as well as heroic. But the slight pieces, Des Grieux's *Tra voi belle* and the *Iris Serenade*, could be lighter and more charming. The CD gives the voice even greater projection, with its full resonance and brilliance admirably caught, but it does also make the listener more aware of the occasional lack of subtlety of the presentation.

'Live': Recital 1: Arias and duets from: VERDI: *La Traviata; I vespri siciliani; Aida.* MASSENET: *Werther.* PONCHIELLI: *La Gioconda.* DONIZETTI: *La figlia del reggimento; L'elisir d'amore.* MEYERBEER: *L'Africana.* BOITO: *Mefistofele.* MASCAGNI: *L'amico Fritz.* PUCCINI: *Tosca.* Recital 2: Arias from VERDI: *La Traviata; Aida; Macbeth; La forza del destino; I Lombardi; Il Corsaro; Falstaff; Un ballo in maschera;* Duet from *Otello (Già nella notte densa).* Arias from PUCCINI: *Turandot.*
(B) **(*) Double Decca 443 018-2 (2) [id.].

Here are two Pavarotti recitals for the price of one, although in the second, mainly a Verdi collection, Katia Ricciarelli, in splendid voice, gets the lion's share of the arias and she and Pavarotti join for only a single duet – from *Otello.* Pavarotti rounds off the programme as usual with *Nessun dorma,* to tumultuous applause. However, applause is not really a problem on the second disc, whereas it is often intrusive on the first. Artistically, however, the partnership of Pavarotti and Freni works well (as we know from their complete recordings). The *Werther* and *Africana* items were new to Pavarotti's repertory at the time; sweet singing from Freni, too, though her delivery at times could be more characterful. Vividly robust recording.

'The essential Pavarotti' (with various orchestras and conductors): Arias from: VERDI: *Rigoletto; Il Trovatore; La Traviata; Aida.* PUCCINI: *La Bohème; Turandot; Tosca; Fanciulla del West; Manon Lescaut.* DONIZETTI: *L'elisir d'amore.* FLOTOW: *Martha.* BIZET: *Carmen.* LEONCAVALLO: *I Pagliacci.* GIORDANO: *Fedora.* MEYERBEER: *L'Africana.* MASSENET: *Werther.* Songs: DALLA: *Caruso.* LEONCAVALLO: *Mattinata.* TOSTI: *Aprile; Marechiare; La Serenata.* CARDILLO: *Core 'ngrato.* ROSSINI: *La Danza.* MODUGNO: *Volare.* DENZA: *Funiculì, funiculà.* DI CURTIS: *Torna a Surriento.* DI CAPUA: *O sole mio!* SCHUBERT: *Ave Maria.* FRANCK: *Panis angelicus.* MANCINI: *In un palco della Scala* (with apologies to Pink Panther). GIORDANO: *Caro mio ben.* BIXIO: *Mamma.*
(M) *** Decca Analogue/Dig. 436 173-2 (2) [id.].

Such a collection as this is self-recommending and scarcely needs a review from us, merely a listing. The first disc opens with *La donna è mobile* (*Rigoletto*), *Che gelida manina* (*La Bohème*), *Nessun dorma* (*Tosca*), all taken from outstandingly successful complete recordings, and the rest of the programme, with many favourite lighter songs also given the golden touch, is hardly less appealing. The second CD includes Pavarotti's tribute to the Pink Panther and ends with a tingling live version of *Nessun dorma,* to compare with the studio version on disc one. Vivid, vintage, Decca recording throughout.

Pavarotti in Central Park (with Harlem Boys' Ch., NYPO (members), Leone Magiera): Arias from: VERDI: *I vespri siciliani; Luisa Miller.* DONIZETTI: *Lucia di Lammermoor.* CILEA: *L'arlesiana.* MASSENET: *Werther.* PUCCINI: *Tosca.* Songs by: LEONCAVALLO; MASCAGNI; BIXIO; ELLINGTON; TRAD.; DI LAZZARO; SIBELLA; DENZA; BIZET/BORNE; DE CRESCENZO; DE CURTIS; DI CAPUA.
**(*) Decca Dig. 444 450-2 [id.].

Pavarotti, with his wide smile and a unique voice still in splendid shape, has a way of turning all his major concerts into great public occasions. This recording readily demonstrates his electrifying effect on the audience. The 77-minute programme, with its high proportion of popular songs and arias that he has recorded and re-recorded, is for the Pavarotti aficionado rather than for the general collector.

Price, Leontyne (soprano)

'The Prima Donna Collection' (with RCA Italiana Op. O, Molinari-Pradelli; New Philh. O, Santi; LSO, Downes; or Philh. O, Henry Lewis): Disc 1: Arias from: PURCELL: *Dido and Aeneas.* MOZART: *Le nozze di Figaro.* VERDI: *La Traviata; Otello* (with C.Vozza). MEYERBEER: *L'Africaine.* MASSENET: *Manon.* CILEA: *Adriana Lecouvreur.* Gustave CHARPENTIER: *Louise.* PUCCINI: *Turandot* (with D. Barioni, Amb. Op. Ch.). KORNGOLD: *Die tote Stadt.* BARBER: *Vanessa.*

Disc 2: HANDEL: *Atalanta.* MOZART: *Don Giovanni.* WEBER: *Der Freischütz.* WAGNER: *Tannhäuser.* VERDI: *Macbeth* (with C. Vozza, E.El Hage). BOITO: *Mefistofele.* DVORAK: *Rusalka.* DEBUSSY: *L'enfant prodigue.* GIORDANO: *Andrea Chénier.* ZANDONAI: *Francesca da Rimini.* PUCCINI: *Suor Angelica.* MENOTTI: *Amelia goes to the ball.*

Disc 3: GLUCK: *Alceste.* MOZART: *Don Giovanni.* VERDI: *I Lombardi; Simon Boccanegra.* FLOTOW: *Martha.* OFFENBACH: *La Périchole.* WAGNER: *Die Walküre.* Johann STRAUSS Jr: *Die Fledermaus.*

BIZET: *Carmen*. MASCAGNI: *Cavalleria rusticana*. MASSENET: *Thaïs*. PUCCINI: *Gianni Schicchi*. POULENC: *Les dialogues des Carmélites*.

Disc 4: HANDEL: *Semele*. MOZART: *Idomeneo*. BERLIOZ: *La Damnation de Faust*. WEBER: *Oberon*. BELLINI: *Norma* (with B. Martinovich, Amb. Op. Ch.). VERDI: *Rigoletto*. WAGNER: *Tristan und Isolde*. LEONCAVALLO: *Pagliacci*. CILEA: *Adriana Lecouvreur*. BRITTEN: *Gloriana*.
(M) *** BMG/RCA 09026 61236-2 (4).

This remarkable anthology is drawn from a series of recitals which Leontyne Price recorded for RCA in London and Rome between 1965 and 1979, including many items made when she was at the very peak of her form. It is irritating that the individual recording dates are not given, but the programme appears to be laid out generally in the order they were recorded, although there are a few exceptions. Some of the very finest performances come on Disc 1. The famous *Lament* from Purcell's *Dido and Aeneas* makes a moving opener, the voice is wonderfully fresh; and the following performances are all gloriously sung – clearly these early sessions with Molinari-Pradelli in Rome were highly productive. But there are many fine things elsewhere. The Sleep-walking scene from Verdi's *Macbeth* on Disc 2 is a disappointment (Lady Macbeth is plainly not one of her best parts), but her *Come in quest' ora bruna* from *Simon Boccanegra* is very fine, and she finds unusual expressive depth in Offenbach's Act III Prison aria from *La Périchole*. She is, not unexpectedly, superb in *Voi lo sapete* from *Cavalleria rusticana* (disc 3), and a highlight from the final disc is the passionately felt *D'amour l'ardente flamme* from Berlioz's *Damnation de Faust*. The languorously played cor anglais solo here is characteristic of the consistent excellence of the accompaniments and, like the voice, they are beautifully recorded. Care has been taken with detail, so that in the long scene from Act I of *Norma* (with *Casta diva* at its centre) there is support from the Ambrosian Chorus, recorded in fine perspective. As she has already recorded a complete *Carmen*, it is good to hear Miss Price singing richly in the subsidiary role of Micaëla, and the programme includes a fair sprinkling of novelties, not least a rare excerpt from Britten's *Gloriana*. In a programme as long as this (approaching five hours of music) there are bound to be minor vocal flaws, but they are suprisingly few, and vocally the performances are amazingly consistent. A feast of opera, very well ordered – each disc makes a satisfying solo recital.

'Grandi voci': Arias from: MOZART: *Don Giovanni*. VERDI: *Aida; Requiem*. PUCCINI: *Tosca*. R. STRAUSS: *Ariadne auf Naxos*. GERSHWIN: *Porgy and Bess*. Songs: SCHUBERT: *Ave Maria*. MOZART: *Exsultate jubilate: Alleluja*. TRAD.: *Sweet little Jesus boy*.
(M) *** Decca 440 402-2 [id.].

Leontyne Price can be heard at her finest here: the Verdi and Puccini arias central to her repertory are superbly done. It is good too to have her represented in Mozart (in Donna Elvira's three key arias) and Strauss, recorded at the peak of her career, though style there is less positive and individual. Nevertheless this very enjoyable recital is more than the sum of its parts, and the programme ends appropriately with an affecting performance of *Summertime* from *Porgy and Bess*. Excellent sound throughout.

Resnik, Regina (mezzo-soprano)

'Golden Jubilee': Arias from BIZET: *Carmen*. TCHAIKOVSKY: *Jeanne d'Arc*. SAINT-SAENS: *Samson et Dalila*. WAGNER: *Die Walküre*. VERDI: *Il trovatore; Don Carlo* (all with ROHCG O, Edward Downes); *Falstaff; Un ballo in maschera*. R. STRAUSS: *Elektra* (with Birgit Nilsson). J. STRAUSS Jnr: *Die Fledermaus*. LEHAR: *Merry Widow*. BORODIN (arr. Wright/Forrest): *Kismet*.
(M) *** Decca 421 897-2 [id.].

This collection was originally issued to celebrate the artistry and range of Regina Resnik, who made her stage début in 1942. Most of the programme derives from a 1961 recital, to which excerpts from complete sets in which she was featured have been added. The *Carmen* and *Delilah* items are magnificent. She is in top form here, and where in the complete *Tristan and Isolde* her Brangäne was decidedly unsteady, she is firmer on this occasion, with the vibrato under better control. The sense of line, too, is commanding, and there is an urgency about the different characterizations. The *Joan of Arc* aria is sung in Russian and in the *Walküre* excerpts Resnik sounds appropriately fierce as the scolding Fricka. She is even more impressive as Clytemnestra in *Elektra* in her scene with Birgit Nilsson (*Ich will nichts hören . . . Ich habe keine güten Nachte*) and makes a memorably saturnine Orlovsky in *Die Fledermaus*. The Offenbach *Can-can*, too, is as racy as anyone could ask. A very well-selected programme (75 minutes) and vivid recording.

Royal music

'The world of royal music': HANDEL: Coronation anthem: Zadok the Priest (King's College Ch., Willcocks). PURCELL: I was glad; Funeral music for Queen Mary: March; Thou knowest, Lord; Canzona (St John's College Ch., Consort of Sackbutts, Cleobury). BLISS: Welcome the Queen (LSO, composer); Antiphonal fanfare. BAX: Fanfare for the wedding of Princess Elizabeth (Philip Jones Brass Ens.). WALTON: Coronation marches: Crown imperial (Simon Preston); Orbe and sceptre (Bournemouth SO, Hill); Coronation Te Deum (Choirs of Salisbury, Winchester and Chichester Cathedrals, LPO Ch., LPO, Solti). PARRY: I was glad (Westminster Abbey Ch., McKie). ELGAR: Imperial march (Carlo Curley). arr. Britten: God save the Queen (LSO, Ch., Britten).
(B) **(*) Decca 432 403-2; 432 403-4.

A well-made concert, effectively drawing from Decca's back catalogue to produce consistently vivid sound-quality. The programme works well, though perhaps Crown imperial should have been offered in an orchestral version – even though Simon Preston's account on the organ of Westminster Abbey produces a fine tonal panoply. Solti's Coronation Te Deum of Walton is a highlight and Willcocks's 1963 King's version of Zadok the Priest has both freshness and impact.

Russian Liturgical Music

St Petersburg Litany – Night Vigil.
*** DG Dig. 445 653-2 [id.]. Priests & Ch. of the Cathedral of the Transfiguration, St Petersburg, Boris Glebov.

Anyone who has attended a Russian Orthodox service will know how impressive an experience it is. With the collapse of the Soviet Union interest in this Church's repertoire has burgeoned, witness the proliferation of recordings of Rachmaninov's Vespers as well as the music of Bortniansky and Kastalsky. In the days of LP, DG recorded the Easter services at Mount Athos, and they have now repeated the process in St Petersburg. The Palm Sunday Vigil lasts some three hours – the present disc runs for 72 minutes. This is a rich panoply of sound, ranging from the ringing of bells, large and small, to the service itself, which is sung throughout without spoken interludes or instrumental accompaniments. It is atmospherically recorded and offers quite an experience.

Schreier, Peter (tenor)

'Great voice': Arias from: MOZART: Così fan tutte; Die Entführung aus dem Serail; Don Giovanni. WEBER: Der Freischütz. TAUBER: Der singende Traum. KALMAN: Gräfin Mariza. RAYMOND: Maske in Blau. Lieder: SCHUBERT: Schwanengesang: Ständchen. Die schöne Müllerin: Ungeduld. Am Brunnen vor dem Tore. SCHUMANN: Dichterliebe: Im wunderschönen Monat Mai. Liederkreis: Schöne Wiege meiner Leiden. TOSELLI: Serenade. CHOPIN, arr. Melichar: In mir klingt ein Lied. SILCHER: Annchen von Tharau; Wenn alle Brünnlein fliessen. TRAD.: Du, du liegst mir im Herzen.
(B) **(*) DG 431 109-2 [id.].

Peter Schreier is a very personable lyric tenor, and it is always a pleasure to have a tenor recital without straining histrionics. He is pleasingly stylish in Mozart, even better in Max's recitative and aria (Durch die Wälder) from Der Freischütz, which is spirited as well as polished. The operetta excerpts perhaps could unleash more sheer passion, but it is good to have the excerpt from Raymond's Blue Mask, a semi-musical from the beginning of the 1930s with a curious stylistic mix, which continues to survive in the German repertoire. Schreier's easy Lieder style in famous songs of Schubert and Schumann is not without depth of feeling, and he is captivating in the lollipops, notably the Melichar arrangement of a very famous Chopin melody and Silcher's delightful Annchen von Tharau. As usual in DG's 'Grosse Stimmen series, there is no proper back-up documentation.

Simionato, Giulietta (mezzo-soprano)

'Grandi voci': Arias and excerpts from: ROSSINI: Il barbiere di Siviglia; La Cenerentola. VERDI: Don Carlos; Il Trovatore (with Mario del Monaco); Un ballo in maschera (with Carlo Bergonzi); La forza del destino. BELLINI: I Capuleti e i Montecchi; Norma. SAINT-SAENS: Samson et Dalila. THOMAS: Mignon. MASSENET: Werther. BIZET: Carmen. DONIZETTI: La Favorita.
(M) *** Decca 440 406-2 [id.].

This provides a superb 77-minute sampler of a singer who bids fair to achieve legendary status, an

Italian mezzo with a firm, finely projected voice who could snort fire to order. The recital begins with four excerpts (from *Il barbiere*, *La Cenerentola*, *I Capuleti e i Montecchi* and *Don Carlos*) recorded in mono in 1954, showing the voice at its freshest – the cabaletta from *Una voce poco fa* is sheer delight – and then covers most of her other favourite roles, with recordings made up until 1961, including a richly sustained *Casta diva* from that year. Her rich middle range and sense of line are eloquently demonstrated in *Printemps qui commence* from *Samson et Dalila* and Mignon's lovely *Connais-tu le pays?*, while the ardour of the *Air de la lettre* from Massenet's *Manon* is very moving, helped by a passionate accompaniment from Previtale. The collection ends with Preziosilla's *Rataplan* from *La forza del destino*, sung with a thrilling military precision seldom encountered on record. Molinari-Pradelli and the Santa Cecilia Chorus and Orchestra add to the *vivo*, and the spectacle is well laced with a splendid side-drum. Here (in early 1955 stereo) as elsewhere the Decca engineers do her proud.

Sinfonye, Stewart Wishart

'Gabriel's greeting' (Medieval carols) including: *Gabriel framevene king; Salva Virgo viginium; Ave Maria virgo virginium; Ther is no rose of swych vertu; Lolay, lolay; Nowell, nowell.*
**(*) Hyp. Dig. CDA 66685 [id.].

Unlike the Taverner Consort who range over many centuries of music, Sinfonye concentrate on vocal and instrumental music from the thirteenth, fourteenth and fifteenth centuries, which usually consists of simple ostinato-like rhythmic ideas with a very distinct melodic and harmonic character. These five singers and instrumentalists present their programme with spirit and vitality, but the range of the music is necessarily limited. Those who take to the repetitive medieval style will undoubtedly find this refreshing, and the recording is pleasingly live and atmospheric.

Souliotis, Elena (soprano)

'Grandi voce': Arias and scenes from: VERDI: *Nabucco; Macbeth; Luisa Miller; Un ballo in maschera; Anna Bolena* (final scene); *La forza del destino.* MASCAGNI: *Cavalleria rusticana.* PONCHIELLI: *La Gioconda.*
(M) *** Decca 440 405-2 [id.].

The charismatic Greek diva Elena Souliotis had a sadly brief (if at times sensational) recording career, and all the excerpts here come from between 1965 and 1967. Rightly, the selection opens with Abigail's venomous scena from *Nabucco*, her finest recording role. The thrilling wildness as she spits fire with extraordinary passion is unforgettable. The same reckless ardour and the vocal power in the chest register make *Voi lo sapete* from *Cavalleria rusticana* equally arresting. (She made her final appearance as Santuzza at Covent Garden in 1973.) As a fiery stage personality she had much in common with Callas, but in these carefully chosen excerpts her upper tessitura is shown as more reliable. *Pace, pace mio Dio* (1967) is finely spun, and the group of Verdi items (a riveting Lady Macbeth, a dominant Luisa Miller, Amelia in *Un ballo*), taken from a 1966 recital, are all most impressive, while the final scene (20 minutes) from Donizetti's *Anna Bolena* is very touching – *Al dolce guidami castel natio* quite lovely. The recital ends with an electrifyingly uninhibited *Suicido!* from *La Gioconda*, again from 1967, showing the sheer power of the voice over the widest range. Some of the singing in this recital may be uneven (though the standard is surprisingly consistent) but the tension never abates. No wonder Alan Blythe comments in his perceptive note: 'She resembled a comet that flashed brightly across the operatic scene and was too soon extinguished.' The Decca recording certainly lights up the sky.

Souzay, Gérard (baritone), Dalton Baldwin (piano)

Mélodies françaises: FAURE: *Chanson du pêcheur; Poème d'un jour, Op. 21; Les berceaux; Le secret; Aurore; Fleur jetée; La rose; Madrigal; 5 Mélodies de Venise, Op. 58; La bonne chanson, Op. 61; Le parfum impérissable; Arpège; Prison; Soir; Dans la forêt de septembre; La fleur qui va sur l'eau; Le don silencieux; La chanson d'Eve, Op. 95, excerpts (Eau vivante; O mort, poussière d'étoiles). Le jardin clos, Op. 106, excerpts (Exaucement; Je me poserai sur ton cœur). Mirages, Op. 113; L'horizon chimérique, Op. 118.* POULENC: *Chansons villageoises; Calligrammes; Le travail du peintre; La fraîcheur et le feu; Airs chantés: Air vif. La grenouillère; Métamorphoses: Reine des mouettes. Priez pour paix.* RAVEL: *5 Mélodies populaires grecques; Epigrammes de Clément Marot; Histoires naturelles; Chansons madécasses; 2 Mélodies hébraïques; Don Quichotte à Dulcinée; Les grands*

vents venus d'outre-mer; Sainte; Sur l'herbe. LEGUERNEY: *20 Poèmes de la Pléiade,* excerpts (*Ma douce jouvence est passée; A son page.* HAHN: *L'heure exquise.* DUPARC: *L'invitation au voyage; Sérénade forentine; La vague et la cloche; Extase; Le manoir de Rosemonde; Lamento; La vie antérieure; Testament; Phidylé; Chanson triste; Elégie;* Soupir. GOUNOD: *L'absent; Sérénade.* CHABRIER: *Les cigales; Chanson pour Jeanne.* BIZET: *Chanson d'avril.* FRANCK: *Nocturne.* ROUSSEL: *Le jardin mouillé; Le bachelier de Salamanque.*
⊛ (M) *** Ph. 438 964-2 (4) [id.].

Now here is something to make the pulse quicken: Gérard Souzay, recorded while still in his prime and in repertoire in which he was unmatched in his day. Only Bernac had as refined an interpretative intelligence and, of an older generation, only Panzera commanded an equal authority and tonal beauty. Souzay's 1963 recording of Fauré's *La bonne chanson* is one of the classics of the gramophone and has been extensively discussed in the *Stereo Record Guide* over the years. It was chosen by RL as one of his 'desert-island' discs in 'The Great Records' ('rich in artistry, imagination and insight'). The recording of the *Deux mélodies hébraïques* is captivating, though Souzay made an even more haunting version for French EMI in the late 1950s; and one is hard pressed to choose between his *Don Quichotte à Dulcinée* and those of Panzera and Bernac. After Souzay's Philips disc with *La bonne chanson* came further recordings of Fauré, an anthology of other French *mélodies* and an LP of the Duparc songs, in every way superior to his later, EMI re-make in the early 1970s. This is treasure-trove which no lover of the French repertoire should be without. It is as essential an acquisition for Souzay admirers as the Schumann *Dichterliebe* – see above, under the composer). Not everyone can afford four CDs all at one go, even at mid-price, and Philips would be wise to re-package the Fauré songs as part of their bargain Duo series, and issue the Duparc separately as well.

'Grandi Voci': Arias (with New SO of London, Paul Bonneau): RAMEAU: *Les Indes Galantes.* GOUNOD: *Philémon et Baucis; Roméo et Juliette.* BERLIOZ: *La damnation de Faust.* BIZET: *Les Pêcheurs de perles; La jolie fille de Perth.* MASSENET: *Le jongleur de Notre-Dame.* OFFENBACH: *Les contes d'Hoffmann.* CHABRIER: *Le roi malgré lui.* GOUNOD: Songs (with Jacqueline Bonneau): *Chanson de printemps; Ce que je suis sans toi; Venise; Ma belle amie est morte; O ma belle rebelle; Viens! les gazons sont verts!; Les deux pigeons.*
(M) ** Decca stereo/mono 440 419-2 [id.].

A strangely disappointing operatic recital from 1956 is here combined with some more memorable performances of Gounod mélodies, recorded three years earlier with Jacqueline Bonneau. The operatic performances are curiously sombre, which suits some items more than others but gives a pervading, gloomy atmosphere. *Coppélius's aria* from *Contes d'Hoffmann* lacks any kind of dramatic force, and easily the finest item is the last, the *Romance du roi* of Chabrier.

Stefano, Giuseppe di (tenor)

'Grandi voce': Arias and excerpts from: GIORDANO: *Andrea Chénier.* PUCCINI: *Tosca; Turandot.* MASSENET: *Werther; Manon.* BIZET: *Carmen; Les Pêcheurs de perles.* GOUNOD: *Faust.* DONIZETTI: *L'elisir d'amore.* PONCHIELLI: *La Gioconda.* VERDI: *La forza del destino.* BOITO: *Mefistofele* (with Cesare Siepi).
(M) *** Decca 440 403-2 [id.].

Flamboyance rarely goes with keen discipline. As Rudolf Bing (among others) has said, if those qualities had been matched in di Stefano, we should have had a tenor to rival Caruso. As it is, a cross-section taken from Decca recordings made between 1955 and 1959 gives a splendid idea not just of his beauty of voice but of his power to project character and feelings. But do not look for stylish restraint in *Una furtiva lagrima* – the tear is anything but furtive – and do not seek a French tenorissimo in *En fermant les yeux* from Massenet's *Manon* but ardour and full timbre. The Puccini excerpts, notably Calaf's *Nessun dorma* and the ringing *Recondita armonia* from *Tosca*, demonstrate there was life before Pavarotti, while the tender opening of *E lucevan le stelle* from the same opera shows that di Stefano could fine his tone down in the most ravishing manner when he needed to. The Decca recordings offer early examples of stereo, but the transfers are remarkably full and vivid.

Sutherland, Dame Joan (soprano)

'Grandi voci': BELLINI: *Norma: Sediziose voci . . . Casta diva . . . Ah! bello a me ritorna. I Puritani: Qui la voce sua soave . . . Vien, diletto* (with ROHCG O, Molinari-Pradelli). VERDI: *Atilla: Santo di patria . . . Allor che i forti corrono . . . Da te questo or m'è concesso* (with LSO, Bonynge).

DONIZETTI: *Lucia di Lammermoor: Ancor non giunse! . . . Regnava nel silenzio; Il dolce suono mi colpì di sua voce! . . . Ardon gl'incensi* (Mad scene). *Linda di Chamounix: Ah! tardai troppo . . . O luce di quest'anima.* VERDI: *Ernani: Surta è la notte . . . Ernani! Ernani, involami. I vespri siciliani: Mercè, dilettte amiche (Boléro).*
🕮 (M) *** Decca 440 404-2 [id.].

Sutherland's 'Grandi voci' disc is one of the most cherishable of all operatic recital records, bringing together the glorious, exuberant items from her very first recital disc, made within weeks of her first Covent Garden success in 1959, and – as a valuable supplement – the poised accounts of *Casta diva* and *Vien, diletto* she recorded the following year as part of the 'Art of the Prima Donna'. It was this 1959 recital which at once put Sutherland firmly on the map among the great recording artists of all time. Even she has never surpassed the freshness of these versions of the two big arias from *Lucia di Lammermoor*, sparkling in immaculate coloratura, while the lightness and point of the jaunty *Linda di Chamounix* aria and the *Boléro* from *I vespri siciliani* are just as winning. The aria from *Attila* comes from 'The age of bel canto' (1963). The sound is exceptionally vivid and immediate, though the accompaniments under Nello Santi are sometimes rough in ensemble.

Sutherland, Joan (soprano), Luciano Pavarotti (tenor)

Operatic duets from: DONIZETTI: *Lucia di Lammermoor; L'elisir d'amore; Maria Stuarda; La fille du régiment.* VERDI: *Rigoletto.* BELLINI: *I Puritani.*
(M) *** Decca 421 894-2 [id.].

Taken from the complete opera recordings they made together from the late 1960s onwards, this collection of duets finds both superstars in glowing form, with Decca recordings of the finest vintage for the period very well transferred to CD. However, this is a straight reissue of a full-priced CD, and the measure (55 minutes 39 seconds) is not now particularly generous.

Tauber, Richard (tenor)

'Opera arias and duos' (with (i) Elisabeth Rethberg; (ii) Lotte Lehmann) from: MOZART: *Don Giovanni.* MEHUL: *Joseph.* OFFENBACH: *Contes d'Hoffmann.* THOMAS: *Mignon.* TCHAIKOVSKY: *Eugene Onegin.* SMETANA: (i) *The Bartered Bride* (with Rethberg). WAGNER: *Die Meistersinger.* PUCCINI: *Turandot;* (i) *Madama Butterfly* (with Rethberg). KORNGOLD: (ii) *Die tote Stadt* (with Lotte Lehmann).
(M)(***) EMI mono CDH7 640292 [id.].

Starting as early as 1922 with Mozart's *Dalla sua pace* from *Don Giovanni*, then immediately following with the 1939 *Il mio tesoro*, this recital charts Tauber's recording career as far as 1945 with the Méhul *Champs paternels* from *Joseph*. Elisabeth Rethberg joins him now and then, notably in the *Butterfly* excerpt, sung in German. The voice is well caught by the transfers, but there are occasionally some noises off. Yet the standard of singing here is so consistently high that one can readily make allowances. For a sampler, try the glorious *Hoffmann* excerpts (1929) or *Lensky's aria* from *Eugene Onegin* (1923).

Tebaldi, Renata (soprano)

Italian songs (with Richard Bonynge): DONIZETTI: *Me voglio fa'na casa.* MASCAGNI: *La tua stella; Serenata.* TOSTI: *Sogno.* ROSSINI: *L'invito.* ZANDONAI: *L'assiuolo.* CIMARA: *Stornello.* PONCHIELLI: *Noi leggevamo insieme.* PAISOTTI (attrib. PERGOLESI): *Se tu m'ami.* PARADISI: *M'ha presa alla sua ragna.* A. SCARLATTI: *O cessate di piagarmi.* GLUCK: *O, del mio dolce ardor.* RICCI: *Il carrettiere del Vomero.* MERCADANTE: *Lo sposa del marinaro.* BELLINI: *Malinconia, ninfa gentile.* PUCCINI: *E l'uccellino.*
(M) ** Decca 436 202-2 [id.].

With the famous voice still in fine fettle in 1972, Tebaldi here turns to a selection of mostly little-known songs, almost all from famous composers. As the rather gusty, if lilting, opening Donizetti number shows, the performances are earthy and direct and have little of the subtlety one usually associates with art singing. She gives a winningly robust portrayal of the carter trying to get his mule to take the wagon up the steep road home to see his girlfriend (Ricci's *Il carettierre del Vomero*), and she obviously has sympathy with the music of Gluck and Alessandro Scarlatti. Indeed the songs that come off best are the lyrical ones, like Mascagni's *Serenata*, most beautifully sung, and the gentle lullaby, *E l'uccellino*, of Puccini which ends the recital memorably. Cimara's fruity *Stornello* is done in appropriate ultra-romantic style, but otherwise the highlight is Zandonai's *L'assiuolo* ('The owl') with its reminder of Verdi's *Willow song* from *Otello*. This has a charming postlude for the piano, which Richard Bonynge plays with graceful sensitivity: most of the other accompaniments are simply a vocal support.

'Grandi voce': Arias and excerpts from: PUCCINI: *Madama Butterfly; La Bohème* (with Carlo Bergonzi); *Turandot* (with Mario del Monaco); *Tosca; Gianni Schicchi; Suor Angelica; La Fanciulla del West* (with Cornell MacNeil); *Manon Lescaut.* VERDI: *Aida; Otello* (with Luisa Ribacci); *La forza del destino.* CILEA: *Adriana Lecouvreur.* GIORDANO: *Andrea Chénier.* BOITO: *Mefistofele.* CATALANI: *La Wally.*

(M) *** Decca 440 408-2 [id.].

Those wanting a single-disc, stereo representation of Tebaldi's vocal art could hardly do better than this. It is good that her early mono complete sets of *La Bohème* and *Madama Butterfly* are now again available, and the selection here rightly concentrates on her stereo remakes of the key Puccini operas in the late 1950s, when the voice was still creamily fresh. *Vissi d'arte* (1959) is particularly beautiful. She could be thrilling in Verdi too, as the splendid *Ritorna vincitor!* vibrantly demonstrates, taken from Karajan's complete *Aida*, made in the same year. With a playing time of 75 minutes, this recital should disappoint no one, for the Decca recordings come up as vividly as ever.

Tenor arias: 'Great tenor arias'

'Great tenor arias' (sung by (i) Luciano Pavarotti; (ii) Jussi Bjoerling; (iii) Mario del Monaco; (iv) Carlo Bergonzi; (v) James McCracken; (vi) Bruno Previdi; (vii) Giuseppe di Stefano): Arias from: (i) FLOTOW: *Martha.* (ii) CILEA: *L'Arlesiana;* (iv) *Adriana Lecouvreur.* GIORDANO: (ii) *Fedora;* (iii; vi) *Andrea Chénier.* (iv) MEYERBEER: *L'Africaine.* VERDI: (iii) *Un ballo in maschera;* (v) *La forza del destino;* (vi) *Il Trovatore.* (vii) MASSENET: *Manon; Werther.* (i) DONIZETTI: *La Favorita.* (v) LEONCAVALLO: *Pagliacci.*

(M) ** Decca 421 869-2.

It is always illuminating to hear the voices of different tenors juxtaposed. Pavarotti with his warm, lyrical line, heard at its most beguiling in the opening *M'apparì* from *Martha*, the heady upper range of Carlo Bergonzi in Meyerbeer's *O paradiso*, and the fine and stylish – indeed melting – line of Giuseppe di Stefano in Massenet. Previdi is more robust in a traditional way, but he is thrilling in *An di all'azzuro spazio* from *Andrea Chénier*, while James McCracken's histrionics in *Vesti la giubba* are hardly less compelling. Mario del Monaco must have been very impressive in the opera house, but on record he is too often too consistently loud, as in his contribution from *Un ballo in maschera*. There are other good things here, but overall this is not an indispensable collection.

Terfel, Bryn (bass-baritone), Malcolm Martineau (piano)

'The Vagabond and other English songs': VAUGHAN WILLIAMS: *Songs of travel (The vagabond; Let beauty awake; The roadside fire; Youth and love; In dreams; The infinite shining heavens; Whither must I wander; Bright in the ring of words; I have trod the upward and the downward slope).* BUTTERWORTH: *Bredon hill (Bredon hill; Oh fair enough; When the lad for longing sighs; On the idle hill of summer; With rue my heart is laden); The Shropshire lad* (6 songs): *Loveliest of trees; When I was one-and-twenty; Look not in my eyes; Think no more, lad; The lads in their hundreds; Is my team ploughing?* FINZI: *Let us garlands bring (Come away, death; Who is Silvia?; Fear no more the heat of the sun; O mistress mine; It was a lover and his lass).* IRELAND: *Sea fever; The vagabond; The bells of San Marie.*

⊕ *** DG Dig. 445 946-2 [id.].

No other collection of English songs has ever quite matched this one in its depth, intensity and sheer beauty. Terfel, the great Welsh singer of his generation, here shows his deep affinity with the English repertory, demonstrating triumphantly in each of the 28 songs that this neglected genre deserves to be treated in terms similar to those of the German *Lied* and the French *mélodie*. The Vaughan Williams songs are perhaps the best known, nine sharply characterized settings of Robert Louis Stevenson which, thanks to Terfel's searching expressiveness and matched by Martineau's inspired accompaniments, reveal depths of emotion hardly suspected.

The five Shakespeare settings by Finzi are just as memorable in their contrasted ways, five of the best-known lyrics from the plays that have been set countless times but which here are given new perspectives, thanks both to the composer and to the singer. The eleven Butterworth settings of Housman are among the finest inspirations of this short-lived composer, and it is good to have three sterling Ireland settings of Masefield, including the ever-popular *Sea fever*, which with Terfel emerges fresh and new. The singer's extreme range of tone and dynamic, down to the most delicate, firmly supported half-tones, is astonishing, adding intensity to one of the most felicitous song-recital records in years. The warm acoustic of Henry Wood Hall gives a glow both to the voice and to the piano.

Tetrazzini, Luisa (soprano)

'The London recordings': Arias from VERDI: *Rigoletto; La Traviata; Un ballo in maschera; I vespri siciliani; Aida; La forza del destino.* THOMAS: *Mignon; Hamlet.* DELIBES: *Lakmé.* MEYERBEER: *Dinorah; Les Huguenots; L'étoile du nord.* DONIZETTI: *Lucia di Lammermoor; Linda di Chamounix.* MOZART: *Le nozze di Figaro; Don Giovanni; Die Zauberflöte.* ROSSINI: *Il barbiere di Siviglia; Semiramide.* GOUNOD: *Roméo et Juliette; Mireille; Faust.* BELLINI: *La Sonnambula; I Puritani.* BIZET: *Les pêcheurs de perles; Carmen.* CHAPI: *Las hijas des Zebedeo* (zarzuela). DAVID: *La Perle du Brésil.* HOSCHNA: *Madame Sherry.* J. STRAUSS: *Voici di primavera* (waltz). Songs: BENEDICT: *Il carnevale di Venezia.* TOSTI: *Aprile; La Serenata.* GRIEG: *Peer Gynt: Solveig's song.* PROCH: *Deh, torna mio bene.* VENZANO: *Ah! che assorta.* BISHOP: *Home, sweet home.* RICCI: *Crispino e la Comare.* LOTTI: *Pur dicesti.* TATE: *Somewhere a voice is calling.* VERACINI: *Rosalinda.* BRAGA: *La Serenata.* Attrib. CIAMPI: *Tre giorni son che Nina.* LEMAIRE: *Vous dansez, Marquise.* LAMA: *Piccolo amor; Cara piccina; 'O mare canta!; Come le rose.* VALENTE: *Nuttata napulitana.* DE CURTIS: *So 'nnammurato 'e te!* DRIGO: *I Millioni d'Arlecchino.* VERACINI: *Rosalinda.*
(M) (***) EMI mono CHS7 63802-2 (2) [id.].

This well-documented EMI set includes all the recordings the great diva made in London between 1907 and 1922. It was a remarkable voice, often radiantly pure; although stylistically her singing was indulgent, she carried the day by her beauty of line and and her personality, which could readily charm. Thus the often slight songs come over appealingly and idiosyncrasies of presentation of well-known arias are forgiven. The transfers are vivid and clean, background noise not really a problem; the effect is less mellow than on the characteristic Nimbus reissues from this period, but this disc has fine presence.

Vienna State Opera Chorus and Orchestra

Vienna State Opera Live Edition

Volume I (1933–1936) (with Viorica Ursuleac, Richard Mayr, Eva Hadrabova, Maria Gerhart, Koloman von Pataky, Charles Kullmann, Toti dal Monte, Luigi Montesanto, Aldo Sinnone, Giacomo Lauri-Volpi, Josef Kalenberg, Rudolf Bockelmann, Gertrude Rünger, Kerstin Thorborg, Julius Pölzer, Ezio Pinza, Lauritz Melchior, Anny Konetzni, Josef von Manowarda, Kirsten Flagstad, Torsten Ralf, Luise Helletsgruber, Ludwig Hofmann, Richard Tauber, Jarmila Novotna): Excerpts from: R. STRAUSS: *Der Rosenkavalier* (cond. Clemens Krauss). TCHAIKOVSKY: *Eugene Onegin.* VERDI: *Aida* (both cond. Hugo Reichenberger). *Otello* (cond. Victor de Sabata). ROSSINI: *Il barbiere di Siviglia.* BELLINI: *La Sonnambula* (both cond. Giuseppe del Campo). WAGNER: *Tannhäuser* (cond. Robert Heger); *Die Meistersinger; Parsifal; Götterdämmerung* (all cond. Felix Weingartner); *Lohengrin* (cond. Hans Knappertsbusch & Josef Krips). D'ALBERT: *Tiefland.* GOUNOD: *Faust* (both cond. Karl Alwin). LEHAR: *Giuditta* (cond. composer).
(M) (**) Koch Schwann mono 3-1451-2 (2) [id.].

Volume II (1938–39) WAGNER: *Parsifal:* excerpts (with Hans Grahl, Herbert Alsen, Anny Konetzni, Hermann Wiedemann, Luise Helletsgruber, Elisabeth Rutgers, Maria Schober, Esther Réthy, Dora Komarek, Dora With; cond. Hans Knappertsbusch). *Die Meistersinger:* excerpts (with Rudolf Bockelmann, Josef von Manowarda, Eugen Fuchs, Erich Zimmermann, Tiana Lemnitz, Rut Berglund, Nürnberger Opernchor; cond. Furtwängler).
(M) (**(*)) Koch mono 3-1452-2 (2) [id.]).

Volume III (1933–42) (with Josef Witt, Else Schürhoff, Else Schulz, Paul Schöffler, Anton Dermota, Herbert Alsen, Hans Hotter, Joachim Sattler, Mela Bulgarinovic, Jakob Sabel, Anny Konetzni, Else

Böttcher, Franz Völker, Elisabeth Rethberg, Josef von Manowarda, Jaro Prohaska, Josef Kalenberg, Hermann Wiedermann, Max Lorenz, Rosette Anday, William Wernigk, Luise Helletsgruber, Henny Trundt, Emil Schipper, Marit Angerer; cond. Richard Strauss; Josef Krips): excerpts from R. STRAUSS: *Salome*. MOZART: *Idomeneo* (new version by Richard Strauss & Lothar Wallerstein). WEBER: *Der Freischütz*. WAGNER: *Die Meistersinger; Siegfried; Götterdämmerung*. (M) (**(*)) Koch Schwann mono 3-1453-2 (2) [id.].

Volume IV (1933–42) (with Jussi Bjoerling, Maria Nemeth, Rosette Anday, Todor Mazaroff, Alexander Swed, Sigurd Bjoerling, Kerstin Thorborg, Ludwig Hofmann, Piero Pierotic, Maria Reining, Piroska Tutsek, Herbert Alsen, Margit Bokor, Friedrich Ginrod, Alexander Kipnis, Esther Réthy, Karl Norbert, Josef Kalenberg, Koloman von Pataky, Nikolaus Zec, Aenne Michalski, René Maison): excerpts from: VERDI: *Aida* (cond. Victor de Sabata); *Don Carlo* (cond. Bruno Walter). LEONCAVALLO: *I Pagliacci* (cond. Karl Alwin & Wilhelm Loibner). GOUNOD: *Faust* (cond. Josef Krips). WAGNER: *Tannhäuser* (cond. Wilhelm Furtwängler); *Der fliegende Holländer* (cond. Robert Heger). PUCCINI: *Tosca* (cond. Leopold Reichwein); *Turandot* (cond. Rudolf Moralt). SAINT-SAENS: *Samson et Dalila* (cond. Hugo Reichenberger).
(M) (**) Koch Schwann mono 3-1454-2 (2) [id.].

Volume V (1933–43) R. STRAUSS: *Die Aegyptische Helena:* excerpts (with Viorica Ursuleac, Franz Völker, Margit Bokor, Alfred Jerger, Helge Roswaenge; cond. Clemens Krauss); *Die Frau ohne Schatten*: excerpts (with Torsten Ralf, Hilde Konetzni, Elisabeth Höngen, Josef Herrmann, Else Schulz, Herbert Alsen, Emmy Loose, Wenko Wenkoff; cond. Karl Boehm); *Daphne* (with Maria Reining, Alf Rauch, Anton Dermota; cond. Rudolf Moralt).
(M) (***) Koch Schwann mono 3-1455-2 (2) [id.].

Volume VI (1933–42) (with Anny Konetzni, Max Lorenz, Margarete Klose, Helena Braun, Sigmund Roth, Paul Schoeffler, Daniza Ilitsch, Elena Nikolaidi, Mathieu Ahlersmeyer, Herbert Alsen, Ludwig Hofmann, Josef Kalenberg, Alfred Jerger, Viorica Ursuleac, Erich Zimmermann): excerpts from: WAGNER: *Tristan und Isolde* (cond. Furtwängler); *Parsifal; Die Walküre; Siegfried* (cond. Hans Knappertsbusch); *Götterdämmerung* (cond. Leopold Reichwin); *Die Meistersinger* (cond. Clemens Krauss). VERDI: *Aida* (cond. Leopold Ludwig).
(M) (**) Koch Schwann mono 3-1456-2 (2) [id.].

Volume VII (1937–44) (with Todor Mazaroff, Ester Réthy, Elsa Brems, Josef Witt, Alfred Jeger, Margit Bokor, Enid Szantho, Anton Dermota, Alois Pernerstorfer, Karl Friedrich, Else Schulz, Maria Nemeth, Kerstin Thorborg, Alexander Sved) excerpts from: BIZET: *Carmen*. PFITZNER: *Palestrina*. VERDI: *Aida* (all cond. Bruno Walter). SMETANA: *The Bartered bride*. SCHMIDT: *Notre Dame* (cond. Rudolf Moralt).
(M) (**) Koch Schwann mono 3-1457-2 (2) [id.].

Volume VIII (1941–2) VERDI: *Un ballo in maschera:* excerpts (with Max Lorenz, Mathieu Ahlersmeyer, Hilde Konetzni, Elena Nikolaidi, Alda Noni, Sigmund Roth; cond. Karl Boehm); *Aida* excerpts (with Set Svanholm, Daniza Ilitsch, Hans Hotter, Elena Nikolaidi, Josef von Manowarda; cond. Vittorio Gui); *Falstaff* (with Georg Hann, Karl Kronenberg, Esther Réthy, Adele Kern, Anton Dermota, Josef Wit, Mela Mugarinovic, Elena Nikolaidi, William Wernigk; cond. Clemens Krauss).
(M) (*(**)) Koch Schwann mono 3-1458-2 (2) [id.].

Volume IX (1933–37) WAGNER: *Der Ring des Nibelungen*: excerpts from: *Das Rheingold* (with Jaro Prohaska, Nikolaus Zec, Herbert Alsen, Anny Konetzni; cond. Josef Krips); *Die Walküre* (with Ludwig Hofmann, Frank Völker, Hilde Konetzni, Rose Merker, Herbert Alsen, Kerstin Thorborg, Dora With; cond. Bruno Walter); *Siegfried* (with Richard Schubert, Gertrude Kappel, Erich Zimmerman; cond. Robert Heger); *Götterdämmerung* (with Gertrude Kappel, Josef Kalenberg, Emil Schipper, Wanda Achsel, Rosette Anday; cond. Robert Heger).
(M) (**) Koch Schwann mono 3-1459-2 (2) [id.].

Volume X (1934–41) (with Jan Kiepura, Esther Réthy, Alfred Jerger, Alexander Kipnis, Ludwig Hofmann, Mathieu Ahlersmeyer, Maria Reining, Maria Cebotari, Martha Rohs, Viorica Ursuleac, Franz Völker, Maria Nemeth, Hilde Konetzni, Elena Nikolaidi, Herbert Alsen, Vera Mansinger, Max Lorenz, Enid Szantho, Georg Monthy, Dora Komarek): excerpts from: MOZART: *Le nozze di Figaro* (cond. Karl Boehm). WAGNER: *Die Meistersinger* (cond. Clemens Kraus). BIZET: *Carmen* (cond. Karl Alwin). PUCCINI: *Turandot* (cond. Hugo Reichenberger). VERDI: *Don Carlo* (cond. Bruno Walter); *Falstaff* (cond. Wilhelm Loibner). NICOLAI: *Das lustigen Weiber von Windsor* (cond. Felix Weingartner). WAGNER: *Die Meistersinger; Siegfried; Götterdämmerung* (cond. Hans

Knappertbusch); *Tannhäuser* (cond. Wilhelm Furtwängler).
(M) (**) Koch Schwann 3-1460-2 (2) [id.].

Volume XI (1941–1943) WAGNER: *Tristan und Isolde:* highlights (with Max Lorenz, Anny Konetzni, Herbert Alsen, Paul Schoeffler, Margarete Klose, Georg Monthy, Karl Ettl, Willy Franter, Hermann Gallos, cond. Wilhelm Furtwängler)
(M) (**(*)) Koch Schwann 3-1461-2 (2) [id.].

Volume XII (1933–6) (with Lotte Lehmann, Maria Jeritza, Helge Roswaenge, Eva Hadrabova, Elisabeth Schumann, Berthold Sterneck, Richard Mayr, Josef Kalenberg, Friedrich Schorr, Eyvind Laholm, Kerstin Thorborg, Ludwig Hofmann, Joel Berglund, Alexander Svéd, Gunnar Graarud, Emil Schipper) excerpts from: R. STRAUSS: *Der Rosenkavalier* (cond. Hans Knappertsbusch); *Salome.* MASCAGNI: *Cavalleria rusticana* (both cond. Hugo Reichenberger). WAGNER: *Tannhäuser* (cond. Robert Heger); *Die Meistersinger* (cond. Felix Weingartner); *Die Walküre* (cond. Clemens Krauss). GOUNOD: *Faust* (cond. Josef Krips). GIORDANO: *Andrea Chénier* (cond. Robert Heger). LEONCAVALLO: *I Pagliacci* (conductor unknown).
(M) (**) Koch Schwann mono 3-1462-2 [id.].

Volume XIII (1937–9) (with Maria Reining, Julius Pölzer, Herbert Alsen, Wilhelm Rode, Josef von Manowarda, Set Svanholm, Wilhelm Schirp, Beniamino Gigli, Maria Nemeth, Rosette Anday, Alexander Svéd, Alfred Jerger, Paul Schoeffler, Margherita Perras, Alfred Piccaver, Elisabeth Schumann, Emil Schipper, Anny Konetzni, Todor Mazaroff, Elena Nikolaidi): excerpts from: MOZART: *Le nozze di Figaro.* SALMHOFER: *Ivan Sergejewitsch Tarassenko.* SCHMIDT: *Notre Dame* (all cond. Wilhelm Loibner). PUCCINI: *La Fanciulla del West* (cond. Hans Duhan). LEONCAVALLO: *I Pagliacci.* MASCAGNI: *Cavalleria rusticana.* VERDI: *Aida* (all cond. Karl Alwin). WAGNER: *Parsifal* (cond. Hans Knappertsbusch); *Der fliegende Holländer; Tannhäuser* (cond. Leopold Reichwein). WEBER: *Der Freischütz* (cond. Rudolf Moralt).
(M) (**) Koch Schwann 3-1463-2 (2) [id.].

Volume XIV (1933) Clemens Krauss conducts WAGNER: *Das Rheingold* (with Josef von Manowarda, Bella Paalen, Hermann Wiedemann, Viorica Ursuleac, Gunnar Graarud, Viktor Madin, Josef Kalenberg, Erich Zimmerman, Franz Markhoff, Luise Helletsgruber); *Die Walküre* (with Friedrich Schorr, Maria Jeritza, Felice Hüni-Mihacsek, Franz Völker, Richard Mayr, Rosette Anday, Aenne Michalski); *Götterdämmerung* (Henny Trundt, Josef Kalenberg, Rosette Anday, Josef von Manowarda, Emil Schipper); *Die Meistersinger* (Rudolf Bockelmann, Nikolaus Zec, Hermann Wiedemann, Viorica Ursuleac, Erich Zimmermann, Karl Ettl, Gertrude Rünger); *Parsifal* (Gunnar Graarud, Josef von Manowarda, Emil Schipper, Gertrude Rünger, Hermann Wiedemann).
(M) (**) Koch Schwann mono 3-1464-2 (2) [id.].

Volume XV (1933–41) R. STRAUSS: *Arabella:* excerpts (with Viorica Ursuleac, Margit Bokor, Alfred Jerger, Adele Kern, Gertrude Rünger, Richard Mayr); *Friedenstag:* complete (with Hans Hotter, Viorica Ursuleac, Herbert Alsen, Josef Wit, Hermann Wiederman, Mela Bugarinovic; both cond. Clemens Krauss); *Ariadne auf Naxos* (with Anny Konetzni), Sev Svanholm, Adele Kern, Else Schulz, Alfred Jerger, Alexander Pichler, Alfred Muzzarelli; cond. Rudolf Moralt).
(M) (**(*)) Koch Schwann mono 3-1465-2 (2) [id.].

Volume XVI (1933–41) (with Viorica Ursuleac, Franz Völker, Gertrude Rünger, Josef von Manowarda, Rosette Anday, Zdenka Zika, Emil Schipper, Richard Mayr, Hilde Konetzni, Anny Konetzni, Wanda Achsel, Karl Hammes, Julius Pölzer, Alfred Jerger): excerpts from: WAGNER: *Rienzi; Götterdämmerung* (cond. Josef Krips & Clemens Krauss); *Lohengrin* (cond. François Rühlmann); *Die Walküre* (cond. Clemens Kraus & Hans Knappertsbusch). LEONCAVALLO: *I Pagliacci* (cond. Karl Alwin). VERDI: *Don Carlo; Otello.* R. STRAUSS: *Die Frau ohne Schatten* (all cond. Clemens Krauss); *Elektra* (cond. Hans Knappertsbusch).
(M) (**) Koch Schwann mono 3-1466-2 (2) [id.].

Volume XVII (1936–1943): Hans Knappertsbusch conducts (with Erna Berger, Maria Reining, Josef von Manowarda, Tiana Lemnitz, Michael Bohnen, Franz Völker, Paul Kötter, Herbert Alsen, Margarethe Teschemacher, Anny Konetzni, Hilde Konetzni, Rose Pauly, Set Svanholm, Max Lorenz, Norbert Ardelli, Margit Bokor, Elisabeth Schumann, Ella Flesch): excerpts from MOZART: *Die Zauberflöte.* WEBER: *Der Freischütz.* WAGNER: *Lohengrin; Götterdämmerung; Tannhäuser.* R. STRAUSS: *Elektra; Der Rosenkavalier.* WOLF-FERRARI: *Jewels of the Madonna.*
(M) (**) Koch Schwann mono 3-1467-2 (2) [id.].

Volume XVIII (1944). WAGNER: *Die Meistersinger:* highlights (with Josef Herrmann, Kurt Böhme,

Erich Kunz, Peter Klein, Maria Reining, Martha Rohs; cond. Karl Boehm); *Lohengrin:* highlights (with Franz Völker, Joseph von Manowarda, Maria Müller, Jaro Prohaska, Margarete Klose; cond. Heinz Teitjen).
(M) (**(*)) Koch Schwann mono 3-1468-2 [id.].

Volume XIX (1941–3) (with Set Svanholm, Hilde Konetzni, Helena Braun, Paul Schoeffler, Alfred Poell, Piroshka Tutsek, Julius Pölzer, Kurt Böhme, Maria Reining, Max Lorenz, Joel Berglund, Maria Nemeth, Todor Mazaroff, Esther Réthy): excerpts from: GLUCK: *Iphigénie in Aulis*. SMETANA: *Dalibor* (both cond. Leopold Ludwig). WAGNER: *Tannhäuser* (cond. Leopold Reichwein); *Die Meistersinger* (cond. Karl Boehm); *Die fliegende Holländer* (cond. Leopold Reichwein); *Die Walküre* (cond. Hans Knappertsbusch & Wolfgang Martin); *Götterdämmerung*. WEBER: *Der Freischütz* (both cond. Hans Knappertsbusch).
(M) (**) Koch Schwann mono 3-1469-2 (2) [id.].

Volume XX (1935–7): Wilhelm Furtwängler conducts WAGNER: excerpts from *Die Walküre* (with Franz Völker, Maria Müller, Walter Grossman, Anny Konetzki, Alfred Jerger, Rosette Andray); *Die Meistersinger* (with Karl Kamann, Herbert Alsen, Max Lorenz, Erich Zimmermann, Maria Reining, Enid Szantho); *Tannhäuser* (with Max Lorenz & Maria Müller, Anna Báthy).
(M) (**(*)) Koch Schwann mono 3-1470-2 (2) [id.].

Volume XXI (1941–4) (with Karl Kronenberg, Paul Schoeffler, Maria Cebotari, Anton Dermota, Alfred Jerger, Erich Kunz, Josef Witt, Hans Hotter, Else Schürhoff, Esther Réthy, Helena Braun, Elena Nikolaidi, Herbert Alsen, Danica Ilitsch): excerpts from: MOZART: *Così fan tutte* (cond. Clemens Krauss). R. STRAUSS: *Capriccio* (cond. Karl Boehm). PFITZNER: *Palestrina* (cond. Rudolf Moralt). ORFF: *Carmina Burana*. BORODIN: *Prince Igor*. EGK: *Columbus* (1st version) (all cond. Leopold Ludwig); *Joan von Zarissa* (ballet; cond. composer).
(M) (*(*)) Koch Schwann mono 3-1471-2 (2) [id.].

Volume XXII (1940–41) (with Hans Hotter, Helena Braun, Josef von Manowarda, Daga Söderqvist, Joachim Sattler, William Wernigk, Mela Bugarinovic, Irma Beilke, Erich Kunz): excerpts from: LEONCAVALLO: *Der Bajazzo* (cond. Anton Paulik). WAGNER: *Der fliegende Holländer; Die Walküre* (cond. Rudolf Moralt); *Parsifal; Siegfried* (cond. Hans Knappertsbusch); *Götterdämmerung* (cond. Leopold Reichwein). MOZART: *Le nozze di Figaro* (cond. Clemens Krauss).
(M) (**) Koch Schwann mono 3-1472-2 (2) [id.].

Volume XXIII (1943): Karl Boehm conducts Wagner & Richard Strauss: WAGNER: *Die Meistersinger:* excerpts (with Josef Herrmann, Erich Kunz, Max Lorenz, Peter Klein, Maria Reining). R. STRAUSS: *Ariadne auf Naxos:* complete (with Maria Reining, Max Lorenz, Alda Noni, Irmgard Seefried, Paul Schoeffler, Josef Witt, Alfred Muzzarelli, Friedrich Jelinek, Hermann Baier, Hans Scheiger, Emmy Loose, Melanie Frutschnigg, Elisabeth Rutgers, Erich Kunz, Richard Sallaba, Marjan Rus, Peter Klein).
(M) (**(*)) Koch Schwann mono 3-1473-2 (2) [id.].

Volume XXIV (1937–1943) Hans Knappertsbusch conducts excerpts from *Der Ring des Nibelungen:* (with Ludwig Hofmann, Enid Szantho, Hans Hotter, Helena Braun, Max Lorenz, Hilde Konetzni, Set Svanholm, Paul Schoeffler, Mela Bugarinovic, Adele Kern, Erich Zimmermann, Josef Kalenberg, Emil Schipper, Elisabeth Schumann, Nikolaus Zec, Anny Konetzni, Fred Destal, Alexander Kipnis).
(M) (**) Koch Schwann mono 3-1473-2 (2) [id.].

This astonishing collection of historic recordings, covering an enormous range of performances at the Vienna State Opera between 1933 and 1943, owes its existence to the fact that a certain Herr May set up primitive recording equipment backstage in the opera house and simply recorded what he could. The excerpts were usually short, but in two instances they cover complete Strauss operas: *Friedenstag* from 1938 in Volume 15 and *Ariadne auf Naxos* from 1943 in Volume 23. Volume 5 is another one to investigate, bringing together highlights from three Strauss operas, all discussed separately, above, under their composer entries. More problematically, the quality of recording varies enormously too, with many of them no better than the primitive cylinder recordings being made at the turn of the last century. The problem was the equipment, which involved recording direct on to a disc, which for best results had to be warmed to a certain temperature. That was often not possible, but the editors of this collection have sifted out the best and most interesting material and have used modern technology to eliminate the worst problems.

Even so, in most instances a 'creative ear' has to be used for full enjoyment, and the series will mainly attract vocal specialists for, not surprisingly, the voices are caught better than the orchestra.

Sometimes, as in two brief excerpts from the Woodbird's music in *Siegfried* (Volume 3), the singer, Luise Helletsgruber, standing in the wings is very much on-stage for the recording machine. Another hazard is that sometimes there is the noise of scene-shifting or stagehands chattering, oblivious to what is otherwise going on. One of the least enjoyable sets of excerpts is of a 1942 performance of Carl Orff's *Carmina Burana* (Volume 21), constantly interrupted by chattering and with any sharpness in the performance under Leopold Ludwig complete blunted by the dim sound. Yet the baritone in that is Karl Kronenberg, one of the little-known singers represented here, who emerges as a fine artist. In the same volume he sings Guglielmo in *Così fan tutte* opposite Anton Dermota (in German), but the rest of the volume is very variable, even if it is good to hear Maria Cebotari in part of the Countess's final monologue from Strauss's *Capriccio* in the Vienna première (March 1944).

More than any other composer, Wagner is well represented in this vast archive of recordings, made on primitive equipment in the wings of the Vienna State Opera. Quite apart from these seven volumes devoted entirely to Wagner, the composer is represented in a high proportion of the rest, often with the most valuable recordings of all. One big snag is that Wagner, more than any other major opera composer, depends on the orchestra, and these recordings convey only a sketchy idea of what orchestral sounds were emerging into the theatre from the pit. The voices on stage are different, and there are many incidental passages which one cherishes, particularly with such Heldentenoren as Franz Volker and Josef Kalenberg hardly known on commercial recordings. Max Lorenz too, the leading Heldentenor of his day, was too little recorded, and he is well represented here, as is the dramatic soprano, Maria Müller. But such conductors as Furtwängler, Walter and Boehm are already represented in the catalogues with recordings covering much of the same material, either complete or in much more consistent excerpts, recorded in far more vivid sound, both in the studio and from live performances. Even so, any Wagnerian curious about the singing tradition of the 1930s – dramatically good but vocally living up to legendary status only occasionally – will find much fascinating material here. For all the horrors of crumbly sound, it is still a compelling experience to listen in on a great opera-house.

Italian operas are almost invariably sung in German, with Volume 8 offering excerpts from Verdi's *Ballo*, *Aida* and *Falstaff* all in German. One fleeting delight comes in Volume 13 when by some improbable casting Elisabeth Schumann as Nedda communes with the birds in an excerpt from *I Pagliacci* under Karl Alwin in May 1937. The magic of the moment is vividly caught. Also in that volume are three examples of Alfred Piccaver's singing, for long a favourite in Vienna but too little recorded. From *Pagliacci* he sings firmly and resonantly in *Vesti la giubba* (in German) but very slowly, while his Turiddu from *Cavalleria rusticana* is most disappointing, and so is Dick Johnson's big aria from Puccini's *Fanciulla del West*, taken very slowly and sentimentally. There are excerpts from Mozart's *Nozze di* (or *Hochzeit von*) *Figaro* in that volume too, but the only really enjoyable performance is from Paul Schoeffler as *Figaro*.

Among the outstanding tenors in the Italian and French repertory is the Bulgarian, Todor Mazarov, always a favourite in Vienna, who had a long career but curiously remained neglected in the world of recording. In *Don Carlo* (Volume 4) he sings in his native language, only later using German. He also appears as Radames in *Aida* and as Don José in *Carmen*, both with Bruno Walter conducting (Volume 7). Yet, fine as he is, he yields before Jussi Bjoerling, who is also heard as Radames, singing in Swedish with Victor de Sabata conducting (Volume 4). The physical thrill of Bjoerling's singing, as well as the expressive variety compared with other tenors, comes over vividly. Other valuable items include the only available recordings made on stage by the legendary Maria Jeritza (Volume 12), all taken from performances in 1933 – Santuzza in *Cavalleria rusticana*, as well as Brünnhilde in *Walküre* and Salome. Far more clearly than her few studio recordings, they explain her extraordinary magnetism. Another unique item, giving an idea of stage presence, is of Toti dal Monte singing a snatch of Bellini's *La Sonnambula* in Italian (Volume 1). As a sampler there is much to be said for Volume 1, which ranges wide over the whole repertory, with many of the most celebrated names represented, a longer list than in other volumes, both of singers and of conductors.

The examples of Mozart are generally disappointing, but in Volume 3 it is interesting to hear Richard Strauss's heavyweight treatment of *Idomeneo* in his own much-edited edition for, though the singing is largely indifferent and the strings lumber along, the woodwind playing is often stylish. In that volume the *Idomeneo* excerpts complete a whole disc of Strauss conducting. The rest is taken from two performances of *Salome*, given in 1942, both with Else Schulz rather raw in the title-role, but with Paul Schoeffler in one and the young Hans Hotter in the other both tellingly characterful and clean-focused as Jokanaan. The other disc in Volume 3 has Josef Krips conducting Weber's *Der Freischütz* (1933) as well as three Wagner operas, *Meistersinger* (1937), *Siegfried* (1937) and *Götterdämmerung* (1933). Max in *Der Freischütz* is sung superbly by Franz Volker, another fine artist too little-known, thanks to his sparse recordings. Max Lorenz, the leading Heldentenor of his day, is predictably a fine Siegfried, but also impressive is Josef Kalenberg both as Siegfried in *Götter-dämmerung* and as Walther in an all-too-sketchy excerpt from the *Prize Song* rehearsal in Act III of *Meistersinger*.

Provided one is prepared to use a creative ear and to sift out the good from the bad, there is much to enjoy in eavesdropping on a great opera-house at a period, often regarded as legendary but which turns out to be more variable than expected in quality of performance.

Vishnevskaya, Galina (soprano)

Russian songs (with (i) Mstislav Rostropovich, piano); (ii) Russian State SO, Igor Markevitch):(i) TCHAIKOVSKY: *None but the lonely heart; Not a word, beloved; Heed not, my love.* PROKOFIEV: *5 Poems of Anna Akhmatova.* MUSSORGSKY: *Songs and dances of death;* (ii) orch. Markevitch: *Cradle song; The dazzling lassie; Night; Where are you, dear star?; Scallywag; The Dnieper.*
(M) *** Ph. 446 212-2 [id.].

The young Vishnevskaya sang many of these songs when she came to the Aldeburgh Festival in 1961 and there is the same intensity here as there was in the Jubilee Hall for that suddenly arranged and most exciting concert. Vishnevskaya even overcomes what one would have imagined were impossible difficulties of transferring the Mussorgsky *Songs and dances of death* from bass to soprano. The result is not always what one imagines the composer intended – but no one could miss how compelling it is. Only occasionally under pressure does the voice grow hard. The singer's mastery of vocal characteriza-tion comes out repeatedly. *None but the lonely heart* shows Vishnevskaya at her most impressive, recognizably Russian in her timbre but steadier than most. Her sensitive singing of the Prokofiev songs shows how completely they follow the broad Russian tradition. The recording is rather reverberant, with the piano sounding unusually close for a song recital. Rostropovich, as at Aldeburgh, seems just as much at home accompanying his wife on the piano as playing his cello, and certainly there is the same consummate artistry. The other Mussorgsky songs, including the com-poser's very first, *Where are you, dear star?*, and the *Cradle song*, a lullaby sung to a dying child, were recorded in Russia a year later with orchestrations by Markevitch, who accompanies with the Russian State Symphony Orchestra. They are hardly less compulsive.

Wedding music

'The world of wedding music': WAGNER: *Lohengrin: Wedding march.* BACH: *Suite No. 3: Air* (Stephen Cleobury). CLARKE: *Prince of Denmark's march (Trumpet voluntary).* PURCELL: *Trumpet tune* (Simon Preston). BACH/GOUNOD: *Ave Maria* (Kiri Te Kanawa). SCHUBERT: *Ave Maria.* MOZART: *Alleluia* (Leontyne Price). *Vespers: Laudate dominum* (Felicity Palmer). KARG-ELERT: *Marche triomphale: Nun danket alle Gott.* BRAHMS: *Chorale prelude: Es ist ein Ros entsprungen.* WIDOR: *Symphony No. 5: Toccata.* MENDELSSOHN: *Midsummer Night's Dream: Wedding march* (Peter Hurford). WALFORD DAVIES: *God be in my head.* Hymn: *The Lord's my shepherd* (Huddersfield Choral Soc., Morris). STAINER: *Love divine.* Hymn: *Praise my soul, the King of heaven* (King's College Ch., Cleobury). BACH: *Cantata 147: Jesu, joy of man's desiring.* Hymn: *Lead us, Heavenly Father, lead us* (St John's College Ch., Guest). HANDEL: *Samson: Let the bright seraphim* (Joan Sutherland).
(B) ** Decca 436 402-2; *436 402-4.*

An inexpensive present for any bride-to-be, with many traditional suggestions, well played and sung, though it would have been better to have omitted the Karg-Elert *Marche-triomphale* in favour of Handel's *Arrival of the Queen of Sheba*, to which many a contemporary bride trips down the aisle. Good sound.

Westminster Cathedral Choir, James O'Donnell

'Adeste fidelis' (with Ian Simcock): WADE: *O come all ye faithful.* TRAD.: *Gabriel's message; O come, O come Emanuel; Ding dong merrily on high; A maiden most gentle; I wonder as I wander; O little town of Bethlehem; In dulci jubilo; The holly and the ivy.* GAUNTLETT: *Once in Royal David's city.* DARKE: *In the bleak mid-winter.* CORNELIUS: *The three kings.* PETRUS: *Of the Father's love begotten.* KIRKPATRICK: *Away in a manger.* WARLOCK: *Bethlehem down.* HADLEY: *I sing of a maiden.* GRUBER: *Silent night.* HOWELLS: *Sing lullaby.* TAVENER: *The Lamb.* PARRY: *Welcome yule.*

MENDELSSOHN: *Hark the Herald Angels sing.*
*** Hyp. Dig. CDA 66668 [id.].

An extremely well-sung traditional carol collection. Although many of the arrangers are distinguished names, the arrangements of traditional carols are essentially simple, and the concert makes a great appeal by the quality of the singing and the beautiful digital recording, with the choir perfectly focused and realistically set back just at the right distance within the cathedral acoustic. The programme is spiced with one or two attractive modern settings, notably Patrick Hadley's ravishing *I sing of a maiden* and John Tavener's highly individual carol, *The Lamb*.

Wunderlich, Fritz (tenor)

'Great voice': Arias and excerpts from: MOZART: *Die Zauberflöte; Die Entführung aus dem Serail.* VERDI: *La Traviata* (with Hilde Gueden); *Rigoletto* (with Erika Köth); *Don Carlos* (with Hermann Prey). TCHAIKOVSKY: *Eugene Onegin.* LORTZING: *Zar und Zimmermann; Der Waffenschmied.* ROSSINI: *Il barbiere di Siviglia.* PUCCINI: *La Bohème* (with Hermann Prey). *Tosca.* Lieder: SCHUBERT: *Heidenröslein.* BEETHOVEN: *Ich liebe dich.* TRAD.: *Funiculi-funicula; Ein Lied geht um die Welt* (with R. Lamy Ch.).
(B) *** DG 431 110-2 [id.].

Of the eight collections in DG's *'Grosse Stimmen'* series, this is easily the most attractive – 70 minutes of gloriously heady tenor singing from one of the golden voices of the 1960s. Mozart's *Dies Bildnis* makes a ravishing opener, and *Hier soll ich dich denn sehen* from *Die Entführung* is equally beautiful. Then come two sparkling excerpts from *La Traviata* with Hilde Gueden and some memorable Tchaikovsky, like all the Italian repertoire, sung in German. The Rossini excerpt is wonderfully crisp and stylish. Wunderlich is joined by the charming Erika Köth in *Rigoletto* and by Hermann Prey for the rousing *Don Carlos* duet (*Sie ist verloren . . . Er ist's! Carlos!*) and the excerpt from *Bohème.* Last in the operatic group comes the most famous *Tosca* aria, *Und es blitzen die Sterne* (not too difficult to identify in Italian) sung without excessive histrionics. The Schubert and Beethoven Lieder are lovely and, if the two final popular songs (with chorus) bring more fervour than they deserve, one can revel in everything else. Excellent recording throughout. It is a pity there are no translations or notes, but with singing like this one can manage without them. A splendid bargain.